THE YEAR'S WORK IN ENGLISH STUDIES 1994

The Year's Work in English Studies

Volume 75 • 1994

Edited by

PETER J. KITSON

and

MACDONALD DALY
MÁIRE NÍ FHLATHÚIN
ANGELA KEANE
LIONEL KELLY
R. E. PRITCHARD
ELAINE M. TREHARNE
(associate editors)

Published for
THE ENGLISH ASSOCIATION

BLACKWELL
Publishers

First published 1997

2 4 6 8 10 9 7 5 3 1

Blackwell Publishers Ltd
108 Cowley Road
Oxford OX4 1JF
UK

Blackwell Publishers Inc.
Commerce Place
350 Main Street
Malden, MA 02148
USA

British Library Cataloguing in Publication Data

A CIP catalogue record for this book is available from the British Library.

ISBN 0-631-20460-1

Typeset in 9 on 10 pt Times New Roman
by Ace Filmsetting Ltd, Frome, Somerset
Printed in Great Britain by T. J. International Ltd., Padstow, Cornwall

This book is printed on acid-free paper.

Preface

The Year's Work in English Studies is a narrative bibliography that records and evaluates scholarly writing on English language and on literatures written in English. It is published by Blackwell Publishers on behalf of the English Association.

The Editor and the English Association are pleased to announce that this year's Beatrice White Prize has been awarded to Stephen Merriam Foley for his article 'Coming to Terms: Thomas Elyot's Definitions and the Particularity of Human Letters' (*ELH* 61. 211–30).

The authors of *YWES* attempt to cover all significant contributions to English studies. Writers of articles can assist this process by sending offprints to the journal, and editors of journals that are not readily available in the UK are urged to join the many who send us complete sets. These should be addressed to The Editor, *YWES*, The English Association, The University of Leicester, University Road, Leicester LE1 7RH.

Our coverage of articles and books is greatly assisted by the Modern Language Association of America, who supply proofs of their annual *International Bibliography* in advance of publication. We should like to record our gratitude for their generous co-operation.

The views expressed in *YWES* are those of its individual contributors and are not necessarily shared by the Editor, Associate Editors, or The English Association.

The Editor

The English Association

This bibliography is an English Association publication. It is available through membership of the Association; non-members can purchase it through any good bookshop.

The object of the English Association is to promote the knowledge and appreciation of the English language and its literatures.

The Association pursues these aims by creating opportunities of co-operation among all those interested in English; by furthering the recognition of English as essential in education; by discussing methods of English teaching; by holding lectures, conferences, and other meetings; by publishing a journal, books, and leaflets; and by forming local branches overseas and at home.

Publications

The Year's Work in English Studies. An annual bibliography. Published by Blackwell Publishers, Oxford and Malden, MA.

The Year's Work in Critical and Cultural Theory. The first issue of this new critical theory volume appeared in 1994. Published by Blackwell Publishers, Oxford and Malden, MA.

Essays and Studies. An annual volume of essays by various scholars assembled by the collector covering usually a wide range of subjects and authors from the medieval to the modern. Published by Boydell and Brewer, Woodbridge, Suffolk.

English. The journal of the Association, *English,* is published three times a year by the English Association.

Use of English. This journal is published three times a year by the English Association.

Primary English. This journal is published three times a year.

Benefits of Membership

Institutional Membership

Full members receive copies of *The Year's Work in English Studies, Essays and Studies, English* (three issues), and three *News-Letters.*

Ordinary Membership covers *English* (three issues) and three *News-Letters.*

Schools Membership covers one copy of each issue of *English,* one copy of *The Use of English,* one copy of *Essays and Studies,* three *News-Letters,* and preferential booking for Sixth Form Conference places.

Individual Membership

Individuals take out basic membership, which entitles them to buy all regular publications of the English Association at a discounted price and three *News-Letters.*

For further details write to The Secretary, The English Association, The University of Leicester, University Road, Leicester LE1 7RH.

Contents

Abbreviations

1. Journals, Series, and Reference Works

A&D	*Art and Design*
A&E	*Anglistik und Englishunterricht*
AAR	*African American Review*
ABäG	*Amsterdamer Beiträge zur Älteren Germanistik*
ABC	*American Book Collector*
ABELL	*Annual Bibliography of English Language and Literature*
ABMR	*Antiquarian Book Monthly Review*
ABQ	*American Baptist Quarterly*
ABR	*American Benedictine Review*
ABSt	*A/B: Auto/Biography Studies*
AC	*Archeologia Classica*
Academy Forum	*Academy Forum*
ACar	Analecta Cartusiana
ACH	*Australian Cultural History*
ACLALSB	*ACLALS Bulletin*
ACM	*The Aligarh Critical Miscellany*
ACS	*Australian–Canadian Studies: A Journal for the Humanities and Social Sciences*
Acta	*Acta* (Binghamton, N.Y.)
ADS	*Australasian Drama Studies*
AEB	*Analytical and Enumerative Bibliography*
Æstel	*Æstel*
AF	Anglistische Forschungen
AfricanA	*African Affairs*
AfrSR	*The African Studies Review*
AgeJ	*The Age of Johnson: A Scholarly Annual*
Agenda	*Agenda*
Agni	*Agni Review*
AH	*Art History*
AHR	*The American Historical Review*
AHS	*Australian Historical Studies*
AI	*American Imago*
AJ	*Art Journal*
AJES	*The Aligarh Critical Miscellany*
AJL	*Australian Journal of Linguistics*
AJS	*American Journal of Semiotics*
AKML	Abhandlungen zur Kunst-, Musik- and Literaturwissenschaft
AL	*American Literature*

ALA	African Literature Association Annuals
ALASH	*Acta Linguistica Academiae Scientiarum Hungaricae*
AlexS	Alexander Shakespeare
ALH	*Acta Linguistica Hafniensia: International Journal of Linguistics*
ALitASH	*Acta Litteraria Academiae Scientiarum Hungaricae*
ALLCJ	*Association for Literary and Linguistic Computing Journal*
Allegorica	*Allegorica*
ALR	*American Literary Realism, 1870–1910*
ALS	*Australian Literary Studies*
ALT	*African Literature Today*
Alternatives	*Alternatives*
AmDram	*American Drama*
AmerP	*American Poetry*
AmerS	*American Studies*
AmLH	*American Literary History*
AmLS	*American Literary Scholarship: An Annual*
AMon	*The Atlantic Monthly*
AmRev	*The Americas Review: A Review of Hispanic Literature and Art of the USA*
Amst	*Amerikastudien/American Studies*
AN	*Acta Neophilologica*
Anais	*Anais*
AnBol	*Analecta Bollandiana*
ANF	*Arkiv för Nordisk Filologi*
Anglia	*Anglia: Zeitschrift für Englische Philologie*
Anglistica	*Anglistica*
AnH	Analecta Husserliana
AnL	*Anthropological Linguistics*
AnM	*Annuale Mediaevale*
Ann	*Annales: Economies, Sociétés, Civilisations*
ANQ	*ANQ: A Quarterly Journal of Short Articles, Notes, and Reviews (*formerly *American Notes and Queries)*
AntColl	*The Antique Collector*
AntigR	*Antigonish Review*
Antipodes	*Antipodes*
ANZSC	*Australian and New Zealand Studies in Canada*
ANZTR	*Australian and New Zealand Theatre Record*
APBR	*Atlantic Provinces Book Review*
APL	*Antwerp Papers in Linguistics*
AppLing	*Applied Linguistics*
APR	*The American Poetry Review*
AQ	*American Quarterly*
Aquarius	*Aquarius*
AR	*The Antioch Review*
ArAA	*Arbeiten aus Anglistik und Amerikanistik*
Arcadia	*Arcadia*
Archiv	*Archiv für das Studium der Neueren Sprachen und Literaturen*

ARCS	*The American Review of Canadian Studies*
ArdenS	Arden Shakespeare
ArielE	*Ariel: A Review of International English Literature*
ArkQ	*Arkansas Quarterly: A Journal of Criticism*
ArkR	*Arkansas Review: A Journal of Criticism*
ArQ	*Arizona Quarterly*
ARS	Augustan Reprint Society
ArtB	*Art Bulletin*
ArthI	*Arthurian Interpretations*
ArthL	*Arthurian Literature*
AS	*American Speech*
ASch	*The American Scholar*
ASE	*Anglo-Saxon England*
ASInt	*American Studies International*
ASoc	*Arts in Society*
Aspects	*Aspects: Journal of the Language Society of the University of Essex*
AspectsAF	*Aspects of Australian Fiction*
ASPR	*Anglo-Saxon Poetic Records*
ASSAH	*Anglo-Saxon Studies in Archaeology and History*
Assaph	*Assaph: Studies in the Arts (Theatre Studies)*
Assays	*Assays: Critical Approaches to Medieval and Renaissance Texts*
ASUI	*Analele Stiintifice ale Universitatii 'Al.I. Cuza' din lasi (Serie Noua), e. Lingvistica*
ATQ	*American Transcendental Quarterly: A Journal of New England Writers*
AuBR	*Australian Book Review*
AuFolk	*Australian Folklore*
AuFS	*Australian Feminist Studies*
AuJL	*Australian Journal of Linguistics*
AUMLA	*Journal of the Australasian Universities Language and Literature Association*
AuS	*Australian Studies*
AuSA	*Australian Studies (Australia)*
AusCan	*Australian-Canadian Studies*
AusPl	*Australian Playwrights*
AuWBR	*Australian Women's Book Review*
AvC	*Avalon to Camelot*
AY	*Arthurian Yearbook*
BakhtinN	*Bakhtin Newsletter*
BALF	*Black American Literature Forum*
BARS Bulletin & Review	(British Association for Romantic Studies) *Bulletin & Review*
BASAM	*BASA Magazine*
BathH	*Bath History*
BB	*Bulletin of Bibliography*
BBCS	*The Bulletin of the Board of Celtic Studies*
BBCSh	BBC Shakespeare
BBN	*British Book News*

BBSIA	*Bulletin Bibliographique de la Société Internationale Arthurienne*
BC	*The Book Collector*
BCan	*Books in Canada*
BCMA	*Bulletin of Cleveland Museum of Art*
BCS	*B. C. Studies*
BDEC	*Bulletin of the Department of English* (Calcutta)
BDP	Beiträge zur Deutschen Philologie
Belfagor	*Belfagor: Rassegna di Varia Umanità*
BEPIF	*Bulletin des Etudes Portugaises et Brésiliennes*
BFLS	*Bulletin de la Faculté des Lettres de Strasbourg*
BGDSL	*Beiträge zur Geschichte der Deutschen Sprache und Literatur*
BHI	*British Humanities Index*
BHL	*Bibliotheca Hagiographica Latina Antiquae et Mediae Aetatis*
BHR	*Bibliothèque d'Humanisme et Renaissance*
BHS	*Bulletin of Hispanic Studies*
BI	*Books at Iowa*
Bibliotheck	*The Bibliotheck: A Scottish Journal of Bibliography and Allied Topics*
Biography	*Biography: An Interdisciplinary Quarterly*
BIS	*Browning Institute Studies: An Annual of Victorian Literary and Cultural History*
BJA	*British Journal of Aesthetics*
BJCS	*British Journal of Canadian Studies*
BJDC	*The British Journal of Disorders of Communication*
BJECS	*British Journal for Eighteenth-Century Studies*
BJHP	*British Journal for the History of Philosophy*
BJHS	*The British Journal for the History of Science*
BJJ	*Ben Jonson Journal*
BJL	*Belgian Journal of Linguistics*
BJPS	*The British Journal for the Philosophy of Science*
BJRL	*Bulletin of the John Rylands University Library of Manchester*
BJS	*British Journal of Sociology*
Blake	*Blake: An Illustrated Quarterly*
BLE	*Bulletin de Littérature Ecclésiastique*
BLJ	*The British Library Journal*
BLR	*The Bodleian Library Record*
BN	*Beiträge zur Namenforschung*
BNB	*British National Bibliography*
Boundary	*Boundary 2: A Journal of Postmodern Literature and Culture*
BP	*Banasthali Patrika*
BPMA	*Bulletin (Philadelphia Museum of Art)*
BPN	*The Barbara Pym Newsletter*
BQ	*Baptist Quarterly*
BRASE	Basic Readings in Anglo-Saxon England
BRH	*Bulletin of Research in the Humanities*

Brick	*Brick: A Journal of Reviews*
BRMMLA	*Bulletin of the Rocky Mountain Modern Language Association*
BSANZB	The Bibliographical Society of Australia and New Zealand Bulletin
BSE	*Brno Studies in English*
BSEAA	*Bulletin de la Société d'Etudes Anglo-Américaines des XVIIe et XVIIIe Siècles*
BSJ	*The Baker Street Journal: An Irregular Quarterly of Sherlockiana*
BSLP	*Bulletin de la Société de Linguistique de Paris*
BSNotes	*Browning Society Notes*
BSRS	*Bulletin of the Society for Renaissance Studies*
BSSA	*Bulletin de la Société de Stylistique Anglaise*
BST	*Brontë Society Transactions*
BSUF	*Ball State University Forum*
BTHGNewsl	*Book Trade History Group Newsletter*
BTLV	*Bijdragen tot de Taal-, Land- en Volkenhunde*
BunyanS	*Bunyan Studies*
BuR	*Bucknell Review*
BurlM	*The Burlington Magazine*
BurnsC	*Burns Chronicle*
BWPLL	*Belfast Working Papers in Language and Linguistics*
BWVACET	*The Bulletin of the West Virginia Association of College English Teachers*
ByronJ	*The Byron Journal*
CABS	Contemporary Authors Bibliographical Series
CahiersE	*Cahiers Élisabéthains*
CAIEF	*Cahiers de l'Association Internationale des Études Françaises*
Caliban	*Caliban* (Toulouse, France)
Callaloo	*Callaloo*
CalR	*Calcutta Review*
CamObsc	*Camera Obscura: A Journal of Feminism and Film Theory*
CamR	*The Cambridge Review*
CanD	*Canadian Drama/L'Art Dramatique Canadienne*
C&L	*Christianity and Literature*
C&Lang	*Communication and Languages*
C&M	*Classica et Medievalia*
CanL	*Canadian Literature*
CAnn	*The Carlyle Annual*
CanPo	*Canadian Poetry*
CapR	*Capilano Review*
CARA	Centre Aixois de Recherches Anglaises
Carib	*Carib*
Caribana	*Caribana*
CarR	*Caribbean Review*
Carrell	*The Carrell: Journal of the Friends of the University of Miami Library*

CaudaP	*Cauda Pavonis*
CBAA	*Current Bibliography on African Affairs*
CBEL	*Cambridge Bibliography of English Literature*
CCRev	*Comparative Civilizations Review*
CCrit	*Comparative Criticism: An Annual Journal*
CCTES	*Conference of College Teachers of English Studies*
CCV	*Centro de Cultura Valenciana*
CD	The Critics Debate
CDALB	Concise Dictionary of American Literary Biography
CDCP	Comparative Drama Conference Papers
CDIL	*Cahiers de l'Institut de Linguistique de Louvain*
CdL	*Cahiers de Lexicologie*
CE	*College English*
CEA	*CEA Critic*
CEAfr	*Cahiers d'Études Africaines*
CE&S	*Commonwealth Essays and Studies*
CentR	*The Centennial Review*
Cervantes	*Cervantes*
CFM	*Canadian Fiction Magazine*
CFS	*Cahiers Ferdinand de Saussure: Revue de Linguistique Générale*
Chapman	*Chapman*
Chasqui	*Chasqui*
ChauR	*The Chaucer Review*
ChH	*Church History*
ChildL	*Children's Literature*
ChiR	*Chicago Review*
ChLB	*Charles Lamb Bulletin*
CHLSSF	*Commentationes Humanarum Litterarum Societatis Scientiarum Fennicae*
CHR	*Camden History Review*
CHum	*Computers and the Humanities*
CI	*Critical Idiom*
CILT	Amsterdam Studies in the Theory and History of the Language Sciences IV: Current Issues in Linguistic Theory
CISh	Contemporary Interpretations of Shakespeare
Cithara	*Cithara: Essays in the Judaeo-Christian Tradition*
CJ	*Classical Journal*
CJE	*Cambridge Journal of Education*
CJH	*Canadian Journal of History*
CJIS	*Canadian Journal of Irish Studies*
CJL	*The Canadian Journal of Linguistics*
CJR	*Christian Jewish Relations*
CL	*Comparative Literature* (Eugene, Oreg.)
CLAJ	*CLA Journal*
CLAQ	*Children's Literature Association Quarterly*
ClarkN	*The Clark Newsletter: Bulletin of the UCLA Center for Seventeenth- and Eighteenth-Century Studies*
CLC	*Columbia Library Columns*

ClioI	*Clio: A Journal of Literature, History, and the Philosophy of History*
CLQ	*Colby Library Quarterly*
CLS	*Comparative Literature Studies*
Clues	*Clues: A Journal of Detection*
CMCS	*Cambridge Medieval Celtic Studies*
CML	*Classical and Modern Literature*
CN	*Chaucer Newsletter*
CNew	*The Carlyle Newsletter*
CNIE	*Commonwealth Novel in English*
CogLing	*Cognitive Linguistics*
ColF	*Columbia Forum*
Collections	*Collections*
CollG	*Colloquia Germanica*
CollL	*College Literature*
Comitatus	*Comitatus: A Journal of Medieval and Renaissance Studies*
Commentary	*Commentary*
Comparatist	*The Comparatist: Journal of the Southern Comparative Literature Association*
CompD	*Comparative Drama*
CompLing	*Computational Linguistics*
ConL	*Contemporary Literature*
Connotations	*Connotations*
ConnR	*Connecticut Review*
Conradian	*The Conradian*
Conradiana	*Conradiana: A Journal of Joseph Conrad Studies*
ContempR	*Contemporary Review*
Cosmos	*Cosmos*
CP	*Concerning Poetry*
CQ	*The Cambridge Quarterly*
CR	*The Critical Review*
CRCL	*Canadian Review of Comparative Literature*
CRev	*The Chesterton Review*
CRevAS	*Canadian Review of American Studies*
Crit	*Critique: Studies in Modern Fiction*
CritI	*Critical Inquiry*
Criticism	*Criticism: A Quarterly for Literature and the Arts*
Critique	*Critique (Paris)*
CritQ	*Critical Quarterly*
CritT	*Critical Texts: A Review of Theory and Criticism*
CrM	*Critical Mass*
CRNLE	*The CRNLE Reviews Journal*
CRUX	*CRUX: A Journal on the Teaching of English*
CS	*Critical Survey*
CSASE	Cambridge Studies in Anglo-Saxon England
CSCC	Case Studies in Contemporary Criticism
CSLBull	*Bulletin of the New York C. S. Lewis Society*
CSPC	Cambridge Studies in Palaeography and Codicology
CSR	*Christian Scholar's Review*

CTR	*Canadian Theatre Review*
CulC	*Cultural Critique*
CulS	*Cultural Studies*
CUNY	*CUNY English Forum*
Current Writing	*Current Writing: Text and Reception in Southern Africa*
CV2	*Contemporary Verse 2*
CVE	*Cahiers Victoriens et Edouardiens*
CW	*Current Writing: Text and Perception in Southern Africa*
CWS	*Canadian Woman Studies*
DA	*Dictionary of Americanisms*
DAE	*Dictionary of American English*
DAEM	*Deutsches Archiv für Eforschung des Mittelalters*
DAI	*Dissertation Abstracts International*
DAL	*Descriptive and Applied Linguistics*
D&S	*Discourse and Society*
Daphnis	*Daphnis: Zeitschrift für Mittlere Deutsche Literatur*
DC	The Dickens Companions
DerbyM	*Derbyshire Miscellany*
Descant	*Descant*
DHLR	*The D. H. Lawrence Review*
DHS	*Dix-Huitième Siècle*
Diac	*Diacritics*
Diachronica	*Diachronica*
Dialogue	*Dialogue: Canadian Philosophical Review*
Dickensian	*The Dickensian*
DicS	*Dickinson Studies*
Dictionaries	*Dictionaries: Journal of the Dictionary Society of North America*
Dionysos	*Dionysos*
Discourse	*Discourse*
DLB	*Dictionary of Literary Biography*
DLN	*Doris Lessing Newsletter*
DM	*The Dublin Magazine*
DMT	Durham Medieval Texts
DNB	*Dictionary of National Biography*
DOE	*Dictionary of Old English*
Dolphin	*The Dolphin: Publications of the English Department, University of Aarhus*
DOST	*Dictionary of the Older Scottish Tongue*
DownR	*The Downside Review*
DPr	*Discourse Processes*
DQ	*Denver Quarterly*
DQR	*Dutch Quarterly Review of Anglo-American Letters*
DQu	*Dickens Quarterly*
DR	*Dalhousie Review*
Drama	*Drama: The Quarterly Theatre Review*
DrS	*Dreiser Studies*
DSA	*Dickens Studies Annual*
DU	*Der Deutschunterricht: Beiträge zu Seiner Praxis und Wissenschaftlichen Grundlegung*

DUJ	*Durham University Journal*
DVLG	*Deutsche Viertejahrsschrift für Literaturwissenschaft und Geistesgeschichte*
DWPELL	*Dutch Working Papers in English Language and Linguistics*
EA	*Études Anglaises*
EAL	*Early American Literature*
E&D	*Enlightenment and Dissent*
E&S	*Essays and Studies*
E&Soc	*Economy and Society*
EAS	*Essays in Arts and Sciences*
EASt	*Englisch Amerikanische Studien*
EC	*Études Celtiques*
ECan	*Études Canadiennes/Canadian Studies*
ECCB	*Eighteenth Century: A Current Bibliography*
ECent	*The Eighteenth Century: Theory and Interpretation*
ECF	*Eighteenth-Century Fiction*
ECI	*Eighteenth-Century Ireland*
ECLife	*Eighteenth-Century Life*
ECon	*L'Epoque Conradienne*
ECr	*L'Esprit Créateur*
ECS	*Eighteenth-Century Studies*
ECW	*Essays on Canadian Writing*
EDAMN	*The EDAM Newsletter*
EDH	*Essays by Divers Hands*
EdL	*Études de Lettres*
EdN	*Editors' Notes: Bulletin of the Conference of Editors of Learned Journals*
EDSL	*Encyclopedic Dictionary of the Sciences of Language*
EEMF	Early English Manuscripts in Facsimile
EHR	*The English Historical Review*
EI	*Études Irlandaises (Lille)*
EIC	*Essays in Criticism*
EinA	*English in Africa*
EiP	*Essays in Poetics*
EIRC	*Explorations in Renaissance Culture*
Éire	*Éire-Ireland*
EiTET	*Essays in Theatre/Etudes Théâtrales*
EJ	*English Journal*
ELangT	*ELT Journal: An International Journal for Teachers of English to Speakers of Other Languages*
ELet	*Esperienze Letterarie: Rivista Trimestrale di Critica e Cultura*
ELH	*Journal of English Literary History*
ELN	*English Language Notes*
ELR	*English Literary Renaissance*
ELS	*English Literary Studies*
ELT	*English Literature in Transition*
ELWIU	*Essays in Literature (Western Illinois Univ.)*
EM	*English Miscellany*

Embl	*Emblematica: An Interdisciplinary Journal of English Studies*
EMS	*English Manuscript Studies, 1100–1700*
EMu	*Early Music*
Encyclia	*Encyclia*
English	*English: The Journal of the English Association*
EnT	*English Today: The International Review of the English Language*
EONR	*The Eugene O'Neill Review*
EPD	*English Pronouncing Dictionary*
ER	*English Review*
ERR	*European Romantic Review*
ES	*English Studies*
ESA	*English Studies in Africa*
ESC	*English Studies in Canada*
ESQ	*ESQ: A Journal of the American Renaissance*
ESRS	*Emporia State Research Studies*
EssaysMedSt	*Essays in Medieval Studies*
ESTC	*Eighteenth Century Short Title Catalogue*
EWhR	*Edith Wharton Review*
EWIP	*Edinburgh University, Department of Linguistics, Work in Progress*
EWN	*Evelyn Waugh Newsletter*
EWPAL	*Edinburgh Working Papers in Applied Linguistics*
EWW	*English World-Wide*
Exemplaria	*Exemplaria*
Expl	*The Explicator*
Extrapolation	*Extrapolation: A Journal of Science Fiction and Fantasy*
FCEMN	*Mystics Quarterly (*formerly *Fourteenth-Century English Mystics Newsletter)*
FCS	*Fifteenth-Century Studies*
FDT	Fountainwell Drama Texts
FemR	*Feminist Review*
FH	*Die Neue Gesellschaft/Frankfurter Hefte*
Fiction International	*Fiction International*
FJS	*Fu Jen Studies: Literature and Linguistics* (Taipei)
FLH	*Folia Linguistica Historica*
Florilegium	*Florilegium: Carleton University Annual Papers on Classical Antiquity and the Middle Ages*
FMLS	*Forum for Modern Language Studies*
FNS	*Frank Norris Studies*
Folklore	*Folklore*
FoLi	*Folia Linguistica*
Forum	*Forum*
FranS	*Franciscan Studies*
FreeA	*Free Associations*
FrontenacR	*Revue Frontenac Review*
Frontiers	*Frontiers: A Journal of Women Studies*
FS	*French Studies*
FSt	*Feminist Studies*

Futures	*Futures*
GAG	Göppinger Arbeiten zur Germanistik
GaR	*Georgia Review*
GBB	*George Borrow Bulletin*
GEGHLS	*George Eliot–George Henry Lewes Studies*
GeM	*Genealogists' Magazine*
Genders	*Genders*
Genre	*Genre*
GEFR	*George Eliot Fellowship Review*
Gestus	*Gestus: A Quarterly Journal of Brechtian Studies*
Gettysburg Review	*Gettysburg Review*
GHJ	*George Herbert Journal*
GissingJ	*The Gissing Journal*
GJ	*Gutenberg-Jahrbuch*
GL	*General Linguistics*
GL&L	*German Life and Letters*
GlasR	*The Glasgow Review*
GLM	*Gazette du Livre Medieval*
Glossa	*Glossa: An International Journal of Linguistics*
GLS	*Grazer Linguistische Studien*
GR	*The Germanic Review*
Gramma	*Gramma: Journal of Theory and Criticism*
Gramma/TTT	*Tijdschrift voor Taalwetenschap*
GrandS	*Grand Street*
Granta	*Granta*
Greyfriar	*Greyfriar Siena Studies in Literature*
GRM	*Germanisch-Romanische Monatsschrift*
GSE	Gothenberg Studies in English
GSJ	*The Gaskell Society Journal*
GURT	*Georgetown University Round Table on Language and Linguistics*
H&T	*History and Theory*
Harvard Law Review	*Harvard Law Review*
HatcherR	*Hatcher Review*
HBS	Henry Bradshaw Society
HC	*The Hollins Critic*
HE	*History of Education*
Hecate	*Hecate: An Interdisciplinary Journal of Women's Liberation*
HEdQ	*History of Education Quarterly*
HEI	*History of European Ideas*
HeineJ	*Heine Jahrbuch*
HEL	*Histoire Épistémologie Langage*
Helios	*Helios*
Hermathena	*Hermathena: A Trinity College Dublin Review*
HeyJ	*The Heythrop Journal*
HFR	*Hayden Ferry Review*
HistJ	*The Historical Journal*
HistR	*Historical Research*
History	*History: The Journal of the Historical Association*

HJR	*The Henry James Review* (Baton Rouge, La.)
HL	*Historiographia Linguistica*
HLB	*Harvard Library Bulletin*
HLQ	*The Huntington Library Quarterly*
HNCIS	Harvester New Critical Introductions to Shakespeare
HNR	Harvester New Readings
HOPE	*History of Political Economy*
HPT	*History of Political Thought*
HQ	*Hopkins Quarterly*
HRB	*Hopkins Research Bulletin*
HSci	*History of Science*
HSE	*Hungarian Studies in English*
HSELL	*Hiroshima Studies in English Language and Literature*
HSJ	*Housman Society Journal*
HSL	*University of Hartford Studies in Literature*
HSN	*Hawthorne Society Newsletter*
HSSh	*Hungarian Studies in Shakespeare*
HSSN	*The Henry Sweet Society Newsletter*
HSt	*Hamlet Studies*
HT	*History Today*
HTR	*Harvard Theological Review*
HudR	*Hudson Review*
HumeS	*Hume Studies*
HumLov	*Humanistica Lovaniensia: Journal of Neo-Latin Studies*
HUSL	*Hebrew University Studies in Literature and the Arts*
HWJ	*History Workshop*
HWS	History Workshop Series
IAN	*Izvestiia Akademii Nauk S.S.S.R.* (Moscow)
I&C	*Ideology and Consciousness*
I&P	*Ideas and Production*
ICS	*Illinois Classical Studies*
IEEETrans	*IEEE Transactions on Professional Communications*
IF	*Indogermanische Forschungen*
IFR	*The International Fiction Review*
IGK	*Irland: Gesellschaft und Kultur*
IJAL	*International Journal of Applied Linguistics*
IJECS	*Indian Journal for Eighteenth Century Studies*
IJES	*Indian Journal of English Studies*
IJL	*International Journal of Lexicography*
IJPR	*International Journal for the Philosophy of Religion*
IJSL	*International Journal of the Sociology of Language*
IJSS	*Indian Journal of Shakespeare Studies*
IJWS	*International Journal of Women's Studies*
ILR	*The Indian Literary Review*
ILS	*Irish Literary Supplement*
IMB	*International Medieval Bibliography*
Indexer	*Indexer*
IndH	*Indian Horizons*
IndL	*Indian Literature*
InG	*In Geardagum: Essays on Old and Middle English*

	Language and Literature
Inklings	*Inklings: Jahrbuch für Literatur und Ästhetik*
Inquiry	*Inquiry: An Interdisciplinary Journal of Philosophy*
Interlink	*Interlink*
Interpretation	*Interpretation*
IowaR	*The Iowa Review*
IRAL	*IRAL: International Review of Applied Linguistics in Language Teaching*
IS	*Italian Studies*
ISh	*The Independent Shavian*
ISJR	*Iowa State Journal of Research*
Island	*Island Magazine*
Islands	*Islands*
ISR	*Irish Studies Review*
IUR	*Irish University Review: A Journal of Irish Studies*
JAAC	*Journal of Aesthetics and Art Criticism*
JAAR	*Journal of the American Academy of Religion*
JAF	*The Journal of American Folklore*
JAfM	*Journal of African Marxists*
JAIS	*Journal of Anglo-Italian Studies*
JAL	*Journal of Australian Literature*
JAmC	*Journal of American Culture*
JAMS	*Journal of the American Musicological Society*
JAmS	*Journal of American Studies*
JArabL	*Journal of Arabic Literature*
JAS	*Journal of Australian Studies*
JBeckS	*Journal of Beckett Studies*
JBS	*Journal of British Studies*
JCAKSU	*Journal of the College of Arts, King Saud University*
JCanL	*Journal of Canadian Literature*
JCC	*Journal of Canadian Culture*
JCF	*Journal of Canadian Fiction*
JChL	*Journal of Child Language*
JCL	*The Journal of Commonwealth Literature*
JCP	*Journal of Canadian Poetry*
JCPCS	*Journal of Commonwealth and Postcolonial Studies*
JCSJ	*The John Clare Society Journal*
JCSR	*Journal of Canadian Studies/Revue d'Etudes Canadiennes*
JCSt	*Journal of Caribbean Studies*
JDECU	*Journal of the Department of English (University of Calcutta)*
JDHLS	*D. H. Lawrence: The Journal of the D. H. Lawrence Society*
JDJ	*John Donne Journal*
JDN	*James Dickey Newsletter*
JDTC	*Journal of Dramatic Theory and Criticism*
JEDRBU	*Journal of the English Department, Rabindra Bharati University*
JEGP	*Journal of English and Germanic Philology*
JEH	*The Journal of Ecclesiastical History*

JELL	*Journal of English Language and Literature*
JEn	*Journal of English* (Sana'a Univ.)
JEngL	*Journal of English Linguistics*
JENS	*Journal of the Eighteen Nineties Society*
JEP	*Journal of Evolutionary Psychology*
JEPNS	*Journal of the English Place-Name Society*
JES	*Journal of European Studies*
JETS	*Journal of the Evangelical Theological Society*
JFR	*Journal of Folklore Research*
JGE	*JGE: The Journal of General Education*
JGH	*Journal of Garden History*
JGN	*The John Gower Newsletter*
JH	*Journal of Homosexuality*
JHI	*Journal of the History of Ideas*
JHLP	*Journal of Historical Linguistics and Philology*
JHP	*Journal of the History of Philosophy*
JHSex	*Journal of the History of Sexuality*
JIES	*The Journal of Indo-European Studies*
JIL	*Journal of Irish Literature*
JIPA	*Journal of the International Phonetic Association*
JIWE	*Journal of Indian Writing in English*
JJ	*Jamaica Journal*
JJA	*James Joyce Annual*
JJB	*James Joyce Broadsheet*
JJLS	*James Joyce Literary Supplement*
JJQ	*James Joyce Quarterly*
JL	*Journal of Linguistics*
JLH	*The Journal of Library History, Philosophy and Comparative Librarianship*
JLP	*Journal of Linguistics and Politics*
JLS	*Journal of Literary Semantics*
JLSP	*Journal of Language and Social Psychology*
JLVSG	*Journal of the Loughborough Victorian Studies Group*
JMemL	*Journal of Memory and Language*
JMGS	*Journal of Modern Greek Studies*
JMH	*Journal of Medieval History*
JML	*Journal of Modern Literature*
JMMD	*Journal of Multilingual and Multicultural Development*
JMMLA	*Journal of the Midwest Modern Language Association*
JModH	*Journal of Modern History*
JMRS	*Journal of Medieval and Renaissance Studies*
JNLH	*Journal of Narrative and Life History*
JNPH	*Journal of Newspaper and Periodical History*
JNT	*Journal of Narrative Technique*
JNZL	*Journal of New Zealand Literature*
JoyceSA	*Joyce Studies Annual*
JP	*The Journal of Philosophy*
JPC	*Journal of Popular Culture*
JPCL	*Journal of Pidgin and Creole Languages*
JPhon	*Journal of Phonetics*

JPJ	*Journal of Psychology and Judaism*
JPrag	*Journal of Pragmatics*
JPRAS	*Journal of Pre-Raphaelite and Aesthetic Studies*
JPsyR	*Journal of Psycholinguistic Research*
JQ	*Journalism Quarterly*
JR	*Journal of Religion*
JRH	*The Journal of Religious History*
JRMMRA	*Journal of the Rocky Mountain Medieval and Renaissance Association*
JRSA	*Journal of the Royal Society of Arts*
JRUL	*Journal of the Rutgers University Libraries*
JSA	*Journal of the Society of Archivists*
JSaga	*Journal of the Faculty of Liberal Arts and Science, Saga University*
JSAS	*Journal of Southern African Studies*
JSSE	*Journal of the Short Story in English*
JTheoS	*The Journal of Theological Studies*
JWCI	*Journal of the Warburg and Courtauld Institutes*
JWH	*Journal of Women's History*
JWIL	*Journal of West Indian Literature*
JWMS	*The Journal of the William Morris Society*
JWSL	*Journal of Women's Studies in Literature*
KanQ	*Kansas Quarterly*
KB	*Kavya Bharati*
KCLMS	King's College London Medieval Series
KJ	*The Kipling Journal*
KN	*Kwartalnik Neoflologiczny* (Warsaw)
KompH	*Komparatistische Hefte*
KPAB	*Kentucky Philological Association Bulletin*
KPR	*Kentucky Philological Review*
KR	*Kenyon Review*
KSJ	*Keats Shelley Journal*
KSR	*Keats Shelley Review*
Kuka	*Kuka: Journal of Creative and Critical Writing* (Zaria, Nigeria)
Kunapipi	*Kunapipi*
KWS	*Key-Word Studies in Chaucer*
L&B	*Literature and Belief*
L&C	*Language and Communication*
Landfall	*Landfall: A New Zealand Quarterly*
L&H	*Literature and History*
L&L	*Language and Literature*
L&LC	*Literary and Linguistic Computing*
L&M	*Literature and Medicine*
L&P	*Literature and Psychology*
L&S	*Language and Speech*
L&T	*Literature and Theology: An Interdisciplinary Journal of Theory and Criticism*
L&U	*The Lion and the Unicorn: A Critical Journal of Children's Literature*

LangF	*Language Forum*
Language	*Language: Journal of the Linguistic Society of America*
Lang&S	*Language and Style*
LangQ	*USF Language Quarterly*
LangR	*Language Research*
LangS	*Language Sciences*
LanM	*Les Langues Modernes*
LB	*Leuvense Bijdragen*
LBR	*Luso-Brazilian Review*
LCrit	*The Literary Criterion* (Mysore, India)
LCUT	*The Library Chronicle of the University of Texas at Austin*
LDOCE	Longman Dictionary of Contemporary English
LeedsSE	*Leeds Studies in English*
Legacy	*Legacy: A Journal of Nineteenth-Century American Women Writers*
LeS	*Lingua e Stile*
Lexicographica	*Lexicographica: International Annual for Lexicography*
Lexicography	*Lexicography*
LFQ	*Literature/Film Quarterly*
LH	*Library History*
LHY	*The Literary Half-Yearly*
Library	*The Library*
LibrQ	*The Library Quarterly*
LIN	*Linguistics in the Netherlands*
LingA	*Linguistic Analysis*
Ling&P	*Linguistics and Philosophy*
Ling&Philol	*Linguistics and Philology*
LingB	*Linguistische Berichte*
LingI	*Linguistic Inquiry*
LingInv	*Lingvisticæ Investigationes*
LingP	*Linguistica Pragensia*
Lingua	*Lingua: International Review of General Linguistics*
Linguistics	*Linguistics*
Linguistique	*La Linguistique*
LiNQ	*Literature in Northern Queensland*
LIT	*LIT: Literature, Interpretation, Theory*
LitH	*Literary Horizons*
LitR	*The Literary Review: An International Journal of Contemporary Writing*
LittPrag	*Litteraria Pragensia: Studies in Literature and Culture*
LJGG	*Literaturwissenschaftliches Jahrbuch im Auftrage der Görres-Gesellschaft*
LJHum	*Lamar Journal of the Humanities*
LMag	*London Magazine*
LockeN	*The Locke Newsletter*
LongR	*Long Room: Bulletin of the Friends of the Library, Trinity College, Dublin*
Lore&L	*Lore and Language*
LP	*Lingua Posnaniensis*

LPLD	*Liverpool Papers in Language and Discourse*
LPLP	*Language Problems and Language Planning*
LR	*Les Lettres Romanes*
LRB	*London Review of Books*
LSE	Lund Studies in English
LSLD	*Liverpool Studies in Language and Discourse*
LSoc	*Language in Society*
LST	Longman Study Texts
LTM	Leeds Texts and Monographs
LTP	*LTP: Journal of Literature Teaching Politics*
LTR	*London Theatre Record*
LuK	*Literatur und Kritik*
LVC	*Language Variation and Change*
LWU	*Literatur in Wissenschaft und Unterricht*
MÆ	*Medium Ævum*
MAEL	Macmillan Anthologies of English Literature
Mana	*Mana*
M&H	*Medievalia et Humanistica*
M&L	*Music and Letters*
M&N	*Man and Nature/L'Homme et la Nature: Proceedings of the Canadian Society for Eighteenth-Century Studies*
M&SA	*Metaphor and Symbolic Activity*
Manuscripta	*Manuscripta*
MAR	*Mid-American Review*
MarkhamR	*Markham Review*
Matatu	*Matatu*
Matrix	*Matrix*
MBL	*Modern British Literature*
MC&S	*Media, Culture and Society*
MCI	Modern Critical Interpretations
MCJNews	*Milton Centre of Japan News*
McNR	*McNeese Review*
MCRel	*Mythes, Croyances et Religions dans le Monde Anglo-Saxon*
MCV	Modern Critical Views
MD	*Modern Drama*
Meanjin	*Meanjin*
MED	*Middle English Dictionary*
Mediaevalia	*Mediaevalia: A Journal of Mediaeval Studies*
MedPers	*Medieval Perspectives*
Melus	*MELUS: The Journal of the Society of Multi-Ethnic Literature of the United States*
Meridian	*Meridian*
MESN	*Mediaeval English Studies Newsletter*
MET	Middle English Texts
METh	*Medieval English Theatre*
MFN	*Medieval Feminist Newsletter*
MFS	*Modern Fiction Studies*
MHL	Macmillan History of Literature
MHLS	*Mid-Hudson Language Studies*

MHRev	*The Malahat Review*
MichA	*Michigan Academician*
MiltonQ	*Milton Quarterly*
MiltonS	*Milton Studies*
MinnR	*Minnesota Review*
MissQ	*Mississippi Quarterly*
MissR	*The Missouri Review*
MJLF	*Midwestern Journal of Language and Folklore*
MLAIB	*Modern Language Association International Bibliography*
MLJ	*The Modern Language Journal*
MLN	*Modern Language Notes*
MLRev	*Malcolm Lowry Review*
MLQ	*Modern Language Quarterly*
MLR	*The Modern Language Review*
MLS	*Modern Language Studies*
MMD	Macmillan Modern Dramatists
MMG	Macmillan Master Guides
MMisc	*Midwestern Miscellany*
MOCS	*Magazine of Cultural Studies*
ModA	*Modern Age: A Quarterly Review*
ModM	Modern Masters
ModSp	*Moderne Sprachen*
Monist	*The Monist*
MonSP	*Monash Swift Papers*
Month	*The Month: A Review Of Christian Thought and World Affairs*
MOR	*Mount Olive Review*
Moreana	*Moreana: Bulletin Thomas More* (Angers, France)
Mosaic	*Mosaic: A Journal for the Interdisciplinary Study of Literature*
MoyA	*Moyen Age*
MP	*Modern Philology*
MPHJ	*Middlesex Polytechnic History Journal*
MPR	*The Mervyn Peake Review*
MQ	*Midwest Quarterly*
MQR	*Michigan Quarterly Review*
MR	*Massachusetts Review*
MRDE	*Medieval and Renaissance Drama in England*
MRTS	Medieval and Renaissance Texts and Studies
MS	*Mediaeval Studies*
MSC	Malone Society Collections
MSE	*Massachusetts Studies in English*
MSEx	*Melville Society Extracts*
MSh	Macmillan Shakespeare
MSNH	Mémoires de la Société Néophilologique de Helsinki
MSpr	*Moderna Språk*
MSR	*Malone Society Reprints*
MSSN	*Medieval Sermon Studies Newsletter*
MT	*The Musical Times*

MTJ	*Mark Twain Journal*
MusR	*Music Review*
MW	*The Muslim World* (Hartford, Conn.)
MysticsQ	*Mystics Quarterly*
Mythlore	*Mythlore: A Journal of J. R. R. Tolkien, C. S. Lewis, Charles Williams, and the Genres of Myth and Fantasy Studies*
NA	*Nuova Antologia*
Names	*Names: Journal of the American Name Society*
N&F	*Notes & Furphies*
N&Q	*Notes and Queries*
Narrative	*Narrative*
Navasilu	*Navasilu*
NB	*Namn och Bygd*
NCaS	New Cambridge Shakespeare
NCBEL	*New Cambridge Bibliography of English Literature*
NCC	*Nineteenth-Century Contexts*
NCE	Norton Critical Edition
NCL	*Nineteenth-Century Literature*
NConL	*Notes on Contemporary Literature*
NCP	*Nineteenth-Century Prose*
NCS	*Nineteenth-Century Studies*
NCS	New Clarendon Shakespeare
NCT	*Nineteenth-Century Theatre*
NDQ	*North Dakota Quarterly*
NegroD	*Negro Digest*
NELS	*North Eastern Linguistic Society*
Neoh	*Neohelicon*
Neophil	*Neophilologus*
NEQ	*The New England Quarterly*
NER	*New England Review*
NewA	*New African*
NewBR	*New Beacon Review*
NewC	*The New Criterion*
New Casebooks	New Casebooks: Contemporary Critical Essays
NewComp	*New Comparison: A Journal of Comparative and General Literary Studies*
NewF	*New Formations*
NewR	*New Republic*
NewSt	*Newfoundland Studies*
NewV	*New Voices*
NF	*Neophilologica Fennica*
NfN	*News from Nowhere*
NGC	*New German Critique*
NGS	*New German Studies*
NH	*Northern History*
NHR	*The Nathaniel Hawthorne Review*
NJL	*Nordic Journal of Linguistics*
NL	*Nouvelles Littéraires*
NL&LT	*Natural Language and Linguistic Theory*

NLH	*New Literary History: A Journal of Theory and Interpretation*
NLitsR	*New Literatures Review*
NLR	*New Left Review*
NLWJ	*The National Library of Wales Journal*
NM	*Neuphilologische Mitteilungen*
NMAL	*NMAL: Notes on Modern American Literature*
NMer	New Mermaids
NMIL	*Notes on Modern Irish Literature*
NMS	*Nottingham Medieval Studies*
NMW	*Notes on Mississippi Writers*
NN	*Nordiska Namenstudier*
NNER	*Northern New England Review*
Nomina	*Nomina: A Journal of Name Studies Relating to Great Britain and Ireland*
NoP	*Northern Perspective*
NOR	*New Orleans Review*
NortonCE	A Norton Critical Edition
Novel	*Novel: A Forum on Fiction*
NOWELE	*North-Western European Language Evolution*
NPS	New Penguin Shakespeare
NR	*The Nassau Review*
NRF	*La Nouvelle Revue Française*
NRRS	*Notes and Records of the Royal Society of London*
NS	*Die Neueren Sprachen*
NSS	New Swan Shakespeare
NTQ	*New Theatre Quarterly*
NVSAWC	*Newsletter of the Victorian Studies Association of Western Canada*
NwJ	*Northward Journal*
NWR	*Northwest Review*
NWRev	*The New Welsh Review*
NYH	*New York History*
NYLF	New York Literary Forum
NYRB	*The New York Review of Books*
NYT	*New York Times*
NYTBR	*The New York Times Book Review*
NZListener	*New Zealand Listener*
OA	Oxford Authors
OB	*Ord och Bild*
Obsidian	*Obsidian II: Black Literature in Review*
OBSP	Oxford Bibliographical Society Publications
OED	*Oxford English Dictionary*
OENews	*Old English Newsletter*
OET	Oxford English Texts
OH	*Over Here: An American Studies Journal*
OHEL	Oxford History of English Literature
OhR	*The Ohio Review*
OL	*Orbis Litterarum*
OLR	*Oxford Literary Review*

OPBS	Occasional Papers of the Bibliographical Society
OpenGL	Open Guides to Literature
OpL	*Open Letter*
OPL	Oxford Poetry Library
OPLiLL	*Occasional Papers in Linguistics and Language Learning*
OPSL	*Occasional Papers in Systemic Linguistics*
OralT	*Oral Tradition*
Orbis	*Orbis*
OS	Oxford Shakespeare
OSS	Oxford Shakespeare Studies
OT	*Oral Tradition*
Outrider	*The Outrider: A Publication of the Wyoming State Library*
Overland	*Overland*
PA	*Presence Africaine*
PAAS	*Proceedings of the American Antiquarian Society*
PacStud	*Pacific Studies*
Paideuma	*Paideuma: A Journal Devoted to Ezra Pound Scholarship*
PAJ	*Performing Art Journal*
P&C	*Pragmatics and Cognition*
P&CT	*Psychoanalysis and Contemporary Thought*
P&L	*Philosophy and Literature*
P&P	*Past and Present*
P&R	*Philosophy and Rhetoric*
P&SC	*Philosophy and Social Criticism*
PAPA	*Publications of the Arkansas Philological Association*
PAPS	*Proceedings of the American Philosophical Society*
PAR	*Performing Arts Resources*
Parabola	*Parabola: The Magazine of Myth and Tradition*
Paragraph	*Paragraph: The Journal of the Modern Critical Theory Group*
Parergon	*Parergon: Bulletin of the Australian and New Zealand Association for Medieval and Renaissance Studies*
ParisR	*The Paris Review*
Parnassus	*Parnassus: Poetry in Review*
PastM	Past Masters
PaterN	*Pater Newsletter*
PAus	*Poetry Australia*
PBA	*Proceedings of the British Academy*
PBerLS	*Proceedings of the Berkeley Linguistics Society*
PBSA	*Papers of the Bibliographical Society of America*
PBSC	*Papers of the Biographical Society of Canada*
PCL	*Perspectives on Contemporary Literature*
PCLAC	*Proceedings of the California Linguistics Association Conference*
PCLS	Proceedings of the Comparative Literature Symposium (Lubbock, Tex.)
PCP	*Pacific Coast Philology*
PCS	Penguin Critical Studies
PEAN	*Proceedings of the English Association North*

PE&W	*Philosophy East and West: A Quarterly of Asian and Comparative Thought*
PELL	*Papers on English Language and Literature* (Japan)
Pequod	*Pequod: A Journal of Contemporary Literature and Literary Criticism*
Performance	*Performance*
Peritia	*Peritia: Journal of the Medieval Academy of Ireland*
Persuasions	*Persuasions: Journal of the Jane Austen Society of North America*
Philosophy	*Philosophy*
PHist	*Printing History*
Phonetica	*Phonetica: International Journal of Speech Science*
PHOS	Publishing History Occasional Series
PhRA	*Philosophical Research Archives*
PhT	*Philosophy Today*
PIL	*Papers in Linguistics*
PIMA	*Proceedings of the Illinois Medieval Association*
PinterR	*Pinter Review*
PJCL	*The Prairie Journal of Canadian Literature*
PLL	*Papers on Language and Literature*
PLPLS	*Proceedings of the Leeds Philosophical and Literary Society, Literary and Historical Section*
PM	Penguin Masterstudies
PMHB	*Pennsylvania Magazine of History and Biography*
PMLA	*Publications of the Modern Language Association of America*
PNotes	*Pynchon Notes*
PNR	*Poetry and Nation Review*
PoeS	*Poe Studies*
Poetica	*Poetica: Zeitschrift für Sprach- und Literaturwissenschaft* (Amsterdam)
PoeticaJ	*Poetica: An International Journal of Linguistic-Literary Studies* (Tokyo)
Poetics	*Poetics: International Review for the Theory of Literature*
Poétique	*Poétique: Revue de Théorie et d'Analyse Littéraires*
PoetryCR	*Poetry Canada Review*
PoetryR	*Poetry Review*
PoetryW	*Poetry Wales*
POMPA	*Publications of the Mississippi Philological Association*
PostS	*Post Script: Essays in Film and the Humanities*
PoT	*Poetics Today*
PP	Penguin Passnotes
PP	*Philologica Pragensia*
PPMRC	*Proceedings of the International Patristic, Mediaeval and Renaissance Conference*
PPR	*Philosophy and Phenomenological Research*
PQ	*Philological Quarterly*
PQM	*Pacific Quarterly* (Moana)
PR	*Partisan Review*

Pragmatics	*Pragmatics: Quarterly Publication of the International Pragmatics Association*
PrairieF	*Prairie Fire*
Praxis	*Praxis: A Journal of Cultural Criticism*
Prépub	*(Pré)publications*
PRev	*The Powys Review*
PRIA	*Proceedings of the Royal Irish Academy*
PRIAA	Publications of the Research Institute of the Abo Akademi Foundation
PRMCLS	*Papers from the Regional Meetings of the Chicago Linguistics Society*
Prospects	*Prospects: An Annual Journal of American Cultural Studies*
Prospero	*Prospero: Journal of New Thinking in Philosophy for Education*
Proteus	*Proteus: A Journal of Ideas*
Proverbium	*Proverbium: Yearbook of International Proverb Society*
PrS	*The Prairie Schooner*
PSt	*Prose Studies*
PsychR	*Psychological Reports*
PTBI	Publications of the Sir Thomas Browne Institute
PubH	*Publishing History*
PULC	*Princeton University Library Chronicle*
PURBA	*Panjab University Research Bulletin (Arts)*
PVR	*Platte Valley Review*
PWC	Pickering's Women's Classics
PY	*Phonology Yearbook*
QI	*Quaderni d'Italianistica*
QJS	*Quarterly Journal of Speech*
QLing	*Quantitative Linguistics*
QQ	*Queen's Quarterly*
Quadrant	*Quadrant* (Sydney)
Quarendo	*Quarendo*
Quarry	*Quarry*
RadP	*Radical Philosophy*
RAL	*Research in African Literatures*
RALS	*Resources for American Literary Study*
Ramus	*Ramus: Critical Studies in Greek and Roman Literature*
R&L	*Religion and Literature*
Raritan	*Raritan: A Quarterly Review*
Rask	*Rask: International tidsskrift for sprog og kommunikation*
RB	*Revue Benedictine*
RBPH	*Revue Belge de Philologie et d'Histoire*
RCEI	*Revista Canaria de Estudios Ingleses*
RCF	*Review of Contemporary Fiction*
RDN	*Renaissance Drama Newsletter*
RE	*Revue d'Esthétique*
ReAL	*Re: Artes Liberales*
REALB	*REAL: The Yearbook of Research in English and American Literature* (Berlin)

RECTR	*Restoration and Eighteenth-Century Theatre Research*
RedL	*Red Letters: A Journal of Cultural Politics*
REED	Records of Early English Drama
REEDN	*Records of Early English Drama Newsletter*
Reinardus	*Reinardus*
REL	*Review of English Literature* (Kyoto)
Ren&R	*Renaissance and Reformation*
Renascence	*Renascence: Essays on Value in Literature*
RenD	*Renaissance Drama*
RenP	*Renaissance Papers*
RenQ	*Renaissance Quarterly*
Rep	*Representations*
RES	*The Review of English Studies*
Restoration	*Restoration: Studies in English Literary Culture, 1660–1700*
Rev	*Review* (Blacksburg, Va.)
RevAli	*Revista Alicantina de Estudios Ingleses*
Revels	Revels Plays
RevelsCL	Revels Plays Companion Library
RevR	Revolution and Romanticism, 1789–1834
RFEA	*Revue Française d'Etudes Américaines*
RFR	*Robert Frost Review*
RH	*Recusant History*
Rhetorica	*Rhetorica: A Journal of the History of Rhetoric*
Rhetorik	*Rhetorik: Ein Internationales Jahrbuch*
RHist	*Rural History*
RHL	*Revue d'Histoire Littéraire de la France*
RHT	*Revue d'Histoire du Théâtre*
Ricardian	*The Ricardian: Journal of the Richard III Society*
RL	Rereading Literature
RLC	*Revue de Littérature Comparée*
RLM	*La Revue des Lettres Modernes: Histoire des Idées des Littératures*
RLMC	*Rivista di Letterature Moderne e Comparate*
RLT	*Russian Literature Triquarterly*
RM	*Rethinking Marxism*
RMR	*Rocky Mountain Review of Language and Literature*
RM	*Renaissance and Modern Studies*
RMSt	*Reading Medieval Studies*
RomN	*Romance Notes*
RomQ	*Romance Quarterly*
RomS	*Romance Studies*
ROO	*Room of One's Own: A Feminist Journal of Literature and Criticism*
RORD	*Research Opportunities in Renaissance Drama*
RPT	Russian Poetics in Translation
RQ	*Riverside Quarterly*
RR	*Romanic Review*
RRDS	Regents Renaissance Drama Series
RRestDS	Regents Restoration Drama Series

RS	*Renaissance Studies*
RSQ	*Rhetoric Society Quarterly*
RUO	*Revue de l'Université d'Ottawa*
RuskN	*Ruskin Newsletter*
RUUL	*Reports from the Uppsala University Department of Linguistics*
SAC	*Studies in the Age of Chaucer*
SAD	*Studies in American Drama, 1945–Present*
SAF	*Studies in American Fiction*
Saga-Book	*Saga-Book (Viking Society for Northern Research)*
Sagetrieb	*Sagetrieb: A Journal Devoted to Poets in the Pound–H.D.–Williams Tradition*
SAJL	*Studies in American Jewish Literature*
Sal	*Salmagundi: A Quarterly of the Humanities and Social Sciences*
S&S	*Sight and Sound*
SAntS	*Studia Anthroponymica Scandinavica*
SAP	*Studia Anglica Posnaniensia*
SAQ	*South Atlantic Quarterly*
SAR	*Studies in the American Renaissance*
SARB	*South African Review of Books*
SatR	*Saturday Review*
SB	*Studies in Bibliography*
SBHC	*Studies in Browning and His Circle*
SC	*The Seventeenth Century*
Scan	*Scandinavica. An International Journal of Scandinavian Studies*
ScanS	*Scandinavian Studies*
SCel	*Studia Celtica*
SCER	*Society for Critical Exchange Report*
SCJ	*The Sixteenth Century Journal*
SCL	*Studies in Canadian Literature*
ScLJ	*Scottish Literary Journal: A Review of Studies in Scottish Language and Literature*
SCLJ(S)	*Scottish Literary Journal Supplement*
SCN	*Seventeenth-Century News*
ScottN	*Scott Newsletter*
SCR	*The South Carolina Review*
Screen	*Screen* (London)
SCRev	*South Central Review*
Scriblerian	*The Scriblerian and the Kit Cats: A Newsjournal Devoted to Pope, Swift, and Their Circle*
Scripsi	*Scripsi*
Scriptorium	*Scriptorium: International Review of Manuscript Studies*
SD	*Social Dynamics*
SDR	*South Dakota Review*
SECC	*Studies in Eighteenth-Century Culture*
SECOLR	*The SECOL Review: Southeastern Conference on Linguistics*
SED	*Survey of English Dialects*

SEEJ	*Slavic and East European Journal*
SEL	Studies in English Literature
SEL	*Studies in English Literature 1500–1900* (Rice Univ.)
SELing	*Studies in English Linguistics* (Tokyo)
SELit	*Studies in English Literature* (Tokyo)
SELL	*Studies in English Language and Literature*
Sem	*Semiotica: Journal of the International Association for Semiotic Studies*
Semiosis	*Semiosis: Internationale Zeitschrift für Semiotik und Ästhetik*
SER	*Studien zur Englischen Romantik*
Seven	*Seven: An Anglo-American Literary Review*
SF&R	Scholars' Facsimiles and Reprints
SFic	*Science Fiction: A Review of Speculative Literature*
SFNL	*Shakespeare on Film Newsletter*
SFQ	*Southern Folklore Quarterly*
SFR	*Stanford French Review*
SFS	*Science-Fiction Studies*
SH	*Studia Hibernica* (Dublin)
ShakB	*Shakespeare Bulletin*
ShakS	*Shakespeare Studies* (New York)
Shandean	*The Shandean*
Sh&Sch	*Shakespeare and Schools*
ShawR	*Shaw: The Annual of Bernard Shaw Studies*
Shenandoah	*Shenandoah*
SherHR	*Sherlock Holmes Review*
Shiron	*Shiron*
ShJE	*Shakespeare Jahrbuch* (Weimar)
ShJW	*Deutsche Shakespeare-Gesellschaft West Jahrbuch* (Bochum)
ShLR	*Shoin Literary Review*
ShN	*The Shakespeare Newsletter*
SHR	*Southern Humanities Review*
ShS	*Shakespeare Survey*
ShSA	*Shakespeare in Southern Africa*
ShStud	*Shakespeare Studies* (Tokyo)
SHW	*Studies in Hogg and his World*
ShY	*Shakespeare Yearbook*
SIcon	*Studies in Iconography*
Signs	*Signs: Journal of Women in Culture and Society*
SiHoLS	Studies in the History of the Language Sciences
SiM	*Studies in Medievalism*
SIM	*Studies in Music*
SiP	Shakespeare in Performance
SIR	*Studies in Romanticism*
SJS	*San José Studies*
SL	*Studia Linguistica*
SLang	*Studies in Language*
SLCS	Studies in Language Companion Series
SLitI	*Studies in the Literary Imagination*

SLJ	*Southern Literary Journal*
SLRev	*Stanford Literature Review*
SLSc	*Studies in the Linguistic Sciences*
SMC	Studies in Medieval Culture
SMed	*Studi Medievali*
SMELL	*Studies in Medieval English Language and Literature*
SMLit	*Studies in Mystical Literature* (Taiwan)
SMRH	*Studies in Medieval and Renaissance History*
SMS	*Studier i Modern Språkvetenskap*
SMy	*Studia Mystica*
SN	*Studia Neophilologica*
SNew	*Sidney Newsletter*
SNNTS	*Studies in the Novel* (North Texas State Univ.)
SOA	*Sydsvenska Ortnamnssällskapets Årsskrift*
SoAR	*South Atlantic Review*
Sociocrit	*Sociocriticism*
SocN	*Sociolinguistics*
SocT	*Social Text*
SohoB	Soho Bibliographies
SoQ	*The Southern Quarterly*
SoR	*The Southern Review* (Baton Rouge, La.)
SoRA	*Southern Review* (Adelaide)
SoSt	*Southern Studies: An Interdisciplinary Journal of the South*
Soundings	*Soundings: An Interdisciplinary Journal*
Southerly	*Southerly: A Review of Australian Literature*
SovL	*Soviet Literature*
SP	*Studies in Philology*
SPAN	*SPAN: Newsletter of the South Pacific Association for Commonwealth Literature and Language Studies*
SPAS	*Studies in Puritan American Spirituality*
SPC	*Studies in Popular Culture*
Spectrum	*Spectrum*
Speculum	*Speculum: A Journal of Medieval Studies*
SPELL	Swiss Papers in English Language and Literature
SphereHL	Sphere History of Literature
Sphinx	*The Sphinx: A Magazine of Literature and Society*
SpM	*Spicilegio Moderno*
SpNL	*Spenser Newsletter*
Sprachwiss	*Sprachwissenschaft*
SpringE	*Spring: The Journal of the E E Cummings Society*
SPub	*Studies in Publishing*
SPWVSRA	*Selected Papers from the West Virginia Shakespeare and Renaissance Association*
SQ	*Shakespeare Quarterly*
SR	*The Sewanee Review*
SRen	*Studies in the Renaissance*
SRSR	*Status Report on Speech Research* (Haskins Laboratories)
SSEL	Stockholm Studies in English

SSELER	Salzburg Studies in English Literature: Elizabethan and Renaissance
SSELJDS	Salzburg Studies in English Literature: Jacobean Drama Studies
SSELPDPT	Salzburg Studies in English Literature: Poetic Drama and Poetic Theory
SSELRR	Salzburg Studies in English Literature: Romantic Reassessment
SSEng	*Sydney Studies in English*
SSF	*Studies in Short Fiction*
SSL	*Studies in Scottish Literature*
SSt	*Spenser Studies*
SStud	*Swift Studies: The Annual of the Ehrenpreis Center*
Staffrider	*Staffrider*
STAH	*Strange Things Are Happening*
STC	*Short-Title Catalogue*
STGM	Studien und Texte zur Geistegeschichte des Mittelalters
StHum	*Studies in the Humanities*
StIn	*Studi Inglesi*
StLF	*Studi di Letteratura Francese*
StQ	*Steinbeck Quarterly*
StrR	*Structuralist Review*
StTCL	*Studies in Twentieth Century Literature*
Style	*Style* (De Kalb, Ill.)
SUAS	Stratford-upon-Avon Studies
SubStance	*SubStance: A Review of Theory and Literary Criticism*
SUS	*Susquehanna University Studies*
SussexAC	*Sussex Archaeological Collections*
SVEC	*Studies on Voltaire and the Eighteenth Century*
SWPLL	*Sheffield Working Papers in Language and Linguistics*
SWR	*Southwest Review*
SwR	*The Swansea Review: A Journal of Criticism*
TA	*Theatre Annual*
Tabu	*Bulletin voor Taalwetenschap, Groningen*
Talisman	*Talisman*
T&C	*Text and Context*
T&L	*Translation and Literature*
T&P	*Text and Performance*
TAPS	*Transactions of the American Philosophical Society*
TCBS	*Transactions of the Cambridge Bibliographical Society*
TCE	*Texas College English*
TCL	*Twentieth Century Literature*
TCS	*Theory, Culture and Society: Explorations in Critical Social Science*
TCWAAS	*Transactions of the Cumberland and Westmorland Antiquarian and Archaeological Society*
TD	*Themes in Drama*
TDR	*The Drama Review*
TEAS	Twayne's English Authors Series
TEBS	*Edinburgh Bibliographical Society Transactions*

Telos	*Telos: A Quarterly Journal of Post-Critical Thought*
TenEJ	*Tennessee English Journal*
Te Reo	*Te Reo: Journal of the Linguistic Society of New Zealand*
Text	*Text: Transactions of the Society for Textual Scholarship*
TH	*Texas Humanist*
THA	*Thomas Hardy Annual*
Thalia	*Thalia: Studies in Literary Humor*
ThC	*Theatre Crafts*
Theater	*Theater*
TheatreS	*Theatre Studies*
Theoria	*Theoria: A Journal of Studies in the Arts, Humanities and Social Sciences* (Natal)
THES	*The Times Higher Education Supplement*
Thesis	*Thesis Eleven*
THIC	*Theatre History in Canada*
THJ	*The Thomas Hardy Journal*
ThN	*Thackeray Newsletter*
ThoreauQ	*The Thoreau Quarterly: A Journal of Literary and Philosophical Studies*
Thought	*Thought: A Review of Culture and Ideas*
Thph	*Theatrephile*
ThreR	*The Threepenny Review*
ThS	*Theatre Survey: The American Journal of Theatre History*
THSLC	*Transactions of the Historic Society of Lancashire and Cheshire*
THStud	*Theatre History Studies*
THY	*The Thomas Hardy Yearbook*
TiLSM	Trends in Linguistics Studies and Monographs
TJ	*Theatre Journal*
TJS	Transactions (The Johnson Society)
TkR	*Tamkang Review*
TL	*Theoretical Linguistics*
TLR	*The Linguistic Review*
TLS	*TLS: The Times Literary Supplement*
TMLT	Toronto Medieval Latin Texts
TMS	Twayne's Masterwork Studies
TN	*Theatre Notebook*
TNWSECS	*Transactions of the North West Society for Eighteenth Century Studies*
TP	*Terzo Programma*
TPLL	*Tilbury Papers in Language and Literature*
TPr	*Textual Practice*
TPS	*Transactions of the Philological Society*
TR	*Theatre Record*
Traditio	*Traditio: Studies in Ancient and Medieval History, Thought, and Religion*
Transition	*Transition*
TRB	*The Tennyson Research Bulletin*
TRHS	*Transactions of the Royal Historical Society*

TRI	*Theatre Research International*
TriQ	*TriQuarterly*
Trivium	*Trivium*
Tropismes	*Tropismes*
TSAR	*The Toronto South Asian Review*
TSB	*Thoreau Society Bulletin*
TSL	*Tennessee Studies in Literature*
TSLang	Typological Studies in Language
TSLL	*Texas Studies in Literature and Language*
TSWL	*Tulsa Studies in Women's Literature*
TTR	*Trinidad and Tobago Review*
TUSAS	Twayne's United States Authors Series
TWAS	Twayne's World Authors Series
TWBR	*Third World Book Review*
TWQ	*Third World Quarterly*
TWR	*The Thomas Wolfe Review*
TYDS	*Transactions of the Yorkshire Dialect Society*
UCrow	*The Upstart Crow*
UCTSE	*University of Cape Town Studies in English*
UCWPL	*UCL Working Papers in Linguistics*
UDR	*University of Dayton Review*
UE	*The Use of English*
UEAPL	*UEA Papers in Linguistics*
UES	*Unisa English Studies*
Ufahamu	*Ufahamu*
ULR	*University of Leeds Review*
UMSE	*University of Mississippi Studies in English*
Untold	*Untold*
UOQ	*University of Ottawa Quarterly*
URM	*Ultimate Reality and Meaning: Interdisciplinary Studies in the Philosophy of Understanding*
USSE	*University of Saga Studies in English*
UtopSt	*Utopian Studies*
UTQ	*University of Toronto Quarterly*
UWR	*The University of Windsor Review*
VCT	Les Voies de la Création Théâtrale
VEAW	Varieties of English around the World
Verbatim	*Verbatim: The Language Quarterly*
VIA	*VIA: The Journal of the Graduate School of Fine Arts, University of Pennsylvania*
Viator	*Viator: Medieval and Renaissance Studies*
Views	*Viennese English Working Papers*
VIJ	*Victorians Institute Journal*
VLC	*Victorian Literature and Culture*
VN	*Victorian Newsletter*
Voices	*Voices*
VP	*Victorian Poetry*
VPR	*Victorian Periodicals Review*
VQR	*The Virginia Quarterly Review*
VR	*Victorian Review*

VS	*Victorian Studies*
VSB	*Victorian Studies Bulletin*
VWM	*Virginia Woolf Miscellany*
WAJ	*Women's Art Journal*
WAL	*Western American Literature*
W&I	*Word and Image*
W&L	*Women and Literature*
W&Lang	*Women and Language*
Wasafiri	*Wasafiri*
WascanaR	*Wascana Review*
WBEP	Wiener Beiträge zur Englischen Philologie
WC	World's Classics
WC	*The Wordsworth Circle*
WCR	*West Coast Review*
WCSJ	*Wilkie Collins Society Journal*
WCWR	*The William Carlos Williams Review*
Wellsian	*The Wellsian: The Journal of the H. G. Wells Society*
WEn	*World Englishes*
Westerly	*Westerly: A Quarterly Review*
WestHR	*West Hills Review: A Walt Whitman Journal*
WF	*Western Folklore*
WHASN	*W H Auden Society Newsletter*
WHR	*Western Humanities Review*
WLT	*World Literature Today*
WLWE	*World Literature Written in English*
WMQ	*The William and Mary Quarterly*
WoHR	*Women's History Review*
Women	*Women: A Cultural Review*
WorcesterR	*Worcester Review*
Word	*WORD: Journal of the International Linguistic Association*
WQ	*The Wilson Quarterly*
WRB	*Women's Review of Books*
WS	*Women's Studies: An Interdisciplinary Journal*
WSIF	*Women's Studies International Forum*
WSJour	*The Wallace Stevens Journal*
WTJ	*The Westminster Theological Journal*
WTW	Writers and Their Work
WVUPP	*West Virginia University Philological Papers*
WW	*Women Writers 1500–1900*
WWR	*Walt Whitman Quarterly Review*
XUS	*Xavier Review*
YCC	*Yearbook of Comparative Criticism*
YeA	*Yeats Annual*
YER	*Yeats Eliot Review*
YES	*The Yearbook of English Studies*
YEuS	*Yearbook of European Studies/Annuaire d'Etudes Européenes*
YFS	*Yale French Studies*
Yiddish	*Yiddish*

YJC	*The Yale Journal of Criticism: Interpretation in the Humanities*
YLS	*Yearbook of Langland Studies*
YM	*Yearbook of Morphology*
YNS	York Note Series
YPL	*York Papers in Linguistics*
YR	*The Yale Review*
YULG	*Yale University Library Gazette*
YWES	*The Year's Work in English Studies*
ZAA	*Zeitschrift für Anglistik und Amerikanistik*
ZCP	*Zeitschrift für Celtische Philologie*
ZDA	*Zeitschrift für Deutsches Altertum und Deutsche Literatur*
ZDL	*Zeitschrift für Dialektologie und Linguistik*
ZGKS	*Zeitschrift der Gesellschaft für Kanada-Studien*
ZGL	*Zeitschrift für Germanistische Linguistik*
ZPSK	*Zeitschrift für Phonetik, Sprachwissenschaft und Kommunikationsforschung*
ZSpr	*Zeitschrift für Sprachwissenschaft*
ZVS	*Zeitschrift für Vergleichende Sprachforschung*

Volume numbers are supplied in the text, as are individual issue numbers for journals that are not continuously paginated through the year.

2. Publishers

AAAH	Acta Academiae Åboensis Humaniora, Åbo, Finland
AAH	Australian Academy of Humanities
A&B	Allison & Busby, London
A&R	Angus & Robertson, North Ryde, N.S.W.
A&U	Allen & Unwin (now Unwin Hyman)
A&UA	Allen & Unwin, North Sydney, N.S.W.
A&W	Almqvist & Wiksell International, Stockholm
AarhusUP	Aarhus UP, Aarhus, Denmark
Abbeville	Abbeville Press, New York
ABC	ABC Enterprises
ABDO	Association Bourguignonne de Dialectologie et d'Onomastique, Dijon
AberdeenUP	Aberdeen UP, Aberdeen
Abhinav	Abhinav Pubns, New Delhi
Abingdon	Abingdon Press, Nashville, Tenn.
ABL	Armstrong Browning Library, Waco, Texas
Ablex	Ablex Pub., Norwood, N.J.
Åbo	Åbo Akademi, Åbo, Finland
Abrams	Harry N. Abrams, New York
Academia	Academia Press, Melbourne
Academic	Academic Press, London and Orlando, Fla.
Academy	The Academy Press, Dublin
AcademyC	Academy Chicago Pubs., Chicago
AcademyE	Academy Editions, London
Acadiensis	Acadiensis Press, Fredericton, New Brunswick, Canada
ACarS	Association for Caribbean Studies, Coral Gables, Fla.
ACC	Antique Collectors' Club, Woodbridge, Suffolk
ACCO	ACCO, Leuven, Belgium
ACP	Another Chicago Press, Chicago
ACS	Association for Canadian Studies, Ottawa
Adam Hart	Adam Hart Publishers Ltd, London
Addison-Wesley	Addison-Wesley, Wokingham, Berks.
Adosa	Adosa, Clermont-Ferrand, France
AEMS	American Early Medieval Studies
AF	Akademisk Forlag, Copenhagen
Affiliated	Affiliated East-West Press, New Delhi
AFP	Associated Faculty Press, New York
Africana	Africana Pub., New York
A-H	Arnold-Heinemann, New Delhi
Ahriman	Ahriman-Verlag, Freiburg im Breisgau, Germany
AIAS	Australian Institute of Aboriginal Studies, Canberra
Ajanta	Ajanta Pubns, Delhi
AK	Akadémiai Kiadó, Budapest
Al&Ba	Allyn & Bacon, Boston, Mass.
Albatross	Albatross
Albion	Albion, Appalachian State Univ., Boone, N.C.
Alderman	Alderman Press, London
AligarhMU	Aligarh Muslim Univ., Uttar Pradesh, India

Alioth	Alioth Press, Beaverton, Oreg.
Allen	W. H. Allen, London
Allied Publishers	Allied Indian Publishers, Lahore
Almond	Almond Press, Sheffield
AM	Aubier Montaigne, Paris
AMAES	Association des Médiévistes Angliciste de l'Enseignement Supérieur, Paris
Amate	The Amate Press, Oxford
AmberL	Amber Lane, Oxford
AMP	Aurora Metro Press, London
AMS	AMS Press, New York
Amsterdam	Amsterdam
AMU	Adam Mickiewicz Univ., Posnan
Anansi	Anansi Press, Toronto
Anma Libri	Anma Libri, Saratoga, Calif.
Antipodes	Antipodes Press, Plimmerton, New Zealand
Anvil	Anvil Press Poetry, London
APA	APA, Maarssen, Netherlands
APH	Associated Pub. House, New Delhi
APL	American Poetry and Literature Press, Philadelphia
APP	Australian Professional Pubns, Mosman, N.S.W.
Appletree	Appletree Press, Belfast
APS	American Philosophical Society, Philadelphia
Aquarian	The Aquarian Press, Wellingborough, Northants
ArborH	Arbor House Pub., New York
Archon	Archon Books, Hamden, Conn.
ArchP	Architectural Press Books, Guildford, Surrey
Ardis	Ardis Pubs., Ann Arbor, Mich.
Ariel	Ariel Press, London
Ark	Ark Paperbacks, London
Arkona	Arkona Forlaget, Aarhus, Denmark
Arlington	Arlington Books, London
Arnold	Edward Arnold, London
ArnoldEJ	E. J. Arnold & Son, Leeds
ARP	Australian Reference Pubns, N. Balwyn, Vic.
Arrow	Arrow Books, London
Artmoves	Artmoves, Parkdale, Victoria
ASB	Anglo-Saxon Books, Middlesex
ASECS	American Society for Eighteenth-Century Studies, c/o Ohio State Univ., Columbus
AshfieldP	Ashfield Press, London
Ashton	Ashton Scholastic
Aslib	Aslib, London
ASLS	Association for Scottish Literary Studies, Aberdeen
ASU	Arizona State Univ., Tempe
Atheneum	Atheneum Pubs., New York
Athlone	Athlone Press, London
Atlas	Atlas Press, London
Attic	Attic Press, Dublin
AucklandUP	Auckland UP, Auckland

AUG	Acta Universitatis Gothoburgensis, Sweden
AUP	Associated Univ. Presses, London and Toronto
AUPG	Academic & Univ. Pubs. Group, London
Aurum	Aurum Press, London
Auslib	Auslib Press, Adelaide
AUU	Acta Universitatis Umensis, Umeå, Sweden
AUUp	Acta Universitatis Upsaliensis, Uppsala
Avebury	Avebury Pub., Aldershot, Hampshire
Avero	Avero Pubns, Newcastle upon Tyne
A-V Verlag	A-V Verlag, Franz Fischer, Augsburg, Germany
AWP	Africa World Press, Trenton, N.J.
Axelrod	Axelrod Publishing Co., Tampa Bay, Fla.
BA	British Academy, London
BAAS	British Association for American Studies, c/o Univ. of Keele
Bagel	August Bagel Verlag, Dusseldorf
Bahri	Bahri Pubns, New Delhi
Bamberger	Bamberger Books, Flint, Mich.
B&B	Boydell & Brewer, Woodbridge, Suffolk
B&J	Barrie & Jenkins, London
B&N	Barnes & Noble, Totowa, N.J.
B&O	Burns & Oates, Tunbridge Wells, Kent
B&S	Michael Benskin and M. L. Samuels, Middle English Dialect Project, Univ. of Edinburgh
BAR	British Archaeological Reports, Oxford
Barn Owl	Barn Owl Books, Taunton, Somerset
Barnes	A. S. Barnes, San Diego, Calif.
BathUP	Bath UP, Bath
Batsford	B. T. Batsford, London
BBC	BBC Pubns, London
BClarkL	Bruccoli Clark Layman
BCP	Bristol Classical Press, Bristol
Beacon	Beacon Press, Boston, Mass.
Beck	C. H. Beck'sche Verlagsbuchandlung, Munich
Becket	Becket Pubns, London
Belin	Editions Belin, Paris
Belknap	Belknap Press, Cambridge, Mass.
Belles Lettres	Société d'Edition les Belles Lettres, Paris
Bellew	Bellew Pub., London
Bellflower	Bellflower Press, Case Univ., Cleveland, Ohio
Benjamins	John Benjamins, Amsterdam
BenjaminsNA	John Benjamins North America, Philadelphia
BennC	Bennington College, Bennington, Vt.
Berg	Berg Pubs., Oxford
BFI	British Film Institute, London
BGUP	Bowling Green Univ. Popular Press, Bowling Green, Ohio
BibS	Bibliographical Society, London
Bilingual	Bilingual Press, Arizona State Univ., Tempe
Bingley	Clive Bingley, London

Binnacle	Binnacle Press, London
Biografia	Biografia Pubs., London
Birkbeck	Birkbeck College, University of London
Bishopsgate	Bishopsgate Press, Tonbridge, Kent
BL	British Library, London
Black	Adam & Charles Black, London
Black Cat	Black Cat Press, Blackrock, Eire
Blackie	Blackie & Son, Glasgow
Black Moss	Black Moss, Windsor, Ont.
Blackstaff	Blackstaff Press, Belfast
Black Swan	Black Swan, Curtin, Utah
Blackwell	Basil Blackwell, Oxford
BlackwellR	Blackwell Reference, Oxford
Blackwood	Blackwood, Pillans & Wilson, Edinburgh
Bl&Br	Blond & Briggs, London
Blandford	Blandford Press, London
Blaue Eule	Verlag die Blaue Eule, Essen
Bloodaxe	Bloodaxe Books, Newcastle upon Tyne
Bloomsbury	Bloomsbury Pub., London
Blubber Head	Blubber Head Press, Hobart
BM	Bobbs-Merrill, New York
BMP	British Museum Pubns, London
Bodleian	The Bodleian Library, Oxford
Bodley	The Bodley Head, London
Bogle	Bogle L'Ouverture Pubns, London
BoiseSUP	Boise State UP, Boise, Idaho
Book Guild	The Book Guild, Lewes, E. Sussex
Borealis	Borealis Press, Ottawa
Borgo	Borgo Press, San Bernardino, Calif.
BostonAL	Boston Athenaeum Library, Boston, Mass.
Bouma	Bouma's Boekhuis, Groningen, Netherlands
Bowker	R. R. Bowker, New Providence, N.J.
Boyars	Marion Boyars, London and Boston, Mass.
Boydell	The Boydell Press, Woodbridge, Suffolk
Boyes	Megan Boyes, Allestree, Derbyshire
Bran's Head	Bran's Head Books, Frome, Somerset
Braumüller	Wilhelm Braumüller, Vienna
Breakwater	Breakwater Books, St John's, Newfoundland
Brentham	Brentham Press, St Albans, Herts.
Brepols	Brepols, Turnhout, Belgium
Brewer	D. S. Brewer, Woodbridge, Suffolk
Brewin	Brewin Books, Studley, War.
Bridge	Bridge Pub., S. Plainfield, N.J.
Brill	E. J. Brill, Leiden
Brilliance	Brilliance Books, London
Broadview	Broadview, London, Ont. and Lewiston, N.Y.
Brookside	Brookside Press, London
Browne	Sinclair Browne, London
Brownstone	Brownstone Books, Madison, Ind.
BrownUP	Brown UP, Providence, R.I.

Brynmill	Brynmill Press, Harleston, Norfolk
BSA	Bibliographical Society of America
BSB	Black Swan Books, Redding Ridge, Conn.
BSP	Black Sparrow Press, Santa Barbara, Calif.
BSU	Ball State Univ., Muncie, Ind.
BuckUP	Bucknell UP, Lewisburg, Pa.
Bulzoni	Bulzoni Editore, Rome
Burnett	Burnett Books, London
Buske	Helmut Buske, Hamburg
Butterfly	Butterfly
CA	Creative Arts Book Co., Berkeley, Calif.
CAAS	Connecticut Academy of Arts and Sciences, New Haven
Cadmus	Cadmus Editions, Tiburon, Calif.
Cairns	Francis Cairns, Univ. of Leeds
Calaloux	Calaloux Pubns, Ithaca, N.Y.
Calder	John Calder, London
CALLS	Centre for Australian Language and Literature Studies, English Department, UNewE, N.S.W.
Camden	Camden Press, London
C&G	Carroll & Graf, New York
C&W	Chatto & Windus, London
Canongate	Canongate Pub., Edinburgh
Canterbury	Canterbury Press, Norwich
Cape	Jonathan Cape, London
Capra	Capra Press, Santa Barbara, Calif.
Carcanet	The Carcanet New Press, Manchester
Cardinal	Cardinal, London
CaribB	Caribbean Books, Parkersburg, Iowa
CarletonUP	Carleton UP, Ottawa
Carucci	Carucci, Rome
Cass	Frank Cass, London
Cassell	Cassell, London
Cavaliere Azzurro	Cavaliere Azzurro, Bologna
Cave	Godfrey Cave Associates, London
CBA	Council for British Archaeology, London
CBS	Cambridge Bibliographical Society, Cambridge
CCP	Canadian Children's Press, Guelph, Ont.
CCS	Centre for Canadian Studies, Mount Allison Univ., Sackville, N.B.
CDSH	Centre de Documentation Sciences Humaines, Paris
CENS	Centre for English Name Studies, University of Nottingham
Century	Century Pub., London
Ceolfrith	Ceolfrith Press, Sunderland, Tyne and Wear
CESR	Société des Amis du Centre d' Etudes Superieures de la Renaissance, Tours
CFA	Canadian Federation for the Humanities, Ottawa
CH	Croom Helm, London
C-H	Chadwyck-Healey, Cambridge
Chambers	W. & R. Chambers, Edinburgh

Champaign	Champaign Public Library and Information Center, Champaign, Ill.
Champion	Librairie Honoré Champion, Paris
Chand	S. Chand, Madras
ChelseaH	Chelsea House Pubs., New York, New Haven, and Philadelphia
Children's Lit. Association	Children's Literature Association
Christendom	Christendom Pubns, Front Royal, Va.
Chronicle	Chronicle Books, London
Chrysalis	Chrysalis Press
ChuoUL	Chuo Univ. Library, Tokyo
Churchman	Churchman Pub., Worthing, W. Sussex
Cistercian	Cistercian Pubns, Kalamazoo, Mich.
CL	City Lights Books, San Francisco
CLA	Canadian Library Association, Ottawa
Clarendon	Clarendon Press, Oxford
Claridge	Claridge, St Albans, Herts.
Clarion	Clarion State College, Clarion, Pa.
Clark	T. & T. Clark, Edinburgh
Clarke	James Clarke, Cambridge
Classical	Classical Pub., New Delhi
CLCS	Centre for Language and Communication Studies, Trinity College, Dublin
ClogherHS	Clogher Historical Society, Monaghan, Eire
Clunie	Clunie Press, Pitlochry, Tayside
CMAP	Caxton's Modern Arts Press, Dallas, Tx.
CMERS	Center for Medieval and Early Renaissance Studies, Binghamton, N.Y.
CML	William Andrews Clark Memorial Library, Los Angeles
CMST	Centre for Medieval Studies, Univ. of Toronto
Coach House	Coach House Press, Toronto
Colleagues	Colleagues Press, East Lansing, Mich.
Collector	The Collector Ltd, London
College-Hill	College-Hill Press, San Diego, Calif.
Collins	William Collins Sons, London
CollinsA	William Collins (Australia), Sydney
Collins & Brown	Collins & Brown, London
ColUP	Columbia UP, New York
Comedia	Comedia Pub. Group, London
Comet	Comet Books, London
Compton	The Compton Press, Tisbury, Wilts
Constable	Constable, London
Contemporary	Contemporary Books, Chicago
Continuum	Continuum Pub., New York
Copp	Copp Clark Pitman, Mississuaga, Ont.
Corgi	Corgi Books, London
CorkUP	Cork UP, Cork, Eire
Cormorant	Cormorant Press, Victoria, B.C.
CornUP	Cornell UP, Ithaca, N.Y.

Cornwallis	The Cornwallis Press, Hastings, E. Sussex
Coronado	Coronado Press, Lawrence, Kansas
Cosmo	Cosmo Pubns, New Delhi
Coteau	Coteau Books, Regina, Saskatchewan
Cowley	Cowley Pubns, Cambridge, Mass.
Cowper	Cowper House, Pacific Grove, Calif.
CPP	Canadian Poetry Press, London, Ont.
Crabtree	Crabtree Press, Sussex
Creag Darach	Creag Darach Publications, Stirling
Cresset	Cresset Library, London
CRNLE	Centre for Research in the New Literatures in English, Adelaide
Crossing	The Crossing Press, Freedom, Calif.
Crossroad	Crossroad Pub., New York
Crown	Crown Pubs., New York
Crowood	The Crowood Press, Marlborough, Wilts
CSAL	Centre for Studies in Australian Literature, Univ. of Western Australia, Nedlands
CSLI	Center for the Study of Language and Information, Stanford Univ.
CSU	Cleveland State Univ., Cleveland, Ohio
CTHS	Editions du Comité des Travaux Historiques et Scientifiques, Paris
CUAP	Catholic Univ. of America Press, Washington, D.C.
Cuff	Harry Cuff Pubns, St John's, Newfoundland
CULouvain	Catholic Univ. of Louvain, Belgium
CULublin	Catholic Univ. of Lublin, Poland
CUP	Cambridge UP, Cambridge, New York, and Melbourne
Currency	Currency Press, Paddington, N.S.W.
Currey	James Currey, London
CV	Cherry Valley Editions, Rochester, N.Y.
CVK	Cornelson-Velhagen & Klasing, Berlin
CWU	Carl Winter Universitätsverlag, Heidelberg
Da Capo	Da Capo Press, New York
Dacorum	Dacorum College, Hemel Hempstead, Herts
Daisy	Daisy Books, Peterborough, Northants
Dalkey	Dalkey Archive Press, Elmwood Park, Ill.
D&C	David & Charles, Newton Abbot, Devon
D&H	Duncker and Humblot, Berlin
D&M	Douglas & McIntyre, Vancouver, B.C.
Dangaroo	Dangaroo Press, Mundelstrup, Denmark
Dawson	Dawson Publishing, Folkestone, Kent
DBAP	Daphne Brasell Associates Press
DBP	Drama Book Pubs., New York
De Boeck	De Boeck-Wesmael, Brussels
Dee	Dee
De Graaf	De Graaf, Nierwkoup, Netherlands
Denoël	Denoël S.A.R.L, Paris
Dent	J. M. Dent, London
DentA	Dent, Ferntree Gully, Vic., Australia

Depanee	Depanee Printers and Pubs., Nugegoda, Sri Lanka
Deutsch	André Deutsch, London
Didier	Didier Erudition, Paris
Diesterweg	Verlag Moritz Diesterweg, Frankfurt-on-Main
Dim Gray Bar Press	Dim Gray Bar Press
Doaba	Doaba House, Delhi
Dobby	Eric Dobby Publishing Ltd, St Albans
Dobson	Dobson Books, Durham
Dolmen	Dolmen Press, Portlaoise, Eire
Donald	John Donald, Edinburgh
Donker	Adriaan Donker, Johannesburg
Dorset	Dorset Publishing Company
Doubleday	Doubleday, London and New York
Dove	Dove, Sydney
Dovecote	Dovecote
Dovehouse	Dovehouse Editions, Canada
Dover	Dover Pubns, New York
Drew	Richard Drew, Edinburgh
Droste	Droste Verlag, Düsseldorf
Droz	Librairie Droz S.A., Geneva
DublinUP	Dublin UP, Dublin
Duckworth	Gerald Duckworth, London
Duculot	J. Duculot, Gembloux, Belgium
DukeUP	Duke UP, Durham, N.C.
Dundurn	Dundurn Press, Toronto and London, Ont.
Duquesne	Duquesne UP, Pittsburgh
Dutton	E. P. Dutton, New York
DWT	Dr Williams's Trust, London
EA	The English Association, London
Eason	Eason & Son, Dublin
East Bay	East Bay Books, Berkeley, Calif.
Ebony	Ebony Books, Melbourne
Ecco	Ecco Press, New York
ECNRS	Editions du Centre National de la Recherche Scientifique, Paris
ECW	ECW Press, Downsview, Ont.
Eden	Eden Press, Montreal and St Albans, Vt.
EdinUP	Edinburgh UP, Edinburgh
Edizioni	Edizioni del Grifo, Lecce
Eerdmans	William Eerdmans, Grand Rapids, Mich.
EETS	Early English Text Society, c/o Exeter College, Oxford
Elephas	Elephas Books, Kewdale, Australia
Elm Tree	Elm Tree Books, London
ELS	English Literary Studies
Ember	Ember Press, Brixham, South Devon
EMSH	Editions de la Maison des Sciences de l'Homme, Paris
Enitharmon	Enitharmon Press, London
Enzyklopädie	Enzyklopädie, Leipzig
EONF	The Eugene O'Neill Foundation, Danville, Calif.
EPNS	English Place-Name Society, Beeston, Notts

Epworth	The Epworth Press, Manchester
Eriksson	Paul Eriksson, Middlebury, Vt.
Erlbaum	Erlbaum Associates, N.J.
Erskine	Erskine Press, Harleston, Norfolk
ESI	Edizioni Scientifiche Italiane, Naples
ESL	Edizioni di Storia e Letteratura, Rome
EUFS	Editions Universitaires Fribourg Suisse
EUL	Edinburgh Univ. Library, Edinburgh
Europa	Europa Pubns, London
Evans	M. Evans, New York
Exile	Exile Editions, Toronto, Ont.
Eyre	Eyre Methuen, London
FAB	Free Association Books, London
Faber	Faber & Faber, London
FAC	Fédération d'Activités Culturelles, Paris
FACP	Fremantle Arts Centre Press, Fremantle, W.A.
FALS	Foundation for Australian Literary Studies, James Cook Univ. of North Queensland, Townsville
F&F	Fels & Firn Press, San Anselmo, Calif.
F&S	Feffer & Simons, Amsterdam
Farrand	Farrand Press, London
Fay	Barbara Fay, Stuttgart
F-B	Ford-Brown, Houston, Texas
FDUP	Fairleigh Dickinson UP, Madison, N.J.
FE	Fourth Estate, London
Feminist	Feminist Press, New York
FictionColl	Fiction Collective, Brooklyn College, Brooklyn, N.Y.
Field Day	Field Day, Derry
Fifth House	Fifth House Publications, Saskatoon, Saskatchewan, Canada
FILEF	FILEF Italo-Australian Pubns, Leichhardt, N.S.W.
Fine	Donald Fine, New York
Fink	Fink Verlag, Munich
Flamingo	Flamingo
Flammarion	Flammarion, Paris
FlindersU	Flinders Univ. of South Australia, Bedford Park
FlorSU	Florida State Univ., Tallahassee, Fla.
FOF	Facts on File, New York
Folger	The Folger Shakespeare Library, Washington, D.C.
Folio	Folio Press, London
Fontana	Fontana Press, London
Footprint	Footprint Press, Colchester, Essex
FordUP	Fordham UP, New York
Foris	Foris Pubns, Dordrecht
Forsten	Egbert Forsten Pub., Groningen, Netherlands
Fortress	Fortress Press, Philadelphia
Francke	Francke Verlag, Berne
Franklin	Burt Franklin, New York
FreeP	Free Press, New York
FreeUP	Free UP, Amsterdam

Fremantle	Fremantle Arts Centre Press
Freundlich	Freundlich Books, New York
Frommann-Holzboog	Frommann-Holzboog, Stuttgart
FSP	Five Seasons Press, Madley, Hereford
FW	Fragments West/Valentine Press, Long Beach, Calif.
FWA	Fiji Writers' Association, Suva
FWP	Falling Wall Press, Bristol
Gale	Gale Research, Detroit, Mich.
Galilée	Galilée, Paris
Gallimard	Gallimard, Paris
G&B	Gordon and Breach, Amsterdam
G&G	Grevatt & Grevatt, Newcastle upon Tyne
G&M	Gill & Macmillan, Dublin
Garland	Garland Pub., New York
Gasson	Roy Gasson Associates, Wimborne, Dorset
Gateway	Gateway Editions, Washington, D.C.
Girasole	Edizioni del Girasole, Ravenna
GL	Goose Lane Editions, Fredericton, N.B.
GlasgowDL	Glasgow District Libraries, Glasgow
Gleerup	Gleerupska, Lund
Gliddon	Gliddon Books Pubs., Norwich
Gloger	Gloger Family Books, Portland, Oregon
GMP	GMP Pub., London
GMSmith	Gibbs M. Smith, Layton, Utah
Golden Dog	The Golden Dog, Ottawa
Gollancz	Victor Gollancz, London
Gomer	Gomer Press, Llandysul, Dyfed
GothU	Gothenburg Univ., Gothenburg
Gower	Gower Pub., Aldershot, Hants
Grafton	Grafton Books, London
Granta	Granta Publications, London
Granville	Granville Pub., London
Grasset	Grasset & Fasquelle, Paris
Grassroots	Grassroots, London
Graywolf	Graywolf Press, St Paul, Minn.
Greenhalgh	M. J. Greenhalgh, London
Greenhill	Greenhill Books, London
Greenwood	Greenwood Press, Westport, Conn.
Gregg	Gregg Publishing, Surrey
Greville	Greville Press, Warwick
Greymitre	Greymitre Books, London
Groos	Julius Groos Verlag, Heidelberg
Grove	Grove Press, New York
GRP	Greenfield Review Press, New York
Grüner	B. R. Grüner, Amsterdam
Gruyter	Walter de Gruyter, Berlin
Guernica	Guernica Editions, Montreal, Canada
Gulmohar	Gulmohar Press, Islamabad, Pakistan
Haggerston	Haggerston

HakluytS	Hakluyt Society, c/o British Library, London
Hale	Robert Hale, London
Hall	G. K. Hall, Boston, Mass.
Hambledon	Hambledon Press, London
H&I	Hale & Iremonger, Sydney
H&M	Holmes & Meier, London and New York
H&S	Hodder & Stoughton, London
H&SNZ	Hodder & Stoughton, Auckland
H&W	Hill & Wang, New York
Hansib	Hansib Pub., London
Hans Zell	Hans Zell
Harbour	Harbour Pub., Madeira Park, B.C.
Harman	Harman Pub. House, New Delhi
Harper	Harper & Row, New York
Harrap	Harrap, Edinburgh
HarvardUP	Harvard UP, Cambridge, Mass.
Harwood	Harwood Academic Publishers, Langhorne, Pa.
Hatje	Verlag Gerd Hatje, Germany
HBJ	Harcourt Brace Jovanovich, New York and London
HC	HarperCollins, London
Headline	Headline Book Pub., London
Heath	D. C. Heath, Lexington, Mass.
Heinemann	William Heinemann, London
HeinemannA	William Heinemann, St Kilda, Vic.
HeinemannC	Heinemann Educational Books, Kingston, Jamaica
HeninemannNg	Heinemann Educational Books, Nigeria
HeinemannNZ	Heinemann Pubs., Auckland (now Heinemann Reed)
HeinemannR	Heinemann Reed, Auckland
Helm	Christopher Helm, London
Herbert	Herbert Press, London
Hermitage	Hermitage Antiquarian Bookshop, Denver, Colorado
Hern	Nick Hern Books, London
Heyday	Heyday Books, Berkeley, Calif.
HH	Hamish Hamilton, London
Hilger	Adam Hilger, Bristol
HM	Harvey Miller, London
HMSO	HMSO, London
Hodge	A. Hodge, Penzance, Cornwall
Hogarth	Hogarth Press, London
Hong KongUP	Hong Kong UP, Hong Kong
Horwood	Ellis Horwood, Hemel Hempstead, Herts
HoughtonM	Houghton Mifflin, Boston, Mass.
Howard	Howard UP, Washington, D.C.
HRW	Holt, Rinehart & Winston, New York
Hudson	Hudson
Hueber	Max Hueber, Ismaning, Germany
HUL	Hutchinson Univ. Library, London
HullUP	Hull UP, Univ. of Hull
Humanities	Humanities Press, Atlantic Highlands, N.J.
Huntington	Huntington Library, San Marino, Calif.

Hutchinson	Hutchinson Books, London
HW	Harvester Wheatsheaf, Hemel Hempstead, Herts.
HWWilson	H. W. Wilson, New York
Hyland House	Hyland House Publishing, Victoria, Australia
Ian Henry	Ian Henry Pubns, Hornchurch, Essex
IAP	Irish Academic Press, Dublin
IBK	Innsbrucker Beiträge zur Kulturwissenschaft, Univ. of Innsbruck
ICA	Institute of Contemporary Arts, London
IHA	International Hopkins Association, Waterloo, Ont.
IJamaica	Institute of Jamaica Pubns, Kingston
Imago	Imago Imprint, New York
Imperial War Museum	Imperial War Museum Publications, London
IndUP	Indiana UP, Bloomington, Ind.
Inkblot	Inkblot Pubns, Berkeley, Calif.
IntUP	International Universities Press, New York
Inventions	Inventions Press, London
IonaC	Iona College, New Rochelle, N.Y.
IowaSUP	Iowa State UP, Ames, Iowa
IOWP	Isle of Wight County Press, Newport, Isle of Wight
IP	In Parenthesis, London
Ipswich	Ipswich Press, Ipswich, Mass.
ISI	ISI Press, Philadelphia
Italica	Italica Press, New York
IULC	Indiana Univ. Linguistics Club, Bloomington, Ind.
IUP	Indiana Univ. of Pennsylvania Press, Indiana, Pa.
Ivon	Ivon Pub. House, Bombay
Iwalewa-Haus	Iwalewa-Haus (University of Bayreuth)
Jacaranda	Jacaranda Wiley, Milton, Queensland
JadavpurU	Jadavpur Univ., Calcutta
James CookU	James Cook Univ. of North Queensland, Townsville
Jarrow	Parish of Jarrow, Tyne and Wear
Jesperson	Jesperson Press, St John's, Newfoundland
JHall	James Hall, Leamington Spa, Warwickshire
JHUP	Johns Hopkins UP, Baltimore, Md.
JIWE	JIWE Pubns, Univ. of Gulbarga, India
JLRC	Jack London Research Center, Glen Ellen, Calif.
Jonas	Jonas Verlag, Marburg, Germany
Joseph	Michael Joseph, London
Journeyman	The Journeyman Press, London
JT	James Thin, Edinburgh
Junction	Junction Books, London
Junius-Vaughan	The Junius-Vaughan Press, Fairview, N.J.
Jupiter	Jupiter Press, Lake Bluff, Ill.
JyväskyläU	Jyväskylä Univ., Jyväskylä, Finland
Kaibunsha	Kaibunsha, Tokyo
K&N	Königshausen & Neumann, Würzburg, Germany
K&W	Kaye & Ward, London
Kansai	Kansai Univ. of Foreign Studies, Osaka

Kardo	Kardo, Coatbridge, Scotland
Karia	Karia Press, London
Karnak	Karnak House, London
Karoma	Karoma Pubs., Ann Arbor, Mich.
KC	Kyle Cathie Ltd, London
KCL	King's College, London
Kegan Paul	Kegan Paul International, London
KeeleUP	Keele University Press
Kenkyu	Kenkyu-Sha, Tokyo
Kennikat	Kennikat Press, Port Washington, N.Y.
Kensal	Kensal Press, Oxford
KenyaLB	Kenya Literature Bureau, Nairobi
Kerosina	Kerosina Pubns, Worcester Park, Surrey
Kerr	Charles H. Kerr, Chicago
Kestrel	Viking Kestrel, London
K/H	Kendall/Hunt Pub., Dubuque, Iowa
Kingsley	J. Kingsley Publishers, London
Kingston	Kingston Pubs., Kingston, Jamaica
Kinseido	Kinseido, Tokyo
Klostermann	Vittorio Klostermann, Frankfurt-on-Main
Kluwer	Kluwer Academic Publications, Dordrecht
Knopf	Alfred A. Knopf, New York
Knowledge	Knowledge Industry Pubns, White Plains, N.Y.
Kraus	Kraus International Pubns, White Plains, N.Y.
KSUP	Kent State UP, Kent, Ohio
LA	Library Association, London
Lake View	Lake View Press, Chicago
LAm	Library of America, New York
Lancelot	Lancelot Press, Hantsport, N.S.
Landesman	Jay Landesman, London
L&W	Lawrence & Wishart, London
Lane	Allen Lane, London
Lang	Peter D. Lang, Frankfurt-on-Main and Berne
LATR	*Latin American Theatre Review,* Center of Latin American Studies
LC	Library of Congress, Washington, D.C.
LCP	Loras College Press, Dubuque, Iowa
LeedsUP	Leeds UP, Leeds
LehighUP	Lehigh University Press, Pennsylvania
LeicAE	University of Leicester, Dept of Adult Education
LeicsCC	Leicestershire County Council, Libraries and Information Service, Leicester
LeicUP	Leicester UP, Leicester
LeidenUP	Leiden UP, Leiden
Leopard's Head	Leopard's Head Press, Oxford
LeuvenUP	Leuven UP, Leuven, Belgium
Lexik	Lexik House, Cold Spring, N.Y.
LF	LiberFörlag, Stockholm
LH	Lund Humphries Pubs., London
Liberty	Liberty Classics, Indianapolis, Ind.

Libris	Libris, London
Liguori	Liguori, Naples
Limelight	Limelight Editions, New York
Lime Tree	Lime Tree Press, Octopus Publishing Group, London
LittleH	Little Hills Press, Burwood, N.S.W.
Liveright	Liveright Pub., New York
LiverUP	Liverpool UP, Liverpool
Livre de Poche	Le Livre de Poche, Paris
Llanerch	Llanerch Enterprises, Lampeter, Dyfed
Locust Hill	Locust Hill Press, West Cornwall, Conn.
Loewenthal	Loewenthal Press, New York
Longman	Longman Group, Harlow, Essex
LongmanC	Longman Caribbean, Harlow, Essex
LongmanF	Longman, France
LongmanNZ	Longman, Auckland
Longspoon	Longspoon Press, Univ. of Alberta, Edmonton
Lovell	David Lovell Publishing, Brunswick, Australia
Lowell	Lowell Press, Kansas City, Mo.
Lowry	Lowry Pubs., Johannesburg
LSUP	Louisiana State UP, Baton Rouge, La.
LundU	Lund Univ., Lund, Sweden
LUP	Loyola UP, Chicago
Lutterworth	Lutterworth Press, Cambridge
Lymes	Lymes Press, Newcastle, Staffs.
MAA	Medieval Academy of America, Cambridge, Mass.
Macmillan	Macmillan Pubs., London
MacmillanC	Macmillan Caribbean
Madison	Madison Books, Lanham, Md.
Madurai	Madurai Univ., Madurai, India
Maecenas	Maecenas Press, Iowa City, Iowa
Magabala	Magabala Books, Broome, W.A.
Mainstream	Mainstream Pub., Edinburgh
Maisonneuve	Maisonneuve Press, Washington, D.C.
Malone	Malone Society, c/o King's College, London
Malthouse	Malthouse Press
Mambo	Mambo Press, Gweru, Zimbabwe
ManCASS	Manchester Centre for Anglo-Saxon Studies, Univ. of Manchester
M&E	Macdonald & Evans, Estover, Plymouth, Devon
M&S	McClelland & Stewart, Toronto
Maney	W. S. Maney & Sons, Leeds
Mansell	Mansell Pub., London
Manufacture	La Manufacture, Lyons
ManUP	Manchester UP, Manchester
Mardaga	Mardaga
MarquetteUP	Marquette UP, Milwaukee, Wisc.
Marvell	The Marvell Press, Calstock, Cornwall
MB	Mitchell Beazley, London
McFarland	McFarland, Jefferson, N.C.
McG-QUP	McGill-Queen's UP, Montreal

McGraw-Hill	McGraw-Hill, New York
McIndoe	John McIndoe, Dunedin, New Zealand
McPheeG	McPhee Gribble Pubs., Fitzroy, Vic.
McPherson	McPherson, Kingston, N.Y.
Meany	P. D. Meany Pubs., Port Credit, Ont.
Meckler	Meckler Pub., Westport, Conn.
MelbourneUP	Melbourne UP, Carlton South, Vic.
Mellen	Edwin Mellen Press, Lewiston, N.Y.
MellenR	Mellen Research UP
MercerUP	Mercer UP, Macon, Ga.
Mercury	Mercury Press, Stratford, Ontario
Merlin	The Merlin Press, London
Methuen	Methuen, London
MethuenA	Methuen Australia, North Ryde, N.S.W.
MethuenC	Methuen, Toronto
Metro	Metro Pub., Auckland
Metzler	Metzler, Stuttgart
MGruyter	Mouton de Gruyter, Berlin, New York, and Amsterdam
MH	Michael Haag, London
MHRA	Modern Humanities Research Association, London
MI	Microforms International, Pergamon Press, Oxford
Micah	Micah Pubns, Marblehead, Mass.
MichSUP	Michigan State UP, East Lansing, Mich.
MidNAG	Mid Northumberland Arts Group, Ashington, Northumbria
Milestone	Milestone Pubns, Horndean, Hampshire
Millenium	Millenium Books, E. J. Dwyer Pty Ltd, Newtown, Australia
Millstream	Millstream Books, Bath
Milner	Milner, London
Minuit	Editions de Minuit, Paris
MIP	Medieval Institute Pubns, Western Michigan Univ., Kalamazoo
MITP	Massachusetts Institute of Technology Press, Cambridge, Mass.
MLA	Modern Language Association of America, New York
MlM	Multilingual Matters, Clevedon, North Somerset
MLP	Manchester Literary and Philosophical Society, Manchester
Monarch	Monarch Publications, Sussex
Moonraker	Moonraker Press, Bradford-on-Avon, Wilts.
Moorland	Moorland Pub., Ashbourne, Derbys.
Moreana	Moreana, Angers, France
MorganSU	Morgan State Univ., Baltimore, Md.
Morrow	William Morrow, New York
Mosaic	Mosaic Press, Oakville, Ont.
Motilal	Motilal Books, Oxford
Motley	Motley Press, Romsey, Hampshire
Mouton	Mouton Pubs, New York and Paris
Mowbray	A. R. Mowbray, Oxford

MR	Martin Robertson, Oxford
MRS	Medieval and Renaissance Society, North Texas State Univ., Denton
MRTS	MRTS, Binghamton, N.Y.
MSUP	Memphis State UP, Memphis, Tenn.
MtAllisonU	Mount Allison Univ., Sackville, N.B.
Mulini	Mulini Press, A.C.T.
Muller	Frederick Muller, London
MULP	McMaster University Library Press
Murray	John Murray, London
Mursia	Ugo Mursia, Milan
NAL	New American Library, New York
Narr	Gunter Narr Verlag, Tubingen
Nathan	Fernand Nathan, Paris
NBB	New Beacon Books, London
NBCAus	National Book Council of Australia, Melbourne
NCP	New Century Press, Durham
ND	New Directions, New York
NDT	Nottingham Drama Texts, c/o Univ. of Nottingham
NEL	New English Library, London
NELM	National English Literary Museum, Grahamstown, S. Africa
Nelson	Nelson Pubs., Melbourne
New Endeavour	New Endeavour Press
NeWest	NeWest Press, Edmonton, Alberta
New Horn	New Horn Press, Ibadan, Nigeria
New Island	New Island Press
NewIssuesP	New Issues Press, Western Michigan University
NH	New Horizon Press, Far Hills, N.J.
N-H	Nelson-Hall, Chicago
NHPC	North-Holland Pub., Amsterdam and New York
NIE	La Nuova Italia Editrice, Florence
Niemeyer	Max Niemeyer, Tübingen, Germany
Nightwood	Nightwood Editions, Toronto
NIUP	Northern Illinois UP, De Kalb, Ill.
NLA	National Library of Australia
NLB	New Left Books, London
NLC	National Library of Canada, Ottawa
NLP	New London Press, Dallas, Texas
NLS	National Library of Scotland, Edinburgh
NLW	National Library of Wales, Aberystwyth, Dyfed
Northcote	Northcote House Pubs., Plymouth
NortheasternU	Northeastern Univ., Boston, Mass.
NorthwesternUP	Northwestern UP, Evanston, Ill.
Norton	W. W. Norton, New York and London
NorUP	Norwegian University Press, Oslo
Novus	Novus Press, Oslo
NPF	National Poetry Foundation, Orono, Maine
NPG	National Portrait Gallery, London
NPP	North Point Press, Berkeley, Calif.

NSP	New Statesman Pub., New Delhi
NSU Press	Northern States Universities Press
NSWUP	New South Wales UP, Kensington, N.S.W.
NT	National Textbook, Lincolnwood, Ill.
NUC	Nipissing Univ. College, North Bay, Ont.
NUP	National Univ. Pubns, Millwood, N.Y.
NUU	New Univ. of Ulster, Coleraine
NWAP	North Waterloo Academic Press, Waterloo, Ont.
NWP	New World Perspectives, Montreal
NYPL	New York Public Library, New York
NYUP	New York UP, New York
O&B	Oliver & Boyd, Harlow, Essex
Oasis	Oasis Books, London
OBAC	Organization of Black American Culture, Chicago
Oberon	Oberon
O'Brien	The O'Brien Press, Dublin
OBS	Oxford Bibliographical Society, Bodleian Library, Oxford
Octopus	Octopus Books, London
OdenseUP	Odense UP, Odense
OE	Officina Edizioni, Rome
OEColl	Old English Colloquium, Berkeley, Calif.
Offord	John Offord Pubns, Eastbourne, E. Sussex
OhioUP	Ohio UP, Athens, Ohio
Oldcastle	Oldcastle Books, Harpenden, Herts.
Olms	Georg Olms, Hildesheim, Germany
Olschki	Leo S. Olschki, Florence
O'Mara	Michael O'Mara Books, London
Omnigraphics	Omnigraphics, Detroit, Mich.
Open Books	Open Books Pub, Wells, Somerset
OpenUP	Open UP, Buckingham and Philadelphia
OPP	Oxford Polytechnic Press, Oxford
Orbis	Orbis Books, London
Oriel	Oriel Press, Stocksfield, Northumb.
OrientUP	Oriental UP, London
Orwell	Orwell Press, Southwold, Suffolk
Oryx	Oryx Press, Phoenix, Ariz.
OSUP	Ohio State UP, Columbus, Ohio
OTP	Oak Tree Press, London
OUCA	Oxford University Committee for Archaeology, Oxford
OUP	Oxford UP, Oxford
OUPAm	Oxford UP Inc., New York
OUPAus	Oxford UP, Melbourne
OUPC	Oxford UP, Toronto
OUPI	Oxford UP, New Delhi
OUPNZ	Oxford UP, Auckland
OUPSA	Oxford UP Southern Africa, Cape Town
Outlet	Outlet Book Co., New York
Owen	Peter Owen, London
Owl	Owl

Pacifica	Press Pacifica, Kailua, Hawaii
Paget	Paget Press, Santa Barbara, Calif.
PAJ	PAJ Pubns, New York
Paladin	Paladin Books, London
Pan	Pan Books, London
PanAmU	Pan American Univ., Edinburgh, Texas
P&C	Pickering & Chatto, London
Pandion	Pandion Press, Capitola, Calif.
Pandora	Pandora Press, London
Pantheon	Pantheon Books, New York
ParagonH	Paragon House Pubs., New York
Parnassus	Parnassus Imprints, Hyannis, Mass.
Parousia	Parousia Pubns, London
Paternoster	Paternoster Press, Carlisle, Cumbria
Patten	Patten Press, Penzance
Paulist	Paulist Press, Ramsey, N.J.
Paupers	Paupers' Press, Nottingham
Pavilion	Pavilion Books, London
PBFA	Provincial Booksellers' Fairs Association, Cambridge
Peachtree	Peachtree Pubs., Atlanta, Ga.
Pearson	David Pearson, Huntingdon, Cambs.
Peepal Tree	Peepal Tree Books, Leeds
Peeters	Peeters Publishers and Booksellers, Leuven, Belgium
Pelham	Pelham Books, London
Pembridge	Pembridge Press, London
Pemmican	Pemmican Publications, Winnipeg, Canada
Penguin	Penguin Books, Harmondsworth, Middx.
PenguinA	Penguin Books, Ringwood, Vic.
PenguinNZ	Penguin Books, Auckland
Penkevill	The Penkevill Pub. Co., Greenwood, Fla.
Pentland	Pentland Press Ltd, Ely, Cambs.
Penumbra	Penumbra Press, Moonbeam, Ont.
People's	People's Pubns, London
Pergamon	Pergamon Press, Oxford
Permanent	Permanent Press, Sag Harbor, N.Y.
Perpetua	Perpetua Press, Oxford
Petton	Petton Books, Oxford
Pevensey	Pevensey Press, Newton Abbott, Devon
PH	Prentice-Hall, Englewood Cliffs, N.J.
Phaidon	Phaidon Press, London
PHI	Prentice-Hall International, Hemel Hempstead, Herts
PhilL	Philosophical Library, New York
Phillimore	Phillimore, Chichester
Piatkus	Piatkus Books, London
Pickwick	Pickwick Pubns, Allison Park, Pa.
Pilgrim	Pilgrim Books, Norman, Okla.
PIMS	Pontifical Institute of Mediaeval Studies, Toronto
Pinter	Frances Pinter Pubs., London
Plains	Plains Books, Carlisle
Plenum	Plenum Pub., London and New York

Plexus	Plexus Pub., London
Pliegos	Editorial Pliegos, Madrid
Ploughshares	Ploughshares Books, Watertown, Mass.
Pluto	Pluto Press, London
PML	Pierpont Morgan Library, New York
Polity	Polity Press, Cambridge
Polygon	Polygon, Edinburgh
Poolbeg	Poolbeg Press, Swords, Co. Dublin
Porcepic	Press Porcepic, Victoria, B.C.
Porcupine	Porcupine's Quill, Canada
PortN	Port Nicholson Press, Wellington, N.Z.
Potter	Clarkson N. Potter, New York
Power	Power Pubns, Univ. of Sydney
PPG	Paperback Publishers Group, USA
PPUBarcelona	Promociones y Publicaciones Universitarias, Barcelona
PrestigeB	Prestige Books, New Delhi
Primavera	Edizioni Primavera, Giunti Publishing Group, Florence, Italy
Primrose	Primrose Press, Alhambra, Calif.
PrincetonUL	Princeton Univ. Library, Princeton, N.J.
PrincetonUP	Princeton UP, Princeton, N.J.
Printwell	Printwell Pubs., Jaipur, India
Prism	Prism Press, Bridport, Dorset
PRO	Public Record Office, London
Profile	Profile Books, Ascot, Berks
ProgP	Progressive Pubs., Calcutta
PSUP	Pennsylvania State UP, University Park, Pa.
Pucker	Puckerbrush Press, Orono, Maine
PUF	Presses Universitaires de France, Paris
PurdueUP	Purdue UP, Lafayette, Ind.
Pushcart	Pushcart Press, Wainscott, N.Y.
Pustet	Friedrich Pustet, Regensburg
Putnam	Putnam Pub. Group, New York
PWP	Poetry Wales Press, Ogmore by Sea, Mid Glam.
QED	Q.E.D. Press of Ann Arbor, Mich.
Quarry	Quarry Press, Kingston, Ontario
Quartet	Quartet Books, London
RA	Royal Academy of Arts, London
Rainforest	Rainforest
Rampant Lions	Rampant Lions Press, Cambridge
R&B	Rosenkilde & Bagger, Copenhagen
R&L	Rowman & Littlefield, Totowa, N.J.
RandomH	Random House, London and New York
RandomHAus	Random House Australia, Vic.
Ravan	Ravan Press, Johannesburg
Ravette	Ravette, London
ReadingUP	Reading University Press
Reaktion	Reaktion Books, London
Rebel	The Rebel Press, London
Red Kite	Red Kite Press, Guelph, Ont.

Reference	Reference Press, Toronto
Regents	Regents Press of Kansas, Lawrence, Kansas
Reichenberger	Roswitha Reichenberger, Kessel, Germany
Reinhardt	Max Reinhardt, London
Remak	Remak, Alblasserdam, Netherlands
RenI	Renaissance Institute, Sophia Univ., Tokyo
Research	Research Pubns, Reading
RETS	Renaissance English Text Society, Chicago
RH	Ramsay Head Press, Edinburgh
RHS	Royal Historical Society, London
RIA	Royal Irish Academy, Dublin
RiceUP	Rice UP, Houston, Texas
Richarz	Hans Richarz, St Augustin, Germany
RICL	Research Institute for Comparative Literature, Univ. of Alberta
Rizzoli	Rizzoli International Pubns, New York
RobartsCCS	Robarts Centre for Canadian Studies, York Univ., North York, Ont.
Robinson	Robinson Pub., London
Robson	Robson Books, London
Rodopi	Rodopi, Amsterdam
Roebuck	Stuart Roebuck, Suffolk
RoehamptonI	Roehampton Institute of Higher Education, London
Routledge	Routledge, London and New York
Royce	Robert Royce, London
RS	The Royal Society, London
RSC	Royal Shakespeare Co., London
RSL	Royal Society of Literature, London
RSVP	Research Society for Victorian Periodicals, Univ. of Leicester
RT	R.T. Pubns, London
Running	Running Press, Philadelphia
Russell	Michael Russell, Norwich
RutgersUP	Rutgers UP, New Brunswick, N.J.
Ryan	Ryan Pub., London
SA	Sahitya Akademi, New Delhi
SAI	Sociological Abstracts, San Diego, Calif.
Sage	Sage Pubns, London
Salamander	Salamander Books, London
Salem	Salem
S&A	Shukayr and Akasheh, Amman, Jordan
S&D	Stein & Day, Briarcliff Manor, N.Y.
S&J	Sidgwick & Jackson, London
S&M	Sun & Moon Press, Los Angeles
S&P	Simon & Pierre, Toronto
S&S	Simon & Schuster, New York and London
S&W	Secker & Warburg, London
Sangam	Sangam Books, London
Sangsters	Sangsters Book Stores, Kingston, Jamaica
SAP	Scottish Academic Press, Edinburgh

Saros	Saros International Publishers
SASSC	Sydney Association for Studies in Society and Culture, University of Sydney, N.S.W.
Saur	Bowker-Saur, Sevenoaks, Kent
Savacou	Savacou Pubns, Kingston, Jamaica
S-B	Schwann-Bagel, Düsseldorf
ScanUP	Scandinavian University Presses, Oslo
Scarecrow	Scarecrow Press, Metuchen, N.J.
Schäuble	Schäuble Verlag, Rheinfelden, Germany
Schneider	Lambert Schneider, Heidelberg
Schocken	Schocken Books, New York
Scholarly	Scholarly Press, St Clair Shores, Mich.
ScholarsG	Scholars Press, Georgia
Schöningh	Ferdinand Schöningh, Paderborn, Germany
Schwinn	Michael Schwinn, Neustadt, Germany
SCJP	Sixteenth Century Journal Publications
Scolar	Scolar Press, Aldershot, Hampshire
SCP	Second Chance Press, Sag Harbor, N.Y.
Scribe	Scribe Publishing, Colchester
Scribner	Charles Scribner's Sons, New York
Seafarer	Seafarer Books, London
Seaver	Seaver Books, New York
Segue	Segue, New York
Self-Publishing Association	Self-Publishing Association
Semiotext(e)	Semiotext(e), Columbia Univ., New York
Seren Books	Seren Books, Bridgend, Mid Glamorgan
Serpent's Tail	Serpent's Tail Pub., London
Sessions	William Sessions, York
Seuil	Editions du Seuil, Paris
7:84 Pubns	7:84 Pubns, Glasgow
Severn	Severn House, Wallington, Surrey
SF&R	Scholars' Facsimiles and Reprints, Delmar, N.Y.
SH	Somerset House, Teaneck, N.J.
Shalabh	Shalabh Book House, Meerut, India
ShaP	Sheffield Academic Press
Shearwater	Shearwater Press, Lenah Valley, Tasmania
Sheba	Sheba Feminist Pubs., London
Sheed&Ward	Sheed & Ward, London
Sheldon	Sheldon Press, London
SHESL	Société d'Histoire et d'Épistemologie des Sciences du Langage, Paris
Shinozaki	Shinozaki Shorin, Tokyo
Shinshindo	Shinshindo Pub., Tokyo
Shire	Shire Pubns, Princes Risborough, Bucks
Shoe String	Shoe String Press, Hamden, Conn.
SIAS	Scandinavian Institute of African Studies, Uppsala
SIL	Summer Institute of Linguistics, Academic Pubns, Dallas, Texas
SIUP	Southern Illinois University Press

Simon King	Simon King Press, Milnthorpe, Cumbria
Sinclair-Stevenson	Sinclair-Stevenson, London
SingaporeUP	Singapore UP, Singapore
SIUP	Southern Illinois UP, Carbondale, Ill.
SJSU	San Jose State Univ., San Jose, Calif.
Skilton	Charles Skilton, London
Skoob	Skoob Books Pub., London
Slatkine	Editions Slatkine, Paris
Slavica	Slavica Pubs., Columbus, Ohio
Sleepy Hollow	Sleepy Hollow Press, Tarrytown, N.Y.
SLG	SLG Press, Oxford
Smith Settle	Smith Settle Ltd, W. Yorkshire
SMUP	Southern Methodist UP, Dallas, Texas
Smythe	Colin Smythe, Gerrards Cross, Bucks
SNH	Société Néophilologique de Helsinki
SNLS	Society for New Language Study, Denver, Colo.
SOA	Society of Authors, London
Soho	Soho Book Co., London
SohoP	Soho Press, New York
Solaris	Solaris Press, Rochester, Mich.
SonoNis	Sono Nis Press, Victoria, B.C.
Sorbonne	Pubns de la Sorbonne, Paris
SorbonneN	Pubns du Conseil Scientifique de la Sorbonne Nouvelle, Paris
Souvenir	Souvenir Press, London
SPA	SPA Books Ltd
SPACLALS	South Pacific Association for Commonwealth Literature and Language Studies, Wollongong, N.S.W.
SPCK	SPCK, London
Spectrum	Spectrum Books, Ibadan, Nigeria
Split Pea	Split Pea Press, Edinburgh
Spokesman	Spokesman Books, Nottingham
Spoon River	Spoon River Poetry Press, Granite Falls, Minn.
SRC	Steinbeck Research Center, San Jose State Univ., San Jose, Calif.
SRI	Steinbeck Research Institute, Ball State Univ., Muncie, Ind.
SriA	Sri Aurobindo, Pondicherry, India
Sri Satguru	Sri Satguru Pubns, Delhi
SSA	John Steinbeck Society of America, Muncie, Ind.
SSAB	Sprakförlaget Skriptor AB, Stockholm
StanfordUP	Stanford UP, Stanford, Calif.
Staple	Staple, Matlock, Derbyshire
Starmont	Starmont House, Mercer Island, Wash.
Starrhill	Starrhill Press, Washington, D.C.
Station Hill	Station Hill, Barrytown, N.Y.
Stauffenburg	Stauffenburg Verlag, Tübingen, Germany
StDL	St Deiniol's Library, Hawarden, Clwyd
Steel Rail	Steel Rail Pub., Ottawa
Steiner	Franz Steiner, Wiesbaden, Germany

Sterling	Sterling Pub., New York
SterlingND	Sterling Pubs., New Delhi
St James	St James Press, Andover, Hampshire
St Martin's	St Martin's Press, New York
St Mut	State Mutual Book and Periodical Source, New York
Stockwell	Arthur H. Stockwell, Ilfracombe, Devon
Stoddart	Stoddart Pub., Don Mills, Ont.
StPB	St Paul's Bibliographies, Winchester, Hampshire
STR	Society for Theatre Research, London
Strauch	R. O. U. Strauch, Ludwigsburg
Studio	Studio Editions, London
Stump Cross	Stump Cross Books, Stump Cross, Essex
Sud	Sud, Marseilles
Suhrkamp	Suhrkamp Verlag, Frankfurt-on-Main
Summa	Summa Pubns, Birmingham, Ala.
SUNYP	State Univ. of New York Press, Albany, N.Y.
SUP	Sydney University Press
Surtees	R. S. Surtees Society, Frome, Somerset
SusquehannaUP	Susquehanna UP, Selinsgrove, Pa.
SussexUP	Sussex UP, Univ. of Sussex, Brighton
Sutton	Alan Sutton, Stroud, Gloucester
S-W	Shepheard-Walwyn Pubs., London
Swallow	Swallow Press, Athens, Ohio
SWG	Saskatchewan Writers Guild, Regina
Sybylla	Sybylla Feminist Press
SydneyUP	Sydney UP, Sydney
SyracuseUP	Syracuse UP, Syracuse, N.Y.
Tabb	Tabb House, Padstow, Cornwall
Taishukan	Taishukan Pub., Tokyo
Talonbooks	Talonbooks, Vancouver
TamilU	Tamil Univ., Thanjavur, India
T&H	Thames & Hudson, London
Tantivy	Tantivy Press, London
Tarcher	Jeremy P. Tarcher, Los Angeles
Tate	Tate Gallery Pubns, London
Tavistock	Tavistock Pubns, London
Taylor	Taylor Pub., Bellingham, Wash.
TaylorCo	Taylor Pub., Dallas, Texas
TCG	Theatre Communications Group, New York
TCP	Three Continents Press, Washington, D.C.
TCUP	Texas Christian UP, Fort Worth, Texas
TEC	Third Eye Centre, Glasgow
Tecumseh	Tecumseh Press, Ottawa
Telos	Telos Press, St Louis, Mo.
TempleUP	Temple UP, Philadelphia
TennS	Tennyson Society, Lincoln
TexA&MUP	Texas A & M UP, College Station, Texas
TextileB	Textile Bridge Press, Clarence Center, N.Y.
TexTULib	Friends of the Univ. Library, Texas Tech Univ., Lubbock

The Smith	The Smith, New York
Thimble	Thimble Press, Stroud, Glos.
Thoemmes	Thoemmes Press, Bristol
Thornes	Stanley Thornes, Cheltenham
Thorpe	D. W. Thorpe, Australia
Thorsons	Thorsons Pubs., London
Times	Times of Gloucester Press, Gloucester, Ont.
TMP	Thunder's Mouth Press, New York
Tombouctou	Tombouctou Books, Bolinas, Calif.
TorSVP	Sister Vision Press, Toronto
Totem	Totem Books, Don Mills, Ont.
Toucan	Toucan Press, St Peter Port, Guernsey
Touzot	Jean Touzot, Paris
TPF	Trianon Press Facsimiles, London
Tragara	Tragara Press, Edinburgh
Transaction	Transaction Pubs., New Brunswick, N.J.
Transcendental	Transcendental Books, Hartford, Conn.
Transworld	Transworld, London
TrinityUP	Trinity UP, San Antonio, Texas
TTUP	Texas Technical University Press, Lubbock
Tuduv	Tuduv, Munich
TulaneUP	Tulane UP, New Orleans, La.
TurkuU	Turku Univ., Turku, Finland
Turnstone	Turnstone Press, Winnipeg, Manitoba
Turtle Island	Turtle Island Foundation, Berkeley, Calif.
Twayne	Twayne Pubs., Boston, Mass.
UAB	Univ. of Aston, Birmingham
UAdelaide	Univ. of Adelaide, Adelaide
UAlaP	Univ. of Alabama Press, Tuscaloosa
UAlbertaP	Univ. of Alberta Press, Edmonton
UAntwerp	Univ. of Antwerp, Antwerp
UArizP	Univ. of Arizona Press, Tucson
UArkP	Univ. of Arkansas Press, Fayetteville
UAthens	Univ. of Athens, Athens, Greece
UBarcelona	Univ. of Barcelona, Barcelona
UBCP	Univ. of British Columbia Press, Vancouver
UBergen	Univ. of Bergen, Bergen
UBrno	J. E. Purkyne Univ. of Brno, Brno, Czechoslovakia
UBrussels	Univ. of Brussels, Brussels
UCalgaryP	Univ. of Calgary Press, Calgary
UCalP	Univ. of California Press, Berkeley
UCAP	Univ. of Central Arkansas Press, Conway
UChicP	Univ. of Chicago Press, Chicago
UCopenP	Univ. of Copenhagen Press, Copenhagen
UDelP	Univ. of Delaware Press, Newark
UDijon	Univ. of Dijon, Dijon
UDur	Univ. of Durham, Durham
UEA	University of East Anglia, Norwich
UErlangen-N	Univ. of Erlangen-Nuremberg, Germany
UEssex	Univ. of Essex Press, Colchester

UExe	Univ. of Exeter Press, Exeter
UFlorence	Univ. of Florence, Florence
UFlorP	Univ. of Florida Press, Florida
UGal	Univ. College, Galway
UGeoP	Univ. of Georgia Press, Athens
UGhent	Univ. of Ghent, Ghent
UGlasP	Univ. of Glasgow Press, Glasgow
UHawaiiP	Univ. of Hawaii Press, Honolulu
UIfeP	Univ. of Ife Press, Ile-Ife, Nigeria
UIllP	Univ. of Illinois Press, Champaign
UInnsbruck	Univ. of Innsbruck, Innsbruck
UIowaP	Univ. of Iowa Press, Iowa City
UKanP	Univ. of Kansas Press, Lawrence
UKatowice	University of Katowice Press, Poland
UKL	Univ. of Kentucky Libraries, Lexington
ULavalP	Les Presses de l'Université Laval, Quebec
ULiège	Univ. of Liège, Liège, Belgium
ULilleP	Presses Universitaires de Lille, Lille
ULondon	Univ. of London, London
Ulster	Univ. of Ulster, Coleraine
U/M	Underwood/Miller, Los Angeles
UMalta	Univ. of Malta, Msida
UManitobaP	Univ. of Manitoba Press, Winnipeg
UMassP	Univ. of Massachusetts Press, Amherst
Umeå	Umeå Universitetsbibliotek, Umeå
UMel	Melbourne University Press, Victoria, Australia
UMichP	Univ. of Michigan Press, Ann Arbor
UMinnP	Univ. of Minnesota Press, Minneapolis
UMirail-ToulouseP	University of Mirail-Toulouse Press, France
UMIRes	UMI Research Press, Ann Arbor, Mich.
UMissP	Univ. of Missouri Press, Columbia
UMP	Univ. of Mississippi Press, Lafayette Co, Mississippi
UMysore	Univ. of Mysore, Mysore, India
UNancyP	Presses Universitaires de Nancy, France
UNCP	Univ. of North Carolina Press, Chapel Hill
Undena	Undena Pubns, Malibu, Calif.
UNDP	Univ. of Notre Dame Press, Notre Dame, Ind.
UNebP	Univ. of Nebraska Press, Lincoln
UNevP	Univ. of Nevada Press, Reno
UNewE	Univ. of New England, Armidale, N.S.W.
Ungar	Frederick Ungar, New York
Unicopli	Edizioni Unicopli, Milan
Unity	Unity Press, Hull
Universa	Uilgeverij Universa, Wetteren, Belgium
UNMP	Univ. of New Mexico Press, Albuquerque
UNott	Univ. of Nottingham, Nottingham
UNSW	University of New South Wales
Unwin	Unwin Paperbacks, London
Unwin Hyman	Unwin Hyman, London
UOklaP	Univ. of Oklahoma Press, Norman

UOslo	Univ. of Oslo, Oslo
UOtagoP	Univ. of Otago Press, Dunedin, New Zealand
UOttawaP	Univ. of Ottawa Press, Ottawa
UPA	UP of America, Lanham, Md.
UParis	Univ. of Paris, Paris
UPColorado	UP of Colorado, Niwot
UPennP	Univ. of Pennsylvania Press, Philadelphia
UPFlor	Univ. Presses of Florida, Gainesville
UPittP	Univ. of Pittsburgh Press, Pittsburgh
UPKen	Univ. Press of Kentucky, Lexington
UPMissip	UP of Mississippi, Jackson
UPN	Université de Paris Nord, Paris
UPNE	UP of New England, Hanover, N.H.
Uppsala	Uppsala Univ., Uppsala
UProvence	Univ. of Provence, Aix-en-Provence
UPValery	Univ. Paul Valery, Montpellier
UPVirginia	UP of Virginia, Charlottesville
UQP	Univ. of Queensland Press, St Lucia
URouen	Univ. of Rouen, Mont St Aignan
URP	University of Rochester Press
USalz	Institut für Anglistik und Amerikanistik, Univ. of Salzburg
USantiago	University of Santiago, Spain
USCP	Univ. of South Carolina Press, Columbia
USFlorP	University of South Florida Press, Florida
USheff	Univ. of Sheffield, Sheffield
Usher	La Casa Usher, Florence
USPacific	Univ. of the South Pacific, Institute of Pacific Studies, Suva, Fiji
USydP	University of Sydney Press
USzeged	Univ. of Szeged, Hungary
UtahSUP	Utah State UP, Logan
UTampereP	University of Tampere Press, Finland
UTas	Univ. of Tasmania, Hobart
UTennP	Univ. of Tennessee Press, Knoxville
UTexP	Univ. of Texas Press, Austin
UTorP	Univ. of Toronto Press, Toronto
UTours	Université de Tours
UVerm	Univ. of Vermont, Burlington
UVict	Univ. of Victoria, Victoria, B.C.
UWalesP	Univ. of Wales Press, Cardiff
UWAP	Univ. of Western Australia Press, Nedlands
UWarwick	Univ. of Warwick, Coventry
UWashP	Univ. of Washington Press, Seattle
UWaterlooP	Univ. of Waterloo Press, Waterloo, Ont.
UWI	Univ. of the West Indies, St Augustine, Trinidad
UWiscM	Univ. of Wisconsin, Milwaukee
UWiscP	Univ. of Wisconsin Press, Madison
UYork	Univ. of York, York
Valentine	Valentine Pub. and Drama, Rhinebeck, N.Y.

V&A	Victoria and Albert Museum, London
VanderbiltUP	Vanderbilt UP, Nashville, Tenn.
V&R	Vandenhoeck & Ruprecht, Göttingen, Germany
Vantage	Vantage Press, New York
Variorum	Variorum, Ashgate Publishing Group, Hants
Vehicule	Vehicule Press, Montreal
Verso	Verso Editions, London
VictUP	Victoria UP, Victoria Univ. of Wellington, New Zealand
Vieweg	Vieweg Braunschweig, Wiesbaden
Vikas	Vikas Pub. House, New Delhi
Viking	Viking Press, New York
VikingNZ	Viking, Auckland
Virago	Virago Press, London
Vision	Vision Press, London
VLB	VLB Editeur, Montreal
VR	Variorum Reprints, London
Vrin	J. Vrin, Paris
VUUP	Vrije Universiteit University Press
Wakefield	Wakefield Press
W&N	Weidenfeld & Nicolson, London
Water Row	Water Row Press, Sudbury, Mass.
Watkins	Paul Watkins, Stamford, Lincs.
WB	Wissenschaftliche Buchgesellschaft, Darmstadt
W/B	Woomer/Brotherson, Revere, Pa.
Webb&Bower	Webb & Bower, Exeter
Wedgestone	Wedgestone Press, Winfield, Kansas
Wedgetail	Wedgetail Press, Earlwood, N.S.W.
WesleyanUP	Wesleyan UP, Middletown, Conn.
West	West Pub., St Paul, Minn.
WHA	William Heinemann Australia, Port Melbourne, Vic.
Wheatsheaf	Wheatsheaf Books, Brighton
Whiteknights	Whiteknights Press, Univ. of Reading, Reading
White Lion	White Lion Books, Cambridge
Whitston	Whitston Pub., Troy, N.Y.
Whittington	Whittington Press, Herefordshire
WHP	Warren House Press, Sale, Cheshire
Wiener	Wiener Pub., New York
Wildwood	Wildwood House, Aldershot, Hampshire
Wiley	John Wiley & Sons, Chichester, New York, and Brisbane
Wilson	Philip Wilson, London
Winter	Carl Winter Universitätsverlag, Heidelberg, Germany
Winthrop	Winthrop Pubs., Cambridge, Mass.
WIU	Western Illinois Univ., Macomb, Ill.
WL	Ward Lock, London
WLUP	Wilfrid Laurier UP, Waterloo, Ont.
WMP	World Microfilms Pubns, London
WMU	Western Michigan Univ., Kalamazoo, Mich.
Woeli	Woeli Publishing Services
Wo-No	Wolters-Noordhoff, Groningen, Netherlands

Wolfhound	Wolfhound Press, Dublin
Wombat	The Wombat Press, Wolfville, N.S.
Woodstock	Woodstock Books, Oxford
Woolf	Cecil Woolf, London
Words	Words, Framfield, E. Sussex
WP	The Women's Press, London
WPC	The Women's Press of Canada, Toronto
WSUP	Wayne State UP, Detroit, Mich.
WVUP	West Virginia UP, Morgantown
W-W	Williams-Wallace, Toronto
WWU	Western Washington Univ., Bellingham
Xanadu	Xanadu Pubns, London
YaleUL	Yale Univ. Library Pubns, New Haven, Conn.
YaleUP	Yale UP, New Haven, Conn. and London
Yamaguchi	Yamaguchi Shoten, Kyoto
YorkP	York Press, Fredericton, N. B.
Younsmere	Younsmere Press, Brighton
Zed	Zed Books, London
Zena	Zena Pubns, Penrhyndeudraeth, Gwynedd
Zephyr	Zephyr Press, Somerville, Mass.
Zomba	Zomba Books, London
Zwemmer	A. Zwemmer, London

I

English Language

KATARZYNA JASZCZOLT, NICOLA WOODS, JULIE COLEMAN,
OLGA FISCHER, WIM VAN DER WURFF, CAROLE E. HOUGH
and JEAN JACQUES WEBER

This chapter has the following sections: 1. General; 2. History of English Linguistics; 3. Dialectology and Sociolinguistics (including Creolistics); 4. Lexicography, Lexicology and Semantics; 5. Morphology; 6. Syntax; 7. Onomastics; 8. Stylistics. Section 1 is by Katarzyna Jaszczolt; sections 2 and 4 are by Julie Coleman; section 3 is by Nicola Woods; sections 5 and 6 are by Olga Fischer and Wim van der Wurff; section 7 is by Carole Hough; and section 8 is by Jean Jacques Weber.

1. General

The Encyclopedia of Language and Linguistics from Pergamon, a long awaited ten-volume reference book on all areas of linguistics, has appeared and is very likely to fulfil the exigencies of the users. R. E. Asher has performed an admirable task of compiling over two thousand articles by top specialists in the particular areas, bound together by a comprehensive glossary, indices and a list of the world's languages. Thematic entries are very thorough, succinct, informative, mostly uncontroversial, and accompanied by an extensive bibliography and cross-references. This is a magnificent achievement, highly commendable for readers of any degree of linguistic initiation. Reference books are in abundance this year. Other commendable issues include *The Cambridge Thesaurus of American English*, edited by William Lutz, and *Atlas of the World's Languages* from Routledge, edited by Christopher Moseley and R. E. Asher. The first is praiseworthy for its user-friendliness: arranged alphabetically and aesthetically laid out, it constitutes a vast improvement in style as compared with *Roget's Thesaurus*. The book contains over 200,000 synonyms and antonyms of contemporary American English. The other reference book is a spectacular collection of maps of languages that combine to form an account of world languages, unprecedented in its scope, accuracy and clarity. Edited by Moseley and Asher, the atlas is in fact a work of many specialists on particular language families or geographical areas. The work consists of colourful maps depicting languages and language families of particular geographical regions, divided into eight sections. Each section is prefaced with a thorough, accurate and authoritative introduction, spelling out the details that could not be fully presented on the maps. The first enterprise of this scale, the atlas is easy to use and truly captivating in the quality and quantity of provided information.

The profusion of works of general linguistic interest does not easily yield to summaries. First, an offer from Pinter: Thomas Sebeok's *An Introduction to Semiotics* is a comprehensive exposition of the study of signs. Written in a witty and captivating style and illustrated with numerous examples, it provides pleasant and informative reading on the features and typology of signs. Sebeok divides signs into signals, symptoms, icons, indices, symbols and names, and exposes various relationships that hold between the signifier and the signified of a sign. The author also conducts a convincing analysis that reveals the eclectic nature of some signs in relation to the defined categories. For instance, a fetish is said to have indexical, iconic and symbolic elements. The analysis of the structure and functioning of a fetish is followed by a discourse on the relation between linguistics and semiotics, a convincing argumentation to the effect that the use of signs is biologically based and functions as converting the external world into the world of a mental representation. Finally, it is concluded that language itself is a modelling system that enables such a sign-based functioning of humans. The work abounds in sweeping conclusions when taken in the light of the achievements of cognitive science, but is readable and stimulating for beginners. *Roman Jakobson: Life, Language, Art* by Richard Bradford proves that the interface between the studies of language and literature can be not only informative but also essential for seeing one's own field of research in a sufficiently broad perspective. The work deals with Jakobson's poetics, work on poetry and literary criticism, but shows at the same time how his views on linguistics (mainly phonology) and post-Saussurean semiotics permeate it all. The monograph presents Jakobson in the broad spectrum of his contemporaries, followers and adversaries, spelling out the importance of his legacy. Links with Saussure, Freud, Lacan, Barthes, Lévi-Strauss and Derrida, as well as Xlebnikov and Majakovskij, elevate the work to the status of a historical vision of an important period in European culture. On a historical note, another proposal from Routledge: Ulrich Ricken's *Linguistics, Anthropology and Philosophy in the French Enlightenment* is a readable contribution to the Routledge History of Linguistic Thought series and presents the history of linguistic ideas in the French Enlightenment, placing it against a broad spectrum of European developments in social sciences, philosophy and anthropology, all enabled by the vision of language as the tool of all human activity. Linguistic debates of the period involved functions of language, the origin of language and writing systems, non-European languages, etymology, grammar, language use (and abuse), and language as a system of arbitrary signs. With its insight into the work of Locke and his French followers and the problem of the relation of language and thought, all enhanced by a succinct style, the book is readable, informative and enjoyable.

The Cultural Politics of English as an International Language by Alastair Pennycook is a rather sensational and unwieldy presentation of the position of English in the world, targeted at teachers of English with the aim of making them sensitive to the culturally, socially and politically motivated requirements of their market in various countries. The author elaborates on such platitudes as the cultural and political effects of teaching English, embellishing the exposition by his personal observations and (it seems, very limited) research on education and life in Singapore and Malaysia. Conclusions and practical solutions are far from being profound: a little experience and common sense should result in no worse a *critical pedagogy*, i.e. a diversified vision of teaching. A more practical tool for English teaching and learning is on offer from Geoffrey Leech and Jan Svartvik – the second edition of their 1975 *A Communicative Grammar of English* continues to enjoy the status of an ideal reference book. It is based on the unbeatable *A Comprehensive Grammar of the English Language* by Quirk et al. and is practical in combining the issues of grammar, meaning and language use illustrated by authentic examples from corpora. Widely used, the work does not need any further appraisal.

A cross-cultural dissertation is offered by Keiko Tanaka in *Advertising Language: A Pragmatic Approach to Advertisements in Britain and Japan*. Using Sperber and Wilson's relevance theory, and in particular the view on covert communication proposed there, the author sets out to prove that understanding advertisements is not merely a matter of decoding information and that advertisers often rely on what is implicated in metaphors, puns and images. Rather disappointing from the linguistic point of view, the account is praiseworthy for its combative criticism of sexist and social prejudices, sometimes resulting in pointed comments on the abuse of words by those socially and economically powerful; one of the most abused words seems to be none other than 'feminism' in Japanese.

Cognitive linguistics and psycholinguistics dominate the arena of general interest language books this year thanks to the plethora of high-quality introductory works aimed at non-specialists. First of all, an American bestseller by Steven Pinker, *The Language Instinct: The New Science of Language and Mind*. The science is not so new any longer, estimated at thirty-five years of age, but an accessible introduction was badly needed. Pinker manages to achieve two goals: to prove that the discoveries in the area can be captivating, and to interweave arguments in favour of innate language abilities and universal grammar, delivered as the current standing doctrine. The gist is this: language is seen as a biological phenomenon, located in the brain and developing spontaneously – as an instinct to learn, speak and understand. Language is thus innate and universal and the ability to communicate has been gained in an evolutionary process. As an expository overview of the state of the art in cognitive science, i.e. psychology, computer science, linguistics, philosophy and neurobiology, the work introduces a lay reader step by step to their achievements. If there is anybody out there who still holds that language is a cultural invention and is acquired by imitation, he or she will inevitably be converted by five hundred pages of argumentation to the contrary. As an extra bonus, the reader is also allowed to form her or his opinion on the existence of language genes – all this embellished by numerous anecdotes and linguistic jokes. For more information on the evolution of human language and its differences from the communication system of non-human primates the reader can refer to Michael Corballis's *The Lopsided Ape: Evolution of the Generative Mind*, whose paperback edition appeared in 1993, too late to be included in last year's review. The author discusses the uniqueness of human language and ascribes it to the specialization of the left hemisphere of the brain. The linguistic discontinuity between humans and other primates is the subject of a thorough and anfractuous analysis that results in the claim that the evolutionary view should not be precluded but rather altered to account for sudden changes in genetic structure, unlike those allowed by Darwinian selection. The conclusion is as follows: our adaptability went beyond the demands of the environment and the consequences of the lopsidedness of the brain got out of hand; we may have to restore the balance in order to survive. More on this topic is in a book by Sue Savage-Rumbaugh and

Roger Lewin, *Kanzi: The Ape on the Brink of the Human Mind*, reporting the results of research on a chimpanzee that acquired some rudimentary syntax. The authors discuss the hypothesis that language and manipulative skills evolved together, supporting it by evidence from the changes of the brain and the vocal apparatus, as well as from the capacity for using tools. Kanzi, a male bonobo chimpanzee, provided some evidence to the effect that language occurred relatively early in the development of *Homo sapiens* and gave rise to arguments that some form of language was available even to *Australopithecus*. Unfortunately, the report on the experiments lacks a strict scientific method, and the sensational findings that, for example, chimps respond with understanding to the questions of the type: *What are you thinking about?* or *Can you go scare Matata* [another ape] *with the snake?* cry for a focused scientific description and theoretical support, being entangled instead in a multitude of anecdotes and opinions on the hostility of the dominant paradigm. Nevertheless, the cognitive capacity of the ancestors of humans was shown to be greater than it was previously assumed, and the gap between human language and primates' communication may thus be smaller than has been thought so far.

The *Handbook of Psycholinguistics* edited by Morton A. Gernsbacher continues the tide of introductions to this area of science. The book hardly lives up to its title: it contains over a thousand pages of rather specialized articles on speech perception, reading comprehension, discourse processing and language acquisition – all of very limited use to a linguist due either to their non-linguistic focus or to their vagueness in handling linguistic theories, and, needless to say, frequently to both. The quality varies, however, over these thirty-four chapters, and two of them are particularly commendable. They deal with figurative language and the psycholinguistic research pertinent to the topic. The proposed tenet is that figurative utterances are not understood as apparent violations of conversational maxims. After all, it is conjectured that metaphor may not be a linguistic entity but rather a conceptual one. Another work on language acquisition will be of interest only to linguists particularly concerned with the *pro-drop* parameter: Lakshmanan's *Universal Grammar in Child Second Language Acquisition* pays particular attention to this phenomenon and apart from that is largely constituted by a rather colourless literature review. To continue on a cognitive note, *A Companion to the Philosophy of Mind* edited by Samuel Guttenplan is an admirable achievement. It consists of alphabetically arranged articles on particular phenomena and known figures in this area of research. The encyclopaedic composition combined with the thorough, informative entries make the book a useful reference for anybody interested in the field. Linguistics and philosophy of language are aptly represented, to mention only entries on Chomsky, Searle and Fodor contributed by these authors themselves. And to demonstrate that it has been a fruitful year for cognitive science, another introductory work: G. F. Luger et al., *Cognitive Science: The Science of Intelligent Systems*, by a group of five scientists from Albuquerque, is a step-by-step introduction to representations, problem solving, machine learning, connectionist networks, language processing and programming. This is a perfect book for those trying to make up their mind on the issue of whether intelligence can exist outside the human mind. Comprehensive, readable and informative, it brings a linguist up to date with the achievements of this interdisciplinary research in which any specialist is bound to be lost at some time or other. Particular attention is given to the clear exposition of connectionism, an approach to learning that steadily gains in popularity. It concerns the interaction of neurons in the process of learning in which the connections between the neurons are strengthened.

Jerry A. Fodor's new book continues the flood of interest in human thought processes. In *The Elm and the Expert: Mentalese and its Semantics,* Fodor undertakes an uncompromising enterprise to reconcile two theses that seem to clash: that mental processes are computational and that semantics is informational; the symbols on which the mind operates are causally related to the world. No compromise is allowed: the previously held idea of a 'narrow content' for computations is rejected. However, the whole enterprise looks more like a reasoning exercise in trying to reconcile the unreconcilable than an epistemologically plausible story of meaning and thought.

Metaphor and Knowledge (eds. F. R. Ankersmit and J. J. A. Mooij) is the third volume of the *Knowledge and Language* series of conference papers from Groningen. As a late arrival of 1993, is has to be included in the present review. It is essentially a mixture of general interest papers and specialized research reports falling into two parts: 'Metaphor and Truth' and 'The Uses of Metaphor'. The volume gives evidence for the diversity of approaches to metaphor, ranging from viewing metaphor as a primary, original vehicle of meaning which only results in literal language when the free creativity is harnessed, to the rather dogmatic accounts of metaphor as comparison or solely as a vehicle of an emotive function, unable to embody thoughts. From the linguistic point of view, it is a rather disappointing compilation of tenets that lack the all-encompassing perspective on meaning and communication, eked out with examples from literature, literary criticism, political and social writing. Another book on the subject, *Aspects of Metaphor* edited by Jaakko Hintikka, published by Kluwer in Synthese Library, presents the subject with slightly more baldness and vigour, although it is also full of platitudes and unwieldy discussions. It is a collection of eight papers representing various approaches to the study of metaphor. Its dominant topics include metaphor discussed with respect to the following areas and phenomena: epistemological writings, simile, conceptualization and semantic fields, cognition, possible worlds, speech acts, truth, language games, creativity, visual art, the perception of the degrees of metaphor, the poverty of language, and the way of life. Although it is broad in its scope of topics, the collection lacks new, controversial arguments and intransigence.

On the semantics and pragmatics front, *Foundations of Speech Act Theory* edited by Savas L. Tsohatzidis is an offer from Routledge and deserves some attention. It is a collection of twenty-two papers that, taken in its entirety, presents the current state of the art in speech act theories. The outcome is rather negative: illocutionary act is no longer a standard doctrine, and the weaknesses of the classificatory approaches to speech acts are exposed in multifarious criticisms or attempts at attaining higher precision by formalizations. Few papers deserve recommendation. Among them are François Récanati's discussion on the battle between analytic philosophy and 'contextualism', i.e. ordinary language philosophy, exposing some faults in reasoning that led contextualism into disrepute; Kent Bach's criticism of Grice's rigid distinction between what is said and what is implicated; and Graham Bird's controversial reconciliation of the formalization of speech act theory with the relevance-theoretic vision of cognition and communication, resulting in assigning to relevance the place of a gap-filler for the under-researched psychological underlay of speech act theory. All in all, the volume does not live up to its title and the concoction does not result in the flavour of the 'foundations' of speech act theory. On a semantic note, Nicholas Asher's *Reference to Abstract Objects in Discourse*, a 1993 book not reviewed last year, is a complete semantic account of abstract entities such as propositions, properties, states of affairs and facts, developed in Discourse Representation Theory, a framework ideal for the enterprise due to its dynamism and context-relativity of meaning. Max Cresswell's new book on possible worlds semantics appeared from CUP, entitled *Language in the World*, conveying a message that the semantics is determined by causal interactions between the utterance and facts in the world. Causation in its turn requires the framework of possible worlds. The book is a series of lectures on semantics and discusses many important and interrelated problems such as isomorphism of interpretations, Putnam's argument that meanings are not in the head, truthfulness, Lewis's account of counterfactuals, causation, an explanation of behaviour in terms of beliefs and desires, and Fodor's narrow content (*nota bene*, rejected in Fodor, *The Elm and the Expert*). Equipped with a crash course on first-order logic, it is accessible to linguists and philosophers of all levels and specializations.

Language in society is always a topic with guaranteed readership. On the general level, a few commendable texts appeared this year. Joanna Channell's *Vague Language* discusses selected phenomena that fall under the label of vagueness, such as approximator and number structures ('about five'), vague quantifiers ('lots of') and 'placeholders' ('thingy', 'whatnot'), approaching them with the focus on applied linguistics. Channell adopts an empirical approach to the topic and discusses spoken and written data that give evidence of the use of vague expressions. She recognizes that vagueness can mean a variety of things in language but boldly proceeds to classify them and define the key notion so that it can be used in the empirical exercise. However, the methodological stance seems at least dubious: one could question the optimistic presumption that vagueness is not a vague notion itself and that an empirical analysis of vague terms is anything more than a forlorn hope. After all, there is a vast philosophical tradition that specifies what constitutes vagueness, as well as a bulk of solutions to the vagueness of expressions of natural language, beginning with the sorites paradox and other ancient puzzles. Moreover, there is the currently fashionable vagueness of sentences, i.e. the underdetermination of semantic representation. All in all, the choice of discussed phenomena is thus rather contentious and subjective, if not aleatory. Moreover, the sweeping statements of the type 'vagueness occurs as much or more than precision' and '[h]uman cognition is well set up to process vague concepts' are on the verge of being uninformative and give evidence that it is a rather misfired undertaking. It is a precarious enterprise to try to classify *whatnot* if *a lot of whatnots* may not be classifiable – we have known that since the early post-Bloomfieldian era. All that does not preclude the possibility that studying vague language in real conversation and through conversational strategies may be successful.

Approaches to Discourse from Deborah Schiffrin is an impressive although not uncontroversial textbook offered in the series Blackwell Textbooks in Linguistics. The author divides the field into speech act theory, interactional sociolinguistics, the ethnography of communication, pragmatics, conversation analysis and variation analysis. The dissection itself involves some reanalyses and regroupings that do not conform to acknowledged standards. But as well as being contentious, the analysis is also revealing of many similarities and the mutual compatibility of the approaches. The paramount asset of the work is thus the fact that it presents a collection of information rarely to be found in one textbook. The main weakness is that the depth of treatment of certain approaches is compromised. For instance, 'pragmatics' receives a rather superficial treatment, seemingly justified by the author's sympathy with an eclectic approach. The compromises are also directly reflected in the gaps in bibliography. On the other hand, the informative definitions of discourse and the clear presentation of collected data make the enterprise a valuable textbook and reference book, as long as the approach is handled with caution and criticism: the reader should be aware of the strong beliefs being smuggled through the seemingly introductory text. A trivial cultural digression at this point: both Schiffrin's and Pennycook's books use Paul Klee's works as their cover illustration: a coincidence, fashion, or rather a deeply motivated symbol? On a discourse note, the paperback issue of Harvey Sack's complete *Lectures on Conversation* should be warmly welcomed, as their readable style and seminal topics of, for example, turn taking, conversational sequencing and adjacency pairs make his a position sought after by many conversation analysts. On the subject of textbooks, Routledge proposes *English Words* by Francis Katamba. This book is more general and less technical in its style and topic. It contains more issues of a wider interest, such as psycholinguistics of the use of words; speech and writing; spelling and etymology – all aimed at non-linguists. The wittily written introduction makes morphology fascinating and practical, as well as relatively easy thanks to comprehensive exercises for beginners. The approach to mental lexicon results in convincing, poignant arguments that words in the mind are structured hierarchically in a network, corroborated by an account of aphasia, as well as malapropisms and other speech errors. On a similar note, Jean Aitchison's *Words in the Mind: An Introduction to the Mental Lexicon* arrived at its second edition this year.

Language change is a topic of unfading interest, and this year April McMahon's contribution *Understanding Language Change* gives evidence of the vast scope of issues researched in this field. Apart from the expected information on topics such as language birth and death, spreading of language, language contact and linguistic variation, the author offers a comprehensive commentary on various theories of these phenomena and adds as a final chord some insightful observations on linguistic evolution.

Linguistics journals grow in number and in the degree of specialization. Nevertheless, some interesting contributions of general interest appeared this year. First, 'Idioms', an article from G. Nunberg, I. Sag and T. Wasow (*Language* 70.491-538). The authors make a common-sensical but so far unaccounted-for distinction between 'idiomatically combining expressions' (e.g. 'take advantage') whose meaning is partly compositional, i.e. distributed among the constitutive parts, and 'idiomatic phrases' (e.g. 'kick the bucket') with no such distribution. They provide tests and arguments in favour of this distinction, concluding convincingly that the syntax of idioms is not as arbitrary as has been claimed so far. Readable and pleasurable, this article can be highly recommended to anyone interested in language on whatever level. Studies of politeness flourish throughout *JPrag*, to mention only contributions such as L. R. Mao's 'Beyond Politeness Theory: "Face" Revisited and Renewed' (21.451–86), dealing with Chinese discourse behaviours and their discrediting power for Anglocentric models of politeness. T. Pavlidou discusses German and Greek politeness and its consequences in the example of telephone conversations on the basis of a vast number of data (21.487–511), and the state of the art in politeness studies is indicated by the abundance listed in the extensive bibliography of the work on the topic to date. Also in *JPrag* 21, D.A. Koike offers an interesting study of suggestions and requests in Spanish and English (513-26), stating that negation in speech acts can convey politeness, but also (and unexpectedly) can mean the opposite. Mira Ariel in 'Interpreting Anaphoric Expressions: A Cognitive Versus a Pragmatic Approach' (*JL* 30.3–42) presents an innovative cognitive account of anaphora, including pronouns, reflexives, lexical noun phrases and zeros, arguing that the accessibility of the mental representation of the noun phrase is signalled by the speaker. Set against neo-Gricean pragmatic proposals that are based on conversational maxims and principles, the theory claims to enjoy greater psychological plausibility and factual accuracy.

To conclude, a brief appraisal for psychologists: *JLSP* 13 offers a special issue on interpersonal deception. Among the bulk of diversified and fascinating contributions, there is one of particular interest to the linguist: Michael Burgoon, Mark Callister and Frank Hunsaker talk about 'Patients Who Deceive' in an empirical investigation of patient–physician interaction (443–68). The gist of the analysis is that patients often lie and exaggerate their symptoms in order to receive the doctor's attention. Now, the question arises of how such deception fits into the Gricean Cooperative Principle. An interesting questionnaire on this topic had been submitted to many Americans and the conjecture was confirmed: deception in the form of equivocation, concealment and falsification belongs to the established pattern of interaction between patients and physicians. A task for speech act theory? Or for the theory of implicature and conversational maxims? In any case, here is more puzzling evidence from language use for language theorists to be accounted for in years to come.

2. History of English Linguistics

Anita R. Riedinger assumes, in 'Lexical Inequities in Marriage: Old English *Wif*, *Wer*, and *Husbonda*' (*SN* 61.3-14), that at some time in the Dark Ages men and women were nearly equal. Inequality within marriage, caused by the Norman Conquest, the twelfth-century renaissance and the church's increasing control, is symbolized by the replacement of *wer* with *husband*. In 'The Rise of a New Conceptualization Pattern: Old English *lippe, weler, tunge* and *muþ* with Reference to Linguistic Action' (in Henk Aertsen and Robert J. Jeffers, eds, *Historical Linguistics 1989*), Louis Goossens accepts the *OED* account of biblical influence in the figurative use of *lip* and *mouth* in Old English, but asserts that these metaphors led to the development of further calques. Kenneth R. Andrews's 'The Semantic Development of *can* and *could* from Old English to the Present' (also in Aertsen and Jeffers) traces the parallel developments of a hypothetical sense in the past and a 'possibility' sense in the present tense, and concludes that modal verbs took on the function of the subjunctive mood.

Roger Dahood discusses the implications of an account of a twelfth-century Anglo-Norman noblewoman calling for help in English in 'Hugh de Morville, William of Canterbury, and Anecdotal Evidence for English Language History' (*Speculum* 69.40–56). He concludes that the anecdote tells us more about English in William's period than in the baroness's. Henk Aertsen's 'The Lexicon and Linguistic Change' (in Aertsen and Jeffers) looks at three types of borrowing within the lexicon with reference to words for 'play' in Middle English: borrowing of the sense of a near synonym, phrasal borrowing, and borrowing from dialects. In 'Language Prescription and Standardization Ideology in Late Middle English' (*NM* 95.229–42), Luis Igelesias-Rábade considers whether the use of French vocabulary in mystery plays, especially the Towneley cycle, is motivated by a desire to represent colloquial speech, a desire to individualize characters, or a scholarly attempt to standardize the local variety under French influence. Alan Fisk's 'Living with Fossilized Ear's' (*Verbatim* 21.ii.20–1) is an irascible account of pronunciation changes observed within his own lifetime, which he considers to represent a continuation of the Great Vowel Shift.

Stephen J. Nagle discusses the use of multiple modals in Irish, Scots, and American Southern English in 'Double Modals in Early English' (in Aertsen and Jeffers) and concludes that the development must have taken place during the early modern period because the most prevalent types are not found in Old English. 'Dr Johnson and the Spelling of *dispatch*' (*IJL* 7.307–10) is Noel Osselton's account of how modern editions of Johnson's letters have given rise to an apparent disparity between Johnson's dictionary and contemporary practice. *Despatch*, the dictionary form, is found to represent Johnson's usual spelling. F. Aarts's 'William Cobbett's *Grammar of the English Language*' (*NM* 95.319–32) assesses the significance of Cobbett's *Grammar*, which, although it was priced above the reach of its target audience, the working classes, sold over 100,000 copies between 1818 and 1836, was little and negatively reviewed at the time and has rarely been mentioned since. John Victor Singler's 'An African-American Linguistic Enclave. Tense and Aspect in Liberian Settler English' (in Aertsen and Jeffers) suggests that the English of Sinoe Settlers is more similar to nineteenth-century black American English of the deep south than contemporary black American English is, largely because of the absence of standardization.

Sarah Dunant's *The War of the Words* contains only one essay dealing with linguistic political correctness: Deborah Cameron's '"Words, Words, Words": The Power of Language'. Cameron identifies the incompatibility between two of the main criticisms of PC language – that it trivializes politics and yet undermines free expression – and argues that the central problem is the definition of neutral language. David Galef discusses the development of spellings intended to represent sounds into independent words in 'Sound and Sense' (*Verbatim* 21.ii.15–16). He also looks at the use of pronunciation spellings for words like *doughnut, women* and *victuals*. Gary Egan's 'Wordplay' (*Verbatim* 20.iv.1–3) considers the use of puns in newspaper headlines and notes that although they are usually used for humour, they are also found in serious reports. In 'Plane Speaking' (*Verbatim* 21.ii.1–3), Steven Cushing looks at miscommunication in air-traffic control. Illustrating his points with anecdotal evidence, he attributes miscommunication to semantic and syntactic ambiguity, to homophony and to assumed shared knowledge.

Jonathon Green's *Slang Down the Ages: The Historical Development of Slang* does not really fulfil the promises of its title. Although it does look at the earliest records of slang, its contents are arranged semantically rather than chronologically, so there is no discussion of the development of slang as such. A two-page introduction precedes a discursive slang lexicon, divided into sections like 'Men', 'Women', 'The Body', 'Defecation', 'Insults', 'Clothing', and so on. Further subdivisions are sometimes misleading. The section 'Police', for instance, is divided into 'the policeman', 'the detective', 'the novice', 'the uniform', 'linguistic terms' (such as backslang and rhyming slang), 'names', 'animals', 'activities' and 'special terms', but anyone looking for *bobby* (named for Robert Peel) or *the sweeney* (from

Sweeney Todd) under 'names' would be disappointed, since they are in 'the policeman' and 'linguistic terms' respectively. Similarly, *plod*, apparently from Enid Blyton's PC Plod, is in 'activities', but *pavement pounder* is under 'uniform'. The index of words does make it possible to locate these terms, however, but a contents page giving a summary of the areas covered would have been a useful addition. Dates of earliest use are given where possible, but they are often specific only to the century. The extent to which a term was actually used is not normally indicated and this, along with the lack of bibliographical references, and indeed of a bibliography, indicates that the book is not intended for an academic audience.

The first volume (A–G) of J. E. Lighter's *Random House Historical Dictionary of American Slang* covers three centuries of American usage, and is the fruit of twenty-six years' work. Pronunciation, etymologies, information on geographical and other restrictions in distribution, usage labels, variant forms and discursive notes are included where relevant, as are useful cross-references to other dictionaries. Illustrative quotations are given from a wide range of sources, including oral citations and questionnaires, and non-North American citations are clearly marked. Expressions found only in word-lists and other dictionaries have generally been excluded. The introduction, which is fully annotated, argues that slang can be as usefully subjected to the historical treatment used in the *OED* as any other register. It claims that slang which achieves widespread usage is unlikely to prove ephemeral, and gives examples of forms declared obsolete by Grose in the late eighteenth century, such as *twaddle* 'nonsense' and *hump* 'to copulate'. The labels *slang, colloquial, standard, nonstandard, dialect, argot* and *jargon* are carefully explained, and a brief account is given of factors likely to promote the evolution and employment of slang. The development of English slang is traced back to the Middle English period, though the concept seems not to have existed before the sixteenth or seventeenth century. Specifically American slang began to appear in the seventeenth century and received appreciation and academic attention rather earlier than slang in Britain did. The select annotated bibliography complements the information contained within the introduction and provides a useful starting point for independent research.

The use of nouns as verbs is an age-old practice which has prompted lively reactions. Robertson Cochrane ('Verbum Sap: To Verb or Not to Verb', *Verbatim* 21.ii.22–3) notes the tendency to label such disliked usages as American. Bill Bryson's account of the history of English in America (*Made in America*) is 'unashamedly discursive', dealing not just with disputed etymologies, including those for *OK, the real McCoy* and *Kilroy was here*, but also with many of the myths of American history. The first few chapters are largely chronological, but later he focuses on subjects such as immigration, food, travel, advertising and the movies. Entertainingly intermingled with accounts of, among other things, the doomed attempt to introduce into America all the birds mentioned in Shakespeare, Bryson manages to include much useful linguistic information, using important historical documents as the basis of his discussion of pronunciation, spelling, vocabulary and, occasionally, grammar. He dismisses the myth that German was ever a serious alternative to English as the national language of America, puts Franklin's interest in spelling reform into perspective and reveals that the Pilgrim Fathers were able to benefit from the help of the native Americans, not because of the settlers' linguistic aptitude, but because Tisquantum, from the local Wampanoag tribe, already spoke fluent English. Trends in suffixation in brand-names are discussed, and a fascinating account of American place-names reveals that many were determined on the whim of railway and post office officials. The final chapter, perhaps predictably, considers the influence of political correctness, but also covers the educational system and literacy levels, and concludes that, despite the large number of Spanish speakers, English is likely to remain unchallenged as the national language of America.

The fifth volume of *The Cambridge History of the English Language*, edited by Robert Burchfield, is the most significant contribution to this section this year. It deals with varieties of English in the British Isles and overseas. J. Derrick McClure, Alan R. Thomas and Jeffrey L. Kallen discuss the spread and development of English in Scotland, Wales and Ireland, respectively, and Ossi Ihalainen deals with English dialects since 1776. The Englishes of Australia, the Caribbean, New Zealand, South Africa and South Asia are treated in chapters by George W. Turner, John A. Holm, Laurie Bauer, William Branford and Braj B. Kachru. Each chapter describes the political, cultural and economic factors influencing the evolution of English in its region. The discussions range from the earliest records to the present day, with some of the contributors hazarding suggestions about future development. The chapters are divided into sections on lexis, grammar, phonology, dialect variation and so on, which facilitates comparison between the national and local varieties of English. Excluded from consideration are African Englishes, because there is little research to rely on, and North American English, which will be covered by volume VI. One of the many praiseworthy features in this thorough and well-written volume is its coherence. The author of each chapter has read the other contributions, so unnecessary repetition is avoided, and some interesting comparisons are made between the varieties of English discussed. Brief lists of further reading and a thorough bibliography should also prove invaluable.

3. Dialectology and Sociolinguistics (including Creolistics)

Sociolinguistic perspectives on the use and spread of English around the world are discussed in several texts this year. First, the fifth volume of the *Cambridge History of the English Language* edited by Robert Burchfield brings together papers written on (1) dialects of England since 1776; (2) the use of English in the former Celtic-speaking countries of Ireland, Scotland and Wales; (3) the settler Englishes of Australia, New Zealand and South Africa; (4) the creole Englishes of the Caribbean; and finally, (5) the non-native Englishes of South Asia. The strengths of the volume include the often compelling and invariably detailed sociohistorical accounts of the spread of English, and the exhaustive descriptions of particularly lexical features of world Englishes. Highlights include Braj B. Kachru's extended analysis of 'English in South Asia'; J. Derrick McClure's fine description of patterns of language shift in Scotland; and Laurie Bauer's account of the Maori language and its influence on New Zealand English (these papers are discussed in greater detail below). On the minus side, many of the linguistic data presented are available elsewhere; there is little discussion of the relationship between the various Englishes represented; and finally, although a number of the papers discuss the importance of language and dialect contact in the spread and development of English, processes such as *levelling* and *focusing* which are a known consequence of speaker contact are given only a sketchy treatment.

Alastair Pennycook's *The Cultural Politics of English as an International Language* takes a critical look at the spread of English and argues convincingly for a new interpretation of the status of English as a world language. Pennycook examines the discourse of English as an international language, and rejects the often-made assumption that the rise of English as a world language has been 'natural', 'neutral' and 'beneficial'. Rather, he argues for a critical interpretation (which involves examination of the political and cultural constraints on English) of what he terms the *worldliness* of English. The first half of Pennycook's text includes discussion of the relationship between language, culture and society: he is critical of traditional sociolinguistic theory, which, he argues, perceives a simple, one-way influence of society on language, rather an interaction between the two in which language also constructs dominant ideologies within society. Against this detailed theoretical background, Pennycook examines the use of English in Malaysia and Singapore, and discusses the pedagogical concerns which emerge from his analysis: he argues for a new role for English teachers as critical educators who understand the role of English in relation to issues of power, authority, access to knowledge and cultural inequality. Pennycook's volume will be of particular relevance to those involved with the teaching of English, but will also be of interest to those in applied linguistics and to any who perceive the importance of examining language in terms of its wider political, cultural and economic context.

J. Phillipson's 'English Language Spread Policy' (*IJSL* 107.7–24) also examines the importance of English as an instrument of state and looks specifically at the external language spread policies of Britain and the US. Phillipson begins by providing an historical account of the colonial inheritance of English and stresses the 'civilizing' role that the English language was perceived to fulfil. He also considers the American promotion of the spread of English, and identifies the role of government agencies in propagating that spread under the 'aegis' of such missions as Peace Corps, Aid Work, and Agencies for International Development. All of these, he argues, legitimize English language teaching as being in the national and international interest. In terms of Britain's role, critical analysis is made of the British Council: for example, in terms of the role it plays in ELT 'aid' projects in Africa and the Middle East.

Here is perhaps the best place to mention the publication of the third edition of P. Trudgill and J. Hannah's *International English: A Guide to the Varieties of Standard English.* This text is updated and expanded this year to include elaborated details on varieties of American English and a detailed account of second language varieties of English (e.g. English in West Africa, India and the Philippines). The volume remains an essential introductory guide to the linguistic characteristics of world Englishes. Finally, on charting patterns of change in the Englishes of the world, we should briefly mention Laurie Bauer's *Watching English Change* and Labov's *Principles of Linguistic Change*, vol. I, *Internal Factors* (reviewed in section 6(b)). We look forward to the second volume of Labov's discussion, which will cover the 'External Factors' relevant to language change.

Looking now at the use of English in specific countries and continents, we should perhaps begin with a consideration of the Canadian context, since there has been a wealth of papers on this area this year – many of which are included in *IJSL*. John Edwards's focus article on 'Ethnolinguistic Pluralism and its Discontents: A Canadian Study, and Some General Observations' (110.5–85) provides an account of the current state of the use of English and French in Canada, and particularly reports on the introduction and maintenance of official bilingualism. As background for his analysis of the Canadian situation, Edwards considers the relationship between language and identity and takes the opportunity to challenge his (many) critics; particularly those who have charged him with being 'anti-ethnic' and 'anti-minority'. On Canada, Edwards provides a thorough account giving a broad overview of the consequences of the conflict between the increasing shift to French in Quebec and the Anglophone development outside of this region. The 'linguistic cleavage' which occurs as a result is considered in the light of the aim to achieve a national identity and internal recognition of this identity within Canada. The remainder of issue 110 of *IJSL* is taken up with critical reviews on Edwards's article, including comments by Nancy Dorian, Suzanne Romaine and Viv Edwards.

IJSL 105/6 is devoted to papers discussing 'French–English Language Issues in Canada'. Richard Bourhis provides an overview of the topic in which he charts the history of English and French from the first French settlements to the most recent legislation on French and English language use (5–36). John de Vries considers trends and patterns of language use between 1971 and 1991 in his paper 'Canada's Official Language Communities: An Overview of the Current Demolinguistic Situation' (37–68). D'Iberville Fortier examines 'Official Languages Policies in Canada: A Quiet Revolution' (69–97), in which he draws on his experience of being the Commissioner of Official Languages in the years 1984–91. Raymond Mougeon and Edouard Beniak's paper on 'Bilingualism, Language Shift, and Institutional Support for French: The Case of the Franco-Ontarians' (99–126) outlines the position and status of this community since the late 1600s, and examines the conditions under which French mother-tongue speakers are shifting to the use of English. Mougeon and Beniak base their study on census data of 1981 and 1986 and report that, of the 475,605 individuals who class themselves as being of French mother tongue, 84 per cent report that they were able to hold a conversation in both the official languages of Canada (very different statistics from Quebec, where only 29 per cent of French mother-tongue speakers claim a similar level of competence in English). The shift to English is measured in two dimensions: (1) the loss of the ability to carry out a conversation in French – 4 per cent of those included in the 1981 census reported this degree of loss of their mother tongue; and (2) the use of English as the language most often spoken in the home – 55 per cent of those who stated French as their mother tongue reported that English was used as the main language of communication in this domain. Factors which have led to the shift include the requirement for English in many professional and work-related domains; the declining influence of the Catholic church; and migration into urban centres, which has led to an increased contact with English speakers. However, although Mougeon and Beniak find the loss of French in the home, they report on legislation which is introducing French into the public domains of society. The authors conclude with a statement of their hope that this increased level of institutional support will stem the tide of the shift to English and the consequent assimilation of the Franco-Ontarians. Josiane Hamers and Kristen Hummel's 'The Francophones of Quebec: Language Policies and Language Use' (*IJSL* 105/6.127-52) discusses the unique place of this French-speaking community, which has its own institutions in French and where French can be used for 'all activities of daily life'. In contrast, Gary Caldwell examines 'English Quebec: Demographic and Cultural Reproduction' (153–80) and paints a picture of *contraction* caused by increased out-migration and the drying up of in-migration. However, although English Quebec is likely to become smaller in the future, Caldwell argues that it may well become more stable: 'Lower turnover will result from fewer newcomers, and, in the eventuality of a renewed federalism as opposed to the accession of Quebec to independence, fewer leavers' (174). Caldwell concludes that this new stability may lead to a stronger locally orientated identification and so to the maintenance of Anglophones in Quebec. This edition (*IJSL* 105/6) on language use in Canada also includes papers by Rodrigue Landry and Réal Allard on 'The Acadians of New Brunswick: Demolinguistic Realities and the Vitality of the French Language' (181–215), and Richard Bourhis on 'Bilingualism and the Language of Work: The Linguistic Work Environment Survey' (217–266).

From Canada to the USA, Carmen Silva-Corvalán's *Language Contact and Change* examines the result of contact between Spanish and English in Los Angeles. The work begins with theoretical preliminaries regarding contact and the sociocultural setting of Spanish in LA. Chapters 2 and 3 discuss changes in tense-mood-aspect morphology in Spanish, and chapter 4 examines the *internal* motivation for change. Here Silva-Corvalán argues that, although changes in a contact situation may be internally motivated (i.e. autonomous to the linguistic system), external factors hold the key to explaining the diffusion and spread of linguistic changes. Chapter 5 includes discussion of external factors leading to change in Spanish, and the final chapter of the volume discusses the role of 'Conflicting Loyalties' in relation to Spanish and English.

Joshua Fishman's 'Yiddish and Voting Rights in New York, 1915 and 1921' (*LPLP* 18.i.1–18) critically examines the English Literary Amendment to the New York State Constitution – an amendment which decreed competence in English to be a necessary prerequisite for the right to vote, and was later overturned by civil rights legislation of the 1960s and 1970s. Fishman's thesis is that this amendment is resurrected in modern-day 'English Only' policies in the US; particularly those which have emerged as a consequence of the Hispanic influx into America in the 1980s. Indeed, Fishman claims that while the main target of restrictive legislation may change from one historical context to another, the aims and objectives of such legislation are invariably the same: to foster the hegemony of English speakers in the American political system at the expense of newcomers who are linguistically, culturally and politically different. Fishman also publishes an article on 'Critiques of Language Planning: A Minority Languages Perspective' this year (*JMMD* 15.91–9).

Barbara Boseker reports on 'The Disappearance of American Indian Languages' (*JMMD* 15.147–60), and examines the reasons as to why only a third of the native American languages remain, and why others are currently declining and in danger of death. Apart from the obvious consequences of slaughter and disease in the early years of white 'settlement', the procedure of assimilating and civilizing native children by forcing them into boarding school education is seen as a key factor in the death of indigenous languages. Reports from Menominee women reveal the cruelty of punishments which ensued from the speaking of their mother tongue. However, Boseker's paper is not all doom and gloom: she reports on the success of a number of maintenance programmes which have been introduced to stem the decline of the native languages; e.g. the Rock Point Community School's bilingual education programme in the maintenance and revival of Navajo, and the Isleta Headstart Computer Programme on the maintenance of the oral language Isleta (a dialect of Tiwa).

On the use of creole languages on the islands around America, Suzanne Romaine reports on 'Hawai'i Creole English as a literary language' (*LSoc* 23.527–54) and examines the sociopolitical factors which determine the perception of

Hawai'i Creole English (HCE) as a literary *dialect* rather than a literary *language*. Romaine gives a history of this variety and examines its literary heritage. She observes that Hawaii has been slow to acknowledge the value of HCE in the literary domain, even perceiving Hawaii to have 'no literature of its own'. However, while it is not the case that Hawaii lacks a literature, HCE does lack a standardized form, which results in its lack of autonomy. Romaine argues that since it is autonomy which facilitates elaboration, then the lack of a standardized HCE acts as a barrier to its increased use in the literary domain. The elaboration of HCE is not unproblematic, however. Not only are the sociopolitical conditions necessary for standardization lacking in Hawaii, elaboration may also bring about unwelcome consequences for the use of HCE as a marker of social identity. For example, Romaine notes that, at present, HCE is represented mainly in first person narrative, and that in this form it functions as an intimate language signalling 'otherness'. The elaboration of HCE into third person narrative may result in HCE becoming a language of *public* rather than *private* discourse, resulting in the loss of this important function. Nevertheless, Romaine concludes that 'reclaiming both Hawaiian and HCE as legitimate languages is essential to decolonization in Hawaii'.

John Holm's paper on 'English in the Caribbean' (in Burchfield, *The Cambridge History of the English Language*) begins with a detailed review of the historical landmarks which influenced the spread of English in this context: the first English settlements of the early seventeenth century and the consequent development of pidgin English; late seventeenth- and early eighteenth-century development of slave communities and the emergence of 'a creole with a structure quite distinct from English' (339); the abolition of slavery in the early nineteenth century and consequent immigration leading to decreolization. This compelling sociohistorical account provides a background against which Holm details the linguistic characteristics of the (basilectal) creole Englishes of the Caribbean. Holm is careful to identify various different strands in the development of creole varieties: for example, while the segmental phonological system of Caribbean creoles are shown to include vowels and consonants from both the superstrate and substrate languages, the phonotactic constraints which operate upon these segments derive from the CV syllabic structure of the substrate languages alone – hence Sranan *bigi* ('big') and *dagu* ('dog').

Also on the Caribbean context, Alison Irvine's 'Dialect Variation in Jamaican English: A Study of the Phonology of Social Group Markings' (*EWW* 15.35–53) examines attitudes towards two variants of Jamaican English : (1) 'Upper St Andrew drawl', which is used by white and light-skinned affluent Jamaicans; and (2) an unmarked variety of Educated Jamaican English. Employing a matched guise technique, Irvine elicits attitudes on both dimensions of status and solidarity and finds, for example, that judges would prefer users of the unmarked Educated Jamaican English as friends, but consider speakers of the 'drawl' variety to be more intelligent. Irvine also examines the phonological correlates of these two varieties and assesses the sociolinguistic significance of such features as nasality, rhoticity and palatalization. She concludes that variation in Jamaica does not necessarily involve a 'mixture' between creole and English, but may be realized within each of these varieties independently. Lise Winer and Mary Rimmer examine 'Language Varieties in Early Trinidanian Novels 1838–1907' (*EWW* 15.225–48). They find several varieties of English represented (e.g. Standard British Literary English, British Dialect English, Victorian Villainous English), as well as other languages (e.g. Trinidanian Creole English, French Creole, Spanish, Latin, African languages). A detailed analysis of four literary texts reveals two particularly significant features of the novels: (1) mutual intelligibility – characters in the novels appear to understand each other no matter which variety of English is used; (2) respect for language differences – characters in the novels reveal an acceptance that not all speakers have the same target language or language varieties.

While on the topic of the relationship between English and creole languages, we should mention, albeit briefly, Belinda Young-Davy's reports on 'Polyfunctional prepositions in Rama Cay Creole' (*EWW* 15.79–100) – an English-orientated creole spoken by the Rama Indians on Rama Cay, an island off the central Atlantic coast of Nicaragua. Young-Davy argues that this creole variety is unique in its number and range of polyfunctional prepositions, and claims that this is a consequence of 'multiple layers of linguistic influence on Rama Cay Creole over the last 150 years or more'. In *JPCL,* John Rickford and Jerome Handler discuss 'Textual Evidence on the Early Nature of Barbadian Speech, 1775–1835' (9.221–56). The authors argue that early Barbadian English exhibited more non-standard features than has traditionally been recognized, and show that while early Barbadian speech comprised a range of varieties, 'creole-like varieties were undoubtedly part of that range'. *JPCL* also publishes two papers on Haitian Creole this year: Viviane Déprez's 'Haitian Creole: A Pro-Drop Language?' (9.1–24), and John Lumsden's 'Possession: Substratum Semantics in Haitian Creole' (9.25–49).

On the use of English in the British Isles, we should first record the publication of the *Survey of English Dialects: The Dictionary and Grammar* (Clive Upton, David Parry and John D. Widdowson). Published by Routledge, this detailed and carefully constructed volume marks a further major development in the reporting of dialect data collected between 1950 and 1961. The volume provides a synthesis of the information provided in the original twelve volumes, and gives a new and accessible overview of regional variation in the pronunciation, distribution and function of regional lexis in the dialects of England. The text is divided into two parts: (1) 'The Dictionary', which lists variation in dialectal forms according to semantic categories – each listing provides head-word, word-class, definition, pronunciation and distribution in that order; (2) 'The Grammar', which details aspects of morphology and syntax recorded in the survey which differ from their counterparts in Standard English (in either form or context of occurrence). The volume is an essential reference guide for those working in the field of English dialects. Ossi Ihalainen's contribution to *The Cambridge History of the English Language* reports on 'The Dialects of England since 1776'. Ihalainen identifies the end of the nineteenth century as a significant landmark in the history of English in England, since this period saw the end of tolerance towards regional varieties – shown, for example, by public schools' explicit aim of eradicating variation. The phonological characteristics of late eighteenth-century and early nineteenth-century dialects are considered, and particular attention is paid to A. Ellis's *On Early English Pronunciation* (Trübner, 1889) which Ihalainen argues provides the first 'coherent picture of the dialectal structure of England' (207). Ihalainen concludes his paper with a note on the importance of London and its environs as the main context of innovation and change in the dialects of England. Gillis Kristensson provides a brief exposition on 'Sociolects in 14th-century London' (*Non-standard Varieties of Language: Papers from the Stockholm Symposium* 11–13 April 1991 [1994], 103–10). Kristensson looks at the differences between Standard English and the regional London dialect, and argues for a theory which is already generally accepted: namely, the significance of a migrant merchant class in the creation of Standard English.

On a more contemporary theme, James Milroy, Lesley Milroy and Sue Hartley discuss 'Local and Supra-Local Change in British English: The Case of Glottalisation' (*EWW* 15.1-33). Observations in different geographical areas (Cardiff, Tyneside, Coleraine, Northern Ireland) reveal that the increase in glottalization takes two forms: glottal replacement and glottal reinforcement. These two trends show different patterns of linguistic and sociolinguistic distribution: in terms of sociolinguistic patterning, for example, sex of is found to be a more significant factor than social class. Specifically, the authors find that while men are the more frequent users of glottal reinforcement (which tends to be confined to local regions), women lead in the use of glottal stops (a change on a supra-local level). These observations are used to cast doubt on the assumption that a simple notion of 'prestige' is adequate to explain women's linguistic behaviour.

The Cambridge History of the English Language, ed. Burchfield, includes J. Derrick McClure's detailed, thorough and engaging account of the spread and development of 'English in Scotland'. McClure begins by distinguishing between Scots and Scottish English, and by reporting on the debate as to whether both varieties should be considered as dialects of English, or whether Scots deserves to be treated as a language in its own right. McClure details the historical, political and social factors which led to the decline of Gaelic and the emergence of Scots, and the later shift from Scots to Scottish English. In charting these patterns of language change, McClure takes issue with the general assumption that the Reformation marked the beginning of the imposition of English. Rather, he argues that the advent of printing in the fourteenth century led to the assimilation of Scots written texts to English models of spelling and grammar. From this point on, English spread unevenly through particular domains and registers: while official prose had a secure position and so succumbed to English slowly, narrative prose 'accommodated' to English norms over a period of time, and poetry was extinguished quite rapidly. Spoken language, on the other hand, remained relatively unaffected, and Scots remained as the spoken tongue of Scotland until the eighteenth century. Throughout his linguistic description, McClure identifies sites of regional, social and stylistic variation, and provides examples of each of these. Also on language use in this region, we should mention Morag MacNeil's 'Immersion Programmes Employed in Gaelic-Medium Units in Scotland' (*JMMD* 15.245–52), in which the author provides a description of the teaching methods used in these programmes, and discusses the views and experiences of both teachers and parents involved in the projects.

Moving from Scotland to Wales, Alan Thomas's discussion of 'English in Wales' (in Burchfield, ed., *The Cambridge History of the English Language*) points specifically to the political and educational factors which resulted in the language shift from Welsh to English. Starting with English settlement in the fourteenth century, Thomas traces the demise of Welsh through the Acts of Union of 1536 and 1542, to the Education Act of 1888 and beyond. As well as identifying these overt external influences on Welsh, Thomas points to the influence of attitudes towards Welsh and English in Wales, and observes that from the mid-nineteenth century, negative attitudes prevailed: Welsh being viewed as a barrier to social mobility, commercial propensity and even 'moral progress'. In his paper 'Development, Dependency and the Democratic Deficit' (*JMMD* 15.101–27), Colin Williams discusses the paradox by which the infrastructure set in place to support the use of Welsh is at the same time creating a 'binding dependency' of Welsh users on the local state. Also in *JMMD* this year, Nikolas Coupland, Angie Williams and Peter Garrett report on 'The Social Meanings of Welsh English: Teachers' Stereotyped Judgements' (15.vi.471–89), in which study is made of the evaluations of teachers from seventy-one schools throughout Wales. Assessment of attitudes reveals that, while Standard British English is considered as the most prestigious dialect, the variety of Welsh English used in south-west Wales is also judged as relatively prestigious, as well as being considered *dynamic*, *pleasant* and *truly Welsh sounding*.

Finally to Ireland, and first to Jeffrey L. Kallen's contribution in *The Cambridge History of English* (ed. Burchfield), in which the author discusses Irish English in two parts: (1) external history, in which Kallen identifies the various patterns of migration and contact which have co-occurred with the development of Ireland and Irish English; and (2) internal developments, in which he considers the formation of Early Irish English (beginning in the fourteenth century), through the rise of Modern Irish English (from the sixteenth century), to English in modern Ireland (the nineteenth century and beyond). Kallen draws consistent and systematic links between these two developments, and thereby highlights the relationship between external and internal factors in the emergence of Irish English. He concludes his paper by considering the intriguing possibility that Irish English arose from neither substratum (i.e. Irish) nor retentionist (i.e. English) influences, but from a third source of 'language universals made manifest in the contact situation' (193). Examining the Irish language itself (and particularly its relationship to English in Ireland's Gaeltacht region), Pádraig Ó Riagáin reports on 'Language Maintenance and Language Shift as Strategies of Social Reproduction' (*JMMD* 15 179–97). Ó Riagáin charts patterns of stability, migration and economy in this region, and links these to the fate of Irish. The main strength of his analysis is that he provides details of precisely *how* these language external factors relate to the fate of Irish: economic factors are seen to influence social network structure and, in turn, differences in social network structure to lead to a change in linguistic behaviour. For example, Ó Riagáin shows that although the Gaeltacht underwent a significant economic shift in the 1920s and 1930s, the social networks stayed strong in this area and bilingual competence in English and Irish was maintained. It seems that bilingual reproduction levels in the western area went into decline only in the 1960s or later. A further shift away from Irish has occurred in the past fifteen years due to frequent interaction with English speakers and young people moving away to work outside of the Gaeltacht area: the social networks are thus shifting and this has served to 'diminish the possibility of maintaining Irish'. Ó Riagáin thus provides a context-dependent account of the notion of social network to explain language use. He concludes that the complex sequence of maintenance, shift and revival of Irish cannot be explained unless patterns of linguistic behaviour are seen in the light of changes in the economic base of the community. Finally, on the position of Irish *vis-à-vis* English, we should mention Thomas O'Donoghue's report on 'Bilingual Education at the Beginning of the 20th Century: The Bilingual Programme of Instruction in Ireland 1904–1922' (*JMMD* 15.491–505).

Few studies are published on the use and status of English in Europe this year. Of most interest to readers of this bibliography might be Jenny Cheshire and Lise-Marie Moser's 'English as a Cultural Symbol: The Case of Advertisements in French-Speaking Switzerland' (*JMMD* 15.451–69). Cheshire and Moser examine the use of English in the media and find that between one quarter and one third of all adverts in a selection of weekly magazines in French-speaking Switzerland are published in the English language. Analysis reveals that the use of English in adverts serves a number of different symbolic functions relating to: (1) its use in English-speaking countries, particularly the USA; (2) its status as an international language; and (3), and perhaps most significantly, its appropriation as a symbol of Swiss national identity. Also worth mentioning is that *IJAL* 4.ii includes two papers on the acquisition of English as a foreign language in two European contexts. The first is Ayse Akyd's account of 'First Language Use in EFL: Planning in Turkish vs. Planning in English' (169–96), in which Akyd examines the function and significance of the language used for planning or pre-writing in Turkish students' composition of English essays; and the second is Angela Hasselgren's paper 'Lexical Teddy Bears and Advanced Learners: A Study into the Ways Norwegian Students Cope with English Vocabulary' (237–58).

Moving to a consideration of southern hemisphere Englishes, we should note George W. Turner's contribution to *The Cambridge History of the English Language* (ed. Burchfield), in which the author discusses the formation and development of 'English in Australia'. Turner pays considerable attention to the pronunciation of Australian English tracing it from early (inconsistent) nineteenth-century comments – 'some hear Cockney everywhere, others note a remarkably pure speech' (283), through the ground-breaking work of A. Mitchell (*The Pronunciation of English in Australia* [Angus and Robertson 1946]) and A. Mitchell and A. Delbridge (*The Pronunciation of English in Australia* [rev. edn Angus and Robertson 1965]) to B. Horvath's *Variation in Australian English: The Sociolects of Sydney* (CUP 1985) account of the sociolects of Sydney. As well as giving considerable detail on segmental phonology, Turner also considers non-segmental characteristics of Australian English: he reports on the distinctive use of high rise terminals, and also on characteristic patterns of stress and rhythm. The discussion of Australian English morphology and syntax is unsurprisingly brief; in comparison to phonology, there is a dearth of research on the grammatical systems of southern hemisphere Englishes. However, Turner provides a full description of Australian English vocabulary in which he identifies items borrowed from Aboriginal languages and the jargon of early convicts. From the consideration of the linguistic, Turner proceeds to the historical, and concludes his paper by describing Australia and the development of its language through the early days, the pastoral era, the goldrushes and the modern period.

On a modern-day issue, Michael Currie and Michael Hogg report on 'Subjective Ethnolinguistic Vitality and Social Adaptation among Vietnamese Refugees in Australia' (*IJSL* 108.97–115). The authors examine social and linguistic factors which influence the educational achievement, occupational aspiration and life satisfaction of Vietnamese refugees living in Melbourne. Results show that 'refugee trauma' and background sociodemographic factors related to life in Vietnam are far less accurate predictors of educational achievement, etc., than is the dimension of cultural vitality and a strong feeling of ethnolinguistic identity. Kees de Bot and Michael Clyne provide an engaging account of 'A 16-year Longitudinal Study of Language Attrition in Dutch Immigrants in Australia' (*JMMD* 15.17–28), in which Dutch migrants interviewed by Clyne in the early 1970s are reinterviewed and tested by Kees de Bot in the late 1980s and early 1990s. Results show that, although the effects of English are observable in some areas of Dutch language use (e.g. adverbial order), there is no evidence that the general linguistic abilities of these speakers has decreased over the sixteen-year period. The authors conclude that migration does not necessarily lead to language attrition.

Other papers on the linguistic and sociolinguistic situation in Australia appear in *JMMD* and *LPLP*. The former includes two articles of interest to readers of this volume. The first is Marianne Bodi's 'The Changing Role of Minority Languages in Australia: The European and the Asia-Pacific Nexus' (*JMMD* 15.219–27), in which Bodi observes that the shift in the direction of 'Asia literacy' (and the consequent prioritizing of languages such as Japanese, Bahsa and Mandarin) has resulted in the diminishing support for some smaller (mostly European) minority languages. And the second is Leo Papademetre's 'Self-Defined, Other-Defined Cultural Identity: Logogenesis and Multiple-Group Membership in a Greek Australian Sociolinguistic Community' (*JMMD* 15.507–25), which reports on aspects of Greek and English language use among second and third generation bilinguals living in the Australian urban setting of Adelaide. The article of interest in *LPLP* is Camilla Bettoni and Barry Leal's 'Multiculturalism and Modern Languages in Australian Universities' (18.i.19–37). Bettoni and Leal report on an apparent inconsistency in the Australian education system, inasmuch as Australia's widespread image as a multicultural and multilingual society contrasts with the minor academic importance it accords to modern (particularly community) languages. Finally, we should mention Ian Malcolm's paper 'Discourse and Discourse Strategies in Australian Aboriginal English', which is published in *WEn* (13.289–306) this year.

Laurie Bauer provides the chapter on 'English in New Zealand' for *The Cambridge History of the English Language* (ed. Burchfield). Bauer begins his paper with a discussion of European settlement in New Zealand, and a discussion of the indigenous Maori people (and their language) with whom these settlers came into contact. In regard to the linguistic characteristics of New Zealand English, Bauer starts with a synchronic description of the variety in its present state, and then outlines the developmental stages which have led to this state. The phonology of the variety is dealt with in four main parts: (1) early developments (e.g. the use of an open vowel in the STRUT lexical set); (2) features noted before World War I (e.g. the centralization of the short vowel in KIT); (3) post-1930 developments (e.g. the use of dark /l/ pre-vocalically); and (4) recent developments (e.g. the merger of the diphthongs in NEAR and SQUARE). While noting that the grammar of New Zealand English is largely the same as Standard British English, Bauer does observe a few characteristically New Zealand forms: for example, the productive use of the *-ie* diminutive as used in *sickie* (absence from work) and *rellies* (relatives). In considering vocabulary, Bauer reports on borrowings from a diverse collection of languages including Maori, Samoan, Scottish, Irish and American English. Throughout his analysis of linguistic features, Bauer considers New Zealand English as, regionally at least, a single homogeneous variety. The fact that there is little regional variation is, as Bauer himself points out, surprising given the diverse mixture of British English dialects spoken by early settlers. The development of homogeneity from heterogeneity may be explained by the levelling and focusing processes known to occur when speakers of different dialects come into contact. However, in considering the possible origins of English in New Zealand, Bauer plays down the role of these processes, and argues that New Zealand English is directly descended from the English used in Australia.

From diachrony to synchrony: Janet Holmes's paper 'New Zealand Flappers: An Analysis of T-Voicing in New Zealand English' (*EWW* 15.195–224) examines a change in progress towards the use of voiced inter-vocalic /t/ in words like *letter* and *butter*. Holmes examines both linguistic and social constraints on the use of this variable, and finds that, in regard to the former, stress, vowel length and word-position exert constraints on the use of voiced /t/, and, in regard to the latter, that social dimensions such as age, gender and social class all influence the use and frequency of voiced forms. The particular aim of Holmes's paper is to detail the extent to which New Zealanders from different social backgrounds use T-voicing or flapping, and she finds that voicing is particularly frequent in the speech of young, male, working-class speakers and of informal speech styles. Miriam Meyerhoff's paper 'Sounds Pretty Ethnic, Eh?: A Pragmatic Particle in New Zealand English' (*LSoc* 23.367–88) provides a sociolinguistic and discourse-based analysis of the use of *eh*. Meyerhoff's analysis provides 'clear support' for the notion that *eh* is correlated with ethnicity: Maori men are the most frequent users of this discourse particle. However, *eh* also correlates with other social dimensions: for example, Pakeha (New Zealanders of European descent) women use the particle more than Pakeha men, and young speakers use it more than older speakers. In explaining this unusual pattern of sociolinguistic variation, Meyerhoff concludes that *eh* fulfils a macro-level intergroup function for male Maori (signalling in-group membership), and a micro-level interpersonal function of Pakeha women (marking personal affiliation).

William Branford's contribution to *The Cambridge History of the English Language* (ed. Burchfield) describes 'South African English'. Branford begins by considering factors unique to the situation in which this variety has developed: the beginnings of the variety marked by the Dutch East India company's settlement; late nineteenth-century step-by-step transference of African ancestral lands to white ownership; twentieth-century struggle and resistance. The various historical stages of the development of South African English, and different patterns of contact which have characterized this development, are reflected particularly in its lexicon. Branford provides a very lengthy and detailed account of South African English vocabulary and also lists the main phonological characteristics of this variety.

JPCL includes two papers on the use of English in Africa which will be of interest to readers: G. Tucker Child's 'Expressiveness in Contact Situations: The Fate of African Ideophones' (9.257–82); and Timothy Lloyd Wilt's 'A Survey of the Linguistic Preferences of Cameroon Pidgin English Speakers' (9.51–64). On English in Nigeria we should note the publication of Edmundo Bamiro's 'Lexico-Semantic Variation in Nigerian English' (*WEn* 13.47–60), and V. O. Awonusi's 'The Americanization of Nigerian English' (*WEn* 13.75–82); in the latter Awonusi discusses emerging Americanisms at both the phonological and lexical levels of use. Finally, *WEn* also includes Jan Bernsten's paper 'English and Shona in Zimbabwe' (13.iii.411–18), in which the author reports on the diglossic nature of urban contexts in Zimbabwe: Shona is used to mark ethnicity, while English identifies speakers as 'educated citizens of the world'.

On the 'new Englishes', we should begin by noting Braj B. Kachru's valuable account of the debates and controversies related to the use of 'English in South Asia' (*Cambridge History of the English Language*). Kachru provides an overview of the region in terms of its geography, history and (diverse) linguistic make-up, and then describes the imposition and spread of English in this multicultural and multilingual context. He outlines four stages in the introduction of English – exploration, implementation, diffusion and institutionalization – and points to the various roles of those responsible for its spread. Kachru concludes that, while the end of the British raj during the 1940s was supposed to initiate the demise of the English language in South Asia, 'the actual picture is one of ever greater social penetration of English' (542). Robert Baumgardner and Audrey Kennedy's paper 'Measure for Measure: Terms of Measurement in Pakistani English' (*EWW* 15.173–93) examines the use of measurement vocabulary from Urdu and other Pakistani languages in the speech of Pakistani speakers' mother tongues and English. It is found that, in spite of the conversion to the metric system, many still use the older terms, and that these terms 'naturally' transfer into the bi- and multilingual speech of users of English.

Ismail Talib examines the use of English in Singapore and reports specifically on 'The Development of Singaporean Literature in English' (*JMMD* 15.419–29). Talib traces the historical development of English literature in Singapore, and examines the sociocultural and political problems which ensue from the use of English in a context where the other languages and the ethnicity of the vast majority of the population are Asian. Talib concludes that, while the increased use of English in literature may be controversial, nevertheless the spread of English into the literary domain together with the popularity of these texts indicates 'the growing importance of English, not only as a lingua franca, but as a cultural medium as well'.

Herbert Pierson reports on 'Ethnolinguistic Vitality during a Period of Decolonisation without Independence: Perceived Vitality in Hong Kong' (*IJSL* 108.43–61). As one of Hong Kong's two official languages (spoken by 2.2 per cent of the 5,522,281-strong population), English is used in government, administration, business, law and education. Pierson discusses the rise in the status of English as Hong Kong has progressed to international status in trade, finance, communications, etc., and reports that while most of the population inherit Cantonese as their mother tongue (88.7 per cent), 'English is the official language of consequence.' Pierson concludes his work by considering whether the elevated status of English will continue when Hong Kong comes under Chinese rule. Also on English in this region, Martha Pennington and Francis Yue discuss 'English and Chinese in Hong Kong: Pre-1997 Language Attitudes' (*WEn* 13.1–20).

Eliezer Ben-Rafael's *Language, Identity and Social Division* (which is published in the Oxford Studies in Language Contact series) examines the linguistic and sociolinguistic situation in Israel and deals in some detail with the status and function of English in this nation. English is one of only four compulsory school subjects, is increasingly used in the media, and is a necessary prerequisite for middle- and high-ranking jobs. The greatest competency in English is displayed amongst the 'privileged strata', and knowledge of English is 'the linguistic variable that best differentiates between classes'. The function of English as a creator of identity is also considered, and it is found that immigrant Jews who have English as their mother tongue (e.g. immigrants from South Africa) are likely to maintain the use of English and, with the exception of that group ideologically committed to Zionism, to use it to reflect their high status. Ben-Rafael's volume is thus of interest at the level of English use around the world. However, to read the volume only for the information it provides on English would be to miss the main value of the text, which lies in its detailed description of the role of language, specifically the role and revival of Hebrew, in the creation of group unity and the development of a national identity. Here is perhaps the best place to mention another publication in the Oxford Studies in Language Contact series: Paul Kerswill's *Dialects*

Converging, a text which does not deal with English, but rather with rural speech and patterns of migration and dialect contact in Norway. Although only deserving of a brief mention in this context, those interested in sociolinguistic study outside of the domain of the English language, and specifically those interested in the social impetus of language change and dialect formation, will find this a most useful volume.

To conclude this discussion of varieties of English around the world, we should mention two papers of general interest. Both appear in *EWW* 15.i. The first is J. C. Chambers's 'An Introduction to Dialect Typography' (35–53), in which typographical methods used in Canada are discussed and explained with the objective that the techniques will be considered useful for dialect study in other areas. The second is Manfred Görlach's paper 'Innovation in New Englishes' (101–26), in which Görlach examines English-language use in various contexts, and looks particularly at neologisms in world Englishes. He considers varieties as diverse as Scottish English, American English, Indian English and certain creole Englishes. Finally, we should report the publication of a special issue of *WEn* (13.ii.) on 'World Englishes in Contact and Convergence'. The volume includes a general paper by Braj Kachru on 'Englishization and Contact Linguistics' (135–54), as well as numerous papers on 'Englishization' in specific countries and contexts: e.g. Martin Jonghak Baik's 'Syntactic Features of Englishization in Korean' (155–66); Anne J. Kishe's 'The Englishization of Tanzanian Kiswahili' (185–202); and Yasufumi Iwasari's 'Englishization of Japanese and Acculturation of English to Japanese Culture' (261–72).

On the wider issue of the relationship between English and other languages, we should recommend John Edwards's *Multilingualism*, which, as well as providing a theoretical analysis of the causes and consequences of multilingualism, also gives examples of direct relevance for those interested in English-language issues: e.g. the use and relationship between English and French in Canada, and the attempt to rescue and revive Irish. Here is the best place to also recommend Suzanne Romaine's *Bilingualism*, which appears in its second edition this year. Finally, I mention Yael Maschler's 'Metalanguage and Discourse Markers in Bilingual Conversation' (*LSoc* 23.325-66), in which Maschler provides an analysis of Hebrew–English bilingual conversation, and concentrates on how language alternation between these two functions as a marker of discourse boundaries in conversation.

Two textbooks on sociolinguistics are published this year. One is Suzanne Romaine's *Language in Society*, which provides an introduction to this subject area including chapters on language and gender, the social motivation of linguistic change, and pidgin and creole languages. The book is written in a clear, accessible and informative style, and so is ideally suited to those beginning the study of sociolinguistics. The other text which should be mentioned is Esther Figueroa's *Sociolinguistic Metatheory*. Unfortunately, the text remains unseen at the time of publication of this review.

On language and gender, *LSoc* publishes Lynette Hirschmann's article 'Female–Male Differences in Conversational Interaction' (23.427–42), over twenty years after it was conceived in her 'Women and Language' seminars at the University of Pennsylvania. Hirschmann's early and original observations – that women use more assent terms, facilitate conversation, and build on each other's statements – have now been supported countless times, of course. *LSoc* publish this paper with a foreword by Deborah Tannen and an epilogue written by Hirschmann in 1993. Also in *LSoc,* Susan Erlich and Ruth King report on 'Feminist Meanings and the (De)Politicization of the Lexicon' (23.59–76). Erlich and King argue that non-sexist innovations have a limited influence because they are often appropriated by sexist speech communities. For example, they claim that neutral generic terms (e.g. chairperson, spokesperson) are often not used or interpreted in their intended (neutral) way, but that rather they are used 'in ways that maintain sexist stereotypes and distinctions'. I note the publication of Janet Holmes's *Women, Men and Politeness*. Unfortunately, this volume remains unseen at the time of publication. We hope to provide a belated review next year.

L&C (14.ii.) has a special issue on 'Language Attitudes' this year, which includes papers by A. C. Cargile, H. Giles, E. Ryan and J. Bradac on 'Language Attitudes as a Social Process: A Conceptual Model and New Directions' (211–36); L. Hosman and S. Siltanen on 'The Attributional and Evaluative Consequences of Powerful and Powerless Speech Styles: An Examination of the "Control over Others" and "Control of Self" Explanations' (287–98); and A. Mulac and T. Lundell on 'Effects of Gender-Linked Language Differences in Adults' Writing Discourse: Multivariate Tests of Language Effects' (299–309).

Although on the periphery of the appropriate content for this section, I briefly mention a selection of the books published on the topic of English discourse. First, I note the publication of John Gibbons's (ed.) *Language and the Law*, which brings together a diverse collection of papers on topics as wide ranging as 'Orality, Literacy and Performativity in Anglo-Saxon Wills' (by Brenda Danet and Bryna Bogoch); 'Ideological Exchanges in British Magistrates' Courts' (by Sandra Harris); 'A Case of Communicative Clash: Aboriginal English and the Legal System' (by Diana Eades); and 'Auditory and Acoustic Analysis in Speaker Recognition' (by Francis Nolan). Longman's Real Language Series gives us another valuable work in Ulrike Meinhof and Kay Richardson's (eds.) *Text, Discourse and Context: Representations of Poverty in Britain.* The volume includes five papers all of which present original and pertinent interpretations of the discourse of poverty. They are: Gunther Kress's 'Text and Grammar as Explanation'; Brian Street's 'The International Dimension'; Ulrike Meinhof's 'From the Street to the Screen: Breadline Britain and the Semiotics of Poverty'; Kay Richardson's 'Interpreting Breadline Britain'; and Roger Hewitt's 'The Beggar's Blanket: Public Scepticism and the Representation of Poverty'. On a very different theme, I also recommend Heidi Ehernberger Hamilton's *Conversations with an Alzheimer's Patient*, in which Hamilton uses an interactional sociolinguistic approach to analyse conversations she had with an Alzheimer's sufferer over a four-year period. I also mention the publication of Vai Ramanathan-Abbott's 'Interactional Differences in Alzheimer's Discourse: An Examination of Alzheimer's Discourse Speech across Two Audiences' (*LSoc* 23.31–58). Finally, for those seeking an introduction to methods in discourse analysis, I recommend Deborah Schiffrin's *Approaches to Discourse*, which presents a detailed and thorough account of theories of discourse from speech acts, through ethnography to variation analysis.

4. Lexicography, Lexicology and Semantics

Walter Nash's *Jargon: Its Uses and Abuses* is described in its publicity material as 'part essay, part discursive dictionary'. Indeed, as the author's interests are in style rather than lexicography, he confesses that the glossary is not a systematic study of jargon so much as 'an amplifying commentary' on the text. Jargon is, of course, something that other people use, and one of the pleasures of the glossary is the occasional irascibility of the author, who claims that with advancing years 'rage is the only fun left'. Political correctness and literary theory are among the objects of this rage. The text itself makes a useful distinction between three types of jargon: shop talk, which is the jargon of profession; sales talk, the jargon of production; and show talk, the jargon of pretension. Shop talk is the jargon of a particular trade or interest, which can exclude as well as include by serving as a badge of belonging. Sales talk, which includes the jargon of politics, is used to manipulate and to deceive. In this section, Nash includes an interesting discussion of the use of sporting metaphors, often used, paradoxically, to signal seriousness of intent, as well as to identify the speaker with the moral integrity characteristically associated with such pastimes. Show talk is often used as a defence by those who fear that if they spoke more clearly people might understand that they had nothing of interest to say.

John Algeo's *Fifty Years Among the New Words: A Dictionary of Neologisms* represents 113 instalments of a column called 'Among the New Words', published in *American Speech* between 1941 and 1991. Its editors, aided by their numerous contributors, set out to provide a descriptive account, illustrated by citations, of words not yet included in general dictionaries of American English. Nonce-words were included only to demonstrate general rules of word-formation. The introduction divides the sources of new words into creating, borrowing, combining, shortening, blending and shifting (in style, grammar or meaning), and deals with each type in some detail. Shortening, for instance, is subdivided into clipping, alphabetism, acronymy, phonetic elision, and back formation. Motivations for neologisms are considered, including social, technical and political change. An alphabetical list of the terms included in the columns over the fifty-year period is cross-referenced to the reprinted columns themselves. The earliest instalments, edited by Dwight L. Bolinger, have a particular charm, including as they do, terms such as *burp* (noun and verb), *snazzy* and *zany*, as well as many relating to current events, such as *appeasement, flack* and *black marketeer*. The column from December 1942 notes with approval the introduction of words for women fulfilling previously masculine roles, such as *sailorette, graduette, legionette* and *bellehop*. Later columns provide citations for *date-rape, dweeb* and *outing*. One respect in which the book is likely to be useful is that it draws many of its citations from newspapers and magazines, which might otherwise be inaccessible to lexicographers and lexicographiles.

Neologisms are also the subject of Gerald Nelson's 'War and the *OED*' (*Verbatim* 20.iv.17–18), which is based on the assumption that neologisms are produced at a steady rate across a single generation. He concludes that although wars may increase linguistic ingenuity, practical problems may undermine the process of documentation. John Algeo argues, in 'Desuetude among New English Words' (*IJL* [1993] 6.iv.281–93), that the emphasis on neologisms has detracted from consideration of word-loss. He finds that 58 per cent of words first recorded between 1944 and 1977 are no longer listed in unabridged dictionaries. He likens this rate of loss to the random mutations of evolution.

In his *The Story of Webster's Third*, Herbert C. Morton gives a fascinating account of the work leading to, and the controversy following, the publication of *Webster's Third* dictionary in 1961. The first section includes short biographies of those involved and a history of the Merriam publishing company. The second section describes the practices of the dictionary, the third its immediate reception, and the fourth its long-term influence. The *Third* was criticized for excluding encyclopaedic information, for reducing the number of usage labels, for including widely used non-standard terms such as *ain't*, for its treatment of trade marks and racial slurs, for giving too many variant pronunciations, and for using illustrative quotations from contemporary speakers and writers, apparently in preference to quotations from the Bible and literary greats. The dictionary was blamed for declining standards in language and, by implication at least, for the impending collapse of civilization. Morton demonstrates that the tone of much of the adverse comment was set by the *Third*'s own pre-publication publicity, which demonstrated little understanding of the dictionary's nature. Its detractors often failed to notice that many of the failings they saw in the *Third* were in accordance with the practices of *Webster's Second*. The *Second*'s adherents even planned to take over the company so that the *Third* could be scrapped altogether and a new prescriptive dictionary developed on the basis of the earlier edition. Reactions in Britain and among academics in the States were, on the whole, positive, as were the long-term responses of its users, but Morton does not ignore the limitations of the work, some of which derive from excessively rigid application of editorial principles.

Juliet Fleming's 'Dictionary English and the Female Tongue' in Richard Burt and John Michael Archer, eds, *Enclosure Acts*, discusses early dictionaries' targeting of women and the association between women and the vernacular. She argues that before class-based differences in language preoccupied prescriptive writers, women were presented as the linguistic outsiders whose extravagance must be curbed. Laurence Urdang's 'The Uses of Lexicography' (*Verbatim* 20.iv.19–20) is an account of the banning of dictionaries for offensive definitions and objectionable words. 'New Dimensions in Vocabulary Studies' (*L&LC* 9.ii.149–54) is Andreas H. Jucker's review article of the second edition of the *OED* on CD-ROM. He demonstrates that although it facilitates research which would previously have been impossible or impractical, the raw data it produces require careful and informed interpretation in light of their limitations.

Laurie Bauer and Paul Nation study the understanding of inflections and affixes in reading, in 'Word Families' (*IJL* [1993] 6.4.253–79), and discuss the significance of this in deciding where, if at all, prefixed derivatives should be listed in second-language dictionaries. Lexicographers are also well served by Henri Béjoint's *Tradition and Innovation in Modern English Dictionaries* and Bo Svensén's *Practical Lexicography*. Although the two books cover much of the same ground, Béjoint's is an account of lexicographical practice and Svensén's more of a manual for dictionary-makers. Béjoint addresses the question of what a dictionary is, what it should be, what it is used for, and whether customer expectations are or ought to be allowed to influence content. He gives an account of the 'lexicographical scene' of various English-speaking countries, and demonstrates the relative influence of the British and American traditions. The origin of the general-purpose dictionary in eighteenth-century social aspiration and linguistic conservatism is discussed, and the use of dictionary definitions as evidence in court is considered in his account of the treatment of racially, sexually and politically sensitive words. Béjoint summarizes previous studies of dictionary use and discusses the implications of their reliance on questionnaires. His brief consideration of the lexicographical expectations of speakers of different languages provides some useful pointers for EFL learning. He also identifies and evaluates assumptions underlying dictionary production, such as the notion that a dictionary can be representative, that the most usefully included words are those most frequently used, that words are discrete units with discrete meanings which can be defined and whose definitions ought to be able to serve as a substitute for the defined word, that definitions ought not to be circular, that defining words should be more frequent than the word defined, and that all words used in a dictionary ought to be defined in it. The final chapter deals with the future of lexicography and discusses the problems of idiomaticity and polysemy.

Svensén considers lexicographical problems from collecting material to deciding on layout and typeface. He discusses the requirements and competence of users of monolingual and bilingual dictionaries, noting that while both look up meanings most often, second language learners rank grammatical information and native speakers spelling next in importance. Lexicons of many types are discussed, from construction and collocation dictionaries to picture dictionaries and dictionaries for children. He considers methods used for collecting and selecting material, and points out that while obvious compounds can be excluded from a monolingual dictionary, they must be included in a dictionary aimed at non-native speakers. The problems of treating new words, technical terms, trade marks and frequently made mistakes are also covered. Svensén also discusses how information on pronunciation, inflection, parts of speech, constructions, collocations and idioms, etymology and register can be included, and considers how much information is necessary for various types of dictionary. Faulty and flawed definitions are provided as examples of the pitfalls of various defining methods, and the use of equivalents is also considered. The book ends with a discussion of the setting up and funding of a dictionary project, from preliminary planning to publication, and considers the lexicographical applications of computer technology in text capture, inputting, editing, sorting and verification.

The use of computers in lexicography is treated in greater detail in B. T. S. Atkins and A. Zampolli's *Computational Approaches to the Lexicon*, which takes the form of a collection of essays on corpora, lexical analysis and methodology, prefaced by a general introduction and discussion of the development of academic lexicography in Europe. The volume follows on from the fifth Pisa International Summer School on Computational Lexicology and Lexicography in 1988. In the first section, corpus creation, encoding, parsing and the notion of lexical substitutability are all discussed, and the second moves on to a consideration of the inclusion of syntactic and grammatical information in lexicons for native and second-language users. Charles J. Fillmore and B. T. S. Atkins's paper, 'Starting where the Dictionaries Stop: The Challenge of Corpus Lexicography', compares the treatment of *risk*, verb and noun, in ten monolingual dictionaries with corpus evidence, and concludes that practical considerations would inhibit the full use of such evidence. The last section, on methodology and tools, considers both the construction of computer-based dictionaries and the use of lexicographical workstations in research.

Richard Lord's *The Words We Use* is a basic introduction to lexicology in the widest possible sense. He begins with the question of what a word actually is, providing reference to Chinese and Japanese to undermine the intuitions of English speakers, and goes on to cover dictionaries, the origins of language, changes in meaning, word-borrowing, neologism, morphology, language acquisition, collocation, the mental lexicon, writing, the use of language in poetry, and words as reality. What is particularly impressive is that he manages to do all of this in 116 pages without once being inaccessible to a non-specialist reader. His coverage is, necessarily, brief, but he succeeds in introducing many important lexicographical disciplines and problems in a book which could be read in an afternoon. Each of the fifteen chapters aims only to suggest the possibilities of its subject, and each is followed by a bibliography of more specialized texts. Chapter 9, on language acquisition, for instance, although it hardly scrapes the surface of the subject, is usefully and interestingly illustrated by reference to personal experience. In the course of this chapter Lord also mentions phonetics and componential analysis, almost casually, but with as much explanation as is necessary in the context. His discussion of semantic change is illustrated with memorable examples of folk etymology, and the treatment of the mental lexicon is brought to life by reference to aphasic patients. As an introductory text aimed at an undergraduate audience, it could not be more accessible.

Garland Cannon's *The Arabic Contributions to the English Language*, on which Alan S. Kaye collaborated, deals with over 2,300 Arabic terms in English, about 93 per cent of them nouns. The introduction is a consideration of previous studies of lexical borrowing in various European languages, of the influence of speakers of Arabic languages, and of the tendency to underestimate the importance of Arabic borrowings in English. The terms listed are all collected from dictionaries and the novels of Sax Rohmer, including those for which Arabic was only an intermediate language rather than the direct or the ultimate source. There is some attempt to consider the degree to which these terms are assimilated into English by taking into account their extent of use and their semantic and morphological productivity. Before the dictionary proper begins, terms are listed and considered under forty-six semantic categories, each containing at least five items. Only 132 words did not fit into these categories. The chapter on phonology concentrates on changes in Arabic words after their borrowing into English, and also considers the problems of transliteration. The dictionary itself provides the information that *assassin* is ultimately from the Arabic for 'those who use hashish', that *algorithm* comes from the name of a ninth-century, Persian mathematician, *carcass* ultimately from Persian 'arrow-bearing', and *racket* from the Arabic for 'palm of the hand'. Dictionary entries include part of speech, date of first use, semantic category, usage label, etymology, definition, and reference to the source dictionary where relevant.

J. Alan Pfeffer and Garland Cannon's *German Loanwords in English: An Historical Dictionary* does much the same thing for terms from German, although different criteria are used for inclusion. German terms entering English through an intermediary language are excluded, but those ultimately from another source are included. Terms from dialects of German, such as Pennsylvanian German, are excluded, as are those from Yiddish, and only terms from (Early) New High German included in the 5,380 loan-words under consideration. A further 621 unassimilated loan-words are included in an appendix. Calques, complete or partial, are included in this number, as are semantic extensions of English items under German influence. Proper names are excluded if their use is purely biographical or geographical. Even so, about 15 per cent of the corpus is onomastic in origin. A semantic overview of loans from German provides discussion by semantic field and a chronological list of relevant terms. The authors cite, in order to disprove, the tradition of considering German loans to be insignificant in number and restricted to technical usage, but the fields of mineralogy, chemistry, biology, geology, botany, biochemistry, philosophy, psychology, zoology and the military together account for about half of the German loans considered. On the basis of their own material, and taking into account that comparative studies of other language sources are not always available, they conclude that the most significant sources of loan-words in English are Latin, then French, followed by German, Greek, Italian and Spanish, in an order yet to be determined, then Old Norse, followed by Hebrew and Portuguese, followed by Sanskrit and Arabic.

Cannon's 'Modern Spanish-Based Lexical Items in English' (*Dictionaries* 15.117-31) looks at 227 Spanish-derived terms entering the language since 1949, which he divides into new borrowings and naturalizations of previously borrowed terms. These are discussed by semantic field, stylistic label, region and part of speech. Cannon teams up with Félix Rodriguez to produce 'Remarks on the Origin and Evolution of Abbreviations and Acronyms' (CILT 113.261-72). They give an account of the history of abbreviation from the classical period to the present day, dealing with extensions, contractions, initializations, acronyms, blends and clippings.

Louise Sylvester's *Studies in the Lexical Field of Expectation* is a by-product of the Glasgow *Historical Thesaurus* project and is based, like the Glasgow *Thesaurus*, on the *OED*. In the introduction Sylvester gives a brief account of the background to her study, explaining that the Glasgow *Thesaurus* aims to provide a classification of words, while Roget's intention was to present a classification of ideas, but it is conceded that it is sometimes difficult to distinguish between the two. The main body of the text, some 180 pages, consists of classifications of the semantic fields of EXPECTATION, PREDICTION, SURPRISE, DISAPPOINTMENT, HOPE, TRUST, FEAR, DESPAIR, CAUTION, COURAGE and RASHNESS, with FEAR terms derived from animal names grouped together in an appendix. The classification, which includes dates of usage and stylistic labels, is based on a form of componential analysis, but the commentary deals with the limitations of this or any kind of semantic classification. Decisions about inclusion or exclusion of individual terms or senses is ultimately dependent on sense divisions in the *OED*. The problems of grammatical classification are also considered. Etymological information about the 4,757 forms studied is provided in detail in tables and pie-charts in the last three chapters, which consider obsolescence as well as accessions of vocabulary.

In his *Aspects of Semantic Opposition in English*, Arthur Mettinger surveys earlier studies of antonymy and criticizes their use of only a small number of examples to illustrate different types of semantic opposition. He tries to rectify this shortcoming by using dictionaries, thesauruses and novels to provide examples of systematic and non-systematic opposition. He focuses mainly on systematic, or linguistically rooted, opposition, although non-systematic opposition, which is largely contextual and relies upon extra-linguistic or encyclopaedic knowledge, also receives some consideration. The novels provide 161 examples of semantic opposition, of which Mettinger finds that 61.5 per cent can be placed within nine 'syntactic frames', such as *neither X nor Y* and *X rather than Y*. Those which cannot be included in these frames are generally accounted for by collocation, syntactic co-ordination or morphological relationship.

Mettinger distinguishes between 'adversality', which represents extra-linguistic reality, 'oppositeness', which takes place on the level of the linguistic system, and 'contrast', which is situated on the level of parole. In his consideration of gradability he discusses cases of 'pseudo-binarity', for instance *looking* and *listening*, in which two members of a multiple-member set are contrasted. He questions the notion of the negative prefix and discusses markedness and unmarkedness in gradable opposites, giving examples of pairs in which one can be at once an opposite and an archilexeme to the other, such as *much* and *little.*

Perspectives on English: Studies in Honour of Professor Emma Vorlat, edited by Keith Carlon, Kristin Davidse and Brygida Rudzka-Ostyn, is a collection of essays divided into three sections: the diachronic, the synchronic and the applied. Although the range of the thirty essays in the volume is wide, many of them deal with semantics in one way or another. Dirk Geeraerts, for example, considers whether what appears to be inductive generalization in English and Dutch is not better seen as metonymy or metaphor. Jacques van Roey looks at the use of acronymic euphemisms and nature metaphors in press reports on the Gulf War. Willy Martin discusses, with reference to the treatment of animal terms in the COBUILD dictionary, the requirement that definitions should be complete, consistent and correct. Kristin Davidse writes about the Kiparskys' factive presupposition from a syntactic and semantic viewpoint, while Johan Vanparys considers Searle's illocutionary taxonomy and the alternatives to it, none of which is found to be adequate. Markedness in English proper and common nouns and in personal pronouns is the subject of Willy van Langendonck's contribution, and Anne-Marie Simon-Vandenbergen examines metaphorical verbal clauses in George Orwell's *Nineteen Eighty-Four*. Maarten Lemmens adopts a synchronic and diachronic approach to the literal and metaphorical use of *abort* and its derivatives, and Brygida Rudzka-Ostyn subjects verbs of answering (*answer, rejoin, reply, respond* and *retort*) to a similar treatment. Register variation in English is discussed by M. A. K. Halliday, not merely as a matter of collocational diversity, but also in terms of grammar and semantics. Michaël Goethals uses theoretical and practical approaches to language teaching to explore the notion of educationally meaningful vocabulary lists, while Susan Kesner Bland considers the importance of providing a systematic approach to relationships between lexical and grammatical knowledge in EFL teaching.

Ronnie Cann's *Formal Semantics* is concerned with Montague semantics and aimed at the linguist rather than the logician or mathematician, but an understanding of logical notation would certainly be an advantage. He discusses in detail the development of a metalanguage which would avoid the problems of ambiguity and undeterminacy in natural languages, and begins by using L_P. After a consideration of negation, co-ordination, and type theory, he introduces the more complex metalanguage L_{type}. This enables him to represent such complexities as verb phrases and verb phrase modifiers. The introduction of the lambda operator allows him to deal with passives and logical quantifiers for noun phrases, and to move on to discuss inference. Time, tense and aspect are treated with reference to the problem of distinguishing between timeless and temporally bound sentences. The last two chapters deal with possible worlds and contexts and with intensionality. His theory, then, accounts for ambiguity, for relations of entailment, and for paraphrase and contradiction. Presupposition, polysemy and homonymy are excluded from detailed discussion, largely because of limitations of space. Each chapter concludes with suggested further reading, and includes exercises to test whether the theoretical steps considered have been fully understood. Most of the answers are, fortunately, given at the back of the book.

I have not seen Donna Lee Berg's *A Guide to the OED* (OUP) or James Hurford's *Semantics* (CUP).

5. Morphology

We start with a big question: does morphology exist? As the reviews in this section over the past few years will have made clear, there have been several recent attempts to 'deconstruct' morphology, in the sense that scholars have tried to show that morphological facts can be made to follow entirely from principles also operative in syntax and/or phonology. However, our reviews have also shown that morphologists have not taken this lying down. This year, Mark Aronoff's *Morphology by Itself: Stems and Inflectional Classes* provides further arguments for recognizing the existence of morphology as a separate, irreducible component of grammar. As an example of an irreducibly morphological fact, Aronoff cites the identity of the perfect and passive participles in English. Other (and much more elaborate) examples come from languages that show rather more inflectional diversity than English; Aronoff discusses verb stems in Latin, gender and nominal inflection classes in various languages, and the system of binyanim in Hebrew. Perhaps not surprisingly, he has little use for the concept of the morpheme as an independent building-block of words; instead, he argues for the existence of realization pairs, consisting of a morphosyntactic feature array plus a morphophonological realization rule. Also relevant to the question of the status of morphemes are data from lexical access to complex words. This issue is considered in Pier Marco Bertinetto's 'Phonological Representation of Morphological Complexity: Alternative Models (Neuro- and Psycholinguistic Evidence)' (*CogLing* 5.91–108). He argues, on the basis of evidence from experimental work, language acquisition and speech disorders, that there are differences in access between regular and irregular inflectional forms, and also between highly frequent and less frequent forms. This means that no viable model of lexical access can posit rule generation of all morphologically complex items.

While we are at it, let us also bring up the general question of whether morphology is an innate module of grammar. A negative answer is given by Wolfgang Dressler, who offers 'Evidence from the First Stages of Morphology Acquisition for Linguistic Theory: Extragrammatic Morphology and Diminutives' (*ALH* 27.91–108). He points at the existence of several types of 'extragrammatical' morphology which do not observe universal structural properties. Examples are: reduplications (e.g. *variables shmariables*), contaminations, abbreviated forms, submorphemes (e.g. *wh-*), and back formations. These are all common in early acquisition, and, according to Dressler, result from general cognitive principles. They can survive the development of morphology proper, which takes place by a self-organized process of dissociation from general cognitive principles. A special survival of this type, found in many languages, is diminutive formation, which often exhibits various non-prototypical properties (being partly derivational, partly inflectional; showing pragmatic rather than conceptual semantic differences from the base-form; lacking head-properties; taking bases that can be nominal, verbal or adjectival; etc.).

A contribution which, while also of a general nature, is focused primarily on English facts is Rolando Bacchielli's 'Syntheticity and Analyticity in the Syntactic Make-up of English' (in Maurizio Gotti, ed., *English Diachronic Syntax*). Bacchielli suggests that we should leave the terms 'synthetic' and 'analytic' alone because they are too elusive, and instead look at linguistic phenomena linearly. He distinguishes four parameters here: (1) premodification or synthesis (the type *milkbottle*, but also OV word order); (2) postmodification or analysis (*lacklustre*, and VO structure); (3) copulative compounding (*soldier-poet*); and (4) inverted premodification (*the world over*). He notes that what is so interesting about English is that it makes use of all types, combining both Germanic and Romance features, and being typologically divided. Dieter Kastovsky goes into these 'Typological Differences between English and German Morphology and their Causes' (in T. Swan et al., eds, *Language Change and Language Structure*) diachronically and in more detail. He first looks at the factors that have triggered the much more severe loss of inflections that has taken place in English than in German. He notes that a number of phonological changes did not affect the two languages in a similar way (such as palatalization, i/j-mutation), and that this had an effect on the morphology such that English changed from a mainly stem-based morphology (but with already some very productive word-based patterns) to a word-based one, whereas German morphology has remained heterogeneous. The point is that i/j-mutation started off as a phonological rule in both languages, but that it quite soon became morphologically conditioned in English, leading to morphological surface opacity, which in turn triggered many analogical changes. It is not surprising that with such an unbalanced system, simplification occurred, leading to invariant stems and to a word-based morphological system.

Arnfinn M. Vonen compares English word-formation processes with those of a Polynesian language in 'Multifunctionality and Morphology in Tokelau and English' (*NJL* 17.155–78). He notes the similar use that is made of conversion in the two languages and draws a number of typological conclusions such as that conversion is more likely to occur in 'basic-form inflection' (as in English) than in 'stem-inflection' languages (such as German), and also in languages where the number of productive, overt morphological patterns is small. Both points are perhaps rather obvious.

Strictly diachronic matters form the topic of Martin Haspelmath's 'The Growth of Affixes in Morphological Reanalysis' (*YM* 1994.1–29). He discusses several types of affix reanalysis (labelling them telescoping, conglutination and secretion). A simple example is that of Old English *opn-ian* > *op-nian*, leading to *berht-nian*. Factors favouring reanalysis appear to be morphotactic opacity (itself often due to phonological erosion), and the creation of optimal syllable structure for the word as a whole. Haspelmath notes that reanalysis, which is paradigmatically based, always increases the segmental size of affixes (i.e. there are no cases like *harp-ist* > *harpis-t*, and hence *drum-t*, *cello-t*), and that it shares this characteristic with the mechanism of grammaticalization, which is syntagmatically based. For more diachronic morphology, we refer the reader to April McMahon's *Understanding Language Change*, which we review in section 6(b) below.

Also diachronic, but concerned with the history of one particular English form only, is Derek Britton's 'On Middle English *she*, *sho*: A Scots Solution to an English Problem'. This paper appeared several years ago (in *NOWELE* 17[1991].3-51) but was not reviewed here at the time. In this article, Britton proposes a new solution to the 'she' puzzle. Essentially the problem has always been the absence of clear evidence for a native phonetic change whereby [h-] developed into [ʃ-]. For this reason, many linguists have rejected this phonetic option and proposed other solutions. This paper remedies this lack of evidence by looking at modern Scots developments, e.g. [ʃudʒ] and [ʃ^k] for *huge* and *hook* 'sickle' respectively. In a well-researched and detailed paper (discussing all Old and Middle English spellings, earlier investigations of the problem, the path of development, and especially the factors that have limited the development of [hj-], the intermediate stage, to [ʃ-]), the author makes clear that this modern Scots development is relevant because it shows that there was no typological impediment to the change in question, i.e. the change must have been phonetically possible in any period of the history of English.

Two articles are concerned with the problem of productivity in word-formation. The first, by Pavol Štekauer ('On Productivity in Word-Formation', *LingP* 1994.67–82), deals first with a terminological issue, namely what exactly the term 'productivity' entails in word-formation studies (especially in relation to the term 'frequency'), and second tackles a methodological issue, i.e. how productivity should be described both synchronically and diachronically, and what factors (both internal and external) affect productivity. This last point is also discussed by Christiane Dalton-Puffer in 'Productive or not Productive? The Romance Element in Middle English Derivation' (in Francisco Fernández, et al., eds, *English Historical Linguistics 1992*); she stresses that it is far from settled what the notion of productivity entails. She argues that it involves an interplay of many different factors such as frequency, transparency, creativity, etc. Pointing out the very low degree of creativity in the occurrence of Romance suffixes (hardly any hybrids occur) in the relevant parts of the Helsinki Corpus, she comes to the conclusion that Romance suffixes did not become a productive part of the word-formation rules in Middle English, as has been generally believed. Still in the area of derivational morphology, Rainer Nagel offers a contribution on 'Das Wortbildungsmorphem *Cyber*' (*ZAA* 42.163–70). He shows how the morpheme *cyber-*, taken from the word *cybernetics* (first coined by Norbert Wiener in 1948, and popularized in science fiction since the 1980s), has become a very productive element of word-formation in science fiction writing. He gives plenty of examples, dividing up its use semantically and by its occurrence in the various parts of speech. Another study of a specific prefix is Ronald Southerland's 'Derivatives in *pre-*: A Persuasive Morphological Resource?' (*AS* 69.168–76). He has collected some one hundred *pre*-forms, and finds that nearly all of them have a verbal base, that their use is often signalled by meta-markers such as scare quotes or phrases like *sort of*, and that about sixty of them are from the field of commercial advertising, where they often convey a suggestion of convenience (because the relevant articles are *precooked*, *predrilled*, *preformatted* or otherwise *pretreated*).

On the topic of inflectional morphology, Pam Peters contributes a study on the 'American and British Influence in Australian Verb Morphology' (in Udo Fries et al., eds, *Creating and Using English Language Corpora*, reviewed in section 6(a)), in which she tries to find some systematicity in the variable forms of irregular verbs, and especially in how far the Australian development can be considered to be independent or not. In the same volume, Terttu Nevalainen deals with 'Diachronic Issues in English Adverb Derivation', showing how English has developed its present morphologically mixed system of using zero suffixes as well as *-ly*.

With the adverb, we have moved on to morphosyntactic matters. There are three contributions here. Michiko Ogura's 'Grammatical Choices in Old and Early Middle English' deals with '[the] choice between a simple verb, the prefix/particle–verb or verb–particle combination, and the "auxiliary + infinitive" construction' (in Fernández et al.) in a number of parallel MSS of Old and Middle English texts. Apart from the general factors influencing the choice of form (such as loss of morphology and the influence of Latin), Ogura finds that there emerges 'a medieval liking for alternative uses' rather than a mechanical change to more and more periphrasis, and that authors, confronted by the choice of prefixed verb or verb–

particle, made use of the subtle shades of meaning both could convey as long as both variants were still tolerated by the language. Maurizio Gotti looks at a number of morphosyntactic features (such as the use of *its* versus *it/his*, *be* vs. *are*, *have* vs. *be* in perfects, *ye* vs. *thou*) in order to assess 'The alleged archaism of morphosyntactic structures in the authorised version of *The Bible*' (in Gotti). By comparing the use of these features with that in contemporary texts, he notes that its language in most respects was similar to that used elsewhere, and that in some ways it was even innovatory. A strictly synchronic study of the morphosyntax of synthetic compounds in present-day English is Hiroyuki Oshita's 'Compounds: A View from Suffixation and A-Structure Alteration' (in *YM* 1994.179–205). Oshita argues that nominalizing *-ing* has in fact three readings: result/concrete, as in *our findings*; simple event/process, as in *swimming, skiing,* and *skating*; and complex event, as in *deliberate planning of the campaign*. It is only in the last case that the verbal head's A-requirements are not nullified by the affix, but must be saturated in the syntax, which means that only this reading yields a synthetic compound. Adjectives like *water-resistant*, *meaning-preserving*, *smooth-driving* (based on a middle verb) and *pleasant-looking* (from an identificational verb) also qualify as synthetic compounds, but nominal compounds in *-er*, and also the bases for back-formed compound verbs like *proof-read*, do not.

Finally, on the borderline between compounds and syntax, we find an article by Marge Landsberg, 'On Some Principles of Serialization underlying Linguistic Freezes' (*GL* 34.1–43). She reviews earlier literature on freezes (i.e. fixed expressions like *wear and tear*, *hook, line and sinker*, *pitter-patter*, *razzle-dazzle*, etc.), and identifies the following phonological and semantic ordering principles, illustrating them with numerous examples: high V before low V, short before long, front before back, C before CC, monosyllabic before polysyllabic, animate before inanimate, positive before negative, strong before weak, important before unimportant, ego before non-ego (the last two, we are sad to say, always seem to imply adult male before anybody else).

6. Syntax

(a) Modern English

Students who want short but comprehensible explanations of (traditional) grammatical terms can now be referred to James Hurford's *Grammar: A Student's Guide*. In it, they will find an A–Z of exactly one hundred grammatical terms, with each entry (two or three pages on average) containing an explanation, examples, contrasts (usually paradigmatic in nature), relationships (syntagmatic), sometimes some additional cross-linguistic facts for interest, and a little exercise. The grammarian's traditional stock-in-trade terms are all included (e.g. under 'I', there are impersonal, indicative, indirect object, indirect speech, infinitive, interjection, interrogative, and much more), the information given mostly consists of widely accepted facts and interpretations, and extensive cross-references are provided. This seems like a handy reference work to us.

If students want to analyse actual sentences, in English or other languages, they might work through Nigel Fabb's *Sentence Structure*. This book (in Routledge's Language Workbooks series) provides a useful introduction to basic concepts and how they can be applied; starting from absolute scratch, readers will get acquainted with the nature and (syntactic) function of word classes, phrases, tree structures, subordination, co-ordination, apposition, types of NP, topicalization, passive, case-forms, the VP and so on. Throughout the text, the general principles of sentence structure are stressed, rather than the 'correct' ways of analysing individual sentence types. The book also includes many exercises, on English sentences but also on material in one of the four mini-corpora given at the back of the book (sentences in Chinese, Madi, Malay and Tamil). Another introductory work on grammatical analysis is Tony Wright's *Investigating English*. Its purpose is not to provide a systematic body of knowledge (the explicit grammatical information given is quite basic and limited), but to raise students' awareness about English. Although the book contains some puzzling questions to the students (e.g. 'Is English your friend or your foe? Can you explain why?' and 'What sort of shape do you think various parts of language have?'), it also contains a great deal of material on topics like verbs and time, modals, passive, adverb(ial)s, nouns and their properties, text organization, written vs. spoken language, lexical choice, adjacency pairs, and many more, and various activities for students, which involve classifying or linking forms, locating examples in texts, choosing appropriate forms, thinking about differences, rewriting sentences, etc.

At a more advanced level, this year's publications include some important book-length presentations of entire grammatical models: two for systemic-functional grammar, and two for generative grammar. To begin with, there is a second edition of *An Introduction to Functional Grammar* by Michael Halliday. The work has not been changed substantially (though, very usefully, an index has been added), and remains the fullest overall exposition of the systemic-functional model of language. After two introductory chapters, there are separate chapters on each of the well-known lines of meaning that Halliday and others have identified in sentences and texts: theme–rheme structure, 'mood' (signalling the clause's status as a form of exchange), transitivity, the structure of groups and phrases (very graphically described, on p. 213, as follows: 'a group is a bloated word, whereas a phrase is a shrunken clause'), clause complexes, intonation and rhythm, cohesion, and (grammatical) metaphor. An exhaustive analysis of a short text is provided in an appendix to show how all these strands of meaning combine and interact to yield a full interpretation, and detailed suggestions for further reading on each of the topics covered are given. Altogether, we think that this work will be read with pleasure not only by *aficionados* of nursery rhymes and *Alice in Wonderland* (Halliday's favourite sources of examples), but by anyone interested in English grammar who missed the first edition. Many of the topics discussed by Halliday are also dealt with (though in less detail) in Suzanne Eggins's more pedagogically orientated *Introduction to Systemic Functional Linguistics*. She first devotes two chapters to the influence of context on language use (using the terms 'genre' and 'register' as convenient and well-defined labels for this), then describes cohesion, and next gives a clear outline, with many examples, of the lexico-grammatical systems of functional grammar. Throughout, the integration of formal analysis and function is emphasized, in such a way that readers may feel induced to explore this particular line of linguistic enquiry further. This year, we have actually not seen many such further systemic-functional explorations: we only found an article on 'The Relevance of Theme in the Textual Organization of BBC News Reports', by María Gómez (in *Word* 45.293–305). The author shows that in the BBC radio news bulletins included in the Lancaster Corpus, usually the theme coincides with the topic, and contains given information in the form of a definite common NP. The occurrence of marked themes is also considered – they are usually circumstantial adjuncts, and often seem to signal a topic switch.

Just like earlier years, 1994 saw a great number of explorations conducted within the model of generative grammar. Some of these develop or apply its most recent version, the so-called minimalist model, but before we turn to such studies, we will review some of the more 'traditional' (i.e. GB or Barriers-inspired) studies (others will be discussed at the appropriate points below). We start by noting two textbook introductions to the field of generative grammar as a whole: Liliane Haegeman's *Introduction to Government and Binding Theory* (2nd edition), and Jamal Ouhalla's *Introducing Transformational Grammar: From Rules to Principles and Parameters*. Compared with the first edition, Haegeman's work has undergone some expansion and reshuffling. In addition to chapters on such well-established staples of the generative diet as the lexicon and sentence structure, X-bar theory, case theory, binding, PRO and control, NP-movement, Wh-movement, empty categories, logical form and barriers, there are new chapters on functional categories and relativized minimality, while much of the material from the chapters on Romance and Germanic syntax has now been integrated in other chapters. As in the first edition, students are shown step by step why certain analyses and derivations have been developed, how they can be represented in the form of tree diagrams, and what aspects are still under investigation; these are no doubt some of the reasons why this book has been – and we think will continue to be – a popular choice as a text for introductory generative courses.

Ouhalla's book deals with many of the same subjects, except that more attention is paid to the shift from the older, rule-based approach to constructions towards the principle-based approach. The book also differs from that by Haegeman in containing a separate chapter on cross-linguistic variation (in which phenomena like pro-drop, word order, incorporation, I-lowering and V-raising are discussed). Perhaps because Ouhalla presents so much material in a work only half as long as Haegeman's, we think it will demand quite careful reading on the part of the student, and will need to be backed up by intensive course work. If this is provided, however, students will certainly learn a great deal from it.

There are also some book-length studies of specific topics in the theory of generative grammar this year. The nature and status of parameters is examined in Priyamvada Bondre-Beil's *Parameter der Syntax*. After a brief sketch of the principle and parameter model, she identifies several problems in parameter theory: the diversity of parameters proposed (what, for example, unifies right–left directionality, the (im)possibility of pro-drop, the size of binding domains, the presence or absence of verb-second, and the choice of bounding domains for subjacency?), the sometimes blurred distinction between description and explanation, and several questions about the interaction between parameters and universal principles. After considering in detail the parameters of pro-drop, long-distance binding and Wh-in-situ, she suggests that in all cases there is parametrization of S-structure properties of functional categories.

Several parameters (though not specifically associated with functional categories) are invoked by Ljiljana Progovac in her *Negative and Positive Polarity: A Binding Approach*, in which she provides a purely syntactic account of the distribution of negative polarity items (NPIs) like *any* and positive polarity items such as *some*. Building on her earlier work on this topic (see *YWES* 73.37; 74.42), she suggests that English NPIs are subject to binding condition A, which means they must be bound by negation in INFL or a polarity operator in COMP (as in conditionals, questions, and complements to adversative predicates). In other languages, NPIs must also be bound, but are subject to condition B, with the result that the negation must be located in a higher clause. Furthermore, in English, a NPI can raise, either to an IP-adjoined position (so that it can be bound by a polarity operator in COMP) or to COMP (so that it can be bound by a higher negative). Other languages allow only one or neither of these raising options. Progovac rejects a semantic approach to NPIs and PPIs (in particular, Ladusaw's account in terms of downward entailment) since it cannot explain the contrast between *I forgot that anyone had called* and **I forgot anyone*.

In *Thematic Structure in Syntax*, Edwin Williams argues against certain elements of received thematic wisdom. For example, he proposes that in sentences like *John seems sick*, there is a process of function composition by which the theta-role of the complement of *seem* is transmitted to the subject of *seem*. As a result, no NP-movement needs to be assumed any more, in this and other structures (such as passive, scrambling, or the case of ordinary IP-subjects, which are often thought to originate in SpecVP). Williams also proposes that argument structure conforms to X-bar theory, and that the assignment of theta-roles involves a binding relation between the argument of V and the external argument of the head of NP. Conversely, binding relations also involve theta-roles. In addition, Williams argues against the existence of short verb-movement, as proposed for French and other languages. Of course, this necessitates a specific analysis of adverb position and negation for both French and English, which Williams provides. For negation in English, he argues that *not* heads a *not*P, with the complement of *not* determining its category.

Much of the material in Williams's chapter on short verb-movement can also be found in his 'A Reinterpretation of Evidence for Verb Movement in French', which appears in a volume entitled *Verb Movement*, edited by David Lightfoot and Norbert Hornstein. Unlike Williams, most of the authors represented do not think short verb-movement is chimerical; on the contrary, they propose sometimes quite elaborate movement analyses for the relevant facts. The book starts with a useful overview by the editors, who place the study of verb-movement in the context of the increasing attention paid to the import of barriers and the ECP for phenomena like incorporation and verb-second. They also consider the diagnostics and possible triggers for verb-movement, and the idea that all languages should have V-to-C at LF. This introduction is followed by articles on verb-movement in Italian, Icelandic and Yiddish, and Scandinavian in general – these are not directly relevant to modern English, which is usually assumed to lack (short) verb-movement, but they do suggest valuable lines of inquiry for the study of earlier English, which has comparable phenomena that have so far gone largely unstudied. Ken Wexler's 'Optional Infinitives, Head Movement and the Economy of Derivations' is specifically concerned with English facts. Wexler asks why English children often drop verbal *-s*. To answer this question, he adduces evidence from the acquisition of French, Scandinavian, German and Dutch, showing that children often use an infinitive, which remains in situ, rather than the appropriate finite form, which undergoes V-to-I movement. He suggests that this is also what English children do; child negatives like *I no want this* provide corroborating evidence for this view. Hilda Koopman's contribution, 'Licensing Heads', also deals with modern English. Koopman argues that causative verbs like *make* and *let* take an embedded IP (i.e. AgrP, TP, etc.), whose head I has to incorporate into the causative verb, because this verb lacks a temporal argument. More generally, she proposes that lexical properties (including thematic structure) are satisfied through incorporation. Although it appears in a different volume (*LIN* 1994.95–106), Samir Khalaily's 'Syntax of Verbs from a Nominal Point of View' is also most conveniently discussed at this point, since it too deals with a possible case of incorporation into a verb. What he argues is that transitive dynamic verbs such as *hit* underlyingly consist of an abstract V° plus a N° *hit*, which incorporates into the abstract V. The difference between, for example, the verb *kiss* and the phrase *give a kiss* is that in the latter case there is no N° but a full NP, making incorporation impossible. Data from Arabic provide further evidence for an incorporation analysis of transitives.

Studies on Scrambling, edited by Norbert Corver and Henk van Riemsdijk, is another collection of generative papers on a specific topic, that of free word-order phenomena. In their introduction, the editors sketch the various logically possible analyses (i.e. scrambling being due to base-generation, or to NP/Wh/other movement, or possibly a combination of these) – interestingly and instructively, each of the possibilities is actually defended in at least one of the volume's papers. As far as the data analysed are concerned, there is a heavy preponderance of Germanic, but there is little from English, which lacks the relevant constructions. In this case too, we would nevertheless recommend the book to generative syntacticians working on English, not only because the disagreement among the papers on very similar or even identical facts brings out very sharply the general theoretical issues at stake, but also because earlier English has comparable facts, which have so far gone largely unstudied. One of these, the pattern *he loves me not*, is mentioned by Viviane Deprez in her 'Parameters of Object Movement'; she suggests that its loss is related to the loss of verb-movement in English, a suggestion that we think intriguing.

As usual, there are also many shorter generative contributions this year. Jan-Wouter Zwart writes about 'Het ontstaan van I" en C" [The Origins of I" and C"]' (*Gramma/TTT* 3.55–70). He points out that the existence of both I' and C' follows directly from X-bar theory, and attributes the somewhat late realization of this fact in the literature to two factors: rather than assuming I' and C', it was long believed that V was the head of S and S-bar and, in addition, the idea that COMP could harbour both a Wh-trace and *that* was used for a long time to explain the *that*-trace filter. It was only when INFL was seen to be a governor, in the early 1980s, that it was analysed as a head. In the same period, head-movement came to be distinguished from XP-movement, which led to the realization that there should be a SpecCP position. Frederick Newmeyer is also concerned with interpreting what has happened and is happening in the field in 'A Note on Chomsky on Form and Function' (*JL* 30.245–51). He argues that, *pace* many critics, Chomsky's views do not at all rule out the possibility that meaning and language use should influence or correspond with linguistic form. Another general piece, which does not fit in well elsewhere, is Edwin Williams's 'Remarks on Lexical Knowledge' (*Lingua* 92.7–34). Williams identifies various more or less abstract patterns in English that cannot be captured under the notion of parameters, but that none the less constitute real knowledge of the language that must be learned. Examples are: *pants*, *jeans*, *shorts*, *cutoffs*, etc., exemplifying the linguistic generalization that an item of lower trunk wear must take the plural form; *trout*, *bass*, *perch*, etc. used as plurals; the fact that present participles, but not past participles, are all formed in the same way; the relative-like construction *what food I had*, which implies the amount is small; and the many expressions of the type *N to N* and *N by N*. Another group of individual items is studied by Aimo Seppänen, Rhonwen Bowen and Joe Trotta, who write 'On the So-Called Complex Prepositions' (*SAP* 29.3-29). The authors reconsider the traditional analysis of syntagms such as *out of*, *in spite of*, *in (the) light of*, etc., as complex prepositions (whereby the following NP functions as a complement), and instead propose that they should be analysed as a head followed by a prepositional phrase, i.e. *in spite [of the war]* rather than *in spite of [the war]*. The only exceptions to this new analysis are *out of* and *on to*, which they see as simple prepositions, and phrases like *on board (the ship)*, which are the only complex prepositions left. In accordance with X-bar theory, they analyse the head of these phrases as a preposition (with some exceptions, and some ambiguous cases) in view of the fact that they form part of a PP (the head of a PP also being a preposition). Their evidence for this new analysis, apart from more general theoretical considerations, comes from a number of constituency tests that they carry out such as fronting, co-ordination, interpolation and ellipsis.

On a more technical question, there is Robert Chametzky's 'Chomsky-Adjunction' (*Lingua* 93.245–64). The author identifies several problems for the idea that adjunction creates a new node with the same label as the non-adjunct. It means that adjunction both creates structure and labels nodes, that there is a labelled node not licensed by any lexical properties, and that complications arise in the definition of the concept of domination. Chametzky therefore proposes that such new nodes should remain label-less. Another paper concerned with questions of tree geometry is Thomas Ernst's 'M-Command and Precedence' (*LingI* 25.327–35). On the basis of binding facts like *She insulted both suitors on purpose in each other's presence*, where the anaphor is not c-commanded by the antecedent, he argues that binding (of anaphors, bound pronouns and NPIs) requires not c-command but m-command plus precedence. This means that Larsonian VP-shells will no longer be necessary to explain binding patterns as in *I showed Mary herself/everyone his paycheck/no one anything*.

Several papers address issues that have to do with movement other than that of verbs. Kunihiro Iwakura looks at 'The Distribution of CP-Trace and the Expletive *it*' (*LingA* 24.122–41). The relevant facts are as follows: *[that he had come], we didn't really find e/*it very surprising* and *they said nobody e/*it would do that [who had any sense]* vs. *we didn't really find *e/it very surprising [that he had come]*. To explain why movement of CP does or does not call for insertion of expletive *it*, Iwakura proposes that nominal CPs (defined as relative CPs, CP complements to N, their traces, and expletive *it*) must be free, while CP-traces which are not nominal CPs must be bound. Other data are also shown to follow from this stipulation. Various types of construction that are usually subsumed under the label of Wh-movement are closely scrutinized in Paul Postal's 'Contrasting Extraction Types' (*JL* 30.159–86). He proposes that topicalization, clefts, and non-restrictive relatives form a group which is distinct from that of Wh-interrogatives, restrictive relatives, pseudo-clefts, negative NP-fronting and comparatives. In particular, the former are banned from several contexts where the latter are not, as shown by the contrasts **such chemicals he knew that there were t in the bottle* vs. *no such chemicals did he know that there were t in the bottle* and **that reason did he resign for t* vs. *what reason did he resign for t*. Postal points out that these contexts happen to anti-trigger pronominals as well (as witness **there are them on the table*, and **I resigned for those reasons but Harry didn't resign for them*), and then proposes that extractions of the first type actually involve null resumptive pronouns. Facts concerning extraction from islands suggest that some (but not all) extractions of the second type also allow resumptive pronouns. In 'Parasitic Gaps and Pseudoparasitic Gaps' (*LingI* 25.63–117), Postal suggests that parasitic gaps also come in two types: real parasitic gaps (which are NPs, and are licensed only by leftward extraction of NPs; they are to be analysed as a control phenomenon) and pseudo-parasitic gaps (which arise when there is rightward extraction, may also be PPs, do not obey island-constraints, and are to be analysed as cases of non-co-ordinate right-node raising). Examples of pseudo-parasitic gaps are: *Albert boasted at the office t after firing the woman who had heard him boasting at home ppg [that his results were fantastic]* and *She mentioned the first problem t without mentioning the second problem ppg [to the professor who taught Greek]*. Postal also considers parentheticals (as in *They should, I am sure he realizes t without me having to tell pg him, leave now*), which he argues have both leftward extraction and right-node raising.

The problem of whether and how lexical properties determine the shape of syntactic trees receives little generative attention this year. The only paper on this that we have seen is Jila Ghomeshi and Diane Massam's 'Lexical/Syntactic Relations without Projection' (*LingA* 24.175–217). They propose that trees are simply created by X-bar rules, with lexical insertion being free. Checking occurs at the post-S-structure level of semantic interpretation. The syntax will therefore generate all of the following sentences: *He shot (at) the duck*, *He baked (*at) a cake*, and *He looked *(at) the duck*. At the level of interpretation, the fact that *bake* has result-focus will rule out any sentences with *bake* lacking a direct object, and the fact that *look* is specified as not allowing result-focus will rule out sentences with *look* taking a direct object. Since *shoot* is not specified for result-focus, neither of the sentences will be ruled out. In this way, the authors capture the idea that a syntactic position has a semantics independently of the verb used. They also present cross-linguistic data that further support their analysis.

In comparison with previous years, there is also little on the nature of projections traditionally called NPs (we discuss studies of binding below, together with non-generative papers on the NP). In 'Saturation, Predication, and the DP Hypothesis' (*LingA* 24.39–61), Thomas Stroik addresses the contrast between *I consider John a fool* and **I consider John the fool*. He explains it by assuming that the predicate phrase has the structure $[_{DP} [_{NumP} [_{NP}]]]$, with the indefinite article being in SpecNumP, and the definite article in D. If, then, a nominal XP within a nominal XP predicate is also a predicate itself, which needs to be saturated (for example by an indefinite article in SpecNumP), the facts follow, since the NP predicate cannot be saturated by a definite article in D-position. Although Stroik adduces evidence to back up his analysis, it will no doubt be felt by some to be rather abstract, since functional projections within the NP-domain are much harder for most people to intuit than those in the clausal domain. That there are also theoretical problems to the idea that NP is embedded in functional projections is made clear by Willy van Langendonck, who asks: 'Determiners as Heads?' (*CogLing* 5.243–59). His answer is negative, since (1) if a phrase is an instance of the head, *the book* must have *book*, and not *the*, as its head; (2) if the head determines the external relations of a phrase, again it must be the noun rather than the determiner that is the head (cf. *they distributed the books/*the streets*, or *I overslept each *(morning)*); (3) languages with Adj-N order usually also have Dem-N, a fact which cannot be captured well unless the noun is taken to be the head of the phrase.

We now come to minimalism, the latest offshoot of generative grammar. A work which, in its pre-publication version, has played a role in the development of the minimalist model, and has to some extent been incorporated in it, is Richard Kayne's *The Antisymmetry of Syntax*. His starting point is the Linear Correspondence Axiom, by which a certain order of sentence elements is enforced. Specifically, it leads to the conclusion that adjunct–head–complement order (with the usual X-bar structure) is universal. Specifiers are to be viewed as adjuncts, and any phrase can only have a single adjunct. No rightward adjunction is allowed. After demonstrating that these are indeed the consequences of the Linear Correspondence Axiom, Kayne analyses in some detail the following constructions, which at first sight all appear to be problematic for his theory: co-ordinate structures (which are actually asymmetric phrases headed by the conjunction; some instances of co-ordination involve right-node raising, itself a result of deletion processes), apparent cases of multiple complements (which are forbidden, and must therefore be reanalysed in terms of small clauses, or Larsonian shells), heavy NP-shift (as in *I gave to Andreas all the pictures that I had painted over the past ten years*, which really involves leftward movement of the PP *to Andreas*, and may feature parasitic gaps only because of right-node raising), right dislocation (as in *He's real smart, John*, which derives from *He's real smart, John is e* by a process of reduction), relative clauses (which actually have raising of the antecedent from inside the relative clause), extraposition of relative clauses (actually due to fronting of the antecedent, with the relative clause being stranded) and several others. Kayne's conclusion is that the Correspondence Axiom is restrictive but not too much so, since, even when it is applied to problematic cases, it does not call for additional machinery beyond what is already in use. Of course, not everybody will agree with Kayne's sometimes quite far-reaching proposals. With respect to the analysis of co-ordination, Robert Borsley argues 'In Defense of Co-ordinate Structures' (*LingA* 24.218–46). He shows that there are all kinds of problems for analyses like Kayne's, which deny that co-ordination exemplifies a special kind of grammatical structure and instead try to assimilate it to structures found elsewhere (i.e. X-bar structure). The problems concern the category of the co-ordinate XP (always the same as the phrases it is made up of), the co-ordination of non-phrasal units, and various aspects of co-ordinate NPs consisting of more than two elements (having to do with the (non-)use of *and* and the availability of distributive and collective readings for sentences containing such NPs). Borsley therefore prefers (a version of) the traditional analysis of co-ordination.

Of the shorter studies within the minimalist framework, several make crucial use of economy considerations. Chris Collins, writing about 'Economy of Derivation and the Generalized Proper Binding Condition' (*LingI* 25.45–61), appeals to the principle of economy of derivation (which entails that Form Chain must be one operation) to explain the impossibility of 'interleaving' A-chains and A-bar chains. Sentences like ??*Who did you say that [pictures of t] were stolen t*, for example, might be formed by first moving *who* out of the underlying object and adjoining it to the embedded VP, then moving the NP *pictures of t* into embedded subject position, and next moving *who* into the matrix SpecCP. No condition would be violated, but economy of derivation will rule out this sentence. He also proposes that economy will exclude sentences such as **Who do pictures of please you*? Eddy Ruys (in *LIN* 1994.223–34) gives 'A Global Economy Analysis of Weak Crossover', appealing to the shortest link condition. He argues that **who$_i$ does his$_i$ mother love t$_i$* is out because there is a sentence with a shorter derivation and the same LF: *whose$_i$ mother loves him$_i$* (which has subject movement, which counts as a shorter link than object movement). For the same reason, the first variant of the following pairs loses out to the second one: **his mother loves every boy* vs. *every boy's mother loves him*, and **which book did John file it without reading t* vs. *which book did John file t without reading it*. Ruys points out that his account also explains the existence of 'weakest crossover', i.e. cases where there should be reduced grammaticality due to weak crossover, but there is not. Thus, an example like *This book I expect its author to buy t* is possible because it has no variant with a shorter derivation.

Norbert Hornstein provides 'An Argument for Minimalism: The Case of Antecedent-Contained Deletion' (in *LingI* 25.455–80). Earlier analyses of sentences like *John kissed [everyone that Fran did [$_{VP}$ e]]*, in terms of quantifier raising or relative clause extraposition, are shown to face technical and empirical problems. Hornstein's solution is simple: at LF, the whole object NP will move to SpecAgrO for case-checking, and at that point the remaining VP [*kissed e*] can be copied into the empty VP without creating a problem of infinite regress. One of the ramifications and consequences of this analysis discussed by Hornstein is that the construction should also be possible with ECM subjects, since these move to the matrix SpecAgrO at LF, and this turns out to be correct (cf. non-ECM **I expect (that) everyone you do [$_{VP}$ e] will visit Mary* with ECM *I expect everyone you do [$_{VP}$ e] to visit Mary*).

Shichiro Tanaka, writing about 'The Nature of Derivation: Evidence from the Distribution of *who*' (*LingA* 24.82–121), makes use of the idea that adjuncts can be attached, by generalized transformation, at a later stage than arguments. This, he argues, will explain why **who brother did you meet t* is impossible, while *who that you know did you meet t* is grammatical. In both cases, *who* is part of a larger constituent; why should its nominative case be licensed (presumably by AgrS) in the one sentence but not the other? The answer can now be that in the second sentence, *who* actually moves through SpecAgrSP to Comp alone, the (adjunct) relative clause being attached to it later. Zeljko Bošković considers 'D-Structure, Theta-Criterion, and Movement into Theta-Positions' (in *LingA* 24.247–86). He first sketches the motivation for doing away with D-structure, the projection principle, and the theta-criterion in the minimalist framework, and then shows how various sentence-types that used to be ruled out by the theta-criterion are to be excluded now (e.g. *John believes [t to like Mary*], in which *John* is case-checked twice). With the theta-criterion gone, it might be possible to have movement into a theta-position, and the writer argues that this is in fact what happens with root modals (analysed as *John can [t swim]*).

In 'Predicate Inversion and Minimality' (*LIN* 1994.1–12), Marcel den Dikken explains the obligatory presence of *to be* in sentences such as *We consider there *(to be) a man in the room*, *I consider the best candidate *(to be) John* and *The best candidate seems *(to be) John* by means of the principle of equidistance. To make raising of the small clause predicate (*there*, *the best candidate*) possible, the head of the small clause (i.e. Agr) has to move to a higher head. This means there must be a TP, and this in turn will require the presence of *be* to check T's tense features. Agr will incorporate in *be* (a possibility not allowed by main verbs). Den Dikken proposes the same type of analysis for *Down the hill rolled a carriage*; here, there will be an AspP (since *roll* is resultative), and Agr can incorporate into that, hence *be* does not need to be inserted. Guido Vanden Wyngaerd writes about 'Reconstruction and Minimalism' (in *LIN* 1994.247-57). The problem he is interested in is why, in *John wondered [which picture of himself] Bill saw t*, the anaphor *himself* can be bound by either *John* or *Bill*. The standard answer is that reconstruction is optional. However, this would incorrectly predict that it should be possible for *Tom* and *he/him* to be co-referential in *John wondered [which pictures of Tom/him] he/Tom liked t*. Vanden Wyngaerd shows that Chomsky's solution to this problem does not work, and he suggests that reconstruction is always obligatory, with the apparent long-distance binding of *himself* resulting from the fact that it can be logophoric. He also suggests that binding, which takes place at LF, depends on visibility, and must therefore be calculated from a case-marked position (the source-position of A-bar movement, and the target position of A-movement). The final minimalist contribution that we will discuss here is Rita Manzini's 'Locality, Minimalism, and Parasitic Gaps' (*LingI* 25.481–508). In it, Manzini reformulates her earlier ideas about locality within the minimalist framework, arguing that they can take the form of an adjacency requirement on minimal domains. She then discusses in detail various kinds of extraction, including parasitic gaps (for which she formulates a requirement that has the effect of banning them from tensed clauses).

We now turn to several studies in the area of tense and aspect, starting with Wolfgang Klein's book on *Time in Language*. The title succinctly describes what the book sets out to do. It starts off with the cognitive notion of time and works out how this can be expressed in language. Thus, not only verbal categories such as tense and aspect are discussed, but also inherent lexical features and various types of adverbials and particles, and how they combine with one another. Furthermore, Klein also tries to be more precise about the notions of tense and aspect. Thus, '[t]ense does not directly specify "the time of situation"; rather, it imposes a temporal constraint on the time [i.e. the description of the situation] for which the assertion is made [i.e. it narrows down the assertion to some particular time]. Aspect is a temporal relation between the "time of the situation" and "the time for which the assertion is made"', which Klein calls 'topic time'. In other words, both tense and aspect can be defined in terms of temporal relations. A great asset of the book is that it is highly readable, not couched in technical machinery, but yet precise and thought-provoking.

Where Klein approaches the problem of linguistic tense from the cognitive notion of time, this is not the route taken by Renaat Declerck in 'The Present Perfect and the English Tense System' (*LB* 83.157–80), a review article of Meyer's book on the subject (see *YWES* 73.39). He does not agree with Meyer's idea that English has only one tense; instead he argues that English has four (putting forth his belief that tense can be distinguished both morphologically, and syntactically by means of auxiliaries), namely past, present and future, while the present perfect realizes 'a temporal schema of its own, and should therefore be considered a tense of its own'. Laura Michaelis also investigates the perfect in 'The Ambiguity of the English Present Perfect' (*JL* 30.111–57). She argues that the perfect is not vague, but ambiguous (i.e. its continuative, existential and resultative interpretations constitute distinct meanings). She then discusses several properties of the resultative perfect: its inability to refer to a pragmatically presupposed event (e.g. **Where have you found my watch*?); its inability to take a time adverbial specifying event time (**He has died in 1970*); its inability to assert the occurrence of an event sequence; and its inability to take a pure manner adverbial (**he has angrily called a halt to the meeting*). Michaelis considers these to be idiosyncratic properties, which have to be learned (though they do have a semantic and discourse-pragmatic basis, to the effect that the event must not get undue salience). Another perfect piece is Scott Schwenter's '"Hot News" and the Grammaticalization of Perfects' (*Linguistics* 32.995–1028). The hot news perfect (as in *Tuition has just gone up!*) is presented as one of the stages in the grammaticalization of the perfect from a present-related function to a (past) perfective function, since it highlights the event itself, and not so much its present relevance. The author gives some early Modern English examples from the Helsinki Corpus that come close to the hot news perfect, and also notes that it is rarer in American English than in British English.

An issue having to do with aspectionality is discussed in Pier Marco Bertinetto's 'Statives, Progressives, and Habituals: Analogies and Differences' (*Linguistics* 32.391–423). He scrutinizes claims that progressives and habituals are statives. For the progressive, such claims have been based on the fact that, in English and other languages, it is formed by means of stative *be*, while in other languages it is formed from a locative, the fact that paraphrases by means of a stative exist (*he is flying* » *he is in flight*), and the fact that both progressives and statives allow *still* (as in *He is still working/angry*) but do not occur in the imperative. Bertinetto shows that some of these supposed similarities are ill founded, some are due to independent factors, and some are language-specific. Besides, there are important empirical differences and conceptually, too, the two categories are different: 'stative' is a category of Aktionsart, and therefore a lexical property, while 'progressive' is a category of grammatical aspect. In the same way, the author shows that habituals are not statives.

From aspectuality, we go to mood, in particular the imperative. Flor Aarts's concern in 'Imperative Sentences in *A Corpus of English Conversation*' (*LB* 83.145-55) is descriptive/taxonomic. He seeks to establish the following points: What types of imperative sentence occur in the corpus, what is their frequency and distribution, and what are their syntactic properties? He distinguishes two main types, i.e. +LET and –LET (the latter the most frequent), and a number of subtypes. Hidemitsu Takahashi looks at the imperative from a pragmatic point of view in 'English Imperatives and Speaker Commitment' (*LangS* 16.371–85). This study deals with the differences between the imperative and other 'hypotheticals', such as the subjunctive and the infinitive, especially in how far they differ in terms of speaker commitment. The author believes that the latter is both unique and central to the meaning of the English imperative and that it forms a continuum ranging from low (*Sleep until noon, and you'll miss lunch*) to high (*Sleep until noon; you are very tired*) commitment. The difference between the subjunctive and the imperative (which seems to us not always clearly made) is that the former can only replace instances of high speaker commitment.

Another 'Latin' category that has been associated with a gradience approach, but then of a syntactic rather than a pragmatic nature, is the gerund. Hans Kirsten provides in his 'Ein Plädoyer für das Gerundium' (*ZAA* 42.16–20) a critical evaluation of the argument that the traditional differentiation between gerunds and participles is not well founded (as suggested by Quirk et al. 1985, and see also Esser in *YWES* 72.53), and concludes, on the basis of a fuller range of examples than Quirk et al. provide, that the distinction remains a useful one. Jürgen Esser in his reply to this ('Zur Terminologie und Analyse von nominalen *ing*-Sätzen ("Gerundien")', *ZAA* 42.21–6) does not agree. He argues that the original Latin terms 'gerundium' and 'participle' are in fact not so useful when applied to English. These terms put too much emphasis on formal characteristics, whereas it is more important to look at the functions that these forms may have. He suggests, therefore, that the term 'nominal *ing*-clause' should be used instead of 'gerund', and describes how corpus linguists try to distinguish between nouns ending in *-ing* and *ing*-clauses. James Blevins has looked at gerunds from a different perspective, and provides 'A Lexicalist Analysis of Gerundive Nominals in English' (*AuJL* 14.1–38), which refines and develops an earlier analysis proposed by Geoffrey Pullum (see *YWES* 72.41). Blevins argues that a phrase like *John('s) claiming immunity* is generated by the phrase rules N" → (NP) H'[VForm PresP] and N" → NP[POSS] H'. Bar-level succession is regular here, but the feature on H' in the former phrase structure rule will override the Head Feature Convention, so that the NP can have a verbal head. Derived nominals, such as *the reading of the poem*, Blevins argues, have a nominal head. There is more on derived nominals, and not only those ending in *-ing*, in John Taylor's '"Subjective" and "Objective" Readings of Possessor Nominals' (*CogLing* 5.201–42). He considers the question why some POSS+N phrases invite a subject interpretation for POSS (e.g. *their avoidance of the cliff*), others an object interpretation (e.g. *the soldiers' fright at the scarecrow*) and still others allow both (e.g. *his dismissal*). He proposes that the choice is determined by the semantics of both the POSS+N construction and the specific derived N (of which there are shown to be various types). POSS, being a reference point, has to be topical (i.e. represent given, accessible information). Moreover, to facilitate identification of N, POSS must be informative with respect to N. In *their avoidance of the cliff*, for example, *their* is more informative than *the cliff*, because if one wanted to verify whether they avoided the cliff, one would inspect the referent of *their* rather than that of *the cliff*; to verify the truthfulness of *the city's destruction by the soldiers*, however, one would inspect *the city* rather than *the soldiers*. This approach yields more or less the same results as the affectedness constraint, which was proposed in the earlier literature to explain facts of this type, but it derives them from more principled considerations.

Interest in auxiliaries and modals has waned somewhat compared with previous years (but also see the section on Early English). Salikoko Mufwene writes 'On the Status of Auxiliary Verbs in Gullah' (*AS* 69.58–70). He defines auxiliary verbs as syntactic heads of VP that are semantically modifiers. After describing the Gullah tense, aspect and mood markers, he suggests, on the basis of etymology, their use as independent verbs, and their modification by verb-modifiers, that most of these markers can indeed be regarded as auxiliaries. The modal (and sometimes not so modal) verbs *need* and *dare* are subjected to detailed investigation in Patrick Duffley's '*Need* and *dare*: The Black Sheep of the Modal Family' (*Lingua* 94.213–43). After briefly reviewing the morpho-syntax of these two verbs, and earlier work on them, Duffley suggests that in their modal uses, they evoke the conceivability of the existence of daring and need, while in their full-verb uses they evoke the existence of a need or of audacity. Blend constructions (common with *dare*) evoke both conceivability and reality at the same time. Duffley also suggests that, since modal verbs in general express the potential existence of an event, they are not expected to take third person singular *-s* (which evokes actuality), or to be followed by a *to*-infinitive (which expresses a subsequent event), or to take *do*-periphrasis (which evokes actual reality or realization). Margaret Mishoe and Michael Montgomery have studied 'The Pragmatics of Multiple Modal Variation in North and South Carolina' (*AS* 69.3–29). In a corpus of 236 authentic examples, they have found a wide variety of combinations (many more than the commonly cited *might can*, *might could*, and *might would*). More than half of the instances are found in embedded clauses, and the subject is usually *I*, *we* or *you*. They occur most often in face-to-face conversations, and are strongly linked to pragmatic indirectness (i.e.

they are typically associated with negotiation, concerns of politeness, and the use of hedges and mitigations). This pragmatic function makes them less likely to turn up in written texts, and this might explain why there are no American examples on record before 1850, even if, as seems probable, they were imported to the USA from Scotland and Ireland in the eighteenth century.

A more general article concerned with the verbal phrase is Leon Stassen's, who discusses, in 'Typology versus Mythology', 'the case of the zero-copula' (*NJL* 17.105–26). He argues on the basis of a typological study of a large number of languages that it is incorrect to state that the copula is empty of semantic content (the so-called Dummy-hypothesis), and a mere carrier of grammatical categories such as tense, aspect, etc. If that were true, he says, then one would expect only a copula when the sentence is marked for TMA. Instead it is found that zero copula also occurs in marked TMA sentences, and full (lexically expressed) copulas in unmarked TMA sentences.

Another typological study, not on the verb phrase but on elements intimately connected with it, is Frank Palmer's new book *Grammatical Roles and Relations*. This study is concerned with the way grammatical roles such as 'Agent', 'Patient', etc. are expressed in a large number of languages, and what their relation is to grammatical functions such as 'Subject', 'Object', etc. The book is not primarily theoretical but in the first place an inventory; it is interested in similarities and differences between languages. The first chapter is devoted to setting out and disentangling the terminology used. The other chapters provide lucid discussion of the (interplay between the) various roles and relations and especially how the arguments (which are primarily notional concepts, and therefore not language-specific) can switch or be remapped in different systems related to notions of transitivity, passivity, reflexivity, the impersonal/personal distinction, etc. It shows how languages use these devices differently and what means they employ to express the various grammatical roles. A separate chapter is devoted to causative constructions. These are also examined by Beth Levin and Malka Rappaport Hovav in 'A Preliminary Analysis of Causative Verbs in English' (*Lingua* 92.35-77). To explain the alternation *The vase broke* vs. *He broke the vase*, they distinguish two types of verb: those with an 'internal cause' (*play*, *speak*, *work*, *blush*, *laugh*, *slouch*, etc.) and those with an 'external causer' (*break*, *blacken*, *bounce*, *close*, etc.). Verbs of the second type can detransitivize (i.e. become unaccusative) if they denote an eventuality that can happen spontaneously. Verbs of the first type are unergative; only those of them that have a meaning compatible with external causation can transitivize (as in *She burped the baby*). Specific rules linking the lexical semantic and syntactic representations are proposed for both types. The nature of such linking rules is also discussed, but at a somewhat more general level, in Lisbeth Falster Jakobsen and Peter Harder's 'Valency in a Hjelmslev-Inspired Functional Grammar: Substance, Form, Expression and Content in a Functional Analysis of Valency' (*ALH* 27.275–84). The approach taken is to start from the 'raw conceptual material', and then to analyse the different levels of form-giving. For DRINK, for example, the conceptual material includes an animate doer, a liquid entity, and a particular manner of ingestion. Abstracting away from the entity yields *This animal does not drink*, incorporating the entity in the verb yields *He drinks like a fish*, etc. A distinction is also made between expression argument (i.e. a formal entity) and content argument (a semantic entity).

A study that can be regarded as an in-depth application of Palmer's comparative approach to grammatical remapping is Susan Olsen's

'Lokativalternation im Deutschen und Englischen' (*ZSpr* 13.210–35). With respect to the well-known sentence pair, *He sprayed paint on the wall* and *He sprayed the wall with paint*, and the similar distinction made morphologically with German verbs such as *schreiben/beschreiben*, Olsen agrees neither with Baker's (1988) point of view nor with that of Rappaport and Levin (1988). Baker argues that the semantic structure of the verb does not change, and that there is only a change in the grammatical realization of the internal verbal arguments, a purely formal operation taking place in the lexicon. Rappaport and Levin believe that a lexical–semantic distinction should be made between two different verbs. Olsen argues that one should make a distinction between a base verb (e.g. *schreiben*) and a derived verb (e.g. *beschreiben*), where the derived verb shows reduced syntactic force ('Wertigkeit'), having a θ-frame in which a structural argument is blocked but can be licensed as an argument-adjunct with the help of a preposition. In 'The Locative Alternation and Multistratalism' (*Linguistics* 32.5–45), Patrick Farrell looks at the locative alternation from the perspective of relational grammar, asking whether the construction shows grammatical relation revaluation or not. He takes dative shift as the prime example of such revaluation (or advancement), and then shows that the locative alternation differs from it in several respects (compare, for example, **What we did a present was give the boss* vs. *What we did with the hay was load the wagon*; **We gave the boss* vs. *We loaded the wagon*; **our offer of the neighbours of help* vs. *the loading of wagons with hay*; **They are hard to sell cars* vs. *The wagon is easy to load with hay*). He concludes that the locative alternation is strictly monostratal. The primary focus of Tanja Mortelmans's 'Understanding German Dative Verbs and their English and Dutch Equivalents: A Contrastive Study in Cognitive Grammar' (*Antwerp Papers in Linguistics* 78.1–124) is on German verbs that take one object which has dative case (e.g. *helfen* 'help', *fehlen* 'miss/lack', *gleichen* 'resemble', and *lauschen* 'listen to'). She views the dative as signalling bilateral involvement, which makes these verbs somewhat different from prototypical transitives with an accusative object, in which the object represents a totally passive entity. Since English and Dutch lack the case distinction, translational equivalents of the German sentences in these languages present a slightly different conceptualization of the event, and are closer to the transitive prototype. This means that they also allow uses of the relevant verbs in which the object is patient-like, and shows no bilateral involvement at all (as, for example, in *I can't help it* and *It helps the pain*).

Another construction that is interesting from the point of view of grammatical roles and relations is the middle. Peter Ackema and Maaike Schoorlemmer have looked at 'The Middle Construction and the Syntax–Semantics Interface' (*Lingua* 93.59–90), and present a pre-syntactic account of it. At Lexical Conceptual Structure, the argument highest on the hierarchy Actor–Patient–Agent–Theme–Goal will become the external argument; middles arise when the Actor is arbitrary, and can therefore fail to project. The affectedness constraint found with many middles (e.g. **This book understands easily*) follows from the fact that the Patient is second in the hierarchy. If there is no Patient, however, some other argument may become external (as in *Greek translates easily*). The authors also analyse such interesting Dutch middles as: (literally) '*This chair sits nicely*' and '*It sits nicely in this chair*'. We will also deal with two pieces on inversion here: Joan Bresnan's 'Locative Inversion and the Architecture of Universal Grammar' (*Language* 70.72–131), and Betty Birner's 'Information Status and Word Order: An Analysis of English Inversion' (*Language* 70.233–59). Bresnan compares English sentences like

In the corner was a lamp and *Among the guests was sitting my friend David* with their Chichewa counterparts, and advances a LFG analysis for them. In both languages, locative inversion can occur if the verb takes a theme and a locative; its function is to (re)introduce the inverted subject on the scene referred to by the preposed locative. In English, the locative is not the subject, because it is not a NP (but it can raise, as in: *On that hill appears to be located a cathedral*). In Chichewa, locative is a gender-class, and it can function as subject. Several earlier analyses of locative inversion are discussed but argued to be incorrect. Birner's paper is particularly concerned with the function of inversions like *Also eliminated is the expense of buying costly chemicals* and *Zooming in on you like a guided missile comes a rival contender*. After discussing some earlier proposals, Birner demonstrates in some detail, on the basis of a corpus of about 700 examples, that the finite verb and the postposed logical subject represent old (i.e. invoked or inferable) information compared to the preposed phrase. This also explains why the verb is always informationally light.

Issues of grammatical function are also prominent in several papers in *FoLi* 28, a special issue on sentence processing and the nature of the human syntactic parser. Markus Bader examines 'Syntactic–Function Ambiguities' (5–66), comparing processing in English (SVO) and German (SOV). He shows that in both languages, syntactic processing (e.g. establishing c-command, binding, etc.) can take place online, except that in German, theta-role assignment has to wait for the verb to appear. Ingeborf Lasser comes to roughly similar conclusions after considering 'What the Parser Needs to Know in Order to Attach a Phrase' (67–100). An immediate-attachment model of parsing, she argues, allows a clear specification of how various types of information (of the input string and of the grammar) are used in parsing; she shows how this works in English and German. A third paper that also considers data from English, in particular 'garden-path' sentences, is Paul Gorrell's 'Structural Relations in the Grammar and the Parser' (101–37). Gorrell proposes a parsing model that incrementally builds trees (at each point choosing the 'simplest' possible one, in terms of precedence and dominance), and that cannot alter or delete structure. All three papers use a GB/Barriers model of syntactic structure; they all agree that structure-building is incremental, and that there can be no temporarily unattached phrases.

We now turn to several studies that look at aspects of NPs that do not directly concern (alternations in) grammatical function. As usual, there are several papers on binding facts. Paul Bloom, Andrew Barss, Janet Nicol and Laura Conway have looked at 'Children's Knowledge of Binding and Coreference: Evidence from Spontaneous Speech' (*Language* 70.53–71). They have found that, in the CHILDES database, even two- and three-year-olds use *me* and *myself* in accordance with binding principles A and B nearly all the time. These production data therefore contrast with comprehension studies, which have shown that children often make binding errors (interpreting, for example, *Is Mama Bear touching her?* as reflexive). The authors attribute these errors to performance factors such as a response bias, limited attention span, and overgeneralization of contrastive stress patterns (as in *I do see ME*). Sergey Avrutin and Rosalind Thornton write on 'Distributivity and Binding in Child Grammar' (*LingI* 25.165–71). They tested four-year-olds on sentences like [*The Smurf and the clown*]$_i$ *dried them*$_i$, and found a tendency to allow this when the subject is collective, but reject it when the subject has a distributive reading. The authors attribute the reflexive interpretation to the possibility of having co-reference without co-indexing (as another example of this in child language, they offer the sentence *Mama Bear*$_i$ *is drying her*$_i$). Such accidental co-reference is impossible with distributed NPs, because these are quantifiers and therefore have no reference (just like the subject in *Every bear*$_i$ *is drying her*$_i$, which children do not allow either). The topic of co-reference in general is addressed by Mira Ariel in 'Interpreting Anaphoric Expressions: A Cognitive versus a Pragmatic Approach' (*JL* 30.3–42). She considers the distribution of zero, reflexives, pronouns and full NPs. Rejecting an account in terms of Grice's quantity maxim, she proposes that referring expressions can be placed on an accessibility hierarchy (zero < reflexive < agreement < clitic < unstressed pronoun < last name < short definite description < long definite description < full name < full name plus modifier), according to how accessible the speaker judges the entity to be to the speaker. We just mention here Mark Janse's 'Clitics and Word Order since Wackernagel: One Hundred Years of Research into Clitics and Related Phenomena' (*Orbis* 37.389-410); this useful addition to the bibliography edited by Zwicky et al. (1992) covers all the titles published between 1992 and 1994 on this topic plus studies missing in the earlier bibliography.

There are two pieces on reciprocals that are very similar to each other. Mary Dalrymple, Sam Mchombo and Stanley Peters study 'Semantic Similarities and Syntactic Contrasts between Chichewa and English Reciprocals' (*LingI* 25.145–63). Their starting point is the recent claim that English *each other* has compositional meaning, with scope ambiguities being due to differences in LF movement and application of binding theory. The authors show that the reciprocal in Chichewa, very similar in meaning to that of English, is formed by a detransitivizing affix, and cannot possibly be analysed syntactically in the same way as *each other*. They conclude that reciprocals have a constant semantics, but may have various morphosyntactic realizations. Basically the same conclusion is reached in 'The Syntax and Semantics of the Reciprocal Construction in Ciyao' (*LingA* 24.3–31) by Sam Mchombo and Armindo Ngunga, on the basis of comparable facts from another Bantu language.

Bas Aarts has investigated NPs of the type *a hell of a problem*, *her nitwit of a husband* and *those fools of doctors*, and reports his findings in 'The Syntax of Binominal Noun Phrases in English' (*DWPELL* 30.1–28). After reviewing earlier analyses, he describes various properties of the construction (in particular the possibilities for modifying the nouns), and argues that criteria for headedness point to the second noun as being the head. He proposes that *hell of a*, *nitwit of a* and *fools of* are pre-modifying NPs, suggesting that this state of affairs is the result of some kind of reanalysis or grammaticalization, and that *of a* may well disappear (as it is in a way doing in *helluva*). Louisa Sadler and Douglas Arnold write on 'Prenominal Adjectives and the Phrasal/Lexical Distinction' (*JL* 30.187–226). They propose that in adjective–noun structures, both the adjective and the noun are zero-level. The adjective can take an X°-adjunct, yielding NPs like *an* $[_N [_A$ *extremely happy] person]*, but not an XP modifier or complement (hence: **a three miles long walk*, **navigable by boat rivers*, **a how large house*, etc.). The fact that a word like *asleep* cannot occur prenominally can be explained by saying that it is an AP, and the fact that a pronoun like *someone* cannot take any prenominal adjectives will follow from its XP status. As for semantics, an adjective–noun structure expresses one coherent property, while a noun–adjective structure, which is analysed as [NP AP], expresses two coherent properties.

Two papers deal with quantitative issues concerning nouns. Richard Hudson reports that 'About 37% of Word-Tokens are Nouns' (*Language* 70.331–9). This holds not only for the Brown and LOB corpora (with the division into common noun, proper noun, and pronoun depending on genre), but also for shorter texts, and for languages other than English. Other word-classes, too, appear to show relatively stable percentages across different texts. Hudson (who is 'as reluctant as any linguist could be to believe it') points out that these are surprising facts that cry out for an explanation. The frequency of plural *-s* marking is investigated by Shana Poplack and Sali Tagliamonte in '*-S* or Nothing: Marking the Plural in the African American Diaspora' (*AS* 69.227–59). They find that zero-plurals in Samaná English, African Nova-Scotian English, and the Ex-Slave Recordings are more frequent than in Black English Vernacular generally. They describe the contexts promoting the (non-)use of the plural marker, and interpret the zero-forms as perpetuations of forms of earlier English, rather than as evidence of a creole system.

Several writers have looked at the form and use of pronouns. Judith A. Quattlebaum has written 'A Study of Case Assignment in Co-ordinate Noun Phrases' (*LangQ* 32.131–47). It deals with the way case is assigned to the co-ordinate NP in instances such as *Sue and he/him will be late*. The problem is that *him* is more frequent in normal usage than *he* but does not follow the regular rule of case assignment. Quattlebaum investigates the choices speakers make before they have had any formal training, and what kind of training might be effective in acquiring the case of prestige usage. In the title of their more formally orientated study of the same construction, Frank Parker, Charles Meyer and Kathryn Riley exclaim: '*Here Us Go Again*' (*AS* 69.435–9). The reason for the exclamation is that Graham Shorrocks has criticized their earlier proposal that only co-ordinate constructions can contain an objective case-form functioning as subject to a tensed verb (see *YWES* 73.43). The authors are not impressed or amused by the counter-examples offered by Shorrocks: some of them, such as *Thee come here*, do not have a tensed verb (this, they imply, is because 'Shorrocks is simply unfamiliar with current syntactic theory'); those really having a tensed verb are restricted to a few regional British dialects; and, anyway, Shorrocks does not present an alternative theory. Another study of pronouns, again concerned with matters of prestige, is Katie Wales's 'Royalese: the Rise and Fall of the "Queen's English"' (*EnT* 10.iii.3–10). She looks at its use of the pronouns *we* and *one* (also at phonetic and lexical matters which we will not discuss here). Three types of *we* are distinguished, the first type, royal *we*, being clearly in decline (except with Margaret Thatcher). The use of *one* is still going strong among royals, who use it in the sense of 'I' (it serves well as a replacement of royal *we*), and even as an object or reflexive pronoun, and in tag questions. This use of *one* has now also acquired connotations of upper-classness. Also interesting in this connection is a note in the same volume of this journal by David Rosewarne on the avoidance of *he* as an anaphoric pronoun to *one* because of the 'necessity' of being sexually neutral in one's language. He notes that in American English, this *one* is now often referred to by *they*, with quite difficult grammatical consequences. This article in turn is a reaction to the use of non-sexist *themself* in Canadian legislative drafting discussed in *EnT* 10 by Donald Revell et al. (10–17).

While on the subject of varieties of English (there will be more on this in section 6(b)), we would like to mention Josef Schmied's article on 'Syntactic Style Variation in Indian English' (in Günther Blaicher and Brigitte Glaser, eds, *Anglistentag 1993 Eichstätt*). This involves a comparison of the LOB corpus with the Kolhapur corpus of Indian English (both containing a wide spread of text types). The aim is to establish types of variation and to account for them stylistically and sociodialectically, but also to measure them quantitatively, and to find out in how far it is true that English used as a second language is often more literary and archaic (due to so-called colonial lag). He looks at constructions that have been tentatively seen as typically Indian, such as a higher degree of sentence complexity, the use of invariable tags, of *-ing* forms with stative verbs, etc. Marjory Meechan and Michele Foley deal with subject–verb concord in existential sentences in Standard Canadian ('On Resolving Disagreement: Linguistic Theory and Variation in *There's bridges*', *LVC* 6.63–85). Using variationist methodology, they find that there is a clear preference for the singular verb in the type mentioned in their title and conclude that this is connected not with the type of determiner preceding the NP but with the form of the copula (full or reduced) and the speaker's level of education. Concord in earlier American English is the subject of Michael Ellis's 'Literary Dialect as Linguistic Evidence: Subject–Verb Concord in Nineteenth-Century Southern Literature' (*AS* 69.128–44). An investigation of some ten southern literary works from the period 1830–60 reveals the use of various types of non-standard concord (e.g. *don't* for *doesn't*, plural *was*, singular *were*). Only one type seems to be uniquely characteristic of southern literary dialect: non-pronominal plural subject plus verb form in *-s*; the author calls for further examination of non-literary materials to establish more precisely the distribution of this type.

There are quite a number of comparative studies this year; we have already mentioned many above. They are often written against a typological backdrop, and they are most useful in order to gain more and fresh insight into a particular phenomenon in one's own native language. Dale A. Koike has written on 'Negation in Spanish and English and Requests: Mitigating Effects?' (*JPrag* 21.513–26). Koike shows that negation in speech acts does not always serve to mitigate an effect (by cancelling a positive belief), but may in fact have the opposite effect, especially in suggestions and requests, such as *Have you thought about reading this book?*, where the negative version is too forceful to be polite in English. It is shown that the pragmatic effect of the negative varies according to the type of speech act in which it is used, and also that languages, in this case English and Spanish, vary in how they use it. The next two contributions, both on voice, are more strictly typological. John Myhill and Zhiqun Xing '[Compare] the Function of Voice in Biblical Hebrew, Chinese, and English' (*LangS* 16.253–83). The idea is to develop a universal typology of voice through a systematic description and comparison of it in three unrelated languages but in similar texts (relatively free translations of the Bible). The authors write that most studies on the universal function of voice have been marred by the fact that they start off with a description of it in only one language. From the present survey it becomes clear that we cannot simply categorize constructions as passive or not passive, but only as more or less passive. This is because what have been generally seen as functions of the passive, such as 'agent-suppression' or 'agent-demotion', consist of many different types with many different realizations in languages. Martin Haspelmath's typological study of 'Passive Participles across Languages' (in Barbara Fox and Paul J. Hopper, eds, *Voice: Form and Function*) is more diachronically orientated. It looks at cross-linguistic similarities and differences of passive participles, and notes first of all that these participles are basically verbal adjectives, which later may become grammaticalized into passive constructions rather than the other way around. Usually this happens via their interpretation as a resultative participle (the verbal adjective expressing a state that results from a previous event) as in *the abused child*.

Another comparative study is Yishai Tobin's *Invariance, Markedness and Distinctive Feature Analysis: A Contrastive Study of Sign Systems in English and Hebrew*, which takes a sign-orientated approach to several constructions and contrasts in English (and Hebrew). Tobin argues that signs have invariant meanings, which are exploited to communicate specific discourse messages. In his analyses of various phenomena, the distinctive feature [semantic integrality] plays an important role; it means that potentially discontinuous entities are perceived in continuous space, time or existence, as part of an integral set. Marked for this feature are, for example: mass nouns (as compared with unmarked count nouns), *much* (vs. *many*), *every* (vs. *each*), *any* (vs. *some*), *as X* (vs. *like X*), *too* (vs. *also*), *X-less* (vs. *without X*), and *X-er* (vs. *more X*). Tobin also shows in some detail how this feature can be used to explain the alternation between the genitive and the *of*-phrase, which has puzzled so many grammarians. In *the journey's end*, for example, the end is being presented as an integral part of the journey; *the end of the journey* is unmarked for this feature. Another area where the feature plays a role is contractions: forms like *you've* signal semantic integrality, whereas *you have* does not. Tobin analyses numerous examples of all these forms, and also shows that in *The Wizard of Oz*, at points in the text where unity and happiness are being expressed, genitives and contractions are indeed very frequent. Another aspect of meaning that Tobin discusses is Process, which is unmarked, and Result, which is a marked feature (compare for this also his earlier work; see *YWES* 74.46). This distinction is relevant, for example, to the verbs *speak* (unmarked) and *talk* (marked). Markedness is also used by Tobin to explain the differences in use between *how come* (marked for Cause), *what for* (marked for Result) and *why* (unmarked for either).

Comparative concerns play an obvious role in the study of code switching, so this may be a good point to deal with the three items on this topic that we noted this year. Eva Eppler's 'Code-Switching in "Emigranto"' (*Views* 3.75–93) is a descriptive study of code switching by Austrian Germans living in Britain. As far as the site of switching is concerned, she finds that it occurs mostly after a determiner or adjective, or at an adverb phrase. A more theory-orientated study is Janice Jake's 'Intrasentential Code Switching and Pronouns: On the Categorial Status of Functional Elements' (*Linguistics* 32.271–98). Jake uses evidence from code switching in various language pairs to show that pronouns can be either content morphemes (like nouns and verbs) or system morphemes (like agreement, determiners, inflections, and other functional morphemes). This (pragmatic/semantic) division therefore cuts across syntactic categories. Also theoretical in outlook is the article 'Code Switching and X-bar Theory: The Functional Head Constraint' by Hedi Belazi, Edward Rubin and Almeida Toribio (*LingI* 25.221–37). In this interesting study, it is proposed that code switching is subject to the following constraint: a complement selected by a functional head must be in the same language. The authors argue that this constraint is an improvement over the well-known government constraint, which was too restrictive. The functional head constraint will allow attested examples like *El profesor dijo that the student had received an A* and *The police officers have seen un ladrón* (where the verb selects the switched complement), but rule out sentences such as *El hombre no wants the book* (in which the functional head Neg selects the switched constituent). We are not sure what the constraint would say about data like those found by Eppler (with switching after the determiner).

As usual, a great deal of attention is paid to verbal complementation. There are quite a number of general, theoretical contributions here to which we will turn first. Anita Steube and Gerhild Zybatow have edited a book wholly devoted to the topic, *Zur Satzwertigkeit von Infinitiven und Small Clauses*. Most of the papers included deal with the interpretation and analysis of infinitival clauses in German. This is therefore not the place to discuss these in detail, but anyone interested in infinitival constructions in English, and especially in their diachronic development, would do well to take a look at the studies here collected, especially the contributions by Peter Suchsland (who writes about the differences between control and raising structures in terms of the use they make of passive and perfective infinitivals) and by Günther Grewendorf (who discusses German accusative plus infinitive constructions – he sees them as CPs, not IPs – and verb-raising phenomena). There are two more general papers, one of which is also concerned with English. This is Chris Wilder's 'Small clauses im Englischen und in der GB-theory'. He discusses all the types of V+NP+Predicate string that have been analysed in the literature as small clauses (where the NP may be either fully lexical or a trace, as in *We drank [the pub dry]* and *She became [t sick]* respectively). He argues that the small clause configuration is by no means as wide-spread as has usually been claimed. He discusses two possible alternative structures, with the predicate adjoined either to VP or to NP. Rudolf Ruicka (still in the same volume) pleads for the preservation of PRO in 'Gegen die Aufgabe von PRO'. He argues that, although one must be careful in postulating elements that one can neither see nor hear, there are still very good reasons for accepting an empty category PRO in view of the fact that quite a number of syntactic processes, such as control, raising, some binding phenomena, etc., fully depend on the appearance and visibility of PRO. As far as we can see he does not really provide new arguments for postulating PRO, but it is useful to see the existing ones stated together in one place.

'Another Look at Small Clauses' is offered by Christian Kreps (*UCWPL* 6.149–77). Like Wilder, he would like to do away with small clauses, but his suggestion is that they should be analysed as IP clauses (or exceptional clauses as found in accusative plus infinitive constructions), with an empty I position followed by a VP complement, in which the verb, if a copula, may be deleted. This analysis solves some of the problems, but in turn creates others, as is admitted. In the same journal there are two more theoretical papers which we will briefly mention. Annabel Cormack and Richard Breheny propose a distinct phrasal projection for all operator heads (in 'Projections for Functional Categories', 35–61) and reject the notion of adjunction as currently used in the Principles and Parameters framework. They argue that their proposal has descriptive and explanatory advantages, especially in connection with the analysis of noun modifiers and predicate adjuncts. Michael Brody, in his 'Phrase Structure and Dependence' (1–33), makes a plea for dependency relations (e.g. anaphoric relations) in syntactic structure, arguing that taking these as basic together with constituent hierarchies (to which precedence has usually been given in generative grammar) leads to a much simpler theory of phrase structure.

We now turn to complementation as a more strictly English concern. A broad perspective, both comparatively and theoretically, is given by Klaus-Uwe Panther's book, *Kontrollphänomene im Englischen und Deutschen aus semantisch-pragmatischer Perspektive*. His main area of interest is obligatory control structures, such as subject and object control, after verbs like *promise* and *convince*. The angle of approach is formed by the following question: how do speakers identify the empty infinitival slot with its antecedent in the matrix clause? The first five chapters are introductory; they initiate the reader into control theory as formulated by Montague grammarians, and more syntactically orientated theories, especially the government and binding approach of the eighties. The relationship between control theory and thematic roles, and the more radically anti-syntactic theories, which endeavour to explain all control features purely on semantic and pragmatic grounds, are discussed. In his own proposal, the author steers a middle course, rejecting the autonomous syntactic approach, but also insisting that not all morphosyntactic features can be pragmatically explained. Earlier semantic transparency gets lost in many cases because of other functional needs that play a role in language or because of changes that have taken place elsewhere on another level. He shows in a detailed study that English and German differ in this respect: with respect to control phenomena, English, through the loss of many morphosyntactic features, has become a more opaque language from a semantic point of view. He hopes to have shown, however, that even though this is true semantically, one can still understand the control structures as used in English in a pragmatically systematic fashion. How children learn the proper interpretation of PRO is the topic of 'A Longitudinal Study of Principles of Control and Pronominal Reference in Child English', by Helen Cairns, Dana McDaniel, Jennifer Hsu and Michelle Rapp (in *Language* 70.260–88). They tested a group of 3–4-year-olds over a period of nine months, to see how they interpreted PRO in adverbial clauses (e.g. *Ernie kisses Cookie Monster before PRO jumping over the fence*, in which children often have object-controlled or arbitrary PRO) and in complements (e.g. *Big Bird tells Ernie PRO to jump over the fence*, in which children sometimes have subject-controlled or arbitrary PRO). In earlier work, the authors had hypothesized that children's grammars go through several stages before reaching the adult system: (1) analysing all PRO clauses as cases of co-ordination; (2) having complement clauses in subordinate position; (3) also analysing adverbial clauses as subordinate, but attaching them to VP; (4) attaching adverbial clauses to S, as in the adult grammar. The results of the experiment confirm the existence of these stages and their developmental order (with stages 1 and 2 taking longest). The idea that stage 1 involves co-ordination also received support. Several further refinements also suggested themselves (e.g. the fact that, of the adverbial clauses, those introduced by *in order to* tended to stay in stage 3 longest).

Complementation after specific verb classes also receives its fair share of attention. Geart van der Meer makes two attempts to throw more light on perception verb complements. His first contribution, 'Complements and the Fiction of "Syntactic Structure"' (*LB* 83.181–95), is quite radical. He objects to the idea of allowing *Bill* in *I watched Bill mend the lamp* to have a double function as long as that notion has not been 'clarified and given empirical backup'. Indeed, he makes the general proposal that there can be no such thing as ambiguity of structure in a linguistic form. He puts forward the idea that structure is encoded into form by the speaker (or read off from form by the hearer), but that structure is not form itself; rather, structure is content. In other words, we do not have to account formally for all relations that we intuit between the form and the things in the world out there. He therefore proposes to do away with all ideas of underlying order, empty slots, nodes, etc., and to have just what is observable, i.e. words, order and intonation. Order in this view depends on the rich and complex content of 'words'. In his second article, 'Verbs of Perception and their Complementation' (*ES* 75.468–80), his focus is narrower. He is interested in two aspects, namely what the difference in meaning is between a present participle and a bare infinitive after perception verbs, and, second, whether they are different syntactically. On the basis of the behaviour of especially co-ordinate constructions he concludes that the *-ing* form is basically static and the bare infinitive dynamic. Although he notes that there are a number of constructions in which only the present participle is possible (indicating that, syntactically, participle and infinitive are not the same), and that the bare infinitive cannot be separated so easily from its NP object, still he concludes that it is better to argue that participle and infinitive have the same structure.

Also concerned with 'The Infinitive and the *-ing* as Complements', but this time after 'verbs of effort', is the paper by Patrick J. Duffley and Rachel Tremblay in *ES* 75 (566–75). It is in a way a follow-up of Duffley's book (see *YWES* 73.34–5), which dealt with the difference between plain and *to*-infinitives. They try to explain (try explaining?) the difference between *to*-infinitive and *-ing* after these verbs, noting that with *attempt* the difference seems minimal, in contrast to e.g. *try*, and also that some verbs do not take *-ing* forms at all. They conclude that 'sameness of time' cannot be the criterion that distinguishes the two forms because with many verbs it does not work. Instead they show that the *-ing* form correlates with NPs used as direct objects and the *to*-infinitive with PPs with an adverbial function, so similar to the difference between *He grabbed her purse/at her purse*. Thus, *to* must be interpreted as a preposition which expresses the notion of movement 'from a before-position to an after-position in time'; *-ing* on the other hand simply 'identifie[s] that which is "verb-ed" in the main verb's event'. Complements to causative verbs are often analysed as being, in a sense, reductions of complex structures (see, for example, Hilda Koopman's article reviewed above), but Suzanne Kemmer and Arie Verhagen do not agree with this idea. In 'The Grammar of Causatives and the Conceptual Structure of Events' (*CogLing* 5.115–56), they argue that causatives of intransitives (as in *Frederike made us work harder*) are modelled on simple two-participant clauses (*We ate the cake*), while causatives of transitives (*They made us finish the work*) are modelled on three-participant clauses (*We gave him the present* or *She broke it with a hammer*). They motivate this conceptually (and cognitively) by pointing out that it would mean that more complex structures (i.e. causatives) are modelled after basic ones (i.e. those for monotransitive and ditransitive event structure). Empirical evidence for the analysis comes from the fact that in many languages the causee receives dative or instrumental marking, from the existence of ditransitives like *show*, which express causative meaning ('cause to see'), and from the identity of causative and ditransitive affixes in some languages. Walt Wolfram writes 'On the Sociolinguistic Significance of Obscure Dialect Structures: The [NP_i *call* NP_i V-*ING*] Construction in African-American Vernacular English' (*AS* 69.339-60). An example of the type of sentence in question is: *They call themselves dancing* (with the implication that it is not actually authentic dancing that they are doing). This pattern, which has not really been noted before, is apparently understood by white speakers, but its active use seems to be restricted to AAVE (yes, please note that this is what political correctness has forced BEV to call himself/herself nowadays; it feels as if we have lost a good friend). Wolfram shows that the construction is not frequent, was already in use in the 1960s, and is typically used in evaluations, sometimes as a form of ritualistic teasing. It can be analysed as featuring a small clause complement, the subject of which is co-referential with the matrix subject (which must be human).

Next, we move from small clauses to fuller clauses. Peter Collins has written on 'The Structure of English Comparative Clauses' (*ES* 75.157–65). He first defines comparative clauses by the way in which they are distinguished from all other subclauses, namely by the fact that they are incomplete, i.e. they show some kind of ellipsis. Then, he distinguishes two primary classes by means of the dimension of 'equality' and 'scalarity'. (In)equality is reflected in the use of *than/as* respectively, whereas scalar comparisons allow three possibilities: either clauses are non-scalar, or if scalar, they indicate degree or quantity. Renaat Declerck considers 'The Taxonomy and Interpretation of Clefts and Pseudo-Clefts' (*Lingua* 93.183–220), a review article of P. Collins's *Cleft and Pseudo-Cleft Constructions in English* (1991). Declerck sees several problems in Collins's work; the main ones are the claim that there are clefts with a zero highlighted element (these, Declerck argues, exemplify another construction), and the failure to deal with clefts and pseudo-clefts in the same way.

It is but a small step from clefts to relatives. In 'Nonrestrictive Relative *that*-Clauses Revisited' (*SN* 61.181–95), Bengt Jacobsson returns to the myth that *that* can only be used in restrictive clauses, and to some minor myths, such as that *that* cannot take stress and therefore cannot be followed by a pause. He illustrates the present position of *that* as found in prose writings between 1960 and 1993, as a follow-up to an earlier article on this topic published in *MSpr* (1963). He comes to the conclusion that the distinction between restrictive and non-restrictive ('pseudo-exact terms' he calls them) may be heuristically useful, but that in actual usage such a binary partition is not possible and leads to a distortion of the facts found. Ilse Depraetere's study ('Factors Requiring, Promoting and Excluding the Use of a (Non-)Restrictive Relative Clause', *LB* 83.433–58) starts off where Jacobsson's ends. She wants to unearth the factors that cause a speaker to produce one relative clause rather than another in order to test whether these clauses are indeed on a cline. The following parameters are found to be important: (1) the emptiness of the antecedent, (2) the context of speaking, (3) the presence of other modifiers and (4) that of particular indefinite determiners, and (5) the use of demonstrative pronouns. Her conclusion is that it is not correct to see the difference as a continuum. In another paper, Depraetere makes 'Some Observations on the Expression of Temporal Relations in Future-Time Relative Clauses' (*Linguistics* 32.459–73). She observes that a present tense in a non-restrictive relative clause (as in *You will meet John, who is wearing a red cap*) can refer to the moment of speech only, while in a restrictive relative clause, a present may refer to a point in the future (i.e. *You will meet a man who is wearing a red cap* is ambiguous). The availability of the two interpretations for restrictives is shown to be subject to several syntactic, semantic and lexical constraints. Flor Aarts has looked at 'Relative *who* and *whom*: Prescriptive Rules and Linguistic Reality' (in *AS* 69.71–9). After outlining the history of grammarians' statements about *who* and *whom*, he presents modern data on their use. It turns out *whom* is still very much alive (in particular in written English), occurring in direct object function, in constructions like *We feed children whom we think are hungry*, and following a preposition. A taxonomic contribution is Edoardo Lombardi Vallauri's 'A Multilevel Functional Classification of Relative Clauses' (*LingInv* 18.321–56). Using the criteria of restrictiveness, presupposition, and thematicity, with binary values, he arrives at a formal–functional taxonomy of relative clauses, and then shows what functional equivalents the various types have. For example, a non-restrictive, non-presupposing, thematic relative clause like *The boy, who cannot walk, (broke the glass)* can be replaced by a NP (*a paralytic*). The same taxonomy is also applied to Italian relative clauses.

Barbara Fox has also written on relative clauses, but the impact of her very interesting article reverberates far beyond that, as the title indicates: 'Contextualization, Indexicality, and the Distributed Nature of Grammar' (*LangS* 16.1–37). Fox wishes to answer the question of what kind of language structure people actually have in their heads, separate from usage, and what kind of patterning in language is actually a product of the methods and practices that give meaning to linguistic expressions in contextual situations (the role played by 'indexicality', i.e. the notion that the sense of ordinary descriptive terms is heavily influenced by the context in which they are uttered). She explores the problems of a form-based, abstract kind of grammar that has no constant interaction with actual language use by looking at *get*-constructions and relative clauses. She notes in both cases that it is impossible to devise an abstract system that will account for all types of *get* and relative structure. There may be a certain kind of core rule, but that is only 'an orderliness wrested by the participants from interactional contingency rather than as automatic products of standardized plans'. It is her belief that grammar and context are interdependent; they continually create one another and thus cannot exist in any complete form without one another. She admits that it is possible that more abstract templates are formed on the basis of the occurrence of more frequent patterns, but according to her these do not determine the creation of simple, core instances, only guide them. It must be clear too, she says, that there are many language phenomena that cannot really be dealt with by abstract grammar rules, such as the use of repetition, where the choice of a repetition of a full NP or a pronoun responds 'to the local pressures of the exact context of utterance'. This brings us to our next topic, repetition.

It is only when the study of grammar crosses the boundary of the sentence that repetition becomes an interesting topic to study. Needless to say, it has already been much investigated in literary language, as the collection of articles gathered together in SPELL 7 testifies. A number of articles here are linguistically orientated, and, not surprisingly, most of them deal with repetition from a pragmatic or discourse point of view. The most narrowly grammatical study is D. J. Allerton's contribution, the title of which almost sums up the article, '"Drop the Verb if You Can. Otherwise Use Proforms (in the Same Way Other People Do), but Do it According to the Rules," or The Non-Repetition of Lexical Verb Structures' (SPELL 7.35–45). Allerton is concerned with the question of what devices English has for avoiding repetition of the lexical verb, and how and when each of these devices is used. He distinguishes between mild (the lexical verb is replaced) and severe reduction (the verb is ellipted). The first type is used for referring back in a neutral way, whereas the second is used to confirm, modify, deny, etc., a previous assertion. He also has a look at the different ways in which proform structures like *do*, *do it*, *do that* and *do so* are used. Jean Aitchison's paper, '"Say, Say it Again Sam": The Treatment of Repetition in Linguistics' (SPELL 7.15–34), provides a comprehensive survey of the uses of repetition in language, and what possible functions it may have. Thus, repetition may be used for intensification, to promote textual cohesion, but also for comprehension ('information is dripped across to the hearer more slowly'), and finally to maintain conversation (a kind of cohesion). She further investigates how far repetition is obligatory or not. Obligatory repetition is usually grammaticalized and is especially prevalent in pidgin languages, showing its origin as an iconic sign. In most cases repetition is optional, but interestingly enough there is also sometimes a constraint against repetition, as in the adverbial form of *ugly*, which is not **uglily*.

Andreas Jucker is interested in how relevant repetitions are ('Irrelevant Repetitions: A Challenge to Relevance Theory', SPELL 7.47–60). The crucial question here is: can repetition be argued to add contextual effects or to reduce processing efforts? This study is restricted to cases of (almost) immediate self-repetition, using actual data. It is found that these repetitions add to the contextual effect in that they may convey something different content-wise or illustrate the commitment of a speaker (although it seems quite difficult actually to distinguish between these two parameters), and that repetition is also employed to reduce processing effort in cases of conversational overlap or false starts. The last contribution in this area is by Andrea Tyler, who writes on 'The Role of Repetition in Perception of Discourse Coherence' (*JPrag* 22.671–88). She wants to show that lexical repetition (including the repetition of semantically related words) is not just the consequence of treating a particular topic, but independently contributes to the coherence of a text. She illustrates this by comparing two short introductory lessons given by a native and a non-native speaker (the latter was 'camouflaged'), and having these judged on clarity and comprehensibility. It is quite clear that repetition patterns, next to other ways of structuring a text (such as the proper use of anaphora), are invaluable to text comprehension.

Hub Prüst, Remko Scha and Martin van den Berg are also concerned with the influence that discourse structure has on reference possibilities in their 'Discourse Grammar and Verb Phrase Anaphora' (*Ling&P* 17.261–327). They argue that VP anaphors cannot be resolved by simply identifying the anaphoric VP with an antecedent VP, but that instead we must establish a syntactic/semantic parallelism between larger discourse constituent units. Thus, while *Three boys donated $10* has two possible readings (a collective and a distributive one), in a co-ordinate structure, *Three boys donated $10 and two girls did too*, one cannot freely combine the possible readings; in fact the reading of the first structure determines that of the co-ordinate one. Likewise, the antecedent of a VP anaphor need not be a single VP or be located in the directly preceding clause. Also written from a discourse angle is Leif Kvistgaard's contribution (in a new journal, *Rask* 1.63–82), which is concerned with 'Variation in the Use of the Definite Article and the Demonstrative as Cohesive Devices'. He considers the factors that motivate the choice for either the definite article or the demonstrative. He finds two constraints on the use of the demonstrative. First, it requires a direct referent (in contrast, with the definite article, the referent may also be inferred); second, the referent must be saliently present in the discourse. When these constraints do not apply, the choice is determined by the degree to which the speaker regards the relation between the antecedent and the pronoun/article as being 'at issue'. Pragmatics also plays an important role in Villy Rouchota's 'On Indefinite Descriptions' (in *JL* 30.441–75). It has been argued that indefinite descriptions are ambiguous between an attributive reading (as in *An expert will come to fix the computer*) and a referential reading (as in *An admirer of yours is waiting for you*). Rouchota argues that the two readings are also available for definite descriptions and even quantifiers, and that there are actually more possible readings (specific, predicative and generic). After examining and rejecting arguments for the existence of ambiguity, the author concludes that indefinite descriptions receive the interpretation they do on the basis of pragmatics, and shows that Relevance Theory offers a useful model for this.

Discourse function is one of the aspects Leonhard Lipka and Hans-Jörg Schmid look at in their discussion of '*To begin with*: Degrees of Idiomaticity, Textual Functions and Pragmatic Exploitations of a Fixed Expression' (*ZAA* 42.6–15). The authors argue, using the LOB corpus, that there is a gradient of idiomaticity between the literal use of *to begin with* and its idiomatic use, as in *To begin with, let me say that* . . . . They analyse the formal properties of this expression (semantic, syntactic, phonological) and show how in its idiomatic use it functions as a discourse signal, a text-structuring device (to announce the beginning of a list), but how it has also developed into a pragmatic device that can be used to 'feign arguing power'. This development may parallel a diachronic one, but this needs further investigation. Finally, they discuss its relation to *to start with*. Another corpus-based study interested in 'Determining the Flexibility of Idioms', but from a 'syntactic' point of view, is a paper by Henk Barkema (in Fries et al.), which shows that the distinction between lexicon and grammar is not clear cut. Idioms are not just inflexible lexicalized expressions: standard morphological and syntactic rules can be used to vary the expression. Such variations also play an important role in the argumentation of Geoffrey Nunberg, Ivan Sag and Thomas Wasow, who have given their contribution the title 'Idioms' (*Language* 70.491–538). The main point to emerge from their article is that many idioms are semantically compositional, because the component parts carry identifiable bits of meaning (as in *pull the strings, the cat is out of the bag, leave no stone unturned*, etc.). Evidence for this view comes from the fact that parts of many idioms can be modified, quantified, topicalized, ellipted and referred to by a pronoun (e.g. *leave no legal stone unturned, touch a couple of nerves, Those strings, I can't pull for you, My goose is cooked, but yours isn't*, and *It's out of the bag*). The compositionality may make us expect there to be families of idioms, and these do indeed exist (e.g. the many idioms with *come* and *bring*). The authors also point out that the compositionality of idioms undermines the many syntactic arguments that have been built on the idea that idioms are non-compositional.

Discourse-based studies are becoming more numerous every year. This is a natural development because the intensive study of sentence-based grammar has not only taught us a lot about grammatical structures but also shown us its limitations. A need is felt to look beyond the confines of the sentence. In a similar way, 'performance' is considered to be worth our while again, and armchair linguistics is being challenged by corpus studies. This is a welcome development as long as we are not carried away by mere data, but approach the increasing number of corpora with an 'armchair-linguistic' mind. Three books have appeared on corpora this year. One is purely diachronic, and will be discussed in the next section. *Creating and Using English Language Corpora*, edited by Udo Fries, Gunnel Tottie and Peter Schneider, is a mixture of synchrony and diachrony. The first part deals with the creation of new corpora. Here two synchronic projects are discussed. Philip Bolt talks about the Hong Kong element in the International Corpus of English project and Stig Johansson and Knut Hofland discuss the setting up of an English–Norwegian parallel corpus. The main part of the book is concerned with how corpora are or can be used. Nancy Belmore shows how a comparison of two different syntactic analyses of the same corpus may improve the analysis itself in 'Contrasting the Brown Corpus as Tagged at Brown with the Brown Corpus as Tagged by CLAWS1'. Mats Eeg-Olofsson and Bengt Altenberg study 'Discontinuous Recurrent Word Combinations in the London–Lund Corpus' – having already investigated the 'continuous' ones intensively – because both types can provide information about the pre-patterned nature of speech. Their article shows, like Barkema's contribution mentioned above, that lexicon and grammar are more closely linked than theoretical linguists are willing to admit (in a way this is also the gist of Fox's contention discussed above). Sylviane Granger and Fanny Meunier survey the usefulness of 'A Grammar Checker for Learners of English'. A more specific study involves the question whether '*See* [is] Becoming a Conjunction', but it also shows how 'The Study of Grammaticalisation [can be] a Meeting Ground for Corpus Linguistics and Grammatical Theory' (Christian Mair).

The other corpus publication is called *Corpus-Based Research into Language*, edited by Nelleke Oostdijk and Pieter de Haan in honour of Jan Aarts. It contains sections on the encoding and tagging of corpora (part I), parsing and databases (part II), and linguistic exploration of the data (part III). Of interest to us here is the report by Geoffrey Leech et al. on the automatic grammatical tagging of the British national corpus, where they describe the strategies and processes used. All other contributions in part II are concerned with the practice of parsing corpora and using parsed corpora. Of more strictly linguistic interest is the paper by Bengt Altenberg, 'On the Functions of *such* in Spoken and Written English', where he discusses whether *such* in examples like *It was such a surprise* and *How could he say such things* functions as a pre-determiner, post-determiner, adjective, adverb, etc. He also investigates whether *such* is equally common in all styles or restricted to certain situations.

The way information is structured in language is another area that is linked to discourse. Maria Luise Thein has written a book-length study, *Die informationelle Struktur im Englischen: Syntax und Information als Mittel der Hervorhebung*, whose main aim is to find out in how far and in which way the informational function and the semantic content of the elements involved in a linguistic expression may be changed by syntactic and intonational variation. In the first four chapters (part I), the author analyses the various models that have been used in the last decades to describe informational structure, such as those used in functional (the Prague School) and generative grammar, in the work of Halliday *cum suis*, and in the mixture of models used in the grammars by Quirk et al. This discussion is conducted in the light of her own model, which is the subject of part II. This model is of a positivist nature. In the first place she is interested in a description and listing of the various syntactic and informational patterns that play a role in information structure in English. Second, she stresses that we must take the spoken language as primary because syntactic ambiguities are usually solved by differences in intonation. Third, it is important to see these elements within the larger context. For these reasons she takes the 'Tonstrecke' (intonational phrase) rather than the clause or sentence as the basic unit, and she devotes a large part of her book to seeing the model actually at work in a number of texts. Another book on this topic is Knud Lambrecht's *Information Structure and Sentence Form: Topic, Focus, and the Mental Representations of Discourse Referents*. The author argues for information structure being a component of grammar in which propositions undergo pragmatic structuring according to the discourse situation, and are then paired with the appropriate lexico-grammatical structures. Syntactic form is therefore motivated by function (but not determined by it). The emphasis is on developing a model for information structure and its relation with grammatical form, rather than on the analysis of actual texts. Among the concepts that play an important role in information structure, and that are discussed at length, are the identifiability of entities, the difference between presupposed and non-presupposed entities, discourse-activeness of elements, topicality (an 'aboutness' relation), and focus (a potential piece of information). Elena S. Maslova is also interested in textual matters, but from a typological point of view. In 'Cognitive Strategies in the Formation of Topic Constructions' (*NJL* 17.127–39), she distinguishes between a cognitive topic (a component which is language-independent) and a surface topic, i.e. the position in the sentence where the cognitive topic emerges. She argues, using typological evidence, that the one may be derived from the other in three different ways, and that the choice depends on the formal properties of the language in question and on a particular discourse situation.

The pragmatics and grammatics of questions are examined in two articles. Diane Blakemore's 'Echo-Questions: A Pragmatic Account' (*Lingua* 94.197–211) uses relevance theory for the analysis of echo-questions. She does not agree with an earlier analysis by Banfield, who had argued that echo-questions always question the style or words used, rather than what they refer to. Blakemore shows that echoes can also question the thought that the utterance represents (as in the dialogue: A – *I was blown over by the wind*; B – *You were blown over by the WIND?* A – *Well, it was blowing at about 80 miles per hour*). Her conclusion is that echo-questions can concern the sounds uttered (i.e. their phonetic properties) as well as the thoughts communicated, and everything in between. Rodney Huddleston is interested in 'The Contrast between Interrogatives and Questions' (in *JL* 30.411–39). He makes a distinction between interrogative (a grammatical form, specifically a clause type, just like declarative, imperative and exclamative) and question (a category of meaning, which can be subdivided into polar, alternative and variable questions). Discrepancies between questions and interrogatives can be found in sentences like *Have you moved or are you about to move?* and *Is it long enough, do you think?*, which consist of two interrogative clauses, but count as one polar question; echo-questions (discussed at some length); in non-interrogative questions like *You are (no doubt) ready?* (cf. **Are you no doubt ready?*) or *I can't remember the kind of pizza she likes*; and in interrogative non-questions like *How do you do?*

Above, we briefly mentioned the paper by Eeg-Olofsson and Altenberg on discontinuous word combinations. Another type of discontinuity is the topic of Richard Hudson's 'Discontinuous Phrases in Dependency Grammar' (*UCPWL* 6.89–120). This is concerned with phrases that become discontinuous through movement rules such as extraposition, raising, etc. It seems clear that such phrases can only be dealt with in Phrase Structure grammars by distinguishing two continuous analyses related by transformation. Hudson advocates a Dependency Grammar analysis which has the advantage of accommodating discontinuous phrases in a *single* structure making use of the observable order of words and abstract relations between them. In 'Derived Constituent Order in Unbounded Dependency Constructions' (*JL* 30.349–409), James Blevins argues that discontinuities due to topicalization, Wh-questioning, clefting, etc., can be sanctioned by phrase structure rules. This would mean that constituency relations in sentences are stable. He develops the machinery needed for this (involving tree structures with crossing lines), and shows how it would account for right-node raising, across-the-board extraction, parasitic gaps, resumptive pronouns, and various other constructions. He suggests that features should be used to restrain discontinuities, so that islands for extraction will indeed be islands.

We round off this section by discussing several items that focus not so much on the properties of English grammar as on the acquisition of these properties for the practical purpose of using and understanding English. Terence Odlin has edited a collection of papers on this topic, entitled *Perspectives on Pedagogical Grammar*. In his introduction, he discusses several general concepts, such as the distinction between prescription vs. description, competence vs. performance, form vs. function, and recursivity, and relates them to the teaching of a second language. He argues that successful second-language acquisition requires time, but can be speeded up somewhat (and prevented from coming to a premature halt) by a certain amount of formal teaching of grammar. This claim receives support from Peter Master's study of 'The Effect of Systematic Instruction on Learning the English Article System'. It describes a carefully controlled, and replicated, experiment involving explicit teaching of the article to high-intermediate learners at UCLA, which resulted in significant improvement in performance. Virginia Yip's 'Grammatical Consciousness-Raising and Learnability' also leads to the conclusion that explicit teaching does make a difference. Yip first discusses the general problem that plentiful input is often not sufficient to eliminate errors, partly because it does not provide the negative data that are needed to exclude certain overgeneralizations. She describes the type of error she has looked at (**It is happened*) as such a case (i.e. an overgeneralization of passive). In a small experimental study, consciousness-raising about the relevant verbs was found to lead to generally better performance, especially by active, interested students. In 'Linguistic Theory and Pedagogic Practice', David Nunan argues that explicit teaching may even be useful if it involves a construction which is 'too difficult' for students, so that it is not to be expected that it will directly improve students' performance. He examines some actual teaching of Wh-questions with *do*-insertion, and finds clear evidence that the teachers were violating the teachability hypothesis. Still, he points out, the lessons were useful, because (1) students might pick up certain formulae from them; (2) they provided continued exposure to the structure, making gestation in the learners' minds possible; (3) comprehension of Wh-questions is very useful for conducting a class.

Some other contributions to Odlin's volume provide suggestions about the teaching of particular aspects of English grammar. Tim Johns goes 'From Printout to Handout: Grammar and Vocabulary Teaching in the Context of Data-Driven Learning', and describes how use is made of concordance print-outs from authentic texts at Birmingham University. Another approach to grammar via words is sketched by David Little in 'Words and their Properties: Arguments for a Lexical Approach to Pedagogical Grammar'. He suggests that grammar can be taught also in communicative approaches, but that the basis for it must be the word; a possible method would be to take some key words from an authentic text, give them to the learners, ask them to write a text with them, discuss this, and later compare their products with the original text. Further practical suggestions (and also theoretical considerations) about teaching are given in Russell Tomlin's 'Functional Grammars, Pedagogical Grammars, and Communicative Language Teaching'. He takes as his starting point the often-noted problems learners have with clause types in their own writing (i.e. the question of whether a piece of information should go in a dependent or independent clause). He suggests that (North American) functionalism may provide help on this problem, in the form of the concepts of foregrounding and backgrounding, which, as Tomlin shows, correlate with clause type. To make learners aware of what material is foregrounded and what backgrounded, the diagnostic could be used that what will figure in a short abstract of a text is foregrounded information.

A very wide-ranging contribution is 'Learning to Function with the Other Tongue: A Systemic Functional Perspective on Second Language Teaching', by Ruqaiya Hasan and Gillian Perrett. Among the subjects covered are the need to focus on the social aspect of language in teaching, the special social position of language learners and their activities, the overall characteristics of the systemic functional model, the way it deals with modality, and the usefulness of this area of grammar for learners. The implications of principles-and-parameters theory for pedagogy are explored in Vivian Cook's 'Universal Grammar and the Learning and Teaching of Second Languages'. After discussing the more theoretical issues of access vs. non-access to UG in second-language learning, possible markedness of certain parameter settings, and the notion of multicompetence, Cook suggests that in teaching, it may be useful to provide concentrated exposure to sentences on the basis of which parameters can be (re)set, to make extra use of intonation to mark syntactic boundaries, and to pay special attention to syntactic properties of lexical items. Philip Hubbard writes on 'Non-Transformational Theories of Grammar: Implications for Language Teaching'. He looks at Relational Grammar, Lexical-Functional Grammar, and Generalized Phrase Structure Grammar, and sketches some salient aspects of each that might be useful for teaching. What they have in common is the importance attached to grammatical function, lexical subcategorization, and the close link between syntax and semantics. The two remaining contributions to the volume deal with general problems in pedagogical grammar. Paul Westney writes about 'Rules and Pedagogical Grammar'. In his opinion, the concept of rule (an umbrella term for what are actually very different entities, such as internal rules, rules formulated by linguists, rules taught, rules learned, rules used, etc.) is not very useful in teaching. He shows with reference to various areas of English grammar, such as the use of *some* vs. *any*, dative shift, the plural of nouns, and non-finite complementation, that it is very difficult to find safe, simple and reliable rules. Odlin's own paper is called 'The Introspective Hierarchy: A Comparison of Intuitions of Linguists, Teachers, and Learners'. He demonstrates that the notion of intuition is problematic: it is actually not so clear what it represents, and it shows inter-subject and intra-subject variability and fluctuation due to various factors. He calls for greater awareness of this problem among teachers. We also mention here Paul Rastall's 'The Prepositional Flux' (*IRAL* 32.229–31), which describes some of the reasons why prepositions are so difficult to learn (the apparent arbitrariness of non-spatial uses, their small communicative value, the many fixed combinations, whether idiomatic or not, and some recent changes in usage – for example, in *disgusted ABOUT something*, and *the willingness BY the students*, *the plan BY Mr Baker*).

The upshot of all this surely is that learning English grammar is not easy. However, there is no need for despair. Apart from the methodological advice given in the contributions reviewed here, teachers and learners can also make use of several excellent substantive works on English grammar. One of these, *A Communicative Grammar of English* by Geoffrey Leech and Jan Svartvik, has now appeared in a second edition. Compared with the first edition, there have been no major changes; some examples have been added or made more natural, and references to the *Comprehensive Grammar of the English Language* (Quirk et al.) have been inserted at the appropriate points, but the contents have remained the same. Part I still provides an introduction to the book and some of its general terminology; part II presents grammar in communicative action, showing how concepts, information, beliefs, (ir)reality, mood, emotion, attitude, textual links, order, emphasis and so forth can be communicated by using grammatical resources; and part III is an A-Z of English grammar (basically, a simpler and very much condensed version of the *Comprehensive Grammar*).

(b) Early English

We will begin this section with a discussion of the third volume that has come out in the Cambridge History of the English Language project, even though quite strictly speaking this volume is more synchronic than diachronic. The first two volumes (and also volumes III and IV when they appear) deal with the history of English in a purely chronological order, giving central place to a discussion of all grammatical levels such as phonology, morphology, syntax, etc. Volume V, which has now appeared, *English in Britain and Overseas: Origins and Development*, edited by Robert Burchfield, is devoted to the geographical spread of English during and after the colonial period. It first of all intends to reflect the differences in development and the amount of variation, while the discussion of what happened diachronically on the various linguistic levels is secondary. Morphology and syntax, therefore, do not get the same treatment in all chapters. Strangely enough, when these areas are mentioned in the table of contents (as is the case with Australian and New Zealand English) there is very little syntax (there is indeed little to discuss here), whereas in those cases where there are important differences (Caribbean, South African, Scottish, Irish and Welsh English), there is no mention of syntax in the contents, but the discussion is quite lengthy. It is not surprising that only in the latter geographical variants are extensive differences found, because in all five cases substratum influence has played a large role. This is most noticeable in Caribbean English. John Holm discusses the divergent tense and aspect systems used here, and he also notes the different means by which plurality and possession is indicated in NPs, i.e. not by inflection but by the use of determiners and word-order. The three varieties based on a Celtic substratum share certain syntactic properties such as special habitual uses of auxiliaries, a different and more frequent use of topicalization and fronting (Welsh and Irish), a more general use of the tag *is it* (also found in English creoles), and differences in complementation patterns, e.g. in the use of *-ing* or *to*-infinitive. Some of the more surface syntactic differences, such as the last one mentioned, are also found elsewhere. Interesting too is the survival of older dialectal forms in the geographical varieties close to Britain, such as the preservation of pronouns (*thou*, *ye*, *hit(s)*), of strong verb forms, double negatives, archaic inflectional endings, etc.

Very recent changes in English are studied in Laurie Bauer's *Watching English Change: An Introduction to the Study of Linguistic Change in Standard Englishes in the Twentieth Century*. Drawing material from dictionaries and a corpus of newspaper editorials, and working within a broadly Labovian framework, Bauer has looked at several changes that have taken place in English over roughly the last one hundred years. His findings are that there has been a decrease in lexical borrowing and native suffixation, but an increase in abbreviations, blends and compounds; that the suffix *-ee* with 'subject' interpretation has become more common (as in *waitee*, *returnee* and *escapee*); that the quite variable use around 1900 of *-er*/*-est* vs. *more*/*most* with disyllabic adjectives such as *remote* and *common* has been regularized over the years; that plural verbs with collective nouns have declined (from 50 per cent of all potential cases to 10 per cent); and that there may have been change in the use of the relative markers, but that it is very hard to be certain. Bauer also discusses the implications of his findings, which are mainly that data can be so messy (e.g. because of possible stylistic differences) that standard concepts, such as actuation, implementation, embedding and evaluation of change, are very difficult to apply. The clearest changes that he has found all involve sound change (involving the realization of some short vowels, stress position, and yod-dropping).

There are a number of general studies on language change that deserve to be mentioned here. R. L. Trask's contribution to Routledge's Language Workbook series is simply called *Language Change*. In fourteen short units, which include exercises, it provides an accessible and easy-to-understand introduction to the basic facts of change. All the usual areas (lexical change, borrowing, word-formation, sound change, grammatical change, semantic change, dialects, language-relatedness and reconstruction, pidgins and creoles, language death, and attitudes) are covered, and further reading and suggestions for project work are provided. This is a book that we would recommend, either as a text in a short and elementary introductory course or as preliminary reading that students can do on their own before starting on a more advanced course on historical linguistics. For such a more advanced course, a very serious candidate textbook has appeared this year: April McMahon's *Understanding Language Change*. It provides an up-to-date overview of the study of language change, covering more or less the same topics as Trask's book, but at much greater depth. As the title indicates, McMahon emphasizes the importance of matters having to do with explanation, and there indeed seem to be few weak points in the studies she cites that have escaped her critical attention. Another strength of the work is the discussion of what modern theoretical models of language have to offer for the study of language change. As far as syntactic change is concerned, there is one chapter on generative approaches, which traces the development from accounts in terms of rule re-ordering and addition, via Lightfoot's Transparency Principle, to recent principles-and-parameters work on change. A second chapter surveys non-generative approaches to syntactic change, such as those based on Greenbergian typology and that of grammaticalization (as developed by C. Lehmann and by E. Traugott). Under morphological change, McMahon first discusses analogy and its possible links to iconicity, Humboldt's Universal, perceptual strategies, and the process of abduction. She then turns to the theory of Natural Morphology, which she regards as potentially illuminating because it allows for interaction between universal and language-specific naturalness, and between synchrony and diachrony.

Also general in scope is Enrique Bernardez's 'Can Catastrophe Theory Provide Adequate Explanation for Linguistic Change?' (in Fernández et al.). Bernardez proposes to apply the idea of catastrophy theory (CT) to syntactic change. One of the advantages of CT is that it necessarily takes into account external factors in change, since the theory asks for biologically based parameters such as those related to human perception, but also to interaction between language users. The advantage of applying CT to language change is, according to the author, that one would be able to build up a typology of change and so get more insight into the parameters involved in change and in the interaction between them. However, this still seems a long way off, as his application of the theory to Middle English word-order change shows. He sees this change in terms of a change in the parameters of speaker orientation and listener orientation, but in this explanation only the change in word-order is considered and not the morphological changes tied up with it, which, no doubt, would make Old English much less speaker orientated as he now defines it. There is a link here with Invisible Hand Theory, in that in both theories the external factors, the way in which communication functions, are of the utmost importance, and both theories try to account for the grey area between a (speaker's) innovation and the structural linguistic change that may result from it.

Rudi Keller's book, *On Language Change: The Invisible Hand in Language*, which is a translation of the 1990 German edition, shows the implications of Invisible Hand Theory for language. He first argues that language is neither a natural system (such as physics or chemistry), nor an artificial system (such as programming languages and mathematics), but rather a 'phenomenon of the third kind' because, unlike in natural systems, covering laws do not apply to it (so prediction is not possible), nor is it completely human-made; indeed, it partakes of both natural and artificial. Like other sociocultural phenomena, language is the result of human actions but not the goal of their intentions. In other words, language change involves a process which runs from the level of individual purposeful actions to a higher level of unintended resulting structure; that is, change begins intentionally, but continues causally, just as in a traffic jam, a driver brakes intentionally if the car in front does, but it is not the driver's purpose to cause a jam, even though that is an automatic result of the intentions of the individual drivers. In order to study linguistic change, therefore, it is necessary to look at the speaker's intentions (this can be done, according to Keller, with the help of Gricean maxims) and at how these affect the structure. Another linguist who is very much concerned with external factors is Erica García. Her article, 'Extra-Linguistic Conditioning of Grammatical Change' (*LingB* 153.341–71), is concerned with Spanish clitic pronouns, but the questions she considers are of general theoretical interest. She concludes that 'sociological considerations matter not only in the "actuation" of a change, they may also bring out paradigmatic "reinterpretation" of linguistic forms, through the relative frequency with which these are observed to satisfy particular communicative needs'. In other words, she argues that the way in which and the frequency with which constructions are used are relevant to change, and for that reason they should not be ignored in synchronic analyses either.

Before we turn to the nitty-gritty of historical research, there are two general works on Old English that should be mentioned. Roger Lass has written a most welcome *Historical Linguistic Companion* to *Old English*. The book is written as a guide for students and it answers in a pleasant and lucid way all the questions students may have when studying Old English, such as what exactly Ablaut is, why there are seven classes of strong verbs, what the difference is between thematic and athematic nouns, etc. The guide has been written to function as a bridge between the elementary Old English grammars and the standard philological handbooks, but it also bridges a diachronic as well as a synchronic gap. Diachronically, it shows the Indo-European and Germanic background from which Old English grew, clarifying why the system of Old English is the way it is, and why some structures can be captured by general rules, whereas others must be seen as relics of an earlier system. Synchronically, much more attention than in the standard handbooks is paid to the interrelatedness of linguistic levels: between morphological systems and how they are affected phonologically, between morphology and syntax, and especially between syllable structure and stress and developments in morphology and phonology. Another way in which the author stimulates the student is in his keenness to illustrate particular historical processes by means of processes in contemporary languages, encouraging the student to see the generality or systematicity of many such processes. Another book on Old English, Fred C. Robinson's *The Editing of Old English*, does not strictly belong here, but neither does it in the section on Old English literature. It is a book that both linguistic and literary scholars of historical documents (and historians too, for that matter) should take to heart because it lucidly describes all the pitfalls of working with and producing printed editions. It shows us how printed editions evolve, how much of the original manuscript context (which contributes to its meaning) is lost, how much of the punctuation and spacing has authorial foundation, what methods are used in emendation, what the interventions of medieval scribes can do to a text, etc.; and many other interesting titbits, such as the practice of 'grammatical glossing', i.e. the habit of Anglo-Saxon scribes of indicating the case of a Latin word by adding an appropriate Old English preposition over the word.

We will now turn to studies that are narrower in scope. First, the verbal phrase. Natalie Schilling-Estes and Walt Wolfram show in 'Convergent Explanation and Alternative Regularization Patterns: *were/weren't* Levelling in a Vernacular English Variety' (*LVC* 6.273–302) that the process of analogical levelling, although it seems relatively straightforward, can be quite complex. It is difficult to define what majority and minority forms are and to predict the directionality of the process. Using a corpus of Ocracoke (North Carolina) English, they show that other factors are involved apart from the purely syntactic one of paradigmatic levelling, such as (phonological) perceptual saliency, and social significance. A discourse-orientated study is Peter Richardson's 'Imperfective Aspect and Episode Structure in *Beowulf*' (*JEGP* 93.313–25). He discusses how also in Old English, as in many other languages, aspect was used for narrative purposes. He looks in particular at imperfective aspect, which in Modern English is expressed by the progressive. In Old English the progressive was rare and most probably performed a different function. According to the author, imperfective aspect was commonly expressed by perception verbs and verbs of motion followed by an infinitive of the type *He seah hine slæpan* 'He saw him sleep', and *Hie gangan cwomon* 'They came walk[ing].' He next looks at the use of these constructions in *Beowulf* and finds that they cluster around the main event of the narrative, i.e. they tend to precede an important event, and thus organize the narrative into segments distinguishing new and significant episodes from lesser, subordinated ones.

Modal verbs still attract a lot of attention. Hiroshi Ogawa provides 'Some Further Considerations' on 'Old English Modal Verbs' (*NM* 95.403–13). These are a follow-up of the author's book published in 1990 (in the Anglistica series) on the same subject. The issue addressed here is the nature of the replacement of the synthetic subjunctive by the analytic modal verb. The author argues strongly against mere substitution in Old English and gives evidence that modal verbs were used to emphasize or specify a particular nuance (i.e. the two forms do not parallel one another), and that the use of modal verbs as a subjunctive post-dates the Old English period. In other words there was no simple temporal progression in the substitution. The question, of course, is: what does one mean by substitution, and how much of the whole process of change does it encompass? Is there ever 'simple temporal progression'? Most change starts in variation, and substitution can only *follow* that. Bengt Jacobsson writes on 'Recessive and Emergent Uses of Modal Auxiliaries in English' (*ES* 75.166–82), which discusses the behaviour of present-day modals, but the emphasis is on change. His main point can best be described in his own words, 'a characteristic feature of the modals [. . .] is their semantic vagueness or even indeterminacy, hence the proliferation of meanings assigned to them. To a large extent context determines meaning.' He notes both that recessive meanings still occur and that new meanings develop which are not covered yet by corpus studies. His conclusion is that the wholesale restructuring of modals in the history of English is a process that is still continuing. And presumably, listening to his arguments, it is unlikely to stop. Leslie Arnovick writes on 'The Expanding

Discourse of Promises in Present-Day English: A Case Study in Historical Pragmatics' (*FLH* 15.175–91). She notes that the mere use of *I will/shall* is no longer enough to count as a promise in present-day English; instead, some further marking (pragmatic expansion) is usually required. She attributes this to the change from epistemic to deontic that these two modals have undergone. Stephen J. Nagle is interested in 'The English Double Modal Conspiracy' (*Diachronica* 11.199–212). He seeks to explain the existence of double modals such as *might could* in some non-standard varieties of English diachronically. He notes that the Middle English double modals are unlike the present-day ones because in Middle English the second modal is always an infinitive, and this type died out before 1700. The modern construction is a new development, which arose through a conspiracy of syntactic and semantic factors, the main fact being that in Scots English (which is seen as the ancestor dialect here) *can* lingered as a full verb allowing the combination *can* (V) + modal, which was later reanalysed as *can* (Aux) + modal. The whole development should be seen in the light of further 'epistimicization' of the modals. Juan Manuel De la Cruz's 'The Modals Again in the Light of Historical and Cross-Linguistic Evidence' (in Fernández et al.) is in a sense another review of Lightfoot's claim that the Old English pre-modals underwent radical restructuring in the sixteenth century. De la Cruz focuses on two aspects, i.e. the co-occurrence of the modals, as in *I shall may go*, and their use in past participle constructions, *I have wold*. Many of the facts he adduces here are not new (cf. e.g. Warner's review of Lightfoot in *JL* 19), apart from his comments on the development of the modals in other Germanic languages. He concludes that Old and Modern English are not so different after all as far as modal behaviour is concerned, and that the modals did not in the end 'regularize' (become more like normal verbs) as they did in German and Dutch, due to the intervention of *do* periphrasis, which enabled the modals to preserve their historical defectiveness.

Talking about *do*, two articles have appeared from this never-exhausted fount. D. Gary Miller and Katherine Leffel write on 'The Middle English Reanalysis of *do*' (*Diachronica* 11.171–98). They believe that there were in fact two reanalyses of *do*: first it became an auxiliary like *have/be*, and only later did it become a modal. They distinguish two types of auxiliary, i.e. INFL (Tense, Modal) and Aux Phrase (Aspect, Voice). It is shown by means of the modal verb *need*, which occurs both as V and INFL, that modern *do* clearly is in INFL, whereas up to the sixteenth century periphrastic *do* does not fit (either structurally or semantically) the INFL node, and does not function as a V. This paper concentrates on the motivation of the first reanalysis from causative *do* to periphrastic *do*. The other article is on 'Interrogative *do* in the Late 16th and Early 17th Centuries' (in Gotti), by R. A. Henderson. Henderson shows on the basis of a corpus of dramatic prose that Leith (in his *Social History of English*) is wrong in regarding the use of interrogative *do* as a feature of lower-class London usage. Although there is little system to be discovered in its use in the data, it is shown that there are some clear lexical preferences for its use or non-use, and that factors like stress and phonetic factors seem immaterial. On the whole, though, this article does not really add much to our knowledge of the behaviour of early *do*.

Other auxiliaries are also discussed. Olga Fischer deals with 'The Development of Quasi-Auxiliaries in English and Changes in Word Order' (*Neophil* 78.137–64). The article concentrates on the development of *have to* from a full verb into a semi-modal. Unlike the authors of most studies that have appeared on this subject, Fischer believes that there was no slow grammaticalization process in which the verb was bleached from a full verb with possessive meaning to a modal, with the bleaching being accompanied by the loss of a variety of syntactic features. Rather, she shows, on the basis of material taken from the Helsinki corpus, that in constructions where *have* was used with an infinitive, *have* continued to be used as a main verb up to the early Modern period, and that it was the change in basic word-order from SOV to SVO, putting the verb *have* and the infinitive always next to one another, which led to the eventual change of *have to* into a semi-modal expressing obligation. David Denison's 'Some Recent Changes in the English Verb' (in Gotti) looks in detail at the non-catastrophic change-over from a system where there were only verbs in the VP to a system (past 1600) where it could consist, next to V, of Modal, perfect *have*, progressive *be*, passive *be* and dummy *do*, and how these elements develop slowly but surely into a tighter and tighter systematic scheme. He pays special attention to how the various combinations of auxiliaries come into being, noting some very interesting sociolinguistic facts on the way: the earliest progressive–passive combinations (*She was being read to*) all centre on members of the same 'social network' (the term originates from the work of Lesley and James Milroy). 'The Rise of the English *get*-Passive' is discussed by T. Givón and Lynne Yang (in Fox and Hopper). Whereas Lakoff (1971) tried to explain the behaviour of the *get*-passive synchronically with reference to reflexive and inchoative constructions, which show a semantic relation, Givón and Yang wish to explain its characteristics (especially the control and responsibility aspects which the subject of the *get*-passive invokes in contrast to that of a *be*-passive) from a diachronic point of view by looking at other constructions with *get*. They show that the development of the *get*-passive does indeed take place via a reflexive (causative) and inchoative stage, but they also make clear that the rise is not a linear one but rather a complex, multistranded development in which analogy plays a large role. Finally Merja Kytö looks at '*Be* vs. *have* with Intransitives in Early Modern English' (in Fernández et al.). The process of this change is studied on the basis of the Helsinki corpus. It is found that *have* was already established with intransitive stative verbs by the 1500s, but that *have* with mutative verbs increases only slowly during the early Modern period. The following (extra-)linguistic factors were found to be of influence: the increasing functional load of *be*, and the earlier occurrence of *have* in the past perfect, perfect infinitive and progressive, which focus on the aspectual part of the activity paving the way for a more general use of *have*.

Moving on to non-finite verbal phrases, Teresa Fanego, in 'Infinitive Marking in Early Modern English' (in Fernández et al.), looks at the influence on infinitive marking of two factors in particular (which were also found to play a role in Middle English), namely separation from the matrix verb and fronting. The data comprise both prose and verse and are based on four Shakespeare plays, and work by Marlowe and Dryden. Only non-co-ordinated infinitivals are considered. It is found that separation itself plays no role, but that the lightness or heaviness of the intervening element (generally the object NP) does, i.e. pronominal objects tend to co-occur with a bare infinitive while nominal objects tend to select a *to*-infinitive. Fronting (both by NP movement in second passives, and by wh-movement) is also seen to play a definite role in regularly selecting the *to*-infinitive. Olga Fischer builds from earlier work on the appearance of accusative plus infinitive constructions in English. There she came to the conclusion that apart from Latin influence, it was mainly structural word-order facts that helped to establish the construction firmly in English, while in German and Dutch, which did not change their basic word-order, the construction remained foreign to the language. In 'The Fortunes of the Latin-Type Accusative and Infinitive Construction in Dutch and English Compared' (in Swan et al.), she considers the question of adoption from another perspective and looks at how the construction was used in Latinate Dutch. She finds further support there for her earlier conclusion that word-order was indeed decisive in the acceptance (in English) or the non-acceptance (in Dutch and German) of the aci construction, because the construction that paved the way for the aci in English, i.e. a passive construction of the type *He ordered the town to be destroyed* (which replaced earlier OV constructions such as *He ordered the town to destroy*), does not occur in Dutch at all. She notes furthermore that the parameters noted by Warner (1982) – which in his view helped to spread the English aci in a non-salient way – are also observed in medieval and Renaissance Dutch, but that they do not result in the acceptation of the aci in Dutch in the long run (the aci is never found outside Latinate texts, and is soon lost again), showing that word-order has been a crucial factor in the acceptance of the Latin aci in English.

Some modal uses of the infinitive are dealt with by Ulrike Demske-Neumann in *Modales Passiv und* Tough Movement*: Zur strukturellen Kausalität eines syntaktischen Wandels im Deutschen und Englischen*. She notes that both Old High German and Old English had the modal passive and tough-movement, and that the two languages did not differ in these constructions. Modern German and Modern English, however, do differ, and Demske-Neumann attributes this to independent grammatical changes in the two languages. She starts by outlining the situation in Old High German and Old English, analysing the modal passive (i.e. constructions of the type *þæt weorc biþ to donne*) as consisting of copular *be* and a verbal adjective, and tough-movement (i.e. *þæt weorc biþ eaðe to donne*) as having a raised NP-subject (originally, she suggests, a fronted accusative NP, which was reanalysed due to case syncretism; this, however, seems to us a somewhat unlikely idea because of the many counter-examples that would work against such reanalysis). In later English, the structure of the modal passive became *be* $[_{IP}$ NP $[_{I}$ to] VP]; the lack of adjacency between *be* and the infinitive blocked reanalysis to a real modal passive (which did take place in German), with the result that a passive infinitive came to be used. Demske-Neumann also proposes that, for some time at least, words like *easy*, when used in tough-movement, could be adverbs as well as adjectives.

Developments in negation usually attract some attention. Ingrid Tieken-Boon van Ostade writes on 'Multiple Negation in Malory's *Morte Darthur*' (in Fernández et al.) but the article is mainly concerned with the 'copye' on which Caxton based his edition ('After a copye unto me delyverd'). She shows (*pace* Vinaver) that the Winchester MS and Caxton's edition of Malory's works are not both collaterally derived from the same source, but that Caxton must have used the Winchester MS to base his version on (as suggested, using only external evidence, by Lotte Hellinga in 1977 in *BLJ*). Her argument for this is based on linguistic evidence involving the addition and removal of negative elements. There are two contributions by Gabriella Mazzon on this topic. The first, 'OE and ME Multiple Negation: Some Syntactic and Stylistic Remarks' (in Fernández et al.), indeed contains '*some* remarks' because we could not really discover a general line of argument. Thus, we are shown the decline of multiple negation from a data collection of Old and Middle English works (showing among other things that the high percentage of multiple negation in Chaucer's *Boece* may be due to stylistic factors but also to its French original), the decline in the use of *ne*, the 'breaking' of the rule of negative attraction, and the tendency to have ever stronger negatives to replace the older ones (the perpetual movement of the 'negative cycle'). In her other article ('OE and ME Incorporated Negation and the "Negative Cycle"', in Gotti), she goes over more or less the same ground, but she focuses this time on contracted negative forms, such as *nat* for *ne wat* 'not know', and the reasons for their disappearance.

There are a number of papers on relative pronouns. Catherine N. Ball writes on 'Relative Pronouns in *it*-Clefts: The Last Seven Centuries' (*LVC* 6. 179–200). She considers a contemporary corpus of written and spoken English, and compares it with data in a diachronic corpus. She shows that there is no structural difference between relative clauses in *it*-clefts and regular relative clauses, i.e. it is not the case that wh-pronouns are rare or unacceptable in the former. Also diachronically, it is clear that the two types of clause share a similar development, which suggests that they have been and are structurally of a kind. Concha Castillo's 'Ø-relatives with Antecedent *þæt* and Free Relatives in OE and ME' (in Fernández et al.) deals with relatives of the type *þu hæfdest þæt þu noldest* 'you had "that" you would not', which according to the author are ambiguous between a zero relative analysis and an analysis as a free relative. We do not really find the distinctions clearly made here, nor is the argumentation very convincing. Hans Peters's 'Relative *who* in Early Modern English' (in Blaicher and Glaser) posits a number of questions on the lateness of relative *who*, such as what caused it, whether relative *which* was a viable alternative, what route leads from the fifteenth-century cases (with *God* as antecedent) to its use with all personal antecedents, and why it hardly becomes established in restrictive relatives. Peters has an alternative suggestion beside the already established ones and that is that *who* began to function as a discourse marker involving such notions as topic and topicality, and that it was also used to avoid discourse ambiguity. Important, too, to its spread was the teaching of seventeenth-century grammarians.

There are two more articles on pronoun use. Axel Hübler looks at the question of what may have induced Old English writers to use both the possessive dative (as in *He feol him to fotum*) and the possessive pronoun (*Feol he to his fotum*) both meaning 'He fell at his feet' ('Possessive Dative and Possessive Pronoun in Old English', in Gotti). He believes that the dative expresses a surplus of meaning which involves the degree of the speaker's 'attachment'; in other words it functions as an *index* in semiotic terms. Derek Britton presents evidence in 'The Etymology of Modern dialect 'en, "him"' (*N&Q* 41.16–18) that dialectal south-western '*en* is not likely to be derived from the old accusative form *hine* (pace the *OED*) because of the pattern of survival in Middle English (he shows that it is rare after 1300 except in Kent, where present-day dialectal '*en* is not found); he argues rather that it is a delabialized variant of *him*.

Studies on the noun phrase are never as numerous as those on the verb phrase, but there are a few this year. Kurt Braunmüller asks himself the question, in 'Some Typological Tendencies in the Development of the Noun Phrase in Germanic Languages' (in Swan et al.), why it is that quite a number of NP constituents in present-day Germanic languages do not harmonize typologically with the prevalent SVO order (he considers German and Dutch as having SVO as their basic order). He hypothesizes that Proto-Germanic must have been typologically ambiguous between SOV and SVO – in fact he postulates that the N" phrase was non-configurational – and that the later restructuring into configurational patterns caused a split between the North and West Germanic languages. Matti Rissanen concentrates on 'Aspects of the Development of the Noun Phrase in English' (in Gotti). He adopts a variationist approach to change, basing himself on the Helsinki corpus, and investigates the variations and developments in the article system, the rise of pronominal *one*, and the combination of a demonstrative and a possessive pronoun. All three developments are shown to be intimately connected with the attrition of inflectional endings and the need to remedy this loss in other ways. There are two other studies that are interested in developments concerning the determiner. Robert McColl Millar's 'Ambiguity in Function. Old English "þæt" and the Demonstrative Systems of Laȝamon's "Brut"' (*NM* 95.415–32) gives a useful description of how and why (eventually) the original neuter article *þæt* came to be used as a deictic pronoun. He looks at its usage in the *Brut*, where it is still essentially an article, to see whether there is any evidence 'for a general slide of words with asexual or abstract connotations' – so away from grammatical gender – towards the use of *þat* as a deictic; whether *þat* is used in any functions in which it would be impossible in Modern English; and to find out the distribution of *þat* vs. *þe* and *þis*. The conclusion is that there was enough ambiguity of *þat* in the *Brut* to explain the later loss of its article function. Still on the article, Penny Stewart and Richard F. Fawcett comment on the disappearance of *an* in '"An" to "A" in American Speech: Language Change in Progress' (*EnT* 10.i.18–27). They show the rate of decline of *an* over the last twenty years, on the basis of an analysis mainly of talk shows on American national television, i.e. a medium used by prestigious speakers of English. Finally, Helena Raumolin-Brunberg investigates 'The Position of Adjectival Modifiers in Late Middle English Noun Phrases' (in Fries et al.), which Hawkins (1983), following Lightfoot (1979), believed was fundamentally post-nominal, a view which this author on the evidence of the Helsinki corpus shows to be basically wrong.

There are fewer contributions on word-order this year. Robert P. Stockwell and Donka Minkova show in 'Kuhn's Laws and the Rise of Verb-Second Syntax' (in Swan et al.) that it is most likely that it was metrical preferences which led to the positioning of light elements at the beginning of the verse line (the clause), and that therefore the theories of Kuhn and Hock, namely that there was a reanalysis whereby the phonologically cliticized auxiliary became reinterpreted as a finite verb leading to general V2-hood, is most unlikely. In other words, syntactically based suggestions about the rise of V2 are more plausible. In the same volume, Toril Swan looks at the effect initial adverbs had on word order in 'A Note on Old English and Old Norse Initial Adverbs and Word Order with Special Reference to Sentence Adverbials'. She shows that already in the earliest periods Old Norse and Old English differed in the occurrence of V2 in connection with adverbs and that these differences are related to present-day differences. Old English already distinguished between regular initial adverbs and sentence adverbs in that the latter usually showed V3 behaviour, thus behaving already as disjunctive adverbs. In Old Norse, no such distinction was made, and all initial adverbs triggered V2. This has more or less remained the case till today, sentence adverbs being distinguished by other means rather than by first position. Concha Castillo studies 'Verb–Particle Combinations in Shakespearian English' (*NM* 95.439–51). This article has a clearly descriptive aim, i.e. to find out how verb–particle combinations are used syntactically in Shakespeare's plays and how this differs from modern usage. She concentrates on the frequency of occurrence of the various positional structures (there are four in all, in fact, all the theoretically possible ones) and how this variety can be explained. It is clear that V(erb)P(article), and after that VxP are the most common orders as in Modern English, and that the P(x)V sequences can be mostly explained in terms of rhythm and rhyme. Most Shakespearian types are still possible in Modern English, except such cases as *He forth walked*, and . . . *that down fell priest and book*, and a few minor types.

Gunnar Bergh and Aimo Seppänen write on 'Subject Extraction in English: The Use of the *that*-Complementizer' (in Fernández et al.). The paper deals with a well-known peculiarity in English, namely that the complementizer *that* may appear in all types of extractions (next to zero) but is not a possible variant in subject-extraction of the type *What men did she say *that/Ø had done it*. The authors look at the diachrony of this phenomenon. They note that the above construction with *that* was perfectly grammatical in Old and Middle English, and then set out to describe (tentatively, this article being part of a larger research project) when, how and why the change took place. Factors seen to be of importance are the general decrease of the complementizer *that*, the corresponding decrease in non-subject extraction, and the relation between the *that*+gap construction and the use of resumptive pronouns. Leiv Egil Breivik's contribution is a more general one. His 'On Comparatives in English and Other Languages' (in Swan et al.) supports Seuren's analysis of unequal comparatives (*Jim is taller than Joe*) as one that involves implicit negation and is related to co-ordinate structures, showing that, diachronically, unequal comparatives derive from semantically more transparent structures involving a negative or adversive element, and paratactic constructions in a number of languages, not all genetically or typologically related.

We finish this section with a review of corpus studies. Douglas Biber, Edward Finegan and Dwight Atkinson report on a new corpus, ARCHER, in 'ARCHER and its Challenges: Compiling and Exploring a Representative Corpus of Historical English Register' (in Fries et al.). ARCHER can in fact be seen as a sequel to the Helsinki corpus, since it covers the late Modern English period. The corpus represents 'both written and speech-based British and American registers across selected social situations' and has been produced with the following aims in mind: to test some of the hypotheses of the authors, such as the historical drift towards oral styles and the more 'involved' style of present-day American registers; and to investigate more generally linguistic evolution across small periods of time, the evolution of written varieties in relation to spoken ones, patterns of dialect and gender, etc. Another book on English diachronic corpora, *Corpora across the Centuries*, has been edited by Merja Kytö et al. It contains a survey of historical corpora that have been or are being developed. We will simply list them here with the names of the compilers following: (1) a corpus of late Modern English prose (David Denison), a small corpus consisting of a selection of letters only, written between 1860 and 1920; (2) a corpus of Irish English (Raymond Hickey), which begins with the earliest texts (fourteenth century) up to the nineteenth and twentieth centuries, where only drama is presented because that represents the Irish English features best, being a form of written speech; (3) a corpus of early American English, currently being prepared by Merja Kytö, which aims at widening the temporal and regional scope of the Helsinki corpus; (4) the Innsbruck Archive of Middle English Texts (Manfred Markus), which differs from the Helsinki corpus in concentrating on prose and giving more than just extracts of texts; (5) the Helsinki Corpus of Older Scots (Anneli Meurman Solin), another supplement to the (6) Helsinki Corpus, which is described here by Matti Rissanen; (7) the Lampeter Corpus of Early Modern English Tracts (Josef Schmied), which is meant for research into socio-stylistic variation; and finally (8,) the Cambridge Leeds

Corpus of Early Modern English (*c*.1600–1800) by Susan Wright and Jonathan Hope. The rest of the book deals with progress reports on historical thesauruses, atlases and dictionaries.

7. Onomastics

The main publishing event of this year in onomastics is Barrie Cox's *The Place-Names of Rutland*, a triple volume in the English Place Name Society (EPNS) series. This is the first time for more than fifty years that the place-names of an entire English county have been treated within a single cover, and the book represents a remarkable achievement. Name scholars and historians will already be familiar with journal articles in which Cox has argued, from the paucity of Scandinavian place-names in the historic county of Rutland (now part of Leicestershire), that the Danes were politically excluded from the area at the division of the Mercian kingdom in 877. Here for the first time the full range of evidence is presented. The introduction to the volume is highly informative, tracing the development of Rutland from prehistoric times to the present day; and the treatment of individual place-name etymologies maintains the high standards of scholarship that have come to be expected of an EPNS publication.

Also by Barrie Cox, *English Inn and Tavern Names* is a welcome addition to an often-neglected area of toponymy. It comprises a detailed historical study of inn names, treating them in fifty-year groupings from 1350 to 1935. Unsurprisingly, the tavern names of Rutland receive particularly comprehensive treatment. Two appendices present a corpus of inn names first documented between 1350–1599 and 1600–1935, and a third discusses tavern names in the diary of Samuel Pepys. The monograph is the first in a new series of publications from the Centre for English Name Studies, University of Nottingham, where a major research project funded by the Leverhulme Foundation is currently in progress under the direction of Barrie Cox and Christine Fell. Reports on the project by Carole Hough appear in *JEPNS* 26.15–26 ('English Place-Names: The Leverhulme Project') and *MESN* 31.9–11 ('The Survey of the Language of English Place-Names').

Kenneth Cameron has a fine piece on 'Stenton and Place Names' in D. Matthew with A. Curry and E. Green, eds, *Stenton's 'Anglo-Saxon England' Fifty Years On*. As well as discussing Stenton's contribution to place-name scholarship, Cameron provides a synopsis of some of the most important developments in place-name studies over the last fifty years. He deals in turn with Celtic names, early Anglo-Saxon names and Danish names, demonstrating that despite some radical rethinking by modern scholars, many of Stenton's conclusions remain fundamentally sound.

It is good to see that onomastic dictionaries are still considered commercially viable by publishers. Adrian Room's *Brewer's Dictionary of Names* (*YWES* 73.66, *YWES* 74.65) has been reissued with a change of title as the *Cassell Dictionary of Proper Names*. The text is unaltered except for a short section of the introduction referring to the title. Also targeting a general readership is a revised edition of Mike Darton's *The Dictionary of Place Names in Scotland: And the Elements that Go to Make them Up*. A four-page introduction provides some very basic information for the uninitiated, and Darton maintains a highly colloquial style throughout. Although rather sloppily written and lacking a bibliography, the format of the dictionary is well conceived, integrating entries on place-names and place-name elements within a single alphabetical sequence. The author is presumably not responsible for the howler on the back cover, where it is claimed that only in Scotland do place-names have a meaningful origin!

Mixed feelings attend the reissue of James B. Johnston's *Place Names of England and Wales* in an attractive and modestly priced paperback volume apparently aimed at the popular market. While this is a boon to the small number of scholars concerned with the history of onomastics, the interested public is unlikely to realize the extent to which the book has become outdated since its first publication in 1915, and may well be misled. The situation is not helped by the misspelling of the author's name as James Johnson on both the cover and the title page.

This year sees the publication of John Insley's 1980 thesis on *Scandinavian Personal Names in Norfolk*, substantially unaltered apart from an expanded introduction and a nine-page appendix of 'Name Forms from Sources Excerpted Subsequent to 1980'. The book comprises an alphabetical corpus of Scandinavian personal names evidenced either independently in Norfolk records from the tenth to the thirteenth centuries, or in Norfolk place-names and field-names. The etymology and distribution of each name listed are discussed in meticulous detail: more thoroughly, indeed, than in Fellows-Jensen's pioneering *Scandinavian Personal Names in Lincolnshire and Yorkshire* (1968), as can be seen from a comparison of the entries for *Hálfdan, Ívarr* and *Ketill.* Insley's scholarship is impeccable and his presentation immaculate. The conclusions outlined in his introduction, concerning regional patterns of name-giving in areas of Scandinavian settlement, place-name evidence for an aristocratic rather than peasant settlement in certain areas of East Anglia, the significance of the survival of the name element *-ketill* in its full form in East Anglia, and the occurrence of Scandinavian personal names in areas with little place-name evidence for Scandinavian settlement, deserve very careful consideration, but could usefully have been illustrated with distribution maps. My main criticism is that there is no place-name index.

In *JEPNS*, Victor Watts reports on progress made towards 'A New Dictionary of English Place-Names' (26.7–14), and Ann Cole writes on 'Baulking: An Anglo-Saxon Industry Revealed' (27–31). The industry in question is that of fulling, a deposit of fuller's earth having been discovered at Baulking, Berkshire, in 1969. Cole makes a good case for understanding the place-name 'the stream with the baths' as an allusion to pools in which fleeces were fulled, indicating that the industry may date back to early Anglo-Saxon times.

Jonathan Kissock provides a very readable introduction to medieval feet of fines, with a discussion of their evidential value in a range of subject areas, including land-use patterns, landscape studies, land transfers, mill rights, place-names and surnames ('Medieval Feet of Fines: A Study of their Uses with a Catalogue of Published Sources' *Local Historian* 24.66–82). Particularly useful is the list of published collections of feet of fines, organized by county, with which the article concludes.

Two articles deal with field-names. W. Elliott has a piece on 'Field-Names in Cleobury Mortimer' in Shropshire (*Cleobury Chronicles* 3.18–25), while P. A. S. Pool presents a detailed analysis of 'The Field-Names of the Manor of Mulfra' (part of the highland area of West Penwith), discussing the effects on field-names of the change of language from Cornish to English between the mid-seventeenth and mid-nineteenth centuries (*Journal of the Royal Institution of Cornwall* n.s. [II]

2.43–73). Also of interest is Trevor Foulds's edition of *The Thurgarton Cartulary*. This contains hundreds of early forms of field-names and street-names in Nottinghamshire, Derbyshire and Lincolnshire, all indexed under the appropriate parish, and is thus a very useful reference tool. David Roffe's translations of the Stamford Ragman Rolls in *Stamford in the Thirteenth Century: Two Inquisitions from the Reign of Edward I* are of less value to the onomast since place-names have been modernized and personal-names occurring as marginalia are omitted; but his introductory account of the historical background and significance of these records is well written and informative.

Nomina 16 (1992–3) was published this year, and includes a conference report and some papers from the First Annual Study Conference of the Society for Name Studies in Great Britain and Ireland, held in Belfast in April 1992. Several contributions focus on Irish names, with papers on 'The Maps of Robert Lythe as a Source for Irish Place-Names' (J. H. Andrews, 7–22), 'The Irish Genealogies as an Onomastic Source' (Nollaig O Muraíle, 23–47), 'Nationality Names in the Irish Annals' (Diarmuid O Murchadha, 49–70), and 'Some Commemorative British Place-Names in Dublin City' (Breandán S. Mac Aodha, 71–7). In the same volume, Patrick Hanks introduces an ongoing survey of 'The Present-Day Distribution of Surnames in the British Isles', based on telephone directories of the early 1980s (79–98), and John S. Moore contributes part I of an article on 'Family-Entries in English *Libri Vitae*, *c.*1050 to *c.*1530' (99–128).

Publication of the December 1993 issue of *Names* (41.iv.), a collection of articles in honour of Leonard R. N. Ashley, was delayed until early this year. Contributions cover topics as diverse as 'Names in the Films of R. W. Fassbinder' (Russell E. Brown, 239–47), 'Welsh Surnames of Occupational Origin' (Robert A. Fowkes, 288–97), and 'Scottish Place Names as Evidence for Language Change' (W. F. H. Nicolaisen, 306–13). Three articles focus on Shakespeare: Grant Smith's 'Shakespeare's Mutes and What They Tell Us' (334–43), Robert F. Fleissner's 'Sizing Up Shylock's Name Again' (282–7), and Dorothy E. Litt's 'The Power of the Name *Essex*' (298–305). The last-named is an attempt to identify the Shakespearian play performed before Queen Elizabeth I on the eve of the execution of the Earl of Essex: Litt puts forward *3Henry VI* on the basis of a textual variant in the 1623 Folio where the place-name *Essex* has been omitted. Frederic G. Cassidy contributes 'A Note of Names and Censors' (262–6), and Grady Clay writes on the evolution of generic place-name terms in 'Place-Framing for Wider Distribution' (267–70). North American names are represented by Irving Lewis Allen's annotated glossary of 'Some Informal Neighborhood and Street Names in Manhattan: From *Alphabet City* to the *Dead End*' (219–27), Gerald Leonard Cohen's examination of legends relating to 'Naming of Fairdealing, Missouri' (271–5), Robert M. Rennick's systematic study of 'The Post Offices of Daviess County, Kentucky' (314–33), and Wilbur Zelinsky's 'Parsing Greater Washington's Namescape' (344–60). In 'Feminization of Unisex Names from 1960 to 1990' (228–38), Herbert Barry III and Aylene S. Harper report on a Pennsylvania-based study supporting previous findings that personal-names tend to evolve from masculine to unisex to feminine. Cleveland Kent Evans discusses the origins of the name *Vanessa*, a literary invention of Jonathan Swift, and suggests that the butterfly genus *Vanessa* may have been named after Swift's character ('How Vanessa Became a Butterfly: A Psychologist's Adventure in Entomological Etymology', 276–81). Frederick M. Burelbach's 'Naming and a Black Woman's Aesthetic' (248–61) argues that characters in the fiction of Zora Neale Hurston and Alice Walker are given ordinary rather than meaningful names as a way of resisting the imposition of analysis.

Other articles on literary onomastics appear in *Names* 42. In 'Designer Selves in Tom Wolfe's *The Bonfire of the Vanities* and Danielle Steel's *Crossings*' (1–11), Hildegard Hoeller discusses the use of brand-names as narrative tools. Elizabeth A. Hait writes on 'Parisian Street Names in George Du Maurier's *Trilby*' (19–25), and Zacharias P. Thundy examines the significance of the title of Umberto Eco's book 'The Name of the Rose' (79–89). Debra Walker King discusses the connotative value of names in the context of African American literature in 'Reading the "Deep Talk" of Literary Names and Naming' (181–99). Elsewhere, Lucas Carpenter suggests that 'The Name "Minette" in *Women In Love*' not only is roughly synonymous with Pussum, the name it replaced to avoid a libel action by one of the people portrayed in the novel, but has pornographic associations which make it particularly appropriate in the context (*ELN* 32.70–3). Kurt Schlüter's 'Onomastic Identity Versus the Convention of Single Naming in Anthony Burgess' *Earthly Powers*' (*Anglia* 112.411–20) provides an insight into the strength of the literary convention whereby a particular name is used for one person only within a fictional text, and investigates some of the consequences of a breach of the convention. In 'Chaucer's Names', Paul Beekman Taylor discusses references in Chaucer's poetry to his own Christian and family names, suggesting that occurrences of his baptismal name are used with particular subtlety and significance (*NM* 95.243–8). Not seen by this reviewer is Claire A. Culleton's *Names and Naming in Joyce*.

Returning briefly to *Names* (42.300–7), a list of 'More Official and Unofficial English Names of Places, Books, Films, and Television Programs with *alley* or *Alley*' is presented as a supplement to a 1985 piece on the 'Figurative Use of *alley* in English-Language Placenames' (see *YWES* 66.104).

The *Proceedings of the Cambridge Antiquarian Society* for 1993 were published this year, and include an extensive 'Gazetteer of Hundred and Wapentake Meeting-Places of the Cambridge Region' compiled by Audrey L. Meaney (92.67–92). The sites of some fifty-six Hundred meeting-places in Cambridgeshire and surrounding counties are discussed, with maps showing their distribution in relation to Domesday Hundreds and Roman roads, and some characteristic features are identified. In *The Councils of 'Clofesho'*, Simon Keynes examines place-name and other evidence for the location of *Clofesho*, the site of several ecclesiastical councils during the eighth and early ninth centuries. He also discusses the location of *Aclea*, another meeting-place where synods were held, but reaches no firm conclusion in either instance.

Barrie Cox investigates 'The Pattern of Old English *burh* in Early Lindsey' (*ASE* 23.35–56), demonstrating that each place-name in *burh* represents an Anglo-Saxon stronghold strategically sited to control a point of entry to the territory of the Lindisfaran. Since many of the place-names are of an early type, containing monothematic personal-names or the archaic *-inga-* formula, Cox argues that the defensive system was probably in place by the early seventh century, and may have been devised in reponse to threats from Northumbria and Mercia.

The interdisciplinary value of place-names is also illustrated by Henry Loyn's *The Vikings in Britain*, which provides a synthesis of different types of evidence for an undergraduate readership. It is substantially based on his 1977 book of the same title. Breaking new ground is John Blair's *Anglo-Saxon Oxfordshire*, a wide-ranging and perceptive study of the political and social development of the

Oxfordshire region from the fifth to the eleventh centuries. Blair makes extensive use of place-name evidence, as well as of recent research in archaeology, church history, and numismatics. His treatment of all these areas is consistently well informed and up to date. It is reassuring to find that the discussion of early topographical vocabulary in the introduction draws on the latest work by Margaret Gelling and Ann Cole, while the use of onomastic and other material in the four main chapters ('The Formation of English Communities', 'A Mercian Frontier Province', 'Oxfordshire in the West Saxon Kingdom' and 'Oxford 900–1066: From Frontier Fortress to Commercial City') is likewise exemplary. Unusually, index entries are not grouped together under 'place-names' but dispersed under individual headings like '*denu* place-names', '*feld* place-names' and '*lēah* place-names'. All such formations receive sensible and discerning treatment in the text, although Blair's interpretation of the names *fildena weg* and *fildena wuduweg* (25–7) may require revision in the light of Peter R. Kitson's recent findings (*YWES* 74.68–9). The book is beautifully presented, and is illustrated by more than a hundred high-quality photographs and maps. It deserves to attract a wide readership among the interested public as well as the scholarly community. A short section is concerned with charter boundaries, a topic which also receives close examination elsewhere. Mary Higham discusses 'The Boundary of Burton-in-Lonsdale Chase' (*Yorkshire Archaeological Journal* 66.91–105), presenting a more detailed treatment of material summarized in a *Nomina* article last year (*YWES* 74.68). Della Hooke's *Pre-Conquest Charter-Bounds of Devon and Cornwall* brings together an important collection of boundary clauses, all freshly transcribed from the surviving manuscripts and accompanied by a translation and proposed solution. It contains a number of inaccuracies which this reviewer has treated in some detail elsewhere (*Nomina*, forthcoming), but the discussions of local topography are generally good and make it possible to identify estate boundaries more precisely than hitherto.

The Reign of Cnut, King of England, Denmark and Norway, edited by Alexander Rumble, comprises an interdisciplinary collection of studies by leading scholars from different fields. Of immediate interest to onomasts is Gillian Fellows-Jensen's 'Danish Place-Names and Personal Names in England: The Influence of Cnut?'. Although less directly concerned with Cnut and his reign than other papers within the volume, the essay provides a lucid account of the long-running debate between historians and name scholars concerning the density of Danish settlement in England, and argues that whereas a small proportion of place-names containing Scandinavian personal-names may have been coined during the eleventh century, perhaps reflecting grants of land by Cnut to his Danish followers, the vast majority appear to date from the early tenth, testifying to Scandinavian immigration into the East Midlands on a large scale. The case is not clear-cut, however, and Fellows-Jensen's treatment of the methodological problems associated with this range of evidence is particularly good. In the same volume, Michael Dennis O'Hara's account of 'An Iron Reverse Die of the Reign of Cnut' includes a discussion of variations in the spellings of moneyers' names on coins, as well as an appendix on 'The Significance of the Moneyer's Name: Thurulfr'. Other contributors include Peter Sawyer, Niels Lund, Simon Keynes, Nicholas Hooper, David Hill, Roberta Frank, M. K. Lawson, John Crook and Kenneth Jonsson.

Finally, it is appropriate to mention Hywel Wyn Owen's *The Place-Names of East Flintshire*, the first in a series of volumes on the place-names of Clwyd. This is a major study on the same lines as the county surveys produced by the English

Place-Name Society, and it includes a detailed glossary of place-name elements as well as an exhaustive and scholarly analysis of all East Flintshire place-names recorded before 1900. Since the area contains many English as well as Welsh names, the volume makes available a range of comparative material that will be of great value in the study of English place-names.

8. Stylistics

This year has seen a dramatic rise in the number of publications devoted to stylistics. Outstanding among the collections of papers is *Literature and the New Interdisciplinarity: Poetics, Linguistics, History*, edited by Roger Sell and Peter Verdonk, which reopens some fundamental debates in stylistics. First there is Henry Widdowson's '"Old song that will not declare itself": On Poetry and the Imprecision of Meaning' versus Nils Enkvist's 'Context' on the question of the distinctiveness of literary discourse. Whereas the former assigns a special status to literary discourse because of what Widdowson calls its representational function, his argument is in fact largely undermined by the latter's discussion of contextualization, the process by which readers construct a world or context for all, literary and non-literary, discourses.

The debate is continued by Adrian Pilkington ('Against Literary Reading Conventions') and Tony Bex ('The Relevance of Genre'), who focus on the question of whether special reading conventions are activated during the processing of literary works. According to Bex, this activation is triggered by generic choices. Pilkington, on the other hand, challenges the existence of all such conventions, and argues that the relevance-theoretic account of weak implicatures and poetic effects provides a satisfactory and psychologically plausible view of literary communication without the necessity of positing any kind of special literary reading conventions.

A large number of linguistic models are drawn upon in these studies. Both Bex and Pilkington rely in their analyses on relevance theory; and it is also the relevance-theoretic account of verbal irony that is critically assessed by Michael Toolan in 'On Recyclings and Irony'. He substitutes a view of irony as 'shifted critical commentary' for Sperber and Wilson's view of it as 'echoic interpretive use'. Peter Stockwell's 'To Be or Not To Be a Phagocyte: Procedures of Reading Metaphors' conflates Gentner's structure-mapping account of metaphor with schema-theoretic approaches into a dynamic model of metaphor comprehension as the mapping of schema networks. Two contributors draw upon Bakhtin's sociolinguistic poetics: Guy Cook ('Contradictory Voices') considers the advantages of the Bakhtinian over the Saussurean view of language in our age of the electronic book, and Alison Tate ('Bakhtin, Addressivity and the Poetics of Objectivity') uses Bakhtin's concept of addressivity to explain the feeling of disorientation often experienced by readers of modernist poetry.

The last few chapters are more of a mixed bag, ranging from Irma Taavitsainen's study in genre and intertextuality ('Characters and English Almanac Literature') via Ingrid Tieken-Boon van Ostade's sociolinguistic analysis of eighteenth-century styles and registers ('Eighteenth-Century Letters and Journals as Evidence') to Ineke Bockting's study in narratological pragmatics ('*Light in August* and the Issue of Unreliability'). Finally, there is Roger Sell's 'Literary Gossip, Literary Theory, Literary Pragmatics', which considers how literary gossip about Donne affects the process of reading his poetry, and Willie van Peer's 'Emotional Functions of Reading Literature', an old-fashioned account of the moral and psychological influence of literature reaching the momentous conclusion that the 'role literature may play in this respect should not be underestimated'.

The contributors of Katie Wales's *Feminist Linguistics in Literary Criticism* share a concern with the nature of a woman's language which would be more suitable for the embodiment of female experience. Marion Lomax ('Gendered Writing and the Writer's Stylistic Identity'), relying on Kristeva's distinction between the symbolic and the semiotic, examines how women novelists disrupt the former and exploit the latter in their search for a positive linguistic identity. In 'Language in Common: Apposition in Contemporary Poetry by Women', Lesley Jeffries studies the uses and effects of noun-phrase sequences, which can be conjoined or appositive or ambiguous between the two. Louise Sylvester ('Women, Men and Words: Lexical Choice in Two Fairy Tales of the 1920s') finds a difference in approach between male and female writers with, in the case of the latter, a 'resistance to systematic coherence', which she too interprets as a drawing on Kristeva's semiotic order.

The last three chapters are the most interesting ones from a stylistic point of view. Clara Calvo's 'In Defence of Celia: Discourse Analysis and Women's Discourse in *As You Like It*' brings out the difference between Celia's conversational strategies in the first and the second half of the play: whereas at the beginning Celia's discourse of friendship is shaped by strategies of positive politeness, these are replaced towards the end by negative and off-record strategies which bring out the often ridiculous nature of Rosalind's behaviour. Both Shan Wareing and Sara Mills use Halliday's systemic-functional grammar in order to examine critically the representation of women in popular fiction and culture. In a fascinating case study ('And Then He Kissed Her: The Reclamation of Female Characters to Submissive Roles in Contemporary Fiction'), Wareing shows how strong and assertive female characters are recuperated into the roles of passive romantic heroines in sexual encounters: in transitivity terms, they are the passive recipients of the male character's actions, and in terms of focalization, they are the fragmented objects of the male gaze. Mills tries to go even further than this: her 'Close Encounters of a Feminist Kind: Transitivity Analysis and Pop Lyrics' advocates a 'more complex form of feminist analysis' which uses transitivity analysis to reveal the contradictions within the ideology of romantic love.

Cynthia Bernstein's *The Text and Beyond: Essays in Literary Linguistics* is a somewhat uneven collection of papers ranging from text-orientated studies of cohesion, foregrounding and reference to more contextualized, discourse-stylistic studies of gender, power and culture. The former include William Chisholm's 'unabashedly Jakobsonian' analysis of 'Lexico-Syntactic Cohesion in Creeley's "I Know a Man"'; M. J. C. Curry's 'Anaphoric and Cataphoric Reference in Dickens's *Our Mutual Friend* and James's *The Golden Bowl*', which uses cohesion as a criterion for distinguishing between realist and modernist texts; and Melissa Monroe's discussion of noun+noun compounds in 'Comparison and Synthesis: Marianne Moore's Natural and Unnatural Taxonomies'.

The most interesting of the pragmatic and discourse-based studies is Rei Noguchi's insightful 'Conversational Style and the Form–Meaning Link in Literary Analysis'. His aim is to examine 'some features of conversational style where the link between form and meaning seems the least arbitrary and, thus, the most promising for relating stylistic description to literary interpretation'. He considers three variables of the exchange unit: length, type and sequence of utterances, including the presence or absence of 'countering speeches' between soliciting and proper responding speech, and discusses the widely shared social meanings attached to these variables.

Two chapters deal with the distinction between powerful and powerless speech. In '"Policewoman", Male Dominance, and the Cooperative Principle', J. M. and T. C. Frazer claim that the empowerment of the heroine in this popular-feminist TV series fails to extend to discourse. Nancy Wilhelmi, on the other hand, finds that Tennessee Williams's plays often depict female characters as 'seizers of powerful language'. In her chapter entitled 'The Language of Power and Powerlessness: Verbal Combat in the Plays of Tennessee Williams', she thus hopes to have proved that 'the language of the powerful is not reserved for men alone'. Were there still people around who thought it was?

The last chapter by Barbara Johnstone ('"You gone have to learn to talk right": Linguistic Deference and Regional Dialect in Harry Crews's *Body*') is an excellent exercise in literary dialectology: she focuses on Crews's representation of discourse-level features of his southern white characters' speech, in particular terms of address and strategies for indirectness.

In *Poetic Voices: Discourse Linguistics and the Poetic Text*, Timothy Austin uses a discourse-based stylistics to study the interaction between text and reader in poems by Wordsworth, Shelley and Tennyson. He insists on the 'naturalness' of speech in poetry, showing how in Tennyson's 'Ulysses' we infer the complex character of the speaker from the formal idiosyncrasies of his speech. Two chapters discuss the literary effects of narrative framing or discourse layering in poetic narratives. Throughout the book, Austin advocates a flexible, eclectic, inclusive stylistic approach, which explores the connections between linguistic structure and discourse context. Austin also keeps coming back to an interpretive crux in Wordsworth's 'Resolution and Independence': namely, how to account for the duplication of both the Narrator's question (about the Leech Gatherer's employment) and the latter's reply. He develops a sensitive reading which reinterprets the poem as a contribution within the Wordsworth–Coleridge literary debate, reading the Narrator as Coleridge and the Leech Gatherer as Wordsworth. The theoretical point is that identifying the first-person narrator of poetic narratives with the poet may be the default option, but certainly not always the only one or even the best one.

Whereas most stylistics textbooks use language and linguistic analysis to provide insights into the nature of literature, Valerie Shepherd's *Literature About Language* inverts this relationship and uses literary texts in order to provide insights into the nature of language. Indeed literary texts frequently thematize a concern with language, focusing upon how language at the same time empowers and constrains its users. Shepherd starts from the well-trodden ground of Golding's *The Inheritors*: Lok and his people are shown to have highly limited linguistic capacities, lacking in particular a capacity to think and express themselves metaphorically, and to organize their experience into a narrative structure. Later in the book (chapters 4 and 5), human creativity through metaphor and narrative is dealt with in much greater detail, but now there is a rather strange asymmetry: metaphor is seen in an essentially negative light, with Shepherd emphasizing how the inevitable partiality of metaphor has the power to mislead, whereas narratives are seen in a totally positive light as '*givers* of life, re-evaluations which permit new perceptions, new ways of seeing that allow us to take increased control of our day-to-day existence'. The author does not seem to notice that this eulogy of narrative would apply equally well to metaphor, if only she were willing to look at the latter from a less restrictive perspective.

In *Lexical Ambiguity in Poetry*, Soon Peng Su presents a two-level approach to ambiguity, showing how potential lexical ambiguity is actualized in context by the reader. The author studies the constraining and disambiguating effects of context, but also examines how it can generate new ambiguities, e.g. when the same word relates to different contexts. The chapter on the reader seems largely redundant, since the reader's role in ambiguity has already been dealt with in the chapter on context, which includes a consideration of such factors as (the reader's) social situation or knowledge of the world. So one wonders why one needs to be introduced to such concepts as the ideal reader, the mock reader, the super-reader, the informed reader, the intended reader, none of which is used in the actual analyses of ambiguity in the poetry of G. M. Hopkins. Later chapters compare ambiguity with cognate phenomena such as indeterminacy, vagueness and obscurity, and discuss a number of potential sources of ambiguity: metaphor and other tropes, lexical innovation, and referential ambiguity. As for the final chapter, it addresses, but all too briefly, the complex question of the aesthetic value of lexical ambiguity.

Forms of Speech in Victorian Fiction by Raymond Chapman is a useful survey, with illustrations taken from a wide range of novels. He shows how the representation of non-standard speech relies on simplified deviance: a few deviant spellings (especially the dropped aspirate and hypercorrection of the wrongly inserted aspirate), along with slang words and non-standard syntax, are used as pointers to low social status and suggest a lack of education. On the other hand, the use of standard speech by an uneducated character is conventionally a pointer to that character's virtue and natural goodness. There are good and entertaining sections on the Victorian novelists' parodies of Evangelical rhetoric and of the affected 'debilitated' drawl of upper-class speech; on the protest speech of the angry and passionate woman, and the strong, self-assertive language of the 'masculine' woman; and on the narrow range of oaths and the wide range of euphemisms to be found in Victorian novels. Other sections are far less convincing, sometimes because of superficiality (e.g. three pages only are devoted to the discussion of the uses and effects of direct, indirect, and free indirect discourse) and sometimes because of an idiosyncratic use of linguistic terminology (e.g. legal and other registers are dealt with in a section entitled 'Occupational Speech', whereas the chapter entitled 'Register' deals exclusively with terms of address).

As for Gerard Steen's *Understanding Metaphor in Literature*, it is likely to disappoint those readers who expect practical analyses of metaphors in particular literary texts, for there are none! The aim of this study is to set up an empirical theory of metaphor in literary reception. Steen describes a number of experiments which investigate how actual readers understand metaphor in literature. He explores such issues as the ways in which the processing of metaphor is affected by the three factors of reader, text and context; the specific nature of the processes of understanding metaphor in literary as opposed to journalistic reception; and the complex relation between metaphorical properties and discourse processes. Last but not least in this surprisingly long list of books on stylistics published this year is Guy Cook's *Discourse and Literature: The Interplay of Form and Mind*, which, however, arrived too late for detailed consideration. Suffice it to say that here Cook puts forward a highly interesting, but also highly controversial view of literature as discourse effecting cognitive change by disrupting or 'refreshing' the reader's mental schemata.

Turning now to journals, we look first at the area of prosodic studies, where Richard Cureton has made substantial contributions to a theory of rhythm with 'Rhythmic Cognition and Linguistic Rhythm' (*JLS* 23.220–32) and 'Rhythm and Verse Study' (*L&L* 3.105–24). In the latter, he defines verse rhythm as a recursive hierarchy of prominence and discusses the complementary co-ordination of the three prominence hierarchies (metre, grouping and prolongation).

Two papers informed by a critical-ideological perspective are Gordon Fulton's 'Dialogue with the Other as Potential and Peril in *Robinson Crusoe*' (*L&L* 3.1–20), a critical-stylistic analysis of the subversive effects of dialogue in the scenes depicting Crusoe's conversion of Friday, and Andrew Cooper's '"Folk-Speech" and "Book English": Re-presentations of Dialect in Hardy's Novels' (*L&L* 3.21–41), which emphasizes the ideological conflicts underlying the literary representation of dialect speech, with particular reference to *Tess of the d'Urbervilles*. Meanwhile, Donna Miller sounds a note of caution about how easy it is to read dialogism into almost any literary work. In 'D. H. Lawrence Revisited: By Way of Bakhtin' (*LeS* 29.305–23), she criticizes David Lodge's reading of *Women in Love* as a dialogic novel and focuses instead on the tension between centrifugal (dialogic) and centripetal (monologic) forces in Lawrence's discourse.

Other studies in pragmatic and discourse stylistics worth mentioning include the following: Peter Stockwell ('How to Create Universes with Words: Referentiality and Science Fictionality', *JLS* 23.159–87) analyses the beginning of Ray Bradbury's *The Martian Chronicles* in an interesting attempt to point the way towards a discourse-procedural theory of reference. David Herman uses Gricean pragmatics and conversation-analytic categories (adjacency pairs, turn-taking procedures, topic boundaries) as a framework for understanding 'The Mutt and Jute Dialogue in Joyce's *Finnegans Wake*' (*Style* 28.219–41), while Mounir Triki and Hasan Taman study 'The Processes of Mystification' in *JLS* (23.200–19). In 'Interactional Silence: Pauses in Dramatic Performance' (*JPrag* 21.171–90), Nathan Stucky discusses the communicative relevance of pauses in Sam Shepard's *True West*. Valerie Lowe's '"Unsafe Convictions": "Unhappy" Confessions in *The Crucible*' (*L&L* 3.175–95) is a careful examination of how asymmetrical power relationships render void Tituba's speech act of confession in Arthur Miller's play. Other articles in *L&L* include 'Mind Style as an Interdisciplinary Approach to Characterization in Faulkner' (Ineke Bockting, 3.157–74) and 'Subjectivity as a Text-Type Marker in Historical Stylistics' (Irma Taavitsainen, 3.197–212).

More narratological in its approach is Toru Sasaki's 'Towards a Systematic Description of Narrative Point of View: An Examination of Chatman's Theory with an Analysis of "The Blind Man" by D. H. Lawrence' (*L&L* 3.125–38), the title of which really says it all. Still on point of view, but this time from the perspective of computational linguistics, Janyce Wiebe's 'Tracking Point of View in Narrative' (*CompLing* 20.233–87) addresses the problem of identifying 'subjective sentences' (sentences that present the thoughts, perceptions or inner states of a character in the story). However thorough and well researched her work may be, she fails to convince the reader that the proposed algorithm can successfully capture all the complexities of psychological point of view. In 'From Empathetic Deixis to Empathetic Narrative: Stylisation and (De)Subjectivisation as Processes of Language Change' (*TPS* 92.55–88), Sylvia Adamson argues brilliantly that free indirect discourse (or 'empathetic narrative') originates, not with the nineteenth-century novel, but with seventeenth-century Puritan subjectivism. She focuses on Bunyan's *Grace Abounding*, where empathetic deixis stylizes (is generalized and conventionalized) into empathetic narrative. Robyn Warhol's 'Narrating the Unnarratable: Gender and Metonymy in the Victorian Novel' (*Style* 28.74–94), a feminist-narratological study, establishes an interesting distinction between a more abstract, 'masculine' mode of metonymic discourse and a more concrete, 'feminine' mode. *Style* also has a special issue this year on 'Second-Person Narrative' (iii), guest-edited by Monika Fludernik and containing nine chapters, but there is no space to review them here. The interested reader would do well in particular to look up the excellent studies by David Herman ('Textual *You* and Double Deixis in Edna O'Brien's *A Pagan Place*', 28.378–410) and by Keith Green and Jill LeBihan ('The Speaking Object: Daphne Marlatt's Pronouns and Lesbian Poetics', 28.432–44).

An outstanding contribution in metaphor studies is Andrew Goatly's 'Register and the Redemption of Theory' (*Pragmatics* 4.139–81), which successfully combines relevance theory with Hallidayan genre and register theory in order to provide a more satisfactory account of metaphor. He analyses metaphors in a number of different genres and shows how the computation of relevance is dependent on the particular purposes inherent in field and tenor, and on the processing conditions dictated by mode. In a similar synthetizing spirit, Anne Pankhurst ('Interpreting Metonymy', *EWPAL* 5.98–108) uses extracts from Dickens and Woolf in order to present a combined linguistic, rhetorical, and relevance-theoretic analysis of the role and functions of metonymy. Paul Werth ('Extended Metaphor: A Text-World Account', *L&L* 3.79–103) claims that his text-worlds model provides a powerful explanatory framework for the 'double-vision' aspect of metaphor. He also introduces the rather formidable notion of 'megametaphors' (fundamental cultural images) to describe the metaphorical undercurrents running through whole passages by E. M. Forster and Dylan Thomas. As for Eli Rosik's 'Poetic Metaphor' (*Sem* 102.49–69), its most interesting contribution for stylisticians is perhaps the lucid account of 'referential associations' evoked by metaphorical expressions (similar to the poetic effects discussed in relevance theory).

In the area of computer-assisted and corpus-based stylistics, I would recommend Michael Stubbs's discussion of ergative verbs and projecting clauses in two geography textbooks ('Grammar, Text and Ideology', *AppLing* 15.201–23) and Gregory Watson's application of Douglas Biber's stylistic model to the novels of the Australian Aboriginal writer M. Nyoongah ('A Multidimensional Analysis of Style in Mudrooroo Nyoongah's Prose Works', *Text* 14.239–85). Watson's paper has a double aim: to reveal a diachronic style shift in Nyoongah's fiction and to point to some inadequacies in Biber's multifeatured approach. In another interesting study ('Lyrical Drama and the "Turbid Mountebanks"', *CHum* 28.63–86), J. F. Burrows and D. H. Craig present statistical comparisons of styles of dialogue in Romantic and Renaissance tragedy. Finally, brief mention should also be made of Louis Milic and Steve Slane's statistical study using ten stylistic variables to estimate the distinctiveness of genres ('Quantitative Aspects of Genre in the Century of Prose Corpus', *Style* 28.42–54); Thomas Merriam and Robert Matthews's 'Neural Computation in Stylometry II: An Application to the Works of Shakespeare and Marlowe' (*L&LC* 9.1–6); and Thomas Rommel's '"So soft, so sweet, so delicately clear": A Computer-Assisted Analysis of Accumulated Words and Phrases in Lord Byron's Epic Poem *Don Juan*' (*L&LC* 9.7–12).

Books Reviewed

Aitchison, Jean. *Words in the Mind: An Introduction to the Mental Lexicon* (2nd edn). Blackwell. pp. 288. pb £14.99. ISBN 0 6311 8921 1.

Aertsen, Henk, and Robert J. Jeffers, eds. *Historical Linguistics 1989: Papers from the Ninth International Conference on Historical Linguistics*. Benjamins (1993). pp. 538. $115. ISBN 1 5561 9560 5.

Algeo, John. *Fifty Years Among the New Words: A Dictionary of Neologisms*. CUP (1993). pp. 257. hb £37.50, pb £16.95. ISBN 0 5214 1377 X, 0 5214 4971 5.

Ankersmit, F. R., and J. J. A. Mooij, eds. *Metaphor and Knowledge*. Vol. 3 of *Knowledge and Language* (1993). Kluwer. pp. 213. £64. ISBN 0 7923 1791 2.

Aronoff, Mark. *Morphology by Itself: Stems and Inflectional Classes*. Linguistic Inquiry Monograph 22. MITP. pp. 210. hb $51.25, pb $25.50. ISBN 0 2620 1136 0, 0 2625 1072 3.

Asher, Nicholas. *Reference to Abstract Objects in Discourse*. Kluwer (1993). pp. 455. £92.50. ISBN 0 7923 2242 8.

Asher, R. E., ed. *The Encyclopedia of Language and Linguistics*. 10 vols. Pergamon. pp. 5782. £1,860. ISBN 0 0803 5943 4.

Atkins, B. T. S., and A. Zampolli. *Computational Approaches to the Lexicon*. OUP. pp. 479. £55. ISBN 0 1982 3979 3.

Austin, Timothy R. *Poetic Voices: Discourse Linguistics and the Poetic Text*. UAlaP. pp. 240. pb $24.95. ISBN 0 8173 0726 5.

Bauer, Laurie. *Watching English Change: An Introduction to the Study of Linguistic Change in Standard Englishes in the Twentieth Century*. Learning about Language. Longman. pp. 200. pb £10.99. ISBN 0 5822 1089 5.

Béjoint, Henri. *Tradition and Innovation in Modern English Dictionaries*. Clarendon. pp. 276. £32.50. ISBN 0 1982 3919 X.

Ben-Rafael, Eliezer. *Language, Identity and Social Division: The Case of Israel*. Oxford Studies in Language Contact. OUP. pp. 289. £40. ISBN 0 1982 4072 4.

Bernstein, Cynthia G., ed. *The Text and Beyond: Essays in Literary Linguistics*. UAlaP. pp. 308. pb $26.95. ISBN 0 8173 0699 4.

Blaicher, Günther and Brigitte Glaser, eds. *Anglistentag 1993 Eichstätt: Proceedings of the Conference of the German Association of University Teachers of English*. Vol. XV. Niemeyer. pp. 555. pb DM 168. ISBN 3 4844 0128 1.

Blair, John. *Anglo-Saxon Oxfordshire*. Sutton. pp. 230. £25. ISBN 0 7509 0147 0.

Bondre-Beil, Priyamvada. *Parameter der Syntax*. Linguistische Arbeiten 324. Niemeyer. pp. 179. pb DM 84. ISBN 3 4843 0324 7.

Bradford, Richard. *Roman Jakobson: Life, Language, Art*. Routledge. pp. 213. hb £37.50, pb £12.99. ISBN 0 4150 7731 1, 0 4150 7732 X.

Bryson, Bill. *Made in America*. Secker and Warburg/Minerva. pp. 479. hb £15, pb £6.99. ISBN 0 4362 0140 2, 0 7493 9654 7.

Burchfield, Robert, ed. *The Cambridge History of the English Language. Vol. V: English in Britain and Overseas: Origins and Developments*. CUP. pp. 656. £70. ISBN 0 5212 6478 2.

Burt, Richard, and John Michael Archer, eds. *Enclosure Acts: Sexuality, Property, and Culture in Early Modern England*. CornUP. pp. 340. hb £33.50, pb £13.50. ISBN 0 8014 2745 2, 0 8014 8024 8.

Cann, Ronnie. *Formal Semantics: An Introduction*. CUP (1993). pp. 344. hb £50, pb £15.95. ISBN 0 5213 7463 4, 0 5213 7610 6.

Cannon, Garland, and Alan S. Kaye. *The Arabic Contributions to the English Language: An Historical Dictionary*. Harrassowitz Verlag. pp. 345. DM 98. ISBN 3 4470 3491 2.

Carlon, Keith, Kristin Davidse and Brygida Rudzka-Ostyn. *Perspectives on English: Studies in Honour of Professor Emma Vorlat*. Peeters. pp. 576. Belgian frs 1250. ISBN 9 0683 1593 5.

Channell, Joanna. *Vague Language*. OUP. pp. 226. pb £14.30. ISBN 0 1943 7186 7.

Chapman, Raymond. *Forms of Speech in Victorian Fiction*. Longman. pp. 263. pb £11.99. ISBN 0 5820 8745 7.

Cook, Guy. *Discourse and Literature: The Interplay of Form and Mind*. OUP. pp. 285. pb £13.90. ISBN 0 1943 7185 9.

Corballis, Michael C. *The Lopsided Ape: Evolution of the Generative Mind*. OUP (1993). pp. 366. pb £13.95. ISBN 0 1950 8352 0.

Corver, Norbert, and Henk van Riemsdijk, eds. *Studies on Scrambling: Movement and Non-Movement Approaches to Free Word-Order Phenomena*. Studies in Generative Grammar 41. MGruyter. pp. 531. hb DM 198. ISBN 3 1101 3572 8.

Cox, Barrie. *English Inn and Tavern Names*. CENS. pp. 116. pb £5. ISBN 0 9525 3430 4.

——. *The Place-Names of Rutland*. EPNS. pp. 483. £72. ISBN 0 9048 8917 3.

Cresswell, Max J. *Language in the World*. CUP. pp. 160. £27.95. ISBN 0 5214 4562 0.

Darton, Mike. *The Dictionary of Place Names in Scotland: And the Elements that Go to Make them Up*. Dobby. pp. 287. £9.99. ISBN 1 8588 2011 1.

Demske-Neumann, Ulrike. *Modales Passiv und* Tough Movement*: Zur strukturellen Kausalität eines syntaktischen Wandels im Deutschen und Englischen*. Linguistische Arbeiten 326. Niemeyer. pp. 294. pb DM 128. ISBN 3 4843 0326 3.

Dunant, Sarah, ed. *The War of the Words: The Political Correctness Debate*. Virago. pp. 188. £7.99. ISBN 1 8538 1834 8.

Edwards, John. *Multilingualism*. Routledge. pp. 240. £19.99. ISBN 0 4151 2011 X.

Eggins, Suzanne. *An Introduction to Systemic Functional Linguistics*. Pinter. pp. 360. hb £40, pb £13.99. ISBN 1 8556 7208 1, 1 8556 7209 X.

Fabb, Nigel. *Sentence Structure*. Language Workbooks. Routledge. pp. 144. pb £6.99. ISBN 0 4150 8569 1

Fernández, Francisco, Miguel Fuster and Juan José Calvo, eds. *English Historical Linguistics 1992*. Current Issues in Linguistic Theory 113. Benjamins. pp. 388. Dfl 170. ISBN 9 0272 3616 X.

Fodor, Jerry A. *The Elm and the Expert: Mentalese and its Semantics*. MITP. pp. 129. £15.95. ISBN 0 2620 6170 8.

Foulds, Trevor, ed. *The Thurgarton Cartulary*. Watkins. pp. 813. £75. ISBN 1 8716 1531 3.

Fox, Barbara, and Paul J. Hopper, eds. *Voice: Form and Function*. Typological Studies in Language 27. Benjamins. pp. 380. hb Dfl 175, pb Dfl 65. ISBN 9 0272 2915 5, 9 0272 2916 3.

Fries, Udo, Gunnel Tottie and Peter Schneider, eds. *Creating and Using English Language Corpora*. Language and Computers: Studies in Practical Linguistics 13. Rodopi. pp. 203. pb Dfl 60. ISBN 9 0518 3629 5.

Gernsbacher, Morton A., ed. *Handbook of Psycholinguistics*. Academic. pp. 1174. hb $105. ISBN 0 1228 0890 8.

Gibbons, John. *Language and the Law*. Language in Social Life. Longman. pp. 476. hb £45, pb £16.99. ISBN 0 5822 2976 6, 0 5821 0145 X.

Gotti, Maurizio, ed. *English Diachronic Syntax*. Guerini (1993). pp. 292. pb L 38,000. ISBN 8 8780 2395 7.

Green, Jonathon. *Slang Down the Ages: The Historical Development of Slang*. Kyle Cathie Ltd (1993). pp. 393. £16.99. ISBN 1 8562 6115 8.

Guttenplan, Samuel, ed. *A Companion to the Philosophy of Mind*. Blackwell. pp. 642. £60. ISBN 0 6311 7953 4.

Haegeman, Liliane. *Introduction to Government and Binding Theory* (2nd edn). Blackwell Textbooks in Linguistics. Blackwell. pp. 701. pb £15.99. ISBN 0 6311 9067 8.

Halliday, Michael A. K. *An Introduction to Functional Grammar* (2nd edn). Arnold. pp. 434. pb £17.95. ISBN 0 3405 7491 7.

Hamilton, Heidi E. *Conversations with an Alzheimer's Patient: An Interactional Sociolinguistic Study*. CUP. pp. 184. £30. ISBN 0 5214 2101 2.

Hintikka, Jaakko, ed. *Aspects of Metaphor*. Kluwer. pp. 263. £76. ISBN 0 7923 2786 1.

Hooke, Della. *Pre-Conquest Charter-Bounds of Devon and Cornwall*. Boydell. pp. 239 + 9 plates. £29.50. ISBN 0 8511 5354 2.

Hurford, James R. *Grammar: A Student's Guide*. CUP. pp. 271. hb £30, pb £9.95. ISBN 0 5214 5409 3, 0 5214 5627 4.

Insley, John. *Scandinavian Personal Names in Norfolk: A Survey Based on Medieval Records and Place-Names*. A&W. pp. 455. pb SEK 228. ISBN 9 1853 5226 8.

Johnston, James B. *Place Names of England and Wales*. Bracken (reprint. 1st edn 1915). pp. 532. pb £2.99. ISBN 1 8589 1133 8.

Katamba, Francis. *English Words*. Routledge. pp. 282. hb £35, pb £12.99. ISBN 0 4151 0467 X, 0 4151 0468 8.

Kayne, Richard S. *The Antisymmetry of Syntax*. Linguistic Inquiry Monographs 25. MITP. pp. 195. pb £15.50. ISBN 0 2626 1107 4.

Keller, Rudi. *On Language Change: The Invisible Hand in Language*. Trans. Brigitte Nerlich. Routledge. pp. 182. ISBN 0 4150 7672 2.

Kerswill, Paul. *Dialects Converging: Rural Speech in Urban Norway*. Oxford Studies in Language Contact. Clarendon. pp. 181. £30. ISBN 0 1982 4826 1.

Keynes, Simon. *The Councils of 'Clofesho'*. Vaughan Paper No. 38. LeicAE. pp. 52 + 2 tables. pb £2.50. ISBN 0 9015 0756 3.

Klein, Wolfgang. *Time in Language*. Germanic Linguistics. Routledge. pp. 243. £40. ISBN 0 4151 0412 2.

Kytö, Merja, Matti Rissanen and Susan Wright, eds. *Corpora across the Centuries: Proceedings of the First International Colloquium on English Diachronic Corpora*. Language and Computers: Studies in Practical Linguistics 11. Rodopi. pp. 212. pb Dfl 65. ISBN 9 0518 3615 5.

Labov, William. *Principles of Linguistic Change*. Vol. I. *Internal Factors*. Language in Society. Blackwell. pp. 641. £19.99. ISBN 0 6311 7913 5, 0 6311 7914 3.

Lakshmanan, Usha. *Universal Grammar in Child Second Language Acquisition*. Benjamins. pp. 162. £26. ISBN 9 0272 2475 7.

Lambrecht, Knud. *Information Structure and Sentence Form: Topic, Focus, and the Mental Representations of Discourse Referents*. Cambridge Studies in Linguistics 71. CUP. pp. 388. £37.50. ISBN 0 5213 8056 1.

Lass, Roger. *Old English: A Historical Linguistic Companion*. CUP. pp. 300. hb £45, pb £17.95. ISBN 0 5214 3087 1, 0 5214 5848 X.

Leech, Geoffrey, and Jan Svartvik. *A Communicative Grammar of English* (2nd edn). Longman. pp. 423. hb £32, pb £13.99. ISBN 0 5822 3827 7, 0 5820 8573 X.

Lighter, J. E. *The Random House Historical Dictionary of American Slang*. Vol. 1. *A-G*. RandomH. pp. 1006. $50. ISBN 0 3945 4427 7.

Lightfoot, David, and Norbert Hornstein, eds. *Verb Movement*. CUP. pp. 388. hb £40, pb £15.95. ISBN 0 5214 5041 1, 0 5214 5661 4.

Lord, Richard. *The Words We Use*. Kahn & Averill. pp. 116. £8.95. ISBN 1 8710 8244 7.

Loyn, Henry. *The Vikings in Britain*. Blackwell. pp. 128. £22.50. ISBN 0 6311 8711 1.

Luger, George F. et al. *Cognitive Science: The Science of Intelligent Systems*. Academic. pp. 666. hb $49.95. ISBN 0 1245 9570 7.

Lutz, William D., ed. *The Cambridge Thesaurus of American English*. CUP. pp. 515. £12.95. ISBN 0 5214 1427 X.

Matthew, D., with A. Curry and E. Green, eds. *Stenton's 'Anglo-Saxon England' Fifty Years on: Papers Given at a Colloquium held at Reading, 11–12 November 1993*. Reading Historical Studies 1. ReadingUP. pp. 134. £15.65. ISBN 0 7049 0448 9.

McMahon, April M. S. *Understanding Language Change*. CUP. pp. 361. hb £35, pb £11.95. ISBN 0 5214 4119 6, 0 5214 4665 1.

Meinhof, Ulrike, and Kay Richardson, eds. *Text, Discourse and Context: Representations of Poverty in Britain*. Longman Real Language Series. Longman. pp. 149. hb £40, pb £10.99. ISBN 0 5821 0214 6, 0 5821 0213 8.

Mettinger, Arthur. *Aspects of Semantic Opposition in English*. OUP. pp. 205. £27.50. ISBN 0 1982 4269 7.

Morton, Herbert C. *The Story of Webster's Third*. CUP. pp. 332. hb £30, pb £14.95. ISBN 0 5214 6146 4, 0 5215 5869 7.

Moseley, Christopher, and R. E. Asher, eds. *Atlas of the World's Languages*. Routledge. pp. 372. hb £39.50. ISBN 0 4150 1925 7.

Nash, Walter. *Jargon: Its Uses and Abuses*. Blackwell (1993). £16.99. ISBN 0 6311 8063 X.

Odlin, Terence, ed. *Perspectives on Pedagogical Grammar*. Cambridge Applied Linguistics Series. CUP. pp. 340. hb £27.95, pb £13.95. ISBN 0 5214 4530 2, 0 5214 4990 1.

Oostdijk, Nelleke, and Pieter de Haan, eds. *Corpus-Based Research into Language*. Language and Computers: Studies in Practical Linguistics 12. Rodopi. pp. 279. pb Dfl 85. ISBN 9 0518 3588 4.

Ouhalla, Jamal. *Introducing Transformational Grammar: From Rules to Principles and Parameters*. Arnold. pp. 332. pb £14.99. ISBN 0 3405 5630 7.

Owen, Hywel Wyn. *The Place-Names of East Flintshire*. UWalesP. pp. 428. £35. ISBN 0 7083 1242 X.

Palmer, F. R. *Grammatical Roles and Relations*. Cambridge Textbooks in Linguistics. CUP. pp. 259. hb £37.50, pb £12.95. ISBN 0 5214 5204 X, 0 5214 5836 6.

Panther, Klaus-Uwe. *Kontrollphänomene im Englischen und Deutschen aus semantisch-pragmatischer Perspektive*. Studien zur Englischen Grammatik. Narr. pp. 225. pb DM 78. ISBN 3 8233 4921 X.

Peng Su, Soon. *Lexical Ambiguity in Poetry*. Longman. pp. 188. pb £10.99. ISBN 0 5821 0114 X.

Pennycook, Alastair. *The Cultural Politics of English as an International Language.* Longman. pp. 365. hb £34, pb £14.99. ISBN 0 5822 34735, 0 5822 3472 7.
Pfeffer, J. Alan, and Garland Cannon. *German Loanwords in English: An Historical Dictionary.* CUP. pp. 381. £60. ISBN 0 5214 0254 9.
Pinker, Steven. *The Language Instinct: The New Science of Language and Mind.* PenguinA. pp. 494. hb £20. ISBN 0 6881 2141 1.
Progovac, Ljiljana. *Negative and Positive Polarity: A Binding Approach.* Cambridge Studies in Linguistics 68. CUP. pp. 168. £27.95. ISBN 0 5214 4480 2.
Ricken, Ulrich. *Linguistics, Anthropology and Philosophy in the French Enlightenment: Language Theory and Ideology.* Routledge. pp. 287. £55. ISBN 0 4150 7679 X.
Robinson, Fred C. *The Editing of Old English.* Blackwell. pp. 212. £45. ISBN 1 5578 6438 1.
Roffe, David, ed. *Stamford in the Thirteenth Century: Two Inquisitions from the Reign of Edward I.* Watkins. pp. 88. hb £17.95, pb £7.95. ISBN 1 8716 1573 9, 1 8716 1562 3.
Romaine, Suzanne. *Language in Society: An Introduction to Sociolinguistics.* OUP. pp. 235. pb £7.99. ISBN 0 1987 5134 6.
——. *Bilingualism.* Language in Society 14 (2nd edn). Blackwell. pp. 384. pb £14.99. ISBN 0 6311 9539 4.
Room, Adrian. *Cassell Dictionary of Proper Names.* Cassell. pp. 610. £14.99. ISBN 0 3043 4447 8.
Rumble, Alexander, ed. *The Reign of Cnut, King of England, Denmark and Norway.* LeicUP. pp. 256. £42.50. ISBN 0 7185 1455 6, 0 8386 3605 5.
Sack, Harvey. *Lectures on Conversation.* Blackwell. pb £35. ISBN 1 5578 6705 4.
Savage-Rumbaugh, Sue, and Roger Lewin. *Kanzi: The Ape on the Brink of the Human Mind.* Wiley. pp. 299. hb $24.95. ISBN 0 4715 8591 2.
Schiffrin, Deborah. *Approaches to Discourse: Language as a Social Interaction.* Blackwell Textbooks in Linguistics. Blackwell. pp. 470. pb £15.99. ISBN 0 6311 6623 8.
Sebeok, Thomas A. *An Introduction to Semiotics.* Pinter. pp. 154. hb £33, pb £10.99. ISBN 1 8556 7193 X, 1 8556 7194 8.
Sell, Roger, and Peter Verdonk, eds. *Literature and the New Interdisciplinarity: Poetics, Linguistics, History.* Rodopi. pp. 257. pb Dfl 50. ISBN 9 0518 3609 0.
Shepherd, Valerie. *Literature About Language.* Routledge. pp. 178. pb £10.99. ISBN 0 4150 6997 1.
Silva-Corvalán, Carmen. *Language Contact and Change.* Oxford Studies in Language Contact. Clarendon. pp. 255. £45. ISBN 0 1982 4287 5.
Steen, Gerard. *Understanding Metaphor in Literature.* Longman. pp. 263. pb £12.99. ISBN 0 5821 0118 2.
Steube, Anita, and Gerhild Zybatow, eds. *Zur Satzwertigkeit von Infinitiven und Small Clauses.* Linguistische Arbeiten 315. Niemeyer. pp. 272. pb DM 118. ISBN 3 4843 0315 8.
Svensén, Bo. *Practical Lexicography: Principles and Methods of Dictionary-Making.* Trans. John Sykes and Kerstin Schofield. OUP (1993). pp. 285. £40. ISBN 0 1986 3116 2.
Swan, Toril, Endre Mørck and Olaf Jansen Westwik, eds. *Language Change and Language Structure: Older Germanic Languages in a Comparative Perspective.* Trends in Linguistics 73. MGruyter. pp. 346. DM 168. ISBN 3 1101 3538 8.
Sylvester, Louise. *Studies in the Lexical Field of Expectation.* Rodopi. pp. 397.

£46.15. ISBN 9 0518 3608 2.

Tanaka, Keiko. *Advertising Language: A Pragmatic Approach to Advertisements in Britain and Japan*. Routledge. pp. 148. £35. ISBN 0 4150 7647 1.

Thein, Maria Luise. *Die informationelle Struktur im Englischen: Syntax und Information als Mittel der Hervorhebung*. Linguistische Arbeiten 323. Niemeyer. pp. 227. pb DM 106. ISBN 3 4843 0323 9.

Tobin, Yishai. *Invariance, Markedness and Distinctive Feature Analysis: A Contrastive Study of Sign Systems in English and Hebrew*. Current Issues in Linguistic Theory 111. Benjamins. pp. 406. Dfl 180. ISBN 9 0272 3614 3.

Trask, R. *Language Change*. Language Workbooks. Routledge. pp. 93. pb £6.99. ISBN 0 4150 8563 2.

Trudgill, P., and J. Hannah. *International English: A Guide to the Varieties of Standard English* (3rd edn). pp. 156. pb £10.99. ISBN 0 3405 8645 1.

Tsohatzidis, Savas L., ed. *Foundations of Speech Act Theory: Philosophical and Linguistic Perspectives*. Routledge. pp. 500. £75. ISBN 0 4150 9524 7.

Upton, Clive, David Parry and John D. Widdowson. *Survey of English Dialects: The Dictionary and Grammar*. Routledge. pp. 506. £90. ISBN 0 4150 2029 8.

Wales, Katie, ed. *Feminist Linguistics in Literary Criticism*. Brewer. pp. 157. £29.50. ISBN 0 8599 1411 9.

Williams, Edwin. *Thematic Structure in Syntax*. Linguistic Inquiry Monograph 23. MITP. pp. 266. hb $48.50, pb $24.25. ISBN 0 2622 3173 5, 0 2627 3106 1.

Wright, Tony. *Investigating English*. Arnold. pp. 182. pb £10.99. ISBN 0 3405 5782 6.

II

Old English Literature

ELAINE M. TREHARNE

This chapter contains the following sections: 1. Bibliography; 2. Manuscript Studies, Palaeography and Facsimiles; 3. Social, Cultural and Intellectual Background; 4. Literature: General; 5. The Exeter Book; 6. The Poems of the Vercelli Book; 7. The Junius Manuscript; 8. The *Beowulf* Manuscript; 9. Other Poems; 10. Prose.

1. Bibliography

The *OENews* (Summer 27.iv) contains the complete bibliographical listings for Old English for 1993, along with 'Research in Progress'. *OENews* 27.ii (Winter) contains the reviews of works published in 1992. *OENews* 27.iii (Spring) includes conference news and abstracts of conference papers, and reports on *Fontes Anglo-Saxonici,* the publication of the *Anglo-Saxon Chronicle: A Collaborative Edition*, and *A Thesaurus of Old English*, with an article by Lynne Grundy on 'The Structure of *A Thesaurus of Old English* Database' (25–7). Christian Kay provides a brief article on the *Glasgow Historical Thesaurus* (28–9). Sarah Larratt Keefer discusses 'Computing in Anglo-Saxon Studies: A Representative Retrospective' (31–4), and Robert Hasenfratz reflects on 'A Decade's Worth of *Beowulf* Scholarship: Observations on Compiling a Bibliography' (35–40). Volume 28.i (Fall) contains reports on the *DOE* and the English Place-Names project. Carol Neuman de Vegvar's 'Images of Women in Anglo-Saxon Art V: Matron as Ring-Giver in Harley 630' (22–4) discusses the image of the woman at f.67v of the Harley Psalter and suggests that she is representative of 'the role of mother as distributor and potential testatrix'. Three occasional papers concerned with the CORPUS project deal with 'Insular, Anglo-Saxon, and Early Anglo-Norman Illuminated Manuscripts: Survey of Research Past, Present, Future'. Thomas Ohlgren talks about 'The CORPUS Project: The Nest and the Egg' (A.1–A.7), Mildred Budny discusses 'The Research Group on Manuscript Evidence: Contributions to the CORPUS Project' (A.8-A.22), and M. J. Toswell writes on 'Anglo-Saxon Psalter Manuscripts' (A.23–A.31). Appendix B (1–16) contains short reports on Anglo-Saxon Studies in Eastern Europe.

2. Manuscript Studies, Palaeography and Facsimiles

The year 1994 sees the publication by MRTS of the first two volumes in the collaborative *Anglo-Saxon Manuscripts in Microfiche Facsimile* series edited by Phillip Pulsiano, with A. N. Doane and Ronald E. Buckalew. This series will be of unlimited value to all Anglo-Saxonists as it is to include all manuscripts which contain Old English, reproduced and described in full. Vol. 1, *Books of Prayers and Healing*, contains descriptions by A. N. Doane and has fiches of ten British Library manuscripts. These are Cotton Caligula A.vii, Galba A.xiv, Nero A.ii, Vitellius C.iii, Harley manuscripts 585, 6258B and 7653, and Royal manuscripts 2.A.xx and 12.D.xvii. It is clear why fiche is the chosen medium: the price of the volumes is so reasonable that individuals can afford to purchase them; the quality of the fiches is clear and they are easy to negotiate. All the descriptions represent new work, follow essentially the same format, and are to be used in conjunction with the fiche. These descriptions offer the following information: the history of the manuscript where it is known; a codicological description detailing physical layout, foliation, script, rubrication; collation; a list of contents by title of text; and a select bibliography. 'Photo notes' provide information about the manuscript for the user which is not visible on the fiche. The second volume, *Psalters I*, with descriptions by Phillip Pulsiano, contains eight manuscripts from the British Library: Additional 37517 (the 'Bosworth Psalter'), Arundel 60 (the 'Arundel Psalter') and 155, Cotton Tiberius C.vi (the 'Tiberius Psalter'), Vespasian A.i (the 'Vespasian Psalter'), Vitellius E.xviii (the 'Vitellius Psalter'), Royal 2.B.v (the 'Regius Psalter'), and Stowe 2 (the 'Stowe Psalter'). The complex descriptions follow the same format as those in the first volume. Both Doane and Pulsiano exhibit meticulous care in describing the manuscripts and are to be congratulated on getting the series off the ground. There is little doubt that this series will open up the field of manuscript studies and will provide the impetus for a great deal of new scholarship on all the manuscripts published.

Two books with the title *The Editing of Old English* have been published this year, illustrating how central the issues of editing and manuscript studies in general have become. The first, *The Editing of Old English: Papers from the 1990 Manchester Conference*, edited by D. G. Scragg and Paul E. Szarmach, contains twenty essays by some of the leading scholars in the field. The initial essays are taken up with theoretical matters while those that follow focus on specific texts or manuscripts and the practice of editing. In his introduction to the volume, Szarmach tells us that these papers address both the theoretical and practical aspects facing the editor of Old English texts. He sees the current editing debate as being between the Old Philology and the New Philology or between Optimism and Recensionism. The papers themselves reflect these approaches, as well as others, making this an indispensable volume which has no single agenda other than that of raising the profile of editing in general and discussing the issues that affect not only editors, but also users of editions. The first essay in this volume is Helmut Gneuss's 'Guide to the Editing and Preparation of Texts for the *Dictionary of Old English*', still one of the most useful articles on editing to have been written. A headnote outlines the methods behind the *DOE* and provides details of recent new editions. This is followed by Marilyn Deegan and Peter Robinson's interesting 'The Electronic Edition', where the authors examine the different elements of the editing process and the ways in which computers can aid this process. They explain the evolution of encoding using SGML; the availability of collation programs; and the benefits of computers in preparing glossaries and in finding sources and parallel texts. They rightly point to the possible alternatives to hard-copy editions in, for example, the electronic hypertext edition.

Alexander R. Rumble's 'Palaeography and the Editing of Old English Texts' provides a definition and contextualization of editing Old English: from Alfred editing Ine's law codes to medieval copying of diplomas and the cataloguing of medieval manuscripts in recent centuries. Rumble calls for cheaper facsimile editions and for the reinstatement of wynn in printed editions. He also presents a timely call for a knowledge of palaeography among prospective editors. David N. Dumville, in 'Editing Old English Texts for Historians and Other Troublemakers', addresses the requirements of non-literary specialists. His comments are wide-reaching: he discusses issues such as the modernization of punctuation and capitalization, and the desirable inclusion of translations, bemoaning the lack of consideration shown by many editors to all users of the texts, and the narrow focus of philologists in their editorial undertakings. Indeed, it is not only historians, archaeologists and so forth, who ought to be catered for by such editions, as Dumville suggests, but students too, and his suggestions could wisely be taken on board by many Old English textual scholars. Michael Lapidge takes up the common Lapidgean theme in 'On the Emendation of Old English texts' (see also *YWES* 74.84): the need for Anglo-Saxonists to tackle their editing with more courage and foresight. 'Now it is the editor's principal duty to establish what the author wrote; and therefore the manuscripts [may] require to be emended.' He discusses the nineteenth-century editors' methods with particular reference to conjectural emendation. Lapidge criticizes those who are conservative in their editing policy and he pleads for a 'more balanced attitude to the transmitted text'. He concludes 'The editor's first duty is not to dictionary-makers, not to beginning students [. . .] but to someone far more important than any of these – the author.' Agree or disagree, Lapidge's view is certainly thought-provoking. Antonette di Paolo Healey looks at the benefits of choosing to use editions over manuscript forms for the compilation of the *DOE* ('The Search for Meaning'). Within the editions, Healey pleads to editors, *contra* Lapidge, 'to show a tolerance for possible forms and an unwillingness to emend them out of existence'. She provides examples from editions where precisely this kind of editorial intervention has obscured unique linguistic data. Aspects of editions desirable for subsequent lexicographical use are also outlined: parsed glossaries, vernacular and Latin source published together, and the provision of cognate terms for rare words. Hugh Magennis's 'Old English Texts for Student Use' states the obvious in that an edition cannot be all things to all readers; rather, the subject of editing needs to be approached from a number of angles and intended purposes. Additionally, new approaches to teaching Old English are required, such as providing editions with *en face* translations, or using electronic editions and computer packages. Editors of student texts, as Magennis sees it, are facilitators who should not overburden their audience with unnecessary explication.

Eleven other essays in this volume will be reviewed in the appropriate sections below, but finally here is Don Scragg's 'Postscript: *Quo vadis, editio*?', which is, as usual, an inspiring reflection. He comments on the concern that Old English editors have, in general, become more conservative in recent decades despite the efforts by scholars such as Lapidge to remedy this prevailing policy. As an accomplished editor himself, Scragg offers food for thought for practising and potential editors: how far should an editor intervene in the text? Intervention ranges from the standardization of forms to the modernization of punctuation and capitalization, to the adoption of a particular typography, and to the emendation of grammatical and lexical items. Scragg illustrates his points with a series of questions that editors should ask themselves – for example, 'Is there a clearly identifiable mechanical error?' – and by showing how to explain and emend a copyist's misreading by looking at all the available manuscript evidence. He calls for a standard set of conventions to be used by all editors which would also extend to the apparatus and glossary. He illustrates how much there is still to be done in the field of editing. Recent discussion and publications, he points out, 'suggest that the subject is now more central to the agenda. It should stay there.' He is right.

The second volume concerned with editorial methodology and processes is Fred C. Robinson's *The Editing of Old English*. This book contains twenty-two essays and shorter articles, the majority of which are reprinted here and which are concerned with the issues facing the editor of Old English. The book is divided into four sections, each of which tackles separate concerns of the editor. The first, 'Text and Manuscript', includes 'Old English in its Most Immediate Context', 'Consider the Source: Medieval Texts and Medieval Manuscripts', and 'Print Culture and the Birth of the Text: A Review Essay'. Each of these essays, linked by a focus on the comparison between the modern editions of texts and the original manuscript, has been published before but include updated bibliographies. In the third essay, Robinson elucidates upon the fluidity of the original Old English work in contrast to the fixed printed text. He provides examples of the kinds of scribal variation to be found in manuscripts which prevent the editor from regarding the material as static. Section two of the volume, 'Textual Criticism', contains seven republished essays concerning *Beowulf* (such as 'Two Non-Cruces in *Beowulf*', 'Is Wealhðeow a Prince's Daughter?' and 'Textual Notes on *Beowulf*') and five essays on other Old English poems, including 'Notes on the Old English *Exodus*' and 'The Old English *Genesis*, Lines 1136–1137'. A new essay on *Genesis B* is reviewed below. This section collates material all of which deals with the types of textual problem facing the editor of Old English verse, and ways in which these problems can be addressed. The third section, 'Linguistic Studies of Old English', contains four essays (such as 'Old English Lexicographical Notes', and 'Latin for Old English in Anglo-Saxon Manuscripts') which discuss the kinds of language problem that must be taken into account in editing Old English. In the fourth and final section, 'Three Editions of Old English Texts', Robinson puts into practice his observations and warnings on editing. Two of the three essays, '"Bede's" Envoi to the Old English History: An Experiment in Editing' and 'The Devil's Account of the New World', are updated reprintings, but the other, 'The Rewards of Piety', is a considerably expanded version of an earlier essay and will be reviewed in section 9 below. In all, this is a welcome and timely collection of related essays, the wide-ranging nature of which reflect Robinson's considerable knowledge and scholarship. Textual critics, editors and other scholars will find it of immense value and interest; but students will also find Robinson's prose lucid and accessible.

Of considerable importance is the publication of some of Bernhard Bischoff's essays in *Manuscripts and Libraries in the Age of Charlemagne*, translated by Michael M. Gorman. This is the first in the new series Cambridge Studies in Palaeography and Codicology, volumes dedicated to the furtherance of manuscript studies from late Antiquity to the Renaissance. In the light of other manuscript studies series such as the *Anglo-Saxon Manuscripts in Microfiche Facsimile* project, it is apparent that the field as a whole is on the ascendant.

Gorman has selected and translated seven essays by Bischoff to make his immense scholarship more widely available. In particular, this book 'is intended to serve as a guide to the world of Carolingian manuscripts', an aim it fulfils admirably. Some bibliographical additions are made by Gorman to the essays to bring the information up to date and he has made a coherent work of the selections, each essay thematically following on from that which precedes it. A bibliography of Bischoff's writings from 1981–1993 is also included. The first essay is 'Manuscripts in the Early Middle Ages', a survey of Latin manuscripts from the late classical period covering the regions of Africa, Spain, Italy, Britain, Ireland, France and Germany. Major centres of production are discussed and the main styles of script are analysed, thereby providing an invaluable survey of this early period. 'Manuscripts in the Age of Charlemagne' details styles of script current in the last third of the eighth century and up to AD 815, and refers to the major writing centres, listing manuscript groups and important individual manuscripts. There is a discussion of Charlemagne's court scriptorium, and of centres associated with the Carolingian period, including those of Alsace, Italy and southeast Germany, and the Germanic-Insular centres influenced by Anglo-Saxon missionaries. The third essay examines 'The Court Library of Charlemagne' and attempts a reconstruction of the library by gathering contemporary references to the books – analysing title pages, dedications, and the recurrence of particular scribes – to further knowledge of this important repository. This is followed by an investigation into 'The Court Library under Louis the Pious'. This library possessed a variety of works from the classical to the contemporary before its dispersal on Louis's death. 'Libraries and Schools in the Carolingian Revival of Learning' illustrates how intellectual life in the Middle Ages owed much to the establishment of this type of library under Charlemagne and Louis. 'Palaeography and the Transmission of Classical Texts in the Early Middle Ages' is a seminal essay defining the practice of palaeography and its relationship to textual transmission, which uses texts such as the *Scriptores historiae Augustae* to illustrate the points. An appendix lists manuscripts attributable to Tours. The final essay, 'Benedictine Monasteries and the Survival of Classical Literature', deals with the transmission of Latin authors' works in the Carolingian era and the monks who copied these texts. Bischoff discusses and illustrates the distinction of the Anglo-Saxons in the interest they showed in classical works. He focuses on the libraries of Aldhelm, Bede and Alcuin and the texts of authors such as Virgil, Juvenal and Lucan which were known to the Anglo-Saxons. The breadth of these essays and the depth of scholarship exhibited in them make this an indispensable tool for Anglo-Saxonists; for the palaeographer of this period, this is surely a most important work.

The second in the Cambridge Studies in Palaeography and Codicology series, Richard Gameson, ed., *The Early Medieval Bible: Its Production, Decoration and Use*, was also published in 1994. It contains eleven essays which examine and reappraise the evidence of the Latin Bible from the late classical period to the thirteenth century. A variety of approaches are employed by the authors – palaeographical, textual, historical and cultural – to provide an extensive study. David Ganz writes on 'Mass Production of Early Medieval Manuscripts: The Carolingian Bibles from Tours', Rosamund McKitterick discusses 'Carolingian Bible Production: The Tours Anomaly', Margaret Gibson examines 'Carolingian Glossed Psalters', and Lesley Smith analyses 'The Theology of the Twelfth- and Thirteenth-Century Bible'. Other studies look at Italian and French bibles, but of most relevance here will be 'The Royal 1.B.vii Gospels and English Book

Production in the Seventh and Eighth Centuries' by Gameson, 'The Old Testament in Late Anglo-Saxon England: Preliminary Observations on the Textual Evidence' by Richard Marsden (to be reviewed in section 10 below), and Patrick McGurk's 'The Oldest Manuscripts of the Latin Bible'. The latter essay includes a discussion of the codicology and reasons behind the production of some of the most famous codices: the Book of Kells, the Lindisfarne Gospels, the Harleian Gospels, and the *Codex Amiatinus*. McGurk also gives an overview of the biblical manuscripts in use in Anglo-Saxon England. Gameson's essay focuses on the eighth-century, possibly Northumbrian, manuscript Royal 1.B.vii, which is associated with King Athelstan. He examines what it can show about the production of manuscripts in the earlier Anglo-Saxon period. Gameson gives a detailed codicological description placing the manuscript in the context of other, comparable books. Textually, the codex shares affinities with the Lindisfarne Gospels, but also with a number of other manuscripts. Decoratively, it is an unpretentious manuscript, lacking, for example, evangelist portraits, but parallels can be drawn between its artistic designs and those in manuscripts such as the Barberini and St Petersburg Gospels. The relevance of this comparison between the *de luxe* volumes and those of more modest appearance is broadened to illustrate the dichotomy in the Anglo-Saxon church of the time, prosperous on the one hand and attempting to support Christianity at a local level on the other.

Mary P. Richards has edited *Anglo-Saxon Manuscripts: Basic Readings* for Garland's Basic Readings series. This volume contains fifteen general and manuscript-specific essays, plus an introduction by Richards. Of these, twelve are classic essays, previously published and now very usefully bound together, some with an updated bibliography. These reprinted essays include P. R. Robinson's 'Self-Contained Units in Composite Manuscripts of the Anglo-Saxon Period', the definitive work on identifying the criteria for booklets; Michael Lapidge's updated 'Surviving Booklists from Anglo-Saxon England', which provides Anglo-Saxonists with a research tool of major importance; and David N. Dumville's 'English Libraries Before 1066: Use and Abuse of Manuscript Evidence', which is a useful overview of scholarship on manuscripts with pointers for the future direction of research. Mary Blockley brings up to date her 'Further Addenda and Corrigenda to N. R. Ker's *Catalogue*'. The manuscript-specific essays will be mentioned below, but also in the volume are three new essays especially commissioned, which occur in the general section of the book. Alexander R. Rumble's 'Using Anglo-Saxon Manuscripts' is an indispensable guide to the procedures required in describing, reading, transcribing and editing manuscripts, fragments and single leaves of the Anglo-Saxon period. Each section of the process is clearly discussed and provided with a brief bibliography. Rumble demonstrates the steps for describing manuscripts from their external features inwards, and he gives the conventions for dating about which many scholars could remind themselves. There are few students who could afford to miss this essay, and all who write about manuscripts should refer to it to refresh and review their own techniques. Kevin Kiernan examines 'Old Manuscripts/New Technologies', particularly the ways in which technology can be applied to manuscript studies. He discusses the various types of equipment (fibre-optic light and the Video Spectral Comparator, for example) and the results gained in reading and photographing illegible or damaged manuscripts with these tools. He surveys the history of employing specialized equipment to help read manuscripts and gives the example of using ultraviolet light to capture letters which are missing to the naked eye in the *Beowulf* manuscript. For all newcomers to this area,

Kiernan's account is accessible and fascinating. Richard W. Pfaff also provides an interesting read in his biographical and professional study of Neil Ker. 'N. R. Ker and the Study of English Manuscripts' outlines Ker's education at Eton and Oxford and details influential palaeographers with whom he had contact, before focusing on his magisterial publications and their inestimable value to all medievalists.

Colin G. C. Tite's Panizzi Lectures for 1993 are published this year as *The Manuscript Library of Sir Robert Cotton*. The book contains much of interest to Anglo-Saxonists. The library established by Cotton and its subsequent history forms the focus of the three lectures, 'The Development of the Manuscript Collection, 1588–1753', 'Librarians and Aspiring Librarians' and 'Cotton House and the Reputation of Sir Robert'. Tite highlights the activities of Cotton in his collection of materials for the library and examines the ways in which Cotton conserved and classified his books, outlining the public interest that Cotton maintained in his work. Of fascinating detail is Tite's detective work, with its accompanying illustrations, which reconstructs the processes behind the creation and shelving arrangement of the library itself. Tite also dwells on the reputation of Cotton in his own time and in subsequent centuries. That Cotton's contribution to the appreciation and preservation of manuscripts is immeasurable is made the clearer by Tite's scholarly and entertaining study.

ASE 23 contains a number of essays related to manuscript studies and palaeography. David N. Dumville continues his work on Anglo-Saxon scripts in 'English Square Minuscule Script: The Mid-Century Phases' (133–64). In this article, Dumville examines the use of Square minuscule in the 940s–960s, particularly at Canterbury. He categorizes the manuscripts and diplomas of the period up to 959 as examples of phase III of the script, and notes that the small number of extant texts show this style of writing to be dominant in Old English and Latin for the two decades preceding. In terms of the material copied, this period is one of 'consolidation rather than of radical extension of the available range of literary works'. From 960 to 963, style IV is distinguishable: a form of Square minuscule bastardized by Caroline forms. The evolution of this script, which Dumville attributes to the influence of a Royal Chancery initially established not later than Athelstan's reign, with its distinctive changes, shows the transition between monarchs: changes in script coming with new political circumstances.

In 'Dry-point Glosses to Aldhelm's *De laudibus virginitatis* in Beinecke 401' (*ASE* 23.195–213), Philip G. Rusche provides an excellent analysis not only of the many dry-point glosses he has discovered in this manuscript, but also of their creators, purpose and implications. Rusche examines the tenth-century dates of the various dry-point glossators' work in relation to ink glossators' and discusses the methods of both. He concludes that some of these dry-point glosses are the result of students writing translations as orally transmitted by their teacher. This article, clearly and intelligently written, has wide-reaching points to make for glossography, manuscript studies, and Anglo-Saxon educational practices in general.

James P. Carley's 'More Pre-Conquest Manuscripts from Glastonbury Abbey' (*ASE* 23.265–81) attributes two more manuscripts (to the two he has already shown) to Glastonbury provenance (see *ASE* 16 [1987]). The first of these is CCCC 340, which is of Continental origin, datable to the end of the ninth or beginning of the tenth century. This manuscript may have arrived at Glastonbury from Saint-Amand via St Augustine's, Canterbury. The second manuscript is the composite BL, Harley 3020, comprised of three booklets and datable to the end of the tenth or beginning of the eleventh century. It contains the name of William Foxe in a hand of the second-half of the sixteenth century; Foxe was associated with Glastonbury. Carley traces the complex history of this hagiographical manuscript's three booklets to conclude that, by the second quarter of the sixteenth century, all three booklets were at Glastonbury, though their origins appear to be Glastonbury, Canterbury and Winchester respectively.

Nicholas Orchard provides a transcription and discussion of 'An Eleventh-Century Missal Fragment' (*ASE* 23.283–9) found in BL, Harley 271's front and back flyleaves. This separated bifolium can be dated to the last decades of the eleventh century (style IV Anglo-Caroline minuscule). The scribe, who seemed to have difficulty in copying his exemplar, misdivides words and shows unusual orthography copied from the source. By collating the variants with over twenty extant missals, Orchard discovers that it is three early fourteenth-century Paris Missals that most closely agree with the fragment. Orchard points out that as the fragmented text is corrupt, 'there is no easy way of escaping the fact that whoever read from this book delivered a form of solemn nonsense to his congregation'.

Linda Nix offers two studies of manuscript layout in the Anglo-Saxon period. The first, 'Manuscript Layout and the Production of the Text in Anglo-Saxon England: A Preliminary Examination' (*GLM* 25.17–23), considers how the design of a manuscript can affect the text, and how the nature of the text itself can affect the manuscript design. The way the text is laid out can also have important implications for its transmission. Nix uses the example of the *Vita Guthlaci* and pays particular attention to CCCC 307 and CCCC 389 to illustrate the ways in which each version of the text can be thought of as 'an alternative text', with 'a different historical existence'. Nix also contributes 'Early Medieval Book Design in England: The Influence of Manuscript Design on the Transmission of the Text' to *A Millennium of the Book*, edited by Robin Myers and Michael Harris. Disconcertingly, this article begins with essentially the same two paragraphs as her article in the *Gazette*, though it turns out to be a very much expanded essay on similar lines of approach. Nix looks at Gospel Books and the layout of the texts in these, followed by an analysis of the transmission of the *Vita Guthlaci* in CCCC 307 and CCCC 389 (again). She also discusses Bede's *Historia ecclesiastica* and other texts in a number of manuscripts, commenting on the physical aspects such as script and embellishment to determine in her conclusion, which echoes that of her other article, that 'in historiated reality [the vehicle and its content] are inseparable'.

David N. Dumville's 'John Bale, Owner of St Dunstan's Benedictional' (*N&Q* 41.291–5) discusses a letter from Bale to Matthew Parker in 1560 concerning 'bokes of antiquite'. The focus is a 'Benedictionarium archiepiscopale Dunstani' to which Bale refers as having been in his possession and which Dumville seeks to identify. Having considered and dismissed some manuscript candidates, Dumville turns to surviving fragments, and concludes that three extant benedictional fragments in a monumental Square minuscule may be from the book which Bale mentions. Also in *N&Q* 41, Hiroshi Ogawa investigates the identity of 'The Retoucher in Mss. Junius 85 and 86' (6–10). Mistakes in the corrections made by this retoucher and his punctuation practices suggest that he may not be a medieval scribe/reader, as noted by some scholars. Ogawa, following up the codicological and palaeographical evidence, demonstrates that the retoucher was a seventeenth-century member of Voss's circle, and may even have been Junius himself.

3. Social, Cultural and Intellectual Background

Rob Meens gives 'A Background to Augustine's Mission to Anglo-Saxon England' (*ASE* 23.5–17), where he draws attention to the *Libellus responsionum*, a letter written by Gregory the Great to Augustine, and used by Bede in his *Historia ecclesiastica*. The *Libellus* provides information on the history of the conversion of Anglo-Saxon England by British missionaries, and it is this aspect which Meens focuses on. Questions concerning ritual purity addressed in the *Libellus*, for example, suggest that these were issues raised during the conversion by Augustine also. Meens proposes that Augustine is referring to beliefs on impurity, held by British bishops and disseminated to English Christians, for which recourse to Papal authority was required for clarification. Ian Wood also deals with 'The Mission of Augustine of Canterbury to the English' (*Speculum* 69.1–17), addressing the difficulties inherent in the traditional narrative of Augustine's mission as told by Bede. For example, Bede's account of Augustine's arrrival in Kent details Æthelbert's fear of the Christian missionary, a strange narrative feature considering Æthelbert's marriage to a Christian. Wood points out that episodes like this seem more likely to be narrative embellishment rather than true accounts, and thus can be seen to reflect contemporary authorial concerns.

Barrie Cox looks at 'The Pattern of Old English *burh* in early Lindsey' (*ASE* 23.35–56), in particular in the territory of the Lindisfaran in Lindsey, and suggests that the pattern of the fortified strongholds in Northern Lincolnshire indicates 'an independent Lindsey guarding against incursions'. This defence system was established in the early seventh century in response to threats from neighbouring kingdoms.

In 'The "Three Orders" of Society in Anglo-Saxon England' (*ASE* 23.103–32), Timothy E. Powell assesses the ways in which the idea of the Three Orders was used differently by pre-Conquest authors, particularly Alfred, Wulfstan and Ælfric. He postulates a non-extant Frankish source for this motif; its use can be seen as 'a model for stability and unity', though the contexts for the incorporation of the idea differ markedly.

Scott Gwara's erudite and important 'Manuscripts of Aldhelm's *Prosa de Virginitate* and the Rise of Hermeneutic Literacy in Tenth-Century England' (*SMed* 35.101–59) examines the role of the hermeneutic style in Anglo-Saxon England and Aldhelm's part in promoting this style. He also discusses the re-emergence of Aldhelm as a 'curriculum author' in the tenth century. He provides a detailed analysis of the seventeen extant manuscripts of Aldhelm's *Prosa de Virginitate*, paying particular attention to the complex glosses within these texts and giving numerous revised accounts of the manuscripts. From his analysis, he proposes that there were two schools of hermeneutic Latin in this period, Glastonbury and Canterbury, and that it is Dunstan who raised the reputation of Aldhelm. In a second article on the same text, Scott Gwara publishes 'Unpublished Old English Inked Glosses from Manuscripts of Aldhelm's *Prosa de Virginitate*' (*NM* 95.267–71). These glosses, missed in previous publications, are *dracena*, *aule*, *geglencgat*, *wilsamhede*, *andresnum*, *cwyst*, *italian*, *rum* and *clæfre*. Andy Orchard has published *The Poetic Art of Aldhelm* in the Cambridge Studies in Anglo-Saxon England series, to be reviewed fully in *YWES* 76.

Frederick M. Biggs writes on 'Alcuin's Use of Augustine and Jerome: A Source and Recollection Identified' (*N&Q* 41.3–6). He looks at Alcuin's *Adversus Felicem Urgellitanum libri vii*, in which Augustine's letter to Prosper and Hilary is cited as a source. Biggs traces the citation to Augustine's *De praedestinatione sanctorum*. In Alcuin's *De animae ratione*, he cites an exchange between Augustine and Jerome, the source of which is a response by Jerome to Augustine mentioned in the latter's *Retractions*.

Stephanie Hollis and Michael J. Wright examine and print four Old English translations from the *Medicina de Quadrupedibus* which appear in the very damaged manuscript, Cotton Galba a.xiv (in 'The Remedies in British Library, MS Cotton Galba A.xiv, fols. 139 and 136r', *N&Q* 41.146–7).

Phillip Pulsiano gives 'Additional Evidence for an Old English "Canterbury Vocabulary"' (*NM* 95.257–65), which extends the lexical data provided by other scholars for the existence of vocabulary in Old English texts associated with Canterbury. Pulsiano gathers his material from the vocabularies of the *Liber Scintillarum*, the *Regularis Concordia* in BL, Tiberius A.iii, and prayers extant in a number of manuscripts. The characterizing feature of this vocabulary is its 'unextraordinary' nature, and it includes items such as *cynehelm*, *inlenda* and its variants, *behydan*, *gyrla*, *ferdwic* and *hunigteare*. In a second article, Pulsiano edits the 'Old English *Nomina ventorum*' (*SN* 66.15–26) from a number of extant manuscripts including BL, Cotton Tiberius C.i, Harley 3667, Harley 1005, Royal 10.A.viii, and CUL, Kk.3.21. He provides parallel lists and diagrams of the names of the winds showing the variant forms found between manuscripts and the confusions which appear in the names given. He demonstrates that the text in the CUL manuscript, the oldest, is the most accurate, and that errors arising in other manuscripts are unsurprising considering the complexity of the material and the different traditions which existed in Anglo-Saxon England. Notwithstanding the difficulties encountered in dealing with this material, the scribes of the period evidently found the texts interesting and worthy of study.

Mechtild Gretsch, in an exemplary article, analyses 'The Language of the "Fonthill Letter"' (*ASE* 23.57–102). This document (for which see *YWES* 73.87), ostensibly dating from the early tenth century, is subjected to a rigorous phonological, lexical and stylistic analysis to ascertain the state of the language at that date and the author's own use of Old English in his composition of the letter. The orthography of the text is shown to be remarkably consistent and representative of phonetic emulation, and perhaps demonstrates that the author was an educated layman rather than a professional scribe. Lexically, a high percentage of *hapax legomena* are legal terms and possibly colloquialisms. Stylistically, the letter is composed of 'pragmatic prose' certainly dictated by, if not written by, Ealdormann Ordlaf.

Alfred Bammesberger discusses *rodi* and *blodæ* as 'Two Archaic Forms in the *Ruthwell Cross* Inscription' (*ES* 75.97–103). He shows that both forms can be paralleled within the dialectal system of early Anglian and can be regarded as linguistically correct.

Ingeborg M. Bajema collates the twenty-seven occurrences of *eam* to ascertain its interpretation in 'The Mother's Brother: An Investigation into the Meaning of Old English *eam*' (*Neophil* 78.633–43). In sixteen of the cases, the term identifies the brother of the mother; in four cases, the exact relationship is indeterminate. In the *Orosius*, it is possible that the term means the brother of a father or mother, a precursor to the semantic generalization that the term was later to undergo.

David W. Porter provides a detailed stylistic analysis of Ælfric Bata's Colloquies in 'The Latin Syllabus in the Anglo-Saxon Monastic Schools' (*Neophil* 78.463–82) to determine what the Colloquies can tell us about the eleventh-century educational system. The main goal of the Colloquies appears to be to teach the students to communicate naturally in Latin. As such, they emphasize fluency of communication over grammatical correctness, using simulated real-life situations which focus on the everyday situations of the monastery.

Mary Clayton's 'Centralism and Uniformity versus Localism and Diversity: The Virgin and Native Saints in the Monastic Reform' (*Peritia* 8.95–106) aims to expand upon the historical implications of the cult of the Virgin and to view this cult against those of other saints in the second half of the tenth century. Clayton's view, that the dominance of the Virgin's cult in the reform period outweighed all others, is at variance with other scholars' work which illustrates the fostering of Anglo-Saxon saints, especially those of royal origin, in the same period. Clayton contends that these readings, however, are compatible in that the fostering of the Marian cult and those of martyred royals both aimed at creating a political and monastic spiritual unity and propaganda for the kings of Wessex, which extended outside of Wessex itself. Subsequently, though, this unity of purpose fragmented as saints, including Mary, became localized in veneration. The cult of Mary as a dominant unifying monastic and political phenomenon was curtailed in the post-Reform period by the encroachment of local cults, apart, it seems, from at Winchester and Canterbury.

4. Literature: General

A much-needed addition to the corpus of affordable student textbooks giving accessible commentary on Old English poetry has been published in the form of the *Companion to Old English Poetry,* edited by Henk Aertsen and Rolf H. Bremmer Jr. This book, more than many others that claim to be addressed to an undergraduate audience, hits the mark. It contains eleven essays on Old English verse, all of which outline major issues involved in studying the poetry and which synopsize scholarship to date on individual poems and different approaches. Four of the essays deal with general issues, while seven address specific texts and will be dealt with in the appropriate sections. The first essay is Allen Frantzen's 'The Diverse Nature of Old English Poetry'. Frantzen provides an overview of the body of verse and of various cultural and critical approaches to it. Having discussed the 'fixed' nature of the verse – its metrical structure, its lexicon, and the tradition of the canon – Frantzen debates the eventfulness of the text, incorporating a précis of recent critical work in this area. He points out, using manuscript evidence, that there is a greater diversity of material than might at first appear to be the case and calls for a more open approach to ways of reading these texts. Mildred Budny offers the second essay, on 'Old English Poetry in its Material Context'. She provides an account of the methods of manuscript production in Anglo-Saxon England, and the subsequent history of the extant codices. She discusses not only the manuscripts but also the other media onto which poetry is inscribed. Importantly for any student coming to these texts for the first time, Budny outlines the methods of textual transference from the manuscript to the printed page, with the numerous alterations that the editorial process has traditionally involved. This is a useful reminder for undergraduates, who all too often take what they see on the page in the textbook as the real and unchallengeable text. In 'The Shorter Heroic Verse', Graham D. Caie begins by warning against the romanticizing of the heroic nature of Anglo-Saxons on the basis of their literature. He ranges widely through verse that is classified as heroic – *Deor*, *Widsith*, *Waldere*, *Beowulf*, *Brunanburh* and *Maldon*, for example. These works, in which Germanic society is enshrined, not only represent a literary recreation of the Anglo-Saxon heritage, but also function as education and entertainment for the contemporary audience as well as a late twentieth-century one. In '*Christ and Satan* and *The Dream of the Rood*', David F. Johnson, beginning with Cædmon, provides the context for the religious verse which dominates the poetic corpus. In discussing the two main texts of the title, he illustrates the combination of innovation and tradition, and demonstrates the variety and quality of the verse.

Garland's Basic Readings in Anglo-Saxon England series includes this year *Old English Shorter Poems: Basic Readings* edited by Katherine O'Brien O'Keeffe. It contains nineteen important and well-selected essays divided into two sections: 'Critical Perspectives' and 'Essays on Individual Poems'. The majority of essays are republished here to provide an excellent volume for students and scholars alike. The texts covered include *The Battle of Maldon*, *The Seafarer*, *The Wanderer*, Riddles, *The Wife's Lament*, *Wulf and Eadwacer* and *Widsið*, and the range of approaches is varied and contemporary. Each of the essays on specific texts will be mentioned below, but here, one of the essays specially commissioned for this volume can be summarized. Roy Michael Liuzza's 'The Return of the Repressed: Old and New Theories in Old English Literary Criticism' might appropriately have begun the volume, as it provides perhaps the best context for the book as a whole. In this essay, Liuzza surveys the prevailing critical approaches of Anglo-Saxonists in the last three decades. 'Theories', Liuzza states, 'make possible our readings; they focus attention on certain areas and repress others.' Among the dominant theories relevant to Anglo-Saxon studies are new criticism, oral-formulaic theory, and exegetics. Liuzza treats each of these, and traces their evolution and practices, focusing on the manner in which theory was foregrounded by some and resisted by other scholars. This balanced study shows how 'readers of Old English literature must realize that their understanding is limited by the very theories that make it possible'. He thus rightly privileges the ambiguities and complexities of the literature over the attempts to define, to delimit and to disambiguate it. Among the most recent theories, for example, post-structuralism is shown to emphasize precisely the elusiveness of meaning; and manuscript studies can be seen to foreground the physical context of texts, which also contributes to this reinvestigation of the uncertainties of the literature. It is this latter approach which Liuzza regards as a 'return to the "most immediate context"' that is the potential way forward for all scholars in the field. In the same section, Gillian R. Overing offers an examination of the metonymic principles at work in poems such as *Beowulf*, *The Wanderer*, *Christ and Satan* and *Daniel*. In 'Some Aspects of Metonymy in Old English Poetry', she demonstrates the immediacy of the poetry for its audience, which was aided by this literary device of contiguity rather than by metaphor. Fred C. Robinson's 'Old English in its Most Immediate Context' and Martin Irvine's 'Anglo-Saxon Literary Theory Exemplified in Old English Poems: Interpreting the Cross in *The Dream of the Rood* and *Elene*' are also reprinted in the 'Critical Perspectives' section of the volume.

From Anglo-Saxon to Early Middle English: Studies Presented to E. G. Stanley, edited by Malcom Godden, Douglas Gray and Terry Hoad, contains eleven essays and a bibliography of Stanley's writings. The essays' range reflects Stanley's own broad base of writings: the literary, the linguistic, the metrical and the cultural aspects of texts in Old and early Middle English are represented. Some of the contributions can be reviewed here; the others will be dealt with in the appropriate sections. Essays that deal with early Middle English are Robert Burchfield's 'Line-End Hyphens in the *Ormulum* Manuscript', Derek Brewer's 'The Paradox of the Archaic and the Modern in Layamon's *Brut*', and Douglas Gray's 'An Early English *Entführung*: A Note on *Floris and Blauncheflur*'. Roberta Frank discusses the differences between poetry and prose before focusing on the vocabulary of each form and, particularly, on poetic vocabulary which was used in prose. In 'Poetic Words in Late Old English Prose', Frank analyses fifteen poetic simplices including *brytta*, *guma*, *folde*, *blican* and *sefa*; their contexts and definitions are given, and critical commentary on them offered. Such an analysis throws light on the longevity of these lexical items, raises issues of style, and helps to clarify their interpretations. Terry Hoad aims to advance the debate on the *-an* ending in the genitive plural of weak adjectives and substantives in 'Old English Weak Genitive Plural *-an*: Towards Establishing the Evidence'. He assesses the examples of this morphological phenomenon as used by Sievers and finds the majority of them to be dubious instances. He then conducts his own survey based on a variety of texts and concludes that there is sound evidence for the occurrence of this form in late Old English at least. In 'The Englishness of Old English', Bruce Mitchell debates the issue of labelling Old English and Middle English as creoles in origin. In assessing the critical arguments for and against this theory, Mitchell points out the continuity between Old and Middle English, aligning himself firmly with the traditional view which emphasizes this continuity. He demonstrates his view convincingly by the use of prose and verse examples to conclude forcefully that 'Old English is where the English language began [. . .] So its place in any University syllabus ought to be assured.' We neglect it at our peril.

Nida Louise Surber-Meyer's study of *Gift and Exchange in the Anglo-Saxon Poetic Corpus: A Contribution Towards the Representation of Wealth* works towards illustrating the literary motif of treasure as non-reflective of real practice in the Anglo-Saxon period. The study is one that applies anthropological, linguistic and literary approaches, as well as gift theory, to the corpus of Old English poetry as defined by the *ASPR*. The volume begins with an historical and legal survey which looks at critics' views of the Anglo-Saxons' gift exchanges and love of wealthy artefacts; wills and charters, for instance, are analysed, and the terms used to denote the types of exchange are examined and listed in an appendix. The second section of the work outlines the theory of gift giving and exchange, before applying this theory to *Beowulf*. The 'Analysis of the Representation of Wealth' ranges broadly through Old English poetic material and historical analogues, dealing with each of the *ASPR* volumes in turn, and surveys the depiction of exchange within the texts (appendices listing Old English terms used are provided for each). *Genesis*, *Andreas*, *Christ* and *Beowulf* feature most prominently among the many poems discussed. The conclusion emphasizes the balance that appears to be highlighted in the poems' depiction of wealth and gift-giving: a balance between having sufficient wealth to be generous, yet avoiding avarice and hoarding by not being too wealthy; a balance between the 'pagan' and 'archaic' treatment of exchange (in *Beowulf*, for example) and 'the mistrust [of] the effects of this gift-giving material' linked with overtly Christian remarks. The poems are, according to the author, 'situated in a commodity-economy' which is therefore not contemporary with the 'gift-giving economy' described in the texts themselves.

Britton J. Harwood and Gillian R. Overing, eds., *Class and Gender in Early English Literature: Intersections*, has evolved from a number of sessions held at

Kalamazoo which examine the interdependency of gender and class in medieval texts. The editors deal with the problems raised by these issues in the foreword and provide a scholarly contextualization for the essays that follow. Three essays concern Old English texts and are dealt with in the appropriate sections below; those concerning Middle English are dealt with in chapter III.

Another gender-based approach to medieval studies can be found in Clare A. Lees's edited volume *Medieval Masculinities: Regarding Men in the Middle Ages*. This book contains ten articles covering Anglo-Saxon Literature, Middle English, and Medieval French, Italian and Spanish subjects from the tenth to the fifteenth centuries. It looks at men from the perspective of gender studies, 'putting them back into the picture [. . .] in order to understand the multifaceted dynamic of male experience'. The three sections of the book examine men in institutions, and epic, and empire. Of interest to Anglo-Saxonists will be Jo Ann McNamara's 'The *Herrenfrage*: The Restructuring of the Gender System, 1050–1150', which explores the results for men and women of the imposition of clerical celibacy. Clare A. Lees offers 'Men and *Beowulf*', which will be discussed in section 8 below.

Allen Frantzen's 'Who Do These Anglo-Saxon(ist)s Think They Are, Anyway?' (*Æstel* 2.1–43) addresses the present and future states of Anglo-Saxon studies and is prompted by a review article of his edited book, *Desire for Origins*. Viewing himself and others as representatives of 'revisionist medievalism', Frantzen challenges those traditionalists whom he seems to regard as the opposition, and who, he believes, regard him as an intruder. While bemoaning the personal nature of the traditionalists' views of his work, he himself engages in a defensive and personal stand. Once past this, though, Frantzen goes on to demonstrate the ways in which Anglo-Saxon studies are advancing – in the area of electronic media, for instance – and he discusses the exciting open-endedness of the field as a whole.

Timo Lauttamus provides a detailed analysis of 'Metrical Structures in Finnish and Old English Prosody: A Diachronic Study of Gemination' (*NM* 95.273–306), in which he investigates the tendency to generalize the heavy syllable to main-stress position at the expense of the light syllable in West Germanic and in vernacular Finnish.

Jonathan Wilcox offers an investigation into 'Anglo-Saxon Literary Humour: Towards a Taxonomy' (*Thalia* 14.9–20), in which he examines the different types and causes of laughter in Anglo-Saxon literature before discussing the humour of Old English texts themselves. Methods of humour can be categorized as litotes, irony, puns, parody and dramatic irony, for example. This survey ranges through texts such as *Apollonius of Tyre*, *Maldon*, the Riddles, *Judith*, the *Prose Solomon and Saturn*, *The Riming Poem* and *Waldere*.

Susan E. Deskis offers a study of 'The Gnomic Woman in Old English Poetry' (*PQ* 73.133–49). She focuses on *Precepts* and *Maxims I* and *II*, where women are, for instance, shown positively in the role of motherhood and as the noblewoman giving gifts and sharing in her husband's decision making. The behaviour of wives is described in a balanced and conservative manner, and is not representative of the misogynistic portrayal of women seen in much Christian Latin literature.

In 'Experienced Time in Old English Texts and Illuminations' (*SN* 66.27–34), Peter Richardson combines an investigation of the use of verbal aspect with an analysis of parallel illuminations that show a sequence of events in the Hexateuch and the translation of Enoch in *Genesis*. He demonstrates how episodes in the illumination correspond with aspectually marked clauses in the text to enhance narratorial technique.

William Vantuono has edited selections of *Old and Middle English Texts with Accompanying Textual and Linguistic Apparatus* which include texts from the Anglo-Saxon period up to the end of the medieval period. The work is aimed towards a history of the language course rather than a literature course, since the excerpts would be insufficient for the latter. Vantuono includes a basic outline of Old English language together with standard declensions and paradigms. The texts are given a brief introduction and have accompanying parsed glosses. *Cædmon's Hymn* is printed, together with eighteen lines of *The Wanderer*, five lines of Ælfric's *Homily on Saint Gregory*, twenty-four verse lines from Alfred's *Boethius*, and eleven lines from *Beowulf*. None of these extracts is edited afresh here, and while the book may serve the purposes of a rudimentary historical survey that operates via translation exercises, its uses outside this curriculum would be very limited.

5. The Exeter Book

Bernard J. Muir's edition of *The Exeter Anthology of Old English Poetry: An Edition of Exeter Dean and Chapter MS 3501* is a reasonably priced two-volume set which aims to present a comprehensive edition of the poems contained in the Exeter Book. The introduction discusses the manuscript's history, description, and previous critical editions and transcripts of its contents. Muir provides a good deal of information about the physical layout of the manuscript: detailed analysis of the gatherings, the preparation of the folios, drypoint drawings, marginalia and glosses are all included in the discussion. He is of the opinion that the anthologist drew the material from a variety of sources. In considering the sectional divisions of the codex, Muir deals first with the critical debate to date. He proposes that the divisions were copied by the scribe from the exemplar(s) but with an overall organizational design in mind, creating a definite sense of an anthology. The first eight poems, for example, are 'related thematically in their concern with different models for Christian living'. Such a theory does not correlate with Conner's careful examination of the composition of the manuscript as three booklets (see *YWES* 74.81–2). Muir gives an overview of the manuscript's language to show that the scribe was 'more conscientious and systematic' than has been noted, a view which he uses to justify his policy of not normalizing the textual editions. He also presents new data regarding the corrections and alterations made to the manuscript by a scribe and/or corrector concerned with, among other things, standardizing the spelling of the manuscript. The question Muir asks in relation to the attempt to standardize, is why so many 'unintelligible forms (or *non*-words) still remain'. His answer that this may be because the 'one scribe, involved somewhere (and perhaps) latterly in the chain of transmission of the texts, may have been a non-native' is not particularly convincing. Muir elaborates on this theory by showing that the scribe was apt to confuse graphs in the exemplar (*s*-*f*, or *m* for *ni*, for example), but very many Old English scribes were prone to these types of misreading. The second volume contains an expansive commentary and a 'Sources and Analogues' section for each poem, and complete bibliography on the texts.

Alexandra Hennessey Olsen's 'Old English Women, Old English Men: A Reconsideration of "Minor" Characters' (in O'Brien O'Keeffe) is a specially commissioned essay which provides a feminist perspective on Anglo-Saxon England aiming to 're-vision' men and women in the period. She seeks to examine the female point of view in Old English poetry, focusing on *Wulf and Eadwacer* and *Deor* to move away from the paradigm of the heroic Anglo-Saxon male and passive female. Olsen sees the heroic reading of *Deor* as less important than an interpretation which foregrounds the misfortune of ordinary men. Likewise in the discussion of *Wulf and Eadwacer*, Olsen, by re-examining and repunctuating the poem, interprets the text as a representation of the female leader's point of view, rather than that of the usual passive and suffering subject. Joyce Hill's '*Widsið* and the Tenth Century' is reprinted in the same volume.

Also in O'Brien O'Keeffe, Edward B. Irving writes a sensitive new essay on 'Heroic Experience in the Old English Riddles'. He proposes an examination of the riddles to gain a new perspective on the heroic experience which is different from that preserved in heroic verse. The playful mode of the Shield riddle, for instance, allows for the safe expression of a 'non-heroic subtext', that of the anonymous defensive soldier experiencing 'meaningless suffering and death'. Similarly, the Anchor and Badger riddles can be read in this way, the latter interestingly illustrating a female defensive fighter. Irving moves through a wide range of riddles (such as the Storm, Sword, Bow, Spear, Ram, Flail, Well Sweep, Ox, Gold and Inkhorn) to illustrate a variety of interpretations denoting another side to the heroic: the object made into a weapon unwillingly (Spear, Ram); the enslaved or abducted (Well Sweep, Ox); or the prisoner of war (Inkhorn). Such readings show, as Irving puts it, 'the darker side of those bright exhilarations of combat and slaughter that infuse heroic poetry'.

Wim Tigges aims at a student audience in a discussion of the riddles in 'Snakes and Ladders: Ambiguity and Coherence in the Exeter Book Riddles and Maxims' (in Aertsen and Bremmer). He looks at the riddles and maxims as examples of the 'heroic, Germanic, didactic, and Christian' which represent 'unity-in-variety'. In so doing, he summarizes scholarship to date and introduces the texts in a reader-friendly manner as illustrative of the Anglo-Saxon scops' and clerics' interest in the variety of God's creation. John W. Tanke proposes a reading of the sexual riddles as 'classifications [which] exert an ideological force whose aim is not simply to represent but to construct a sexual order' (in '*Wonfeax wale*: Ideology and Figuration in the Sexual Riddles of the Exeter Book', in Harwood and Overing). He focuses, in particular, on riddles 25 and 12, to look at problems of class, ethnicity and gender, and the 'ideological dimensions of the double-entendre' riddle.

In Aertsen and Bremmer, T. A. Shippey analyses '*The Wanderer* and *The Seafarer* as Wisdom Poetry'. He gives the definitions and types of the group of poems often classed as wisdom poetry. He concentrates on *The Wanderer* and *The Seafarer*, showing the critical debate on, for example, the number of voices in each text, and the ways in which they might be interpreted and classified. He offers his own view of the substance of the poems, concluding that as we know little of the poems' intended audience, both may be regarded essentially as 'uncluttered by presupposition'.

Republished in O'Brien O'Keeffe are three important essays on *The Seafarer*: John C. Pope's 'Second Thoughts on the Interpretation of *The Seafarer*'; Stanley B. Greenfield's 'Sylf, Seasons, Structure and Genre in *The Seafarer*'; and John F. Vickrey's 'Some Hypotheses Concerning *The Seafarer*'. O'Brien O'Keeffe has also selected Martin Green's 'Man, Time, and Apocalypse in *The Wanderer*, *The Seafarer*, and *Beowulf*' and Gerald Richman's essay, 'Speaker and Speech Boundaries in *The Wanderer*'.

Andrew Galloway attempts to discover the intellectual tradition behind Anglo-

Saxon dream theory in 'Dream Theory in *The Dream of the Rood* and *The Wanderer*' (*RES* 45.475–85). In *The Dream of the Rood*, for example, the defining feature of the dream is that the voice speaks when all human noise is quietened. This can be paralleled with Gregory's comments on dreams in his *Moralia in Job*. With regard to *The Wanderer*, Galloway applies Gregorian dream theory to illustrate the poem's 'false vision', a *vana illusio*. Galloway also examines the awakening of the dreamers within their texts in relation to Gregory's comments.

Helen T. Bennett's 'Exile and the Semiosis of Gender in Old Elegies' (in Harwood and Overing) begins by discussing the ostracism of women from heroic literature, a supression 'enhanced' by scholars until recently. She looks at the gendered nature of 'sign creation' and 'sign reception' in *The Wanderer*, *The Seafarer*, *The Wife's Lament*, and *Wulf and Eadwacer* to demonstrate that while male exiles are yet able to engage with the symbolic codes that yield meaning, female exiles 'constitute a challenge to social and linguistic structure'.

In 'Of Graves, Caves, and Subterranean Dwellings: *Eorðscræf* and *Eorðsele* in the *Wife's Lament*' (*PQ* 73.267–86), Paul Battles, commenting on the multitude of interpretations of the *Wife's Lament*, sees the narrator's dwelling as central to the debate. The *eorðscræf* and *eorðsele* have variously been read as a cave, a grave, a sunken dwelling, or a metaphorical reflection of the narrator's state of mind. Battles suggests the terms actually refer to a *souterrain*, an underground dwelling, used as a secret hideaway by a fugitive, known archaeologically to have existed, and mentioned in several literary and historical sources. He takes this reading and applies it to a full interpretation of the poem in this light. A quite different interpretation and context for the text are provided by Shari Horner in her article, 'En/Closed Subjects: *The Wife's Lament* and the Culture of Early Medieval Monasticism' (*Æstel* 2.45–61). In this intelligent reading, Horner situates the poem in the context of early monasticism and its Christian framework. She examines the 'discourse of enclosure' in the text to illustrate how it engenders the subject: the speech of the narrator shows her to operate within the cultural and physical confines representative of those of a female religious.

Henk Aertsen addresses students in his '*Wulf and Eadwacer*: A Woman's *Cri de Coeur* – For Whom, For What?' (in Aertsen and Bremmer) where he provides the text with an extensive and helpful discussion of its possible meanings and various interpretations.

'Women's Words as Weapons: Speech as Action in *The Wife's Lament*' by Barrie Ruth Straus, 'The Situation of the Narrator in the Old English *Wife's Lament*' by Karl P. Wentersdorf, Peter S. Baker's 'The Ambiguity of *Wulf and Eadwacer*' and Marijane Osborn's 'The Text and Context of *Wulf and Eadwacer*' are all republished in O'Brien O'Keeffe.

Rolf H. Bremmer Jr looks at 'Changing Perspectives on a Saint's Life, *Juliana*' (in Aertsen and Bremmer). He offers a simplified account of saints and their *vitae*, and the transmission of their cults. This includes a brief survey of the *Old English Metrical Calendar*, and of the poetic saints' lives, particularly those by Cynewulf. In his discussion of *Juliana*, Bremmer illustrates the conventions of hagiography, likening the genre to the folktale and Propp's paradigm of the fairytale. He also elaborates on certain aspects of the text such as familiar oral narrative techniques and allegorical interpretation.

Jane Roberts investigates the use of the A3 verse form, the examples of anacrusis and hypermetric half-lines in *Christ III* in 'Some Reflections on the Metre of *Christ III*' (in Godden et al.). She looks at the combinations of verse types to show how frequently patterns repeat themselves, and the way in which the poet is able to exploit available rhythms.

Thomas D. Hill proposes an Augustinian analogue for a Christian paradox explicit in Cynewulf's *Christ II* in 'The Anchor of Hope and the Sea of this World: *Christ II*, 850–66' (*ES* 75.289–92). Hill notes the paradox in Cynewulf's description of the Christian's present hazardous journey and yet present salvation in Christ's harbour. This ambiguity occurs in Augustine's commentary on I John, but is adapted and expanded by Cynewulf to include Anglo-Saxon seafaring imagery, thereby synthesizing the Christian-Germanic literary traditions.

6. The Poems of the Vercelli Book

Margaret Jennings's '*Rood* and Ruthwell: The Power of Paradox' (*ELN* 31.3.6–12) suggests that the paradoxes of the poem and the portions of text inscribed on the Ruthwell Cross lie in the religious context influencing both. The central paradox surrounds the nature of the cross as instrument of death and giver of life, and its use as a symbol of the 'divine/human antithesis'. The Ruthwell Cross concretely illustrates the paradox as it is reflected in the poem.

In 'Text as Revelation: Constantine's Dream in *Elene*' (*Neophil* 78.645–53), Antonina Harbus examines the adaptations made by Cynewulf in the episode where the Cross is revealed to Constantine. The poem contains a psychological aspect and an emphasis on symbols which can be regarded as especially meaningful to the Anglo-Saxon audience. The poem itself, and its inclusion of the dream, foreground the process of revelation which might lead to an 'imaginative and contemplative reaction' in its audience. This aim is heightened by the parallels that Cynewulf draws between his former state of mind and Constantine's before his dream, and illustrates Cynewulf's concerns with the spiritual aspects of the legend.

7. The Junius Manuscript

Barbara Raw's important 'The Construction of Oxford, Bodleian Library, Junius 11' (in Richards) is an analysis of the physical make-up of the codex which demonstrates the original plan behind the manuscript's creation and how the codex was added to and altered during the course of its early history.

'Oppositions and their Operation in the Old English *Exodus*' (*Neophil* 78.165-70) by Steven F. Kruger discusses how the *Exodus* poet sets up the central oppositions of the narrative to give rise to the poem's unique treatment of the Old Testament story. For example, the poet establishes the Israelites as 'sea-faring' people, while the Egyptians are land-dwellers, in order to show the sea as the salvation of the former and damnation of the latter. Good and evil are clearly delineated in a manner which directs the reader to allegory, and aids the moral resolution of the poem. Kruger explains, though, that the distinction between good and evil is blurred by the humanity of the Israelites and Egyptians, which forces the reader to focus on the 'process of human beings making moral choices'. William Helder's 'Abraham and the Old English *Exodus*' (in Aertsen and Bremmer) examines *Exodus* in the general context of Anglo-Saxon Old Testament verse and surveys the critical scholarship on the poem. He goes on to explore the significance of the *topos* of Abraham, referred to seven times in the poem. This motif is one that reinforces the poem's 'essential thematic unity [derived from] the typology of the *ecclesia*'.

Andrew Breeze, in 'The Book of Habakkuk and the Old English *Exodus*' (*ES* 75.210–13), proposes that the Book of Habakkuk is a source of portions of the Old English poem; for example, a reading of 'nets of death' for *wælnet* at line 202a can be supported by Habakkuk 1:14–17.

Peter J. Lucas's 1977 edition of *Exodus* has been reprinted in an updated form this year: emendations have been made to the text and the notes, and bibliographical additions are given. The edition contains a very good introduction examining the manuscript context, a palaeographical discussion, with an analysis of style, metre, language, sources, date and origin. Given that the text is just under £11, it still remains a reasonably priced complete edition.

Antonina Harbus looks at 'Nebuchadnezzar's Dreams in the Old English *Daniel*' (*ES* 75.489–508). She compares the poem to its source to investigate the changes made by the poet and the ways in which these adaptations reflect contemporary concerns. The major change is the poet's focus on Nebuchadnezzar rather than Daniel and the reduction in the significance of dreams in the Old English. In the poet's retelling of the first of Nebuchadnezzar's dreams, for example, the Vulgate version is dramatically adapted: Daniel himself interprets the king's dream, which itself is different from its source; Daniel's prophetic role later in the poem is thus anticipated by the poet at this point. Harbus's overall examination shows that the poet is more interested in the failings of Nebuchadnezzar than in concentrating on Daniel; that dreams as signifiers of divine providence are useful only if heeded; and the result is something more akin to a commentary on the biblical text rather than a translation. The audience expectation as deduced from authorial adaptation is one of didacticism concerning 'active atonement [rather than] Old Testament prophecy'.

Phyllis Portnoy reassesses the relationship between *Daniel* and *Christ and Satan* and the liturgy for Holy Saturday in '"Remnant" and Ritual: The Place of *Daniel* and *Christ and Satan* in the Junius Epic' (*ES* 75.408–22). Placing the texts firmly in the context of the lections for Holy Saturday, Portnoy shows that the texts illustrate a 'final representation and resolution' to the alternatives of 'faith and apostasy, judgement and deliverance'.

Robert Emmett Finnegan studies 'Christ as Narrator in the Old English *Christ and Satan*' (*ES* 75.2–16) to show that the major theme and subject as well as the narratorial voice are Christ. This proposal is illustrated by examples of the first-hand knowledge of the narrator that permits him to describe events in the poem without reference to sources or authorities. The narrator, for example, suggests that he has spent time in hell, has heard and seen Satan himself, and can recount Eve's words because he was present. Christ also speaks as man in the poem, identifying himself as a sinner, and directing the audience to salvation. By such a narratorial technique, Christ instructs his Christian audience in a direct and effective manner.

In 'Eve's "Weaker" Mind in *Genesis B*, Line 590' by Fred C. Robinson (in Robinson), the interpretation of the phrase *wacran hige* is investigated. It describes Eve's failing in succumbing to the tempter. Usually, the phrase is translated as 'weaker mind' but Robinson shows that by analysing the occurrences of *wac* in Old English and in the cognate Old Saxon, a meaning of 'wanting in courage' is the more appropriate.

8. The *Beowulf* Manuscript

E. G. Stanley's volume, *In the Foreground: 'Beowulf'*, is cited on the book-jacket as 'a book that no scholar or critic of Old English can afford to ignore': rightly so. This volume, which is much broader in scope than the title might suggest, represents decades of formidable scholarship and intellectual engagement. It is divided into three sections: 'What is Said of *Beowulf*: *Beowulf* in Literary History', 'What is Known of *Beowulf*', and 'Indexes' (of bibliographical citations, of authors of writings, of words and phrases, and a general index). The book as a whole offers a review of, a challenge to, and a way forward in scholarship on *Beowulf* certainly, but also on Old English verse in general – ranging across much of the poetic corpus as it does. The first section deals with the poem and its critical history 'Up to the Second World War', and 'In the Last Fifty Years'. Stanley discusses the beginnings of criticism on the poem, which was at once recognized as heroic though numerous other classifications apply and have been applied. All the great names of *Beowulf* scholarship are mentioned – Grimm, Müllenhoff, Kemble, Grein – as the evolution of critical publications is traced. The last five decades of work on *Beowulf* are treated thematically: with regard to 'Etymology and wordplay', for example; as 'Oral poetry'; as 'Fact and fiction'; as an allegory, and with regard to its date. Stanley's erudition, as well as his sharp wit, are everywhere apparent in this section. Of some scholars, he comments: 'Silence is a valuable present from the critic to the reader when the critic's foundations are weak in scholarship and critical good sense seems out of reach.' The second section is comprised of chapters III–VI: 'Uncertainties of the Date and Transmission of *Beowulf*' opens this section and deals with the impossibility of studying Old English verse with any sense of chronology, as so little is actually known. What can be discerned, though, is a sense of what constitutes good and bad poetic achievement: '*Beowulf* [. . .] is good', but far too much other verse is also praised. *Beowulf*'s transmission is considered for the information it can yield, along with the language of the poem and its verse style, as well as other Old English works. Stanley moves on to 'Some Metrical Considerations, Poetic Diction and Ornamentation' in a lengthy chapter IV, and 'Prayers, Praise, and Thanksgiving' in chapter V. In themselves, these two chapters form an immensely rich discussion of details of metre, for example; of possible onomatopoetic effect; of compounding; dialectal features; and figurative devices. The texts examined include *The Phoenix*, *Brunanburh* and *Daniel*, as well as *Beowulf*, and numerous others. The chapter becomes, then, a survey of the fundamental elements of Old English verse. Chapter V looks at the issue of 'Pagan and Christian?' and begins by focusing, first, on Cædmon, and then on 'The ubiquity of prayer' in Old English writings, narrowing to a consideration of *Beowulf* (in particular, its prayers and sermons). In sum, Stanley is always empathetic to the Anglo-Saxon milieu, to the shifts in scholarship, to the lunacies of some criticism; but above all, he is sensitive to the literature and rightly sees it as the centre of all else.

J. R. Hall's 'The First Two Editions of *Beowulf*: Thorkelin's (1815) and Kemble's (1833)' (in Scragg and Szarmach) examines background material to Thorkelin's edition and discusses Sharon Turner's studies of Cotton Vitellius A.xv. Hall analyses the edition, its layout, editorial conventions, and additional material such as appendices, and notes the many textual errors made within the edition. Kemble's conservative edition and its contents are related to Thorkelin's, the former having fewer inaccuracies but showing a greater contempt for the manuscript's scribes. Both scholars, Hall concludes, while 'objects of curiosity' for modern scholars, are nevertheless 'source[s] of inspiration'.

T. A. Shippey examines the work of earlier critics of *Beowulf* in 'Local Patriotism and the Early Interpretation of *Beowulf*' (in Flemming G. Anderson and Lars Old Sauerberg, eds, *Traditions and Innovations: Papers Presented to Andreas Haarder*). Shippey shows that following Thorkelin's rediscovery of *Beowulf*, critics such as Nicholas Outzen, Karl Müllenhoff and John Kemble approached the text from subjective nationalistic viewpoints. Outzen, for example, made a determined effort to locate the poem in his own 'fatherland' of South Jutland. Interpretations of the poem became associated with contemporary nationalistic concerns. For Kemble's part, he attempted to secure the poem's German affiliations, as opposed to the Danish. These concerns to locate the poem in the critic's favoured area are, Shippey points out, still very much with us in contemporary criticism.

James W. Earl has published a wide-ranging and accessible volume which draws on fifteen years of his own considerations about *Beowulf*. *Thinking about 'Beowulf'* is organized into six chapters, with 'Two Introductions' summarizing the themes and aims of the work, which brings together portions of revised essays published in disparate books and periodicals with new work. The book is divided methodologically into two parts: the phenomenological approach of chapters 1–3 and the psychoanalytic approach of 4–6 ending with Earl's contemplations on the 'creative autonomy' of both the poet of *Beowulf* and the poem's readers. Introducing himself as a nominalist, Earl challenges those who claim to know what *Beowulf* means, seeing instead an act of originality and creativity that defies certainties. The uncertainties of the poem include, of course, its date, and Earl recognizes that this primary issue is insoluble and thus provides no basis for interpretation; its possible oral origins, a theory with which Earl does not wholly concur; and its historicity. Earl debates these and other issues fully in his six chapters: 'The Birth and Death of Civilization', 'Transformation and Chaos', 'Oral-Literate: Two Case Histories', which also discusses Cædmon and Alfred's *Meters of Boethius*, '*Beowulf* and the Men's Hall', 'Two Psychoanalytic Excursions' and '*Beowulf* and the Origins of Civilization'. The volume as a whole is infused with Earl's considerable patristic knowledge, his theoretical astuteness, and an inviting and friendly style of expression. His aim is to reach a wide audience with his intellectual musings: there is no reason why this aim should not be fulfilled.

Kevin Kiernan's controversial and influential 'The Eleventh-Century Origin of *Beowulf* and the *Beowulf* Manuscript' is republished this year in Richards. In this essay, which no Anglo-Saxonist can afford to neglect, Kiernan outlines the codicological and palaeographical evidence to support the theory that the eleventh-century date of the manuscript's production is the same as that of the poem's creation.

D. R. Howlett's 'New Criteria for Editing *Beowulf*' (in Scragg and Szarmach) focuses on the numerical artistry of the poem, with comparative reinforcement from the opening of the Greek and Latin Gospels of St John. Howlett explains the criteria for the mathematical composition of texts and advises any editor of the poem simply to listen to the author, 'to note the parallels and chiastic shapes of his verse paragraphs and fits and groups of fits', and to the numerical structuring of lines, words and syllables.

Talking of new criteria for editing *Beowulf*: two new student editions have been published this year. George Jack's *'Beowulf': A Student Edition* prints the text with a select *en face* glossary, frequently occurring words being placed in the end glossary. (Jack also edits *The Fight of Finnsburh.*) Jack's aim is to make this an edition that will be useful for all Old English students, including those who are at an early stage of their studies; this being the case, an *en face* select glossary of words in their head form does not help beginners much, since they still require a knowledge of declensions and paradigms which Jack does not give, or, at the very least, they would require a parsed form of the word used in the text. Usefully, though, copious notes in the apparatus help the student with the numerous difficult sentences in the poem. In his introduction, Jack chooses not to discuss the structure or interpretation of the poem, but instead gives a lengthy bibliography of such critical work. He does discuss manuscript context, the history of the manuscript, and transcripts of the poem. He also summarizes scholarship pertaining to the date of the codex, which would, however, be way beyond the understanding of a beginner. The introduction includes details of narrative elements, style and diction. While this is not an edition for a new student of Old English, therefore, it certainly could be used by a student who had studied elementary Old English, though still, parsed words in the facing glossary would be more useful than the head-words supplied. The second student text of *Beowulf* is E. L. Risden's translation, *'Beowulf': A Student's Edition.* This is aimed both at the student (non-specialist presumably) and the general reader, and for both of these envisaged audiences this is a useful text. The introduction provides a brief summary about the manuscript, the poem and the translation, which, while superficial, would suffice for a casual reader or student on a survey course. The translation attempts to emulate the form of Old English verse without sounding stilted, and it manages this well.

Two representative approaches to *Beowulf* are incorporated into Aertsen and Bremmer's edited volume. Joseph Harris's 'A Nativist Approach to *Beowulf*: The Case of Germanic Elegy' calls for the student of the poem to return to studying the 'common heritage, "tradition", of early Germanic oral literature'. Harris discusses the Old Man's Lament, the Lament of the Last Survivor, and their relationship to analogous Old Norse elegies to demonstrate less obvious common elements of *Beowulf* and the Germanic tradition. In 'The Christian Language and Theme of *Beowulf*', Thomas D. Hill explains to the prospective student the problem of determining the nature of *Beowulf*: Christian or pagan? His method of interpreting the poem sees it as a 'radical synthesis of pagan and Christian history'. He gives the context of the poem itself with the framework of the Anglo-Saxon mentality – looking back to the 'old' meant the pagan heritage, even if the contemporary was a Christian milieu. The *Beowulf* poet himself existed in this mindset and composed a humanistic work which recognized the value of the pagan past and that of the Christian contemporary. Such a tolerance of past and present Hill believes to be an integral part of the early medieval heritage.

Clare A. Lees's 'Men and *Beowulf*' (in Lees) concerns the nature of *Beowulf* criticism, how it utilizes masculinity as an interpretative starting point, and how we might reappraise the masculinity of the patriarchy, informing an understanding of the poem. She treats criticism of the poem (such as Tolkien's, Earl's and Overing's) as part of the continuing process of poetic interpretation. Tolkien's '*Beowulf*: The Monsters and the Critics', for example, can itself be seen to focus on Beowulf the man and Beowulf the hero to the exclusion of the feminine. While Lees says she recognizes this essay as 'very much a product of its time', this statement seems forgotten in her general analysis. Her focus on Earl's '*Beowulf* and the Origins of Civilization' and Overing's *Language, Sign, and Gender in Beowulf* highlights the importance of examining one's own critical constructs in reading the poem. Lees herself explores the patrilineal family and the 'institutionalized aggression of its warrior class' to illustrate the operation of patriarchal and masculinist ideologies.

Paul Dean has published two articles on '*Beowulf* and the Passing of Time: Part I' (*ES* 75.193–209) and '*Beowulf* and the Passing of Time: Part II' (*ES* 75.293–302). By a careful explication of the central episodes in the poem, how they relate back to and forward to events told by the poet, Dean exposes a philosophy of time influenced by Boethian and Augustinian writings. His study concerns the poem as 'about history, and even about philosophy of history'. Believing that critical appreciation of the poem has been misdirected in ceasing to see the poem as a poem, Dean proposes a focused approach to the text itself to glean the poet's own views of the past he is depicting. Dean takes us through the poem, highlighting the vagueness and the shifting of time. He dwells on the depiction of *wyrd* as an 'executant of God's design'; discusses in depth the Finn episode; and talks about the sword with which Grendel's mother is killed and Hrothgar's sermon as a gloss on the pictures on the hilt of the sword. The second section of the poem (line 2200 forward) relates 'the contrast between things of this world and of the world to come' where the first section ended with a vision of ideal relationships. In all, the poem serves to show that all human experience is subsumed in God's eternal vision.

In 'Speech as Gift in *Beowulf*' (*Speculum* 69.993–1022), Robert E. Bjork utilizes stylistic and rhetorical and gift theory to analyse the crucial nature of the direct discourse in the poem. The fragile system of gift exchange demonstrated in Germanic culture is illustrated by reference to Eddic poetry, and is coterminous with the importance of linguistic exchange seen in many Old English poems. Bjork looks at the words–deeds theme which recurs in the text to show that words had the prestige of objects to the Anglo-Saxons, but were liable to suffer the same fate. He provides a detailed analysis of the speech in parts 1 and 2 of the poem (appendices give a breakdown of speaker, line references, and types of direct discourse) outlining the differences in the parts. For example, customs are very much a part of action and speech in part 1, but become sparse in part 2 as the fabric of society disintegrates; boasts play an important and cohesive role in part 1; and boundaries of speech preserved in part 1are loosened in part 2. Bjork's sensitive and scholarly reading underlines the importance of speech to the Anglo-Saxon community and paves the way for further studies using this interesting approach.

Fred C. Robinson asks 'Did Grendel's Mother Sit on Beowulf?' (in Godden, et al.), basing his consideration on line 1545a, 'Ofsæt þa þone selegyst'. The various interpretations of this half-line offered by commentators are examined before Robinson concentrates on the definition of *ofsittan*. By analysing its occurrences in the Old English corpus, Robinson concludes that 'set upon' is the most appropriate meaning in this context. Keith P. Taylor refers to the description of Grendel's mother as *ides aglæcwif* ('lady, monster-woman') in his article '*Beowulf* 1259a: The Inherent Nobility of Grendel's Mother' (*ELN* 31.iii.13–25). He surveys critical interpretations of the phrase, which usually assume it to work in apposition to 1259b, *Grendles modor*. Taylor believes that 1259a might refer to the poet's description of Grendel's mother as innately noble. To support this view, he analyses *aglæcwif* not in apposition to the following half-line, but as a reiteration of what the poet has already said about the character: that she is both a woman (*wif*) and an *aglæca*. If *ides* is brought into the equation, the nobility of Grendel's mother is emphasized. She is one worthy of being regarded as noble in her attempts to avenge her son's death.

Christopher Manes discusses 'The Substance of Earth in *Beowulf*'s Song of Creation' (*ELN* 31.4.1–5), proposing the rejection of Klaeber's emendation of *eorðan worhte* to *eorðanworh* at line 92b. Retaining the original reading, Manes interprets the phrase as showing that the features of God's creation are created for all of humanity's sake. Mark Griffith's '*Beowulf* 1495: *Hwil dæges* = momentum temporis?' (*N&Q* 41.144–6) looks at line 1495b, concluding that its usual interpretation of 'a good part of the day' gives the hero a superhuman ability to swim for hours underwater. Griffith, thus, on the grounds of other occurrences in Old English of *hwil* and *dæg,* suggests that here *hwil* may be used in a definite sense with *dæg* in an indefinite one, resulting in the interpretion of 'a very brief space of time'.

Ruth P. Lehmann asks 'Ecgþeow the Wægmunding: Geat or Swede?' (*ELN* 31.iii.1–5). She reconstructs Beowulf's genealogy and looks at evidence in the poem to suggest that Ecgþeow was a Swede. She concludes that if this were indeed the case, then a number of problems in the text would thus be solved. Finally, Sehchi Suzuki looks at the use of variants of the A-type verse line to produce rhythmic variation in 'On the Combination of Type A Verses into Lines in *Beowulf*: A Further Consideration' (*N&Q* 41.437–9).

I turn now to work on *Judith*. Karma Lochrie's 'Gender, Sexual Violence and the Politics of War in the Old English *Judith'* (in Harwood and Overing) concerns the terms of rank and gender in the text, which become increasingly blurred as the narrative progresses, gender ultimately displacing rank with Holofernes's decapitation. Previous readings have tended to allegorize the heroine, thereby diminishing the contemporary political impact of the poem, though Lochrie paints an overly bleak picture of the results of source study of *Judith*. She chooses to concentrate on the crisis caused by the juxtaposition of the poem's violence and politics of war, and the ideology behind this. The feminist reading offered by Lochrie couches in theoretical terms the familiar: the excess of Holofernes's feast ('hypertrophied masculinity'), the violent and tyrannical implications of the golden net (representing the power of the 'masculine gaze'), and the 'interchangeability of war and sexual violence in Anglo-Saxon cultural codes' illustrated by Judith's appropriation of 'the masculine fantasies of rape and violence in the decapitation of Holofernes' and call-to-arms of the Bethulians.

9. Other Poems

Katherine O'Brien O'Keeffe's essay, 'Orality and the Developing Text of Caedmon's *Hymn*' is republished in Richards. It traces the variations in the copying of the *Hymn* into the Latin and Old English versions of Bede's *Historia ecclesiastica*. O'Brien O'Keeffe's 'Editing and the Material Text' (in Scragg and Szarmach) examines the 'materiality' of Old English verse and its implications for editing, particularly when the text is extant in two manuscripts, as is the case with *Solomon and Saturn I* found in CCCC 422 and CCCC 41. The 'transitional' nature of the literacy that such texts preserve needs to be addressed when presenting the verse in edited form, since an edition effectively disembodies them and thus limits their 'optimum recovery'. She looks at editorial scholarship on these poems, which is ultimately unsatisfactory in that it does not address the manifestation of the 'realized' text; this she rectifies in a discussion of her own approach to editing them: presenting an *en face* critical edition with an 'archaeological' diplomatic version, along with the inclusion of manuscript context – texts accompanying the subject text. Such an edition preserves the living nature of the Old English verse and allows subsequent dialogical study by the student/scholar. In 'Source, Method, Theory, Practice: On Reading Two Old English Texts' (*BJRL* 76.i.51–73), the Toller Memorial Lecture, O'Brien O'Keeffe addresses the interaction between source studies and postmodern criticism. She views the current status of source studies and attempts to provide a definition for 'source' – a word which diminishes the importance of the Old English text itself, for which the label 'target' text is proposed instead. Source studies involves the seeking of similarities and differences, and from this O'Brien O'Keeffe extends her discussion into a contextual and practical application of source scholarship and theoretical positioning with reference to the two verse texts, the dialogues of Solomon and Saturn. She traces the history of editions and studies of the texts, which has concerned itself with subjective source analysis and studies of literary analogues which essentially close the text. Challenging these approaches, O'Brien O'Keeffe proposes five principal *desiderata* for the pursuit of objective source studies which she regards as 'vital to the sources enterprise'.

Graham D. Caie's important contribution to the Scragg and Szarmach volume is 'Text and Context in Editing Old English: The Case of Poetry in CCCC 201'. In it, he focuses on the catechetical poetic works *Judgement Day II*, *An Exhortation to Christian Living*, *A Summons to Prayer*, *Lord's Prayer II* and *Gloria I*. Caie warns against the dangers of editing texts in isolation, extracted from their codicological context. He illustrates this point by showing how the five verse texts can be better understood when they are studied as a group; indeed, they were probably intended to be regarded as a unified series of texts for instruction. Caie also shows how misleading some titles provided by editors become when those texts are edited in isolation; *Judgement Day II*, for example, might more appropriately be entitled 'Pilgrimage of Penance'. This essay is a clear, well-illustrated and useful discussion of the importance of taking manuscript context into account in the processes of editing. Fred C. Robinson also discusses the verse texts in CCCC 201 in '"The Rewards of Piety": "Two" Old English Poems in Their Manuscript Context' (in Robinson). He, like Caie, demonstrates the dangers inherent in an editorial removal of individual Old English verse texts from their manuscript context, especially when there is little division between texts, and no supplied title, lineation or capitalization. The texts upon which Robinson focuses are *An Exhortation to Christian Living* and *A Summons to Prayer*, which are usually regarded as separate poems. They are, however, linked, not only by manuscript context but by style, theme and orthography. Robinson believes the texts are one continuous verse and demonstrates that the *Summons* follows on directly from the *Exhortation*. To show their unity, he renames the text 'The Rewards of Piety' and edits it with an *en face* translation, thereby convincingly providing a unified verse which is 'better' than its dislocated predecessors.

Jan Geir Johansen, like Caie and Robinson, closely examines manuscript context and thematic links in his article on 'The Cohesion of the Worcester Fragments' (*PLL* 30.157–67). Because of the trimming of lines from f. 63 of Worcester Cathedral F.174, the texts, the 'Bede Fragment' and 'The Departing Soul's Address to the Body', have traditionally been regarded as individual works. Johansen, however, provides interesting and convincing thematic evidence to suggest that the text is a single, unified work: the lamenting speaker and the lost soul are both 'abandoned, *forloren* and *forleten*, because good education is lacking' in the early thirteenth century.

In '*The Fight at Finnsburh*: Pragmatic Aspects of a Narrative Fragment' (*NM* 95.207–27), Jan-Ola Östman and Brita Wårvik apply pragmatic methodology and discourse analysis to Hickes's text of the *Finnsburh Fragment* in order to provide a re-interpretation of the poem. They discuss the traditional interpretations of the text before introducing pragmatics into their analysis: this includes close examination of the adverbial *þa*, the 'action marker' *ac*, and the other pragmatic particles *oð*, *nu* and *þonne*. They also analyse the referential problems in the poem, focusing on deixis to attempt a resolution of interpretative ambiguities in the poem.

A. N. Doane's 'Editing Old English Oral/Written Texts: problems of method (with an Illustrative Edition of Charm 4, *Wið Færstice*)' (in Scragg and Szarmach) presents an edition of the charm in Harley 585 that reflects the suprasegementals and, in Doane's judgement, better reflects the vocal nature of the text. He points out that editors of scholarly texts have focused on the layout of the text to the detriment of the manuscript format and the performative aspect. Doane discusses many aspects of the editing of verse and analyses the options available to the editor: his edition is preceded by a manuscript facsimile and followed by explanatory notes, so that it forms, in full, an example of the editing methodology investigated in his preliminary comments.

Three previously published essays on *The Battle of Maldon* are reprinted in O'Brien O'Keeffe. These are: Helmut Gneuss's '*The Battle of Maldon* 89: Byrhtnoð's *ofermod* Once Again', Mary P. Richard's '*The Battle of Maldon* in its Manuscript Context' and W. G. Busse and R. Holtei's '*The Battle of Maldon:* A Historical, Heroic, and Political Poem'.

10. Prose

There are a number of important editions of prose texts published this year, including works by Ælfric as well as anonymous authors. Jonathan Wilcox's *Ælfric's Prefaces* for Durham Medieval Texts represents one of the best introductions to Ælfric and his work to date. Students and scholars alike can ill afford to neglect the eighty-five-page introduction, which provides an erudite and extensive examination of the historical and intellectual background, and an analysis of Ælfric's overall works, style, and purposes in composing his *Prefaces*. In terms of the *Prefaces* themselves, Wilcox gives an accessible and detailed account of their nature, function and importance, especially for determining Ælfric's self-conscious approach to his writing. Ælfric attempted 'to claim authoritative fixed status for his works', an aim which ultimately failed as his works and their contexts were altered by later copyists. This 'sense of his own mission' evident in the *Prefaces* is reinforced by the comments that Ælfric incorporated into his *Catholic Homilies I* and *II*, and *Lives of the Saints*, which Wilcox also edits. In total, the *Prefaces* to the *Catholic Homilies*, the *Grammar*, the *Translation of Genesis*, the *Lives of the Saints*, the *Admonitio ad filium spiritualem* and the *Vita S. Æthelwoldi* are presented in this edition, along with the Letters to the Monks of Eynsham, to Sigeweard, to Sigefyrth and for Wulfstan. The edited texts are clearly laid out on an uncluttered page, and are followed by variant forms, explanatory notes and a glossary. This makes for a complete edition aiming to bring the *Prefaces* to a wider audience. The book could certainly be used by students, but is especially useful for scholars as it brings this important material together in an inexpensive and accurate volume.

Clare A. Lees's 'Whose Text is it Anyway: Contexts for Editing Old English Prose' (in Scragg and Szarmach) looks at the relationship between teaching and research, and more particularly between editorial theory, practice and canonicity, to examine the contexts for Old English texts. Lees discusses the implications of including or excluding certain texts, such as prose hagiography, in textbooks, and the consequences of such editorial selection. The stability of the Old English literary canon, unquestioningly accepted by many, is demythologized by Lees; the canon's place in perpetuating a narrow view of Anglo-Saxon culture is addressed; and the gender bias and named-author bias of prose selection are criticized. She widens the discussion to a consideration of the text in manuscript form by looking at Ælfric's *Prefaces* and their relationship to the *Lives of the Saints*' manuscripts, before concluding that we need to recognize 'the processes that create the contexts for these [edited] texts' more than we need to argue for or against the ownership of a text by author, or editor.

Joyce Hill continues her work on the eventful text, focusing on Ælfric in 'Ælfric, Authorial Identity, and the Changing Text' (in Scragg and Szarmach). She cogently summarizes the position of the conservative and emendatory editor and introduces reader-reception issues into the debate. She looks at the aspects of Ælfric as author and proposes that 'modern concepts of authorship and textual integrity are not applicable to the Anglo-Saxon period, even when they appear to be present, and thus [. . .] editorial activity should properly be extended to revisions, derivatives, and composites'. She exemplifies this with reference to Ælfric's own sense of his writings in his *Prefaces* and the Pastoral Letters. She convincingly argues that later copies of original texts must be the focus of editorial interest, for they are also important witnesses to their milieu and additionally reflect Anglo-Saxon literary and cultural attitudes like their predecessors.

In the same edited volume, Theodore H. Leinbaugh explains the interrelationship of the *Lives of the Saints* I with a number of analogous texts such as Belfour IX, *De Creatore et Creatura*, a Latin homily from Boulogne-sur-Mer 63 and Alfred's version of Boethius. In 'Ælfric's *Lives of the Saints* I and the Boulogne Sermon: Editorial, Authorial and Textual Problems', Leinbaugh attempts to demonstrate how the complexity of these textual relationships has important implications for editing Ælfric's *Lives of the Saints*.

Also in Scragg and Szarmach is Kathryn Sutherland's 'Editing for a New Century: Elizabeth Elstob's Anglo-Saxon Manifesto and Ælfric's St Gregory Homily'. This concerns the publication in 1709 of Elstob's edition of the Gregory homily, and the social and political circumstances informing its production and background. Among other work, Elstob published in 1715 the first Old English–Modern English grammar, and Sutherland points out that 'Elstob's Saxon researches have an analogue in her concern to establish a scholarly tradition and a place in history for women'. Elstob's relationships with other Saxonists and antiquarians are outlined, before Sutherland discusses Elstob's editing policy and methods, particularly her use of page layout, which informs the reader of Elstob's *modus operandi* as much as her own, open, editorial statements do.

Peter Clemoes's two essays reprinted in Richards are extracts from longer works which now become accessible to a much wider audience. They are 'History of the Manuscript and Punctuation (from *Ælfric's First Series of Catholic Homilies* –

British Library Royal 7.C.xii, fols. 4–218)' and 'The Production of an Illustrated Version (from *The Old English Illustrated Hexateuch*)'.

Mary Clayton's 'Ælfric's *Judith*: manipulative or manipulated?' (*ASE* 23.215–27) questions the need to reconcile the two Ælfrician comments on his own translation of *Judith*: as a typological exemplar for nuns, and as a call-to-arms against the heathen. She examines the difficulties faced by Ælfric in translating the text and sees both authorial interpretations of *Judith* as reflecting 'a desire to make safe the text'. Malcolm Godden looks at the writings of Ælfric and Wulfstan for the political and topical information they yield in the face of the contemporary Viking threat. In 'Apocalypse and Invasion in Late Anglo-Saxon England' (in Godden et al.), Godden shows that Ælfric's early work often uses an apocalyptic setting, though it does not refer to the Viking threat; in his later work such as the *Lives of the Saints*, the Viking threat becomes rather more prominent. Godden concentrates on a number of texts including *De oratione Moysi* and the *Maccabees* to illustrate this trend and the problems of interpreting it. Wulfstan, influenced by Ælfric, shows the same tendencies in his early writings as Ælfric did in his. Wulfstan's major discussion of the Viking threat, the *Sermo ad Anglos*, was rewritten a number of times and exists in three versions, all of which, Godden argues, are Wulfstan's own. He analyses the text's history, showing the increasing number of references to the Vikings which are placed within the apocalyptic framework. By the twelfth century, and the inclusion of the text in Bodley 343, the *Sermo* becomes an end-of-the-world sermon rather than one concerning the Vikings, demonstrating the longevity and reuse of such writing long after its creation.

Richard Marsden has published two pieces on the Old Testament. The first, in *ASE* 23 (229–64), concerns 'Old Latin Intervention in the Old English *Heptateuch*'. He examines the translations in the vernacular *Heptateuch* which appear to be derived from pre-Vulgate Old Latin texts rather than Vulgate exemplars. Marsden outlines the manuscripts of the Old English versions and the transmission of the Old Latin translations of the Old Testament text, which often come into Anglo-Saxon England through their inclusion in biblical, liturgical and patristic writings. Ælfric's *Heptateuch* and the anonymous *Heptateuch* provide the cases of transmission that Marsden analyses for their debt to Old Latin sources, though, as Marsden is careful to explain, an assessment of their derivation is complex. He shows that biblical translation in Anglo-Saxon England is not simply a question of mechanical use of the Vulgate, but that 'contamination' from Old Latin texts complicates the picture considerably. In the second piece, 'The Old Testament in Late Anglo-Saxon England: Preliminary Observations on the Textual Evidence' (in Gameson), Marsden surveys the evidence for the history and transmission of the Vulgate Old Testament in and following the period of the monastic revival. He surveys the relatively scarce extant manuscripts from Anglo-Saxon England and places them in the context of continental and English manuscript transmission. His main focus is on BL, Royal 1.E.vii–viii, an Old Testament manuscript which was at Christ Church, Canterbury, after the Conquest but which probably originated at one of the houses associated with Athelwold and Winchester. This manuscript, together with other Anglo-Saxon Old Testament fragments, shows the major influence on this textual tradition to be that of the known continental Carolingian tradition (such as the Alcuinian), though other traditions are also evident, such as that of Fleury.

Roy M. Liuzza has published the first volume in his two-volume edition of *The*

Old English Version of the Gospels for EETS. This one, the introduction and text, follows the standard format of EETS editions: information is provided in the introduction which details the manuscripts and their relationships, and the editorial policy statement is given. What makes this volume stand out, however, is the amount of new scholarship that Liuzza includes, especially with regard to the palaeography of each of the manuscripts. The detail and precision of the manuscript descriptions read like a handbook to the script of Old English texts and in itself will be of considerable value to manuscript historians. The relationship of the manuscripts too demonstrates the accuracy and knowledge that Liuzza brings to bear on this volume; he shows, for example, by a meticulous analysis of variant and shared textual forms, that BL Royal 1.A.xiv's version of the Gospels is copied from Bodley 441. He is able to state that the copyist of Hatton 38 (s.xii/s.xiii) read his exemplar with understanding and did not merely copy mechanically. This is an important point of evidence to counter those who believe that Old English was little understood by the end of the twelfth century. Liuzza bases his edition of the Gospels on CCCC 140 with corrections from Bodley 441 and Otho C.i, volume 1, and provides numerous variants in the apparatus. The language analysis in Liuzza's second volume promises to be of substantial importance for assessing the evolution of English via the copying process through the eleventh and twelfth centuries. This first volume is already, though, a major contribution to our understanding of textual transmission in the late Old English and early Middle English periods, transcending the usual 1066 or 1100 chronological boundaries imposed by scholars.

Hugh Magennis's edition of *The Anonymous Old English Legend of the Seven Sleepers* is a good one for student use. He edits this popular legend, freely translated from a Latin exemplar probably in the second half of the tenth century, from the version contained in BL, Cotton Julius E.vii with variants from the damaged Otho B.x. Magennis provides useful linguistic data and an interesting lexical analysis, where the vocabulary emerges as 'solidly West Saxon'. He also gives a thorough discussion of 'Genre and Treatment' which emphasizes the illustration of God's providential purpose in the Old English. The legend is untypical of many hagiographies of the period in its highlighting of the passive acceptance by the saints of their lot. Other features of the Old English show that it is adapted from the Latin rather than merely translated; for example, the Old English author foregrounds the humanity of the saints, introducing 'a greater variety of treatment and a greater sense of dramatic impact'. The text is accompanied by an apparatus which contains textual and manuscript emendations, and variants from Otho B.x follow. The textual notes are succeeded by an analogous Latin text from Egerton 2797 with an *en face* translation. The glossary concludes this valuable addition to editions of anonymous prose texts.

Mary Clayton and Hugh Magennis have published *The Old English Lives of St Margaret* in the CSASE series. This edition provides access to the eleventh- and twelfth-century versions of the life extant in BL, Cotton Tiberius A.iii, CCCC 303, and known to have existed in the burnt Cotton Otho B.x. The editors give an analysis of the transmission of the legend, concentrating particularly on the Latin versions of the text, which extends to a brief consideration of the saint's inclusion in martyrologies and epitomes. A chapter on the Mombritius and pre-Mombritius traditions of the legend highlights and discusses in detail the version most closely allied to the Old English texts, which emphasizes Margaret as triumphant conqueror of the devil, in *imitatio Christi*. In looking at the Old English versions,

Clayton and Magennis suggest that the Tiberius life belongs to the Casinensis tradition, while the CCCC 303 life is, generally, 'closer to the standard Latin version', *BHL* 5303, though some elements of the text which depart from this version cannot be paralleled in any Latin or vernacular text (yet the editors state at p. 7 that this standard version, *BHL* 5303, is the source of CCCC 303's life). The manuscript CCCC 303 itself is variously dated: at p. 41, the manuscript is early twelfth-century, while at p. 92, it is dated to the first half of the twelfth century. The life in CCCC 303 is interesting in that the vernacular author appears to have emphasized Margaret's intense and personal devotion to God, consonant perhaps with the late eleventh- and early twelfth-century development of Anselmian spirituality (though similar spiritual concerns are known from Anglo-Saxon prayers, for example). The editors go on to discuss the cult of Margaret in England before turning to an examination of the manuscripts. The life extant in the Tiberius manuscript is complicated by numerous corrections added by the two scribes. The original scribe's text is therefore irrecoverable. What the editors choose to supply are two texts, 'one of the vita as it was copied into the manuscript by the first scribe', as an appendix; and the other, a composite text following the corrections of the two scribes. The latter they regard as an Old English edition of an Old English text, though there is little attempt made to ascertain the status and authority of either of these two scribes, and almost four pages of editorial justification are required before the presentation of this text. The appendix text is presented 'semi-diplomatically', as it is closest to the 'authorial text', while the main text is 'much more thoroughly edited'. This represents at best a catch-all editorial policy, and at worst an indeterminate one, made the more so since the volume seems aimed at a generalist audience, there being no glossary. The CCCC 303 life is more straightforward, though *drihten* abbreviated to *driht* should be added to their list of manuscript abbreviations at p. 93, and a number of erasures in the manuscript itself (e.g. p.162, paragraph 13, line 4, *wel . . . fæmne* written over an erasure) have been omitted. A useful corrected Latin version of the *passio* is supplied from Paris, BN, Lat. 5574 with variant text from a Saint-Omer manuscript. All in all, this is a valuable addition to the corpus of editions of Old English religious prose.

D. G. Scragg's 'The Compilation of the Vercelli Book' (in Richards) has been republished with updated information. It is an important piece which examines the possible sources of the codex to attempt to determine the nature of its compilation and place of origin. While the linguistic forms point to Kent, the evidence yielded by investigating the scribe's sources suggests that there was no predetermined plan for the book's contents.

Malcolm Godden looks at the problems of producing prose editions in 'Editing Old English and the Problem of Alfred's *Boethius*' (in Scragg and Szarmach). He first discusses W. J. Sedgefield's 1899 collated edition of Alfred's translation of the *Consolation of Philosophy*, in which, for example, the page layout is so cluttered that it is difficult to follow the text. Godden examines the opening pages of the manuscripts of the work, Bodley 180 and the damaged Cotton manuscript, to show how different the two are, and to exemplify how great the need is for his new edition which treats the extant versions separately. He gives some examples of a hypothetical edition of the Cotton manuscript and talks about the possibility of providing a reconstructed edition which is closer to Alfred's original than either of the two surviving versions. Janet Bately analyses lexical items in the Old English translation of the *Consolation of Philosophy* in 'An Alfredian Legacy? On the Fortunes and Fates of Some Items of Boethian Vocabulary in Old English' (in

Godden et al.). Bately brings up-to-date information to bear on these items by looking at these philosophical words, their definition, and their later synonyms in the Old English corpus. She then looks more closely at *providentia* and *praedestinatio* and their vernacular renderings to show that Alfred and his group had at their disposal a vocabulary that was well able to cope with a range of abstract and intellectual concepts. Another Alfredian translation, of Gregory's *Pastoral Care*, is the focus of Kenneth Sisam's 'The Publication of Alfred's *Pastoral Care*', which is reprinted in Richards.

John William Houghton's 'The *Old English Benedictine Office* and its Audience' (*ABR* 45.431–45) summarizes the circumstances of the production of this Old English text and argues, *contra* Milton McG. Gatch and Helmut Gneuss, that the text was composed for the use of the secular clergy. Houghton describes the manuscripts, which often provide only 'sketchy' descriptions of the elements of the *Office*. This suggests to him that the composition was intended for the use of 'someone who knew what has been omitted', that 'someone' being a teacher, a monk to instruct the secular clergy. Detailed textual analysis of the Prime-Capitular Office sequence furnishes further evidence of the secular nature of the text.

Turning to legal prose, Carole A. Hough writes on 'The Early Kentish "Divorce Law": A Reconsideration of Æthelberht, Chs. 79 and 80' (*ASE* 23.19–34). These two sections of Æthelberht's code have previously been considered as evidence for the independence of divorced women in early Kentish society. Here, though, Hough reinterprets these chapters using convincing linguistic and comparative legal evidence to suggest that rather than dealing with divorce, these clauses demonstrate the legal status of the widow and her inheritance. In the same volume of *ASE*, Simon Keynes looks at 'The "Dunstan B" charters' (165–93) in detail. He provides an edition and contextual examination of the two recently discovered charters dating from King Edgar's reign, which now survive as modern transcriptions. He provides a stimulating discussion of their importance within the group of Dunstan B charters and within their historical and political milieux.

Richard Dammery, in his very valuable 'Editing the Anglo-Saxon laws: Felix Liebermann and Beyond', traces the history of editing the laws from the *Archaionomia* to Liebermann, focusing on the latter's achievements and flaws. Inaccuracies in Liebermann are attributed by Dammery to the failure of the editor to consult all the manuscript evidence himself; to pay close attention to manuscript punctuation when the manuscripts are consulted; and to divide and number adequately the clauses of the laws. His summary points to the need for a more accessible edition of the laws, a conclusion his essay certainly illustrates.

J. D. Pheifer shows us 'How Not to Edit Glossaries' (in Scragg and Szarmach) in this erudite and detailed essay. By providing clear examples and comprehensible commentary, Pheifer demonstrates that editors of glossaries have essentially failed to treat with sufficient respect the historical and textual history of 'extract-glossaries' such as the Epinal and St Gallen Glossaries. The tradition of editing glossaries is examined and samples of collated texts are provided with translations, to show the relationship between Vatican 1469 and Monte Cassino 90 and their relevance for Anglo-Saxon glossaries. By such means, Pheifer exemplifies that much editorial work is still required which takes into account previous editors' work and scholarship. Helmut Gneuss edits and discusses the glossary in folios 150r–152v of Harley 3826, a manuscript dated to the end of the tenth or beginning of the eleventh centuries, in 'A Grammarian's Greek–Latin Glossary in Anglo-

Saxon England' (in Godden et al.). He describes the text's continental and Anglo-Saxon transmission and the analogous versions, before looking at the text itself, which is comprised of 128 lemmata in four parts, Poetry, Grammar, Versification, and Punctuation and the sentence. The text, partially derived from Isidore's *Etymologies*, might have come to England in the tenth century from France.

M. J. Toswell identifies 'A Further Old English Gloss in Paris, Bibliotheque Nationale MS lat. 8846' (*N&Q* 41.10–11). This gloss occurs at f.69v, Psalm 38, where it reads *ma ic ne bio* for 'amplius non ero'. The closest Old English parallel to this is that in the Eadwine Psalter. The language of the glosses in the twelfth-century Paris Psalter suggest mechanical copying, perhaps directly from the Eadwine Psalter. In a second article, Toswell explores in detail the devices of the Old English verse-writer of the Psalms. In 'The Translation Techniques of the Old English Metrical Psalter, with Special Reference to Psalm 136' (*ES* 75.393–407), Toswell aims to show how the Psalter 'fits, or fails to fit, in the poetic and prosaic tradition'. This excellent article looks closely at Psalm 136, *Super flumina*, in comparison to a Latin version from the Vespasian Psalter. Toswell illustrates the translator's methods – the use of a stock of alliterative filler words, for instance or the occasionally 'plodding style', or the relatively high frequency of end-stopped lines – showing that the poet works within his poetic criteria with some degree of skill and competence. The Metrical Psalter is seen to be a companion work to the Latin Psalter, rather than a replacement text, and can be linked to other religious didactic verses.

Books Reviewed

Aertsen, Henk, and Rolf H. Bremmer Jr, eds. *Companion to Old English Poetry*. VUUP. pp. 216. £14. ISBN 9 0538 3116 9.

Clayton, Mary, and Hugh Magennis, eds. *The Old English Lives of St Margaret*. CSASE 9. CUP. pp. 239. £37.50. ISBN 0 5214 3382 7.

Earl, James W. *Thinking About 'Beowulf'*. StanfordUP. pp. 204. £25. ISBN 0 8047 1700 1.

Gameson, Richard, ed. *The Early Medieval Bible: Its Production, Decoration and Use*. CSPC 2. CUP. pp. 242. £40. ISBN 0 5214 4540 X.

Godden, Malcolm, Douglas Gray and Terry Hoad, eds. *From Anglo-Saxon to Early Middle English: Studies Presented to E. G. Stanley*. Clarendon. pp. 233. £35. ISBN 0 1981 1776 0.

Gorman, Michael M., trans. *Bernhard Bischoff, Manuscripts and Libraries in the Age of Charlemagne*. CSPC 1. CUP. pp. 193. £40. ISBN 0 5213 8346 3.

Harwood, Britton J., and Gillian R. Overing, eds. *Class and Gender in Early English Literature: Intersections*. IndUP. pp. 156. £9.99. ISBN 0 2532 0858 0.

Jack, George, ed. *'Beowulf': A Student Edition*. OUP. pp. 244. hb £35, pb £6.99. ISBN 0 1987 1043 7, 0 1987 1044 5.

Lees, Clare A., ed. *Medieval Masculinities: Regarding Men in the Middle Ages*. UMinnP. pp. 193. $17.95. ISBN 0 8166 2426 7.

Liuzza, Roy M., ed. *The Old English Version of the Gospels*. EETS 304. OUP. pp. 202. £25. ISBN 0 1972 2306 0.

Lucas, Peter J., ed. *Exodus*. UExe. pp. 208. £10.95. ISBN 0 8598 9383 9.

Magennis, Hugh, ed. *The Anonymous Old English Legend of the Seven Sleepers*. Durham Medieval Texts 7. Durham. pp. 128. £7. ISBN 0 9505 9896 8.

Muir, Bernard J., ed. *The Exeter Anthology of Old English Poetry: An Edition of Exeter Dean and Chapter MS 3501.* 2 vols: Vol. I *Text*; Vol. 2 *Commentary.* UExe. pp. 817. £45. ISBN 0 8598 9436 3.
Myers, Robin, and Michael Harris, eds. *A Millennium of the Book: Production, Design, Illustration, 900–1900.* Oak Knoll Books, Delaware. pp. 192. $30. ISBN 1 8847 1807 8.
O'Brien O'Keeffe, Katherine, ed. *Old English Shorter Poems: Basic Readings.* BRASE 3. Garland. pp. 426. $67. ISBN 0 8153 0097 2.
Orchard, Andy. *The Poetic Art of Aldhelm.* Cambridge Studies in Anglo-Saxon England 8. CUP. pp. 355. £40. ISBN 0 5214 5090 X.
Pulsiano, Phillip, with A. N. Doane and Ronald E. Buckalew, eds. *Anglo-Saxon Manuscripts in Microfiche Facsimile.* MRTS. Binghamton. Vol. I: *Books of Prayers and Healing*, desc. A. N. Doane. MRTS 136. pp. 164, mss. 10. $40. ISBN 0 8669 8141 1; Vol. 2: *Psalters I*, desc. Phillip Pulsiano. MRTS 137. pp. 68, mss. 8. $40. ISBN 0 8669 8141 2.
Richards, Mary P., ed. *Anglo-Saxon Manuscripts: Basic Readings.* BRASE 2. Garland. pp. 401. $62. ISBN 0 8153 0100 6.
Risden, E. L., trans. *'Beowulf': A Student's Edition.* Whitston. pp. 99. $6.50. ISBN 0 8787 5455 5.
Robinson, Fred C. *The Editing of Old English.* Blackwell. pp. 212. £45. ISBN 1 5578 6438 1.
Scragg, D. G., and Paul E. Szarmach, eds. *The Editing of Old English: Papers from the 1990 Manchester Conference.* Brewer. pp. 317. £39.50. ISBN 0 8599 1413 5.
Stanley, Eric Gerald. *In the Foreground: 'Beowulf'.* Brewer. pp. 273. £35. ISBN 0 8599 1394 5.
Surber-Meyer, Nida Louise. *Gift and Exchange in the Anglo-Saxon Poetic Corpus: A Contribution Towards the Representation of Wealth.* Slatkine, Geneva. pp. 256. ISBN 2 101302 0 [*sic*.].
Tite, Colin G. C. *The Manuscript Library of Sir Robert Cotton.* The Panizzi Lectures 1993. BL. pp. 116. £16. ISBN 0 7123 0359 6.
Vantuono, William, ed. *Old and Middle English Texts with Accompanying Textual and Linguistic Apparatus.* Berkeley Insights in Linguistics and Semiotics 12. Lang. pp. 177. $20. ISBN 0 8204 2346 7.
Wilcox, Jonathan, ed. *Ælfric's Prefaces.* DMT 9. UDur. pp. 202. £7. ISBN 0 9505 9897 6.

III

Middle English: Excluding Chaucer

CATHERINE BATT, ALAN J. FLETCHER, GILLIAN RUDD and GREG WALKER

This chapter has the following sections: 1. General and Miscellaneous; 2. Alliterative Poetry; 3. The *Gawain*-Poet; 4. *Piers Plowman*; 5. Romances; 6. Gower, Lydgate, Hoccleve; 7. Middle Scots Poetry; 8. Lyrics and Miscellaneous Verse; 9. Malory and Caxton; 10. Other Prose; 11. Drama. Sections 1, 5, 6 and 9 are by Catherine Batt; sections 3, 10 and 11 are by Alan J. Fletcher; and sections 2, 4, 7 and 8 are by Gillian Rudd. Supplementary material is provided by Greg Walker.

1. General and Miscellaneous

Several studies this year make critical use of a highly developed self-consciousness about the practice of late twentieth-century approaches to medieval literature, in order to define how the nature of our engagement with past cultures informs our reading and understanding. Gayle Margherita's *The Romance of Origins: Language and Sexual Difference in Middle English Literature* brings psychoanalyis (especially the work of Freud, Lacan and Kristeva) to bear in an investigation of (among a wealth of other foci) the relationship between literary representation and loss, and how anxieties about linguistic instability are projected onto representations of the female body. Margherita addresses different manifestations of these issues first in texts she deems transgressive and (some might think surprisingly) 'extracanonical': there are chapters on Margery Kempe, who works through a 'corporealising' of language and an interest in the maternal to create her own space for articulation; the Harley lyrics, where the argument turns on the absence of the Lady and the consequently complex nature of the lyric voice; and the Early Middle English *Juliana*, in which the text is read as (*inter alia*) a championing of English ethnicity against Anglo-Norman hegemony. Chapters on Chaucer are reviewed in chapter IV. The final chapter is an assured reading of *Sir Gawain and the Green Knight*, investigating its debt to the *Aeneid*, specifically in its worries over patrilineal origins, and the way in which Morgan especially draws attention to ambivalence of discourse. As a discussion of the interrelation of body and metaphor, of language and historicity, and of how we formulate the past, this book opens up some valuable areas for debate, and will no doubt excite much controversy, though occasionally one may want a closer fit between its sophisticated theoretical arguments and the literary material.

Feminist Readings in Middle English Literature: The Wife of Bath and All Her Sect, edited by Ruth Evans and Lesley Johnson, constitutes a valuable textbook for students both of Middle English and of women's studies, not least because, as its introduction makes clear, it gives a sense of the historical conditions of feminist critical investigation of literature (a sense illustrated by the inclusion of essays by Mary Carruthers, Sheila Delany and Susan Schibanoff, originally published in 1979, 1983 and 1986 respectively), as well as demonstrating the variety and creativity of feminist approaches. Four of the essays address Chaucer's representation of women: Mary Carruthers writes on 'The Wife of Bath and the Painting of Lions'; Felicity Riddy contributes 'Engendering Pity in the *Franklin's Tale*'; Lesley Johnson looks at 'Reincarnations of Griselda: Contexts for the *Clerk's Tale*?'; and Sheila Delany, in 'Sexual Economics, Chaucer's Wife of Bath and *The Book of Margery Kempe*', offers a Marxist reading of the Wife in which the oppressions of class and gender are paramount, but sees Chaucer's portrayal as insufficient in comparison to the portrait of a 'historical' woman in the person of Margery.

A different perspective on Margery Kempe is offered by Julia Long in 'Mysticism and Hysteria: The Histories of Margery Kempe and Anna O.', where she compares Bertha/Anna's relationship to psychoanalysis with Margery's relation to masculine ecclesiastical culture. Ruth Evans, 'Body Politics: Engendering Medieval Cycle Drama', concentrates on the representation of Christ in the York Crucifixion play to pose questions about the implications of the protagonist's feminization for interpretation, and the different sexualized responses of women and men to the Passion. In 'Lady Holy Church and Meed the Maid: Re-envisioning Female Personifications in *Piers Plowman*', Colette Murphy gives an accessible reading of the significance of female personification in the poem, tracing in its instances both the dynamic aspect of allegory and how the femaleness of such as Holi Church or Mede is integral to masculine perceptions of, and responses to, what they represent. Jocelyn Wogan-Browne, in 'The Virgin's Tale', investigates what is positive for women in the virgin martyr legends, showing how such tales allow their female protagonists a certain autonomy and, moreover, offer a critique of female roles in secular romance. The last essay in the collection, Susan Schibanoff's '"Taking the Gold out of Egypt": The Art of Reading As a Woman', compares the Wife of Bath and Christine de Pisan's responses to misogynist material, and goes on to consider the complexities of access to and control of literacy. The introduction offers a careful analysis of the arguments of these essays and of their critical perspectives, which serves as a helpful guide to the student without being prescriptive.

One could possibly think a volume devoted to *Medieval Masculinities: Regarding Men in the Middle Ages*, edited by Clare A. Lees, a retrograde step, but the introduction, and the essays themselves, negotiate fairly successfully the possible charge of simply reprivileging the masculine, by means of a pluralistic approach that emphasizes the broader cultural implications of their project, although the volume as a whole does not have the same theorizing trenchancy with regard to constructing sexuality and gender difference as does *Framing Medieval Bodies* (see below). Some essays deal with aspects of masculine identity in particular historical situations. Vern L. Bullough's 'On Being a Male in the Middle Ages' is the most general account, and at the culmination of a discussion about male sexual anxiety argues that in the Middle Ages sexual potency defines masculinity, and is man's most vulnerable aspect. Jo Ann McNamara identifies a crisis of masculine identity around the issue of enforced clerical celibacy, and consequently the constraining of secular married men's status and the oppression of women, in 'The *Herrenfrage*: The Restructuring of the Gender System, 1050–1150'. Susan Mosher Stuard, 'Burdens of Matrimony: Husbanding and Gender in Medieval Italy', traces the relationship between male power and the upholding of particular social and political formations, in a city such as Venice as in the household. Stanley Chojnacki, 'Subaltern Patriarchs: Patrician Bachelors in Renaissance Venice', finds an ambivalence in the position of the unmarried man in this society. John Coakley's 'Friars, Sanctity and Gender: Mendicant Encounters with Saints, 1250–1325' draws on Italian evidence to suggest that the mendicant friars construct different forms of sanctity for men and women saints, and through their contact with women vicariously partake of the latter's particular relationship with God.

The other essays in the collection draw on specific literary evidence: Clare R. Kinney, 'The (Dis)Embodied Hero and the Signs of Manhood in *Sir Gawain and the Green Knight*', scrutinizes the fluctuations of masculine identity which this poem brings into play. Harriet Spiegel sees 'The Male Animal in the Fables of Marie de France' as the focus for the woman writer's perceptions of the masculine as 'other', and the fable form as a locus for her ambivalent look at men and women. Christopher Baswell, 'Men in the *Roman d'Eneas*: The Construction of Empire', looks at how this work is primarily concerned with men, and how although it occasionally incorporates, for example, a 'feminine' discourse, it ultimately defines the feminine as marginal in relation to masculine interests in the construction of empire and manhood. Louise Mirrer, 'Representing "Other" Men: Muslims, Jews, and Masculine Ideals in Medieval Castilian Epic and Ballad', shows how the language of these texts equates Christians with the 'manly' and aggressive, set against Jewish and Muslim men, made passive, and excluded from attitudes specifically defined as masculine.

In *Class and Gender in Early English Literature: Intersections*, Britton J. Harwood and Gillian R. Overing edit eight papers addressing the links between class and gender in Old and Middle English literature (see Chapter II for the essays on Old English). The terms 'class' and 'gender' are themselves subject to a certain fluidity of definition across the collection, and the essays also show varying degrees of 'theorizing' prefatory to and informatory of textual discussion. Two essays are concerned with *Piers Plowman*; David Aers, in 'Class, Gender, Medieval Criticism and *Piers Plowman*', urges a fuller engagement with these critical approaches the better to understand the nature and subtlety of Langland's writings. Clare A. Lees, 'Gender and Exchange in *Piers Plowman*', focuses on the significance of Mede as female, in a theoretically informed piece which compares with Colette Murphy's essay (in Evans and Johnson, above) on the same subject. Two essays concern Chaucer: Britton J. Harwood's imaginative 'Building Class and Gender into Chaucer's *Hous*', and Allen J. Frantzen, '*The Pardoner's Tale*, The Pervert, and the Price of Order in the World', a reading informed by Marxism and gender criticism. For Harriet Hudson's essay on romance, see section 5. This interesting set of readings should stimulate new discussion of its political terms, and of the texts it presents.

Lynn Staley, *Margery Kempe's Dissenting Fictions*, brings a range of current critical perspectives, among them questions of gender, to bear on *The Book of*

Margery Kempe, distinguishing between 'Kempe' as writer and 'Margery' as subject of the narrative, in her exploration of the text as 'sacred biography'. For Staley, it is the analysis of the community that is more important to the *Book* than is the idea of autobiography: thus it can function as the site of social criticism, and a challenge to the hierarchies of institutionalized religion, with women shaping an alternative 'ecclesia' in response to religious authority. Staley also considers the relation between the vernacular and the political constructions of nationhood as a context for Kempe's own appropriation of the vernacular for a new sense of community in her text. The *Book* emerging from this reading is one that carefully negotiates the conventions of religious writing to address fundamental social and spiritual questions.

The elegance and scholarly sophistication of *Framing Medieval Bodies*, edited by Sarah Kay and Miri Rubin, disproves any notion that there is little new to say about the corporeal in the middle ages. The articles, some of them consolidating their authors' previous work, address different perceptions and constructions of the body in a fruitful combination of theoretical rigour and sound analysis of specific material. Walter Simons, 'Reading a Saint's Body: Rapture and Bodily Movement in the *Vitae* of Thirteenth-Century Beguines', discerns a marked ambivalence on the part of commentators to the bodily frenzies of these saintly women. Jocelyn Wogan-Browne, 'Chaste Bodies: Frames and Experiences', follows through the images of enclosure, architectural as of the body, in English anchorite literature, but shrewdly sets the material in the historical context of female experience of religious communities during the medieval period. Roberta Gilchrist, using archaeological evidence, gives a fascinating insight into the segregation of women and of lepers in secular and religious society, in 'Medieval Bodies in the Material World: Gender, Stigma and the Body'.

Michael Camille's 'The Image and the Self: Unwriting Late Medieval Bodies' uses examples from medieval iconography to illustrate the nature of links between the body and cosmos and the body and politics, perspectives on the body of Christ, and on the female body as dangerous, concluding with an account of what distinguishes the work of the fourteenth-century artist Opicinus. Miri Rubin, 'The Person in the Form: Medieval Challenges to Bodily "Order"', illuminates the 'fluidity' of the sexual body, and the nature of anxieties focused on the body, by considering cases of hermaphroditism, torture, and ideas of Jews' investments in bodies. Anna Abulafia, 'Bodies in the Jewish–Christian Debate', expands on the association of the Jewish and the corporeal with an elegant essay that demonstrates this to be the common link between Christian thought on the nature of Jewish belief (seen to depend on a wilfully literal interpretation of Scripture) and Christian society, which constructed the Jews as interested only in material gain, a link which served to intensify anti-Jewish feeling.

Rita Copeland contributes a clever essay on 'The Pardoner's Body and the Disciplining of Rhetoric', showing how Chaucer's Pardoner embodies the metaphors medieval rhetoricians use to invent rhetoric 'through constructions of sexual transgression'. The exposition of the language of sexuality and gender in discussions of rhetoric's nature suggests a wealth of related material that would reward further exploration. Shulamith Shahar examines the stereotypes of 'The Old Body in Medieval Culture', from the 'neutral old male' and the 'harmful old female' to the metaphorical uses of the body in allegorical/religious writings, and finds the old body often set negatively in opposition to ideas of youthfulness. Mark Chinca, 'The Body in Some Middle High German *Mären*: Taming and Naming', analyses the literary representation (and mutilation) of the body in some of these thirteenth-century tales in terms of what they reveal of powerful and influential men's perception of women, whom they relegate to the social margins.

Sarah Kay's magisterial study of 'Women's Body of Knowledge: Epistemology and Misogyny in the *Romance of the Rose*' considers the 'authoritative' figures of La Vielle and Nature against the background of the intellectual debates in Paris in the 1270s, and the questions philosophical writings raise about cognition: she concludes that the interaction of the body, knowledge and gender in Jean de Meun is part of his elaborate play with recent developments in the fields of philosophy and epistemology. In 'Dante and the Body', Robin Kirkpatrick proposes that frame for the understanding of the constitution of the individual set up by such as Foucault is in fact inadequate for an appreciation of how Dante deploys his understanding of the unity of body and rational soul in the individual. In the course of the *Commedia*, Dante's poetic, philosophical and local interests mean that 'the body' evades generalization as to its significance. Sarah Beckwith, 'Making the World in York and the York Cycle', connects culture, politics and work in an examination of the fraught politics of different groups' participation in the Corpus Christi pageants, and shows how the Crucifixion pageant produces a Body of Christ the treatment of which, rather than emblematizing unity, projects the divisions of the social world.

Tim William Machan, in an analysis of the practices of textual editing, argues cogently in *Textual Criticism and Middle English Texts* that most editing is undertaken according to a humanist paradigm that both claims a transhistorical status and equates the 'authoritative' text with 'authorial' intention. Machan has recourse to manuscript and literary evidence across the range of medieval literature to suggest this particular theoretical underpinning of textual criticism serves to valorize an approach inimical to medieval cultural perceptions of vernacular literature, particularly in that approach's insistence on lexical exactness and the authority of the individual writer.

Partly related to Machan's inquiry into how one defines the medieval 'author' is Gregory B. Stone's *The Death of the Troubadour: The Late Medieval Resistance to the Renaissance*, which defines the anonymous voice of the medieval lyric as a deliberate move to resist individualism. Stone's attractively provocative thesis ranges from troubadour poetry and Marie de France to a discussion of *lai*, and to Chaucer's use of lyric in the *Book of the Duchess*, in an argument that, while it provides some imaginative literary readings, ultimately fails to convince, because its discussion of 'lyric resistance' in narrative frames seems anxious to section off lyric from narrative (and to place the dominance of one and then the other on a historical time-scale that the evidence does not support) rather than to give full value to the sophistication and range of their interplay in both early and late medieval texts.

There is some interest this year in the relation of language to literature. David Burnley and Matsuji Tajima in *The Language of Middle English Literature*, which forms volume I of *Annotated Bibliographies of Old and Middle English Literature*, offer useful summaries of work on (non-Chaucerian) Middle English language, which is listed in 'Early' and 'Later' Middle English sections, with a supplementary list of doctoral theses: especially helpful is the introduction, which both reviews the nature of work already undertaken in this field, and suggests ways in which further research might both consolidate present trends and take new directions. The bibliography is largely composed of work that applies linguistic analysis to medieval literature in ways that fruitfully describe literary effect. Obviously this work is just one resource among several, but as part of the compilers' declared aim is to promote research into what a 'literary' text might owe to 'non-literary' sources, it might also have been useful to include in the introduction a fuller discussion of linguistic method and of seminal work in the area of Middle English language study in general.

Andrew Galloway's 'The Making of a Social Ethic in Late-medieval England: From *Gratitudo* to "Kyndenesse"' (*JHI* 55.365–83) is exemplary as an essay that synthesizes semantic and historical scholarship: he provides evidence from philosophical, historical, social and literary material of a fascinating shift in interest from the concept of 'gratitude' (developed from feudal relationships) to a different concept of social cohesion and reciprocity characterized by 'kyndenesse', which has implications for how we understand, for example, Langland's and Gower's visions of society in particular, and late medieval notions of community in general. Gloria Cigman, 'The Medieval Self as Anti-Hero', in *Heroes and Heroines in Medieval English Literature*, edited by Leo Carruthers (a collection of literary essays that illuminate heroism and anti-heroism in Old and Middle English texts), begins by noting that the term 'hero' is not in general use in Middle English, and proposes from consideration of homiletic and romance literature that the notion of anti-hero more nearly represents medieval consciousness of the self than does the positive term. (The essays relating to Malory in this volume are reviewed in section 9.)

Joyce E. Salisbury's *The Beast Within: Animals in the Middle Ages* is an entertaining guide to attitudes to animals from the fifth to the fifteenth centuries, its central thesis being that the earlier period is anxious to emphasize distance between human and animal, while from the twelfth century onwards the boundaries between what constitutes animal and what human blur. Salisbury draws on social, cultural, legal, iconographic and literary evidence to discuss how animals are regarded as property, as food, in sexual terms, and how later their various anthropomorphizations can turn them into human 'exemplars'. The organization of this neat argument makes for description rather than in-depth analysis of particular evidence (for a fine example of such analysis see Felicity Riddy, 'The Speaking Knight: Sir Gawain and Other Animals', in *Culture and the King: The Social Implications of the Arthurian Legend*, edited by Martin B. Shichtman and James P. Carley), but the book opens up the subject while also leaving much room for further investigation.

Paul Acker provides information on another aspect of medieval mentality and culture by tracing, through a range of sources, the process by which algoristic arithmetic takes over from classical arithmetic, in 'The Emergence of an Arithmetical Mentality in Middle English Literature' (*ChauR* 28.iii.293–302). For 1993, Kathleen Ann Kelly, '"Blue" Indians, Ethiopians and Saracens in Middle English Narrative Texts' (*Parergon* 11[1993].i.35–52), garners evidence from writings on physiognomy and encyclopaedic works to show that such a designation was commonly used to evoke these peoples as 'other'.

Jill Mann's 'Allegorical Buildings in Mediaeval Literature' (*MÆ*63.191-210) looks at how writers try to make the image of the allegorical building dynamic, in a selection of texts, from Prudentius' *Psychomachia* to Grosseteste's *Chasteau d'Amour*. *Piers Plowman* is the main focus of the discussion, and Mann provides a solid general appraisal of how Langland uses images of closure and release in architecture to inform, especially in Christ's Harrowing of Hell, a vision of positive virtue.

The Rusted Hauberk: Feudal Ideals of Order and their Decline, edited by Liam O. Purdon and Cindy L. Vitto, both seeks to define the nature of feudalism as a concept, and to relate literary and documentary accounts of feudalism and chivalry to social reality, taking special account of the notion of decline. The essays cover a broad stretch of ground, from historical conditions in the Low Countries in the twelfth and thirteenth centuries, and a consideration of rape trials in England in the early thirteenth century, to epic, the rewriting of Arthurian romance, and Chaucer's revision of feudal values. Cindy L. Vitto, 'Feudal Relations and Reason in *Cleanness*', claims that in this poem feudal reciprocity is the principal means to stabilize society. Daniel F. Pigg, 'Imagining Feudalism in *Piers Plowman*: Attempts to Restore Order', also sees his poet as conservative, with Langland seeking to assert order through a social model of feudal custom and practice. John W. Schwetman, 'Feudal Chivalry in Popular Medieval Battle Poems', finds in the descriptions of battle in fourteenth- and fifteenth-century poems (some on the border wars between Scotland and England, some by Laurence Minot, some in chronicles), a tendency to treat chivalry as part of 'a hyperbolic, fantasized world', but not as a code directly implemented in the serious business of war. Jane Chance offers an interesting 'Afterword: Chivalry and the Other', noting the elasticity of medieval chivalry as a metaphor for social order, which reinvents itself throughout the Middle Ages in order to accommodate different perspectives and social conditions. Cynthia Ho's essay on *The Knight of the Tour d'Landry* is mentioned in section 9.

Paul Zumthor, in a general essay on 'The Medieval Travel Narrative' (*NLH* 25.809–24), surveys the diverse nature of travel writing, from the fourth to the sixteenth centuries, and makes brief mention of the popularity of John Mandeville's work and his interest in the social condition.

Those interested in literary approaches to the natural sciences will welcome Richard Kay's *Dante's Christian Astrology*, which complements such studies as J. D. North's *Chaucer's Universe* (OUP, 1988), though this present work claims only to be a preliminary study. Kay argues that Dante's organization of material in the first twenty-two cantos of the *Paradiso* is largely informed by awareness of the properties of the planets, and while illuminating the use of astrology in the *Commedia*, Kay opens up for further discussion the relation of astrology to cosmology in Dante's work.

The Medieval Translator IV, edited by Roger Ellis and Ruth Evans, is the latest in the series, arising from Roger Ellis's conferences on translation, and by definition its studies of translation emphasize the international and intertextual nature of much medieval literature. Roger Ellis's introduction offers a review of the essays and the issues they raise with regard to the difference between original and translation, and modes of production and reception. Ruth Evans's 'Translating Past Cultures?' sets the work of this volume in the broader context of translation studies as a whole, focusing especially on Rita Copeland's conservative discussion of translation and authority in *Rhetoric, Hermeneutics and Translation in the Middle Ages* (CUP, 1991), and moving from this important work to suggest how other approaches, such as colonial discourse theory and gender issues, can also inform discussion of translation.

Several essays in the collection take up these more recent critical perspectives: Jocelyn Wogan-Browne's 'Wreaths of Thyme: The Female Translator in Anglo-Norman Hagiography' considers the anonymous nun of Barking, Clemence of Barking and Marie of Chatteris as writers of saints' lives, discussing especially the literary implications for such works of their production for female religious communities, and their possible interrelation. Rina Drory's 'Al-Harízí's Maqámát: A Tricultural Literary Product?' offers a fresh perspective on this text, which is traditionally seen as paradigmatic of Arabic influence on Hebrew literature, and suggests from a study of the author's milieu and the dedications prefacing his work that his book is part of a competitiveness on the part of Hebrew writings for areas of written communication traditionally occupied by Arabic in the medieval Spanish Jewish community, and that the shift in language function is made possible by the complex linguistic and cultural conditions obtaining in Christian Spain in the thirteenth century. Helen Phillips, in '*The Complaint of Venus*: Chaucer and de Graunson', analyses the three lyrics Chaucer translates from de Graunson, but in which he substitutes a female for a male voice, and suggests the constrained female voice acts as a disingenuous marker of the more limited nature of the translator's role in respect to that of the 'original' poet. Ian Johnson's 'Tales of a True Translator: Medieval Literary Theory, Anecdote and Autobiography in Osbern Bokenham's *Legendys of Hooly Wummen*' draws on Genette's concept of 'paratext' to consider how Bokenham adapts an Aristotelian prologue to comment on his own function as both *auctor* and translator in a collection that seeks to fulfil a spiritual purpose.

Mary-Jo Arn, 'Charles of Orleans: Translator?', sensibly defends Charles against charges of 'mistranslating' his own poems from French to English, pointing out that it is more appropriate to term the English poems 'versions' rather than translations. Veronica Lawrence, 'Richard Whitford and Translation', places the work of this early sixteenth-century Brigittine monk within a monastic context with a firm tradition of translation. Scott D. Westrem, 'A Medieval Travel Book's Editors and Translators: Managing Style and Accommodating Dialect in Johannes Witte de Hese's *Itinerarius*', looks at three translations into Dutch of a Latin travel book, and concludes, from a consideration of the freedom and fluidity with which redactors and writers might regard the notion of translation, that they have a common origin.

Anne Savage's lively 'The Translation of the Feminine: Untranslatable Dimensions of Anchoritic Works' targets ambivalence as central to such texts as *Hali Meiðhad*, *Ancrene Wisse* and the accounts of virgin martyrs in the *Katherine*-group, an ambivalence on the part of modern (female) translators and readers as much as of the male authors about the subject of the feminine, and of the original anchoritic audience in the reception of the text, and concludes that there is no 'ultimate' translation, but that it is always a continuing process of interpretation. Denis Renevey, in 'Encoding and Decoding: Metaphorical Discourse of Love in Richard Rolle's Commentary on the First Verses of the Song of Songs', demonstrates some of the complexity of Rolle's use of erotic vocabulary to inform a perception of the Divine, and the problems of reconciling the spiritual and the language of carnal love. In conclusion, René Tixier's 'Le Théologien et le Poète: Deux Traductions en Français Moderne de *The Cloud of Unknowing*', discusses two translations, one by Maurice Noetinger from 1925, heavily freighted with critical commentary, and the other by Armel Guerne, which appeared first in 1953. Tixier characterizes the first as an act of interpretation by a theologian (Noetinger used a translation of the orignial text), and the second, which tries to let the text speak without editorial 'interference', as the work of a poet: the two usefully demonstrate extremes of interpretation that translation can encapsulate. Together, these essays provide a wealth of sound scholarship and critical approaches to translation that should interest non-medieval as well as medieval specialists.

The lack of an accessible, readable, moderately priced modern translation of *The Romance of the Rose* is made good by Frances Horgan's work, which also includes an introduction summarizing the poem(s) and drawing attention to some of the central issues raised.

William Calin, *The French Tradition and the Literature of Medieval England*, raises questions about cultural and literal translation in its survey of interrelations between England and the Continent. This is a huge task, and Calin is necessarily selective of his material (and inevitably sometimes sketchy in his analysis), and some of the questions go unanswered: how *does* one account, in cultural terms, for a 'division' in English literature between those texts deemed 'not part of a French tradition' and those dependent on it? Calin considers the evidence in blocks, from 'Anglo-Norman Narrative' and 'The Continental French Legacy' to 'English Court Poetry' and 'Middle English Romance'. In the course of this literary history, Calin especially emphasizes the debt of English court poets, from Chaucer and Gower onwards, to an international poetic heavily dependent on French models, but never quite formulates what distinguishes the production of literature in English (as distinct from in French). In the same way, the Middle English romances are seen as especially dependent on Anglo-Norman and French models, but the analysis is limited by a traditional view of the nature of English reworkings of their originals, and the assertion that aspects of Malory's approach to his material previously considered unique to him can be shown to be present in his sources does not lead to a fresh perspective on the *Morte*. Although, therefore, Calin is careful to assert, in his tracing of French influence on English literature, that this is not an exercise in transcultural 'point-scoring', the constraints of the format, which tends towards descriptive summary rather than cultural analysis, often lead to Calin's subscribing to the same kinds of value-judgements he elsewhere vigorously argues against. This is useful as a reference work in its summarizing of French influences on English literature, and the importance of Anglo-Norman, but it also exposes a pressing need to develop a new critical vocabulary to appreciate fully the nature of the multilingual culture of medieval England.

Rather more concerned with a political positioning of the written English vernacular is Steven Justice's deeply felt *Writing and Rebellion: England in 1381*, which reconstructs social contexts (concentrating especially on medieval communities) for the six texts known collectively as 'John Ball's Letters', and examines how vernacular writing is recognized as and used as a political weapon. His ingenious argument draws into its ambit the work of such as Wyclif, Chaucer, Langland and Gower, not only positioning them within a historical context, but also attempting to formulate how responses to these authors' material depended on political and social forces beyond their control: some aspects of the discussion (such as the supposed relations between Chaucer and Gower) reformulate familiar ideas, but other issues, such as the conditions of Langland's revision of *Piers Plowman*, will no doubt prompt lively critical debate. In 'Inquisition, Speech, and Writing: A Case from Late-Medieval Norwich' (*Rep* 48.1–29), meanwhile, Justice proposes that the scribe John of Exeter's occasional use of the vernacular in his Latin account of heresy trials arises primarily from a desire to make his work less tedious, and argues for the advantages for interpretation and understanding (particularly here of Lollardy as informing a way of life) of incorporating commonplace observation into critical practice.

In the field of manuscript studies: interesting in the light of both Machan and Calin's work (cited above) is Bernadette McMasters's resistance of the author-based literary model in a detailed championing of the importance of the scribe in medieval literary production, in 'Anglo-Norman in Context: The Case for the Scribes' (*Exemplaria* 6.167–203). McMasters identifies the apparent 'syllabic instability' of Anglo-Norman poetic manuscripts as indicative of an insular style (one obtaining also in Middle English and Latin verse), not as sustained evidence of scribal incompetence, and relates her findings in this context to medieval aesthetic practice in general. N. M. Diekstra, 'British Library MS 37049, Fol.96r-96v: A Mutilated Tract on God's Mercy and Justice and Material for its Reconstruction' (the information that this is an Additional MS is absent from the title) (*ES* 75.214–22), reconstructs an incomplete text (printed in the article) from a fifteenth-century religious miscellany by reference to treatises in BL MS Harley 6571 and BL MS Additional 30944, all of which are thought to derive from a common Latin source. Kari Anne Rand Schmidt, in '*The Index of Middle English Prose* and Late Medieval English Recipes' (*ES* 75.423–9), demonstrates how the indexing procedures for recipes and recipe collections are inadequate for researchers, and proposes as a solution the production of a first-line index of individual recipes. O. S. Pickering, 'Irish Saints in Twelfth-century Shropshire? Middle English and Latin Evidence' (*Anglia* 112.115–22), builds on his earlier research into the topic, unearths Middle English and Latin manuscript evidence for the burial of Irish saints in Shropshire, and considers the possible political and ecclesiastical background to the story.

Joel Fredell, 'Decorated Initials in the Lincoln Thornton Manuscript' (*SB* 47.78–88), reconstructs, from a study of the nature and placement of the illuminated initials in the manuscript showing evidence of professional piecework, a conscious, planned programme of decoration on Robert Thornton's part that assigns privileged status in the collection to the *Alliterative Morte Arthur* and, later, to the *Prose Alexander*. Phillipa Hardman's more meticulous and extensive investigation of Thornton's attitude to literature, in 'Reading the Spaces: Pictorial Intentions in the Thornton MSS, Lincoln Cathedral MS 91, and BL MS Add. 31042' (*MÆ* 63.250–74), comes to the same conclusion as Fredell that, from the Lincoln MS, Thornton seems especially interested in kingship and political power in Alexander's and Arthur's stories. Hardman also, however, examines the choice of texts in the London MS, and argues both for an important devotional role for the illustrations, and for how the heterogeneity of the texts, from religious lyrics to romances, demonstrates the width of the range of material the devout fifteenth-century reader could use to devotional purpose. In 'The Appearance of Saint George above the English Troops at Agincourt: The Source of a Detail in the Historical Record' (*N&Q* 41.304–7), John Schwetman traces the source of this event, reported in the *Brut*, to a scribal misunderstanding of a description of the banner of St George at the battle in an earlier poem on Agincourt.

Manifestations of what many (very loosely) term 'medieval' appear in the whole range of modern cultural experience, from the superficial and depressing appropriation of the nomenclature of Arthurian legend by a lottery company to earnest attempts to inform the present with what are construed as the values of the past. The essays in *Medievalism in North America*, edited by Kathleen Verduin, represent this variety well. In '"The History is Concisely This": Thomas Paine's Account of the Peasants' Revolt', Roger Wood shows how both Burke and Paine view the events of 1381 according to their respective ideologies. Kymberly N. Pinder, 'The Reception of Toby E. Rosenthal's *Elaine*: Medievalism in San Francisco', traces in the enthusiasm for the picture, and the response to its theft and restoration, aspects of an urban American eagerness to adopt a European cultural history.

Erica E. Hirshler, 'A Quest for the Holy Grail: Edwin Austin Abbey's Murals for the Boston Public Library', discusses the murals' British and American cultural contexts and their major debt to the Pre-Raphaelite movement. Alan Lupack's 'Visions of Courageous Achievement: Arthurian Youth Groups in America' charts the popularity of these organizations (not uniquely boys' clubs) from the nineteenth to the second half of the twentieth century. In 'Fra Albertus and the Roycrofters: Medievalism in East Aurora', Charlotte H. Osberg assesses what Elbert Hubbard and his artists' colony did to popularize a cultural appreciation of the medieval in America.

Raymond H. Thompson finds, in 'The Arthurian Legend in Canada', a large amount of Arthurian-inspired literary fantasy, as well as realist fiction, but he notes that Arthuriana is one set of influences among many: he appends a useful bibliography of Canadian 'Arthurian' literature. Stan Galloway, in 'The Greystoke Connection: Medievalism in two Edgar Rice Burroughs Novels', explores the escapist nature of this author's chivalric fantasies. Robin Blaetz's 'Cecile B. DeMille's *Joan the Woman*', meanwhile, shows how the director trivializes the power and importance of this medieval figure. Robert D. Peckham's 'Dark Laughter in the Chambers of the King: François Villon in America', looks at the various characterizations of a mercurial figure more suited to the requirements of different American audiences than fashioned with regard to historical accuracy. Jeff Rider's 'Roger Sherman Loomis: Medievalism as Antimodernism' argues for the scholar's anti-modernism as the chief impulse behind his attraction to, and the nature of his research of, medieval literature. Klaus P. Jankofsky, '"Launcelot in Hell": John Ciardi's Medievalism', examines the Dantean as well as Arthurian influences on this poem.

Mary Morse traces the influence of the medieval Spanish exemplum tradition on modern Mexican culture in 'The Medieval Roots of Two New Mexican *Cuentos*'. Pamela S. Morgan, '"One Brief Shining Moment": Camelot in Washington, D.C.', reconsiders the widespread association of the Kennedy presidency with Camelot, and especially the contribution the musical *Camelot* made to the popularization of the metaphor. Susan Aronstein and Nancy Coiner, 'Twice Knightly: Democratizing the Middle Ages for Middle-class America', use Eco's definitions of medievalism to anatomize American popular cultural appropriation of (debased) medieval motifs and themes in, for example, Disneyland, and argue further that the modern American myth has its roots in the myth of the Middle Ages. Finally, Jonathan M. Elukin's note on 'Medieval Language and Politics: Making the World Safe for Feudalism' assesses the damaging obfuscatory aspects of an unthinking deployment of medieval terms by Western journalists and politicians in the Gulf War.

Representations of the Feminine in the Middle Ages (Academia, 1993) and *Proceedings of the Medieval Association of the Midwest, II* (Emporia State Univ., 1993) were not available for review.

2. Alliterative Poetry

Stephen Knight's eminently readable book on Robin Hood (*Robin Hood: A Complete Study of the English Outlaw*) is a perpetuator of, as well as testament to, the fact that Robin Hood himself is 'a long existing potent myth', so to ask when or, indeed, whether Hood actually existed is to limit the scope of the figure. Nevertheless, such questions have tended to be at the core of discussions of Hood and the various answers offered are given due space in Knight's book, though he aims to put an end to the desire to find the man behind the myth. This is not a study of the outlaw but of the traditions and ideas behind this particular outlaw, for Knight repeatedly makes clear how fruitless and mistaken it is to search for or believe in a single Robin Hood. His attitude towards historians is therefore rather guarded, to say the least: they are too reliant on empiricism and not aware enough of the mediations of literature, which may defy the idea of real people lurking behind the names of heroes. Robin is thus presented as the focus of anti-authority feeling, whether that authority be represented by church or by secular institutions. Hence the combined forces of outlawry and friars may be pitted against those of law and monks. Despite this, Robin the romantic hero is convincingly debunked by this study; 'taking from the rich and giving to the poor is never a function of the genuinely radical Robin Hood'. The multiplicity of Robins emerges as Knight takes us through Robin in the ballads, on through the plays and up to twentieth-century treatments and exploitation of the theme. The influence of performance in particular is interesting here. Knight suggests that drama is essentially conservative, where ballads may be more easily rebellious and satiric. It was the Elizabethan stage which ennobled Robin, giving him the rank of Earl of Huntingdon, which allowed for this potent figure to be brought into the circle of the social establishment, while simultaneously accentuating the social divide: 'our' Earl of Huntingdon, 'your' Robin Hood. This act of gentrification was then perpetuated and established through later performances, down to the films of the 1990s.

It comes as somewhat of a surprise to find that Robin Hood was adopted as a national figure only in the eighteenth century, and then only gradually. Knight provides a succinct and constantly interesting account of the creation of the background and personal history of Robin Hood, which are now so familiar. The ease with which the family tree was accepted indicates how strong is the desire to be sure of a single Robin Hood. Knight also touches on why novels have not contributed as much to the myth as one might assume. A few do add to the legend, such as Peacock's *Maid Marion*; some do not. Scott's *Ivanhoe* is rather surprisingly numbered among the latter, but Knight makes clear the effects of restricting Hood to a particular role in a greater text, which takes a Lancelot figure as its main protagonist, and his argument is largely convincing. Less so is his decision to omit any real discussion of the versions of the myth written for children. It is in such books as Roger Lancelyn Green's *The Adventures of Robin Hood* that we find the greatest attempts to mould the disparate stories found in the Gestes into a single coherent narrative, and for those of us who encountered these tales in childhood, these overarching and chronological 'histories' colour our expectations and reading of Robin Hood tales for ever after. It is a particularly odd omission given the space allotted to films and television shows, but it may be a result of Knight's apparent love of the more transgressive elements of the legend, which still live on to his evident delight. The sheer enjoyment with which he recounts the appearance of the graffito 'The Sheriff Strikes Back' on boards blocking up the accidentally broken window of the exhibition shop of Nottingham's Tales of Robin Hood epitomizes the character of this book as a whole, and also proves its central thesis that 'the myth repeats itself because of the simple power of its structures'.

Also testifying to the power of historical myth is the volume *The Text and Tradition of Layamon's 'Brut'*. Seventeen essays are brought together by Françoise Le Saux with the expressed aim of offering both contributions which would provide readers with a yardstick for the current state of *Brut* scholarship, and more controversial pieces. The result is acceptable, but rarely exciting. Jane Roberts's introduction to the idea of manuscript discussion is very brief, and only touches on interesting points about the way dating may be regarded in a different light if Layamon is regarded as an archaizing poet rather than an archaic one. While Marshal Grant and Douglas Moffat develop this theme rather more in their piece concentrating on the prefix *To-*, one is left wishing for a clinching and confident assertion of this school of thought. Similarly Iyeiri's essay on negation is something and nothing. One of the somethings is the all too fleeting point that the alliterative style of the text, which makes extensive use of 'ne', 'never' and 'no', rather than of 'noht', marks a kinship with *Gawain* and the *Alliterative Morte*, and raises the possibility that alliterative poetry may in some ways be more conservative in its use of language than prose, and that the *Brut* may be later or more progressive than we often suppose. The consequences of these observations are never pursued and are finally ducked at the conclusion of the piece. The next essay, by Stanley, also points to a later date for the *Brut*, the case being made this time on syntactic grounds. Arthur Glowka's flirtation with the idea of Layamon as a precursor to Whitman is a more upbeat affair, which presents the text as a work of 'poetic glitz' and gives it an appropriately showy treatment. This is followed by an informative contribution from S. K. Brehe on rhythmical alliteration and the possible origins of the *Brut*'s metre. Brehe endorses Blake's theory of a continuum of alliterative forms without firm boundaries between verse and prose, and his discussion allows for reflection on the poem and its literary context and genealogy. Laudably, he also brings the lyrics in for consideration as a significant part of the poetic tradition and development of form, suggesting that 'inconsistency' was not as disturbing for medieval writers and readers as it is now for us, who are accustomed to categories and preconceptions absorbed from classical and continental models. Above all Brehe must be praised for the view 'as much as we may revere Chaucer, we are not obliged to adopt every one of his opinions'. No, indeed.

Attention to the manuscripts of *Brut* continues in the essays by Elizabeth Bryan and Carole Weinburg. Bryan advocates using the manuscripts in ways other than attempts at reconstructing the original, preferring to see them as products of certain types of reading. O's marginalia are seen as marking the process of rule from British to English, while C's focus on institutional interests is as likely to lead the reader from the text into other information already stored in the memory as to trigger recall of *Brut* itself. Reading is thus presented as a 'memorial process'. Additionally, she points out that the notes of O highlight instances of betrayal which simultaneously caution one about and advocate heroic values. Weinburg concentrates on the Latin marginal glosses in the Caligula MS and offers an explication of them. In doing so, she creates a group of affinitive texts for the Caligula *Brut*, listed on p.113, and declares the Layamon's serious historical idea is acknowledged by the majority of the Latin glosses. Acknowledgement of his creative imagination seems to rest rather more tenuously on gloss 10 alone. This largely descriptive contribution has its uses none the less, not least in providing a handy copy of all the glosses on pp. 119–20. Rosemund Allen's essay, 'The Implied Audience of Layamon's *Brut*', marks itself out as one of the trendier pieces by its use of *Rezeptionsästhetik*. The challenge issued by *Rezeptionsästhetik* to posit oneself as an audience is also one issued by *Brut*, whose created audience is in fact that of the solitary reader, behind whom is the implied audience of the larger group. This lively piece asserts that the most nearly concrete construct of the poem is the project, object, subject and hero of the text, namely, 'þis londe'. She also takes into account the effect of reading this text as performance, with its 600-line chunks and concomitant awareness of the effect of the passing of time. This is a sound idea, which works well, though the idea itself seems to be one of consensus rather than actual experience. There is a good focus on formula variant, a trick which may work best in oral delivery, and is wisely not applied to the simply written text. The tentative suggestions about the actual audience of *Brut* seem rather out of place at the end of this essay, and perhaps indicate a degree of uncertainty about the worth of such ahistorical treatments of a highly historical text. Lesley Johnson suffers no such anxieties in reverse as she cogently argues for the classification of *Brut* as a national, not providential, history. For her it is emphatically a textual book seeking its own authority through other books. Johnson highlights the use of place names to elicit particular responses and encourage readers to consider connections between earlier and later episodes in the text. This truly literary piece of criticism is most welcome in this volume.

The two subsequent offerings by Neil Wright and James Noble turn the attention to the question of the relative merits of the Angles and Saxons in the text. Wright heartily debunks Kirby's claim that Layamon always characterized the Saxons as cruel and the Angles as 'true' Englishmen. Tracing his argument through Wace and Geoffrey of Monmouth, Wright points out that Layamon makes use of no such distinction; rather he made 'thoughtful use of the geographical origin of the Saxons in *Angles*' to explain the change of Britain to England. The increased sympathy for the English evident at the end of the poem is then regarded as the result of an understanding of historical process, by which one nation rises and becomes the embodiment of civilization while another falls. Noble continues this theme, seeking to resolve Layamon's ambivalence about the Angles and Saxons by focusing on his expansions of Wace, which tend to put the Saxons in an increasingly bad light. Noble regards the *Brut* as largely anti-Norman; it is the Normans who disrupt a pattern of arrival and settlement, it is they who invade and are to be seen as the new Saxons. Despite all the crime and punishment in the text, and Layamon's position as a priest, Françoise Le Saux maintains that moral considerations are not foremost in the *Brut*. Secular justice is paramount and the actions most strongly condemned are those which lead to civil unrest. This piece falters when it is too easily asserted that the villains are primarily male, and the female criminal is treated surprisingly leniently. The gender aspect seems rather grafted on to the better general argument, from which the *Brut* emerges as a pragmatist text. For Kelley Wickham-Crowley it is an historical proto-novel. Taking a Bakhtinian approach, Wickham-Crowley draws out the dialogic nature of the text in a way which provides a quite detailed consideration of the prophecy in the *Brut* and suggests that the audience is encouraged to seek the completion of the prophecies beyond the text. In contrast, Marie-Françoise Alamichel asserts the 'highly symbolical' nature of the text and proceeds to trace the different kinds of space to be found in it, including encirclement. Many of her observations are unsurprising (the sea figures largely and is ambiguous), but it is a pleasant enough piece to read. Herbert Pilch presents a comparison of *Sir Gawain and the Green Knight* and two of its Breton analogues in the hope of creating a model by which to interpret the *Brut*'s relation to its analogues. Like Wickham-Crowley, Pilch regards the *Brut* as novelesque and highlights the role of Welsh plot tradition in moulding Layamon's text. Finally, James McNelis III demonstrates that the *Brut* did not drop quite so far out of sight as has been previously assumed. Much that has been attributed to the influence of Geoffrey of Monmouth or Wace could in fact have been the result of encountering Layamon.

While it is not of strict relevance to alliterative poetry, readers might find something to interest them in the collection of essays produced in honour of Robert W. Frank, *Art and Context in Late Medieval English Narrative*, edited by Robert Edwards. Much of this book refers to Chaucer, and those essays dealing primarily with Langland will be found reviewed under section 4 below, but Mary Hamel's piece, 'The *Descriptio Navalis Pugnae* in Middle English Literature', has some claim to be considered here. In it, Hamel argues that there is a discernible rhetoric of medieval sea-battles which may be seen in *The Alliterative Morte Arthure*, in Chaucer's tale of Cleopatra in *The Legend of Good Women* and even in Froissart. Accounts of sea-battles in chronicles, pre-medieval Latin texts and Middle English tales contain consistent elements, frequently in a recognizable pattern. One can expect trumpets, ship-to-ship fighting, missile exchange, grappling irons, the defeated jumping or being thrown overboard, and much more. Lucan and Vegetius are regarded as substantially influential, but Hamel notes that the topos is based on real naval practices. She does not, however, tackle the question of how much the actual practice might have been influenced by the literary depictions of battle.

Helen Barr has followed her Everyman edition of *Pierce the Ploughman's Crede, Richard the Redeless, Mum and the Sothsegger* and *The Crowned King* (*YWES* 74) with an extended critical study of the texts. *Signes and Sothe: Language in the 'Piers Plowman' Tradition* further establishes Barr's claim for the desirability of regarding these poems as being in the poetic tradition of *Piers Plowman*. It is the attitudes towards, and use of, language which define this tradition, and which account for electing to name it after the texts rather than their widely accepted author. This idea of tradition causes Barr some unease, which she seeks to allay by tackling it head on in her first two chapters ('Locating Tradition' and 'Reading Tradition'). Such unease may be inevitable in a study of this kind, but is not, I believe, necessary. For the kind of kinship Barr is asserting between these texts, the apposite word clearly is 'tradition'. If her readers agree with the argument they are unlikely to quibble over the term; if they dislike the term the chances are they will also wish to rebut the argument. None the less, the topic is intrinsically interesting, and Barr's discussion of it suggestive, as she balances Blake's assertions that Middle English can have no real sense of tradition with Axton's idea of textual force. However, these areas of debate are rather overwhelmed by tangling with a definition of tradition which is largely author-based. It is perhaps inevitable that books dealing with *Piers Plowman* and its inheritors make reference to Chaucer, but I am not convinced that it is desirable. In this case the comparison with an author so clearly eager to leave his mark in his texts skews the argument by making the comparative absence of a looming, named, authorial presence in *Piers* seem more remarkable than would have been the case had the comparison been made with one of the many other late medieval texts written by someone possessed of a less large textual ego. Since the main thrust of Barr's case is that it is *Piers* the *poem* which provides the material and inspiration for a tradition, this long and not entirely clear consideration of the Author seems rather tangential. Once it is left behind, the nitty-gritty of textual analysis begins and with it the excitement.

As her title indicates, Barr's main interest lies in the relation between what is said, how it is expressed, and where truth may lie. Much of what is good here is the close study which goes into explaining how each text uses the discourses appropriate to its own subject to criticize that very subject matter. The explications are often illuminating, tending to illustrate how the text undermines intended meaning (a term which does not seem to cause the same degree of anxiety as 'tradition') and reveals more than expected about the close relation between one sphere of discourse and another. An example is 'pickis', used of *Richard the Redeless*'s porter, which is revealed to be both a cutting remark on the porter's footwear (ludicrous and upwardly mobile) and actual pikes. Anti-puns, too, play a part, neatly illustrated by playing through the various possibilities of 'mete', itself a significant word in *Piers*. There is nothing exactly new here for those who have read A. V. C. Schmidt's *The Clerkly Maker: Langland's Poetic Art* (Brewer, 1987) or M. C. Davlin's *A Game of Heuene* (Brewer, 1989), but much to strengthen the central claim for a tradition of language use. Reading such passages, one has the sense of a tradition moving on from its foundation, of actually being a tradition rather than a series of imitations. This sense is confirmed in the final chapter, where the prominence of legal diction is taken to indicate the textual force of *Piers*, while the rather different deployment of this language in the later texts is evidence of departure from the founder text. Here one is aware of the presence of J. A. Alford's work on legal diction, just as one was aware of Ann Hudson's work on Wycliffite texts in the previous chapter. In each case the presence is a fruitful one, as Barr selects from the mass of information and argues her own particular application of the material with a conviction which in the end carries the day.

Susanna Greer Fien has detected an alliterative stanza buried in the prose of Rolle's *Form of Living* ('A Thirteenth-Century Alliterative Stanza on the Abuse of Prayer from the Audelay MS', *MÆ* 63.i.61–74). Fien suggests that the prose contains a trigger, 'Rebul' which has resulted in the verse being included, having been recalled from memory. As the manuscript has the distinction of having belonged to the first named carol writer, and as the stanza deals with criticisms often levelled at clergy, namely neglecting prayers and holy service (singling out particularly the bad habits of skipping and mumbling), it 'becomes another bit of evidence for piecing out a history of an interesting poetic movement'. The stanza and surrounding Rolle text are supplied in an appendix.

Finally Monica Brzezinski Potkay suggests that the legal system which provides the grounding of *The Owl and the Nightingale* is the theoretical one of natural law ('Natural Law in *The Owl and the Nightingale*', *ChauR* 28. 368–83). Neither bird defines either nature or laws; instead, they present conflicting definitions in their speeches. Potkay traces the origins of these definitions through Stephen of Tournai, Gratian and Peter Damian and supports the view that the author of the poem was trained in canon law. The Owl's charge of the bestial lechery of the Nightingale touches on the major question of this text, and indeed any other animal fable, which is how far animal tales furnish moral examples for humans. Potkay regards love as the unique aspect which marks off the human and animal, but she does not interrogate this claim, and it is one which current eco-critics, especially eco-feminists, might wish to dispute. Similarly, reason is regarded as a solely human preserve, a superior faculty inappropriate for animals. While it is likely that this is an accurate reflection of medieval views, it would be interesting to see how interpretation of this text changes when these apparent givens are questioned: it is after all a text of questioning and debate. Potkay also leaves the matter of inappropriateness hanging when the birds resolve to adopt human laws in preference to the avian ways. The comic elements of the poem are stressed throughout, and regarded as undermining the concept of natural law as the rule of the animal kingdom. This engaging piece also offers a clear tour round the complicated notion of natural law, and as such will be of value to those more interested in that than in *The Owl and the Nightingale* itself.

3. The *Gawain*-Poet

In 'The Play World and the Real World: Chivalry in *Sir Gawain and the Green Knight*' (*PQ* 72[1993].403–18), Victoria L. Weiss deftly argues that the pageants of medieval chivalry straddled game and earnest, and in this ambivalence lies a potentially confusing ambiguity for anyone seeking self-definition through pageantry's means. She makes intelligent use of historical details of thirteenth- and fourteenth-century mummings and disguisings to support her case. The perplexing question ever before Gawain is how seriously he should take the situations in which he finds himself.

Carolyn Dinshaw's gender-orientated criticism is brought to bear in 'A Kiss is Just a Kiss: Heterosexuality and its Consolations in *Sir Gawain and the Green Knight*' (*Diac* 24.205–26). Dinshaw seeks to trace what she believes is the poem's attempt to suppress diversity of meaning in favour of meaning that is monovalent. In a series of (for the larger part) provocative reflections, she argues that heterosexuality becomes one of the text's principles of intelligibility, and the homosexual inverse is gestured at in order to be suppressed rapidly. Arthur G. Lindley makes a case that Gawain's reorientation is essentially a private matter in '"Ther he watz dispoyled, with spechez of myerthe": Carnival and the Undoing of Sir Gawain' (*Exemplaria* 6.67–86). Constituted by his social world at the beginning, by the end Gawain has reconstituted his mental world as a way of reconstituting himself. The larger fiction of the heraldic world has been deconstructed. In 'The Wanting Words of *Sir Gawain and the Green Knight*' (*Exemplaria* 6.305–38), Elizabeth D. Scala contends that *Sir Gawain and the Green Knight* stages a confrontation with its own textuality. This it does, she believes, in order to stake its claim to value and viability.

Bella Millett wonders 'How Green is the Green Knight?' (*NMS* 38.138–51). She examines the history of the scholarship on the Green Knight's vegetation aspects down to the most recent, ecologically powered criticism about what he and Green Men in general have to say about the rapacious and exploitative nature of modern industrialized society. But she questions whether or to what extent the Green Knight should be linked with nature and the Green Man tradition, and makes an interesting case for believing that the text he inhabits may be more closed, less multivalent, than critics have hitherto tended to suppose.

J. J. Anderson considers '*Sir Gawain and the Green Knight*, 1008–1009' (*N&Q* 41.443) and what these lines have to reveal about the nature of Sir Bertilak's feast: the poet is saying, Anderson maintains, that a general description of the feast would be hard enough, and a detailed description would be endless.

In 'The Dreamer Redeemed: Exile and the Kingdom in the Middle English *Pearl*' (*SAC* 16.119–42), Jim Rhodes attempts to reclaim a central role for the dreamer in the social and theological discourse of *Pearl*. He proposes in this thoughtful and informed piece that the poem may be regarded as constructed around a Bakhtinian dialogic, in which both parties have equal authority, instead of around a traditional Boethian dialogue, in which the Maiden is superior to the dreamer. Earl R. Anderson comments on '*Pearl* 755: *Ostriys* "Chamber"' (*ELN* 32.10–13), and advances the possibility that this crux means 'chamber' (< Medieval Latin *hosteria*).

4. *Piers Plowman*

The facsimile of Bodley 851, the Z-Text of *Piers Plowman* (C. Brewer and A. G. Rigg, *Piers Plowman*), is produced to the same high standard as the facsimile of MS Douce 104 (*YWES* 73). Rigg provides a clear and detailed description of the whole manuscript of which the Z-Text forms a part. As well as furnishing the textual and historical beef for the Z-Text claim, it also enables even a fairly untutored reader to grasp some idea of the kinds of thing these manuscripts are, with their mixture of contents and gradual additions as they pass down the years. As one would expect given the history of the reception of the claim for the existence of the Z-Text, Charlotte Brewer's introduction is an adamant, firmly worded restatement of the arguments in favour of a 'rolling text' of *Piers*, which begins by reminding us of the huge influence that Skeat's judgement of the history of the poem has had (and continues to have) on its reception, and goes on to advocate close scrutiny of editorial practices and principles. With unshaken confidence, Brewer presents the Z-Text as an authorial text. Central to this argument is the point that an author may cut when revising as well as expand. Though this possibility is eminently sensible in itself, and also suggested with regard to Langland as early as 1813 by Whitaker, Brewer points out that it has been largely ignored in studies of the text. A salutary paragraph in her introduction exposes how easily rational views may lie unattended for no good reason. Both Brewer here and Mann in her contribution to this year's *Yearbook of Langland Studies* ('The Power of the Alphabet: A Reassessment of the Relation between the A and the B Versions of *Piers Plowman*', *YLS* 21–50) highlight the unargued nature of the assumption that progress is from simplest and shortest to longest and most complicated. This is the linchpin of Brewer's argument, and is convincing. There are, however, other aspects which are less secure in her introduction. There is no scrutiny of the terms used when discussing different readings of the text: what does it mean to say that one is superior to another? Nor is there satisfactory consideration of the relative merits of collation versus single-text editorial practice. The final note of this introduction is the recognition of the importance of the scribe; with it comes an acknowledgement that once the search for authenticity is abandoned its concept becomes irrelevant. It is possible to see Skeat as an inheritor of this role of scribe. With a nice touch of irony he is awarded a triumphal fanfare by Brewer, but it is relegated to the penultimate footnote.

Jill Mann's discussion has a slightly different focus, as she has no particular text to defend but a thesis to present. It is good to see this highly interesting paper in print. Not only does she remind us of the ease with which we accept apparent chronologies, but she also points out that not all that Langland wrote need be good in poetic terms; likewise, not all the good stuff need be written by Langland. She cites John But's pastiche of Passus XII as a case in point. For Mann, B is the first and primary text, with A being an abridgement for less Latinate readers, who are also protected from or denied most sexual material. C may be a partial revision intended for another audience again and Z yet another abridgement. Taking account of views put forward by Doyle, Adams and Meroney, she suggests that A is the latest text, not the earliest.

In *Managing Language in 'Piers Plowman'*, Gillian Rudd draws on medieval and modern theorizing about language to explore the shifts in language's function in this difficult poem. Her close reading of portions of the different versions of *Piers* shows how Langland's work is invested with an awareness of the word as (Divine) *logos* and (human) *verbum*, and takes us through ways in which Langland uses language to explore themes of authority, interpretation and perception in a quest for spiritual wisdom and cognitive understanding, and the interrelation of different kinds of knowledge. Rudd emphasizes how *Piers* capitalizes on reading and writing as acts of interpretation, and urges readerly engagement – and re-engagement – with its linguistic complexity. Discussion of particular aspects of Langland's ambiguity is pleasingly nuanced, though for a study of language and perception, some aspects of language and communication, and the bounds of Langland's inquiries, seemed too readily taken on trust: one missed, for example, detailed investigation of what personification reveals about how an individual conceptualizes the abstract, and consideration of how social and political forces shape Will's language. [CB]

This year's volume of the *Yearbook of Langland Studies* consists mainly of proceedings of the Langland conference held in Cambridge in July 1993. The plenary addresses, of which Mann's is one, are printed here, some in slightly edited form. George Kane's paper addressed the topic of reading *Piers Plowman* at all. It begins with a lively attack on post-structuralism, which also reveals Kane's feeling of possession of the text, through references to 'our poem'. Barthes et al. might make an open-minded critic re-examine her or his assumptions, and so serve a useful purpose. (It is noticeable, though, that such re-examination does not include Kane's abandoning the use of the generic 'he' for a large group of critics which is including an increasing number of women.) The first nine pages are a disquisition on text and author, which concludes with the wonderfully appropriate point that 'to speak of an author's "ownership" of his text seems less precise than to think of him haunting it as what has been called an "unquiet presence"'. For the final term, Kane directs us to Séan Burke's *The Death and Return of the Author*, just as elsewhere he makes frequent reference to Barthes, while defining his own position as 'historicist humanist'. Kane then moves on to the topic of reading; we read *Piers* at least in part because of its canonical position. The meaning of the poem is partly the craftsmanship of its author, partly the preoccupations of the author and partly the response of the reader, who becomes 'a function of that meaning'. This is illustrated, wickedly, through mistakes made by respected critics of the poem, as Kane asserts the responsibility critics have for accurate reading: 'we read ourselves into the poetry we read'. Perhaps most interesting is the final acknowledgement of the need so many have to discover or create the author behind this poem, a need which Kane describes as compulsive and which ends this deeply personal piece, which otherwise has no conclusion.

Also revisiting familiar territory are Robert Adams (on the *ordinatio*), Anne Hudson on the Peasants' Revolt, David Aers dealing with *Piers* and theological politics, D. Vance Smith dealing with Meed in terms of reward and salvation, and Christopher Dyer providing an historical perspective on ploughmen with regards to *Piers*. Adams rehearses and further develops his contestation that the rubrics of the poem are not authorial in the light of Clopper's recent defence of them. His position is summed up by his own précis of the argument as it stood in 1985 when it was 'far from evident (and remains so) why the *Do* triad . . . should . . . hold the key to the structural significance of the entire poem. On the other hand, it was plain why a medieval editor – or a modern one, for that matter – might be tempted to use them for such a role: their refrain-like quality and minimal semantic content make them invitingly malleable.' This appeal may also lead to the layout of one manuscript being adopted by another whose text does not quite fit the division offered or imposed by the *ordinatio*. The case is argued through the A, B and C-Text traditions as Adams notes, for instance, that Vernon has no rubrics except for the announcement at the beginning of Passus 9 that a new section concerned with Dowel, Dobet and Dobest is about to commence, while the existence of two different and equally strong demarcations of the Dobet section in the C version is used to question the notion that the C rubrics are less corrupt than the B. In all, the resuscitation of the debate by Clopper and restatement of his position by Adams attest to the continuing desire to impose a regulated structure on the poem. Adams's appendices, which provide, amongst other things, a graphic correlation of two variant C *ordinatio*s and two from B and then a list of C manuscripts' rubrics, will provide future fuel for the debate for any who wish to embark upon it. Meanwhile, Hudson wishes to recover the sense of surprise which she feels is due to the evident connection of the poem with the Peasants' Revolt. More than simply a text roped in for effect in the letters of the revolutionaries, *Piers* may well have been a vehicle for communication between the leaders. Its use as a 'rallying cry' may actually tell us something about the way the poem was read in the decade following its dissemination: '[m]ost obviously *Piers* is being read as a social document, a critique of contemporary church and state', but need that mean it is actively inciting revolt? Hudson almost teasingly suggests that Langland's text is deliberately 'coded to the point of unintelligibility' and as such is akin to revolutionary writing. She further argues that the B-Text may contain elements of Langland's reaction to having his poem adopted by the Revolt; B.15.564–7 in particular may be seen to echo Wyclif's analysis of social ills in *De Blasphemia* and the demands of Ball and Wat Tyler during the revolt. Other phrases, too, take on greater resonance if we accept the idea that the Revolt and its use of A may have been the spur behind writing the B version, with the C version being the result of mixed feelings about that use and its outcome. Being responsible for a reformatory text which becomes a revolutionary one would indeed be, as Hudson describes it, 'an unsettling experience'.

Aers looks at the representations and use of the humanity of Christ, with particular reference to Caroline Walker Bynum's claim that biology and subordination made women (and enabled them to be) more powerful representations of the suffering aspect of Christ, which is usually invoked when the humanity of Christ is being considered. To Bynum's work, Aers seeks to add dimensions of political theology and the broader canvas of plural representations of Christ's humanity, thereby adding also to our understanding of the *imitatio Christi*. He points out that the women who practised the extremes that form the basis of Bynum's study, and who provide the context for Lochrie's study of Margery Kempe, were not in fact the political subversives of their times. He accords that role to the like of Lollards, Cathars and Waldensians. Clearly we have a different definition of political subversion here, one which firmly places the Lollard desire to reform thoroughly the practices of the church as central to any discussion of this nature. The kinds of change that interested the Lollards also meant a shift of focus away from the individual experience and suffering of Christ and on to his ministry. Imitating

Christ's example also changes from enduring suffering, especially self-inflicted suffering, to living a worthy life. It is this form of *imitatio*, rather than the dominant one exemplified in Bynum and Lochrie's works, which is central to *Piers Plowman*, the command to live and work for the betterment of others which demands involvement in the social, not retirement from it into asceticism or self-abjection. 'The emphasis is on the way divine power, through the Incarnation, is identified *with* the cause of humankind.' The fact that Langland does not encourage the devotion to Christ which includes, even requires, personal suffering, omitting it even when dealing with the Crucifixion, indicates that he chose to follow a model of Christ's life which would have wider political, theological, individual and collective ramifications. Aers's assertion that it deserves to be studied in such a context tallies well with the general bent of this volume.

The most interesting element of Vance Smith's treatment of 'The Labors of Reward: Meed, Mercede, and the Beginning of Salvation' is that in order for the grammatical analogy employed by Conscience in C.3 to work in the terms of the poem it is not only necessary to assume an antecedent for the relation between pronoun and referent, but also to know what that antecedent or beginning is. Labour provides the answer, as the nature of work here is not only 'the work of material production but also the work of recuperating the origin of relation'. Historical and ideological context is supplied by a consideration of the account in Favent's chronicle of the Merciless Parliament of 1388, which attributes the evils and uncertainties of Richard's reign less to individual events and more to doubts about the integrity of Richard's original oath. Precedent plays an equally vital part in evaluating Meed, whose birth is debated and who is affected by entering the B-Text hard on the heels of Fauel. These implications are further developed in the C-Text, where it is made explicit that those who begin a relation by inquiring about the eventual reward are starting in the wrong place. Developing further the use of grammatical relation in the poem, Smith posits that Langland deliberately used the concept of relation because it is one which relies on the notion of absence and so allows him to draw analogies with social relations; a ploy which Smith describes as 'not merely a feat of ingenuity; his reliance on general theories of relation current in the fourteenth century gives a theoretical underpinning to his argument that human society and individual piety must refer to a foundation to be meaningful'. The desire to recover that foundation by recovering the beginning is, however, doomed to disappointment. It is unclear whether this means that the poem must now be regarded as fundamentally defeatist, with the espousal of the belief that seeking that beginning is in itself a 'most ethical activity', a poor palliative in the face of insuperable odds.

Dyer's historical perspective on ploughmen and *Piers* provides a different kind of food for thought by reminding us of the precise details scattered throughout the poem and telling us how accurate each one of them is. He also sets us right in our likely mental picture of Langland's rural landscape. We should be envisioning woodland and small enclosed fields, not strip cultivation of large open fields. Similarly, there is more to the choice of ploughman as protagonist than the metaphorical relation to preaching. Ploughing was a skill, an admirable and central task, demanding co-operation and social responsibility, unlike the frequently solitary occupation of shepherding. This is an engaging essay, providing much information about ploughing and how it was regarded which sheds real light on the figure of Piers. It is one of the most rewarding reads of this year's crop. It is followed by a note by John Friedman on the portrait of the friar found in MS

Douce 104, now, of course, available for more general consumption via facsimile. Friedman suggests that this portrait may be more than a straightforward picture of Sir Penetrans-Domos, the friar with alleged medical abilities who corrupts Unity. The illustrator may also have been alluding to the friar-glutton referred to as this 'iurdan' earlier in the poem, which in turn may be a reference to friar William Jordan, or even (additionally?) to Henry Daniel, a Dominican physician responsible for a diagnostic compilation on urine in 1379. In addition to some appealing speculation on such precise historical referents for the illustration, Friedman also directs our attention to a mid-fifteenth-century *horae* from Provence, which depicts a bespectacled rabbit holding up a uroscopy flask towards a pair of dogs, one on crutches. Rather tenuously, Friedman uses the association of dogs and Dominicans to link this joke on doctors with anti-mendicant feeling, and then suggests a similar link may lie behind the Douce friar. I suspect that this is a step too far.

A further four essays on *Piers* are to be found in *Art and Context in Late Medieval English Narrative*, edited by Robert Edwards. Three of these are useful additions to the pool of information and views of the poem. Anna Baldwin continues to explore the application of law to the text by elaborating the relation of debt law and narrative in *Piers*. The source of much of Langland's imagery was the thirteenth-century action of 'Account', which was largely obsolete in the later fourteenth century. The new law gives precedence to writing over a tally of debt, though merchants were allowed to use the old tally in common law courts. Baldwin makes no comment, but could this in part account for the exemption of merchants from the law as laid down in that crucially written text, the Pardon? Baldwin is more interested in positing that English debt law is a parallel to the law of Christ, since acceptance of the debt of sin is a sign of freedom to participate in one's salvation. The Pardon scene is allowed to remain obdurately difficult in Elizabeth Kirk's piece 'Langland's Narrative Christology', because of the problem of the image – where exactly does that piece of paper come from? It is a familiar question in these days of an increased volume of official documents with mysterious origins: a position perhaps not unlike that of a time when church magnates would be only names to a large proportion of the populace. The main focus of this piece is, however, the Passion. Kirk convincingly demonstrates how Langland's use of a nexus of images questions views which found the central action of B.18 in a way that is similar to the layout of a glossed Bible: the discussion literally surrounds the main point. In an equally detailed contribution ('The Chilling of Charity: Eschatological Allusions and Revision in *PP* C.16–17'), M. Teresa Tavormina deals with the ramifications of the phrase 'charite at chield is now' (C.17.49). The associations with the Last Days underpins the alterations from B to C-Texts of Anima to Liberum Arbitrium and in the details of the infected tree of the church. The emendations of the C-Text are defended as showing 'a great deal of careful and often effective poetic decision-making' as Liberum Arbitrium prepares the way for the Tree of Charity more fully than Anima's discourse in B. The whole piece is tightly argued and while the changes Tavormina notes are of degree rather than kind, this in itself may tell us something about the nature of poetic revision.

It is a shame that the first essay in this collection should be so regrettable. Larry Benson's piece, 'The Frustration of Narrative and the Reader in *Piers Plowman*', is an exercise in frustration itself, infuriatingly perpetuating the notion of Langlandian difficulty and the habit of discussing Langland only through comparison with Chaucer. While it means running the risk of being regarded as a humourless and crusty Langlandian, it is difficult to resist the temptation to dismiss this piece out of hand. Many holes may be picked in its assertions – more people may teach more of Langland than Benson believes, and the comparison with Chaucer cannot be maintained, as few indeed teach all of Chaucer's works. *Piers* is not so unlike much of medieval literature, though it may well seem unlike what we often choose to teach. Towards the end there is some calmer, more serious consideration of *Piers*: whether the reader calms down likewise is debatable, and for anyone relatively new to Langland the damage may well have already been done. This is a pity, as there are some interesting suggestions buried here concerning the way the reader's reaction is built into the text, thereby involving him or her in the complexities and moral questions of the poem. The respite is short-lived, however. The 'new techniques' Benson declares we need for teaching and reading Langland's texts, arising from the recognition that this is not a novel or 'purely narrative poem', have in fact been in place for some time.

In an interesting article, Hugh White compares the difference in use of original sin in Langland and Milton ('Langland, Milton and the *Felix Culpa*', *RES* 45.179, 336–56). Where Milton acknowledges the necessary and *felix* nature of the sin, but yet ends *Paradise Lost* on a negative tone, Langland points 'unambiguously forward' as Conscience rejoices at recommencing the journey which is, in *Piers* the best activity possible and a good in itself. For Langland mutability, a chief result of original sin, is a positive thing as it engenders love and a desire to know God (Elde's experience being cited as a case in point). Moreover, the Incarnation adds to God's knowledge, and, again, the acquisition of knowledge is regarded here as a certain good for Langland. None of this is the case for Milton, who sees the knowledge gained at the Fall as incremental and mutability as a cause for regret. Langland exploits and celebrates the creative condition of the Fallen world.

5. Romances

Romance, once considered something of a poor relation in Middle English studies, is now flourishing, especially as the focus of investigations into medieval culture as a whole. *Readings in Medieval English Romance*, edited by Carol M. Meale, brings together essays from the third conference on 'Romance in Medieval England', held at the University of Bristol, 31 March–2 April 1992, which demonstrate a range of critical approaches to their subject, from close readings to considerations of medieval texts in terms of modern critical theory. The most thought-provoking essays in the collection consider romance, and the concept of romance as a genre, in the context of its interrelation with other literary forms and what it can reveal of broader cultural issues. Maldwyn Mills, '*Sir Isumbras* and the Styles of the Tail-rhyme Romance', reviews the diversity of the extant manuscript texts of this highly popular romance in its own time, and shows how different redactors exploit the stylistic range offered by tail-rhyme, in both six- and twelve-line stanza forms, to augment and modify aspects of the romance. J. A. Burrow, in 'The Uses of Incognito: *Ipomadon A*', examines the function of the hero's tournament disguises in this fourteenth-century tail-rhyme romance, and argues that the assuming of various disguises makes possible an incremental presentation of the hero's valour, which, in this highly conservative romance, is essential to his definition as the worthiest knight in the world. Donna Crawford, '"Gronyng wyth grysly wounde": Injury in Five Middle English Breton Lays', builds on Elaine Scarry's recent theoretical work on physical injury, *The Body in Pain* (OUP, 1985), making use especially of the notion of the 'referential instability' of the wounded body, to summarize the disturbing instances of violence in *Sir Launfal*, *Sir Degaré*, *Sir Gowther*, *Sir Orfeo* and *The Earl of Toulouse*. This approach is fruitful in showing how injury can be integral to the narrative process, which leads ultimately to restitution and the confirmation of the social order with which (with the exception perhaps of *Launfal*) the lays are primarily concerned; and yet wounds also, as Crawford notes, stand as the measure of a loss for which there is no restoration. The observations on different uses of violence, and especially on violence against women in the definition of knightly prowess, would reward fuller development than is possible in a short article. A. S. G. Edwards's 'Gender, Order and Reconciliation in *Sir Degrevant*' notes the important conciliatory role played by women in this romance, as a counter to masculine values, and postulates that women's prominence here, the interest the poem shows in the relationship between gender and conduct, and the complexities of 'trawth' as a social value may owe something to a primarily female audience for the work.

Arlyn Diamond, 'Unhappy Endings: Failed Love/Failed Faith in Late Romances', sets *Sir Gawain and the Green Knight* and Chaucer's *Knight's Tale* in the context of medieval romance conventions of courtly discourse, and finds in Chaucer a refusal to allow desire a creative power, and in the *Gawain*-poet a manipulation of conventions culminating in Gawain's bitterness against women which is part of an occlusion of women's voices. In working against certain conventions, Diamond challengingly argues, these poets gesture towards a 'loss of faith in the social structures within which romance narratives were generated'.

In '"Bet . . . to . . . rede on holy seyntes lyves . . .": Romance and Hagiography Again', Jocelyn Wogan-Browne argues powerfully for the advantages of a broad cultural appreciation of medieval literature that recognizes interests common to hagiography and romance – for example, a concern with 'exemplary biography', and with the encyclopaedic as vehicle for religious and social instruction – taking for discussion the story of Pope Clement, which features in Middle English collections of saints' lives and in an Anglo-Norman version, and which contains many features found also in romance. This discussion is especially interesting for its observations on romance and hagiographic uses of female sexuality and integrity. John J. Thompson, 'The *Cursor Mundi*, the "Inglis tong", and "Romance"', also investigates romance in broader cultural terms, through what the prologue to this compilation of biblical stories, and the manuscript history of the collection, reveals of attitudes towards literature in general, and romance in particular: he also positions the *Cursor*-Poet's achievement in the context of a rich trilingual literary culture.

Two essays, Thorlac Turville-Petre, '*Havelok* and the History of the Nation', and Diane Speed, 'The Construction of the Nation in Medieval English Romance', offer complementary analyses of this early romance. Turville-Petre concentrates especially on how the poem can be read as 'historical' in impulse, and compares its account of its hero's career leading to the consolidation of disparate groups into one nation with the different approaches to ethnicity in the chronicle material. Speed both assesses the cultural significance of composing in English during this period, and intriguingly reads *Havelok* in the context of modern critical theory about nationalism, suggesting that the rise of romance as a literary form is commensurate with an interest in constructing a national literature. John Scattergood, meanwhile, considers an example of the local rather than the national concerns of romance, in '*The Tale of Gamelyn*: The Noble Robber as Provincial

Hero', where he interprets the relationship between violence and law in this poem against the background of contemporary documentation regarding legal corruption, the claims of the gentry, and the incidence and justifiability of violent lawlessness. For Colin Richmond's work on 'Thomas Malory and the Pastons', see section 9. Carol Meale's adroit survey of the challenges and clues the extant manuscripts of romance offer as regards receptions of, and audiences for, romance material, '"Gode men / Wiues maydnes and alle men": Romance and its Audiences', completes the volume.

Havelok is also the subject of Roy Michael Liuzza's 'Representation and Readership in the Middle English *Havelok*' (*JEGP* 93.504–19): Liuzza compares its depiction of details of non-aristocratic life with the realism of the late thirteenth-century Latin *Meditations on the Life of Christ*, and examines how in each the validation of bourgeois experience is a means to engagement with the text's larger themes, of social harmony and of contemplation respectively. In passing, he notes the inadequacy of working according to a strict notion of genre, as do several contributors to romance scholarship this year.

In 'The Rite of Vassalage in *Havelok the Dane*' (*M&H* 20.25–39), Liam O. Purdon argues that the poem is structured around examples of both complete and incomplete rites of vassalage, the former involving the doing of homage and leading to the establishment of secure social and political structures, the latter omitting the element of homage and permitting usurpation and the tyrannical misuse of power by those sworn to authority.

Timothy Jones, 'Geoffrey of Monmouth, *Fouke le Fitz Waryn*, and National Mythology' (*SP* 91.233-49), further emphasizes the benefits of reading across different kinds of text with his demonstration of how the Anglo-Norman author presents the one-time outlaw hero in the context of historicized feudal values, and appropriates and displaces Geoffrey of Monmouth's Brutus myth, replacing it with an ancestor's confrontation with a demon not unlike St Margaret's dragon, to construct an epic, Christian genealogy for his hero. Roger Pensom, 'Inside and Outside: Fact and Fiction in *Fouke le Fitz Waryn*' (*MÆ* 63.53–60), also looks at genre in this text, but sees its deployment as more formalized, the story depending for its effect on a reader's consciousness of the distinction between the three basic narrative types Pensom identifies (chronicle, folktale and the marvellous), and the nature of their interaction in a story centrally concerned with history and legality. John K. Bollard, '*Hende Wordes*: The Theme of Courtesy in *Ywain and Gawain*' (*Neophil* 78.655–70), cuts through some of the more negative assessments of English redactions of French material with an analysis of the care with which the English author uses the term 'hende', noting both the word's semantic range and the skill with which its thematic importance is woven into the narrative.

Kathleen Coyne Kelly, 'The Bartering of Blauncheflеur in the Middle English *Floris and Blauncheflеur*' (*SP* 91.101–10), debunks critical assessment of this romance as 'charming' in favour of a darker interpretation that draws on Gayle Rubin's critique of Lévi-Strauss, and stresses the importance to the story of Blauncheflеur's status as object of exchange, a slave: Kelly thus points out unresolved tensions rather than resolution in the fate of the poem's heroine. Shearle Furnish , 'The Modernity of *The Erle of Tolous* and the Decay of the *Breton Lai*' (*MedPers* 8[1993].69–77) sees this text, in its formal difference from other *lais* and in its interest in human agency and political life, as evolving from *lai* to novella. Robert Cook, 'Chaucer's Franklin's Tale and "Sir Orfeo"' (*NM* 95.333–6), suggests that the earlier poem provides the material for the visions of courtly entertainments the magician produces for Aurelius in Chaucer's text.

Matthew Hearn, in 'Twins of Infidelity: The Double Antagonists of *King Horn*' (*MedPers* 8 [1993].78–86), relates the romance to its historical thirteenth-century context by reading the Saracens as displacements of political anxieties about feudalism: in working against Fikenhild, Horn proves his integrity as loyal knight, while his defeat of the Saracens proves his worthiness to be king. Daniel F. Pigg, 'The Implications of Realist Poetics in the Middle English *Athelston*' (*ELN* 32.1–8), is a somewhat terse and densely argued evaluation of the poem as concerned with the multivalency of signs and the difficulty of establishing truth in society, at the same time as it is highly aware of the power relations between church and royal court.

Harriet E. Hudson, 'Construction of Class, Family, and Gender in Some Middle English Popular Romances' (in Harwood and Overing), relates differences among literary treatments of these issues in four romances spanning a hundred-and-fifty-year period (from *Sir Eglamour of Artois*, *c.*1350, and *Torrent of Portyngale*, *c.*1400, to *Paris and Vienne*, *c.*1478, and *The Squire of Low Degree*, *c.*1500) to the specific interests of their gentry audience. Hudson concludes that the later romances tend to confirm, rather than explore the implications of, conservative family structures, but that in their contradictory constructions of class and gender they also conveniently blur the contradictions in the lives of their audiences.

The romance essays in *Oral Poetics in Middle English Poetry*, edited by Mark Amodio, are rather more traditional in their approach to the subject. Nancy Mason Bradbury, in 'Literacy, Orality, and the Poetics of Middle English Romance', challenges what she sees as modern literate critics' prejudices about the oral aspects of this material, and urges a proper appreciation of the cultural position of 'memorial transmission'. Alexandra Hennessey Olsen, 'Oral Tradition in the Middle English Romance: The Case of *Robert of Cisyle*', uses the Vernon manuscript (*c.*1390) of the poem as a base-text, and argues that differences between it and later manuscript versions that substitute different wordings but follow the sense of the earlier text are more likely to be the result of the transcription of oral performances than of scribal emendation. Dave Henderson, meanwhile, in 'Tradition and Heroism in the Middle English Romances', assumes romances are 'oral-derived', and determines the degree of 'traditionality' (or 'closeness to hypothetical oral provenance') of a romance according to the characterization of the hero. Horn and Havelok are what Ong would call 'heavy' characters, lacking in complexity: *Amis and Amiloun* is similarly a 'traditional' romance, in terms of character, but is complicated by the intrusion of 'religious allegory'. *Sir Gawain*, however, is furthest removed from the oral, as evidenced by the complexity of the hero and its ambiguity.

In *Culture and the King: The Social Implications of the Arthurian Legend: Essays in Honor of Valerie M. Lagorio*, Martin B. Shichtman and James P. Carley have edited an interesting collection of articles. Among them is Edward Donald Kennedy's 'The Stanzaic *Morte Arthur*: The Adaptation of a French Romance for an English Audience', which argues that the changes to the French text the English author makes, in what is a reinterpretation rather than a translation, recast Arthur in the more positive mould of the English chronicle tradition. In the same volume, Elspeth Kennedy's 'The Knight as Reader of Arthurian Romance' concentrates on the reception of Arthurian literature in thirteenth-century non-Arthurian writings, and surveys the diversity of response to and use of Arthurian romance in, for example, discussions of chivalric ethics. Ad Putter, 'Finding Time for Romance:

Mediaeval Arthurian Literary History' (*MÆ* 63.1–16), investigates how various French and English writers locate their tales in an 'historical' Arthurian regnum as outlined by, for example, Geoffrey of Monmouth, and uses the example of Robert Mannyng of Brunne's consolidation of the heterogeneity of Arthurian material into one historical account to show to what extent romance and chronicle writers share perspectives on a historical Arthur.

Edward E. Foster's revised edition of Larry D. Benson's *King Arthur's Death: The Middle English Stanzaic 'Morte Arthur' and Alliterative 'Morte Arthure'* (first published in 1974) updates the original in line with the editorial practices of the TEAMS Middle English Texts series. It offers a lightly modernized and regularized spelling text, based primarily on J. D. Bruce's EETS edition of the *Stanzaic Morte* (e.s. 88, 1903) and Edmund Brock's EETS edition of the Alliterative text (o.s. 8, 1871). The text itself is clearly set out with footnotes and marginal glosses, a separate glossary and textual and critical endnotes. The prefatory material is aimed squarely at the teacher of introductory-level courses in Middle English, explaining the editorial methodology in pedagogical rather than purely scholarly terms, and the text should make a valuable addition to the TEAMS texts series, fulfilling its intention of bringing two important Middle English texts before readers 'who have had little or no training in Middle English'.

There are some textual notes on romances. Bengt Lindström (*N&Q* 41.11–14) offers 'Eight Notes on *Havelok*', questioning the wisdom of various editorial emendments to the text, and in general proposing more sensible and straightforward solutions. A. S. G. Edwards's 'Stanzaic *Morte Arthur*, line 3651' (*N&Q* 41.10–11) points out that 'Oure wylle hathe be to sore bought solde' is presumably a scribal anticipation of a collocation, and should rather read 'to sore sold'. Frank Stubbings has written up his discovery, in a sixteenth-century binding, of 'A New Manuscript of *Generydes*' (*TCBS* 10[1993].317–40): to be catalogued as Emmanuel College MS 405, the text consists of thirty-six stanzas of Version B of the romance, in a late fifteenth-century hand, together with fragments of other writings.

Of related interest to readers of English romance are Matilda Tomaryn Bruckner, *Shaping Romance: Interpretation, Truth, and Closure in Twelfth-century French Fictions*; and *Cyclification: The Development of Narrative Cycles in the Chansons de Geste and the Arthurian Romances*, edited by Bart Besamusca et al. Bruckner's book depends on informed close readings of familiar and not-so-familiar French works, taking us from (fairly traditional) interpretations of the Tristan legend in the *Folie Tristan d'Oxford* and Thomas's surviving fragments of the story, to more exciting readings of Chrétien de Troyes' *Chevalier de la Charrette* (focusing particularly on Lancelot as a meeting-point of the contradictions and conflicts of Arthurian romance), gender and genre in *Partonopeu de Blois*, and the importance of an awareness of story-collection in Marie de France's *Lais*. The emphasis throughout is on romance fictions as sites of experimentation, in terms of both form and ideas, and in the process Bruckner explores the interplay in romance of oral and written, and of author, narrator and reader, the instability of signifying systems, and the importance of the genre as an investigation of the forms of human perception.

The essays and discussion notes in *Cyclification* examine more closely the development into narrative cycles of those romances (especially in prose) that Bruckner's analyses suggest are a natural consequence of the earlier romances' implicit invitation to narrative continuation. Emmanuèle Baumgartner, in 'Le roman de *Tristan* en prose et le cercle des bretthes estoires', offers a resumé of the narrative techniques of the prose *Tristan* – its intercalation with the Arthurian prose cycle, its use of lyric, for example – and sees the principal forms of augmentation as those of continuation and of what she calls a 'decentring', whereby Tristan is no longer the central focus as hero, but one site of interest among several. In 'Les techniques de la formation des cycles dans les chansons de geste', Michael Heintze detects related methods of cyclic production and continuation in this material, and though he notes that a *chanson de geste* might make brief reference to Arthurian material, these interpolations are never enough to interfere with the distinctive character of the *chanson de geste* cycle. Jane H. M. Taylor, 'Order from Accident: Cyclic Consciousness at the End of the Middle Ages', distinguishes between 'sequential' cyclicity, the linking of narratives, perhaps involving one hero, in linear time, and 'organic' cyclicity, which involves a sense of the place of such narratives in an overarching world history. Taylor emphasizes an increasing interest on the part of compilators of cyclic material in genealogy and in Biblical eschatology, and traces the subsuming of sequential into organic cyclicity from the thirteenth century onwards. Povl Skårup, in 'Un cycle de traductions: *Karlamagnus saga*', considers how the Old Norse translations of disparate material relating to Charlemagne might be said to constitute a cycle. Bart Besamusca's discussion of 'Cyclification in Middle Dutch Literature: The Case of the *Lancelot* Compilation' compares a Dutch compilation of verse translations of the latter part of the French Vulgate Cycle, into which are woven translations of seven other Arthurian romances, with French compilations of Arthurian material to determine the scale of the Dutch compiler's orthodoxy and innovativeness.

Discussion notes in the volume are organized around the topics of typological, codicological, biographical, 'genetic', and structural and thematic aspects of cyclification, and together offer a series of pathways into issues of cyclical organization, demonstrating how much there is still to be explored in a form of literature which, as Donald Maddox's thoughtful contribution suggests, demands a deal of concerted interdisciplinary effort to explain its production, reception and cultural value.

Norris J. Lacy looks at the phenomenon of 'Emergent Direct Discourse in the Vulgate Cycle' (*ArthI* 4.19–29), that is, the shifts from narration to indirect discourse and back again, even within sentences, the effect of which is, he claims, to merge the cycle's voices into the governing voice of the 'conte'. At the same time, Lacy's concluding notes on how modern punctuation can obscure the rich ambivalence of who is speaking when, and the way in which the technique makes us aware of the production and transmission of voice, suggest more varied ways of interpreting its incidence.

6. Gower, Lydgate, Hoccleve

The work of all three writers in this section is increasingly being discussed within parameters that seek to define and account for its possible cultural, social and political positionings and contexts. Larry Scanlon, in *Narrative, Authority, and Power: The Medieval Exemplum and the Chaucerian Tradition*, ambitiously sets out to contextualize these authors' productions in an investigation of the political and ideological issues, particularly the questions of authority and power, raised by the exemplum and its handling by writers in Latin and the vernacular. The book sketches an outline of the ideological and cultural conditions of the exemplum in

Latin – Scanlon distinguishes between the 'sermon' exemplum and the 'public' exemplum – to inform a study of the *Canterbury Tales*, Gower's *Confessio Amantis*, Hoccleve's *Regement* and Lydgate's *Fall of Princes*, all predicated for Scanlon (in varying degrees) on concerns with vernacular lay, as opposed to clerical, authority. Scanlon argues that Chaucer appropriates ecclesiastical authority in his authorization of his own fictions, the *Canterbury Tales* serving as an exploration and affirmation of secular narrative (though the discussion seems to assume an uncharacteristic overdefensiveness on Chaucer's part).

The claims of vernacular literary authority through Chaucer established, Scanlon offers a challenging reading of the *Confessio Amantis*, in which Gower is seen to combine a more explicit anti-clerical critique with a celebration of lay political authority, concentrating especially on kingship. The later poets modify these positions in their writings, moving away from anti-clericalism, but Scanlon suggests also that they are accordingly more dependent on the secular power of the moment. Thus, Hoccleve's *Regement* is a legitimizing of the future Henry V's rule which also shows the poet deriving his authority from the prince. The bold analysis of Lydgate's *Fall of Princes*, in the context not only of Lydgate's poetic promulgation of moral order, but of how Lydgate's treatment of the hero might be said to anticipate the operations of Renaissance drama, offers much food for thought. One might have reservations about the ways in which 'authority' is defined in this study, and about the implicit assumptions made concerning the role and nature of the vernacular, but the author offers it as a 'stimulus to further discussion' of the issues it raises, and it will certainly achieve that.

Russell A. Peck, 'The Phenomenology of Make Believe in Gower's *Confessio Amantis*' (*SP* 91.250–69), offers an alternative approach to Gower in a densely argued piece that traces in the poet's treatment of the fictions and ideologies of the past a receptiveness to empirical semantics that reflects the late medieval interest in empirical sign theory as central to theories of perception and the interiority of representation. Charles A. Owen Jr, 'Notes on Gower's Prosody' (*ChauR* 28.405–13), provides us with exactly that: observations on how aspects of Gower's style serve to reinforce his meaning, and how the poet's revisions of his work bear witness to his technical accomplishment.

There are other political readings of Lydgate's position: for 1993, Lee Patterson's contribution to *New Historical Literary Study: Essays on Reproducing Texts, Representing History*, edited by Jeffrey N. Cox and Larry J. Reynolds, entitled 'Making Identities in Fifteenth-century England: Henry V and John Lydgate', argues for a certain resistance to Lancastrian rule on the part of the Lydgate who writes *The Siege of Thebes*, even as its author appears to be consolidating a literature (his own included) that celebrates the monarch as representative of English integrity. The essay traces Henry V's meticulous political self-fashioning, and the role of the English vernacular within that construction of identity, but also points out its inherent contradictions; it thus reconstructs a political and literary background against which Lydgate's *Siege of Thebes* emerges, in terms of both its fraught historical theme and its authorship by a Benedictine, as an assertion of the claims of poetry against political power, and an expression of anxiety over late medieval historical constructions of political legitimacy, which has much in common with Chaucer's *Troilus and Criseyde*. Nicholas Watson has a different assessment of Lydgate's attitude to Chaucer in his wittily executed 'Outdoing Chaucer: Lydgate's *Troy Book* and Henryson's *Testament of Crisseid* as Competitive Imitations of *Troilus and Criseyde*', in *Shifts and Transpositions in*

Medieval Narrative: A Festschrift for Elspeth Kennedy, edited by Karen Pratt. Watson argues that Lydgate, in his *Troy Book*, by associating Chaucer with feminine perfidy, contains and then displaces the earlier poet's concerns and refashions the Troy story for his own moralizing interests. By contrast, Henryson stands in more complex relation to Chaucer's creation, capitalizing on the ambiguities of *Troilus and Criseyde* in the production of his own poem.

Karen A. Winstead, 'Lydgate's Lives of Saints Edmund and Alban: Martyrdom and *Prudent Pollicie*' (*Mediaevalia* 17[1994 for 1992].221–41), contextualizes Lydgate's work in what she identifies as fifteenth-century developments in hagiography, shifts in emphasis Lydgate himself helped to bring about: thus, Lydgate's literary treatment of the two saints' lives, influenced by French and Latin models, shows a greater interest in history, but also in moral complexity, the reconciliation of the spiritual and temporal, a tolerance of human weakness and the interests of community, elements with which fifteenth-century piety is generally concerned. Bryan Crockett, 'Venus Unveiled: Lydgate's *Temple of Glas* and the Religion of Love' (in *New Readings of Late Medieval Love Poems*, edited by David Chamberlain [1993]), summarizes recent critical evaluations of the poem in the course of his interpretation of it as intellectually playful, and an ironic treatment of frustrated love, part of a long tradition of such approaches to love in medieval literature.

Hoccleve too is receiving more serious critical attention. In a slim volume on *Thomas Hoccleve* in the Variorum 'Authors of the Middle Ages' Series, John Burrow offers an overview of the life of Thomas Hoccleve, reconstructed from the available evidence: in an appendix Burrow brings together material from contemporary documents relating to Hoccleve, and the bibliography lists the extant manuscripts of Hoccleve's works, according to their contents. Unfortunately, the bibliography is not without error; for example, on p. 55, the Ashburnham and Phillipps MSS both appear as San Marino, CA Huntington Library MS HM 111 (though the correct reference for Ashburnham is given on p. 52), and Rosenbach Museum & Library MS 1083/30 appears as Rosenbach Foundation MS 1983/10. This suggests information needs to be carefully checked against other sources: in general terms, however, this remains a useful preliminary reference text for the Hoccleve scholar.

Ethan Knapp brings together Hoccleve the civil servant and Hoccleve the poet in a short article on 'Bureaucratic Identity and Literary Practice in Lancastrian England' (*MedPers* 9.63–72), arguing that the petitionary language of the often-neglected *Formulary*, the collection of administrative documents copied out by Hoccleve, offers clues to the construction of Hoccleve's poetic identity. Knapp is especially interesting on how the cultivated anonymity of the bureaucratic petitioner can prompt an oppositional emergence of a conception of the self. Derek Pearsall, in 'Hoccleve's *Regement of Princes*: The Poetics of Royal Self-representation' (*Speculum* 69.386–410), considers the nature of good counsel in this poem within the constructions of Lancastrian propaganda. In his argument that Hoccleve presents Chaucer as exemplar of literary nationhood as a correlative to the presentation of the future Henry V as ideal ruler, and that anti-Lollard orthodoxy plays a large part in these fashionings of writer and monarch, Pearsall suggests Hoccleve's concerns are subsumed by the political interests of the Prince.

7. Middle Scots Poetry

The only book I have been able to see on the subject this year is Rosemary Greentree's study of Henryson's *Moral Fables*, entitled *Reader, Teller, and Teacher*, which is a competent if uninspiring treatment of the tales, dividing the power of the narrator into the three roles of her title, to rather limiting effect. The initial claim that as 'reader and teller, the narrator serves as the window through which the audience may gain an experience of the fanciful world of the tales' would benefit hugely from some consideration of whether or not this window distorts. The presentation is overdirective, though the defence of the Bassandyne order is reasonable and the brief consideration of the Bannatyne manuscript in the appendix has some merits. The area has been better served by articles, with William Stephenson detecting an acrostic in lines 58–63 of Henryson's *Testament*, which reads 'FICTIO' ('The Acrostic "Fictio" in Robert Henryson's *The Testament of Cresseid* [lines 58–63]', *ChauR* 29.163–5). This occurs at the very point where Henryson refers to the 'vther quair', which, with the use of 'fenȝeit' in the following stanza, leads Stephenson to the conclusion 'one can hardly doubt that his reference to the "vther quair" is involved in a pretence'. Edward Wheatley discusses Henryson's fables through comparison with educational texts, a context which he points out has been oddly overlooked given Henryson's position as a schoolmaster. 'Scholastic Commentary and Robert Henryson's *Morall Fabillis*: The Aesopic Fables' (*PQ* 73.70–99) begins with a discussion of the commentaries which the 'Romulus' collection of Aesopic fables acquired in the Middle Ages, in which Wheatley points out that much of what Rita Copeland says of Latin commentaries of more philosophical texts could be applied to the commentaries on the fables. Detailed reading of the passages given by Henryson to his narrator reveals that Henryson is satirizing Priscian, the role of the schoolmaster who sets his pupils to translate and abridge 'Aesop', and the topos of translation myths (such as those which preface the 'Romulus' collection), and even taking the odd poke at the narrator figure himself. In addition, he used the fables as vehicles for different forms of academic discourse, rather than leaving them at the level of simple rhetorical models for children, the role assigned them by Priscian. Wheatley goes on to present attentive readings of some of the fables, illustrating how the choice of material and voice for the *moralitas* provides evidence for the kind of close engagement with scholarly discourse and discussions that he perceives in Henryson's work. Likewise, his choice of a particular animal for voicing particular views can be seen to be affected by his knowledge of the scholastic commentaries of Walter's fables. Wheatley thus debunks the notion that Henryson delighted in being perverse, stating that those elements of the *Fabillis* which modern critics find unsettling are the result of his delight in the variety available in the scholastic fable tradition, to which Henryson has added a few embellishments of his own.

In 'Nationalism in Barbour's *Bruce*' (*Parergon* 12.89–107), Diane Watt reads the *Bruce* in the light of the Declaration of Arbroath. Questioning the notion that nationalism was essentially a post-medieval phenomenon, she reads Barbour's text as a persuasive document aimed at all Scotsmen, nobleman to serf, figured as the 'imagined political community' of the nation.

Several essays in *Selected Essays on Scottish Language and Literature*, a festschrift for Allan H. MacLaine edited by Steven R. McKenna, deal with Middle Scots material. In '"The Hurt Off Ane Happie The Uther Makis": Henryson's Construction of His Audience', Rosemary Greentree and Steven R. McKenna discuss the morally didactic functions of cruel humour in the *Fables*. Humour also provides a focus for David Parkinson's chapter, 'Prescriptions for Laughter in some Middle Scots Poems', which considers the 'ballettis mirry and uthir solacius consaittis' of the Bannatyne manuscript, and chiefly the works of Dunbar and Henryson's 'Sum Practysis of Medecyne'. Parkinson draws parallels between the treatment of 'venomous' invective and that of more literal poisons and sicknesses in these texts. Taking its cue from Kennedy's dismissal of Dunbar as a 'Golyas' in 'The Flyting of Dunbar and Kennedy', Joanne S. Norman's 'William Dunbar: Scottish Goliard' discusses the similarities and dissimilarities between the poet's life and work and those of the original Goliardic writers. Norman suggests that the poet's much-commented-on 'two voices' of invective and panegyric, and the unstable poetic persona which he fashioned, were a reaction to his position of court poet, allowing him to free himself from what she sees as the limitations imposed by an 'official' point of view. In '"Self Aboif the Sternis Styld": Dunbar, Skelton, and the Beginning of the British Renaissance', James A. McGoldrick reads the satirical poems and flytings of Skelton and Dunbar in the light of Stephen Greenblatt's formulation of the concept of 'self-fashioning'. He suggests that in the abusive language and strategies of the flytings in particular 'the language of Renaissance nationalism is being formed'.

8. Lyrics and Miscellaneous Verse

Though dealing mainly with the French troubadour tradition, Gregory B. Stone's book *The Death of the Troubadour: The Late Medieval Resistance to the Renaissance* has much which could also be applied to lyrics written in English. He uses the lyrics and songs to illustrate his central thesis that the Renaissance's preference for *self*-expression and the birth of the individual ego were not necessarily a positive event. He acknowledges that it is, in fact, possible to question whether Burckhardt's distinction between the medieval and Renaissance subject as that between the individual as part of a generalized group (medieval) and as able to voice a sole opinion (Renaissance) is valid, but sets this aside in favour of what is perhaps a more interesting project. For Stone, late medieval 'anonymity . . . is a deliberate, mature rejection of the new Renaissance model of the self-determining singular ego', a model with which it is familiar but which it regards as wrong: '[t]he Middle Ages consciously insists that *I* am *they*'. It is this effort to perpetuate the value of the collective individual which forms the resistance of which the subtitle speaks. The 'I' of Troubadour song speaks for no one historical individual, and so for everyone who cares to be so spoken for. It is, after all, the plight of the courtly lover to find that he (or occasionally she) is just one of many and to find himself giving voice to a situation which has already happened many times and will be repeated many times again: it is this very fact that makes it worthy of repetition and furnishes a context as well as content for the songs. For Stone, the story, with its individual narrative and process, seeks to repress song, and it is the rearguard action that he depicts here. The vernacular song is seen as engaging with the nature of grammar and language itself, and in his first chapter he discusses it as *langue*, as a form which enshrines an abstract code, ruled by the notion of lyric subjectivity. The language of the love lyric is shown to be collective rather than individual, the use of the personal pronoun allowing all to adopt or have access to its subject. We are then led through the confusion and ambiguity of the voice in these lyrics, an ambiguity which recalls the way the dreamer in Chaucer's *Book of the Duchess* is able to overhear a personal lament without having to leap to the conclusion that it has personal application. The applications to those lyrics, which blend secular and religious aspects and are thus both love lyrics and addresses to Mary, are discussed in the chapter 'Lyric Secrecy', which again furnishes food for thought by reference to texts written in English, Latin or Macaronic verse, as well as those in French. The final chapter tackles a recurring theme directly in discussing Chaucer's *Book of the Duchess* and the tussle between narrative and lyric in it. While this text is in many ways ideal for this treatment, there are many verses which could also benefit from this kind of reading, from 'I have a yonge suster' to 'Noe goth sonne under wod'.

Meanwhile Andrew Breeze continues to direct our attention to Welsh texts and influences. In 'Two Bardic Themes: The Virgin and Child and *Ave*-Eva' (*MÆ* 63.17–33), he discusses the unusual development of these two themes in Welsh poetry. Friar Madog ap Gwlater is credited with the earliest poem on Christ's nativity: he may well have been writing as early as *c.*1250, while no English poem on this subject has been found before 1372. Madog's verse proves the existence of a vernacular Nativity lyric tradition which does not owe its existence to drama. The 'simplicity' of the verse is shown to be the result of careful use of longstanding literary themes which highlight the paradox of the Lord of Creation being born in a stable. Breeze acknowledges the influence of Franciscanism here. There is an interesting contrast with a twelfth-century Welsh poem found in MS Llanstephan 27 where the glory of Christ is described in highly feudal terms, leading to the perception of a shift in emphasis from twelfth to thirteenth century in the role of Mary, from revered power to loving mother. Turning to the *Ave*-Eva theme, Breeze concentrates on the poetry of Rhys Goch Enyri which plays on the Welsh 'awen' (poetic inspiration) with 'Ave' and 'nef' (heaven) to yield a claim for divine inspiration: 'awen' can be regarded as the result of 'ave' and 'n'. It is not an entirely secure claim, but it allows Breeze to assert that Rhys's poem 'shows bards able to extract powerful arguments from unpromising material, producing a nimble, serious debate on poetry and the role of the poet which would be famous if had not been written in a minority language such as Welsh'. This subtle use of language by Welsh writers is further attested by Scott Gwara's note in the same number, where the use of a pun on the Latinized Welsh name Ioruert (Iorwerth) allows for the dual interpretations of the name as 'worthy, truthful' or 'turned', with the 'Ior' element being possibly 'eager' rather than 'lord'.

Wendy Scase seeks to rename the satirical poem entitled 'On the Corruption of Public Manners' by Wright, preferring 'Proud Gallants and Popeholy Priests' as more accurately reflecting the subject of this text. Her article, '"Proud Gallants and Popeholy Priests": The Context and Function of a Fifteenth-century Satirical Poem' (*MÆ* 63.275–86), puts the case for this poem to be read seriously rather than relegated to the margins as a piece of light satire which provides some information about dress, but little more. Scase's research shows that the elements of popular song, noted by Fairholt and Owst as akin to a quatrain in the *Brut*, have been grafted on to a piece on popeholy priests. This has been done with some skill, creating a coherent new poem, not just a yoking together of two disparate halves. Scase contests that the anti-gallant satire and criticisms of popeholy priests have some common ground which explains the experiments with the material evidenced by this text. The main link is criticism of apparel, with both target groups being accused of being too caught up in a love of good, even showy clothing. In the case of the priest, an additional factor is that the codes of dress which applied to clergy served to differentiate lay and religious in a way intended to invest the religious with authority. Priests who criticized gallants for obsession with dandy clothes, yet who themselves transgressed the clerical dress codes, were thus not only hypocritical but also liable to undermine the authority they were supposed to represent. By exploiting popular song for the purposes of satirically joining in the public discourse on the authority of the clergy, this text 'negotiates independence' from the expected forms of discourse and gives rise to several related texts which are not only defined against the official discourses, but also contribute to them.

In *Fortunes Stabilnes: Charles of Orleans's English Book of Love*, Mary-Jo Arn provides a splendidly comprehensive scholarly edition of BL MS Harley 682, with full critical apparatus of paraphrases at the foot of the page, textual and explanatory endnotes, glossary, bibliography, indices of first lines, *ballade* refrains, French counterparts of English poems and proper names, and an appendix of poems attributed to Charles of Orleans not found in Harley 682. The 129-page introduction sets the roundels, ballades, lyrics and narrative stanzas of this highly eclectic manuscript firmly in their codicological, linguistic, literary and historical context. The text itself is presented with only the minimum of regularization, but the punctuation is modernized, considerably facilitating its comprehensibility. Taken together, the constituent parts of this mammoth project make a cogent and persuasive case for a critical re-evaluation of Duke Charles and the acceptance of his *magnum opus* as an innovative, experimental and surprisingly playful poetic text.

9. Malory and Caxton

Some good work on Malory this year draws out his historical and literary/linguistic contexts. Colin Richmond's delightfully written contribution to *Readings in Medieval English Romance*, edited by Carol M. Meale, 'Thomas Malory and the Pastons', uses primarily epistolary evidence to sketch in the nature of the milieu to which Malory and this family belonged (though there is no evidence to suggest Malory knew the Pastons directly), and in the process both refines the definition of the 'fifteenth-century gentleman', and locates some of the mystery of Malory's literary work in the conditions of his existence in 'a world [he] made as little sense of as we do ours'.

Several engaging pieces on Malory appear in Shichtman and Carley. Martin B. Shichtman's own contribution is a highly competent (if somewhat tersely expressed) account of the breakdown of signs and the instability of meaning in the English author's handling of the Grail legend: 'Politicizing the Ineffable: The *Queste del Saint Graal* and Malory's "Tale of the Sankgreal"'. Where Shichtman sees the French source as an attempt to mediate the problems between the Cistercians and the chivalric classes, for him as for Richmond, Malory's work is 'a product of the chaos of fifteenth-century English culture'. Bonnie Wheeler's '"The Prowess of Hands": The Psychology of Alchemy in Malory's "Tale of Sir Gareth"' cogently suggests that Malory uses the language of alchemy in the description of the processes of Gareth's maturation. Maureen Fries, 'How Many Roads to Camelot: The Married Knight in Malory', draws on fifteenth-century debate about marriage to show that in Malory's world marriage is not finally compatible with masculine knightly honour. In the same collection, David R.

Carlson uncovers political uses for Malory's text in 'Before and After the Revolution: The Blome-Stansby Edition of Malory (1634) and *Brittans Glory* (1684)': the editors of the former work use the Arthurian legend to criticize the monarchy, while the later text celebrates the unity of the Arthurian court and through Arthur recommends strong monarchical rule as the means to political stability.

Gael Milun, 'Le bon chevalier loup-garou et la mauvaise femme: l'histoire de Sir Marrok dans *La Mort d'Arthur* [sic] de Thomas Malory' (*MoyA* 100.65–80), contextualizes Malory's brief mention of the werewolf knight who appears in the list of those who attempt to heal Sir Urry, tracing his tale especially in Breton legend, and drawing out motifs (such as sympathy for the lycanthrope) common to retellings of the werewolf story.

In 'From the Lady to the Tramp: The Decline of Morgan le Fay in Medieval Romance' (*ArthI* 4.1–18), Maureen Fries charts the dip in Morgan's fortunes, from her positive appearance as a healer in the *Vita Merlini* to her later associations with malign forces, while the benevolent figure of the Lady of the Lake (who has some of the aspects of the early Morgan) becomes more prominent in Arthurian story. Fries summarizes Morgan's role in Malory's text, and concludes that she is largely foiled by the Lady of the Lake (whom Fries here treats as a composite character) – a helper to Arthur and Arthurian heroes – yet the latter is herself only a minor figure in a book that privileges the masculine.

Some articles pay attention to specific aspects of Malory's language: Ingrid Tieken-Boon van Ostade, '"After a Copye unto Me Delyverd": Multiple Negation in Malory's *Morte Darthur*', in *English Historical Linguistics: Papers from the Seventh International Conference on English Historical Linguistics*, edited by Francisco Fernandez et al., examines differences and similarities in the use of the double negative between the Winchester and Caxton *Morte*s, in linguistic support of Hellinga's proposition that the Winchester MS is, together with an intermediate copy, the basis of Caxton's edition. Joy Wallace, 'Transposing the Enterprise of Adventure: Malory's "Take the Adventure" and French Tradition' (in Pratt), carefully follows through the semantic shifts of Malory's French-derived term, seeing the taking of adventure as positive with regard to Fair Unknowns such as Gareth, but gaining more negative overtones (particularly of recklessness) when applied to the behaviour of such as Balin and Lancelot: this thesis is particularly interesting in its analysis of the 'dislocations' of the last books of the *Morte*. Terence McCarthy, in 'Beowulf's Bairns: Malory's Sterner Knights' (in Carruthers), invokes the word 'stern' (a term identified with the alliterative tradition) in arguing that the spirit of Malory's work owes much to what he sees as the martial values specific to English epic and alliterative verse (and in passing, McCarthy displays an odd sense of humour with respect to violence against women [e.g. pp. 153, 154]). Alan J. Fletcher, 'King Arthur's Passing in the *Morte Darthur*' (*ELN* 31.iv.19–24), gives a close reading of another of Malory's expressions, the note that King Arthur 'chaunged hys lyff', and makes judicious use of both internal and external semantic evidence to show the resonances of this phrase, its simultaneous expression of the king's mortality and immortality.

Other studies dwell on general cultural contexts. Robert Kelly's 'Penitence as a Remedy for War in Malory's "Tale of the Death of Arthur"' (*SP* 91.111–35) offers a valuable reading of the historical and political importance of penitence both in Malory's text and in contemporary practice, and uses the English translation of Alain Chartier's *Treatise of Hope* to illuminate Malory's perspective, concentrating especially on his treatment of the characters of Lancelot and the Archbishop of Canterbury, to suggest that ultimately Malory's message is one of spiritual hope and comfort. Michael Murrin, in his rich book on *History and Warfare in Renaissance Epic*, which considers the effect of technical innovation on warfare in European epic narratives 1483–1610, gives some thought to Malory's reworking of romance battle material regarding Arthur's rise to power, to make it closer to contemporary warfare, and concludes that the introduction of realism serves in fact to expose the lack of fit between romance and history in this respect. He also notes the contradictions in Malory's treatment of war in the last books, as set in the past but also belonging to the present, but does not develop this line. Gayle Margherita's notes on the intrusion of a painful present on a fictional past in this context (pp. 155–7 of *The Romance of Origins*) offers a more explicit comment on what she characterizes as the 'historical problematic' of Malory's work.

Paul R. Rovang's study of 'Malory's Treatment of the Marvelous: A Comparison With his Sources' (*FCS* 21.279–302), concludes that while Malory's allusive style strengthens the literary effect of the incidence of magic in the *Morte*, he generally employs the marvellous insofar as it serves the human (especially chivalric) interests with which he is more concerned. Craig R. Davis also looks to Malory's French sources in 'Biblical Typology in Malory's *Morte Darthur*' (*Mediaevalia* 17[1994 for 1992]. 243–58), and, noting Malory's incorporation of biblical reference into his Grail narrative, finds the English author, like his French antecedents, endorses a biblical historical typological programme of what Davis identifies as 'election, supplantation, redemption' to inform his vision of Arthurian history.

William Calin's notes (in Besamusca et al.), 'The Prose *Lancelot* and Malory's *Morte Darthur*: Two Examples of Cyclification and the Problems they Pose', reproduce aspects of his argument in his book *The French Tradition and the Literature of Medieval England.* He thinks Malory decentres the original Lancelot story by having Tristram's romance occupy a third of his text, which lessens the unity of the original, and sees him following in the steps of earlier English adapters who abbreviate their source in the interests of emphasizing story and ethics. James Wimsatt also undertakes comparative research in his 'Type Conceptions of the Good Knight in the French Arthurian Cycles, Malory and Chaucer' (in Carruthers). Wimsatt traces the evolution of the 'good knight' from the Lancelot of the core of the Vulgate Cycle, who is 'displaced' by Galahad, to the *Tristan*, in which no single knight embodies the ideal, but where it is social interchange that defines it; Malory's treatment of the material endorses this viewpoint, while Chaucer too is intent on showing good knighthood in society rather than in one individual.

Cynthia Ho's essay, 'As Good As Her Word: Women's Language in *The Knight of the Tour d'Landry*' (which Caxton translates as *The Book of the Knight of the Tower*) (in Purdon and Vitto), concentrates on the way in which Landry inculcates in his daughters a loyalty to a feudal system, through the stress on the importance of the marriage vow and a general emphasis on a woman's moral duty to keep her word, that restricts their own fulfilment. Ho notes that Caxton's introduction reassures his readership that women as well as men approve the work's precepts.

Catherine Batt's '"Hand for Hand" and "Body for Body": Aspects of Malory's Vocabulary of Identity and Integrity with Regard to Gareth and Lancelot' (*MP* 91.269–87) takes as its central point the way that 'threats to the wholeness of a character's moral and social identity are often figured in physical terms'. Batt concentrates on Gareth and Lancelot in her discussion of Malory's vocabulary of battle. She reveals the subtlety of Malory's choice of terms; 'body for body' indicates judicial combat or a fight undertaken as an obligation, usually with an unknown or unspecified opponent. She points out that the roots of these connotations are to be found in French texts, such as the Vulgate Arthurian romances, and are to be found in Layamon, the fifteenth-century prose *Merlin* and Andrew of Wyntoun. In contrast, encounters of a more individual nature, where the knight is also in more control of events, are signalled by the more precise phrase 'hand to hand'. Batt convincingly demonstrates the precise connotations that lie behind allusions to knights' hands in the text, with Gareth being her main example. In all, Batt's piece directs our attention to aspects of the tales which are easily overlooked, because easily understood in ways more simplistic than that which she demonstrates they deserve. Her argument is precise and clear-headed, and includes some interesting passing remarks on magic. [GR]

Norman Blake's 'MS. Chetham 6709 and Some Manuscript Copies of Caxton Prints', in *Language and Civilization: A Concerted Profusion of Essays and Studies in Honor of Otto Hietsch, I & II*, edited by Claudia Blank (Lang) from 1992, has not been made available for review.

10. Other Prose

M. Teresa Tavormina has presented a formidable study of the mathematical propensities of the author of *Dives and Pauper* in 'Mathematical Conjectures in a Middle English Prose Treatise: Perfect Numbers in *Dives and Pauper*' (*Traditio* 49.271–86). She bases her discussion primarily on his arithmological strategies of interpretation, and his comments about perfect numbers. For any student of *Dives and Pauper*, this is not to be missed.

Manfred Görlach has edited *The Kalendre of the Newe Legende of Englande*, first printed in 1516 by Wynkyn de Worde as a distillation of his *Nova Legenda Anglie* that appeared in the same year. The *Kalendre* is a vernacular summary of the legends of 168 British saints, and was the last enterprise of its kind in England before the Reformation. Görlach's introduction includes discussion of the evolution of the *Kalendre* from earlier collections, its treatment of its immediate source (de Worde's *Nova Legenda Anglie*), a description of the surviving copies and analysis of matter of linguistic interest, as well as discussion of the contents and choice of saints. A standard editorial apparatus is included. Students of saints' lives will welcome Görlach's edition. Also welcome is *A Study and Edition of Selected Middle English Sermons* by Veronica M. O'Mara. Three sermons are edited, with discussion and apparatus: Richard Alkerton's Easter Week sermon of 1406 (London, British Library, MS Additional 37677, fols. 57–61); a sermon on Sunday observance (Durham, University Library, MS Cosin V.IV.2, fols. 125–8v); and finally a nunnery sermon for the Assumption (Cambridge, University Library, MS Hh.1.11, fols 128–32v). This is a useful volume which would have been substantially more so had it included an index, no matter how rudimentary. Andrew Galloway discusses 'A Fifteenth-century Confession Sermon on "Unkyndeness" (Cambridge University Library MS Gg. 6. 26) and its Literary Parallels and Parodies' (*Traditio* 49.259–69). His edition of the sermon, found on fols 22v–3r of the manuscript, makes an especially welcome supplement to what he has to say about its literary thematic congeners.

Karen A. Winstead reviews 'The Conversion of Margery Kempe's Son' (*ELN* 32.9–13), and finds a parallel between it and Margery's own conversion: God converted Margery, and Margery converts her son. Winstead sees the web of parallels working boldly to constitute Margery as a holy woman who has a leading role in God's plan for the world. In 'The Comfort of Voice, the Solace of Script: Orality and Literacy in *The Book of Margery Kempe*' (*SP* 91.50–69), Diana R. Uhlman argues that Margery's Book is couched within the interdependent relation between oral and literate cultures, and that it takes advantage of both cultures in order to communicate and to legitimate itself as mystical writing. Thus it follows for Uhlman that to emphasise oral over written or vice versa is to neglect the complicity between the two which the Book establishes.

One of the chapters in *Spiritual Discourse and the Meaning of Persons*, by Patrick Grant, will be of interest to students of Julian of Norwich. Grant fluently illustrates how Julian's *Showings* are permeated with an uneasy tension between the individuality of her experience and her awareness of the orthodox categories by which it would in its day have been assessed.

In 'Public Revisions or Private Responses? The Oddities of BL, Arundel MS. 197, with Special Reference to *Contemplations of the Dread and Love of God*' (*BLJ* 20.55–64), Margaret Connolly illustrates how the devotional texts in this manuscript have been substantially rewritten, and ventures that the manuscript's textual oddities may be evidence of a scribal response to the text, 'private notes which have survived by chance, which happen to have become public'. Finally, Gloria Cigman casts light upon a baffling passage in a unique Middle English sermon in Oxford, Bodleian Library, MS Rawlinson C. 751 in her note 'Bounden as a Sheep' (*N&Q* 41.15). I have not seen Georgia R. Crampton, ed., *A Book of Showings to the Anchoress Julian of Norwich* (MIP).

Undergraduate study of the English visionaries of the thirteenth and fourteenth centuries has always been hampered by the lack of a single, authoritative and readily available anthology of their works. In *English Mystics of the Middle Ages,* Barry Windeatt fills that gap, bringing together generous selections from the writings of Richard Rolle, Walter Hilton, Julian of Norwich, Margery Kempe and the author of *The Cloud of Unknowing*. To these are added material from a number of English translations of continental mystical texts, which provide a wider context for the domestic contemplative tradition. The texts, some presented complete, others in extracts, are newly edited from manuscripts and lightly modernized, thus thorn is replaced by 'th' and yogh by 'gh', 'y' or a final 'z'. Punctuation and paragraphing have also been modernized for clarity, and the editor provides an introductory essay, textual and critical notes and glossary. The result is a clear and readable edition of these intense and challenging texts. It is to be hoped that CUP quickly progress to a paperback edition and so bring the collection within the price range of an undergraduate readership.

11. Drama

An invaluable guide to the state of the art in medieval drama criticism has appeared this year in *The Cambridge Companion to Medieval English Theatre*, edited by Richard Beadle. This attractively produced volume will be an essential addition to both undergraduate and postgraduate bibliographies. Its twelve chapters give respectively an introduction to medieval English theatre (William Tydeman), to the theatricality of the plays (Meg Twycross), to the plays of York (Richard Beadle), Chester (David Mills), Towneley (Peter Meredith) and N-Town (Alan J. Fletcher), to the non-cycle plays and the East Anglian tradition (John C. Coldeway), to Cornish drama (Brian O. Murdoch), to morality plays (Pamela M. King), to saints' plays (Daryll Grantley), and to medieval plays in modern performance (John Marshall); and finally there is included a select guide to criticism (Peter Happé). The misprints I noted are few, and doubtless will be eliminated in the *Companion*'s second edition, plans for which are already under way.

J. Alan B. Somerset's edition of *Records of Early English Drama: Shropshire* builds another magnificent landmark in the field of historical theatre studies which is being so heroically tilled by the 'Records of Early English Drama' project. We are offered in Somerset's collection another treasury of information that historians of drama can by no means afford to neglect; in fact, the same claim could with justice be made for every volume that has appeared in the REED series to date. Shropshire, though comparatively short on records of dramatic activity and entertainment in the private households, makes up for this deficit in other areas. As might be expected, Shrewsbury has the lion's share of the entries and Ludlow comes in second place. After them follows a host of the smaller towns. The net result is a rich and complex series of records, the general complexion of which is described in Somerset's introduction. We must be forever grateful that the Social Sciences and Humanities Research Council of Canada has been enlightened enough to underwrite the REED project. We trust that its support will continue until the project can be brought to completion, for its long-term prospect is the promise of no less than a total revolution in our understanding of the nature of drama and the performing arts in the British Isles before 1642.

The seven-chapter study of *Medieval Theatre in the Round – The Multiple Staging of Religious Drama in England* by Sydney Higgins makes a timely contribution to the relatively underdeveloped critical literature on the Cornish drama. After a brief introductory chapter, Higgins considers Cornish theatre in the round in the general context of what is known about in-the-round performance in the British Isles and on the Continent. Chapter 3 seeks to interpret the stage plans of the Cornish rounds, contriving as it proceeds to enlist Giotto in a novel way as stage evidence. Chapter 4 investigates the nature of the *platea*, and chapters 5 and 6 between them trace the two-day action of the *Beunans Meriasek*. The final chapter investigates where the audience would have been located. In all, this study is a well-considered approach to its topic.

N-Town has fared well this year. In '"This game wel pleyd in good a-ray": The N-Town Playbooks and East Anglian Games' (*CompD* 28.221–34), Douglas Sugano shows himself sensitive to the heterogeneity of N-Town, and proposes some appropriate critical approaches for dealing with it. He will be interested to see how closely he has agreed with some of the points which Fletcher has made in his discussion of N-Town in the *Cambridge Companion* reviewed above. Gail McMurray Gibson takes a leisurely look at the question of why the *Woman Taken in Adultery* was thought a fit choice for representing Christ's earthly ministry in dramatic form in 'Writing Before the Eye: The N-Town *Woman Taken in Adultery* and the Medieval Ministry Play' (*CompD* 27[1993–4].399–407). The answer she proposes is, essentially, that the play is much less about things said than things unsaid, about 'unspoken words, icons traced emblematically in the dust'. In 'Maculating Mary: The Detractors of the N-Town Cycle's "Trial of Joseph and Mary"' (*PQ* 73.11–29), Alison M. Hunt attempts a sensitive historicizing of the detractors in the N-Town Trial of Joseph and Mary play. She illustrates how socially disruptive they may originally have seemed; they were underminers of the shared beliefs that held the community together. Her examination of some of the categories of contemporary anti-Lollard polemic in arriving at her assessment is particularly satisfying.

Medieval English Theatre makes a welcome return after a period in abeyance. *METh* 14 (1992) contains the following essays. Philip Butterworth ponders 'The York *Crucifixion*: Actor/Audience Relationship' (67–76), and draws upon his recent experience of directing the York *Crucifixion* to make some astute observations about the nature of medieval performance. In 1978, Meg Twycross proposed that the stations of the York Corpus Christi play were all located on the left-hand side of the pageant route. Now, as new evidence has accumulated (including Eileen White's splendid analysis of playing in York, published in 1987 [see *YWES* 68.172]), Twycross has written 'The Left-hand-side Theory: A Retraction' (77–94). She adds to her retraction her reflections, arising from practical experience, on the permutations and possibilities of manoeuvring pageants in the York streets. In 'God: One Intention of the Author in the York Old Testament Plays from *The Fall of the Angels* to *The Expulsion*' (102–19), Anthony G. Corbett gives detailed consideration to the question of the extent of God's physical movement in the opening plays of all the cycles, and notes how static God can be. Corbett convincingly correlates the nature of God's physical stage movement with received medieval theological opinion on God's role in the Creation and Fall. W. R. Streitberger shows how 'Court Performances by the King's Players, 1510–1521' (95–101) refashioned the earlier, more formal revels of Henry VII into revels of a different order, ones in which the young Henry VIII himself actively participated.

John Scattergood's absorbing investigation of 'Skelton's *Magnyfycence* and the Tudor Royal Household' (*METh* 15[1993].21–48) seeks to redress an imbalance in Skelton criticism, by emphasizing not so much the occasions and inceptions of Skelton's poems as their broader implications, cultural, moral and philosophical. *Magnyfycence* is presented by Scattergood as a morality devised to contain the behaviour of the youthful Henry VIII, and to remind the king of the proper way of running his royal household. Another piece on *Magnyfycence* has been written by Peter Happé. 'Fansy and Foly: The Drama of Fools in *Magnyfycence*' (*CompD* 27[1993–4].426–52) begins by pointing out how many fools inhabit this play, and proceeds to discuss the theory of folly and the ways in which this theory displays itself in dramatic and other texts. Happé illustrates too Skelton's effectiveness and limitations in rendering folly on stage. In '*Fulgens and Lucres*: An Historical Perspective' (*METh* 15[1993].49–86), Olga Horner considers how practical performance of this play may transform initial impressions of it which are based solely on literary perusal, and proceeds to mesh the play into its historical moment, making a case for believing that Medwall may have modelled his Lucres on the person of Lady Margaret Beaufort, mother to Henry VII.

John Marshall investigates 'A Scene from the Life of St Edmund: Dramatic Representation in an English Medieval Alabaster' (*TN* 48.85–102). He plausibly suggests why it should be that no unequivocal artistic depictions of early drama have survived in England, and proceeds to make a paradigm case, built principally on a fifteenth-century English alabaster depicting the martyrdom of St Edmund, of how pictures might be interrogated for evidence of technical details of theatrical production. Also by him, '"Fortune in Worldys Worschyppe": The Satirising of the Suffolks in *Wisdom*' (*METh* 14[1992].37–66) rehabilitates and persuasively expands an earlier suggestion of W. K. Smart that there may be some connection between *Wisdom* and the de la Pole family. Marshall illustrates how that family is satirized in the play. This satirical element tends to rule out certain of the suggestions that have been made about the likely auspices of the play's early performance.

Margaret Rogerson writes on 'The Medieval Plough Team on Stage: Wordplay and Reality in the Towneley *Mactacio Abel*' (*CompD* 28.182–200), seeking to establish, by recourse to some recent historical research and medieval art, that the plough team of the *Mactacio Abel* was comprised not of eight beasts, as has traditionally been thought, but of two, a horse called 'Don' and a mare called 'Molly'. Maris G. Fiondella, in 'Derrida, Typology and the Second Shepherds' Play: The Theatrical Production of Christian Metaphysics' (*Exemplaria* 6.429–58), employs Derridean theory, reading the Towneley plays against the grain of analogical realism and rewriting them as mechanisms of Christian metaphysical production. In 'Spectacle and Sacrament: A London Parish Play in the 1530s' (*MP* 91.449–54), Mary C. Erler draws attention to a previously unknown play produced in the 1530s at the church of St Mary Magdalen, Milk Street, London, and comments on its likely nature and function. Alexandra Reid-Schwartz writes on 'Economics of Salvation: Commerce and the Eucharist in *The Profanation of the Host* and the Croxton *Play of the Sacrament*' (*Comitatus* 25.1–20), in which she illustrates late medieval perceptions of the host which debase it to pseudo-currency. The *Play of the Sacrament*, along with the Eucharistic presentation in Uccello's *The Profanation of the Host*, aim to recuperate the sense of the host's sanctity, yet she believes that finally they do not succeed. Kevin J. Harty, *The Chester Mystery Cycle: A Casebook* (Garland), was not seen.

Books Reviewed

Amodio, Mark, ed., with Sarah Gray Miller. *Oral Poetics in Middle English Poetry*. Albert Bates Lord Studies in Oral Tradition 13. Garland. pp. 304. $45. ISBN 0 8153 0830 2.

Arn, Mary-Jo, ed. *Fortunes Stabilnes: Charles of Orleans's English Book of Love: A Critical Edition*. MRTS 138. SUNYP. pp. 624. n.p. ISBN 0 8669 8147 0.

Barr, Helen. *Signes and Sothe: Language in the 'Piers Plowman' Tradition*. Piers Plowman Series X. Brewer. pp. 188. £35. ISBN 0 8599 1419 4.

Beadle, Richard, ed. *The Cambridge Companion to Medieval English Theatre*. CUP. pp. 372. hb £35, pb £13.95. ISBN 0 5213 6670 4; 0 5214 5916 8.

Benson, Larry D., ed., rev. Edward E. Foster. *King Arthur's Death: The Middle English Stanzaic 'Morte Arthur' and Alliterative 'Morte Arthure'*. TEAMS Middle English Texts Series. MIP. pp. 292. n.p. ISBN 1 8792 8838 9.

Besamusca, Bart, Willem P. Gerritsen, Corry Hogetoorn and Orlanda S. H. Lie, eds. *Cyclification: The Development of Narrative Cycles in the Chansons de Geste and the Arthurian Romances*. RNAAS. pp. 244. Fl 78. ISBN 0 4448 5781 8.

Brewer, C. and A. G. Rigg. *Piers Plowman: A Facsimile of the Z-Text in Bodleian Library, Oxford, MS Bodley 851*. Brewer. pp. 46 + folios 5, 124–40. £75. ISBN 0 8599 1396 1.

Bruckner, Matilda Tomaryn. *Shaping Romance: Interpretation, Truth, and Closure in Twelfth-century French Fictions*. UPennP. pp. 292. £37.95. ISBN 0 8122 3169 4.

Burnley, David, and Matsuji Tajima. *Annotated Bibliographies of Old and Middle English Literature I: The Language of Middle English Literature*. Brewer. pp. 280. £39.50. ISBN 0 8599 1405 4.
Burrow, J. A. *Thomas Hoccleve*. Authors of the Middle Ages: English Writers of the Late Middle Ages 4. Variorum. pp. 60. £10. ISBN 0 8607 8419 3.
Calin, William. *The French Tradition and the Literature of Medieval England.* UTorP. pp. 588. hb £49, pb £19.50. ISBN 0 8020 0565 9, 0 8020 7202 X.
Carruthers, Leo, ed. *Heroes and Heroines in Medieval English Literature: A Festschrift Presented to André Crépin on the Occasion of His Sixty-Fifth Birthday*. Brewer. pp. 172. ISBN 0 8599 1415 1.
Chamberlain, David, ed. *New Readings of Late Medieval Love Poems*. UPA (1993). pp. 350. n.p. ISBN 0 8191 8911 1, 0 8191 8912 X.
Cox, Jeffrey N., and Larry J. Reynolds, eds. *New Historical Literary Study: Essays on Reproducing Texts, Representing History*. PrincetonUP (1993). pp. 337. £9.95. ISBN 0 6910 1546 5.
Edwards, Robert, R. ed. *Art and Context in Late Medieval English Narrative.* Brewer. pp. 205. £35. ISBN 0 8599 1407 0.
Ellis, Roger, and Ruth Evans, eds. *The Medieval Translator IV*. UExe. pp. 256. £27.50. ISBN 0 8598 9412 6.
Evans, Ruth, and Lesley Johnson, eds. *Feminist Readings in Middle English Literature: The Wife of Bath and All Her Sect*. Routledge. pp. 258. £12.99. ISBN 0 4150 5819 8.
Fernandez, Francisco, Miguel Fuster, and Juan-Jose Calvo, eds. *English Historical Linguistics: Papers from the Seventh International Conference on English Historical Linguistics, Valencia, 22–26 September, 1992*. Current Issues in Linguistic Theory 113. Benjamins. pp. 390. £62. ISSN 0304-0763.
Görlach, Manfred, ed. *The Kalendre of the Newe Legende of Englande*. Middle English Texts 27. Universitätsverlag C. Winter. pp. 253. DM128. ISBN 3 8253 0217 2.
Grant, Patrick. *Spiritual Discourse and the Meaning of Persons*. Macmillan. pp. 202. £35. ISBN 0 3335 6581 9.
Greentree, Rosemary. *Reader, Teller, and Teacher: The Narrator of Robert Henryson's 'Moral Fables'*. Scottish Studies 15. Lang. pp. 121. ISBN 3 6314 6552 1.
Harwood, Britton J., and Gillian R. Overing, eds. *Class and Gender in Early English Literature: Intersections.* IndUP. pp. 156. £9.99. ISBN 0 2532 0858 0.
Higgins, Sydney. *Medieval Theatre in the Round – The Multiple Staging of Religious Drama in England.* Università degli Studi di Camerino. pp. 168. n.p. ISBN not available.
Horgan, Frances, trans. and ed. *Guillaume de Lorris and Jean de Meun: The Romance of the Rose*. WC. OUP. pp. 350. £6.99. ISBN 0 1928 2689 1.
Justice, Stephen. *Writing and Rebellion: England in 1381*. UCalP. pp. 289. $40. ISBN 0 5200 8325 3.
Kay, Richard. *Dante's Christian Astrology*. UPennP. pp. 395. £44.50. ISBN 0 8122 3233 X.
Kay, Sarah, and Miri Rubin, eds. *Framing Medieval Bodies.* ManUP. pp. 287. £45. ISBN 0 7190 3615 1.
Knight, Stephen. *Robin Hood: A Complete Study of the English Outlaw*. Blackwell. pp. 308. hb £45, pb £13.99. ISBN 0 6311 7219 X, 0 6311 9486 X.
Lees, Clare A., ed. *Medieval Masculinities: Regarding Men in the Middle Ages.*

Medieval Cultures Volume 7. UMinnP. pp. 194. hb £27.50, pb £11.95. ISBN 0 8166 2425 9, 0 8166 2426 7.

Le Saux, Françoise, ed. *The Text and Tradition of Layamon's 'Brut'.* Arthurian Studies xxxiii. Brewer. pp. 272. £29.50. ISBN 0 8599 1412 7.

Machan, Tim William. *Textual Criticism and Middle English Texts.* UPVirginia. pp. 250. £35.95. ISBN 0 8139 1508 2.

Margherita, Gayle. *The Romance of Origins: Language and Sexual Difference in Middle English Literature.* UPennP. pp. 214. hb £32.95, pb £13.95. ISBN 0 8122 3217 8, 0 8122 1502 8.

McKenna, Steven R., ed. *Selected Essays on Scottish Language and Literature.* Mellen. 1992. pp. 263. $89.95. ISBN 0 7734 9597 5.

Meale, Carol, ed. *Readings in Medieval English Romance.* Brewer. pp. 246. £29.50. ISBN 0 8599 1404 6.

Murrin, Michael. *History and Warfare in Renaissance Epic.* UChicP. pp. 371. £25.95. ISBN 0 2265 5403 1.

O'Mara, Veronica M., ed. *A Study and Edition of Selected Middle English Sermons.* Leeds Texts and Monographs. New Series 13. Leeds Studies in English. pp. 245. £10.95. ISBN 0 9022 9623 X.

Pratt, Karen, ed. *Shifts and Transpositions in Medieval Narrative: A Festschrift for Elspeth Kennedy.* Brewer. pp. 206. £35. ISBN 0 8599 1421 6.

Purdon, Liam O., and Cindy L. Vitto, eds. *The Rusted Hauberk: Feudal Ideas of Order and their Decline.* UPFlor. pp. 340. hb £39.95, pb £12.99. ISBN 0 8130 1281 3, 0 8130 1282 1.

Rudd, G. *Managing Language in 'Piers Plowman'.* Brewer. pp. 246. £35. ISBN 0 8599 1392 9.

Salisbury, Joyce E. *The Beast Within: Animals in the Middle Ages.* Routledge. pp. 238. £12.99. ISBN 0 4159 0769 1.

Scanlon, Larry D. *Narrative, Authority, and Power: The Medieval Exemplum and the Chaucerian Tradition.* Studies in Medieval Literature 20. CUP. pp. 390. £40. ISBN 0 5214 3210 3.

Shichtman, Martin B., and James P. Carley, eds. *Culture and the King: The Social Implications of the Arthurian Legend: Essays in Honor of Valerie M. Lagorio.* SUNYP. pp. 324. hb £47, pb £16. ISBN 0 7914 1863 4, 0 7914 1864 2.

Somerset, J. Alan B., ed. *Records of Early English Drama: Shropshire.* UTorP. 2 vols. pp. 833. £114. ISBN 0 8020 0648 5.

Staley, Lynn. *Margery Kempe's Dissenting Fictions.* PSUP. pp. 224. hb £31.50, pb £15.50. ISBN 0 2710 1031 2, 0 2710 1030 4.

Stone, Gregory B. *The Death of the Troubadour: The Late Medieval Resistance to the Renaissance.* UPennP. pp. 229. hb £29.95. ISBN 0 8122 3214 3.

Verduin, Kathleen, ed. *Studies in Medievalism VI: Medievalism in North America.* Brewer. pp. 238. £29.50. ISBN 0 8599 1417 8.

Windeatt, B., ed. *English Mystics of the Middle Ages.* CUP. pp. 311. £37.50. ISBN 0 5213 2740 7.

IV

Middle English: Chaucer

VALERIE ALLEN and MARGARET CONNOLLY

This chapter is divided into four sections: 1. General; 2. *Canterbury Tales*; 3. *Troilus and Criseyde*; 4. Other Works.

1. General

There are the usual bibliographical attempts to keep pace with the prolific industry of Chaucer scholarship. With the help of a team of regular and *ad hoc* contributors, Mark Allen and Bege K. Bowers have compiled and edited 'An Annotated Chaucer Bibliography 1992' (*SAC* 16.311–94); the complete *SAC* bibliography is also online at the University of Texas at San Antonio; Bege K. Bowers has also produced 'Chaucer Research, 1993, Report No. 54' (*ChauR* 29.207–25). Three further bibliographical studies should be noted. James D. Johnson's 'Identifying Chaucer Allusions, 1981–1990: An Annotated Bibliography' (*ChauR* 29.194–203) is a continuation of his earlier annotated bibliography of Chaucer allusions for 1953–80 which was published in *ChauR* in 1984 (*YWES* 65.136). His present list, comprising some thirty-seven annotated entries, includes some pre-1980 references which were overlooked in the previous study. Jackson Campbell Boswell and Sylvia Wallace Holton provide a more specific list of 'References to Troilus, Criseyde, and Pandarus' (*ChauR* 29.93–109), culled from the preparations for a more extensive list of references to Chaucer and his work, published between 1475 and 1640. They give a brief update on the progress of this reference work, but no indication of its likely date of completion; in the interim, however, their working list brings to light thirty-one hitherto unknown references to the main characters of *Troilus and Criseyde*. Finally William H. Watts and Richard J. Utz consider some 'Nominalist Perspectives on Chaucer's Poetry: A Bibliographical Essay' (*M&H* 20.147–73), observing how sloppily the term has been applied to Chaucer's work and restoring some philosophical specificity to it. The received view of Ockham as a radical sceptic is challenged in the light of his emphasis on divine omnipotence. The essay concludes that Chaucer can only be called a nominalist by analogy rather than by nature. The greater part of the essay is devoted to reviewing the criticism on the subject of Chaucer and nominalism, and there is a useful bibliography given at the end.

There are several books and collections of essays to be considered. An interesting but hard-to-get-hold-of publication from last year is *Computer-Based Chaucer Studies*, edited by Ian Lancashire, which contains the proceedings from a conference in 1992 and comprises eleven papers and an afterword. Murray McGillivray considers the 'Electronic Representation of Chaucer Manuscripts: Possibilities and Limitations' in the context of a project to produce a hypertext parallel edition of the MSS of the *Book of the Duchess*. His comments on the possibilities and limitations of the project are, however, general. Eventually, what is envisaged is a virtual reality experience in one's own university library of turning the pages of Bodleian MS Fairfax 16. Even with a more modest medium, however, certain specific difficulties are created in reproducing a MS: the irreducible physicality of the MS; the lack of standard character set; and the multiple producers of the MS. Willard McCarty compares 'Handmade, Computer-assisted, and Electronic Concordances of Chaucer', by which he refers specifically to the 'handmade' Tatlock and Kennedy and the computer-assisted Oizumi concordances, and their interactive concording in an electronic format that contains not only both concordances but also a database of the source text. He admits that while the analytic possibilities of interactive concording are much superior to the printed object, the software becomes obsolete so fast that the printed concordance remains a necessary adjunct to scholarship. David Burnley describes 'The Sheffield Chaucer Textbase: Its Compilations and Uses' as the attempt to reconstruct Chaucer's linguistic milieu, using core texts from the City of London and Westminster written in English between 1330 and 1435, although French and Latin texts are also planned to be added to this 'linguistic architecture of the period'. In its complexity and size, such a project is really only possible with the use of electronic technology, yet it offers a reading of Chaucer which is primary and fundamental because it reads him in the context of his historical and cultural milieux rather than in linguistic abstraction. Larry Benson, in an essay on 'A Lemmatized Concordance of Chaucer', takes the opposite view from McCarty and pronounces the printed concordance obsolete. By 'lemmatized', Benson means the kind of complete glossarial concordance Furnivall envisioned in the nineteenth century. The result is a database which is half simple dictionary, half concordance. Stephen R. Reimer engages in 'Differentiating Chaucer and Lydgate: Some Preliminary Observations', mostly concentrating on the much-neglected Lydgate. In comparison to Chaucer, Lydgate tends to use long and complex syntactic structures, and certain characteristic words and phrases. Patricia J. Erble, in an afterword, points out the analogies between medieval intertextuality (interlinear glosses, etc.) and the contemporary electronic capacity to read many texts at the same time. The other five essays in the collection are reviewed in the appropriate sections below.

Robert Myles's *Chaucerian Realism* is a close examination of realism not as a literary style but as a position within medieval philosophy of language. His first chapter offers a tiresomely dogmatic denunciation of critics who have associated Chaucer with nominalism. One such critic wins the wooden spoon by being singled out under the heading 'Major Misunderstandings: Robert M. Jordan'; but there are runners up, making sheepish appearances under 'Major Misunderstandings: Nine More Critics'. Describing many kinds of realism – foundational, epistemological, ethical, semiotic and linguistic, and intentionalist – Myles outlines four main positions discernible in medieval debates on universals: realism, the belief that universals exist *ante rem*; moderate realism, the belief that universals exist *in rem*; extreme nominalism, the belief that universals exist *post rem*; and moderate nominalism, the belief that universals, although not possessing an extra-mental reality, none the less correspond to the world of things, a kind of *juxta rem*. Since 'no one of importance in the Middle Ages' was an extreme nominalist, this leaves only moderate nominalism, which is close enough to moderate realism to be called conceptual realism, thereby enabling Myles to assert that basically everyone including 'scholastic nominalists are realists'. While his challenge to the 'misequation of Cratylism with realism, and linguistic conventionalism with nominalism' is entirely to the point, his depiction of Chaucer as holding basically the same views of language as Augustine and Dante, and of the entire fourteenth century as conservative on matters of language, renders the period problematically homogeneous. Finally in this chapter, since he complains that Marcia Colish's *Mirror of Language* (UNebP, 1983) does not appear in the bibliography of Robert Jordan's *Chaucer's Poetics and the Modern Reader* (*YWES* 68.178), one might reply by asking how his own could omit Sheila Delany's *Chaucer's House of Fame: The Poetics of Skeptical Fideism* (see below) and, more seriously, how discussion of the *House of Fame*, one of Chaucer's most important statements about language, could be left out entirely from his discussion, save for a glancing reference at p. 19.

Myles's argument gets under way in chapter 2, which is a discussion of medieval and modern intentionality. The term (*intentio*) originates in medieval philosophy, despite its primary associations with contemporary phenomenology; Myles describes it as the directed nature of the relationship between *verbum* and *res*. Where in the act of creation the intentionality of the divine thought and utterance 'Let there be light' is causative (for 'there was light'), human intentionality is not, which is not to say that there is no difference between meaning and not meaning what one says (a problem which would clearly relate to the Pardoner's 'intentions'). Myles argues that Chaucer sees language as simultaneously mind-related and world-related and thus as a tool for interpreting the speaker's intent. The consequence of this emphasis on psychological intent is a recuperation of 'character' rather than 'subject'. Chapter 3, on Judaeo-Christian semiological metaphysics, addresses the ontological relationship between speaker and their words, in both the divine and human instances. Chapter 4 is on the correlation between modern 'modes of presentation' and the Augustinian distinction between *uti* and *frui*. The way in which Chaucer's text gets dipped into piecemeal for the odd key word (*entente*, *longen*, etc.) leaves one with a growing suspicion that the book is only tangentially about Chaucer, at least until the final two chapters, where Myles finally discusses the role of *intentio* in the curses, contracts and promises of the *Friar's Tale*. This has some nicely observed detail in, for example, the exchange between the summoner and the devil, where the summoner's suspicion that the devil is lying (when in point of fact he is telling the truth) is a perfect inversion of the Liar paradox. And by linking the summoner of the *Tale* to the pilgrim, Myles brings in the sodomitical theme of 'improper couplings' – a sexual metaphor which pertains also to the grammatical sin of mismatching word to deed. The consideration of the *Friar's Tale* is detailed and scholarly, but, in a book on Chaucer in general, one expects some consideration of other clearly relevant cruces in his work. Whether or not one agrees with Myles's conclusions, his book will be something for champions of the radical instability of medieval language to chew on.

In Michael Calabrese's *Chaucer's Ovidian Arts of Love*, the influence of the Latin poet is seen to be pervasive. The medieval *accessus*, serving as the proto-Norton anthology headnote, formed the context in which Ovid's poems were read, and from them the reader would have learned of his tragic exile. Chaucer's acquaintance with Ovid as the poet of love was thus intimately connected with him as a poet of exile also. Not all 'biographies' of Ovid were sympathetic, however, and the tensions Calabrese delineates between the acceptance of Ovid as an authority and the censure of his carnality are elaborated in an ambivalence in Chaucer's own treatment of him, resolved only in the dismissal of Ovid at the ending of *Troilus*. Two chapters on *Troilus* follow closely the literary relations between Ovid, Boccaccio and Chaucer. Pandarus, 'Uncle Amoris', is the most Ovidian of the poem's characters, but Calabrese finds him less assured, operating within an uncertain moral universe. Troilus, ignorant and innocent in matters of Ovidian love, comes to grief when he mistakes Ovidian stratagems as the guide to truth in love. Where Criseyde consoles herself with the ultimate Ovidian remedy – taking a new lover – the *remedia amoris* Troilus finds do not lie in Pandarus's distracting ploys but in the closing Olympian vision of the poem, where carnal love is repudiated. The doubleness of Ovid is seen both as the authority for an anti-feminist tradition and as a wily counsellor to the Wife of Bath in matters of love. At once the Wife's adversary and benefactor, Ovid is both one of the authorities in Jankyn's book of *wikked wyves* and the source of Alice's wiles. Feigning Ovid's tricks are the Wife's only recourse against gendered hierarchies constructed by anti-feminism, yet she is motivated by a vision of marriage that could be free of such fencings. And finally, Calabrese deals with the *Retraction* as a closing statement on Chaucer and Ovid, where the two poets' biographies diverge in a contrasting experience of exile. The Parson is the 'Ovid' who offers the pilgrim the final consolation of heaven. But unlike Ovid, his muse is grace, and he offers the poet a way back from the spiritual exile signified by the very act of pilgrimage.

Niall Rudd's *The Classical Tradition in Operation* is a collection of five essays which were originally given as the Robson Classical Lectures in 1992. The first alone concerns Chaucer: in it, Rudd compares Chaucer's treatment of Dido in the *House of Fame* and the *Legend of Good Women* with Virgil's presentation of Dido in the *Æneid*, and Ovid's in *Heroides* 7, concluding that Chaucer worked from a Latin source, rather than a translation, and that he used his source material freely. Also dealing with matters of source and influence, David Anderson's article 'The Italian Background to Chaucer's Epic Similes' (*Annali d'italianistica* 12.15–38), examines instances of the extended simile in the *Knight's Tale* and in *Troilus and Criseyde*. He rejects a simplistic tracing of the poet's models, contending that Chaucer vernacularized rather than translated, producing an English version of the classical form, and proving himself a master of rhetoric. Several items link Chaucer and Spenser. In '"Neither of idle shewes, nor of false charmes aghast": Transformations of Virgilian Ekphrasis in Chaucer and Spenser' (*JMRS* 23[1993].345–63), John Watkins examines the two poets' treatment of a single episode from Virgil, accusing Chaucer of a sceptical anti-Virgilianism. Craig A. Berry writes on 'Borrowed Armour/Free Grace: The Quest for Authority in *The Faerie Queene* 1 and Chaucer's *Tale of Sir Thopas*' (*SP* 91.136–66), but has more to say about Spenser than Chaucer. And in 'The Art of Naming: A Study of Fictional Names as an Element of Style in Chaucer, Spenser, and Shakespeare' (*PoeticaJ* 41.59–83), Nobuyuki Yuasa confines his interest in Chaucer to the *Canterbury Tales*, examining the names of the pilgrims when these are known, but only some of the names of the characters within the tales.

Art and Context in Late Medieval English Narrative, a volume of twelve essays edited by Robert R. Edwards and presented in honour of Robert Worth Frank, includes five items which take Chaucer as their central concern. In 'The Triumph of Fiction in the *Nun's Priest's Tale*', Monica E. McAlpine rejects the binary simplicity of previous critical approaches to the tale, arguing that Chaucer here transforms satire into a vision of human experience. Mary Carruthers considers the use of memory systems in 'Seeing Things: Locational Memory in Chaucer's *Knight's Tale*', finding that memory structures account for features of the tale's design. A different sort of structure is examined by Kathryn L. Lynch in 'Partitioned Fictions: The Meaning and Importance of Walls in Chaucer's Poetry'; Lynch traces Chaucer's predilection for enclosed fictions from his early dream visions to the *Canterbury Tales*, showing how the metaphor of the wall may represent both the loss of the Golden Age and the conditions of civilized life. The subject of Carolyn P. Collette's contribution, 'Chaucer's Discourse of Mariology: Gaining the Right to Speak', is the authority of feminine speech, particularly the authority claimed by the Prioress and the Second Nun through reference to the figure of the Virgin. And in 'The *Descriptio Navalis Pugnae* in Middle English Literature', Mary Hamel looks at the battle scene in the tale of Cleopatra in the *Legend of Good Women*, as well as at descriptions of naval warfare in other medieval texts. Two further essays which focus more especially on late medieval English narrative and social practice also refer to Chaucer: Paul Strohm's contribution, '"Lad with revel to Newegate": Chaucerian Narrative and Historical Meta-narrative', draws parallels between the brief narrative of Perkyn's revelry in the *Cook's Tale* to official contemporary discourse related to civil unrest; and Peggy Knapp's exploration of the different senses of the word 'Thrift' involves discussion of *Troilus and Criseyde* and some of the *Canterbury Tales*.

Chaucer's Knight: A Man Ther Was is a slim collection of six essays written at various points during Virginia Walker Valentine's career. The volume is beautifully produced, and a fine reproduction of Blake's picture of the Canterbury pilgrims adorns the dust jacket, but despite the packaging this is not really a book about Chaucer. In the essay which gives the book its title, Valentine argues against Robinson's judgement that the Knight is a completely idealized figure, using as evidence the Knight's asides and use of *occupatio*, as well as examining the differences between Boccaccio's narrative and Chaucer's. If her discussion seems outmoded, this is explained by the paper's original date of composition, though as it was also read at conferences in the early 1980s, one wonders why it has not been revised to take account of Terry Jones's stance. The only other essay which deals with Chaucer, the brief 'Apologia pro Criseyde', was written even longer ago (1951). Here, Valentine takes up two points about *Troilus and Criseyde*: the issue of courtly love, which she finds to be a substantial but not comprehensive presence in the poem, and Chaucer's complex attitude to his heroine.

Jean E. Jost has edited *Chaucer's Humor: Critical Essays*, of which ten of the nineteen are original. The volume includes a selected annotated bibliography at the end but lacks the by now expected list of contributors. Jost's introduction offers a 'practical method' for investigating Chaucerian humour under the categories of time, place, circumstance, discourse and tone. No rationalization is given for the categories, and they do not bring the reader any closer to a theoretical understanding of what humour consists of. Original essays on specific poems are reviewed in the appropriate sections below. The first essay in the collection, 'The Voice of the Past: Surveying the Reception of Chaucer's Humor', is written by Jost. Since literary criticism as a formal discipline is only a century or so old, it is not so surprising that Jost submits that humour is only analysed seriously from the twentieth century onwards and that earlier references do not go much beyond laughing at jollity or frowning at scurrility. The essay consists mostly of a chronological sampling of comments through the ages and, although it is useful as a reference piece, does not provide a very thought-provoking opening. Howard Rollin Patch's 1939 'The Idea of Humor' (*YWES* 20.41) is of special historical interest in its formal and ideological differences from contemporary criticism, and he offers a definition of humour as being essentially based on a 'sense of harmless incongruity between the transitory and the permanent'. G. K. Chesterton, in an excerpt from *Chaucer*, claims Chaucer as the seed of a quintessentially English sense of humour. Paul G. Ruggiers, in the reprinted 'A Vocabulary for Chaucerian Comedy: A Preliminary Sketch' (*YWES* 58.114), considers Chaucer's humour in terms of Aristotelian plot and character analysis, and notes how all Chaucerian comedy involves the momentary transgression and escape from law. Thomas J. Garbáty's 'Chaucer and Comedy' leaves one wondering why it was ever reprinted from Paul Ruggiers's *Versions of Medieval Comedy* (*YWES* 58.111). Surely something more searching can be found to be said about Chaucer's fabliaux than that he writes 'harmless stories' which 'don't pretend to probe much below the surface' – an observation which might be more aptly applied to Garbáty's essay? In his reprinted 'Comedy' (*YWES* 67.170), Derek Pearsall observes how rooted the fabliaux are in the here and now, and how Chaucer's perspective on the characters resembles 'a clinical analysis of the inhabitants of a zoo'. In his reading of each fabliau, Pearsall argues for a comic as distinct from a moral justice and for the difference between Chaucerian comedy and the more classical notion of comedy as a social corrective. He also dissociates it from any 'realist' project, and argues against the opinion that the fabliaux are lower-class, particularly given that the butts of the jokes are so repeatedly those very members of the petite bourgeoisie. The intruder (inevitably male), who completes the *ménage-à-trois* is usually from a different class, and thus, as a predator upon the more settled and familial values of the bourgeois, bears an implicit alliance with aristocracy.

In the same volume, John Michael Crafton examines '*Paradoxicum Semiotica*: Signs, Comedy, and Mystery in Fragment VI of the *Canterbury Tales*'. Pointing out that a 'Canterbury Tale' meant a tall story or lie in the Middle Ages, Crafton draws attention to how, in Chaucer's discourse, *sentence and solas* or *ernest and game* are not true dichotomies but inextricably connected. Everything both is as it appears to be, yet is not. Linking this playful misspeaking to Freudian theories of humour and to the radical undecidability of deconstructive writing, Crafton also examines Chaucer's comedy in the light of the late medieval debates between realists and nominalists. The *Tales* are seen to caricature both extremes of the philosophy of language, and Crafton argues that Chaucer's comedy here is less to be associated with nominalism than it is with the new humanistic rhetorical attitudes expressed by Boccaccio and Petrarch. Drawing from folk traditions of festive comedy, the carnivalesque, the saturnalian, etc., Alfred David's 'The Comedy of Innocence' is reprinted from its former appearance in *The Strumpet Muse* (*YWES* 57.89). Alan T. Gaylord's 'Chaucer's Dainty "Dogerel": The "Elvyssh" Prosody of *Sir Thopas*' is reprinted (*YWES* 60.112–13). The tail-rhyme is seen to epitomize the mingling and confusing of royal romance with popular idiom; the *Tale* is ultimately seen to be 'in some measure about the poetic craft, about true and false rhetoric, and about the tension between ornamentation and sincerity'. Daniel F. Pigg addresses the unlikely subject of comedy in the religious tales: 'The Semiotics of Comedy in Chaucer's Religious Tales'. Here he understands comedy as a divine comedy, as a movement from *tristia* to *gaudium*, in which the Canterbury pilgrimage prefigures the journey to the New Jerusalem: 'The signs of earth become the things of heaven.' The Man of Law leaves the impression that there is unending joy for Constance; the characters of the *Clerk's Tale* are not 'real' people, but allegories; the story of Virginia's beheading anticipates a comedy of the future – 'a comedy of silence in which earthly signs are unnecessary'; the Prioress participates in the boy's martyrdom and resurrection; and in the Second Nun's story of St Cecilia we reach, as it were, the end of things and the closure of the human discourse of earthly signs. In a funny and profound essay, Judith Tschann considers 'The Mind Distended: *The Retraction*, *Miller's Tale*, and *Summoner's Tale*'. Focusing on how the 'stink of mortality' lingers in Chaucer's two tales, Tschann elaborates on the associations between the faecal and death, and between the fart and the escape of the animus from the body. Despite their life-affirming comedy, the tales bear an implicit relation to that most pregnant *memento mori* of Chaucer's, the *Retraction*. The reference to the 'mind distended' is taken from Augustine and alludes to the paradoxical relationship between past, present and future; just such a paradox informs the relation between Chaucer's revokable tales (the smutty ones) and the penitential *Retraction*.

'Chaucer's Creative Comedy: A Study of the *Miller's Tale* and the *Shipman's Tale*' by A. Booker Thro is reprinted here (*YWES* 51.113). Its focus is on Chaucer's celebration of creative ingenuity rather than of cuckoldry. And the final essay in the volume, John M. Steadman's 'Felicity and Mutability: Boethian Framework of the *Troilus*', also reprinted (*YWES* 53.117), is the one piece not on the *Canterbury Tales*. Acknowledging the poem's conventional structure of tragedy, Steadman none the less traces within it elements of comedy, elegy and encomium. For an expensive volume that runs to almost five hundred pages, there are far fewer delights than one would expect for the time and money, especially at the beginning, where a more searching theorization of the comic is needed.

On the language side of Chaucer studies, W. Rothwell investigates the relationship of Latin, French and English, in 'The Trilingual England of Geoffrey Chaucer' (*SAC* 16.45–67), using examples from the *Canterbury Tales* to illustrate the interaction of the three languages in the usage of contemporary literate society. He first explores the non-Latinate nature of later medieval Latin, and then considers the French element in Chaucer's vocabulary, arguing that this stems from insular rather than continental influences. As he rightly comments in conclusion, the complex linguistic situation obtaining in Chaucer's England will be properly understood 'only when medievalists become themselves trilingual and, just as important, are both able and willing to handle all three languages in their interrelated complexity and in conformity with the medieval view of language'. 'Chaucer's Names' are studied by Paul Beekman Taylor (*NM* 95.2.243–8), who notes that while the actual family name 'Chaucer' is mentioned in the *Tales* only once, there is a much greater frequency of reference to 'Malin', also a family name, descending from Robert Malin le Chaucer, the poet's paternal grandfather. Malyn, in fact, is the most frequently cited fictional name in Chaucer's work, and Taylor suggests that Chaucer plays the name game in these citations, especially since the French *maligne* means not only 'malign' but also 'cunning' or 'astute'. Taylor sees an even richer range of associations within the use of Chaucer's baptismal name, 'Geoffrey', and its Latinate variants. One form of the name in Anglo-Saxon was 'Walfrid', and both the Germanic and Latin forms mean either 'ruler of love' or 'servant of love'. Some playful resonance, then, can be detected in the *Troilus* narrator's reference to himself as 'I, that God of Loves servauntz serve'.

Furthermore, Taylor suggests that the reference to the *Englyssh Gaufride* in the *House of Fame* refers to Chaucer rather than to Geoffrey of Monmouth. 'The Great Vowel Shift in the North of England, and Some Forms in Chaucer's *Reeve's Tale*' (*NM* 95.4.433–7) are the consideration of Jeremy Smith, who notes that in the Hengwrt and Ellesmere MSS, certain unusual spellings occur in the *Reeve's Tale*: <heem>/<ham>, respectively, for 'home', and similarly, <gane><geen> for 'gone', and <naan><neen> for 'none'. The <ee> forms were dismissed by Tolkein as the result of scribal confusion and they have generally been perceived as 'vaguely dialectal'. Smith explains their occurrence with more specificity, arguing that the fact that they only appear in the *Reeve's Tale* suggests that they represent the attempt on the part of the author or scribe (assuming that both MSS were copied by the same hand) to capture a northern dialect in writing. If this is the case, then some explanation is needed for the <ee> orthography. Since current opinion is that the Great Vowel Shift occurred in the north of England earlier than in the south, Smith suggests that the forms represent early sporadic indications of raising and diphthongization of long vowels (i.e. the Great Vowel Shift) in northern, as opposed to southern, Middle English. Smith makes an important qualification in his argument: that the <ee> form is the southern attempt to approximate northern pronunciation rather than spelling, reminding us that the text which we now read in silence was more likely to have been originally a text for reading aloud. James R. Andreas, in '"Wordes Betwene": The Rhetoric of the Canterbury Links' (*ChauR* 29.45–64), takes Mikhail Bakhtin as his inspiration for understanding the links between the tales, arguing that they are the moments in which the dynamic, heteroglossic and inherently social nature of language is emphasized. Medieval and postmodern poetics are brought together in the recognition of the generative power of language or, in Chaucerian terms, of *newe corn* from *olde feldes*. Central to Andreas's reading is the oral and performative nature of the *Tales* — a point highlighted by the frequency with which speakers are interrupted in the links.

Finally, some general studies of a literary nature. In 'Chaucer and the Rhetoric of the Body' (*ChauR* 28.216–36), Patrick J. Gallacher considers Chaucer's manifold representation of the human body by looking at brief selections from the tales of the Knight, Clerk and Reeve, the prologue to the *Second Nun's Tale*, and *Troilus and Criseyde*. Sarah Stanbury's article, 'Women's Letters and Private Space in Chaucer' (*Exemplaria* 6.271–85), explores the accounts that Chaucer gives us of women reading and writing letters, dwelling especially on the descriptions of Criseyde, May and Donegild when so engaged. In answer to her own questions as to what these private actions show about female autonomy in the domestic sphere, and about the medieval sense of the private self, Stanbury finds anxieties about public exposure and private autonomy; she also notes that Chaucer pays particular attention to spatial detail when looking into the closed spaces in which women read and write. Looking into another closed space, Joseph A. Dane asks 'Who is Buried in Chaucer's Tomb? – Prolegomena' (*HLQ* 57.99–123), but his title poses a question which his discussion then fails to address: although he makes a comprehensive survey of the descriptions of Chaucer's tomb, he uses this only to consider the preliminary matter of the tomb's inscriptions.

2. *Canterbury Tales*

Roy Vance Ramsey offers an impassioned and extensive defence of *The Manly–Rickert Text of the Canterbury Tales*, proving that he is indeed one of the apologists of Manly–Rickert (so labelled by George Kane). He begins by surveying the current state of *Canterbury Tales* editorial scholarship, in particular lamenting what he sees as an overdependence on the text of the Ellesmere manuscript (elsewhere outlining his reasons for preferring Hengwrt), arising from an unnecessary deference towards Robinson's work. He is rightly critical of editors who neglect the evidence of the original manuscripts, but his insistence that they focus on Manly–Rickert as a resource of almost equal value seems a little overzealous. His account of the 'enormous drudgery' of Manly and Rickert's labours, and of the pressures under which they worked, makes interesting if depressing reading, though this chapter, even more than the rest of the book, is burdened by repetition, a feature which contributes to the volume's excessive length. In general, Ramsey urges that a study of the original manuscripts, their scribes and their modes of production should form the foundations of textual scholarship, a foundation which he sees as lacking from current editions of the *Tales* which 'are not what they could be and thus what they should be'. He dismisses Tatlock's theory that the text of the *Canterbury Tales* proceeds from a single manuscript, and disagrees with Doyle and Parkes's judgement of the relationship between Ellesmere and Hengwrt; for his own part he suggests that Thomas Chaucer owned the exemplar for MS Cambridge Dd.4.24, that Hengwrt was made for Lewis Chaucer, and that the unknown Adam Scriveyn (about whom he writes a great deal), was the scribe of Ellesmere. He has benefited from Charles Moorman's statistical studies (*YWES* 74.149), and from work undertaken for the Variorum Chaucer Project; it seems astonishing, therefore, that he never once mentions the other *Canterbury Tales* Project based at Sheffield under the direction of Norman Blake (*YWES* 74.148). Blake, however, is one of those singled out for special disapprobation in the appendices (others include Germaine Dempster and George Kane, against whom Ramsey is particularly vitriolic). This book is simultaneously a defence of Manly–Rickert and an attack on those who have criticized, misunderstood or neglected their work; its argument is supported by some twenty-five charts, but ironically, the volume suffers its own collation problems, with the section from pp. 605 to 630 mistakenly repeated.

John H. Fisher is also interested in editorial issues, and provides a clear exposition of the 'Historical and Methodological Considerations for Adopting "Best Text" or "Usus Scribendi" for Textual Criticism of Chaucer's Poems' (*Text* 6.165–80). Although he regards Blake as very much on the right track in his assessment of Hengwrt, Fisher suggests the *Equatorie of the Planetis* as a different linguistic model to be used in the preparation of 'a new kind of text of Chaucer's poems'; he also offers his own services to this venture, obviously undeterred by the labours so copiously described by Ramsey. Charles A. Owen Jr is troubled by 'an undercurrent of discomfort' which he discerns in the witnesses of the *Parson's Tale* and the *Retraction*, and his investigation of 'What the Manuscripts Tell Us about the *Parson's Tale*' (*MÆ* 63.239–49) leads him to suggest that Chaucer may have intended it as an independent work, the *Treatise on Penitence*, with the *Retraction* designed as its conclusion. His suggestion goes against the almost universal acceptance of the tale as Chaucer's ending for the *Canterbury Tales*, an acceptance which he derides as based on an assumption that a closer relation existed between author and manuscripts than is warranted by the evidence; this position conveniently allows him to discount the fact that the majority of manuscripts present the tale in precisely that context.

One of the most important and thought-provoking publications to appear this year is Larry Scanlon's book *Narrative, Authority, and Power: The Medieval Exemplum and the Chaucerian Tradition*. Scanlon argues against a simplistic interpretation of medieval authority, redefining the exemplum as 'a narrative enactment of cultural authority', and showing how Chaucer and other writers used the form both to explore the differences between clerical authority and lay power, and to establish their own cultural authority through a validation of the vernacular tradition. His discussion is divided into three sections. The introduction, comprising three chapters, explores the issues of exemplarity and authority, beginning with an analysis of the most authoritative of the *Canterbury Tales* – the Parson's – and also briefly considering the *Retraction* which follows it; a short second chapter then offers the redefinition of the exemplum, which Scanlon arrives at via current theoretical notions of ideology, hegemony and subjectivity; and the third chapter examines the terms *auctoritas* and *potestas* in more detail. In the next section, Scanlon moves on to investigate what he calls the 'Latin Tradition', considering the sermon exemplum and the classical or, as he prefers, the 'public' exemplum of the *Mirrors of Princes* genre; though recognizing that these are two distinct modes, he finds in both evidence of the church's efforts to extend its control of secular life. In the final and most substantial section of the book, Scanlon presents the supporting evidence for his theories from the 'Chaucerian Tradition'. He identifies up to twelve of the *Canterbury Tales* which may be regarded as exempla, focusing on two tale-sequences (though admitting the insecurity of relying on tale-order), to demonstrate how Chaucer moves from anti-clericalism to lay affirmation. He discusses the anti-clerical tales of the Friar and Summoner, and the public exemplum of the *Clerk's Tale* with its lay heroine; the second stage of his discussion covers the anti-fraternal *Pardoner's Tale*, the *Tale of Melibee*, the *Monk's Tale*, which is a miniature exemplum collection, and the *Nun's Priest's Tale*, which is more than a fable – the latter three are seen as variously centred on the figure of the monarch. Subsequent chapters discuss the exemplum collections of Gower, Hoccleve and Lydgate, placing this book in the currently popular 'Chaucer and After' school. The volume appears as part of the Cambridge Studies in Medieval Literature, and is characterized by the high level of scholarship we have come to expect from this series.

Susan Crane's intelligent and detailed study of *Gender and Romance in Chaucer's Canterbury Tales* has specific if not systematic reference to the *Knight's*, *Wife of Bath's*, *Squire's* and *Franklin's Tales* and to the *Tale of Sir Thopas*. Pointing out the etymological relation between gender and genre, Crane lays out her definitions in the introduction, distinguishing gender from sex on the one hand, yet refusing on the other to read sex as a biological or empirical fact; quoting Denise Riley, she argues that 'the body is a concept'. Chapter 1 demonstrates how masculine gender is constructed in romance around difference from the feminine, which is located outside chivalric rule. Even 'feminine' virtues such as pity are masculinized. Despite received perceptions of the emergence of the individual in romance, the social constitution of the (male) individual is fundamental, and narrative crisis takes the form less of social resistance than of self-regulation. Homoerotic and sodomitical relations are also examined as the context into which heterosexual courtship, ostensibly the central stuff of the narrative, is inscribed, thereby incorporating love into a prior economy of brotherhood. Chapter 2 considers the inscription of female subjectivity into a genre which both figures yet negates them. Drawing from contemporary French feminism, Crane presents woman as 'the sex which is not one', and as the lack within an identity which is always already masculine. From there, she interprets classic moments of female behaviour within romance as instances of a divided identity which can only articulate itself obliquely. Dorigen's 'playful' promise to Aurelius is symptomatic of a world in which women have no vocabulary of refusal. The persistently hierarchical nature of gender difference is then examined, and here Crane draws out the analogies between estates literature and romance. Both conceive of hierarchy as natural and assert the correspondence between outer status and inner worth, witnessed in the knight whose aristocratic lineage is hidden from him but who yet wins renown through noble deeds. Crane links gender and class in a reading of the *Franklin's Tale* in which the ambivalent social status of the Franklin corresponds to the ambivalence of Dorigen's social position, which is paradoxically superior yet subordinated. Vavasours in romance are associated more with the domestic and familial than with the chivalric, thereby linking them with the sphere of the feminine. In another chapter, uncanny women – women with special or fairy powers in romance – are linked with Freud's uncanny (*das Unheimliche*). Uncanniness comes to mark the contradictions inherent in the representation of femininity itself, and this essential strangeness is never erased, not even in domesticization (such as the Wife's loathly lady being transformed into a beautiful and biddable wife). And finally, the concept of 'aventure' – particularly in its later association with chance rather than in its earlier association with destiny – is seen to be both the defining characteristic of romance and associated with the feminine. Adventure in romance is described as the 'masculine experience of a mysterious and often overtly feminine unpredictability'. Crane's study is comprehensive and scholarly.

Ruth Evans and Lesley Johnson's *Feminist Readings in Middle English Literature* brings together a collection of feminist essays, of which a number are on the *Canterbury Tales* and are discussed under the individual tales below.

Peter Brown finds a common failing amongst introductory works on Chaucer, namely that they 'leave precious little room for the learning experience of the stumbling student'; in trying to avoid this failing, Brown bases his approach in *Chaucer at Work: The Making of the Canterbury Tales* primarily on sources and contexts, both literary and pictorial. He discusses the *General Prologue* and seven of the tales: those of the Knight, Miller, Wife of Bath, Merchant, Franklin, Pardoner and Nun's Priest, adopting for each chapter a regular pattern of close textual analysis and discussion of the source or context. He works from particular details towards general interpretation, seeking interaction from the reader by including questions at regular intervals, and also giving discussion points and suggestions for further reading at the end of each chapter; these are good strategies for an introductory guide such as this, although the format can get a little tiresome after a while, and the book works best when read in parts. Sometimes Brown's line of approach is unsurprising; for example, in the chapter on the *Knight's Tale*, he looks at ideas of imprisonment, fortune and love, and refers us to the *Teseida*, Boethius and the *Romance of the Rose*; similarly his discussion of the *Wife of Bath's Prologue* and *Tale* is based on attitudes to women and the concept of *gentilesse*. Elsewhere, he is more inventive: he uses medieval calendar illustrations with the *Merchant's Tale*; he juxtaposes the Noah play with the *Miller's Tale* to reveal the tale's potential as domestic drama; and with the *Franklin's Tale* he successfully demonstrates its central concept by drawing comparisons with *Patience*. This is a slim, attractive volume, generously illustrated; it will prove a good introduction at the sixth-form or undergraduate level (though the price may dissuade from purchase), and will also be useful to those teaching Chaucer for the first time.

Helen T. Bennett draws links between 'Pope Gregory's *Liber Regulae Pastoralis* and Chaucer's *Canterbury Tales*' (*MedPers* 9.24–40), arguing that Chaucer may have had direct knowledge of Gregory's text, and finding in the *Canterbury Tales* particular applications of Gregory's pastoral strategy. In the same issue, Dansby Evans explores some affinities between 'Chaucer and Eliot: The Poetics of Pilgrimage' (41–7), arguing that the Chaucerian allusion at the beginning of *The Waste Land* invites the reader to consider that poem as a modern pilgrimage.

The date on which the pilgrims assembled at the Tabard Inn is the subject of Sigmund Eisner's article, 'The Ram Revisited: A Canterbury Conundrum' (*ChauR* 28.330–43). Eisner does not offer a new solution to this old problem, but seeks to bolster up one which was previously 'proposed and ignored, proposed again and rejected, then resurrected and again ignored'; that is, that in referring to the Ram in the opening lines of the *Canterbury Tales*, Chaucer was making a distinction between the sign and the constellation of Aries. In following the history of this debate, Eisner is lucid, but his discussion subsequently becomes too mathematical for this reviewer. Mindful of Chaucer's position as justice of the peace for Kent, Mary Flowers Braswell argues in 'Chaucer's "Court Baron": Law and *The Canterbury Tales*' (*SAC* 16.29–44) that the *Canterbury Tales* is built upon a legal palimpsest. She draws parallels between the assemblage of medieval manor courts and the pilgrims' meeting, regarding the characters as defined by aspects of the law, though she does not reduce them to legal principles, and she is quick to acknowledge that Chaucer creates characters for whom there is no manorial precedent. Her essay makes an interesting case for Chaucer's legal influences, and also explores ideas of judgement and representation.

The sense of disappointment engendered by the ending of the *Canterbury Tales* is pondered by Phyllis Portnoy in 'Beyond the Gothic Cathedral: Post-modern Reflections in the *Canterbury Tales*' (*ChauR* 28.279–92). Working from an image proposed by Robert Jordan, Portnoy argues that the fictional pilgrimage ends in a lack of spiritual fulfilment, and that rather than pointing towards God in Gothic fashion, the *Retraction* defines more sharply the gap between human intention and achievement.

Charles A. Owen, in 'Chaucer's Witty Prosody in *General Prologue*, Lines 1–42' (in Jost, *Chaucer's Humor*), includes prosodic wit within Chaucer's comic vision, and adds to an earlier examination of witty prosody in the *Prologue's* portraits, noting that he had not taken any examples from the key opening lines of the poem.

Terry Jones's radical reassessment of *Chaucer's Knight: The Portrait of a Medieval Mercenary* first appeared in 1980 (*YWES* 61.107), and a revised edition with a new preface followed in 1985; this year Jones offers a further revised edition, which is based on the text of the 1985 version, but which includes some new material. This basically means that the volume has a full new introduction, complete with an exhortation by the author: 'Why I think you should read this edition rather than any previous edition', although two sections of the commentary on the Knight's description in the *General Prologue* have also been rewritten. Jones is concerned to take account of some of the criticisms levelled against his book, admitting that he originally overstated and oversimplified his case, but this is no retraction: he still affirms the central points of his argument. In particular he takes note of the counter-arguments of Maurice Keen (*YWES* 64.151), but seems unaware of those of John Pratt (*YWES* 68.185), whose name does not even appear in the additional bibliography. Shunichi Noguchi's article 'Prayers in Chaucer's *Knight's Tale*' (*PoeticaJ* 41.45–50) is disappointing because it scarcely goes beyond describing their contents, and making comparisons with Boccaccio.

A few pieces deal with language in the *Knight's Tale*. Mark A. Sherman considers 'The Politics of Discourse in Chaucer's *Knight's Tale*' (*Exemplaria* 6.1.87–114), arguing that the erotic impulse with which the poem opens is sublimated lest it undermine ideological hierarchies upon which the religious (the pilgrimage) and social (the Knight's opening of the story-telling) rituals of the poem depend. The Knight's enemy, that is, is not the infidel so much as the erotic impulse. Taking his cue from Lee Patterson's critique of chivalric self-consciousness (*YWES* 73.154), Sherman sees this self-consciousness constituting a privileged mode of subjectivity, in opposition to which the presence of Femenye represents the threat of the Other. Femenye, whose presence is systematically erased from the poem, is situated as an historical perspective which is ultimately antagonistic to the providential scheme of the Canterbury poem. The way in which erasure of Femenye is effected through chivalric discourse is exemplified by the Knight's abundant use of *occupatio*, that most epical and aristocratic of devices, when he announces that the conquest of Femenye is a tale too long to recount. In this way, the Knight also becomes an exclusionary and revisionary historiographer of the real consequences of experience. The Knight's overwriting of the erotic impulse is depicted in the fact that Theseus constructs his theatre on the very site of the grove where Palamon and Arcite fight. The theatre is read as a psychomachia-like reconstruction of Theseus's conquest of Femenye and transmuting of Emelye's body into the realm of the symbolic. It also represents the chastening of the primal erotic passions of the two knights and, by consequence, becomes a motif of the aristocratic attempt to discipline the erotic impulse throughout the *Tales*.

Jean E. Jost's 'Potency and Power: Chaucer's Aristocrats and their Linguistic Superiority' (in Liám O. Purdon and Cindy L. Vitto, *The Rusted Hauberk*) is a consideration of the *Knight's Tale* and the *Squire's Tale*, with greater attention paid to the former. She sees Chaucer's use of language as the index of a certain anxiety, informing the entire late feudal period, about the status of chivalry and the justice of the aristocratic claim to privilege. This crisis is traced by contrasting the two tales: in the *Knight's Tale*, the artistic symmetry and poetic control of language constitute a generally successful attempt to valorize order; but in the *Squire's Tale*, poetic control runs riot, reflecting the decadence of a class born to privilege, but no longer deserving of it. Both assert the linguistic superiority of their class in the face of the threat of the rising parvenu, represented by the Franklin. The essay relies overmuch on a synthesis of other critics' arguments to develop its own. In the same collection (Purdon and Vitto), Lois Roney considers the decline of the binding force of oaths to be a symptom of the decline of the feudal order in 'Chaucer Subjectivizes the Oath: Depicting the Fall from Feudalism into Individualism in the *Canterbury Tales*'. Arguing that 'feudalism was gone' from England by Chaucer's time, Roney presents the characters of the *Canterbury Tales* as subjectivized individuals more than as exemplars of an estate. Oaths in the *Tales* take on a similar relativism of value. Describing the *Knight's*, *Franklin's* and *Clerk's*

Tales as 'Chaucer's most feudal tales', she shows how each respectively exhibits a crisis in the interpretation of oaths, in the validity of intention, and in the problematics of fulfilment. In the *Knight's Tale*, Palamon and Arcite's quarrel over supremacy between Palamon's prior claim and Arcite's more powerful one demonstrates the opposition between positive and natural law. In the *Franklin's Tale*, Dorigen's innocence of intention conflicts with the requirements of an adulterous oath. And in the *Clerk's Tale*, Griselda's dilemma is that, in fulfilling her oath of obedience to her husband, she violates a different, maternal bond. For Marta Powell Harley's consideration of allusions to Proserpina in the *Knight's Tale*, see below under *Merchant's Tale*.

'Newer Currents in Psychoanalytic Criticism, and the Difference "It" Makes: Gender and Desire in the *Miller's Tale*' (*ELH* 61.473–99), by H. Marshall Leicester Jr, begins by quoting one of Freud's more colourful essays. From it, Leicester notes specific tendencies in Freud – biologism, and a positivist tendency to define woman by some essence – and how later psychoanalysts (Lacan, Irigaray) have emphasized the constructedness of sexual difference and that the unconscious is a process in language. By asking what difference 'It' makes, Leicester points to the importance of these latter psychoanalytic insights for criticism, in that they draw attention to the processes by which gender and power relations are constructed. The argument that gender is introduced into the clash between the Miller and Knight as soon *as som bettre man* is called for seems tenuous, however, as it is not clear whether *man* is marked or unmarked. Much of the essay is devoted to Alisoun, and Leicester notes that in all the extant analogues of the story, the would-be lover kisses the backside of the actual lover, never of the woman. The confusion of sexes in this scene points to an inherent undifferentiatedness of sexual orientation which is repressed in the constructing of gender. The force of Absolom's rage, Leicester argues, is from 'having to choose and to play the role of something as arbitrary as one's "proper gender"'. Karma Lochrie considers 'Women's "Pryvetees" and Fabliau Politics in the *Miller's Tale*' (*Exemplaria* 6.2.287–304). Her analysis is of gender politics where cuckoldry is central. Understanding cuckoldry to be primarily a transaction between men (the husband and the lover), she places it within a homosocial economy of *quiting*. The *Tale*, in its multiple references to *pryvetees*, employs a poetics of secrecy by which cuckoldry operates: the woman must first be concealed (John keeps Alisoun *narwe in cage*) before she can be thieved and circulated. The sphere of the private is also examined by William F. Woods in 'Private and Public Space in the *Miller's Tale*' (*ChauR* 29.166–78), in which he draws concentric spheres within the tale; Alisoun, the house, the town and the country stand for the domains of the personal, domestic, societal and natural, and set up an interplay between private and public, self and society, and society and nature. Similar sets of concentricities, parallels and oppositions are detected in the *Knight's Tale*. Each of the men comes to grief through violating the tale's principle of plenitude: Nicholas, by penetrating *Goddes pryvitee*, John by caging Alisoun up, and Absolom by being squeamish about farting – although the logic of this final reason was still no clearer after two or three readings.

Robert W. Hanning, in '"Parlous Play": Diabolic Comedy in Chaucer's *Canterbury Tales*' (in Jost), reviews the role of the devil in cycle drama and finds parallels and analogies in a number of Chaucer's *Tales*, amongst which the most sustained are those of the *Miller's Tale*. The association of the devil with farting is a comic and obscene parody of God's Word, and thus the flatulent Nicholas is a diabolic figure who usurps God's *pryvitee*. In that Nicholas plays God in the tale, by commanding the flood and directing the carpenter–Noah, Absolom is also a diabolic figure who makes an obscene 'up yours' gesture with the poker to 'God' (i.e. Nicholas), and thus brings about the 'fall' of humanity, represented by John in the tub in the roof. A crux from 'Chaucer's *Miller's Tale*, 3770: Viritoot' (*ChauR* 29.204–6) continues to excite linguistic interest for the second year running, but A. C. Breeze, who here offers the topographical gloss 'fairy toot' for the term, seems unaware of Jeffrey L. Singman's note proposing an entirely different definition last year (*YWES* 74.154). In fairness to Breeze, his article was probably at press when Singman's appeared; Breeze also discusses other instances from the Miller's and Friar's tales where 'viry-' may mean 'fairy'.

Peter G. Beidler writes about 'Chaucer's *Reeves' Tale*, Boccaccio's *Decameron*, IX, 6, and Two "Soft" German Analogues' (*ChauR* 28.237–51). By a 'hard' analogue, he means a text to which Chaucer would most likely have had access, given what we know of its provenance, date and proximity to Chaucer's own work; a 'soft' analogue, by contrast, is either post-Chaucerian or not likely to have been available to Chaucer. Beidler offers Boccaccio's *Decameron* as a 'hard' analogue, in support of which he notes a dozen minor points where there are similarities between the *Tale* and the *Decameron* but not in the French *Le meunier et les .II. clers* (the recognized 'hard' analogue for the *Tale*). Two German versions of the cradle-trick story are offered as 'soft' analogues: *Das Studentenabenteuer* and Rüdiger von Munre's *Irregand und Girregar*. Since there is no reason to suppose that Chaucer knew German, these stories were not likely to have been known to him, although the former, *Das Studentenabenteuer*, is the more similar of the two. Susan Yager, in '"A Whit Thyng In Hir Ye": Perception and Error in the *Reeve's Tale*' (*ChauR* 28.393–404), continues the discussion of optics and Chaucer in the Miller's wife's reference to a *whit thyng in hir ye* and finds it less of an academic joke than a serious comment on the limits of human perception. The philosophers, when discussing sight and perception, often use examples of white as indicators of error. Distinguishing between the powers of perception in faculty psychology, Yager argues that the wife's 'perception' is a classic confusion between a correct perception (she was certain that she saw a white thing in her eye) and an incorrect judgement (that what she saw was the *volupeer* of the clerk).

Pamela E. Barnett's '"And shortly for to seyn they were aton": Chaucer's Deflection of Rape in the *Reeve's* and *Franklin's Tales*' (*WS* 22[1993].2.145–62) emphasizes the importance for feminists of recuperating not only what is articulated but also what is not articulated in texts. These two tales of Chaucer's, she argues, narrate acts of rape upon women, the violence of which is deflected through playful rhetoric, through humour, and through presenting the act as (dubiously) consensual. This is a hard-nosed piece that refuses to be sidetracked in its redescription of the *Reeve's* and *Franklin's Tales* as straightforward cases of rape. 'There is no textual evidence with which to suppose the daughter's [Malyn's] receptivity.' Barnett sees the possible shadings of meaning, from sexual violation to theft of property, within *raptus* as so much patriarchal kicking up of sand. Without diminishing the need to critique oppression in all its forms, one could ask whether the thresholds and boundaries of 'violence', 'consent', 'liberty', etc., are historical constants. The essay, unfortunately, is the sort of piece that gets feminism a bad name amongst medievalists and vice versa.

In '"Pennannce profytable": The Currency of Custance in Chaucer's *Man of Law's Tale*' (*Exemplaria* 6.1.141–66), Laurel L. Hendrix looks at the 'semiotic of exchange' which informs the *quiting* theme of the *Canterbury Tales* and notes the mercantile metaphors which permeate religious discourse. Noting the growing crisis in the church over the blurring of distinction between spiritual and monetary exchange arising out of penitential practices, Hendrix observes that just as Christ is commodified through the rise of indulgences so Constance is handled by the Man of Law as a saleable object as he tells his *thrifty tale*. Her earthly tribulations are *pennannce profytable*, which pay off substantial spiritual dividends.

As always, the Wife of Bath commands much critical attention, with five articles about her appearing in *ChauR* alone. Peter M. W. Robinson, in 'An Approach to the Manuscripts of the *Wife of Bath's Prologue*' (in Lancashire), notes that, despite popular perception of the eighty-three extant Chaucer MSS being relatively consistent with each other, they contain variants of 'apocalyptic proportions'. In his examination of the MSS of the Wife's *Prologue*, Robinson concludes that there are stable groups of MSS, corresponding roughly to Manly–Rickert's 'constant' groups, but that there is considerable instability between the four vital early MSS, suggesting, perhaps, a possible record of an 'early cooperative editorial effort to recover Chaucer's text'. Robinson also discusses the merits of cladistic analysis of MSS relations as opposed to traditional stemmatics. Where the latter creates the double bind of being unable to create the stemma until having the archetype, but being unable to find the archetype until having the stemma, cladistics seeks to identify not only the readings ancestral at the top of the genealogical tree, but also those at every ancestral node.

Mary Carruthers's well-known 'The Wife of Bath and the Painting of Lions' (*YWES* 60.110–11), is reprinted in Evans and Johnson along with an afterword. In the afterword, she lists the varying critical reactions her essay has received, most notably the Marxist-informed criticism of Sheila Delany, identified by Carruthers as a kind of 'Socialist realism' which substitutes for the idea of a timeless art a notion of 'timeless politics, revealed in "metahistorical" patterns of struggle against dominance, whether colonialism, capitalism, or patriarchy'. As a characterization of dialectical materialism, this seems seriously misguided, but, on the strength of it, Carruthers argues for literature as an autonomous ontological category, in terms of which the Wife has 'power as a fiction' to invoke an imaginative and emotional reality, and the world of economics or politics invoked in the tale has primarily a metaphoric existence. Conveniently, one of the main foci of Carruthers's critique, Sheila Delany's 'Sexual Economics, Chaucer's Wife of Bath, and *The Book of Margery Kempe*', is here reprinted from a 1983 anthology.

In '"Space to Speke": The Wife of Bath and the Discourse of Confession' (*ChauR* 28.252–74), Jerry Root suggests that the theme of confession may prove an instructive frame for interpreting the *Wife of Bath's Prologue*. Using an analysis based on Foucault, Root considers medieval confessional practice with regard to the Parson, Friar and Summoner, as well as the Wife, and demonstrates how the Wife's action in appropriating a space in which to speak puts experience in the place of authority. In 'Trade as Pudendum: Chaucer's Wife of Bath' (*ChauR* 28.344–52), Stewart Justman regards Chaucer's portrayal of the Wife as an indirect satire on the bourgeoisie; with her shameless propensity to trade in husbands and to transact love, she is a parody of men's economic desires, and a cunning image of the emerging commercial class, not just an anti-feminist stereotype. 'False Texts and Disappearing Women in the *Wife of Bath's Prologue* and *Tale*' (*ChauR* 29.179–93), by Thomas A. Van, is less of an analysis or argument than it is a descriptive commentary, illustrating that the theme of the *Prologue* and *Tale* combined is how to love well. The disappearing women are presumably the dancing ladies whose vanishing implies that, until the knight learns how to love well, woman in all her fullness will never be apparent to him. And once the knight learns that lesson, the foul hag, whose foulness was not objective so much as in his beholder's eye, also disappears.

Dorothy Yamamoto explores what may be meant by '"Noon Oother Incubus But He": Lines 878–81 in the *Wife of Bath's Tale*' (*ChauR* 28.275–8); she rejects the standard explanation usually attached to these lines, and provides textual examples which show that the assault of an incubus was associated not just with pregnancy but with extreme violence. Alan Spearman, in '"How He Symplicius Gallus . . .": Alison of Bath's Name-Calling, or "The Taming of the Shrewed"' (*ChauR* 29.149–62), tells us that the more expected form of the name that Alisoun uses was 'Sulpicius Gallus'. Circumstantial evidence would suggest that Chaucer's form of the name was, if not intentional, at least not unconscious. Spearman isolates the word 'simple' in the form 'Symplicius' and glosses it as, in this instance, 'ignorant'. The Wife thus casts aspersions on the man who rules his domestic roost so tyranically as a fool. This 'onomastic manipulation' is part of a larger design of the Wife, namely, to retell the masculine discourse of antifeminist authorities.

Isamu Saito considers the ironies involved in the depiction of 'Chaucer's Kneeling Friar' (*PoeticaJ* 41.51–8), but in spite of the brevity of the article, its points are somewhat laboured, and the discussion rather pedestrian.

Judith Bronfman's *Chaucer's 'Clerk's Tale': The Griselda Story Received, Rewritten, Illustrated* tracks the Griselda story from its (unknown) origins, through Chaucer, to present-day representations of her and to contemporary critical interpretations of the *Tale*. Beginning with the Boccaccian account, she examines possible sources for the story, and records its subsequent popularity prior to Chaucer's *Tale*. Two chapters are given to its critical reception, from Kittredge's integration of it into a marriage debate, to allegorical, feminist, hagiographical and political readings of it. The fourth chapter records retellings of the story in English literature from Chaucer through to the twentieth century, and Bronfman finally considers illustrations, from medieval to nineteenth-century, of Griselda. The book is useful mostly for reference as there is not any specific interpretation of the *Tale* put forth, and the conclusion that its charm lies in the variety of interpretations it has generated is bland.

Lesley Johnson also considers the heterogeneity of interpretations in 'Reincarnations of Griselda: Contexts for the *Clerk's Tale*?' (in Evans and Johnson), and sees such multiplicity as an integral part both of the Griselda story and of Chaucer's text in particular. She notes how, even from its first known appearance in Boccaccio's *Decameron*, in which the interpretation of the Griselda narrative is avidly discussed by the ladies present, the story specifically lacks an evident unity of meaning, but yet how criticism has persistently attempted to 'master' the popular narrative and Chaucer's text and to invoke a unified medieval response. In resistance to this attempt at mastery, Johnson speaks of the 'surplus discursive value' of the story. She examines, in particular, contemporary political and hagiographical interpretations of Chaucer's *Tale* and points out how each suppresses inconsistencies within the text in order to maintain itself. In 'The Transcription of the "Clerk's Tale" in MS HM140: Interpreting Textual Effects' (*SB* 47.89–103), William McClellan examines one version of the *Clerk's Tale* within what he calls the 'problematic archaeology' of MS HM140; he also discusses the limits of such codicological analysis in determining intention or in assisting interpretation. In '"She Should Have Said No to Walter": Griselda's Promise in *The Clerk's Tale*' (*ES* 75.303–21), Robert Emmett Finnegan considers the terms and implications of Griselda's vow, arguing that in obeying Walter unconditionally, she 'makes of herself an accomplice to homicide'. See the *Knight's Tale* section above for Lois Roney's discussion of oaths in the *Clerk's Tale*.

In 'January's "honeste thynges": Knighthood and Narrative in the *Merchant's Tale*' (*RMSt* 20.37–49), Rosalind Field asks why January's social status as a knight has so often been ignored by critics. By extracting details from the description of January's household she shows that he is well-bred but lacking in gentility, and so demonstrates how the *Merchant's Tale* forms an integral part of Chaucer's debate about *gentilesse*. In addition, the tale satirizes the idea of privacy: January is ridiculed in private, but in public his honour is maintained. In this respect, as in others, he is truly a Janus-like figure, as the tale thus 'exposes (or claims to) the hollowness behind knightly pride'. Field argues that this aspect of the tale's satire may be easily missed by a modern audience accustomed to finding intimacy in literature. In a second article published this year, '"Superfluous Ribaldry": Spurious Lines in the *Merchant's Tale*' (*ChauR* 28.353–67), Field further considers the *Merchant's Tale*, but not as we know it, centring her discussion on a set of three passages, comprising fourteen lines in total, which augment the pear-tree episode, and which were rejected by Tyrwhitt in 1775 as non-authorial material. Her conclusion, that the insertion of these lines creates another version of the entire tale, is overbold, but her discussion of their influence on the text's reception and production is revealing, and her points are strengthened by a detailed consideration of the language used in the spurious lines. In Eric Jager's *The Tempter's Voice: Language and the Fall in Medieval Literature* (1993), one chapter on the *Merchant's Tale* is presented as a satire on Augustinian semiotics and its relation to the 'fallen' word: 'The Carnal Letter in Chaucer's Earthly Paradise'. Juxtaposing the tale with Dante's story of Paolo and Francesca (*Inferno*, Canto V), Jager draws attention to the seductive role of the word in the Fall and to the abundance of the Merchant's references to and images of writing. In the act of bodily revelation brought about by Damien lifting up May's smock, the orthodox hermeneutic revelation of spiritual truth, achieved in casting off the 'smock' or veil of the carnal letter, is flagrantly reversed. Jager sees in the tale a study of the abuse of the sign and an intensified anxiety about the irremediable fallenness of language; the *Retraction* to the *Canterbury Tales* offers a final, penitential recognition of that fallenness.

Marta Powell Harley's 'Chaucer's Use of the Proserpina Myth, in *The Knight's Tale* and *The Merchant's Tale*', appearing in *Images of Persephone: Feminist Readings in Western Literature* (edited by Elizabeth T. Hayes), takes as its keynote the composite Diana–Lucina–Proserpina figure depicted in the Knight's temple of Diana. She shows how, through the common element of Proserpina in both narratives, Emelye and May are brought into a relation with each other which is something more serious than parody or antithesis. In the two tales, Chaucer brings out the association of Proserpina with the innocence she possessed prior to her ravishment by Pluto. Powell Harley points out the respects in which both Emelye and May can be identified with Diana's chastity, Lucina's brightness and Prosperpina's vulnerability (the identification of May with chastity being tenuous, by even her own admission). This makes for a more complex picture of May, although both tales, romance and fabliau alike, ultimately conform to the anti-feminist constraints of genre. The underlying myths of the triple goddess thus raise the issue of female vulnerability and protest, but finally undermine the figures of

May and Proserpina in the tale. In 'Chaucer's May, Standup Comics, and Critics' (in Jost), Susan K. Hagen observes the analogies between the Merchant and a stand-up comic. Both capitalize upon generally held, but implicit and unconscious, cultural assumptions – in this case, that an old man cannot sexually satisfy a healthy young woman. Both also establish a sense of community with their audience, as the Merchant does in exaggerating his marital woes. And finally, just as the stand-up comic's playing upon implicit cultural values holds a more serious interrogative function, so the Merchant's comedy questions the societally sanctioned marriage of young women to old men by showing how unsuccessful it is in practice. Frederick B. Jonassen's 'Rough Music in Chaucer's *Merchant's Tale*' (in Jost) is a consideration of the ancient custom of 'charivari', which is a serenade of 'rough music' (using instruments such as kettles and pans) directed at some behaviour that a community finds shameful. The objects of censure in this festive rite can range from quack physicians and perjurers to incontinent widows, but by far the favourite object was some form of marital disorder, including marriage between parties who differ greatly in age. The rough music of the charivari custom aptly mirrors the discord of the marital bond. Jonassen finds the description of January's marriage, with its pointed reference to the musical accompaniments, just such an instance of an implicit festive judgement. And in a brief account which also focuses on the scene of the wedding feast, Robert Boenig shows how 'January's Trumpets' (*ELN* 32.i.19–23) are inappropriate instruments for this setting. (See the *Knight's Tale* section above for Jean E. Jost's comments on the *Squire's Tale*.)

In 'Carnival Food Imagery in Chaucer's Description of the Franklin' (*SAC* 16.99–117), Frederick B. Jonassen examines the passage in the *General Prologue* which describes the food offered at the Franklin's table, suggesting that the distinction drawn there between meat and fish conforms to ecclesiastical guidance on feasting and fasting; he also finds the passage as a whole influenced by popular European folklore concerning the Battle of Carnival and Lent, and the Land of Cockaigne. Felicity Riddy considers the project of 'Engendering Pity in the *Franklin's Tale*' (in Evans and Johnson). She shows how the word *gentilman*, by denoting the lowest class of the gentry, raises issues of the precarious and changing boundaries between classes; and how affective rhetoric or pity, as the specific marker of *gentilesse*, has to do ultimately with class relations between men rather than with any unisex notion of refinement. This makes for an interesting counter-argument to Jill Mann's identification of pity as specifically feminine (*YWES* 73.152). Gender and class are intriguingly connected in Riddy's examination of the representation in the *Roman de la Rose* of Daunger – the opposite of womanly pity for her suitor – as a peasant brandishing a club, where woman's power to withhold herself from man becomes insidiously linked with social sedition. The perceived threat of the Peasant's Revolt, the hierarchy of man's power over woman, and the entire ideology of *gentilesse* all hinge on the maintenance of the distinction between thraldom and freedom. Riddy finds the *Tale* complicit with such a maintenance and speculates on its silent female medieval readers, who 'may not have agreed that women are to be pitied and that only men are "free"'. Interestingly, Riddy's speculation is organized around the possibility that the Auchinleck MS was known within Chaucer's family circle, and Robert Cook picks up the theme when he compares 'Chaucer's *Franklin's Tale* and *Sir Orfeo*' (*NM* 95.333–6). Cook wants to add to Laura Hibbard Loomis's argument that Chaucer's ideas about the Breton lay derive from his reading of the MS, dating from around 1340, which contains a copy of *Orfeo*. He notes that the four separate illusions shown to Aurelius and his brother by the magician compare closely with the series of scenes Orfeo sees during his exile, leading up to his vision of Heurodis. Although there are differences in the basic narrative situation and minor differences between the visions, Cook suggests that the passages are united by their hallucinatory quality and by the manner of their appearance.

Along with Lois Roney's discussion of oaths (see the section on the *Knight's Tale* above) is another piece which considers the role of promises in the *Franklin's Tale*. Leslie K. Arnovick, in 'Dorigen's Promise and Scholars' Premise: The Orality of Speech in the *Franklin's Tale*' (in Mark C. Amodio, *Oral Poetics in Middle English Poetry*), argues that the ambiguous nature of Dorigen's promise to Aurelius in part lies in the oral nature of the exchange; it is a speech-act in writing, and therefore the pragmatic or contextual circumstances of her promise become of paramount importance. Arnovick's analysis is based on speech act typology, and she finds that in Dorigen's initial rejection of Aurelius, psychological state correlates with the form of her utterance, thus fulfilling the basic criteria for an illocutionarily successful speech act. Dorigen's 'playful' promise, however, loses its illocutionary force when she contradicts it by then asserting that she knows it will not come to pass. But although the initial sincerity condition is not met, Dorigen nevertheless later chooses to accept responsibility for the expression of an intention she never possessed. Such disjunctions arise out of the mixed nature of oral and literate composition in the *Tale*. Joe Green trots out a lot of recycled ideas about the Franklin's overindulgence and showy concern for appearances in 'Chaucer's Genial Franklin' (*PVR* 21[1993].1.6–16). The most recent of the four critical works he cites is from 1977.

The *Physician's Tale*, along with the *Second Nun's Tale*, is touched on briefly in Jocelyn Wogan-Browne's discussion of virginity in 'The Virgin's Tale' (in Evans and Johnson). Finding saints' lives to offer an important critique of courtly love for their female readers, Wogan-Browne describes Chaucer as an imaginative and thoughtful reworker of hagiographical material. In comparison with other saints' lives, his description of the virgins' bodily mutilation tends to be decorous and understated, and, in the *Physician's Tale*, he positions Virginia's martyrdom within a 'nuanced awareness of the political and the social'.

The *Physician's* and *Pardoner's Tales* are considered in opposition to each other by Marc M. Pelen (*ChauR* 29.1–25). He finds that each attempts to deny the apparent point of the other without proposing any alternative. The Physician's identification of purity with sacrifice is countered by the Pardoner's gross materialism, and in turn the Pardoner's own tale is contradicted by its overt morality. Pelen sees the source of Chaucer's opposition between murder and immortality in the conflicting positions assumed by Raison, Genius and Nature in the *Roman de la Rose*.

The *Pardoner's Tale* comes into Richard W. Ireland's study of 'Chaucer's Toxicology' (*ChauR* 29.74–92), where he notes the common association of poison with sin and diabolical presence. The references to poison in the tale thus create a more sinister effect than previously appreciated, and are foreshadowed in the inherent opposition between medicine and poison suggested by the *Physician's Tale* coming immediately before in the ordering of the *Tales*. In the second half of the essay, Ireland considers the reference made by the Parson to poison used for abortive purposes, and suggests that, in a context where secular justice seemed tentative on the subject of abortion, the Parson's forthright condemnation is especially significant. Allen J. Frantzen writes about '*The Pardoner's Tale*, the

Pervert, and the Price of Order in Chaucer's World' (in Britton J. Harwood and Gillian R. Overing, *Class and Gender in Early English Literature*) using a 'mix of Marxism and gender criticism'. The opening equation he makes between gender as involving the personal, and class the public, sets up a false distinction cut across by the medieval category of estate. Similarly, the representation of the church, the estate of those who pray, as consumers of a surplus produced by those who labour sets up a producer/consumer division that is too easy an economic rationalization of late feudalism. Rather than seeing the Pardoner as lack (by dint of his eunuchry), Frantzen argues that what the Pardoner lacks is lack itself. In other words, by flouting the estates ideal of the common good, the Pardoner breaks the rules and gets away with it. His final humiliation has nothing to do with any natural justice, but is rather the revenge of a system which cannot forgive his exposure, through his self-sufficiency, of its manipulations. The epithet of 'pervert' in the title is taken from Deleuze and Guattari's designation of one who is more artificial than the society he is transgressing, and this perversion, ironically, emerges as the very condition for an understanding of the 'normal'. The sexualization of the Pardoner continues in 'Claiming the Pardoner: Toward a Gay Reading of Chaucer's *Pardoner's Tale*' (*Exemplaria* 6.1.115–39), in which Steven F. Kruger frames his argument within the story of an AIDS sufferer's perception of the Pardoner as 'the first angry homosexual'. Kruger, 'a gay man living in 1992', wants to retain the significance of the Pardoner for gay culture, but 'to arrive at a more fully historicist gay reading'. By this is meant the recognition, articulated from Michel Foucault onwards, that sexuality is itself an historically specific notion – a recognition Kruger illustrates by a distinction between (modern) homosexual identity and (pre-modern) homosexual behaviour. The problem, however, remains in the very term 'homosexual' and is unfortunately not addressed by Kruger, who, after summarizing the criticism on the subject, simply concludes that the Pardoner is a possible homosexual. The Pardoner is inscribed within a homophobic perspective and Chaucer sees only disruption and danger in the Pardoner's 'anger' and 'camp sensibility'. The anger and campness, however, are positive in themselves, and the very violence with which the Pardoner is treated itself reveals the insecure need to contain the queer. There is a subtle but significant distinction between medieval male sodomy and modern homosexuality, and to elide them, as Kruger does, both narrows the understanding of the latter and misleadingly abstracts the former from other related manifestations of violations against nature.

William F. Woods, in 'Metaphoric Comedy: *The Shipman's Tale*' (in Jost), renarrates the story in the light of the idea that its dominant ethic is the quid pro quo of mercantile exchange, and that it is not the individual merchant who is the focus of comedy but the whole merchant class.

Three items consider the *Prioress's Tale* in some detail. In 'Cultic Anti-Judaism and Chaucer's Litel Clergeon' (*MP* 91.413–27), Denise L. Despres explores the relationship between eucharistic symbolism and anti-Judaism in an attempt to show how the Prioress's vision of purified community could have resonance for a post-expulsion fourteenth-century audience wholly unacquainted with Jews. Daniel F. Pigg, on the other hand, claims that critical preoccupation with the tale's anti-Semitism misses the point. In 'Refiguring Martyrdom: Chaucer's Prioress and Her Tale' (*ChauR* 29.65–73), he argues that the tale is an appropriate discourse for a nun because it illustrates medieval notions of martyrdom (which he briefly surveys), and authorizes the monastic life as a means of achieving that martyrdom. For him the tale is 'an act of ritualistic devotion', and its teller 'far more complex and mysterious than readers have appreciated'. In 'Gender-crossing in the *Prioress' Tale*: Chaucer's Satire on Theological Anti-Semitism?' (*Cithara* 33.ii.11–17), Wolfgang E. H. Rudat concentrates not on the titular topics but on phallic imagery, voicing surprise that 'nobody seems to have pursued this idea further', although in fact he himself has covered this ground before in his monograph, *Ernest Exuberance in Chaucer's Poetics*, published last year (*YWES* 74.149–50); here, as there, he takes things altogether too far, suggesting a pregnancy and abortion for the Prioress, and reading her tale as Chaucer's attack on the church's sexual repression of women.

In 'The *Thopas–Melibee* Sequence and the Defeat of Antifeminism' (*ChauR* 29.26–39), Celia R. Daileader sees the two tales as continuing the Wife of Bath's attempt to deconstruct anti-feminism. The *Tale of Sir Thopas* inaugurates the authority of audience over author and shows Chaucer letting himself get caught with his 'authorial pants down' in order to interrogate an *auctoritee* of which he himself is a part. In the *Tale of Melibee*, Prudence, acting as the voice of the mutilated body of Sophie, defends woman before the council of men from the stereotype of the wicked wife. Both her story and that of the Wife of Bath end with the transformation of a misguided man through the counsel of a woman. The same two tales are considered by Seth Lerer in '"Now holde youre mouth": The Romance of Orality in the *Thopas–Melibee* Section of the *Canterbury Tales*' (in Amodio), for whom Thopas dramatizes the pitfalls of orality in literary presentation while *Melibee* is actively disengaged from the phenomenon of voice, being a text about other texts. The narrator intrudes continuously into the *Thopas* narrative to such an extent that the story collapses; what the Host is objecting to in the tale is not so much its trite content as how it sounds. In reaction, *Melibee* is not told so much as written. Lerer links this turning from one mode of presentation to another with the Augustinian casting off of romances and recitations in favour of the more responsible readings of a man, thereby linking orality to (Chaucer's elvish) childishness and writing with maturity. Matters oral are further discussed by Ward Parks in 'Oral Tradition and the *Canterbury Tales*' (in Amodio). Parks muses for a while on the relationship between Chaucer and an oral tradition, and reviews the received scholarship on what technically constitutes such a tradition, submitting that Chaucer's *Tales* are not only intertextual but also 'interperformative', by which is meant that the poet operates in a 'literary' tradition which is preserved through memory and is not recuperable in the way that books make possible. It is in *Thopas* that Parks sees the vestigial presence of an oral tradition most visibly at work. Two aesthetic sensibilities are operative and their incompatibility explains at least in part the perceived farcical formulae (e.g. *stile and stoon*) of the *Tale*. The narrative disorganization of *Thopas* shows the ineptitude of a narrator who can no longer order the stock materials of his story. Finally, Parks explains Chaucer's apology in the *General Prologue* that he had not ordered the portraits correctly in terms of the oral–traditional depiction of the poet as the reteller of tales.

In a detailed account, Jane Dick Zatta examines the Monk's catalogue of tyrannic despots in 'Chaucer's Monk: A Mighty Hunter before the Lord' (*ChauR* 29.111–33), and finds them resonant of the political crises in England in the late fourteenth century. The reference to Nimrod implied in the *Prologue*'s description of the Monk as a hunter is significant because Nimrod was also identified by Augustine with the origin of tyranny. The irony is that, while the Monk produces all the right examples of tyranny, he is unable to interpret their vice aright. The essential political function of the clerical estate is to interpret the events of history, but the Monk fails in it through his seeking of personal gain rather than *commune profit*. Vincent DiMarco speculates on the source of the second stanza of the Monk's vignette of Nero in 'Nero's Nets and Seneca's Veins: A New Source for the *Monk's Tale*?' (*ChauR* 28.384–92). Finding the present candidates for sources unsatisfactory, DiMarco points us to a version of the legend that Nero disliked used clothing in the *Alphabetum narrationum*, probably composed in 1308, and extant in over ninety MSS from the fourteenth and fifteenth centuries. Although a critical edition of the work is currently in preparation, there has not been an edition made of it yet, and DiMarco transcribes the relevant passages from a Latin MS and its Middle English translation. One of the persuasive details he records is that the *Alphabetum* describes Seneca as having slit both his veins, a detail Chaucer mentions but which does not occur in the usually assumed source for Chaucer, Vincent of Beauvais' *Speculum historiale*. DiMarco suggests that the *Alphabetum* should at the very least be considered as a close analogue for the *Monk's Tale*. Electronic technology is applied by Thomas H. Bestul to 'Chaucer's "Monk's Tale": Sources and Analogues in the Age of Computing' (in Lancashire). Since his opening sentence is that 'no new sources for Chaucer's "Monk's Tale" have recently been discovered', he might want to go back to the drawing board after reading DiMarco. Despite seeing theoretical difficulties with the hierarchical orderings implied in the relationship between a source and an analogue (not to mention between 'soft' and 'hard' analogues), Bestul still sees a need for a computerized database of such texts, and describes how a computerized organization of the *Tale*'s sources and analogues could provide a schema *in parvo* for a similar organization of those of the whole of the *Canterbury Tales*.

Two analyses of Chaucer's sole explicit reference to the Peasants' Revolt appeared this year, of which the first, Richard W. Fehrenbacher's '"A Yeerd Enclosed Al Aboute": Literature and History in *The Nun's Priest's Tale*' (*ChauR* 29.134–48), presents the rhetorical excesses of the *Tale* as an attempt to contain the force of the political. The conclusions of Stephen Knight and Lee Patterson, both of whom see Chaucer retreating from the very dissent he has eloquently voiced through the Miller and the Wife, are the guiding star of Fehrenbacher's argument. The *Nun's Priest's Tale* re-enacts, clearly unsuccessfully, Chaucer's attempts to dehistoricize. History returns with a vengeance in such attempts, as in the narrator's invocation of Vinsauf, where the allusion to rhetoric as the politically disinterested gift of eloquence is undercut by the naming of Richard I. R. James Goldstein analyses the 'political unconscious' of Chaucer's jokes in 'Chaucer, Freud, and the Political Economy of Wit: Tendentious Jokes in the *Nun's Priest's Tale*' (in Jost). 'Tendentious' here means jokes which aim to offend or expose, and Goldstein finds them in the joking allusions to peasantry and to women. The real target of attack, which has been repressed within the *Tale* only to return in the form of jocular asides, is the peasant class, whose seditiousness is recognized in Chaucer's only explicit allusion to the Peasants' Revolt.

Ian Lancashire examines 'Phrasal Repetends and *The Manciple's Prologue* and *Tale*' (in Lancashire) and finds that there is a far higher quantity of repetends than one might expect. Since these findings correspond to earlier research done on the *General Prologue*, Lancashire surmises that the *Manciple's Tale*'s findings are fairly typical of Chaucer's other tales. The conclusion he does not jump to is that repetends are indicative of an oral tradition. Rather, he notes that the phrasal repetends are not themselves evenly distributed throughout Chaucer's *Tales* but tend to cluster in two or more of the *Tales* at a time. Lancashire suggests that the statistics might well indicate the tales' proximity of composition to each other.

In a brief item, John C. Hirsh considers a phrase which relates to Chaucer's Parson, 'General Prologue 526: "A Spiced Conscience"' (*ChauR* 28.414–17), examining what this may tell us about the Parson's religiousness.

3. *Troilus and Criseyde*

For a list of references to Troilus, Criseyde, and Pandarus, published between 1475 and 1640, see section 1 above. The first item to be discussed here, Stephen A. Barney's *Studies in Troilus: Chaucer's Text, Meter, and Diction* (1993), should have been reviewed last year. This volume of six essays consists, by Barney's own admission, of 'partly apologetic, partly reflective, partly corrective, partly argumentative spillings over' from his work editing *Troilus* for the Riverside Chaucer. For the most part his arguments are directed against Barry A. Windeatt's edition (*YWES* 65.153), which appeared as he was preparing his own; whilst insisting that Windeatt's work is 'magisterial', he nevertheless lists errors (in the notes, glossary, variant readings, treatment of final *-e*) and suggests corrections, to such an extent that at times the volume resembles a lengthy – and belated – review of Windeatt's edition. He accepts Windeatt's views on metre, but calls at the same time for a deeper study of Chaucer's metre, complaining that real investigation of this matter ceased with Kitteredge. He is right in claiming that such an assessment would require a complete collation of the spellings of all the textual authorities, but his faith that 'mechanical word-processing' will magically provide this, and his cry 'let computers do it for us', show a lack of understanding of the very real labour involved in assembling a computer database. Aware of the technical nature of his subject, it is Barney's stated aim to be 'inviting' to the general student of Chaucer, a mission which he manages only partially to fulfil; his introduction gives a brief survey of the *Troilus* manuscripts and a beginner's guide to the technical terms of textual criticism, but subsequently his discussion inevitably becomes more complicated, and a good deal less inviting to non-specialists. However, with so much editorial energy being expended on the *Canterbury Tales* at present, it is good to see some directed towards *Troilus* for a change. There is also some interest in linguistic issues. In '"As she that": Syntactical Ambiguity in Chaucer's *Troilus and Criseyde*' (*PQ* 73.151–68), Susan Yager notes that this phrase, which occurs frequently towards the end of the poem, may be read either as a phrasal calque or as a clause of comparison, or sometimes as both – a range of interpretative possibilities which accords with the thematic ambiguity of the poem itself. Yoshiyuki Nakao offers 'A Note on the Affectivity of Criseyde's *pite*' (*PoeticaJ* 41.19–43), in which she examines Chaucer's use of the term *pite* and a number of semantically related terms. Karen Arthur reviews 'A *TACT* Analysis of the Language of Death in *Troilus and Criseyde*' (in Lancashire), showing how text-retrieval systems such as *TACT* can be used to analyse thematic material. She makes a number of observations, including how Pandarus's vocabulary of death increases dramatically in Book II as he coerces Criseyde into seduction, and how the language of mortality shifts in Book V from courtly hyperbole to Christian and salvific notions of death.

The one essay by Gayle Margherita appears in two forms, in *Exemplaria* 6.243–69 and as the chapter 'Historicity, Femininity, and Chaucer's *Troilus*' in her *The*

Romance of Origins: Language and Sexual Difference in Middle English Literature. She opens her chapter with a strong critique of the historicism represented by such critics as Lee Patterson, Paul Strohm and Steven Knight, arguing that their commitment is to a history shaped primarily by the public and collective. Inevitably, in this scenario, the private is associated with the feminine, resulting in a false opposition between public and private, and in a privileging of the former over the latter. She points out the etymological relation between 'private' and 'privation', and counters that the boundary between public and private, and between past and present, is not empirically fixed. She defends the feminist and psychoanalytic reading of Chaucer's texts on the grounds of their ability to problematize gaps and absences in the poem. Instead of asking what Chaucer could have known about the unconscious, she asks rather how we could ever think to keep the Middle Ages (and Chaucer) from 'knowing what we know', in that our preoccupations and complexes determine the very questions we ask of history. Her reading of Criseyde, like that of Blaunche, presents woman as embodying the losses and fractures which are the origin of masculine poetic subjectivity and historicism. Margherita's work is not an easy read, but its commitment to psychoanalysis and feminism and to their relation to the past is thoughtfully posed. A different approach is followed in 'Questions of Gender in Chaucer, from *Anelida* to *Troilus*' (*LeedsSE* 25.83–110), where Alcuin Blamires finds Chaucer resistant to medieval gender stereotypes; Blamires considers instances of role reversal in both texts, dwelling in particular on the extent to which Troilus is cast as the blushing bride in the consummation scene with Criseyde. Nancy Mason Bradbury investigates Chaucer's textualization of folkloric materials in *Troilus and Criseyde* in 'Gentrification and the *Troilus*' (*ChauR* 28.305–29). She proposes the term 'gentrification' as a counterpart to 'popularization', arguing that Chaucer was influenced as much by English popular culture as by an international scholarly tradition. This is a strand of influence which has been very much overlooked, probably, she suggests, because although Chaucer's use of proverbial language and non-literary allusions would have been readily accessible to a contemporary audience, they are less so to us.

The area of *Troilus* studies which seems to be attracting most attention is the poem's relationship with its successors. In 'Outdoing Chaucer: Lydgate's *Troy Book* and Henryson's *Testament of Cresseid* as Competitive Imitations *of Troilus and Criseyde*', Nicholas Watson shows how Chaucer's poetic descendants treated his work as both source and challenge, simultaneously canonizing and subverting his authority by 'complex acts of literary theft'. Although Watson seems to ignore a number of relevant recent studies, readers should note the final footnote, which explains when the article was completed; it appears in *Shifts and Transpositions in Medieval Narrative: A Festschrift for Elspeth Kennedy*, edited by Karen Pratt, where it is the only contribution, of thirteen, to discuss Chaucer. Watson concentrates on Lydgate, somewhat at the expense of Henryson, but two other studies redress the balance. In 'Cresseid Reading Cresseid: Redemption and Translation in Henryson's *Testament*' (*ScLJ* 21.ii.5–22), Susan Aronstein argues that Henryson's agenda in the *Testament of Cresseid* is 'to reassert the pre-Chaucerian Criseyde of earlier misogynist tradition and thus to recover a social order based on that tradition'. She sketches the literary history of the story of Troilus and Criseyde from Benoit to Chaucer, and briefly reviews the history of medieval prostitution and attitudes towards it, showing how by the late fifteenth century the function of the brothel was to serve as an instrument of penitence for the fallen woman. Henryson, influenced by contemporary attitudes, returns the story of Criseyde to its original purpose, that is, as a warning to both sexes about the infamy of women. Unlike Chaucer, whose ambiguous attitude towards his heroine allows for a flexibility of interpretation, Henryson's poem seeks to prevent the danger of misreadings based upon sympathy, by eliminating the ambiguities of Chaucer's version. And in a brief article, William Stephenson argues that the occurrence of 'The Acrostic "Fictio" in Robert Henryson's *The Testament of Cresseid* (lines 58–63)' (*ChauR* 29.163–5) is an indication of the fictional nature of the 'uther quair', Henryson's supposed source for the poem.

4. Other Works

In *American Dream Visions: Chaucer's Surprising Influence on F. Scott Fitzgerald*, Deborah Davis Schlacks draws a surprising comparison between medieval and modern. The discussion is confined to Fitzgerald's early works. An introductory chapter outlines Fitzgerald's interest in the medieval era and what is termed the 'Chaucer–Fitzgerald connection'; four subsequent chapters then attempt to show in more detail how Fitzgerald uses 'the enticing models provided by Chaucer's dream visions'. The second and third chapters focus primarily on the *House of Fame*, drawing out similarities with three of Fitzgerald's short stories and his unsuccessful play; two further chapters concentrate on *The Great Gatsby*, in which Schlacks finds echoes of all four of Chaucer's dream visions, in particular the *Book of the Duchess*. The structural comparisons drawn are less than persuasive, which partly undermines the book's conclusion, and the suggestion that the theme of artistic creativity is one which links both authors also fails to convince. This volume will probably be of more interest to American literature specialists than to Chaucerians.

Helen Phillips's excellent edition of *The Book of the Duchess*, first published by Durham Medieval Texts in 1982 (*YWES* 63.109), was reissued in a revised format in 1993, a fact which escaped the notice of this reviewer. The first edition is out of print, so the appearance of the second is to be welcomed, although there is not much that is different about it: there are some revisions and corrections, and a brief account of recent criticism of the poem; the bibliography has been brought up to date and rearranged, though some inconsistencies in layout remain; and the appendix which promises 'Latin and French Sources and Analogues' in fact covers French material only. Despite some additions the second edition is fourteen pages shorter than the first, thanks to improvements in the preparation of camera-ready copy, which have also greatly enhanced the volume's overall appearance.

Ardis Butterfield makes the *Book of the Duchess* the Middle English focus of her wide-ranging article 'Pastoral and the Politics of Plague in Machaut and Chaucer' (*SAC* 16.3–27), in which she considers the transposition of the pastoral between France and England. She argues that the fourteenth-century *dits amoureux* may be seen as versions of pastoral, and makes a fresh case for the significance of the *Jugement dou Roy de Navarre* to Chaucer's poem, based on the instance of royal female death through plague which is a defining factor in both works, even though the *Book of the Duchess* omits any specific reference to the cause of Blanche's death. In '*The Book of the Duchess* as a Memorial Monument' (*ChauR* 28.205–15), Phillipa Hardman argues that the poem is the verbal equivalent to the tomb commissioned for Blanche, Duchess of Lancaster, in 1374 and completed by 1376. This leads her, incidentally, to some interesting thoughts about the dating of the poem, but her main purpose is to draw comparisons between the structure and functions of late fourteenth-century memorial tombs and those of Chaucer's text. Her treatment of various contemporary images is sensitive and detailed, and although she has to rely upon a seventeenth-century engraving for details of her most important image (the original double tomb of Blanche and Gaunt perished in the Great Fire of London), her discussion is nevertheless compelling. In a second, equally excellent, article published this year, 'Chaucer's Man of Sorrows: Secular Images of Pity in the *Book of the Duchess*, the *Squire's Tale*, and *Troilus and Criseyde*' (*JEGP* 93.204–27), Hardman considers the portrayal of the Man in Black, arguing that he functions as a secular *imago pietatis*, which solicits an active response from its readers. Her detailed consideration of the text leads her into analogies with both lyric poetry and contemporary illustrations, as, undeterred by the apparently scanty evidence of the image's currency in fourteenth-century England, she investigates how Chaucer might have encountered the image of the Man of Sorrows. Despite the title, the article is mainly about the *Book of the Duchess*; the other works are treated much less fully, leaving room for development here, especially with regard to *Troilus and Criseyde*.

It does not look as if Chaucer was too good at chess, according to Margaret Connolly in 'Chaucer and Chess' (*ChauR* 29.40–4), an essay which focuses mostly on the *Book of the Duchess*. She points out that, until the rules of the game were changed in the fifteenth century, the queen was actually the weakest piece on the board, so that the narrator's puzzlement at the Black Knight's grief is perfectly understandable. But there are other problems, such as why the Knight should be lamenting at all since the Queen is in the opposing colour, and how the lovers' relationship could be analogized through that between a Knight and Queen. She argues that Chaucer is borrowing the chess analogy from the *Roman de la Rose*, but applying it to less apt particulars. Gayle Margherita's chapter 'Originary Fantasies and Chaucer's *Book of the Duchess*', in *The Romance of Origins: Language and Sexual Difference in Middle English Literature*, is a revision of an essay from last year (*YWES* 74.164). For the other chapter in her book dealing with Chaucer, see section 3 above.

Durham Medieval Texts, which last year provided a revised version of Helen Phillips's edition of *The Book of the Duchess* (see above), this year gives us a new edition of *The House of Fame*, edited by Nicholas R. Havely. Havely's text is based on MS Bodley Fairfax 16, but he also collates evidence from the other two manuscript witnesses and from the early printed editions of Caxton and Thynne; he records all variant readings which significantly affect sense or metre, which means that his list of variants, whilst not exhaustive, does give more information than that of the Riverside edition. A brief introduction considers the textual witnesses, the poem's date, language and metre, possible sources, and some of the poem's concerns, namely poetics and folly. Havely also provides fifty pages of line-by-line commentary, on-the-page glossing and a select glossary at the end of the volume, an index of proper names, and a reasonably extensive bibliography, which are all features which students will find useful.

Sheila Delany's *Chaucer's House of Fame: The Poetics of Skeptical Fideism* is reprinted in paperback form, with a new foreword by Michael Near. Initially published in 1972, the book's footnotes do not, of course, reflect the critical interest the poem has attracted in the last twenty odd years, but Delany's scholarship remains as pertinent as ever, and it is good to have the book within the price range of students.

Marilynn Desmond's *Reading Dido: Gender, Textuality, and the Medieval Æneid* carries a chapter, entitled '*Sely* Dido and the Chaucerian Gaze', on the *House* and on the *Legend of Dido*. Primarily focusing on the *House*, Desmond finds the narrator to be incontrovertibly masculinist. She associates the power of the written letter with masculine discourse and the oral with the feminine, and finds the bookish narrator to be engaging in a 'gender of technology' which renders woman as object of representation rather than as representing subject. Given the importance she attaches to issues of literacy, some qualification of her equation of private reading with silence (as distinct from public reading which is performed aloud) would be appropriate. Desmond details the convoluted ekphrasis by which text and image are merged in the depiction of Dido's story, and concludes that the gendered dynamics of the narrator's male gaze render female desire unrepresentable except as representation. But in the *Legend of Dido*, Chaucer bestows Dido with a subject position which enables her to articulate a 'female, heterosexual desire'. Desmond finds Chaucer's modification of the Dido story in making her pregnant especially significant as a marker of the physical realities of her body. Desmond's analysis of the power of the specular is heavily indebted to psychoanalytic paradigms of castration, the fetish, voyeurism, etc., although it is not clear that the same narrative shapes the power of the iconic and of 'showings' in medieval textuality and visual depiction. In 'Building Class and Gender into Chaucer's *Hous*', Britton J. Harwood (in Harwood and Overing) argues both for the independence of the two categories, with neither as the antecedent cause of the other, and yet also for their interdependence. He sees the *House* as motivated by 'an ideological project coordinating class interest with a gender one'. Gender in the poem is apparent in the relation between the feminized cage of twigs, read by Harwood as a *moder*-like structure in which the tidings maturate and then burst forth towards the castle of Fame. Fame, in this schema, performs the paternal function of assigning names to the tidings. And class is also apparent in the relation between the castle and the cage of twigs, the former resembling the manorial castle and the latter a peasant house, while the tidings, the 'production' of the cage, function as the feudal rent. In Harwood's reading, gender and class are linked through these images of production and reproduction. Much of the essay is devoted to a more general discussion of forces and relations of production, and the transitions between it and the reading of the poem seem, at times, disjointed. R. J. Schoeck's brief article '*The Hous of Fame* Revisited' (*Connotations* 3.ii.110–14) really constitutes an addendum to John Steadman's essay published in the same journal last year (*YWES* 74.164). Schoeck agrees with Steadman's view that the work's lack of coherence and continuity are symptoms of its performative or, as Schoeck prefers, its 'presentational' nature; this allows him to reiterate his own point, made several decades ago, that the poem was designed for revels at the Inns of Court. He also insists that the poem's structure embodies 'a sense of playfulness', but his failure to be more specific means that the poem continues to be 'a game for which we have lost the rules'. In 'The Bret Glascurion and Chaucer's *House of Fame*' (*RES* 45.63–9), Andrew Breeze dismantles Robinson's identification of Glascurion as a tenth-century Glamorgan bard, suggesting instead another candidate, Gwydion son of Dôn.

The *Parliament of Fowls* has provoked almost no discussion this year, one of the two exceptions being an article by Ordelle G. Hill and Gardiner Stillwell which argues that the poem constitutes 'A Conduct Book for Richard II' (*PQ* 73.317–28). Whilst concurring with the accepted view that the poem's central topic is love, Hill and Stillwell call attention to several references to law-breaking, and find in the work's emphasis on nature an implicit warning against deviant behaviour. They make more claims than they can substantiate, stopping just short of stating that John of Gaunt commissioned the poem for Richard's instruction, and their reference to the supposed date of Richard's death makes for a weak conclusion. The *Parliament of Fowls* is considered by Judith H. Anderson as an important and generally unappreciated source for Spenser's *Faerie Queene* in 'The "Couert Vele": Chaucer, Spenser, and Venus' (*ELR* 24.638–59). Her particular interest is in the Temple of Venus in Spenser's fourth book, and she cites Chaucer's description of the Temple from the *Parliament* (as opposed to those from the *Knight's Tale* or the *House of Fame*) as its dominant literary ancestor. In both accounts, the figure of Venus wears a skimpy veil, only in Spenser's case its purpose is to hide her hermaphroditic doubleness. The Spenserian Venus bears resemblance to two other figures in the *Faerie Queene*, the goddess Nature and Acrasia, who themselves are both veiled and both allude to the *Parliament*. Spenser's Venus, set thus between a corrupt Acrasia's Bower and an idealized bower of Nature, captures the very dilemma of Chaucer's dream poem – the choice between two loves, the one virtuous, the other vicious, yet both inescapably interconnected.

Don Chapman, in his study of 'Neologisms in Chaucer's *Boece*' (in Lancashire), takes a conservative date of composition, 1385 rather than the possible 1380, for the work. Comparing its vocabulary against the *MED*, Chapman defines a word in *Boece* as a neologism if there is no earlier recording of it. By far the largest concentration of neologisms, he discovers, occurs in this work. Chaucer, it appears, was more apt to borrow a word from French than Latin; he used several alternatives for translating Latin terms; he created more neologisms in Book V than anywhere else; and, finally, he most frequently used these neologisms in other works which are themselves translations, thus suggesting, perhaps, a distinct idiom for translations.

Sheila Delany's *The Naked Text: Chaucer's Legend of Good Women* brings together previous and new research on the poem. The title is ironic, for nakedness (of text, body, thought or meaning) is impossible. Delany argues, as a general context for reading the poem, that it was perceived early on as a serious and instructive work in defence of women (*pace* William Quinn below), but also that it was designed to provoke debate (see Alastair Minnis below). Where the *Tales* is a poem about writing and the *House* is a poem about reading, the *Legend* is transitional between them. Delany's review of critical debate over the chronological and aesthetic priority of G or the 'juicier' F Prologues is done in a 'metacritical' spirit, to show how what we inherit is not one poem as such but a series of rewritings. Furthermore, in its preoccupation with doubts about the power of authority, experience and perception, the poem is deeply sceptical in tone and takes nothing on trust as purely naked. Thus its hagiographic depiction of the saintly women is not, of course, properly hagiographic at all, but an ironic, learned parody which nevertheless does not diminish its object of imitation. In a neat comparison of Christine de Pisan and Chaucer, Delany shows how the writing of each is gender marked. For Chaucer, an unambiguous praise of woman would be an oversimplification of a complex reality – to write such poetry is punishment; for Christine, it is that (misogynistic) 'reality' that is distorted – to read such poetry is punishment. In the third chapter, Delany considers the resonant metaphor of a naked text, showing its association with the unrestrained dangers of a divine scripture denuded of its allegorizations, Latin veils and glosses (although it is a pity she does not qualify the image in the context of the equally common hermeneutic image of clothing as suspect rhetorical adornment). If such an image is threatening, it is also utopian, imagining an unmediated transparence of meaning and language which experience does not bear out. Chaucer's naked text is knowingly veiled. The presence of orientalism in the *Legend* is then examined as the site of difference and is read in the context of historical and political dealings with the East. Rather than equating the exotic orient with gender, Delany sees them as separate in Chaucer; where the feminine offers a deconstructable difference, the orient does not. Delany also surmises from Chaucer's unhistorical mythologizing of the orient a distinctively English point of view, and that he 'probably thought England's resources could be more usefully disbursed domestically than in military adventures abroad'. In her conclusion, Delany compares Chaucer's poem to the roof bosses of medieval churches and asks the same question: 'For whom were they created?' Just as the bosses' intricacy of detail and visual inaccessibility seem too complex to be explained away as required for a *lewed* congregation, so the depth and complexity of the *Legend* seem to go beyond its ostensible occasion and dedicatee (Queen Anne). The ambivalence she traces in Chaucer is no more than that which Delany notes in other writers of the period, be it Boccaccio or Christine de Pisan. Delany's book is elegantly conceived and thorough in its scholarship.

William Quinn's *Chaucer's 'Rehersynges': The Performability of the Legend of Good Women* argues that the poem is a performance piece and a 'script to be applauded' rather than a 'text to be footnoted', which leads to a technical distinction in Quinn's view between the terms 'script' and 'text'. *Rehersynge* refers to the actual recital of the poem. He speculates on the first 'performance' of the *Legend* at a May feast in the presence of Queen Anne, with a mixed audience of thirty to fifty courtiers, and possibly recited over the space of an entire day. Quinn thus aims to take the performing 'I' of the F Prologue quite literally, and maintains that the notion of a live rendition of the poem both resolves many of the poem's ambiguities and heightens its comic effect. Quinn addresses the problem of the relationship between the two Prologues (F and G): namely, that despite a preponderance of evidence to suggest that G is a revision of F, critics tend to agree that F, the earlier, is the more aesthetically satisfying. He tries to get away from this compulsion to rate the Prologues, arguing that Chaucer is doing two different things in them. F shows no sign of ever having been intended for anything other than being the script for a performance, while the G revision suggests that Chaucer expected it to be read as an independent text. Only the F Prologue is a proper *rehersynge*. Quinn's support for this argument rests on stylistic evidence. This performative theory of the *Legend* resolves outstanding ambiguities such as that of the first *Legend*, on Cleopatra, which has always been seen as unsuccessful. Quinn suggests that its inappropriateness is comic and designed to highlight the absurdity of Cupid's command. The naval battle is read as a study of obscene innuendo, and the *Legend*'s alliteration as a conspicuous 'bumpkin' style that undercuts its apparent serious intention. The next *Legend*, on Thisbe, represents the first choice the narrator supposedly makes for himself, yet it still fails to fulfil Cupid's requirements, as Pyramus proves to be just as faithful as Thisbe. By comically misreading Cupid's intentions, Chaucer reasserts a masculine perspective and momentarily gets the last word. Not until Dido is there some (more serious) attempt to portray men as false lovers; however, Quinn envisages the

Legend as being played for laughs, with the narrator imposing his ironic attitude on her most tragic lines – an imposition possibly helped by a narratorial and comic miming of Dido's gestures of kneeling and tearing her hair. The analysis continues, partly through comparison with his sources and partly through speculation on the tone and mode of oral delivery. Quinn reads the stories ironically and the women as the narrative victims of the 'comic conflict between Chaucer's program and his patron's charge'. Certainly there are some interesting observations *en passant* on the relation between Chaucer and his sources, and Quinn's rereading does draw attention to the editorial constructedness of the Riverside punctuation, and to the blurred boundary between telling and reading; but the critical conclusions seem weak, and the thesis speculative, even by his own admission. *De gustibus non disputandum est.*

Alastair Minnis, on the other hand, in 'Repainting the Lion: Chaucer's Profeminist Narratives' (in Roy Eriksen, *Contexts of Pre-novel Narrative*), rejects the argument that the *Legend* is one big literary joke. He suggests that the radical revisions Chaucer makes of his sources are part of the design of the poem as debate, that the poem is intended to provoke discussion and judgements amongst the audience. The hagiographic strategies employed in the *Legend* undergo some significant qualifications in order for Chaucer to construct his pro-feminist narratives. Where the usual martyrdom tale celebrates virginity, the *Legend's* heroines are married, or implied to be married, and are happy to be so. Moreover, the misogynist tradition is more precisely a misogamist tradition, so that Chaucer's foregrounding of the *wyves* as sexually active takes on an added significance. To the anti-feminist tradition's question: 'Where is the virtuous woman?' Chaucer responds: 'Where is the faithful man?' For Marilynn Desmond's thoughts on the *Legend of Dido*, see above under the *House of Fame*.

In 'Chaucer's *Complaint of Venus* and the "Curiosite" of Graunson' (*EIC* 44.171–89), John Scattergood begins by listing John Shirley's remarks about the poem's courtly context, but then leaves aside speculations about contemporary scandal to investigate more precisely the relationship between Chaucer's translation and the Graunson ballades on which it is based, and in particular to consider Chaucer's response to Graunson's intricate workmanship.

Kari Anne Rand Schmidt's tome on *The Authorship of The Equatorie of the Planetis* (1993) is not for the fainthearted, despite its cachet as a sort of Chaucerian whodunnit. In her opening chapter, Schmidt reviews the fluctuating fortunes of the *Equatorie* since first coming to public attention in 1952, when it was let into the Chaucerian canon, and when put out. First identified and largely accepted as a holograph in Chaucer's own handwriting because of its 'Radix Chaucer' note, Peterhouse MS 75.I fell somewhat from favour once J. D. North argued that, although a holograph, it was not from Chaucer's hand (*YWES* 50.119–20). Opinion has remained divided ever since, and Schmidt's consideration of the merits of the arguments of each is cautious, thorough and disinterested. Distinguishing between the separate issues of whether the MS is a holograph and whether Chaucer's holograph, she notes the main arguments in favour of it being an autograph: that it is in a single, informal hand; and that the consistency in spelling and phonology suggests the absence of scribal tampering. The MS gives the impression of being a draft, and the presentation is clear but messy. Finally in Part I, some of the criteria by which the text has been adjudged as Chaucerian (or not) are reviewed: the comparison of hands with those of other texts which are possible candidates for Chaucer's own writing; whether the *Equatorie* is in what are thought to be Chaucer's own dialect and idiolect; and frequency of syntactical habits. Part II, far the most technically complex section of the book, involves a statistical analysis of the style of the *Equatorie*. An analysis such as this requires control data, that is, texts on a similar subject yet by different authors, with which the key text can be compared and contrasted. *The Shippe of Venyse* and *The Newe Theorik of Planetis* are used to represent non-Chaucerian but meaningfully comparable texts. Next, the distinguishing criteria for such an analysis have to be determined and, in this case, are: the use and extent of vocabulary and single frequent words; syntax; and punctuation. Schmidt's conclusions are that the *Equatorie*, while a holograph, cannot be identified with any surety as Chaucer's. Its hand differs in significant ways from the other putative Chaucer manuscripts (which all themselves differ from each other); although it is in the type of London dialect Chaucer could well have used, there is nothing convincing to identify it as his; and its syntactic constructions similarly fail to produce conclusive results. Schmidt is careful not to pronounce definitively against the motion for authorship, but argues that there is still reasonable doubt. A facsimile of the *Equatorie* (71v–78v in the MS) with transcription on the facing page follows in Part III, prefaced with a detailed description of the Peterhouse MS. Editorial emendation has been conservative. One of the manuscript's erasures is interesting as, when viewed under ultraviolet light, it partially reveals a word which has been speculated on as a proper name, possibly of Nicholas of Lynn or of Robert of Leicester. Also given are transcriptions of an unpublished MS of *A Treatise on the Astrolabe*, the unpublished *Newe Theorik of Planetis* and the incomplete *Shippe of Venyse*. And finally, in Part IV, Schmidt gives a concordance in KWIC (key word in context) format. The scholarship in this book is meticulous if cautious, and will be indispensable for anyone working on these texts.

Gregory M. Sadlek discusses Chaucer's *Romaunt of the Rose* in 'Interpreting Guillaume de Lorris's *Oiseuse*: Geoffrey Chaucer as Witness' (*SCRev* 10[1993].i.21–37), although the piece is really as much, if not more, about the *Book of the Duchess*. Sadlek notes that there is some contention about the meaning of *Oiseuse* in the French *Roman*, whether it signifies leisurely inactivity or laziness; some critics even see it as a secular parallel to religious contemplation. Chaucer translates *Oiseuse* as *Ydelnesse*, rather than *Folie* or *Vanitee*; however, this does not initially further the inquiry much, as Middle English *ydelnesse* could mean 'vanity' just as well as 'inactivity'. The *Book of the Duchess* sheds some light in that it mentions *ydelnesse* three times in a courtly context. Sadlek shows that there is not, even in this one poem, any one specific meaning, and he suggests that by it, the Black Knight means 'leisure' and perhaps 'vanity'. On the whole, Chaucer seems to suspect corrupting effects from *ydelnesse*, and certainly does not appear to celebrate it as a virtue, courtly or otherwise.

Books Reviewed

Amodio, Mark C., ed., with Sarah Gray Miller. *Oral Poetics in Middle English Poetry*. Albert Bates Lord Studies in Oral Tradition 13. Garland. pp. 304. $45. ISBN 0 8153 0830 2.

Barney, Stephen A. *Studies in Troilus: Chaucer's Text, Meter, and Diction*. Medieval Texts and Studies 14. Colleagues (1993). pp. 167. $28. ISBN 0 9371 9145 0.

Bronfman, Judith. *Chaucer's 'Clerk's Tale': The Griselda Story Received, Rewritten, Illustrated.* Garland Studies in Medieval Literature 11. Garland. pp. 162. $28. ISBN 0 8153 1640 2.

Brown, Peter. *Chaucer at Work: The Making of the Canterbury Tales.* Longman. pp. 186. hb £28, pb £10.99. ISBN 0 5822 3719 X, 0 5820 1319 4.

Calabrese, Michael A. *Chaucer's Ovidian Arts of Love.* UPFlor. pp. 170. $29.95. ISBN 0 8130 1301 1.

Crane, Susan. *Gender and Romance in Chaucer's Canterbury Tales.* PrincetonUP. pp. 233. hb $39.50, pb $15.95. ISBN 0 6910 6952 2, 0 6910 1527 9.

Delany, Sheila. *Chaucer's House of Fame: The Poetics of Skeptical Fideism* (2nd edn). UPFlor. pp. 134. pb $16.95. ISBN 0 8130 1259 7.

—— *The Naked Text: Chaucer's Legend of Good Women.* UCalP. pp. 259. $45. ISBN 0 5200 8119 6.

Desmond, Marilynn. *Reading Dido: Gender, Textuality, and the Medieval Æneid.* Medieval Cultures 8. UMinnP. pp. 296. hb $44.95, pb $17.95. ISBN 0 8166 2246 9, 0 8166 2247 7.

Edwards, Robert R., ed. *Art and Context in Late Medieval English Narrative.* Brewer. pp. 205. £35. ISBN 0 8599 1407 0.

Eriksen, Roy, ed. *Contexts of Pre-novel Narrative: The European Tradition.* Approaches to Semiotics 114. Gruyter. pp. 397. DM188. ISBN 3 1101 3883 2.

Evans, Ruth, and Lesley Johnson, eds. *Feminist Readings in Middle English Literature: The Wife of Bath and All Her Sect.* Routledge. pp. 258. hb $59.95, pb $16.95. ISBN 0 4150 5818 X, 0 4150 5819 8.

Harwood, Britton J., and Gillian R. Overing, eds. *Class and Gender in Early English Literature: Intersections.* IndUP. pp. 156. hb $25, pb £9.99, $11.95. ISBN 0 2533 2734 2, 0 2532 0858 0.

Havely, Nicholas R., ed. *Chaucer: The House of Fame.* Durham Medieval Texts 11. Durham Medieval Texts. pp. 216. pb £10. ISBN 0 9520 0782 7.

Hayes, Elizabeth T., ed. *Images of Persephone: Feminist Readings in Western Literature.* UFlorP. pp. 212. $29.95. ISBN 0 8130 1262 7.

Jager, Eric. *The Tempter's Voice: Language and the Fall in Medieval Literature.* CornUP (1993). pp. 336. $42.50. ISBN 0 8014 2753 3.

Jones, Terry. *Chaucer's Knight: The Portrait of a Medieval Mercenary* (2nd rev. edn). Methuen. pp. 322. pb £9.99. ISBN 0 4136 9140 3.

Jost, Jean E., ed. *Chaucer's Humor: Critical Essays.* Garland Studies in Humor 5. Garland. pp. 477. $62. ISBN 0 8153 0618 0.

Lancashire, Ian, ed. *Computer-Based Chaucer Studies.* Centre for Computing in the Humanities, University of Toronto (1993). pp. 205. ISBN 0 1183 790 X.

Margherita, Gayle. *The Romance of Origins: Language and Sexual Difference in Middle English Literature.* UPennP. pp. 214. hb $36.95, pb $14.95. ISBN 0 8122 3217 8, 0 8122 1502 8.

Myles, Robert. *Chaucerian Realism.* Chaucer Studies 20. Brewer. pp. 153. £29.50. ISBN 0 8599 1409 7.

Phillips, Helen, ed. *Chaucer: The Book of the Duchess* (2nd rev. edn). Durham Medieval Texts 3. Durham Medieval Texts (1993). pp. 224. pb £7. ISBN 0 9505 9892 5.

Pratt, Karen, ed. *Shifts and Transpositions in Medieval Narrative: A Festschrift for Elspeth Kennedy.* Brewer. pp. 206. £35. ISBN 0 8599 1421 6.

Purdon, Liam O., and Cindy L. Vitto, eds. *The Rusted Hauberk: Feudal Ideals of*

Order and their Decline. UPFlor. pp. 340. hb $44.95, pb $19.95. ISBN 0 8130 1281 3, 0 8130 1282 1.

Quinn, William A. *Chaucer's 'Rehersynges': The Performability of the Legend of Good Women*. CUAP. pp. 253. $55.95. ISBN 0 8132 0791 6.

Ramsey, Roy Vance. *The Manly–Rickert Text of the Canterbury Tales*. Mellen. pp. 691. $139.95. ISBN 0 7734 9128 7.

Rudd, Niall. *The Classical Tradition in Operation*. UTorP. pp. 204. $55. ISBN 0 8020 0570 5.

Scanlon, Larry D. *Narrative, Authority, and Power: The Medieval Exemplum and the Chaucerian Tradition*. Cambridge Studies in Medieval Literature 20. CUP. pp. 390. £40. ISBN 0 5214 3210 3.

Schlacks, Deborah Davis. *American Dream Visions: Chaucer's Surprising Influence on F. Scott Fitzgerald*. Studies on Themes and Motifs in Literature 5. Lang. pp. 234. $44.95. ISBN 0 8204 2246 0.

Schmidt, Kari Anne Rand. *The Authorship of The Equatorie of the Planetis*. Chaucer Studies 19. Brewer (1993). pp. 436. £39.50, $71. ISBN 0 8599 1370 8.

Valentine, Virginia Walker. *Chaucer's Knight: A Man Ther Was*. Axelrod. pp. 94. $25. ISBN 0 9364 1743 9.

V

The Sixteenth Century: Excluding Drama after 1550

CERI SULLIVAN and STEPHANIE J. WRIGHT

This chapter has three sections: 1. General; 2. Sidney; 3. Spenser. Section 1 is by Ceri Sullivan and sections 2 and 3 are by Stephanie J. Wright. Section 1 is broken down into bibliographical and textual studies, early sixteenth-century work, late sixteenth-century prose, late sixteenth-century verse, and miscellaneous studies.

1. General

(a) Bibliographical and Textual Studies

The *Crisis in Editing: Texts of the English Renaissance* that Randall McLeod's contributors perceive is a recognition that the platonic – ideal and unitary – text is no longer available as a bibliographic concept. Responses to this include a sardonic critique of the editorial rhetoric of revolution and reaction by Gary Taylor, based on his experience as editor of Shakespeare. Nicolas Barker recasts stemmata as circular movements where manuscript and print copies fertilize each other without reference to the author. Suspicious and well-illustrated essays by Stephen Orgel, Antony Hammond and Random Cloud physically demonstrate how the reader experiences, even in the prints' composition and line length, the editor's 'textual desire' (using Herbert's 'Easter Wings' and Elizabethan play texts). Jonathan Goldberg goes further and celebrates the 'more text' which results from this, using *Romeo and Juliet*.

Two articles in a collection on *The Construction of Authorship* from the sixteenth to the twentieth century (edited by Martha Woodmansee and Peter Jaszi) take up this theme of shifting author/text *loci*. John Feather discusses the copyright practices of Stationers' Company members and suggests that copy was seen as property by the stationers, but only attached to the author, as at present, in James's reign. Max W. Thomas uses the compilation of commonplace notebooks to question the validity of modern notions of authorship in early modern criticism, clashing Pierre Macherey's theorizing of constituent conditions for the forms of writing and reading against a notebook by John Lilliat from the turn of the century. In 'Mantuan's Eclogues in the English Reformation' (*SCJ* 25.623–32) Lee Piepho looks at how English humanists adopted Baptista Mantuan's attacks on the Papal

Curia into the grammar school curriculum, making us aware of how polemical literary education was. Ceri Sullivan echoes this in a note on Elizabethan editing techniques (*N&Q* 41.445–6).

A sceptical look at the use of books as self-advertisements for the learning and income of their authors is given by David Carlson in *English Humanist Books: Writers and Patrons, Manuscript and Print, 1475–1525*. Noting that print was at this point only one of the means of distribution a humanist in search of a patron might select, he shows the attempts of six humanists (Filippo Alberici, Pietro Carmeliano, Bernard Andre, Erasmus, Robert Whittington and Thomas More) to squeeze money from the system through a variety of media, such as presentation copies for powerful patrons, printed works (Carlson also discusses the public relations disaster of piracy), and ephemeral manuscripts aimed at friends or rivals. Carlson's learned and wry story of the reality of professional ruthlessness, not the humanists' self-promoted image of disinterested wisdom, will be recognized by those who have to publish for research assessment exercises.

A similar lack of innocence pervades Lisa Ferraro Parmelee's 'Printers, Patrons, Readers, and Spies: Importation of French Propaganda in Late Elizabethan England' (*SCJ* 25.853–72). Works which were 'anti-League, anti-Guise, anti-Jesuit, anti-papal, and anti-Spanish' were funnelled into Britain to allay nearly every source of Elizabethan anxiety. On the topic of patronage, David Wiles gives a transcript of 'A Poor Man's "What Shall I Do?"' appealing for a military position, which he attributes to Robert Carey (*N&Q* 41.453–5). In '"To scape the Rod": Resistance to Humanist Pedagogy and the Sign of the Pedant in Tudor England' (*SP* 91.270–82), Sidney Logan Sondergard traces the shift in literature from approving to pejorative connotations of the term 'pedant', paralleling the establishment's suspicion of exoteric humanism. Marcy North, in 'Ignoto in the Age of Print: The Manipulation of Anonymity in Early Modern England' (*SP* 91.390–416), challenges the idea that the self-publicity associated with print meant a decline in the importance of the figure of the unknown author.

Given the importance of the Italian presses for humanist work in Britain, Brian Richardson's *Print Culture in Renaissance Italy: The Editor and the Vernacular Text, 1470–1600* should be mentioned. Richardson describes in detail the role of editor in guiding the work of author, commentator and printer of the Venetian and Florentine presses, showing how the editor established a popular Tuscan-based scholarship. The editor mediates between the learned text and its commentary, and the common reader, with responsibility for copytext and contents.

In 'Coming to Terms: Thomas Elyot's Definitions and the Particularity of Human Letters' (*ELH* 61.211–30), Stephen Merriam Foley engagingly delineates the way Elyot's *Dictionary* played its part in 'Henrician cultural stagecraft', making the court 'an almost mythical source of learning and wisdom, magically supplying every want of a grateful nation'.

Researchers in devotional literature will find the revised edition of A. F. Allison and D. M. Rogers's *The Contemporary Printed Literature of the English Counter-Reformation between 1558 and 1640* indispensable. This annotated bibliography lists all known Catholic books printed abroad or in England, split between works in English and in other languages. The bibliographical and historical annotation has been expanded since the first edition, many authors of anonymous texts have been identified, and additional entries and locations have been added. Indices include title, publishers and printers, a year-on-year handlist, and authors. Nearly a thousand editions of recusant texts were published in English during this period, and this authoritative bibliography should do much towards correcting the Protestant bias of Renaissance criticism.

Other useful annotated bibliographies included 'Recent Studies in Women Writers of Tudor England, 1485–1603' to 1993 by Georgiana M. Ziegler; 'Recent Studies in Samuel Daniel' to 1990 by W. L. Godshalk, and 'Recent Studies in Neo-Latin Literature' by Richard F. Hardin (*ELR* 24.229–42, 489–502, 660–98).

(b) Early Sixteenth-century Work

An injured innocence fills *Rethinking the Henrician Era*, edited by Peter C. Herman. Pointing out that 'early Tudor' tends to be seen as synonymous with 'minor Tudor', this volume sets out to rescue the 'previously slighted' – though as this category here includes John Skelton, Wyatt and the Earl of Surrey, some special pleading does take place. Herman notes the irony that the Elizabethans themselves were happy to acknowledge their debts to Henrician culture. Essays examine the literature produced by the court, including pageants, love lyrics by Mary Shelton and Margaret Douglas, the use of the Bible in producing the image of the monarch, and the concept of courtly poet as a prophetic voice (Skiles Howard, Paul Remley, John N. King, W. A. Sessions); More's gendering of *Utopia* (Janel Mueller); Skelton as a marginal poet defining the boundaries between church and state, and the female economy of Elynour Rummynge (W. Scott Blanchard, Peter C. Herman); Wyatt's use of religious verse to express political concerns, his perception of women in Petrarchanism, and the latter's use in writing about the New World (Alexandra Halasz, Barbara Estrin, Roland Greene); Bale's *King Johan* as an attempt to authorize the new Protestant nation (David Scott Kastan); and Shakespeare's presentation of the Henrician court in *Henry VIII* (Bill Readings). The collection's aim of shifting 'a syllabus or two' from concentration on Golden Age work is likely to be realized through the synergy of the piece as much as by the quality of the individual contributions.

In fact, there is a clutch of shorter articles on the period. A transcript of Surrey's 'O happy Days' by Helen Baron, and a note and an article by Raymond Southall and Baron (*RES* 45.314–15, 316–17, 318–35), conclude independently that the poem in the Devonshire manuscript was transcribed by Mary Fitzroy, and reflect on whether this or the Tottel text is likely to be closer to the author's. H. A. Mason challenges the authority of the Egerton manuscript of Wyatt's poetry over a textual crux (*N&Q* 41.443–5). W. R. Streitberger discusses 'Court Performances by the King's Players, 1510–1521', and speculates on how the change in patronage from father to son changed their style (*METh* 14[1992].95–101). In 'Transubstantiation and the Sign', Julia Houston studies Thomas Cranmer's turning the miracle into drama (*JMRS* 24.33–52). The career in Poland of the early humanist Leonard Coxe is described by Henryk Zins (*RS* 8.13–39). Two minor early Tudor devotional and patience poems have been found and transcribed by Oliver Pickering (*LeedsSE* 25.159–66). Andrew Hadfield contributes a note on Skelton's influence on John Bale (*N&Q* 41.19–20), while David N. Dumville discusses a liturgical book Bale may have owned (*N&Q* 41.291–5). In '"One Man in His Time Plays Many Parts": Authorial Theatrics of Doubling in Early English Renaissance Drama' (*SP* 91.359–89), John W. Sider discusses Bale's *King Johan* and *Three Laws of Nature* in view of the doubling schemes he produces. Spanning the gap between gender studies and religious prose is Amanda Shephard's *Gender and Authority in Sixteenth-century England*, which concentrates on the debate generated by John Knox's *First Blast of the Trumpet against the Monstrous Regiment of Women*, and its five major refutations by John Aylmer, Richard Bertie, John Leslie, David Chambers and Henry Howard.

Alistair Fox's *Utopia: An Elusive Vision* starts with a sensible guide for students to the text's historical context, a chronology of More's life, and *Utopia*'s critical reception. The overview which follows ascribes the multiple critical versions of *Utopia* – as joke, approving political philosophy, or satire on contemporary states – to More's wish to provoke speculative dialogue after the book had been read. More's text is organized as a training in deliberation on public affairs by denying the reader a purchase on the 'right' way to read it. This is a clearly written introduction to the concept of Renaissance scepticism. A special issue of *Moreana* (31.118–19) on 'Utopia Revisited' includes essays by William A. McClung on the physical design of the city, John Freeman on rural practice in *Utopia* and England, and George M. Logan on the deliberative rather than demonstrative rhetoric of the text. Also included is a survey of criticism between 1987 and 1993. More and Skelton are linked by an attack on the young heretic Thomas Bilney, which Greg Walker suggests is an establishment plan (*Parergon* 9[1991].i.75–85).

The quincentenary of William Tyndale's birth occurred in 1994, and saw two works on him. John A. R. Dick and Anne Richardson edited a collection of essays, *William Tyndale and the Law*, concerned with the way Tyndale interprets divine and secular law. Rudolph P. Almasy discusses conflicting authorial voices, and John Dick discusses Tyndale's views on the King's great affair, in Tyndale's *Practice of Prelates*; Anne Richardson studies his written protests against abuse of the helpless; Donald Dean Smeeton and Peter Auksi reconcile the paradox of Tyndale's belief in faith and obedience to God's law by reference to Lollard writings and the 'natural law' tradition respectively. Gerald Hammond deals with the relationship of the Old and New Testaments; James Andrew Clark with the fine line between permissible and impermissible licence in the translation of the Bible, and Richard Y. Duerden with the conflict of human and divine laws in *The Obedience of a Christian Man*. John T. Day looks at Tyndale's will. David Daniell contributes an essay on Tyndale's view of copyright, and has also brought out this year *William Tyndale: A Biography*. This is the first full-scale biography for over half a century, and concentrates on Tyndale's skill as a translator more than his image as martyr or theologian. 'A weak translator goes for paraphrase, or worse, for philological purity . . . With a difficult word or phrase, [Tyndale] understands the alternatives presented by technical semantics, or changes of tone or feeling, and goes for what makes sense.' Daniell shows how the writer's craftsman-like feeling for language was formed, and analyses the translations and tracts in detail. This is an unsentimental and thorough literary biography.

Barbara L. Estrin's *Laura: Uncovering Gender and Genre in Wyatt, Donne, and Marvell* counters the Lacanian critics who regard the pursuit and fixing of 'Laura' by male poets as objectifying her. Estrin focuses not on the force driving these poets to pursue the lady, but on her subjectivity as allowed by the poems: a 'Daphne' who denies sexuality, an 'Eve' who returns the poet's love, and a 'Mercury' who reinvents her own life. Moreover, 'what the woman does (the story as genre) depends on what the woman wants (the story as gendered)'. Determining what the Laura figure wants determines how the poem is to be read. Estrin describes Wyatt's 'They flee from me', 'The long love', and 'Whoso list to hunt' as poems which are baffled by the way the woman wants to read the situation – an uncertainty which shakes the self-enabling poetic Wyatt has assumed in his Petrarchan translations. This is a fascinating, though at times overwritten, challenge to the critical truism of sonnet-as-fragmentation. Finally, in *The Usurer's Daughter*, Lorna Hutson produces a subtle and learned argument on the representation of women in humanist literature as signs of friendship. The topos of *amicitia* is removed from the medieval code of gift-exchange as a pledge of future aid, to become an affective relationship sprung from persuasive texts. Renaissance drama's focus on women, despite their extra-literary social condition, is dependent on their use as signs of credit between men. This is peculiarly so in humanism, where the 'claim to be able to "fashion" women by addressing them through persuasive fictions of themselves lent a special social credibility to the masculine activity of authorship'.

(c) Late Sixteenth-century Prose

Peter E. Medine has produced a workmanlike modern-spelling edition of a popular Renaissance handbook, Thomas Wilson's *The Art of Rhetoric*, published eight times before 1585. Wilson was one of those humanists who published for patronage, and was unlucky in that this companion piece to *The Rule of Reason* came out just before the death of Edward VI. Despite the Ramist titles of the two pieces, Medine shows how Wilson's was one of the first vernacular rhetorics to deal with all five parts of the art, and also take on deliberative and epideictic speech. His notes give sources and analogues rather than discussion. The edition should be most useful to undergraduates who want to get a swift, clear view of Renaissance rhetoric. I was unable to obtain a copy of William Barker's edition of Richard Mulcaster's *Positions Concerning the Training Up of Children* (UTorP) published this year.

D. Allen Carroll has edited Greene's *Groatsworth of Wit* of 1592, attributed to Henry Chettle and Robert Greene. The usual careful editing of the MRTS series means this edition will replace the last annotated version of the text, by Grosart. The pamphlet describes the death-bed repentance of the popular writer, ostensibly in his own words, and Carroll weighs up how far the possibility of profiting from his death made this a publisher's project concocted by Chettle. Appendices deal with, among other things, the references to the 'Upstart Crow', Christopher Marlowe, and Thomas Nashe. Carroll, in 'The Player-Patron in Greene's Groatsworth of Wit (1592)' (*SP* 91.301–12), speculates about the identity of the actor who recruits Roberto (Greene) into the business of playwriting as possibly being Anthony Munday.

Non-fictional prose first: *Reading Holinshed's Chronicles* rescues Holinshed from simply providing examples for the study of the Tudor myth, or source materials for canonical authors. Annabel Patterson's radical, crisply stated argument centres on the text's stated aim of 'indifference', or dispassion in dealing with events. The *Chronicles* accept that there is diversity of opinion, demonstrated and even created by past dissent about major themes (Patterson grasps a taxonomic nettle and divides them firmly into religion, economics, law, and government); in other words, that 'political liberalism was in fact worked out in the second half of the sixteenth century in England, and that it found expression in the largest definition of the nation produced at that time, Holinshed's *Chronicles*'. This liberal attitude is reinforced by the *Chronicles*' collaborative authorship and history of revisions. Patterson links 'spiritual and political consciousness-raising' in the project (rather oddly paralleled with American liberalism), where the reader is to gain a just understanding of different perceptions, and think beyond the status quo. Her study moves on the grand scale of interpretations offered overtly by the text, and also on the detail of style, such as analysing the contrasting digressions inserted into the text.

New World Encounters, edited by Stephen Greenblatt, brings together essays mainly published before in *Representations* on the theme of negotiation with the 'muffled voices' of the New World. The collection insists that the construction of the other as either victim or savage denies it historical specificity, and aims to show how this discourse of colonization does much of the actual work of the process. Three articles deal with sixteenth-century literary texts: Louis Montrose and Mary C. Fuller talk about Ralegh's *Discoverie of Guiana*, where piety masks greed, the economic failure of the expedition is covered by a rhetoric of deferral into the future, and the country is subdued by feminizing it; and Jeffrey Knapp relates the rarefied product, tobacco, and the spiritual tone taken by English imperialism in its literature. Margo Hendricks and Patricia Parker, in *Women, 'Race', and Writing in the Early Modern Period*, theorize the parallels made by the public voice of early modern culture between the two 'minorities', but note that such homogenization depends on their definition as 'other' to a DWEM (dead white European male) centre – still a charge which can be made of white academic feminism. The book largely concentrates on the seventeenth century, though general essays which refer to literature include one on cannibalism and homosociality by Carla Freccero. Lynda E. Boose discusses the width of reference which the term 'other race' had in Renaissance literature (Irish, Venetians, Moroccans and Jews) before moving on to look at how the narrative of the black woman/white man upsets notions of the womb as mere receptacle, so that possibilities of 'contamination' are dealt with in literature. Still on the theme of nationalism, *Literature, Politics and National Identity* by Andrew Hadfield concentrates on how Renaissance writers moved to regarding literature as a sphere of ideology rather than one of genre boundaries. He sites this discussion in literature dealing with the emerging concept of the favoured nation. Chapters on Skelton, John Bale, *A Mirror for Magistrates*, rhetorical handbooks, Sidney and Spenser describe establishing a vernacular literature as part of a national identity. His strength lies in not homogenizing forms of nationhood throughout the century – Skelton's assumption that he can speak for England against the Protestants and humanists is in ironic contrast with Spenser's vision, for instance, particularly given the latter's reuse of Skelton's authority.

John R. Knott, in *Discourses of Martyrdom in English Literature, 1563–1694*, looks at the rhetorical aspects of Protestant hagiography, ranging from the *Actes and Monuments* and writings by the Marian exiles, through the responses of the Elizabethan Puritans, to Milton's use of John Foxe, John Bunyan and Quaker texts. Relevant here is the first half of the book on Foxe, which argues that he created an image of heroic suffering, a faith defined by acts of resistance and patience, rather than an icon of an elect nation governed by a godly prince. The examples studied are Foxe's account of one of the martyrdoms (of John Rogers), his responses to stories of early Christian martyrs, and his ideal of a holy community of Christians (the Marian exiles). Though the plot is a foregone conclusion, each martyrdom provides a contest between different ideas of power and sincerity. In '*A Solemne Contestation of Diverse Popes*: A Work by Foxe?' (*ELN* 31.iii.35–42), Thomas Freeman analyses the anonymous 1560 collection of polemical quotations and attributes it to Foxe.

Prose fiction received some attention this year. Literature as an indicator of rank is examined by Peter Holbrook in *Literature and Degree in Renaissance*

England. Linking Nashe, 'bourgeois' tragedy (such as *A Woman Killed With Kindness* and *A Warning for Fair Women*) and Shakespeare, he notes the techniques they use to promote status differences. Holbrook argues that Nashe is 'knavish' towards high discursive modes, and perpetually sees himself as a marginal figure. His varied tones – clown, humanist scholar, would-be courtier – assert his independence from symbolic modes and yet provide proof of his ability to manipulate them with sophistication. Holbrook's discussion handles the tricky fault lines of early modern rank, class and genre with precision, and he gives detailed examples.

Fashioning Authority: The Development of Elizabethan Novelistic Discourse by Constance C. Relihan looks at the role of the market and the non-aristocratic reader in fashioning prose fiction. Thomas Deloney, Philip Sidney, John Lyly, Nashe, and particularly Barnabe Riche in *Farewell to Militarie Profession* are shown to write in a way that takes advantage of – and even creates – new modes of textual consumption, moving from the public reading of a text towards the individual alone with the book. They take advantage of the freedom from traditional modes of consumption, in the new genre of prose romances, novellas, court fictions and cony-catching pamphlets. Relihan is interested in how the shift down-market in the audience leaves certain features of prose fiction as 'other' to literary and social authority, such as the use of poetry to gain artistic authority, the stress on subjectivity, the thematic concentration on women, the sense of place, and the East.

Roy Eriksen's essay, in his collection on the development of *Contexts of Pre-novel Narrative*, argues that George Gascoigne's *The Adventures of Master F. J.* is part of the move from High Renaissance centripetal, ordered and moral ground-plots to centrifugal and transgressive narrative strategies, full of willed difficulty and characteristic of Mannerism. Nashe's work is cited as an analogue of Gascoigne's complex, unstable structures. Philip Schwyzer's 'Summer Fruit and Autumn Leaves: Thomas Nashe in 1593' (*ELR* 24.583–619) argues that *The Unfortunate Traveller* and *Christs Teares*, written in the same year, are based on the same strategy of deferral of the signs of redemption because of the assurance that it has already taken place. On the topic of deliberately unstable narrative structures, Edward T. Bonahue Jr relishes the authorial construct 'G.B.', in '"I know the place and the persons": The Play of Textual Frames in Baldwin's *Beware the Cat*' (*SP* 91.283–300).

Rosemary Kegl's *Rhetoric of Concealment: Figuring Gender and Class in Renaissance Literature* looks at political 'gestures' in a number of Renaissance literary texts, including Puttenham's *Arte of Poesie*, the *Arcadia*, *The Merry Wives of Windsor* and *Jack of Newberry*. These gestures are formal and repeated properties of the text: for instance, riddling disclosure as a figure in Puttenham's work, both as pun and as metaphor. These, Kegl claims, participate in rather than simply act as an image of social struggle. In Puttenham's case, she considers how far struggle at court, in the handbook for behaviour which the *Arte* is said to be, can be considered representative of the whole society. Her thesis is interesting but somewhat obscured by her anxiety to refer to twentieth-century social theory.

(d) *Late Sixteenth-century Verse*

Maurice Evans's useful 1977 teaching edition of *Elizabethan Sonnets* has been revised by Roy J. Booth. *Pamphilia to Amphilanthus*, some sonnets by Robert Sidney, Spenser's 'Epithalamion' and the homoerotic sonnets of Richard Barnfield have been added to sequences from Philip Sidney, Samuel Daniel, Michael Drayton, Spenser, Henry Constable, Thomas Lodge and Barnabe Barnes (the latter two represented only selectively), as well as more minor sonneteers. The additions allow a reader to understand how the genre is based on answering and inverting formal and thematic features of previous sequences. The edition's concentration on Golden Age writing makes clear the fashionable status of the sonnet.

Marc Shell has edited Elizabeth I's *The Glass of the Sinful Soul*, a translation of Marguerite of Navarre's work done in 1544, published by Bale and published again three times during the Queen's reign. This edition comprises a photo-reproduction and transcription of the text, Bale's dedicatory epistle and conclusion, a glossary of names in Bale, and heavy historical annotation by Shell. His introduction teases those who use Elizabeth as a 'role model for "juveniles" growing up in unsettled circumstances'. Elizabeth's work provides a model for politically aware 'extraordinary kinship' – introducing Elizabeth as national mother and wife – which she was certainly aware of when she authorized its reprinting. Shell's concentration is on the political and religious rather than literary import, but it is good to have the text available. Additionally, Steven M. May and Anne Lake Prescott give transcriptions of 'The French Verses of Elizabeth I (Text)' (*ELR* 24.9–43). These are a devotional translation from an unidentified meditation, and were not included in Bradner's edition of her verse.

Formal aspects are stressed in Robin Sowerby's study of *The Classical Legacy in Renaissance Poetry*. Referring to the highly rhetorical nature of Elizabethan grammar school education, which resulted in a formidable classicism in its pupils' poetry, Sowerby attempts to remedy the gap in students' knowledge left by twentieth-century schooling, along the lines of Isabel Rivers's *Classical and Christian Ideas in English Renaissance Poetry* (*YWES* 60.188). Organizing by genre, he works through the epic, tragedy, history and old and new style comedy, the lyric, pastoral and georgic, the epyllion, love elegy, heroic epistle, and satire. Each section starts with Greek and Roman examples of the genre and goes on to discuss their application by a very wide range of Renaissance authors. This is a clear and thorough teaching text.

Some work was done on the relationship of early modern literature and the other arts. Judith Dundas, in *Pencils Rhetorique: Renaissance Poets and the Art of Painting*, discusses the views of Sidney, Spenser, George Chapman and Inigo Jones, Shakespeare, Jonson and Milton on the topos of *ut pictura poesis*. Each goes beyond the vague notion of imitation of nature, of art as mirror, to make technical use of visual art as allusion and ekphrasis, thus reflecting back on his own craft. Dundas sees the relationship between the two arts at this period as agonistic: they compete to show their relative effectiveness in carrying conviction to the reader/viewer; their moral superiority in presenting a truth or an ideal; their professionalism; their relative social ranking; and their ability to provide advice on daily life. Dundas's work is additionally useful in recognizing another quarry for the rather scarce literary criticism (as opposed to the plentiful literary theory) by contemporary writers. Her work pairs off neatly with Norman E. Land's *The Viewer as Poet: The Renaissance Response to Art*, which looks at the effect the literary structure of ekphrasis had on art criticism and practice. The concentration is on Italian theory, as was the sixteenth century's. Michael Bath's *Speaking Pictures: English Emblem Books and Renaissance Culture* is the first extended study of such books for nearly five decades, since Rosemary Freeman's. Bath moves on from this more descriptive guide to the genre to examine its two phases: the production of moralizing emblems based on classical and humanist topoi and influenced by rhetorical invention, and later devotional works created under pressure from the revival in formal meditation. Understanding language as natural or conventional impacts on this art, as does the emblem's relationship with the ethos of self-presentation in the *impresa*. Four chapters discuss these topics thematically. One chapter concentrates on Thomas Palmer's use of rhetorical commonplace, hieroglyph and biblical parable, and then looks at the process of interpretation a viewer goes through in understanding Geoffrey Whitney's *Choice of Emblemes*. Further chapters discuss seventeenth-century authors: Henry Peacham, George Wither, Francis Quarles and Henry Hawkins.

Robin Headlam Wells starts *Elizabethan Mythologies: Studies in Poetry, Drama and Music* with verve, by attacking new historicism as dependent on, yet contemptuous of, traditional studies of the environment of the poet. He suggests that studies which start with a desire to uncover power will conclude by finding it. Wells examines the Orpheus myth in the Renaissance, the belief in the transforming power of the arts which could, in Sidney's phrase, 'lead and draw us to as high a perfection as our degenerate soules . . . can be capable of'. In doing so, he challenges the idea of author as 'discursive construct with no capacity for generating original meaning'. Headlam's work discusses Spenser, Shakespeare, John Dowland, and the Tudor court lyric and lute song. This is a crisply expressed, well-substantiated and even-handed attempt to back Renaissance studies out of the cul-de-sac of new historicist power-broking without reverting to nineteenth-century empiricism or the formalism of new criticism. S. K. Heninger's *The Subtext of Form in the English Renaissance: Proportion Poetical* shares the alarm of Robin Headlam Wells over current literary criticism – at present 'we have only arguments that refute other arguments' – though he puts this down to 'mistaking epistemological problems for ontological certainties', making us jump from the difficulty of knowing the past in detail to assuming there is only a 'turbulence of competing discourses'. He is 'concerned to devise a means of recuperating sixteenth-century English culture in such a way as to legitimize interpretation', by analysing the early modern sense of the immanence of form. The subtext of form expresses the Neoplatonic ideas underlying the transient world. With the challenge of the new science to this ontology, of objective, observable nature, came a new aesthetic. The sonnet, companion poems (which answer each other), and the introduction of perspective in painting are used to show this shift. Heninger's work is a model of close reading, demonstrating his easy familiarity with formal aspects of the verse, though I found his use of examples drawn from twentieth-century art engaging rather than explicatory.

In *Conceived Presences*, Raphael Falco traces the audacious attempt by sixteenth-century poets to disclaim their medieval forebears and to conceive of a literary genealogy by looking to the Continent and, ultimately, the classics. Their own sense, challenged today, that they were distinct from all previous English writers led them into a trope of succession, a 'serial fable'. Competition between poets for particular literary fathers acts as a tournament of families before a patron, and reflects backwards on the humanist project of resuscitation. The rather disparate first chapter deals with Thomas Elyot's attempt to import a foreign culture, George Puttenham and Francis Meres as social critics, and John Rainolds and Stephen Gosson on the utility of poetry. Later, more strongly argued chapters deal with the poetic identities of Spenser, Sidney, Jonson and Milton.

In Jeffrey N. Nelson's 'Lust and Black Magic in Barnabe Barnes's *Parthenophil and Parthenope*' (*SCJ* 25.595–608), unrequited lust is discussed in terms of – and relieved by – black magic, which violates the necessary distance of the Petrarchan dyad. Karen Batley discusses whether Robert Southwell's 'New Heaven, New Warre' is a single poem (*Expl* 53.7–10).

(e) Miscellaneous Studies

A lively, discursive collection of essays on *Renaissance Rhetoric* has been edited by Peter Mack, proceeding from a conference held at the European Humanities Research Centre at Warwick. The essays focus on the length of rhetoric's reach: writers, artists, pedagogues and politicians using it in a wide range of situations. Pieces discuss the reception and transmission of classical rhetoric in editions and schools (Larry Green, Dilwyn Knox, Brian Vickers); its relationship with dialectic (Lisa Jardine, Kees Meerhoff) and political arguments (David Norbrook); and its use in art, drama and romances (Pat Rubin, George Hunter, Peter Mack). In *Renaissance Argument*, Mack has also produced a learned critique of Valla's *Repastinatio dialecticae et philosophiae* and Agricola's *De inventione dialectica*, of interest to sixteenth-century English scholars where it discusses their influence on ideas of language in Erasmus, Vives and Ramus. Quentin Skinner delivered the F. W. Bateson Memorial Lecture on 'Moral Ambiguity and the Renaissance Art of Eloquence' (*EIC* 44.267–92). Skinner considers the anxiety which reflective literature expressed about the shifting referents for evaluative terms about human behaviour. He aligns this rather with the revival in the art of rhetoric than with the interest in Pyrrhonian scepticism – a tricky distinction, deftly made.

Three critics have concentrated on the rhetoric of social hierarchies in the early modern period. Victoria Kahn's closely argued *Machiavellian Rhetoric from the Counter-Reformation to Milton* starts by discussing Machiavelli's divorce of ethics and politics in his own work. The later construct of the Machiavel, the crafty rhetorician, provides a discourse of power for Renaissance writers thinking about politics (Kahn concentrates on Stephen Gardiner, Walter Ralegh, Francis Bacon, Shakespeare and a group of Henrician disputants writing about the strains between church and state). She contends that skill in arguing both sides of a question made for social consensus but not necessarily on the side of the status quo – unfixing political statements from truth allowed radical discussion. Kahn ends this complex, well-substantiated thesis with a study of the strategies of 'virtuous indeterminacy' in Milton. (Incidentally, on the topic of Ralegh, Peter R. Moore wonders 'Did Ralegh try to kill Essex?' in a recommendation to Robert Cecil in dealing with the Essex revolt [*N&Q* 41.463–7]). The search for the early modern individual continues in Kevin Dunn's *Pretexts of Authority*, which examines the creation of the authorial ethos in prefaces. Rather than the topos of modesty expected of the author as 'an unmotivated function of the case' of classical and medieval prefaces, Dunn recognizes the self-authorizing rhetoric of Renaissance prefaces. Sadly, a convoluted style obscures his interesting argument that these prefaces show the evolution of the bourgeois public sphere as a designation of rank (engagement in the ability to speak for and to the people) as well as an economic concept (the ownership of lands in common rather than privately). Kenneth Graham provides a corrective to an idea he assigns to Stanley Fish, that 'epistemological sophistication and conviction are incompatible', in a study of the plain style, *The Performance of Conviction*. Graham concentrates on the problem that the plain style has the authority of sincerity, but expressing it opens that claim to question.

Renaissance scepticism finds the plain style a tempting topos: the contrast between conviction and opinion, the origin of public or private belief, and the political ethos of the plain style. Graham focuses on Thomas Wyatt, Fulke Greville, Roger Ascham, revenge tragedy and *King Lear*, *Coriolanus*, and *Timon of Athens*.

There have been increasing numbers of studies which move away from monographs on literary features towards examining 'the production of culture' located in literary 'artefacts'. David Lee Miller, Sharon O'Dair and Harold Weber's collection of essays, *The Production of English Renaissance Culture*, studies artefacts from specific institutions which shape knowledge for public consumption. While expressing unease at the unlimited horizons of study which new historicism claims for its disciplinary site, this collection concludes that literary studies cannot return to colluding with the 'mystification of value' characteristic of traditional criticism. Three essays look at sixteenth-century texts: Richard Lachmann, Joseph F. Loewenstein and Clark Hulse discuss witchcraft trials, the Stationers' Company, and the cult of Thomas More as struggles for economic and 'symbolic capital'. The editors' point of view can be contrasted this year with those of Robin Headlam Wells and S. K. Heninger.

Much provocative discussion came from the field of gender studies. Betty S. Travitsky and Adele F. Seeff edited the proceedings of a 1990 conference held at the University of Maryland on *Attending to Women in Early Modern England*. Keynote speakers included Margaret Hannay on methods of accessing information about women (picked up again by Keith Moxley), Nanette Salomon on Elizabeth's control of her image, Lisa Jardine on the handling by women of institutional narratives, Heather Dubrow and Retha M. Warnicke on death as a public testimony of what was expected (and hence created) of the female image, and Susan Amussen on 'exceptional women'. Louise Schleiner's *Tudor and Stuart Women Writers* concentrates on the obstacles women overcame to enter the public sphere. She quotes extensively from manuscript sources, and provides an appendix of unpublished Latin poems. Specifically, she sets strategies used by serving women such as Isabella Whitney, Margaret Tyler and Aemilia Lanyer against those used by aristocratic women, such as the Countesses of Pembroke and Oxford, and 'activists' such as the Cooke sisters. The jargon of cultural semiotics badly obscures her interesting general question of how these women 'found motivation and positioning to write anything beyond the sheerly personal'. An essay by Wendy Wall in Carol J. Singley and Susan Elizabeth Sweeney's *Anxious Power: Reading, Writing, and Ambivalence in Narrative by Women* sees Mary Sidney and Lanyer as reversing the critical trope that male writers overcome the social stigma of publication by using women's bodies as images for writing. The idea that Mary Sidney refines masculine modes of writing is also present in Margaret P. Hannay's '"House-confined maids": The Presentation of Women's Role in the *Psalmes* of the Countess of Pembroke' (*ELR* 24.44–71), which notes the additions and deletions that Sidney makes to her source and the scholarly commentaries she uses when they touch on female experience. 'The Sonnets of the Countess of Oxford and Elizabeth I: Translations from Desportes' by Rosalind Smith (*N&Q* 41.446–50) extends a caveat against taking John Soowthern's attributions of them to the two women in *Pandora*.

A witty collection of essays edited by Valeria Finucci and Regina Schwartz looks at literary manifestations of *Desire in the Renaissance*, following the way early modern assumptions about the inner life create the external landscape – either in social structures or in literature. The Ovidian themes of mistaken identity, doublings, memory, voyeurism, mourning, incest and the uncanny are traced to their literary manifestations as ways of repeating, controlling and exorcising anxieties. Essays look at *The Changeling*, *The Faerie Queene*, *As You Like It*, Jonson's 'On my First Sonne', and *Paradise Lost*, as well as Petrarchanism, Castiglione, Ariosto and Machiavelli.

A selection of essays edited by Jonathan Goldberg, *Queering the Renaissance*, is interested in driving back the assumption of universality in 'straight' readings of early modern literature. The policing of sexuality by later critics of, say, devotional poetry '(when "they couldn't have meant that")' is energetically refuted in a number of literary sites. Appropriately, Alan Bray on the exaltation and excoriation of the signs of male friendship begins the volume. Specifically sixteenth-century essays include Dorothy Stephens on the Britomart–Amoret pairing and Carla Freccero on Margaret de Navarre, who see writers seeking sites of evasion which allow female eroticism; Donald N. Mager on John Bale's *Comedy Concernynge thre lawes, of Nature, Moses, & Christ* featuring a character called Sodomy; and Elizabeth Pittenger on Nicholas Udall, the Master of Revels who selected the boys who served the Queen. Work on Bacon, Shakespeare, Beaumont and Fletcher, and the seventeenth-century religious lyric is also contributed.

More tangentially relevant to gender studies in literature of this period are the following books. Frances E. Dolan's *Dangerous Familiars: Representations of Domestic Crime in England, 1550–1700* uses trial transcripts, ballads, popular plays such as *Arden of Faversham*, and Shakespearean texts to show how legal and literary narratives contain the threat of dependents, particularly women. A glance at the illustrations is illuminating: 'a mother who has killed her children commits suicide', 'a father drowns his daughters', 'petty tyrants kill their wives'. Two essays in Richard Burt and John Michael Archer's *Enclosure Acts: Sexuality, Property, and Culture in Early Modern England* deal with Book VI of *The Faerie Queene* and Spenser's efforts to break into the closed circle of the court (Michael Schoenfeldt), and early dictionaries' attempts at exclusion of the speech of women and other 'unskillful persons' beyond the linguistic 'pale' (Juliet Fleming). The rest of the book is primarily concerned with enclosure as a critical trope in discussions of popular literature, Marlowe, Shakespeare, Marvell and the Cavalier poets.

2. Sidney

William Craft's *Labyrinth of Desire: Invention and Culture in the Work of Sir Philip Sidney* begins with an attempt to define culture by linking Fulke Greville's term 'labyrinth of desire' with Sidney's notion of the poet's 'zodiac of his own wit'. This, Craft claims, constitutes the Daedalian maze within which both poet and reader have to work. He also identifies a bifurcation in critical opinion on Sidney, as either a 'politically and generically hamstrung poet' or a 'noble ornament', both views rendering him 'the prisoner of his age'. In the book's five chapters, Craft seeks to rescue Sidney from this position by examining Sidney's major works as experiments by which he empirically tested certain Elizabethan ideas. Craft focuses mainly upon the *New Arcadia* and says, in his concluding chapter, 'This last and best of his poems puts justice on trial, like the first version: it puts eros on trial, like the sonnet sequence: but it also tests invention itself, and with the experience of confronting the "endless overthrow" (*NA* 136) of our contingent, unsettled, mortal life.' Ultimately, Craft offers a rather conservative reading of Sidney's texts, although he makes some gestures towards more modern critical thinking at the end of the book: 'Presently, we will most likely trip on Sidnean assumptions about gender and class', apparently suggesting that Sidney's readers should not problematize these issues, as Sidney did not consider them problematic himself.

The second chapter of Kegl's *The Rhetoric of Concealment* looks at *The Countess of Pembroke's Arcadia.* Here, Kegl gives a thorough analysis of the rhetorical gestures through which Sidney articulates rebellion, that is, 'the logic of dismembered bodies and crumbling buildings'. She argues that in comparing the rebellion of the lower orders with a falling steeple, Sidney's text demonstrates the predetermined nature of the social order, in that the parts remain identifiable, even when the structure has crumbled. Kegl then compares this type of rebellion with that of Sidney's female characters, in which, she argues, 'it is not merely the mortar that crumbles, but the very parts themselves'. When discussing her choice of the *Old Arcadia* as the focus of a chapter in *Pastoral and the Poetics of Self-contradiction: Theocritus to Marvell,* Judith Haber anticipates charges of being idiosyncratic by arguing that this text most clearly demonstrates the difficulties confronting Renaissance pastoralists. She argues that there is a fragmentation of the pastoral form in the Renaissance and that Sidney, more obviously than other English poets, sees the pastoral as 'inherently problematic'. Throughout the chapter, Haber compares the *Old Arcadia* with Sannazaro's *Arcadia* and Montemayor's *Diana* to highlight Sidney's reworking of a central tenet of classical pastoral, that is, that the continuity of a problem is that problem's solution.

This year saw the publication of two articles which took very different approaches to the issue of gender in Sidney's major works. Mary Ellen Lamb's 'Apologizing for Pleasure in Sidney's *Apology for Poetry*: The Nurse of Abuse Meets the Tudor Grammar School' (*Criticism* 36.499–519) identifies an anxiety about masculinity in Sidney's text. Taking account of the perceived feminizing and infantilizing threat posed by poetry to the male reader (particularly those adolescent males still at school), Lamb suggests that the *Apology* attempts to reconcile the pleasurable teaching afforded by poetry with the grammar school education and socialization of boys into masculine adulthood. Katherine Roberts's 'Realism in Sidney's *Astrophil and Stella*: The Creation of Stella' (*SNew* 12[1993].2.30–41) identifies a deviation by Sidney from Petrarchan conventions in his characterization of Stella as 'neither the cruel mistress nor the plaster saint'. However, Roberts's reading of Stella is somewhat optimistic, as she claims that 'Stella's voice comes to the reader directly without being interpreted by the poet/lover', apparently missing the fact that Stella's voice exists solely in the literary medium supplied by the poet/lover.

A rather marginalized section of the Sidney oeuvre is given some attention by Paul A. Marquis in 'Rereading Sidney's *Certain Sonnets*' (*RS* 8.i.65–75). Arguing for a reconsideration of this collection, Marquis focuses upon its range and diversity, taking the reader on a journey through the miscellany. Marquis ultimately proposes that, in the *Certain Sonnets*, Sidney seized an opportunity to experiment and thus transformed the miscellany 'into a genre with remarkable rhetorical force'. Robert H. F. Carver's '"Valiant Aristomenes": A Messenian Hero in Sidney's *Old Arcadia*' (*N&Q* 41.26–8) offers an identification of some source material for Sidney's use of Aristomenes in the *Old Arcadia* and also suggests that his appearance implies a subtle critique of Musidorus, which is consistent with Sidney's tempering his commendation of his central characters with criticism. Carver's subsequent note 'Sidney's Emperor's' (*N&Q* 41.29–30) presents evidence to suggest that the text which Sidney recommends in his letter to Edward Denny is volume III of *Varii Historiae Romanae Scriptores*, published by Henri Estienne in 1568. Carver describes this as 'a monument to the notion of historical continuity between the power structures of the Renaissance and those of the ancient world', offering ideal patterns of behaviour for young men such as Denny.

3. Spenser

Two distinct but related areas received a considerable amount of attention this year: Spenser's identity as a poet and his relationship with Ireland. Gary Waller's *Edmund Spenser: A Literary Life* takes a refreshingly new approach to the task of constructing the life of a poet. Waller divides his text into seven chapters, the first of which considers the very problem of the 'literary life'. Chapter 2 identifies three 'worlds' in which Spenser might be seen to have existed – the English court, Ireland and the metaphorical world of poetry. Chapter 3 considers Spenser's experience of the difficult relationship between Protestantism and poetry, relating this to his early poems and *The Shepheardes Calendar*. The following three chapters focus more closely upon *The Faerie Queene*, although chapter 6 pays particular attention to the *Mutabilitie Cantoes*, which, claims Waller, 'are among the closest places in which Spenser comes in his literary life to his material life'. Here, Waller also discusses the way in which *Amoretti* creates an alternative to Petrarchism, providing 'a Protestant critique of the persuasiveness of Petrarchan modes of thought and expression'. Of particular interest is Waller's care to locate Spenser as an outsider to the English court, due not only to his social inferiority, but also to his prolonged stay in Ireland. Waller thereby problematizes the construction of Spenser as an English court poet and highlights Spenser's own anxieties about his relationship to the centre of power.

Waller notes Spenser's interest in fashioning his own poetic identity, an issue which is also discussed by Falco in *Conceived Presences*. Chapter 2 deals with Spenser's elegies for Sir Philip Sidney, 'The Ruines of Time' and 'Astrophel', and opens thus: 'Spenser's contribution to Elizabethan literary genealogy has the deceptive appearance of self-sacrifice.' Falco uncovers the deception to show that Spenser uses the elegiac mode to fashion his own place in the literary genealogy of Renaissance England, at once creating the image of Sidney as a poetic precursor and distancing himself from that image by stating his own revised poetic agenda. 'Astrophel' is also given attention by Theodore L. Steinberg in 'Spenser, Sidney, and the Myth of Astrophel' (*SSt* 11.187–201), in which he defends the text against accusations that it is a cold, insipid failure. Steinberg relates the poem to Spenser's other works, which results in the essay metamorphosing into a defence of Spenser's authorship of the 'Dolefull Lay of Clorinda' against the claims made for Mary Sidney's authorship.

Spenser's anxiety about his social origins are seen to appear in his characterization of Red Crosse Knight and his use of *The Tale of Sir Thopas*, according to Craig A. Berry's article 'Borrowed Armor/Free Grace: The Quest for Authority in *The Faerie Queene* 1 and Chaucer's *Tale of Sir Thopas*' (*SP* 91.136–66). Berry wants to trace 'the process by which Spenser's interpretation of his own circumstances participates in the ongoing creation of a poetic career', and does so by identifying the opening stanzas of *The Faerie Queene* and Arthur's dream encounter in Canto 9 (adapted from Chaucer) as Spenser fashioning a poetic self by acknowledging and then discarding his own lowly origins. Berry gives us a brief account of these origins at the beginning of his article, and Donald Bruce provides similar details in 'Edmund Spenser: The Boyhood of a Poet' (*ContempR* 264.70–9). This article is largely speculative, musing upon the effects that the geographical location of East Smithfield may have had upon the young poet. However, Bruce does make a note of the pageants and displays in London during Spenser's boyhood, and the appearance of similar events in *The Faerie Queene* and *The Shepheardes Calender*.

Historical evidence relating to Spenser's life is also the concern of Jean R. Brink's note 'Documenting Edmund Spenser: A New Life Record' (*ANQ* 7.201–8). In this she gives details of three Chancery Bill records, and suggests that some nineteenth- and twentieth-century critics have not taken enough care in interpreting historical evidence, resulting in the portrayal of Spenser as 'a land-hungry unscrupulous villain'. Brink's apparent concern to redeem Spenser's reputation is also central to her essay 'Constructing the *View of the Present State of Ireland*' (*SSt* 11.203–28). In a detailed account of the entries in the Stationer's Register and the various extant MSS of the *View*, Brink presents the case that the text, which she argues is unfinished, was neither suppressed by the censors, nor written by Edmund Spenser. Of particular interest is her comment that four new MSS were identified in 1980, but have been neither described nor collated against the standard edition. Brink does not suggest an alternative author for the *View*, but states that whilst '[s]cholarship abhors a vacuum' it is better to acknowledge uncertainty than construct interpretations on weak foundations.

Andrew Hadfield also surveys the evidence provided by the Stationer's Register in 'Was Spenser's *View of the Present State of Ireland* Censored? A Review of the Evidence' (*N&Q* 41.459–63), but does not question Spenser's authorship. Acknowledging the unsatisfactory nature of the evidence, Hadfield comes to the tentative conclusion that the *View* may have been intended for circulation only in MS and that the attempt to publish was not Spenser's doing. The article ends by asserting that his tentative and speculative conclusions are 'less dangerous and misleading' than the assumption that the *View* was censored specifically because it was an especially offensive and transgressive text. Hadfield's second piece on the *View*, 'Spenser, Ireland, and Sixteenth-century Political Theory' (*MLR* 89.1–18), refutes the claims of earlier critics that Irenius's comments are self-contradictory, and suggests that '[t]he implied reader of the *View* is manipulated into accepting Irenius's arguments'. Reading the *View* in relation to the *Mutabilitie Cantoes*, Hadfield argues that the poetry says what the *View* can never consider, that Ireland 'is the site where (the English) language turns against itself and ceases to be able to transform its "other" '.

The role of Ireland in Spenser's choice of poetic language is the subject of Willy Maley's 'Spenser's Irish English: Language and Identity in Early Modern Ireland' (*SP* 91.417–31). In this historically detailed article, Maley argues that Spenser found a ready-made archaic store of English dialect in Elizabethan Ireland, where 'a marginal and marginalized English colonial community jealously guarded its identity by preserving earlier forms of the metropolitan dialect'. Therefore, perhaps Spenser's 'Chaucerian English' should more accurately be described as 'Irish English'. E.K'.s attempts to clarify Spenser's use of English are defended by Jeffrey N. Nelson 'In Defense of E.K'.s Gloss on "Neighbour towne" ' (*ANQ* 7.129-30), which, he argues, is not useless or confusing, but rather part of the Elizabethan attempt to prove that the English language is the equal of Greek and Latin.

The Faerie Queene had two books devoted to it this year. Sheila T. Cavanagh's *Wanton Eyes and Chaste Desires: Female Sexuality in The Faerie Queene* is a feminist re-reading of the whole text. In five wittily titled chapters, Cavanagh presents the case, stated in chapter 1, that '[w]omen are rarely portrayed as truly "present" in the epic'. This chapter illustrates that virtuous women are generally perpetually in flight. However, when women are static, actual or metaphorical disrobings take place which 're-mystify female bodies even as they seem to de-mystify them'. Sightings of female genitalia are conspicuous by their absence. Chapter 2 deals with the appearance of women in dreams, particularly nightmares. The identification of evil female characters as nightmarish and non-human offers the male characters some kind of control and allows them to retain their Neoplatonic ideals. Chapter 3 questions the relative value given to beauty and chastity throughout the text, whilst chapter 4 focuses upon the stories of Mirabella, Pastorella and Belphoebe. Here, Cavanagh uses psychoanalytic theories of eroticism and sexual domination to argue that Spenser tries to create an agenda for correct responses to male desire by beautiful and chaste women. The final chapter deals with the cross-dressed Britomart, in which Cavanagh argues that despite being the titular knight of chastity, Britomart does not appear committed to defending that quality in any woman other than herself. This characteristic is partly explained by Britomart's characterization as naive and dull-witted, although Cavanagh finally concludes that 'Britomart's complicated and contradictory behavior merely reflects the impossible nature of the virtue she represents.' A version of Cavanagh's chapter 2 also appeared as 'Nightmares of Desire: Evil Women in *The Faerie Queene*' (*SP* 91.313–38).

Darryl J. Gless's *Interpretation and Theology in Spenser* deals with the first book of *The Faerie Queene*. Although this may seem a limited scope for a critical work of 273 pages, Gless analyses the 'Legend of Holiness' in the context of the theological debates contemporaneous with Spenser's literary career. Drawing upon the common feature of literary texts and theological texts – that both are subject to a multiplicity of interpretations – Gless situates the 'Legend' within the unresolved doctrinal debate of post-Reformation English Protestantism. Chapter 1 offers a discussion of the various theological views of holiness, whilst chapter 2 invites the reader to eschew the simplistic interpretation of the allegory, claiming that 'the multiple generic signals [which] readers received as they begin to encounter the poem prepare for a complex response'. Following Spenser's text closely, the subsequent four chapters deal with evil, sin, heroism and holiness. The final chapter, entitled '"Spenser" and Dogmatic Mutability' claims that Red Crosse Knight's pursuit of virtue in Book I never actually reaches closure and thus Gless looks forward briefly into the rest of *The Faerie Queene*, especially Book II, in which Guyon's virtue is identified as a synecdoche of Red Crosse Knight's. Tamara A. Goeglein's 'Utterances of the Protestant Soul in *The Faerie Queene*: The Allegory of Holiness and the Humanist Discourse of Reason' (*Criticism* 36.1–19) identifies two dialogues in Book I, which 'dramatize aspects of the protestant soul engaging in self-debate': Red Crosse Knight's conversations with Despair and with Contemplation. The former, argues Goeglein, pulls Red Crosse into himself and therefore towards self-destruction, and the latter leads him outwards to fulfil his quest, but ultimately the 'dialogic utterances of [Red Crosse Knight's] soul merge together, to become a protestant "voice"'.

Books I and II of *The Faerie Queene* received further attention in Maren-Sofie Røstvig's *Configurations: A Topomorphical Approach to Renaissance Poetry*.

Røstvig uses the practice of perceiving 'the unifying patterns by observing the placing of topoi within the body or morphe of the text', hence the term in her title. In a substantial and detailed chapter, she identifies the various patterns of linkage within and between individual stanzas and whole cantos. Røstvig also provides forty-six diagrams which illustrate the different ways in which stanzas can be linked, for example by simple symmetry or by groupings into biblically significant numbers, such as thirty-three or nineteen. In 'An Instance of Number Symbolism in Spenser's *Faerie Queene* I.6' (*N&Q* 41.30–2), David Ormerod notes the importance of the number thirty-three in Richard Douglas Jordan's interpretation of the Satyrs as the Jewish people and Sylvanus as Moses. Ormerod supplements Jordan's interpretation by suggesting that the mixed parentage of Satyrane, together with his role in bringing Una/Divine Truth from the Satyrs/Jews into the wider world, might allow for an indentification of him as St Paul.

Book III of *The Faerie Queene* is examined by Susan Frye in 'Of Chastity and Violence: Elizabeth I and Edmund Spenser in the House of Busirane' (*Signs* 20.49–78). She argues that the violence present in Spenser's treatment of heterosexuality arises from the conflict between his definition of chastity as male possession of the female body and Elizabeth I's definition of her own chastity as 'self-possessed'. Identifying Amoret and Britomart as versions of Elizabeth I, she demonstrates the way in which Spenser underplays the rape of Amoret, and suggests that Busirane is 'the figure of all the displaced violence that Spenser feels toward his Queen'. Michael Steppat's essay 'Social Change and Gender Decorum: Renaissance Courtesy' (in Jacques Carre, *The Crisis of Courtesy: Studies in the Conduct-book in Britain, 1600–1900*) is also concerned with Spenser's discontent. Setting Book VI of *The Faerie Queene* in the context of other Renaissance conduct books and noting the educative aim which Spenser claims for his great work, Steppat argues that Spenser locates courtesy's home as being no longer in the court. He also identifies a criticism of Elizabeth I by relating Mirabella's practice of rejecting and recalling her suitors to Elizabeth's own behaviour, and points to the denial of closure effected by the poem's refusal to quell the Blatant Beast.

Lesley Brill, in 'Other Places, Other Times: The Sites of the Proems to *The Faerie Queene*' (*SEL* 34.1–17), sees the Proems as a 'coherent subset' of the whole poem. However, in comparing them with the main body of the text, she identifies the lack of allegorical discourse in the Proems. As such, Brill argues, they exist in a 'sort of historical present tense' and their speaker both 'is and is not Spenser, is and is not the speaker of the cantos'. Spenser's debts to other writers are the concern of Lawrence F. Rhu's 'Romancing Eliza: The Political Decorum of Ariostan Imitation in *The Faerie Queene*' (*RenP*[1993].31–9) and Kerri Lynne Thomsen's 'Spenser's Use of Claudian's *De Raptu Proserpinae*' (*N&Q* 41.456–9). Rhu sets Spenser's borrowings in the context of the Elizabethan court, where Elizabeth's godson, Sir John Harrington, irreverently presented his partial translation of *Orlando Furioso*. He demonstrates that Spenser's marginal position necessitated that his 'recurrent imitations' of Ariosto were employed very cautiously. Thomsen argues for a deeper relationship between the *Mutabilitie Cantoes* and Claudian's text. Making a close comparison between the two texts and pointing to Spenser's specific reference only to Pluto and Proserpina, Thomsen argues that Spenser 'completes and then improves' Claudian's work, by identifying the poet and reader as the figures who will be snatched away by death or mutability. *Approaches to Teaching Spenser's Faerie Queene* (MLA) was not available for review.

Books Reviewed

Allison, A. F., and D. M. Rogers, eds. *The Contemporary Printed Literature of the English Counter-Reformation between 1558 and 1640*. 2 vols. Scolar. pp. 291, 250. £116. ISBN 1 8592 8060 9.

Bath, Michael. *Speaking Pictures: English Emblem Books and Renaissance Culture*. Longman (1993). pp. 310. hb £39, pb £16.99. ISBN 0 5820 6197 0, 0 5820 6196 2.

Burt, Richard, and John Michael Archer, eds. *Enclosure Acts: Sexuality, Property, and Culture in Early Modern England*. CornUP. pp. 340. hb £33.50, $42.95, pb £13.50, $16.95. ISBN 0 8014 2745 2, 0 8014 8024 8.

Carlson, David R. *English Humanist Books: Writers and Patrons, Manuscript and Print, 1475–1525*. UTorP (1993). pp. 275. pb $21.95. ISBN 0 8020 7796 X.

Carre, Jacques, ed. *The Crisis of Courtesy: Studies in the Conduct-book in Britain, 1600–1900*. Brill. pp. 210. £45.65. ISBN 9 0041 0005 9.

Carroll, D. Allen, ed. *Greene's Groatsworth of Wit*. MRTS. pp. 164. $20. ISBN 0 8669 8167 5.

Cavanagh, Sheila T. *Wanton Eyes and Chaste Desires: Female Sexuality in The Faerie Queene*. IndUP. pp. 226. hb £25, pb £10.99. ISBN 0 2533 1367 8, 0 2532 0889 0.

Craft, William. *Labyrinth of Desire: Invention and Culture in the Work of Sir Philip Sidney*. AUP. pp. 163. £25. ISBN 0 8741 3522 2.

Daniell, David. *William Tyndale: A Biography*. YaleUP. pp. 429. $30. 0 3000 6132 3.

Dick, John A. R., and Anne Richardson, eds. *William Tyndale and the Law*. SCJ Publishers. pp. 135. $35. ISBN 0 9404 7426 3.

Dolan, Frances E. *Dangerous Familiars: Representations of Domestic Crime in England, 1550–1700*. CornUP. pp. 253. pb $15.95. ISBN 0 8014 2901 3.

Dundas, Judith. *Pencils Rhetorique: Renaissance Poets and the Art of Painting*. AUP (1993). pp. 292. £32.50. 0 8741 3459 5.

Dunn, Kevin. *Pretexts of Authority: The Rhetoric of Authorship in the Renaissance Preface*. StanfordUP. pp. 198. £25. ISBN 0 8047 2284 6.

Eriksen, Roy, ed. *Contexts of Pre-novel Narrative: The European Tradition*. MGruyter. pp. 397. £73.35, $144.65. ISBN 3 1101 3883 2.

Estrin, Barbara L. *Laura: Uncovering Gender and Genre in Wyatt, Donne, and Marvell*. DukeUP. pp. 345. hb $49.95, pb $18.95. ISBN 0 8223 1500 9, 0 8223 1499 1.

Evans, Maurice, ed., rev. Roy J. Booth. *Elizabethan Sonnets*. (Everyman) Dent. pp. 289. pb £5.99. ISBN 0 4608 7363 6.

Falco, Raphael. *Conceived Presences: Literary Genealogy in Renaissance England*. UMassP. pp. 235. £29.50, $32.50. ISBN 0 8702 3935 X.

Finucci, Valeria, and Regina Schwartz, eds. *Desire in the Renaissance: Psychoanalysis and Literature*. PrincetonUP. pp. 273. hb £32, $37.50, pb £14.95, $14.95. ISBN 0 6910 0100 6, 0 6910 3403 6.

Fox, Alistair. *Utopia: An Elusive Vision*. Twayne. pp. 127. pb £6.95. ISBN 0 8057 8570 1.

Gless, Darryl J. *Interpretation and Theology in Spenser*. CUP. pp. 273. £32.50, $49.95. ISBN 0 5214 3474 2.

Goldberg, Jonathan, ed. *Queering the Renaissance*. DukeUP. pp. 388. hb £52, pb £16.95. ISBN 0 8223 1381 2, 0 8223 1385 5.

Graham, Kenneth J. E. *The Performance of Conviction: Plainness and Rhetoric in the Early English Renaissance*. CornUP. pp. 232. £25.50. ISBN 0 8014 42871 8.

Greenblatt, Stephen, ed. *New World Encounters*. UCalP (1993). pp. 344. hb £40, pb £12.95. ISBN 0 5200 8020 3, 0 5200 8021 1.

Haber, Judith. *Pastoral and the Poetics of Self-contradiction: Theocritus to Marvell*. CUP. pp. 218. £32.50, $49.95. ISBN 0 5214 4206 0.

Hadfield, Andrew. *Literature, Politics and National Identity: Reformation to Renaissance*. CUP. pp. 265. £37.50. ISBN 0 5214 4207 9.

Hendricks, Margo, and Patricia Parker, eds. *Women, 'Race', and Writing in the Early Modern Period*. Routledge. pp. 383. hb £40, pb £14.95. 0 4150 7777 X, 0 4150 7778 8.

Heninger, S. K., Jr. *The Subtext of Form in the English Renaissance: Proportion Poetical*. PSUP. pp. 214. hb £32, pb £14.95. ISBN 0 2710 1070 3, 0 2710 1071 1.

Herman, Peter C. *Rethinking the Henrician Era: Essays on Early Tudor Texts and Contexts*. UIllP. pp. 312. hb $44.94, pb $17.95. ISBN 0 2520 2034 0, 0 2520 6340 6.

Holbrook, Peter. *Literature and Degree in Renaissance England: Nashe, Bourgeois Tragedy, Shakespeare*. AUP. pp. 204. £27. ISBN 0 8741 3474 9.

Hutson, Lorna. *The Usurer's Daughter: Male Friendship and Fictions of Women in Sixteenth-century England*. Routledge. pp. 295. £40. ISBN 0 4150 5049 9.

Kahn, Victoria. *Machiavellian Rhetoric from the Counter-Reformation to Milton*. PrincetonUP. pp. 314. £23.50. ISBN 0 6910 3491 5.

Kegl, Rosemary. *The Rhetoric of Concealment: Figuring Gender and Class in Renaissance Literature*. CornUP. pp. 194. £24.95. $32.50. ISBN 0 8014 3016 X.

Knott, John R. *Discourses of Martyrdom in English Literature, 1563–1694*. CUP (1993). pp. 278. £40. ISBN 0 5214 3365 7.

Land, Norman E. *The Viewer as Poet: The Renaissance Response to Art*. PSUP. pp. 216. £35.95. 0 2710 1004 5.

Mack, Peter. *Renaissance Argument: Valla and Agricola in the Traditions of Rhetoric and Dialectic*. Brill (1993). pp. 395. £63.75. ISBN 9 0040 9879 8.

——, ed. *Renaissance Rhetoric*. St Martin's. pp. 188. £42.50. ISBN 0 3121 0184 8.

McLeod, Randall, ed. *Crisis in Editing: Texts of the English Renaissance*. Papers given at the Twenty-fourth Annual Conference on Editorial Problems, University of Toronto, 4–5 November 1988. AMS. pp. 306. £44.50. ISBN 0 4046 3674 8.

Medine, Peter E., ed. *Thomas Wilson: The Art of Rhetoric (1560)*. PSUP. pp. 321. $45. ISBN 0 2710 0941 1.

Miller, David Lee, Sharon O'Dair and Harold Weber, eds. *The Production of English Renaissance Culture*. CornUP. pp. 326. hb £29.50, $37.50, pb £12.50, $15.95. ISBN 0 8014 2961 7, 0 8014 8201 1.

Patterson, Annabel. *Reading Holinshed's Chronicles*. UChicP. pp. 339. hb £34.50, pb £13.50. ISBN 0 2266 4911 3, 0 2266 4912 1.

Relihan, Constance C. *Fashioning Authority: The Development of Elizabethan Novelistic Discourse*. KSUP. pp. 178. £21.50. ISBN 0 8733 8495 4.

Richardson, Brian. *Print Culture in Renaissance Italy: The Editor and the Vernacular Text, 1470–1600*. CUP. pp. 265. £35. ISBN 0 5214 2032 6.

Røstvig, Maren-Sofie. *Configurations: A Topomorphical Approach to Renaissance Poetry*. ScanUP. pp. 582. £39.50. ISBN 8 2002 1909 7.

Schleiner, Louise. *Tudor and Stuart Women Writers*. IndUP. pp. 293. hb £32.50, pb £13.99. ISBN 0 2533 5098 0, 0 2532 0886 6.

Shell, Marc. *Elizabeth's Glass: With 'The Glass of the Sinful Soul' (1544) by Elizabeth I, and 'Epistle Dedicatory' and 'Conclusion' by John Bale (1548)*. UNebP (1993). pp. 365. $40. ISBN 0 8032 4216 6.

Shephard, Amanda. *Gender and Authority in Sixteenth-century England: The Knox Debate*. KeeleUP. pp. 217. pb £15.95. ISBN 1 8533 1055 7.

Singley, Carol J., and Susan Elizabeth Sweeney, eds. *Anxious Power: Reading, Writing, and Ambivalence in Narrative by Women*. SUNYP (1993). pp. 400. hb $64.50, pb $21.95. ISBN 0 7914 1389 6, 0 7914 1390 X.

Sowerby, Robin. *The Classical Legacy in Renaissance Poetry*. Longman. pp. 415. hb £39, pb £16.99. ISBN 0 5820 5549 0, 0 5820 5548 2.

Travitsky, Betty S., and Adele F. Seeff, eds. *Attending to Women in Early Modern England*. AUP. pp. 384. hb £34.50, pb £14.95. ISBN 0 8741 3519 2, 0 8741 3549 4.

Waller, Gary. *Edmund Spenser: A Literary Life*. Macmillan. pp. 211. pb £9.99. ISBN 0 3335 2358 X.

Wells, Robin Headlam. *Elizabethan Mythologies: Studies in Poetry, Drama and Music*. CUP. pp. 287. £37.50, $59.95. ISBN 0 5214 3385 1.

Woodmansee, Martha, and Peter Jaszi, eds. *The Construction of Authorship: Textual Appropriation in Law and Literature*. DukeUP. pp. 462. hb £42.75, pb £16.95. ISBN 0 8223 1382 0, 0 8223 1412 6.

VI

Shakespeare

BENJAMIN GRIFFIN, DERMOT CAVANAGH, PAULINE KIERNAN, DEBORAH CARTMELL and SUSAN BRUCE

This chapter has four sections: 1. Editions and Textual Scholarship; 2. Shakespeare in the Theatre; 3. Shakespeare on Screen; 4. Criticism. Section 1 is by Benjamin Griffin; section 2 is by Dermot Cavanagh; section 3 is by Deborah Cartmell; sections 4(a) and (e) are by Pauline Kiernan, sections 4(b) and (c) by Susan Bruce, and section 4 (d) by Deborah Cartmell.

1. Editions and Textual Scholarship

The Oxford Shakespeare series, as it gets older, is also getting fatter. Two new editions, *Anthony* [*sic*] *and Cleopatra* and *Coriolanus*, are imposingly big. *Anthony* is edited by Michael Neill. He faces stiff competition, because (in addition to the New Variorum) the NPS and the recent NCaS editions are both excellent; but the strengths of this edition are sufficiently unique to merit inclusion in the first rank. Neill eschews a 'survey' of criticism as such, choosing to offer his own perceptive analysis. For Neill, the play's paradoxes, oppositions and anti-climaxes flow from a deep concern with the nature of personal identity. He provides an outstanding discussion of revivals and adaptations from Dryden to recent years, which focuses on the difficulties the play presents on stage. As for the spelling of the characters' names, especially Antony's: I am bound to question Shakespeare's supposed preference for the inclusion of the letter 'h'. If there were reason to think the Folio text derived from authorial papers, that would be something; but Neill is sceptical, wisely I think, about the exact nature of the copy. It is proposed that 'Anthony' is a useful reminder of the 'Elizabethanness' of these seeming-Romans; but is this not a modernized edition? Neill's text is accurate, and it incorporates several excellent new emendations – it is interesting how often he is able to get sense from the Folio text simply by repunctuating. It is courageous to have Cleopatra 'yon *ribanded* nag of Egypt' at III.x.10, but I still think something like 'ribald' is meant. A very fine edition.

R. B. Parker's Oxford *Coriolanus* is likewise a thick volume – the introduction is 150 pages by itself. Here too there is real competition, because Philip Brockbank's New Arden edition is excellent, but much has changed since 1976, and Parker frequently contrives to make Brockbank's edition look a little old.

Increased attention is given to the 1607/8 Midlands risings and the relation to Jacobean politics generally. Parker offers the 'survey' of contemporary criticism which Neill avoids, and the results are not terribly stimulating: Volumnia is 'struggling to interpret motherhood in terms of her society', Coriolanus may be 'suffering from paranoid aggression'. Parker is better the further he gets from all this; in particular he shows himself sensitive to the play's language. Unfortunately, the introduction is dogged by the spirit of error. A line from Jonson's *Epicoene* is misquoted three times in as many places; Plutarch's *Life of Coriolanus* is dated 'about AD 2'; the fable of the belly is misreferenced to the wrong part of *Policraticus*; and there are other slips, too many. The text itself is accurate. Parker's view on the Folio copy is that, 'on the principle of Occam's razor', it is not necessary to postulate some level of theatrical influence; all the text's anomalies derive from the hand of Shakespeare. Parker's approach to theatrical copy-text is distinctly out of date. Perhaps surprisingly, he admits more traditional emendations than Brockbank. Less surprisingly, in view of the length of the introduction, the source material from Plutarch is presented only in excerpts (Brockbank prints the whole *Life*). On the whole, this would not be my first choice.

'*Titus Andronicus* is not everyone's favourite play', writes Alan Hughes in the preface to his NCaS edition. There is more convention than truth in that statement; in fact, for quite a while now, a readiness to assert the virtues of *Titus* has been a major Shakespearean shibboleth. Hughes's view of the play is the familiar one: that it has been underrated because critics have neglected its theatrical virtues by concentrating on its poetic deficiencies; *Titus* 'reads badly' but 'plays well'. There is an important qualification to this theory: it plays well 'only when the actors believe in the reality of the characters and the truth of the action'. This might be called the 'Tinkerbell' theory of value. In the introduction and notes Hughes discusses the ways in which actors and directors may try to avert the hilarity that tends to accompany the play's grosser horrors; and he suggests rhetorical contexts which validate such speeches as Marcus's long set piece when he discovers the mutilated Lavinia. I find Hughes's apologetics unconvincing. To insist that where readers and viewers consistently find absurdity, there must be something wrong with their response, is bardolatry. It amounts to denying Shakespeare the freedom to write in bad taste. Critics used to distance the play from Shakespeare by denying his authorship; now they distance the play from the audience, by suspecting our responses and rating 'dramatic craftsmanship' over real impact. Hughes's stage history is full and interesting, blending theatrical chronicle with reflections on audience response and literary quality. Unfortunately, the text itself is full of errors, to a degree that is shocking in a major series; and the annotations are not reliable.

Jay L. Halio has edited *The First Quarto of King Lear* in a new offshoot of the NCaS, a supplementary series called 'The Early Quartos'. The idea is to make available the earlier published forms of the plays, in an edited, modern-spelling form, which yet retains the distinctive readings of those early printings. The value of this edition, however, is seriously compromised by its extravagant admission of Folio variants; some of these are necessary where Q is incomprehensible, but others take the place of perfectly viable Q phrases – the very things the edition is intended to preserve. The result is, not to mince words, a conflated text. In addition to incursions from F there are many editorial emendations; it is especially disappointing to see the adoption of 'thy flaxen biggin threats' at IV.ii.55, one of the Oxford edition's least happy creations. The edition is without commentary – it is meant to be used with Halio's 1992 Folio-based edition of *Lear* in the NCaS main series. So this is essentially a rather expensive appendix, a confused venture whose purpose and usefulness seem very uncertain.

Something similar could be said of the edition of *Hamlet* with supplementary literary theory edited by Susanne L. Wofford. The series from which this comes is called 'Case Studies in Contemporary Criticism', and the clinical-sounding title is entirely appropriate. The 'case' (*Hamlet*, reprinted from the Riverside edition) has had mountains of criticism piled on it, and trying to retrieve it is like leaping into the grave. Each section contains a chin-stroking 'What Is?' introduction (e.g. 'What Is Feminist Criticism?'), a 'Selective Bibliography', and 'A Perspective' (e.g. Showalter's 'Representing Ophelia') – plus yet another bibliography. Repeated five times for five schools of criticism (feminist, psychoanalytic, deconstructive, Marxist, and new historicist), with the addition of two quite separate notes on the text, this quickly becomes fussy and mechanical. If it does reach its student audience, it is going to reinforce the absurd idea that reading should be done through the lenses of a pre-formed 'perspective'. Reading this edition, one feels surprise that the play is still at the beginning of the volume; it might as well have been relegated to an appendix.

Weighing in at six pounds and with a bibliography of just under fifty pages, Gordon Williams's *Dictionary of Sexual Language and Imagery in Shakespearean and Stuart Literature* firmly gives the lie to the self-righteous platitude that 'swearing is the sign of a limited vocabulary'. This triple decker spans the alphabet from *abbess* ('proprietress of a nunnery [brothel]') to the innocuous *zone*, which, we are assured, is a euphemism for 'vaginal region'. Linguistically, it straddles ('term describing the gait of syphilitics with painful nodes') the Latinate *tu quoque* ('To be called a cunt is an old insult') and the Anglo-Saxon *horn*, via French, *callibistris* ('priuie parts'), Dutch, *Hans in kelder* ('jack in the cellar, i.e. the child in the womb'), and Greek, *didymis* ('testicular ducts'). Stylistically, we move from the gross and explicit *trench* to the more obscure and charming *nugging house* ('brothel').

In his introduction Williams attributes this plethoric slang to a rural way of life: 'in an agrarian culture, geared to seasonal change, human sexuality is perhaps dominantly acknowledged as part of that cyclic process which governs life at every stage'. He ascribes a rise in the language of obscenity to the invention of printing and anti-Catholic literature, though the implication that the Reformation resulted in 'a fresh concern with the rights of subordinates, wife and children' seems a little cavalier. Williams is more persuasive on Restoration indecency when he notes its common tone of filthy disgust and self-loathing, such as Rochester's writing displays: 'there is a new dimension to the harping on natural emissions, which become the repulsive suppurations of disease.' This, he suggests, has its roots in the humiliation of defeat: 'What the sexual language of Restoration court society illustrates above all is a maimed elite, still reeling from the shock of being challenged – and defeated – by a bunch of farmers and shopkeepers.'

Williams assures us that these sixteen hundred pages represent only the tip of the iceberg. The greatest joy of this collection is the generosity of primary material. Williams is scrupulous about illustrating his definitions with quotations which are referenced via a detailed and full bibliography. Urquhart's Rabelais and the work of Greene, John Day, Nashe, Jonson and Rochester are, predictably enough, commonplace, but there are plenty of lesser-known writers drafted in to demonstrate the ubiquity of early modern obscenity. Occasionally the choice of authorities is a little eccentric. Barry Humphries, John Updike, Susan Sontag and Edna O'Brien are among modern writers who also appear.

Omissions are inevitable given the polyphony and openness of carnival; nevertheless, some are surprising. Pistol's curse, *foutre*, is missing as is the verb *to stir* meaning 'to excite sexually', as in *Pericles* when the Bawd instructs Marina on the ways of prostitution, 'men must comfort you, men must feed you, men must stir you up' (IV.ii.90), or *As You Like It* in which Rosalind disguises herself as a boy in order to prevent sexual harassment: 'so shall we pass along, / And never stir assailants' (I.iii.109–10). *Jakes* is defined perversely as 'prostitute' though its prevalent use is toiletry, as in Harington's punning title, *The Metamorphosis of Ajax* (which, oddly enough, appears in the bibliography). However, these faults are trivial compared to the achievements of the dictionary and the purchase of these three full volumes of smut, conscientiously edited and engagingly illustrated, is a must for any scholar of the period. Whether any scholar will be able to afford them is a rather more delicate matter. [Reviewed by Peter J. Smith]

This year there are signs of the Return of the Author, in that 'textual-discrepancy' studies are yielding to authorship studies. Charles Hamilton, his publishers inform us, has made 'dozens of notable discoveries' in his sixty-year career as a handwriting expert. His latest discovery, that *The Second Maiden's Tragedy* is Shakespeare and Fletcher's *Cardenio*, is not one of them. That the play's plot is not clearly based on Cervantes's tale of Cardenio, that the play has no discernible relation to Theobald's *Double Falshood* (which Hamilton accepts as a revision of *Cardenio*), and that there are no marks of Shakespeare's or Fletcher's hands in the text are objections which seem to carry no weight here. The case rests on Hamilton's conviction that Shakespeare's last will and testament is entirely autograph (one of his previous 'discoveries'). The will itself is said to be in the same writing as the MS of *The Second Maiden's Tragedy*, which, in turn, is an authorial draft. Further complicating matters is Hamilton's curious belief that Fletcher's style is nearly indistinguishable from Shakespeare's. Distinguish Fletcher's share from Shakespeare's – in a play by Middleton? I should think it *is* difficult. Hamilton has no time for the linguistic paraphernalia of modern authorship studies; the way to prove authorship, he thinks, is to determine whether the play is 'tightly knit, redolent with power'. It is all wildly implausible, though I might mention that the book is lavishly illustrated with facsimile handwriting samples of the Tudor–Stuart period (most of them quite unconnected with either Shakespeare or *The Second Maiden's Tragedy*).

The obverse side of authorship studies – solid, statistical – is represented by Jonathan Hope's *The Authorship of Shakespeare's Plays*. Hope uses sociohistorical linguistic evidence to discriminate between the styles of Shakespeare and his putative collaborators. The premise is that authors maturing at different times and in different social circumstances manifest different linguistic forms. That sort of evidence encourages the expectation that, for example, 'Fletcher will use more incoming prestige variants than Shakespeare.' The idea, I believe, is that these sociolinguistic variants are likely to be 'constants' in an individual's style, not varying over lifetime and circumstances. They should thus be a good anchor for Hope to lean upon. As bar-graphs make for less than compelling reading, even by authorship-study standards, the best thing for me to do is probably to repeat, telegraphically, some of Hope's conclusions. *Henry VIII*: by Shakespeare and Fletcher, but less Shakespeare than previously thought. *Two Noble Kinsmen*: Shakespeare and Fletcher. *Double Falshood*: probably not a 'forgery' as such, and if a Shakespeare–Fletcher collaboration, then earlier scenes more like Shakespeare. *Timon of Athens*: partly non-Shakespearean, but the collaborator is not obviously Middleton. *Pericles*: support for Wilkins–Shakespeare collaboration. *Yorkshire Tragedy*: not Shakespeare, not clearly Middleton. *Edward III*: could be Shakespeare, may be collaborative. *Edmond Ironside*: equivocal.

The general public, as every Shakespearean knows, thinks 'authorship studies' means the question of whether Marlowe or Bacon or Oxford, or someone, actually wrote the canonical works. If you have ever wished for a book you could recommend on this subject, there is now *Shakespeare, in Fact* by Irvin Leigh Matus. It is a study of who Shakespeare was not, with the reasons for not thinking so. Matus possesses a peculiar advantage for taking on this assignment: he is not a professional scholar and can thus side-step the usual charge of complicity in an academic conspiracy to protect the illiterate player. Professional or not, his scholarship is good. The concentration is on the Oxfordian claim. For three hundred pages Matus turns the wheel, as pieces of broken butterfly float in every direction. And that raises the only doubt about the enterprise: these theories are such sorry things to begin with, does one really need to see them 'dismantled'? They appear to be self-dismantling. But if you do want this, or know someone who ought to, *Shakespeare, in Fact* could hardly be better.

Kristian Smidt's *Unconformities in Shakespeare's Later Comedies* is the fourth and final volume in his series covering the whole of Shakespeare's dramatic works. 'Later' comedies here means from *Much Ado* through *The Tempest*. 'Unconformities' is meant in its geological sense of discontinuities in subterranean strata, indicating ancient upheaval; Smidt pursues the analogous disturbances in Shakespeare's text. The volume functions as a compendium, each chapter covering the textual problems of a single play. If you want to know if Feste is a late addition to *Twelfth Night*, or if Posthumus's dream is a late addition to *Cymbeline*, this is a resource. But the short-tempered should be warned that some of the 'unconformities' are the sort of thing that modern commentators almost never countenance – Quiller-Couch-type worries about the suddenness of character-conversions like Bertram's in *All's Well*. Too often, Smidt tolerates the assumption that Shakespeare wrote naturalistic drama centred on character. The Shakespeare presented here is definitely a reviser, but he is presented without any of the vertiginous anxiety we are often told we feel about the revising author; on the other hand, Shakespeare the reviser can be hard to tell from Shakespeare the ditherer. Smidt is never dogmatic about which is which. An appendix lists places where words and phrases are duplicated in passages which seem 'superfluous or imperfectly integrated in [their] context', a possible guide to textual disturbance.

Giorgio Melchiori's *Shakespeare's Garter Plays* brings together several of the author's projects over the last few years. The book is not purely concerned with textual matters. Its literary thesis is that Shakespeare's plays on English history, from *Edward III* through the second tetralogy to *The Merry Wives of Windsor*, are to be seen as a sextet, not a tetralogy, united by 'the recurrent theme' of the Order of the Garter and by Shakespeare's treatment of the values it represented. Melchiori revives the theory that Shakespeare originally wrote *Henry IV* as a single play, and that the fuss over 'Oldcastle' necessitated a thoroughgoing remake, in the course of which the expansion of Falstaff's role made the new wine burst the old bottle. He attempts a more complete excavation of the ur-*Henry IV* than has hitherto been done. Melchiori's boldness in textual reconstruction is intoxicating, but it can also be a stumbling-block. Reading chapter 2, I was just on the point of conceding the validity of the ur-*Henry IV* theory, when the argument suddenly vaulted to new heights: despite the utter loss of the ur-play, Melchiori is able to tell us that it was 'in the region of 3500 lines'; that it was 'mainly, but not all', in verse; what happened in each of its scenes; and that it was less 'subversive of Renaissance authority' than the remake. Stung, I retreated into narrow scepticism. Melchiori's section on *The Merry Wives of Windsor* is altogether more ponderable: the 'Fairy Queen' passage at the play's end is an embedded fossil of a masque written by Shakespeare for the Garter feast in April 1597. This, Melchiori proposes, featured a 'comic antimasque' centred on 'the figure of a knight unworthy of the Order because of his sexual uncleanness'. Melchiori reminds us that in *1 Henry VI* the knight who is stripped of his Garter for cowardice is 'Sir John Falstaffe', though editors routinely change it to Fastolf. The suggestion is that, when Shakespeare came to write an entertainment for the Garter feast, he thought back to the disgartered knight, and it was *Henry VI*'s Sir John Falstaff who reappears in *The Merry Wives* – not the Histories' 'Oldcastle'. It is all an attractive genetic solution to the question of why the Falstaff of Windsor is so different from the Falstaff of the Histories, and to the problems about the play's date. But even granting the existence of a Garter entertainment (of which no record seems to survive), there is nothing to show that Falstaff formed a part of it. For Melchiori, the Garter itself, with the principle of honour for which it stands, ties together all the plays; a problem here is that *Edward III* never mentions it. Editors and textual researchers are bound to be stimulated by this pugnacious book.

The *Wives* is also the subject of an article on revision. Barbara Freedman confronts the way the play's undoubted topicality 'seems to have complicated rather than clarified accounts of its textual and theatrical history' ('Shakespearean Chronology, Ideological Complicity, and Floating Texts: Something is Rotten in Windsor', *SQ* 45.190–210). Observing that all other theories of 'Shakespeare's occasional plays' have perished, Freedman tries to finish the job by freeing *The Merry Wives* from the 1597 investiture of Shakespeare's patron, Hunsdon, as a Knight of the Garter. It is odd Freedman should be so tough on the 'occasionalist' theory of the play's genesis when she is so trusting of 'topical' references. To my mind, the evidence linking *Wives* with Hunsdon – through the common factor of Shakespeare – is strong.

The bad quartos are now frequently taken to represent the way plays were performed in the theatre. Querying this assumption, Janette Dillon asks 'Is There a Performance in this Text?' (*SQ* 45.74–86). She works into this question by way of the edition of the First Quarto of *Hamlet* published in 1993 in the Harvester series (*YWES* 74.195). Dillon exposes the claims of post-structuralist un-editing: where they claim to favour a pluralist dissemination of different texts, they really argue for the superiority of one marginalized form (in this case the 1603 Quarto). The supposed theatricality of the reported text makes a special appeal to a generation of scholars for whom the plays purportedly exist 'for the stage'. Dillon turns the tables and deconstructs the Harvester editors' polarization of the 'stage' and the 'author': for 'this too is a false polarity, based on a denial of the material conditions of the theater'. Dramatists are *authors* who write for the theatre: 'the theater cannot offer an escape from authorship'. Neither can the agency of the actors be circumvented by postulating a world of 'theatre practice': yet academics 'desire to encounter not actors but something called "the Jacobean stage", addressing an apparently material theater practice as if it did not have agents', as if actors enjoyed a condition of inherent authority. Dillon's article is a brilliant reinvestigation of play-text authority, building on all the important work in the field.

Ann R. Meyer's interesting article on 'Shakespeare's Art and the Texts of *King Lear*' (*SB* 47.128–46) argues that the effort to present the author's intentions requires a conflated text. The Oxford editors 'do not fully account for the possibility of non-authorial influence' on the Folio text. Shakespeare need not be the theatrical personage who cut the mock trial in III.vi. Meyer gives bibliographical reasons to see Q omissions, not F revisions, in the final scene. E. Pearlman's 'Shakespeare at Work' (*ELR* 24.315–42) attempts a coherent account of Shakespeare's compositional process as reflected in the texts of *Romeo and Juliet*, but runs into problems. Pearlman thinks Shakespeare started with the 'traditional-1590s' design of choruses between the act breaks, but then became experimental and abandoned that design after 'the juncture of the first and second acts'. But the 'acts' in question are editorial additions; the early quartos are undivided. I would say the prologue-and-choruses device was *itself* the experiment and the departure; Shakespeare had never used it before, but was to use it again.

Linguists and statisticians are having trouble distinguishing Fletcher from Shakespeare, which shows that the human ear still has its uses. The new crop includes Thomas B. Horton, 'Distinguishing Shakespeare from Fletcher through Function Words' (*ShakS* 22.314–35), and Gerard Ledger and Thomas Merriam, 'Shakespeare, Fletcher and *The Two Noble Kinsmen*' (*L&LC* 9.235–48). These are inconclusive studies, probably of interest more to those following developments in stylometry than those interested in Shakespeare's canon itself. Thomas Merriam, 'Evidence from Forker's Three Listings' (*N&Q* 41.482–6), tries to compromise on the dating of Hand D's additions to *Sir Thomas More* by suggesting they are 'the product of two separate periods of writing'. M. W. A. Smith, '*Sir Thomas More*, *Pericles* and Stylometry' (*N&Q* 41.55–8), exposes the weaknesses of Merriam's methods. R. J. C. Watt has a persuasive note for editors of *King John*, '"My Mother's ——"' (*N&Q* 41.479–81).

Two new editions from OUP, *Twelfth Night* (eds Roger Warren and Stanley Wells) and *A Midsummer Night's Dream* (ed. Peter Holland), are not reviewed here on account of the publisher's failure to provide review copies. My attention was drawn too late to Kathleen Irace's *Reforming the Bad Quartos* (UDelP, AUP); it is hoped to review this next year.

2. Shakespeare in the Theatre

Dennis Kennedy has produced the most exciting and original book of the year in *Looking at Shakespeare*. Kennedy's aim is to study 'the relationship between scenography and international Shakespeare performance in the modern and postmodern eras', and this project is carried out brilliantly. The book reconstructs the spectacle of performance from visual evidence and locates this in a detailed account of the changing modes of Shakespeare production, from Victorian 'pictorialism' to contemporary 'intercultural' approaches. The accompanying stills and illustrations are a delight and contribute to an outstanding essay in the social and cultural uses to which Shakespeare has been put. Kennedy ranges widely in European and American production modes – if not beyond – and makes one look anew at the meaning of the visual field of performance. The book concludes with an incisive chapter on the 'postmodern' and is a compelling account of twentieth-century Shakespeare in 'the realm of the seen'.

In *Modern Hamlets and their Soliloquies*, Mary Z. Maher analyses the performance of the play's seven soliloquies by eleven actors, from Gielgud in 1936 to Kevin Kline in 1990. Maher treats the speeches 'contextually', by detailing the intentions of each production; the meaning of the soliloquies is determined by specific performance settings. The principal distinction she makes is between 'externalized' delivery, where explicit contact is made with the audience, and an 'internalized' style, where Hamlet is overheard speaking to himself. An 'externalised' address tends to dilute the madness of the prince, who appears more witty and objective about his own condition and his relationship with the other characters; an 'internalized' soliloquy emphasizes his disturbance and the painful intimacy of his feelings towards those around him. (Maher acknowledges that these modes can be combined, but argues that one always predominates.) The study is written lucidly and contains methodical accounts of individual productions. Most chapters are enriched by an interview carried out with the actor; these include David Warner, Ben Kingsley, Derek Jacobi and Anton Lesser. Kingsley provides a luminous and often moving account of his role in Buzz Goodbody's 1965 production – horribly overshadowed by the suicide of the director – and is exceptionally perceptive on the concern with acting in the play: the 'extraordinary coinciding of my own feelings as an actor with Hamlet's'. At times Maher tends to present her material in an overly passive way and the book would have benefited from a more emphatically defined argument. In particular, her sense of 'context' simply as the particular performance is limiting, and differing acting styles and directorial approaches are not perceived in terms of wider social and cultural influences. However, the book is consistently engaging and Maher is attentive to the nuances of actor–director relationships, the demands of different theatrical spaces and competing performance traditions.

NTQ continues to publish a range of stimulating articles on staging Shakespeare. In 'The Weyward Sisters: Towards a Feminist Staging of *Macbeth*' (30.167–77), Lorraine Helms hypothesizes a production where the witches embody the improvisational 'rough theatre' of travelling players. In this staging, they would respond to, rather than create, the tragic violence of the play. Helms envisions a comic deployment of 'carnivalesque androgyny' that would provide a critical commentary on the play's dominant hierarchies of rank and gender. Jan Kott pursues an analogous interest in the carnivalesque aspects of Shakespearean production. In 'Bottom and the Boys' (36.307–15), he argues, intriguingly, that the mechanicals in *A Midsummer Night's Dream* might well have been played by boys – perhaps the troupe of George Carey, who, as Lord Chamberlain, had recently been the patron of Shakespeare's company – and that their 'children's theatre' would have enhanced both their indecency and their power of travesty. Three essays analyse the implications of some recent traditions of performance. Kent Hagglund examines the upsurge of interest in *A Midsummer Night's Dream* in Sweden: 'Issues of Sexuality and Power: Five Swedish "Dreams", 1989–90' (29.23–33). Hagglund perceives these as being partly stimulated by a lively new translation of the text, but also as indicative of a growing social preoccupation with sexual violence and the oppression of women. In 'Not Only a Question of Money: Shakespeare and the Ego Decade', Liisa Hakola attempts to explain the 'unremarkable Shakespeare' of the 1980s in England (33.37–43). Hakola argues, somewhat reductively, that Shakespearean production thrives in conditions of frequent political change, or else stagnates into banal spectacle and superficial 'star performances'. Suresh Awashti offers a telling analysis of why a specific production – the Kathakali *King Lear* – failed to engage both Indian and European audiences in 1990. In 'The Intercultural Experience and *King Lear*' (34.172–8), Awashti provides a fascinating account of Kathakali as a non-verbal theatrical tradition with a fixed performance 'score', inflected by intuitive improvisation and based on character types expressed through formalized make-up, facial expression and stylized movement. The articulation of *King Lear* in this mode was disastrous, leading to a garbled version of the text that relied on stereotyping and which made no attempt to merge two distinct cultural traditions. Elsewhere, Randall Louis Anderson provides a detailed account of a much more successful, if controversial production: 'Shakespeare at the Guthrie: *The Tempest* Through a Glass Darkly' (*SQ* 44.87–92). This essay analyses Jennifer Tipton's 1991 production of the play at the Guthrie Theater, Minneapolis. Tipton's forceful emphasis on the coercive manipulation inherent in Prospero's authority sought to confront and overwhelm 'the traditional assumptions and generic expectations one brings to the play'.

Robert A. Pearson and William Urrichio have made a useful contribution to *Reclamations of Shakespeare* (ed. A. J. Hoenselaars). In '"Shrieking from below the Gratings": Sir Herbert Beerbohm Tree's *Macbeth* and his Critics', they concentrate on 'the broader cultural dynamics of conditions of production and reception' as they affected early twentieth-century theatrical and cinematic versions of Shakespeare. Their essay analyses a growing disparity between educated and popular tastes. Increasingly, academics and critics expressed disdain for commercial theatrical treatments of Shakespeare and admiration for performances governed by close textual analysis, 'archaeological' discoveries and an austere 'Elizabethan' style. Beerbohm Tree was a useful focus for such suspicions in his pursuit of spectacular visual pleasure and emphatic textual editing. These qualities made him an eager, if much criticized, participant in the filming of *Macbeth* in America in 1916.

Henk K. Gras's 'Direct Evidence and Audience Response to *Twelfth Night*: The Case of John Manningham of the Middle Temple' (*ShakS* 21.109–54) is an ambitious attempt to uncover the significance of 'historical response'. Gras returns to the diary kept by the lawyer, John Manningham, in 1601–3 with its well-known and tantalizingly brief reference to the *Twelfth Night* that he saw in 1602. Gras locates this fragment in relation to the interests – and, he believes, anxieties – that recur throughout Manningham's journal. In particular, he examines the text's preoccupation with friendship and sexuality and finds, not only a pervasive misogyny, but a bawdily assertive masculinity that masks a fear of failure. This is used to explain Manningham's interest in the Malvolio plot; the triangular situation in which one man is made a laughing-stock because of his sexual failure recurs, particularly in the form of jokes, throughout the diary. Gras also speculates that Manningham does not record the Orsino plot-line precisely because of its unsettling erotic ambiguities. The latter phase of the essay is highly conjectural – and perhaps overly Freudian – but this is a resourceful reappraisal of a familiar allusion that suggests new ways of exploring the social (and psychological) context of related observations.

3. Shakespeare on Screen

As a measure of its increasing prominence in Shakespeare criticism, 'Shakespeare on Screen' now has its own separate entry in this volume. Significantly, the last paper in Russ McDonald's excellent collection, *Shakespeare Reread*, is Barbara Hodgdon's 'The Critic, the Poor Player, Prince Hamlet and the Lady in the Dark', in which three readers of Shakespeare are compared: F. R. Leavis, Ian McKellan and Mel Gibson. Examining how close reading accommodates and constructs the body in performance, Hodgdon focuses on Gibson's bodily reading of Hamlet in Zeffirelli's film. Drawing on a host of references, including *Lethal Weapon, Star Trek, Fatal Attraction* and *The Addams Family,* Hodgdon wittily demonstrates just how tragedy should activate relations between 'high' and 'popular' culture and thereby reflect 'the body of the time his form and pressure'. This is, arguably, the purpose of Shakespeare on screen.

Four major books have been produced this year: *Shakespeare and the Moving Image: The Plays on Film and Television*, edited by Anthony Davies and Stanley Wells; *Screen Shakespeare*, edited by Michael Skovmand; *Shakespeare Films in the Classroom: A Descriptive Guide*, by Jo McMurtry; and *Walking Shadows: Shakespeare in the National Film and Television Archive*, edited by Luke McKernan and Olwen Terris. *Shakespeare and the Moving Image* is an excellent collection of essays (many previously published in *ShS* 39), covering television and cinema as well as including essays on comedies, histories and tragedies. Clearly it aims to introduce readers to the benefits of considering Shakespeare on screen, and thus includes a selective filmography (compiled by Graham Holderness and Christopher McCullough) to guide us through the volume. The other collection, *Screen Shakespeare*, fails where *Shakespeare and the Moving Image* succeeds. Although including a few distinguished essays (notably, Bernice W. Kliman's 'Welles's *Macbeth,* a Textual Parable' and Michael Mullin's 'Peter Brook's *King Lear*: A Reassessment'), the majority are lack-lustre and poorly edited (for instance, Derek Jacobi's name is misspelt in Suzanne Fabricuius's '"The Face of Honour": On Kenneth Branagh's Screen Adaptation of *Henry V*', and in '"Knowing I Lov'd My Books": Shakespeare, Greenaway, and the Prosperous Dialectics of Word and Image' Claus Schatz-Jacobsen is eight years off in his dating of the BBC *Tempest*). Certainly the most useful and impressive of the three books published this year must be *Walking Shadows.* Coinciding with a 'Shakespeare on Screen' season at the National Film Theatre, the book provides a remarkably extensive annotated catalogue of the National Film and Television Archive holding, an invaluable guide for anyone working in the area. It will, however, need to be supplemented, as the selection is limited to the contents of the archive. If information is required on, for example, Branagh's *Henry V*, not in the collection, one would have to consult another book-length filmography, such as the excellent *As You Like It: Audio Visual Shakespeare,* edited by Cathy Grant (British Universities Film & Video Council, 1992). The most user-friendly of the 'Shakespeare on film' reference books to date is Jo McMurtry's *Shakespeare Films in the Classroom,* which provides impressive, detailed commentary on mainstream Shakespeare films, with purchase and rental information.

Five years after its release, Branagh's movie continues to generate critical attention. In an outstanding essay, '"When Blood is their Argument": Class, Character and Historymaking in Shakespeare's and Branagh's *Henry V*' (*ELH* 61.27–52), Robert Lane considers what he calls the chinks in Henry's ideological armour when (Shakespeare's) Henry's efforts at self-legitimization backfire. Lane argues that Branagh's version evades the problematic product of male comradeship in war and instead celebrates war as a means of masculine fulfilment. W. P. Shaw compares Olivier and Branagh's versions of *Henry V* and asks why both circumvent the play's ambiguities. Shaw regards Olivier's film as keeping the text while repressing the tone, while Branagh's has the tone without the text ('Textual Ambiguities and Cinematic Certainties in *Henry V*', *LFQ* 22.117–28). Similarities between Branagh and Kurosawa are noted by M. Manheim in 'The Function of Battle Imagery in Kurosawa's Histories' (*LFQ* 22.129–35).

Perhaps undeservedly, Branagh's name continues to crop up in Shakespeare criticism. Ellen Edgerton ingeniously notices how Branagh self-consciously converts play to screen in *Much Ado About Nothing,* beginning with the opening sequence in which we are presented with the lines of the text, followed by a voice speaking those lines, a picture of the landscape, and finally music and motion. ('Your Answer Sir, is Cinematical: Kenneth Branagh's *Much Ado About Nothing'*, *ShakB* 12.42–5). Finally, this review should take note of the 'Shakespeare on Screen Newsletter', included in *ShakB,* revealing how Shakespeare on screen undoubtedly has a major impact on both Shakespeare scholarship and the teaching of Shakespeare in schools and universities. It is not at all unlikely that this year's major Shakespeare film, Disney's *The Lion King* (an animated adaptation of *Hamlet*), will be featured next year, contributing to the debate as to whether screen adaptations serve to trash or treasure the Bard.

4. Criticism

(a) General

Teaching With Shakespeare: Critics in the Classroom (eds Bruce McIver and Ruth Stevenson) is a really good idea: 'to explain to our students the bases and nature of critical procedures and to put these procedures into practice in follow-up workshops'. The book, then, offers lectures examining different approaches in interpretation by six Shakespeare scholars, with each lecture followed by a workshop using the critical procedures examined in the lecture. Particularly helpful is the way Leah Marcus tackles the difficult subject of teaching textual variation in a lecture called 'Disestablishing Shakespeare', using *Hamlet* and *King Lear* in the follow-up workshop. R. A. Foakes shows how 'Cutting the Bard Down to Size' can be achieved by five current approaches: deconstructive, new historicist, feminist, performance and textual. Patricia Parker uses Pyramus and Thisbe to examine wordplay; and in '"A Political Thriller": The Life and Times of Henry V', Annabel Patterson provides a 'test case' of issue-orientated cultural criticism to expose how Shakespearean text can be and has been altered for ideological purposes. In her 'review' of all the practical teaching applications of the book's contributors which concludes the volume, Patterson suggests that while such an approach can expand the boundaries of literature and literary inquiry 'to show how Shakespeare can be used to promote partisan political views', it may mean that a student can so incorporate the norms of issue-orientated criticism as to be 'unable to see the play as anything but a critique of social injustice'. I cannot praise this book too highly.

Stanley Wells has written a useful guide for theatre-goers and general readers with *Shakespeare: A Dramatic Life*. Not surprisingly, the book is particularly strong on the plays as theatrical texts, and it does not ignore the poems and the later collaborations.

Bruce Smith's *Roasting the Swan of Avon: Shakespeare's Redoubtable Enemies and Dubious Friends* is the profusely illustrated 'book of the exhibition' mounted at the Folger Shakespeare Library in 1994, which displayed 'the backside of Bardolatry' and in which all the 'mockers, debunkers, and deconstructors, not to mention fans who don't equate admiration with reverence' get to have their say. The book offers much that is familiar (and perhaps not so familiar) but it is presented in such an entertaining way that it is a joy to take down from the shelf.

In *Shakespeare in the Stratford Records,* Robert Bearman examines the thirty-one records relating to Shakespeare that are held at the Shakespeare Birthplace Trust, including two recent items: his purchase of 107 acres near the town in 1602, and a recently discovered document that relates to the settlement of these lands on his daughter, Susanna, and the lease of part of the 'Birthplace' in Henley Street let as an inn. In his conclusion, Bearman proposes Anthony Nash as the likeliest candidate for Shakespeare's 'local man of business'. The new findings are the subject of two notes: Mairi McDonald's 'A New Discovery about Shakespeare's Estate in Old Stratford' (*SQ* 45.87–9) and 'Lewis Hiccox and Shakespeare's Birthplace' by Jeanne E. Jones (*N&Q* 41.497–502).

The year 1994 could be described as The Year of Shakespeare the Globetrotter. In *Shakespeare and the Geography of Difference*, John Gillies demonstrates how Shakespeare's geographic imagination is informed by a 'rich geographic tradition that is already moralised, already inherently "poetic" in the sense of being alive with human and dramaturgical meaning: specifically with the meaning of human difference'. Gillies argues that the new Renaissance geography generated 'a new poetry to make sense of its radically incongruous world-image', but that it was 'still enthralled to the imagery of the past', and he provides illuminating examples of the way in which each imagined geography invites a reading in terms of the 'poetic' energies of the other geography: classical contexts and the Renaissance discovery and idea of the New World join together in Shakespeare's mental map. There is much of interest here on Renaissance map-making, on the exotic and barbarian in Shakespeare, especially on his inventive 'imitation' of Ovid in *Titus Andronicus,* and also on the distinction between the Venetian reality (and myth) and the Venice which represented the *idea* of the world maritime capital, which Elizabethan merchants had in mind for London. This is an original, well-researched study, offering depth and scope, with a very useful selection of twenty plates showing maps, titles and frontispieces of atlases, and other examples of cosmographic iconography.

Shakespeare in the New Europe, edited by Michael Hattaway, Boika Sokolova and Derek Roper, offers twenty new essays on how the interpretation and production of Shakespeare have been affected by changes to the political map of Europe since 1989, by scholars from Croatia, Cracow, Bulgaria, Berlin, Prague and Seville. The section 'Subversive Shakespeare, East and West' includes a stimulating piece called 'Shakespeare in Czech: An Essay in Cultural Semantics', in which Martin Hilský shows how Shakespeare was used to oppose the obviously corrupt subjective art of the 'bourgeois' writers ('It is surprising how little refashioning Shakespeare needed to be integrated into the official Marxist doctrine of realism') and how he was 'almost fiendishly good' at surviving – even the Prague Spring reforms, when the masque of the Muscovites in *Love's Labour's Lost* became a dangerous political joke. As Hilský nicely puts it: 'Shakespeare was subversive, and, which is more interesting, he had no other choice.' Other essays in the volume include Mark Sokolyansky's engaging discussion of Shakespearean irony and recent Russian experience; Alexander Shurbanov and Boika Sokolova on Bulgarian appropriations of Shakespeare; Manfred Pfister on Hamlets made in Germany East and West; and Rafael Portillo and Manuel J. Gomez-Lara on 'Shakespeare in the New Spain'. Another welcome volume to follow the excellent *Foreign Shakespeare* of last year (see *YWES* 74.199–200; 207).

Shakespeare and Cultural Traditions: The Selected Proceedings of the International Shakespeare Association World Congress, Tokyo, 1991 (eds. Tetsuo Kishi, Roger Pringle and Stanley Wells) is, as its title suggests, a multicultural assessment of Shakespeare. The four plenary lectures are here: Stephen Greenblatt on witchcraft and *Macbeth*; Germaine Greer's analysis of the proletariat in Shakespeare's plays; Ruth Nevo's examination of Freudian perspectives on *Hamlet*; and Takashi Sasayama's study of tragedy and emotion in Shakespeare and Chikamatsu. In other papers relevant to this section, Alexander Leggatt considers the question: 'What did Bearbaiting Mean to Shakespeare?'; E. A. J. Honnigmann offers a new reading of Shakespeare's will; Dennis Bartholomeusz discusses how 'Shakespeare Imagines the Orient: The Orient Imagines Shakespeare'; Tetsuo Kishi writes on the question of Japanese translation and different cultural contexts; and Werner Habicht examines the competing claims of Romanticism and anti-Romanticism and the German Shakespeare tradition. One worry I have is that the volume reflects a current trend for twenty-minute paper conferences which often seems to result in a less than satisfactory book, either because the essays have been too ambitious for their length, or too little is argued too thinly. A question which conference organizers and delegates might be encouraged to address?

The declared aim of *Shakespeare's Italy: Functions of Italian Locations in Renaissance Drama* (eds. Michele Marrapodi et al.) is to 'supply a fresh approach to a much discussed subject'. The subtitle refers to the chapters on 'Italian Vices' and Italy staged in English Renaissance drama, while chapters specifically devoted to Shakespeare plays include three on *Romeo and Juliet:* Angela Locatelli's 'The Fictional World of *Romeo and Juliet:* Cultural Connotations of an Italian Setting', Sergio Rossi's 'Duelling in the Italian Manner', and Giorgio Melchiori's '"In fair Verona": *commedia erudita* into Romantic Comedy'. The volume also includes Harry Levin's 'Shakespeare's Italians', 'Agostino Lombardo's 'The Veneto, Metatheatre and Shakespeare', Roberta Mullini's 'Streets Squares and Courts: Venice as a Stage in Shakespeare and Jonson', and Leo Scalingar's 'The Idea of Venice in Shakespeare and Jonson'. This is a useful collection on an important Shakespeare topic. For this reader, though, the material in the volume could have been perhaps a little fresher, and the subjects tackled with more weight.

Two volumes that arrived too late to be included in *YWES* 74 are Dirk Delabastita's *There's a Double Tongue: An Investigation into the Translation of Shakespeare's Wordplay with Particular Reference to 'Hamlet'*, and Dirk Delabastita and Lieven D'hulst (eds), *European Shakespeares: Translating Shakespeare in the Romantic Age.* In the first, Delabastita provides a thorough examination of Shakespeare's punning and its translation, concluding with an anthology of the puns in *Hamlet*, with a selection of diverse translations. The second volume gathers together a valuable collection of essays examining translations of Shakespeare in Hungary, eighteenth-century Italy and West Slavic literatures, and others. As a non-expert on the subject, I found many helpful insights in both books.

In a wide-ranging essay, 'Shakespeare in the Tropics: From High Modernism to New Historicism' (*Rep* 45.1–25), Richard Halpern argues that the twentieth century's reading of Shakespeare has been 'fundamentally mediated by a primitivist discourse whose disciplinary language is anthropology' even when this influence is not immediately apparent, and usefully traces the persistence and transformation of modernism's colonial allegory in new historicist criticism. In the same volume, the relationship between anthropology and literary criticism is examined by one of the subjects of Halpern's discussion, Stephen Greenblatt ('The Eating of the Soul', 97–116). A suggestive essay which, at the same time, functions as a kind of defence of new historicist procedures, it considers the treatment of death – natural and unnatural – in the tragedies and the numerous instances of 'unvoiced, unexplained extinction' and of the 'missing mothers' in Shakespeare.

In his full-length study, *A Buddhist's Shakespeare: Affirming Self-Deconstructions*, James Howe describes his book as 'a partial record of one American Buddhist's transaction with particular Shakespearean texts', and suggests that the insights of Buddhism resemble those of Derrida and Foucault but are 'more affirmative' and have 'less agonistic' implications. Shakespeare, Howe says, frequently performs the Dharmic/Derridean function of dissolution: he often subverts not only the apparent meanings of his texts but also their authority as texts, thereby disrupting their 'normal' relations with their audience (or reader), and changing his role as author by making it visible.

Shakespeare: The Jacobean Plays is the companion volume to Susan Bassnett's *The Elizabethan Plays* (*YWES* 74. 205). Philip C. McGuire examines only seven of the twelve Jacobean plays, but particularly commendable is the emphasis on the effects of performance tradition, editorial practice and critical consensus on audience and reader reception to the plays. Giving less attention to current critical approaches than does Bassnett, McGuire helpfully considers the significant differences between the Elizabethan and Jacobean plays, as well as the impact of the King's Men acquiring performance rights at the indoor playhouse, Blackfriars, in 1608, when they were required to perform plays effectively in both the indoor theatre and the Globe, for both old and new audiences.

Most of the eighteen essays collected in *Reclamations of Shakespeare* (ed. Hoenselaars) were originally presented as papers for a conference on 'Shakespeare: The Myth and the Makers', which aimed to assess the degree to which appreciation of Shakespeare has been an engagement with the myths rehearsed in the plays, and how readers, critics, directors and so on have extended the act of myth making. Of the chapters relevant to this section, C. C. Barfoot gives an account of *Antony and Cleopatra* by way of its messengers, providing useful tables on 'Entries of Named and Unnamed Messengers', 'Reactions to Messengers', 'References to Letters' and so on. M. T. Jones-Davies examines 'Shakespeare and the Myth of Hercules'; Mark Berge writes on the theme of irresolution in *King Lear*; and Pierre Eselin discusses myth, memory and music in *Richard II*, *Hamlet* and *Othello*. Andrew Gurr offers an entertaining and thought-provoking essay on a hitherto neglected topic – the significance of hats on Shakespeare's stage – in an attempt to recapture the 'body language' of hats as 'signifiers of social status and social courtesies' that we have lost, and which leads to an intriguing new reading of Hamlet's cry at Ophelia's graveside, 'This is I, / Hamlet the Dane'. Other chapters examine Asimov, Wilde and Burgess as the makers of 'The Myth of Sweet Master Shakespeare'(Paul J. C. M. Franssen); while Art Balk writes suggestively on Jules Laforgue's rewriting of Shakespeare's *Hamlet*, to argue that the French novella constitutes a self-conscious direct charge against Shakespeare's authority. Robert E. Pearson and William Uricchio have provided a fascinating and thoughtful essay on the cultural dynamics of the conditions of production and reception of Shakespeare by focusing on the critical and popular responses to Beerbohm Tree's theatre productions and his (lost) tercentenary film of *Macbeth*.

Shakespeare Reread: The Texts in New Contexts (ed. Russ McDonald) aims, with varying degrees of success, to find ways of close reading making use of recent critical methods. Of the essays relevant to this section, Barbara Hodgdon examines 'the performing and performed body' in 'The Critic, the Poor Player, Prince Hamlet and the Lady in the Dark', and George Wright looks closely at the relationship between metre and characterization.

In *Shakespeare's Christian Dimension* Roy Battenhouse has edited an anthology of ninety-two pieces of commentary on twenty-six plays, reprinted mostly from the 1950s to the late 1980s, to 'reappreciate the Christian roots of Shakespeare's art'. Battenhouse first traces the development of Christian critical approaches, then introduces the commentaries on the influence of the Christian heritage in the shaping of Shakespeare's plays. Each section is introduced by Battenhouse with a supplementary bibliography and all the commentaries have been abridged (usually to two or three pages).The longest sections, are, as one might expect, on *Merchant of Venice* and *Hamlet*. Influential studies of the last fifty years, including Battenhouse's own 1969 *Shakespearean Tragedy*, are represented here, though judging by some absences, such as Roy Walker's 1948 study in which Hamlet's decision to return to Elsinore is compared to Christ's decision to go to Jerusalem (an interpretation very different from Battenhouse's), it is difficult to assess how comprehensively the book satisfies Battenhouse's belief, stated in the preface, that 'today's students deserve an alternative' to 'modern day approaches' which question whether Shakespeare's art is for all time 'so that informed debate may be possible'. Battenhouse also has a piece on Christian sources in Shakespeare in *Connotations* 3.iii.226–42.

Linda Woodbridge takes issue with psychoanalytical criticism's 'overemphasis' on the sexual, and with new historicists for 'reducing history to politics', in *The Scythe of Saturn: Shakespeare and Magical Thinking*, to argue that Shakespeare is *not* our contemporary, but shared a magical mindset with his contemporaries. Woodbridge makes a distinction between conscious magical belief, which accepts the possibility of human supernatural agency, sometimes aided by divine or demonic forces, and magical thinking, which is the unconscious residue of such belief. She locates the themes of dismemberment, fertility and rivalry between generations that are to be found in the plays under the ambiguous sign of Saturn, and the scythe which was the harvesting tool of a fertility god, lord of seedtime and harvest; but which was also related to the sickle with which Cronos castrated his father. An informative and interesting study.

Shakespeare as Prompter: The Amending Imagination and the Therapeutic Process by Murray Cox and Alice Theilgaard is a remarkable book which shows how theatre and therapy are alike in endeavouring to 'call into existence that which was not there before'. It demonstrates how Shakespeare can be used in therapy as a prompter, to help patients in their process of recovery. There is much in this book for critics, directors and students of Shakespeare.

Three essays seeking to 'engage afresh with the relation between Shakespeare and materalist feminism' make up *The Weyward Sisters: Shakespeare and Feminist Politics* by Dympna Callaghan, Lorraine Helms and Jyotsna Singh. Singh argues that the sexual labour of the prostitute in early modern England is predicated on the repression of female desire, drawing on contemporary narratives to examine prostitutes' roles in *1 and 2 Henry IV*, *Measure for Measure* and *Othello*; Callaghan discusses 'The Ideology of Romantic Love: The Case of *Romeo and Juliet*' to develop 'an explicitly Marxist understanding of the new formations of sexual love that nascent capitalism required'; while Helms, working against what she calls 'the interpretive restrictions that the conditions of the maculinist stage enforce as well as those inscribed in the play texts', describes her hypothetical production of *Macbeth* in which the Weyward Sisters appear as a troupe of clowns and acrobats.

With *Daemonic Figures: Shakespeare and the Question of Conscience*, Ned Lukacher has provided us with an important study on the influence of Shakespeare's works on Heidegger and Freud's interpretations of conscience, arguing that Shakespeare overturns traditional interpretations and suggests a new concept of the relation of language to self-consciousness: a scholarly work which productively examines Plato, the Pauline Epistles, Kant and Hegel, Nietzsche and Foucault on the subject.

ShS 46 is on 'Shakespeare and Sexuality', a collection which might have been rather more inspiring than the title promised (and surely someone could have come up with a more original idea for its dust jacket than a still of a reclining Claire Higgins in the 1992 RSC production of *Antony and Cleopatra*, which is reviewed inside). Besides an introduction by Ann Thompson, and essays from Juliet Dusinberre on *As You Like It*, John Astington on *Twelfth Night*, Catherine Bates, Thomas Clayton (both on *Othello*) and Kenneth C. Bennett on *The Winter's Tale*, Lawrence Danson writes on the ideology of marital possessiveness, with perhaps too much reliance on uncritical footnotes (69–79); Russ McDonald argues that the complex verse patterns of the late plays are intimately related to Shakespeare's 'imaginative recovery of the feminine', focusing on *Coriolanus* and *Antony and Cleopatra* (19–106); William C. Carroll suggests that female sexuality in Shakespeare is articulated as linguistic transgression (107–19); and Michael Hattaway analyses misogyny in Shakespeare's works (121–35). Two notable contributions are provided by Michael Dobson who writes entertainingly on 'Bowdler and Britannia: Shakespeare and the National Libido' (137–44), and by Margret de Grazia, who examines the history of the Sonnets' reception to argue that 'The Scandal of Shakespeare's Sonnets' is the denial of homosexuality in them by post-Renaissance cultures, and goes on to put forward the view that for contemporaries the real scandal in the Sonnets would have been the risk of miscegenation with a dark lady (35–49).

In 'Breaking the Illusion of Being: Shakespeare and the Performance of the Self', Emily C. Bartels takes Robert Weimann's terms of the *locus* and *platea* styles and spaces of acting to examine 'Hamlet's impulse to reinscribe or reiterate conventional roles and use them as the passion and cue for acting and being'. I am not sure I learned very much from this.

(b) Comedies and Late Plays

Michael Cordner, Peter Holland and John Kerrigan introduce their volume of essays on *English Comedy* by lamenting the paucity of comic theory compared with that devoted to tragedy, but their own introduction does little to remedy this state of affairs. A couple of the essays are more concerned with individual plays than with comedy in general; of the others, Stephen Orgel's 'The Comedian as the Character C' understands comedy very broadly, as 'the largest condition of drama', which enables him to talk (for instance,) about *Coriolanus* and *Titus Andronicus* as well as *The Tempest* and *The Winter's Tale*. Orgel does not really seem to want to write about comedy as such in this essay, and is more interested in meditating on matters such as the relations between handwriting, forgeries and character, about which he is characteristically interesting. Jonas Barish's examination of 'Mixed Verse and Prose in Shakespearean Comedy' remarks that the prose is often more highly structured than the poetry, concluding that alternations between the two 'usually have more to do with local contrast . . . than with any fixed principle such as social degree, sex, or presumed level of politeness'. Adrian Poole and Eric Griffiths write, respectively, about 'Laughter, Forgetting and Shakespeare", and 'Ludwig Wittgenstein and the Comedy of Errors'.

This is a patchy collection; so too is another edited collection, Frances Teague's *Acting Funny: Comic Theory and Practice in Shakespeare's Plays*. Teague's introductory essay also begins by lamenting the paucity of theory on comedy, going on to give, for students, a decent summary of the main contributions thus far. Again like *English Comedy*, Teague's conception of comedy is broad: her own essay concerns *Othello* and examines what she calls the play's 'fundamentally comic structure', pointing out analogues between '*Othello* and New Comedy' (some of which seem to be rather incidental). Of the remainder of essays concerning general comedy, Susan Baker's 'Comic Material: "Shakespeare" in the Classic Detective Story' starts off by detailing similarities between detective fiction and Shakespearean comedy, but turns into an essay which is much more concerned with listing instances where Shakespeare appears in detective stories. M. Arogyasami promises us 'an Indian Perspective' on 'Shakespeare's Treatment of Comic Sentiment' but writes about *Hamlet*, *Macbeth* and *Antony and Cleopatra*, and in an unfocused way. Ejner J. Jensen argues in 'Knowing Aforehand: Audience Preparation and the Comedies of Shakespeare' that Shakespeare creates within his plays the 'condition of our response' to them, repeating conventions in order to shape our response to characters.

Much more directed is Jean Howard's treatment of cross-dressing in her *The Stage and Social Struggle in Early Modern England*. Cross-dressing, Howard argues, may seem to question strict notions of sexual difference, but in fact often acts to reinscribe the old, conservative *mores:* the 'telos of the dramatic narrative' of *Twelfth Night*, she claims, is to 'release the woman from the prison of masculine attire and to return her to her proper . . . position as a wife'; *The Merchant of Venice* and *As You Like It* she acknowledges as somewhat more progressive, but apparently almost despite herself.

As far as I know, no journal articles appeared on *The Comedy of Errors* this year, but together with *The Taming of the Shrew* the play was the subject of a chapter of Lorna Hutson's book, *The Usurer's Daughter*. For Hutson, Shakespeare solves the problem of representing women within the mode of the Terentian plot by identifying the 'dramatic productivity' of 'error' with the representation of women rather than men; in Shakespeare, female sexuality becomes the 'space of opportunity itself' so that men are free to err, the moral accountability of their financial and sexual misconduct being displaced onto the sexual misconduct of women. Hutson's argument is very densely written: I found myself wishing she had spent a little more time unpacking it. I was surprised that she did not make any explicit connection between the thesis of her book and that of Eve Kosofsky Sedgwick's *Between Men* (CUP, 1993), with which, in its theory, *The Usurer's Daughter* has much in common. But this is an important and challenging book.

One of the better essays in *English Comedy* is Richard Beadle's 'Crab's Pedigree', which examines the history and function of the dog Crab in *Two Gentlemen of Verona* and traces the iconography of weeping dogs in Middle English culture. In an often perceptive article entitled ' "O Me, the Word Choose!": Female Voice and Catechetical Ritual in *The Two Gentlemen of Verona* and *The Merchant of Venice*' (*ShakS* 22.122–40), Lori Schroeder Haslem examines private conversation between women in the two plays, concluding that whilst in *Two Gentlemen of Verona* female speech operates only as an illusion of counteraction to the patriarchal world of the plays, in *The Merchant of Venice* it is allowed to play a more challenging role. A different interpretation of Shakespeare's politics is offered by Jean Howard's treatment of *Much Ado About Nothing* in *The Stage and Social Struggle*. Comparing it with Dekker's *The Whore of Babylon*, Howard argues that Shakespeare's play much more effectively 'performs the work of ideology' in which what is arbitrary passes as inevitable, and through which contradictions are mystified and iconoclastic or resistant voices suppressed: almost everything in the play is designed to shore up a 'hierarchical, male-dominated social order'.

The most substantial journal essay on *Much Ado About Nothing* this year was Marta Straznicky's 'Shakespeare and the Government of Comedy' (*ShakS* 22.141–71), which also addresses the play's politics but which comes to very different conclusions about them. Straznicky examines the 'nongovernmental power relations' (specifically, those encapsulated in language) she believes overlooked by new historicist critical concentration on monarchical power; these forms of power, she argues, 'promote a particular kind of social equilibrium' which benefits the welfare of the community, frustrating more self-interested behaviour that tends to be exhibited most often by aristocratic men. Much less substantial is Barbara Everett's '*Much Ado About Nothing*: The Unsociable Comedy' (in Cordner et al., *English Comedy*), which does not really go very far, and has a tendency to declare things which one might have thought were fairly obvious: that seriousness and laughter are both essential to Shakespearean comedy, for example. Ian House, in '*Much Ado About Nothing*: A Line Restored to its Speaker' (*N&Q* 41.487), argues that Leonato and not Benedick should stop Beatrice's mouth at the end of the play.

Another note, this time on *The Taming of the Shrew* and *The Merchant of Venice*, is offered by Anthony Brian Taylor, who examines 'Shakespeare's Debts to Golding' (*N&Q* 41.477–9) in those two plays. Hoping to liberate the play from the accusations of sexism to which it has been subjected, G. A. Wilkes reads the ending of *The Taming of the Shrew* as a continuation of a game initiated earlier in the play in which Katherina and Petruchio operate as a team ('The Stupefied Bystander: Complicity in *The Taming of the Shrew*?', *SSEng* 20.117–20). Annabel Patterson takes up a similar question rather more successfully in her contribution to *Shakespeare and Cultural Traditions* (eds Tetsuo Kishi et al.). She argues that the frame, in this play and in *The Rape of Lucrece*, mediates the two texts' more overt political messages; she has interesting things to say as well about the way in which a network of linkages between the words 'comedy' and 'commodity' signifies in *The Taming of the Shrew*. Also interested in the semantics of the play is Lynda E. Boose's '*The Taming of the Shrew*, Good Husbandry, and Enclosure', which appeared in the extremely good collection *Shakespeare Reread* (ed. Russ McDonald), one of whose aims (and achievements) is to re-establish the practice of good close reading. Boose situates her historicist discussion of the play in an examination of popular protest about enclosure in the 1590s; the word 'shrew', she argues, underwent a semantic shift between the fourteenth and seventeenth centuries, which transformed its origins in class invective into its more contemporary gendered usage. Finally, like Patterson, P. J. Gabriner is also interested in the Induction to the play in his cogently and economically argued article, 'Hierarchy, Harmony and Happiness: Another Look at the Hunting Dogs in the "Induction" to *The Taming of the Shrew*' (in Hoenselaars, *Reclamations of Shakespeare*). Gabriner connects the conversation about the hunting dogs with a similar dialogue in *A Midsummer Night's Dream*; both, he points out, discourse on hierarchy in nature, and appear in comedies whose thrust will be to clarify proper forms of social order.

Nothing terrifically exciting appeared on *A Midsummer Night's Dream* this year. Rick Bowers takes issue with the suggestion that 'Pyramus and Thisbe' includes lines criticizing Thomas Phaer, the translator of Virgil ('Thomas Phaer and the London Literati', *N&Q* 41.33–5); whilst in a rambling piece that goes nowhere slowly, Harry Guest says he wants to talk about 'Aspects of the *Dream:* Shakespeare, Purcell and Britten' (in Holger Klein and Christopher Smith, eds, *The Opera and Shakespeare*). Jane Galligani Casey also addresses musical aspects of the *Dream* ('"Hounds and Echo in Conjunction": Musical Structure in *A Midsummer Night's Dream*', *StHum* 21.31–44). Casey argues that there is an integral relation between sight and sound in the play, and details analogies between the structures of the play and of polyphonic secular song forms such as the madrigal.

Hounds seem to have struck a critical chord this year, in fact: I am suddenly conscious that I have already mentioned three articles which are wholly or partly about dogs. Yet another is Bruce Thomas Boehrer's 'Bestial Buggery in *A Midsummer Night's Dream*' (in David Lee Miller et al., eds, *The Production of English Renaissance Culture*). Boehrer thinks that Theseus's 'dewlapp'd hounds' are a reference to the male member. The play, he declares, is 'patently about bestiality' and 'a bit like a Protestant marriage manual constructed out of animal pornography'. There is actually a more interesting argument embedded in this essay, that anxieties concerning the corruption of human nature by bestial and/or female others underlie the representation of the 'bestial prodigy' of Bottom and Titania, but this argument has a tendency to get swamped in what would appear to be iconoclasm for its own sweet sake; after which it was something of a relief to move on to Peter Holland's examination of 'Theseus' Shadows in *A Midsummer Night's Dream*' (*ShS* 46.139–51). This opens with an interesting discussion of the point of source studies in general, and goes on to make some intelligent comments on the 'sources' of *A Midsummer Night's Dream* in particular, concluding that the operation of a source remains a matter for critical debate, as it is almost impossible to delimit the sphere of its influence. One of the better articles in Teague's *Acting Funny* is Marcia McDonald's 'Bottom's Space: Historicizing Comic Theory and Practice in *A Midsummer Night's Dream*', which reads the play as an intervention in a literary debate about the status of comedy in Elizabethan England, and argues that Bottom represents the stage itself, being protean, unpredictable in its effects and ambiguous in its relation to authority. Finally, William Empson's two essays on the play, one ('Elizabethan Spirits') a response to Frances Yates, the other a longer version of an essay first published in Empson's *Essays on Shakespeare*, have this year been issued in Empson's *Essays on Renaissance Literature* (ed. John Haffenden).

Love's Labour's Lost saw one note and one long article devoted to it this year, in addition to a republication of Anne Barton's 1953 essay in her *Essays, Mainly*

Shakespearean. Brian Striar's 'Note on *Love's Labour's Lost* v.ii.417–418' argues that the line in question is a translation from the *Aeneid* (*N&Q* 41.33), whilst Ursula Hehl uses Freud and contemporary psychoanalytic theory to examine 'Elements of Narcissistic Personality Disorders in *Love's Labour's Lost*' (*L&P* 40.48–70). Hehl argues that the play's 'failure' to provide a conventional ending is contiguous with a recurrent theme of failure in the play, and that this emphasis on failure is symptomatic of the narcissistic personality disorder to which most of the men in the play, and especially Navarre and Berowne, appear to be subject. This is a well-written and generally convincing application of theory to the text.

Psychoanalytic theory, this time on mothers, brothers and female psychosexual development, is also invoked by William Kerrigan in his discussion of 'Female Friends and Fraternal Enemies in *As You Like It*' (in Valeria Finucci and Regina Schwartz, eds, *Desire in the Renaissance*). Like Hehl, Kerrigan also notes a difference between male and female behaviour, but his conclusions are less optimistic than hers: *As You Like It*, he argues, effects a banishment of a dual heterosexual male dread – of women and of homosexuality. Some of Kerrigan's conclusions are shared by Susanne L. Wofford, whose complex essay, alive to the paradoxes and contradictions in the play, examines the connections between speech acts and sexual politics in *As You Like It* ('"To You I Give Myself, For I am Yours": Erotic Performance and Theatrical Performatives in *As You Like It*', in McDonald, *Shakespeare Reread*). The play's cross-dressing, she argues, serves to 'contain the threat of a powerful female figure': a woman can 'only return herself to those who already possess her, enacting in her performative the social possibility that preceded her utterance'. Henk Gras's 'Enchanting Metadrama: Shakespeare's Use of the Boy Actor in *As You Like It*' (in Hoenselaars, *Reclamations of Shakespeare*) is somewhat misleadingly titled, since he touches on this subject only sporadically over the course of his essay, preferring to 'sketch several aspects of the literary and theatrical contexts'. Similarly unrewarding is Donald A. Bloom's 'Dwindling into Wifehood: The Romantic Power of the Witty Heroine in Shakespeare, Dryden, Congreve and Austen' (in Gail Finney, ed., *Look Who's Laughing*); Bloom thinks that 'like much of Shakespeare . . . *As You Like It* can be confused by excessively subtle readings, which, fascinating though they may be, lose track of its fundamental simplicity'. A note by Steven Doloff links 'Jaques's "Weeping" and Ovid's Cyparissus' (*N&Q* 41.487–8), and one by Fred Somkin speculates on a possible spoof of Aquinas in Act IV of *Twelfth Night* ('A Note of the Wit of the Hermit of Prague', *N&Q* 41.489). The two plays are discussed together by Anne Barton in her '*As You Like It* and *Twelfth Night*: Shakespeare's Sense of an Ending' (again, reprinted in her *Essays, Mainly Shakespearean*).

Laurie E. Osborne offers a performance history of the way in which different promptbooks (1791–1883) have responded to the problem of *Twelfth Night*'s unreconciled Antonio, reading those responses in terms of the increase in the persecution of homosexuality in early nineteenth-century England ('Antonio's Pardon', *SQ* 45.108–14). And Robin Headlam Wells's *Elizabethan Mythologies* includes a chapter on the function of love and song in *Twelfth Night*: music in the play, he argues, reflects an idea 'not of social harmony and discord, but of mutability', the brevity of the songs reflecting the ephemeral, transitory resonances of their content.

Two journal articles appeared this year on *The Merchant of Venice*, one extremely good, the other not so. J.Auffret's 'The Merchant of Venice – From Tyre to London' was the latter (*CahiersE* 46.23–58). Charles Spinosa's 'The Transformation of Intentionality: Debt and Contract in *The Merchant of Venice*' (*ELR* 24.370–409) is in another class of criticism altogether, and in my view was one of the most important articles on Shakespeare published this year. This learned and challenging piece argues that the current legalist consensus on the play is deficient in that it 'fails to concern itself with how legal change is motivated by . . . broader changes in social practices', practices which Spinosa details through painstaking historicist research. The Venetians are exemplary citizens in that they 'cast their own intentions from the point of view of the other'; Shylock, conversely, 'conducts his business by instinct and gets results by developing relationships' with others. This is only part of the argument of an essay which is at once wide-ranging, original and consistently thought-provoking, and equally at home with the text and its context. One other essay on the play appeared in an edited collection. This was Avraham Oz's ' "Which is the Merchant Here? And Which the Jew?": Riddles of Identity in *The Merchant of Venice*', which accounts for the play's representation of 'ethnoreligious identity' through a discussion of the two conflicting conceptions of private property which Oz believes underlie the play (in Kishi et al., *Shakespeare and Cultural Traditions*).

Like Spinosa, Rosemary Kegl also uses contemporary legal records, as well as domestic conduct books, to underpin her Marxist argument about *The Merry Wives of Windsor* (' "The Adoption of Abominable Terms": Middle Classes, Merry Wives, and the Insults that Shape Windsor', *ELH* 61.253–78, and also in her *The Rhetoric of Concealment*). Shakespeare's 'abominable terms', she argues, 'promote collective identities – "townsmen" and "gentlemen" ' whose 'very different positions within the feudal and emerging capitalist modes of production . . . [and] within very different structures of oppression' have been obscured by conventional critical accounts of the play's 'middle class' or 'bourgeoisie'. The play's middle class is 'not a *thing* to be defined, but, instead, a *process* of constructing alliances among groups characterized by their multiple and often contradictory . . . interests'. Patricia Parker's 'Interpreting Through Wordplay: *The Merry Wives of Windsor*' is the most obviously 'academic' of the contributions to McIver's and Stevenson's *Teaching With Shakespeare* (the other contributions are more clearly aimed at students). She addresses the question of the link between the Act 4 grammar lesson and the rest of the play, arguing ingeniously that a network of wordplay provides these links: 'translation' meaning not only the translation of words, but also the purloining of property and women. Anthony Brian Taylor's ' "Let Vultures Gripe Thy Guts": Pistol Cursing Falstaff in Particularly Apt Terms' (*N&Q* 41.37–8) speculates on a possible allusion here to the *Aeneid*, and Anne Barton's essay on 'Falstaff and the Comic Community' is reprinted in her *Essays, Mainly Shakespearean*, as are two essays on the late plays and tragi-comedies. Helen Wilcox's 'Gender and Genre in Shakespeare's Tragicomedies' (in Hoenselaars, *Reclamations of Shakespeare*) argues that myths about the tragicomedies and romances are 'particularly strongly gendered', 'constructed by generations of critical readings as dramas of lonely male figures', and that tragicomedy 'may be characterised as a maternal form', for example; her essay also includes a thoughtful and perceptive discussion of motherhood in the plays, and her contention that the links between sexuality and dramatic form are worth pursuing further seems right.

To some degree, this is what Mary Bly attempts to do in 'Imagining Consummation: Women's Erotic Language in Comedies of Dekker and Shakespeare'(in Finney, *Look Who's Laughing*). Bly locates *All's Well* at the peak of a brief dramatic experiment with overtly desiring heroines, and argues that the play's fusion of Petrarchan verse with the open expression of female desire is one reason behind its designation as a problem play. Its use of the bed-trick facilitates its negotiation of this experiment by allowing a sexual act to be undertaken by women for chaste motives. Two other articles on *All's Well* also appeared this year. Like Bly, Mary Free concentrates on the text's genre ('*All's Well That Ends Well* as Noncomic Comedy', in Teague, *Acting Funny*). She argues that two elements 'hold the comic at bay' in the play: its use of marriage as an expression of power, and what she calls a 'metalanguage of power' underlying the hierarchies that the play presents. The other article is Lynne Simpson's psychoanalytic treatment of the text ('The Failure to Mourn in *All's Well That Ends Well*, *ShakS* 22.172–88). This was so poorly written that I often had difficulty following it, but I think she is arguing that Helena's inability to mourn derives from unresolved Oedipal guilt, and that the cure for her failure to mourn is effected in the play by the gratification of her wish for a baby from her father, this gratification itself effected by two 'substitutions': impregnation by Bertram, and the exchange of a hymen for a wedding ring.

Several articles came out this year on *Measure For Measure*. Two essays which took different routes to rather similar conclusions were published in *PQ*. In one of them, Karl F. Zender offers a thoughtful examination of 'Isabella's Choice' (*PQ* 73.77–93), arguing that Isabella's failure to denounce Angelo derives not only from the absence of an impartial authority figure whom she could petition, but also from her desire not to speak, seen as reflective of an increasing focus within the comedies on 'more problematic interior restraints' rather than on external obstacles. I quite liked the unabashedly humanist tenor of Zender's article (he is very interested in what he calls Isabella's 'moral growth') but I found similar moves in Mark Taylor's '"Farther Privileges": Conflict and Change in *Measure For Measure*' (*PQ* 73.169–93) much harder to take. In this piece, Taylor fuses an interest in characters' growth with a psychological model adopted from Karen Horney's *Our Inner Conflicts*, arguing that the Duke's proposal in the play can be understood by reading the play as critical of the sexual abstinence it portrays. Critical it may indeed be, but I was unconvinced by Taylor's analysis of Angelo and the Duke as, respectively, 'aggressive' and 'compliant' types, and very dubious about some of the sexual readings Taylor offers.

Carolyn E. Brown offers some somewhat more convincing readings in her 'The Wooing of Duke Vincentio and Isabella of *Measure For Measure*: "The Image of It Gives [Them] Content"' (*ShakS* 22.189–219), but, like Taylor, slips into some unfortunately naive terms in defence of her adoption of psychoanalytic models to discuss the play ('the human nature [Shakespeare's creative genius] captured has not changed'). For Brown, Isabella and the Duke's involvement in the bed-trick gratifies their common fantasizing about sexual intercourse; Isabella is made 'to recognize the latent sexual import of her actions, to recognize that she seduced Angelo' by the conclusion of the play. In a rather better essay on the play, Julia Briggs examines the prose sources (such as Boccaccio and Sidney) for the bed-tricks of *All's Well* and *Measure For Measure*. She argues that in his transcription of these sources, Shakespeare exaggerates the conflict between desire and marriage, and that he uses the bed-trick to bring transgression and marriage together, and to force sexual dissidents back into the community ('Shakespeare's Bed-Tricks', *EIC* 44.293–314). Stephen Derry offers a (rather unconvincing) note on 'Time and Punishment in *Measure For Measure* (*N&Q* 41.489–90), arguing that the discrepancy between Claudio's assertion that the laxity has lasted nineteen years, and the

Duke's that it has lasted fourteen, derives from the fact that each refers to a different period of time. Finally, the play's genre is treated by Robert. N. Watson in his *The Rest Is Silence*; he argues that the play's relations to tragedy, comedy and tragicomedy emerge through its treatment of death and sexuality: subverting the binarism between procreative love and death, the play is tragicomic because mortality 'remains imperfectly refuted at the centre of [its] resolution'.

The Winter's Tale generated considerable interest from critics this year. B. J. Sokol's *Art and Illusion in The Winter's Tale* claims that for Shakespeare 'appreciation of the traditions of the great Italian artists . . . was important . . . but . . . in *The Winter's Tale* [he] was neither an uncritical nor an unconscious partaker of these traditions'. Sokol's title is somewhat misleading, since much of his interest in this book is devoted to the psychology of the play's characters: whilst he situates his examination of the statue in a discussion of the painted statue in early seventeenth-century England, for example, his discussion of Leontes leaves the world of art behind, invoking instead a variety of different theoretical models such as Kleinian psychoanalysis and Mary Douglas's anthropology. This results in the book's chapters seeming more like separate essays, a problem exacerbated by the periodic adoptions of different kinds of psychoanalytic theory which are inadequately reconciled with each other; there are, however, a number of fruitful discussions.

The three articles which appeared this year on *The Winter's Tale* are all, to a greater or less degree, source studies. Janet S. Wolf argues that whilst traditional accounts of the relationship between the play and the myth of Persephone align Persephone with Perdita and Demeter with Hermione, it is also possible to read Paulina as Demeter, and Hermione as Persephone ('"Like an Old Tale Still": Paulina, "Triple Hecate", and the Persephone Myth in *The Winter's Tale*', in Elizabeth T. Hayes, ed., *Images of Persephone: Feminist Readings in Western Literature*). Sara Hanna offers a convincing examination of the relevance of Plutarch's *Life of Dion* and Sophocles' *Antigone* to the play in her 'Voices Against Tyranny: Greek Sources of *The Winter's Tale*' (*CML* 14.335–44), and Barbara A. Mowat examines 'Rogues, Shepherds and the Counterfeit Distressed: Texts and Infracontexts of *The Winter's Tale* 4.3' (*ShakS* 22.58–76). Despite the jargon-ridden preamble, perseverance rewards one with a decent and convincing historicist account of the way in which the figure of Autolycus resonates within the contemporary discourse of the itinerant underclass.

In a note on the significance of 'cipher', Michael W. Price examines 'Shakespeare's *The Winter's Tale* 1.2.1–9' (*Expl* 52.140–2). John Pitcher offers a perceptive comment on the play's bear, connecting it with the lost melodrama *Cox of Collumpton* ('"Fronted with the Sight of a Bear"', *N&Q* 41.47–53). M. W. A. Smith continues an old argument, also in *N&Q*, about the authorship of *Sir Thomas More* and *Pericles* ('*Sir Thomas More*, *Pericles* and Stylometry', *N&Q* 41.55–8).

Cymbeline saw three journal articles devoted to it this year, including Elena Glazov-Corrigan's complex, lucid essay, 'Speech Acts, Generic Differences, and the Curious Case of *Cymbeline*' (*SEL* 34.379–99). This very fine piece examines *Cymbeline*'s genre by way of an analysis of its language, the 'hidden mechanism', Glazov-Corrigan argues, for the play's lack of unity. She first distinguishes between tragic and comic usages of language: tragedies employ 'a language that binds . . . unconditionally', she argues, whilst comedies, conversely, 'concern themselves with . . . a multiplicity of fracturing and misadventure' which lies between speech and action. In *Cymbeline* these two modes are 'emphatically left behind', and 'all . . . progressions [of words into actions] are ruptured or deferred'. The play diverges from tragedy 'because the play's players direct action without subduing it'; and from comedy 'because devoid of authority, they cannot initiate unauthorized patterns of enactment'. I found this a difficult article, and one to which I will have to return, but I thought it was wonderful. Christy Desmet's 'Shakespearean Comic Character: Ethos and Epideictic in *Cymbeline*' (in Teague, *Acting Funny*) also addresses the play's lack of unity, suggesting that an adoption of ethical rather than psychological categories in our analysis of Shakespearean character can help us make sense of the disjointed characterization of *Cymbeline*. Carmine Di Biase's 'Ovid, Pettie and the Mythic Foundation of *Cymbeline*' (*CahiersE* 46.59–70), offers a convincing argument for a source in Ovid.

The Tempest garnered most interest of all amongst the plays in this section this year, with ten articles, one book chapter, and a note. The best of all these was Richard Halpern's ' "The Picture of Nobody": White Cannibalism in *The Tempest*' (in Miller et al., *The Production of English Renaissance Culture*), which approaches the play through Retamar's theory of the *mestizo*. This entails a wide-ranging and frequently provocative examination of the various manifestations of utopian politics in the play, its diverse invocations of Golden Age myths, arcadias, and other ideal commonwealths. This was amongst the best articles of this year's batch. 'The Utopian Structure of *The Tempest*' was also the subject of a clearly written but rather less adventurous piece by Thomas Bulger (*UtopSt* 5.38–47), who, like Halpern, believes that the 'utopian possibilities' introduced in the main body of the play are qualified by the play's final act, although he differs from Halpern in his belief that the ending of the play exhibits 'a testament to the enduring vitality . . . of the concept of the utopic community'.

The play continues its hold on the attentions of those interested in matters of race and colonialism. Chantal Zabus's 'Prospero's Progeny Curses Back: Postcolonial, Postmodern, and Postpatriarchal Rewritings of *The Tempest*' (in Theo D'haen, ed., *Liminal Postmodernisms: The Postmodern, the (Post-)Colonial, and the (Post-) Feminist*) is a descriptive rather than analytic piece, which lists different literary and filmic engagements with *The Tempest* from Aimé Césaire to Iris Murdoch, George Lamming to Derek Jarman. Geraldo U. de Sousa and William M. Hamlin both react against what Hamlin calls 'colonialist' readings of the text. De Sousa believes that interpretations which cast Prospero as the oppressor obscure the fact that he was himself oppressed when he arrived on the island, and that Prospero's withdrawal from public life into the 'domestic world' of the island mirrors a movement in the play from tragedy to comedy ('*The Tempest*, Comedy, and the Space of the Other', in Teague, *Acting Funny*). William M. Hamlin thinks that 'ethnographic contextualisation' of the play's racial discourse offers more enlightenment than do 'colonialist readings', which, he argues, are too invested in political ends (is ethnography, Renaissance or otherwise, really any the less 'political'?). He concludes that the ambiguity of Caliban's representation reflects 'genuine uncertainty regarding the human status of cultural aliens that emerges as a pervasive motif in the early modern period' ('Men of Inde: Renaissance Ethnography and *The Tempest*', *ShakS* 22.15–44).

Ambiguity in the play is also the structuring principle behind John S. Hunt's examination of 'Prospero's Empty Grasp' (*ShakS* 22.277–313). 'Grasp' in this essay becomes a catch-all term which includes, for example, wanting things as well as literally holding them; Hunt's conclusions are very similar to Bulger's in that he sees the ending of the play as 'opening up new possibilities of mutual dependency', primarily due to Prospero's increasing self-consciousness about power. Two more essays on *The Tempest* both examine magic in the play. Mark Fortier offers some dubious observations on connections between magic and technology in the play ('in capabilities and function Ariel has much in common with a U.S. attack helicopter'); the quotation in the title of his paper originates from a colleague who commented on the degree to which these ideas relate to the play itself ('"In No Recognizable Way": *The Tempest*', in Daniel Fischlin, ed., *Negation, Critical Theory, and Postmodern Textuality*).

David Snelling tells us that he is going to offer a 'detailed examination' of Act I scene ii of the play, and its relation to experiments in alchemy, but he does not fulfil this promise; the end of this rather poor article argues that Rudolph II is the model for Prospero ('Prospero on the Coast of Bohemia' (*Prospero* 1.4–16). Roslyn L. Knutson proposes that Caliban is modelled on Caddi-biah, the son of a Liberian king brought to England by traders ('A Caliban in St. Mildred Poultry' in Kishi et al., *Shakespeare and Cultural Traditions*). In a note on the text, B. J. Sokol examines the function of 'Numerology in the Time Scheme of *The Tempest*' (*N&Q* 41.53–5), concluding that it 'confirms that while Prospero manages to abide as a white mage, this is a near thing'. Julia Muller argues that music can 'underline or undermine' the plot of plays such as *The Tempest*; in the main, her article investigates different Restoration performances of the play ('Music as Meaning in *The Tempest*', published in both Klein and Smith, *The Opera and Shakespeare* – where it is mispaginated with Harry Guest's 'Aspects of the Dream' – and Hoenselaars, *Reclamations of Shakespeare*). Robin Headlam Wells also examines music in *The Tempest* in his chapter on the play in his *Elizabethan Mythologies*; he sees music in *The Tempest* as an 'omnipresent agent of reconciliation and rehabilitation'.

(c) Poems

Probably the best essay on the Sonnets this year was Helen Vendler's contribution to the remarkable collection *Teaching With Shakespeare: Critics in the Classroom* (eds McIver and Stevenson). The seminar and workshop Vendler offered in the series of classes by different critics which make up this book are extraordinary: her close reading of Sonnets 94 and 105 is quite dazzling, and the workshop she led on the poems breathtaking for the sheer energy, enthusiasm and intelligence displayed by both teacher and students. Vendler provides here an exemplary model for the teaching of what is very difficult material. I much preferred this essay to Vendler's other contribution on the sonnets this year, 'Reading Stage by Stage: Shakespeare's *Sonnets*' (in McDonald, *Shakespeare Reread*). This is punctuated by occasional humour ('there is even a man in the *Variorum* who thinks the Dark Lady was a wine bottle') and ubiquitous dazzling close readings, as well as intelligent questions, but it lacks the verve of the *Teaching With Shakespeare* essay.

Also very good was Elizabeth Harris Sagaser's 'Shakespeare's Sweet Leaves: Mourning, Pleasure and the Triumph of Thought in the Renaissance Love Lyric' (*ELH* 61.1–26). Sagaser examines Sonnets 29, 30 and 122, arguing that they are examples of what she calls 'anticipatory elegy', '[answering] to love's most terrible apprehensions by fostering in advance the creative, narcissistic spirit of traditional mourning elegy'. This was a sensitive and thoughtful piece, and, beautifully written, a pleasure to read.

Close reading was the methodology adopted by David Thatcher in his 'What a Lark: The Undoing of Sonnet 29' (*DUJ* 86.59–66), which argues against Rowse's claim that the sonnet is mimetically transparent. Robert Ellrodt examines the vocabulary of the Sonnets to claim that the low percentage of words expressing the feelings of the conventional Petrarchan lover, and the high one of vocabulary expressing 'negative values', are proof that Shakespeare discarded prevailing authorial conventions ('The Inversion of Cultural Traditions in Shakespeare's *Sonnets*' in Kishi et al., *Shakespeare and Cultural Traditions*). David Schalkwyk takes issue with the way criticism on the Sonnets concentrates on the speaker's subjectivity alone, and usefully analyses the use of sonnets in *Love's Labour's Lost* and *Twelfth Night* to claim that as an 'instance of social action' the sonnet 'always addresses a particular audience', however 'disembodied' or 'aestheticized' it may be. The 'split subject . . . [of] the poet of the *Sonnets* is', he concludes, 'combined . . . in the figure of Viola/ Cesario' ('"She Never Told Her Love": Embodiment, Textuality and Silence in Shakespeare's Sonnets and Plays"' (*SQ* 45.381–407). A note on the word 'complexion' in 'Shakespeare's Sonnet 18' (*Expl* 53.10–11) was offered by Robert H. Ray; and one on verbal echoes connecting 'Shakespeare's Sonnets 153 and 154' (*Expl* 53.11–14) by Richard A. Levin.

The Phoenix and the Turtle was treated only by Christiane Gillham this year, in an ongoing debate over the relation between the poem and the Song of Solomon. ('Single Natures–Double Name: A Reply to Peter Millward and James H. Sims', *Connotations* 3.123–8).

Mieke Bal's '*The Rape of Lucrece* and the Story of W' was one of the best essays in *Reclamations of Shakespeare* (ed. Hoenselaars), and also the best on *The Rape of Lucrece* this year. This was a complex piece on the representation of rape in general, as well as its particular treatment in the poem. Bal is specifically interested in the connections between rape and 'self-murder', in the way in which the poem intertwines its attention to rape with attention to the visual and to the competitive, and in the way in which rhetoric operates in the text, about all of which she is frequently illuminating. Not so adventurous is Joyce Green McDonald's examination of 'Speech, Silence and History in *The Rape of Lucrece*' (*ShakS* 22.77–103), which situates its discussion of these topics in the context of Renaissance conduct books and biographical accounts, and which argues that 'Lucrece finds her . . . voice only to encounter its limitations in a poem deeply informed by Renaissance assumptions about silence and segregation as indices of female chastity'. The third essay on the text, also feminist in its approach, reaches some different conclusions: unlike Bal, who argues that the play exposes the connections between sexual violence and male competition, Jane O. Newman sees the poem as furthering 'an ideology of gender that represses traditions of female political agency' ('"And Let Mild Women To Him Lose Their Mildness": Philomela, Female Violence and Shakespeare's *The Rape of Lucrece*', *SQ* 45.304–26). Shakespeare's substitution of a suicide for the bacchic murder of his source tales in Livy and Ovid, she argues, is, like other parts of the text, a 'response to the potentially dangerous message of legitimate female violence as part of a mechanism of political renewal'. Finally, John Roe, in a rather poorly argued essay, disagrees: reading the poem as an interrogation of Augustine and Petrarch, he argues that through its use of the revenge theme, and through an experiment in which lyric poetry's emphasis on chastity is 'tested by exposure to [the] different mode of narrative', the poem exonerates Lucrece ('"Pleasing the Wiser Sort": Problems of Ethics and Genre in *Lucrece* and *Hamlet*', *CQ* 23.99–119).

Venus and Adonis was discussed in a note by Goran R. Stanivukovic, who argued for its influence on Gale's *Pyramus and Thisbe* ('Shakespeare, Dunstan Gale, and Golding', *N&Q* 41.35–7); and at more length by Sayre N. Greenfield, who uses Shakespeare and Spenser as vehicles for an argument about allegory in his 'Allegorical Impulses and Critical Ends: Shakespeare's and Spenser's *Venus and Adonis*' (*Criticism* 36.475–98).

(d) Histories

Two collections of essays – *Shakespeare Reread: The Texts in New Contexts*, ed. Russ McDonald, and *Enclosure Acts: Sexuality, Property, and Culture in Early Modern England*, edited by Richard Burt and John Michael Archer – demonstrate how the histories are firmly entangled in interdisciplinary studies, making it increasingly problematic for the reviewer of a single genre, 'the history play'. The former volume contains two essays (almost exclusively) on Shakespeare's histories: 'Hydra and Rhizome' by Harry Berger Jr and '"Word Itself against the Word": Close Reading after Voloshinov' by James R. Siemon. The title of Berger's essay reflects his interest in the discursive latencies of the two Henry plays ('rhizome') and the narrative manifestations of those hidden possibilities ('hydra'); Berger's argument is a disguised plea for close reading, or in his words 'a deterritorialized flow', 'an interpretive standpoint outside the direct or indirect influence of the stage'. In the same volume, James R. Siemon looks at *Richard II* against John Hayward's *History of Henry VIII*, documents relating to the Essex rebellion, and a close reading of the queen's famous identification of herself with Shakespeare's Richard. Siemon stresses how the practice of close reading offers a useful method for social interpretation and suggests it as a possible alternative to current modes of analysis. Siemon seems to have had a productive year. His essay 'Landlord Not King: Agrarian Change and Interarticulation' is the leading piece of *Enclosure Acts*. Early modern commentaries on the vexed subject of enclosure are considered in relation to the garden scene of *Richard II* and Alexander Iden's garden in *2 Henry VI*. Thomas Cartelli, in the same volume ('Jack Cade in the Garden: Class Consciousness and Class Conflict in *2 Henry VI*'), concentrates on Cade's interaction with Alexander Iden, which, he argues, serves to demystify the conception of a private place where all are equal, thereby providing evidence of 'a deep and divisive consciousness of class'. No one now seems to dispute the position that the histories are uniquely discourses of patriarchal dominance, and this is developed by Phyllis Rackin in the next essay, 'Foreign Country: The Place of Women and Sexuality in Shakespeare's Historical World'. Rackin describes the distinctions drawn between Shakespeare's feminized theatrical spaces (such as the Boar's Head) and the masculine domain of the powerful history makers (the court). Deborah Willis provides another twist to the popular thesis that patriarchal discourse requires for its survival the repression of women, in 'Shakespeare and the English Witch-Hunts: Enclosing the Maternal Body'. Willis suggests that Shakespeare's foregrounding of the links between witch and mother in the histories can be explained by contemporary representations of witches, which she argues are organized by fantasies of maternal persecution.

Book-length studies of a single play are somewhat rare these days, with the exception of the casebook or performance study. The two histories that do not belong to a related cycle of plays are the subjects of book-length performance studies: Geraldine Cousin's *King John* and Hugh M. Richmond's *King Henry VIII*; and accordingly, these texts do not suffer from the problem of Barbara Hodgdon's *2 Henry IV* (*YWES* 73.193) – in the same Shakespeare in Performance series – in separating the dramas from productions of related plays. *King John's* theatre history is comprehensively related by Geraldine Cousin, focusing on the nineteenth century, mid-twentieth century RSC productions of the 1970s, the 1984 BBC version and Deborah Warner's productions of 1988 and 1989. Cousin is most readable when she describes productions which she seems to have seen herself; however, there is a tendency to patronize attempts at 'finding' *King John* as if the author herself holds the secret to Shakespeare's intentions. She seems to possess unique insight, informing us that 'Shakespeare understood that anger is a vital component of grief' and that he 'understood, too, the helplessness of Constance as a woman'. Hugh M. Richmond's study of *King Henry VIII* is more self-consciously subjective; Richmond often draws from his own experiences in staging the play and is thus more sympathetic to the various productions of *Henry VIII*. He traces early performances of the play and concentrates on five major twentieth-century productions. He sees a developing trend, commencing with the performance of Sarah Siddons in the eighteenth century, of shifting the emphasis of the play away from the king and towards Queen Katherine. Richmond manages to make the play seem interesting, unlike Maurice Hunt, who has to search for comparable episodes in other plays to enliven his all too familiar argument that in *Henry VIII*, deeds speak louder than words. As the give-away title of his article, 'Shakespeare's *King Henry VIII* and the Triumph of the Word' (*ES* 75.225–45), announces, the spoken word is ultimately victorious in the vision of Elizabeth I, liberator and protectress of God's English.

In an attempt to locate *Richard II* in terms of genre, John Halverson labours to demonstrate the absurdities in Richard's speeches and concludes that the drama is more comical than tragical; here we have another title which tells all, 'The Lamentable Comedy of *Richard II*' (*ELR* 24.343–69). Leaving aside the fact that Halverson assumes his responses to be shared by his readership (unfortunately, this reader found most of the speeches dismissed as ludicrous to be rather touching), there is an assumption throughout that genre classification alone is itself of interest. Somewhat late in coming is his suggestion that the carnivalesque elements in *Richard II* may have contributed to Elizabeth's notorious objection to the play. Inappropriate festivity is the subject of Charles Whitney's essay in the same issue ('Festivity and Topicality in the Coventry Scene of *1 Henry IV*', 410–48). Convincingly, Whitney argues that through the anti-heroism and festivity evident in the representation of Falstaff's lean recruits, Shakespeare daringly touches on contemporary horrors, glancing at the perseverence of the plebeian community despite exploitation, war and famine. Thelma N. Greenfield looks on the brighter side of Falstaff; rather than urging the audience to reform, Falstaff's pronounced fleshiness is seen to endorse his audience's shared instinct for self-preservation. The Hostess's description of his death subtly monumentalizes his animal appetites; she felt him from the feet upward and discovered all 'cold as any stone' ('Falstaff: Shakespeare's Cosmic [Comic] Representation', in Teague, *Acting Funny*).

Among Shakespeare's histories, *Henry V* continues to be the most discussed play. In 'Nostalgia and the Not Yet Late Queen: Refusing Female Rule in *Henry V*' (*ELH* 61.523–50), Katherine Eggert argues that the play's pointedly masculine monarch is an assertion of the power of patriarchy over and against female rule. In the elimination of Katherine of France as Elizabeth's female forebear, the play reflects the late Elizabethan unrest over the state of its monarchy and the fantasy of the return of legitimate male rule. In 'Broken English and Broken Irish: Nation, Language, and the Optic of Power in Shakespeare's Histories' (*SQ* 45.1–32),

Michael Neill argues that Ireland functions in the history plays as a recurrent point of reference. Henry V's conquest of France, ultimately embodied in the 'Englished' Katherine, is seen in the context of the Elizabethan myth of nationhood and the desire of the colonizer to transform and possess the Irish body. In '*Henry V* and the Paradox of the Body Politic' (*SQ* 45.33–56), Claire McEachern considers the employment of 'personableness' in critical responses to Henry V in relation to the Elizabethan vocabulary of corporate identity and the opposition between hegemony and mutuality, or power and personhood. Her complex argument concludes with an analysis of Henry's courtship of Katherine which, she argues, 'accommodates the body to hegemony and vice versa'. As the year's work testifies, Henry's courtship of Katherine is not, as P. K. Ayers claims, a moment which receives little attention. In 'Fellows of Infinite Tongue: *Henry V* and the King's English' (*SEL* 34.253–78), Ayers sees Henry as (yet again) a man of 'infinite tongues', going no further than describing how Henry's 'plainness' breaks from the past of his father and achieves an English which is associated with London while, none the less, 'under erasure'. Following Stephen Greenblatt's challenge to readings of *Henry V* as subversive, Judith Mossman compares Plutarch's account of Julius Caesar with Shakespeare's *Henry V* and suggests that the play is modelled like a Plutarchan life in order to elevate a national hero ('*Henry V* and Plutarch's *Alexander*', *SQ* 45.57–73).

E. A. Rauchut's note, 'Hotspur's Prisoners and the Laws of War in *1 Henry IV*', also appears in *SQ* 45 (96–7). Rauchut observes that King Henry's insistence that Hotspur surrender his prisoners ignores the law of arms and cheats Hotspur of war's greatest gain; this is added to the evidence incriminating Henry as a thief. Hotspur's words are read as revealing unconscious conflicts underlying his phallocentricity by Marvin B. Krims ('Hotspur's Antifeminism', *L&P* 40.118–32). Hotspur's repression of femininity in himself and others is explained by Krims (who fails to see the irony in Hotspur's self-presentation) as an extension of his fear of infantile helplessness, ultimately revealing a latent wish to be the victim he eventually becomes. Shakespeare's histories are the subject of three chapters of another interdisciplinary study, Daniel J. Kornstein's *Kill All the Lawyers?: Shakespeare's Legal Appeal*. It is disappointing that the discussion of the relationship between Shakespeare's histories and the law is, for the most part, limited to a debate as to whether legal practices are given a good or bad press by Shakespeare.

Two outstanding articles on the subject of history in the first tetralogy have appeared this year. Shakespeare's representation of Eleanor Cobham is examined in the context of fifteenth- and sixteenth-century accounts of her fall by Nina S. Levine ('The Case of Eleanor Cobham: Authorizing History in *2 Henry VI*', *ShakS* 22.104–21). Levine argues that Shakespeare dramatizes the paradigm of the virago-witch-traitor while also showing the duchess to be an unwitting pawn. Shakespeare's strategies of representing Eleanor Cobham and, implicitly, powerful women are seen to reflect the social and political unease characteristic of the 1590s. The convergence of spectacle and market, subjectivity and history, is explored by Christopher Pye ('The Theatre, the Market and the Subject of History', *ELH* 61.501–22). Concentrating on a formative moment in Shakespeare's career and in the history cycle – *1Henry VI*, I.iv – Pye's new-historicist reading demonstrates how Shakespeare alerts his audience to their own condition as economic and theatrical beings. The best entry on the histories in *N&Q* this year is on the first tetralogy: Maurice Pope's 'My Kingdom for a Horse', (41.272–7). Pope proposes two interpretations for the famous line – sardonic and heroic – and suggests that the contradictory appearances of the line are due to textual corruption.

Jean Howard takes a broader view of the histories in 'Kings and Pretenders', the final chapter of *The Stage and Social Struggle in Early Modern England.* Theatricality in the first tetralogy is seen as opposed to legitimate authority, as theatrical impostors threaten monstrous rule throughout. In the second tetralogy, theatricality becomes interior to kingship, and Howard argues that this shift in the representation of the theatre reflects a more modern approach in so far as the sacred aura of kingship is demystified.

Catherine Gira and Adele Sceff's monumental *Henry IV Parts 1 and 2: An Annotated Bibliography* has appeared this year. Covering 1,534 items, it includes work from 1940 to 1985; its chief defect is that it stops at 1985 and, thus, its usefulness is limited to research on Shakespeare's critical heritage. In the same endangered series is Deborah T. Curren-Aquino's *King John: An Annotated Bibliography*, in which it is proven that the seemingly forgotten Shakespeare play is not forgotten in the least. This impressive survey covers published work from 1940 to 1990 and includes 1,568 items, with detailed and useful annotations.

(e) Tragedies

There is little on *Romeo and Juliet* in the journals this year. In '"Draw if you be men': Saviolo's Significance for *Romeo and Juliet*' (*SQ* 45.162–89), Joan Ozark Holmer helpfully demonstrates direct parallels between the 1595 translation of Saviolo's fencing treatise and Shakespeare's tragedy in both its language and its treatment of the ethics of fencing, to illuminate the tragic complexity of the fatal duels in the play, and there are several well-produced illustrations reproduced from the treatise. E. Pearlman examines the sources of passion in the play in *ShSA* 6.22-8; and Jonathan Goldberg's discussion of heterosexuality and gender in the play, '*Romeo and Juliet*'s Open Rs', is printed in Jonathan Goldberg, ed. *Queering the Renaissance*.

Hamlet receives its perennial spotlight attention. In the preface to *Hamlet's Perfection* William Kerrigan explains that his title alludes to 'Hamlet's attempts to perfect himself [. . .] and to the perfection of Shakespeare's art'. The first chapter gives an overview of the history of *Hamlet* in criticism; an examination of the play's treatment of the division of day from night, good from evil, in relation to the Senecan tradition is followed by a somewhat rambling descanting on 'the virgin/whore split', explained by Kerrigan thus: 'Men have trouble getting love and desire to lie down together', which he says poses the 'toughest test' for men when confronted with the problem of marriage. An uncomfortable read for those playgoers and readers who think the play invites its audiences to share the emotions of a woman whose mind fractures under the pressure of such a split. Ophelia, we may need reminding, commits suicide.

The declared aim of *New Essays on Hamlet* (eds. Mark Thornton Burnett and John Manning) is to 'contextualize the play in terms of the plurality of discourses characteristic of the English Renaissance and contemporary changes in critical practice that have overtaken literary and cultural studies'. For me, the best thing about the book is the way its contributors argue over metatextual questions and explore the play's interest in theatrical representation. The book begins with two notes by Alastair Fowler on textual cruces of the play. He suggests a Gavin Douglas poem as a source for Horatio's description of morning succeeding night (the 'russet mantle' of I.i.171), and discusses Shakespeare's use of chronographia and the ornate and archaic to begin *The Murder of Gonzago*; while John Manning analyses '*Symbola* and *Emblemata*' in the play. In a section on 'Politics and Performance', Burnett traces patterns of concealment and exposure in the play and links these to the rapid development of espionage which coincides with *Hamlet*; in 'Hamlet's Thing', Bill Readings examines the enigma of *Hamlet* as a visual play caught between 'the lure of representation and the grip of (the obligation to) the heard command of the Father'; Andrew Mousley discusses the play as dramatizing the failure of ideologies to 'speak through' the individual; and Robert Barrie, reviewing the figures of the Fool and the Vice and the fortunes of Will Kempe and the Lord Chamberlain's Men, argues that 'Hamlet, as his own Fool, can be seen to subvert *Hamlet* so thoroughly as to reduce to laughter the very idea of serious tragedy.' Essays on 'Psychoanalysis and Language' are provided by Elizabeth Oakes, who offers a Jungian reading of sacrificial themes, by Joanna Montgomery Byles, who examines the play in the light of the concept of the superego, by Valeria Wagner, using Lacan's seminar 'Desire and the Interpretation of Desire in *Hamlet*' to examine the play's relationship to critical commentary, and by Lisa Hopkins discussing 'the systematic tracing of the patterns of linguistic doubling which riddle the play'. A section on 'Renaissance Feminisms' provides two of the most stimulating pieces in the book. Alison Findlay's '*Hamlet*: A Document in Madness' is one of the best feminist studies of the play I have read in a long time. Examining the relationship between words, madness and the desire for order in the play, to consider how madness 'produces and is produced by a fragmentation of discourse', Findlay relates Ophelia to Burton's *Anatomy of Melancholy* and less familiar seventeenth-century writings about mental disorder, to purposeful effect. Kay Stanton, in another thought-provoking essay on the play ('*Hamlet*'s Whores'), observes that Hamlet is 'very skilled in detecting whorishness in women; he is less good (though not completely inept) in detecting it in himself', and provides the important insight that the only time Hamlet is happy is when he is planning *The Mousetrap*: 'It is his great love, the one thing he values more highly than his father.' In the latter half of the volume, the essays focus on different aspects of 'Hamleticism'. Martin Wiggins examines eighteenth-century attempts to mitigate what critics saw as the 'horror' of Hamlet's gloating vision of Claudius being propelled into hell in the Prayer scene, to argue that commentators who internalize the action of *Hamlet* are 'not discussing Shakespeare's play at all, but a palimpsest created through repression in the middle of the eighteenth century'. Christina Britzolakis examines the Modernist appropriation of the play, how Eliot and Joyce both read the play as an allegory of the aesthetic process with Hamlet as a protoype of the artist. The late, great Angela Carter's novel *Wise Children* is one of the most provocative pieces of *Hamlet* commentary of this century, so it is particularly pleasing to recommend Kate Chedgzoy's essay on cultural legitimacy and the reproduction of *Hamlet*, which takes the key themes of the novel as a starting point for a re-reading of 'the historical vicissitudes of the Freudian and Shakespearean myths of the family which finally converge in Carter's text'. The final section of the volume, 'Nation and Culture', focuses on the political ramifications of the rewriting of *Hamlet*. Michal Kobialka examines the source of Jan Kott's arguments about the play (in *Shakespeare Our Contemporary*), Stanislaw Wyspianski's 1904/5 essay on *Hamlet*, which influenced actors and directors staging revolutionary critiques of nationalist policies, a subject that is discussed in Marta Gibińska's essay in Hattaway et al., *Shakespeare in the New Europe*. Heiner O. Zimmermann provides a fascinating history of German appropriations of the play to show how thoroughly 'the recipient's historical position and interests can predetermine the meaning distilled from a text'. From the early writings that shaped the myth (Goethe and the Schlegel brothers) to Heiner Müller's production of *Hamlet*, and his *Hamletmachine*, Zimmermann shows how far the history of a text in another culture can acquire an 'autonomous momentum'.

The best of the journal output on *Hamlet* this year is Steven Mullaney's 'Mourning and Misogyny: *Hamlet*, *Revenger's Tragedy* and the Final Progress of Elizabeth, 1600–1607' (*SQ* 45.138–62), which examines Elizabethan and early Jacobean revenge tragedy as an interplay of mourning and misogyny around the ageing and posthumous body of Elizabeth. The essay suggests that in Hamlet, mourning for a dead king, even revenge itself are 'displaced' or 'complicated' by a misogyny towards a queen who is too sexually vital and transgresses her age. Hamlet's scene with Yorick's skull is read as a turning point: after this, Mullaney states, Gertrude is no longer presented as a sexual transgressor, but as a victim of Claudius's lust, and Hamlet reveals a new assurance of the working of divine providence. Mullaney also notes that Yorick must have died when Hamlet was the age of 'breeching' (7 years old), when boys passed from their mother's care into their father's. Stuart M. Kurland, 'Hamlet and the Scottish Succession?' (*SEL* 34. 279–300), reconsiders Lilian Winstanley's (1921) identification of Hamlet with Essex and King James VI of Scotland to argue that the late Elizabethan succession question – fears that James would assert his rights to the throne by force – figure importantly in the political world of the play, and points to Horatio's recurrent concern with an unsettled populace. He argues that the political ills depicted in the play, cannot all be traced to Claudius. Kurland is not arguing for specific correspondences, but rather reminds us of the immediacy with which a contemporary audience might have perceived the anxious war preparations of the opening scene.

Richard Mallette takes up the vexed question of Hamlet's understanding of the divine to examine the play's concerns with free will in the context of Calvinist determinism, arguing that the play 'transcends the Reformation controversy about the nature of the will' (*JEGP* 93.336–55). Louise Cary ('Hamlet Recycled' *ELH* 61.783–804) examines textual variants of the falconer's call at I.v.117–18 to provide a linguistic analysis of 'Hillo ho ho ho'. It makes much of what Cary calls the 'graphic' H: 'the vertical strokes are identical, yet different because of where (and when) they occur. We might expand them into the birth and death, the beginning and the end of the letter.' Perhaps those more sympathetic to this approach will find this more helpful than I did.

Some of the most suggestive insights on the play this year have been provided in notes. The most fascinating and important is by Robert Painter and Brian Parker on 'Ophelia's Flowers Again' (*N&Q* 41.42–4), pointing out what commentators seemed to have ignored. Rosemary, for example, was 'often given as a token of remembrance between lovers, not merely remembrance of the dead'; pansies were associated with the erotic and fennel with fickleness in love; rue was used to abate carnal lust; the daisy was identified with dissembling love and also with testicles. Even more suggestively, they note that many of the flowers Ophelia refers to were used in contraception: perhaps with one exception, they were all anti-fertility drugs. In the same journal, Charles Edelman suggests that 'hangers and carriages' in the exchange between Hamlet and Osric at V.ii.136–60 refers to testicles (*N&Q* 41.136–46), and Peter Moore (48–9) suggests Ben Jonson's *The Case is Altered* as a source for 'Ophelia's False Steward' at IV.v.172–3. Also in *N&Q* (41.41), Richard Levin's 'More Nuns and Nunneries and Hamlet's Speech to Ophelia' adds to R.V. Holdsworth's note on 'nun' from last year (*YWES* 74.217); Levin states that the earliest use of 'nun' to mean 'whore' is in Gosson's 1579 *The School of Abuse,* but also cites lines from *The Witch of Edmonton.* Charlotte F. Otten suggests, in '*Hamlet* and *The Secret Miracles of Nature*' (*N&Q* 41.38–41), that there is 'more than random consonance' in the verbal correspondence with the Dutch physician Levinus Lemnius, particularly in Hamlet's 'There are more things in heaven and earth' and 'To be' speeches. In 'Androgynous "Union" and the Woman in *Hamlet*' (*ShakS.* 23.71–99), James W. Stone argues that 'the woman in Hamlet is as much a threat to him as the invaginating "mother" – "*hysterica passio* " – is to Lear, the inextricable "woman's heart" is to Posthumus and (s)mothering Volumnia is in Coriolanus', and that 'it is the misogynistic representation of woman as duplicitous masquerader that marks the focal point of *Hamlet* as a tragedy'. Shakespeare, we are told in a confused and not very convincing argument, 'plays out the poisonous consequences of androgyny'. R. Chris Hassel Jr, in 'Hamlet's "Too, Too Solid Flesh"' (*ScLJ* 25.608–22), writes suggestively on Hamlet's desire for perfect knowing as the Lutheran spiritual illness of 'prudence or wisdom of the flesh'; and Hassel explores the play's treatment of the relationship between God and the human race in '"How Infinite in Faculties": Hamlet's Confusion of God and Man' (*L&T* 8.127–39). Naomi Conn Liebler reads Hamlet's lament for the hobby horse in terms of nostalgia for tradition (*CahiersE* 45.33–45); Kenneth Gross looks at rumour and slander in the play (*Raritan* 14.43–67); and Lansing Evans Smith (*SN* 66.35–46) examines the image cluster in the play concerning 'breeding, brooding, and birthing', which, he argues rather thinly, operates as 'a metaphor of the political, psychological and aesthetic processes of conception, action and poetic composition'. In 'Hamlet's Heroism' (*CLQ* 30.291–7), Bert G. Hornback starts by stating: 'Of course Hamlet isn't delaying' and goes on to argue that he 'does not even try' to take revenge, in what seems to be more an assertion than a demonstration of his point; while more fruitfully, Martha C. Ronk examines Gertrude's speech on the dying Ophelia as an act of *allegoresis* in 'Representations of Ophelia' (*Criticism* 36.i.21–44)

HSt 16 includes 'A Review of Periodical Articles 1992–3' by W. Hutchings (95–104); John Hardy writes on 'Hamlet's "Modesty of Nature"' (42–56); and Elizabeth Jenkins, in a source study of the play's treatment of melancholy, explains 'Why I Would Not Vote for Hamlet' (71–5). Michael Andrews examines criminality in '"Foul Play" in *Hamlet* ' (75–82); and David Arnett applies a cognitive aproach to the play in 'What Makes Hamlet Run? Framing Cognition Discursively' (24–41). In the same number, Gertrude is the subject of Lisa Hopkins's '"That's Wormwood": Hamlet Plays His Mother' (83–5), which examines the Player Queen in the dumb show; and Elizabeth Oakes provides two notes on Gertrude (85–8). Also in *HSt* 14, William Collins Watterson considers Yorick as 'a merry father' providing a direct contrast to the father figures in the play ('Hamlet's Lost Father', 1–23); and John Halveson ('The Importance of Horatio' 57–70) argues that Hamlet and Horatio could not have known each other that well before the play begins because Hamlet first addresses Horatio as 'you'.

Othello came in for a lot of attention this year. *Critical Essays on Shakespeare's Othello* (ed. Anthony G. Barthelemy) is a useful collection of reprinted essays (mostly recent) on the play. It includes Barthelemy's own 'Ethiops Washed White: Moors of the Nonvillainous Type', and Karen Newman's '"And Wash the Ethiop

White": Femininity and the Monstrous in *Othello*'; Michael Neill's '"Unproper" Beds: Race, Adultery and the Hideous in *Othello*', as well as Ania Loomba's 'Sexuality and Racial Difference'; Eldred Jones's essay from *Othello's Countrymen: Africans in English Renaissance Drama*; Lynda Boose's essay on the symbolism of Othello's handkerchief; Joel Fineman's study of the relationship of the play's sound imagery to desire; Julia Genster's essay on the play's treatment of rank and its relationship to self and to social and sexual identity. Carol Thomas Neely's essay on men and women in the play is reprinted along with A. C. Bradley's 'The Peculiarity of Othello'.

The first part of Virginia Mason Vaughan's *Othello: A Contextual History* is a straightforward and informative survey of the Jacobean contexts of the play at its 'point of production', which include the romantic ideal of military service, the discourse of racial difference, discussions of narratives contemporary with *Othello* (such as the Geneva Bible's depiction of blackness as the visual signifier of eternal sin), and texts examining jealousy (such as Thomas Wright's *Passions of the Mind*). Where the study comes seriously adrift is in the second part, when the personal lives of actors and directors are brought in as evidence to support an argument. If criticism of an actor-director's sex life – we are told that Orson Welles 'engaged in countless affairs' and 'bedded his Italian mistress' – is what constitutes a criticism of cultural contexts, I am afraid I will have to pass. Macready's interpretation of the play, with his Othello played as a noble, loving husband, we are told, domesticized the character because the actor was a happily married family man (and since this is a book on *Othello*, we cannot expect to be told how this loving father approached the role of Macbeth). The chapter on Paul Robeson's Othello is informative on the implicit racism in the reviewers who praised his performance, and is good on describing how the audience was protected from the full brutality of the murder. It would have been interesting to have a comparison with the cultural contexts of Ira Alridge's interpretation, which is the subject of Joyce Green MacDonald's engaging essay 'Acting Black: *Othello*, *Othello* Burlesques, and the Performance of Blackness' (*TJ* 46.231–49); this argues that the transgressive power of black Shakespeare lay in its public contradiction of the supposedly rigid and absolute ideologies of racial difference.

Ruth Vanita ('"Proper" Men and "Fallen" Women: The Unprotectedness of Wives in *Othello*', *SEL* 34.341–56) argues that Emilia and Desdemona 'die similar deaths for similar reasons': that the tragedy is shown at every point to be avoidable and finally occurs because those who should intervene fail to do so. In examining the play's presentation of societal collusion in husbandly violence, she argues that the play forcefully combats racism (which 'posits blacks and whites as essentially different') precisely by its presentation of Othello as not at all different from any white husband. She points out that most Indian women students perceive Othello's behaviour as normal, husbandly, manly behaviour. *Othello*, she argues, is the only one of Shakespeare's major tragedies in which 'the innocent victim is put to death before our eyes after systematic physical and mental torture' in the presence of witnesses – and the theatre audience – and 'this is possible because she is a wife'. In a related piece, Vanita's 'Men Beware Men: Shakespeare's Warnings for Unfair Husbands' also looks at the treatment of wives (*CompD* 28.201–20).

Patricia Parker examines 'Fantasies of "Race" and "Gender": Africa, *Othello* and Bringing to Light' in Margo Hendricks and Patricia Parker, eds, *Women, 'Race', and Writing in the Early Modern Period*. David Lucking employs a semantic approach to the play in '"Putting Out the Light": Semantic Indeterminacy and the

Deconstruction of Self in *Othello*' (*ES* 75.110–22). In 'The Humiliation of Iago' (*SEL* 34.323–39) Karl F. Zender draws attention to a seemingly inconsequential episode which explores Iago's 'complete freedom to make any signifier means anything he wills it to'. Brian Cheadle (*N&Q* 41.491–3) relates the legal implication of 'process' (at I.iii.142) to the play's repeated emphasis on Brabantio's insistence that Othello as an outsider is always on trial. Three items on the play's influence on Verdi are provided by James Aldrich-Moodie in *CompD* 28.324–47; by Lisa Hopkins on '*Othello*' as Operatic Text (*ShY* 4.61–70); and, in the same journal, by George Hyde's '*Othello/Otello*', while Roberta Montemorra Marvin notes the play's influence on Rossini.

The best of the journal output on *King Lear* this year is Martin Mueller's thought-provoking 'From *King Leir* to *King Lear*' (*PQ* 73.195–217), which offers what he calls 'frankly speculative thoughts' about the shape and direction of Shakespeare's career. Mueller suggests a complex itinerary of source influence which examines the old play as a decade-long pervasive presence in the plays, and goes on to demonstrate how it helped shape the formal and thematic structure of several quite different plays, so that we find *Leir* echoes in *Richard III*, *The Merchant of Venice*, *As You Like It* and *Hamlet*. Mueller further suggests strong links between *King Leir*, Lodge's *Rosalynde*, and the Ur-*Hamlet* which may have been Shakespeare's 'pet bundle' for thinking about generational struggles. There are many suggestive parallels here: for example, *As You Like It* as an anti-Lear, or Lear on the heath as a bad-weather version of Duke Senior in the forest of Arden.

Philip Armstrong ('Uncanny Spectacles: Psychoanalysis and the Texts of *King Lear*', *TPr* 8.414–34) ponders questions of blindness and sight, doubling and mirroring, in terms of a Freudian case study of the Uncanny and examines the scene at 'Dover' as a staging of the delusion behind the 'reality' as presented by both the theatre and the visual art of its day. Other articles on the play may be briefly noted. Robert S. Miola examines the play's relationship to New Comedy: I particularly valued the discussion of the parodying of the New Comedic discovery of offspring at II.ii.80–5 (*PQ* 73.329–46). Robert Matz writes on the play's treatment of torture and political authority (*Exemplaria* 6.223–41); and David Lowenthal examines its treatment of kingship (*IJPR* 21.391–417). A. P. Reimer examines '"The Promised End": Some Last Words on *King Lear*' (*SSEng*. 20:3–19), and Michael Pavese writes '"On the Five Nevers"' (*High Plains Literary Review* 9.47–61).

There are some good notes on the play this year. Stephen Doloff's 'Foolish Death in *King Lear*' (*ELN* 32.2.17–19) suggests the utterance 'Alas my poor fool is hang'd!' (V.iii.305) connects to the thematic pattern concerning the fools in the larger context of the play, and allows its implications to encompass the disappearance and murder of *both* the Fool and Cordelia and even Lear himself; and Doloff suggests as a source for 'The Barbarous Scythian' (*N&Q* 41.493) a book on classical scepticism popular in the Renaissance, in which Sextus Empirius' outline of Pyrrhomis gives the association of 'Scythian' with patricide. In the same journal, William Gulstad writes on Scot's *The Discoverie of Witchcraft* as a source for 'The Mock-Trial or Witch-Trial in *King Lear*' (494–7); and John Breen (493–4) considers the usage of the term 'banish'd' in its Renaissance association with the defence of the state. Alan Smith examines the use of *double entendre* at I.i.90 in *Expl* 52.iv.201–2.

The Scottish play is the subject of political journalist Gary Wills's *Witches and Jesuits: Shakespeare's Macbeth*, which gives a lively account of the Gunpowder

Plot but uses much material that has been well rehearsed in *Macbeth* criticism. In 'The Historiographical Evolution of the Macbeth Narrative' (*ScLJ* 21.5–23), Kenneth D. Farrow examines the early Scottish sources of the Macbeth story, providing an intriguing insight into the ways in which history gets rewritten. In 'Close Reading without Readings' Stephen Booth analyses *Macbeth* (in McDonald, *Shakespeare Reread*).

There are few pieces on the classical tragedies this year, and they are for the most part disappointing. In 'Theatre, Identity and Brutus' Grand Illusion' (*SELit* 70.129–47), Fumio Toshioka explores the use of spectacle and theatrical illusion in *Julius Caesar*; and in *Expl* 52.iii.135–7, Susan Hines in 'Shakespeare's *Julius Caesar*' suggests there is a functional significance involved in the removing of Caesar's body from the stage: Antony can then 'cast the body back into the dramatic production'. She argues that by calling attention to Caesar's body Shakespeare 'advances a political theory that is, in essence, theatrical'. A. M. Kinghorn writes entertainingly on '"All joy o' the Worm", or, Death by Asps or Asps Unknown in Act V of *Antony and Cleopatra*' (*ES* 75.104–9); G. A. Wilkes examines theatricality as a central concern in *Antony and Cleopatra* ('Excellent Dissembling: A View of *Antony and Cleopatra*', *SSEng* 19.31–9). In '"To the Very Heart of Loss": Renaissance Iconography in Shakespeare's *Antony and Cleopatra*' (*ShakS* 30.97–112) Peggy Muñoz Simonds seeks to demonstrate that 'a fatally addicted Antony' and others in the play describe Cleopatra in terms of the attributes widely associated with the goddess Fortuna, that Antony's 'foolish trust in Fortune's continuing love for him' allows him to be 'caught like a fish sacrificed to honour and glory', and that 'although a bereft Cleopatra attempts in the end to immortalise her own brilliant performance of Fortune in the great theatre of the world as a transcendent art work of marble statuary, the play does end tragically – if somewhat ambiguously so – for both the lovers'. I have to confess that I could barely recognize Shakespeare's play strapped into this moralizing straitjacket. In '"Narcissus in thy face": Roman Desire and the Difference it Fakes in *Antony and Cleopatra*' (*SQ* 45.408–25), Jonathan Gil Harris uses the tale of Narcissus as told (in 1595) by Thomas Edwards to challenge orthodox understandings of gender in the play; the play 'stages an orientialist discourse of the Other' revealing its '"exotic" object of "heterosexual" desire to be a chimera conjured up and misrecognized by the narcissistic male gaze'. I found this a rather overdetermined reading. A Macmillan New Casebook on *Antony and Cleopatra* (ed. John Drakakis) reprints mostly recent essays on the play, including Margot Heinemann's thoughtful analysis of order and disorder in the play; and, at last, L. T. Fitz's (now Linda Woodbridge) splendid 1977 *SQ* (*YWES* 58.152) article on 'Egyptian Queens and Male Reviewers: Sexist Attitudes in *Antony and Cleopatra* Criticism' is anthologized.

There was very little on *Coriolanus* this year. Tetsuya Motohashi's 'Body Politic and Political Body in *Coriolanus*' (*FMLS* 30.97–112) argues that the 'Hydra-like Body Politic finally devours the body of this political viper'; and Pradip Datta examines 'The Paradox of Greatness and the Limits of Pragmatism in Shakespeare's *Coriolanus*' (*CLAJ* 28.97–107).

Titus Andronicus receives more attention than usual this year. Naomi Conn Liebler ('Getting it All Right: *Titus Andronicus* and Roman History', *SQ* 45.263–78) examines Nicholas Smyth's (*c.*1550) translation, *The History of Herodian*, as a 'con-text' for the treatment of dynastic and political issues in Shakespeare's play. In the same journal, Katharine A. Rowe ('Dismembering and Forgetting in *Titus*

Andronicus', *SQ* 45.297–303) argues that 'to read the play's severed parts as exclusively phallic risks eliding their specific range of reference as hands, tongues, and heads', and drawing on Renaissance emblems (rather shakily) and Freudian 'Fetishism' (more fruitfully) suggests that the play 'insists on hands as the central emblem of effective political action'. In 'Textual Politics in *Titus Andronicus*: "Record", Maxim and an Icon of Justice' (*AUMLA* 81.1–19), Heather Kerr examines the play's presentation of the conflict between law and authority in the context of legal theory; and Nanette Jaynes (*Expl* 52.iii.132–3) takes issue with critics who have praised Aaron's 'manly worth' in his attitude to his son, and concludes 'no child escapes the brutality of objectification and incorporation' in this play.

Of the reissues out this year, Anne Barton's *Essays, Mainly Shakespearean* is a collection of this fine scholar's work written over the last twenty-five years. The volume includes the ground-breaking essay on the night-before-battle scene in *Henry V*, and her study on realism in the last plays, as well as the essays on *Antony and Cleopatra* and *Coriolanus*, and the most recent essays, 'Parks and Ardens' and 'Wrying But a Little', an essay on *Cymbeline* (published here for the first time). In these Barton answers her own call, made in the preface, for the emergence of 'a style of criticism which is open to historical circumstance without losing touch with the general shape as well as the details of the play'.

It is good to be able to report that the paperback edition of Jonathan Bate's *Shakespeare and Ovid* has been published so quickly (*YWES* 74.204). Brian Vickers's *Appropriating Shakespeare*, also published last year, is now in paperback (*YWES* 74.202–3). Published in paperback this year as well is Leah Marcus Scragg's 1988 *Discovering Shakespeare's Meaning*. The second edition of *Political Shakespeare* (*YWES* 66.217) contains two new chapters by its editors: Jonathan Dollimore discusses current critical approaches to questions of gender and sexuality in 'Shakespeare Understudies: The Sodomite, the Prostitute, the Transvestite and their Critics', and ends the chapter by offering his services to direct a camp production of *Antony and Cleopatra* 'in the service of queer politics and creative vandalism'. Alan Sinfield discusses 'Heritage and the Market, Regulation and Sublimation' in a meandering essay which might have been more effective if the argument had been more focused.

The revised editions of Casebooks on *Macbeth* and *Othello*, both edited by John Wain, begrudgingly tack on some new chapters with little discernible thought: the *Othello* volume has reprinted essays by Christopher Norris, Karen Newman and Anthony Brennan, and the *Macbeth* adds reprints of essays by Malcolm Evans, Graham Holderness and Germaine Greer.

Books Reviewed

Barthelemy, Anthony G., ed. *Critical Essays on Shakespeare's 'Othello'*. Hall. pp. 234. $47. ISBN 0 8161 8866 1.

Barton, Anne. *Essays, Mainly Shakespearean*. CUP. pp. 386. £40. ISBN 0 5214 1444 4.

Bate, Jonathan. *Shakespeare and Ovid*. Clarendon. pp. 292. pb £12.95. ISBN 0 1981 8324 0.

Battenhouse, Roy, ed. *Shakespeare's Christian Dimension*. IndUP. pp. 520. hb £27.50. ISBN 0 2533 1122 5.

Bearman, Robert. *Shakespeare in the Stratford Records*. Sutton. pp. 88. pb £6.99. ISBN 0 7509 0632 4.

Burnett, Mark Thornton, and John Manning. *New Essays on Hamlet*. AMS. pp. 328. $57.50. ISBN 0 4046 2311 5.

Burt, Richard, and John Michael Archer, eds. *Enclosure Acts: Sexuality, Property, and Culture in Early Modern England*. CornUP. pp.340. hb £33.50, $42.95, pb £13.50, $16.95. ISBN 0 8014 2745 2, 0 8014 8024 8.

Callaghan, Dympna, Lorraine Helms and Jyotsna Singh. *The Weyward Sisters: Shakespeare and Feminist Politics*. Blackwell. pp. 164. hb £35, pb £10.99. ISBN 0 6311 7797 3, 0 6311 7798 1.

Cordner, Michael, Peter Holland and John Kerrigan, eds. *English Comedy*. CUP. pp. 323. £37.50, $59.95. ISBN 0 5214 1917 4.

Cousin, Geraldine. *King John*. SiP. ManUP. pp. 176. £35. ISBN 0 7190 2753 5.

Cox, Murray, and Alice Theilgaard. *Shakespeare as Prompter: The Amending Imagination and the Therapeutic Process*. Kingsley. pp. 454. pb £22.50. ISBN 1 8530 2159 8.

Curren-Aquino, Deborah T. *King John: An Annotated Bibliography*. Garland. pp. 894. $120. ISBN 0 8240 6626 X .

Davies, Anthony, and Stanley Wells, eds. *Shakespeare and the Moving Image: The Plays on Film and Television*. CUP. pp. 266. hb £37.50, pb £13.95. ISBN 0 5214 3424 6, 0 5214 3573 0.

Delabastita, Dirk. *There's a Double Tongue: An Investigation into the Translation of Shakespeare's Wordplay with Special Reference to 'Hamlet'*. Rodopi (1993). pp. 522. $112. ISBN 9 0518 3495 0.

——, and Lieven D'hulst, eds. *European Shakespeares: Translating Shakespeare in the Romantic Age*. Benjamins (1993). pp. 256. $59. ISBN 9 0272 2130 8 (Eur.), 1 5561 9486 2 (US).

D'haen, Theo, ed. *Liminal Postmodernisms: The Postmodern, the (Post-)Colonial, and the (Post-)Feminist*. Rodopi. pp. 357. £72.05. ISBN 9 0518 3756 9.

Dollimore, Jonathan, and Alan Sinfield, eds. *Political Shakespeare: Essays in Cultural Materialism* (2nd edn). ManUP. pp. 304. hb £35, pb £10.99. ISBN 0 7190 4351 4, 0 7190 4352 2.

Drakakis, John, ed. *Shakespeare: Antony and Cleopatra*. Macmillan New Casebook. Macmillan. pp. 341. hb £37.50, pb £10.99. ISBN 0 3335 5531 7, 0 3335 5532 5.

Empson, William. *William Empson: Essays on Renaissance Literature. vol. 2.: The Drama*. Ed. John Haffenden. CUP. pp. 292. £37.50, $49.95. ISBN 0 5214 4044 0.

Finney, Gail, ed. *Look Who's Laughing: Gender and Comedy*. G&B. pp. £25, $39. ISBN 0 8812 4644 3.

Finucci, Valeria, and Regina Schwartz, eds. *Desire in the Renaissance: Psychoanalysis and Literature*. PrincetonUP. pp. 273. hb £32, $37.50, pb. £11.95, $14.95. ISBN 0 6910 0100 6, 0 6910 3403 6.

Fischlin, Daniel, ed. *Negation, Critical Theory, and Postmodern Textuality*. Kluwer. pp. 331. £59.50, $99. ISBN 0 7923 2833 7.

Gillies, John. *Shakespeare and the Geography of Difference*. CUP. pp. 255. hb £37.50, pb £12.95. ISBN 0 5214 1719 8, 0 5214 5953 6.

Gira, Catherine, and Adele Sceff. *Henry IV Parts 1 and 2: An Annotated Bibliography*. Garland. pp. 616. $92. ISBN 0 8240 7097 6.

Goldberg, Jonathan, ed. *Queering the Renaissance*. DukeUP. pp. 388. hb £52, pb £16.95. ISBN 0 8223 1381 2, 0 8223 1385 5.
Halio, Jay L., ed. *The First Quarto of King Lear*. The Early Quartos, NCaS. CUP. pp. 141. £29.95. ISBN 0 5214 1811 9.
Hamilton, Charles, ed. *Cardenio, or the Second Maiden's Tragedy*. Glenbridge. pp. 275. $25. ISBN 0 9444 3524 6.
Hattaway, Michael, Boika Sokolova and Derek Roper, eds. *Shakespeare in the New Europe*. ShaP. pp. 384. £42.50. ISBN 1 8507 5474 8.
Hayes, Elizabeth T., ed. *Images of Persephone: Feminist Readings in Western Literature*. UPFlor. pp. 212. £26.95, $33.50. ISBN 0 8130 1262 7.
Hendricks, Margo, and Patricia Parker, eds. *Women, 'Race', and Writing in the Early Modern Period*. Routledge. pp. 383. hb £40, pb £14.99. ISBN 0 4150 7777 X, 0 4150 7778 8.
Hoenselaars, A. J., ed. *Reclamations of Shakespeare*. Rodopi. pp. 317. pb $31. ISBN 9 0518 3639 2.
Hope, Jonathan. *The Authorship of Shakespeare's Plays*. CUP. pp. 188. £30. ISBN 0 5214 1737 6.
Howard, Jean. *The Stage and Social Struggle in Early Modern England*. Routledge. pp. 184. hb £35, pb £11.99. ISBN 0 4150 4258 5, 0 4150 9553 0.
Howe, James. *A Buddhist's Shakespeare: Affirming Self-Deconstructions*. FDUP. pp. 273. £35.50. ISBN 0 8386 3522 9.
Hughes, Alan, ed. *Titus Andronicus*. NCaS. CUP. pp. 66. hb £29.95, pb £5.25. ISBN 0 5212 2157 9, 0 5212 9372 3.
Hutson, Lorna. *The Usurer's Daughter: Male Friendship and Fictions of Women in Sixteenth-Century England*. Routledge. pp. 295. £40, $69.95. ISBN 0 4150 5049 9.
Kegl, Rosemary. *The Rhetoric of Concealment: Figuring Gender and Class in Renaissance Literature*. CornUP. pp. 194. £23.50, $32.50. ISBN 0 8014 3016 X.
Kennedy, Dennis. *Looking at Shakespeare*. CUP. pp. 399. £45. ISBN 0 5213 4655 X.
Kerrigan, William. *Hamlet's Perfection*. JHUP. pp. 179. £22.50. ISBN 0 8018 4719 2.
Kishi, Tetsuo, Roger Pringle and Stanley Wells, eds. *Shakespeare and Cultural Traditions: The Selected Proceedings of the International Shakespeare Association World Congress, Tokyo, 1991*. AUP, UDelP. pp. 379. £49.50, $59.50. ISBN 0 8741 3462 5.
Klein, Holger, and Christopher Smith, eds. *The Opera and Shakespeare*. *ShY 4*. Mellen. pp. 378. np. ISBN 0 7734 9016 7.
Kornstein, Daniel J. *Kill All the Lawyers?: Shakespeare's Legal Appeal*. PrincetonUP. pp. 274. £24.95. ISBN 0 6910 3217 3.
Lukacher, Ned. *Daemonic Figures: Shakespeare and the Question of Conscience*. CornUP. pp. 228. pb £13.50. ISBN 0 8014 8223 2.
Maher, Mary Z. *Modern Hamlets and their Soliloquies*. UIowaP. pp. 218. $32.95. ISBN 0 8774 5380 2.
Marrapodi, Michele, A. J. Hoenselaars, Marcello Capuzzo and L. Falzon Stantucci, eds. *Shakespeare's Italy: Functions of Italian Locations in Renaissance Drama*. (1993). ManUP. pp. 324. £40. ISBN 0 7190 4089 2.
Matus, Irvin Leigh. *Shakespeare, in Fact*. Continuum. pp. 331. $29.50. ISBN 0 8264 0624 6.
McDonald, Russ, ed. *Shakespeare Reread: The Texts in New Contexts*. CornUP. pp. 296. hb £39.95, pb £15.95. ISBN 0 8014 2917 X, 0 8014 8144 9.

McGuire, Philip C. *Shakespeare: The Jacobean Plays*. Macmillan. pp. 217. hb £37.50, pb £10.99. ISBN 0 3334 4257 1, 0 3334 4258 X.
McIver, Bruce, and Ruth Stevenson, eds. *Teaching With Shakespeare: Critics in the Classroom*. AUP, UDelP. pp. 269. £30, $41.50. ISBN 0 8741 3491 9.
McKernan, Luke, and Olwen Terris. *Walking Shadows: Shakespeare in the National Film and Television Archive*. BFI. pp. 269. hb £35, pb £13.99. ISBN 0 8517 0414 X, 0 8517 0486 7.
McMurtry, Jo. *Shakespeare Films in the Classroom: A Descriptive Guide*. Archon. pp. 249. $39.50. ISBN 0 2080 2369 0.
Melchiori, Giorgio. *Shakespeare's Garter Plays: 'Edward III' to 'Merry Wives of Windsor'*. UDelP, AUP. pp. 155. £23. ISBN 0 8741 3518 4.
Miller, David Lee, Sharon O'Dair and Harold Weber, eds. *The Production of English Renaissance Culture*. CornUP. pp. 326. hb £29.50, $37.50, pb £12.50, $15.95. ISBN 0 8014 2961 7, 0 8014 8201 1.
Neill, Michael, ed. *Anthony and Cleopatra*. OS, WC. OUP. pp. 388. hb £40, pb £3.99. ISBN 0 1981 2909 2, 0 1928 1447 8.
Parker, R. B., ed. *Coriolanus*. OS, WC. OUP. pp. 388. hb £45, pb £3.99. ISBN 0 1928 1452 4, 0 1981 2923 8.
Richmond, Hugh. M. *King Henry VIII*. SiP. ManUP. pp. 160. £29.99. ISBN 0 7190 3657 7.
Scragg, Leah. *Discovering Shakespeare's Meaning: An Introduction to the Study of Shakespeare's Dramatic Structures*. Longman. pp. 237. pb £8.99. ISBN 0 5822 2930 8.
Skovmand, Michael, ed. *Screen Shakespeare: Academic Essays on Shakespearean Films*. AarhusUP. pp. 148. $19.95. ISBN 8 7728 8375 8.
Smidt, Kristian. *Unconformities in Shakespeare's Later Comedies* (1993). Macmillan. pp. 239. £37.50. ISBN 0 3335 8450 3.
Smith, Bruce. *Roasting the Swan of Avon: Shakespeare's Redoubtable Enemies and Dubious Friends*. Folger, UWashP. pp. 75. pb $14.95. ISBN 0 2959 7364 1.
Sokol, B. J. *Art and Illusion in The Winter's Tale*. ManUP. pp. 283. £40, $69.95. ISBN 0 7190 3857 X.
Teague, Frances. *Acting Funny: Comic Theory and Practice in Shakespeare's Plays*. FDUP, AUP. pp. 190. £29.95. ISBN 0 8386 3524 5.
Vaughan, Virginia Mason. *Othello: A Contextual History*. CUP. pp. 243. £30. ISBN 0 5214 6069 7.
Vickers, Brian. *Appropriating Shakespeare: Contemporary Critical Quarrels*. YaleUP. pp. 508. pb £11.95. ISBN 0 3000 6105 6.
Wain, John, ed. *Shakespeare: Macbeth* (rev. edn). Macmillan. pp. 289. hb £37.50, pb £9.99. ISBN 0 3335 3355 0, 0 3335 3356 9.
——, ed. *Shakespeare: Othello* (rev. edn). Macmillan. pp. 231. hb £37.50, pb £9.99. ISBN 0 3335 3353 4, 0 3335 3354 2.
Watson, Robert N. *The Rest Is Silence: Death as Annihilation in the English Renaissance*. UCalP. pp. 416. £40, $52. ISBN 0 5200 8494 2.
Wells, Robin Headlam. *Elizabethan Mythologies: Studies in Poetry, Drama, and Music*. CUP. pp. 287. £37.50, $59.95. ISBN 0 5214 3385 1.
Wells, Stanley. *Shakespeare: A Dramatic Life*. Sinclair-Stevenson. pp. 403. £20. ISBN 1 8561 9423 X.
Williams, Gordon. *A Dictionary of Sexual Language and Imagery in Shakespearean and Stuart Literature*. 3 vols. Athlone. pp. 1616. £350. ISBN 0 4851 1393 7.

Wills, Gary. *Witches and Jesuits: Shakespeare's Macbeth.* OUP. pp. 223. pb £14.50. ISBN 0 1950 8879 4.
Wofford, Susanne L., ed. *Hamlet*. CSCC. Macmillan. pp. 418. £6.99. ISBN 0 3335 9492 4.
Woodbridge, Linda. *The Scythe of Saturn: Shakespeare and Magical Thinking.* UIllP. pp. 390. hb $47.50, pb $17.95. ISBN 0 2520 2080 4, 0 2520 6370 8.

VII

Renaissance Drama: Excluding Shakespeare

MICHAEL JARDINE, SARAH POYNTING, PETER J. SMITH, EMMA SMITH, STUART HAMPTON-REEVES and JULIE SANDERS

This chapter has three sections: 1. Editions and Textual Scholarship; 2. Theatre History; 3. Criticism. Sections 1(a) and 3(c) are by Michael Jardine; section 3(b) is by Stuart Hampton-Reeves; section 1(b) is by Sarah Poynting; section 2 is by Peter J. Smith and Stuart Hampton-Reeves; section 3(a) is by Emma Smith; and section 3(d) is by Julie Sanders. Material concerning the year's work for 1993 which was submitted too late for inclusion in *YWES* 74 is included this year.

1. Editions and Textual Scholarship

(a) Publications (1993)

Three welcome additions to the Revels series represent the most significant publications for this year, maintaining the high standards expected in this series. Christopher Marlowe's *Doctor Faustus*, edited by David Bevington and Eric Rasmussen, makes a particular splash by being the first modernized edition to contain both extant versions of the play, and by arguing that the A-text is 'close to the Marlowe original' while the B-text is a stagy and incoherent revision. They thus challenge the long-held view of the A-text as a memorial reconstruction, arguing for its being based on authorial papers of a collaborative nature, the collaborator being responsible for the comic scenes. They also claim 'intermittent playhouse influence' in the copy for the B-text, which they see as a 'compilation of materials written and revised at different times'. As these texts present possibly 'the most complex and obscure textual problem in Elizabethan dramatic literature' it was felt necessary to publish a companion volume, by Eric Rasmussen, entitled *A Textual Companion to Doctor Faustus*, in order to present the full case for the rehabilitation of the A-text. This represents a total refutation of Greg's 1950 thesis in his *Parallel Texts* edition, which damned the A-text as a bad quarto and made the B-text Marlowe's original, and hence the copy-text. A version of the first chapter of the companion has also been published as 'Rehabilitating the A-text of Marlowe's *Doctor Faustus*' (*SB* [1992] 46.221–38), in which Rasmussen undermines Greg's position, arguing for revision as against memorial contamination.

Further chapters in the companion examine the two versions, review questions of authorship (using function-word frequency tests and arriving at Henry Porter as possible collaborator) and discuss in detail the process of revision, concluding that there is a strong case for treating the versions as separate plays, which 'require different interpretations and separate reading editions'. It is to Rasmussen's credit that even the non-specialist reader will find his detective work an invigorating narrative and his painstaking reasoning both lucid and meticulous.

It is revealing of current disputes within textual scholarship that within the same series we can move from an edition which attacks the practice of conflation to one which is dependent upon it. Ten years of editorial work were needed in preparation for the edition of Thomas Middleton's *A Game at Chess*, by T. H. Howard-Hill. This is a major editorial enterprise also necessitating a separate (forthcoming) publication to contain additional textual commentary. The editorial challenge facing the production of a conflated copy-text can be seen from the fact that the play's early forms are six transcripts by different scribes, plus two distinct early printed editions, allowing unusual access to the text of a play as it evolved during a hectic period of notoriety. Howard-Hill admits that the grounds for his base-text can only be 'informed eclecticism', and the fact that this is a modernized edition disguises some of the editorial problems, as the variant sources have a plethora of orthographic diversity. However, if one accepts the legitimacy of modernized editions this must stand as one of the most valuable of its type, particularly in its detailing of historical context and explication of the 'moral-religious allegory'. Perhaps the appearance of this long-awaited edition will result in this no longer being a play 'more notorious than read'. Of the three other editions to appear in 1993, Albert Tricomi's of Robert Knightley's *Alfrede or Right Reinthron'd* is a 1659 translation of a 1619 Latin play, *Aluredus sive Alfredus*, by William Drury. Tricomi is to be thanked for making available what is a very readable play, and one of considerable literary historical significance. Working from manuscript copy, Tricomi's edition is what he calls a 'conservative transcription', with some of the accuracy of a diplomatic transcription, but with certain concessions to readability. One point further to note is the editor's unusual citing of contemporary critical theory (two references to post-structuralism) in a welcome, if half-hearted, attempt to bridge the yawning gap between textual and critical scholarship. Dana Sutton's edition and translation of *Thomas Legge: The Complete Plays* comes in two volumes; the first volume consists of his *Richard III*, while the second contains his *Solymitana Clades*, each being made up of trilogies on the same historical topic. This is the first translated critical edition and contains a biographical essay with both critical and textual commentary, and the Latin original text is given with a parallel translation based on a collation of available manuscript versions. Legge had a considerable contemporary reputation, being mentioned as one of 'our best for tragedy' by Francis Meres, and the availability of these plays in translation is a very welcome stimulus to our understanding of the important role played by Latin drama in the English Renaissance period. Sutton's textual commentary is well informed, particularly in the historical detail, and goes beyond glossing, for example in noting an intriguing drift from classical, particularly Senecan, models towards realism. Another welcome addition of a neglected play is George Cheatham's edition of the anonymous *A New Wonder, a Woman Never Vext*. Eschewing modernization, Cheatham chooses to offer this 1632 text in an old-spelling format, and it is equipped with a full critical commentary.

In the only remaining full-length publication for 1993, the RETS has gathered together a series of previously published articles from the 1980s on a range of textual matters, designed to illustrate the current diversity of bibliographical approaches. The volume, edited by W. Speed-Hill and entitled *New Ways of Looking at Old Texts*, mainly concerns non-dramatic texts, but some articles focus on early modern drama, those by A. R. Braunmuller, John Pitcher, John Jowett and Margreta de Grazia being of particular interest. The last's 'What is a Work? What is a Document?' is a notable blend of critical theory and bibliographical knowledge which explores the close relationship between new historicism, new textualism and poststructuralism, arguing that 'a single authorial consciousness [. . .] may not be sufficient to account for the complexity and anomalies of texts'. This is a point of debate which underlies many of this year's contributions, in particular G. Thomas Tanselle's 'Editing Without a Copy-Text' (*SB* 47.1–22), a seminal paper which engages with the giants of Renaissance bibliography, McKerrow, Greg and Bowers, on the crucial issue of the role of the 'copy-text'. Tanselle in reviewing this issue asks whether we need critical editions at all, or whether the informed guesswork of editors in emending texts is a skill worth preserving. In the context of a resurgence in preference for facsimile or diplomatic editions, or even computerized 'hypertexts', he concludes that although the role of the editor needs rethinking, there will continue to be a need for the critical edition, though with clear procedures to be followed in making critical judgements. In his view the security of the 'best-text' principle, enshrined in Greg's concept of the copy-text, is no longer sustainable, killed off along with the Barthesian author, leaving us in a postmodern world of 'inherently unstable material'. This lively article is a call for 'an active embracing of judgement', not a giving up in the face of the hypertext.

The most significant of the rest of the articles this year is Thomas O. Calhoun and Thomas L. Gravell's 'Paper and Printing in Ben Jonson's *Sejanus*' (*PBSA* 87.13–64). They reach the conclusion that earlier textual work on *Sejanus* erred as a result of not referring to sufficient copies, in particular missing vital evidence relating to the paper used, which was the more expensive, and therefore rare, English variety. The deduction offered is that, given the proximity of the Gunpowder Plot, and Jonson's concern following his arrest for his part in *Eastward Hoe*, this paper was chosen, with its royal watermarks, in order to advertise Jonson's patriotism. They conjecture that the publication may, indeed, have had the sanction of the king himself. The other main conclusion is that there is evidence of speed in the printing, particularly in the early stages, presumably in order to gain advantage from Jonson's notoriety. Finally, they observe that no two copies studied are the same, meaning that 'there is virtually no chance that Jonson could have retained an exemplary copy [. . .] to serve as authority for the 1616 *Works*'. As a result of this research they conclude that 'an ideal copy of the 1605 quarto can now be constructed and future textual study should follow from it'. Bibliographical interest in Jonson's works also accounts for James A. Riddell's 'The Concluding Pages of the Jonson Folio of 1616' (*SB* 47.147–54). Riddell tackles the thorny problem of which were the original and which the corrected versions of the final two pages of the Folio. He sets out to demonstrate that only one version of the ending can have been the revised one, concluding that the original version of *The Golden Age Restored* placed a speech by Astraea last, and that someone intervened to shift the previous speech by Pallas to the end, not the reverse as has been argued. He thus undermines a number of recent interpretations of the text and of Jonson's politics, and exposes the folly of using dubious textual scholarship on which to rest interpretations of Jonson's political leanings. Jonson also figures prominently in John W. Velz's 'From Authorization to Authorship, Orality to Literature: The Case of Medieval and Renaissance Drama' (*Text* 6.127–36). After surveying the two periods, Velz concludes that Jonson's 1616 Folio marks the point at which plays stopped being drama and became 'literature'.

There are four articles which address problems of authorship, three by means of statistical analysis. 'Neural Computation in Stylometry: An Application to the Works of Shakespeare and Fletcher' (*L&LC* 8.iv.203–10), by R. Matthews and T. Merriam, deploys pattern recognition technique inspired by neurological research, with a sample of 1,000 words from core canon works by Fletcher and Shakespeare, resulting in claims that *The Double Falsehood* and *The London Prodigal* have strongly Fletcherian characteristics, that *Two Noble Kinsmen* shows signs of collaboration between the two, and that *Henry VIII* is Shakespearean. Thomas Merriam uses stylometric analysis in another article, 'Marlowe's Hand in *Edward III*' (*L&LC* 8.ii.59–72), focusing on two scenes (III.i and III.ii), and concluding that 'Marlowe's authorship [. . .] is not beyond the bounds of literary credibility', thus challenging the orthodoxy which points to Shakespeare as probable author. He also conjectures that if this ascription is correct it points to a closer professional relationship between the two authors than previously allowed by scholars. M. W. A. Smith refers back to 1980s debates over authorship in his '*Edmund Ironside*' (*N&Q* 40.202–5), using stylometrics to deny Shakespeare's authorship, 'while simultaneously not diminishing the claims for such an elevation of *Edward III*'. Tirthankar Bose supports the case for Dekker's authorship in '*The Noble Spanish Soldier* and *The Spanish Contract*' (*N&Q* 40.226–7), but argues that these are one and the same play, the latter being an alternative title when the play was taken on tour to Norwich in 1624. A competing conjecture is that it may have been a midway revision between *The Noble Spanish Soldier* and another play by Dekker entitled *The Welsh Embassador*.

The remaining work is made up of a series of small items, the most substantial of which is R. V. Holdsworth's 'Notes on *Women Beware Women*' (*N&Q* 40.2, 215–22), which is offered as a supplement to recent editions of the play and constitutes an invaluable additional commentary on the text. The notes are impressively thorough and reflect Holdsworth's extensive knowledge of early modern drama and his sensitivity to the richly allusive nature of this play. T. W. Craik does a similar, though briefer, job in 'Notes on the Text of Marston's *Antonio and Mellida*' (*N&Q* 40.206–7), again as a supplement to recent editions. The cruces identified here, however, are more open to interpretation, and at times Craik's preferred emendations are not wholly convincing. A number of notes are concerned with tracing sources for plays, the most detailed of which is Michael G. Brennan's 'Christopher Marlowe's *The Jew of Malta* and Two Newsletter Accounts of the Siege of Malta (1565)' (*N&Q* 40.157–60), which offers the first evidence that Marlowe had available at least two English-language versions of newsletters about the siege when he wrote this play. Maureen Godman, in 'Stow's *Summarie*: Source for Marlowe's *Edward II*' (*N&Q* 40.160–3), argues that Stow's text has been overlooked as a source for this play though it is 'very likely' to have been used as 'a starting point', lending an outline for the whole action and providing a 'map' for Marlowe which is so obviously a source that it has been hitherto ignored. In 'Medwall's *Fulgens and Lucres* as a Probable Source for Middleton and Rowley's *A Fair Quarrel*' (*N&Q* 40.214–15), Swapan Chakravorty notes similarities between a 'duel of flatulence' in each text, and argues for a 'wider link' as both plays are concerned with the same theme, the source of true nobility. In '*The Changeling* and Thomas Watson's *Hecatompathia*' (*N&Q* 40.222–40), Douglas Bruster claims to be the first to note the influence of Watson's text on Rowley's part of the play. Bruster traces numerous borrowings before proceeding to claim that Middleton's contribution was also under Watson's influence. Finally, two notes comment on problematical words, Antony Telford Moore's '"Shey" in Jacobean and Caroline Drama' (*N&Q* 40.228-9) and Derek Britton's 'The Meaning of *Geances* in Jonson's *A Tale of a Tub*' (*N&Q* 40.226-9). Moore's is a particularly interesting note which exposes the fallibility of editors in ignorantly altering text which is correct (i.e. 'shey' meaning 'say' or 'say ye'). Britton's definition of 'geances' as referring to small Genoese coins again corrects widespread editorial error and also has the effect of defending the questioned authenticity of Jonson's representation of Middlesex dialect.

(b) Publications (1994)

The publisher's introduction to the Clarendon Press edition of Marlowe's *Edward II* tells us that there has been no 'critical edition of the play with full scholarly apparatus for twenty-five years'. This omission has now been put right not only by OUP, but also by ManUP, which has published a new critical edition of Marlowe's play this year as well. However, although both editions use the 1594 quarto (the only authoritative early edition) for their copy-text, in other ways they are so different from each other that they may be seen as complementary rather than competitive. Richard Rowland's edition, the third volume of the Oxford *Complete Works*, is an old-spelling edition with a bare twenty pages of critical introduction and the commentary banished to the back pages, while Charles Forker's follows the usual Revels format of a modernized text, with an old-spelling collation and critical commentary on the same page as the text, and an introduction that is in itself the length of a short book. The differences, however, are deeper than those simply of presentation (which may in any case affect our reading of the text). The two editions present us with differing textual information, critical interpretation, collation, division of the text, and even slightly different extracts from Holinshed.

Both editors quote from the expanded 1587 edition of Holinshed, but Rowland, in his stimulating introduction, places its additions, particularly the new pages of the *Historie of Scotland,* at the centre of his consideration of the contemporary resonances of the play, in the context of which his discussion of genre, dramaturgy, style and critical interpretation is firmly sited. Staging and audience response are also briefly considered, with attention paid particularly to Jacobean revivals. Forker's much more detailed, and perhaps more conventionally 'literary', introduction relegates topicality to a footnote, but is thorough in its analysis of Marlovian and Shakespearean cross-influences and echoes, Marlowe's treatment of his sources, critical reception of the play from Charles Lamb onwards, and its twentieth-century stage history.

The 1594 quarto, with its lack of act or scene divisions, presents editors with an unavoidable decision as to how to present the text. Rowland has opted for a simple division into twenty-three scenes, while Forker prefers a full five-act structure. The quarto text requires little emendation, and, in keeping with the practice of the Oxford series, Rowland records at the foot of each page only those substantive variants adopted from other editions. He has, though, made use of the fuller punctuation introduced in later Jacobean quartos in order to clarify the text.

The Revels edition, while, as usual, not presenting a full historical collation, does provide a collation of significant nineteenth- and twentieth-century texts, as well as an appendix listing additional variants from the editions of 1818.

Both editions, of course, provide their readers with full commentaries, but we learn different things from each of them. Rowland, for example, tells us about Marlowe's use of the word 'favourite', while Forker informs us about 'minion'; the former, in his comment on 'Hylas', directs our notice to Propertius and Spenser, the latter to Drayton. Rowland pays particularly close attention to the relationship between *Edward II* and the works of Nashe, a useful addition to Forker's discussion of Marlowe and Shakespeare. Forker and Rowland both, finally, provide us with excerpts from Holinshed, to which Forker adds extracts from Stowe, Fabyan, Grafton and Churchyard.

The Malone Society edition for this year is Samuel Daniel's *Hymen's Triumph*, a page-for-page near-diplomatic transcription by John Pitcher of the sole remaining manuscript, which was supervised and corrected by Daniel, and is now in Edinburgh University Library. Until – and, indeed, after – such time as his full critical edition of the play is published (as part of the complete poetry and drama edition from Oxford English Texts), this makes a very useful addition to the Malone Society's collection, and it is, as one would expect, a scrupulous transcription, with textual notes recording everything that cannot be shown in the text, from corrections in a different hand to ink dots. There is a thorough and enlightening textual introduction. It is particularly interesting on the work of the two scribes responsible for the manuscript, and an unexpectedly lively picture emerges of the scribes copying even as Daniel was finishing his work on the lyrics of the play's choruses. John Pitcher has also escaped, to an extent, from the austerely textual limits once placed on Malone introductions, and provides us with a welcome discussion of the performance of the play and its historical context.

The new contributor to this section took it over very late in the year and has been unable, owing to the constraints of time, to include any discussion of articles of textual interest. We apologize for this omission, as well as the absence of any editions which may have been missed. These will be included in next year's issue.

2. Theatre History

In a weighty article, Daryl W. Palmer investigates the interrelationship between physicality and the wielding of political power. 'Edward IV's Secret Familiarities and the Politics of Proximity in Elizabethan History Plays' (*ELH* 61.279–315) suggests that this particular reign offered chronicle historians an interpretative puzzle: how to celebrate the union of the house of Tudor without foregrounding 'the continuity of discords, sects and factions'. Palmer goes on to illustrate attitudes to the shaping of history through erotic intimacy and looks in particular at the cases of Edward IV and Jane Shore. Palmer ends his article with a comparison of Heywood's and Shakespeare's treatments of relations (sexual and political) which straddle divisions of social class. Heywood's histories, Palmer argues, are more democratic, beginning 'nearer the bottom of the social ladder'.

In '"One Man in His Time Plays Many Parts": Authorial Theatrics of Doubling in Early English Renaissance Drama' (*SP* 91.359–89), John W. Sider offers diagrammatic schemes and explanations of doubling in a number of sixteenth-century plays in an effort to establish some common practices, but this thirty-page article with two appendices is all much ado. Sider's citation of Wever's *Lusty Juventus* (1550) actually illustrates the nonchalance with which doubling seems to have been treated: 'Foure may play it easely, taking such partes as they think best: so that any one take of those partes that be not in place at once.' Sider proposes a number of significant doublings for several of the plays, based on character contrasts or parallels, but eventually is forced to concede the flimsiness of his suggestions.

D. Allen Carroll explores the problems surrounding the identification of 'The Player-Patron in *Greene's Groatsworth of Wit* (1592)' (*SP* 91.301–12). He notes that several candidates have been advanced, including Shakespeare and Edward Alleyn, both of whom Carroll dismisses because they would have been too young. Carroll goes on to advance Anthony Munday as 'the most interesting of all possibilities'. This prospect depends on 'the whole of *Groatsworth* [being] a hoax', having been composed by Henry Chettle but, as Carroll concedes, 'the basis for an identification of Munday here is, finally, too weak and fleeting to carry conviction'. In 'Property or Performer?: Animals on the Elizabethan Stage' (*TheatreS* 39.45–59), Matthew Bliss considers the use of animals in performance. Of the stage direction, '*His dogs bark: bow wow*' (in *The Staple of News*), Bliss ponders 'Is "bow wow" a simple woof or a continued baying at the intruders?' The account of Crab in *The Two Gentlemen of Verona* is nearer the mark, especially when it notes that it is the unpredictability of the dog that demands of the actor playing Launce the capacity to improvise.

Shifting from creatures canine to avian, we have Allan Pritchard's interesting piece on ducks and drakes. In 'Puritans and the Blackfriars Theater: The Cases of Mistresses Duck and Drake' (*SQ* 45.92–5), he explores the anti-theatrical sentiment of two spiritual biographies of the later 1640s. Margaret Duck was a follower of the anti-theatre Puritan divine, William Gouge, though her husband, Arthur, had been appointed chancellor of the diocese of London by none less than Archbishop Laud. Pritchard resolves, wisely, that such a situation 'illustrates how problematic the term *Puritan* can be'. Joan Drake was married against her will and her 'suffering was aggravated by a mismanaged childbirth'. She was then ministered to by a number of Puritan clergy including Dr John Dod. Drake herself seems to have treated the divine with contempt, 'likening him unto *Ananias*, one whom at a play in the Black-Friers shee saw scoft at, for a holy brother of *Amsterdam*', which suggests that she had seen a performance of *The Alchemist*.

There is an appropriately complimentary review of Richard Dutton's *Mastering the Revels* (*YWES* 72.192–3) from T. H. Howard-Hill in his 'Reveling in the Masters: Court, Censorship, and Comedians in the English Renaissance' (*Rev* 16.271–80). Howard-Hill notes that what has survived from the period is the censored version. Therefore, any 'topical references so identified by the modern critic [which] have survived to the printed text [. . .] can be used as evidence of what censors would tolerate [. . . However] we cannot be certain that the censorial reader ever noticed the topical allusions that the ingenious modern critic, perhaps for the first time, has detected in them.'

Two short notes on theatre buildings and the personnel involved: Mary Edmond's 'Hudson and the Burbages' (*N&Q* 41.502–3) provides a picture from various surviving sources of Richard Hudson, a building worker known to the Burbages and associated with the Chamberlain's/King's Men. He may, Edmond ventures, have been 'one of the men employed by Peter Street to dismantle the Theatre and use the timber to build the Globe in 1599'. Chris Sutcliffe, in 'Robert

Armin: Apprentice Goldsmith' (*N&Q* 41.503–4), notes that John Lonyson, Master of Works at the Royal Mint, to whom Armin was apprenticed, came from Lynn, as did his apprentice, and would have been a contemporary of Armin's father.

Lynda E. Boose's 'The 1599 Bishops' Ban, Elizabethan Pornography, and the Sexualization of the Jacobean Stage' (in Richard Burt and John Michael Archer, eds, *Enclosure Acts: Sexuality, Property, and Culture in Early Modern England*) is reviewed below, section 3(a). In '"Mummerset": The Delineation of a Popular Genre' (in Claudia Blank, ed., *Language and Civilization*), Martyn F. Wakelin examines the phonological and grammatical features of the dialect in a number of appropriate extracts from texts spanning *Gammer Gurton's Needle* to Defoe's *Tour Thro' the Whole Island of Great Britain*. He notes that the language of Alfred's Wessex was eclipsed by Anglo-Norman and the later rise of Standard English and, as a result, was increasingly associated with vulgarity. Barbara D. Palmer also insists on the importance of the provinces' contribution in challenging the metropolitan bias of our view of Renaissance performance. 'Early Entertainment Patterns in Northern England' (*BJRL* 74[1992].175–87) establishes four important principles: first, the cultural influence of the great households; second, the blurring of the line between religious and secular entertainments; third, that the rigid separation of 'professional' and 'amateur' will not hold; and finally, that travel between northern and southern England and the level of communication as a result of it have 'been seriously underestimated and undervalued'. Her essay concludes with the call to revise the 'map of early English entertainment' in the light of documentary evidence.

Documentary evidence is thin on the ground in Max W. Thomas's '*Kemps Nine Daies Wonder*: Dancing Carnival to Market' (*PMLA* 107 [1992].511–23). Thomas reads Kemp's record of his London to Norwich dance as an incipient commodification of a traditional and hitherto communal pastime, the morris dance, but relies too heavy-handedly on a vocabulary of economic determinism, according to which the dance (and the book-of-the-dance) are reified into the weapons of a capitalist conspiracy.

'The Seasons of the Globe: Two New Studies of Elizabethan Drama and Festival' (*Connotations* 2 [1992].234–56) is a prolix review article that runs to over twenty pages, in the course of which Thomas Pettitt considers only two books: François Laroque's *Shakespeare's Festive World* and Sandra Billington's *Mock Kings in Medieval Society and Renaissance Drama* (both 1991). Pettitt identifies two approaches in the study of Shakespeare and the carnival. The first, represented by E. K. Chambers and C. L. Barber is historically based but 'does not inevitably make for exciting reading'. The second, represented by Bakhtin, is that 'in which historical scholarship [. . .] is largely waived in favour of an immediate plunge into sociocultural interpretation of Elizabethan theatre and drama in terms of festive perspectives'. Pettitt goes on, 'It is greatly to their credit that both of the works under review here are firmly in the Chambers–Barber tradition.' Pettitt, rightly, makes some factual corrections to both books, but a good deal of this overlong piece is off target. [PJS]

In the light of recent archaeological discoveries and of modern research into provincial playing, the question of how early modern playhouses were built now begins to inform our sense of their social and political situation, to an extent that this year, those works which deal primarily with the nuts and bolts of early modern theatre do more to open up its material reality than those works which explore it from an exclusively sociological perspective.

Accordingly, the best book of the year is Alan H. Nelson's *Early Cambridge Theatres: College, University and Town Stages, 1464–1720*, which manages to yield real insights into the politics of playing in a university town through a study of its playing places. The meat of Nelson's book is a study and a taxonomy of Cambridge stages, which are reconstructed through the application of traditional carpentry methods rather than the classical architectural theories which have previously guided research into building practice. Perhaps the most surprising speculation for those interested in these matters is Nelson's assertion that the Trinity College Hall was designed with its playing area integral to the building. A chapter on university commencement stages makes use of some unpublished research as well as permitting some thoughts on the 'theatre' of degree ceremonies. However, the real charm of this book is its digressions and anecdotes, in the main drawn from Nelson's voluminous research for REED. Nelson makes much of his methodological revolution of classical theory in favour of the ancient tradition of carpentry, but his reliance on one source runs the risk of reintroducing a uniformity to a practice that we now tend to acknowledge as complex and diverse. Such a risk is confronted by John Orrell in his article, 'The Architecture of the Fortune Playhouse' (*ShS* 47.15–28). Orrell knows full well that early modern playhouses were not built according to classical virtues, but he also knows that the complexity of social pressures did not preclude such influence. The playhouse was built as a copy of the Globe, but it was set square, an interesting diversion which, along with the terms and satyrs which Street and Alleyn introduced into the English theatre, reflected Alleyn's desire to give expression to the virtues of fit proportion and contained energy. Although Alleyn's venture may not be reckoned much of a commercial success, Orrell argues that its design was to have a lasting influence on English playhouse architecture.

In his article 'Drama and the Resistance to Institutions in Somerset' (*RORD* 33.153–64), James D. Stokes seeks a re-evaluation of court records as an important source of resistance to the regulation and suppression of ancient entertainments and rituals between the 1530s and the 1630s. The court records for Somerset are richly detailed, and give the impression that local resistance was substantial through the century. At the end of the article, Stokes makes a teasing connection between the dwindling resistance to reform in the 1630s and the civil war of the 1640s, a sociopolitical point that seems worthy of elaboration. Another pressure on local traditions of playing may have been the commercial activities of the touring player, who is the subject of Alan Somerset's '"How Chances it they Travel?": Provincial Touring, Playing Places, and the King's Men' (*ShS* 47.45–60). Somerset argues that touring was an economic and diverting alternative to the London theatres, as it allowed the players the luxury of playing on mainly indoor stages with a limited repertory, saving them from the arduous task of regularly rehearsing new plays.

Jean E. Howard's *The Stage and Social Struggle in Early Modern England* and Laura Levine's *Men in Women's Clothing: Anti-Theatricality and Effeminization, 1579–1642* deserve to be read alongside each other, as texts which reflect upon the current state of new historicism, and as texts which explore cross-dressing on the Renaissance stage in comparable ways. The advance which both Levine and Howard make (apparently independently of each other) is to turn the tables on the theatre, by studying some surprising echoes of the anti-theatricalist terror of effeminization in the drama of Shakespeare, Jonson, Dekker and Marlowe, among others. It is at this point that the two scholars differ: Levine analyses these episodes as satirical send-ups of such sexual anxieties and a deliberate rebuttal of the theatre's critics, whilst Howard prefers to see both the pamphleteer and the dramatist in opposition to the fluid, effeminizing and beguiling power of the stage. In Howard's view, the discourse of theatricality staged the struggle between the forces of change and conservatism, in a time of rapid social development. The theatre's enemies, such as Gosson and Stubbes, attacked it as an agent of social change, in some sense symbolic of all that was fallen and sinful about their age. Howard is prepared to give a surprising amount of weight to this anti-theatrical ideology, as she goes on to explore its appearances in plays by Dekker, Jonson and Shakespeare, who harbour similar anxieties. The tenor of Howard's book is reflective, especially in the early chapters, where much space is devoted to a valuable and clear restating of the new historicist mode of materialist analysis.

Laura Levine gives more credit to the dramatist by reading scenes of voyeurism in Shakespeare as anti-anti-theatrical moments, in which the epistemological framework of the theatre's critics is rehearsed and tested. In her study of the pamphleteers, Levine emphasizes their restricted universe of pure referentiality, in which signs are equivalent to things, so that transvestism is considered as an actual adulteration of the male, with the women's clothing having the power physically to feminize the body. This 'magical thinking' is staged by Shakespeare and Jonson in order to render it fictional and absurd. Where Howard explores the contradictions within the theatrical institution, Levine prefers to see it in direct opposition to conservative tendencies. This method exchanges a complex social analysis for a complex textual analysis, which registers nuances of irony and agenda in the plays but relies upon a sense of the negotiation between theatre and society which is too easy. That Howard's and Levine's work is finally incompatible raises a legitimate question about their materialist methodology. A fault which both works share is an insufficient grounding in the actual material conditions of the theatre and the period: many of their generalizations and assumptions are based on a construct of the early modern theatre which is rapidly becoming obsolete.

Those readers who feel that Howard and Levine do not go far enough in pursuing gender constructions and give too much away to history and theory will enjoy reading Frances E. Dolan's absorbing study, '"Gentlemen, I have one more thing to say": Women on Scaffolds in England, 1563–1680' (*MP* 92.157–78). Strictly speaking, the scaffold is not a theatre, but Dolan insists that it is a stage, which occasionally gave the main part to a woman, who found herself in the unique position of being in public and having nothing to lose, to be able to have her say and have her voice recorded. Consequently, the scaffold was not only a *locus* of power in action, but a theatre of slippages, especially when the condemned refused to follow the script and performed extempore. By contrast, the theatre appears as a timid agent, a social galvanizer which silently executes its characters offstage.

In 'Edward Alleyn and the Rose Playhouse: Biography and Repertoire' (*THStud* 14.85–93), Leslie du S. Read draws a portrait of Alleyn during his tenure at the Rose playhouse in the 1590s. The career and biography of another actor, Joseph Taylor, is reconsidered in 'Shakespeare and Joseph Taylor' by David Farley-Hills (*N&Q* 41.58–61). Taylor joined the King's Men after Burbage's death and took over many of the leading roles in Shakespeare's plays. Farley-Hill argues that Shakespeare may have personally instructed Taylor when he was a boy actor.

Andrew Gurr offers a cautionary warning against exceeding the limits of historical methodology in 'The Bare Island' (*ShS* 47.29–44), which, following the current trajectory of Gurr's work, seems to be more concerned with exposing the extent of our ignorance than curing us of it. Prospero's 'bare island', which he departs from at the end of *The Tempest*, is still obscure to theatre historians. Gurr asks what it was bare of, going on to reflect how little we know of the Shakespearean *mise-en-scène* and how indefinite our sense of the 'geography of the stage' still is, in spite of all our advances in understanding the building practice and the social role of the playhouses. Gurr would have some sympathy with Caroline Gardiner, who set herself the unenviable task of comparing Shakespeare's latterday audiences with his original ones in 'From Bankside to the West End: a Comparative View of London Audiences' (*NTQ* 10.70–86). The rich archive of statistical evidence for modern audiences which Gardiner is able to draw on dwarfs the pitiful and inconsistent evidence for their early modern ancestors. Gardiner's conclusion is that the West End audiences are more socially diverse than Bankside audiences, but they attend the theatre less frequently.

Finally, Kathleen O. Irace's *Reforming the 'Bad' Quartos: Performance and Provenance of Six Shakespearean First Editions* re-evaluates the famous bad quartos as texts which have been performed and recorded by either actors or audience; for Irace, they are authentic records of actual performances, which offer a tantalizing window on the business of staging and adapting plays in Shakespeare's theatre. The textual corruptions of these 'first editions' are then thought of as a consequence of the vagaries and practicalities of their performance, rather than the faulty memory of an actor. [SHR]

3. Criticism

(a) General

The most significant work to be published this year is, without doubt, Jean Howard's *The Stage and Social Struggle in Early Modern England*. Howard's book opens by presenting 'a brief for political criticism', and proposes to examine the politics of the representation of the stage and its practitioners in a range of dramatic texts and in anti-theatrical and anti-feminist pamphlets which she designates as a 'genre of anxiety'. She is sensitive to local nuances, arguing that the early modern theatre was neither essentially subversive nor recuperative, but that it 'could and did serve a variety of competing class and gender interests'. The gap between the experience of the staged play and the ostensible sentiments of the scripts being performed presents one of the many ideological inconsistencies of the institution of theatre, in which practices such as cross-dressing can be accommodated to a conservative or radical telos. This study is an invaluable addition to the literature on the fractured ideological role of the theatre and its representational strategies, and although its sourcing of attitudes to gender might be considered selective, its reading of play texts and the theatre as text is an important contribution to the field.

Questions of gender and sexuality are addressed in numerous articles and books. Marjorie Garber puts a characteristically contemporary gloss on Middleton's *The Changeling* in 'The Insincerity of Women' (in Valeria Finucci and Regina Schwartz, eds, *Desire in the Renaissance*), in which she suggests that Beatrice-Joanna learns 'how to fake it' in Alsemero's laboratory, and compares the representation of her repeated 'O's with the notorious 'faking it' scene in the 1989 film *When Harry Met Sally*. . . . Garber equates this 'insincerity of women' with the intrinsic insincerity of the theatre, whose representation of female pleasure 'is itself a changeling'. Jean Howard's contribution to the collection, *Women, 'Race', and Writing in the Early Modern Period*, edited by Margo Hendricks and Patricia Parker, considers 'An English Lass Amid the Moors: Gender, Race, Sexuality, and National Identity in Heywood's *The Fair Maid of the West*'. Her essay places the play within the contemporary emerging and tentative discourse of national identity defined partly by geography and partly by a perceived difference from other imagined communities, arguing that the weighted binary opposition of English/Spanish is triangulated by the third term of Moor. She traces Bess's character as an exploration of the ambivalent role of gender in nationalism, as the 'English lass' both resolves tension and renders it ultimately irresolvable.

Heywood's negotiations of gender are also discussed in three overlapping essays on *A Woman Killed with Kindness*: Nancy Gutierrez's 'Exorcism by Fasting in *A Woman Killed with Kindness*: A Paradigm of Puritan Resistance?' (*RORD* 33.43–62), Cynthia Lewis's 'Heywood's *Gunaikeion* and Woman-Kind in *A Woman Killed with Kindness*' (*ELN* 32.24–36), which suggests that in both texts, Heywood dissents from the received tradition of patriarchal domination, and Jennifer Panek's 'Punishing Adultery in *A Woman Killed With Kindness*' (*SEL* 34.357–78), which also refers to *Gunaikeion*, alleging, somewhat contentiously, that this work 'can reasonably be taken to contain Heywood's personal views on female adultery and its punishment'. Panek's essay suggests that the play is a negative exemplum of how not to treat a repentant adulteress, although her conclusions may be undermined by unsubstantiated generalizations such as her claim that the idea of 'companionate marriage [. . .] was generally accepted in Renaissance times'. Gutierrez's references to beliefs about marriage and religion carry more authority, and her article suggests that Anne's death by fasting is both religious salvation and political resistance. Gutierrez seems, however, to use 'Puritan' and 'puritan' without distinction, and her portentous final sentence, which describes the play as encoding 'the strained undercurrents that will later in the century disrupt the larger world of the state', threatens to drag down her whole argument with its unsupported weight. Lena Cowen Orlin's discussion of Heywood's play in her highly suggestive study *Private Matters and Public Culture in Post-Reformation England* offers a more sophisticated reading in the context of her overall thesis that early modern culture located the private in property. She analyses Heywood's meticulous evocation of the household through stage business, arguing for the importance of the domestic setting in the conceptual history of the private. Orlin also reads *Arden of Faversham* and related archival material to reveal the early historicization of the story as a complex interplay of extra-domestic hostilities, in which public and private lose their distinction. At times her method may seem overly concerned to make plays stand as documentary evidence – early in the study she explains that 'the texts I treat here serve as a public laboratory for intellectual investigation of disorders in the private sphere' – but her readings are careful and her narrative a useful one. Also concerned with the domestic genre is ' "Arden lay murdered in that plot of ground": Surveying, Land, and *Arden of Faversham*' (*ELH* 61.231–52), in which Garrett A. Sullivan Jr examines the play's 'ethics of ownership' in the context of early modern surveying and the cultural function of land. His ultimate conclusion on the play is very close to Orlin's: that it collapses the categories of public and private.

There is yet more attention to Heywood in Richard Rowland's ' "Thou teachest me humanitie": Thomas Heywood's *The English Traveller*' (in Michael Cordner,

Peter Holland and John Kerrigan, eds, *English Comedy*). Rowland argues that the play is a riposte to William Prynne's attack on the stage, and is a self-reflexive comic investigation into the instability of generic conventions. Kathleen E. McLuskie looks at Heywood alongside one of his contemporaries in *Dekker and Heywood: Professional Dramatists,* in which she argues that both playwrights' primary relationship to their art was dominated by the marketplace. McLuskie is particularly good at drawing out the commercially successful mixture of stage tradition and innovation which marks the dramaturgy of Dekker and Heywood, arguing that both writers represented popular political concerns, and that their roles for women create new possibilities for the staging of the domestic realm. The importance of the two playwrights is their engagement in explicit debate on issues of cultural politics over a long period of social and political change. One unanswered question in McLuskie's study is, however, why Dekker and Heywood might benefit from being considered together, and the format of alternate chapters on each author suggests that in fact this double focus cannot easily be synthesized.

Beaumont and Fletcher's collaboration makes them more obvious candidates for a joint study, and their partnership is the subject of two books and two articles. Sandra Clark's *The Plays of Beaumont and Fletcher: Sexual Themes and Dramatic Representation* discusses the neglect of these authors, and suggests that their *oeuvre* is ripe for reconsideration by both critics and directors. Clark is interested in illuminating the dramatic conditions of performance, arguing that meaning is produced through reading and performance, rather than being inherent in the text. It is the representation of gender which is the focus of her book, and in this area Clark offers a measured contribution to theories of the significance of stage transvestism, keeping a distance from the critical debate to which she alludes. 'Beaumont and Fletcher' becomes, however, a strange portmanteau term, as Clark discusses their separate collaborations with other playwrights and does not really address the issues of joint authorship. The treatment of these questions is a particular strength, though, of Jeffrey A. Masten's essay (in Martha Woodmansee and Peter Jaszi, eds, *The Construction of Authorship*) on the history of the concepts of authorship, copyright and intellectual property. Masten attempts a prequel to Roland Barthes's famous concept of the death of the author by examining the collaborative texts of the early modern theatre. He argues for a rethinking of collaborative literature as a profound unsettling of author-centred methodologies, positing that multiple authorship is not merely a doubling of existing author-figures but also acts to disperse the authors and authority of the text. In another essay (in Jonathan Goldberg, ed., *Queering the Renaissance*), Masten concentrates on the homoerotic dynamic of the 1647 Beaumont and Fletcher Folio, which presents the plays as the strange progeny of 'two Masculines espous'd'. Masten reads the anxieties about the status of the joint work in the commendatory verses and other prefatory material, and uses Aubrey's famous recollection of the Beaumont and Fletcher household to discuss the intersecting phobias of homoeroticism and collaboration. As in the Folio, which bears a picture of Fletcher and gives him the lion's share of the attention of the commendatory verses, Gordon McMullan's *The Politics of Unease in the Plays of John Fletcher* reconsiders the epistemological challenge of collaborative texts with a focus on an individual. McMullan looks at the ways in which, through collaboration, generic instability and politics, Fletcher's output is characterized by a doubleness which defies standard critical practices. Arguing that collaboration is central to the early modern theatre and not only to those texts which have more than one named author, he is particularly erudite in tracing the influence of Shakespeare's plays on Fletcher's work, seeing Fletcher's early analysis of sexual politics as deriving from *The Taming of the Shrew* and later plays reworking the themes of *The Tempest*. Also concerned with genre limits is Martin Butler's '*A New Way to Pay Old Debts*: Massinger's Grim Comedy' (in Cordner et al., *English Comedy*) which reinstates the play in the context of war fever in 1623. Butler contends that the play is preoccupied with preserving the status quo, but that it rehearses a split in the ideology of deference during the 1620s.

Like McMullan, Lisa Hopkins also reconsiders an often overlooked dramatist in her *John Ford's Political Theatre*, which discusses Ford's work under the two categories of politics and religion. Hopkins begins with a dazzling reconstruction of the links between Ford and his dedicatees, which is both fascinating in its connections, and convincing in situating Ford within a 'Catholic coterie'. Her facility in elucidating personal friendship and familial ties is also demonstrated in her note 'A Source for John Ford's *'Tis Pity She's a Whore*' (*N&Q* 41.520–1). In her book she goes on to consider *Perkin Warbeck* as a Stuart succession play, and links aristocratic nostalgia for the past with a yearning for certain aspects of Catholicism in many of Ford's plays. Protestant and Catholic attitudes to food, language and the body are discussed, and Hopkins concludes this valuable study by describing Ford's serious aesthetic, religious and political agenda as dictating both his artistic successes and failures. In another note on Ford, she suggests that *'Tis Pity She's a Whore* is not a glorification of incest but an investigation of insanity ('John Ford's *'Tis Pity She's a Whore* and Early Diagnoses of *Folie à Deux*', *N&Q* 41.71–4).

George K. Hunter's 'Rhetoric in Renaissance Drama' (in Peter Mack, *Renaissance Rhetoric*) begins with a somewhat uneasy denial of a simple link between 'modern literary criticism' and Renaissance rhetoric, and goes on to describe what he calls the 'ethical polyphony' of Dekker and Webster's *Westward Ho!*. This approach is derived from rhetorical analysis without reference to the collaborative status of the play, and although Hunter's institutional context for the study of literature is an interesting one, it seems to lack confidence in its self-reflexivity. Karin S. Coddon's '"For Show or Useless Property": Necrophilia and *The Revenger's Tragedy*' (*ELH* 61.71–88) finds that the play's theatricalization of disguise and desire decentres the revenger, and confounds the boundaries of subject and object. In parodying death through the eroticized skull of Gloriana, *The Revenger's Tragedy* intervenes in contemporary notions of the body as object of desire and investigation. The play is also considered in Annette Drew-Bear's survey *Painted Faces on the Renaissance Stage: The Moral Significance of Face-Painting Conventions*, in which she uses it to illustrate the link between cosmetics, poisoning and sexual corruption. Drew-Bear traces stage face-painting back to the Tudor interludes, and, more sketchily, to biblical precedents, such as Mary Magdalene. Her theme is the restating of Dekker's 'there's knavery in dawbing', and while she discusses many examples of face-painting, her work is disappointingly uninformed by critical debates about theatricality and disguise, or the production of gender. She ventures only rarely outside dramatic literature, in a study which might have benefited from references to, say, social history, fashion or sermon literature.

In *The Bed-Trick in English Renaissance Drama*, Marliss C. Desens asserts that this significant dramatic convention has not received due critical attention. She traces its biblical, classical and folkloric antecedents, and argues that in the drama it is a strategy usually sanctioned by a male authority figure and an attempt to reconcile the idealized and the sexual woman. Desens has little to say about the extra-dramatic context, for example the difficulties of defining legitimate marriage vows and promises in the period with which she is concerned, and there are inconsistencies in her argument, particularly when she censures previous critics for centring the dramatic bed-trick convention on Shakespeare, while going on to present her material as a mere context to 'better appreciate Shakespeare's individual achievement'. This is a slight work which frequently declares the neglected importance of the bed-trick without ever quite demonstrating it, although its appendix of bed-tricks in forty-four plays between 1594 and 1630 is a useful overview. A more successful discussion of a dramatic convention, which also lists its occurrences in an appendix, is Alison Findlay's *Illegitimate Power: Bastards in Renaissance Drama*. This work discusses the 'production of illegitimacy as a cultural phenomenon' through non-dramatic literature such as pamphlets and parish records, as well as plays. Findlay analyses the figure of the bastard in relation to notions of crisis and disorder, linking him – bastards seem invariably to be male – to discourses of witchcraft, anti-Catholicism, malcontents, masterless men and rebellion. In an accessible style, the book allies the bastard with a feminine world as a threat to patriarchal society, and the final chapter is a lucid and interesting investigation of the staging of the bastard, his particular relationship to the performance arena and the audience as the summation of his ideological, verbal and spatial detachment from legitimate society. Also on outsiders is Rosemary Gaby's 'Of Vagabonds and Commonwealths: *Beggar's Bush*, *A Jovial Crew* and *The Sisters*' (*SEL* 34.401–24), which investigates how these plays by Fletcher, Brome and Shirley present communities of rural vagabonds as a kind of utopia, expressing defiance and embracing liberty.

Three essays consider Elizabeth Cary's play *Mariam*: two of these, Marta Straznicky's '"Profane Stoical Paradoxes": *The Tragedie of Mariam* and Sidnean Closet Drama' (*ELR* 24.104–34) and Laurie J. Shannon's '*The Tragedie of Mariam*: Cary's Critique of the Terms of Founding Social Discourse' (*ELR* 24.135–53), in a special edition of *ELR* devoted to Renaissance women's writing, and the other, 'Re-reading Elizabeth Cary's *The Tragedie of Mariam, Faire Queene of Jewry*' by Dympna Callaghan, in Hendricks and Parker, *Women, 'Race', and Writing*. As Callaghan's full citation of the play's title suggests, her essay is concerned with Cary's representation of 'race' (the 'scare-quotes' remind the reader of what the editors of the volume recognize as the instability of the term, especially in the early modern context), but, like the *ELR* essays, this 're-reading' is concerned to promote criticism of *Mariam* which escapes the hermeneutics of biography that reduce the play's action and characterization to Cary's projection of her own life. For Callaghan, second-wave critical attention to the play places its depiction of an idealized and degraded femininity in relation to its portrayal of 'race'. Both gender and 'race' are mechanisms for the construction and negotiation of difference. Shannon's essay also criticizes an exclusively biographical approach to the text, while providing a useful survey of previous criticism. She chooses rather to focus on Cary's intervention in the debate about the morality of unjust laws and authorities, while seeing in her dedicatory sonnets to female friends a 'feminist wisdom' exiled from the text proper. Straznicky's corrective to readings of the play as Cary's own personal history attempts to insert it in a reconstruction of the political-interest network of the Sidney circle. She makes interesting suggestions about the gendering of stoical rhetoric, and proposes that Cary's rewriting of the stoic ethic presents the disempowered female protagonist with a discourse of politicized heroism.

The most provocative article this year must be Theodore B. Leinwand's 'Redeeming Beggary/Buggery in *Michaelmas Term*' (*ELH* 61.53–70), which delights in the bawdy wordplay of Middleton's drama, and places it in the context of the play's evocation of, and appeal to, a 'homoerotic and misogynistic London'. Leinwand's essay will make it impossible to ignore the implications of the names Rearage and Cockstone, though his suggestion that Quomodo's two spirits are really spurts of seminal fluid might be more easily dismissed. There is something very suggestive, however, in his linking of beggary, or class, with buggery, or sex, and his relating of sodomitical discourse with discourses of economic corruption and status infraction. Social status also is an important aspect of James R. Siemon's essay 'Sporting Kyd' (*ELR* 24.553–83). Siemon takes his title from Jonson's description of Kyd, using a formalist equation of form and social interaction to argue that 'sporting' can refer to both artist and art. He elaborates certain binaries in *The Spanish Tragedy* such as native/foreign, and scholar/gentleman, and links these to Kyd's humanist education, which confronts the tension between birth/education. William Empson found other tensions in Kyd's play. His reprinted *Essays on Renaissance Literature. Vol. 2: The Drama* (ed. John Haffenden) show him struggling with the idea that the inconsistencies and uncertainties in *The Spanish Tragedy* are evidence of censorship because of the sensitivity of Elizabeth's French marriage negotiations. Sometimes this thesis looks highly speculative, as is admitted by its author, who, asserting that Andrea murdered for love, adds that 'it is peculiar for the text never to say it'. In the face of this difficulty, Empson supplies his own invention of the missing lines. Elsewhere, Empson is suggestive on atmosphere, seeing in Webster's *The Duchess of Malfi* a precursor of the Gothic fiction of Monk Lewis and Ann Radcliffe, but his 1950s historicism seems schematic and oversimplified in the context of more recent research on religious, social and theatre history. Also concerned with issues of censorship is Lynda E. Boose in 'The 1599 Bishops' Ban, Elizabethan Pornography, and the Sexualisation of the Jacobean Stage' (in Burt and Archer, *Enclosure Acts*). She considers the effect of the order to the Stationers Company to burn books by, and stop future printing of, proscribed authors including Marston, Marlowe and Nashe. This ban, she argues, brought satire and sexual representation from print onto the stage, and led to a misogynized Jacobean theatre.

Various notes work on a smaller scale to elucidate aspects of the drama. A number are concerned with Middleton: in *N&Q* 41, John Jowett's 'Middleton's Song of Cupid' (66–77) unravels the sociopolitical and sexual innuendo in the song fragment from the lost *Masque of Cupid*, and R. V. Holdsworth traces 'A Middleton Oath in *A Yorkshire Tragedy* and *The Bloody Banquet*' (70), which may support Middleton's authorship of *A Yorkshire Tragedy*. Holdsworth returns to this attribution in 'Middleton's Authorship of *A Yorkshire Tragedy*' (*RES* 45.1–25), in which he proposes Middleton as the play's sole author. Murray Biggs takes on 'The Questionable Ending of Middleton's *A Trick to Catch the Old One*' and asks 'How seriously can we take the palinodes?' (*N&Q* 41.507–9), suggesting that the final soliloquies do tell of a true intention to reform which should be brought out in performance. Jerzy Limon finds '"A Silenc'st Bricke-Layer": An Allusion to Ben Jonson in Thomas Middleton's *The Inner Temple Masque*' (*N&Q* 41.512–14), A. A. Bromham throws light on 'The Significance of Names in Middleton and Rowley's *The Old Law*' (*N&Q* 41.509–12), and Swapan Chakravorty offers 'A

Note on *Women Beware Women* II. ii. 469–77' (*N&Q* 41.514) on wormwood as a remedy for seasickness. Chakravorty also finds in 'Deloney's *The Gentle Craft* and Middleton and Rowley's *The Changeling*: An Unnoticed Borrowing' (*N&Q* 41.514–15).

(b) Marlowe

The modern, energetic pursuit of Marlowe and his work seems to have stalled this year. With no major new study and only a handful of significant articles produced, the trajectory of much current research is towards consolidating approaches to Marlowe in relation both to his work and to his society.

Christopher Marlowe: The Plays and their Sources, edited by Vivien Thomas and William Tydeman, is an anthology of extracts and translations of Marlowe's major sources, including nearly complete texts of Perondinus's *Life of Tamburlaine* and the *English Faust-book*. As the title suggests, this is not just a source book, it is also a comparative analysis aimed at shedding some light on Marlowe's creative process. In their introduction, the editors express a wish to see the writer in his 'cultural milieu', managing and condensing various sources into the marketable product demanded by the theatre. The sections on *Tamburlaine* and *Doctor Faustus* argue for Marlowe's impressive skills as an editor, whilst a section on *Edward II* teaches us how Marlowe's approach to his sources was dictated by the demands of the theatre. The editors' commentary sustains what would otherwise be a fragmentary collection, and I doubt there are many scholars who would not find some value in this work.

In 'Economic and Ideological Exchange in Marlowe's *Jew of Malta*' (*TJ* 46.157–70), David H. Thurn begins by contrasting two different perspectives on the function of Marlowe's theatre in a general economy of power: the theory of containment preferred by new historicists and the exchange theories of negotiated power amongst autonomous social areas which is nowadays offered as a critique of new historicism. Thurn turns this theoretical impasse to a study of *The Jew of Malta*, exploring its strategy of ideological containment in its cultural scripting of the Jew against its preoccupation with the liberal circulation of semiotic value. In this analysis, the play registers the tension between the two social forms. Barabas represents plenitude and excess under the sign of 'the pre-history of capitalism', but both his wealth and his schemes to recover his lost wealth are constantly betrayed by writings (letters, proclamations and so on) that enclose and contain him as 'the Jew'. However, Thurn argues, the liberal semiotic economy of the play erupts and breaks through its ideological constraints; in other words, Barabas subverts his stereotyping through an excessive and violent Jewishness – a model of power negotiation which combines both the processes of containment and exchange.

Unfortunately, most of the published scholarship on Marlowe this year has approached Marlowe indirectly, in the context of some other argument, so that our knowledge of Marlowe has not advanced very much, whilst Marlowe is being used to advance knowledge in other areas. This inevitably leads to a reliance on an established set of assumptions, even though the work of Thurn, Tydeman and Thomas clearly shows that much of our received understanding of Marlowe is open to question. Viewing Marlowe in this way is not without its compensations, as Maurice Charney's essay 'Marlowe's *Edward II* as Model for Shakespeare's *Richard II*' (*RORD* 33.31–41) demonstrates. This paper argues that *Edward II* was used by Shakespeare as a 'prototype' for *Richard II*, in which the subject of sodomy somehow 'escapes' from Marlowe's play and manifests itself in Shakespeare's play. Charney's article is published alongside Nina Taunton's 'Biography, a University Education, and Playwriting: Fletcher and Marlowe' (*RORD* 33.63–97), which reinforces doubts about Fletcher's university education by comparing his work with Marlowe's, who is here taken as the model for the classically trained playwright. The main interest for Marlowe scholars is an extended digression on the use of theological disputation and Ramusian logic in *Doctor Faustus*, in which Marlowe's thinly disguised worrying about predestination is located in Cambridge theology. However, Taunton's interest in Marlowe as a certain kind of exemplary university wit to be contrasted with Fletcher is necessarily reductive, and abrogates a complex view of Marlowe in relation to his university education. Roy Kendall's comprehensive article 'Richard Baines and Christopher Marlowe's Milieu' (*ELR* 24.507–53) is a fascinating study of the career of the man who pointed an accusing finger at Marlowe in 1592. In 1582 Baines painted a distressingly similar picture of himself in an oral and a written confession, both of which are presented here in new translations by Christopher Upton. Kendall dwells on the similarities between the documents of 1582 and 1592, and on Baines's bizarre attempt to poison a whole seminary, which, as Kendall repeatedly reminds us, has a parallel with *The Jew of Malta*. If it was Kendall's intention that we should read correspondences between Baines's life and Marlowe's work as having genuine historical value, then this essay begins to look tenuous. An unusual perspective is brought to bear on *Doctor Faustus* by Roslynn D. Haynes in *From Faust to Strangelove: Representations of the Scientist in Western Literature*. Haynes's work is a history of the scientist in literature from the early modern period. Marlowe has an important, transitional place in this history. It seems that his treatment of the Faust legend in *Doctor Faustus* developed the old stereotype of the alchemist into a complex, modern figure, with an innovative sense of tragic waste and of the follies of intellectual curiosity that pre-empted many subsequent caricatures of the scientist.

Thomas Healy's *Christopher Marlowe* and William Zunder's *Elizabethan Marlowe* are both clear, concise introductions to Marlowe's life and works, and both adopt a contemporary approach. Healy is fresh and flexible, exploring different analytic possibilities, moving from a post-colonial reading of *The Jew of Malta* to a study of *Edward II*'s sexual politics, without ever being baffling or unapproachable. In his introduction, Healy is dismissive of approaches which seek to ground a reading of Marlowe in the life and biography of the author, preferring to think of Marlowe as a 'cultural agent', exploring representations of a society which is complex and dynamic. There is little which is new in any of this, of course, but there are some gems in Healy's writing, and a study of the two *Tamburlaine* plays which emphasizes their differences is well worth reading.

William Zunder's work is a much more conventional attempt to service one of the key concepts of new historicism, that of intertextuality, to the practice of what is in fact a very old kind of historicism. For Zunder, Elizabethan society is a stable and locatable historical fact, and the modern tenor of his language cannot hide the fact that a straightforward laying out of text against contemporaneous political, social or cultural events is a dusty, traditionalist mode of analysis. Surprisingly, it is not without fruit: there is an entertaining and evocative account of *The Jew of Malta*'s relationship to the mystery play cycles, and the book ends with a chapter on *Hero and Leander* which affords a rare (these days) opportunity to read Marlowe's poetry alongside his dramatic work. However, the book has some faults which cannot be ignored. Statements such as the claim that *Edward II* 'registers the radical decline of feudalism by the 1590s' seem outdated, whilst one of Marlowe's most interesting plays, *Dido*, is not mentioned once in 113 pages.

Finally, *N&Q* published three brief notes which should be of interest to Marlowe scholars. In 'A Possible Source for Marlowe's Pageant of the Seven Deadly Sins' (*N&Q* 41.451–2), Lisa Hopkins observes that the Seven Deadly Sins episode from *Doctor Faustus* does not follow Marlowe's main sources. Hopkins refers us to the exorcism of one Richard Mainy, who, at the climax of his possession, gave an apparently entertaining solo performance of the seven deadly sins. Ceri Sullivan poses the possibility of recusancy language being reflected in the line, 'Strike off their heads, and let them preach on poles' (I.i.118 and III.i.20) in 'Marlowe's *Edward II* and Recusant Phrasing' (*N&Q* 41.451); whilst in 'Marlowe's Translation of Ovid's *Amores* I.xv.19' (*N&Q* 41.450–1), Wolfgang Riehle worries about Marlowe's substitution of the poet Accius by Plautus, a mistake which Jonson typically did not repeat in his translation. Riehle defends Marlowe by arguing that if Marlowe had made a mistake then he had made a common Renaissance error, but that it was more likely Marlowe deliberately replaced an obscure poet with a well-known one for the benefit of his readers.

(c) Jonson (1993)

The ever-increasing domination of Shakespeare as market leader continues to have a baleful effect on the study of his contemporaries, particularly Jonson, who is the subject of only one book and a handful of articles in 1993. However, *Licensed by Authority: Ben Jonson and the Discourse of Censorship* by Richard Burt is a particularly notable addition to both Jonson and Renaissance studies. The book seeks to redefine censorship in such a way as to challenge a wide range of critical approaches from early to postmodern, using Jonson as provider of a series of 'exemplary paradoxes' which support a redefinition of censorship that attempts to shift the focus away from the power of the state and relocate it in the neurotic individual, exemplified by Jonson, whose writings are said to be the product of a personal agon between repressive self-censorship and expressive licence. This approach runs the risk of explaining away all the dangerous bits in Jonson and serving him up as a postmodern man for whom dissent is a purely private matter. This is the inevitable result of Burt's deconstructive approach, which collapses difference between (consensual) criticism and censorship in his drive to deny the enlightenment narrative which he detects throughout modern literary criticism. It is, then, a highly political book that makes a lively and well-informed contribution to a crucial contemporary political debate, locating 'censorship' in the form of 'political correctness' at the centre of current conflict between left and right. It is a work which should refocus Jonson studies and stimulate a rethinking of the function of the critic.

In another thought-provoking piece, Bruce Boehrer's 'The Poet of Labor: Authorship and Property in the Work of Ben Jonson' (*PQ* 72.289–312) locates Jonson's epochal significance in his invention of the modern concept of the author as owner, said to be 'Jonson's single most revolutionary contribution to Western literary history'. This perception allows Boehrer to turn the tables neatly on the Shakespeare industry by arguing that it was only because of Jonson's promotional efforts that Shakespeare was able to be deified. Jonson heralds the age of the professional writer, and not for the first time note is made of 'the real irony of Jonson's model of authorship', which is 'that Shakespeare, not he, should be retroactively constructed as its representative *par excellence*'. This irony is explained by Boehrer as a result of the clearly laboured character of Jonson's writing, which denies it the very quality of naturalness and hence universality which has been ascribed to Shakespeare, with 'work' becoming a two-edged sword, raising the status of the author, while denying the spontaneity which attaches to the term 'play', and detaching Jonson from both his social superiors and inferiors: as Boehrer puts it, 'He must distinguish himself. . .from the Johnsons.' Jonson's insistence on ownership of his works is also the subject of Tobin Nellhaus's 'Self-Possessed Jonson: Reason, Will, Ownership, Power' (*JDTC* 8.5–18). As with the last two critics, Jonson is again seen as a precursor of the modern, in Nellhaus's view creating 'a new concept of the self' characterized by 'self-possessed individuality', which is made up of a combination of reason, will and ownership. The need to set Jonson against Shakespeare is here also, with Jonson's notoriously undeveloped characters being seen as the product of this brand of individualism. Unlike Shakespeare's relative self-effacement, 'Individual speeches may be uttered by particular characters, but the plays were "by Jonson".' All this is set in the context of the rise of capitalism, which encourages notions of property, and the appearance of print, which has the same effect. In words reminiscent of Burt, Nellhaus concludes that 'Jonson opposed the notion of public domain, insisting on his private possession of his text.' Jonson emerges from this article in the now too familiar guise of the modern who turns out also to be a reactionary.

In some ways the most stimulating of this year's material is Kristen McDermott's 'Versions of Femininity in *Bartholomew Fair*' (*RenP* 22.91–116), as it makes a pleasant change to move from the epochal reading to a close one which gives credit to Jonson's sensitivity to the use and abuse of language. McDermott's approach to the play is to focus on the eight female characters and in so doing to offer readings of neglected aspects of the play. As the title suggests, there is not so much a thesis in this article as a series of meditations on the representation of females in *Bartholomew Fair*. McDermott makes the large claim that Jonson explores 'every possible aspect of adult femaleness available to the Jacobean mind', and argues that he either perverts or subverts each stereotype during the course of the action. For McDermott the manifest disorder of the fair is not depicted in terms of social relations, but is located in 'disordered personal identity', and she is acutely sensitive to the role of market forces commodifying the females and transforming them from the identities in which they first appear. McDermott is to be valued for giving much-needed attention to Jonson's depiction of women, avoiding a too easy representation of him as a misogynist while showing how sensitive he was to the difficulties faced by women in a man's world. The play in this view is again an alternative to Shakespeare, being 'an anti-green, anti-romantic world, in which female desire is [. . .] frustrated and corrupted', in which Grace itself can only survive by embracing cynicism. Douglas Bruster's *Drama and the Market in the Age of Shakespeare* contains a chapter entitled 'The Farce of Objects: *Othello* to *Bartholomew Fair*', in which he explores a similar line of enquiry to McDermott's, focusing on commodities in the fair and positing that 'fetishistic desire propels the play from the beginning'. His discussion of the play is carefully argued, moving persuasively from the local to the general, drawing suggestive conclusions about the period in terms of the impact of developments in early capitalism.

Two minor contributions complete this survey. The first, 'Venetian Local Color at the End of *Volpone*' (*Expl* 51.ii.81–3), by D. McPherson, notes again the care taken by Jonson in researching for *Volpone*, and the accuracy of the local detail in the play. Christopher Baker in '*The Alchemist* and Shakespeare's Sonnet 129' (*N&Q* 41.211–12) queries Herford and Simpson's claim that Jonson ignored Shakespeare's Sonnets and observes a close correspondence between the two named texts.

(d) Jonson (1994)

The year 1994 did not witness the publication of many extended monographs on Jonson but produced a veritable wealth of articles on his drama. A number of these articles appeared in the first volume of the new *Ben Jonson Journal* (henceforth *BJJ*). Much is to be hoped for Jonsonian scholarship from such a journal, but it was perhaps somewhat surprising and disappointing that the first edition seemed rather slim on essays on Jonson himself, and that the essays on Jonson were workmanlike rather than inspirational. Of those that were Jonson-related, Susanne Woods on 'Aemilia Lanyer and Ben Jonson: Patronage, Authority, and Gender' (*BJJ* 1.15–30) was more focused on its female poetic subject and failed as a result to offer any genuinely new observations on Jonson and gender. The article, perhaps inevitably, compares the strategies of Jonson's 'To Penshurst' and Lanyer's 'Description of Cooke-ham', seeing them as masculinist and feminist in their respective approaches to the country-house genre. Richard Harp's essay 'Jonson's "House of Wisdom"' (*BJJ* 1.1–13) also treats with 'To Penshurst', seeing this poem about the Sidney family estate as less about nature than about art and traces related presences and resonances within the 1616 masque *The Golden Age Restored*, which has been the focus of a number of articles this year. The year 1616, also that of *The Devil is an Ass,* is, it would seem, the one for 1994's Jonson scholars.

Sara van den Berg, by contrast, involves herself with the late Elizabethan era in 'The Passing of the Elizabethan Court' (*BJJ* 1.31–61). She sees that moment of passing as distinguished by three events: the funeral of Queen Elizabeth I, a severe outbreak of plague, and the entertainments that welcomed the new monarch. Berg discusses the literature produced in response to these events as enactments of both the anxieties and the desires of the contemporary political community, and claims for Jonson an investment in the restoration of the language of patriarchy, a discourse relied upon heavily by the king himself in his writings and his speeches. Implicit in this argument is the notion that Jonson rejected the feminine rule of Elizabeth and instead placed his hopes (not least for promotion) on the masculine rhetoric and emphases of the Jacobean court. Also in *BJJ* 1, John Mulryan looks at 'Mythic Interpretations of Ideas in Jonson's *Pleasure Reconciled to Virtue*' (63–73) and the dramatist's creative use of sources. Five mythological figures are argued for as being crucial to the masque – Atlas, Hercules, Comus, Mercury, and Daedalus – and all are seen as being involved in the struggle between pleasure and virtue. Possible emblematic sources for these representations are suggested, as well as a discussion being made of their interrelation within the masque. A very specific numerological argument is proffered by David McPherson in his 'Exact Numbers in the Ages of Man: A Debate in Renaissance England' (77–103), in which he details the numerical variations on the Ages of Man in classical texts. Jonson in *The Alchemist* is seen to be working on a structure involving multiples of five rather than the 'seven ages' more familiar from Shakespeare's *As You Like It*. In 'Ben Jonson, Neostoicism, and the *Monita* of Justus Lipsius' (105–23), Robert C. Evans (almost omnipresent in this year's catalogue of work on Jonson) offers an account of the importance of Justus Lipsius' practical text on political conduct and ethics, viewing his theories on patience as particularly influential upon Jonson's *The New Inn*.

Perhaps, though, the most salient event in 1994 for teachers and scholars of Jonson was the publication of Peter Happé's edition of *The Devil is an Ass* for the Revels series. The edition offers an excellent and fluid version of the playtext, and whilst at times Happé underplays or underestimates the potential for more radical politics within it, his introductory essay is on the whole erudite and revealing, exhibiting in particular an admirable empathy for, and understanding of, the sophisticated gender politics of the play. Happé's version of the playtext is now also generously available in a student budget-friendly Drama Classics edition, as is the text of the Revels *Volpone*. Of necessity these editions lack any of the introductory essays, textual annotation or appendices so indicative of a Revels volume, but the alternative introductions they do offer are invariably valuable.

The Devil is an Ass also provides the basis for one of the strongest essays in Robert C. Evans's *Jonson and the Contexts of his Time*, the single Jonsonian monograph this year. Evans's book asserts an ostensibly anti-new historicist approach in its opening pages; whilst claiming an investment in the 'micropolitical' aspects of Jonson's work and career, Evans nevertheless rejects new historicism's interest in patterns of power, and by extension the 'macropolitical', suggesting that these are largely relational. The author's bold resistance to reading Jonson from an ideological standpoint regrettably does not always enhance the coherence of his collection. As a book *Jonson and the Contexts of his Time* remains steadfastly an assemblage of previously published, largely discrete essays; a gathering of component parts, some of which, predictably, are better than others. Whilst the book's title and Evans's own overview introduction do offer some arguments for the interrelation of the contents – not least a Leah Marcus-inspired focus on 'local' readings – this remains a somewhat unsatisfying collection. The local and historicized reading of *Devil*, for example, is highly persuasive and offers an important contribution to the all-too slim body of critical work on that remarkable play. By contrast, the chapter on 'Thomas Sutton: Jonson's Volpone?' seems to lose all sight of the play in its microscopic focus on one possible (and previously much-discussed) source for the characterization of Jonson's protagonist. Many of the individual points are interesting and carefully researched – witness the chapters on Joseph Webbe and on *Pleasure Reconciled to Virtue* – but the transitions from chapter to chapter, and occasionally even within chapters, are often abrupt and unexplained.

Certainly it is within individual essays and articles that the most impressive work is to be found on Jonson this year. Most noteworthy amongst those is Helen Ostovich's 'The Appropriation of Pleasure in *The Magnetic Lady*' (*SEL* 34. 425–42), a lucid and confident article which not only reclaims for attention the much-neglected late drama *The Magnetic Lady* but subjects Jonson to rigorous theoretical scrutiny, in this case from the standpoint of gender critique. It is to be noted that the methodological and theoretical upheavals and progresses of recent decades seem frequently to have avoided Jonson. Even new historicism, which would seem to have a particular stake in Jonsonian negotiations with questions of authorship, state and society, has remained steadfastly silent on his plays within the canonical texts of its own discipline.

Redressing this critical imbalance, Ostovich adeptly engages with matters of gender and class in *The Magnetic Lady*. Her overriding thesis is that Jonson is relying on 'blanket binaries' within the play, subjecting women to a reductive equation that views them as the 'nature' to men's 'culture', and inhibiting the potential scope of his female characterizations: they represent either male fantasies or degraded mothers. Whilst I am not always in wholehearted agreement with Ostovich's reading of Jonson, her article nevertheless challenges us to consider the role of gender in this play in an intellectually rigorous way, and her examination of the subversive role of independent female sexuality in the play and of related motifs of witchcraft and embroidery is deep and revealing. As ever, Ostovich's prose is cogent and her article is an important contribution to Jonson studies this year.

Questions of gender, sexuality and performance also dominate Laura Levine's treatment of Jonsonian drama in her excellent book *Men in Women's Clothing*, specifically *Epicoene* and *Bartholomew Fair*. The former may be built on the 'key tropes of popular anti-theatricality' – homophobia, effeminization, and androgyny – but Levine argues that Jonson is thematizing this stance rather than endorsing it: this may establish a potential for reading the female characterizations in *The Magnetic Lady* from this angle. Genuine anxieties about theatre, and in particular the figure of the boy actor, are then deliberately played out on the Jonsonian stage and absolutism is in the process subtly criticized. Levine makes here a crucial intervention in the current debate over the extent to which Jonson is merely staging his asserted absolutist authorial control. Her discussion of *Bartholomew Fair* continues in the same vein, adopting as its focus the moment when the Puppet Dionysius lifts his skirts, at Zeal-of-the-Land Busy's instruction, only to reveal the puppet's wooden frame. Once again, Levine observes, Jonson is actually defending theatre against the attacks of its detractors. A central feature in that defence is his suppression of the homosexual aspects of Marlowe's 'Hero and Leander', not as an act of homophobia, but precisely to remove those elements of the puppet-play which Busy could justifiably attack, thus rendering his anti-theatricality misplaced and risible.

The puppet-show in *Bartholomew Fair* and attendant questions about the Jonsonian relationship with theories of authorship also concern Scott Cutler Shershow in his 'The Mouth of "Hem All": Ben Jonson, Authorship, and the Performing Object' (*TJ* 46.187–212). The article is heavily influenced by theory, from Barthes to Foucault, but it is Mikhail Bakhtin's theories of the carnivalesque which most openly shape Shershow's argument, that the puppet-play in *Bartholomew Fair* and its parodic version of the Hero and Leander myth embodies Jonson's problematic engagements with the potentially destabilizing forms of popular culture, revealing in the process a Jonson who is engaged with his audiences, albeit in a mode of anxiety and debate.

Rewriting the general understanding of the Jonsonian attitude towards audiences is the project undertaken by John Creaser in his eloquent article 'Enigmatic Ben Jonson' (in Cordner et al., *English Comedy*). Reviewing the critical tradition which regards Jonson as an author constantly seeking control of his texts and their meaning, and therefore scornful of popular theatre audiences, Creaser suggests that we need instead to recognize a Jonson whose 'dramaturgy is founded not on distrust but on confidence in the audience'. Proffering numerous examples from plays such as *Every Man Out of His Humour*, *Epicoene*, *The Alchemist* and *Bartholomew Fair*, Creaser produces an engaging and thought-provoking version of Jonson which sees him as an author engaged, however anxiously, with his audiences on every level. This is an exciting essay which opens up new areas of debate within Jonson scholarship.

Another article which locates Jonson in the midst of positive audience interaction and acknowledgement is Bruce Thomas Boehrer's '*Epicoene*, Charivari, Skimmington' (*ES* 75.17–33). This essay represents a cogent engagement with critical theory on popular culture and folk ritual. Boehrer convincingly examines how *Epicoene* participates in patterns which emerge from folkloric rituals such as the charivari or skimmington and argues that there is space to view the playtext as a saturnalian comedy in which youth triumphs over age.

Historical revisionism's contribution to the refashioning of Ben Jonson is extensively considered in a number of essays in the interdisciplinary collection entitled *Culture and Politics in Early Stuart England*, edited by Kevin Sharpe and Peter Lake. Notable amongst these are Blair Worden's 'Ben Jonson Among the Historians' and Martin Butler's 'Ben Jonson and the Limits of Courtly Panegyric', although Jonson receives many mentions elsewhere in the volume. Worden examines at length the close associations between Jonson, William Camden and John Selden, suggesting that the three men shared common political perspectives and political anxieties, which throw a grim light upon the public life of late Elizabethan and Jacobean England. Exploring the ways in which Jonson, under Camden's influence, strove for 'historical truth' in his plays, Worden examines in detail the two Roman tragedies *Sejanus, His Fall* and *Catiline, His Conspiracy*. *Sejanus* in particular is seen to reflect those political anxieties Jonson shared with his historian companions. Martin Butler's article is on panegyric and praise; in evaluating the impact of historical revisionism on studies of the Jacobean and Caroline period, Butler observes that one of its significant contributions has been to transform attitudes towards the literature of compliment, so that it is now regarded less as mere poetic time-serving than as a genuine attempt to dignify the business of Whitehall politics. Butler takes as his particular focus a number of the Jacobean masques: *Pleasure Reconciled to Virtue* is seen in relation to the activities of courtly self-fashioning, and a significant earlier dating of *The Golden Age Restored* is offered as confirmation of the matrix of complex topical allusions to the Sir Thomas Overbury scandal to be found in the masque.

This work on the Overbury scandal is expanded upon by Butler in his joint article with David Lindley, 'Restoring Astraea: Jonson's Masque for the Fall of Somerset' (*ELH* 61.807–27). Commenting on the importance of registering the 'local and specific historical embeddedness' of masque, Butler and Lindley concern themselves here with decoding the rhetoric of *The Golden Age Restored* but also with recognizing the political and economical contingencies which operated upon the masque, during both its composition and performance, and provide an erudite account of the complex intersection of politics and aesthetics in Stuart culture and the Jonsonian canon.

It is heartening this year to see new attention being paid to the less canonical texts of the Jonsonian *oeuvre*. Ostovich's work on *The Magnetic Lady* and Evans's on *The Devil is an Ass* are cases in point, as is work on masques other than the critically well-served *Masque of Blackness*. There would still seem to be valuable and valid critical work to be done on the last, however, as two articles in the excellent volume of essays *Women, 'Race', and Writing* (eds Hendricks and Parker) indicate: Lynda E. Boose's '"The Getting of a Lawful Race": Racial Discourse in Early Modern England and the Unrepresentable Black Woman' and Kim F. Hall's '"I Rather Would Wish to Be a Black-Moor": Beauty, Race, and Rank in Lady Mary Wroth's *Urania*'. Both have innovative statements on the *Masque of Blackness*.

Canonical plays such as *Volpone* are still well served by this year's criticism. James D. Redwine Jr's 'Volpone's "Sport" and the Structure of Jonson's *Volpone*' (*SEL* 34.301–21) is more classical in its approach than its title might suggest, analysing how Jonson adheres to the strict classical dramatic structure of protasis, epitasis and catastasis in constructing his dark comedy. In arguing for a moral understanding of the play Redwine does not seem to be saying anything strikingly new, but some of his comparisons with Thomas More's *Utopia* are enlightening: he describes *Volpone* as a dystopian satire on Renaissance society almost a century after More. James Tulip writes on 'The Intertextualities of Ben Jonson's *Volpone*' (*SSEng* 20.20–35). Despite his asserted interest in the Marlovian-Shakespearean-Jonsonian theatrical and textual interaction, Tulip becomes overpowered by what he himself describes as the 'overpowering' Shakespearean model and offers instead a catalogue of Shakespearean influences upon Jonson, suppressing the two-way flow of ideas in favour of tracing elements of *Othello*, *Richard III* and *King Lear* in *Volpone*. On the same play are Michael Cameron Andrews's 'Jonson's *Volpone*' (*Expl* 52.145–7) and Elizabeth Lee-Caulfield's 'Jonson's *Volpone*' (*Expl* 52.202–4), the latter treating questions of materialism and disorder.

Richard Harp discerns the influence of apocalyptic language and theories of millenarianism in *The Alchemist* in 'Ben Jonson's Comic Apocalypse' (*Cithara* 34.34–43), suggesting that the precise date of the play's action, All Souls Day, is part of this particular discourse. Another textually specific article is John Bak's consideration of the signification of particular terminology and vocabulary in Jonsonian masque in his '"Firedrake" and "Oregon": A Gypsy's Pun in a Song From Ben Jonson's *The Gipsies Metamorphos'd*' (*ShY* 4.329–34). Claiming for the terms 'firedrake' (fiery dragon) and 'ore-gone' (overgone) a second, alchemy-related meaning, Bak demonstrates how this successfully subverts the masque's panegyric by causing the performing courtiers to expose themselves as charlatans (since the familiar Jonsonian association of alchemy was with deceit).

To finish then, a cluster of notes on allusions, both by and to Jonson. Jerzy Limon detects a reference to Jonson in Thomas Middleton's *Inner Temple Masque* in '"A Silenc'st Bricke-Layer": An Allusion to Ben Jonson in Thomas Middleton's *The Inner Temple Masque*' (*N&Q* 41.512–14). Robert E. Jungman in 'Ball-Playing in Jonson's *Volpone*' (*N&Q* 41.64–6) finds in Volpone's reference during his Scoto performance to playing at ball an allusion to Cicero's *Pro Archia*, suggesting that the protagonist (and possibly his creator) is claiming oratorical power. Kurt R. Niland and Robert C. Evans in 'Bolton on Jonson: An Ungathered Allusion' (*N&Q* 41.517) find in Edmund Bolton's allusion to Jonson, in an appendage to his 1624 text on Nero, possible confirmation that Jonson was still on friendly terms with the Duke of Buckingham at this time, since the same text was dedicated to Villiers. With Neil P. Probst, Evans also discerns proof of the influence of the thinking of Flemish intellectual Justus Lipsius on the dramatist: see 'Jonson, Seneca, Homer, and Lipsius: Unreported Allusions in *The King's Entertainment at Welbeck*' (*N&Q* 41.519–20). It seems apt to end on an example of Evans's ubiquitous research for this year.

Books Reviewed

Bevington, David, and Eric Rasmussen, eds. *Christopher Marlowe: Doctor Faustus. A and B-Texts*. Revels. ManUP (1993). pp. 298. hb £35, pb £10.99. ISBN 0 7190 1554 5, 0 7190 1643 6.

Blank, Claudia, ed. *Language and Civilization*. 2 vols. Lang (1992). Sfr. 230. ISBN 3 6314 1627 X.

Bruster, Douglas. *Drama and the Market in the Age of Shakespeare*. CUP (1992). pp. 164. £32.50. ISBN 0 5214 1664 7.

Burt, Richard. *Licensed by Authority: Ben Jonson and the Discourse of Censorship*. CornUP (1993). pp. 227. $33.50. ISBN 0 8014 9772 8.

——, and John Michael Archer, eds. *Enclosure Acts: Sexuality, Property, and Culture in Early Modern England*. CornUP. pp. 340. hb £33.50, $42.95, pb £13.50, $16.95. ISBN 0 8014 2745 2, 0 8014 8024 8.

Cheatham, George, ed. *A New Wonder, a Woman Never Vext*. Lang (1993). pp. 264. $42.95. ISBN 0 8204 1916 8.

Clark, Sandra. *The Plays of Beaumont and Fletcher: Sexual Themes and Dramatic Representation*. HW. pp. 198. £37.95. ISBN 0 7450 1569 7.

Cordner, Michael, Peter Holland and John Kerrigan, eds. *English Comedy*. CUP. pp. 323. £35. ISBN 0 5214 1917 4.

Desens, Marliss C. *The Bed-Trick in English Renaissance Drama: Explorations in Gender, Sexuality, and Power*. AUP. pp. 175. £25. ISBN 0 8741 3476 5.

Drew-Bear, Annette. *Painted Faces on the Renaissance Stage: The Moral Significance of Face-Painting Conventions*. AUP. pp. 139. £23. ISBN 0 8387 5230 6.

Empson, William. *William Empson: Essays on Renaissance Literature. Vol. 2: The Drama*. Ed. John Haffenden. CUP. pp. 292. £37.50, $49.95. ISBN 0 5214 4044 0.

Evans, Robert C. *Jonson and the Contexts of his Time*. BuckUP. pp. 226. £29.50. ISBN 0 8387 5268 3.

Findlay, Alison. *Illegitimate Power: Bastards in Renaissance Drama*. ManUP. pp. 282. £35. ISBN 0 7190 3991 6.

Finucci, Valeria, and Regina Schwartz, eds. *Desire in the Renaissance: Psychoanalysis and Literature*. PrincetonUP. pp. 273. hb £32, $37.50, pb £11.95, $14.95. ISBN 0 6910 0100 6, 0 6910 3403 6.

Forker, Charles, ed. *Edward II by Christopher Marlowe*. Revels. ManUP. pp. 369. £45. ISBN 0 7190 1536 7.

Goldberg, Jonathan, ed. *Queering the Renaissance*. DukeUP. pp. 388. hb £52, pb £16.95. ISBN 0 8223 1381 2, 0 8223 1385 5.

Happé, Peter, ed. *The Devil is an Ass, by Ben Jonson*. Revels. ManUP. pp. 256. hb £45, pb £12.99. ISBN 0 7190 1556 1, 0 7190 3090 0.

——, ed. *The Devil is an Ass, by Ben Jonson*. Hern. pp. 256. £3.99. ISBN 1 8545 9268 8.

——, ed. *Volpone, by Ben Jonson*. Hern. £3.99, $6.95. ISBN 1 8545 9194 0.

Haynes, Roslynn D. *From Faust to Strangelove: Representations of the Scientist in Western Literature*. JHUP. pp. 417. hb £45.50, pb £16.50. ISBN 0 8018 4801 6, 0 8018 4983 7.

Healy, Thomas. *Christopher Marlowe*. WTW. Northcote. pp. 186. pb £6.99. ISBN 0 7463 0707 1.

Hendricks, Margo, and Patricia Parker, eds. *Women, 'Race', and Writing in the Early Modern Period*. Routledge. pp. 383. hb £40, pb £14.99. ISBN 0 4150 7777 X, 0 4150 7778 8.

Hopkins, Lisa. *John Ford's Political Theatre*. Revels CL. ManUP. pp. 208. £45. ISBN 0 7190 3797 2.

Howard, Jean E. *The Stage and Social Struggle in Early Modern England*. Routledge. pp.184. hb £35, pb £11.99. ISBN 0 4150 4258 5, 0 4150 9553 0.

Howard-Hill, T. H., ed. *Thomas Middleton: A Game At Chess*. Revels. ManUP (1993). pp. 223. hb £35. ISBN 0 7190 1546 4.

Irace, Kathleen O. *Reforming the 'Bad' Quartos: Performance and Provenance of Six Shakespearean First Editions*. UDelP, AUP. pp. 232. £35. ISBN 0 8741 3417 4.

Levine, Laura. *Men in Women's Clothing: Anti-Theatricality and Effeminization, 1579–1642*. CUP. pp. 185. hb £35, pb £10.95. ISBN 0 5214 5507 3, 0 5214 6627 X.

Mack, Peter. *Renaissance Rhetoric*. Macmillan. pp. 188. £40. ISBN 0 3121 0184 8.

McLuskie, Kathleen E. *Dekker and Heywood: Professional Dramatists*. Macmillan. pp. 200. pb £10.99. ISBN 0 3334 6237 8.

McMullan, Gordon. *The Politics of Unease in the Plays of John Fletcher*. UMassP. pp. 338. £31.50. ISBN 0 8702 3892 2.

Nelson, Alan H. *Early Cambridge Theatres: College, University and Town Stages, 1464–1720*. CUP. pp. 194. £35. ISBN 0 5214 3177 8.

Orlin, Lena Cowen. *Private Matters and Public Culture in Post-Reformation England.* CornUP. pp. 309. £26.95. ISBN 0 8014 2858 0.

Pitcher, John, ed. *'Hymen's Triumph': Samuel Daniel*. Malone. pp. 74. ISBN 0 1972 9032 9.

Rasmussen, Eric. *A Textual Companion to Doctor Faustus*. ManUP (1993). pp. 114. £35. ISBN 0 7190 1562 6.

Rowland, Richard, ed. *Edward II. The Complete Works of Christopher Marlowe*, vol. III. OUP. pp. 150. £40, $59. ISBN 0 1981 2278 0.

Sharpe, Kevin, and Peter Lake, eds. *Culture and Politics in Early Stuart England.* Macmillan. pp. 382. hb £45, pb £14.99. ISBN 0 3335 7850 3, 0 3335 7851 1.

Speed-Hill, W., ed. *New Ways of Looking at Old Texts. Papers of the Renaissance English Text Society, 1985–1991*. Medieval and Renaissance Texts and Studies 107. MRTS (1993). pp. 320. $25. ISBN 0 8669 8153 5.

Sutton, Dana, ed. and trans. *Thomas Legge: The Complete Plays*. 2 vols. Lang. pp. 387, 613. $49.95, $62.95, $89.95 (per set). ISBN 0 8204 1754 8, 0 8204 1825 0, 0 8204 1826 9 (set).

Thomas, Vivien, and William Tydeman, eds. *Christopher Marlowe: The Plays and their Sources*. Routledge. pp. 416. £50. ISBN 0 4150 4052 3.

Tricomi, Albert H., ed. *Robert Knightley: Alfrede or Right Reinthron'd* . MRTS. pp. 170. $25.00. ISBN 0 8669 8113 6.

Woodmansee, Martha, and Peter Jaszi, eds. *The Construction of Authorship: Textual Appropriation in Law and Literature*. DukeUP. pp. 462. hb £42.75, pb £16.95. ISBN 0 8223 1382 0, 0 8223 1412 6.

Zunder, William, *Elizabethan Marlowe: Writing and Culture in the English Renaissance*. Unity. pp. 113. £7.99, $26. ISBN 0 9523 1800 8.

VIII

The Earlier Seventeenth Century: Excluding Drama

MELANIE OSBORNE

This chapter has three sections: 1. General; 2. Poetry; 3. Prose.

1. General

James Doelman's '"A King of Thine Own Heart": The English Reception of King James VI and I's *Basilikon Doron*' (*SC* 9.1–9) examines how English readers responded to the work, and, in particular, how they attempted to use it to advise and direct James by quoting the book back to him. For Doelman, James's strategy facilitated the possibility that English readers might be able to govern the king by his own words, so that whilst the aim of the *Basilikon Doron* was to promote majesty it also, paradoxically, gave James's subjects the power to interpret and direct their own king. In 'Wit, Will and Governance in Early Modern Legal Literature' (*Mosaic* 27.iv.15–34), Mary Polito explores how two law books, *Doctor and Student* (1532) and *The Lawes Resolutions of Women's Rights* (1632), provided knowledge about the legal subject for the edification of a lay reading public. For Polito, both texts 'paradoxically claim to berate while acting to restrain their implied readers, soliciting voluntary acts of self-governance for the good of the English realm', a claim that is effected in these texts by the employment of different literary devices. Through her close examination, Polito attends to the rhetoricity and literariness of these legal treatises as well as to the way in which the gendered inflections of their governmental strategies can be made visible. J. D. Alsop endeavours to reconstruct aspects of the family and community milieu of Winstanley's childhood and adolescence in 'A High Road to Radicalism? Gerrard Winstanley's Youth' (*SC* 9.11–20). Through close examination of archival materials, Alsop concludes that, contrary to recent historiography, Winstanley's seemingly undistinguished early life offers few clues to comprehending how he developed into one of the most radical writers of his century. That it was tobacco that interested the English, even more than people from the new world, is the contention of Janine Hartman in 'Dangerous American Substances in Jacobean England' (*CE* 46.1–8). As her reading of Jonson and Middleton illustrates, tobacco as a visible symbol of the new world was primarily concerned with consumption, a consumption that was both physical and material.

Frances E. Dolan's fascinating '"Gentlemen, I have one thing more to say": Women on Scaffolds in England, 1563–1680' (*MP* 92.157–78) addresses the hitherto neglected focus upon gender in the scholarship on public executions. Dolan analyses the way in which different generic representations of executions of women constructed them as subjects, and she further explores how they represent women's speech. Equally thought-provoking is Betty S. Travitsky's '"A Pittiless Mother"?: Reports of A Seventeenth-Century English Filicide' (*Mosaic* 27.iv.55–80), which carefully analyses the three extant documents relating to the filicide by Mrs Margaret (Day) Vincent in 1616 of two of her three children, and her subsequent trial and execution. It is argued that these documents provide evidence of the patriarchal bias of the period; and from this perspective, they suggest to Travitsky that Vincent 'might more accurately be termed a "pitiable mother" reacting with violence to the stress of the institution of motherhood and the institution of religion – and to the institution of patriarchy which bound them both'. In '"Being Stirred to Much Unquietness": Violence and Domestic Violence in early modern England' (*JWH* 6.ii.70-89), Susan Dwyer Amussen discusses a range of different texts in order to question Early Modern attitudes to violence. In an essay broad in scope, Amussen notes the usual texts of interest to this field, from *The Lawes Resolution of Women's Rights* to William Heale's *Apologie for Women*, and argues that acceptance of violence 'depended on both the context and the adherence by participants to a certain set of rules and limits. There was a moral economy of violence.'

On the subject of emblems this year, Michael Bath's *Speaking Pictures: English Emblem Books and Renaissance Culture* examines the emblem's importance in the literary and epistemological systems of English Renaissance culture. Introducing his study with a preliminary account of the various contexts within which the emblem circulated in English culture, Bath proceeds to a discussion of the way in which emblems drew upon a whole host of analogous signifying systems, and subsequently describes and analyses their use by a variety of different authors, including Wither and Quarles. Jane Fransworth's 'Robert Farley's *Kalendarium Humanae Vitae*: A Study in Emblematic Strategies' (*Embl* 7.79–98) explores the emblematic strategy of this 1648 text. The text employs, she argues, a complex strategy that both invests with new significance the common device of the calendar, with its comparison of human life to the seasonal cycle, and, simultaneously, challenges the formal and thematic limits of the calendar to suggest a vision of eternity. In 'Ben Jonson and Van Dyck: A Study in Allegorical Portraiture (*Embl* 7.61–78), Judith Dundas traces the use by both Jonson and Van Dyck of simile and metaphor drawn from a conventional symbolic language to characterize members of the nobility and particularly examines their focus on name-punning, a device that exemplifies, above all, their own wit. Examining a range of emblem books, Ayers Bagley's 'Some Pedagogical Uses of the Emblem in Sixteenth- and Seventeenth-Century England' (*Embl* 7.39–60) focuses upon the 'opposition' of decorative and pedagogical uses of the emblem. Bagley questions this dichotomy, querying the truth of 'the alleged estrangement' between the two and the adequacy of the implicit definitions.

2. Poetry

Seventeenth-Century English Poetry: The Annotated Anthology (eds Terence Dawson and Robert Scott Dupree) aims to be 'a sound introduction to the great English lyric tradition of the seventeenth century'. With spelling modernized and the poetry briefly annotated, this edition is more representative of the earlier period than the later, following, of course, the traditional chronological division of 1600–60. The edition is, no more and no less, a useful student text, but it is a shame to include, yet again, only Lanier's 'The Description of Cookham' when selections from *Salve Deus Rex Judaeorum* are being studied with other religious poetry of the period; furthermore, giving four poems by Carew, three by Suckling and only two by Traherne is just a little limiting for adequate teaching of seventeenth-century poetry. Students' unfamiliarity with classical studies, particularly as they inform Renaissance culture, is addressed by the publishing of *The Classical Legacy in Renaissance Poetry* by Robin Sowerby. In this useful student text, the opening chapters introduce broader and more fundamental aspects of the classical tradition concerning the dominating influence of Latin and the difficulty of Greek, the reception of classical texts in a prevailing Christian culture, the theory and practice of literary imitation, and the rules of art. Subsequent chapters are devoted to discussion of the classical heritage as it affected Renaissance culture; they include analysis of the work of Wyatt, Shakespeare, Marlowe, Jonson, Marvell, Carew, Rochester, Cowley and Dryden. The book is clear and informative throughout and therein will lie its appeal to students of English Renaissance literature.

Barbara L. Estrin's *Laura: Uncovering Gender and Genre in Wyatt, Donne, and Marvell* is a sensitive and complex reading of the way in which Petrarch and his English imitators, Wyatt, Donne and Marvell, imagine, desire and yet deny that desire for the ideal woman, Laura. Estrin's interpretations of the work of these poets resist traditional perspectives that posit Laura as the object of the male gaze and, instead, focus upon the subjectivity of the imagined woman and the imaginative space of the poems that she occupies. Drawing upon and contributing to postmodern reassessment of the Renaissance period, Estrin shows how genre and gender in the Petrarchan tradition work together to undermine the stability of these very concepts, and furthermore illustrates how early modern poets formulated questions about sexuality, society and poetry. Estrin's study is, undoubtedly, an important contribution to Renaissance studies and women's studies as well as to postmodernist approaches to Early Modern literature.

In *Cavaliers, Clubs, and Literary Culture: Sir John Mennes, James Smith, and the Order of the Fancy*, Timothy Raylor explores the lives of Mennes and Smith, younger sons from moderately prosperous gentry backgrounds, and their attempt to enter courtly circles via their ability to turn witty verses. Through such exploration, Raylor investigates the clubs and fraternities in which they were involved in the 1620s and 1630s, and in particular the Order of the Fancy, a club centred on the Blackfriars Theatre. In the final section of this study, Raylor offers an interpretation of the verse of Mennes and Smith, verse which mainly took the form of burlesque epistles and mock-poems, much of which was published in the 'drolleries' (verse miscellanies with a royalist bias) *Musarum Deliciae* (1655), *Wit and Drollery* (1656) and *Wit Restor'd* (1658).

James Doelman's 'The Accession of King James I and English Religious Poetry I' (*SEL* 34.19–40) considers the impact of a new cultural activity, brought about by James's accession, upon the poetry of Joshua Sylvester, John Davies of

Hereford and John Harrington. Assessment of this impact, Doelman argues, reveals how 'James's accession was viewed as the beginning of a new poetic era, one in which religious poetry would be valued and the relationship between poet and royal patron raised to a higher level'.

The only edition of Donne's poetry this year is *The Works of John Donne*, in the Wordsworth Poetry Library. The very brief introduction and scant bibliography is followed by the poetry and indexes. In 'Preaching Pastor versus Custodian of Order: Donne, Andrewes, and the Jacobean Church' (*PQ* 73.417–30), Daniel W. Doerksen questions the association made between Donne, Andrewes and William Laud. By comparison of Donne's sermons with those of Andrewes, Doerksen rebuts claims for Donne's Anglo-Catholicism and concludes that 'while Andrewes and the Laudians tended to think of themselves primarily as custodians of order, Donne found his fulfilment as a preaching pastor'. In 'Sexual Transgression in Donne's Elegies' (*MP* 92.14–35), Diana Treviño Benet argues that the Elegies reveal Donne's interest in the potential fluidity of gender identities and that this interest produced a major thematic emphasis on the sexual transgressions of the masculine woman and the feminine man. Through close examination of these poems, Benet illustrates that Donne was more inclined to explore sexual transgression than to pass any particular judgement on it. Also on the Elegies, Dandy Feinstein's 'Donne's "Elegy 19": The Busk between and Pair of Bodies' (*SEL* 34.61–78) considers the changes in women's fashions in the sixteenth century in order to consider the significance of the reference to details of the woman's dress in the poem. On studies of individual poems, Theresa M. Dipasquale's 'Cunning Elements: Water, Fire, and Sacramental Poetics in "I am a little world"?' (*PQ* 73.403–16) explores the psychological dynamics of the self-referential poetics at work in the poem. For Dipasquale, Donne's poem reveals the poet's sense of salvation from the fear of losing the grace of baptism, that the answer to his fears about sacramentality is sacrament, and that poetic utterance remedies the despair that was spoken into being through poetry. In 'Donne and the Court of Wards' (*ANQ* 7.130–3), M. Thomas Hester considers Donne's relationship to the association of Protestant sectarianism (and its enforcement) with the practice of the English Court of Wards and the English penal laws against Catholic recusants, as it is expressed in 'Satyre III'.

Peter Porter introduces a reprinting of T. S. Eliot's *George Herbert*; the introduction provides a clear account and critical contextualization of Eliot's thesis, and briefly incorporates Porter's own readings of Herbert's poetry. In 'The Conquering Laurels and Creeping Ivy: The Tangled Politics of Herbert's *Reditum Caroli*' (*GHJ* 17.i.1–23), Jeffrey Powers-Beck argues that Herbert's oration was his attempt 'to bring his own hatred of war, his respect for James's prerogatives in foreign policy, and his mollifying affection for Prince Charles to bear on a political situation that was muddled'. Analysing Herbert's involvement in the politics of the Spanish Match, Powers-Beck also considers Herbert's harsh anti-war rhetoric, his unusual failure to praise the Duke of Buckingham and a possible connection between the oration and his poem 'The Answer'. Daniel W. Doerksen continues the Laudian debate in 'The Laudian Interpretation of George Herbert' (*LH* 3.ii.36–54). In this article, Doerksen concentrates on the discrepancies between Herbert's own final pronouncements on his poems (as reported by Walton) and the quite different readings given (in effect) by Ferrar's 'The Printers to the Reader', Harvey's *The Synagogue*, and Walton's *Life of George Herbert* as a whole. For Doerksen, 'Herbert was indeed a conformist, but a non-Laudian one.'

On studies of individual poems, Kathleen Lynch's 'George Herbert's Holy "Altar", Name and Thing' (*GHJ* 17.i.41–60) explores the way in which this poem functions as an emblematic title page for 'The Church' and, therefore, how the possible reconciliation of name and thing might be played out in the narrative of this text. Because Herbert's 'The Church' is itself a representation of his position in the politics of the Church of England, Lynch also considers the practices and controversies revolving around the use of an altar in the early seventeenth century in the Church of England. In 'George Herbert's "Vertue": An Easter Poem?' (*GHJ* 17.i.61–9), Suzanne McDonald focuses on Christ's death and resurrection as an important context for a reading of this poem. Susannah B. Mintz argues in '"He my succour is": A Language of Self in Herbert's "The Holdfast"' (*GHJ* 17.ii.1–19) that this poem proceeds as a deeply human, individualized catechism wherein the speaker survives the appropriate responses of the doctrinal other, and reveals that the place from which he speaks is not owned by doctrine. Thus, Mintz illustrates how a sense of identity outside the limits set down by his 'catechist' emerges from the speaker's process of defining his individual practice of faith. The tracing of 'configurations' in Herbert's 'Denial' and 'Christmas' is the subject of Chauncey Wood's 'Configuring Herbert's "Christmas"' (*GHJ* 17.ii.21–35), a tracing that includes the consideration of these poems with reference to Paul's letter to the Ephesians, John Donne's 'Good Friday, 1613. Riding Westward', and Henry Herbert's use of Ephesian imagery from St Paul in his unpublished spiritual meditation in prose, *The Golden Harpe*. In 'Herbert's "Love" Sonnets and Love Poetry' (*GHJ* 17.ii.37–49), Anthony Martin concentrates not upon the question of the evocation of eroticism in secular poetry but, instead, upon Herbert's ambiguous attitude towards eroticism itself. From this perspective, Martin argues that it is therefore possible to read these sonnets not simply as attacks on secular poetry (and thus problematic for Herbert's own poetry), but rather as texts which reproduce the energies and ambivalences of love poetry. Finally, for Herbert, Richard F. Kennedy's 'More Allusions to Herbert in Joshua Poole's *The English Parnassus*' (*GHJ* 17.ii.51–4), adds a further nineteen citations of George Herbert's poetry to the fifteen already listed by Robert Ray in his *Herbert Allusion Book*.

The Poetry of Robert Tofte 1597–1620: A Critical Old-Spelling Edition, edited by Jeffrey N. Nelson, offers a biographical and critical introduction to his edition of Robert Tofte's texts 'Laura', 'Alba', 'The Fruits of Jealousie' and 'An Indian Nimphe'. For Nelson, Tofte's original poetry in English reveals both a manipulation of and an increasing disillusionment with the conventions of late sixteenth- and early seventeenth-century England, and, taken as a whole, the poetry illustrates 'the ways in which major literary models are employed by a gentleman who attempts to cope with a changing England'. A selection of Thomas Carew's love poetry edited by Anthony Astbury, *Thomas Carew: Love Poems*, appeared this year.

The printing of John Westwood's only known poem is the subject of 'A Manuscript Poem on the Royal Progress of 1634: An Edition and Translation of John Westwood's "Carmen Basileuporion"' (*SC* 9.173–95) by Timothy Raylor, with a 'Linguistic Introduction and Translation' by Jackson Bryce. Raylor notes that it is not its literary merit but rather its historical importance that underlies this publication, for the poem provides the most complete account of the royal visit to the Cavendish seat of Welbeck Abbey in the summer of 1634, an account which throws new light upon the entertainment at Bolsover which concluded that visit.

In 'A Horatian Influence on the Verse of Samuel Danforth (1626–1674)' (*ELN* 32.37–9), Michele Valerie Ronnick posits that the image in the final line of the seventh stanza of 'The Almanack for the Year of Our Lord 1647' derives from the second poem in Horace's first book of *Odes*.

On Vaughan, Jonathan Nauman analyses Vaughan's 'peculiar mode of reading Herbert' in 'Herbert the Hermetist: Vaughan's Reading of *The Temple*' (*GHJ* 17.i.25–40). In this sharply argued article, Nauman maintains that Vaughan's reading is similar to that with which he read the scriptures: truths consistent with the hermetic physical universe were assumed to be available in *The Temple* even as refutations of Aristotle were assumed to be available in the Epistle to the Romans. Consequently, Naumann argues that, instead of seeing in Herbert's texts signs of a rival cosmology, Vaughan took the hermetic cosmos to be pervasively present in them.

In 'Robert Herrick's Fathers' (*SEL* 34.41–60), Roger B. Rollin interprets the poems of the *Hesperides* as constituting an unconscious search for the father, and as a psychical struggle to come to terms with him. Adopting a psychoanalytic approach, Rollin suggests new insights into the poet's 'unifying personality' and creative imagination, and further attempts to bring to light latent patterns of order and meaning in the collection of poetry as a whole.

3. Prose

Samuel G. Wong's 'Some Baconian Metaphors and the Problems of Pure Prose' (*TSLL* 36.233–58) discusses the metaphors employed in the dedication, 'To the King' in *The Advancement of Learning*, questions the status and influence of the treatise, and finally shows how analysis of Baconian metaphor illuminates problems inherent in traditional readings and stylistic classifications of Renaissance prose. For Wong, this emphasis reveals how the project of advancement is borne on the imagined glory of the prince and how Bacon copes with his own difficult status as author and servant.

In 'Legislating "Middle-Class" Morality in the Marriage Market: Ester Sowernam's *Ester hath hang'd Haman*' (*ELR* 24.154–83), Megan Matchinske considers the 'connections in Sowernam's text between an emerging understanding of marriage as a *legal* (largely "middle-class") *institution* and the financial and moral imperatives that seem to insist on its construction'. Identifying the way in which Sowernam's text turns marriage into a system of fair market exchange, Matchinske succinctly illustrates how this account 'reveals current cultural anxieties about marriage as a reorganization of mercantile property and also foreshadows a later concretization of those anxieties in emended civil legislation'.

The bequeathing of an unsettling legacy to contemporary feminist criticism, as well as to Elizabeth Jocelin's daughters, is the subject of Teresa Feroli's '"Infelix Simulacrum": The Rewriting of Loss in Elizabeth Jocelin's *The Mothers Legacie*' (*ELH* 61.89–102). By identifying that legacy to Jocelin's child, a legacy that is one of despair and aggression couched in terms of maternal love, Feroli calls into question an unproblematic revering of early modern women writers by feminist critics in order to suggest, instead, how Jocelin's 'violence' might, in fact, express a complex and unsettling female subjectivity, a subjectivity that challenges not just patriarchy but also feminist readers. In 'A Pack of Lies in a Looking Glass: Lady

Mary Wroth's *Urania* and the Magic Mirror of Romance' (*SEL* 34.79–108), Jennifer Lee Carrell illustrates how Wroth's *Urania* counters in content, and through her own authoring of them, Vives's statements on romance. For Carrell, 'the ending of Wroth's book suggests that her understanding of romance is quite the opposite of Vives's; the looking glass of romance fictions acts not to dupe women into illicit lust by the telling of lies, but to lead men into constant love by the telling of (partly, or perhaps potentially) truthful fictions'. It is this opposition, together with Wroth's occupation of a liminal space between fact and fiction, that enabled her to bid for control, a bid that was to prove so threatening to Jacobean male readers.

Continuing recent scholarship on the problematics of subjectivity in the work of Margaret Cavendish, Sandra Sherman's 'Trembling Texts: Margaret Cavendish and the Dialectic of Authorship' (*ELR* 24.184–210) argues that 'Cavendish's retreat from contemporary discourse into a world of her own imagining, implying a self anterior to any text, is continually undermined by an appeal to the judgement of history, implying a self determined by discourse and entirely intertextual.' For Sherman, Cavendish's texts are a site upon which images of monarchy contend with a rhetoric of submission. Stephen Clucas's 'The Atomism of the Cavendish Circle' (*SC* 9.247–73) investigates the effect of the continental atomist Gassendi on the atomistic theories of the 'Newcastle' or 'Cavendish Circle'. Exploring the work of, and relationships between, Walter Warner, Margaret Cavendish, Thomas Hobbes, Walter Charleton and Kenelm Digby, Clucas considers some of the difficulties which the seventeenth-century concept of 'atomism' creates for historians of science, and suggests that 'these difficulties might perhaps be resolved by eschewing categorical criteria for the definition of atomism and instead viewing atomism as a series of overlapping and idiomatically constituted conceptual fields determined by the philosophical predilections of its seventeenth-century exponents'. Tombs, and their memorial expressions, are the focus of Graham Parry's 'Cavendish Memorials' (*SC* 9.275–87), an article that explores the inscriptions of the Cavendish family memorial tombs.

Books Reviewed

Astbury, Anthony, ed. *Thomas Carew: Love Poems*. Greville. pp. 15. pb £6.50. ISBN 0 9068 8756 9.

Bath, Michael. *Speaking Pictures: English Emblem Books and Renaissance Culture*. Longman (1993). pp. 310. hb £39, pb £16.99. ISBN 0 5820 6197 0, 0 5820 6196 2.

Dawson, Terence, and Robert Scott Dupree, eds. *Seventeenth-Century English Poetry: The Annotated Anthology*. HW. pp. 592. £13.58. ISBN 0 7450 1504 2.

The Works of John Donne. Wordsworth, PPG. pp. 300. £2, $6. ISBN 1 8532 6400 8.

Estrin, Barbara L. *Laura: Uncovering Gender and Genre in Wyatt, Donne, and Marvell*. DukeUP. pp. 345. hb $49.95, pb $18.95. ISBN 0 8223 1500 9, 0 8223 1499 1.

Nelson, Jeffrey N. *The Poetry of Robert Tofte 1597–1620: A Critical Old-Spelling Edition*. Garland. pp. 293. $82. ISBN 0 8153 1091 9.

Porter, Peter, ed. *George Herbert (T. S. Eliot)*. St Mut (1990). £40. ISBN 0 7463 0741 1.

Raylor, Timothy. *Cavaliers, Clubs, and Literary Culture: Sir John Mennes, James Smith, and the Order of the Fancy*. UDelP. pp. 335. £36.50. ISBN 0 8741 3523 0.

Sowerby, Robin. *The Classical Legacy in Renaissance Poetry*. Longman. pp. 415. hb £39, pb £16.99. ISBN 0 5820 5549 0, 0 5820 5548 2.

IX

Milton

JOAD RAYMOND

In a year which saw a great deal of publishing on Milton, let me begin with the winner of the 1994 James Holly Hanford Prize of the Milton Society of America. Sharon Achinstein's *Milton and the Revolutionary Reader* is likely to have a significant beneficial impact on Milton studies. This is an important interdisciplinary study of the pamphlet culture of the 1640s and 1650s as a context for reading Milton. Its excellence lies in its attention to many obscure pamphlets as objects worthy of interest in themselves; Milton is, in fact, largely peripheral. Achinstein argues that the so-called English revolution was a revolution in reading. This is not a sociology of reading, as the evidence used is entirely printed, but it does constitute a very nuanced picture of the generic shifts in the two decades, which must have influenced the writing of *Paradise Lost*. Just how is another question: we remain uncertain of the means and extent of Milton's access to pamphlets. While some of the particular connections Achinstein draws seem arbitrary, it seems to me that this picture of Milton writing within a public sphere of popular political print is an accurate one, and more conducive to understanding his works than Parker's Milton-as-recluse or even Hill's Milton-as-enthusiastic-boozer.

The model of a public sphere, upon which Achinstein's argument relies, is discussed in a most important article by David Norbrook, '*Areopagitica*, Censorship, and the Early Modern Public Sphere', in *The Administration of Aesthetics* (ed. Richard Burt). In the wake of Foucaultian readings, theoretically historical and historically ahistorical, it is now not uncommon to see *Areopagitica* cited as a defence of censorship. Norbrook suggests that a modified version of Jürgen Habermas's model of an emergent public sphere can be used to understand the communicative spirit of the 1640s; and that in this context Milton attacked pre-publication licensing because it impinged upon an atmosphere which might lead, through conflict, to the rhetorical production of truth. The Hellenistic allusions evoke a space in which ideas of freedom and civic duty offer a reconfiguration of the relationship between private and public: one which, Norbrook suggests, can be attuned to the role of women in political debate.

Also addressing the question of Milton's reading and his sensitivity to the reading public is Stephen B. Dobranski's '"Where Men of Differing Judgements Croud": Milton and the Culture of the Coffee Houses' (*SC* 9.35–56), which suggests that Milton found access to printed pamphlets of news and politics in local coffee houses. The article includes very useful appendices detailing London coffee houses corresponding to Milton's residences.

Martin Dzelzainis's scholarly contributions are accreting to a strong view of Milton's place in revolutionary England. In 'Juvenal, Charles X Gustavus and Milton's Letter to Richard Jones' (*SC* 9.25–34), he suggests that the 'princely victories' satirically referred to in the Milton–Jones correspondence of 1656 may be those of the King of Sweden, which Milton was publicly supporting in his letters of state, in line with government policy. Hence we should be cautious about assuming that Milton endorsed the views expressed in his official compositions. In 'An Allusion to Milton in *The Transproser Rehears'd* (1673)' (*N&Q* 41.172–3) Dzelzainis shows how the paraphrase of Milton discussing the forcing of conscience in *The Transproser Rehears'd* alludes to the first edition of *The Readie & Easie Way*, but only as paraphrased by *The Censure of the Rota* (1660).

Some of the most powerful and original readings of *Paradise Lost* appear in Jason P. Rosenblatt's *Torah and Law in Paradise Lost*. Rosenblatt's premise is that Milton had an impressive and deliberated knowledge of rabbinical commentaries through his own scholarship and particularly his friendship with the pre-eminent Hebraic scholar and Jewish-sympathizer John Selden. Rosenblatt takes the reader through *Paradise Lost* in a gentle and scholarly *tour de force*. He illuminates the Hebraic representation of Eden, tracing parallels with the philo-Judaic tracts of 1643–5, in which the Mosaic law is seen not as the repressive system we find in the commentaries of Paul, but as the beneficial, easeful Torah, through which our general parents lived. After the Fall the law is ruptured into a Pauline dualism, and the impossibly harsh Mosaic law causes the body to sin. These sources may have some bearing on the debate over *De Doctrina Christiana*, with its intensely Pauline tendencies. Rosenblatt also examines the narrator's voice, initially Mosaic in tone and linked to Adam and Eve; which after the fall moves towards Christian typology, in conflict with the symbolic modes of the Hebrew Bible. Rosenblatt also traces this conflict through Adam's soliloquy (*Paradise Lost* 10:720–844) in which Adam undergoes a personal Reformation. The last two books adopt a more Pauline theology, in which Torah has become Mosaic law and Adam has some harsh lessons to learn, notably through typology. Rosenblatt's subtle close readings offer a powerful interpretation of Milton's sensitivity to Torah, its repeated and varied conflicts with Pauline Christianity, and Milton's ability to separate the two. Books 11 and 12 become dark tragedies indeed.

Michael Lieb's *Milton and the Culture of Violence* argues that Milton's writings were characterized by a 'sparagmatic sensibility', that is, an obsession with ritualistic dismembering violence: 'Violence was his signature.' Milton fears assault on the purity of his body, yet conceives that moments of violence, under the hand of providence, can lead to creative renewal. The mythic and psychoanalytic basis of this argument and its sometimes exotic vocabulary lies in Northrop Frye, René Girard and Carl Gustav Jung.

The first part, 'Rending the Body', is concerned with corporal punishments, and the use of violence in *Areopagitica*, Sonnet 18, 'Ad Patrem', 'Lycidas' and the proem to *Paradise Lost* Book 7. Lieb argues that Milton's obsession with Orpheus follows a pattern of pagan violence being transcended by Christian renewal, and outlines some of the real violence Milton had witnessed. In the second section, 'Gendering the Body', Lieb shows how, in the 'Sixth Prolusion', *A Maske* and the description of Belial in *Paradise Lost*, Milton relates that violence to gendering and especially the crossing of gender. A connection between femininity and 'bisexuality' and the fear of dismemberment established in relation to the earlier works is followed through to *Paradise Lost*. The extended analysis of the allusion to the rape of the Matron (Judges 19 and *Paradise Lost* 1.505) in chapters 5 and 6 is the most powerful section of the book. The third section, 'Staging the Body', explores the polemical violence of the 1650s tracts, and particularly Milton's attempt to preserve his body pure and intact ('repristinated') against attacks, including the poems appended to *Clamor*. Lieb relates this to Milton's feminized presentation of himself as 'The Lady'. Milton is seen to enact, within a 'theater of assault', a mutilation upon Alexander More, as a means of exorcising the impurities imputed against his own body. The study concludes with a chapter on the renewing violence of *Samson Agonistes*. The vituperative jocularity of Milton's assault on 'Morus' is imbued with a tragic self-awareness in *Samson*, but the exulting in violence, especially in the exchange between Samson and Harapha (a figuration of Milton and Salmasius), ultimately leads to regeneration through destruction.

In this study we find decapitated bodies and dismembered limbs, extensive Biblical and classical contexts, and ingenious readings. Yet the connections between the imaginary violence of *sparagmos* and the real violence known to Milton is sometimes tenuous, even clumsy. Lieb rejects a crude biographical reading of Milton's comments on the 'evil days' and 'dangers compassed round' in the invocation to *Paradise Lost* 7, on the grounds that it has 'no basis in demonstrable fact', then proceeds to accept the common historical assumptions anyway, explaining 'I am creating my own historical fiction in order to provide a biographical and psychological context.' Without the disputed historical reading the psychological reading equally has no factual basis. This suggests a rather belle-lettristic attitude towards the dictates of literary theory, and Lieb's erudition and interpretative skill can stand without it.

Less coherent and insightful is Clay Daniel's *Death in Milton's Poetry*, which argues first that in Milton's poetry death is caused by sin, and second that lust is repeatedly associated with death. The book is divided into two parts; the first on the later poems which prove the thesis, the second on the early poems which apparently counter it. Slightly more space is devoted to the latter. The chapter on *Paradise Lost* is a tirade against lust: anything that is pointy, big, swells, moves upward, or moves at all is a phallus; flying is sexual activity. Most encounters are rape: so when the Son throws Satan from heaven this is a form of rape; Eve rapes Satan by looking good, etc. Satan tempts man to disobedience in order to improve his own sex life. Daniel argues that *Paradise Regained* is primarily concerned with Satan's continuing disobedience and consequent death. Chapter 4 (prev. pub. *SCRev* [1994]) is a tirade against Samson, who dies because he is lustful. Milton is a pacifist and Samson a psychopath. The second half of the book traces these pseudo-associations between lust, violence, and death back to the earliest poems. This, of course, blunts the nature of Milton's possible stance against violence in *Samson*, ignoring his later affiliations with Quakers, and tries to efface the impact on Milton's thought of anything that happened after Diodati's death in 1638. The readings of the earlier poems, including the *epicedia*, are more plausible, though pedestrian, and offer some knowledgeable elaborations on classical allusions. Daniel argues that classical and Christian imagery clash as Milton explores the possibility of consolation, in which a providential view of death ultimately triumphs over the random pagan killer. Daniel speculates too often, and repeatedly conflates chastity with virginity.

The final section of Victoria Kahn's excellent *Machiavellian Rhetoric: From the Counter-Reformation to Milton* contains three chapters on Milton: on the prose tracts, *A Maske* and *Paradise Lost*. The study concerns readings of Machiavelli, and argues against any hypothesis of secularization; Kahn believes that *The Discourses* and *The Prince* are complementary works, both concerned with rhetoric, reality and political practice, which became increasingly useful during the civil wars of Britain. Kahn's chapters on Milton are concerned with the relationship of interpretation to decision making: and she provides powerful and illuminating readings of the role of Providence in *A Maske* and of the Sin and Death allegory in *Paradise Lost*.

A more theoretically orientated version of hermeneutics is the centre of *Milton and the Hermeneutic Journey*, by Gale H. Carrithers Jr and James D. Hardy Jr. This examines Milton's poetry to find a unifying theme in the hermeneutic progress towards understanding divine love and grace. The inferential cyclical movement of understanding between past and present which characterizes hermeneutics they find both in Milton's own beliefs and practices and their own approach. They write with one eye on the contemporary context of postmodern theory and the Milton industry.

Dayton Haskin, in *Milton's Burden of Interpretation*, argues that Milton passes through three stages in his 'interpretative career': in the first he regards the Bible as clear and open, in which spirit he avers his vocation in *The Reason of Church Government*; following this is a decisive break in which he recognizes that biblical texts can only be understood by diligent compiling and conferring. The second, less dramatic shift occurs in the last books of *Paradise Lost* and the 1671 volume: Milton comes to recognize that not all cruces can be understood by comparison with clear places in Scripture, and of these it is best to be silent. This 'burden' of interpretation, the duty to understand in order to reassure one's conviction of redemption, is manifested, according to Haskin, in Milton's continuing interest in the parable of the talents, and in contemporary concern over predestination and the idea of a deceiving, temporary faith. Haskin's historical specificity and periodization of Milton's 'interpretative career' is at best casual: sometimes he intends it to be chronologically exact, at others non-chronological. Though Haskin offers valuable and insightful scriptural and exegetical contexts for the divorce tracts, *Paradise Lost*, *Paradise Regained* and *Samson Agonistes*, some readers may find that his tirades against the waywardness of the past twenty years of Miltonism a little off-putting.

In *Pretexts of Authority*, Kevin Dunn analyses the place of Milton's self-presentation in a tradition of post-Reformation prefaces which negotiate the position of the authorial voice in a relationship between public and private spheres. In 'Milton among the Monopolists: *Areopagitica*, Intellectual Property and the Hartlib Circle' (in Mark Greengrass, Michael Leslie and Timothy Raylor, eds, *Samuel Hartlib and Universal Reformation*), Dunn explores Milton's comments on literary property in the context of Hartlibian discussions of information, suggesting that Milton espouses not so much a nascent possessive individualism as a humanist contextualism.

In *Creating States: Studies in the Performative Language of John Milton and William Blake*, Angela Esterhammer uses Ferdinand de Saussure, Emile Benveniste, J. L. Austin and John R. Searle to consider two kinds of performative language: the phenomenological, or purely creative, and the sociological. Chapter 3 (also partly in *Spokesperson Milton*, discussed below) examines the significance of the language of inspiration and prophecy, of the oath-as-performative in *Reason of Church Government*. Chapter 4 (also partly in *ESC* 20) explores the creative powers of language in *Paradise Lost*, tracing connections between the language of God and the narrator/Milton. Esterhammer offers some insightful comments on the role of delimitation in creation and in language (relating to Milton's theology of creation *ex deo*), on naming by God and Adam and on the prefiguring power of language.

SEL continues the debate over the authorship of *De Doctrina Christiana*, with contributions by Maurice Kelley, Christopher Hill and William B. Hunter. In 'The Provenance of John Milton's *Christian Doctrine*: A Reply to William B. Hunter', Kelley (34.153–63) responds to Hunter's articles of 1992 and 1993, clarifying Daniel Skinner's relation with Trinity College, Cambridge, and the welcomeness of Arian heterodoxies in the 1650s. Kelley's gives a narrative of the provenance, plus a series of rejoinders to Hunter; Picard's hand is seen to be the real clincher. Kelley dismisses the implication that Miltonists have been the victims of an historical con-trick. In 'Professor William B. Hunter, Bishop Burgess, and John Milton' (34.165–93), Christopher Hill questions the doctrinal incongruity between *De Doctrina Christiana* and Milton's 'canonical' works which has been propounded by Hunter. Using common sense and his usual breadth of reference, Hill identifies with broad strokes numerous parallels between *De Doctrina* and (other?) works by Milton. Hunter's 'Animadversions upon the Remonstrants' Defenses against Burgess and Hunter' (34.195–203) restates some of these doctrinal inconsistencies; namely in the areas of cited authorities, the Incarnation, and the authority of the Old Testament laws. Most interestingly he identifies discrepancies between the uses of proof-texts. He suggests that the author of *De Doctrina* was an acquaintance of Leuwe Van Aitzema, the Dutchman who in 1655 sponsored the Dutch translation of *The Doctrine and Discipline of Divorce*. We await computer analysis of the Latin prose, perhaps to break the impasse.

Jacques B. H. Alblas, 'Milton's *The Doctrine and Discipline of Divorce*: The Unknown Dutch Translation (1655) Discovered' (*MiltonQ* 28.35–9), identifies the long-sought-for Dutch translation of Milton's tract. Alblas has located two copies (in Amsterdam and the Hague), which have eluded Miltonists, first because the tract does not identify its author (and does not admit to being a translation), and second because the title-page bears little resemblance to the English title-pages. Oddly, the translator used the first, 1643 edition rather than the expanded 1644 text which Milton recommended to Van Aitzema.

De Doctrina continues to be a basis for interpretations: Jane Melbourne, in 'Self-Doubt in the Wilderness in *Paradise Regain'd*' (*SEL* 34.135–51), argues that the three temptations in *Paradise Regained* are balanced by three covert temptations, which play on Jesus's self-doubt; and that this presentation of Jesus is consonant with the Nestorian heresy (the Incarnation as the union of two persons rather than two natures) found in *De Doctrina*.

Many of the shorter Milton contributions appear in two collections of essays. The superior, more unified volume, with the more substantial pieces, is Diana Treviño Benet and Michael Lieb, eds. *Literary Milton: Text, Pretext, Context*, a collection of essays for John Shawcross, linked by the influence of his *Intentionality and the New Traditionalism* (1991). Regina M. Schwartz, 'The Toad at Eve's Ear: From Identification to Identity', pursues an extended parallel between psychoanalysis and theology and literature. It is a complex and diffuse piece: Schwartz shows Milton's concern over identity, identification and imitation as human states and activities; and suggests how Milton's mediation of his concerns ultimately resembles the psychoanalyst's control of transference. In 'That Old Man Eloquent', Annabel Patterson considers the sonnets as a sequence, suggesting that they play with the ambiguities of biography. Some of the adjustments from manuscript to print deliberately broaden the historical moment of their occasions, and open up the ideal community which they imply. Their use as biographical documents is not only problematic, but misses their aesthetic intentions, which address the political history of their times. Mary Ann Radzinowicz, 'Forced Allusions: Avatars of King David in the Seventeenth Century', considers the various uses of allusions to I Samuel, and the relative merits of Saul and David in writings by Thomas Hobbes, Abraham Cowley and Milton. She suggests that the multivalency of the biblical texts undermines the strained application of them to contemporary politics, through the repressed, unusable material and implicit counter-interpretations. She concludes with a meditation on the fragile nature of allusion.

Diane McColley, in '"The Copious Matter of My Song"', a compact and learned essay, surveys the density and breadth of allusion in two passages from *Paradise Lost*: the angelic hymn of Book 3 and Raphael's creation narrative. She shows how the verse compounds a tissue of allusion, not necessarily pointed, to liturgy, music, and natural and moral philosophy. The detailed comments on the musical form of the angelic hymn are particularly interesting. Diana Treviño Benet, 'Hell, Satan, and the New Politician', argues that the diabolic conclave of Book 2 should not be understood as a commentary on the earthly politics of 1642–60. Satan is not simply a tyrant in a staged debate, but a new kind of politician, a figure mediated in a number of popular political pamphlets, a loquacious politician who must struggle to maintain his position of command. There is much of merit in Benet's argument: though the pamphlets she cites (far from exhaustively) centre specifically around 1647–8 and 1660; and Benet simply assumes Milton's familiarity with them. The nature and extent of Milton's access to such pamphlets is presently a pivotal issue in Milton studies. In '"Two of Far Nobler Shape": Reading the Paradisal Text', Michael Lieb reads closely the first sight of Adam and Eve, and the failure of appearance to converge with reality. He shows how the Pauline theology which appears to underwrite the inequality of the sexes in that passage (mediated via Satan and the Narrator) is itself made problematic in *Tetrachordon*. Both intratextual and intertextual readings resist the fixing of the male–female hierarchy in this passage central to feminist readings of *Paradise Lost*. Joseph Wittreich contributes a brilliant, sometimes fierce, and sometimes rambling essay, '"Inspired with Contradiction": Mapping Gender Discourses in *Paradise Lost*', exploring the conflicting interpretations of Milton which develop out of his conflicting source materials: namely Genesis 1 and 2, and different cosmologies. *Paradise Lost* shows how competing interpretations emerge, above all in relation to discourses of gender, though truth itself may be unified. Wittreich is ultimately suggesting something familiar, that Milton is challenging a patriarchal orthodoxy closely related to Restoration politics; but Wittreich's deft handling of Genesis blows away cobwebs and commonplaces.

Stephen M. Fallon, 'Intention and its Limits in *Paradise Lost*: The Case of Bellerophon', suggests that the two appearances of Bellerophon (representing heroic chastity, superhuman feats and eventual overreaching) in Milton's works, in the Sixth Prolusion and the invocation to Book 7, mark a trajectory of interpretation which reflects the poet's own career, from unqualified poetic confidence to a poetic confidence which acknowledges the potential for error. The essay follows Shawcross in distinguishing between the potential of the author's text and the specifics of the reader's text, with its capacity to run counter to the author's signposts. Fallon concludes with a reading of an exemplary reader's text: Marvell's 'On Mr. Milton's *Paradise Lost*'. In his insightful '*Paradise Lost* and the Materialism Debate' (*1994 Annual of Hermeneutics and Social Concern* [New York: Continuum] 174–203), Fallon illustrates Milton's engagement with seventeenth-century metaphysics debates. The material being of Milton's angels rejects both Cartesian dualism and Hobbesian determinism, which philosophies are variously voiced by Satan and shown to be flawed by the War in Heaven. In an essay largely reproduced in *Torah and Law*, Jason P. Rosenblatt shows how the Pauline theology of Adam's post-Lapsarian soliloquy tries to suppress the preceding Hebraic evocation of Eden, with its positive conception of Torah, by turning Torah into Law, a burden on mankind.

Barbara K. Lewalski, 'Milton and the Hartlib Circle: Educational Projects and Epic Paideia', argues that Milton's *Of Education* shares certain broad principles with the educational reform proposals of John Dury and Jan Amos Comenius (using printed sources rather than the Hartlib archives), and that the epics try both to illustrate these principles and to put them into practice. Also concerned with the relationship between theory and practice is Mary F. Norton, 'The Praxis of Milton's Truth: *Proairesis* and Qualification in the Civil Liberty Tracts' (*MiltonQ* 28.47–56), which outlines the presentation of *proairesis* (the process of intelligent decision making) in Milton's prose. She shows how integral qualifications are to the *proairesis*, promoting the virtues which are necessary to the recognition and enactment of truth, or proscribing vices which prevent it. This is an interesting and stimulating account, despite its neglect of close political circumstances.

The other volume of essays, edited by Charles W. Durham and Kristin Pruitt McColgan, is *Spokesperson Milton: Voices in Contemporary Criticism*. The essays are shorter and of varying quality, and the volume has little coherence. In the introductory 'Spokesperson Milton', John T. Shawcross outlines the uses of Milton as a voice for diverse causes from the eighteenth century to the present, suggesting that at the root of this flexibility is Milton's notion of liberty. A twentieth-century (liberal and positive) view of liberty lies at the heart of this presentation, and Shawcross tries to salve Milton's occasional offence with the balm of liberalism, William Empson's being the only invalid view.

In 'The Fruitless Tree in *Paradise Lost*: Symbol of Sin', Alice M. Matthews analyses the presentation of the fig tree in Book 9. It is both barren and fecund, prefiguring corruption by lust. The East and West Indies are conflated, and Adam and Eve are presented as noble savages, through which their redemption is promised, by the fruit, the Son of Man. In 'No Fortunate Fall, No "Unfeared Second Fate": Satan and the Critique of Melioration, *Paradise Lost*, Book 2' (and see *YWES* 74.257), Catherine Gimelli Martin suggests that the inference of the *felix culpa* is an erroneous cliché. Milton tries to break this optimism to advocate self-denying fortitude. While this may be true it seems to come more by way of a premise than a conclusion. Also rejecting the *felix culpa* is John F. Tanner's '"By Faith to Stand": Faith in the Theodicy of *Paradise Lost*', a revised section from his *Anxiety in Eden* (1992). More persuasively, and more concerned with practical humanity, Tanner considers the end of *Paradise Lost*, and the role of philosophy and theology in consolation.

Samuel Smith argues that Christ's struggle against Satan in the Desert in

Paradise Regained is a type of the apocalyptic struggle. Smith uses a ragbag of historical examples, establishing the contemporary context largely through the theology of Thomas Taylor and William Perkins. Hence a rather odd emphasis on dragons, and the unusual title 'Dodging the Dragon's Tail: Apocalyptic Content in *Paradise Regained*'. In '*Jubilee* in Scripture and History: Reading Milton's "At a Solemn Music"', Stephen M. Buhler claims that the ideas of diaspora and discord are reflected in the formal qualities of the poem, in which Milton resists harmony and represents a sense of historical process. Milton deploys the year of Jubilee in association with personal liberty and apocalypse, thus signalling his early (theological) radicalism.

In 'Milton's Royalist Reflex: The Failure of Argument and the Role of Dialogics in *Eikonoklastes*', Jane Hiles analyses what she sees as the rhetorical failure of *Eikonoklastes*, largely argued from the perspective of Wilson's *Arte of Rhetorique* (1553). *Eikonoklastes* is 'unrhetorical' because it fails to look to the point: criticism of style prevails over criticism of ideology. Hiles ends by flourishing Bakhtin, suggesting that as the point of Milton's literary criticism is to invoke heteroglossia, it is 'inherently subversive'. Discussing rhetoric, the article falls short of Elizabeth Skerpan's *The Rhetoric of Politics in the English Revolution 1642–1660* (1992); discussing readers and literary genres, it is inferior to Achinstein's book, discussed above.

In 'The Cardinal and the King: Milton's State Letters to France', Robert Thomas Fallon demonstrates that there are many more Miltonic state papers than hitherto acknowledged. The substantive point, in brief, is that the governments of Heaven, Hell, Chaos and Earth all have co-rulers, and the exercise of power in them is modified by family ties; this reflects the political structure of France, with Cardinal Mazarin's administration for the young Louis XIV, for whom Milton repeatedly composed dual letters. In '"Under Thir Head Embodied All in One": Milton's reinterpretation of the Organic Analogy in *Paradise Lost*', Steven Jablonski shows how Milton rejects the body politic analogy in which the king is the head of the state as Christ is the head of the church. Analysing both *Paradise Lost*, mainly through the discussion of authority in Book 5, and *The Readie & Easie Way*, Jablonski shows how Christ's assumption of headship involves humility, such as the atonement, and does not correspond to claims to unaccountable authority as asserted by Satan and Charles I. In 'A Fissure in the Milton Window?: Arnold's 1888 Address', David Boocker investigates Matthew Arnold's place in the history of Milton criticism: Arnold inherited an eighteenth-century Tory distaste for Milton's politics and a Romantic admiration of the poetry. He consequently separated not only the poetry from the prose, but also the aesthetics from the politics. Angela Esterhammer's 'Meddling with Authority: Inspiration and Speech Acts in Milton's Prose' can also be found in her *Creating States*, discussed above. Albert W. Fields, 'The Creative Self and the Self Created in *Paradise Lost*', provides an account of Adam's self-consciousness as a form of Renaissance self-fashioning, with a few gestures to Milton's self-fashioning as author. Self-knowledge and self-consciousness were difficult in Renaissance England (illustrated by a handful of quotations from elite culture) because people did not conceive of the self as a unified thing. Yet through a process of revelation, reflection and introspection they (including Adam) made it. In 'Conflicts of Authority: Interpretation of Events in *Paradise Regained* and *Samson Agonistes*', Daniel T. Lochman examines providential patterns to suggest that the continuities between the works in the 1671 volume are greater than the contrasts. Jane Collins, in 'Authorial

Providence and the Dramatic Form of *Samson Agonistes*', argues that *Samson* should be read as a drama: as an interplay of voices without a narrator, stimulating expectation of a physical conflict, and rooted in ritual and communal ceremony. Moreover, it must be read with the kind of restless scepticism which Milton recommended for scripture, as an investigation of the description and scrutiny of behaviour rather than a providential narrative about the attainment of a state of grace. Elsewhere, George F. Butler, in 'New Light on Samson's Darkness: *Samson Agonistes* and Suicide in the Seventeenth Century' (*CLAJ* 27.443–52), considers Samson as a meditation on suicide and its motives.

Going back to *Spokesperson Milton*: in '*Comus*: Milton's Re-Formation of the Masque', J. Andrew Hubbell argues that '*Comus*' is closer to the politics of 1633 than some Miltonists allow, largely because the anti-masque represents England. Hubbell suggests that the masque is concerned with poetic vocation. Most of the article is familiar from David Norbrook's article in David Lindley, ed., *The Reformation of the Masque* (*YWES* 65.306), though some of the endnotes are helpful. In '"Nature Taught Art": The Topos of Art and Nature in *Paradise Regained*', Peter M. McClusky analyses the art–nature *topos* in the Banquet temptation scene in *Paradise Regained* Book 2. He suggests that the line 'Nature's own work it seem'd (Nature taught Art)' contains a purposeful ambiguity (is the grove natural or artificial?) which at once presents the grove in a suspicious light without indicating that Christ is deceived by it.

In 'Beneficent Hierarchies: Reading Milton Greenly', Diane McColley offers a close and sensitive examination of the beneficent, flexible, reciprocal and environmentally friendly nature of hierarchies in *Paradise Lost*. Focusing largely on idealized types of exchange and communication in Eden, she delineates an optimistic model of a generous and open society, uncorrupted by dominion and its linguistic counterparts. In a similar essay, 'Abundant Gifts: Hierarchy and Reciprocity in *Paradise Lost*' (*SCRev* 11.75–86), Kristin Pruitt McColgan argues that in the pre-Lapsarian relationship between Adam and Eve, Milton envisages a mutuality of hierarchy and reciprocity. Adam and Eve exalt each other, reciprocity leading to greater equality within the hierarchy, in what McColgan describes as a 'humanist' view of marriage. Raphael's response to Eve reflects his challenge to Adam to articulate his position, but also indicates his own limitations; this indicates his own masculinist position, and not Milton's, who proceeds to pen Adam's insightful defence of his partner.

Returning to *Spokesperson Milton*, in '"Gratefull Digressions" and "Casual Discourse": Eve's Rapport-Talk', Joan F. Gilliand uses Deborah Tannen's typology of male and female conversation patterns, in which male report-talk (informative, status-orientated) is opposed to female rapport-talk (conversational, consensus-building), to analyse Adam and Eve's relationship. Hope Parisi's 'Discourse and Danger: Women's Heroism in the Bible and Dalila's Self-Defense' champions Dalila as a collocation of textual fragments (not a character), worked through a contrast between the relative toleration of ancient Israel and the repressive patriarchy of seventeenth-century Europe. Challenging the supposedly monolithic nature of scriptural attitudes to women, Parisi makes seventeenth-century society utterly monolithic. Finally, in 'Milton's Vergilian Epigraphs of 1637 and 1645', Natalie Joy Woodall intelligently reads Milton's epigraphs, modified from Vergil, to the 1637 *A Maske* and 1645 *Poems*, suggesting that they show a developing concern over paganism, particularly as a threat to the godly poet. Her reading offers a different sense of motivation from that of Richard

M. Johnson, in 'The Politics of Publication: Misrepresentation in Milton's 1645 *Poems*' (*Criticism* 36.45–71), who explores the contradictory materials of the frontispiece and title-page of the 1645 *Poems*, suggesting that the discrepancies of the portrait reflect Marshall's sceptical representation of a 38-year-old as a 21-year-old; that Milton countered the royalist caricature with the inscription, and defiantly gestured towards his own vocation as a Puritan, vatic poet in the Vergilian epitaph on the title-page. In 'The Enclosure of Virginity: The Poetics of Sexual Abstinence in the English Revolution' (in Richard Burt and John Michael Archer, eds, *Enclosure Acts*), John Rogers argues that, notwithstanding a broader historical movement in favour of a bourgeois ideology of domestic love, mid-seventeenth-century England witnessed a radical current in favour of virginity, which, especially in males, is seen to possess an apocalyptic power. Rogers suggests that Milton's 1637 revision of the Lady's speech praising chastity in *A Maske* is a proleptical anticipation of this new cult of virginity.

John K. Hale, 'The Audiences of Milton's Italian Verse' (*RS* 8.76–88), examines the four potential audiences of Milton's six Italian sonnets (which he dates to 1629–30) within each poem: namely Italian, English, himself, and ultimately Milton's idea of Dante. R. E. Pritchard, 'Milton and Constable' (*N&Q* 41.166–7), persuasively identifies the 'diffuse influence' on Milton's sonnet 'Methought I saw' of the *Spirituall Sonettes*, circulated in manuscript, of Henry Constable (1562–1613). The relatively neglected Sonnet 14 receives two articles this year. In 'Milton *in parvo*: Mortalism and Genre Transformation in Sonnet 14' (*MiltonQ* 28.1–10), A. E. B. Coldiron endeavours to enhance the reputation of the sonnet on Catherine Thomason, first by considering its mixture of forms as a sonnet-elegy, and second by an analysis of its apparent opposition to the mortalism of *De Doctrina Christiana*. The merits of the argument are diminished by its pretentious and opaque form. Thomas C. Martin's 'Milton's *Sonnet 14*' (*Expl* 52.147–9) is a formalist account of the theme of separation and joining in Milton's sonnet, with Christian Platonism in the background. Michael W. Price's 'Milton's *Sonnet 18: On the late Massacre in Piedmont*' (*Expl* 52.70–2), suggests that the theme of vengeance overrides the formal movement of the sonnet towards resolution, leaving the perpetrators unregenerate and the sonnet in a state of tension.

Helping to render manageable this excess of Miltonism, though ultimately likely to increase it, is Edward Jones's *Milton's Sonnets: An Annotated Bibliography, 1900–1992*, a useful and well-organized bibliography of criticism on the sonnets, divided into sections on general criticism, the Italian sonnets, translations, and one on each of the English sonnets. Within each section the entries are listed chronologically. Sonnets 10, 17 and 21 have apparently received no substantial attention. Jones covers books, articles, chapters, some editions and a few theses. Editions of the works or selected poems are, unfortunately, not listed. The synopses enable readers to identify the 90 per cent dross written on any given sonnet. There are also author, sonnet and subject indexes. Another useful scholarly tool for Miltonists is Samuel J. Rogal's *An Index to the Biblical References, Parallels, and Allusions in the Poetry and Prose of John Milton*. This index is divided into four sections, one each for the Old and New Testaments for both the poetry and prose, and each section is organized according to the books of the Bible listed in conventional order. Milton's prose is, most oddly, referred to by book, chapter and paragraph, rather than to any specific edition. Hence the reader has to count paragraphs through the text to find the allusion, which is an unnecessarily irksome task.

Stella P. Revard, 'The Tangles of Neaera's Hair: Milton and Neo-Latin Ode', in Ann Moss et al., eds, *Acta Conventus Neo-Latini Hafniensis*, outlines the possible influence on young Milton's poetry of the work of neo-Latin poets. Revard suggests their presence in the imagery and generic choices of 'On the Death' and 'On the Morning', and makes an interesting case for the use of the monody form and of the name 'Lycidas', employed frequently in neo-Latin poems. In the same volume, Philip C. Dust offers in 'Otium in Milton's Latin Poetry and "Il Penseroso"' a brief communication considering the influence of Milton's own *otium* on his representation of it in his poetry, namely through the quantity of reading he had leisure for.

In 'The Political and Liturgical Subtext of Milton's "On the Death of a Fair Infant Dying of a Cough"' (*ANQ* 7.18–21), John T. Shawcross identifies echoes of the Feasts of Saint Joachim and Anne, parents of the Blessed Mary (26 July), in the Book of Common Prayer, in Milton's 'On the Death'. These strengthen the argument for a political reading of the poem, placing it as a gesture of 'opposition to monarchic hegemony' in early 1628. Also identifying liturgical subtexts is Anne Barbeau Gardiner, 'Milton's Parody of Catholic Hymns in Eve's Temptation and Fall; Original Sin as a Paradigm of "Secret Idolatries"' (*SP* 91.216–31), which analyses the sin of Eve as an ironic prefiguration of the Eucharist, noting in Eve's hymn to the tree a number of allusions to Catholic prayers and hymns. Gardiner suggests that the poem is already taking the harder line on Catholic worship seen in *Of True Religion*; Eve is 'the first Roman Catholic', Satan the 'counter-revolutionary' and prelatical author of her idolatry. Sung Ryol Kim, 'Milton's Sons of God: A Reconsideration' (*MiltonQ* 28.61–8), examines the exegetical tradition behind the Sons of God episode, deriving from Genesis 6.1–4, to argue that Milton's presentation is not misogynistic. He blames the disobedience on the Sethite men, not the women, and the episode is meant as an example of general human corruption rather than as a miniature repetition of the Fall.

Margo Swiss, in 'Satan's Obduracy in *Paradise Lost*' (*MiltonQ* 28.56–61), argues against a lenient reading of Satan by showing his hard-heartedness, a quality which runs against Milton's presentation of open communion and receptiveness as the path to grace. Paul Cheshire, 'Satan as Toad – God's Uses of Adversity' (*MiltonQ* 28.39–41), shows that in an alchemical tradition the toad is literally and symbolically used to precipitate putrefaction followed by renewal and creation. He suggests that Satan's adoption of the toad form prefigures God's plan for human regeneration, in effect an antetype of Milton's *felix culpa*. In his interesting 'Milton's War in Heaven as Apocalyptic Drama: "Thy Foes Justly Hast in Derision"' (*MiltonQ* 28.28–35), Paul Rovang argues that the derisive laughter of the war in Heaven is apocalyptic in nature, deriving, with other aspects of the war, from the second Psalm, and expressing contempt at the powerless. Rovang ties some of the emotional impulses of the war to the Restoration context.

Notwithstanding the vogue for historicism and politics, gender and psychoanalytic criticism still have their place. In '"Embraces Forcible and Foul": Viewing Milton's Sin as a Rape Victim' (*MiltonQ* 28.11–16), Alexander A. Myers suggests that Milton's representation of Sin is a nuanced, psychologically insightful one, and that Sin is offered as a sympathetic character, separate from the allegorical idea behind her, not actually guilty of sin. Passive she may be, and she may indeed not ask for it, but this case for her innocence falls short of explaining away the allegory and the problem of who says what to whom in this passage. Larry L. Langford's 'Adam and the Subversion of Paradise' (*SEL* 34.119–34) builds upon the now common view that Eve's character is defined by a sense of lack and a capacity to imagine alternatives: Langford, treating Adam and Eve as characters independent of the poem and its author, shows how Adam's sense of completeness derives from the very different interventions God makes in his life, enabling Adam's integrity, at the cost of the sense of possibilities he experiences earlier. The tendency to reify the gaze into an active male voyeur and a passive female victim is challenged by Regina Schwartz in her witty and digressive 'Through the Optic Glass: Voyeurism and *Paradise Lost*' (in Valeria Finucci and Regina Schwartz, eds, *Desire in the Renaissance*). While veering into Lacan and film analysis, Schwartz explores the ways of seeing in *Paradise Lost*, suggesting that the binary opposition between viewer and viewed collapses as objects look back at the looker, and (modern) expectations of the camera's eye are confounded. Schwartz shows that the text's voyeurs are exhibitionists, and that Eve never relinquishes her right to be a viewer.

Two items in Roy Eriksen, ed., *Contexts of Pre-novel Narrative*, reluctantly address the possibilities of theory in Milton studies. Thomas N. Corns, in '"That prerogative over human": *Paradise Lost* and the Telling of Divine History', rejects as inappropriate Bakhtin's definition of epic as a history set in an unreachable past, then uses Bakhtin's accounts of the dialogic novel to analyse the complex plotting of *Paradise Lost* as a narrative of voices existing in different relationships. Dialogism upholds authority and holds the apparently fractured structure in a tight unity. The article is brief, prefatory and breathless. In the same volume, Gordon Campbell's 'Pragmatism and Narratology: The Case of *Paradise Lost*' tries to bring together narratologists and traditional scholars (like the volume, and its preceding conference). In the spirit of an after-dinner talk, Campbell argues (via Genette, Plato and Aelius Donatus) that the technical vocabulary of narratology can help identify different voices in *Paradise Lost*, for which the more genteel language of traditional literary criticism is inadequate.

Campbell makes a more characteristic contribution in the December *MiltonQ*, an issue entirely given to 'Edward King, Milton's "Lycidas": Poems and Documents', which he has edited with Norman Postlethwaite. This is an edition of Edward King's extant poetry (ten Latin occasional poems in all), plus four commemorative poems which did not appear in *Justa Edouardo King*, including two by Clement Paman, plus the texts of the 1630 Royal Mandate appointing King a fellow of Christ's College, his will, and an inventory of his goods. In their introduction Postlethwaite and Campbell point to King's learning and suggest that Milton's friendship with him may have been genuine. This is an interesting and most scholarly volume.

Two eminent literary critics make avowedly nonconformist interventions in chapters in weighty tomes. In her very substantial *Configurations: A Topomorphical Approach to Renaissance Poetry*, Maren-Sofie Røstvig argues that the concept of unity adumbrated by Augustine, involving a symmetry reflecting God's creation as a ratio of 2:1, was observed by many Renaissance poets, including Milton. Røstvig considers the ten-book structure of the 1667 edition, identifying a complex structure of three triads around a centre, related according to theme. Some of this form is carried over into the simpler symmetry of the twelve-book edition, but Røstvig suggests that there are considerable losses, and indicates many numerological significances within the epic. Harold Bloom's *The Western Canon: The Books and School of the Ages* contains a brief chapter on Milton, which presents Satan as a Shakespearean character in the mould of Iago, Edmund and Hamlet, and *Paradise Lost* as a struggle against Shakespeare. Satan, more exactly Lucifer, is the hero of the poem, and Milton demeans himself in so fiercely demeaning the declining Satan. This poetic flaw results 'from Milton's refusal or inability to dramatize the Christian argument of his poem properly'. There is little new here, though Bloom's enthusiasms are infectious: unfortunately the admiration of the long epic is partly expressed through deprecating the 1671 poems.

There are numerous shorter interventions. Willy Maley's 'Rebels and Redshanks: Milton and the British Problem' (*ISR* 6.7–11) discusses Milton's patriotic *Observations upon the Articles of Peace* in the historical moment of the political opportunities of 1649. A. M. Cinquemani, in 'Foolish Monk and Barbarous Declamation' (*MiltonQ* 28.16–17), suggests that the 'barbarous Declamation' written by the 'foolish Monk' alluded to in *An Apology for Smectymnuus* is not the *Invectiva contra Fr. Petrarchum* by Jean de Hesdin, and that Milton's allusion suggests that he was familiar with most of the documents exchanged between Hesdin and Petrarch over clerical corruption and the love of French wines. Martin R. Kalfatovic, 'A Note on Milton's *Lycidas*' (*ANQ* 7.208–9), comments on the appropriateness of Milton's use of Camus to mediate between Christian and classical learning: both are found at Cambridge. In 'Milton's Two Poets' (*SEL* 34.109–18), a lean and purple reading of the conflicting voices in 'Lycidas', Russell Fraser attacks both unnamed Miltonists and Generation X for being unprepared to read poems.

Michele Valerie Ronnick gives three philological notes: 'Milton's *Reason of Church Government* 1.5' (*Expl* 52.210–11) suggests that the poppies derive from Livy, with connotations of the tyrannical nature of the house of Tarquin. 'The Phrase "*Nerone Neronior*" in Walter of Châtillon, John Milton, and John Adams' (*N&Q* 41.169–70) suggests that John Adams borrowed this phrase derived not directly from Walter of Châtillon but via Milton's *Defensio Prima*. 'On Milton's Use of the Noun Wind-Egg' (*N&Q* 41.168–9) notes that Milton's use of 'wind-egg' begins a shift in its English usage towards metaphorical application (i.e. the sterile product of an unfertilized mind).

Erik Gray's 'An Echo of Joannes Secundus in Milton's "Elegia Tertia"' (*N&Q* 41.167–8) provides what the title offers. Edward Le Comte, 'Spirits Odorous' (*MiltonQ* 28.17–18), adds to David Reid's comments (*YWES* 72.228) on seventeenth-century boasts of sweet-smelling bodies. C. Harold Hurley, in 'Milton's *L'Allegro*, 67' (*Expl* 52.207–9), argues that the disputed phrase 'tells his tale' means 'telling stories' rather than 'counting sheep' as most commentators would have it: L'Allegro is, after all, trying to enjoy himself. John K. Hale's 'Milton's *Preface to Samson Agonistes*' (*Expl* 52.73–5) explores the diversity of the meanings of 'temper and reduce' in Milton's account of Aristotelian catharsis prefaced to *Samson*. Anne Lohrli, '"Fresh Fields and Pastures New"' (*N&Q* 41.351–2), outlines the misquotation of the concluding line of 'Lycidas' in the Victorian periodical *Household Words*, and in Mark Pattison's *Milton* (1879).

Much amusement can be offered by the history of the transmission of Milton. Elizabeth K. Hill's splendid 'Naughty Milton; Text and Context of *Liobov' Mil'tona*' (*MiltonQ* 28.23–8) is a brief synopsis of the translation and reception of Milton's works in Russia, up to the early nineteenth century, followed by an account of *Liobov' Mil'tona* (1837), or 'Milton's Sweetheart'. This anonymous Moscow play contains a sympathetic and highly idiosyncratic account of Milton's courtship of Mary Powell, written in the sentimental Russian Romantic style, with Milton as a charming, girl-crazed free-liver.

Harry Redman Jr's *Major French Milton Critics of the Nineteenth Century* is an amusing and curious volume which presents fifteen separate studies, from Abel François Villemain to Augustin Filon. Many of the repeated themes are very much familiar today: Milton's Hellenism; the importance of the Italian trip; genre criticism; uneasiness over the supernatural elements of the epic; the relationship of the poetry to the prose. The weaknesses of this book lie in its lack of in-depth analysis of either Milton or nineteenth-century French intellectual culture. It is not suggested why, other than for elusive reasons of 'taste', the French found the Sin and Death allegory so offensive. On the other hand the identification, first noted by Pongerville, of echoes of Anne D'Urfé's *Hymne des anges* in *Paradise Lost* is useful. As a survey structured episodically it is repetitive when read from cover to cover.

In 'Milton, Pope and the Missionary Position: Yet Once More' (*ANQ* 7.133–6) Patrick J. Cook considers Pope's apparent allusion to *Paradise Lost* in *Rape of the Lock* V, in Belinda's sex-role reversal. He suggests that Milton queries the perceived domination of female by male, and that in the bower 'Milton is careful to avoid vertical positioning': both Adam and Eve are, in effect, on top.

The following are of limited interest. Barbara Pavlock, 'Horace's Influence on Renaissance Epic' (*Classical World* 87.427–41), looks at the influence of Horace's Odes on the representation of male-female relations in the epics of Ariosto, Tasso and Milton. The brief Milton section identifies echoes in the exchanges between Adam and Eve; and in it we learn that *Paradise Lost* was 'published in 1674' and that Milton was the author of such works as 'the *Divorce Tracts* and *Tetrachordon*'. In 'John Milton and the Word of God: Truth in *Paradise Lost*' (in John C. Hawsley, ed., *Reform and Counterreform*), an essay which those who accept C. S. Lewis uncritically may find challenging, Elizabeth Rossettini summarizes some recent work on representations of Eve, who is the victim of a conspiracy by Adam to make her feel guilt and shame. Milton thus transcended his word and 'presented us with God's Truth'. Inger Christensen, '"Thy Great Deliverer": Christian Hero and Epic Convention in John Milton's *Paradise Lost* and C. S. Lewis' *Perelandra*' (in Andrew Kennedy and Orm Øverland, eds, *Excursions into Fiction*) suggests that there are deep structural and thematic affinities between *Paradise Lost* and *Perelandra* (1943). This is not inherently improbable given that Lewis had delivered his lectures on Milton in 1941. Christensen's comments on the epic are vague and the parallels banal and uninformed.

Books Reviewed

Achinstein, Sharon. *Milton and the Revolutionary Reader*. PrincetonUP. pp. 272. £27.50, $35. ISBN 0 6910 3490 7.

Benet, Diana Treviño, and Michael Lieb, eds. *Literary Milton: Text, Pretext, Context*. Duquesne. pp. 274. $48. ISBN 0 8207 0259 5.

Bloom, Harold. *The Western Canon: The Books and School of the Ages*. HBJ. pp. 608. hb £20, pb £10. ISBN 0 1510 0133 2, 0 3336 4813 7.

Burt, Richard, ed. *The Administration of Aesthetics: Censorship, Political Criticism, and the Public Sphere*. UMinnP. hb £35, $49.95, pb £15.95, $21.95. ISBN 0 8166 2365 1, 0 8166 2367 8.

——, and John Michael Archer, eds. *Enclosure Acts: Sexuality, Property, and Culture in Early Modern England*. CornUP. pp. 340. hb £33.50, $42.95, pb £13.50, $16.95. ISBN 0 8014 2745 2, 0 8014 8024 8.

Carrithers Jr, Gale H., and James D. Hardy Jr. *Milton and the Hermeneutic Journey*. LSUP. pp. 256. £32.95, $35. ISBN 0 8071 1876 1.

Daniel, Clay. *Death in Milton's Poetry*. BuckUP. pp. 183. £26.50. ISBN 0 8387 5248 9.

Dunn, Kevin. *Pretexts of Authority: The Rhetoric of Authorship in the Renaissance Preface*. StanfordUP. pp. 198. £25. ISBN 0 8047 2284 6.

Durham, Charles W., and Kristin Pruitt McColgan, eds. *Spokesperson Milton: Voices in Contemporary Criticism*. SusquehannaUP. pp. 284. £37.50. ISBN 0 9456 3665 2.

Eriksen, Roy, ed. *Contexts of Pre-novel Narrative: The European Tradition*. MGruyter. pp. 397. $144.65. ISBN 3 1101 3883 2.

Esterhammer, Angela. *Creating States: Studies in the Performative Language of John Milton and William Blake*. UTorP. £29, $45. ISBN 0 8020 0562 4.

Finucci, Valeria, and Regina Schwartz, eds. *Desire in the Renaissance: Psychoanalysis and Literature*. PrincetonUP. pp. 273. hb £32, $37.50, pb £14.95, $14.95. ISBN 0 6910 0100 6, 0 6910 3403 6.

Greengrass, Mark, Michael Leslie and Timothy Raylor, eds. *Samuel Hartlib and Universal Reformation: Studies in Intellectual Communication*. CUP. pp. 372. £40. ISBN 0 5214 5252 X.

Haskin, Dayton. *Milton's Burden of Interpretation*. UPennP. pp. 314. £40. ISBN 0 8122 3291 X.

Hawsley, John C., ed. *Reform and Counterreform: Dialectics of the Word in Western Christianity since Luther*. MGruyter. pp. 243. £32, $61.55. ISBN 3 1101 4016 0.

Jones, Edward. *Milton's Sonnets: An Annotated Bibliography, 1900–1992*. MRTS. pp. 147. $20. ISBN 0 8669 8127 6.

Kahn, Victoria. *Machiavellian Rhetoric: From the Counter-Reformation to Milton*. PrincetonUP. pp. 314. £24, $29.95. ISBN 0 6910 3491 5.

Kennedy, Andrew, and Orm Øverland, eds. *Excursions into Fiction: Essays in Honour of Professor Lars Hartveit on his 70th Birthday*. Studia Anglistica Norvegia, 6. NovusP.

Lieb, Michael. *Milton and the Culture of Violence*. CornUP. pp. 273. £25.50, $32.50. ISBN 0 8014 2903 X.

Moss, Ann, Philip Dust, Paul Gerhard Schmidt, Jacques Chomerat and Francesco Tateo, eds. *Acta Conventus Neo-Latini Hafniensis: Proceedings of the Eighth International Congress of Neo-Latin Studies*. MRTS. $60. ISBN 0 8669 8173 X.

Redman Jr, Harry. *Major French Milton Critics of the Nineteenth Century*. Duquesne. pp. 390. £48. ISBN 0 8207 0249 8.

Rogal, Samuel J. *An Index to the Biblical References, Parallels, and Allusions in the Poetry and Prose of John Milton*. Mellen. pp. 241. $20. ISBN 0 7734 2390 7.

Rosenblatt, Jason P. *Torah and Law in Paradise Lost*. PrincetonUP. pp. 274. £32.50, $39.50. ISBN 0 6910 3340 4.

Røstvig, Maren-Sofie. *Configurations: A Topomorphical Approach to Renaissance Poetry*. ScanUP. pp. 582. £37.50. ISBN 8 2002 1909 7.

X

The Later Seventeenth Century

STUART GILLESPIE, JAMES OGDEN and ROGER POOLEY

This chapter has three sections: 1. General; 2. Dryden; 3. Other Authors. Sections 1(b), 2(b), and 3(b) are by James Ogden; sections 1(c) and 3(c) are by Roger Pooley; and the rest is by Stuart Gillespie. Sections 1(b) and 3(b) cover work published in 1993 as well as 1994 because these sections did not appear last year.

1. General

This year's compilers of 'Some Current Publications' in *Restoration* 18 were Roxann Wheeler (48–72) and Gary Layne Hatch (113–27). Richard Wendorf reviewed 'Recent Studies in the Restoration and Eighteenth Century' for *SEL* (34.649–87). A very different kind of reference work was brought to a conclusion with the issue of the final volume (as it happens, volume I) in the second edition of Donald Wing's *Short-Title Catalogue*, a work too well known to require comment here.

The only other item received this year on the period's literature in general was J. A. Downie's *To Settle the Succession of the State: Literature and Politics 1678–1750*. This appears in the Macmillan 'Context and Commentary' series, which seeks to show how literature and history 'interweave', or how the work of creative writers intersects with the history of a period. This seems a laudable aim, and undergraduates usually need more context for what they read, but a better expression for the subtitle would have been 'political literature', for this is all Downie is really dealing with. For example, Marvell's sole significance here is as the author of *An Account of the Growth of Popery*, from which a two-page quotation is included, and a poem by John Tutchin gets another couple of pages as 'a particularly fine example of English xenophobia'. This volume would do no harm as a primer on the period's political history, but it gives a curiously slanted picture of its literature.

(a) Poetry

Two books and one article call for attention in this section. Alastair Fowler subtitles *The Country House Poem* 'a cabinet of [. . .] estate poems and related items', so evidently it would be inaccurate to describe its genre as that of an 'anthology' or 'collection'; but it is as comprehensive a printing of this kind of material as we will ever see. There is a surprising amount of post-Restoration work here, by such as Waller, Mildmay Fane, Henry Vaughan, Richard Lovelace, Thomas Stanley, Margaret Cavendish, Charles Cotton, Thomas Otway, and of course Denham and Marvell. But in the last case there are three texts rather than one; everywhere Fowler finds more than we might expect, from whole poems to new pieces of information on those we already knew. The principal purpose of this handsome and well-illustrated volume is of course to place the seventy-seven specimens side by side, and in this respect alone it is indispensable for anybody with interests in the area. But Fowler does so much more that we may adapt Cowley (also included) and say that he has 'with large Bounty open set / All the bright Stores of his rich *Cabinet*'.

David Hopkins's article 'The London Odes on St Cecilia's Day for 1686, 1695, and 1696' (*RES* 44.486–95) usefully supplements our knowledge of the Restoration Cecilian celebrations on a number of counts. Hopkins provides, from original broadsheets, new texts of the odes used in the three years to which he refers. Two of them constitute hitherto unknown poems; the third is now ascribed to Peter Motteux. One of the new odes is an addition to the *oeuvre* of Thomas Flatman; the other cannot be attributed. In Claude Rawson's *Satire and Sentiment 1660–1830*, a collection containing some new and some old essays, the items relating most strongly to our period are two long *TLS* and *LRB* reviews on Rochester and Oldham respectively from the 1980s. This is as much as to say that the book's main interest lies elsewhere, but the appearance of these two pieces here (in revised form) does help to preserve them for future use.

(b) Drama

Interest in women dramatists remains high. *Female Playwrights of the Restoration: Five Comedies*, edited by Paddy Lyons and Fidelis Morgan (see *YWES* 72.233 for the contents), was reprinted. The editors explain how these comedies succeeded in the theatre in their time, and assert that they can succeed today; certainly such anthologies can shift them from the study to the seminar.

Two books, Pat Gill's *Interpreting Ladies* and Nancy Lyn Tippetts's *Sisterhood, Brotherhood, and Equality*, viewed Restoration comedy from feminist perspectives. Pat Gill argues that the comedy of manners defended aristocratic masculinity against foppish and bourgeois alternatives, and distinguished ladies from loose women by showing that the former actually or apparently do not understand sexual innuendo. But 'by suggesting that virtuous and immoral women cannot always be told apart, the dramatists undercut their arguments that satiric and salacious dialogue can be distinguished'. These general ideas are supported by detailed analyses of the plays of Etherege, Wycherley and Congreve. Finally Aphra Behn rises over the ruins of patriarchal comedy, with heroines who know the facts of life and seek 'reciprocal enjoyment'. Nancy Lyn Tippetts believes that 'literary critics for nearly three centuries proclaimed gender equality for characters in the Restoration comedy of manners based on witty repartee between gallants and ladies', but critics now deny such equality either in the plays or in the society they represent. She offers a compromise, maintaining that sisterhoods and brotherhoods modify the effects of patriarchy. So in this book the male dramatists emerge more favourably; perhaps Behn attacks patriarchy more pointedly and desperately than anyone, but Etherege repeatedly challenges its power, Wycherley and Congreve reject 'simplistic morality', Vanbrugh is acutely sensitive to the plight of women, and Farquhar persistently challenges stereotypes. Unfortunately there is much solemn application of modern sociology to the plays, or translation of lively dialogue into deadly jargon; for example, when in Farquhar's *Constant Couple* Clincher Senior tells his younger brother to call him 'Sir', Tippetts tells us 'horizontal connection is rejected'. Gill writes more forcefully, her insights arise from thought as well as theory, and her book is the more stimulating; Tippetts has the wider range. Neither critic communicates a strong sense that the plays can be very funny in the theatre.

Two essays related to Restoration drama were included in Gail Finney's collection *Look Who's Laughing: Gender and Comedy*. Donald A. Bloom's 'Dwindling into Wifehood' celebrates 'the romantic power of the witty heroine' in *As You Like It*, Dryden's *Secret Love* and *Marriage à la Mode, The Way of the World* and *Pride and Prejudice*. This is a lucid and perceptive if predictable essay: 'Even Millamant, even Rosalind, wonderful as they are, pale in comparison' with Elizabeth Bennet. It is a truth universally acknowledged, that a male critic in possession of any imagination must be in love with a witty heroine. Suz-Anne Kinney's 'Confinement Sharpens Invention' compares Behn's *The Rover* with Centlivre's *The Busy Body*, and shows that the endings of these plays with marriages may seem harmonious and conventional, but the unmarried characters Angellica and Marplot create discord and significance. Both dramatists stood for female friendship and independence against male attitudes and arrangements, but social changes made it harder for Centlivre to attack the patriarchy. Finney's collection struck me as a promising start to a series of 'Studies in Humor and Gender', which hopes to match interdisciplinary scholarship and lively prose.

The feminist perspective broadens to the cultural-historical in Paula Backscheider's *Spectacular Politics*, which brings together three studies of 'theatrical power and mass culture': first, the early Restoration, when Charles II used street pageants and propaganda plays to impose his view of monarchy, though some of these expressed the rival idea of Liberty; second, the 1695–6 London theatre season, when one-third of the new plays were by women or adapted from works by women, and presented revolutionary ideas about what men, women and marriage ought to be; third, the late eighteenth-century Gothic drama, when George III was judged 'hopelessly mad', and the theatre expressed the anxieties of the public. The general idea is to explain how theatre and spectacle help to create and sometimes destroy ideologies and 'hegemonies' (a term considered pompous by my history teacher Mrs Mathers forty years ago). Backscheider offers illuminating analyses of the pageants, Robert Howard's *The Committee*, John Tatham's *The Rump*, the work of Katherine Philips, and some of the plays and prose works of Aphra Behn, and supplies context for the plays of Delarivière Manley, Catherine Trotter and Mary Pix. Altogether, rather an attractive combination of theory, scholarship and enthusiasm.

With Brian Corman's *Genre and Generic Change in English Comedy 1660–1710* we return to more familiar subjects and methods. Corman avoids the extremes of comprehensiveness and idiosyncrasy by confining himself to three five-year periods, from which he chooses the more successful plays: by Thomas Shadwell, Wycherley, Buckingham, Betterton (*The Amorous Widow*) and Crowne (1670–5); by Dryden, Mountfort (*Greenwich Park*), Durfey and Congreve (1690–5); and by Vanbrugh, Farquhar, Cibber, Centlivre and Charles Shadwell (*The Fair Quaker*) (1705–10). These plays follow what Dryden called 'the mixt way of Comedy', mixing elements of the Jonsonian-punitive and Fletcherian-sympathetic traditions, often with awkward results, even in a play as unified as *The Country Wife*. The attention to neglected plays is welcome, and the comments on well-known masterpieces and comparisons between plays are generally judicious, but before we reach Corman's 'inescapable conclusion' we may well have thought we were not going to escape it. The truth is there was no 'generic change' at all, only changes of topic and attitude. By the end of the period the 'humane comedy' of Farquhar and others had ousted the relatively subtle but harsh and incredible comedy of their rivals, but that is no great surprise either. This book will certainly be recommended to students, and they will certainly read it selectively.

Now for some essays on various genres at several times. Paul Cannan's 'New Directions in Serious Drama on the London Stage, 1675–1678' (*PQ* 73.219–42) complains that drama historians ignore or dismiss most serious plays of these seasons. Dryden, Lee, Otway, Behn, Settle and Durfey initiated 'the several kinds of tragedy–horror villain, historical, adaptive, and operatic' that flourished in the next thirty years. They shared an impulse towards spectacle, especially when writing for the Dorset Garden Theatre. Susan J.Owen's 'Interpreting the Politics of Restoration Drama' (*SC* 8[1993].67–97) argues that the plays of the 1678–9 season – especially Dryden and Lee's *Oedipus*, Lee's *Caesar Borgia* and *Massacre of Paris*, John Bancroft's *Sertorius*, and Crowne's *Ambitious Statesman* – are less simply partisan, and more profoundly political, than critics have thought. This substantial essay is part of a projected book, and Owen sketches the development of partisan plays in later seasons. Christopher J. Wheatley's 'Thomas Durfey's *A Fond Husband*, Sex Comedies of the Late 1670s and Early 1680s, and the Comic Sublime' (*SP* 90[1993].371–90; *YWES* 74.268) shows how the association of daring, adultery and sublimity was taken seriously in *A Fond Husband* and Aphra Behn's *Sir Patient Fancy*, but mocked or rejected by Thomas Shadwell, Dryden, 'Rawlins', Edward Ravenscroft, Thomas Otway, John Leanerd and finally Durfey himself in *A Virtuous Wife*. Karen Overbye's 'From "Hell in the shape of Heav'n" to the "Spotless Soul"' (*Restoration* 17[1993].104–10) analyses women characters in six tragedies of the 1695-6 season: George Powell's *Bonduca*, Robert Gould's *Rival Sisters*, John Banks's *Cyrus the Great*, Catherine Trotter's *Agnes de Castro*, Delarivière Manley's *Royal Mischief* and Mary Pix's *Ibrahim*. She finds that the male dramatists portray women as fools, villains or virtuous victims; the female dramatists portray them with greater psychological insight and 'an implied questioning of the contemporary gender ideology and status of women'. This essay overlaps with Backscheider's book. Richard Braverman's 'Politics in Jewish Disguise: Jacobitism and Dissent on the Post-Revolutionary Stage' (*SP* 90[1993].347–70) remarks on the association of 'giddy Jews' and revolutionary dissenters. John Crowne's *Caligula* supports the Act of Toleration and is therefore 'philo-semitic', but George Granville's *The Jew of Venice* supports the Jacobite succession and is therefore anti-Semitic.

Theatre history was much advanced by the completion of Highfill, Burnim and Langhans's *Biographical Dictionary* of Restoration and eighteenth-century theatre people. In the last two volumes, biographies of special interest to students of Restoration drama include: Cave Underhill, who created the role of Sir Sampson Legend; Sir John Vanbrugh; Jack Verbruggen, who created the role of Loveless in *Love's Last Shift* and *The Relapse*; Mrs Verbruggen (formerly Mrs Mountfort), famous for breeches roles in many comedies; John Webb, who designed the scenery for *The Siege of Rhodes*; and Robert Wilks, who created the role of Wildair in *The Constant Couple*. This great work advances not only theatre history: it is remarkable how often a glance at *The London Stage* for a cast list, followed by a consultation of the dictionary, will together provide a new perspective on a play. Any supplement will have to incorporate recent work on the acting profession, which proceeds vigorously. Robert D. Freeburn's 'Charles II, the Theatre Patentees and the Actors' Nursery' (*TN* 48.148–56) describes the training of actors by George Jolly and John Coysh in London and Norwich, and by Joseph Ashbury in Dublin. Laura J. Rosenthal's '"Counterfeit Scrubbado": Women Actors in the Restoration' (*ECent* 34[1993].2–22) is more speculative and challenging. Rosenthal notes that on the Restoration stage the roles of wealthy young women of great respectability were taken by poorly paid actresses of dubious status. The effect was 'to blur the distinction between marriageable and unmarriageable women, ladies and whores, and even marriage and prostitution itself'. In the hope of sustaining such distinctions actresses were regarded as whores, though in fact many of them may not have been.

Many useful articles on the Restoration theatre appear in *Theatre Notebook*. Rob Jordan's 'Addendum to *The London Stage 1660–1700*' (*TN* 47[1993].62–75) corrects, amplifies and supplements this primary reference work. Two points seemed noteworthy: the Duchess of Newcastle, 'her breasts all laid out to view in a play house with scarlet trimd nipples', caused a sensation in 1667; the *Marriage à la Mode* première could have been in May 1672 after all. Other articles illuminated the stage and staging more directly. John H. Astington's '*The Wits* Illustration, 1662' (*TN* 47[1993].122–40) is an illustrated account of this well known but badly misunderstood document, concluding that although it is meant to evoke 'the theatre', the illustration (probably by John Chantry, a commercial engraver) is merely 'a visual collage, a *jeu d'esprit*, showing a theatre that never was', so it cannot be relied on as historical evidence. Dawn Lewcock's 'Computer Analysis of Restoration Staging' came out in three parts, covering 1661–72, 1671–82, and 1682–4 (*TN* 47[1993].20–9, 141–56; 48[1994].103–15). Lewcock analyses the staging of plays by the Duke's and King's companies, and questions the theory that for staging spectacular shows Dorset Garden was better than Drury Lane, though later the United Company sometimes preferred Dorset Garden for plays with elaborate or difficult staging. At both theatres dramatists became accustomed to 'integrating the scenery into their texts', and to using the full depth of the stage. The combination of sliding shutters and forestage resulted in a type of theatre that was unique to the period from 1661 to 1694. These articles together make a valuable contribution to our understanding of the Restoration stage. Frans Muller's 'Flying Dragons and Dancing Chairs at Dorset Garden' (*TN* 47[1993].80–95) reconsiders evidence about the design of this theatre, and suggests how Thomas Betterton and Henry Purcell's opera *Diocletian* may have been staged there. Muller modifies Langhans's reconstruction of the theatre (*YWES* 53.253), develops Robert D. Hume's ideas (*YWES* 60.224), and draws his own reconstruction of the stage. William Kendall's 'Did the Apron-Stage Retreat?' (*TN* 47[1993].76–9) shows that during the century and a half after Wren's design for Drury Lane, 'the proportions he suggested of one third of the stage depth for the scene and two-thirds for the players were broadly reversed'. The players did not retreat into the scene, but the scene advanced upon the players.

Questions about the Restoration audience were raised in two studies of the stage history of Jacobean plays and an article on portraits as props. In *Othello: A Contextual History* Virginia Mason Vaughan has a good chapter on the Restoration *Othello* based on her *ThStud* article (*YWES* 71.275). It was a successful King's Company play, so the Duke's Company replied with Thomas Porter's *The*

Villain and Henry Nevil Payne's *The Fatal Jealousie*. Comparisons with these plays suggest that audiences liked to see the nobility of the aristocratic hero (played by Hart or Betterton) contrasted with the deformity of the lower-class villain (played by Sandford). My idea that they would see the funny side of the hero (*N&Q* 39[1992].464) either came too late or seemed too fanciful. In 'The Political Appeal of Beaumont and Fletcher's *A King and No King* on the Restoration Stage' (*ELWIU* 20[1993].171–96) Stephen R. Flores bases much speculation on the fact that the play was popular in our period, and the belief that Restoration audiences, being apt to question the authority of monarchs, may have found it more topical than their Jacobean predecessors did. Flores says hardly anything about how Restoration audiences actually did respond, so it seems fair to set against his assertion that 'as its title so aptly indicates, *A King and No King* inquires into the nature of kingship' Thomas Rymer's view that 'this Title gives no more light into the design, then had they call'd it *Hocus Pocus*'. Rymer is not among the twenty or so critics quoted. In 'Portraits and Spectators in the Late Restoration Playhouse' (*ECent* 35.119–34) Cynthia Lowenthal remarks that Aphra Behn's *The Rover* and Delarivière Manley's *The Royal Mistress* both use portraits as props and so 'participate in and comment on the gendering of the spectatorial economy by bringing to light the mediating force the theatre exerts in allowing and prohibiting the representation of *female* desire'. Manley's scene is especially interesting because she has a woman looking at a portrait of a man.

Studies of Purcell and other musicians often relate to drama, for instance the lively but endless controversy on the date of *Dido and Aeneas*. The work's interpretation may well be influenced by what we know of its first performance: at court, in a theatre, or – the first known performance – at Josias Priest's girls' school in 1689? In '"Unscarr'd by Turning Times"?' (*EM* 20[1992].373–90) Bruce Wood and Andrew Pinnock argue that Tate's libretto and Purcell's music were written before the reign of William and Mary, so the opera did not refer to this royal pair, as Curtis Price (*YWES* 65.321) and others have supposed. Tate borrowed from his own *Brutus of Alba* (1678) and Purcell from John Blow's *Venus and Adonis* (performed at court around 1682, at Priest's school in 1684). *Dido* was probably first performed at court in 1684 – so in the preface to *Albion and Albanius* Dryden could have had in mind Blow's and Purcell's operatic works. But in correspondence John Buttrey (*EM* 20[1992].703) and Martin Adams (*EM* 21[1993].510) dispute some of these arguments, and in '*Dido and Aeneas*: Questions of Style and Evidence' (*EM* 22.115–25) Curtis Price declares that '*Dido* inhabits an entirely different operatic world from *Venus and Adonis*', and finds no evidence that Purcell's work was transferred from court to school like Blow's. Arguments based on Purcell's musical style cannot prove that *Dido* was written in 1684. Price concedes that Tate's libretto 'had no specific political purpose', but believes his prologue could refer to the events of 1689. In correspondence Wood and Pinnock (*EM* 22.365–7) drily remark that 'when a shower of cold water descends from professorial heights, up goes the umbrella', and maintain that *Dido* is likely to have been written before 1689, even if their arguments for 1684 are untenable. In 'The Dating of *Dido and Aeneas*' (*EM* 22.469–81) Andrew R. Walkling proposes that the work was written in 1687–8 to celebrate James II's Declaration of Indulgence. I was not convinced by this conclusion, but Walkling certainly clarifies the issues and promises further proof. In 'The Earliest Notice of *Dido and Aeneas*' (*EM* 22.392–400) Mark Goldie quotes a newly discovered letter which does not help with the date but suggests that Priest's operatic performances generally, and perhaps *Dido* particularly, were deplored by Whiggish parents. He points out that Durfey's *Love for Money* satirizes Priest's school. With '*The Fairy Queen*: A Fresh Look at the Issues' (*EM* 21[1993].45–62) Wood and Pinnock caused less controversy and again illuminated performance history and hence interpretation. They argue that the manuscript score in the Royal Academy of Music is the original version. In 'Newly Discovered Sources of Music by Henry Purcell' (*M&L* 75.16–32) Richard Charteris notes among other things songs, masques and excerpts from operas now in the Hamburg Stadtbibliothek. And in 'Matthew Locke: Three Newly Discovered Songs for the Restoration Stage' (*M&L* 75.200–13) Lynne Hulse reports on songs for the Duke of Newcastle's *Triumphant Widow* and Thomas Tomkis's *Albumazar* now in Nottingham University Library. They confirm that Locke was a leading composer for the Duke's Company.

Restoration drama is rather well represented in London and provincial theatres right now. *Theatre Record* reprints reviews from daily and weekly papers of productions in 1993 of *The Country Wife* (Stratford) and *The Basset Table* (London), and in 1994 of *The Beaux' Stratagem* (touring), *Venice Preserved* (Manchester), *The Wives' Excuse* (Stratford), *The Country Wife*, *The Man of Mode, The Provoked Husband, The Rover* and *Sir Martin Mar-all* (London). *The Man of Mode* at the Royal Court Theatre was preceded by *The Libertine*, a play about Rochester by Stephen Jeffreys, not a play about Don Juan by Shadwell. *TR* is required reading for the theatrically minded critic.

(c) Prose

The most important book in the field this year is Steven Shapin's *A Social History of Truth: Civility and Science in Seventeenth-Century England.* It crosses several boundaries – those between sociology, history of ideas, and history of science among them – to explore the link between gentlemanly conversation, honour and the standards of truthfulness that early modern science began to establish. Central to Shapin's argument is Boyle's ideal of the Christian Virtuoso, the gentleman scholar, and the subsequent hagiography. The book offers a more socially grounded account of the new science than Kroll's recent *The Material Word* (*YWES* 72.234); its wary, inclusive, well-documented, argumentative style generates massive conviction. It successfully changes the teleology of 'the rise of science' by being critically aware of contemporary practice as well as revaluing its 'origins'.

In 'Assessing the Revolution: Ideology, Language and the Rhetoric in the New Philosophy of Early Modern England' (*ECent* 35.99–118) Robert E. Stillman criticizes recent analyses by Vickers and Kroll for undertheorizing the 'problematic insinuations of desire into language'. He discusses Hooke's *Micrographia* and Wilkins's *Principles and Duties of Natural Religion*, and is particularly good on the tension between the desire for certain knowledge and the language of probability in Hooke. Much more relaxed, theoretically, is Robert E. Glass, 'The Image of the Sea Officer in English Literature, 1660–1710' (*Albion* 26.583–600), which investigates the origins and limitations of Macaulay's officer/tar clichés in Pepys, Wycherley, Halifax and a number of minor tracts.

N. H. Keeble's anthology, *The Cultural Identity of Seventeenth-Century Woman*, brings together a large number of extracts, both prose and poetry, about the nature and roles of women as they were perceived by men and women of the century. As a collection of primary materials and a guide to further research it has considerable value, and Keeble shows notable cunning in negotiating the ideological minefields. The arrangement of the book, with a section of 'Feminisms?' at the end in particular, argues that women's self-definition in the period was almost entirely in response to prior, male-established categories – probably true, but the editorial principles might have been argued more out in the open. On a similar topic, a chapter by Jane Spencer in *Contexts of Pre-novel Narrative*, edited by Roy Eriksen, comments on the late seventeenth-century view that 'history is to fiction as masculine is to feminine'. In 'Not Being a Historian: Women Telling Tales in Restoration and Eighteenth-century England', she comments on three texts by women: *She Ventures, and He Wins,* an almost unknown play by 'Ariadne', Behn's novella *The Fair Jilt*, and *The Female Quixote* by Charlotte Lennox. There are some interesting links made here between the novel as anti-romance, and the deceiving woman figure in a text written by a woman narrator. *Counterfeit Ladies*, edited by Janet Todd and Elizabeth Spearing, brings together 'The Life and Death of Mal Cutpurse' (Mary Frith) and 'The Case of Mary Carleton'. Though the editors resist the description of 'female rogue' literature, their substantial introduction does place both texts in the context of Restoration prose genres as well as their individual histories (very complex, in Carleton's case). The Frith text is also one of the first that I know that has used forensic computer tests to uncover what seems to be multiple authorship of the piece, though surprisingly little is made of this.

William M. Spellman, in 'Between Death and Judgement: Conflicting Images of the Afterlife in Late Seventeenth-Century English Eulogies' (*HTR* 87.49–65), surveys a large number of funeral sermons and other works on the afterlife. He argues that the desire to make comforting remarks about the immediate state of the soul after death led to confusion about the importance of the resurrection of the body, and gave occasion to mortalist and annihilationist theologies.

The reissue of *The Cambridge History of Political Thought 1450–1700* (eds J. H. Burns and Mark Goldie) in paperback brings this essential resource within sight of a wider range of scholars. The sections on Locke, Hobbes and his reception, and English republicanism are of particular significance to students of the prose writers of this period. Paul Hammond's review article, 'The Language of the Hive: Political Discourse in Seventeenth-Century England' (*SC* 9.119–33), is wide ranging and astute.

2. Dryden

Eric Griffiths delivered the 1992 Chatterton Lecture on Poetry at the British Academy, and it is published this year as 'Dryden's Past' (*PBA* 84.113–49). Griffiths first explores Dryden's sense of 'the cultural past of the English language', which resulted in his 'hearing his own verse as a long time-tunnel, extending back to Latin and Greek avatars'. This is intimately related to the poet's 'sense of civility', of the nature of the 'civilisation we carry in ourselves', as set against the barbaric; Griffiths is especially acute on several of the translations, in which Dryden confronts the violent worlds of Virgil, Ovid, Chaucer and others. Eventually, through the poem on Congreve with which he set out, Griffiths rounds on critics (Harold Bloom, Walter Jackson Bate) whose ideas about the bearing of the literary past on poets 'ignore the essentially plural character' of a writer's confrontation with the past, which may be a liberation instead of a burden. This is a refreshingly original essay, and inclines one to hope that its author might turn his attention to Dryden again. A version of the chapter on Dryden and Corneille in David Bruce Kramer's *The Imperial Dryden: The Poetics of Appropriation in Seventeenth-Century England* was noted last year (*YWES* 74.266). The remaining chapters deal more widely with Dryden's debts to foreign literatures, especially French, in his plays and elsewhere. There are new insights here, but Kramer's work suffers from his weak understanding of contemporary notions about such 'appropriation', so that what he imagines to be radical in Dryden's practice is often conventional, and what troubles him in Dryden's work is in seventeenth-century terms perfectly legitimate. He is overkeen to convict Dryden of misquotation and misappropriation, and attaches undue importance to many of the instances he finds.

(a) Poetry

Keith Walker has edited *John Dryden* for the Oxford Poetry Library. The glossary and the brief notes on factual and semantic matters are adequate; the startling thing about this 270-page volume is the selection of poems, some nine-tenths of which are translations printed in full. This makes it ideal for those teachers and students who wish to concentrate their attention here, and reflects the rising tide of interest in this part of Dryden's poetic corpus. Yet it clearly does not represent the shape of Dryden's poetry fully, and many teachers will look in vain for a complete text of, say, *Absalom and Achitophel.*

In 'John Dryden: A New Work from his Cambridge Days' (*TCBS* 10[1993].340–58), Hilton Kelliher documents a Latin verse tribute Dryden wrote on the death in 1652 of John Smith, the neo-Platonist author of *Select Discourses*, whom the young Dryden probably knew. The poem of thirty-nine lines belongs to the genre of *carmina lapidaria* and is the only extant specimen of Dryden's Latin. Kelliher includes useful discussion of the circumstances and significance of his find. Half of Jean LeDrew Metcalfe's 'The Politics of Panegyric: Poetic Representations of Oliver Cromwell' (*Restoration* 18.1–16) is on Dryden's poem from the other end of the 1650s, *Heroique Stanza's*. This account tends to repeat what others have said: that the poem qualifies itself ironically, acknowledging 'deficiency' in Cromwell. Jon Thomas Rowland also writes on Dryden's panegyrical verse, as part of his wider study *Faint Praise and Civil Leer: The "Decline" of Eighteenth-Century Panegyric*. His treatment of *Annus Mirabilis* is meant to show 'how panegyrical writing developed into mock-panegyric and satire, increasingly as much in response to versions of events as to the events themselves'.

There were three papers on *Absalom and Achitophel.* David Gelineau's 'Allusion, Legitimacy, and Succession: Milton's Hands Suit Ill with Dryden's Voice' (*ECent* 35.28–45) is a rambling paper having to do with the line 'But Esau's Hands suit ill with Jacob's voice'. Gelineau makes a very great deal of this allusion, which he takes as a starting point for a discussion of the significance of the poem's use of Milton and of theories of poetic succession as enunciated by Harold Bloom, but to tell the truth I was not always confident I could follow his drift. Anne K. Krook's 'Satire and the Constitution of Theocracy in *Absalom and Achitophel*' (*SP* 91.339–58) also has a rebarbative title, but in some ways it is really only a detailed treatment of Dryden's presentation of the figure of David. Dryden 'deploys satire', Krook says, 'to preserve the differences between David and all the other characters', thus orchestrating a defence of Charles II, yet this becomes 'problematic' and 'the abrupt close . . . confirms the extent to which satire not only preserves but also constitutes David's place in the theocracy'. In 'Two Allusions in Dryden's

Portrait of Corah' (*N&Q* 41.174–5), J. A. Richardson refines somewhat on what past editors have said about biblical references in Dryden's depiction of Corah/Oates, specifically the passage where he is referred to as a brazen serpent.

Two other items which have taken an extra year to come to my attention happen both to be on *The Cock and the Fox*. In 'Dryden and Milton in "The Cock and the Fox"' (*MiltonQ* 27[1993].109–18), Taylor Corse draws together and extends information about Dryden's use of *Paradise Lost* in translating Chaucer, and argues for the significance of several verbal echoes. Milton's Satan, and the discussions of Adam and Eve on free will, are particularly important. The echoes are palpable, but there is some danger of making unduly heavy weather of all this, of turning a poem entirely dependent on witty lightness of touch into something that sounds ponderous: 'As God oversees the created universe, so Dryden's narrator [. . .] grapples with the same problem of free will versus predestination that Milton wrestled with.' Similar tendencies are apparent in Stephanie Trigg's 'Singing Clearly: Chaucer, Dryden, and *A Rooster's Discourse*' (*Exemplaria* 5[1993].365–86), which at one point describes Dryden's Chanticleer as a 'phallocentric misogynist'. Fortunately the article is not all like this, and it is obviously very appropriate to 'focus on the sexual politics' of this particular 'text'. Still, she goes wrong in discerning much of an 'alliance' between 'Dryden's implied author and his Chanticleer'; perhaps some of the jokes are lost in translation to American, since anyone who has to call the poem's protagonist a rooster rather than a cock is likely to overlook several important things. This article is heavily overburdened with theory, much of it Foucaultian.

(*b*) *Plays*

Two volumes of Dryden's plays have appeared in the California edition. Volume XII comprises *Amboyna, The State of Innocence* and *Aureng-Zebe,* edited by Vinton A. Dearing, and Volume XIV *The Kind Keeper, The Spanish Fryar, The Duke of Guise* and its *Vindication*, edited by Dearing and Alan Roper. For *Amboyna* and *The State of Innocence* the only tolerable earlier edition was the Scott-Saintsbury, and both present formidable textual problems. *Amboyna* was written to rouse the English against the Dutch, and has been dismissed as hack work, but for Dearing it is 'a dignified and affecting tragedy'. Dryden wrote it in blank verse but unfortunately published it in prose; Congreve partly recovered the verse and Dearing thought about wholly recovering it, 'so that the play's true nature would no longer be so much hidden', but finally editorial conservatism prevailed. *The State of Innocence* exists in many manuscripts, seven of which have been collated. Dearing's commentary on this splendidly irreverent version of *Paradise Lost* is cautious, compared with that on *Amboyna*, though he notes that it has received much appreciative criticism. *Aureng-Zebe* was the last of the heroic plays, and by common consent the best, 'largely because it is the least extravagant in its language'; Dearing does not seriously dispute this judgement, but uses computer analysis to dispose of some erroneous impressions of earlier critics. He and Roper point out that *The Kind Keeper* was Dryden's 'most salacious' play, *The Spanish Fryar* his 'most popular for many years', and *The Duke of Guise* his 'strongest defense of the Stuart monarchy'. *The Spanish Fryar* is surely one of Dryden's best plays, and Dearing's commentary makes good use of recent scholarship and criticism, including Milhous and Hume's chapter in *Producible Interpretation* (*YWES* 67.300). Texts of *The Spanish Fryar* (in Saintsbury's old Mermaid edition) and *The Kind Keeper* (in Norman Jeffares's Folio anthology) have been reasonably accessible, but for *The Duke of Guise* the standby was again Scott-Saintsbury. Written in collaboration with Nathaniel Lee, this tedious political play needed vindication because the Whigs wrote pamphlets against it, two of which are reprinted in an appendix; the text of the *Vindication* is especially valuable because it is not in the standard collections of Dryden's prose by W. P. Ker and George Watson. Roper's commentary explains what Dryden and Lee may have intended, and what the Whigs apprehended, and hence has a general interest for students of theory. As usual in this excellent edition all the texts are highly readable and reliable (though at vol. XII, p. 128, 'presuade' looks like a misprint for 'persuade') and the editorial commentaries are very liberal and learned (though at vol. XIV, p. 503, a loose errata sheet has been found necessary). The commentaries cover stage history, critical reputation, sources, general interpretation and particular points of interest; the textual apparatuses list variants and record emendations.

I found only two essays on Dryden's plays. In 'Fighting Women and Loving Men: Dryden's Representation of Shakespeare in *All for Love*' (in Jonathan Goldberg, ed., *Queering the Renaissance*) Marcie Frank is mainly concerned with Dryden's additional scenes between Octavia and Cleopatra and Antony and Ventidius. When I read that the former scene marks 'an early and transitional moment on the way to Edelman's paradigm' (fighting between women represents love between men), and that Dryden is an 'oedipal critic who prefers homoerotic scenes',

> Now will old *Dryden*'s Ghost be pleased to hear
> His Fame augmented, and his Work made queer,

I mused. In 'The Politics of John Dryden's *The Spanish Fryar; or, The Double Discovery*' (*English* 43.97–113) Susan J. Owen finds that this play combines 'popular though not inflammatory anti-popery and cautious, moderate royalism'. This conclusion seemed perfectly sound but was not particularly surprising, much resembling Roper's in the California edition.

(c) *Prose*

Anne Cotterill's 'The Politics and Aesthetics of Digression: Dryden's *Discourse Concerning the Original and Progress of Satire*' (*SP* 91.464–95) is the only item under this heading. Cotterill requires us to read the *Discourse* by substituting 'Dorset' for 'Horace' (the servile court poet), 'Dryden' for 'Juvenal' (the witty satirist), and 'William' for 'Augustus' (the usurper). She then asks us to imagine that a satire on *Religio Laici* published in 1688 was by Dorset, even though Hugh MacDonald and Brice Harris reject the ascription; and that Dryden's praise of Dorset's verse is all ironic. If we elect to do all that, the *Discourse* will certainly become a work of 'politics' rather than 'aesthetics'. How fortunate for Dryden that Dorset saw none of this – but on the other hand, how implausible that seems to make it.

3. Other Authors

(a) *Poets*

Rochester accounts for a fair proportion of the work under this heading, as usual.

Frank H. Ellis's edition of *The Complete Works* would now be my choice of student text every time, even in a crowded marketplace. It is enormously good value for money: for one thing, it offers more information, of all kinds, than any competitor, and more too than one has a right to expect from a popular paperback edition – including a glossary and a very extensive biographical dictionary. Ellis's predilections as an editor are suggested by his epigraph, a quotation from Robert Ferguson: 'No text hath any more than one determinate Sense, otherwise it could have no sense at all.' I judge Ellis's use of this quotation not to be tongue-in-cheek, for his notes, which occupy a hundred pages of the edition, usually offer a decisive reading of a poem or a passage. As a result they are lively but make little attempt at neutrality. Two articles on Rochester by Harold Love deserve attention: 'Two Rochester Manuscripts Circulated from the Charterhouse' (*Library* 16.225–9) and 'But Did Rochester *Really* write *Sodom*?' (*PBSA* 87[1993].319–36). The first is a short, specialized piece on material in the Panshanger manuscripts on deposit in the Hertfordshire Record Office. Love's general point is that these provide an example of how a new mode of Rochester editing would be possible in which texts are selected from manuscript copies with close connections to Rochester's circle rather than from the tidy versions of professional scribes. His other article is a judicious treatment of the question its title poses. Dare one hope it will settle the issue? Probably not, since Love's answer (in the negative) is uncongenial to many of those currently interested in Rochester – for example, J. W. Johnson (*YWES* 68.329), whose attribution is forcefully rebutted here but has already been eagerly seized upon in a paperback edition of Rochester (a point to which my review of that edition drew attention, *YWES* 74.270). Love himself looks forward to a time when 'stylometric tests' will provide unanswerable confirmation of his views – the only unconvincing notion in his essay.

Gillian Manning's title is self-explanatory: 'Rochester's "Fling this Useless Book Away": An Unlisted Manuscript Copy' (*N&Q* 41.173–4) documents a version of this poem in an Edinburgh University Library MS which may, however, be merely a transcription of an early printed text. But Susan Bruce's '"Rolling about from Whore to Whore": Rochester's Satirico-Sexual Self and the Art of Conspicuous Consumption' (*FMLS* 30.305–15) made my head spin, being composed of sentences such as this: 'For Rochester, the construct of the wit exists only as the symbolic representation of an ideal whose power disintegrates on realisation; just as Rochesterian phallocentrism eventually exposes the impotence of the libertine, so too Rochester's apotheosis of the wit ultimately transforms him into his opposite.' For all its apparent sophistication, I doubted whether this account was sufficiently careful to discriminate between Rochester and the speaker of his poems.

Several articles on women poets come next. Patricia M. Sant and James N. Brown discuss and transcribe 'Two Unpublished Poems by Katherine Philips' (*ELR* 24.211–25). The texts are found in a manuscript at Balliol College together with three others known to be by Philips, and there is other good external and internal evidence of the authorship. Both works seem to be characteristic social or 'friendship' poems. Another scholarly duo, Claudia A. Limbert and John H. O'Neill, write on a Philips poem which has been published in 'Composite Authorship: Katherine Philips and an Antimarital Satire' (*PBSA* 87[1993].487–502). This poem is 'A marry^{d} state', No. 130 in Patrick Thomas's recent edition. What prompts Limbert and O'Neill's discussion is the incorporation of this text into a later and longer anti-marital satire sometimes called 'Advice to Virgins'.

Philips may have written both poems or neither, but the favoured hypothesis is that her poem was developed by a person or persons unknown shortly after her death. For some reason this discussion is tricked out with references to Foucault's ideas about authorship.

The principal literary point of P. A. Hopkins's 'Aphra Behn and John Hoyle: A Contemporary Mention, and Sir Charles Sedley's Poem on his Death' (*N&Q* 41.176–85) is to document a contemporary reference to the liaison between Aphra Behn and John Hoyle, the lawyer whose best-known achievement is an indictment for buggery. This reference tends to confirm both that there was such a liaison, and that Behn was kept by Hoyle in the mid-1670s. Hopkins also discusses Sedley's 'A Ballad, to the Tune of Bateman', showing it to be 'obliquely' a satirical comment on the politics of the 1690s. I found only one other item on Aphra Behn for this year's entry, but immediately wished I had not. Rosemary M. Nielsen and Robert H. Solomon's 'Rescuing Horace, Pyrrha and Aphra Behn: A Directive' (*Ramus* 22[1993].60–77) treats with ponderous solemnity Behn's 'In Imitation of Horace'. The poem 'addresses all women's needs [. . .] and it marginalizes males as lovers and as sole possessors of the erotic tradition'. Behn was herself tremendously serious too: 'neither secondhand knowledge of Latin satisfied Behn, nor secondbody [*sic*] accounts of female sexuality'. Then they discuss bits of 'The Disappointment', which for no discernible reason they construe as another 'imitation' of Horace's 'Pyrrha' Ode. A more sophisticated article, Kathryn R. King's 'Jane Barker, *Poetical Recreations*, and the Sociable Text' (*ELH* 61.551–70), takes issue with what King sees as the usual ways of reading Barker and other women writers. Finding to her alarm that Barker 'brings out the ambiguities' in 'relations of domination' rather than condemning such relations *tout court*, and that she even on occasion 'sought connections' with men, King concludes that 'a major challenge to feminist criticism today is to find ways to combine the ongoing deconstruction of inherited patriarchal codes with a historical narrative that more fully acknowledges women's participation in male-dominated culture – without re-encoding male domination'. If we have the energy for this task after getting to the end of King's sentences, we will stand some chance of perceiving why Barker's poem 'A Virgin Life' represents 'such a remarkable moment in the history of female re-visioning'.

I wish David Hopkins's and Tom Mason's edition of *Abraham Cowley: Selected Poems* had been available years ago, when undergraduates seemed more willing to stray from the beaten track in reading seventeenth-century poetry: it does as much as can easily be imagined to make Cowley accessible and congenial to the young explorer. The editors have done an excellent job in the short compass available with their introduction (extensive), notes, selection, and ordering (thematic) of texts. Who now reads Cowley? Well, with this paperback anyone who wants to try has the means easily available. Who now reads Traherne? N. I. Matar does, but his article 'The Political Views of Thomas Traherne' (*HLQ* 57.241–53) is overhasty in interpreting him. Matar tries to show that Traherne became critical of Charles II and his policies after the Restoration, and thus to counter some of Julia Smith's views (*YWES* 69.324). Unfortunately, all the evidence Matar adduces is either much more equivocal than he would have us believe, or simply no evidence at all: for example, any negative comment on kings or kingship written by Traherne is interpreted as specific criticism of Charles. Much more solid work is done by Oliver Pickering to shed light on Henry Hall (*c*.1656–1707), whose output of predominantly light verse has usually been wrongly assigned to his son, also Henry

Hall. Pickering's 'Henry Hall of Hereford's Poetical Tributes to Henry Purcell' (*Library* 16.18–29) helpfully sets out some of the main facts on this writer. The article proceeds to analyse Hall's 'To the Memory of my Dear Friend Mr. Henry Purcell', published in *Orpheus Britannicus* (1698), in terms of Hall's earlier poems on Purcell, preserved in manuscripts in the Brotherton Collection.

(b) Dramatists

The comic dramatists again did well on the academic stage. It is some fifteen years since I last wrote this section, and I notice that the old troupers Etherege, Wycherley and Congreve now share the bill with Behn, Shadwell and Southerne.

Etherege upstaged his Restoration rivals in a collection of essays on *English Comedy* edited by Michael Cordner and others. Cordner's 'Etherege's *She Would if She Could*: Comedy, Complaisance and Anti-Climax' compares this play with Sedley's *Mulberry Garden*, and contrasts both with Dryden's *Secret Love*, to suggest that Etherege and Sedley 'seem to be at one in a desire to set limits to female freedom'. Etherege celebrates Courtall's arts of pleasing, which may help him and Freeman to avoid the ultimate anti-climax of marriage. But elsewhere these essays have little to say about Restoration comedy, except incidentally in Peter Holland's contribution on Nöel Coward. There were three quite good essays on *The Man of Mode* in the learned journals. David K. Sauer's 'Apart from Etherege: Stage Directions in *The Man of Mode*' (*RECTR* 8.ii[1993].29–48) distinguishes speeches spoken *aside* to the audience (generally reliable) from those spoken *apart* to other characters (generally unreliable). The prevalence of the latter in this play helps to create its ambiguous ending. This essay would certainly assist a director, and its line of enquiry might usefully be extended to other Restoration plays. Michèle Plaisant's 'Modes et Modèles Amoureux dans *The Man of Mode*' (*BSEAA* 37[1993].39–50) compares the play with authentic or fictional memoirs of the French and English courts, to conclude that it is 'la transmutation artistique d'une expérience vécue au quotidien à la cour et à la ville', but it also has 'un éclat rare'. Paul Walsh's 'Performance, Space and Seduction in *The Man of Mode* (Dorset Garden Theatre, 1676)' (*EiTET* 11.ii[1993].123–52) 'considers how the ambiguous signs of Etherege's script assume and can be amplified by an understanding of the performance space for which [it] was written'. Asides would be seen by most of the audience as directed to the side boxes 'as if to equals', and Harriet and Young Bellair's fake foreplay in III.i upstages and fools their parents, but is seen by the audience as a sequence of 'ambiguous signs'. I was not convinced that such effects were peculiar to Dorset Garden, but I enjoyed Walsh's frequent asides about Jean Baudrillard, who has discovered 'the secret of all seduction', lucky fellow.

Wycherley was the subject of W. Gerald Marshall's *A Great Stage of Fools*. Marshall's interest in 'theatricality and madness' was familiar, as three chapters have appeared in learned journals: on obsessive characters in *The Plain-Dealer* (*YWES* 61.233), on social eccentricities in *The Gentleman Dancing-Master* (*YWES* 64.285), and on psychological disorders in *The Country Wife* (*YWES* 70.346). The book adds an introduction, a chapter on *Love in a Wood*, and a selective index. Marshall is now under the influence of Aubrey Williams, and has found that in *Love in a Wood* the divine plan ensures enlightenment and retribution. Here Wycherley 'falls into the tradition of the moral satirist, but in the other three plays his satires are more probing and complex, focusing ultimately upon the realm of the mind and the imagination'. Marshall believes earlier critics have not appreciated Wycherley's concerns with the Divine Impresario, rites of passage, dramas of madness, and the nature of the dramatic genres themselves, so they have failed to see that he was the greatest of the Restoration comic dramatists. It would be hard to say whether the latest critics have done better. Douglas Ford's '*The Country Wife*: Rake Hero As Artist' (*Restoration* 17[1993].77–84) finds that Horner 'functions as Wycherley's self-reflexive device', whose 'manipulation of signifiers is analogous to the operations performed with words by the poet or playwright', and so becomes – when Ford follows Bloom rather than Barthes – 'a symbol of authorial anxiety'. Sparkish is a dull critic whose 'floating chain of signifieds' gets him into trouble, and Harcourt the rival poet who 'swerves' from his predecessor's poem. A. Velissariou's 'Gender and the Circulation of Money and Desire in Wycherley's *The Plain-Dealer*' (*Restoration* 18.27–36) sees Wycherley as exposing gender 'for what it is: a category designed to promote cohesive links in authoritarian discourses', but the dramatist's apparent radicalism is 'circumscribed by his own gender, class and political position within conflicting discourses'. Velissariou's own position within conflicting discourses apparently makes it impossible for him to be a plain-dealer.

Congreve attracted much better criticism. Arthur Hoffman's *Congreve's Comedies* offers thorough discussions of each play and a substantial concluding chapter. The first two comedies are related to their immediate circumstances (but not seen as wholly determined by them): the attempted abduction of Mrs Bracegirdle and the murder of Mountfort delayed the performance of *The Old Batchelor* and may have darkened the tone of *The Double-Dealer*. With the last two comedies the emphasis falls on the 'maturity and seriousness' of 'ethical vision' in *Love for Love* and especially *The Way of the World*, which was Congreve's most effective answer to Jeremy Collier. The conclusion traces the development of his conception of marriage, which is enriched by allusion to Shakespeare and other predecessors. The book is not meant as an 'overview' of Congreve, as Hoffman seeks to augment what is already understood or agreed, but it could function as a stimulating introduction for an intelligent student. It is fully annotated but lacks a bibliography and an index. Curiously, all the recent articles on Congreve were in French, but I found them easier reading than articles in jargon. Josette Hérou's 'Le Théâtre de la Restauration est-il Immoral? Est-il Amoral? Le cas de *The Way of the World*' (*EA* 46[1993].398–406) maintains that in this play Congreve may seem to compromise with the demands of Collier and other moralists, but really he saw human problems in a manner we appreciate better than his contemporaries. 'La pièce est-elle morale? Oui, mais à sa manière'. Michèle Plaisant's '*The Way of the World*, Comédie "Noire"?' (*BSEAA* 37[1993].51–60) focuses on the struggle for love and money in the suffocating atmosphere of the Wishfort family; despite scenes of comic relief, the play 'n'en apparait pas moins comme un huis-clos'. However, Congreve believed, and showed in the characters of Mirabell, Millamant and Sir Wilfull Witwoud, that 'le train du monde n'exclut pas le souci d'authenticité'. Jean-Claude Loreau's 'Jeu, Mots et Maux dans *The Way of the World*' (*BSEAA* 37[1993].61–71) presents the play as a game of words in which the players seek to hide their weak points; Mirabell is the winner but – if I understand Loreau rightly – he plays so seriously that all the fun goes out of the game. Gisèle Venet's 'Bibliographie Sélective' of *The Way of the World* (*BSEAA* 37[1993].7–18) is useful. Pierre Degott's 'De Congreve à Haendel: Les Métamorphoses de Sémelé' (*BSEAA* 39.215–25) discusses Congreve's adaptation of Ovid, Hamilton's of Congreve, and Handel's setting of the text. Congreve's contribution was to introduce ironic, dramatic and moralistic elements into the story. Degott concludes that Jupiter's being forced to kill Semele perhaps allegorizes Handel's feeling obliged to destroy the English version of Italian opera.

The court wits may have convinced Shadwell that Etherege's *She Would if She Could* was 'the best Comedy that has been written since the Restauration of the Stage', but by the time of *The Libertine* and *The Man of Mode* the two dramatists inhabited 'incompatible moral universes', according to Christopher Wheatley's *Without God or Reason*. Wheatley believes commentators on Restoration comedy err by applying their own ethical assumptions, whereas a complex ethical system is needed merely 'to make sense out of an ordinary writer (Shadwell)'. In his plays neither God nor 'universalizable principles of rationality' are assumed; their ethical system is based on individual responsibility and recognition of social roles determined by birth, education and talent. Society's demand for chastity in women and permission of rakishness in men is a problem that may be solved by mutual love, and Shadwell regularly satirizes rakes, promiscuous women, and heavy fathers. His ethical relativism explains the popularity of his plays when the philosophical ideas of Hobbes, Halifax and Charleton were influential, but left him without straight answers to moral questions. The plays appear as more interesting than readers of Dryden have thought, but not as ready for revival. Wheatley's 'Thomas Shadwell's *The Volunteers* and the Rhetoric of Honor and Patriotism' (*ELH* 60[1993].397–418) argues that the 1688 Revolution posed dramatists the problem of convincing audiences that 'honor consisted of loyalty to abstractions', and that this play solves it. The point that patriarchy had to be replaced by patriotism is well made, but the idea that before the Revolution honour was primarily associated with rank rather than merit seems ill-considered. Hotspur, the son of an earl, would pluck bright honour from the pale-faced moon.

Behn's politics are a great source of interest, if not embarrassment, to her critics. Susan J. Owen's '"Suspect my Loyalty when I Lose my Virtue": Sexual Politics and Party in Aphra Behn's Plays of the Exclusion Crisis' (*Restoration* 18.37–47) offers detailed discussions of five plays. Rather alarmingly, dates of premières are only 'probable': *The Feigned Courtesans*, early 1679; *The Young King*, autumn 1679; *The Revenge*, early 1680; *The Second Part of the Rover*, January 1681; *The Roundheads*, autumn 1681. Broadly, the crisis obliged Behn to subordinate her feminism to her Toryism, but, perhaps because it was produced at a time of apparent Whig ascendancy, *The Second Part of the Rover* questioned cavalier libertinism as effectively as any Restoration comedy; *The Roundheads* belongs to the period of Tory triumphalism. This view of the latter play is not fully shared in Elizabeth Bennett Kubek's '"Night Mares of the Commonwealth"' (*Restoration* 17[1993].88–103), which analyses its 'somewhat bewildering' mixture of 'royalist passion and female ambition'. Behn herself must have been uneasy with the ending in which her forceful heroine is promised a royal pardon. Nancy Copeland's 'Female Conduct and Politics in Aphra Behn's *The City Heiress*' (*RECTR* 8.i[1993].27–49) finds that here 'the comic ending is destabilized as the considerable social and moral power of the chaste woman is challenged by the erotic power of the libidinous woman'. Lady Galliard's challenge also threatens the order celebrated by her Tory husband. Margo Hendricks's 'Civility, Barbarism, and Aphra Behn's *The Widow Ranter*' (in Margo Hendricks and Patricia Parker, eds, *Women, 'Race', and Writing*) argues that while satirizing English colonial government and idealizing American Indian rulers, Behn also suggests that the Indians, as shown by their comic religion, are inferior to the English, as represented by her noble hero. But this argument is obscured by jargon and I may have misunderstood it. Two comparatively apolitical essays were Julie Nash's 'Visual Pleasure in Aphra Behn's *The Rover*' (*Restoration* 18.77–87) and Lynne Taetzsch's 'Romantic Love Replaces Kinship Exchange in Aphra Behn's Restoration Drama' (*Restoration* 17[1993].30–8). Nash effectively applies feminist film theory to the relations between male and female characters, and the responses of male and female spectators, to conclude that women can derive genuine if limited satisfaction from Hellena's masquerade. Taetzsch considers relationships among the chief characters of the two parts of *The Rover* and *The Lucky Chance* as signs of 'the historical transition' from forced marriage to romantic love. Heidi Hutner's anthology *Rereading Aphra Behn* (*YWES* 74.273) includes four essays on the plays: Catherine Gallagher's 'The Prostitute and the Playwright', reprinted from *WS* (*YWES* 69.327), on the comedies generally; Hutner's 'Revisioning the Female Body', on both parts of *The Rover*; Jane Spencer's 'Comic Plot and Female Action', on *The Feigned Courtesans*; and Susan Green's 'Semiotic Modalities of the Female Body', on *The Dutch Lover*.

Southerne and Vanbrugh had the benefit of excellent essays by Helga Drougge. In 'Female Sexuality in Southerne's Comedies' (*SEL* 33[1993].545–63) Drougge sees *Sir Anthony Love, The Wives' Excuse* and *The Maid's Last Prayer* as conveying approval of female sexuality, unlike most earlier Restoration comedies. Southerne learns from Wycherley and Behn, goes well beyond them and Vanbrugh in portraying rakish women, and moves towards 'an ever darker picture of sexual relations'. In 'Love, Death, and Mrs Barry in Thomas Southerne's Plays' (*CompD* 27[1993–4].408–25) Drougge remarks that Mrs Barry's roles as Mrs Friendall in *The Wives' Excuse* and Lady Malepert in *The Maid's Last Prayer* both placed tragic heroines in comic situations, and created characters with whom female spectators could identify. But this fusion of feeling and action was perhaps 'inherently alarming' to the actual audience, so in *The Fatal Marriage* and *Oroonoko* Southerne dissociated female masochism in the main plots from tomboyishness in the sub-plots; these plays were inferior but more successful. In '"The Deep Reserves of Man": Anxiety in Vanbrugh's *The Relapse*' (*SEL* 34.507–22) Drougge finds a play full of men fearing women: some their exclusion from Hoyden's matriarchy, others their inclusion in Amanda's womb or grave. This essay is more original and stimulating than summary can suggest, and all three are lucid and lively. In 'Politicizing Sexuality/Sexualizing Politics: Body and Language in Vanbrugh's *The Provoked Wife*' (*Restoration* 18.104–12) You-me Park is sure that this play was conceived in the Bastille, and argues that it is about modes of escape from conventional rules governing sexuality. Sir John Brute emerges as the Houdini of the piece. In 'An Unrecorded Epilogue for *The Recruiting Officer*' (*EA* 47.312–16) Paul Cannan records an 'Epilogue Spoken by Mr. Estcourt' for his own benefit in 1710, which comments satirically on *The Tatler* and throws light on Sir Richard Steele's activities.

The tragic dramatists still play to thin houses. In 'Patriarchal Politics under Cultural Stress: Nathaniel Lee's Passion Plays (*RECTR* 8.ii[1993].1–28) Stephen P. Flores suggests that *The Rival Queens, Mithridates* and *Theodosius* may well seem to blame political conflicts on sexual passions, but ultimately 'the court's patriarchal politics have structured sexual and gender relations'. In 'Lee's *Lucius Junius Brutus* V.ii and Bacon's "Of Seditions and Troubles"' (*N&Q* 41[1993].323–4) Harold Love notes that Brutus's speech justifying the execution of his sons as traitors draws on Bacon's essay. In 'The Interested Heart and the Absent Mind: Samuel Johnson and Thomas Otway's *The Orphan*' (*ELH* 60[1993].611–23) Jessica

Munns examines Johnson's criticism of Otway's plays and compares *Rasselas* with *The Orphan*. This essay helpfully defines changing ideas about the relations of body and mind, though it predictably concludes that where the seventeenth century had feared physical anarchy, the eighteenth feared mental vacuity. In '"Power like new Wine": The Appetites of Leviathan in Durfey's *Masaniello*' (*SECC* 22[1992].231–51) Christopher Wheatley describes historical and literary contexts to show that Durfey does not relate the rebellion in Naples of 1647 to the situation of England in 1700, and that this can only be called a Tory play in the sense that it questions the idea of justifiable rebellion. Like *Venice Preserved* it suggests that some political problems have no solutions. In 'Mary Pix's Nebulous Relationship to *Zelmane*' (*N&Q* 41.186–7) Annette Kramer reports that there is 'very little textual evidence' to show that this play was written by Mary Pix rather than William Mountfort.

Miscellaneous articles mainly on tragicomedy and adaptations make my afterpiece. In 'The Production and Reception of Davenant's *Cruelty of the Spaniards in Peru*' (*MLR* 89.832–41) Janet Clare argues that this masque, if that is the right term, is not merely propaganda for Cromwell's colonialism; its idealized picture of Peruvian civilization before it was disrupted by civil war would appeal to Royalists in the audience. It may be worth adding that John Evelyn in 1659 dismissed 'a new Opera' as a silly distraction from politics. A. D. Harvey's 'Virginity and Honour in *Measure for Measure* and Davenant's *The Law against Lovers*' (*ES* 75.123–32) holds that 'either Davenant had no sympathy for Shakespeare's Isabella, or he thought his audience would not have'. Richard Gale's 'William Clerke's *Marciano* and Restoration Scotland' (*RECTR* 8.ii[1993].57–72) attributes scholarly neglect of the provincial theatre to 'the Shakespearean cannon' (at the mouth of which the bubble reputation was sought?), and supplies a context for Clerke's royalist tragicomedy, produced at Edinburgh in 1662. But *Marciano* has not been wholly neglected, as Nancy Maguire has an appreciative account in *Regicide and Restoration* (*YWES* 73.266–7). Beth S. Newman's 'Setting the Record Straight on John Crowne' (*RECTR* 8.i[1993].1–26) shows that Crowne was born in London in 1641; his management of money was better than has been thought; and he switched political sides like the Vicar of Bray, only not so shamelessly. Ben Ross Schneider Jr's 'Granville's *Jew of Venice* (1701): A Close Reading of Shakespeare's *Merchant*' (*Restoration* 17[1993].111–34) maintains that Granville was closer to Shakespeare than almost all modern critics. Influenced by classical moralists, both dramatists emphasized friendship as a primary virtue, but Granville made it more a unifying theme. Schneider overstates his case, quoting Rowe's view that 'there is something in the friendship of Antonio to Bassanio very great, generous and tender', but not his belief that the role of Shylock 'was designed tragically by the author'. Richard Braverman's 'Politics in Jewish Disguise' (section 1(b) above) also discusses *The Jew of Venice*.

(c) Prose

It has been a quieter year than usual for Behn's fiction. However, Janet Todd, in '"The hot brute drudges on": Ambiguities of Desire in Aphra Behn's *Love-Letters between a Nobleman and his Sister*' (*WW* 1.277–90) gathers a number of insights; in particular, she establishes the relationship between Behn's interest in scepticism and the novel's lack of faith in the transcendentals of love, family and state, and characterizes the differences in technique between Book I and Books II and III as 'devices for desires'. Chapter 3 of David Richards's virtuoso study, *Masks of Difference: Cultural Representations in Literature, Anthropology and Art*, compares

Oroonoko with Captain John Stedman's accounts of Surinam in the 1770s. He brings out particularly well the implications for the novella of the scenes of different races looking at each other. Also focused on race is Margaret Ferguson's essay on *Oroonoko* (in Hendricks and Parker, *Women, 'Race' and Writing*). A strong, though chatty, theoretical opening leads into an interesting refiguring of the race, gender and class issues between hero, heroine and narrator. Bernard Dhuicq, in 'Aphra Behn's Reflections of Morality, or, Seneca Unmasqued' (*N&Q* 41.175–6), explains the discrepancies in numbering between the 1675 edition of La Rochefoucauld's *Maximes* and Behn's 1685 translation, with some remarks about her reinterpretation of them.

Robert Markley reviews some recent work on the early Robert Boyle, particularly the moral essays, in order to reshape his position in that increasingly wobbly narrative, 'the rise of science' ('Robert Boyle In and Out of his Time', *ECent* 35.280–6). Lotte Mulligan, in 'Robert Boyle, "Right Reason", and the Meaning of Metaphor' (*JHI* 55.235–57), argues for the parallel between Boyle's not separating out theology from science and his use of metaphor (particularly that of the 'Two Books' of Nature and Scripture): a lucid and substantial contribution. Edward B. Davis, in 'The Anonymous Works of Robert Boyle and the *Reasons why a Protestant Should not Turn Papist*' (*JHI* 55.611–29), firmly attributes this work to David Abercromby rather than Boyle.

BunyanS has revived after a three-year lapse, with a Festschrift for James F. Forrest. There are four substantial articles. The most interesting and far-reaching is Juliet Dusinberre's 'Bunyan and Virginia Woolf: A History and a Language of Their Own' (5.15–46). She argues for the parallels between the two writers as coming from their search for empowerment: as Bunyan finds a language and a history in Foxe and the English Bible, so Woolf reconstructs a history of women writing. Woolf's debt to Bunyan is traced with deft scholarship. Thomas S. Freeman's 'A Library in Three Volumes: Foxe's *Book of Martyrs* in the Writings of John Bunyan' (5.47–57) notes a number of borrowings and takes a useful parallel line to the discussion of Bunyan and Foxe in John R. Knott's *Discourses of Martyrdom in English Literature*. Arleane Ralph's ' "They do such Musick make": *The Pilgrim's Progress* and Textually Inspired Music' (5.58–67) links various remarks about music in Bunyan's work with a brief history of music inspired by Bunyan, most notably Vaughan Williams's. The account is confined to remarks by composers and reviewers – more to be done here, perhaps. Finally, Maxine Hancock, in 'Bunyan as Reader: The Record of *Grace Abounding*', provides a lively reworking of a much-discussed topic, with particular reference to marginal notes. Also on Bunyan, a brief but suggestive essay by Sayre N. Greenfield, 'Bunyan, Non-conformism, and the Limits of Allegory' (*SVEC* 303[1992] .439–41) argues that 'allegory strives too much for system to encompass the complexities of radicalism', and consequently the allegory fades into exemplary fiction or something else, such as, at moments, Vanity Fair or the doctrinal debates, where Bunyan is most nonconformist. Ralph Stewart notes that Bunyan's view of literature as 'vicarious experience' is unusual for a seventeenth-century author, in 'Bunyan's *The Pilgrim's Progress*, "The Author's Apology for His Book" ' (*Expl* 52.211–14). Tamsin Spargo's 'The Purloined Postcard: Waiting for Bunyan' (*TPr* 8.79–86) takes its occasion from the postcard of Bunyan in prison sent to Terry Waite as a hostage to deliver an improvisatory reflection on the way texts go 'astray', and on *The Pilgrim's Progress* as a male, imperialist text (David Livingstone makes an appearance).

Stephen Clucas's 'The Atomism of the Cavendish Circle: A Reappraisal' (*SC* 9.247–73) is valuable for a brief yet critical general discussion of arguments about atomism in the period, as well as a reassessment of Margaret Cavendish. Sandra Sherman's 'Trembling Texts: Margaret Cavendish and the Dialectics of Authorship' (*ELR* 24.184–210) corrects Gallagher's influential formulation of the 'absolutist' model of the self in women writers of the period, and detects in Cavendish a more unstable construction, subject to the judgements of history, addressing the public even while seeming to exclude it. The essay is richly illustrated and carefully argued.

Richard Ollard has written about 'Clarendon and the Art of Prose Portraiture in the Age of Charles II' in a volume mostly concerned with the visual arts, *Art and Patronage in the Caroline Courts: Essays in Honour of Sir Oliver Millar* (ed. David Howarth). He sees 'context' and 'proportion' as the main features distinguishing Clarendon from other character writers, and he does not simply concentrate on the usual anthology pieces; the tone is urbane, even old-fashioned.

Barbara Arneil, in 'Trades, Plantations and Property: John Locke and the Economic Defense of Colonialism' (*JHI* 55.591–609), notes a number of parallels between tracts by Mun and Childs defending the English colonial enterprise in America and Locke's *Two Treatises*. The links between economic liberalism and the colonies are thus underlined.

Lisa M. Zeitz examines the rhetoric and the revisions and expansions of a once influential work in 'Natural Theology, Rhetoric and Revolution: John Ray's *Wisdom of God,* 1691–1704' (*ECLife* 18.120–33). The article contributes to a growing sense of the importance of 'physico-theology', as well as emphasizing the collaborative, inclusive ambitions of early scientific thinking.

Books Reviewed

Backscheider, Paula R. *Spectacular Politics: Theatrical Power and Mass Culture in Early Modern England.* JHUP (1993). pp. 335. £33, $39.95. ISBN 0 8018 4568 8.

Burns, J. H., and Mark Goldie, eds. *The Cambridge History of Political Thought 1450–1700.* CUP. pp. 816. pb £24.95. ISBN 0 5214 7772 7.

Cordner, Michael, Peter Holland and John Kerrigan, eds. *English Comedy.* CUP. pp. 323. £35. ISBN 0 5214 1917 4.

Corman, Brian. *Genre and Generic Change in English Comedy, 1660–1710.* UTorP (1993). pp. 168. $60. ISBN 0 8020 2885 3.

Dearing, Vinton A., ed. *Amboyna, The State of Innocence, Aureng-Zebe.* Vol. XII of *The Works of John Dryden.* UCalP. pp. 555. $75. ISBN 0 5200 8247 8.

——, and Alan Roper, eds. *The Kind Keeper, The Spanish Fryar, The Duke of Guise and The Vindication of The Duke of Guise.* Vol. XIV of *The Works of John Dryden.* UCalP (1992). pp. 638. $75. ISBN 0 5200 7561 7.

Downie, J. A. *To Settle the Succession of the State: Literature and Politics 1678–1750.* Context and Commentary. Macmillan. pp. 176. hb £40, pb £12.99. ISBN 0 3334 9596 9, 0 3334 9597 7.

Ellis, Frank H., ed. *The Complete Works of John Wilmot, Earl of Rochester.* Penguin. pp. 464. pb £9.99. ISBN 0 1404 2363 1.

Eriksen, Roy, ed. *Contexts of Pre-novel Narrative: The European Tradition.* MGruyter. pp. 397. $144.65. ISBN 3 1101 3883 2.

Finney, Gail, ed. *Look Who's Laughing: Gender and Comedy*. Studies in Humor and Gender. G&B. pp. 363. £25, $39. ISBN 0 8812 4644 3.

Fowler, Alastair, ed. *The Country House Poem: A Cabinet of Seventeenth-Century Estate Poems and Related Items*. EdinUP. pp. 433. £50. ISBN 0 7486 0440 5.

Gill, Pat. *Interpreting Ladies: Women, Wit, and Morality in the Restoration Comedy of Manners*. UGeoP. pp. 209. $35. ISBN 0 8203 1664 4.

Goldberg, Jonathan, ed. *Queering the Renaissance*. DukeUP. pp. 388. £52, $54.95. ISBN 0 8223 1381 2.

Hendricks, Margo, and Patricia Parker, eds. *Women, 'Race', and Writing in the Early Modern Period*. Routledge. pp. 383. hb £40, pb £14.99. ISBN 0 4150 7777 X, 0 4150 7778 8.

Highfill, Philip H. Jr, Kalman A. Burnim and Edward A. Langhans. *A Biographical Dictionary of Actors, Actresses, Musicians, Dancers, Managers and Other Stage Personnel in London, 1660–1800*. SIUP (1993). Vol. 15. pp. 377. $60. ISBN 0 8093 1802 4. Vol. 16. pp. 375. $60. ISBN 0 8093 1803 2.

Hoffman, Arthur W. *Congreve's Comedies*. *ELS*. VictUP (1993). pp. 144. pb $9.50. ISBN 0 9206 0468 4.

Hopkins, David, and Tom Mason, ed. *Abraham Cowley: Selected Poems*. Carcanet. pp. 101. pb £6.95. ISBN 1 8575 4119 7.

Howarth, David, ed. *Art and Patronage in the Caroline Courts: Essays in Honour of Sir Oliver Millar*. CUP (1993). pp. 252. £40. ISBN 0 5214 3185 9.

Keeble, N. H., ed. *The Cultural Identity of Seventeenth-Century Woman: A Reader*. Routledge. pp. 306. £16.99. ISBN 0 4151 0482 3.

Kramer, David Bruce. *The Imperial Dryden: The Poetics of Appropriation in Seventeenth-Century England*. UGeoP. pp. 188. $40. ISBN 0 8203 1543 5.

Lyons, Paddy, and Fidelis Morgan, eds. *Female Playwrights of the Restoration: Five Comedies*. Dent. pp. 363. pb £5.99. ISBN 0 4608 7427 6.

Marshall, W. Gerald. *A Great Stage of Fools: Theatricality and Madness in the Plays of William Wycherley*. AMS (1993). pp. 121. $37.50. ISBN 0 4046 1724 7.

Rawson, Claude. *Satire and Sentiment 1660–1830*. CUP. pp. 290. £37.50. ISBN 0 5213 8395 1.

Richards, David. *Masks of Difference: Cultural Representations in Literature, Anthropology and Art*. CUP. pp. 348. pb £13.95. ISBN 0 5214 7972 X.

Rowland, Jon Thomas. *Faint Praise and Civil Leer: The "Decline" of Eighteenth-Century Panegyric*. UDelP. pp. 190. £25. ISBN 0 8741 3543 5.

Shapin, Steven. *A Social History of Truth: Civility and Science in Seventeenth-Century England*. UChicP. pp. 483. £13.50. ISBN 0 2267 5018 3.

Tippetts, Nancy Lyn. *Sisterhood, Brotherhood, and Equality in the Restoration Comedy of Manners*. Lang. pp. 216. £28. ISBN 0 8204 2255 X.

Todd, Janet, and Elizabeth Spearing, eds. *Counterfeit Ladies: The Life and Death of Mal Cutpurse and The Case of Mary Carleton*. P&C. pp. 165. £25. ISBN 1 8519 6087 2.

Vaughan, Virginia Mason. *Othello: A Contextual History*. CUP. pp. 243. £30. ISBN 0 5214 6069 7.

Walker, Keith, ed. *John Dryden*. OUP. pp. 269. £5.99. ISBN 0 1928 2264 0.

Wheatley, Christopher J. *Without God or Reason: The Plays of Thomas Shadwell and Secular Ethics in the Restoration*. BuckUP, AUP (1993). pp. 201. $36.50. ISBN 0 8387 5243 8.

Wing, Donald, John J. Morrison, Carolyn W. Nelson et al., eds. *Short-Title Catalogue of Books Printed in England, Scotland, Ireland, Wales, and British America and of English Books Printed in Other Countries, 1641–1700. Vol. I: A to England.* MLA. pp. 954. $400. ISBN 0 8735 2661 9.

XI

The Eighteenth Century

ALAN BOWER and NIGEL WOOD

This chapter has five sections: 1. General; 2. Poetry; 3. Prose; 4. Novel; 5. Drama. Sections 1, 3 and 5 are by Nigel Wood and sections 2 and 4 are by Alan Bower.

1. General

The most valuable conclusion (out of many contenders) to be gleaned from Howard D. Weinbrot's *Britannia's Issue: The Rise of British Literature from Dryden to Ossian* is that all the time spent relating eighteenth-century enthusiasms to extensions (at some point) of classical myths and models may well have been earnest myopia. Out of the appropriation of the past came not anxiety at these 'strong' authors but rather a quiet native confidence. The Augustan Age disappears here, and those who still cling tenaciously to source-studies simply confuse 'the small part with the larger whole', and ignore the basic contemporary conviction that 'Augustus was the enemy not the friend of the republic and liberty.' Here, for the first time, is an entirely convincing summation of the counter-Augustan argument: that the anxiety of influence was more a latter-day critical rationalization than an early-century impulse, a rhetorical *diminutio* rather than a creative glass ceiling: 'The new blend is an often discordant *concordia discors* that can stimulate literary greatness.' To this end, Weinbrot re-reads many texts and liberates them for a northern libertarian potency, inclusive of Scottish Celtic as well as Hebraic irregularity. His Neander wins the debate in Dryden's *Essay*, Pope's *Rape of the Lock* and *Windsor Forest* repudiate classical martial heroism, and the Hebraic models found in Dryden, Handel and Smart acquire a vital contemporaneity. Acts of union were hardly just political in scope. Although it is unlikely that each author would trace the association readily, Weinbrot's revisionism is shared by J. C. D. Clark, in his lively *The Language of Liberty, 1660–1832: Political Discourse and Social Dynamics in the Anglo-American World*. Ever since his work of the mid-80s, Clark has challenged exclusively political explanations of social change. By delving into various legal and religious discourses, he sketches the deep interrelations between the two, and so provides an enhanced role for the cultural workings of Protestant dissent in its constant difference from Anglican hegemony. The American Revolution may have been a military and apparently secular success, yet its bases were religious and promoted group identity, evangelical citizenship and a written constitution. Whilst other differences follow, they are drawn from the same nexus. Clark's research in mid-century apologetics and devotional literature is alive to nice distinctions, and the construction of common features of resistance is not unduly tendentious. Certainly, there is a lot of convincing to do; Robert E. Stillman's orthodox ramble through 'Assessing the Revolution: Ideology, Language, and Rhetoric in the New Philosophy of Early Modern England' (*ECent* 35.99–118) almost erases religious effects altogether (see below).

If there is a ruling passion about the year's eighteenth-century offerings, then it could be found in a series of enlightened and theoretically adroit studies of literature in the market-place. Just as Weinbrot sketched a gathering self-consciousness in the country at large, Colin Nicholson's *Writing and the Rise of Finance: Capital Satires in the Early Eighteenth Century* concentrates on notions of the metropolis and its extension into apparently unconnected areas of literary consumption. Nicholson's examples are exclusively Augustan – *The Rape of the Lock*, the complex of pamphleteering and improving essays surrounding matters of investing and the money market *c.*1720, Gulliver's Travels, *The Beggar's Opera*, Pope's poetry of the 1730s, culminating in *The Dunciad* – and his contextualizing is similarly drawn from contemporary models: Defoe and Mandeville, both of whom engage with the radical effects on 'political subjectivity' of a market society: 'the conflict between traditional forms of civic personality grounded in real property and endowed with classical virtue and market-oriented perceptions of individuality where passion and fantasy are encouraged to operate in constant flux'. Nicholson writes with more virtue than fantasy himself, as we might well have anticipated many of the contours of this study and occasionally wish for more controversial matter, especially where Pope is concerned. There are (acknowledged) shades of H. T. Dickinson, Isaac Kramnick and especially J. G. A. Pocock, but, whereas Nicholson synthesizes these sources, there are several passages where the mix could have been far less cosy with a little tincture of J. C. D. Clark or even E. P. Thompson. This aside, Nicholson is an astute and always perceptive commentator on hidden assumptions and psychic reflexes. His 'Introduction' is an excellent summation of much varied recent research, and, in broad outline, his treatments of Swift and Gay are valuable re-readings of often generalized conclusions. His Pope is still the individual energized by the very dullness he condemns and, as such, is mightily familiar.

W. A. Speck's micro-study, *The Birth of Britain: A Nation at War and Peace, 1700–1710*, comes up with some unexpected nuggets amidst otherwise well-tilled ground. In his ten chapters, one for each year of the decade, there is inevitably some familiar narrative, yet the gradual progress on a number of fronts (political, foreign, financial) actually pays off: the act of union with Scotland is never rendered as inevitable and as the brainchild or craven responsibility (depending on your vantage point) of any one set of individuals. Taken alongside the welcome second edition of Roderick Floud and Donald McCloskey's *The Economic History of Britain since 1700* (vol. I, *1700–1860*), Speck's straightforward account, however, seems a little two-dimensional. Floud and McCloskey have assembled an enviable variety of economic historians, from monetarists to Marxists, to provide lucid and up-to-date accounts of business and trade. The most valuable for literary work will be chapters on 'The Pattern of Work as the Eighteenth Century Began' (Ann Kussmaul), 'The Industrial Revolution' (Nick Crafts), 'British Population Change, 1700–1871' (Roger Schofield), 'Agriculture during the Industrial Revolution'

(Robert Allen), 'The Finance of Business during the Industrial Revolution' (Larry Neal), 'Mercantilism and Overseas Trade, 1700–1800' (Stanley L. Engerman), and 'Central Government and the Economy, 1688–1815' (Patrick O'Brien). In asserting the vitality of social scientific models of explanation, the contributors end up questioning quietly the no less totalizing humanism of much historiography. In Peter Earle's *A City Full of People: Men and Women of London, 1650–1750*, London takes centre stage, and here the theatrical metaphor is apposite, for he constantly returns to the effects of civic spectacle and public self-consciousness embedded in everyday urban existence. In part I, 'Structures of Life and Work', Earle provides accessible vignettes amongst the data to flesh out outlines of education and both male and female labour. I would especially recommend 'Living by One's Pen', 'Living Space' and 'Neighbourhood'. Part II dwells on 'Voices of Londoners', and allows just that: space for documented accents to speak for themselves, albeit with a (minimal) editorial ordering. Here is the plenitude represented as anarchistic polyphony by Augustan moralists.

This might be read alongside the contributions to Haydn Mason's Festschrift, *The Secular City* (eds T. D. Hemming, E. Freeman and D. Meakin), which, whilst concentrating on Paris, still offers suggestions that cross-channel urban culture had an eye on London. The introductory 'Topographies of the Secular City' by D. Meakin is more than a mere prelude, and tackles large-scale problems of definition head-on. Thereafter, there is only one chapter that is truly anglophone: Roy Porter's 'Enlightenment London and Urbanity', which seizes on the efforts to find 'Rus in Urbe', and the self-conscious urbanity of St James's and the West End. V. A. C. Gatrell provides a social commentary of a more drastic kind in his *The Hanging Tree: Execution and the English People, 1770–1868*. The point to the terminal date of the title is that Gatrell notes that executions were largely all carried out away from the public gaze from that point. The journey to the abolition of public executions involves large changes in sensibility and techniques of political control. This book's five hundred pages or so include first-hand testimony and a deeper immersion in the 'choking, pissing, and screaming than taboo, custom, or comfort usually allow'. Impatience with the exclusively forensic approach to the topic, content only with legislation and statistics, motivates this occasionally uncomfortable read. Gatrell hardly mentions Foucault on account of his underplaying the role of 'feeling and culture', and instead resorts to Elias and Freud. The result is an accessible account of daily life in the shadow of Newgate that should be compulsory reading for anyone worrying about the 'realism' or otherwise of eighteenth-century portrayals of city life, Defoe or Gay in particular. In parts I and II ('The Scaffold and the Crowd' and 'The Plebeian Texts') the emphasis is on the potential victims, and their carnivalistic unruliness. Bawdy ballads and Gallows Emblems all betoken more than a lowly people at play, for Gatrell is skilful in tracing their undertow, a recognition of the popular as possessing a vitality and function far beyond authority's power to sanction.

J. A. Downie, in his largely introductory *To Settle the Succession of the State: Literature and Politics, 1678–1750* (a volume in the reliable and occasionally suggestive Context and Commentary series), proceeds cautiously through 'The Popish Plot and the Exclusion Crisis' to 'The Rage of Party' and 'Public Virtues, Private Vices' to end with a coda on 'The Forty-Five'. Downie brings disparate material together, and is lucid on the Revolution Settlement and the opposition to Walpole. There is a rudimentary chronology and bibliography. Although it is not at all fair to compare full-blooded monographs on allied themes with what was designed as a student textbook, it is likely that if Downie had had access to two excellent studies of oppositional politics during the early years of the century, he would have had to redesign his selection quite radically. In Robert Harris's multifaceted *A Patriot Press: National Politics and the London Press in the 1740s*, there is a concerted revisionist zeal to place the 1740s at the forefront of explanations of cultural change, this in the face of several convincing voices to the contrary (J. C. D. Clark and Evelyn Cruickshanks argue for the 1750s). Harris traces the roots of Wilkite opposition as much earlier than the 1760s. Here the apparent decline in the decade's adversarial political language is glossed as a corresponding search for the moral high ground once Walpole had fallen. The excellent opening chapter, 'Press, Parliament and Popular Opinion', is possibly the most pertinent for literary scholars, and there is a sensitively argued section on the variety of 1740s political definitions in the second.

Expectations were high for two long-announced treatments of satire: Dustin Griffin's *Satire: A Critical Reintroduction* and Claude Rawson's *Satire and Sentiment, 1660–1830*. Each in its individual way demands more detailed attention than I have room for here, but there are general comments worth making. The most worldly of forms, satire would seem to require exhaustive immersion in context and historicist reconstruction. That both Griffin and Rawson afford us some relief from this relentless footnoting should be some cause for rejoicing. Griffin's aims are complex and involve a two-eyed stance, directed at the initial impetus behind the affront successful satire produces and also at how we now eavesdrop on this localized form of attack. For the generation of Kernan, Frye and Paulson, the satirist emerged as the moralist, setting her or his stall out to discourage deviancy; after Bakhtin, Griffin is surely accurate in depicting our view of satire as rather less one-way traffic. Sensitive to the prominence of Menippean formlessness in most contemporary accounts of the satirist's art, this study attempts to recover its dialogic dimension. Here we can find a full description of satiric heritage and, in the chapter entitled 'Inquiry and Provocation', a trenchant reminder that 'the satirist's point of departure' is its apparent bipolar divisions between good and bad, and not 'the destination'. Satire is a display of verbal dexterity, which talent opens up the thesis overtly indicated to the point of *aporia*. In the chapter on 'Satiric Fictions and Historical Particulars', however, Griffin finds an elegant way to evade the consideration that satire is parasitic on actual events and so behoves critics to be so too: 'Our interpretive task as readers is not simply to identify the victim; it is also to identify the principles of selection and distortion that shape the satirist's "facts". The ensuing call for a more culturally aware approach in the closing chapters is somewhat vitiated by the almost common-sensical briskness of the foregoing treatment, and Griffin's light hand at identifying historical differences between varied forms. For those who agree with him that politics is invariably about transient forces (almost a form of '*ars longa, vita brevis*'), I suspect that this often formalistic approach will not strike many false notes (even if the media associated with satire are still predominantly textual). Conversely, for those who have paid close attention to Bakhtin's earlier work on art as social acts (see Stallybrass and White, *The Politics and Poetics of Transgression* [*YWES* 67.55–6] for example), the dialogic can only be located in the instant and by the registering of an instinctive reaction within the act of reading/seeing, something Griffin elsewhere has understood and written about most clearly – but not here.

Compared to Griffin's excursions into literary theory, Rawson's collection of essays may seem individualistic, even idiosyncratic. Not that this is a totally new venture by Rawson: here are eight essays that originally appeared in *TLS* and *LRB* fleshed out by an introduction and essay already published in a recent collection. Two new chapters appear here: a supplement to his study of Byron and Shelley's mock-heroic, 'Swift, Pope, and Others', and a long and exciting excursus into 'Revolution in the Moral Wardrobe: Mutations of an Image from Dryden to Burke', which dips sure-footedly through the near and far, the historically precise and the dictates of our present reading preferences. There is a clear virtue in this collection: Rawson has attempted to mould disparate notions into some more global cogency, even though he shows on one level an antipathy to easy generalities. He parts company with Griffin on many counts. Here is a study of 'the energies of a patrician culture in decline'. Hence he establishes his understanding of 'lordly accents' (Rochester, Oldham) in the first two chapters, and then reproduces his excellent understanding of the mock-heroic in familar examples (Augustans), and not so familiar ones (Byron et al.). Clothing imagery occupies Rawson in the long and involved new fifth chapter, which takes Burke's fear that the Revolution might tear away 'all the decent drapery of life'. Anti-cultural yahooisms occupy Rawson along with satire's incessant habit of not only breaching taboos, but also reinforcing and trading off them at the same time. Chapters 6–11 adopt sentiment as their focus, and involve triangulation points as apparently far afield as Steele's journalism, Boswell's *Life*, and the innovations of Austen in her minor works and in *Persuasion*. Here there is the essayist's art to render the once familiar and fixed as newly permeable and strange, and we ought to attend as closely to these (relatively) new examples as to Rawson's more canonical earlier comments; but this is not literary history, as many now have come to regard it, and Rawson's sweeping synoptic views often elide quite distinct historical considerations of motive and local aesthetic codes for well-hidden, even occult, resemblances and textual similarities. Themes derived from notions of empire that might occupy Swift as early as 1704 are taken to tax him when exiled in 1726; sentiment as a bourgeois reflex might well have been Richardson's project in the 1740s, yet its Tory credentials recommended it to many apolitical writers well into the 1780s (e.g. Burke himself), and so on. It might make for less of a sweep, but footnotes such as these have their place too.

In two allied treatments of publishing in the century, there emerge clear problems as to how to define the 'author-figure', as Foucault termed it, and the ensuing relation to printed texts. In Martha Woodmansee's *The Author, Art, and the Market: Rereading the History of Aesthetics*, there is a refreshing materialist riposte to those whose account of aesthetics is actually bounded by those texts that share the same metaphysical discourse, culminating in Kant's third critique. Here, in an increasingly insistent repudiation of Terry Eagleton's *Ideology of the Aesthetic* (Blackwell, 1990), Woodmansee widens her focus to take in those marginal texts, such as Adam Bergk's *The Art of Reading Books* (1799) or Fichte's *Proof of the Illegality of Reprinting* (1793), to demonstrate the deepest material motives behind the most philosophical and removed of concerns. Where others accept the self-definitions of influence and genre, Woodmansee returns to Addison, Batteux and Coleridge, amongst many others, to resist their vocative ploys. There is powerful intellectual ambition here, and sometimes one might have wished for extra explanation or corroboration, such as in her fifth chapter, 'Engendering Art', where a thesis worth a whole study to itself is despatched in one densely packed chapter. Occasionally, the range seems a little too compacted, especially where larger, more nationalistic themes might have deserved consideration (see Weinbrot above).

One could not have complained of this in Woodmansee's second contribution, a co-editing with Peter Jaszi of *The Construction of Authorship: Textual Appropriation in Law and Literature*, in the new series of Post-Contemporary Interventions. This meeting of literary theoretical and legal minds is a heady mix of the deconstructive treatment of notions of authorship from the literature camp with an unsurprised assent from the lawyers (who give the impression that they had dealt with that one some time ago). Woodmansee's 'On the Author Effect: Recovering Collectivity' is a succinct summary of how hybrid literary creation could be with special reference to Samuel Johnson's ghostwriting for Chambers and occasional projects set against his parallel concern with 'authenticity' in the Ossian debate. This is taken up by Peter Jaszi in his 'On the Author Effect: Contemporary Copyright and Collective Creativity', where questions of intention come in for some tough interrogation in a varied examination of the link between 'the ideology of "authorship" and the formation of particular doctrinal structures in the law of copyright'. Romantic investment in the imaginative transcendence of the writerly ego is still alive. Mark Rose turns the spotlight on 'The Author in Court: Pope v. Curll (1741)' mainly because it became the first time that a writer turned to law to defend her or his legal stake in what had been written, and so promoted a rudimentary formulation of intellectual property. Could a text (i.e. in this case, letters) be possessed as a commercial property? William Warburton's *Letter from an Author Concerning Literary Property* (1747) attempted to enshrine 'Utility' as well as ascertainable possession as a dual test, a verdict directly attributable to the 1741 case. Marlon Ross's 'Authority and Authenticity: Scribbling Authors and the Genius of Print in Eighteenth-Century England' sees the advent of print from an almost Augustan humanist perspective, as a downgrading of 'non-possessible knowledge'. Following Walter Ong's association of print with the privatization of discourse, Ross is amusing as well as interesting in writing of *The Dunciad* (no small talent, you might agree), and points to positive as well as negative perspectives on 'scribbling'. Two sections on Walpole and Chatterton close the essay, and Ross reminds us that it is not 'status, but print, that will have the final word'. The collection includes some striking arguments in favour of author protection in the postmodern world, and I would direct any literary scholar to the clarity of Alfred C. Yen's 'The Interdisciplinary Future of Copyright Theory'. Turning more to past understandings of ownership, Mark Rose in his *Authors and Owners: The Invention of Copyright* traces the crucial semantic shifts in the term 'copyright' from medieval to modern, with especial reference to the years 1710 to 1774. The material is never less than interesting, although the overall pattern is still left undisturbed. There are two welcome appendices, the one a transcription of Pope's 'Bill of Complaint', the other Curll's 'Answer' with Lord Hardwicke's decision. Compared to more specialized work, this seems a little too ambitious, especially when he moves outside eighteenth-century matters.

Dustin Griffin's work on eighteenth-century patronage is always worth surveying. His latest essay on the topic, 'Fictions of Eighteenth-Century Authorship' (*EIC* 43.81–94), is a more generalized contribution, its main aim being to debunk easy sociological assumptions about authorship. Griffin doubts that there ever was a realistic sense of a 'Republic of Letters', and so he tears holes in the Scriblerian assumption that the world of commercial print signified a fall from grace. As for its being a bondage, Griffin turns that assumption on its head by fostering the notion that many writers were liberated by the new public sphere. He concludes, however, that more recent notions of community, especially Habermas's 'public sphere', elevate coffee-house culture far above its actual status. At least, the public fora for the dissemination of alternative cultural debate were open to widespread contestation (when otherwise ?). In Howard D. Weinbrot's account of 'Enlightenment Canon Wars: Anglo-French Views of Literary Greatness' (*ELH* 60.79–100), there is a similar preoccupation with notions of national literary identity. Early eighteenth-century English assumptions about correctness were directed less by a clear and full understanding of the classical past than by a gathering prejudice at French ways; reciprocally, the French thought they understood academic virtues yet found good reasons to distrust English anarchy. In time, these positions gradually reversed, and Weinbrot is skilful in drawing our attention to many unsung French notions smuggled in as native wit and fire.

Keith Maslen and Herbert Davis's study of *An Early London Printing House at Work: Studies in the Bowyer Ledgers* has been eagerly awaited. The microfiche edition of the documents themselves has been available since 1991, and Maslen's occasional papers have whetted the appetite, yet here, newly collected and edited, is an invaluable insight into the economics of the book trade. Here is an account of costs of printing, the working conditions of compositors and pressmen, joint work between publishers and negotiations with authors, amongst many other topics, all summarized in recently added chapters. A full account is impossible here, but suffice it to say that it supplements many of the tentative propositions about the world of print found in the studies noted immediately above, in illustrating the clear pragmatism surrounding the 'author-figure' and the enhanced role of printers and booksellers.

ECS celebrates its relaunch with a special number on 'Eighteenth-Century Culture and the Disciplines' (28), in which some of the year's most brainstorming writing occurs. As Bernadette Fort, Mary Sheriff and James Thompson have it, in their opening manifesto, 'Introduction: The Editorial Function', interdisciplinarity might be a rediscovery of the encyclopaedic project itself, 'the unity of human knowledge and the difficulty of articulating the order and connection of its parts'. Not all of the contributors share this view wholeheartedly. Lynne Hunt is aware of the necessity of learning new disciplinary languages, yet is against the creation of a completely 'new and different interstitial space', if for no better reason than that one's primary dialogue is principally with politically and historically 'disciplined' colleagues ('The Virtues of Disciplinarity' [1–7]). Juxtaposed to this is the futuristic 'Redesigning the Image of Images: A Personal View' (9–16), where Barbara Maria Stafford stresses the multivalency in all image making, and Michael McKeon's 'The Origins of Interdisciplinary Studies' (17–28), which is placed as a fundamental Enlightenment activity and achievement. Counter to this division and rule, on the other hand, is an alternative current stressing the entwined nature of all perception. Drawing on Swift, Pope and Addison, amongst others, McKeon discovers the multiplicity of histories (*à la* Althusser) that underlie all knowledges. We must beware 'the thickening of epistemology into ontology, methodological procedure into condition of being', which is actually a blindness to this hidden and conditioning imperative. Closing this first section on the disciplines, Madelyn Gutwirth explores the 'deliberate method' of gender study, in her 'Changing the Past: A Feminist Challenge' (29–36). In forsaking the disciplinary guild system, she charts the thrill of genuine knowledge creation that is the core of feminist historiography.

The next section, on the 'Sublime', is presumably indicative of the type of offering the new editors would like to receive, and it awakens a deep ambivalence in me. Whilst the opening theoretical musing looks forwards boldly, the practice returns to much of the same old territory, willing it to put forth a new face. Clifford Siskin's 'Gender, Sublimity, Culture: Retheorizing Disciplinary Desire' (37–50) is a complex piece, in the main to do with the realization that disciplinary divisions were initially produced on gender lines in the educative texts of the century. Siskin's choices are relevant – Mary Astell's *Serious Proposal to the Ladies* and Burke's *Philosophical Enquiry* – and yet the historicity of the enterprise does not only oblige us to find a level at which things cohere. Studies on 'The Revolutionary Sublime' (Marie-Helene Huet [51–64]), the Kantian Sublime ('Taking Stock of the Kantian Sublime', Peter Fenves [65–82]) and its alternatives ('The Sublime Adverse and its Sadian Reverse: Kant, Sade, Schiller', Jean-Pierre Dubost [83–93]) all strive to take stock of what the sublime can signify, especially in a postmodern episteme: all-encompassing subjectivity or mere Romantic aspiration? Whilst never mentioned, Paul de Man hovers over most of the passages of close analysis.

In the third section, 'Culture and Politics: International Views', there are two rather miscellaneous pieces. Margaret C. Jacob provides 'The Mental Landscape of the Public Sphere: An International View'(95–113), not a recipe, one might expect, for ready solutions, especially as the starting premise is that there was a European 'public sphere'. With Dustin Griffin's caveat in mind (see above), Jacob seems to take a great deal on trust, although her conclusion, that civil society as we now have come to know it was forged by such assumptions, is entirely possible, if not capable of proof. Christopher M. S. Johns contributes 'Portrait Mythology: Antonio Canova's Portraits of the Bonapartes' (115–29), a densely argued and illustrated study of how the trappings of classicism could play a propagandist role whilst apparently clearing his treatment of any partisan taint whatsoever. One is left with the notion that the editors have had to work particularly hard to create the universality in this collection that they would have liked, yet one can still be thankful for enthusiasm and a commitment to encyclopaedic breadth. Running parallel to this is an almost new-historicist reinterpretation of academic divisions and professional 'expertise', which was mounted explicitly in Leo Damrosch's *The Profession of Eighteenth-Century Literature* (*YWES* 73.300) for a more holistic comprehension of literary history. Those wishing to read on in this debate might like to consult the work of John Bender, 'Rehearsing the Eighteenth Century: The (Re)Production of Professional Knowledge' (*ECent* 35.86–95), which is quietly polemical in its understanding of what keeps a profession stable and 'professional' – and one of the casualties is feminism, and any conviction that elides difference and hierarchy to recast old certainties.

At the same time, Joel Reed has drawn on a similarly interdisciplinary theme for his edition of a special number of *ECent* (35), 'Academic Cultures'. On the whole, this collection is actually less eclectic, and also rather less exciting. Reed himself supplies an overview of the subject, and demonstrates quite why academic culture emerged with such force throughout Europe, its centralizing and nationalistic impulses at sometimes conscious war with the immediate cultural past ('Introduction' [195–202]). Albert Boime extends this critique to 'The Cultural Politics of the Art Academy' (223–40) and provides a precise anatomy of national conservatism, where, as soon as 'high' standards and formal ways by which talent is to be recognised emerge, exceptional art (that posterity has eventually come to recognize) departs its precincts and yet is also thus defined. Robert Markley supplies the other anglophile essay, 'Robert Boyle In and Out of his Time' (280–6), and attempts to reclaim Boyle for his ethics as well as his science. Markley's essay should be read in conjunction with his arresting and remarkable *Fallen Languages: Crises of Representation in Newtonian England, 1660–1740*. Refusing to sketch the familar account of the growth of Newtonian science, Markley marks how indebted the Royal Scientists were to notions of 'physico-theology', a 'single system of representation that articulates its equally strong commitment to experimental philosophy and to theology'. The legitimacy of scientific representation emerged less as a guarantor of empirical truth than as a way to solve an otherwise vexed problem within ethics and theology as to how its propositions could be grounded on natural philosophy. Boyle and Newton are the real heroes of this narrative, in their refusal to extricate God from the picture as a central and governing source of revelation.

In quick succession after the Markley study, I encountered Jules David Law's *The Rhetoric of Empiricism: Language and Perception from Locke to I. A. Richards* and James L. Larson's *Interpreting Nature: The Science of Living Form from Linnaeus to Kant*. Both accounts stress the figuration of a discourse that strove to escape the figurative. Law finds the eighteenth century hardly at ease with itself in its goal of strong elemental forms as its models often came up against almost atomistic exceptions. Larson discusses the way biology from 1740 to 1790 assumed experimental force, and began to alter conceptions of heredity away from ideas of divine origin that stressed numinous seeds of preformation. Both Law and Larson open early science to non-empirical forces, and, in so doing, describe currents of thought often disguised in standard accounts.

Perhaps this is the best position in the section to mention Susan Rosa's review essay, 'Religion in the English Enlightenment: A Review Essay' (*ECS* 28.145–9), which should definitely be read alongside other, apparently weightier tomes on the subject. I have already mentioned Robert E. Stillman's 'Assessing the Revolution: Ideology, Language, and Rhetoric in the New Philosophy of Early Modern England' (*ECent* 35.99–118) in relation to studies of political change. Its full impact might rather be in understanding the relation between the paradigms of humanism and religion, language theory and emergent philosophies. Drawing on Richard Kroll's *The Material Word* (*YWES* 72.236), Stillman examines texts by both Hooke and Wilkins for their ideological motives, and for their distinct signs of non-empirical assumptions lodged in language and the work it has in representing scientific discoveries for particular ideological purposes. I do not quite trace the novelty that Stillman obviously believes he has located, yet there is a well-written summary of many definitions of post-Marx notions of ideology, and a sensitive synthesis of Kroll and Brian Vickers's contribution to *Rhetoric and the Pursuit of Truth: Language Change in the Seventeenth and Eighteenth Centuries*, ed. Thomas F. Wright (*YWES* 67.70).

In Joel Weinsheimer's ambitious *Eighteenth-Century Hermeneutics: Philosophy of Interpretation in England from Locke to Burke* there is a similar desire to direct critical theory (here Hans-Georg Gadamer's hermeneutics) onto earlier philosophy. Gadamer caters for those who would examine the validity of propositions from their communicative detail, and their effect on the process of reading as the primary process of cognition. This study devotes chapters to Locke, Toland, Bolingbroke, Hume, Reid, Blackstone and Burke (not quite all 'in England', alas), and foregrounds factors in understanding that are by definition unprovable: sympathy, common sense, taste, prudence and equity. The yardstick for their success, or lack of it, to speak across the ages emerges from their ability to equate the dictates of reason and historical change, conserving a common goal whilst being open to different contexts. As most of the above writers set out their stall to accommodate such a goal in any case, one might have expected an unnecessary duplication and exposition, yet Weinsheimer is a particularly astute writer and an experienced historian of ideas. There are gaps, however, in his review of the eighteenth century. Johnson could certainly have made a more telling appearance, especially in the survey of Blackstone's influence, and Weinsheimer's Hume seems rather less interested in historical difference than should have become evident from a more detailed assessment of his *History of England*. The real gains, though, are in the serious treatment of Burke's political and ethical commentaries, which rescues his notions of prejudice from twentieth-century dismissal, and also in the excellent placing of Hume and Reid in a significant relationship when discussing sympathetic reading.

Laura Brown's *Ends of Empire: Women and Ideology in Early Eighteenth-Century English Literature* has already attracted admirers but just as many detractors, so it is rather difficult to escape its advance billing (fostered in part by Brown's own 'self-consciously politicized position') to get to what it actually says. The first page glances at the title and identifies it for us as a 'political pun': to 'evoke the ways in which the literature of the eighteenth century served the purposes of empire, and also the ways in which a radical critique might recruit that literature to uncover the operations of imperialism in the eighteenth century and help put a stop to empire in the twentieth'. This is a large claim, although Brown's recent work has helped place such thinking on the agenda, and in seeing imperialism and commodification as entwined with the gathering force of mercantile capitalism she surely has a point (although a Political Science 101 course might well have alerted many to this). The real power in this study lies in its linking of the figures attached to and derived from the female body to an implicit questioning of an 'incomplete ideological hegemony'. Feminist aesthetics is arrayed against 'traditional' theories of beauty and form, which attempt to transcend the material bases of their production. In its stead, Brown reminds us that history can enter a text in many 'untraditional' ways, not as some naive backdrop, material merely for mimetic display, but rather in patterning and preliminary artistic choices. Her reading of Pope is the best example of this, and in chapter 4, 'Capitalizing on Women: Dress, Aesthetics and Alexander Pope', Brown's analysis of the fetishism in *The Rape of the Lock* amongst several allied texts should by now be both familiar and definitive. I was less prepared for the revelatory chapters on Defoe's Amazons, which is focused on *Roxana* and *Captain Singleton*, and Swift's poetry (in the main, although there is a suggestive application to *Gulliver*). Defoe's attempts at exculpating Roxana have not been taken particularly seriously and Brown is aware of why we need Defoe to be an identikit Whig apologist to keep our account of early-century politics comprehensible, yet Defoe's determination to reveal a new self-fashioning impulse in his Amazons also involves an anatomy of an inimical patriarchy. To some degree, the keynote for this is struck in the earlier chapter on 'Staging Sexuality: Violence and Pleasure in the Domestic She-Tragedy', where Brown traces the emergence of a new heroine, 'whose victimization provides the essential material of the plot'. In Nicholas Rowe's work she locates an 'affective engagement with female suffering', where the body and its sexual needs are almost commodified, as persuasive tools. Rowe is probably a suitable example, but this proto-sentimentality is hardly the whole picture. With Farquhar in the wings, and

Southerne (*The Wives' Excuse*) and Vanbrugh (*The Provoked Wife* or *The Relapse*) as more probable influences, Rowe is not exactly original in this quarter, or a particularly complex example. The leap to questions of class will appeal to some and not to others, depending on prior frames of reference, but the last chapter on Swift, 'Imperial Disclosures', has an urgency and centrality that few will deny. To conclude that Swift teaches us 'the appropriateness of defeatism and despair' takes a particularly perverse form of bravery, when all throughout the last decade the very reverse has been proposed. Not one to miss an opportunity for political analogues, Brown turns this 'criticism of withdrawal' (the refusal to join in and so to compromise) into a precise reflex which eventually endorses virtues of interdependence, then as now. There may be a certain violence of means here, and some partisan writing, but this is a study of genuine novelty and commitment, and a standard lesson in how materialist feminism might actually make a difference.

The above virtue of a forceful and gradually unfurled conviction is not, however, present in two further collections from this year. Here the surprise is a little muted and the novelty rather strained. Perhaps I have read too many such titles to expect great things from them, but in Beth Fowkes Tobin's *History, Gender and Eighteenth-Century Literature* (see also section 5 below) and Veronica Kelly and Dorothea von Mücke's *Body and Text in the Eighteenth Century*, the coherence that we are led to expect by the opening rationale is often rather token. Tobin provides the 'Introduction: Feminist Historical Criticism' and concentrates exclusively on American topics and writers, which ensures its only partial success. The project of interrogating any possible historicist model of feminism, and posing striking questions as to how to marry a political agenda with the desire to recuperate faithfully earlier feminisms, is described lucidly. Thereafter, Shawn Lisa Maurer supplies a piece on the *Tatler* and *Spectator*, Dianne Dugaw writes on Gay's Polly, Susan Staves on Fielding's 'Comedy of Attempted Rape', Jan Fergus on the marginal in Jane Austen, and then Joseph Lew more particularly on *Mansfield Park*. Of more general interest are seven essays more or less on challenges to canonical assumptions. Jill Campbell associates in her letters from Turkey 'Lady Mary Wortley Montagu and the Historical Machinery of Female Identity' and, in so doing, uncovers a distinctive voice, consciously exploring the exotic and forbidden with an eye for aesthetics and sexuality. More than most, Campbell does keep to the organizing rubric. Janice Farrar Thaddeus styles 'Mary Delany, Model to the Age' in her typical slavery to patriarchal assumptions. Married off when 17 to a 60-year-old (one Alexander Pendarves), Mary Granville's life is read alongside Clarissa's as an instructive example: Richardson's tragic narrative portrays characters capable of good intentions, 'too nice to be indulging in a flesh-trade' such as is found in this history. The eventual happiness derived from marriage to Swift's friend, Dr Patrick Delany, is almost providential. Beth Kowaleski-Wallace spends 'A Night at the Opera: Class and Art in *Evelina* and Frances Burney's Early Diaries' to help set up several correspondences between Burney's own beleaguered heroines and the artist herself, both involved in a process that Ruth Perry's focus on 'Bluestockings in Utopia' anatomizes – the creation of female utopias, in particular those described by Sarah Scott in her *Millenium Hall* (1762) and by Lady Mary Hamilton in *Munster Village* (1778). Both depict inherited wealth put to philanthropic use, and are an implicit reproach to slavery.

Beth Fowkes Tobin is interested in the economic 'discourse on agriculture' in her 'Arthur Young, Agriculture, and the Construction of the New Economic Man'. This emergent, ideologically loaded 'Man', such as the professional estate manager, is a type to set against the perceived weaknesses of an effete aristocracy. In Young's calculations of profitable land, and the energetic husbandry it required, a suitable masculine potency was captured and so defined. A similar deft linkage between discourse and the base is attempted by Kathryn Kirkpatrick in her 'Sermons and Strictures: Conduct-Book Propriety and Property Relations in Late Eighteenth-Century England'. Dwelling on Fordyce's *Sermons* (1766) and Hannah More's *Strictures on the Modern System of Female Education* (1799), there emerges a strange proprietorial relationship between women and their reputations. Large digressions into wide questions of capital and class make this an ambitious and rather long-winded affair, and we get to the point that middle-class women saw emancipation as an exclusive affair well before the actual conclusion. Finally, Mitzi Myers unearths some unexpected material on More and her circle in '"A Peculiar Protection": Hannah More and the Cultural Politics of the Blagdon Controversy', and hopes that More's Sunday School work might best be seen in relation to the female Evangelical movement and the divided loyalties it fostered, not least in More herself. In all, this is a collection containing several model materialist essays, but also some rather puzzling inclusions, where the full implications of a link between materialism and gender studies is left rather unresolved.

The same could be said of Kelly and von Mücke's *Body and Text in the Eighteenth Century*. An excellent attempt at explaining how 'body' could be both figurative and visceral at the same time in the editors' introduction is taken up by several contributors – indeed, challenged and extended by some – but as an overriding principle it has to be remarkably capacious to include quite as many emphases as are represented here. Still, one cannot look always to compilations for the cohesion of single-authored monographs, and there is a fine variety of examples. Starting off part I, 'Discursive Shifts and Realignments', Elizabeth Heckendorn Cook nods towards Foucault more than once in an exciting essay principally on Montesquieu's *Persian Letters* (1721), 'The Limping Woman and the Public Sphere', which takes up the figure of the deformed woman as indicative of the anonymous author, open to an unforgiving gaze. Whilst not a literature essay itself, it is a model of how the application of Foucault's remarks on the body (from *Discipline and Punish*) can lead to a most unformulaic set of conclusions. Neil Saccamano writes an entertaining piece on wit in Sterne and as defined by Addison ('Wit's Breaks'). For Sterne, the exceptions are far more enlightening than the rules, but Addison is rather more taken with negative examples, 'false wit', than with any clear sense of what the polite and so familiar might be. For Addison, the entangling of witty transformations with bodily miscegenation tells us much about the economy of form and taste that he strove to inculcate: what he pitchforked out the front door crept inexorably in at the back. We return to Swift's unconscious in Veronica Kelly's 'Locke's Eyes, Swift's Spectacles'. For Locke, the conscious self affected all sallies at comprehending the textual self; what we comprehended with our judgement filtered and graded what we felt about ourselves. As Kelly puts it, using Johnson's *Life of Swift* as the main example, 'the task of biography . . . is to hold the subject, who is after all only a virtual image, within a moral code that is extrapolated from the law of optical perspectives and that suffers from marginal aberrations caused by the body'. Johnson fought with his own fear of madness in reaching the chapter where Swift's final dementia had to be understood, and found that a clear perspective needed subjective intervention where he had thought that impartiality was the only reliable mode. Kelly's point is taken well before she comes to a close.

In part II, 'Technologies of Seeing', Peter de Bolla looks beyond 'The Charm'd Eye' to demonstrate how seeing was culturally taught, using William Shenstone's gardens at the Leasowes and his own 'Unconnected Thoughts on Gardening' as his main texts. Far from expecting some tourist influx from the heritage industry, Shenstone anticipated the interested gaze of improvers like himself, whose 'visuality' incorporated the immediate penetration of the 'male' glance, followed by the softer, more yielding satisfactions of contemplation. Deidre Lynch holds in view 'Overloaded Portraits: The Excesses of Character and Countenance'. For Lynch, facial detail, its 'overloaded' appearance, derived from the subject's age, experience or even deformity, and often marked a clear generic boundary – that unplatonic marks were basically popular, the hallmark of the caricaturist. Examining Hogarth's thoughts on character in art and the Royal Academy's advice on how to leave well enough alone in portraiture, in order to avoid a descent into lampoon, Lynch extends this eighteenth-century dilemma into matters of theatrical performance, namely, Garrick's habit of the 'grimace', which excited so much rapt attention. Finally, amongst the more English subjects, there is Tassie Gwilliam's 'Cosmetic Poetics: Coloring Faces in the Eighteenth Century', which traverses the popular and academic in the matter of cosmetics: unofficial delight at almost Ovidian transformation meets moralistic pronouncements on distinction and worth.

If the above studies promised and, on the whole, delivered fresh views on gender, there is one offering that is an unexpected success: Betty Rizzo's *Companions Without Vows: Relationships Among Eighteenth-Century British Women*. This is an approach which can be taken either as not touching on literary matters at all or as informing all literary depictions of women. From domestic companions to genteel mistresses to scheming false friends to independent-minded confirmed spinsters, Rizzo traces a variety of female society. Especially of interest to Augustan specialists might be the third chapter, 'Satires of Tyrants and Toadeaters [richly left women who did not wish to share their wealth]', where the fates of Sarah Fielding and Jane Collier are discussed at length. Lucid and effective without preaching, this is a study that gradually depicts a quite alien sexual climate, and also the plights of many whose choice of life was constantly opened up to vilification. This could be read alongside Lawrence Stone's *Broken Lives: Separation and Divorce in England, 1660–1857*, in part a continuation of his earlier *Uncertain Unions* (*YWES* 73.279), both of which remind us of how unromantic the technicalities of marrying and separating could be. Proceeding by means of several case studies, Stone depicts how unequal the realities of marriage could be for women of each social class.

This year's studies in fine art have provided the best cultural criticism of how gender portrayal ran deep within many apparently dissociated discourses. In Gill Perry and Michael Rossington's collection, *Femininity and Masculinity in Eighteenth-Century Art and Culture*, there is a concerted bid to render what could have been an almost overwhelming subject as amenable to a textbook format. To a degree, they have proved successful; essays represent most commonly studied topics and those deserving of wider publicity. A tightly argued 'Introduction' by the editors proves a contribution in its own right and covers female education, sensibility and colonialist signs. Gill Perry uncovers the deeper structures in the academic female form of the 'Grand Style'; Wendy Wassyng Roworth extends some of her recent work on Angelica Kauffman to take in a fascinating variety of painterly and sculptural styles where nudity is concerned; Colin Cunningham examines the architectural designs of Robert Adam to display how the new creation of the private domain affected gender roles; Duncan MacMillan finds history painting undergoing some radical reform in the work of Gavin Hamilton, where the example of Lucretia inspired the provision of a new breed of female heroes; Wendy Frith comes at her subject, Lady Mary Wortley Montagu, in a variety of ways. Using a monument to her at Wentworth Castle as the focus, Frith analyses several examples of Montagu's transgressions, and her novelty of outlook in the depiction of the exotic in her usually unsung *Turkish Embassy Letters*; and Susan Khin Zaw treads familiar ground by building on the widespread antagonism felt by Wollstonecraft in her *Vindication* for Burke's *Reflections*. Zaw teases out a further critique of his *Philosophical Enquiry* – its appropriation of 'sensibility' for a masculinist agenda. The result is genuinely revisionist, and should provoke further work (and possible disagreement). Chloe Chard provides a combative piece on the hidden agenda of several commentators on classical male sculptures.

If collections such as this excavate quite unexpected material about how far assumptions could be shared in the sister arts, then it would be as well if literary scholars took heed of visual culture very much more than is usually the case. In Marcia Pointon's admirably detailed *Hanging the Head: Portraiture and Social Formation in Eighteenth-Century England* and David H. Solkin's *Painting for Money: The Visual Arts and the Public Sphere in Eighteenth-Century England*, there are many cultural assumptions about the period in common with literary approaches: that the new market economy assailed ideas of public virtue; that the London art market created its own ecosystem of dealers and hacks, and that apparently mimetic touches drew in discursive associations actually constructed by a gradually self-conscious and self-regarding bourgeois preöccupation with ownership and the commodity. This we knew already, and in Solkin's case there is little else (especially after John Barrell) to report. His ranging of Shaftesburian civic humanism with Hutcheson and Hume's ideas on fine feeling on one side, with an almost Grub Street populism on the other, is deftly expressed, but little extra new information on the art scene is advanced. It may seem churlish to mention it at this juncture, but one glance at Lawrence E. Klein's *Shaftesbury and the Culture of Politeness: Moral Discourse and Cultural Politics in Early Eighteenth-Century England* (see below, section 3) and Paul Monad's succinct 'Painters and Party Politics in England, 1688–1732' (*ECS* 26.367–98) would have indicated that a term such as 'civic humanism' does not quite render the full and contradictory complexion of early-century culture. Pointon, however, reads a myriad of carefully argued conclusions from the minutiae of portrait fashions. Commencing with a revealing opening chapter on 'Spaces of Portrayal' and the business of a portrait painter in the 1780s, she tackles matters of likeness and genre, and the collection of sculptured heads, rather as a cultural historian, without ever forsaking historicist values. The second part of the work, 'The Portrait and its Subject', leads Pointon to consider what the preoccupation with wigs tells us about the sitter and also how Lady Wortley Montagu's Turkish adventures were suggested (politely) in her portraits. All in all, this book goes about its work quietly and thoroughly.

In Stephen Copley and Peter Garside's *The Politics of the Picturesque: Literature, Landscape and Aesthetics since 1770*, the virtues of interdisciplinary research are clearly demonstrated. The collection offers to update the generic investigations of Hussey and Hipple – not a bold undertaking, one might have concluded, as they hail from 1927 and 1957 – and replace them with a more materialist investigation, to 'provide a comprehensive theorization of the Picturesque aesthetic'. To a large degree, this is exactly what the editors have achieved. There are essays that can be categorized within the age-old disciplinary formats, yet they are in the minority. The most ambitious projects can be found in David Punter's 'The Picturesque and the Sublime: Two Worldscapes' and David Worrall's 'Agrarians against the Picturesque: Ultra-Radicalism and the Revolutionary Politics of Land', both of which move effortlessly between the volume agenda and their own. Punter centres his own investigations on aspects of framing, which open out from a Jungian perspective brought into temporal focus (momentarily) by Blake's 'The Tyger'. How do we frame? Is it ultimately to validate all frames or to undermine all such by ironizing their use? This 'discourse of boundaries' places the picturesque on one side of the divide (the quest for apt renditions of a personal view) and the sublime on the other (a rejection of all limitations of choice where the 'frame of conscious experience' is itself threatened). The shaping imagination is a contradiction in terms if the latter perception is explored. The conclusion in which nothing is concluded (sorry, framed) is an attempt at enacting what Punter is at pains to point out: that the very impulse to supply boundaries is at best only an arbitrary one. For Worrall, using an alternative methodology, such critical divisions seem very much a side issue. The opening contention that 'Land is the basis of the Picturesque' leads to the introduction of the ideas of Thomas Spence, that violent redistribution of land be a political reality, and their application (via Bate's 'green' criticism) to Wordsworth's ideas. In a largely Romantic volume, it is heartening to see studies that derive many of their conclusions from the consideration of a continuity with earlier ideas.

Stephen Daniels and Charles Watkins question the prejudice against Price's aesthetics (that it was merely a matter of decorative display) with a thorough and lucid examination of how in practice considerations of estate management weighed heavily in the balance, a model for practical improvers. Stephen Copley similarly revises our estimate of Gilpin's picturesque theories by tracing how influential he was in formulating a particular kind of tourism and thus also how the aspect of economic activity in the landscape could be evaded. In just one instance, the necessary description of Seathwaite's black-lead mine in the Lake District, Copley lifts the veil on how Gilpin's perception of the ugly yellow disfiguring of the view by the mine involves an affective transcendence as well as a refusal to observe the actual categories of human land division he perceives. Michael Charlesworth approaches Rievaulx Abbey through the prescriptions formulated in Thomas Dunham Whitaker's *A Series of Views of the Abbeys and Castles in Yorkshire* (1820) which he then compares with Arthur Young's *Six Months' Tour* (2nd edn, 1771). The result is a varied and detailed test of the relative status awarded perception of an archetypal picturesque site. Ann Bermingham involves us in the female fashion industry in order to demonstrate how interchangeable picturesque terms could be in fine art and matters of dress. Her analysis includes Price and Gilpin but rapidly moves on to Austen and Burke, and supplies an excellent summary of how concepts of the fashionable were inextricably bound to the aesthetics of nature. For Vivien Jones, in a sensitive and engaged application of Wollstonecraft's critique of Burke, the evasion of such aesthetic labelling is exactly the project of three novels: Charlotte Smith's *The Old Manor House*, Sydney Morgan's *The Wild Irish Girl* and Austen's *Mansfield Park*. The 'decadent libertine aesthetic' of the picturesque is embraced in the first two, but its offer of relativized subject positions in Austen's work is 'ruthlessly minimised'. Peter Garside deals with Scott's *Guy Mannering* in terms of its project of defining figures in the landscape both sharply and as foci of their own. John Whale looks at 'Romantics, Explorers and Picturesque Travellers' with an eye for the peculiarly Romantic desire to escape through travel and how this supposed autonomous realm may be threatened by those items that it strives to accommodate.

In Gilpin's and Payne Knight's work, there is a split between an admiration of the 'roughness' at the heart of the picturesque and an anxiety that it disturbed all categorization. The result is 'aesthetic consumerism', and an art of popular evasion, even eventual cosiness, that often returns the traveller to his or her preconceptions rather than the real origins of the view, in picturesque energy. This reflection also informs Raimonda Modiano's 'The Legacy of the Picturesque: Landscape, Property and the Ruin', which glances once again at the pastoralism in rustic depictions. Taking a lead from more avowedly psychoanalytical models (Freud, Melanie Klein), Modiano lays bare the ideological trick of finding the destitute to be sturdy beggars, self-sufficient and unknowable. In fact, they are often projections of narcissistic ego ideals. Progressing to more Victorian topics, Anne Janowitz provides a 'Chartist Picturesque', and Malcolm Andrews a more allusive, even parodic, variety in 'The Metropolitan Picturesque'. Throughout this is a well-edited and often inspiring collection, a genuinely radical re-visioning. I might just tag on at this juncture David Morgan's 'The Rise and Fall of Abstraction in Eighteenth-Century Art Theory' (*ECS* 27.449–78), a provocative demonstration that the most liberal theories, aimed at the most democratic of goals, can founder once academies take over.

The attempt to cross boundaries is evident (clearly) in Barbara Maria Stafford's *Artful Science: Enlightenment Entertainment and the Eclipse of Visual Education*, an ambitious (and I am afraid not always clear) study of how a culture dominated by the icon could be supplanted by one subservient to text. The maturity awarded to verbal demonstration supplied a surplus of distrustful timorousness where the visual was concerned. Spectacle gave place to formulae, spectators to readers. Strangely enough, this process can be seen as both satirized and upheld by Hogarth, whose later work is both displayed and analysed by Ronald Paulson's third volume in his *Hogarth (Art and Politics, 1750–1764)*. This revision of his 1971 biography is extensive, but here works its way through rather sobering material: when Hogarth became a legend in his own lifetime, a text and no longer the powerful iconoclast.

2. Poetry

Murray G. H. Pittock's *Poetry and Jacobite Politics in Eighteenth-Century Britain and Ireland* is a formidable account of resistance to the process by which 'Revolution Politicks' mutated, as Pittock terms it, 'incrementally' into Whig history. He acknowledges the encouragement of Howard Erskine-Hill and that group of revisionist historians of Jacobitism who have been so industrious for more than a decade. Here he seeks 'to liberate eighteenth-century literary history', in a book that is a treasure trove of verse, non-canonical in every sense, and from the marginalized regions of a Britain being forged in the Hanoverian image, contextualizing the more familiar figures from Dryden to Burns and beyond who were engaged or at least implicated in the 'struggle for control of the language of authority'.

> The argument that Jacobite typology 'did not spring from an oral tradition' but was 'manufactured by educated men' ignores the mediated quality of many of these educated manufactures. Not only were balladeers used to provide an organized distribution pattern by Jacobite printers, but oral culture itself was already in a phase where it was naturally influenced by written culture: and that written culture itself (as in the case of the Scots vernacular revival) was defending its identity by attempting to enter and use both folk and popular forms.

Alert to every nuance, Pittock also incorporates those marginalized by Tory disaffection from the 'wee, wee German lairdie', so Swift and Johnson join Pope, Allan Ramsay, James Macpherson, and the hosts of lesser Scots, Irish or Welsh writers whose voices have been silenced by the victors' history. As Pittock concedes, 'This book may be accused of overestimating the force of Jacobitism. Much of the evidence adduced will be, by the nature of things, provisional, codified, uncertain. But there will be a great deal of it.' Indeed there is. The sheer weight and breadth of the materials Pittock commands speak for themselves; he makes no extravagant claims for those who would have called down a plague on both royal houses; and if there must be some doubt about the encoding of Jacobite 'cipher and allusion' in *all* the references to Greeks and Trojans he deconstructs, this is, overall, a persuasive work of revisionist literary history. So too, in its very different fashion, is Malcolm Kelsall's Freudian reading of 'Totemism and Totalitarianism: Pope, Byron and the Hanoverian Monarchy' (*FMLS* 30.329–40), which positions the two satirists as framing and defining 'the Hanoverian epoch . . . [since] it is the arbitrariness and indefinability of the divide between the speakable and the unspeakable which explains the evasions and confrontations of their rhetorical strategies'.

Pittock spends only a paragraph on Anne Finch, and even that links her both with Matthew Prior and with Mary Astell, another for whom 'the feeling of being an outsider by virtue of gender led to identification with the Stuart cause'. That leaves much more to be said, of course, and Charles H. Hinnant says it at considerable length in *The Poetry of Anne Finch: An Essay in Interpretation*. Two cheers are appropriate here. Such a monograph is the seemingly inevitable and generally welcome outcome of the enterprise which has foregrounded those female poets who survived so long on the margins of the male canon, and Hinnant certainly embraces the 'Tory feminist' agenda with the same earnest enthusiasm he brings to his textual analysis. That approach does have its virtues, particularly when it exemplifies 'the complexity of texts that might appear to be simple, or even commonplace in outlook'. For example, a chapter on Finch's 'Apologies for Poetry' concludes with a persuasive explication of 'Glass'. This neatly grounds Hinnant's thesis in 'the devices by which sensuous experience is converted into images or representations . . . [of] transparent pane, reflective mirror, drinking bowl, and spyglass or telescope'; it also gives the poet her due for an extraordinarily individual 'sonnet' that even her more recent champions have neglected. Yet such conjunctions are rare, and they tend to be overwhelmed by remorselessly wordy insistence on Hinnant's own version of 'perspective'. Few readers will need his guidance (let alone his parenthesis) on the point that 'If a major poet is defined as one who has produced a work of extended length and epic scope – like *The Faerie Queen, Paradise Lost*, or *The Dunciad* – then it is obvious that Finch is not a major poet.'

If Hinnant's study might thus have been improved by more vigorous copy-editing, Bernard Tucker could with profit have opted for a more interventionist interpretation of his role as textual editor for *The Poetry of Mary Barber, ?1690–1757*. This semi-facsimile edition of the 1734 *Poems on Several Occasions* – minus all but two of the collection's poems by other hands – offers a modest biographical introduction, a few diffident judgements, and light annotation. The consequence is a range of opportunities only half grasped, as when the irony in 'RATCLIFF's Genius . . . Heighten'd by Learning and Humanity' ('To Dr. Richard Helsham. Upon My Recovery from a dangerous Fit of Sickness') is glossed by a reference to the 'fashionable royal physician . . . referred to . . . disparagingly by Swift', which stops short of mentioning the well-known partisan joke that seems the basis for Mary Barber's allusion, namely, Garth's retort that for the overweening Radcliffe to found an Oxford library was 'as inappropriate, as for an eunuch to found a seraglio'. 'Without wishing to insult the intelligence of readers I have provided a number of footnotes [in fact they are endnotes] for mythological, Irish and other references', writes Tucker, but readers investing around £40 in this volume might wish he had been less courteous. Recently 'rediscovered', turn-of-the-century female verse is also the subject of 'Jane Barker, *Poetical Recreations*, and the Sociable Text' (*ELH* 61.551–70), in which Kathryn R. King explores Barker's poetry through its network of social contexts to remind other feminist critics that individual female writers could avoid stereotypical entrapment as isolated spokeswomen for patriarchy. Perhaps one of those to whom King addresses this word of companionable caution is even now preparing the retort that Barker's poetic 'recreations' might have been indulged precisely because they were contained within the extended 'family' of a coterie audience – and citing evidence from King's other article this year, on Jane Barker's most widely disseminated novel (see section 4 below).

Elsewhere Kathleen M. Oliver is more convinced than convincing about the steel in the backbone of a poem by Mary Barber's friend and countryman. 'Swift's "Mrs. Harris's Petition"', she proposes, is 'not as benign as the critics suggest' (*Expl* 52.iv.216–19); and Alexander Lindsay reports briefly on Portland manuscripts that contain 'An Unpublished "Character" [of a parvenu] by Matthew Prior' (*N&Q* 41.185–6); but the most sustained (and surprising) essay on poetry in the early years of the century is Carson Bergstrom's '[Thomas] Purney, Pastoral and the Polymorphous Perverse' (*BJECS* 17.149–63). Bergstrom makes no claims for the quality of the Newgate cleric's pastorals – 'the narrative borders on the inane . . . while his imitation of pastoral language . . . assaults the ear' – but he justifies the attention he gives to such versifying in a consistently thoughtful investigation of pastoral as 'a valid poetic form in which to explore the new Enlightenment emphasis on the importance of sense and sexuality in human affairs'. The interpolated pastoral of Thomson's *Summer* is one of Bergstrom's comparators, and that more gifted poet's *Liberty* is one of William Levine's subjects in a solid (and rather stolid) old-style historicist reading of 'Collins, Thomson, and the Whig Progress of Liberty' (*SEL* 34.553–77): *Liberty* certainly sprawls, but, according to Levine, in 'the allusive, compressed style of the Pindaric Collins succeeds in problematizing matters for which a more conventional, fully described blank verse narration . . . is not suited'.

Most of the canonical poets mentioned thus far are also represented in *Eighteenth-Century English Poetry: The Annotated Anthology*, edited by Nalini Jain and John Richardson. The apparent hubris of that titular article must have been chosen with marketing in mind, for the editors make no claims to definitiveness. On the contrary, theirs is a genuinely modest proposal; to introduce the poetry of 'a period which today is neither popular nor fashionable', aiming at 'students rather than scholars', including those beyond the geographical or cultural bounds of the 'British and American educated elites'. The anthology will therefore be of potential use rather than illumination to readers of this *YWES* chapter. That said, for a book aimed at young readers, whatever their country of origin, this is a curiously conservative selection. The three token female poets (Finch, Montagu and Leapor) are those who might have appeared in any pre-Lonsdale school text, the list of 'further reading' contains nothing published after 1984, and Pope is given over a quarter of the space available.

Pope's domination of scholarly attention is even more pronounced, though first mention this year must be accorded the two 1993 books devoted to one poem that arrived too late for review last year; Harry Solomon's *The Rape of the Text: Reading and Misreading Pope's 'Essay on Man'*, and Michael Srigley's *The Mighty Maze: A Study of Pope's 'An Essay on Man'*, astringent chalk to mild cheese. Anyone with more than a passing interest in a poem found so problematic for so long by so many may be persuaded to sample both books: they should read Solomon. Srigley offers an urbane, loose-jointed and often repetitive Ovidian reading that has much in common with the mode in which he believes the poem itself works, 'a conversation . . . something of the character of the serpentine walks that wound through the groves and wildernesses of Pope's own garden . . . [for] the ever-present garden . . . imagery of the poem . . . is the message, and the garden is the theodicy'. Solomon, on the other hand, engages in remorseless excoriation of the *Essay*'s 'deformation' by misreadings from Jean Paul de Crousaz in 1738 to A. D. Nuttall in 1984 (*YWES* 65.360), as slum clearance to clear the ground for his project to 'naturalize' the philosophical poem. Reactions to Nuttall provide a handy measure of the tonal and intellectual difference between the two books. According to Srigley, the 1984 'cross-examination is conducted with great skill, and . . . provides many valuable [if unspecified] insights'. Solomon goes straight for the jugular by turning back on Nuttall the latter's summation that Pope's *Essay* represents the 'nadir of Augustan poetry': 'If this is the nadir of modern criticism of Augustan poetry . . . [Nuttall] is simply giving a more audacious rendering of our logocentric impatience with ambiguity and our critical addiction to the vanity of dogmatizing.' There are points of agreement between the two critics, not least in their refusal to accept what Solomon condemns as the 'trivializing' corruption of (mis)readings which either dismiss the philosophy as irrelevant to the aesthetics or regret the philosophical fudges necessarily introduced by the poetry. But Srigley wanders amiably from chaos theory to *Metamorphoses*, like a defence counsel *on* the defence: Solomon challenges the validity of the trial and is forever on the offensive, as he marshals expertise in the history of philosophy combined with a formidable capacity to manipulate deconstruction theory, particularly in his superbly sustained argument that a 'thick' intertextual receptivity is necessary to make available again the glories of a poem beloved by Voltaire, Hume, Rousseau and Kant: 'With binocular irony, metaphor, and paradox, with a "darkly wise" epistemology, and with an eclectic methodology of middle-state Academic Skepticism, Pope brilliantly articulates the constituting dichotomy of all philosophical poetry.' No review within *YWES* bounds could do justice to Solomon's own 'thick' but lucid discourse, though that will be required reading for any subsequent critic of the *Essay* who wishes to avoid crossing swords with an impassioned champion whose relish for (very personal) critical combat even Pope himself might have approved.

This year there is only one paper devoted to Pope's companion *Essay*, and that is a very singular approach, though driven by commitment to dialogism. In 'Alien Voices, Ancient Echoes: Bakhtin, Dialogism and Pope's *Essay on Criticism*' (*PLL* 30.57–72), Mary Ellen Bellanca is so unswervingly determined to prove Bakhtin's applicability (despite his prescriptions) that she reaches far beyond the text, from the poem's 'various voices – internal and external, past and present – and in its subtle evolution through revision . . . [to] dialogue with both the ancient critical tradition and the "passionate communication" of Pope's day'. *Windsor Forest* and *Eloisa* are similarly represented by discrete offerings. Arthur Sherbo's note on 'Pope's "Fox Obscene": Some Precursors and Some Successors' (*N&Q* 41.187–9) is content to contextualize a 'striking image' in usages from Ovid to Goldsmith, but in 'Pope's *Eloisa* Reconsidered in the Light of Ovidian Disequilibrium' (*CML* 15.25–43), Katherine R. Allison works much harder with her Ovidian parallel, as she reads the poem's 'pendulum-like movements' against the *Heroides* to subsume both sympathetic and hostile responses to Pope's 'generic' yoking together of sexual innuendo and spirituality. She cannot, though, resist a coda on 'Abelard's mutilation . . . [as] a parallel to the deformity of his own small body, and Eloisa's . . . struggle for control over her passion . . . [as] a voice for his own unanswered longings', and thus revisits in a more familiar formulation the old chestnut of an issue Helen Deutsch explored last year in a thoughtful (if clogged) essay on Pope's lifelong manipulation of himself as the physical and rhetorical 'figure' of authorship ('The "Truest Copies" and the "Mean Original": Pope, Deformity and the Poetics of Self-Exposure', *ECS* 27[1993].1–26). Again in *CML* (14.167–81), Steven Shankman follows Abraham Cowley's lead to another classical model for another poem ('"Art with Truth Ally'd": Pope's *Epistle to a Lady* as a Pindaric Encomium') and to sympathetic identification between the poet and his androgynous model, here offered as an ameliorating guide to reader response. This is an ingenious mediation, combined with delighted analysis of Pope's technical brilliance, but neither its generic argument nor its specific explications seem likely to deflect hostile critics of 'male stereotyping' from condemnation of 'the kinds of difficulties that make [the poem] . . . a touchy one for modern readers'.

Advertisements for *Alexander Pope and his Eighteenth-century Women Readers* by Claudia N. Thomas (SIUP) promised another perspective, but it was unavailable for review. However, I did see '"Tis a sort of . . . tickling": Pope's *Rape* and the Mock-Heroics of Gallantry' (*ECLife* 18.59–74), the first of three busy essays from Richard Terry which together bear all the marks of another book in the making. Terry begins disarmingly – 'When a critic subtitles a recent article "Feminism and The *Rape of the Lock* Reconsidered – Yet Again," [*YWES* 72.257] another essay on the poem's treatment of women might seem likely only to cause fatigue' – but this disclaimer is the prelude to a stimulating analysis that squares the circle of Laura Brown's commodified *Rape,* unifying 'form and content by arguing that the poem's representation . . . articulates a pervasive male discourse of gallantry or "fair-sexing," a discourse that contains inherent mock-heroic properties'. Womanhood is here constructed 'through an uneasy coexistence of antithetical positions: of politeness and rhetorical brutality, of eloquently winning blandishment and sexual suggestiveness'. Terry's second essay, '"Ill Effects from Good": The Rhetoric of Augustan Mockery (with Illustrations from Pope and Fielding)' (*BJECS* 17.125–37), ranges even more broadly to extend consideration of such binary conjunctions into an Augustan 'habit of mind' which helps explain the rise and decline of mock-heroic burlesque. The 'crucial point . . . is that the dominant model for . . . parodic or mockwriting was not distortion or exaggeration so much as reversal'; virtue was defined by 'operation' rather than intention; good and bad (like wit and dullness) were bordering counterparts; thus 'Pamela's devotion to her "virtue" and Shamela's devotion to her self-interest are not true opposites, so much as a single behavioural pattern viewed from opposite angles.' By coincidence, the contradictory male apprehensions swirling around tea and Addison's 'tea-table talk' adduced in Terry's first essay also provide the exclusive concern for Beth Kowaleski-Wallace in a brisk essay that cites verse on tea by Motteaux, Cowper, and Young as instrumental in the 'cultural definition of womanhood' ('Tea, Gender, and Domesticity in Eighteenth-Century England', *SECC* 23.131–45).

Philip Mallett will not be deflected by such cultural materialist digressions. 'If Pope Be Not a Satirist' (*FMLS* 30.316–28) asserts an elegant, very traditional relevance in a *Rape* that 'stands somewhat apart' from the other satires because Pope 'chooses to undermine rather than insist on the binary structure'. Indeed, Mallett is boldly counter-revisionist enough to claim that 'perhaps the best way to read' the *Rape* is as a poem 'written by an adept to tease its young hero and heroine into the better understanding of the games people play'. And Mallett's is by no means a solitary voice. Robin Grove writes an equally enthusiastic (and often stylistically mimetic) appreciation of the canon, from *Rape* to *Dunciad*, on the older theme of constraint and licence, or 'Pope as the high Augustan . . . directing, spotlighting, orchestrating effects . . . [and] the other Pope, the Avignon contender, challenging authority and challenged by insurrection' ('Pope's Shaping Powers', *CR* 34.22–32); while Jacob Fuchs offers the third of the *CML* essays to assert the primary relevance of the ancients when he links the *Dunciad*'s dissection of contemporary teaching of classical literature – reduced to the mechanical operation of words – with science declined to categorization and history to antiquarianism in Pope's anatomy of commodification ('Words Alone: Pope on the Teaching of the Classics', 14.149–56). Laura Brown is once more taken (gently) to task for refusing to allow that Pope might have understood something of the economics that possessed him; but feminist theory *and* scholarship are disposed by Marilyn Francus to reject any such temporizing in a polemic against Scriblerian 'intensification' of the ancient misogynistic paradigm ('The Monstrous Mother: Reproductive Anxiety in Swift and Pope', *ELH* 61.829–51) as 'largely a function of the politics of literary culture, in which mass publication, literary paternity and female authorship are sites of conflict'. It is characteristic of the convolutions in the annual disputes that Francus should support her feminist argument by appeal to an exclusive polarity that even her older-fashioned antagonists might have thought discarded with the Saintsbury style of literary history ('The fear of these writers is that creativity and artistry reside within the imagination, which in the Augustan age lies within the female province'), and that James McLaverty, in 'Naming and Blaming: The Poetics of Mock Epic' (*Rev* 16.221–36) should give generous plaudits to Colomb's study of the mock-heroic (*Designs on Truth*, *YWES* 73.284) before admitting deep suspicion of new historicism and objecting to the extinction of comic seriousness in solemnity: 'Pope's satire [in the *Dunciad*] is more concerned to cast out than to blame, and laughter allows a sort of readmittance.' Other disputes rumble on – for example, A. D. J. Brown returns to his long-running disagreement with Felicity Rosslyn over 'Pope's Shakespeare' (*CQ* 22[1993].184–

6) – but calm descends as we move away from the major texts. Shef Rogers, 'An Attribution for *The Age of Dullness*' (*N&Q* 41.207–8), gathers evidence to identify William Popple III as the author of some hack verses subtitled 'A Satire. By a Natural Son of the Late Mr. POPE'; Kevin McCabe reproduces a mildly excremental parody not unreasonably ascribed to Richard West in 'West's Burlesque Imitation of Pope's Verses on his Grotto' (*Scriblerian* 27.1–2); and Michael Brennan reports on research into a newly discovered collection of manuscripts at Badminton House, which flesh out 'Pope's personal and literary contacts with one of the most influential and cultured groupings of noble women in England' ('Alexander Pope and the Somerset Family', *RES* 45.357–69). There is a tantalizing coda to this last paper, on an occasional poem inscribed 'Verses made by Mr. Pope' by one of the Somerset ladies who knew him well; but that is as far as the evidence goes.

Fakes are always worth their weight in forensic copy, and the journal *Angelaki* (1) devotes almost all the second issue of its first volume to an eclectic assortment of essays on one of the most celebrated in literary history. Nick Groom starts the ball rolling with a piece of Lyotardian theoretical virtuosity, 'Forgery or Plagiarism: Unravelling Chatterton's *Rowley*' (41–54), and he is followed by Jonathan Barry's straightforward account of how the earnest William Barnett's project, 'The History and Antiquities of the City of Bristol' (55–81), was blighted by the Chatterton affair. Michael F. Suarez SJ investigates Chatterton's shrewdness in 'successfully placing his work with seven different periodicals' during his short time in London, despite the disaster of an ineptly 'clever' overture to Dodsley ('What Thomas Knew: Chatterton and the Business of Getting into Print', 83–94). Paul Bains returns readers to rhetorical riddles by associating 'The Macaroni Parson and the Marvellous Boy: Literature and Forgery in the Eighteenth-Century' (95–112), and the trial of Dr Dodd, that same 'macaroni parson', is investigated by Randall McGowen for the light it throws on contemporary fears about economic consequences following 'Forgery Discovered: Or the Perils of Circulation in Eighteenth-century England' (113–28). John Goodridge then moves the literary focus into the next century with 'Identity, Authenticity, Class: John Clare and the Mask of Chatterton' (131–48). Finally, Nick Groom returns to review the six-volume *Thomas Chatterton: Early Sources and Responses* (*YWES* 74.284), and to his interrogation of slippery categories, in the observation that this modern venture in print, no less than the fictional layering of Peter Ackroyd's postmodern novel, 'is itself a part of the narrative of forgery, especially if that narrative is a plot to get into print'. The point is well taken, particularly in respect of volumes costing £295 for what Claude Rawson has described as 'no better than a set of Xeroxes'.

Another celebrated forger/plagiarist (or simply 'poet') shares space with two very different mid-century writers in S. H. Clark's *Mark Akenside, James Macpherson, Edward Young: Selected Poetry*. Any inexpensive text of these often-mentioned but little-read poets would be welcome, but this edition is a curate's egg of a benefaction. On the positive side of the balance, a sizeable part of *The Pleasures of the Imagination* is here, as are a respectable number of *The Poems of Ossian*, plus nine *Night Thoughts*, all with sprightly introductions and annotation. In the other scale, Clark's sceptically sympathetic overview of the 'poetry of sensibility' is too gnomic when condensed into six pages, and some textual information does not appear at all (for example, when, where, and why Clark departs from his 'usual' copytexts). It is therefore ironic that four journal essays on Akenside and Young positively bristle with bibliographical scrupulosity, though for most readers that will impact on the poetry at best tangentially. Robin Dix and Clyde Binfield, respectively, pursue their scholarly detective work (and a Quaker connection) in 'Mark Akenside: Unpublished Manuscripts' and 'The Pleasures of the Imagination: A Conundrum and its Context' (*DUJ* 86.ii.219–26 and 227–40). Robin Dix also collaborated directly with Trudi Laura Darby to explore 'The Bibliographical Significance of the Turned Letter' (*SB* 46[1993].263–9) in editions of Akenside, for what such errors tell editors about printing-house practice, and in the same issue of *SB* ([1993].270–82) James E. May marshalled evidence to hypothesize a collaborative enterprise between Young and Dodington, with the former's hand discernible in the printed version of his friend's work ('Young's Corrections to Dodington's *Epistle to Bute*: Evidence from the Yale Manuscript').

This year it is Gray as a scholar, beyond the poetry, who receives half the laurel from David Mannings in 'Jonathan Richardson, Thomas Gray, and the Genealogy of Art' (*JHI* 55.405–20): he too 'can claim pioneering status in the development of eighteenth-century taste' by virtue of categorizing paintings during his travels in France and Italy from 1739 to 1741. Elsewhere, there are extended notes on matters of textual detail in Collins and Johnson: John Bishop takes the *OED* to task and broadens the associations of 'genial' in two of the major odes ('The Genial William Collins', *ELN* 31.iv.33–40); while Nalini Jain, on 'The Vanity of Human Wishes' (*N&Q* 41.198–9), tracks 'China to Peru' to Glanvill's *The Vanity of Dogmatizing*, as an established collocation that signified the range of knowledge in all its forms.

Cowper fares much better, not least in James Sambrook's paperback edition of *William Cowper: THE TASK and Selected Other Poems*. If there is reason to be less than entirely happy about other editions this year, Sambrook's work provides a timely model of what can be done without sacrificing accessibility; indeed, of how accessibility can be enhanced by scholarship. The texts are secure, the annotation is tactful but full wherever necessary, and the 53-page introductory essay is Sambrook at his learned, lucid best. Yet the core of the canon is included: most of the anthologized favourites, some well-chosen Olney Hymns, parts of the blank verse translations, and (best of all) *The Task* entire. Even impoverished students will thus have no excuse for failing to turn back to the poems from Richard Terry's third, perhaps most important, and certainly most original essay on the century's mock-heroic. ' "Meaner themes": Mock-Heroic and Providentialism in Cowper's Poetry' (*SEL* 34.617–343) explores a mode moving towards 'gradual attenuation and diffusion' as satiric intent largely disappears.

Elsewhere the annotators are again at work in *N&Q* 41: Pat Rogers seems to encourage – but does not explicitly invite – a search for variants on one of *The Task*'s most famous lines (II.206) in addition to those he cites ('"With All Thy Faults": Cowper and Bolingbroke', 217); and Michael A. G. Haykn identifies 'Ossborn' – who could not be traced by King and Ryskamp – as a deacon of Sutcliff Baptist Church ('Thomas Osborn, an Eighteenth-Century Deacon in Olney, Buckinghamshire', also 217). Also in *N&Q* 41, David Chandler corrects Lonsdale on a 'memorable poem . . . clearly designed as a message of hope to political malcontents' printed in the *New Oxford Book of Eighteenth-Century Verse* as an original poem by William Taylor, when in fact it was one of the four versions of 'free translation' Taylor sent to various publications ('William Taylor's *The Vision* and its Source in Johann Gleim's Preussiche *Kriegeslieder*', 218–19), while E. W. Pitcher assembles a checklist and reproduces one poem ('The Summer's Evening') to support a brief and balanced survey of Edmund Rack, 1735(?)–87, an indefatigable contributor to contemporary journals and an occasional poet ('The Essays and Poems of Edmund Rack: Sources and Additions to the Canon', 211–17). That leaves only one, more substantial journal contribution to notice, a packed and plastic essay by Leith Davis on 'Birth of the Nation: Gender and Writing in the Work of Henry and Charlotte Brooke' (*ECLife* 18.27–47), which fortuitously returns this review of work on poetry to its starting point in marginalized, Celtic (and female) resistance to Hanoverian hegemony. In Henry Brooke's 'authorized' work, 'ancient Ireland is praised because it anticipated the virtues of Enlightenment England'. Charlotte, though addressing the same Anglo-Irish readership – and therefore, of necessity, doubly deferential – nevertheless contrives to affirm a very different agenda in her *Reliques of Irish Poetry* (Dublin, 1789), which concludes with her own verse-story 'Maon: an Irish Tale'. The *Reliques* in fact asserted that 'Irish poetry had its own character long before interaction with England', and in the reversal of normal gender roles for Charlotte's 'Tale' is 'demonstrated a cultural nationalism more sensitive to issues of difference. As a woman and as the daughter of Henry Brooke, she was acutely aware of marginalization and silencing.'

3. Prose

There is little doubt that Swift's politics still stirs critical judgements. In the two most extensive studies of Swift's work this year, political loyalties are taken to be an index of the more aesthetic and moral Swift. For Warren Montag, in his *The Unthinkable Swift: The Spontaneous Philosophy of a Church of England Man, 1688–1730*, a wealth of inconsistencies lie in wait for all those who conclude that Swift merely espoused the centrality of a 'balance of power' in the public realm. What about his praise of Charles I (the most painstaking opponent of 'the will of the people') taken together with his portrayal of the venial Hanoverians as cruel despots? Montag discovers this contradiction deep within Swift's religion: 'But how do we explain, in the light of his apparent denunciations of absolutism, [his] lifelong attempts to restore the Church to what it was . . . and could only be as an apparatus of an absolutist state?' This is not a new observation, and Montag's sketch of such a context in his opening chapter is rather introductory. He is surely correct in pointing to Sancroft's influence as a fundamental one, and that many such Tories were similarly divided in their aims. No, the value of the book is on account less of its biographical information than of its deployment. He gets to the reading that formalists have long asserted, that Swift's irony was symbolic of an intolerable impasse, armed with careful religious distinctions. This is truest of the chapter on the *Tale*, where 'All is Meer Outside' puts an original spin on what materialism meant to Swift, a persistent fear of the natural, that links it to *Gulliver's Travels* – all of a piece throughout. Despite its rather introductory format, which is very selective in its test cases (no great emphasis on Swift's Irishness), the sensitive reworking of Althusser's concept of just what a 'spontaneous philosophy' might be is a genuine contribution to the Marxist debates on the literary and religious within a divided ideology, and consequently to a comprehensive review of political issues in Swift's writings.

Certainly, if Montag's work suffers a little from a lack of ambition, then it could be argued that Ian Higgins's *Swift's Politics: A Study in Disaffection* provides the opposite: a powerful, yet rather overstated, claim that all roads through Swift's kaleidoscopic work are eventually Jacobite ones. Certainly, Higgins never believes that there is a formal belief in Jacobitism there in the background, but in roughly the same spirit as Montag, he rather depicts Swift as spontaneously Jacobite, hankering after the terra firma (notional and increasingly utopian, alas) of a seamless metaphysics of power, rather than the pragmatic politics of actual rule. As Higgins himself makes clear, his close and instructive readings of Jacobites such as Lansdowne and high churchmen such as Sancroft provide only an 'association' with Jacobitism, not proof positive. Despite consulting some new manuscript sources and applying them plus comprehensive contextual studies in his two ingenious and intelligent chapters on the *Tale* and *Gulliver*, Higgins never quite gets Swift to cough up. We learn how fashionable Jacobitism could be throughout Tory ranks, and also how Swift waxed nostalgic about Queen Anne's reign, but there is still some doubt as to where the full political character, spontaneous or not, actually lies. On a considerable plus side, Higgins supplies succinct and often sparkling reviews of a range of ideological perspectives from Swift's context. There is also material for all those working on his fellow Scriblerians.

In *The Converting Imagination: Linguistic Theory and Swift's Satiric Prose*, Marilyn Francus manages to supply a novel and refreshing approach to how Swift set about encoding meaning. Francus's comprehension of knotty linguistic controversies and their pertinence for literary matters moves from a careful investigation of how Swift actually encountered linguistic theories in formal education at a formative age (Kilkenny and Trinity, Dublin), as well as those on Locke from his own reading, to how our own linguistic premises form (and perhaps obscure) our investigations into Swift's creation of meaning. Early translation exercises would seem to have altered Swift's own sense of how the self could be fashioned, and thus of how implicit rhetorical devices to stabilize meaning could be achieved. And yet . . . Francus's author is also acutely aware of how his own stated notions could be perverted by this same translatability: 'Linguistic communication is therefore an endlessly recursive spiral in which writing initiates reading, and reading instigates writing, causing textual authority to be established, usurped, reestablished, and usurped ad infinitum.' This is familiar enough as a conclusion, and Francus does go down the same road throughout this study, sometimes to the detriment of some of her textual criticism. Her notion of the 'rhetoric of satire' derives almost exclusively from her psychoanalytical approach, and receives less support than it should from sideways glances at satirical tradition, especially readings of Erasmus and Montaigne.

Joseph McMinn has provided us with a welcome array of illustrative matter (engravings, paintings, watercolours and maps) in his *Jonathan's Travels: Swift and Ireland*, which 'describes Swift's experience of Ireland'. Here is no heavily theorized anatomy of Irishness *à la* Fabricant, but rather a straightforward account of just what formed Swift's hybrid form of affection for his own Ireland. It is no scholarly blockbuster (and it was not intended so to be), but rather a genuinely informative survey, for which Swift enthusiasts must be particularly grateful.

Aside from *SStud*, this has been a rather thin time for Swift essays. Felicity Rosslyn supplies a lucid exploration of 'Deliberate Disenchantment: Swift and Pope on the Subject of Women' (*CQ* 23.293–302). Here, 'disenchantment' means the undoing of a spell, Swift's instinct for resisting all forms of seduction by demonizing its source. The essay is rather more on this tendency in Pope, but there are suggestive comments on 'Cadenus and Vanessa' and 'The Lady's Dressing Room'. In the same number of *CQ*, there is reproduced its prize essay (chosen from those dissertations submitted for Cambridge finals) on 'Johnsonian Biography and the Swiftian Self' by S. P. T. Keilan (23.324–47). In the main about Johnson's *Life of Swift*, the essay is remarkably mature in its history of Swift mythography, and then moves to a deft application of Said's theories of Swift as Tory anarchist in his reading of the *Verses*. Clive Probyn revisits Swift's excremental figures in 'Surfacing and Falling into Matter: Johnson, Swift, Disgust, and Beyond' (*Mattoid* 48.37–43), and also assesses Johnson's (and others') fascinated rejection of Swift's 'materialism'. Richard Terry's 'Swift and Lying' (*PQ* 73.243–65) takes the long and wide view (Sidney and other early modern apologists for imaginative fiction) on Swift's indulgence in counterfeiting. Lying is 'one of Swift's salient thematic topics', in that he realizes that literature is near neighbour to lying, and part of his 'robust and uncluttered counterpointing of truth and falsehood'. Terry is very good indeed on *Examiner* 14 and *Gulliver*, but any revisionist grasp of the straightforward Swift must fumble whenever it demonstrates his 'uncluttered' procedures.

Marilyn Francus seems to be treading extremely familiar ground in her 'The Monstrous Mother: Reproductive Anxiety in Swift and Pope' (*ELH* 61.829–52). The monster of fertility seems alive and well before Mary Shelley, but this is not as hand-me-down as it may appear. Francus extends this set of figures into far wider issues, such as how both Augustans regarded the 'feminization' of literature. The study mainly draws its examples from *The Battle of the Books*, where Swift is concerned. Mass reproduction threatened authorship (as Walter Benjamin believed of much later ages), and Swift habitually saw this as both figurative of gendered fecundity and a regrettable effect of printing. Sarah Wintle writes lucidly and succinctly of book IV of *Gulliver*, in her 'If Houyhnhnms were Horses: Thinking with Animals in Book IV of *Gulliver's Travels* ' (*CR* 34.3–21). Wintle examines Swift's actual experience of horses in order to lay bare some of the basic information his readers would have had and thus how seriously he predicted the basic hypotheses of book IV would have been regarded. Veronica Kelly approaches Swift via Johnson's *Life*, in her 'Locke's Eyes, Swift's Spectacles' (in *Body and Text in the Eighteenth Century*, eds Kelly and von Mücke), and advances some basic and original ideas about eighteenth-century biographies in general: how 'Locke's introspective empirical philosophy invents the subject of consciousness in the optical metaphor of the reflexive "I" '. Johnson hangs much of his account of Swift's life on metaphors of seeing (his refusal to wear glasses, for example), and often (given his concern with the later madness) on the physical spectacle of how he is seen. Neil Saccamano also takes up the difficulties Swift seemed to have with the figurative in his 'Knowledge, Power, Allegory: Swift's Tale and Neoclassical Literary Criticism' (from *Enlightening Allegory: Theory, Practice, and Contexts of Allegory in the Late Seventeenth and Eighteenth Centuries*, ed. Kevin L. Cope: see also section 5 below). A prevalent subtext of Swift's work is his pervasive anxiety about the paradigm of the plain text, and how it itself provoked rather enigmatic allegory: 'allegorical personification makes meaning visible but only in a recognisably figurative way'. The nub of Saccamano's argument is contained in the one word 'recognisably', for Swift digs deep to root out structural or other implicit figuration. Although not directly on Swift, there is a suggestive account in the same collection of the varied definitions of allegory (and some that challenge Rosemund Tuve's longstanding dicta) in Thomas Maresca's 'Personification versus Allegory', where there are plentiful examples from the *Tale* and *The Battle of the Books*.

SStud continues its invaluable work, and provides, as has become usual, a mixture of bibliographical and interpretative essays. There are four detailed accounts of poetic rediscoveries. A. C. Elias Jr, John Irwin Fischer and James Woolley all combine to give us 'The Full Text of Swift's On Poetry: A Rapsody 1733' (*SStud* 9.17–32), a restoration of the longer 1762 text after the common currency of the shorter 1735 version. There are also illustrations of salient pages with a list of variants between the two editions. A. H. de Quehen's 'St Patrick's Verses by Jonathan Swift' (9.42–50) is an involved investigation of how Swift's way with political and nationalistic myths might illuminate a work such as 'Verses occasioned by the sudden drying up of St Patrick's Well'. K. Richard Wade provides an intelligent reading of *Cadenus and Vanessa*, which contrasts throughout, formally as well as thematically, Swift's desire for poetic delight with a realist's knowledge ('Of "Weighty Arguments" and "Rational Delight": Swift's Comical Strategy in *Cadenus and Vanessa*' [9.65–75]), and then Hermann J. Real considers '"The Most Fateful Piece Swift Ever Wrote": The Windsor Prophecy' (9.76–99), in a reassessment of the 1711 context that goes some way to explaining just why Swift turned his hand to such a scurrilous piece. There are three bibliographical notes. Joao Fraes inspects 'Additional Passages in Swift's Letter to William Pulteney, March 1737' (9.33–41), in which he also recovers detailed comments on England's policy in Ireland from the Gratz MS found in the Historical Society library of Pennsylvania that were not included in the final missive reproduced in the Williams edition (transcribed from the British Library copy). James O'Toole locates 'A New Book from Swift's Library' (9.113–17), namely Hugo de Groot's *De iure belli ac pacis libri tres* (1670), uncovered from St Patrick's College in Tipperary, and Michael Dinning supplies 'Swift in Russia: An Annotated Bibliography I' (9.100–12). The most expansive contribution comes from Patrick Reilly ('A Mighty Impotence: The Satire of Swift', 9.51–64), who ranges far and wide to gain sufficient purchase on Swift's pervasive trope of suggesting matters too deep or emotional for mere words.

This year saw the completion of Bruce Redford's edition of Johnson's correspondence, with volumes IV and V (*The Letters of Samuel Johnson*). The undertaking has been a massive and timely one. New letters have come to light (although previously hinted at in scattered notes, it is useful having them collected), and new light has been shed on darker areas of Johnson's personal as well as literary relations. Volume IV covers the years 1782–4, prefaced by a reproduction of a stern chalk drawing of the man by Thomas Trotter just before death. It serves as a grim reminder of the fortitude Johnson showed in these years not only in the face of his own mortality, but also in the face of his dwindling store of companions. For those who would want to eavesdrop on this private pain, I would recommend the letters of July 1784, signalling the decay of his always understated understanding with Hester Thrale. Volume V is one of *Appendices and Comprehensive Index*, the latter organized on thematic as well as biographical lines. The most helpful appendices are the listings of correspondents with dates of letters, and the tabling of letters of uncertain date (of which there are surprisingly few).

Everyman has published a new edition of *Rasselas* alongside Ellis Cornelia Knight's *Dinarbus* (1790). Lynne Meloccaro's editing has been kept to a minimum – few notes, basic text – yet the juxtaposition is of some interest. There is a table of dates and bibliography for both writers, a rather unequal distribution which becomes clear when you actually read both works in rapid order. Johnson was penning a moral allegory that grew out of its original conception; Knight's work never quite departs from an oriental romance.

Pat Rogers's edition of *Johnson and Boswell in Scotland: A Journey to the*

Hebrides is one of those projects that must have seemed immensely promising at the planning stage: to combine an interleaved edition of Johnson's *Journey* on the right-hand page with edited (yet still generous) portions of Boswell's *Journal* on the left. There is sanction for this, as Boswell revised his text with Johnson's account before him, yet the end result appears confused, without any of the virtues of flexibility that a hypertext reproduction would promise. This 'stereoscopic' format hardly illuminates either text, as they were quite different undertakings in any case. Entwining them in this way actually discourages detailed consultation, I would imagine, but does help rather more casual remarking of differences, even if the Boswellian departures are in fact far less striking than we might have expected. While we peruse Johnson's *Journey* it might be helpful to have a periodical essay at one side, Martin Wechselblatt's 'Finding Mr Boswell: Rhetorical Authority and National Identity in Johnson's *A Journey to the Western Islands of Scotland*' (*ELH* 60.117–43). This is a sustained attempt to do two things: to put into interpretative practice Donald Greene's perception that Johnson's political views and his literary style were interdependent facets of his work, and then further to interrogate the *Journey* for any ironic shades of significance and subtext that supply an allegorical impetus to the account. Wechselblatt proceeds to isolate those passages where Johnson appears to separate the figurative force of his address to the reader and the depiction of Scotland in particular from the literal annal of his journey. He moves inexorably from journey to *Journey*, from the original motive for the undertaking (forgotten and contingent) to the literary categorization (discovered and visited on him by the need to write up his reflections for a reading public). Boswell thus becomes the pretext for the writing (his companionship was welcome) and his Scottishness a provocation of his nationalistic sensitivity. The result is a fascinating reading, powered by theoretical (deconstructive) concerns, but which is put to work in close reading and sensitive biographical interests.

Rather more valuable in the seminar room is Thomas Woodman's *A Preface to Samuel Johnson* in the Longman Preface series. Woodman's is a task that is particularly difficult to do well, and yet he is capable of the right balance of relevant comment and clear description. Part I, 'The Writer in his Setting', contains a full chronology and life. Part II on the 'Intellectual Background' is a reliable guide to Johnson and reason. There are further sections on religion, politics, commerce, happiness and language, and an attempt which veers a mite to the diagrammatic in the mapping of the literary background, but which furthers the cause of teaching Johnson successfully with detail and occasional inspiration. The 'Critical Survey' section is possibly the most helpful here. Lines 135–64 of *Vanity* provide a model illustration of the varieties of heroic couplet, there is a sympathetic, yet undemonstrative, reading of Levet, and there is an apposite choice of chapter XVII from *Rasselas* to depict Johnson as a dynamic moralist. All in all, this is a preface that for once is more than prefatory.

AgeJ 6, edited by Paul Korshin, has as its theme, 'Johnson and America', and it provides a very varied and always carefully prepared set of studies. There is hardly space here to do justice to Korshin's collection, but I might pick out five essays as a main focus. James G. Basker glances at 'Johnson and the American General Reader' (3–30) in a spirited attempt to rescue his subject from those who still regard him as the xenophobe. Taken in isolation, the occasional comments about convicts and lack of libraries that would seem to typify Johnson's relations with America can also be explained by his fear of cultural anarchy, on the one hand, and, on the other, as atypical given his other comments on the bases of cultural authority (*vide* 'Taxation No Tyranny'). Barry Baldwin tackles 'The Mysterious Letter "M" in Johnson's Diaries' (131–46), those entries for 10 January 1765 to 10 January 1766 in particular; taken together with J. D. Fleeman's 'Johnson's Secret' (147–50), this tries to decipher his liberal use of the cryptic letter to denote some irregular activity. Is this an oblique reference to masturbation, an offshoot of melancholia, as Donald Greene has ventured? Baldwin agrees that it has no single meaning, and is not convinced that it even has a sexual connotation, as he elsewhere uses euphemistic Greek to denote such matters. Fleeman is convincing when he finds it far more likely that it implies micturition, given Johnson's fascination with diagnostics. Mark E. Wildermuth goes out of his way to typify Johnson's prose style in his 'Johnson' s Prose Style: Blending Energy and Elegance in *The Rambler*' (205–36). Wildermuth sees a clear progression from *The Idler*, wherein Johnson grew to manage effects of grand generalization with the occasional disarming simplicity of domestic detail. His great desire was to combine elegance with energy, a mixed style which enacted a *concordia discors*. Finally, Thomas M. Curley's 'Johnson and America' (31–74) almost reinvents a pioneering spirit for his subject, involving a love for homeland and a distrust of imperialism and exclusive reasoning that bear comparison with the way early Americans viewed themselves. Kevin P. van Anglen casts new light on Johnson's religion by dwelling on resemblances to Milton's (if it indeed *be* his) *De Doctrina Christiana* ('"The Tories, We . . . ": Samuel Johnson and Unitarian Boston", 75–98); Stephen Swords finds Johnson as a ghostly presence in his 'Emerson and the Ghost of Johnson', which also has some interesting things to say about his relationship with Carlyle (99–130); Aaron Stavisky has Johnson interested in the location of man's essential goodness in 'Savage and the Noble Savage'. From 1744 to 1784 (and the *Life of Thomson*), there is greater toleration if less tragedy in his views.

In A. D. Horgan's *Johnson on Language: An Introduction*, I expected a rather more integrated survey of contemporary debates about the *Dictionary* and other lexicographical matters. Instead, we have here a study (based on undergraduate lectures) which proceeds almost exclusively from Johnson's own estimate. This is introductory material, true, but the guiding premise that Johnson observed in *Adventurer* 115, that language split into the poetic and the scientific, is hardly challenging. A good index helps the reader gain a more sophisticated grasp of several of the themes covered here, but we are hardly surprised at many of Horgan's conclusions, even if they are enthusiastically and lucidly expressed. For a more complex account of Johnson's evolution as a lexicographer, we would have to turn to Anne McDermott's 'The Defining Language: Johnson's *Dictionary* and *Macbeth*' (*RES* 44.521–38). Here McDermott supplies a warning about the misuse of illustrative quotations from the *Dictionary*. The sources Johnson quoted were not simply mouthpieces for Johnson himself, and therefore not to be 'picked up and transported, without modification, to another context'. This is especially true of his treatment of Shakespeare, for, whilst Johnson's work on *Macbeth* in particular predated the inclusion of *Dictionary* material, it did not mean that he simply transferred earlier work to the later. McDermott shows that Johnson's critical and analytical work on *Macbeth* was not a season's endeavour, but a process that took in his own edition of Shakespeare through to the fourth edition of the *Dictionary*. She also goes some way towards demonstrating that, in the more complex definitions, the definitions might gloss the quotations rather than vice versa.

Edward Tomarken's work on Johnson has always been interesting and theoretically ambitious. In his *A History of the Commentary on Selected Writings of Samuel Johnson, 1788–1993*, he offers an 'interpretive history' rather than a simple chronicle, in the service of a 'New Humanism' (a term of Ralph Cohen's) wherein literary criticism might be regarded as a genre in its own right, an 'attempt at conversation, an admission that humanity is historicized'. The result did not really need quite so many first principles. Proceeding by way of sections on most of the principal Johnson texts (the only striking omission being the *Dictionary* [again], and no consideration of biographical witness), Tomarken is comprehensive and has wide-ranging sympathies. It is especially welcome to have sections on *Irene* and the periodical essays. The organization by genre or work dilutes an account of another kind, namely, of more synchronic influences that cut across such boundaries and reflect more general estimates of Johnson himself. On the other hand, certain genres do have their own histories. *The Lives of the Poets*, for example, is a critical invention of recent times, especially the last thirty or so years, and the Shakespearian criticism is taken much less seriously over the same period.

More futuristic in its theoretical orientation is Charles H. Hinnant's *'Steel for the Mind': Samuel Johnson and Critical Discourse*. Like Tomarken, Hinnant writes in terms of 'dialogue', which more often than not is given a Bakhtinian spin. Instead of as finished and closed works, this means that Johnson regarded his writing as a series of 'performances', prefiguring particular audience reactions and the dictates of particular historical moments. Hinnant is particularly pertinent when attempting to deliver this less dogmatic (and Boswellian) author from his most dogged admirers, who require Johnson to be rather more cocksure than he actually was. The perceptions are original, and the writing combative yet also balanced in its generous quotation from alternative viewpoints. The four central chapters (2–5) provide a timely revision of hoary old numbers on Johnson's critical exclusivity, in examining his work from several perspectives that integrate (and explain) the eighteenth-century context with more contemporary critical concerns. The result is mutually illuminating: Johnson tests and furthers an examination of less mimetic modes of inquiry, and in turn a wide range of texts is read with an enhanced sense of audience and intertextuality.

Johnson's reputation, his regrettable status as a legend in his own lifetime, is well documented, yet in Howard D. Weinbrot's 'Samuel Johnson, Percival Stockdale, and Brick-bats from Grub Street: Some Later Responses to the *Lives of the Poets*' (*HLQ* 56.105–34) and then in his 'Censoring Johnson in France: Johnson and Suard on Voltaire: A New Document' (*RES* 45.230–4) there are new nuggets of information. The former concentrates on Stockdale's *Lectures on the Truly Eminent English Poets* (1807) and his *Memoirs* (1809), where his own love-hate relationship with Johnson flourished. In place of Johnson's quest for some universal standard for canonization, Stockdale's own *Poets* were there merely because they excited a response. The latter essay glances at a similar relationship with France, and volume IV of Suard's mixed translations, *Varietés Littéraires* (1768–9), wherein Johnson's severe estimate of Voltaire is excised and the *Preface to Shakespeare* is gallicized. Jean I. Marsden focuses on a similar confrontation between feeling and reason in her 'The Individual Reader and the Canonized Text: Shakespeare Criticism after Johnson' (*ECLife* 17.62–80). Johnson's balanced reasoning in the *Preface* actually confused his first readers, including George Colman. Marsden is at her best when drawing on the contradictions in Elizabeth Griffith's *The Morality of Shakespeare's Drama Illustrated* (1775) surrounding the conflicting claims of dialogue and fable, and thus of text and performance. This same nexus interests Jonathan Brody Kramnick in his 'Reading Shakespeare's Novels: Literary History and Cultural Politics in the Lennox–Johnson Debate' (*MLQ* 55.429–53). In this section of his thesis, Kramnick supplies a basic difference of opinion between Charlotte Lennox in her *Shakespeare Illustrated* (1753), whose paradigms were taken from ideas of novelistic probability, and Johnson's, who found plot to be of only secondary importance. The annotation is chunky and impressive, and this essay establishes Johnson as one who seemed well aware that the novel might have no literary status whatsoever. Proof that Johnson's criticism could deviate from official norms is also provided by Jessica Munns in 'The Interested Heart and the Absent Mind: Samuel Johnson and Thomas Otway's *The Orphan*' (*ELH* 60.611–23). Otway's work is a test case for how Johnson understood 'the discourses of desire', and in his *Lives* his 'domestic tragedy' is praised for its work upon the passions. Munns then contrasts this level of sensitivity with the tougher, more masculine themes of *Rasselas*. We conclude that Otway's 'passionate' play is excused not on account of some overriding textual power, but rather because it is in a lower literary sphere: that of 'feminized' desire.

An altogether less angst-ridden Johnson emerges from Gregory Scholz's lucid and timely 'Sola Fide? Samuel Johnson and the Augustinian Doctrine of Salvation' (*PQ* 72.185–208). Objecting to Donald Greene's seminal verdict that Johnson's Anglicanism was Augustinian in inspiration, that is, emphasizing grace by faith alone, Scholz knocks down Greene's understanding of eighteenth-century theology with disarming ease, and re-establishes a positive ideal of moral endeavour in its place, whereby the individual can still enjoy 'some measure of pre-lapsarian freedom and dignity'. The same spirit of revision imbues Pat Rogers's 'The Rambler and the Eighteenth-Century Periodical Essay: A Dissenting View' (*PSt* 16.116–29). Rogers finds W. J. Bate's determination to read Johnson's *Rambler* journalism as one long gloss to *The Vanity of Human Wishes* dangerously innocent of its generic signs as a paper. Far from a species of moral inquiry, the journal manifests clear signs of Addison's influence, and an evolving attempt to frame the expectations of the intended readership.

The Yale Boswell project has not been idle. An imposing research edition of *The General Correspondence of James Boswell, 1766–1769* (Volume I [1766–7]), ed. Richard C. Cole, with Peter S. Baker and Rachel McClellan, with the assistance of James J. Caudle, has appeared, and who could question its accuracy and impressive appearance of scholarly effort? As a research edition, as opposed to a reading edition, the annotation and range of reference are fuller, and only time will tell how it will alter our view of Boswell. There is another research edition provided in three volumes, the *Catalogue of the Papers of James Boswell at Yale University*, eds Frederick A. Pottle, Marion S. Pottle and Claude Colleer Abbott, which has been eagerly awaited. It is clear and informative. There are separate entries for each genre of document, the most numerous being journal, memoranda and letters.

A less critically intensive environment is provided by Roger Craik in his *James Boswell, 1740–95: The Scottish Perspective*, which has as its aim that of informing 'the school child in Auchinleck's Main Street' about one of its major products. Craik accomplishes his goal with a thickly illustrated account of the early Boswell especially, and then finishes with a sideswipe against Victorian estimates in his summation of 'Boswell and Scotland: The Legacy'. It is an accessible narrative, although an integral part of Boswell's personality was manifested in England. There is an interesting discovery by Philip Mahone Griffith in his 'Boswell's Johnson and the Stephens (Leslie Stephen and Virginia Woolf)' (*AJ* 6.151–64): that the Bloomsbury set could take to Boswell quite as much as to Johnson. In the same volume, Thomas E. Kinsella returns us to the *Life* with redoubled attention to Boswell's imaginative involvement with his subject ('The Convention of Authority: Boswell's Revision of Dialogue in *The Life of Johnson*' (*AJ* 6.237–64). With a fresh look at his drafts for the *Life*, Kinsella concludes that Boswell's desire was less with 'accuracy' than with 'authenticity'. Orrin N. C. Wang is hardly concerned with Johnson's speech at that remove in his 'The Politics of Aphasia in Boswell's *Journal of a Tour to the Hebrides*' (*Criticism* 36.73–100). Wang plays with the figurative expanse of Johnson's conversation as well as the expansiveness of its copious linguistic force – but only in order to isolate those moments in the *Tour* when conversation falters, and dialogue with those they meet stalls. When Wang gets into his stride, he is persuasive, but mostly there is so much contextualizing (in a sort of throat-clearing exercise) that we are sometimes led to expect a little more. Moments such as the failed conversation with the Erse woman and Boswell's amused withdrawal from the scene are mined successfully, yet the analogies with Anglo-Scots history seem strained. David R. Sorensen's 'Carlyle, Boswell's *Life of Johnson* and the "Conversation" of History' (*PSt* 16.27–40) attempts a colloquy across a century between Carlyle's view of historiography and Boswell's desire to create it in his biography. It helped me more with Carlyle than with Boswell. Donna Heiland has unearthed a correspondence between Anna Seward and Boswell during 1784, which points to a much greater warmth to their early relationship than is usually deduced from sources already published ('Swan Songs: The Correspondence of Anna Seward and James Boswell', *MP* 91.381–7).

Burke's *Pre-Revolutionary Writings* have been expertly edited by Ian Harris as one of the Cambridge Texts in the History of Political Thought, a series that is both clear to read and yet also informatively annotated. The text is supported by a 'Biographica' or biographical glossary and a full bibliography, plus indexes of both persons mentioned and themes treated. In short, it is a pleasure to encounter such interest in Burke's earlier work, and here there is a full text of *A Vindication of Natural Society*, the meat of the second edition of the *Philosophical Enquiry* and the seminal *Thoughts on the Present Discontents*. The *Reflections* have appeared in WC, edited unobtrusively and annotated succinctly by L. G. Mitchell. There is an appendix containing his *Letter to a Member of the National Assembly* (1791). Burke has also been well served by two stimulating and fruitfully argued monographs. Stephen H. Browne's *Edmund Burke and the Discourse of Virtue* tries to do many things with, and to, Burke's rhetoric. Browne is more convinced by the collections of themes than by a stable philosophy, and he comes up with a deliberately unfashionable thesis: that 'reading Burke as a rhetorical artist means making no apologies for his partisan motives'. The 'Discourse of Virtue' is captured in certain moments, and most usefully in genuine re-readings of the *Present Discontents*, his *Speech on Taxation* and the *Letter to a Noble Lord*. Burke's 'Virtue' is always 'an attribute of action', and gains worth from a community, from relationships, not from Stoic withdrawal. The end result is to reclaim Burke for serious liberal consideration – no mean feat. Richard V. McLamore takes this strange resemblance up in his ' "To Forge a New Language": Burke and Paine' (*PSt* 16.179–92). Paine's hope that the creation of a new discourse would eradicate error is described in an orthodox manner, but there are some firm links forged between the two antagonists, and a revelatory set of common allusions unearthed that help highlight distinctions and similarities. Mary Jane Corbett is unyielding in her search for Burke's favourite figurative recourse to family symbols throughout his work. Her conclusion is startling: his 'insistence on the importance of the family . . . has a double valence: not only is it necessary, along with the state, for the restraint of masculine "avarice, ambition, and sexuality", but it also provides a check on what would otherwise be the untrammeled forces of feminine sexuality'. This is then turned on Maria Edgeworth's *The Absentee* with detail and some eloquence, and both writers turn out to reinscribe a certain colonialist sensibility in the subservient Irish, which works to underpin empire itself ('Public Affections and Familial Politics: Burke, Edgeworth, and the "Common Naturalization" of Great Britain', *ELH* 61.877–97).

Addison may be making something of a comeback, or at least his involvement in the *Spectator* may. Charles A. Knight provides a short piece on 'The Spectator's Generalizing Discourse' (*PSt* 16.44–57), which gets under the skin of the rhythm of the prose, tracing a Lockeian progression always from the particular to the idealized. Knight also supplies a more extensive piece on 'The Spectator's Moral Economy' (*MP* 91.161–77), which alights on Habermas's concept of the public sphere to help illuminate the rather divided personae that infiltrate the paper, half respectful of the mercantile interest and yet mindful of their need too to make new money old rather quickly. Silences about the evils of mercantilism were evident, and in the place of a fuller account Addison pursued a veneration for the trader hero, who was given moral prominence for his active service for the community. This may seem standard stuff, but Knight knows when to apply close reading to wider issues. Timothy Dykstal's 'The Politics of Taste in the Spectator' (*ECent* 35.46–63) is similarly structured by Habermas (or maybe Eagleton's reading of him). 'Taste' becomes the watchword for all sorts of theatrical and creative metaphors, and then a most unexpected turn in the argument sees Dykstal use Addison and Steele against the materialism of both Eagleton and Hannah Arendt and the assumptions both make about eighteenth-century economies.

David Hume makes a welcome entrance as an essayist into the ranks of the affordable (and so prescribable) with Stephen Copley and Andrew Eager's edition of his *Selected Essays* for WC. This is a generous selection, sparingly annotated but with a full list of variants and original notes, and an up-to-date bibliography. The introduction could also have been longer, as it is an ambitious survey. Still, one could always prescribe it alongside Adam Potkay's *The Fate of Eloquence in the Age of Hume*, which is not as turned as other studies to the *Treatise* or the *Enquiries*, but rather to the *Essays*, that on 'Eloquence' in particular. Whilst eloquence had classical sanction, Hume and many others are shown writhing in its net; the new world would have to know when to dispense with it. Hume thus domesticates and popularizes it: 'Athens' sympathetic fire becomes the amiability of fireside conversation.'

The same star may well have reigned at the birth of Klein's *Shaftesbury and the Culture of Politeness*, which sees Shaftesbury, too, popularizing aristocratic perspectives, especially 'gentlemanliness'. Thus, the *Characteristicks* is subjected to a sustained ideological analysis, sometimes with a verve and depth I feel cannot have been Shaftesbury's. Klein occasionally jumps the rails and teams his protagonist up with Pocock's 'civic humanism' and 'virtue', and one believes Klein until one actually reads a lot of Shaftesbury – but I am prejudiced. On matters to do with his aesthetics, I favour more the ironic persona, and in Richard B. Wolf's 'Shaftesbury's Just Measure of Irony' (*SEL* 33.565–86), a fresh and timely look at 'raillery' helps Wolf create a liberal out to free the reader from rabid religious orthodoxy.

Lady Mary Wortley Montagu's prose has long been a connoisseur's delight, and rarely given an airing in undergraduate courses. With Malcolm Jack's edition of *The Turkish Embassy Letters* it is now a lot easier to demonstrate her variety and control. Often regarded as a footnote to Pope, she often writes wittier prose (I would stress, prose), and here, from 1716 to 1718, she appears at her best, alive to the exotic yet never overwhelmed. An entertaining essay by Anita Desai forms the introduction. My hopes were high for Cynthia Lowenthal's *Lady Wortley Montagu and the Eighteenth-Century Familiar Letter*, perhaps too high, as this is a largely descriptive venture, tying in the life with the letters in a lucid and careful manner. Lowenthal is very persuasive in drawing out Lady Mary's 'performative selves', and, I believe, covers genuinely new ground in her chapter on 'Reading, Writing and the Novel', which concentrates on the work from 1739 on. This period is also where Isobel Grundy takes up the story in her contribution on Lady Mary for *AJ* (6.321–46), 'Lady Mary Wortley Montagu's "Italian Memoir" ', which lasted from 1746 to 1756. It is a depressing tale, for here is not the transgressive role playing of the *Embassy Letters*, but a rather more prosy style, an enactment of 'silencing'.

Two very welcome contributions to our knowledge of the art of correspondence have also come to light. *The Early Journals and Letters of Fanny Burney* has reached volume III (*The Streatham Years: Part I, 1778–1779*), eds Lars E. Troide and Stewart J. Cooke. The annotation is readable as well as simply informative, and some new material is here published. There are also two appendices: an extended note that suggests strongly that Dr Charles Burney was proprietor of Gregg's Coffee House in Covent Garden from 1769 to 1784, and then Charles Burney Junior's lines on *Evelina* (full of tears and the softer passions). This edition coincides with volume III (1799–1804) of *The Piozzi Letters. Correspondence of Hester Lynch Piozzi, 1784–1821,* eds Edward A. Bloom and Lillian D. Bloom. It is handsomely produced, although a little lacking in annotation and introductory apparatus, but the material here unearthed, all in Piozzi's 'chit-chat language', is diverting and something to show those who still think she dwindled away after her friendship with Johnson had finished.

4. Novel

After a couple of decades in which scholar-critics have surveyed the new world of the novel from the heights of retrospection, Joseph F. Bartolomeo lets the eighteenth century speak much more clearly for itself in *A New Species of Criticism: Eighteenth-Century Discourse on the Novel.* First come the novelists' prefaces, Congreve to Godwin, then the commentators. What emerges with striking regularity is the way that writers and readers of the 'new species' – like playwrights and audiences at the turn of the sixteenth century – constantly encouraged and challenged each other into formulation and reformulation: Defoe, for example 'tangled in contradictions', or Richardson, moving chameleon-like through authorial personae, or Johnson content to live with the clash between what his receptive literary instincts told him and what his conservative morality demanded. (Eighteenth-century writers needed no professionalized theory to teach them 'Inconsistencies . . . cannot both be right, but, imputed to man they may both be true.') The second vivid memory readers will take from Bartholomeo is just how solidly univocal all this male heteroglossia became against threatening outsiders from the lower classes, or women of any caste. Charting the defensive lengths to which female novelists were driven begins, this year, with Kathryn R. King's analysis of a characteristically interpolated tale in Jane Barker's most popular fiction, 'The Unaccountable Wife and Other Tales of Female Desire in Jane Barker's *A Patch-Work Screen for the Ladies*' (*ECent* 35.155–72). We might dispute King's proposal that 'The Unaccountable Wife' has specifically 'protolesbian content' but be inclined to agree that where the modern feminist critic detects 'resistance to an oppressive masculinist order, the [contemporary] narrator sees a dangerous threat to the social system that depends upon continued subordination of the "lower orders"'. However, Ian Campbell-Ross builds a powerful case for a subversive Sarah Butler, whose *Irish Tales: or, Instructive Histories for the Happy Conduct of Life* deftly manipulated historical manuscript material to craft what now seems an unmistakable if coded account of Irish, Catholic, Jacobite resistance to English, Protestant, Hanoverian domination ('"One of the Principal Nations in Europe": The Representation of Ireland in Sarah Butler's *Irish Tales*', *ECF* 7.1–16). Here is added support, from fiction, for Murray G. H. Pittock's thesis about the century's marginalized Jacobite poetry (see section 2 above). In an age so sensitized to polemic garbed as historical fiction, it might at first seem remarkable that 'Sarah Barker ... [could write] an open history so challenging as to seem merely a romance with an unusual setting', but one possible solution to this puzzle might be extrapolated from an investigation by P. N. Furbank and W. R. Owens into the authorship and dissemination of a fiction published in London a year after the collapse of the 1715 uprising, 'A True Account of the *Proceedings at Perth*: The Impact of an Historical Novel' (*ECF* 6.233–42). The 'Account' was neither 'True' nor by Defoe (as some have claimed in our century), but *this* work of fiction, designed 'to make propaganda for the Septennial Act', was promoted by the Hanoverian press to such effect that even a recent historian of the Jacobite rebellion was persuaded to accept its 'eyewitness report' at something close to face value.

An Everyman edition of *A Journal of the Plague Year*, aimed at the student market, offers minimalist concern for scholarly matters but the novelty of an introduction by John Man, a writer and maker of documentaries on 'human endurance in extreme circumstances'. By contrast, Michael Shinagel fights the good textual fight through the thickets of Defoe printings, and to good effect, in the new (second) edition of *Robinson Crusoe* for Norton. He also persuades a clutch of eminent Defoe scholars to abridge their own previously published work for the extensive collection of 'Twentieth-Century Criticism'. The single new essay devoted to the same novel which I have found in the year's journals is Geoffrey M. Sill's psychoanalytical reading, grounded in a 'fusion of Puritan narrative and Galenic psychology ... [that] produced the fundamentals of psychological realism'. Galenic melancholy translates into Crusoe's Freudian 'punishment dream', and the goat-in-the-cave sequence ('one of the more puzzling hermeneutic problems of the book' to several of Shinagel's collaborators) into 'the completion of the Oedipal process, through which the child separates himself from the parents' authority' ('Crusoe in the Cave: Defoe and the Semiotics of Desire', *ECF* 6.215–32). Many other citations lead rather to post-colonial critics on Coetzee's 'radical rethinking of Daniel Defoe's desert island myth' (Peter E. Morgan, '*Foe*'s Defoe and *La Teune Née*: Establishing a Metaphorical Referent for the Elided Female Voice', *Crit* 35.81–110); but there would be no end to this review if all such increasingly decentred possibilities were pursued. Robert Markley takes us in the opposite direction with '"So Inexhaustible a Treasure of Gold": Defoe, Capitalism, and the Romance of the South Seas' (*ECLife* 18.148–67), though there is precious little romance in this determined Marxist approach to a dozen 1711 issues of the *Review* and *A New Voyage Round the World*, 'to investigate the complex relations among capitalism, ecology, and identity' seen in 'a more ideologically revealing form' here than in *Crusoe*. Markley concedes that these non-canonical texts are unlikely to attract readers and (perhaps unsurprisingly) seems disinclined to pursue the implication down a looming ideological cul-de-sac.

William E. Hummel begins more bullishly, confident about broadening the debate on the later novels beyond the 'joint Marxist and feminist axis' by applying a 'theory of gift exchange' ('"The Gift of my Father's Bounty": Patriarchal Patronization in *Moll Flanders* and *Roxana*', *RMR* 48.119–41), but his wordy survey of what 'the symbolic and real struggle that giving between genders reveals', in terms of 'the sexual aspirations and economic designs of Defoe's male characters', is more ingenious than illuminating. Lincoln B. Faller needs no such help from twentieth-century sociology to illuminate exchanges between the men and women who tell their criminal stories. To pun on the title of his earlier study, he turns his unrivalled knowledge of contemporary criminal narratives to good account for *Crime and Defoe: A New Kind of Writing*. This works its way into the heart of Defoe's fictions by exploring the many ways he 'sets his texts apart from and "against" the general run of criminal biography, indicates they are in need of interpretation, and opens them up to a variety of more or less "legitimate" meanings'. Readers were thus forced to confront the inadequacy of established simplification; and one of Faller's many achievements is the way he smuggles old-fashioned explication into a Bakhtinian concern for the templates against which contemporaries were reading. The result is ethically complex dialogism; indeed, when Defoe further complicates things by refusing yet other conventional pleasures, such as the equation between theft and trade, there is trialogue. Moll's encounter with the mercer and his journeyman, when she is falsely accused of shoplifting, is here a case in point. Faller's sustained and persuasive analysis points the unresolved tensions that compel both engagement with and distancing from all involved. This is criminal biography transmuted into 'a new kind of writing', extended again in *Roxana*, 'Defoe's most psychological and . . . most pointedly moral' criminal fiction, precisely because Defoe refuses either protagonist or reader the catharsis of punishment when they reach the nadir of a process 'showing . . . how the self can ruin itself quite spectacularly though in an utterly private way'. Malinda Snow is also committed to reader-response theory but superimposes it on a template from Aristotelian rhetoric ('Arguments to the Self in Defoe's *Roxana*', *SEL* 34.523–36): 'Roxana tells how, through deliberation, she created the self that speaks at the narrative's end . . . Moll acts with less self-scrutiny [so] *Moll Flanders* lacks the polyvocal rhetorical structure'. Rhetoric is at issue again, in Troy Boone's 'Narrating the Apparition: Glanvill, Defoe, and the Rise of Gothic Fiction' (*ECent* 35.173–89), but here it is rhetorical anxiety about the generic status of occasional 'apparition narratives', which situates Defoe as a transitional figure in the evolution of a politicized 'oppositional discourse' confident enough to take on rationalism in the later eighteenth century.

Clinton Bond's 'Representing Reality: Strategies of Realism in the Early English Novel' (*ECF* 6.121–40) is an efficient piece of new historicism on a *Clarissa* at the intersection of humanist and bourgeois ideologies, with more than a glance at Defoe, and cross-reference to Renaissance texts (with consequent homage to Stephen Greenblatt). Though no less conscious of the struggle between previously dominant and emerging ideologies, Lois E. Bueler offers a much more original approach to both Richardson and his novel in *Clarissa's Plots*. She identifies three of these: the Tested Woman, from Renaissance drama; Don Juan, most immediately available from Shadwell's *The Libertine*; and the Prudence plot from Puritan spiritual biography. Richardson's precursors in that last mode closed the theatres in 1640, as workshops of the devil that traded in lying fictions, and, as Bueler points out, the bourgeois novelist's attack on the theatres of his own time (in *The Apprentice's Vade Mecum*) proved that he thought them no place for a good drama. However, if the ancient lionized by his class enemies had instructed the world that plot (rather than story, mere 'fable') was 'the soul of drama', there was every reason to appropriate and transform a few morally instructive plots to dramatize the epic struggle for Clarissa's soul. It will come as little surprise when readers find themselves following Richardson through such contradictions or such competing models: much more unusual is the elegant, discriminating lucidity with which Bueler guides them through the interpretative clamour.

Tom Keymer detects a more pragmatic sort of bourgeois plot in an extended note on 'Clarissa's Death, *Clarissa*'s Sale, and the Text of the Second Edition' (*RES* 45.389–96): 'To put it bluntly, the final instalment was not printed with the purpose of preparing for the second edition; the second edition was printed with the purpose of getting rid of the final instalment.' The prospect of an unhappy ending was, it seems, too much for an audience that wanted a sequel to *Pamela* and voted with its feet, or at least its closed purse. That earlier blockbuster is treated to a witty *tour de force* of an essay by James Grantham Turner which, coincidentally, also returns us to the drama. 'Novel Panic: Picture and Performance in the Reception of Richardson's *Pamela*' (*Rep* 48.70–96) surveys the spectrum of the 'Pamela craze that swept through eighteenth-century Europe and inspired emulation in virtually every medium'. Richardson's 'retailing of the production', defences, parodies, visual representations, plays and translations are here brought together in support of Turner's contention that the author and his supporters shared with his detractors the same critical discourse from a shared set of assumptions:

> both camps assumed that 'Pamela' (text and character) could be discussed as an autonomous embodied person; that the author's representation is something *done* to that person, marking that body or procreating from it sexually; that the successful novel approaches the condition of painting and theater; that its most significant moments can be identified as *scenes*; and that dramatic immediacy operates directly to arouse the spectator, male or female.

Even in this respect the focus does not stray long from *Clarissa*: according to Lisa Hopkins, 'the gendered gaze of the [BBC television] camera' resulted in stereotyping voyeurism ('The Transference of *Clarissa*: Psychoanalysis and the Realm of the Feminine', *CS* 6.218–25). At least *Sir Charles Grandison*'s heroine also gets her one moment under the spotlight, and in an essay as supple as the narrative that Betty A. Schellenberg finds imposed on yet embraced by Harriet in the text ('Using "Femalities" to "Make Fine Men": Richardson's *Sir Charles Grandison* and the Feminization of Narrative', *SEL* 34. 599–616), though this 'final statement about the feminization of discourse and its socializing function' is not without its problems and self-betrayals for an author who 'sees his authorial self . . . dependent upon . . . feminine . . . creative energy in producing his own narrative, yet needing to activate, authorize, and censor that energy'.

Bernard Harrison's 'Gaps and Stumbling-Blocks in Fielding: A Response to [Lothar] Černy, [Brean S.] Hammond, and [Nicholas] Hudson' (*Connotations* 3.ii.147–72) details the four previous contributions to a dispute about 'reader participation' in *Tom Jones*. Andrew Varney regrets his non-contribution to 'the ongoing debate' in the prologue to his immediately preceding paper, 'Brightness and Beauty, Taste and Relish: Advertising and Vindicating Eighteenth-Century Novels' (133–46); but this apology begins to look like a wry joke as he gathers pace in a briskly intelligent survey which relates marketing materials to the concern with prefaces he shares with Joseph Bartolomeo (above): 'Title pages are bait luring the reader to the hook; prefaces tend to justify him (or her) for having taken it. Both are unreliable.' Varney's wider aim is to complicate Michael McKeon's developmental categories. He is particularly sharp on Defoe – no 'naive empiricist' here – but he does concede McKeon's 'extreme scepticism' in *Tom Jones*'s 'Bill of Fare', where the 'fictional tradition that began as a power game has descended to charades'. John Allen Stevenson plunges into the body of the narrative – and picks up another dominant thread of this year's writing, of all kinds – in '*Tom Jones* and the Stuarts' (*ELH* 61.571–95). Breezily convinced by revisionist historians that 'Britain . . . faced a choice between illegitimacies' after 1688, Stevenson revisits Jacobite codification here mapped on to the romance plot, but he is (justifiably) less assertive when he concludes that 'Fielding's political playfulness in *Tom Jones* can . . . be seen as a bit of revenge on the intellectual straitjacket offered him by his patrons in the political world.' Emily A. Hipchen also recycles the familiar, though she makes her own bold claims about 'erotic potential . . . and the conflict over the ownership of [Sophia's] body', when she revisits the sexual innuendoes of the heroine's 'muff' ('Fielding's *Tom Jones*,' *Expl* 53.i.16–18). Finally (in every sense), James M. Harding reverses Andrew Varney's polarity in a heavily theorized paper which unpicks the novel's transgressive reprieve of its hero as the necessary summation to which everything drives ('"He's a Gallus un": Excess, Restriction, and Narrative Reprieve at the Gallows in *Tom Jones*', *ECLife* 18.15–35). Sophia's muff also gets a mention here – along with all else – and shortly thereafter Harding seems to assay his own pun; 'Sheathing the signification of sexuality within a reference to the death penalty, the phrase "born to be hang'd" blurs the distinction between sexual functions and killing.' Indigestible prose does something similar.

Henry Fielding: Authorship and Authority returns to Ian Bell's struggle with a Fielding uncertain no less of his authority than of the trustworthiness of his audience, here compounded by the problems of the very monograph enterprise in which Bell is engaged. This occasions such theoretical angst that Bell expends nearly a quarter of his book (its first chapter) on the search for an escape (that Bakhtin might have approved) from the dilemma of writing about a construct which people might mistake as a real author. He springs himself loose after smuggling film theory into his conceptual prison: '"auteurism" . . . [has that] particular configuration of individual creativity, the material circumstances of production, and the mediation of personal expression through awkward and resistant forms [which] makes it especially relevant, I believe, to Fielding, writing as he was at the moment of the rapid and unprecedented technological development of the early novel'. Bell is thus (confusingly) free to read the historical author through chapters on sequential texts; but the anxieties of an escapee cannot be denied. He consistently finds strife in precisely the dialogism others read as liberating, from *Pamela* to *Amelia*, and he pursues his agenda so determinedly on

Tom Jones that the issue of interpretation so fundamental to the text becomes something akin to a failure of class-conscious nerve on Fielding's part. In 'Fielding, Neo-Classicism and the Lower Orders' Robert Clark might almost have been writing an immediate riposte: Clark certainly takes Bell's previous book to task in his contribution to *Logomachia: Forms of Opposition in English Language/ Literature*, edited by E. Douka-Kabitoglou. Clark positively embraces the dialogism of Fielding's 'new species of writing' and finds density of narrative the source of consistency in the project 'to reform the way of the great in order that they should be able to justify their social superiority . . . Neo-classicism provides one model of containment but he mocks the abuse of classical learning as he prides himself on his own refined application.' Judith Frank agrees, if from a thoroughly opposed cultural materialist perspective. 'The Comic Novel and the Poor: Fielding's Preface to *Joseph Andrews*' (*ECS* 27.217–34) reads that text as 'crucially concerned with evoking the difference between aural/visual and literary modes . . . to resist the novel's mass-cultural appeal, and yet to avoid repudiating altogether . . . the monstrous and chaotic, yet mirthful and benevolent realm of popular culture'.

On the cusp between Fielding as playwright and as novelist, Alexander Pettit asks 'What the Drama Does in *Jonathan Wild*' (*ECF* 6.153–68) and concludes that it 'is used to indicate its own limitations'. Pettit writes persuasively on detail but (here again) homage to Bakhtin, on the novelization of reformulated genres, leads to a dubious critical (and literal) closure. If in *Jonathan Wild* Fielding blurs generic boundaries in what looks like an enthusiastic overture to prose fiction, and a measured, affectionate and decisive farewell to the drama, what are we to make of all those richly comic, and thoroughly dialogic, theatrical set pieces in *Tom Jones*? The last essay on Fielding is a *tour de force* of connectivity no less pyrotechnical than James Grantham Turner's performance on *Pamela*. Albert J. Rivero's 'Figuration of the Dying: Reading Fielding's *The Journal of a Voyage to Lisbon*' (*JEGP* 93.520–33) explores metaphors of eating and drinking, conveying, motion, mastery, evacuating natural fluids and giving birth, all radiating from the core book/body trope, and weaves them together with thinkers from Homer and Montaigne to Benjamin Franklin and Wittgenstein, to encompass 'the last work of an author who, recognizing death to be near, engages in the writing of a text which will literally take his place in the world'. Rivero's *Voyage* resists any singular generic categorization, but 'fictionalized narrative' will have to suffice.

David Oakleaf's introduction to his paperback edition of Eliza Haywood's *Love in Excess* could stand alone as a model of the appreciative survey. It blends all the required 'introductory' business with a blessedly jargon-free and perceptive appraisal. Details focus illuminatingly on issues that tempt others into verbose impenetrability; for example, the way 'Haywood's narrator helps the reader's memory (and signals her controlling design) through alliterative doublings' for her complicating love triangles, or 'the garden in which Haywood stages so much passion . . . just inside the realm of public scrutiny'. Oakleaf does not need to labour his points. The lucid progress of his analysis amply justifies those even-handed opening discriminations with which he maps out the territory: 'Haywood . . . wrote from the surest of spurs to professional industry: she had to support herself and two children . . . Naturally enough . . . her writing is sometimes pedestrian. But it is more commonly lively and it is necessarily deeply engaged with the changing demands of an emergent readership.' Three decades later Haywood returned not only to the novel with *Betsy Thoughtless* (1751) and *Jemmy and Jenny Jessamay*

(1753), but also to the 'subversive fictions inside framing narratives' which are the subject of a somewhat routine essay on the 'challenge to Richardson' by Deborah J. Nestor ('Virtue Rarely Rewarded: Ideological Subversion and Narrative Form in Haywood's Later Fictions', *SEL* 34.579–98). These 'Histories' were on the bookstalls alongside Sarah Fielding's pioneering novel for children: Judith Burdan, deploying Locke and Foucault with equal ease, construes its 'narrative use of observation and confession as a way of both realizing and controlling female character . . . [to] accomplish the subtle disciplinary project of rendering authority invisible and therefore completely "natural"' ('Girls *Must be* Seen *and* Heard: Domestic Surveillance in Sarah Fielding's *The Governess*', *CLAQ* 19.8–14). An alternative form of 'naturalness' characterized *The Female Spectator* – one of the many projects with which Haywood busied herself in the 1740s – and provides Clifford Siskin with a key stage in his closely worked survey of 'Eighteenth-Century Periodicals and the Romantic Rise of the Novel' (*SNNTS* 26.26–42): Haywood's essays 'helped to articulate class as well as gender differences, by inducting . . . a multiplicity of middle orders into an increasingly univocal conversation'.

Tom Keymer's second extended note, 'Readers and Stage-Coaches in Fielding and Sterne' (*N&Q* 41.209–11), extends the reader-response debate about *Tom Jones* to Sterne's major fictions by way of coaching metaphors, one of them in *A Sentimental Journey* an echo of *Joseph Andrews* as yet unnoticed by the indefatigable editors of the Florida edition. Scholarship and studies of transmission are also the twin concerns of this year's *Shandean* (6). Three of its essays investigate attempts to characterize Sterne and his writing in other media: René Bosch, '"Character" in Reynolds' Portrait of Sterne' (9–23), contextualizes that portrait in contemporary art theory and tracks its caricaturing progress through successive imitations; Paul Goring, 'Illustration of *A Sentimental Journey* in the 1920s' (54–65), traces the concern with 'erotic possibilities' privileged by illustrators in that decade's 'surge of publication'; and Peter de Voogd, 'Robert Dighton's Twelve "Tristram Shandy" Prints' (86–98), surveys a 1785 series as one that kept its promise to represent both 'sentimental, and humorous Scenes'. It is one of the perennial Shandean delights of the *Shandean* that it contrives to maintain such high (even extravagant) production values that such combinations of literary with art history can be read against close approximations. This year, when Goring writes about Véra Willoughby's 1927 designs, the 'vignettes of pencil illustration . . . contained within elaborate Baroque cartouches' are not only available on the facing page but also in 'a bold cherry pink ink' to match the originals; and de Voogd's analysis can be cross-referenced against a stitched, facsimile booklet tucked into a flap on the volume's back cover. Back in the text, translations provide another theme this year. Luis Pegenaute's 'The Unfortunate Journey of Lawrence Sterne through Spain: The Translations of his Works into Spanish' (24–53) amply justifies its title and also takes those translations as a focus for thoughts on translation theory in relation to the culture and politics of pre- and post-Franco life. By contrast, Anne Bandry stays close to her immediate concern with 'The First French Translation of *Tristram Shandy*', which is more than can be said for those who produced their own 'variation on Sterne's text' by suppressing its indelicacies and enhancing its sensibility. Such is the fate of all writing, according to some theorists, so it is appropriate that after all this *Shandean* scholarship, and hard against the closing flurry of 'Notes, Queries, Reviews, &.-', comes a supple, theoretically sophisticated (and even witty) essay by Carol Watts on 'The Modernity of *Tristram Shandy*' (99–118) that takes as its starting point the oxymoronic summary by a bibliographer of postmodernism; 'a thoroughly postmodern work in every respect but the period in which it is written'.

Predictably enough, a counter-attack was already on another press. J. T. Parnell's 'Swift, Sterne, and the Skeptical Tradition' (*SECC* 23.221–42) reaffirms the traditions of humanist and fideistic scepticism to align Sterne with those for whom satire on rationalism and 'systems' was a literal act of faith. 'It is surely', concludes Parnell, 'in part, our desire to use texts to confirm current theoretical orthodoxies which prevents us from acknowledging them to be informed by world-views uncongenial to our own', and he has heavyweight support from Martin C. Battestin and Marcus Walsh. The latter enlists *Tristram Shandy* among the 'humanist parodies of scholastic methods' by particular reference to 'the waxen nose' trope 'which had so long-established and familiar a connection with . . . textual and more especially scriptural interpretation . . . [in] crucial post-Reformation theological argument' ('Goodness Nose: Sterne's Slawkenbergius, the Real Presence, and the Shapeable Text', *BJECS* 17.55–63). Concerns no less proper for a mid-eighteenth-century churchman also direct Battestin's thinking in 'Sterne Among the *Philosophes*: Body and Soul in *A Sentimental Journey*' (*ECF* 7.17–36). He reads that novel as one influenced by and designed to address the French materialist philosophers, not least Diderot, with whom Sterne shared an improbable but warm and enduring friendship. The critical pressure thus established begins to drop in the last journal essay I have to note. Martha F. Bowden's 'The Interdependence of Women in *Tristram Shandy*: A Chapter of Eyes, Sausages and Sciatica' (*ELN* 31.iv.40–7) follows her three 'patterns of allusion and connection . . . from character to allegorical figure, to digression, and back to the characters again' – and to the unsurprising conclusion that women are important presences in the novel.

That leaves Melvyn New, the doyen of Sterne scholars, who demands the last word for his extraordinary, combative, at times quite dazzling volume for the Twayne Masterworks series, '*Tristram Shandy*': *A Book for Free Spirits*. Other Sterneans will already know this book – W. G. Day devotes two pages to a review in the *Shandean* (6) – so I need do little more here than note its combination of the old with the startlingly original. New's *Tristram Shandy* remains an eighteenth-century satire wilfully misread by all those appropriating postmoderns, but here it is re-read in part by application of the schema used by Stuart Gilbert for Joyce's *Ulysses* and throughout by reference to Nietzschean philosophy (hence New's allusion in his title to *Human, All Too Human*, Nietzche's own 'book for free spirits'). Earlier in his review of New's book, Day remarked that the author 'is a stakhanovite among Sterneans'. So he is: expense of so much energy on his major critical venture does not prevent him adding more '"Scholia" to the Florida *Tristram Shandy* Annotations' (*Scriblerian* 26.254, 27.93–4).

Robert D. Spector's *Smollett's Women: A Study in Eighteenth-Century Masculine Sensibility* (Greenwood) was unavailable for review, and I was unable to consult *BSEAA* – with no fewer than seven pieces on Smollett, between November 1993 and June 1994. Despite that lacuna, there is more Smollett scholarship to report than usual. There is also a logical slippage in the title of the first item, Leslie A. Chilton's 'Not Quite Proven: Tobias Smollett's *The Devil on Crutches*' (*N&Q* 41.206–7) – and inconclusive evidence in the body text to confirm Smollett as the anonymous translator of Lesage's *Le Diable Boiteux* printed in 1749. Careless presentation (for example, on Smollett 'fulmigating' against either praise or censure) distracts in John Skinner's '*Roderick Random* and the Fiction of Autobiography' (*ABSt* 9.98–112), but Skinner works stolidly enough through parallels between letters and text to revisit the complaint that novel-centred criticism continues to disparage autobiography despite the 'ontological conflation' revealed by deconstruction. Altogether more accurate and critically sophisticated is Andrew Varney's 'From Tennis-Ball to Fruit Tree: Smollett's Story of the Scottish Self' in a special issue of *SwR* ('Writing Region and Nation', 549–60). The violent and restless discourse of a novel 'displaced in the culture of the period . . . an intervention from the outside' is here an appropriate representation of 'life as Smollett perceived it . . . resistant to the kind of organization which facilitates the articulation of meaning through story', and nowhere more obviously so than in a providential 'happy ending' which returns Roderick 'to an ahistorical world of idealized feudalism', the passing of which Smollett had earlier mourned in *The Tears of Scotland.* Daniel Punday's 'Satiric Method and the Reader in *Sir Launcelot Greaves*' (*ECF* 6.169–88) is less original. Punday defends that novel against the charge that it is 'sloppy and piecemeal' on the grounds that the apparent confusion of romance with the picaresque is a function of a satiric method that 'both uses and criticizes the romantic conventions embodied by Greaves'; but he seems not to know that Robert D. Spector has been arguing this case (and more vigorously) for some time.

Three papers on *Humphry Clinker* take very different lines of approach. Peter Miles, in 'The Bookhood of *Humphry Clinker:* The Editor, The Publisher, and the Law' (*ECLife* 18.48–63) pursues a relentlessly narratological reading of a text that is transformed by the opening letters by Dustwich and Davies: physical production processes and the law on issues such as copyright, libel and assault 'enter, through the framework structure, into the experience of reading the novel'. Two others focus, from utterly opposed perspectives, on Lesmahago's capture by Indians: Andrew Sharp contextualizes the tale by appeal to humanist thought ('Scots, Savages, and Barbarians: *Humphry Clinker* and the Scots Philosophy', *ECLife* 18.65–79); Charlotte Sussman employs all her post-colonial/cultural materialist toolkit to find in it Smollett's vision for the future: 'a nascent fantasy of disconnection – a means by which England could disentangle itself from the cross-cultural connections of mercantilism' ('Lesmahago's Captivity: Transculturation in *Humphry Clinker*', *ELH* 61.597–618). 'England', here must be an abstrusely coded irony or a slip of the pen, for 'Scottishness' is an inescapable issue in *Roderick Random*, and it is so again, according to Maureen Harkin, if we are to understand another generically unstable novel published in the same year ('Mackenzie's *Man of Feeling*: Embalming Sensibility', *ELH* 61.317–40). This paper would have been improved by pruning of its exegetical concern with features 'typical' of the sentimental novel, to foreground the kernel of its argument about a text which is 'a complex valediction to sentimental fiction', less of a failed model of community than self-conscious about 'limits to the social usefulness of a sentimental sympathy'.

Mary Hays's *The Victim of Prejudice* (1799), edited by Eleanor Ty, squeezes into 'the eighteenth century' only by the accident of chronology, but it warrants mention here as the second inexpensive novel from Broadview in a welcome publishing venture. Burney's work has been receiving its textual due for some time, but Margaret Anne Doody is the best scholar-critic currently writing on her novels, and her splendid Penguin Classics edition of *Evelina* fulfils every expectation. The same novel's Captain Mirvan receives thoroughgoing new historicist treatment by David Hart when he mines the mezzotints for characteristics drawn from those 'tensions, divisions and incongruities . . . specific to the 1770s' ('Frances Burney's *Evelina*: Mirvan and Mezzotint', *ECF* 7.51–70). The now-provocative usage of 'Fanny' in the title of Arno Löffler's '"The World . . . What it Appears to a Girl of Seventeen": Fanny Burney's *Evelina* als Satirischer Roman' (*Anglia* 112.50–74) may also signal a more traditional style of historicism; but it will require a reader with better command of academic German than this reviewer to pursue that speculation. That reader will find English sufficient for the *JEGP* essay by Elisabeth Rose Gruner, 'The Bullfinch and the Brother: Marriage and Family in Frances Burney's *Camilla*' (93.18–34), a busy if rather routine feminist analysis of a novel marked by 'compendiousness . . . generic indeterminacy [and] a number of stories which together revise the familiar metaphor of courtship for self-discovery, and explore the nature of female identity within a family and a world controlled by men'.

John Wiltshire would privilege the journals over any Burney novel, and 'Love unto Death: Fanny Burney's "Narrative of the Last Illness and Death of General d'Arblay"' (*L&M* 12[1993].215–34) over even 'Mastectomy'. Burney enthusiasts may disagree; but few will share with habitual readers of the serial in which Wiltshire is published an overriding interest in the medical ethics of his preferred narrative. No critic gives exclusive attention to *Cecilia* this year, but it is the latest of the 'novels of sensibility' chosen by Patricia Meyer Spacks (the others are Frances Sheridan, *Memoirs of Miss Sidney Bidulph*, 1761, and Frances Brooke, *History of Lady Tulia Mandeville*, 1763) to support her well-argued contention that female writers who interrogate the gendered oppression of sensibility in everyday life must be distinguished from their male counterparts: the three Franceses 'recognize, know, and understand . . . much about exactly those forms of moral and psychological ambiguity that twentieth-century critics perceive in an undifferentiated "literature of sensibility"' ('Oscillations of Sensibility', *NLH* 25.505–20). *Munster Village* (1778) is accorded the rare privilege of a separate essay by Alessa Johns. In 'Mary Hamilton, Daniel Defoe, and a Case of Plagiarism in Eighteenth-Century England' (*ELN* 31.iv.25–33), she reproduces parallel texts but justifies Hamilton's 'reordering' of Defoe's *Political History of the Devil* as one which counters the male construction of witchhood; Hamilton's 'recognition of gender inequality leads her to recontextualize the stolen anecdote. She may appropriate Defoe's words, but in the end she rejects the gendering of his voice.' That seems an appropriate enough last word for a review of the eighteenth-century novel this year, 1994; a year that problematized the calumny visited on a number of 'plagiarisms' and in which the problematic relationships between male and female writers was a matter of constant concern.

5. Drama

Claire Tomalin, *Mrs Jordan's Profession: The Story of a Great Actress and a Future King* is a revealing account of life on the road for a jobbing actress and eventually the Queen of Drury Lane. The narrative is bright and clear, with plentiful verbal and engraved illustrations. Dora Jordan comes over as a vulnerable yet brave personality, whose wisdom overcame precarious circumstances. The most theatrical sections are those early chapters on Drury Lane, and her early favour with the Prince of Wales. Tomalin worked under the constant difficulty of not having any great autobiographical record from her subject, and so her interpretative powers were turned on her letters – sharp and well-turned.

The only full-length academic study of dramatic representation in the period this year came from Jones DeRitter in *The Embodiment of Characters: The Representation of Physical Experience on Stage and in Print, 1728–1749*. DeRitter takes the 1730s London stage alongside the 1740s English novel and attempts to draw a series of analogies, new historicist in inspiration, between stage and other representations. The limited sweep is sometimes an advantage, helping us to appreciate synchronic forces that break free of normal generic boundaries, yet the opening chapter sometimes narrates the period chosen in a rather generalized fashion. Artaud and Derrida are called upon, yet Fielding hardly at all. When DeRitter gets into his stride, in two powerful and succinct chapters on *The Beggar's Opera* and *The London Merchant*, he is capable of incisive writing. His understanding of physical transgression in performance and the economy of the playhouse is developed and original, but the extended associations with novelistic experiment that form the subject of the latter chapters (Fielding and Richardson) seem forced, and in a relatively slim book they need more urgent explication to be totally convincing.

Diane Dugaw attempts 'An Anatomy of Heroism: Gender Politics and Empire in Gay's *Polly*' in Tobin, *History, Gender and Eighteenth-Century Literature* (see also section 1 above). Gay based his sequel to *The Beggar's Opera* on Dryden's *All for Love* and balladry's mythical female warrior, and the result is a deliberate dislocation in heroic ideals: '*Polly* exposes this heroic ideal as an ethos of [gender] slavery.' Far from its being a musical in the modern sense, Dugaw makes a perfectly plausible case for this as a most unlyrical experience, the escape to a 'Third World of . . . hopeful Otherness', a desperate expedient. Janet Wolf 's ambitious study 'Political Allegory in the Later Plays of John Gay' (in Cope, *Enlightening Allegory*: see also section 3 above) advances a seldom rehearsed case that Gay, in works such as *Polly* or the second series of *Fables*, aimed directly at Walpole. Gay rarely kept company with *Craftsmen* contributors, though he doubtless shared some of their sentiments, but Wolf makes some pertinent and provoking attempts to crack Gay's theatrical codes.

Of the remaining essays this year, Joseph R. Roach's review article 'The Theatre of Gender' (*ECent* 35.190–2) is of most general interest. Roach criticizes critics who take at face value those in the period who suspected the theatre, and put forward large doses of anti-theatrical prejudice. George Winchester Stone Jr provides an 'Anatomy of a Theatrical Season for Covent Garden, 1758–59' (*TN* 48.i.11–18). Building on his discovery at the Garrick Club of account books for the relevant season, Stone carefully assembles a full picture of how much of a knife-edge the management of a successful repertory was. Helen Burke's '*The London Merchant* and Eighteenth-Century Law' (*PQ* 73.347–66) goes some way towards explaining the play's immense contemporary popularity. The closing gallows scene, left out of the initial performance and not inserted until its fifth edition, was an important ingredient in Lillo's attempt to 'manage' the anxiety at widespread and increasing capital punishment in the late 1720s. It also supplied hints of how a propertied class might relish harsh laws for the poor (both deserving and the undeserving), thus evading any uncomfortable questioning about their existence in an advanced capitalist economy. The best-researched piece of the year, however, is Peter Holland's 'Unpublished Scenes in David Garrick's Lethe' (*HLQ* 57.301–10). Underpinning Holland's work is the warranted assumption that theatrical work cannot always be represented accurately on the printed page, and that certain pieces are simply not designed to have such a consistent existence. His example here is one of Garrick's first pieces, which was restaged regularly throughout his career and always updated to suit contemporary concerns. A group of characters come up to Aesop and ask for a measure of oblivion gained from the waters of Lethe. This rather loose-leaf construction is designed to be changed to suit the theatrical event, and Holland's researches in the Huntington's Larpent collection provide us with a 1740 and a 1748 version, both quite distinct in their details.

Books Reviewed

Bartolomeo, Joseph F. *A New Species of Criticism: Eighteenth-Century Discourse on the Novel*. UDelP. pp. 209. $36.50. ISBN 0 8741 3488 9.

Bell, Ian A. *Henry Fielding: Authorship and Authority*. Longman. pp. 248. hb £30, pb £10.99. ISBN 0 5820 8162 9, 0 5820 8163 7.

Bloom, Edward A., and Lillian D. Bloom, eds. *The Piozzi Letters. Correspondence of Hester Lynch Piozzi, 1784–1821*. Vol. III (1799–1804). UDelP (1992). pp. 536. £55. ISBN 0 8741 3392 0.

Brown, Laura. *Ends of Empire: Women and Ideology in Early Eighteenth-Century English Literature*. CornUP. pp. 224. hb £25.50, pb £9.50. ISBN 0 8014 2850 5, 0 8014 8095 7.

Browne, Stephen H. *Edmund Burke and the Discourse of Virtue*. Studies in Rhetoric and Communication. UAlaP (1993). pp. 160. £25.50. ISBN 0 8173 0676 5.

Bueler, Lois E. *Clarissa's Plots*. AUP, UDelP. pp. 183. £23.50. ISBN 0 8741 3496 X.

Clark, J. C. D. *The Language of Liberty, 1660–1832. Political Discourse and Social Dynamics in the Anglo-American World*. CUP (1993). pp. 422. £14.95. 0 5214 4957 X.

Clark, S. H., ed. *Mark Akenside, James Macpherson, Edward Young: Selected Poetry*. Fyfield Books. pp. 191. £9.95. ISBN 0 8563 5927 0.

Cole, Richard C., Peter S. Baker, Rachel McClellan and James J. Caudle, eds. *The General Correspondence of James Boswell, 1766–1769*. Vol. 1. 1766–7. YaleUP (1993). pp. 328. $65. ISBN 0 3000 5803 9.

Cope, Kevin L., ed. *Enlightening Allegory: Theory, Practice, and Contexts of Allegory in the Late Seventeenth and Eighteenth Centuries*. Studies in the Eighteenth Century 18. AMS. pp. 405. £35.95. 0 4046 3518 0.

Copley, Stephen, and Andrew Eager, eds. *David Hume. Selected Essays*. WC. OUP (1993) pp. 448. £5.99. ISBN 0 1928 3072 4.

——, and Peter Garside, eds. *The Politics of the Picturesque: Literature, Landscape and Aesthetics since 1770*. CUP. pp. 304. £35. ISBN 0 5214 4113 7.

Craik, Roger. *James Boswell, 1740–95: The Scottish Perspective*. HMSO. pp. 208. £12.95. ISBN 0 1149 4226 9.

DeRitter, Jones. *The Embodiment of Characters: The Representation of Physical Experience on Stage and in Print, 1728–1749*. New Cultural Studies. UPennP. pp. 192. £27.50. ISBN 0 8122 3256 8.

Doody, Margaret Anne, ed. *Frances Burney: Evelina or The History of a Young Lady's Entrance into the World*. Penguin. pp. 505. £5.99. ISBN 0 1404 3347 3.

Douka-Kabitoglou, E., ed. *Logomachia: Forms of Opposition in English Language/Literature*. Thessalonika, Hellenic Association for the Study of English. pp. 456. n.p. ISBN 9 6024 3184 9.

Downie, J. A. *To Settle the Succession of the State: Literature and Politics, 1678–1750*. Context and Commentary. St Martin's. pp. 176. hb £40, pb £12.99. ISBN 0 3334 9596 9, 0 3334 9597 7.

Earle, Peter. *A City Full of People: Men and Women of London, 1650–1750*. Methuen. pp. 352. £25. ISBN 0 4136 8170 X.

Faller, Lincoln B. *Crime and Defoe: A New Kind of Writing*. CUP (1993). pp. 263. £35. ISBN 0 5214 2086 5.

Floud, Roderick, and Donald N. McCloskey. *The Economic History of Britain since 1700*. CUP. 3 vols. £50. 0 5214 5961 3.

Francus, Marilyn. *The Converting Imagination: Linguistic Theory and Swift's Satiric Prose*. SIUP. pp. 260. $35.95. ISBN 0 8093 1890 3.

Gatrell, V. A. C. *The Hanging Tree: Execution and the English People, 1770–1868*. OUP. pp. 520. £20. ISBN 0 1982 0413 1.

Griffin, Dustin. *Satire: A Critical Reintroduction*. UPKen. pp. 256. $27. ISBN 0 8131 1844 1.

Harris, Ian, ed. *Edmund Burke. Pre-Revolutionary Writings*. Cambridge Texts in the History of Political Thought. CUP (1993). pp. 336. hb £32.50, pb £ 12.95. ISBN 0 5213 6227 X, 0 5213 6800 6.

Harris, Robert. *A Patriot Press: National Politics and London Press in the 1740s*. Oxford Historical Monographs. OUP. pp. 304. £40. ISBN 0 1982 0378 0.

Hemming, T. D., E. Freeman and D. Meakin, eds. *The Secular City*. UExe. pp. 256. £25. ISBN 0 5898 9416 9.

Higgins, Ian. *Swift's Politics: A Study in Disaffection*. Cambridge Studies in Eighteenth-Century English Literature 20. CUP. pp. 225. £37.50. ISBN 0 5214 1814 3.

Hinnant, Charles H. *The Poetry of Anne Finch: An Essay in Interpretation*. AUP. pp. 289. £32.50. ISBN 0 8741 3469 2.

——. *'Steel for the Mind': Samuel Johnson and Critical Discourse*. UDelP. £25.95. ISBN 0 8741 3492 7.

Horgan, A. D. *Johnson on Language: An Introduction*. St Martin's. pp. £37.50. ISBN 0 3121 2150 4.

Jack, Malcolm, ed. *Lady Montagu. Turkish Embassy Letters*. PWC. P&C (1993). pp. 288. £35. ISBN 1 8519 6028 7.

Jain, Nalini, and John Richardson, eds. *Eighteenth-Century English Poetry: The Annotated Anthology*. Wheatsheaf. pp. 560. £12.95. ISBN 0 7450 1607 3.

Jaszi, Peter, and Martha Woodmansee. *The Construction of Authorship: Textual Appropriation in Law and Literature*. Post-Contemporary Interventions. DukeUP. pp. 480. £42.75. ISBN 0 8223 1382 0.

Kelly, Veronica and Dorothea E. von Mücke, *Body and Text in the Eighteenth Century*. StanfordUP. pp. 349. £32.50. ISBN 0 8047 2269 2.

Klein, Lawrence E. *Shaftesbury and the Culture of Politeness: Moral Discourse and Cultural Politics in Early Eighteenth-Century England*. CUP. pp. 224. £30. ISBN 0 5214 1806 2.

Larson, James L. *Interpreting Nature: The Science of Living Form from Linnaeus to Kant*. JHUP. pp. 256. £33. ISBN 0 8018 4840 7.

Law, Jules David. *The Rhetoric of Empiricism: Langauge and Perception from Locke to I. A. Richards*. CornUP (1993). pp. 280. £28.50. ISBN 0 8014 2706 1.

Lowenthal, Cynthia. *Lady Wortley Montagu and the Eighteenth-Century Familiar Letter*. UGeoP. pp. 264. £35.95. ISBN 0 8203 1545 1.

Man, John, ed. *Daniel Defoe: A Journal of the Plague Year*. Dent. pp. 235. £4.99.

ISBN 0 4608 7462 4.

Markley, Robert. *Fallen Languages: Crises of Representation in Newtonian England, 1660–1740*. CornUP. pp. 288. £29.50. ISBN 0 8014 2588 3.

Maslen, Keith, and Herbert Davis. *An Early London Printing House at Work: Studies in the Bowyer Ledgers: With a Supplement to the Bowyer Ornament Stock (1973), an Appendix on the Bowyer-Emonson Partnership, & Bowyer Paper Stock Ledger*. BSA. pp. 256. $50. ISBN 0 9149 3016 8.

McMinn, Joseph. *Jonathan's Travels: Swift and Ireland*. Appletree. pp. 160. £15.99. ISBN 0 8628 1453 7.

Meloccaro, Lynne, ed. *Rasselas and Dinarbus*. Dent. pp. 256. £2.99. ISBN 0 4608 7308 3.

Mitchell, L. G., ed. *Edmund Burke. Reflections on the Revolution in France*. WC. OUP (1993). pp. 352. £5.99. ISBN 0 1928 1844 9.

Montag, Warren. *The Unthinkable Swift: The Spontaneous Philosophy of a Church of England Man, 1688–1730*. Verso. pp. 152. £39.95. ISBN 1 8598 4900 8.

New, Melvyn. *'Tristram Shandy': A Book for Free Spirits*. Twayne's Masterworks. Twayne. pp. xii + 152. hb £23.95, pb £13.95. ISBN 0 8057 8358 X, 0 8057 4450 9.

Nicholson, Colin. *Writing and the Rise of Finance: Capital Satires in the Early Eighteenth Century*. Cambridge Studies in Early Eighteenth Century English Literature and Thought, 21. pp. 236. £37.50. ISBN 0 5214 5323 2.

Oakleaf, David, ed. *'Love in Excess: Or, The Fatal Enquiry' by Eliza Haywood*. Broadview. pp. 297. £7.95. ISBN 1 5511 1016 4.

Paulson, Ronald. *Hogarth. Vol. III: Art and Politics, 1750–1764*. RutgersUP (1993). pp. 680. hb $70, pb $24.95. ISBN 0 8135 1698 6, 0 8135 1699 4.

Perry, Gill, and Michael Rossington, eds. *Femininity and Masculinity in Eighteenth-Century Art and Culture*. ManUP. £15.99. ISBN 0 7190 4228 3.

Pittock, Murray G. H., *Poetry and Jacobite Politics in Eighteenth-Century Britain and Ireland*. CUP. pp. 254. £35. ISBN 0 5214 1092 4.

Pointon, Marcia. *Hanging the Head: Portraiture and Social Formation in Eighteenth-Century England*. YaleUP (1993). pp. 288. £45. ISBN 0 3000 5738 5.

Potkay, Adam. *The Fate of Eloquence in the Age of Hume*. Rhetoric and Society. CornUP. pp. 272. £28.95. ISBN 0 8014 3014 3.

Pottle, Frederick A., Marion S. Pottle and Claude Colleer Abbott, eds. *Catalogue of the Papers of James Boswell at Yale University*. 3 vols. Yale Editions of the Private Papers of James Boswell. YaleUP, EdinUP. pp. 1440 (set). £150 ($275) set. ISBN 0 3000 5410 6.

Rawson, Claude. *Satire and Sentiment, 1660–1830*. CUP. pp. 290. £45. ISBN 0 5213 8345 1.

Redford, Bruce, ed. *The Letters of Samuel Johnson*. PrincetonUP. Vol. IV.*(1782–1784)*. $39.50. ISBN 0 6910 6977 8. Vol V. *Appendices & Comprehensive Index*. $39.50. ISBN 0 6910 6978 6.

Rizzo, Betty. *Companions Without Vows: Relationships Among Eighteenth-Century British Women*. UGeoP. pp. 432. £49.50. ISBN 0 8203 1541 9.

Rogers, Pat. *Johnson and Boswell in Scotland: A Journey to the Hebrides*. YaleUP. pp. 288. £25. ISBN 0 3000 5210 3.

Rose, Mark. *Authors and Owners: The Invention of Copyright*. HarvardUP. pp. 190. hb £25, pb £9.50. ISBN 0 6740 5308 7, 0 6740 5309 5.

Sambrook, James, ed. *William Cowper: THE TASK and Selected Other Poems*. Longman. pp. 333. hb £36, pb £14.99. ISBN 0 5820 8728 7, 0 5820 8727 9.

Shinagel, Michael, ed. *Daniel Defoe, Robinson Crusoe: An Authoritative Text, Contexts, Criticism*. Norton. pp. 436. £9.95. ISBN 0 3939 6452 3.

Solkin, David H. *Painting for Money: The Visual Arts and the Public Sphere in Eighteenth-Century England.* Yale UP (1993). pp. 320. £45. ISBN 0 3000 5741 5.

Solomon, Harry M. *The Rape of the Text: Reading and Misreading Pope's 'Essay on Man'*. UAlaP (1993). pp. 245. £31.50. ISBN 0 8173 0696 X.

Speck, W. A. *The Birth of Britain: A Nation at War and Peace, 1700–1710. A History of Early Modern Britain.* Blackwell. pp. 256. £27.50. ISBN 0 6311 7544 X.

Srigley, Michael. *The Mighty Maze: A Study of Pope's 'An Essay on Man'*. Uppsala (1993). pp. 178. £14.75. ISBN 9 1554 3329 4.

Stafford, Barbara Maria. *Artful Science: Enlightenment Entertainment and the Eclipse of Visual Education.* MITP. pp. 380. £24.95. ISBN 0 2621 9342 6.

Stone, Lawrence. *Broken Lives: Separation and Divorce in England, 1660–1857.* OUP (1993). pp. 388. £16.95. ISBN 0 1982 0254 7.

Tobin, Beth Fowkes. *History, Gender and Eighteenth-Century Literature.* UGeoP. pp. 309. £44.95. ISBN 0 8203 1577 X.

Tomalin, Claire. *Mrs Jordan's Profession: The Story of a Great Actress and a Future King.* Viking. pp. 474. £18. ISBN 0 6708 4159 5.

Tomarken, Edward. *A History of the Commentary on Selected Writings of Samuel Johnson, 1788–1993.* Cambden House, B&B. pp. 160. £37.50. ISBN 1 8797 5194 1.

Troide, Lars E., and Stewart J. Cooke, eds. *The Early Journals and Letters of Fanny Burney*. Vol. III. *The Streatham Years: Part I, 1778–1779*. OUP. pp. 477. £55. ISBN 0 1981 2581 X.

Tucker, Bernard, ed. *The Poetry of Mary Barber, ?1690–1757*. Mellen. pp. 246. £39.95. ISBN 0 7734 9465 0.

Ty, Eleanor, ed. *'The Victim of Prejudice' by Mary Hays.* Broadview. pp. 197. £7.95. ISBN 0 9211 4937 9.

Weinbrot, Howard D. *Britannia's Issue: The Rise of British Literature from Dryden to Ossian.* CUP. pp. 538. £37.50. ISBN 0 5213 2519 6.

Weinsheimer, Joel. *Eighteenth-Century Hermeneutics: Philosophy of Interpretation in England from Locke to Burke.* YaleUP. pp. 272. £25. ISBN 0 3000 5280 4.

Woodman, Thomas, *A Preface to Samuel Johnson*. Preface Books. Longman. hb £35, pb £13.99. ISBN 0 5820 8666 3, 0 5820 8665 5.

Woodmansee, Martha. *The Author, Art, and the Market: Rereading the History of Aesthetics.* ColUp. pp. 200. $29.50. ISBN 0 2311 0601 7.

XII

The Nineteenth Century: Romantic Period

DUNCAN WU, DAVID WORRALL, JOHN WHALE and ROBERT MILES

This chapter has three sections: 1. Poetry and Drama; 2. Non-Fictional Prose; 3. Fictional Prose. Section 1 is by Duncan Wu and David Worrall (Blake material); section 2 is by John Whale; and section 3 is by Robert Miles.

1. Poetry and Drama

This section has two categories: (a) Editions and General Studies; (b) Individual Authors.

(a) Editions and General Studies

One of the most exciting aspects of contemporary critical discussion in the field must be the increasing tendency to question the traditionally held views by which Romantic studies have, until recent years, been circumscribed. This tendency is evident throughout this first section of my survey of the year's work.

One of the most important scholarly achievements this year was the publication of William McCarthy and Elizabeth Kraft's *The Poems of Anna Laetitia Barbauld.* This edition is long overdue, as Barbauld is not just a writer of exceptional significance, but one of interest to those working on eighteenth-century literature as well as the Romantic period. In a helpful and perceptive introduction the editors argue for her importance as a forerunner of women's rights, and more generally as a political writer. It is in this light that Romanticists are coming to regard her, 'The Rights of Woman' being one of her most frequently anthologized works at present. The editors have wisely attempted to present her poetry in chronological order by date of composition, and alongside published works they have added a number of poems hitherto unpublished, or not previously attributed to her. Not everyone will agree with all the scholarly decisions they have made, but the edition is informed by an encyclopaedic knowledge of the available manuscripts, printed editions, and so forth, and it is hard to imagine the job being better executed for a long time. Whatever its shortcomings on a scholarly level, this edition is a milestone in the contemporary study of women poets, and stands alongside Stuart

Curran's edition of Charlotte Smith's poems (*YWES* 74.350) as one of the most vital recent contributions to an expanding canon.

The excellent Woodstock books series of facsimile reprints enables us to see the works of women writers much as they appeared to their contemporaries. This year saw the appearances of Susanna Blamire's *The Poetical Works, 1842*, Sara Coleridge's *Phantasmion 1837*, Isabella Lickbarrow's *Poetical Effusions 1814*, Caroline Norton's *A Voice from the Factories 1836*, Anna Seward's *Llangollen Vale 1796*, Helen Maria Williams's *Poems 1786*, Ann Yearsley's *Poems on Various Subjects 1787*, Joanna Baillie's *Poems 1790* and Mary Robinson's *Poems 1791*. Besides the obvious importance of some of these volumes, a number of them are of significance from a scholarly perspective. The Blamire volume is the first important edition of the works of this neglected writer, and it continues to provide a copytext for many anthologists of her work. Lickbarrow's volume appeared only once, and its list of subscribers includes a number of interesting names – not least those of Wordsworth, De Quincey and Southey. Also, as its title-page indicates, it was published by the Branthwaites – the same people who published the *Westmorland Advertiser*, in which Lickbarrow's poetry first appeared. Yearsley's volume contains her interesting preface, which documents the disagreement between her and Hannah More. Facsimiles do not provide us with the same amount of information as critical editions, admittedly, but the uniqueness of their contents, which includes not merely such materials as lists of subscribers and prefatory materials, but such features as typography, layout, format and so forth, speak eloquently in their own way of the nature of publication for women writers of the time. In addition, each of the Woodstock facsimiles contains a helpful introduction by Jonathan Wordsworth, which in many cases comprises the only available critical writing on these neglected works.

Jonathan Wordsworth was busy this year with women Romantics: for one thing, he was co-author, with Stephen Hebron, of the catalogue published to accompany an exhibition on the subject at Dove Cottage, *Romantic Women Writers*. This useful volume contains reproductions (nineteen in colour) of portraits of many of the women poets of the period, along with much scholarly comment. Blamire is among them, and she is the subject of a pamphlet, *Susanna Blamire: Poet of Friendship 1747–1794*, which contains the text of a lecture delivered by Prof. Wordsworth at Carlisle Cathedral. Besides his shrewd observations on Blamire, this useful work contains texts of poems edited from family manuscripts, hitherto unpublished.

This year saw the appearance of two anthologies. Jennifer Breen's *Women Romantic Poets 1785–1832* was first published in 1992 (*YWES* 73.340), and was issued in a lightly revised form. It has received considerable criticism for its contents, but in fact I find this a useful selection, as it contains a number of works otherwise hard to obtain. Its main drawback is its size: within 182 pages (including introduction, index and notes) no editor could expect to make a reasonable selection of all the various works. The question confronting all anthologists of materials such as these must be: is it possible, within the number of pages allowed by the publisher, to include complete texts of the important works or volumes by women Romantics? Sooner or later some publisher must be prepared to permit their editor the freedom to reprint such works as Mary Tighe's *Psyche*, Hemans's *Records of Woman*, Landon's *The Improvisatrice* and Robinson's *Sappho and Phaon* in their entirety. For that purpose allowances of less than 400 pages simply will not do. *Romanticism: An Anthology*, ed. Duncan Wu, includes many women

Romantics alongside the canonical six male writers. Its main strategy is, in fact, to publish complete versions of the works it contains. Thus, it is unusual among books of its kind for containing a complete text of *The Thirteen-Book Prelude*, *Prometheus Unbound*, *Lyrical Ballads*, both *Hyperion*s, *Manfred* and *Don Juan* Canto I. All texts have been freshly edited either from early printed sources or from the appropriate manuscripts.

This year saw the launch of the OPL series. These paperback volumes, which are essentially cut-down versions of the Oxford Authors series, are intended to compete with similarly priced volumes published by Penguin. Authors include Wordsworth, Coleridge, Keats, Byron and Blake. The reader may have qualms about the brevity of some of the selections. For instance, it is a shame to have only extracts from *Home at Grasmere* in the Wordsworth volume (ed. Stephen Gill and Duncan Wu), extracts from *Beppo* in the Byron (ed. Jerome J. McGann), and extracts from *Milton* and *Jerusalem* in the Blake (ed. Michael Mason). But such is the nature of paperbacks which run to little more than 300 pages. In this respect, it is not surprising that Keats (ed. Elizabeth Cook) and Coleridge (ed. Heather Jackson) do comparatively well. The Keats volume contains all the Odes, both *Hyperion*s, and a good helping of sonnets and other poems. The Coleridge volume contains virtually all the poems any general reader could ever want, along with Heather Jackson's exemplary scholarly materials, and, at 201 pages, this is one of the shorter volumes in the series. Each of these volumes is, needless to say, up to the minute in scholarly terms, and they contain useful annotations; it would be hard to imagine a better introduction to the writers concerned.

Collections of essays remain popular among critics, and a number were published this year – two of the best geared to a serious revaluation of the work of women writers. *Romantic Women Writers: Voices and Countervoices,* eds Paula R. Feldman and Theresa M. Kelley, contains work by Isobel Armstrong, Susan Wolfson, Stephen Behrendt, Mitzi Myers, William McCarthy, Anthony Harding, Judith Pike, Jeanne Moskal, Richard Sha, Moira Ferguson, Catherine Burroughs, Susan Levin and Judith Pascoe. The range of authors covered here reflects the extent of the current overhaul of the traditional Romantic canon; it includes Mrs Barbauld, Felicia Hemans, Lady Morgan, Janet Little, Joanna Baillie, Harriett Abrams and Mary Robinson. The overall quality of contribution is very high, and a number of these essays, including Armstrong's 'The Gush of the Feminine' and Harding's study of Hemans, will become standard critical fare for anyone seriously interested in the subject. *Re-Visioning Romanticism: British Women Writers, 1776–1837*, edited by Carol Shiner Wilson and Joel Haefner, has several subjects – and contributors – in common with *Romantic Women Writers* (see also sections 2 and 3 below). It is no less diverse, and includes important work by Linda Peterson, Susan Allen Ford, Katharine Rogers, Marlon Ross, Jane Aaron, Susan Wolfson, Carol Shiner Wilson, Judith Pascoe, Jerome J. McGann, Julie Ellison, Joel Haefner and Catherine B. Burroughs. There are exemplary essays here on Mary Robinson (by Stuart Curran), Mrs Hemans (by Susan Wolfson and Jerome McGann), and Joanna Baillie (by Catherine Burroughs). What both collections underline is that one of the most compelling issues for Romanticists at present must be the introduction into the canon of hitherto marginalized writers. And if that is so, Romanticists are rightly asking themselves whether aesthetics are affected by gender. An entire section of the Wilson and Haefner volume is given over to this important debate, and no doubt there will be a good deal more discussion along these lines in years to come. For another useful essay on Mrs Robinson, see Susan

Luther's 'A Stranger Minstrel: Coleridge's Mrs Robinson' (*SIR* 33.391–409); the same volume also contains William Keach's exemplary article on Mrs Barbauld's *Eighteen Hundred and Eleven*, 'A Regency Prophecy and the End of Anna Barbauld's Career' (569–78), and Anne K. Mellor's 'Joanna Baillie and the Counter-Public Sphere' (559–68).

Mary A. Favret and Nicola J. Watson's collection, *At the Limits of Romanticism: Essays in Cultural, Feminist, and Materialist Criticism*, is important for other reasons (see also section 2 below). The editors propose that the gender division that has perpetuated the male-dominated canon is the result of the line that has been traditionally drawn between the material and the theoretical in Romantic studies. Indeed that division is found to be responsible for a general limiting of Romanticism along other lines too. By rethinking literary and cultural history, the contributors hope to break down those intellectual barriers and remake academic Romanticism. To this end John Rieder provides a powerful critique of 'Wordsworth and Romanticism in the Academy' and Peter T. Murphy goes back to the Byronic view of Romanticism that values the work of Samuel Rogers. Anne Janowitz proposes the ingenious notion of a 'unified field' of Romantic literature in which it is 'the literary form of a struggle taking place on many levels of society between the claims of individualism and communitarianism'. Lucinda Cole and Richard Swartz discuss literacy in the context of an important essay on Ann Yearsley; Kurt Heinzelman discusses Romantic representations of labour; Sonia Hofkosh takes another look at Hazlitt's Keswick escapade; Nanora Sweet discusses Hemans and the post-Napoleonic moment; Nicola J. Watson examines Byron's relationship with Lady Caroline Lamb; Mark L. Shoenfield examines Hogg's literary persona as mediated through his writings; Andrea Henderson discusses the intellectual background to the Gothic; Jan B. Gordon analyses gossip in Scott's novels; and Marjorie Levinson proposes a new kind of autopoietic discourse through her memorable discussion of Wordsworth's *Old Man Travelling*. This is unquestionably one of the more important collections to arise out of recent critical debates concerning the future of Romantic studies.

Characteristically, these volumes see themselves as breaking down definitions, or building bridges between one set of assumptions and another; *Borderwork*, edited by Margaret R. Higonnet, adds an extra dimension, working out its feminist objectives against the numerous challenges that arise in the discipline of comparative literature. The range of writers dealt with is wide, and there is a good deal of purely theoretical discussion. It contains two important essays about Romantic women: 'Modifications of Genre: A Feminist Critique of "Christabel" and "Die Braut von Korinth"', by Lore Metzger, who uses works by Goethe and Coleridge to 'problematize the normative and regulative function of genre'; and an essay in which Chris Cullens performs an impressive comparative analysis of late eighteenth-century women's novels in England and Germany. Another collection, *Men Writing the Feminine: Literature, Theory, and the Question of Genders*, edited by Thaïs E. Morgan, sets out to examine how 'male authors write the feminine by speaking in the voices and describing the innermost thoughts and feelings of women'. It includes an important essay by Susan J. Wolfson, '*Lyrical Ballads* and the Language of (Men) Feeling: Writing Women's Voices', that shows how implicated in gender discourse the *Lyrical Ballads* project was from its inception.

As so often during the present decade, a number of collections have been issued related to bicentenary celebrations. *Romantic Discourses*, edited by Horst Höhne, is the belated result of a conference held in Ahrenshoop in 1992 to commemorate

Shelley's birth (see also section 3 below). Many of the essays here are thus preoccupied with Shelley, including contributions by Horst Meller, Gerd Rohmann, Kevin Cope, Wolf Hirst, John Freeman, Annette T. Rubinstein and Chris Hopkins. Frederick Burwick's paper on 'Shelley's Narratives of Madness and the Romantic Reception of Tasso' is one of the gems of the collection, providing what must be one of the first detailed examinations of Tasso's influence on Shelley; also of considerable importance must be Christopher Salvesen's 'Hazlitt and Byron: Intermittent Affinities'. Although the strength of the volume lies in its concentration on Shelley, it is no less valuable for its diversity. It is a pleasure to read the editor's discussion of Byron's *Cain*, alongside Karl Heller's essay on music, Angus Calder's discussion of Thomas Campbell, and Philip Cox's brief but provocative analysis of Romantic pastoral.

This year marked the bicentenary of the birth of John Clare, and several collections were issued in celebration. Perhaps the most successful was *John Clare in Context*, eds Hugh Haughton, Adam Phillips and Geoffrey Summerfield. It begins with Mark Storey's survey of critical responses to Clare over the years, and continues with a long and brilliantly argued essay by Hugh Haughton, which characterizes and elucidates Clare's poetry without appearing to reduce it; John Goodridge and Kelsey Thornton's persuasive analysis of trespassing in Clare's work; a superb discussion of Clare's qualities as a poet by Seamus Heaney; what must be the most important essay to date on Clare's politics, by John Lucas; Adam Phillips on Clare's renown as a poet; Nicholas Birns on landscape in Clare; James McCusick on Clare's resistance to Romanticism in its Bloomian form; Clare's interest in botany, discussed by Douglas Chambers; Roy Porter on Clare's madness; and Marilyn Gaull in fine form on Clare and science. The collection is prefaced by a useful and informative introduction by Hugh Haughton and Adam Phillips, and can be regarded as setting the agenda for future critical discussions. One of the features of the books on Clare is the sheer dedication and belief in his work that they all share – a quality not always found in monographs on the canonical writers. This is evident in the other two collections of essays in Clare's memory, *The Independent Spirit*, ed. John Goodridge, and *John Clare: A Bicentenary Celebration*, edited by Richard Foulkes. Both contain top-drawer material, including John Lucas's essay on Bloomfield and Clare, and John Goodridge on the enclosure elegies, in the first volume; and Kelsey Thornton on Clare's complexity, Greg Crossan's 'John Clare: Our Contemporary', and Tom Paulin's 'John Clare: A Bicentennial Celebration', in the second. All three books do credit to the poet in whose memory they are published, and it is to be hoped that they will provide further stimulus for a flourishing body of critical materials. Besides these useful volumes, one of the most important articles to appear this year on Clare was James McKusick's 'John Clare and the Tyranny of Grammar' (*SIR* 33.255–77).

Milton, the Metaphysicals, and Romanticism, edited by Lisa Low and Anthony John Harding, brings together a number of distinguished contributors in a volume that claims to undertake 'a long overdue revaluation of the interrelationship between Romanticism and the seventeenth century, especially in the context of new strategies of reading'. This has an obvious relevance to the essays that open the volume – those by Tilottama Rajan and George Anthony Rosso Jr – but I cannot see in what sense it fully accounts for the largely excellent work here by the other contributors, most of whom are more interested in extending or adapting familiar strategies of reading than in exploring new ones. John T. Shawcross's fine essay on the non-influence of Vaughan on Wordsworth could have been published thirty years ago for all it has to say about new strategies of reading – and is none the worse for that. The truth is that this volume brings together a wide range of critical approaches and techniques, and its coherence derives primarily from its concentration on two distinct historical periods. Besides Milton's influence on Blake, Beckford, Wordsworth, Shelley, Radcliffe and Keats, it examines the relationships between other seventeenth-century writers (Donne, Marvell, Herrick, Cowley, Rochester and Dryden) and the Romantics. Contributors include E. S. Shaffer, Annette Wheeler Cafarelli, Nicola Zoe Trott, Michael Chappell, Beth Lau, Frederick Burwick and Anya Taylor. On a related topic, an entire issue of *The Wordsworth Circle*, guest-edited by Joseph Nicholes, Kenneth R. Johnston and Thomas Prasch, entitled 'Cavaliers and Roundheads First', deals with the reverberations of the Civil War in the nineteenth century; it contains valuable contributions by D. J. Trela, Nicola J. Watson, Terence Hoagwood, Greg Kucich, Steven Jones, Claire A. Simmons, William Levine, Kenneth Campbell, Thomas Prasch and Edward Morris (*WC* 25.iii).

Two Romanticists feature in a volume dedicated to *English Comedy*, edited by Michael Cordner, Peter Holland and John Kerrigan. This is a tribute to Anne Barton, and its contributors are either friends or colleagues. Most of the contributions here focus on Renaissance drama, but subjects extend to Coward and even Wittgenstein. Jonathan Wordsworth writes informatively on 'Wordsworthian Comedy', taking the line that his poet follows in the tradition of Sterne and Burns, combining the sublime and the direct, the tersely rhymed and the genially relaxed. Analysing such features as ballad form, mock-epic and manner, he reveals the wit, charm and tact in this poet's work. Jonathan Bate's 'Apeing Romanticism' extends this line of thought in a comparison of Wordsworth and Byron, arguing that transcendence demands insulation from the deflating effects of comedy. This collection also contains excellent contributions from Barbara Everett on *Much Ado About Nothing*, John Creaser on Ben Jonson, Gillian Beer on rhyming, and John Kerrigan on comic noses.

The explosion of conference activity in the 1990s is reflected in the contents of almost every issue of this year's *Wordsworth Circle*. *WC* 25.i contains a selection of papers delivered at the 1993 meeting of the North American Society for the Study of Romanticism (NASSR), which are on the theme of Romanticism and the ideologies of genre, eds Tilottama Rajan and Angela Esterhammer. Contributors include Clifford Siskin, Scott Harshberger, Robert Leigh Davis and Ruth A. Solie; subjects range from John Thelwall to Quintilian to Whitman. *WC* 25.ii contains papers from two conferences: the first being that on money and Romanticism at the University of Durham, 1993, eds Pamela Clemit and Fiona Robertson. Contributors include Stephen Copley, Jacqueline M. Labbe (an exceptionally good essay on Charlotte Smith, Mary Robinson and the marketing of poetry), David Eastwood (very good on Southey), Lisa Hopkins, Paul Hamilton, James Chandler and Gary Kelly. The second is the Wordsworth Summer Conference at Grasmere, 1993, and includes lectures by Frederick Burwick, W. J. B. Owen, J. Robert Barth, Desmond King-Hele and James Holt McGavran Jr. The proceedings of this year's Wordsworth Winter School in Grasmere, comprising lectures by Mary Wedd, Gordon K. Thomas and Duncan Wu, appeared in *ChLB* 88.

If this year saw the publication of numerous studies questioning the traditional boundaries of the subject, it also saw the appearance of one in which those boundaries are reiterated in a European context. Maurice Cranston's posthumously published *The Romantic Movement* begins by nominating Rousseau as its progenitor, and proceeds to analyse its flowering in Germany, England, France, Italy and Spain. Despite its virtues, this volume is not without lapses. Did Wordsworth really 'make his name' with *An Evening Walk* (1793)? Wordsworth did not think so. Nor would it be correct to say, as Cranston does, that while Wordsworth was in France (1791–2), Coleridge was 'lecturing about the French Revolution in provincial English dissenters' meeting places' (Cranston's chronology is decidedly wrong). Even more striking is his claim that Wordsworth returned to Britain from France after becoming disillusioned with the Revolution; all the evidence (and there is quite a lot of it) indicates that disillusionment came well after Wordsworth's return to England. More surprisingly (given his background as a political scientist), Cranston's elucidation of the primary and secondary imaginations is completely erroneous (it bears little relation to any of the proposed interpretations currently in circulation), and he fails to convey any of the political implications of Keats's status as a Cockney ('cockney' being taken to mean, in his discussion, no more than 'Londoner'). Cranston's coverage of American Romanticism, in his final chapter, is far too brief to be any use; although it mentions Crane it ignores Hawthorne, Melville, Whitman and Poe. Such errors and oversights are highly regrettable, because a volume such as this needs to be watertight in its scholarship – far more so than in the case of monographs – for any teacher to feel confident about recommending it to a student readership. Its best chapters deal with French and German Romanticism (not surprisingly, given Cranston's work in those areas), and they at least will provide students with a useful introduction. Those seeking guidance on the other national literatures dealt with here are advised to look elsewhere.

If one had the sneaking feeling that Cranston's book was twenty years too late, that sense was only underlined by comparison with one of the most provocative and exciting general studies to be published this year, Michael Macovski's *Dialogue and Literature*. It begins by proposing a general theory of literature. In his own words, Macovski 'conceives of literary discourse as a composite of voices – interactive personae that not only are contained within the literary text but extend beyond it, to other works, authors, and interpretations'. Such a notion carries with it a number of important implications for Romantic criticism. For one thing it questions not merely the concept of literary originality and authorial intention, but the prevailing belief in the solipsistic Romantic 'self', the 'I' of such works as *The Prelude*. Macovski proposes that every interior dialogue is predicated on the existence of answering voices – voices of an 'other', or of the speaker's past, present or future – which are occasionally incorporated into that of the speaking 'I'. All literary works, therefore, whatever their form, and whatever their content, are inherently dialogic. This is by now fairly familiar; dialogic readings of the Romantics have been common currency for at least a decade, and with good reason: they have an obvious appropriateness in the case of Wordsworth and Coleridge. What is new is that Macovski concocts a new blend of theories, drawing from the work of Bakhtin, Gadamer, Ong and Foucault, which lead to a reconsideration of such topics as the history of the autotelic self, the dissemination of lyric orality, and the nineteenth-century critique of rhetoric.

Macovski is an agile and stimulating writer; if his analyses of *Tintern Abbey* and *The Rime of the Ancient Mariner* will not win general assent, they do offer valuable new perspectives on these well-known poems. His approach seemed to me to be more satisfactory when applied to *Frankenstein* and *Wuthering Heights* – perhaps in part because the theorists on whose work he depends were themselves working within the context of prose fiction. For a distinguished article which also approaches Wordsworth's poetry from a dialogic perspective see Brooke Hopkins, 'Wordsworth's Voices: Ideology and Self-Critique in *The Prelude*', which appeared this year in *SIR* 33.279–99.

A general study by Marjean D. Purinton, *Romantic Ideology Unmasked: The Mentally Constructed Tyrannies in Dramas of William Wordsworth, Lord Byron, Percy Shelley, and Joanna Baillie*, begins with the assertion that Romantic drama tends to be politically charged and therefore ideologically based. It mediates such things as economic issues, gender relations, class struggles, family dissolutions, political revolutions and religious scepticism. Purinton aims to 'unmask' these embedded layers of ideology and reveal the various fictions that ideology perpetrates as truths. For her, meaning lies in the variety of tyrannies symbolized or inscribed within each work. Against the tendency of past critics, who have suggested that the Romantic closet drama is a form of political quietism, she suggests that readers actively participate in this process, as they are compelled to 'unmask' the ideology which underlies each work. Examining Wordsworth's *The Borderers*, she suggests that political tyranny and the ideology of revolution, spawned by the French in 1789, are privileged above other embedded layers of tyrannies and revolutions, going back to the Barons' Revolt of 1258 and the English Civil War. The play questions the ideology that initiates the revolution–restoration cycle. In the case of Byron's *Manfred* and *Werner* tyrannies arise out of familiar and social conflicts; in this light, they criticize reforms instigated in Regency England. Religious and political tyranny is the subject of *The Cenci* and *Prometheus Unbound*, which are pitched against an ideology based on bifurcated thinking opposed to social and moral reform. Baillie's *Count Basil* and *De Monfort* are preoccupied with gender relations and female emancipation. They illustrate the mental oppression to which women of the time were subject, and from which economic and physical constraints were extrapolated. This is a sound study; I suspect that its arguments are less contentious than its author thinks, and in any case it breaks little ground in theoretical terms. Perhaps its most useful contribution to criticism is the chapter on Joanna Baillie, which provides a fairly lucid ideological reading of two important Romantic dramas that are beginning to attract the attention they deserve. The author misses a number of tricks, often through some inexplicable lapses. I do not understand why, for instance, having done such a thorough job of contextualizing *The Borderers* within the revolution debate, and particularly in the terms established by Godwin and Mary Wollstonecraft, Purinton then discusses the play in its later, much-revised, 1842 text, as opposed to that of 1797–9, which is far closer to the political context she is discussing. This is all the more puzzling given that her quotations are taken from Robert Osborn's Cornell edition, which provides both versions in a parallel text.

From a theoretical and scholarly perspective Ralph Pite's *The Circle of Our Vision: Dante's Presence in English Romantic Poetry* is a more sophisticated affair. Dante's influence on the Romantics has for too long been neglected; oddly, since they all knew his work – some, such as Wordsworth, encountering it at university. Pite suggests that the vividness and realism of Dante's poetry were what really fascinated Romantic writers; these qualities were particularly useful in the composition of poetry that dealt not so much in transcendence as in the self-questioning that arises out of the delusions of any fixed position. It would be wrong, however, to suggest that Pite is interested in the psychology of influence;

the subtitle directs us to Dante's 'presence' – a less specific quality, but perhaps a rather more pervasive one. The advantage of such an approach is that it places so much more emphasis on the discerning abilities of the critic, and Pite reveals an enviable acuity in nosing out Dante in the most unlikely places. Who else would have found Dante in Coleridge's tendency to 'pause' in the 1818 revised version of *The Friend*, for instance? Who, in the same work, would have detected Dante's presence in Coleridge's 'employment of the forms of attention and self-attention, at once engaged and detached, that are required of symbolic prose'? Subtle this may be, but in context it is unimpeachable. Pite is sure-footed in his tracking down of Dante partly because he knows his Dante so well. It would be hard to contest his argument that, for instance, 'Dante's bringing together of clarity and involvement governs Keats's descriptions of suffering in *The Fall of Hyperion*'; once this has been illustrated, one sees that Pite really has illuminated a particular aspect of Keats's writing – an aspect that is indisputably present – that would otherwise have gone unnoticed. Such is his rigour that his study represents a good deal more than what it claims; it is the most perceptive and sensitive analysis I have read of Romantic poetry for a long time, and will be tremendously useful to all Romanticists. It is beautifully written, to boot. I have only one quarrel with it: that although he deals with the work of Coleridge, Shelley, Keats, Byron and Blake (though mainly as an illustrator), Pite has nothing to say about Wordsworth. This is an omission, and rather a serious one at that. If Dante is 'present' in *Hyperion*, I do not see why he should not also be present in *The Excursion*, say, or *Tintern Abbey*. Indeed, should not a discussion of that literary relationship be the basis of the Keats chapter? Or it may be that Dante and Wordsworth form the subject of Pite's next book; certainly, the definitive study on that topic has yet to be written.

Joan Baum's *Mind-Forg'd Manacles: Slavery and the English Romantic Poets* examines the Romantics' response to slavery. Why, she asks, do they rarely speak directly against the harsh truths of the slave trade and colonial slavery – and on the rare occasions when they do, manage it to no great effect? Her answer is that they realized that political solutions had failed, and that political poetry was not poetry at all, but versified propaganda with no enduring value as literature. Radicals, she reveals, felt that the fight against slavery was a distraction from the more important battles against the slavery of the working class at large. Although radicals and poets used much the same language, only the poets realized that everyone was implicated in slavery – that oppressors too were victims of their oppression. I wonder whether it is always fair to apply the moral standards of our own times to those who lived 200 years ago. She criticizes John Wordsworth, the poet's brother, on the grounds that he 'did not like Jews or Negroes'; much though one may share her contempt for such prejudices today, I doubt whether John Wordsworth was untypical of either his class or his time in espousing such views, and I wonder whether there might be more to be gained by contextualizing them rather than by citing them as evidence against those concerned. More importantly, Baum's case depends largely on the argument that such poems as Wordsworth's sonnet on Toussaint L'Ouverture, though effective as literature, are useless as agitprop. This may or may not be true, but it would be dangerous to use the failure of Romantic poetry to effect political change to prove that its authors had no desire to see slavery abolished. After all, the close relationship of the Wordsworths and Coleridge with Thomas Clarkson during the 1800s – a time when Clarkson was talking about little else but abolition – and their reading of his books on the subject, in manuscript and proof, would suggest that they were rather more interested in slavery than she allows. None the less, Baum's writing is lively and engaging, and she has tracked down some compelling illustrations for this volume that help make it a particularly enjoyable read. [Duncan Wu]

(b) Individual Authors

The two annual bibliographies of William Blake's art and writing published in *Blake* make an indispensable starting point for any study. The spring 1995 issue breaks with earlier practices and includes both Robert N. Essick's 'Blake in the Marketplace, 1994' and G. E. Bentley Jr's (with the assistance of Keiko Aoyama) 'William Blake and his Circle: A Checklist of Publications and Discoveries in 1994' (*Blake* 28[1995].120–41 and 142–86).

Robert Essick's annual sales checklist is highly authoritative, not least because Essick is a considerable buyer as well as a considerable scholar. Although there is no published catalogue, researchers would do well to remember Essick's collection when considering how to locate items. Past issues of 'Blake in the Marketplace' will provide a ready source to monitor the growth of this collection. For 1994, Essick reports the purchase for his collection of recto and verso proof impressions of plates eleven and seventeen of *Europe*. Blake's art reported lost and found at Yale University Medical School Library includes (lost) a stolen study for 'Pestilence: The Death of the First-Born' and (found) 'Two Types of Insanity' (noted by Butlin as 'untraced since 1949'). A fifth copy of the rare etching of Blake and Thomas Stothard 'in Custody by the Medway' has also come to light (Essick collection), annotated in pencil by Mrs A. E. Bray, the early biographer of Stothard. Blake and Stothard had been arrested on suspicion of spying during a boating expedition. Essick also lists the sale of Cold War spy Anthony Blunt's gift copy of his *Art of William Blake* (1959), which was given by Blunt to Guy Burgess's *mother* in order to elude an incautious connection.

Bentley's checklist for 1994, as well as being a finding list for the year's work in Blake, is a useful mini-supplement to his *Blake Books Supplement* (Clarendon, 1995), which will be reviewed in next year's coverage, if you happen to have one but not the other to hand. The highly technical endorsements and revisions to the bibliographical history of the illuminated books necessitated by Joseph Viscomi's *Blake and the Idea of the Book* (*YWES* 74.321-2) are detailed in Bentley's updating for this year's *Blake*, along with Bentley's own comments. Usefully, this checklist also includes photographs of electrotypes taken from some of those few of Blake's original copper plates that briefly survived his death, which process reveals plate-makers' marks: a sure clue to how Blake recycled the backs of the copper plates. In turn, this has become a new point of investigation for scholars. An item which also came to light this year is the letter-book of Joseph Johnson, the radical publisher friend of Blake, Godwin, Wollstonecraft, Paine, Wordsworth and Coleridge. The letter-book (reportedly now with P&C), quite apart from its intrinsic interest in recording Johnson's experiences of imprisonment for sedition, includes details of payments made to William Hayley on behalf of Blake's engravings for the *Life of Cowper* (Clare Tomalin, *TLS* 4783.15–16).

Blake spent three difficult years at Felpham living under the patronage and protection of Hayley. Philip Cox's 'Blake, Hayley and Milton: A Reassessment' (*ES* 75.430–41) examines the relationship between Blake's *Milton* and William Hayley, author of *The Life of Milton* (1794). By re-reading the literary qualities in Hayley's *Life of Milton*, Cox modifies J. A. Wittreich's influential work in this area. Cox notes how tropes of retirement, mildness, moderation and benevolence are Hayley's favoured touchstone terms for Milton, tantamount to a systematic depoliticizing of Milton's life, which Hayley framed to suit his own response to the revolutionary travails of the 1790s. Cox reminds us that Hayley had considered writing a pamphlet to temper Burke's *Reflections* but, significantly, abandoned it in order to give more time to his domestic affairs. Blake's *Milton* is a decisive rejection of this mild domesticity. Nevertheless, the historical record of these times is fraught with unexpected reversals when it comes to deciding political allegiances. Cox refers to lawyer Thomas Erskine's quoting of Milton to support his courtroom defence of Tom Paine in 1793, but, three years later, the same man quoted *Paradise Lost* to similar effect in order to prosecute him for *The Age of Reason*.

Further information about Blake's later life is included in David Linnell's *Blake, Palmer, Linnell and Co.: The Life of John Linnell*. David Linnell, a descendant, reminds us of how closely the younger and older watercolourists were connected; they visited exhibitions, and shared friendships with Samuel Palmer and the Varley brothers. Blake was on the scene when Linnell publicly embarrassed the Duke of Argyll over the non-payment of a bill. It was also Linnell who arranged (and paid for) Blake's funeral: the cortege and interment details are listed here, all procured from a funeral-directing cabinet maker only a few doors up from the site of Blake's baptism at St James's, Piccadilly. Fascinating although this book is, its value is severely compromised by its lack of anything approaching a modern scholarly apparatus. The original sources are in the holdings of the Linnell Trust or else amongst the Ivimy manuscripts, but none is precisely differentiated or noted. Those interested further should start at the National Register of Archives, Quality Court, Chancery Lane, London.

At the other extreme to this rather vague narrative lies a study as technically accomplished as Joseph Viscomi's '*A Breach in the City the Morning after the Battle*: Lost or Found?' (*Blake* 28.44–61). This kind of inquiry is daunting: old layers of art-historical narrative (mainly based upon loose stylistic deductions) have to be stripped away like so much varnish. For the independent scholar, emulation of Viscomi is nigh on impossible: the version of *A Breach* he redates is in his own university's Ackland Art Museum at Chapel Hill. In short (for the logic is exceedingly fine), Viscomi redates this picture to the early 1780s rather than to the hothouse 1790s whilst, very tentatively, he also suggests that the Ackland *Breach* is a mistitled picture Blake exhibited at the Royal Academy in 1784. The implicit questions the article raises about dating on stylistic grounds, dating on configurations of signature, and dating on the cumulative wisdom of tradition and provenance all make this fine essay required reading. The processes of extrapolation involved are pertinent to much of Blake's verbal and visual art and scholars would be misleading themselves if they were to think Viscomi's conclusions are a dry cul-de-sac of art history.

Nevertheless, before Blake scholarship 'goes critical' on the technicalities, Eugenie R. Freed's *'A Portion of his Life': William Blake's Miltonic Vision of Woman* recaptures something of the holistic Blakean study we are in danger of losing. Laid out with plenty of pictures, familiar and unfamiliar, from Blake's illuminated books as well as obscure alchemical sources, Freed's study is rich in its primary references to Blake's text and to a wide range of modern scholarship. Knotty problems are not ducked: there are two chapters on the subject of Blake's complex idea of Ololon in *Milton*. Precisely because the details of Blake's text and art are difficult to master, *'A Portion of his Life'* is not only a book one would recommend to graduates and abler undergraduates but also to those of us who, periodically, miss the wood for the trees.

David Stewart's 'The Context of Blakean Contraries in *The Marriage of Heaven and Hell*' (*ELWIU* 21.43–53) also returns us to areas known but not yet fully understood by examining Blake's debt to Jacob Boehme, whose presence in that book Stewart argues lies behind Blake's more obvious attack on Swedenborg. The essay's best qualities are its close, detailed readings and cross-references to Boehme's texts; although the essential connections established between ideas of contrariety in Blake and Boehme have been made before and in a similar fashion. Despite the title of Stewart's article, there is little attempt to contextualize Boehme into late eighteenth-century English dissent otherwise, apart from a reference to an interesting enough letter about Newton's doctrine of attraction and repulsion written by William Law in the early 1780s.

The figure of Newton holds a terrible fascination for Blakeans. A brief note by David Simpson in the pages of *Blake* is startlingly original and provocative in suggesting that the subject of the *Newton* colour print is Reverend John Newton, slaver, divine and friend of Cowper ('Which Newton for the British Library?', *Blake* 28.77–8). Simpson points out that John Newton was better known to Blake's generation than Isaac and that, suggestively for the image shown in *Newton*, John Newton's *Authentic Narrative* (1764) of being shipwrecked onto an island off Africa contains a recollection, which prefigured his conversion, that he would often 'take [himself] to remote corners of the island by the sea side, and draw my diagrams [from Euclid] with a long stick upon the sand'. Wordsworth also reports this incident in *The Prelude*, Book VI. With Eduardo Paolozzi's giant 'Newton' sculpture currently being completed for the new St Pancras British Library site, it is intriguing to think that Blake's original image might pose a further dualism about science and belief.

The fuller context of Newton in Blake's work is discussed in Stuart Peterfreund's 'Blake and the Ideology of the Natural' (*ECLife* 18.92–119). Following in the vein set out by Essick in *William Blake and the Language of Adam* (*YWES* 70.87–8), Peterfreund examines the extended roles of metaphor and metonymy not only in Blake but also in Newton and Locke. The essay repays careful reading. Peterfreund suggests that an 'ideology of the natural' is established by the various attempts of seventeenth- and eighteenth-century natural philosophers to explain the immanent principles structuring the universe (a project Blake typified by his memorable adage that 'every Natural Effect has a Spiritual Cause'). In the seventeenth century they consciously employed metaphors and metonymies to explain natural phenomena. Locke knew his '*semeiotike*, or *the Doctrine of Signs*', and Newton was happy to think of light as corpuscular knowing that white light was always refractable into minute colours, a purity supplemented by fractions of light implicitly imbued with immanent principles. Peterfreund shows that Blake brilliantly deconstructs Newtonian corpuscles by insisting that the universe is composed of globules of red blood, an unrefractable colour common to the universe (the sun) and to humanity (the son). Peterfreund's is a very perceptive essay which combines a high level of theoretical acumen within a safely historicist methodology.

In a comparably historicist mode is the present writer's co-edition of essays with Steve Clark, *Historicizing Blake*. The volume is reviewed by Jason Whittaker (*BARS Bulletin & Review* 9[1995].19), who says of it that 'although there is a common agenda to this collection, there is also a considerable diversity in the approach to individual texts which makes *Historicizing Blake* an absorbing anthology'. Essays by Iain McCalman and Jon Mee focus first on the turncoat William Hamilton Reid; Whittaker describes these 'as an entry-point into the murky society of British radicalism, whilst Mee's discussion of the religious ideas of the hyper-Calvinist, William Huntingdon, and the radical engraver, Garnet Terry, provides the necessary context without which some of Blake's religious ideas seem isolated'. In addition, there are essays by Edward Larrissy on 'alchemy and the fate of the "bound"', Mary Lynn Johnson on atomism, Andrew Lincoln on 'Blake and the Reasoning Historian', Philip Cox on *The Four Zoas* and the pastoral of commerce, Detlef Dörrbecker on engravers and the Royal Academy, Helen Bruder's feminist review of *Thel* criticism and John Beer's inquiry into Blake's use of the apocryphal Book of Enoch. Whittaker wrote in conclusion that *Historicizing Blake*'s 'achievement is to draw our attention to the diversity of that society often neglected by orthodox history'.

Amidst all this contextualization, Jeanne Moskal's *Blake, Ethics, and Forgiveness* is a brave and important study of Blake's moral framework, a matter which it would be folly to ignore. There are two principal subsets to Moskal's ideas: first that after 1803, when Blake stood trial for sedition, he tended to reformulate error into a more invasive force of evil. Second, Moskal distinguishes forgiveness into two types, the intrapsychic and the intersubjective. Crucial to these definitions are what Blake calls 'states': 'Distinguish therefore States from Individuals in those States'. Intrapsychic forgiveness might, for example, involve a recognition of the contraries of good or evil at play within an individual. Intersubjective forgiveness might involve the forgiveness of individuals who are collectively composed into states (churches, nations, classes, even genders). Englishmen might forgive Frenchmen (intersubjective); Blake might forgive the patrician Hayley (intersubjective); Blake might also distinguish within himself Los, Urthona, Luvah and Tharmas (intrapsychic) as well as Satan and the Spectre (*both* intrapsychic and intersubjective), all of whom require forgiveness. There are also helpful individual commentaries; amongst many others, on the watercolour 'The Woman Taken in Adultery' (Moskal reminds us that in John's gospel she had been brought to Jesus in order that the Pharisees might 'accuse him'); on Blake's asking the reader to 'forgive what you do not approve' (*Jerusalem*); and on the role of accusation in the complex classes of Elect, Redeemed and Reprobate in *Milton*.

Moskal's taxonomies of Blakean morals are usefully systematic. So too, but more limited, are William Crisman's classifications of different types of song and different types of poetic purpose in the *Poetical Sketches* ('Songs named "Song" and the Bind of the Self-Conscious Lyricism in Blake', *ELH* 61.619–33). Crisman discusses the social role of the literary lyric and touches on the role of sociability in the eighteenth century. Nevertheless, although Crisman reads, reviews and adjudicates between modern judgements of these early Blake poems very skilfully, there is something ahistorical in suggesting that, in Blake's time at least, prophetic form was socially distanced or negative while lyric speech 'is a model for joining people'.

Jules van Lieshout's *Within and Without Eternity: The Dynamics of Interaction in William Blake's Myth and Poetry* is difficult to summarize. There are many close readings of individual poems informed by a modification of a Bakhtinian concept about the role of language and writing – Blake's text as a prime site of heteroglossia, as it were. *Within and Without Eternity* also does an admirably methodical job of, *inter alia*, reviewing the 1980s wave of deconstructionist criticism, to which Lieshout's work is moderately sympathetic. It may be objected that some of the theoretical insights (although the book is not overtly led by theoretical exposition) are not without their drawbacks. For example, Lieshout asserts that Blake's illuminated books are to be read by scanning, rather in the way in which our eyes habitually 'graze' television or advertising. It is difficult to think of Blake's age as being as oversupplied with the bulk delivery of visual images as our own. Lieshout also pays scant attention to the chronology or differing formats of Blake's work. However, in so far as Lieshout presents new ideas, novel and refreshing ways of thinking about Blake's text (particularly that the reader-writer relationship is one of process), *Within and Without Eternity* has plenty to offer.

Far less helpful are some studies which add little to our knowledge. Michael Holley's 'Blake's Atlantis' (*CLQ* 30.109–18) is not without the benefit of close readings or biographical details, but the occasional foray into Erdman and, alas, Jung tells us little new about this mythic trope from Blake's *America*. Similar too, although characterized by an up-to-date appreciation of Viscomi's work and the Blake Trust facsimiles, is Mark Epstein's 'The Two William Blakes' (*NewC* 13.10–22). Epstein's essay is personal (recalling how in 1966 'students high on mescaline intoned Blake's Lambeth prophecies'), but the two Blakes are 'sweet William' and 'mad, bad Willie'. Expect little from both. Martin Bidney's 'A Song of Innocence and of Experience: Rewriting Blake in Brodkey's "Piping Down the Valleys Wild"' (*SSF* 31.237–45) is very difficult to assess because there is so little attempt to contextualize (or canonize) the Harold Brodkey short stories, *First Love and Other Sorrows* (1954), which Bidney finds 'allusively signal' the presence of Blake's *Songs* in their treatment of human contrary states.

Much more useful are two studies of Blake's reception in the late nineteenth and early twentieth century. June Sturrock's essay 'Protective Pastoral: Innocence and Female Experience in William Blake's *Songs* and Christina Rossetti's *Goblin Market*' (*CLQ* 30.98–108) does not attempt to trace historical connections or influences between these two texts, which were both aimed at children, but, rather, it argues that Blake and Rossetti present similar versions of pastoral which depict protected worlds of feminized, Christian innocence. Also recuperative of overlooked female artistic endeavour is Claire Hardisty's essay 'Edna Clarke Hall 1879–1979: A Feminist Interpretation of her Life and Work' (*Women* 5.73–80). Clarke Hall was a painter (mainly) and poet (sometimes – she published two collections) who identified her early life with that of William Blake and Charlotte Bronte. Her life appears to have been as obscure and lowly as Blake's but just as emotionally intense and full. A lot of her pictures, with their vivid mastery and quickness of impression, were destroyed by enemy action during World War II. Revealingly, many of the surviving drawings are in the Tate Gallery *store room*. Sturrock makes out an interesting and sympathetic case for why we should re-examine her work, which is now scattered across many English art galleries.

One of the year's best excursions into contextual recovery is the well-produced and wide-ranging essay by Michael Phillips, 'Blake and the Terror 1792–93' (*Library* 16.263–97). Using many primary sources located in manuscript, scarce pamphlets, and ephemera supported by colour and black-and-white photographs, Phillips fully narrates the dramatic psychological effects in Lambeth and its surrounding districts of Pitt's 'terror' with its closing down of freedoms of speech and writing. The reactionary Loyalist Association's influence in Lambeth, as well as the more ad hoc oppositional forces of Thomas Spence, Daniel Isaac Eaton, William Godwin and many others, are discussed for the months leading up to the more famous treason trials of 1794. Closing by examining the unique copy L of

Blake's 'Song of Liberty' (see *YWES* 74.323), Phillips has gathered a wide contextual survey which provides a political and psychological snapshot of Blake's Lambeth when the artist was at the height of his powers. This is first-rate historical research.

Blake experimented with just about all the contemporary methods of engraving available to him. He would have loved the Internet with its ease in transmitting and distributing text and image. Inevitably, Blake is available in cyberspace. An electronic conference in San Francisco, California (which appears to have begun in this year), can be accessed via email at: blake-request@albion.com. There might be ten new messages a day ranging from the cranky to the latest news in Blake studies, thoughtfully entered in by some of the best-known scholars in the field. It is a site for enthusiasts more than a source of comprehensive information, but this service should be added to those resources available to scholars. Next year these pages will give further information on world-wide web sites about Blake, set up by Morris Eaves, Nelson Hilton and Joe Viscomi. These can be most conveniently accessed by first visiting the University of California Santa Barbara 'Romantic Chronology' site at either: http://humanitas.ucsb.edu/projects/pack/rom-chrono/ chrono.htm, or: http://humanitas.ucsb.edu/projects/pack/romchrono/chrono_text.htm. These are exciting times, electronically speaking. [David Worrall]

Angela Esterhammer's writings on speech-act theory and its usefulness in addressing the distinctiveness of visionary language, particularly in the case of Blake, are well known for their originality and intelligence, and these qualities are what make her new volume, *Creating States: Studies in the Performative Language of John Milton and William Blake*, so important. Esterhammer has one of the most formidable theoretical minds in the business, and her first chapter establishes, with admirable thoroughness, the background to her discussion. The central point of her book is to demonstrate the significance of the sociopolitical and phenomenological performative, of the scene of discourse and subjectivity in language, through readings of Milton and Blake. In the case of Blake she reveals how he inherits a paradigm of performative language from Milton and the Bible which conflicts with the operation of language in his social and political environment. Esterhammer traces this tension in *Songs of Innocence and Experience*, *Urizen* and *The Marriage of Heaven and Hell*, and concludes by arguing that a compromise of sorts is reached in *Jerusalem*. Her arguments are well grounded and backed up by some of the sharpest readings of Blake I have seen in a long time; this is a contribution of enduring value to all those working on this difficult writer.

Last year Peter Kitson was able to confirm Wordsworth's popularity among the authors of monographs. Amazingly, although numerous articles on this poet appeared in collections or in periodicals, only two monographs appeared in 1994: Judith Page's *Wordsworth and the Cultivation of Women* and David Collings's *Wordsworthian Errancies: The Poetics of Cultural Dismemberment.* Against the tendency of most feminist critiques, which portray him as a mercenary exploiter of women, Page's unexpected but welcome study attempts a more rounded view. Page is every inch a feminist, but she finds in 'Wordsworthian sublimity a paradoxical yearning for relationship, a tension that in the later poetry resolves itself in images of beauty and domesticity constructed from a masculine point of view'. This tension is traced in the poetry of the great decade, as well as in *The White Doe of Rylstone* and *The Excursion.* But perhaps the most impressive work here is to be found in the final chapter and the conclusion, which deal primarily with Dora Wordsworth and her relationship with her father. Page finds that the later poetry 'endorses an ideology of womanhood that limits and constrains women's achievements by emphasizing virtues associated with home and hearth', frequently through the figure of daughters. In the conclusion, Page uses published and unpublished writings to examine Dora's readings of her father's work. To her credit, she is interested in doing more than merely confirm a prepared agenda; her enthusiasm and sensitivity for the poetry are evident at every point of this useful study. It is to be hoped that it will stimulate further work on Dora Wordsworth, whose importance as a writer and reader is only slowly coming to be realized.

For David Collings, the outbreak of war between France and Britain in 1793 was a cataclysmic event in Wordsworth's life, which had a formative influence on the poetry of the succeeding decade; for Collings, the starting point for Wordsworth's career was his decision 'to read culture as the scene of its own undoing'. Out of this impulse he generated his own poetics of errancy, a hyperbolic poetics with 'immense implications for his conception of masculine identity and sexuality'. In short, he becomes preoccupied with masochistic desires, which recur throughout his work in such works as *The Ruined Cottage*, *The Thorn*, *The Borderers*, and the 1799 and 1805 *Preludes*. Most of the volume traces such preoccupations through these works – with, it has to be said, varying success. I suspect that few readers will take easily to the notion that the boat-stealing episode in *The Prelude* 'conflates murder and sex, oedipal violence and anal intercourse, as if being stabbed, castrated, and penetrated are versions of the same event that demonstrates beyond doubt the father's vengeful love'. Besides the waywardness of some of Collings's interpretations, it seems to me that his attention is wasted on the poetry of 1793–1804; if his theory is correct, the proof for it will surely be found in the writing of 1792–3, and specifically *Descriptive Sketches* and the *Letter to the Bishop of Llandaff.*

A number of articles on Wordsworth appeared this year. Working from unpublished juvenilia Duncan Wu attempted to psychoanalyse the young poet in 'Wordsworth and Helvellyn's Womb' (*EIC* 44.6–25); David Perkins discussed technique in 'Wordsworth, Hunt, and the Romantic Understanding of Meter' (*JEGP* 93.1–17); James Shokoff examined the Wordsworthian attitude to death in 'Wordsworth's Duty as a Poet in "We are Seven" and "Surprised by Joy"' (*JEGP* 93.228–39); Evan Radcliffe analysed ideological matters in 'Saving Ideals: Revolution and Benevolence in *The Prelude*' (*JEGP* 93.534–59); Stephen Gill's important study of the Victorian Wordsworth continued in 'Wordsworth and "Catholic Truth": The Role of Frederick William Faber' (*RES* 45.204–20); Alan G. Hill examined the poet's use of pagan mythology in 'Wordsworth, Boccaccio, and the Pagan Gods of Antiquity' (*RES* 45.26–41); and Nicholas A. Joukovsky resurrected a hitherto neglected prose work in 'Wordsworth's Lost Article on Byron and Southey' (*RES* 45.496–516).

The scholarly event in the Coleridge world this year was the publication of James Engell's edition of *Coleridge: The Early Family Letters*. Fewer than half have been published previously, though all have been available, for many years, at the British Library. None is by or to S. T. Coleridge himself, and he is rarely mentioned in them, but they reveal a good deal about his family history, which none of his biographers has yet dealt with in any detail. It is interesting to learn, for instance, that John and Frank Coleridge, the poet's older brothers, committed suicide as young men in India. Among the other siblings, William and George were teachers in Hackney, Luke was a doctor at the London Hospital, and all adored their sister who, thanks to family poverty, was compelled to take a job as a milliner's assistant in Exeter. Coleridge's relationships with these various siblings must have been important – as important, in their own way, as that of Wordsworth with his sister – and this welcome volume is a first step towards further research in this area.

Jack Stillinger's *Coleridge and Textual Instability: The Multiple Versions of the Major Poems* is an application of principles enunciated in his thought-provoking study of last year, *Multiple Authorship and the Myth of Solitary Genius* (*YWES* 72.272–3). In his latest work Stillinger argues that there can exist more than one authoritative version of a text and that it is only by viewing the collective versions of the poem that a better understanding of the meaning of the texts can be achieved. Stillinger establishes and documents the existence of the several different, yet authoritative, versions of Coleridge's 'major' poems: 'The Eolian Harp' (sixteen versions), 'The Rime of the Ancient Mariner' (eighteen versions) as well as for 'This Lime-Tree Bower My Prison', 'Frost at Midnight', 'Kubla Khan'. 'Christabel' and 'Dejection: An Ode' (ninety-four versions all told for the seven poems under consideration). Stillinger is a superb textual scholar and his descriptions and discussions of the poetic texts issued by Coleridge are painstakingly thorough. This book is required reading for serious scholars of the poetry, although it will no doubt infuriate undergraduate readers who want to know which text they should study. Stillinger deftly journeys through the various versions of the poems with an extended commentary on each, before printing a reading text of each poem with variations. This is an indispensable study for those working with Coleridge's poetry. [Peter J. Kitson]

Patrick J. Keane's *Coleridge's Submerged Politics: The Ancient Mariner and Robinson Crusoe* was one of the best-researched, and weightier, critical volumes on the poet to be issued this year. At a time when the pressure on critics to align themselves with a school has never been greater, you have to admire Keane's dogged individuality. Although his principal concern is with ideology it would be rash to brand him as a new historicist. His intellectual forebears are the likes of C. L. R. James and E. P. Thompson, and in truth his methods are never more obscure or recondite than theirs. More to the point, he attacks Coleridge's constantly increasing corpus with infectious enthusiasm, meditating, for the first 165 pages, on the Defoe marginalia. His central task is to ask why Coleridge remained silent on the issue of Crusoe's – and Defoe's – attitude to slavery. To an extent, the answer he offers – that the Romantics regarded the imagination as somehow separate from radical politics – reveals him as a new historicist at heart. But he is too artful, and too wise, to be content with that. 'A man haunted by that material world', he writes, 'specifically by the French Revolution and its seismic and atmospheric repercussions in England in the 1790s – could not simply turn off the current of political ideas and images.' Political elements are to be found in *The Ancient Mariner*, but they are definitely 'under the surface'. There are several remarkable things about this book. Perhaps the most important is that Keane manages to 'recontextualize' Coleridge without diminishing him; in the tradition of all great studies of this poet, *Coleridge's Submerged Politics* is erudite, expansive, and full of pleasure in the sheer act of reading good poetry. Not everyone will agree with its thesis, nor will everyone think politics a necessary element in our reading of Coleridge's poem, but Keane is always engaging and provocative; and those qualities alone make this a book worth reading.

Leonard Orr's *Critical Essays on Samuel Taylor Coleridge* is a welcome addition to secondary literature on the poet. It combines already-published criticism by John Beer, Stuart Peterfreund, Paul Magnuson, Andrew M. Cooper, Anne K.

Mellor, Kathleen M. Wheeler, Lawrence Buell and Jerome Christensen with new essays by James McCusick and James Engell. The result is a well-rounded volume, representing many major contemporary writers on the subject, with much of value on the poetry and *Biographia Literaria*. Coleridge scholarship received a boost in *N&Q* this year, which contained three hitherto uncollected marginalia from De Quincey in a useful note by Daniel Sanjiv Roberts (*N&Q* 41.329–35). Also in *N&Q* 41 are the following interesting notes relating to Coleridge's works: Tomoya Oda's 'The Book of Bowles's Poems that Coleridge sent to Mary Evans' (329); Lynda Pratt's 'Coleridge, Wordsworth, and *Joan of Arc*' and her 'A Coleridge Borrowing from Southey' (336–7); David Chandler's 'Coleridge: An Early Claim that the "Law of Association" came from Aristotle' (338–9); and Chris Jones's 'John Newton and Coleridge's "Fears in Solitude"' (339–41).

This was a good year for Shelley criticism. Karen Weisman's new reading of the poet in *Imageless Truths: Shelley's Poetic Fictions* centres on his changing constructions of poetic fictions. Shelley's understanding of language in general, and in particular of fictions and their rhetorical tropes, underwent continual change during his career. It is in his self-consciousness over these transformations, Weisman suggests, that the primary motivating factor in his philosophical and literary development can be found. For her, the Shelley canon represents a developing quest for a mode of fiction-making sensitive to the poet's ill-defined belief in what she calls 'a metaphysical ultimate'. According to her argument, Shelley's awareness of fictionality is a major element in his work, but it comes with an uneasy awareness of the limits of fiction. That double-bind is what marks Shelley out among the Romantic poets. Confronting deconstructionist free play, she suggests that the relentless fictionalizing tendencies of Shelley's poetry articulate a profound anxiety about ontological and epistemological absolutes. Angst and guilt permeate his use of poetic language.

This is an energetic and witty reworking of the standard deconstructionist line, and it is most persuasive in the cases of *Adonais* and *Mont Blanc*, which conform rather well to her basic thesis. But what makes her case so plausible is that it allows for inconsistencies in the poet himself. Her Shelley is a poet of conflicts and anxieties; the same character that emerges out of letters, memoirs and biographies. Bryan Shelley's portrait of the poet, in his *Shelley and Scripture: The Interpreting Angel*, is more surprising. He resists both the early misconceptions of Shelley as a Christian, and the more recent claims that he was an atheist. Assessing Shelley's poetic theory and practice in relation to Gnostic heresies of the early church period and the Enlightenment critiques of Scripture, he argues that the poet's attitude to biblical interpretation was heterodox and revisionist. In appropriating scriptural elements in his poetry, Shelley is shown to have sought out ethical content and its ideals of the kingdom of heaven. Bryan Shelley's analysis is intriguingly consonant with Weisman's, in so far as he finds the later Shelley to have been an increasingly spiritualized self who realizes that his true element is elsewhere. This exceedingly useful volume deals, once and for all, with Shelley's religious beliefs. He was consistent only in remaining inconsistent in his religious views throughout his life. The real point of this study is that it underlines the fact that, like all the Romantics, Shelley was extremely well versed in the Bible and its teachings, which had a formative effect on all his poetry. This exceptionally sound and well-written volume is especially good on such subjects as Shelley's Christ – the 'Jacobin Jesus' – and the later Shelley.

Steven E. Jones's *Shelley's Satire: Violence, Exhortation, and Authority* must be the first book-length examination of the poet's satirical works. A self-professed new historicist, Jones sets out to place such works as *Peter Bell the Third* and *The Mask of Anarchy* in the broad context of popular, political and material culture. For Jones, they comprise 'an important countervoice within Shelley's work and within Romanticism as a whole'. That voice is contradictory, incorporating expressions of curse and revenge. Shelley exhorts and persuades through inherited forms of authority to which he is both attracted and opposed. This rhetorical conflict shapes the satires and is one of their foremost concerns. The larger project of the study is to demonstrate how social determinants control the poet's voice. This is naturally an important issue within Shelley studies, particularly as he is so preoccupied with the desire to change the world for the better. This is a carefully thought-out work, and is characterized by an imaginative use not just of published texts but of Shelley's manuscripts. The chapter on *The Mask of Anarchy* is especially illuminating; it would be hard to fault Jones's case that the poem was Shelley's 'deliberate bid for a representative popular voice'.

In *The Shelley–Byron Conversation* William D. Brewer argues that the two poets were less opposed than has previously been thought, and that they were in fact collaborators. In search of evidence that they have not been given sufficient credit for their willingness to learn from each other, he shows how their personal and literary dialogues ranged from discussions of social-activist goals to perceptions of the benighted state of humanity. Brewer's argument is backed up by close readings of the poetry produced by the two poets during their two periods of close collaboration, in 1816 and 1818. Refreshingly unencumbered by theoretical baggage, Brewer discusses the poetry with insight and passion, and shows the full extent to which Byron and Shelley were indeed, in their different ways, Promethean figures who possessed the unusual ability to inspire each other. This fine work contains two appendices, one on Byron and Shelley in Mary Shelley's *The Last Man*, the other on money and the Byron–Shelley relationship.

David Duff's *Romance and Revolution: Shelley and the Politics of a Genre* takes a new approach to two well-known Shelley poems, *Queen Mab* and *Laon and Cythna*, showing how they emerged from the revival of romance as a literary form and the imaginative impact of the French revolution. Central to Duff's argument is his conviction that the use of romance in revolutionary writings was appropriate to a moment at which history 'seemed to enter the domain of the miraculous'. Drawing on a wide variety of texts, Duff explores the myth-making power of romance metaphors in revolutionary discourse; this section of his study culminates with a remarkable analysis of Wordsworth's 'French Revolution, As It Appeared to Enthusiasts at Its Commencement' (an extract from *The Prelude* published in *The Friend*, 1809), showing how its ideas and language relate to the revolutionary debate as well as to romance concepts. Duff's discussion of *Queen Mab* is in many respects exemplary; it is rightly concerned with the poem's political exploitation of romance, and pays careful attention to such matters as its title-page and its relation to Southey's *Thalaba*. Duff sees *Laon and Cythna* as much more closely related to the work of Spenser and Wordsworth, while at the same time he argues that it is a 'perfect' example of the internalization of the romance genre. This careful, learned volume is full of feeling for its subject, and Duff succeeds in establishing the revolutionary romance as a subgenre about which a good deal remains yet to be said.

A number of useful articles on Shelley appeared this year, besides those already mentioned. The *KSJ* published Kyle Grimes's 'Censorship, Violence, and Political

Rhetoric: *The Revolt of Islam* in its Time' (43.98–116), John Morillo's 'Vegetating Radicals and Imperial Politics: Shelley's *Triumph of Life* as Revision of Southey's *Pilgrimage to Waterloo*' (43.117–40), Susan Fischman's '"Like the Sound of His Own Voice": Gender, Audition, and Echo in *Alastor*' (43.141–69), and an exemplary essay by Scott McEathron, 'Death as "Refuge and Ruin": Shelley's "A Vision of the Sea" and Coleridge's "The Rime of the Ancient Mariner"' (43.170–92).

There were, apparently, no critical books dedicated exclusively to Byron in this year, the main consolation being publication of the long-awaited supplementary volume to Byron's letters and journals, *What Comes Uppermost*, ed. Leslie A. Marchand. It contains, among many other items of interest, two substantial letters to Edward Long, one to Madame de Staël, four to Murray, eight to Kinnaird, and several to Galignani and to John Hunt. The annotation is not always as comprehensive as it should be, but this is a welcome addition to the Byron canon, which no Byronist can afford to be without. Among those articles published this year on the noble Lord, Michael Scrivener's '"Zion alone is forbidden": Anti-semitism in Byron's *The Age of Bronze* is particularly intriguing, being an attempt to historicize the poet's antisemitism (*KSJ* 43.75–97).

Perhaps because they were holding fire until the bicentenary year, few Keatsian monographs appeared this year. The most important was Andrew Bennett's *Keats, Narrative and Audience: The Posthumous Life of Writing*. Bennett focuses on what he regards as a neurotic obsession with audience among the Romantics; in Keats's case this resulted in 'instabilities' in the poetry, observable in his solecisms: linguistic vulgarity, grammatical dislocations, and other rhetorical improprieties. Another important product of this obsession – in some ways the most important, from Bennett's point of view – is the way in which reading is 'figured' in Keats's poetry as something necessarily deferred to a time after the poet's death. Reading is thus the posthumous life of writing. This is an intricate, witty and learned volume, and it must be one of the most accomplished of the recent studies on Romantic readerships.

Rodney Stenning Edgecombe's *Leigh Hunt and the Poetry of Fancy* is the first full-length study of Hunt's verse. Edgecombe bravely admits that the poetry is minor but argues that it be read on its own terms; to this end he elucidates Hunt's distinctive aesthetics, urging that his 'rococo' manner be allowed to define our approach to his decorative and escapist tendencies. It is a shame, I think, that Edgecombe has not offered a chronological assessment of Hunt's work, instead adhering to the loose generic categories originally organized by Hunt and later amplified by H. S. Milford in his 1923 edition of the works. This work is avowedly a defence of Hunt, but the case looks shakier when presented through the distorting lens of these unhelpful categories. Not one of the books about other authors reviewed here adopts anything other than a chronological approach to the poetry, making Edgecombe seem distinctly out of step with current critical thinking. None the less, he is an enthusiastic apologist, and a reading of his book leaves one wishing for a Woodstock reprint of *Foliage*, probably Hunt's most accomplished work. Edgecombe is responsible also for a note, 'On First Looking into Chapman's Musaeus: A Note on a Possible Influence' (*KSJ* 43.26–43)

Besides the collections of essays mentioned above, two small booklets appeared this year devoted exclusively to John Clare. John Lucas's *John Clare*, in the WTW series, is the introduction we have been waiting for. Lucas follows Clare's career from his humble beginnings to his valedictory sonnet to himself, written a few years before his death. Along the way he describes the intellectual world in which Clare lived and moved, and provides some of the most compelling criticism thus far published of Clare's best poetry. Besides a useful chronology the volume contains an invaluable annotated bibliography; this volume is highly recommended for anyone either teaching or studying the work of this neglected poet. *The Life and Times of John Clare* by David Powell is a useful booklet published by Northamptonshire Libraries and Information Services in honour of the county's most distinguished Romantic poet. It is lavishly illustrated and beautifully written, and is evidently aimed primarily at sixth-formers. None the less, it will serve as an excellent basic introduction for anyone with an interest in Clare's life and work, and provides a good foundation for a reading of Lucas's volume.

James Hogg enthusiasts will by now be aware of *SHW*, that excellent periodical published by the James Hogg Society. This year's issue (*SHW* 5 – see also section 3 below) contains, oddly, reviews of the first three titles in EdinUP's new edition of Hogg's works, not due for publication until 1995, alongside articles by Valentina Bold, Murray Pittock, Ian Duncan, Andrew Monnickendam, Penny Fielding and Peter Garside. In some ways its most important element is a facsimile reprint of Hogg's little-known *The Royal Jubilee: A Scottish Mask* (1822), with annotations by Valentina Bold. The James Hogg Society is to be congratulated on a periodical publication that continues to do enormous credit to the author it commemorates.

In the field of drama this year saw the welcome publication of Sheridan's *The Rivals* in Hern's series of drama classics. At £2.99 this volume is not merely affordable; its conveniently small size makes it essential for use in rehearsals, playgoing, or just reading on the hoof. Like other volumes in the series it contains invaluable prefatory matter – in this case, short passages on the author, drama and society, what happens in the play, comedy, love and money, the Georgian stage, and a brief, very select, bibliography. At the rear of the volume readers will also find a useful dictionary of malapropisms and a glossary of eighteenth-century slang.

2. Non-Fictional Prose

De Quincey figures prominently in this year's work and Josephine McDonagh's *De Quincey's Disciplines* maintains the momentum and high quality of recent studies. By deploying a Foucaultian methodology McDonagh is able to explore the relationship in De Quincey's writings between the 'disciplines' of political economy, literary criticism, linguistics and aesthetics. There are extended analyses of his writings on Ricardo, his famous distinction between the 'literature of knowledge' and the 'literature of power', his writings on murder, and the better-known autobiographical works. McDonagh's focus on De Quincey's output in the 1830s and early 1840s is particularly helpful and revealing. For her, De Quincey presents a puzzle in that he is a writer who articulates two seemingly different and opposed aesthetics. These fault-lines she defines as 'representation as contagion' and 'representation as compulsion'. In her final chapter on 'Opium Eaters' she identifies the logic which derives from the 'discursive economy' which generates these apparent contradictions. She shows how a failure of will relates to a violent imposition of will, how a transcendent aesthetic espousing the ideal exists alongside the strategic and material. McDonagh intelligently and responsibly draws attention to the agonies as well as the horrors of De Quincey's political and aesthetic vision. The book's central argument provides a powerful unifying strategy which valuably opens De Quincey up to wider Victorian cultural debates, most importantly to the dissemination and popularization of Romantic aesthetics in the mid-century.

McDonagh's 'Debt and Desire: De Quincey and the Psychology of Economics' (*WC* 25.86–9) overlaps with some of the material in her book dealing with De Quincey and Ricardo. She starts with De Quincey's forays into the streets of London in the 'Pleasures of Opium' section of the *Confessions*, and then poses his autobiographical writings against his economic ones to find in the latter 'a similar kind of exchange', where it is thought that the magnificent glories of the capitalist system compensate for the ravages that the market inflicts on the consumer's tortured body. Accounting for De Quincey's apparently eccentric appropriation of Ricardo, McDonagh argues that his interest was motivated by imaginative appeal, 'the structure of [Ricardo's] thought' rather than the text's political messages. In 'Leeches and Opium: De Quincey Replies to "Resolution and Independence"' (*MLR* 89.572–80) Julian North traces a network of allusions between *Confessions of an English Opium-Eater*, 'Resolution and Independence', and Coleridge's Verse Letter to Sara. He argues for the presence of a creative 'Oedipal subtext' in De Quincey's parodying of Wordsworth which confirms him as an urban 'Opium-Eater' against the poet's 'happy child of the earth'. In 'De Quincey and the Portico Library' (*BJRL* 76.179–86) Grevel Lindop details the connections between De Quincey and the Manchester library referred to in the first edition of the *Confessions* as the 'Porch'. Claire B. May's 'Thomas De Quincey's *Spanish Military Nun*: Questions of Historical Authenticity and Plagiarism' (*MLN* 109.38–45) delves briefly into source material 'which seems to verify that Erauso [the nun in question] was a historical person and that the life in Ferrer's edition is substantially accurate'. May then identifies some of De Quincey's changes to the story, including the sympathetic nature of his characterization and his removal of 'suggestions of lesbianism'. De Quincey's refashioning of the work of others is also the subject of Frederick Burwick's 'How to Translate a Waverley Novel: Sir Walter Scott, Willibald Alexis, and Thomas De Quincey' (*WC* 25.93–100 – see also section 3 below). Burwick engages with English repugnance to German Romantic irony and argues that the essential difference that De Quincey imposes upon his English version of *Walladmor* (1825) lies in its effort to purge the finale of its mocking self-reflexivity. De Quincey is also featured in Nicola J. Watson's 'Domestic Revolutions: Fictions of National History, 1788–1830' (*WC* 25.129–33) when she focuses on his dream of the Civil War in *Confessions of an English Opium-Eater*. There are also two brief bibliographical pieces on De Quincey in *N&Q* 41. In 'De Quincey's "Immortal Druggist" and Wordsworth's "Power of Music"' (*N&Q* 41.329–35) Grevel Lindop cross-references connections between De Quincey's *Confessions* and Wordsworth's poem; and Daniel Sanjit Roberts's 'Three Uncollected Coleridgean Marginalia From De Quincey' (*N&Q* 41.341–3) is concerned with the response of the two English writers to Herder and Kant.

De Quincey, Burke and Paine are featured in *Combative Styles: Romantic Writing and Ideology: Two Contrasting Interpretations*, eds John Coates and Bruce Woodcock, but much of the material has already been covered by this section in previous years. The book consists of four published essays, a conference paper and preliminary biographical sketches and chronologies for the four writers – Burke, Paine, Blake and De Quincey – who are supposed to represent the 'Romantic Writing' of the title. In the unpublished essay on Paine and Blake, Bruce Woodcock tentatively explores some of the shared cultural milieu and ideas of the two writers before concluding that they 'epitomise the two poles of a revolutionary dialectic between political pragmatism, action, rational planning . . . and . . . the constant need for visionary flexibility'. According to its authors, the aim of this volume is to 'juxtapose two interpretations of the French Revolution as it affected some leading writers of the Romantic period', but the juxtaposition does not amount to a coherent argument and the 'style' referred to in the title is never adequately defined in relation to ideology.

This year's collections of critical essays contain a modest amount of material dealing with prose. *Re-Visioning Romanticism: British Women Writers, 1776–1837*, eds Wilson and Haefner, contains two pieces which provide some extended consideration of prose, though both are ultimately more interested in poets (see also sections 1(a) above and 3 below). In 'Configurations of Feminine Reform: The Woman Writer and the Tradition of Dissent', Marlon B. Ross pays particular attention to Hannah More's views on satire, theory and practice in order to define better the pressures of the gendering of genre informing the writing and the reception of Barbauld's *Eighteen Hundred and Eleven*. In the same volume Jane Aaron's 'The Way Above the World: Religion and Gender in Welsh and Anglo-Welsh Women's Writing, 1780–1830' also uses More as a measure against which to define the distinctively Calvinist features of Welsh Methodist women's position in the Romantic period.

There are two valuable contributions on prose writing in *At the Limits of Romanticism: Essays in Cultural, Feminist, and Materialist Criticism*, eds Favret and Watson (see also section 1(a) above). Half of Lucinda Cole and Richard G. Swartz's ' "Why Should I Wish for Words": Literacy, Articulation, and the Borders of Literary Culture' is given over to a consideration of Dorothy Wordsworth's 'English(ness)' and, in particular, her involvement in the feminized activity of charity school education and her descriptions of Erse speakers in her *Recollections of a Tour Made in Scotland*. In a very intelligent and careful consideration of Yearsley and Wordsworth, Cole and Swartz focus on the positive attempts of these two women to 'appropriate, subvert, and otherwise negotiate the idioms of [. . .] official literary culture', while recognizing how their works 'are symptomatic of struggles within literary culture to police, protect, and promote the bounds of literariness itself'. Their essay responsibly complicates Wordsworth's involvement with 'the peculiarly Romantic trope of inarticulation'. In the same volume, Sonia Hofkosh in 'Sexual Politics and Literary History: William Hazlitt's Keswick Escapade and Sarah Hazlitt's Journal' takes the infamous incident of sexual violence involving Hazlitt and a young village woman in the Lake District as the starting point of her inquiry into literary history and the occlusion of woman's position. Her analysis of Sarah Hazlitt's journal reveals an alternative (and critically chastening) point of view to William's in *Liber Amoris*, one which registers its difference not only through reference to a culturally constrained body, but also through its deployment of 'conflicting stories'.

As one might expect, *The Politics of the Picturesque*, eds Stephen Copley and Peter Garside, contains many passing references to and analyses of picturesque theorists such as Gilpin and Price. In the same volume, David Worrall's 'Agrarians against the Picturesque: Ultra-Radicalism and the Revolutionary Politics of Land' details Spencean ideas of 'Nature' as land in common for providing food and the revolutionary strategies for bringing it about, which, he argues, have been occluded by dominant histories of Romantic ecology. The most contentious and most influential of this year's contributions on Wollstonecraft is likely to be Susan

Gubar's 'Feminist Misogyny: Mary Wollstonecraft and the Paradox of "It Takes One to Know One"' (*FSt* 20.453–73). Gubar focuses on what she terms 'a perverse contradiction' in Wollstonecraft's writing – her representation of femininity as a malady, which replicates the language of her contemporary satirists. Claiming not to 'diminish or disparage her achievements', Gubar identifies a challenging and disconcerting inheritance from Wollstonecraft's pioneering feminist texts as she exposes their 'derogations of the feminine', which she reflects back on the contradictions within contemporary feminism.

Deirdre Coleman's 'Conspicuous Consumption: White Abolitionist and English Women's Protest Writing in the 1790s' (*ELH* 61.341–62) explores the problematic intersection of slavery and women's writing in order to break down recent suggestions that late eighteenth-century writings on the subject are more 'positive' and 'open-minded' than their more racist Victorian successors. Coleman uses Coleridge's lecture on the slave trade as a springboard for a fascinating inquiry into the gendering of sugar and the relationship between woman and slave in abolitionist discourse. She handles a wide range of authors (including Wollstonecraft, John Gabriel Stedman, Hannah More and Jefferson) in her quest to illustrate how the 'recuperative features of abolitionism always coexist with a panicky and contradictory need to preserve essential boundaries and distinctions'.

Mary Kitts's 'Mary Wollstonecraft's *A Vindication of the Rights of Woman*: A Judicious Response from Eighteenth-Century Spain' (*MLR* 89.351–9) focuses on a favourable review of the French edition of Wollstonecraft's second vindication in the daily newspaper *Diario de Madrid* in 1792, which was written by its co-editor Julián de Vasco. In the face of repressive censorship of the periodical press under the government of Charles IV, de Vasco plays down some of the more radical aspects of Wollstonecraft's text (including her critiques of the aristocracy, the army and the church) and concentrates on a sympathetic and reasonably accurate rendering of her discourse on female virtue. In '"A More Godlike Portion": Mary Wollstonecraft's Feminist Rereadings of the Fall' (*MLN* 109.28–38), William Richey illustrates how Wollstonecraft employs a 'rhetoric of indirection' in order to camouflage her reworking of Genesis by 'embedding it in an attack on Rousseau', and also how she drops her mask of orthodoxy to articulate her radical views, in which she sees the Fall myth as part of a 'patriarchal conspiracy to subjugate women'. Deborah Kennedy continues the relatively recent increase of interest in the writings of Helen Maria Williams. Her 'Spectacle of the Guillotine: Helen Maria Williams and the Reign of Terror' (*PQ* 73.95–113) addresses Williams's 'mythical representation' of the victims of the Terror and shows how, by concentrating on the victims' 'noble contempt of death', she can evade the facticity of execution. Kennedy argues that Williams 'emphasiz[es] the family loyalty and affection among the victims of the Revolution', and claims that she is concerned to maintain the apocalyptic interpretation of the Revolution in order to offset conservative reaction against it.

Deirdre Lynch's 'Nationalizing Women and Domesticating Fiction: Edmund Burke and the Genres of Englishness' (*WC* 25.45–9) prompts us to recognize Romantic-era narratives of desire and generation that are not organized by the principle of the nation-state and to go beyond 'the Oedipal story' for an understanding of Burke's representation of women. She attempts to identify a project common to many women writers in the period which involves issues of surrogate mothering, divorce and artificial insemination and asks the questions: what belongs to home? what belongs elsewhere?

Highlights from this year's issues of *ChLB* include Joseph Rosenblum's 'Lost Lambs; or, The Dispersal of Charles Lamb's Library: An Essay in Reconstruction' (*ChLB* 86.47–55), the bibliographical content of which is self-explanatory; and Pamela Clemit's 'Lamb and Godwin's *Antonio*' (*ChLB* 85.13–18), in which she uncovers the extent of Lamb's involvement in the production of Godwin's blank verse play of 1800, finding that he wrote the prologue and collaborated with the author on this as well as Godwin's third play *Faulkener* in 1807.

In a rather disappointing year for Hazlitt, Stanley Jones offers further identifications in 'More Hazlitt Quotations: The Bible, Milton, Dryden, Rochester, Boileau/John Dennis' (*N&Q* 41.343–4).

Marcus Wood's *Radical Satire and Print Culture 1790–1822* is an important addition to recent work on popular radicalism in the Romantic period. The collaborative verbal and visual productions of William Hone and George Cruikshank form the heart of Wood's study, but he extends his inquiry well beyond these two in order to establish the historical precedents and origins of early nineteenth-century radical print culture. Throughout he provides ample evidence to suggest that there are significant continuities between radical satire in the Regency and radical tracts and prints in the early eighteenth and even in the early seventeenth century. This uncovering of a 'satirical inheritance' is central to his important argument about the historical self-consciousness of radical culture. After an opening chapter on advertising which shows how radical writers infiltrated and exploited polite culture through parody, Wood cleverly weaves a series of historical precedents around his detailed presentation of the works of his chosen authors, Hone and Cruikshank. Along the way we are provided with a wealth of richly illustrated examples. In addition to advertisements, Wood also supplies fascinating evidence of radical culture's parodic exploitation of broadsides, chapbooks, handbills, graffiti, medals, tokens and emblems in order to demonstrate its rich and daring heterogeneity. Wood's book would have benefited from a more sophisticated sense of parody and satire, but, overall, it fulfils its aim of stressing 'the daring and even joyous nature of much radical propaganda' with admirable enthusiasm and precision.

Gregory Claeys's 'The Origins of the Rights of Labour: Republicanism, Commerce, and the Construction of Modern Social Theory in Britain, 1796–1805' (*JModH* 66.249–90) is the most impressive and sustained of this year's articles on political prose writing. With admirable lucidity, Claeys presents an overview of the ways in which 'the 1790s constituted a watershed in European thinking about the relations between government, commerce, and property rights'. He structures his case around an opposition between the commercial republicanism of Paine and Thelwall and the anti-commercial republican thinking of Godwin and Charles Hall, as all four writers are forced to rethink the relationship between employer and labour in the face of the threat of poverty. Hall emerges as a key thinker, since it is his neo-classical republicanism with its awareness of the growing power of the capitalist which provides 'the theory of industrial development that, through Marxism and other forms of socialism [. . .] would predominate in nineteenth- and twentieth-century radicalism'.

The *SIR* forum on 'Romanticism and its Publics' (*SIR* 33) contains two items which have a particular bearing on the study of prose: Kevin Gilmartin's 'Popular Radicalism and the Public Sphere' (*SIR* 33. 549–57) and Mary A. Favret's 'Coming Home: The Public Spaces of Romantic War' (*SIR* 33. 539–48). In the former, Gilmartin intelligently questions Habermas and Jon Klancher in his quest for a methodological position which can register the complicated nature of the public sphere and its strategic deployment by radicals in the Romantic period. De Quincey's *The English Mail-Coach* features prominently in the latter, as it illustrates in its 'perverse dream of domestic comfort' Favret's contention that in this period 'war itself was labelled "private"'.

3. Fictional Prose

The majority of this year's monographs on Romantic fictional prose focus on the Gothic. The 1990s have been deluged with critical works on the Gothic, to the same degree, it seems, as the 1790s were with the novels themselves. It is hard to account for this phenomenon, exactly, but a few possibilities suggest themselves. The robustness of feminist criticism is the most obvious: as the first genre dominated by women writers, the Gothic novel was bound to leap up the critical agenda. More recently, a 1990s syndrome has come into it: in the original concern for spectral appearances, divided subjects and dysfunctional families we seem to catch echoes of our own preoccupation with postmodernism and its assorted fragmentations. The Gothic monographs published this year are all – more or less – inflected by these concerns.

The best, and also least inflected, is Jacqueline Howard's *Reading Gothic Fiction: A Bakhtinian Approach*. Howard cautions against the hermeneutic circle of reading generic expectations into a text. 'From this [. . .] can flow aesthetic judgements which deny a text's specifically historical, social, cultural, or political meaning and significance.' Howard deploys Bakhtin's theories of dialogism in the novel in order to scupper the anachronistic model of romance applied to the Gothic by such influential feminist critics as Gilbert and Gubar. Reading back from contemporary romance, Gilbert and Gubar found themselves implicitly trapped within the assumption that writing by women was bound by female experience: cut off from the wider world, and deprived of hegemonic language, women adopted a fictional form where they said one thing, but meant another; where they represented convention, while concealing subversion. Howard argues that the Gothic is not a holistic genre organically shaped by 'fantasy', but, in the manner of the novel itself, an inherently disjunctive one ineluctably composed of contemporary discourses. Howard persuasively argues that female Gothic writers of the 1790s did not think of themselves as sequestered within the ghetto of women's writing. On the contrary, with the same alacrity as their male counterparts they engaged in public debate of politicized issues. Women writers were as inventive, and interventionist, as their male colleagues. It is by chasing down the contemporary resonance of the discursive practices echoed within these inventive interventions that Howard seeks to recoup the historical meanings of her chosen texts.

Howard is at her best when pursuing her polemic against existing critical practice. She persuasively argues the need, in the Gothic novel, to 'treat questions of gender as complex political constructs', as opposed to simple sites of anti-patriarchal protest. She effectively challenges Rosemary Jackson's influential claims regarding the fantastic's inherent subversion and the Gothic's inherent conservatism, mainly by pointing out that matters are not so simple. Beginning with the common-sense observation that subversion is in the eye of the observer, she carefully makes a case, on a text-by-text basis, of why a particular opposition of a particular set of discursive practices might .or might not be considered subversive.

Howard's book is less convincing when pursuing its Bakhtinian methodology, largely owing, I suspect, to a disjunction between the genre Bakhtin has in mind (however indeterminate) and the Gothic itself. Howard quotes Bakhtin on the 'social speech types' on which the Gothic, as a site of heteroglossia or 'dialogue of languages', might be said to draw: 'social dialects, characteristic group behaviour, professional jargons, generic languages, languages of generations and age groups, tendentious languages, languages of the authorities, of various circles and passing fashions, languages that serve the specific socio-political purposes of the day'. By this Bakhtin seems to indicate the novel, meaning, in the language of the 1790s, a text 'formed in imitation of real life for the delineation of passions and characters, such as might combine probability with interest'. Howard is quite right to dismiss modern notions of romance (meaning escapist love stories produced and consumed by women) when historically considering the Gothic 'novel'; but it remains a discursive fact of the 1790s scene, acknowledged by writers and critics alike, that distinctions between novels and romances (and hybrids) obtained, and not just in nomenclature but in aesthetic fact. Novels courted Bakhtin's 'dialogue of languages', whereas romances – set in another age, dominated by 'chivalry and enchantment' – did not; at least, not so directly, and not in the same way. This is implicitly acknowledged by Howard, who immediately follows up the quotation from Bakhtin with a list of what, discursively, we are to seek in the Gothic 'novel': 'discourses of the sublime, of Sentimentalism, realism, superstition, myth, legend, folk- and fairy-tale'. Instead of the immediacy of ideologically inflected voices drawn from the contemporary scene we are to look for discourses that are themselves second-order abstractions, such as literary genres, aesthetic categories and complex cultural fads. By 'discursive practice' Howard appears to mean something closer to Foucault than Bakhtin, but the difference is never cleared up. This methodological uncertainty impacts most on Howard's study by narrowing her focus: I frequently felt that a frank acknowledgement of the Foucaultian nature of her subject would have widened the historical context she attempts to survey.

At this juncture I should declare an interest. My own *Gothic Writing 1750–1820: A Genealogy* was published in 1993 (although not covered in *YWES* 74). As the subtitle suggests, it does interpret Bakhtin's heteroglossia in a Foucaultian manner; so it may be that my dissatisfaction on this point is the natural consequence of a different perspective. Be that as it may, Howard's book seemed to me to cut short its contextual pursuits owing to a fuzziness in the conceptualization of her project. For example, her examination of the word 'Gothic' prior to Walpole is cursory and general, as if she is unaware of the dense ideological significance of 'Gothic' as a construction of Englishness (she quotes Mark Madoff, but not Kliger's *The Goths in England*, on which Madoff draws). Similarly, in her otherwise excellent exploration of *Northanger Abbey*, Howard skimps on the richness of her discursive material. The same may be said for her discussion of Radcliffe. She notes the argument between Humphry Repton and William Payne Knight, where Repton reads landscape gardening based too much on a taste for the wild as Jacobinical, with Payne Knight replying that close-trimming improvers were dictatorial destroyers of the genius of the place. Howard then uses the debate to situate Radcliffe's *Mysteries of Udolpho* on the Jacobinical, Payne Knight side of the argument, as evinced by the clash between sensible, idealized St Aubert and the insensible, affected materialist Quesnel. Howard leaves matters with the suggestion that Radcliffe's position could have been considered subversive: but the figure over which the debate turns, a decayed oak – which the improver Quesnel would chop, and St Aubert maintain – was also clearly implicated within Burke's rhetoric of organic accretion. If Radcliffe is signalling radical sympathies, she does so by playing a deep game; for one could as easily see Quesnel as the improving vandal (albeit of an 'oeconomical' rather than Jacobinical kind), and St Aubert as the conserving, Burkean hero.

If Howard's ostensible purpose is to improve feminist criticism of the Gothic by putting it back on to firmer historicist lines, her secret one is to refute utterly Elizabeth Napier's argument that the Gothic novel is incoherent (although in this Napier simply reworks the older charge that the genre is 'schizophrenic'). Howard's studies of dialogism in *The Monk* and *Frankenstein* (apart from texts already mentioned) will become the standard reference works for an opinion that has already hardened into consensus: that Gothic novels were not (always or simply) schizoid products of incoherent fantasy, or expressionist versions of feminine anger, but a part of the novel's mainstream: and at their best, multivocal, ironic and dissonant. The nature of the discourses out of which they are composed is likely to prove more controversial.

Steven Bruhm's *Gothic Bodies: The Politics of Pain in Romantic Fiction* is a case in point. Bruhm applies the familiar post-structuralist concerns with spectacle and the body to the Gothic, and, in a welcome diversion from the norm, covers poetry and theatre as well as the novel. Although Bruhm's conclusions are conventional enough – the displayed 'Gothic body' becomes another formulation for the post-structuralist 'fragmented subject' – much of the preceding discussion is original in its concentrated attention on the problematics of representing pain in the French revolutionary era. For Bruhm, the pained body is above all else a discursive site, in the full Foucauldian sense, and much of the most interesting discussion focuses on medical, legal and penitential discourses as they intersect Bruhm's chosen Gothic representations, with Radcliffe, De Sade, Godwin, Lewis, Coleridge, Byron, Wordsworth and P. B. Shelley providing the bulk of the textual examples. That said, the study is less 'materialist' than it often promises to be, with the Foucauldian, quasi-new historicist project constantly giving way to what might be called a 'deconstructive reflex'. Bruhm instinctively reaches for the ready binary opposition, as, for instance, between 'the public and private, the expressed and the ineffable, the othered and selved, the imaginative and the corporeal, the dispersed and the centred'. The point of Bruhm's discussion often seems to be the discovery of a moment in which a privileged term collapses, or an excluded one returns; and as these oppositions appear rigged (in the sense of being the residue of something more complex) the force of the argument is dissipated. For Bruhm, the pained body is a visual aporia at the centre of a nexus of conceptual antinomies; a nexus, in its turn, at the heart of the Romantic project (here largely linked with sensibility and its Romantic aftermath). Hence Bruhm's need to manoeuvre his material into binarisms, always already deconstructable.

Bruhm's achievement, nevertheless, has been to theorize the representation of the body in Romantic literature while giving us a firm handle on visualization in the Gothic via the theatre (in this respect his book should be read in tandem with Paula Backsheider's *Theatrical Power and Mass Culture in Early Modern England* [*YWES* 74.287]). By looking at his historical material – by situating the body within its discursive web – Bruhm succeeds in making his case that the represented body is the site of many of the anxieties defining the culture of the period. This allows him to collapse the difference between the Romantic and the Gothic body: the same discursive tensions obtain in both, the only non-substantive difference being that in the latter they are placed *in* (articulate) *extremis*. Bruhm thus succeeds in challenging the standard canonical boundaries between Romantic and Gothic, centre and margin. However, by privileging the deconstructive moment of the Gothic body, Bruhm strives to collapse yet another difference, this time between Romanticism and the present, as if the fragmented Gothic body were an (un)dress rehearsal for the postmodern present.

If this is a claim too far, it is at least tentatively put: not so Vijay Mishra's in *The Gothic Sublime*. 'As far as I am aware, the Gothic has not been read systematically through a hermeneutic that effectively considers this form as an earlier moment of the postmodern.' Mishra's point is that Lyotard's postmodern sublime, and the Gothic sublime, both turn on a crisis of representation. The postmodern sensibility, and the Gothic sensibility of the 1790s, are haunted by a sense of the spectral, of surfaces without substance or meaning; and in both cases the sublime comes to be associated with a failure of transcendence, where representation itself is threatened. Mishra manoeuvres himself into this position by following the timeworn tradition of elevating Kant into a kind of patriarch of the sublime. Where the Romantic sublime holds on to the possibility of Kantian transcendence, the Gothic nihilistically lets go, free-falling into the postmodern. Where Bruhm cautiously seeks to question the boundaries between Romanticism and Gothicism, Mishra endeavours to turn the world upside down. If the end of the eighteenth century witnesses Foucault's disruptive entry of the modern, it is in Gothic – and not Romantic – literature that we find it.

The analysis that would support this historical argument never materializes. To put the questions in their crudest terms, are the similarities noted by Mishra epiphenomena of capitalism; generic recrudescences; or *fin de siècle* nightmares? 'Though almost artless in its simplicity – that as the latent underside of any literary history or discursive formation the Gothic signifies a break in the continuum of history – the argument of this book, nevertheless, requires us to develop strategies that would both express the nature of the Gothic sublime and connect it to the historical postmodern.' This is disingenuous in the extreme. By arguing that the Gothic is just such a 'break' Mishra dodges the question at issue. We cannot question whether the Gothic sublime is a precursor of the postmodern, as the Gothic, by definition, dissolves such historicity. This allows Mishra to affirm without evidence the very thing that needs to be proved (that the Gothic sublime is indeed the crisis of representation we subsequently find rehearsed in postmodern aesthetics) while maintaining the appearance of sound historical credentials.

Mishra is careful not to commit the cardinal sin of assuming that there is only one, or indeed several, sublimes; and so we get an infinite variety. Two pages chosen at random gives us the positive Romantic, the Gothic, the Indian, the palaeographic, the melancholy, the proto-oceanic, and the sentimental sublimes. This proliferation suggests, not multiplicity and complexity, but something like the reverse. Although the number of non-transcendent (e.g. non-Romantic) sublimes appear to be legion, they all amount to the same thing: a moment of dissolution where difference and hence meaning is lost. As Mishra puts it, 'the Gothic sublime is an archesublime voraciously feeding on other sublimes'. The bloated animal produced by all this ingestion looks suspiciously like the loose, baggy monster previous critics insistently warned us against. Mishra's Gothic 'archesublime' includes – and ranges between – the Lacanian imaginary, Freud's oceanic bliss,

Freud's uncanny, a 'kind of primal awe', and a postmodern effacement of difference. Once the dust has settled, however, by far the most common feature of Mishra's 'archesublime' is something very familiar: the old-fashioned Freudian unconscious, read as a vertiginous, labyrinthine topos ruled by an Oedipal master plot of incestuous desire (troped by Mishra as the obliteration of difference and identity). In effect, Mishra simply maps the clichés of the Gothic novel, such as the labyrinth, directly onto an unchallenged concept of the unconscious; so that in the welter of post-structuralist formulations one finds strangely pre-theoretical (not to say banal) utterances, such as the following: 'In rendering the Gothic sublime as a compulsion to repeat the mysteries of the unconscious, Lewis predicated the sublime on the necessity to lift the lid on repressed sexuality.' At this point Mishra's historical consciousness has been consigned to its own dustbin.

Jack G. Voller's *The Supernatural Sublime: The Metaphysics of Terror in Anglo-American Romanticism* covers much the same territory as Mishra's book, as one might expect given the titles. But whereas Mishra gets caught up in the dizzy vortex of his own terminology, Voller's procedure is grounded in method and caution. This caution is responsible for the book's weaknesses, but also its strengths. Students unfamiliar with the criticism of the sublime will find it a useful reference work. By concentrating on the supernatural sublime Voller is able to include 'Gothic' poetry as well as fiction, and as with Bruhm's study, this generic expansion enriches his book. His comparative study of English and American Gothic also rewards. The difficulty is that in meticulously mapping the supernatural sublime Voller never gets out of the shadow thrown by the critics he refers to.

For the purposes of his discussion Voller breaks the sublime down into three – roughly historical – stages: a conventional eighteenth-century sublime, followed by the supernatural and the Romantic. Voller argues that the conventional and Romantic sublimes are alike in being at ease with an irony inherent in the sublime: the more ineffable, the better; for the more an experience escapes our powers of comprehension, the more it validates itself as transcendental. To put it in the opposite way, a transcendental experience susceptible of description is not one worth having. Hence Romantic irony, which affirms the possibility of the noumenal object on the grounds of the impossibility of its apprehension. But in the supernatural sublime this irony falters, leaving us with a glimpse into the abyss. The 'proto-nihilism' of the supernatural sublime tends, not to existential angst, but to the terrifying realization that there is indeed a metaphysical power, only the wrong one; that is to say, a power that is indifferent, at best, and actively malign at worst.

Voller carefully refers his arguments back to the seminal works of G. R. Thompson, David B. Morris, Thomas Weiskel and Peter Thorslev Jr; but this back reference restricts his originality. He interestingly suggests that Romanticism nowhere expresses its belated nature more than in its subtle recuperations of the metaphysical fault lines exposed by the earlier supernatural sublime. He also codifies the supernatural sublime with some sensitivity. He refuses to map the radical and conservative modes of the supernatural sublime directly onto the explained and unexplained supernatural. Instead both modes operate within each 'branch'. Voller identifies conservative instances within the radical mode of the unexplained supernatural (Clara Reeve) as well as radical practitioners of the conservative explained (Charles Brockden Brown). But this freshness of approach is offset by the need to slot Matthew Lewis and Ann Radcliffe into their familiar radical and conservative positions.

Gothick Origins and Innovations, eds Allan Lloyd Smith and Victor Sage, derives from the first International Gothic Conference, held at the University of East Anglia in 1991. The collection contains a number of important essays, the best of which follow a materialist and/or ideological line. Jerrold E. Hogle and Emma Clery investigate the mutual imbrications of literary pastiche, the rise of commodity culture, historical consciousness and authenticity in *The Castle of Otranto.* Tim Marshall sets *Frankenstein* in the context of the 1832 Anatomy Act, with special reference paid to the conflict between the professionalization of medicine and traditionary beliefs of the poor (the latter paying the price of the former through their corpses). Richard Haslam's study of the Calvinist sublime in Maturin makes a welcome contribution to a neglected topic. Particularly brilliant – if frustratingly brief – is John Allen Stevenson's '*Tom Jones*, Jacobitism, and the Rise of the Gothic', which, to my mind, succeeds in vindicating its central claim that the 'key revolution' for the 'development of the Gothic novel' was not the French but 'the two English Revolutions of the seventeenth century', events registering in the public mind as an anxiety about the ghostly longevity of 'illegitimate' claims. Stevenson shows how this anxiety survived long into the eighteenth century, permeating as unlikely a 'Gothic' text as *Tom Jones*. But in this Stevenson merely agrees with the views adduced by Maurice Levy in a magisterial essay which fronts the volume like a great intimidating basilisk. For Levy, as far as fiction is concerned, 'Gothic' is culturally and historically specific: it refers to a late eighteenth- and early nineteenth-century genre in which the English bourgeoisie cryptically revisited the originary scene of their cultural power: the Glorious Revolution of 1688. Levy then bemoans the loose application of the term to foreign literatures (especially American) and to modern instances. The rest of the volume compounds just that, more or less, investigating American, Victorian and Modern Gothic, with contributions from the editors, William Veeder, Alison Milbank and David Punter.

There were two general essays on the Gothic: Troy Boone's 'Narrating the Apparition: Glanvill, Defoe, and the Rise of Gothic Fiction' (*ECent* 35.173-189) and Fred Botting's 'Power in the Darkness: Heterotopias, Literature and Gothic Labyrinths' (*Genre* 26.253–82). Both focus on the endemic (and familiar) ambiguity of the genre. For Boone, instability was inherent in the act of narrating supernatural stories. Protestant writers, such as Glanvill and Defoe, exploited the audience for the supernatural tale while distancing themselves from it, an ambivalence reconstituted in the romance/novel debate, where romance was read as giddy, supernatural and Catholic, and the novel as a rationalist, Protestant mode of discourse. Always already ideological, the Gothic became a site of ludic intervention for liminal characters, such as Walpole. Botting visits similar territory, but gains far greater leverage on the problem of the genre's engrained doubleness. I say 'problem' because it remains an open question whether the genre is intelligibly multiple, or just confused. Botting provides an original answer through a highly resourceful application of Foucault's theory of the heterotopia, 'real places on the subordinated or excluded fringes of a particular social formation'. The ready figure for the heterotopia, as topos, is the labyrinth. Just as the centre needs the margin for its definition and stability, so does order need disorder. But, Botting argues, the Gothic novel is not only topologically labyrinthine, but also phenomenologically so: the experience of reading (especially a Radcliffe) Gothic novel is that of being led into a maze of supernatural conjecture before being conducted safely back to a normative order. Gothic fiction thus enjoys a 'reciprocal rather than oppositional relationship to enlightenment values'. Each needs the other in a dance of containment. Over the dual function of the labyrinth/heterotopia Botting maps oppositions between feudal mysteries and the panopticon; concealment and visibility; Catholic and Protestant; romance and novel; ancient and modern. He convincingly argues that Gothic novels should be understood not as being for or against these things, but, in the manner of Foucaultian power, as both at the same time. The distinction of Botting's essay, however, is not its conclusion, which has been made before, but the fresh and compelling light it sheds on a textual feature darkened through overfamiliarity.

Mary Shelley remains the object of much critical attention, with the highlight of the year's work undoubtedly being Marilyn Butler's peerless edition of *Frankenstein.* Butler uses the 1818 text, which she contextualizes in a long introduction through reference to the vitalist controversy that simmered and raged before and after *Frankenstein's* publication. Crudely put, the controversy was a tale of bad science versus good, of the establishment John Abernathy versus the radical William Lawrence, a Godwinian known to both Shelleys. Bad science subscribed to a vital principle, or soul (possibly electricity, or something analogous to it); it was egotistical, male-orientated, Faustian, and inextricably linked to the established order. Good science was materialist; and because it was also evolutionary in its outlook it was able to accommodate the failed revolution in a larger, progressive scheme of things. *Frankenstein* offended contemporary sensibilities, not because it dared to speculate about the spark of life, but because it spoofed it. It is a clever satire of bad science, told from the perspective of the good; and while Mary Shelley's sympathies with Lawrence's anti-vitalist outlook were initially sufficiently hidden by the book's complex framing ironies, they became more apparent after publication, when, fortuitously, Lawrence's materialist views provoked a reactionary storm. Butler suggests, persuasively, that Mary Shelley's toned-down 1831 version echoes the sanitization subsequently forced upon Lawrence. Coincidentally, two historians also published their work on the neglected topic of *Frankenstein's* relationship to contemporary science (Frank A. J. L. James and J. V. Field, '*Frankenstein* and the Spark of Being', *HT* September.47–53). In comparison to Butler's, their treatment is introductory and cursory.

That Mary Shelley's texts have a special affinity with the theoretically minded appears to be borne out by the rest of the year's crop of essays on her. Tilottama Rajan's 'Mary Shelley's *Matilda*: Melancholy and the Political Economy of Romanticism' (*SNNTS* 26.ii.43–68) uses the one text to assess, not just Shelley's *oeuvre*, but her conflicted relation to her family, her circle, their texts, and finally Romanticism itself. For Rajan, *Matilda* is the 'textual abject', a phrase with a theoretical provenance in Kristeva, but also Lacan, Nicholas Abraham and Maria Torok. Rajan effectively identifies a tension between introjection and incorporation, where introjection (the dynamics of melancholy, of irrecoupable negativity) is seen as a strategy of psychic resistance against incorporation into the Symbolic. Rajan argues that *Matilda*'s tension between resistance and participation typifies conflicts elsewhere in Mary Shelley's personal and cultural life.

In the short but dense 'Compounding the Crime: Ingratitude and the Murder Conviction of Justine Moritz in *Frankenstein'*, William G. Sayres argues that Mary Shelley dramatizes the inadequacy of Godwin's rationalist rejection of gratitude as an instrument of justice, a rejection Sayres frames with Foucault's account of late eighteenth-century disciplinary practices (*ELN* 31.iv.48–54). Foucault makes another appearance in Thomas Dutoit's 'Re-specting the Face as the Moral (of) Fiction in Mary Shelley's *Frankenstein*' (*MLN* 109.847–71); as the title suggests, an essay based in deconstructive punning. The French equation (made by Foucault and Derrida) of 'monstre' and 'montre', monstrosity and show, is here inverted, so that monstrosity becomes the face that cannot be shown, where face slides easily (and, some might add, too readily) into figure, and figure into figuration. The monster thus becomes the effaced, the unfigurable, or even the (dis)figured. In an interesting article, William D. Brewer investigates a recurring double-bind in Mary Shelley's work: trauma compels her characters to speak, but utterance affords no relief. On the contrary, vocalization often renders her characters vulnerable, an attitude towards language in explicit contrast to Percy's ('Mary Shelley on the Therapeutic Value of Language', *PLL* 30.387–407). The conference volume *Romantic Discourses*, ed. Höhne (see also section 1(a) above), contains two contributions on Shelley: 'Shelleyan Ideas in *Frankenstein*', and 'Mary Shelley's *Frankenstein* and J.W. Polidori's *The Vampyre*'.

Not noticed last year was H. W. Malchow's important article 'Frankenstein's Monster and the Images of Race in Nineteenth-Century Britain' (*P&P* 139[1993].90–130), which makes a persuasive case for seeing Frankenstein's creature as a reflection of contemporary fears of the racial 'Other'. This is a major article [Peter J. Kitson].

Radcliffeans will have been looking forward to Deborah D. Rogers's *The Critical Response to Ann Radcliffe*. Rogers includes material from the first reviews of *The Castles of Athlin and Dunbayne* in 1789 to the present. Given this scope, much has had to be cut, so that, for instance, Terry Castle's great essay 'The Spectralization of the Other in *The Mysteries of Udolpho*' is pared to two pages. As a consequence the book falls between the two stools always flanking a project of this kind. Its compilation of early reviews is too patchy to meet the needs of Radcliffe scholars (not only are reviews incomplete, but some are missing, such as the significantly negative one in *The Anti-Jacobin*), while the modern criticism is not sufficiently present to compel student interest. However, having said that, Rogers has economized on the ends in order to make room for the neglected middle – the century of responses from 1850 to 1950 – and this gives the collection a welcome continuity in its coverage.

Radcliffe's centrality for the conceptualization of the female Gothic is the lesson of the special issue I edited for *Women's Writing: The Elizabethan to Victorian Period* (1.131–250). The brief was to reconsider the category 'Female Gothic', first coined by Ellen Moers some twenty years ago, a task contributors found nearly impossible without recourse to the 'Great Enchantress'. Five of the seven contributors consider Radcliffe's work, albeit paired with something else: Alison Milbank links her with Milton and Sheridan Le Fanu; Kate Ferguson Ellis with Catholicism; Elisabeth Bronfen with hysteria, phantasy, and the family romance; Fred Botting with *Dracula*; and E. J. Clery with de Sade. Only David Punter (on Poe's *Ligeia*) and Anne Williams (on the female Gothic's underlying 'myths') escape Radcliffe's gravity.

Cannon Schmitt's 'Techniques of Terror, Technologies of Nationality: Ann Radcliffe's *The Italian*' (*ELH* 61.853–76) was the only other Radcliffe article published in this year. Schmitt links the internalized surveillance Foucault identifies as the mark of modernity with the Gothic novel's technologies of terror. For Radcliffe, bourgeois identity, nationalism, Englishness, and a vocation for self-surveillance are all of a piece. The foreign settings of the Gothic mode allow

Radcliffe to identify the antitheses of bourgeois nationalism – localism and cosmopolitanism – while providing the occasion for the terror tactics that chasten the heroine into a modern, Foucaultian subjectivity.

The much-neglected topic of the role of poetry in the Romantic novel is addressed by Mary A. Favret in one of the year's most significant articles ('Telling Tales About Genre: Poetry in the Romantic Novel', *SNNTS* 26.ii.153–72). Favret contextualizes her project by referring to the charge, levelled by Clifford Siskin, Jerome McGann and Alan Liu, that Romantic criticism too readily surrenders to Romantic poetry's own 'lyric turn' away from history. For the writer of the Romantic novel, the problem is not the elevation of the lyric, and its inescapable grip, but something like the reverse. Paying particular attention to the novels of Charlotte Smith and Ann Radcliffe, Favret begins by noting how these writers worked, generically, within a contradictory genealogical paradigm: genres exhibit hierarchy, are differentially arranged by class, and yet belong to literature's single (albeit extended) family. To combine lyric and novel was, generically, to threaten the illicit congress of classes and siblings, misalliance and incest, frequently the very plot lines pursued by the Romantic novels in question. The lyric, in this respect, was the feminized orphan that did not belong within the quotidian world of the novel, a misplaced outcast uncomfortably raising questions of legitimacy. From 'an understanding of genre based on the ideology of family and title' Favret moves to 'one based on the ideology of gender', and from there to the presentation of the lyric within the novel as a 'visible and desirable commodity'. The problem, then, is not that the emerging hegemonic status of the lyric throws the host romance into the shade, but that the uneasy coexistence of novel and feminized lyric ends by making readable the secret ideological business of both genres, whether it be the politics of the woman writer, or the socially profound transitions to a commodity culture of which Romantic novels (and women readers) were a small yet significant part. Regrettably, Favret's fine article is marred by a printing error whereby an entire page has been missed out.

In their important collection, *Re-Visioning Romanticism: British Women Writers, 1776–1837,* Wilson and Haefner comment that critical 'assumptions about what is high Romantic art have long privileged poetry over fiction' (see also sections 1(a) and 2 above). The context of the remark is the critical effort that has been made over the last decade to escape from the 'Romantic ideology' that perpetuates six male poets as the spine of a single, coherent Romanticism, in favour of a discrimination of Romanticisms in which women writers are once again recognized. The collection carries this work forward, and will be indispensable for anyone interested in the topic. It also contains distinguished contributions from Marlon B. Ross, Stuart Curran and Jerome McGann. Unfortunately it does not, in any central way, attempt to revision Romanticism(s) that might include the novel. Susan Allen Ford investigates incest, society and power in *A Simple Story, The False Friend* and *Matilda*, while Katherine M. Rogers demonstrates how, in comparison to Radcliffe, Charlotte Smith engages more sympathetically – more Romantically – with the revolutionary currents of the 1790s. However excellent these contributions are, the collection's focus on poetry tends to replicate the very genre bias it identifies as problematic.

A far more useful contribution on the topic is to be found in Anne K. Mellor's 'A Novel of Their Own: Romantic Women's Fiction, 1790–1830', in *The Columbia History of the British Novel*, eds John Richetti, Deidre David, John Bender and Michael Seidel. The gist of Mellor's argument is an extension of that deployed by

Jacqueline Howard (discussed above). That is, Mellor argues that women writers did not passively accept (then secretly subvert) the patriarchal construction of the 'proper lady': on the contrary, they exploited the novel's gift for 'heteroglossia' and 'dialogism' to create open vehicles for 'ideological contestation and subversion'. Mellor differs from Howard in extending this to the mainstream of the women's novel (while arguing that the women's novel was itself the novel's mainstream). Mellor briefly discusses Mary Wollstonecraft, Ann Radcliffe, Mary Hays, Helen Maria Williams, Mary Brunton, Jane Austen, Maria Edgeworth, Susan Ferrier and Mary Shelley to make her point that it is here that one finds the true defining energies of the novel during the Romantic period, and not in the Austen/Scott axis, where it is usually assumed to reside.

The task of mapping fully the forgotten geography of the novel, and the contribution of women writers to it, continues apace, with essays appearing on many of the writers instanced by Mellor. Judging from the number of articles on her, Maria Edgeworth is consolidating her position as one of the more significant landmarks. However, her critics seem unsure whether Edgeworth is a conservative, in the alleged Austen mode, or a Jacobinical fellow traveller. For Mary Jean Corbett, Edgeworth is very much in the former camp. In 'Another Tale to Tell: Postcolonial Theory and the Case of *Castle Rackrent*' (*Criticism* 36.383–400) and 'Public Affections and Familial Politics: Burke, Edgeworth, and the "Common Naturalization" of Great Britain' (*ELH* 61.877–97), Corbett argues that what goes for more exotic sites of colonialism also goes for those closer to home; the same overlap between imaginative appropriation and economic exploitation found in England's dealings with Asia, Africa or the Caribbean is found in England's commerce with Ireland. By using post-colonial theory to read *Castle Rackrent* Corbett hopes to 'recover the heterogeneity that has been suppressed within British studies itself'. Corbett argues that the 'colonial' status of Edgeworth's text has been obscured (naturalized) by the canon; to see Edgeworth fresh is to see her as a conservative implicated in the colonial appropriation of Ireland. Moreover, colonial pacification is mirrored in marriage, where domestic ideology is supported as a means of quelling the insurgency of women. Heather Macfadyen also sees social conservatism dominating Edgeworth's purposes. In 'Lady Delacour's Library: Maria Edgeworth's *Belinda* and Fashionable Reading' (*NCL* 48.423–39) Macfadyen more or less accepts *Belinda*'s moralizing at face value. The real purpose of the novel is to bring the egregious Lady Delacour back into the fold of 'domestic ideology'. In Macfadyen's view, the unappreciated aspect of Edgeworth's art is her use of textual referents to signify feminine impropriety (thus introducing a self-reflexive element into her art) and her tendency to invert theatrical motifs. The novel ends with Lady Delacour virtuously staging her domestic recuperation, where 'virtuously staging' is not the oxymoron it is for others. In 'Maria Edgeworth and the Construction of Gentlemanly Reading: Forester, Robinson Crusoe, and Benjamin Franklin' (*ESC* 20.395–411) Macfadyen takes the novella *Forester* as a work typifying Edgeworth's conservative, gentlemanly values; or at least ones based on the civil and domestic virtues of the middle class.

Marjorie Lightfoot sees Edgeworth's art quite differently. In '"Morals For Those That Like Them": The Satire of Edgeworth's *Belinda,* 1801' (*Éire* 29.iv.117–31) Lightfoot argues that Edgeworth's true *métier* is subversive (as opposed to conservative) satire, and to prove her point concentrates on Edgeworth's rarely understood tactics of subversion. Teresa Michals's 'Commerce and Character in

Maria Edgeworth' (*NCL* 49.1–20) helpfully accounts for this split in the criticism, couched here as Jacobinically tinged individualist versus hierarchically minded paternalist. Michals points out how Edgeworth liberally adapts the conservative, Burkean language of class and ancestry to bourgeois needs; so although Edgeworth eschews the Jacobinical language of individualism, it is in order to empower those classes who have not benefited from the language of class (where class is understood as a self-validating order enduring through time). From our perspective it is easy to be beguiled by Edgeworth's conservative accents; but hearing them in the context of the time restores Edgeworth's radical notes. Michals's argument is echoed, and historically framed, by Gary Kelly's 'Class, Gender, Nation and Empire: Money and Merit in the Writing of the Edgeworths' (*WC* 25.89–93), the most impressive of all the Edgeworth essays published during the year. To read it after the others is to experience mists clearing. Kelly sketches out how Edgeworth's father brought the pre-revolutionary, revolutionary middle-class ideology of the direct link between merit and money to class-bound, semi-feudal Ireland. Maria Edgeworth, in turn, sought to introduce this middle-class ideology to the feminine sphere of novel writing during an obviously wracked period. Kelly's essay largely concerns itself with the contradictions – of politics and gender – that afflicted Edgeworth's efforts; but by doing so he puts her novels into a clear perspective.

The argument over Edgeworth's political position is itself an obvious echo of the debate that has rumbled, and rumbles, through the Austen criticism. The year's only monograph on Austen was Roger Sales's *Jane Austen and Representations of Regency England*. Sales's book is doubly directed: its clear style and informing mission will suit the student reader, while its historical engagement will interest the Austen scholar. Sales aims to extend the recent contextualization of Austen within the political debates of the 1790s while correcting the unconscious tendency of the less historically informed criticism to read her as a proto-Victorian. Sales does both by highlighting the Regency crisis of 1810–11. He accepts that many of Austen's ideological attitudes were formed in the 1790s, but shows how they were modified by the later crisis. Once the particularity of Regency values is grasped, Austen's difference from the emerging Victorian sensibility becomes easier to discern. The Austen that emerges is a condition-of-England novelist whose meanings lie closer to the surface than has generally been allowed. Sales uses the discrepancy between the received Austen – that is, the Austen of her nephew's memoir, the cleaned-up letters, the heritage industry – and the facts as we have them to pinpoint Austen's discomfiting difference. As a condition-of-England novelist, Austen is neither a Tory anti-Jacobin, nor a cryptic (Wollstonecraftian) feminist. Her novels, rather, simultaneously echo both positions, as Regency politics find themselves mimicked in domestic microcosm. Sales's method helps the student pick out the mimicry, seeing *Mansfield Park*, for instance, as a replay of the Regency crisis. Although historically nuanced, this account rests on a notion of representation largely untroubled by recent literary-theoretical discussion. While this gives his project a certain solidity, the free play of meaning is inevitably restricted. To put it another way, the more Austen appears a condition-of-England writer, the less she appears an elusive ironist.

Aside from Sales's book, the year's major Austen publications are reprints of one kind or another. Routledge/Thoemmes Press have reprinted the first editions of Austen's novels, including Austen-Leigh's *Memoir* and Lord Brabourne's edition of the *Letters*, but obviously excluding the juvenilia, or anything else not contemporaneously published. Although the enterprise might suspiciously be viewed as a product of the academic heritage industry, having access to facsimiles of the first editions serves an obviously useful purpose. The project was edited by Louise Ross; David Gilson provides short, informative introductions. The collection is, in itself, a handsome object.

Robert Clark's Macmillan New Casebook, on *Sense and Sensibility* and *Pride and Prejudice*, admirably fulfils the series' stated intention of introducing the student to 'new critical approaches' while illuminating the 'rich interchange' between recent critical theory and critical practice. Clark focuses on new historical and feminist readings of Austen's texts. After placing his critical foci in their historical context he expertly charts the emerging debates, with their eddies of agreement and disagreement, in a theoretically astute, yet clear way. A number of the extracts derive from seminal monographs by Alistair Duckworth, Marilyn Butler, Mary Poovey and D. A. Miller. The remaining selections, from Isobel Armstrong, Angela Leighton, Judith Lowder Newton, Julia Prewitt Brown, Rachel M. Brownstein and Karen Newman, for the most part are chapters, articles or introductions.

One of the above, Duckworth's *The Improvement of the Estate,* was also reprinted this year, with a new introduction in which Duckworth responds to changes in Austen criticism since his book was first published in 1971. Like Clark, Duckworth argues that the new, dominant methodologies in Austen criticism have been 'feminist, new historicist, and cultural materialist readings'. Indeed, the two introductions echo each other in their concern to plot out the historical subtleties involved in the debate between those who hold to a conservative Austen and those who see her texts concealing latent, possibly feminist, subversion.

Several interventions aimed to resolve the debate in favour of Austen's feminism. Sarah Morrison's solution is to argue that Jane Austen's feminism falls outside the scope of the usual conservative-versus-subversive split ('Of Woman Borne: Male Experience and Feminine Truth in Jane Austen's Novels', *SNNTS* 26.337–50). That is, we should not see Austen as a secret social critic with instinctive feminist sympathies, and still less as a conservative one. Rather, Austen is difficult 'to label because her art succeeds in presenting a truly feminine version' in which the male characters are – beyond the necessities of plot – marginal figures. Tiffany F. Potter takes the supernumerary character of Austen's men even further in '"A Low but Very Feeling Tone": The Lesbian Continuum and Power Relations in Jane Austen's *Emma*' (*ESC* 20.ii.187–203). Anticipating the controversy ignited by Terry Castle's recent intervention in the *LRB,* Potter employs Adrienne Rich's 'lesbian continuum' to argue that *Emma* is conditioned by a lesbian subtext, and that 'intentionally or not' *Emma* is a subversive work. Potter takes it as a given that all relationships between women in Austen exist somewhere along the lesbian continuum; and once that assumption is made, it becomes clear (as indeed it must) that all intra-feminine talk is a lovers' discourse. Conversations between women are loaded with endearments; and as the subject frequently turns on – by skirting round – heterosexual attachments not yet sanctioned by a public declaration, such interlocutions are liberally punctuated with blushes. For Potter, such endearments are not mere form, while the ostensible heterosexual love interest is only a cover: the young women blush for each other. Once the given is granted, the argument makes sense; it is also buttressed with references to the diaries of Ann Lister, and by the theories of Judith Butler. Nevertheless it becomes clear that the only Austenian irony envisaged by Potter is the lesbian subtext shadowing all interactions between females in the book. The reduction of Austen's irony to something merely diatonic is the point on which this essay is likely to meet resistance.

Potter maintains that in marrying Knightley, Emma falls victim to a repressive heterosexual order, a conclusion supported by Frances L. Restuccia's 'A Black Morning: Kristevan Melancholia in Jane Austen's Emma' (*AI* 51.447–69), albeit from a completely different direction. Restuccia argues that '*Emma* can be read, on the model of Kristeva's theory in *Black Sun,* as a melancholic/masochistic text, whose addiction to the "maternal Thing" operates both at the level of the story [. . .] and the level of the functioning of the narrative.' Whereas Kristeva plots out a possible route back to the Symbolic for the female melancholic, *Emma* spurns the chance. Instead of just such a rapprochement, Emma's marriage to Knightley represents an intensification of the power of the patriarchal order, the cost of maintaining the addiction to the maternal Thing. In 'Rehabilitating Mary Crawford: *Mansfield Park* and the Relief of "Throwing Ridicule" ', Eileen Gillooly reads Mary Crawford as a kind of feminist subversive offering vicarious mockery of the patriarchal order. Gillooly's essay is collected in *Feminist Nightmares,* eds S. O. Weisser and J. Fleischner.

In 'Jane Austen's Rejection of Rousseau: A Novelistic and Feminist Initiation' (*PLL* 30.215–34) Paula Marantz Cohen attempts to resolve the vexed question of Austen's feminism by taking Austen's changing attitudes to Rousseau as an index of her developing consciousness. Although she initially rejected his sentimental style, she implicitly accepted the gender roles embedded in his educational theory. But between *Northanger Abbey* and *Pride and Prejudice* Austen rejected these roles. Rousseau championed the rights of love over class even as he insisted on the inequality between the sexes. It is this inequality Austen comes to dispute in her later work, a dispute made visible in her independent, equality-minded heroines. The trouble with Cohen's thick-grained analysis is that the politics of romantic love were a commonplace during the period, too nebulous and pervasive to pin down to Rousseau; and once he is stripped out as an influence, one is left with the issue of bourgeois individualism on which the Austen controversy frequently teeters. Linda C. Middleton, 'Anxious Spectators and Voluntary Spies: The Novel Hauntings of *Northanger Abbey*' (*Genre* 27.105–20), situates the famous formal inconsistencies and contradictory voices of Austen's novel in the context of the Gothic genre, but as her direct acquaintance with the Gothic genre appears to be somewhat fleeting, her analysis lacks subtlety. In 'Jane Austen and Money' Lisa Hopkins avoids the issue altogether, but through close observation of changing attitudes towards money she establishes a case for Austen's increasing openness towards Romanticism (*WC* 25.76–9). In his extended note, ' "Caro Sposo": Mrs Elton, Gurneys, Thrales, and Noels' (*RES* 45.70–5), Pat Rogers uses evidence from journals and letters to establish that Mrs Elton's use of the phrase *caro sposo* marks her as not only pretentious but out of date in her fashionable slang.

Interest in Sir Walter Scott continues after last year's bumper crop. Paul J. deGategno's *Ivanhoe: The Mask of Chivalry* is a clearly written and accessible student guide to Scott's seminal work, covering background, general context, recent criticism and 'artistic legacy'. DeGategno is particularly good at highlighting the romance's distinctive aesthetic, ideological and cultural aspects. As for articles, Frederick Burwick tells a story of intrinsic literary interest in 'How to Translate a Waverley Novel: Sir Walter Scott, Willibald Alexis, and Thomas De Quincey' (*WC* 25.93–100 – see also section 2 above). Burwick begins by noting how

German Romanticism's politicized preference for 'organic' British writing (as against the 'mechanical' French) laid the ground for Scott's enthusiastic reception. Capitalizing on this, Willibald Alexis produced a fake Waverley novel (*Walladmor*) 'translated' into German, a hoax De Quincey translated 'back' into English. Burwick uses the self-reflexivity inherent in this cultural exchange to highlight differences between German and English Romantic irony. In '*The Heart of Midlothian* and the Masculinization of Fiction' (*Criticism* 36.521–40) Beth Newman examines how Scott's anxieties regarding the novel play out in gender terms. Newman portrays *The Heart of Midlothian* as Scott's attempt to resist the common prejudice that novels were feminine, and novel reading effeminate. In Scott's novel, fiction is shored up with the masculine bulwarks of the professions, especially law, but despite these supports the genre slumps back, stubbornly, into the feminine. There were two further essays I was unable to see: J. R. Heller's 'Walter Scott and the Contract Between Playwrights, Actors and Theater Audiences' (*NCP* 21.17–32), and J. Calder's 'Story and History: R. L. Stevenson and Walter Scott' (*CVE* 40.21–34).

SHW 5, ed. Gillian H. Hughes, came too late to my attention to do anything other than note its contents (see also section 1(b) above). The journal (ISSN 0960-6025) contains three articles relevant to this section: Ian Duncan, 'The Upright Corpse: Hogg, National Literature, and the Uncanny'; Andrew Monnickendam, 'The Paradigm of Borders in *The Private Memoirs and Confessions of a Justified Sinner*'; and Penny Fielding, 'Living, and Life-Like: Stories and Things in *The Three Perils of Man*'. Otherwise, I could find only one essay on James Hogg, Michael Steig's interesting, but elusive, 'Unearthing Buried Affects and Associations in Reading: The Case of the Justified Sinner', in *Self-Analysis in Literary Study*, ed. Daniel Rancour-Laferriere. The essay relates Steig's pedagogical practice of basing seminar discussion on his students', as well as his own, associative responses to texts. The narrative of the story is Steig's inability to write successfully on Hogg's novel, a blockage he was finally able to break through by bringing its origins into the seminar discussion. These origins involve Steig's private Oedipal struggles; and while these are not, in themselves, edifying, the unflinching integrity of Steig's approach leads to some illuminating discussion of Hogg's vexed fiction.

Books Reviewed

Baillie, Joanna. *Poems 1790*. RevR. Woodstock. pp. 194. £30. ISBN 1 8547 7175 2.

Baum, Joan. *Mind-Forg'd Manacles: Slavery and the English Romantic Poets*. Archon. pp. xiii + 253. $29.50. ISBN 0 2080 2187 6.

Bennett, Andrew. *Keats, Narrative and Audience: The Posthumous Life of Writing*. CUP. pp. 254. £30. ISBN 0 5214 4565 5.

Blamire, Susanna. *The Poetical Works, 1842*. RevR. Woodstock. pp. 320. £35. ISBN 1 8547 7165 5.

Breen, Jennifer, ed. *Women Romantic Poets 1785–1832*. Dent. pp. 182. £5.99. ISBN 0 4608 7456 X.

Brewer, William D. *The Shelley–Byron Conversation*. UPFlor. pp. 189. £27.95. ISBN 0 8130 1300 3.

Bruhm, Steven. *Gothic Bodies: The Politics of Pain in Romantic Fiction*. UPennP. pp. 181. £28.50. ISBN 0 8122 3291 7.
Butler, Marilyn, ed. *Mary Shelley: Frankenstein. 1818 Text*. P&C (1993). pp. 261. £28.50. ISBN 0 1928 2283 7.
Clark, Robert, ed. *Sense and Sensibility and Pride and Prejudice*. New Casebooks. Macmillan. pp. 208. hb £37.50, pb £10.99. ISBN 0 3335 5016 1, 0 3335 5017 X.
Clark, Steve, and David Worrall, eds. *Historicizing Blake*. Macmillan. pp. 188. £40. ISBN 0 3335 6819 2.
Coates, John, and Bruce Woodcock. *Combative Styles: Romantic Writing and Ideology: Two Contrasting Interpretations*. HullUP. pp. 151. £8.95. ISBN 0 8595 8621 9.
Coleridge, Sara. *Phantasmion 1837*. RevR. Woodstock. pp. 400. £42. ISBN 1 8547 7166 3.
Collings, David. *Wordsworthian Errancies: The Poetics of Cultural Dismemberment*. JHUP. pp. xii + 287. £33. ISBN 0 8018 4848 2.
Cook, Elizabeth, ed. *John Keats*. OPL. OUP. pp. 260. £4.99 ISBN 0 1928 2291 8.
Copley, Stephen, and Peter Garside, eds. *The Politics of the Picturesque*. CUP. pp. 304. £35. ISBN 0 5214 4113 7.
Cordner, Michael, Peter Holland and John Kerrigan, eds. *English Comedy*. CUP. pp. 323. £35. ISBN 0 5214 1917 4.
Cranston, Maurice. *The Romantic Movement*. Blackwell. pp. 169. hb £35, pb £11.99. ISBN 0 6311 9471 1, 0 6311 7399 4.
deGategno, Paul J. *Ivanhoe: The Mask of Chivalry*. TMS 125. Twayne. pp. 119. hb $23.95, pb $13.95. ISBN 0 8057 9438 7, 0 8057 8379 2.
Duckworth, Alastair. *The Improvement of the Estate: A Study of Jane Austen's Novels*. 1971, reprint. JHUP. pp. xxxii + 239. £12.50. ISBN 0 8018 4972 1.
Duff, David. *Romance and Revolution: Shelley and the Politics of a Genre*. CUP. pp. xii + 276. £35. ISBN 0 5214 5018 7.
Edgecombe, Rodney Stenning. *Leigh Hunt and the Poetry of Fancy*. FDUP. £30. pp. 276. ISBN 0 8366 3571 7.
Engell, James, ed. *Coleridge: The Early Family Letters*. Clarendon. pp. 113. £25. ISBN 0 1981 8244 9.
Esterhammer, Angela. *Creating States: Studies in the Performative Language of John Milton and William Blake*. UTorP. pp. 245. £29. ISBN 0 8020 0562 4.
Favret, Mary A., and Nicola J. Watson. *At the Limits of Romanticism: Essays in Cultural, Feminist, and Materialist Criticism*. IndUP. pp. 291. hb £37.50, pb £12.99. ISBN 0 2533 2156 5, 0 2532 0853 X.
Feldman, Paula R., and Theresa M. Kelley, eds. *Romantic Women Writers: Voices and Countervoices*. UPNE. pp. 336. £38.95. ISBN 0 8745 1711 7.
Foulkes, Richard, ed. *John Clare: A Bicentenary Celebration*. LeicUP. pp. 96. £4. ISBN 0 9015 0746 6.
Freed, Eugenie R. *'A Portion of His Life': William Blake's Miltonic Vision of Woman*. BuckUP. pp. 159. £45. ISBN 0 8387 5265 9.
Gill, Stephen, and Duncan Wu, eds. *William Wordsworth*. OPL. OUP. pp. 252. £5.99. ISBN 0 1928 2269 1.
Goodridge, John, ed. *The Independent Spirit: John Clare and the Self-taught Tradition*. The John Clare Society and the Margaret Grainger Memorial Trust. pp. 240. £6.50.ISBN 0 9522 5412 3.
Haughton, Hugh, Adam Phillips and Geoffrey Summerfield, eds. *John Clare in*

Context. CUP. pp. 313. £37.50. ISBN 0 5214 4547 7.

Higonnet, Margaret R., ed. *Borderwork: Feminist Engagements with Comparative Literature*. Reading Women Writing. CornUP. pp. 321. hb £35.50, pb £13.50. ISBN 0 8014 2869 6, 0 8014 8107 4.

Höhne, Horst, ed. *Romantic Discourses*. Blaue Eule. pp. 355. n.p. ISBN 3 8920 6543 8.

Howard, Jacqueline. *Reading Gothic Fiction: A Bakhtinian Approach*. OUP. pp. 307 £40. ISBN 0 1981 1992 5.

Jackson, Heather, ed. *Samuel Taylor Coleridge*. OPL. OUP. pp. 201. £5.99. ISBN 0 1928 2266 7.

Jones, Steven E. *Shelley's Satire: Violence, Exhortation, and Authority*. NIUP. pp. 215. £30. ISBN 0 8758 0186 2.

Keane, Patrick J. *Coleridge's Submerged Politics: The Ancient Mariner and Robinson Crusoe*. UMissP. pp. 419. £35. ISBN 0 8262 0942 4.

Lickbarrow, Isabella. *Poetical Effusions 1814*. RevR. Woodstock. pp. 154. £25. ISBN 0 8547 7167 1.

Lieshout, Jules van. *Within and Without Eternity: The Dynamics of Interaction in William Blake's Myth and Poetry*. Rodopi. pp. 207. £21.75. ISBN 9 0518 3681 3.

Linnell, David. *Blake, Palmer, Linnell and Co.: The Life of John Linnell*. Book Guild. pp. 413. £50. ISBN 0 8633 2917 9.

Lloyd Smith, Allan, and Victor Sage, eds. *Gothick Origins and Innovations*. Rodopi. pp. 237. $50. ISBN 9 0518 3636 8.

Low, Lisa, and Anthony John Harding, eds. *Milton, the Metaphysicals, and Romanticism*. CUP. pp. 271. £35. ISBN 0 5214 4414 4.

Lucas, John. *John Clare*. WTW. Northcote. pp. 86. £6.99 ISBN 0 7463 0729 2.

Macovski, Michael S. *Dialogue and Literature: Apostrophe, Auditors, and the Collapse of Romantic Discourse*. OUP. pp. 231. £28. ISBN 0 1950 6965 X.

Marchand, Leslie A., ed. *What Comes Uppermost: Byron's Letters and Journals. Supplementary Volume*. Murray. pp. 102. £13.99. ISBN 0 7195 5610 4.

Mason, Michael, ed. *William Blake*. OPL. OUP. pp. 311. £5.99. ISBN 0 1928 2305 1.

McCarthy, William, and Elizabeth Kraft, eds. *The Poems of Anna Laetitia Barbauld*. UGeoP. pp. 399. £58.50. ISBN 0 8203 1528 1.

McDonagh, Josephine. *De Quincey's Disciplines*. Clarendon. pp. 209. £27.50. ISBN 0 1981 1285 8.

McGann, Jerome J., ed. *Lord Byron*. OPL. OUP. pp. 218. £5.99. ISBN 0 1928 2267 5.

Miles, Robert. *Gothic Writing 1750–1820: A Genealogy*. Routledge (1993). pp. 258. £40. ISBN 0 4150 7748 6.

Mishra, Vijay. *The Gothic Sublime*. SUNYP. pp. 342. $21.95. ISBN 0 7914 1748 4.

Morgan, Thaïs E., ed. *Men Writing the Feminine: Literature, Theory, and the Question of Genders*. SUNYP. pp. 207. $16.95. ISBN 0 7914 1994 0.

Moskal, Jeanne. *Blake, Ethics, and Forgiveness*. UAlaP. pp. 226. £23.95. ISBN 0 8173 0678 1.

Norton, Caroline. *A Voice from the Factories 1836*. RevR. Woodstock. pp. 48. £21. ISBN 1 8547 7169 8.

Orr, Leonard. *Critical Essays on Samuel Taylor Coleridge*. Hall. pp. 194. £30.95. ISBN 0 8161 8867 X.

Page, Judith. *Wordsworth and the Cultivation of Women*. UCalP. pp. 200. £28. ISBN 0 5200 8493 4.
Pite, Ralph. *The Circle of Our Vision: Dante's Presence in English Romantic Poetry*. Clarendon. pp. 267. £30. ISBN 0 1981 1294 7.
Powell, David. *The Life and Times of John Clare*. Northamptonshire Libraries and Information Services. pp. 24. £2.95. ISBN 0 9053 9116 0.
Purinton, Marjean D. *Romantic Ideology Unmasked: The Mentally Constructed Tyrannies in Dramas of William Wordsworth, Lord Byron, Percy Shelley, and Joanna Baillie*. UDelP. pp. 212. £28. ISBN 0 8741 3499 4.
Rancour-Laferriere, Daniel, ed. *Self-Analysis in Literary Study: Exploring Hidden Agendas*. NYUP. pp. 240. $45. ISBN 0 8147 7439 3.
Richetti, John, Deidre David, John Bender, and Michael Seidel, eds. *The Columbia History of the British Novel*. ColUP. pp. 1,200. £54. ISBN 0 2310 7858 7.
Robinson, Mary. *Poems 1791*. RevR. Woodstock. pp. 260. £30. ISBN 1 8547 7191 4.
Rogers, Deborah D., ed. *The Critical Response to Ann Radcliffe*. Critical Responses in Arts and Letters 7. Greenwood (1993). pp. 262. £53.95. ISBN 0 3132 8031 2.
Ross, Louise, ed. *Jane Austen: Novels, Letters and Memoir*. 19 vols. Routledge, Thoemmes. pp. 5,918. £1,125. ISBN 0 4151 1562 0.
Sales, Roger. *Jane Austen and Representations of Regency England*. Routledge. pp. 270. £13.99. ISBN 0 4151 0920 5.
Seward, Anna. *Llangollen Vale 1796*. RevR. Woodstock. pp. 62. £30. ISBN 1 8547 7171 X.
Shelley, Bryan. *Shelley and Scripture: The Interpreting Angel*. Clarendon. pp. 212. £25. ISBN 0 1981 2284 5.
Sheridan, Richard. *The Rivals*. Hern. pp. 98. £2.99. ISBN 1 8545 9099 5.
Stillinger, Jack. *Coleridge and Textual Instability: The Multiple Versions of the Major Poems*. OUP. pp. 288. £32.50. ISBN 0 1950 8583 3.
Voller, Jack G. *The Supernatural Sublime: The Metaphysics of Terror in Anglo-American Romanticism*. NIUP. pp. 271. £15. 25. ISBN 0 8758 0194 3.
Weisman, Karen A. *Imageless Truths: Shelley's Poetic Fictions*. UPennP. pp. 227. £32.95. ISBN 0 8122 3222 4.
Weisser, Susan O., and Jennifer Fleischner, eds. *Feminist Nightmares. Women at Odds: Feminism and the Problem of Sisterhood*. SUNYP. pp. 405. hb £44, pb £15.25. ISBN 0 8147 2619 4, 0 8147 2620 8.
Williams, Helen Maria. *Poems 1786*. RevR. Woodstock. pp. 422. £42. ISBN 1 8547 7173 6.
Wilson, Carol Shiner, and Joel Haefner, eds. *Re-Visioning Romanticism: British Women Writers, 1776–1837*. UPennP. pp. 329. hb £37.95, pb £15.95. ISBN 0 8122 3231 3, 0 8122 1421 8.
Wood, Marcus. *Radical Satire and Print Culture 1790–1822*. Clarendon. pp. 318. £35. ISBN 0 1981 1278 5.
Wordsworth, Jonathan. *Susanna Blamire: Poet of Friendship 1747–1794*. Privately pub. pp. 20. n.p. ISBN 1 8726 6526 8.
——, and Stephen Hebron. *Romantic Women Writers*. The Wordsworth Trust. pp. 70. No details.
Wu, Duncan, ed. *Romanticism: An Anthology*. Blackwell. pp. 1,142. hb £60, pb £14.99. ISBN 0 6311 9195 X, 0 6311 9196 8.
Yearsley, Ann. *Poems on Various Subjects 1787*. RevR. Woodstock. pp. 216. £55. ISBN 1 8547 7196 5.

XIII

The Nineteenth Century: Victorian Period

INGA BRYDEN, WILLIAM BAKER, KENNETH WOMACK, EMMA FRANCIS and VICTOR EMELJANOW

This chapter has four sections: 1. Cultural Studies and Prose; 2. The Novel; 3. Poetry; 4. Victorian Drama and Theatre. Section 1 is by Inga Bryden; section 2 is by William Baker and Kenneth Womack; section 3 is by Emma Francis; section 4 is by Victor Emeljanow.

1. Cultural Studies and Prose

This year's work concerning Victorian prose and cultural issues was marked by an interest in the textuality of Victorian culture itself. Works focused on the different methods by which culture was recorded and on the resulting tensions inscribed in the writing process. Critics investigated the related issues of subjectivity and intertextuality, viewing, for example, the Victorian writer or critic as 'subject' and the genre of autobiography as intertextual. The emphasis on the ways in which Victorian writing erects boundaries between subject and object was particularly related to the notion of reform. In attempting to cure social ills of one kind or another, the reformer might produce a text which represses the 'other' as much as it advocates change or observes social practices. Other of this year's works stressed a cultural-materialist approach to analysing Victorian texts. To varying degrees they addressed the question of how late twentieth-century literary critics define the notion of 'Victorianness'.

This year saw two articles (both by Joseph W. Childers) on Edwin Chadwick's 1842 *Report on the Sanitary Condition of the Labouring Population of Great Britain*. In the more lengthy and comprehensive of these, 'Observation and Representation: Mr Chadwick Writes the Poor' (*VS* 37.405–32), Childers is concerned with the textuality of the poor, with the kinds of connections or contiguities between 'the two nations' being forged (and the tensions which attend them) in the act of writing. The desire to observe and faithfully represent the 'reality' of poverty for middle-class readers is simultaneously a bridge and a barrier: as Childers points out, language itself is the altruistic hand and the '*cordon sanitaire*'. Chadwick is both reformer and repressor, playing to the gallery of a middle-class audience's voyeurism and repulsion, yet Childers is just as interested in how the poor write themselves in the *Report*. The complex issue of sanitation highlights these points of resistance, rendering them indicators of class cultural difference. Workers in Chadwick's text 'in their refusal to accept dirt as a comment on their character, and in their figuring of cleanness as a potential violence to the body . . . discursively establish the corporal presence of the Great Unwashed'. Textual moments of resistance are, however, increasingly co-opted by middle-class ideology, an act made possible, Childers argues, through the replacement of metonymy by metaphor. The *Report* defines individual members of the 'other' class in terms of their immediate environment, and any acknowledgement of degeneracy allows metaphor to convey the essentialism of poverty: the poor as beasts.

In his article 'Feminine Hygiene: Women in Edwin Chadwick's Sanitation Report' (*PSt* 17.23–37) Childers focuses on the interrelations of gender and class discourses in Chadwick's *Report on the Sanitary Condition of the Labouring Population of Great Britain* and on the ways in which Chadwick's depictions of working-class women reveal the limitations of the middle-class domestic ideology which informs the *Report*. The instance of a working-class woman whose change in external appearance is seen to be caused by the deteriorating conditions of her dwelling place, yet who is not morally depraved, or dead, cannot easily be contained within the 'marriage plot' of middle-class fictions. Again it is the issue of cleanliness which in Chadwick's exploitation of domestic ideology both empowers and polices the working classes. Childers argues that the 'potential agency' of working-class women (as moral guides and as economic contributors to, and managers of, the home) foregrounds them in the representation of the labouring classes. Interestingly, if working-class power were thus 'feminized' in the Report, middle-class readers' fears of the 'masculine' revolutionary mob might be defused. Both 'Observation and Representation: Mr Chadwick Writes the Poor' and 'Feminine Hygiene: Women in Edwin Chadwick's Sanitation Report' amply demonstrate how vestiges of working-class culture (both 'discursive' and 'material') are contained in Chadwick's rewriting of the poor. Ultimately Childers's work is about the difficulties inherent in speaking about or for the 'other'.

Joseph Salter was a multilingual missionary working among non-Europeans in London for over forty years. His memoirs *The East in the West; or Work Among the Asiatics and Africans in London* (1895) and *The Asiatic in England; Sketches of Sixteen Years' Work Among Orientals* (1873) are examined in Ruth H. Lindeborg's 'The "Asiatic" and the Boundaries of Victorian Englishness' (*VS* 37.381–404). Lindeborg reads these autobiographies as reflections of the contradictory sites of late nineteenth-century scientific, missionary and racial discourses in fascinating detail. The texts reveal the constant negotiation of boundaries: Salter must demarcate the Asiatic's presence on English soil and extend the welcoming hand of the Christian community, whilst keeping his subject position apart from those of potential converts. Moreover, the memoirs construct poverty as a distinctly foreign condition. 'Salter's no-man's land', Lindeborg argues, 'consists of the suppressed questions of discursive and cultural mutability and hybridity, specifically those of English territories and Christian texts.'

As Childers points out, even for 'feminist' political economists like Harriet Martineau, the notion of public and private labour colours their consideration of female subjectivity across classes. In 'Harriet Martineau's Political Economy of Everyday Life' (*VS* 37.223–51) Ann Hobart offers a reading of Martineau's sociological text *Society in America* (1837) in conjuction with her domestic novel

Deerbrook (1839). Hobart aims to show how Martineau's paradoxical relationship with political economy left its mark on these texts. She contends that Martineau attempts to appropriate political economy as a kind of 'feminist' theory which will exhort women to participate in the productive economy whilst accepting as 'natural' the gendered division of labour and property within the discourse of political economy. Thus, the private sphere in Martineau's writing is frequently figured not as a domestic haven, but as 'a disruptive or deadening liability, an arena where domesticated women, absorbed by the minutiae of daily life, play out petty jealousies to the detriment of any standard of the general good'. As with Mary Wollstonecraft, Martineau espouses women's rights whilst simultaneously warning women to work to reform themselves.

A number of critics were concerned with the philosophical and ideological positions adopted by Matthew Arnold in his social writings, particularly with the significance of the terms 'Hellenism' and 'Hebraism' as used by Arnold. Chapter 4 of *Culture and Anarchy* alerts readers to a precise historical connection between 'philhellenism' and 'anti-Judaism', argues Lionel Gossman in 'Philhellenism and Anti-Semitism: Matthew Arnold and his German Models' (*CL* 46.1–39), an admirable if rather convoluted attempt to locate Arnold within the contexts of the Greek revival in England and nineteenth-century attitudes towards Jews. Gossman shows how the 'neo-humanist' movement within German culture espoused philhellenism with its emphasis on Greece as the ideal, harmonious state whilst attacking what it regarded as Jewish spiritualism and dualism. He goes on to discuss the political context and significance of Arnold's *Culture and Anarchy*: Arnold invokes the antithesis of 'Hellenism' (related to culture, order, and the ideal of a unified state) and 'Hebraism' (signifying the individual will, conflict, and division), although he hopes for a balance between the two positions. Thus Arnold's 'Hebraism' is defined in terms of his resistance to anti-Judaism in continental scholarship.

Eugene Goodheart, in a more illuminating, lucid and inquiring critique of Arnold's social criticism, is also concerned with the function of Hebraism (a 'figure of will') and the relation of individual bias to an objective whole. However, 'Arnold, Critic of Ideology' (*NLH* 25.415–28) offers a riposte to those literary critics (Goodheart cites Marxist literary critics mainly) who continually seek to 'demystify' Arnoldian cultural criticism and thereby expose its ideologies. Goodheart contends that this apparent 'disinterestedness' is not (in theory) a naive practice or a 'fixed site'. Rather, 'disinterestedness . . . represents the psychological and moral condition . . . that makes objectivity possible': for Arnold it is 'the very condition of culture'. The subject of Arnold's social criticism is thus 'bias' itself. The article concludes with the thought-provoking assertion that 'Genuine thinking is an activity against the grain of ideological formulas that petrify the mind.'

William Baker's 'note', 'Matthew Arnold's Burnt Hand: An Unpublished Early Matthew Arnold Letter' (*N&Q* 41.358–9), draws attention to a rare 1837 letter sent by an adolescent Arnold from Winchester which mentions a 'Mr Wickham' who appears to have saved Arnold's middle finger and forefinger (Arnold had burned his hand after playing with a firearm). Since we do not know which hand was hurt, Baker proposes tantalizingly that this 'Mr Wickham' (probably Reverend Frederick Wickham) possibly saved the writer for posterity.

Laurel Brake continues to transform our knowledge of Victorian attitudes to literary practice in her accessible study *Subjugated Knowledges: Journalism, Gender and Literature in the Nineteenth Century*. Working within historical bibliography and cultural materialism, she is interested in tracing the relations between printed texts (articles, periodicals and part-issues) and modes of production in the nineteenth century and in demonstrating that late twentieth-century notions of 'literature' are predicated on the 'devaluation and invisibility as subjects' of those printed texts. Brake's crusade, then, is to make the invisible visible: after all, the majority of Victorian writers were involved with the periodical press. A very useful opening chapter outlines contemporary debates concerning the definitions of 'literature' and 'journalism' (which was viewed as being 'consumed' rather than 'read'). Brake goes on to discuss the 'cultural, economic, aesthetic, and ideological underpinnings of Victorian criticism', amply illustrating that criticism displayed its author's unease about the critic's identity. Throughout, the book maintains a balance between the analysis of individual periodical texts and discussion of the material and cultural factors affecting their form. Gender issues, both material and textual, are foregrounded in relation to notions of authorship and the politics of biography. Chapter 4 challenges the concept of the 'free, unique artist', examining the construction of the 'authors' Walter Pater, Matthew Arnold and Oscar Wilde in the context of publishing patterns. The essay always 'inscribes its history' and Brake's text acknowledges its own role in this process.

The construction of Walter Pater as a subject is also explored by Laurel Brake as part of the Writers and their Work series published by Northcote in association with the British Council. In keeping with the series philosophy, *Walter Pater* is a concise reassessment of Pater's work in biographical, cultural and recent critical contexts. Brake gives an account of Pater's academic life in Oxford before discussing his work for periodicals ('work expressive of those periodicals') and texts such as *Appreciations*, *Greek Studies* and *Imaginary Portraits*. She combines a cultural-historical approach with literary and cultural theory, and this lends weight to her insistence on the intertextuality of Pater's work: 'It might even be said that Pater's great subject is the meeting of competing discourses.' 'The "Outing" of Walter Pater' (*NCL* 48.480–506) by William F. Shuter presents itself as a biographical and critical project aiming to assess the manner in which evidence concerning Pater's sexuality has been interpreted. Shuter re-reads Pater's writing in opposition to the 'practitioners of gender discourse' who continually 'decode' the texts, yet in attempting to rehistoricize or 'open up' the texts Shuter does not advance a new perspective or a fresh cultural-historical model by which Pater's works can be read.

The two books to emerge from the political material (journalism and lectures) of the last two decades of William Morris's life were *Hopes and Fears for Art* (1882) and *Signs of Change* (1888), published either side of Morris's commitment to socialism in 1883. These texts are usefully presented in one volume, enabling the reader to assess the developments in Morris's social and cultural thinking, in the Thoemmes Press William Morris Library. Here we can view the polymath Morris as writing in the tradition of social criticism set out by Thomas Carlyle, Matthew Arnold and John Ruskin. Peter Faulkner points out in his lucid and pertinent introduction that *Hopes and Fears* 'marks a striking new emphasis in [Morris's] writing career as he moves from poetry to prose, and from fiction to direct social criticism'. The five lectures comprising *Hopes and Fears* employ historical-cultural relativism to critique the commercial and mechanical present. With more of an acute sense of urgency in the context of current environmental debates, we might note that Morris deemed the English middle class to be most complacent and dangerous. In *Signs of Change* the aim to unnerve and revolutionize the middle class takes centre stage.

A special issue of *JWMS* was this year devoted to the subject of 'Morris and Education'. This collection of essays, which includes Morris's 'Thoughts on Education under Capitalism' from *Commonweal*, is testament to the variety and 'breadth of educational vision' which Morris offers us. The subjects discussed range from utopian education to story-telling, and from technical education to current debates surrounding the teaching of English. In 'William Morris and "Education Towards Revolution": "Making Socialists" versus "Putting Them In Their Place"' (*JWMS* 11.i.49–58), Stephen Coleman identifies one aspect of Morris's educational work which has been significantly underestimated. Morris deliberately rejected, Coleman points out, state paternalism or 'benevolent elitism' in favour of dedicating himself to winning workers' minds.

The Politics of the Picturesque, edited by Stephen Copley and Peter Garside, is a volume of interdisciplinary essays drawing on a variety of historical and theoretical approaches to the concept of the picturesque in the late eighteenth and nineteenth centuries. The introduction clearly accounts for the critical history of the term 'picturesque'; rather than adhering to totalizing aesthetic theorization, recent critics of the picturesque are more concerned with its ideological implications. It can be argued, the editors point out, that 'the cultural importance of the Picturesque stands in direct proportion to the theoretical imprecision of its vocabulary'. This volume is concerned with the protean nature of the aesthetic and with its continuance as a focus for political debate. David Punter's wide-ranging essay 'The Picturesque and the Sublime: Two Worldscapes' employs a discourse of boundaries and frames to interpret the picturesque from a psychoanalytic perspective. Punter argues that the picturesque represents the enclosing moment – 'roughness subjected to symmetry' – whereas the sublime represents the outward movement; the abandonment of control. Yet if the picturesque is not just about perception, but about activity, it demands historicization. Anne Janowitz focuses on the Chartists, arguing in 'The Chartist Picturesque' that the Chartist poetic landscape was a kind of 'invented nostalgia' for a landscape to which Chartists actually had a contradictory relationship. Malcolm Andrews refreshingly works with definitions of the picturesque in the context of Victorian urban life. 'The Metropolitan Picturesque' considers the picturesque of Victorian London as an architectural principle and assesses its relations to tourism and conservation. Ruskin especially was influential in advocating a reconstructed picturesque whereby the reader/viewer would experience an ethical response to scenes of urban decay.

The mathematical physicist George Green (1793–1841) was the subject of a 'substantial' biography published last year, Green's bicentenary. Green went to Cambridge when he was 40 to study mathematics. He did not receive public recognition in his own lifetime; it was left to Kelvin to see the importance of Green's 'function technique'. D. M. Cannell in *George Green: Mathematician and Physicist (1793–1841)* aims to interest both the lay reader and the scientific specialist. There is no analysis of Green's works, although the main points of 'An Essay on the Application of Mathematical Analysis to the Theories of Electricity and Magnetism' (1828) are discussed by M. C. Thornley in an appendix. Instead the biographer, left 'with the facts culled from official sources, a dozen letters, and a few personal statements', is as much interested in Green the person as in Green the inventor. Social, intellectual and educational contexts are taken into account and a very useful series of appendices includes mathematical papers, a family tree, and a time chart of contemporary scientists and mathematicians. In the end the reader is left rather with the sense of the mysteries involved in writing the biography of someone who could be termed a self-educated genius.

In contrast to the relations between the figure of Green and his biographer, the figure of Lord Curzon, Viceroy of India, seems a dazzling public hero to Nayana Goradia. Despite this tendency Goradia's biography, *Lord Curzon: The Last of the British Moghuls* manages to anatomize Curzon's narcissism. Goradia reads the body of the hero almost as an analogue for the health of the state, arguing that the flawed Curzon, accustomed to praise in every social context and with sado-masochistic tendencies, embodied the glitter, but also the decadence, of British imperialism.

A fresh perspective on various aspects of Victorian intellectual, cultural and religious life is afforded the reader of Margaret Pawley's biography of Ambrose de Lisle, *Faith and Family: The Life and Circle of Ambrose Phillipps de Lisle*. Pawley sees Ambrose de Lisle as an 'inveterate collector of ideas', almost as a visionary or a prophet who, in his determination to increase both the influence of Roman Catholicism in England and the involvement of lay persons in church affairs, attracted much criticism. Ambrose de Lisle advocated the medievalizing of existence, in religious and architectural terms, and Pawley details his relationships with Pugin, members of the Oxford Movement, and the Young Englanders. The changes within the Roman Catholic community in the 1850s and 1860s were Ambrose de Lisle's 'personal history also'.

The 'autobiographical pressure' was found in all forms of Victorian writing. As dominant cultural discourses concerned the forging of links with formative histories of one kind or another, so individuals, products of a rapidly industrializing nation, attempted to make sense of their lives in autobiography. However, as Robin Gilmour noted in a study last year, this was the site of paradox in Victorian culture: 'The prophets of progress saw the backward glance of autobiography as regressive, its surrender to introspection as a failure to measure up to the active, public virtues of a new civilisation' (*YWES* 74.370–1). Clinton Machann in *The Genre of Autobiography in Victorian Literature* treats individual self-histories as extreme or exaggerated examples of general developments in English history (see also section 2(a) below). His work is a chronological comparative study of eleven autobiographies by British writers (including Cardinal Newman, John Stuart Mill, Harriet Martineau, John Ruskin, Charles Darwin, Herbert Spencer and Sir Walter Besant), which aims to be both an introduction to Victorian autobiography and an account of the ways in which as a genre it is intertextual and historically determined. The Victorian autobiographer struggles to show how the 'protagonist' becomes the author-narrator who is known to the public as a different person. In addition, the text refers to a world beyond itself in the sense that it becomes 'a key to understanding and evaluating the author's published oeuvre'. Machann is concerned with how the autobiography as non-fiction invites the reader to move between the co-ordinates of text and world (culture). He examines a variety of recurring motifs and structural devices (such as advice to young writers) which work to conflate the inner and outer developments. *The Genre of Autobiography in Victorian Literature* is a refreshing move to rehistoricize Victorian autobiography, although the tracing of 'cultural continuities' is sometimes obscured by the attention to intertextual paradigms.

Autobiography as an 'act of revenge' forms part of the Subversive Women series published by Thoemmes Press, a series of five 'radical texts' deemed too dangerous at their time of writing for public circulation. Rosina Bulwer-Lytton's *A Blighted Life: A True Story* (1880) is reprinted with a brief introduction by Marie Mulvey Roberts. *A Blighted Life* can be read as a personal attack on Edward Bulwer-Lytton, husband, novelist and politician, or as a representative account of the female hysteric's situation in Victorian England; as a narrative of resistance or as a narrative of defeat. In any reading it is significant as a document in the contexts of Rosina's writings on the position of married women in Victorian Britain and the campaign for women's rights espoused by Rosina and inherited from her mother Anna Wheeler.

The potentially fascinating topic of 'Women's Magazines in the 19th Century' – which could tell us a great deal about cultural-historical relativities – is treated in an untheorized manner by Lee Jolliffe (*JPC* 27.iv.125–140). Jolliffe actually discusses 'suffrage' magazines (focusing on Lucy Stone's *Woman's Journal* [1870]) in nineteenth-century America. Part I asserts, unsurprisingly, that women gained power 'as a cultural force' with the growth of a new mass medium. An interesting discussion of the contents and targets of the *Woman's Journal* follows. Yet the cultural implications, such as the increasing percentage of pro-suffrage magazines and the relations between the suffrage movement, its own magazines and women's magazines in general, are not addressed. The rhetorical and political strategies adopted by nineteenth-century women as they attempted to articulate the emerging feminist consciousness of the age are discussed by Annette Kolodny in 'Inventing a Feminist Discourse: Rhetoric and Resistance in Margaret Fuller's *Woman in the Nineteenth Century* (1845)' (*NLH* 25.355–82). Kolodny convincingly reminds us of Fuller's rhetorical daring (as critic, intellectual, and teacher of 'conversation' to girls) and her questioning of accepted gender categories as she tried to avoid the 'combative' nature of male rhetoricians.

This year witnessed the publication of Michael Mason's magnificent *The Making of Victorian Sexuality*, a comprehensive and original work which effectively explodes late twentieth-century myths about the nature of Victorian sexual culture (see also section 2(a) below). Mason manages a considerable range and variety of sources with wit and insight. He commences chapter 1, 'Locating Respectability', by anatomizing the hostility we feel towards the 'alien Victorians'. 'Victorian', as we use the label, is unique among historical appellations 'in the amount of meaning it can carry beyond the chronological' and in its association with moral restrictiveness. The guiding purpose of this study is to indicate how far the notion of Victorian sexual moralism is rooted in late eighteenth- and early nineteenth-century culture. Furthermore, Mason's aim is to document the way that issues of sexual behaviour presented themselves to Victorian men and women 'as issues to be judged according to a secular, rational, and progressive code rather than in the light of the deliverances of moral and religious authority'. Interestingly, Francis Place's 'theory' of respectability in his *Autobiography* sets an agenda for the investigation of Victorian sexual culture in chapters 2 and 3. The majority of the volume is concerned with sexual practices; the remainder with sexual attitudes. Attuned to the difficulties of connecting practices with attitudes, Mason none the less advances a number of conclusions, for instance that married and unmarried couples of different classes adopted artificial contraceptive methods as early as the 1860s.

J. B. Bullen's *The Myth of the Renaissance in Nineteenth-Century Writing* continues the recent work in Victorian studies on how and why the Victorians remodelled the Renaissance past in the context of a cultural desire to reinvent a whole range of pasts. In this informative and elucidating work, Bullen examines the 'Renaissance' as a nineteenth-century literary myth or construct, and as a product of historical discourse. The introduction, drawing on the work of Roland Barthes and Hayden White, clearly sets out the connections between historical discourse and myth. Bullen discusses the genesis of the concept of the Renaissance in French historiography, although he mainly focuses on how the concept affected English intellectual life and how it was refashioned in texts by John Ruskin, Augustus Welby Pugin, Walter Pater, George Eliot, Robert Browning and Matthew Arnold. In Victorian England, religious and political debates polarized attitudes towards the Renaissance myth, and the historiography of the Renaissance was intertwined with the progress of 'self-culture'. One of the major implications which emerges from this work is that while in the mid-nineteenth century the 'Renaissance' signified the rebellion of the individual against a drab, conformist society, the textual use of the term acknowledged 'connections between remote elements in a culture; it is to think of history as cultural history'.

A dominant theme in this year's work was the undercurrent of social and cultural disorder in Victorian writing and the ways in which the texts manage or circumscribe it. This sense of disorder or fragmentation might relate to sexuality, evolution or class, and it is represented in various bestial forms such as the female body and the political crowd. Miriam Bailin's *The Sickroom in Victorian Fiction: The Art of Being Ill* discusses the ways in which the sickroom functioned as a symbolic and imaginative space in Victorian literature, referring to non-fictional records of illness to highlight the gendered power relations of the sickroom in fiction by Charlotte Brontë, Charles Dickens and George Eliot (see also section 2(a) below). Crucial to Bailin's argument is the 'realist commitment to the mediation of private and public spheres'. In this scenario invalidism became 'an antidote for the very disorders it signified'. That realism itself might be an illness is a fascinating proposition. Bailin is more convincing in dealing with the sickroom as a literary response to formal, structural 'disorders' than she is in clearly explaining its imaginative relation to specific social and cultural 'disorders'.

P. R. Horne's 'Autocensorship in the Age of Victoria: The Case of Gabriele Rossetti and Charles Darwin' (*MLR* 89.341–350) is a case study of the interaction between context, author and text. It examines the social, practical and ideological factors affecting the delayed publication and content of 'controversial' works by Darwin (his theory of natural selection) and Rossetti (*Mistero*).

Darwin's attempts to describe the Victorians' exercise of sexual choice in historical terms in *The Descent of Man and Selection in Relation to Sex*, and the resulting ideological contradictions, are explored by Rosemary Jann in 'Darwin and the Anthropologists: Sexual Selection and its Discontents' (*VS* 37.287–306). Both Darwin and the anthropologists who influenced him aligned social power with the ability to choose a sexual partner. In using bourgeois gender roles as the model for their genealogies of 'natural' selection they simultaneously normalized Victorian conceptions of female nature. Jann summarizes the anthropological narratives circulating in Victorian culture and demonstrates that the construction of a biological rationale for gendered behaviour was contingent on the projection of 'a patriarchal model of the family back into the no-(hu)man's land between biology and culture'.

The trope of the political crowd in nineteenth-century writing is thoroughly discussed by Nicholas Visser in 'Roaring Beasts and Raging Floods: The

Representation of Political Crowds in the Nineteenth-Century British Novel' (*MLR* 89.289–317). Visser points out that the crowd, often depicted as bestial, represents a 'general threat to authority', although in specifically addressing cultural and historical contexts he is able to locate and explicate the shifting ideological signification of the fictional crowd. Post-1789 fiction tends to endorse 'hegemonic perceptions of revolutionary crowds', whereas by the 1840s the crowd is on the whole depicted by writers as a threat to civilization itself.

'Beauty and the Beast', a popular tale among Victorians, is the starting point for a fascinating and thought-provoking investigation of the figuring of women in nineteenth-century writing. In 'Beauty and the Victorian Body' (*EIC* 44.102–16) Dinah Birch draws on a range of references to show that the central 'doubleness' of femininity is closely linked to contradictory ideas about women's bodies. Particular attention is paid to different and contradictory images of women's bodies in Ruskin's writing. Interestingly, Dickens's heroines are read in the light of Ruskin's definition of the grotesque in *The Stones of Venice*. The grotesque 'fallen' body is always on the verge of transformation: 'The appetites of the fallen world constantly threaten to mutate Dickens's child-women.' Indeed it is women's bodies themselves, Birch argues, which 'signify a falling apart', threatening to devour 'law and literature and culture itself'.

Edward Lear's limericks have much to tell us about social fragmentation in Victorian Britain, according to Thomas Dilworth. 'Society and the Self in the Limericks of Lear' (*RES* 45.42–62) charts how Lear's attitude towards society darkens in the later limericks ('picture-limericks'). Dilworth argues that this is because the price of the 'accommodation' of the individual (artist) into society is conformity. Employing reader/viewer-response theory, he goes on to show that the tension between the individual and the social is echoed on a conceptual level: 'This may be the ultimate revelation of the greatest nonsense, the difference between the infinite freedom of conception and the relatively severe limits of imagination.'

Robert M. Polhemus, in 'John Millais's Children: Faith, Erotics, and *The Woodman's Daughter*' (*VS* 37.433–50), takes the Pre-Raphaelite artist Millais's representation of children as an example of the developing 'faith in the child' in Victorian culture. *The Woodman's Daughter*, read alongside the poem by Coventry Patmore which inspired it (the essay's interdisciplinarity is patchy), figures an 'iconographic and sacrificial role for the child'. Polhemus is concerned with the psychological dimension of Millais's text, although in relating this to Victorian culture he makes some odd generalizations.

Peter Mendes's *Clandestine Erotic Fiction in English 1800-1930: A Bibliographical Study* aims to trace the bibliographical history of erotic fiction in English (including translations into English) published 'clandestinely' between 1885 and 1930 (a survey of the period 1800 to 1885 is appended). 'Clandestine' refers to books whose publishers and printers attempted in a number of ways to hide their identities: the title pages of these books are to a degree mysteries. Given that speculation is largely part of erotic bibliography, Mendes cites his intention to demystify. He clearly locates, classifies and describes titles of the period whilst also trying to establish, with some reference to typography, the identities of printer, publisher, advertiser, distributor and author.

'*The Illustrated London News* and the Invention of Tradition' (*VPR* 27.1–24) is concerned with the ways in which the *ILN* played a major role in creating the 'myth of modern monarchy'. Virginia McKendry carefully discusses selected *ILN* images where the members of the royal family are depicted as both ordinary and 'dynastic symbols of nationhood'. Representations of Victoria which conflated notions of gender, class and power are the main focus of the essay. More attention to the processes of the 'myth's' generation and the power relations of the production machine – the 'media steeped in middle-class values' – might have strengthened this analysis.

Victorian crime and its different 'reader' configurations are discussed in John Springhall's lively article '"Pernicious Reading"? "The Penny Dreadful" as Scapegoat for Late-Victorian Juvenile Crime' (*VPR* 27.326–49). 'Is it possible to ascertain the power of penny dreadfuls either to entertain or to corrupt?' poses Springhall. The essay tests the allegation that sensation fiction aimed at the young provoked juvenile crime, by looking at the public reporting of selected criminal prosecutions and showing how the term 'penny dreadful' was constructed 'from above' by middle-class journalists. As Springhall comments, 'urbanised and commercialised popular culture' itself was on trial.

2. The Novel

(a) General

This year is marked by splendid editions of correspondence. Ongoing editions of the letters of Dickens, Gissing and Stevenson are complemented by editions of Anne Thackeray Ritchie's journals and letters, George MacDonald's correspondence, and Edgar F. Harden's supplement to Gordon N. Ray's seminal edition of Thackeray's letters. However, the nature of the recent critical, historical and biographical analyses regarding the Victorian novel remains similar to the commentary examined in recent surveys in the *YWES*. In addition to forays into feminism, deconstruction, new historicism, and textual and bibliographical study, recent criticism of the nineteenth-century novel features philological, linguistic and postmodernist examinations, among a host of other critical pursuits. Additionally, the Victorian fictive canon continues to remain relatively stable, perennially including such predominant novelists as Dickens, Charlotte and Emily Brontë, George Eliot and Hardy. It is refreshing to see the great diversity of work on the Victorian novel, particularly on such major figures as Thackeray, Trollope, Mrs Gaskell, Stevenson and Gissing, in addition to welcome attention to the writings of Stoker, Wilde, Conan Doyle, Carroll and Thomas Hughes, amongst others.

Drawing upon a variety of theoretical approaches, the essays in Nikki Lee Manos and Meri-Jane Rochelson's *Transforming Genres: New Approaches to British Fiction of the 1890s* explore the transformational powers of British fiction in the late nineteenth century. Selections include Manos and Rochelson's introduction; Ann L. Ardis's 'Shakespeare and Mrs Grundy: Redefining Literary Value in the 1890s'; Margaret Diane Stetz's '*New Grub Street* and the Woman Writer of the 1890s'; Teresa Mangum's 'Style Wars of the 1890s: The New Woman and the Decadent'; R. B. Kershner's 'Modernism's Mirror: The Sorrows of Marie Corelli'; Claudia Nelson's 'Fantasies de Siècle: Sex and Sexuality in the Late-Victorian Fairy Tale'; William J. Scheick's 'Ethical Romance: Kipling's "The Man Who Would Be King"'; Corrine McCutchan's 'Whom Is Kim?'; Lynn Thiesmeyer's 'Imperial Fictions and Nonfictions: The Subversion of Sources in Mary Kingsley and Joseph Conrad'; Lynne Hapgood's 'Regaining a Focus: New Perspectives on the Novels of Richard Whiteing, 1888–1899'; Ronald R. Thomas's 'Reevaluating Identity in the 1890s: The Rise of the New Imperialism and the Eyes of the New

Detective'; Frederick L. De Naples's 'Unearthing Holmes: 1890s Interpretations of the Great Detective'; and Linda Gertner Zatlin's '"The Story of a Confession Album": The Literary Precursor of Aubrey Beardsley's Fascination with Triangles'. Patrick Brantlinger's 'The Case of the Poisonous Book: Mass Literacy as Threat in Nineteenth-Century British Fiction' (*VR* 20.117–33) includes special attention to the promulgation of the sensation novel by Dickens, Wilde and Mary Elizabeth Braddon, among others.

Paul Thomas Murphy's *Toward a Working-Class Canon: Literary Criticism in British Working-Class Periodicals, 1816–1858* surveys the nature of British working-class literacy, affording particular attention to the working-class autobiographies and journalism of the era. Murphy distinguishes working-class periodicals from the other 'cheap' periodicals available during that time in the journalistic marketplace. He explores the literary aspects of these works, especially in the poems and fictional efforts often published in periodicals. Drawing upon works by Dickens and George Eliot, Jeff Nunokawa's *The Afterlife of Property: Domestic Security and the Victorian Novel* investigates the ways in which Victorian novelists imagined women as items of property. Nunokawa addresses the way the categories of economics, gender, sexuality, race and fiction functioned together to commodify women in an uncertain marketplace during this era. In *Revolution in the Form of the English Novel, 1790–1825: Intercepted Letters, Interrupted Seductions*, Nicola J. Watson traces the development of the English novel during the late eighteenth and early nineteenth centuries, including analysis of the evolution of the sentimental and epistolary narrative forms, as well as historical fiction. Watson assesses the writings of a range of epistolary authors, including Sir Walter Scott, Jane West, Helen Maria Williams, Mary Wollstonecraft and Maria Edgeworth. In *The Stone and the Scorpion: The Female Subject of Desire in the Novels of Charlotte Brontë, George Eliot, and Thomas Hardy*, Judith Mitchell draws upon a variety of psychoanalytic insights in her analysis of the representations of desire and femininity in the narratives of Brontë, Eliot and Hardy. Lisa Surridge's 'Dogs'/Bodies, Women's Bodies: Wives as Pets in Mid-Nineteenth-Century Narratives of Domestic Violence' (*VR* 20.1–34) discusses the depiction of female characters engaged in marital conflict in works by Dickens, Eliot and the Brontës, among others.

Michael Mason's *The Making of Victorian Sexuality* (see also section 1 above) demonstrates the inaccuracy of popular conceptions of sexuality during the Victorian age, using data collected from demographic analysis, the travel writing of foreign visitors to England, and nineteenth-century medical texts. Mason argues that the lives of the wealthy and the poor alike were marked by a Victorian moralism that they consciously embraced as a humane and progressive vision of the future of society. In *The Making of Victorian Sexual Attitudes*, his companion volume to *The Making of Victorian Sexuality*, Mason features individual portraits of such figures as the Swedenborgians, Henry James Prince and 'Baron' Renton Nicholson. Christopher Craft's *Another Kind of Love: Male Homosexual Desire in English Discourse, 1850–1920* traces images of male homosexual desire and its representations in English texts of the nineteenth and early twentieth centuries. Craft also examines the modern binary of homosexual and heterosexual desire and its relation to the extant concepts of 'sexual inversion' and 'sodomy' in such texts as Wilde's *The Importance of Being Earnest* and Bram Stoker's *Dracula*, among others. In *Love's Litany: The Writing of Modern Homoerotics*, Kevin Kopelson examines the relationship between erotic philosophy and homosexuality in the modern period, arguing that nineteenth-century conceptions of love shaped contemporary conceptions of lesbian and gay subjectivity. Drawing upon the works of Oscar Wilde, among a host of others, Kopelson addresses the experimental and influential erotic theories embedded in these texts, while challenging the critical undervaluation of love in contemporary constructions of sexuality. In *Engaging with Shakespeare: Responses of George Eliot and Other Women Novelists*, Marianne Novy traces images of Shakespeare and Shakespearean engagement in the works of George Eliot, Jane Austen, Charlotte Brontë, and twentieth-century women novelists such as Virginia Woolf, Willa Cather, Iris Murdoch and others.

In *The Sensation Novel: From 'The Woman in White' to 'The Moonstone'*, Lyn Pykett identifies the principal features of the sensation novel, affording particular emphasis to its social significance and the cultural context in which the genre achieved renown. In addition to focusing upon the works of such writers as Wilkie Collins, Mary Elizabeth Braddon, Ellen Wood and Rhoda Broughton, Pykett discusses the manner in which the genre that dominated the literary scene of the 1860s continues to arouse critical interest in the post-structuralist era. *Critical Reconstructions: The Relationship of Fiction and Life*, edited by Robert M. Polhemus and Roger B. Henkle, offers a collection of essays that examines the relationship between fiction and life in the works of Robert Louis Stevenson and Charles Dickens, among others. Selections include Polhemus's 'Comic and Erotic Faith Meet Faith in the Child: Charles Dickens's *The Old Curiosity Shop* ("The Old Cupiosity Shape")'; Henkle's 'The Crisis of Representation in *Dombey and Son*'; and George Dekker's 'James and Stevenson: The Mixed Current of Realism and Romance'. In *The Power of Lies: Transgression in Victorian Fiction*, John Kucich draws upon works by Anthony Trollope, Wilkie Collins, Elizabeth Gaskell and Thomas Hardy, in his discussion of Victorian England's fascination with lying and transgressing ethical boundaries. Primarily concerned with the transgression of socially and symbolically conceptual boundaries, Kucich's study reveals the ways in which equivocation functioned in all phases of Victorian culture as a social mechanism impinged upon by the middle-class elite, particularly the professionals, cultural intellectuals and writers.

Using works by Charles Dickens, Elizabeth Gaskell, Benjamin Disraeli, Charles Kingsley, Frances Trollope and Elizabeth Tonna, Constance D. Harsh's *Subversive Heroines: Feminist Resolutions of Social Crisis in the Condition-of-England Novel* investigates the social implications and potential power of women in Victorian-era narratives. Harsh also reveals through close readings of these works a covert feminism that redefined the fundamental gender struggles of the time. In *Degeneration, Culture, and the Novel, 1880–1940*, William Greenslade confronts the late nineteenth-century belief among many affluent and educated people that destitution, insanity, criminality and homosexuality were symptoms of the degeneration of the human race. Drawing upon the contrasting, progressive texts by such writers as Hardy, Gissing, Conan Doyle, Conrad, Wells, Forster and Woolf, Greenslade examines the propagation of 'degenerationism' in the work of popular authors such as Warwick Deeping and John Buchan. Drawing upon the works of Charlotte Brontë, Charles Dickens and George Eliot, Miriam Bailin's *The Sickroom in Victorian Fiction* discusses the place of the sickroom and the significance of illness in nineteenth-century life and literature (see also section 1 above). Using non-fictional accounts of illness by Julia Stephen, Harriet Martineau and others, Bailin argues that the sickroom functions within Victorian fiction as a compositional response to the conflicts and contradictions that existed in that society.

In 'From a Past Contemporary: Three Victorian Novelists' (*ContempR* 265.102–4), Amelia Edwards discusses the narratological similarities between the novels of Dickens, Trollope and Thackeray. Russell Poole's 'Constructions of Fate in Victorian Philology and Literature', featured in Geraldine Barnes, Margaret Clunies Ross and Judy Quinn's *Old Norse Studies in the New World: A Collection of Essays to Celebrate the Jubilee of the Teaching of Old Norse at the University of Sydney, 1943–1993*, explores the treatment of fate by Victorian novelists and its associations with Old Norse literature. Rosemary Jann's 'Animal Analogies in the Construction of Class' (*NCS* 8.89–103) discusses the treatment of animals as metaphors for the ills of society during the nineteenth century by Victorian novelists. In 'Narrating the Unnarratable: Metonymy in the Victorian Novel' (*Style* 28.74–94), Robyn R. Warhol addresses the issue of whether male and female novelists write differently, through an analysis of several works of Victorian fiction. Russel J. Perkin's 'Locking George Sand in the Attic: Female Passion and Domestic Realism in the Victorian Novel' (*UTQ* 63.408–28) discusses the Victorian realist novel's debt to the fictions of George Sand, particularly regarding the narrative treatment of passion and domesticity by British writers. Betty Kushen's '"Dreams," "Reveries," and the Continuity of Consciousness in Three Nineteenth-Century Novelists' (*JEP* 15.122–8) investigates the representations of dreams in the works of George Henry Lewes and Elizabeth Gaskell, among others. Jane Aaron's 'Nature's Daughters: Representations of Welshwomen in English Popular Fiction, 1870–1910' (*SwR* 99–112) discusses the education of young women in Wales in a variety of Victorian novels.

Rebecca F. Stern's 'Gothic Light: Vision and Visibility in the Victorian Novel' (*SCRev* 11.26–39) explores images of Gothicism and light imagery in such works as Charlotte Brontë's *Jane Eyre*, George Eliot's *Daniel Deronda* and Elizabeth Gaskell's *Ruth*, among other works. Dinah Birch's 'Beauty and the Victorian Body' (*EIC* 44.102–16) discusses the treatment of the human body, particularly regarding representations of women and children, in the works of a variety of Victorian novelists. In 'Varieties of Textual Change in the Victorian Era' (*Text* 6.225–47), Allan C. Dooley discusses the value of bibliographical and textual criticism to the understanding of works from the Victorian period. Jacqueline Banerjee's 'Girls' Education and the Crisis of the Heroine in Victorian Fiction' (*ES* 75.34–45) examines representations in various Victorian novels of the education of young women. Drawing upon the theoretical insights of modern linguistics, Raymond Chapman's *Forms of Speech in Victorian Fiction* examines the manner in which Victorian writers employed dialogue in the presentation of their characters and the relationships between them. In addition to exploring the Victorian usage of slang, regional dialects, evangelical speech and euphemisms, Chapman discusses the effect of the ways in which language conventions governed the writing and the circulation of fiction during the Victorian era.

In *Fallen Women in the Nineteenth-Century Novel*, Tom Winnifrith examines the complexities underlying the betrayal of the fallen woman in texts by Charlotte Brontë, George Eliot, Thackeray, Dickens and Hardy. Winnifrith also attempts to historicize the manner in which these novelists continue the prevailing narratological polarization of female characters into angels and whores. He offers close studies of such novels as *Jane Eyre*, *Romola*, *Vanity Fair*, *Nicholas Nickleby* and *The Return of the Native* in his volume. Robert Fraser's *Proust and the Victorians: The Lamp of Memory* surveys Proust's reactions to Victorians ranging from Carlyle, Darwin, Emerson and Ruskin to George Eliot, Hardy, Stevenson, Wells and

Wilde. Additionally, Fraser features discussion regarding the connection in Proust's mind between literary and art criticism, as well as to his delayed response to the Ruskin-Whistler trial of 1878. Fraser argues that Proust's adoption of the fruits of Victorian thought enabled him to move from one historical aesthetic to the other that marked the narrative of such works as *Du côté de chez Swann*. Paul Goldman's well-illustrated and indexed *Victorian Illustrated Books, 1850–1870: The Heyday of Wood-Engraving* discusses the role of Victorian artists in the explosion in British publishing and illustration during the mid-Victorian decades. Goldman features close analyses of works by such engravers as G. J. Pinwell, J. W. North and Thomas Morten, among a host of others, and the interrelation between their artistic work and the novels they illustrate. Goldman's is an important work. Donald E. Hall's collection of essays, *Muscular Christianity: Embodying the Victorian Age*, addresses the places of masculinity and the male body in works by Charles Kingsley, Dickens, Thomas Hughes and George MacDonald, among others. Selections include Laura Fasick's 'Charles Kingsley's Scientific Treatment of Gender'; Dennis W. Allen's 'Young England: Muscular Christianity and the Politics of the Body in *Tom Brown's Schooldays*'; John Pennington's 'Muscular Spirituality in George MacDonald's Curdie Books'; David Faulkner's 'The Confidence Man: Empire and the Deconstruction of Muscular Christianity in *The Mystery of Edwin Drood*'; and Patricia Srebrnik's 'The Re-subjection of "Lucas Malet": Charles Kingsley's Daughter and the Response to Muscular Christianity'.

Susan Sage Heinzelman and Zipporah Batshaw Wiseman's *Representing Women: Law, Literature, and Feminism* features a diversity of essays devoted to mapping the intersections of Anglo-American common law, literature and feminism, including Christine L. Krueger's 'Witnessing Women: Trial Testimony in Novels by Tonna, Gaskell, and Eliot'. Roger Walton Jones's *Larry McMurtry and the Victorian Novel* explores the influence of Victorian fiction – particularly such works as George Eliot's *Middlemarch* and Thomas Hardy's *The Woodlanders* – upon the works of the late twentieth-century American novelist Larry McMurtry. In addition to offering close readings of such McMurtry novels as *The Last Picture Show* and *Lonesome Dove*, Jones examines the Victorian sense of moral responsibility and philosophy that mark McMurtry's fictive worlds. In *Strangers and Secrets: Communication in the Nineteenth-Century Novel*, R. A. York focuses upon the sociological nature of communication in such novels as Emily Brontë's *Wuthering Heights*, Charlotte Brontë's *Jane Eyre*, Elizabeth Gaskell's *North and South*, Anthony Trollope's *Barchester Towers*, Wilkie Collins's *The Woman in White*, Dickens's *Great Expectations* and George Eliot's *Middlemarch*. In addition to investigating elements of secrecy and knowledge and their roles in defining the nature of communication, York examines the power of communication as a tool for overcoming xenophobia and secrecy and fomenting sympathy and community. Marysa DeMoor's 'Women Authors and their Selves: Autobiography in the Work of Charlotte Yonge, Rhoda Broughton, Mary Cholmondeley, and Lucy Clifford' (*CVE* 39.51–63) explores the treatment of the self and its autobiographical elements in the works of four Victorian-era women writers.

Michiel Heyns's *Expulsion and the Nineteenth-Century Novel: The Scapegoat in English Realist Fiction* addresses the place of scapegoats in the fictional communities of such novels as Dickens's *Our Mutual Friend* and Eliot's *Daniel Deronda*. Heyns argues that the scapegoat figures in these novels function as victims of external, social plot pressures, rather than aligning their authors with established structures of authority. In *The Genre of Autobiography in Victorian Literature*, Clinton Machann investigates the intertextual and historical elements inherent in Victorian autobiographies (see also section 1 above). Using works by John Stuart Mill, Anthony Trollope, John Ruskin and Charles Darwin, among others, Machann identifies the stylistic variations and structural nuances of these texts, and also reveals further similarities in their plots of self-development. Kimberley Reynolds and Nicola Humble's *Victorian Heroines: Representations of Femininity in Nineteenth-Century Literature and Art* offers a feminist interpretation of the Victorian heroine and the dichotomy between the 'angel in the house' and the sexually aware Victorian woman. Reynolds and Humble employ texts by Charlotte Brontë, Mary Elizabeth Braddon, George Eliot and Wilkie Collins in their study of Victorian heroines. In *The Dialogics of Dissent in the English Novel*, Cates Baldridge discusses issues of genre history through close readings of such works as Elizabeth Gaskell's *North and South* and various novels by Dickens. Baldridge also explores the interstices between the working class and the liberal bourgeoisie in the Victorian-era narratives of Gaskell and Dickens.

The Columbia History of the British Novel, edited by John Richetti, features several essays addressing nineteenth-century novelists, including Patrick Brantlinger's 'The Nineteenth-Century Novel and Empire'. Brantlinger argues that in the 'imperialist context, the history of nineteenth-century British fiction falls into three main periods': 1789 to the 1830s; the 1840s to the 1880s; and the late Victorian period to World War I. Among the novels considered in the early and mid-Victorian period are Bulwer-Lytton's *The Caxtons*, Charles Reade's *It's Never to Late to Mend* and Henry Kingsley's *Recollections of Geoffrey Hamlyn*. Amongst other novelists considered are George Lawrence, James Grant, Flora Annie Steel and Meadows Taylor. A similarly impressive range of fiction is considered in Brantlinger's analysis of fiction from the 1870s to World War I. For Brantlinger, 'from the time of the Crimean War and the Indian Mutiny, even the most overtly patriotic, imperialistic novels often sound notes of warning or anxiety about the internal and external enemies of the Empire'. David Trotter's 'The Avoidance of Naturalism: Gissing, Moore, Grand, Bennett, and Others' considers the reaction and resistance to French naturalism in English fiction in the last decades of the nineteenth century. Trotter discusses Gissing, Moore, the forgotten Margaret Harkness (as John Law) – who published the Zolaesque novels *A City Girl*, *Out of Work*, *In Darkest London* and *A Manchester Shirtworker* – Arthur Morrison's *Child of the Jago* and, amongst other largely forgotten works, Sarah Grand's *The Heavenly Twins* and Moore's *Esther Waters*.

Drawing upon the works of Jane Austen, Charlotte Brontë, George Eliot, Elizabeth Bowen, Muriel Spark and Fay Weldon, Regina Barreca's *Untamed and Unabashed: Essays on Women and Humor in British Literature* explores the manner in which each writer employs humour in her fiction. In this way, Barreca offers a feminist perspective on gender and comedy, while also revealing the ways in which such writers use humour to critique the dominant ideologies that control and oppress them. Claudia Nelson and Lynne Vallone's *The Girl's Own: Cultural Histories of the Anglo-American Girl, 1830–1915* includes essays that explore nineteenth-century British and American representations of the adolescent girl. Selections include Christina Boufis's '"Of Home Birth and Breeding": Eliza Lynn Linton and the Girl of the Period'; Leslie Williams's 'The Look of Little Girls: John Everett Millais and the Victorian Art Market'; and Carol Mavor's 'Dream-Rushes: Lewis Carroll's Photographs of the Little Girl'. In *God between their Lips: Desire between Women in Irigaray, Brontë, and Eliot*, Kathryn Bond Stockton investigates the interrelationships between spirituality and desire and between sex and sorrow in such novels as Charlotte Brontë's *Villette* and George Eliot's *Middlemarch*. Stockton explores Victorian notions of the body and 'God' in terms of post-structuralist feminist theory, while also discussing the nature of feminine relationships – particularly regarding the differences between 'lesbianism' and 'female friendship' – in the novels of Brontë and Eliot.

Josef L. Altholz's *Anatomy of a Controversy: The Debate Over 'Essays and Reviews'* discusses the religious controversy that followed the publication in 1860 of *Essays and Reviews* by seven authors – including six Anglican clergymen – and, ultimately, England's first significant exposure to biblical criticism. Altholz's case study of the culmination and final act of the Broad Church movement reveals both the textual nature of the greatest Victorian crisis of faith and the beginning of an era of protracted religious doubt. Altholz illuminates the subtext of many Victorian novels. Indulging in polemics and drawing upon a number of divergent critical, fictional and political ideas by such figures as Derrida, Margaret Thatcher, Marx, Matthew Arnold, Wordsworth and Wilkie Collins, Julian Wolfreys's *Being English: Narratives, Idioms, and Performances of National Identity from Coleridge to Trollope* traces the evolution of 'Englishness' and its significance in regard to national identity. Wolfreys in his readings of Dickens, George Eliot and Trollope examines a variety of English fictional and cultural constructs, including such nationalistic euphemisms as 'the gentleman' and 'our countrymen'. Finally, Tim Youngs's *Travelers in Africa: British Travelogues, 1850–1900* places the writings of nineteenth-century British travellers in Africa in an historical and cultural context, providing readers with an analysis of the manner in which social change and literary form can impact upon racial images in these narratives. Youngs features detailed studies of such issues as Henry Morton Stanley's controversial Emin Pasha Relief Expedition, African eating habits, and the anxieties over British social change and cultural identity endemic to these travelogues. He concludes with a reading of Conrad's *Heart of Darkness* as a travel narrative, contrasting Marlow's Congo with the Africa of Stanley's travelogue.

(b) Individual Novelists

The year's work in Gaskell studies includes Nancy S. Weyant's useful *Elizabeth Gaskell: An Annotated Bibliography of English-Language Sources, 1976–1991*, which assembles a wide array of contemporary scholarship devoted to Gaskell's work. In addition to her expansive critical and biographical introduction, Weyant includes comprehensive international listings of bibliographies, biographies, correspondence, criticism, and masters and honours theses regarding Gaskell's life and work. Gaskell also receives treatment in Peter Preston's essay, 'Manchester and Milton-Northern: Elizabeth Gaskell and the Industrial Town', included in Preston and Paul Simpson-Housley's *Writing the City: Eden, Babylon, and the New Jerusalem*. Adrienne E. Gavin's 'Language Among the Amazons: Conjuring and Creativity in *Cranford*' (*DSA* 23.205–26) discusses Gaskell's representations of female rhetoric as a mechanism for promoting freedom and self-reliance. Richetti's *Columbia History of the British Novel* includes Mary Poovey's 'Disraeli, Gaskell, and the Condition of England'. Poovey assesses the novels of the 1840s such as Disraeli's *Coningsby* and Elizabeth Gaskell's *Mary Barton*, and other Gaskell writings. Poovey concludes that while 'novelists of the 1840s also addressed the "Condition-of-England" question in terms of individual freedom and national prosperity, the conventions of their genre returned the issue of gender to the fore'. Andrew H. Miller's 'Subjectivity Ltd.: The Discourse of Liability in the Joint Stock Companies Act of 1856 and Gaskell's *Cranford*' (*ELH* 61.139–58) reads Gaskell's novel in terms of Parliament's 1856 act limiting liability in failed stock investments. In 'Elizabeth Gaskell's *North and South*: A National *Bildungsroman*' (*VN* 85.1–8), Patricia E. Johnson addresses Gaskell's emergence as a female progenitor of the industrial novel in *North and South*, while Dorice Williams Elliott's 'The Female Visitor and the Marriage of Classes in Gaskell's *North and South*' (*NCL* 49.21–49) examines Gaskell's depictions of Victorian-era labour relations in the context of the female philanthropic visitor to the impoverished. Elliott argues that Gaskell's novel also encompasses the domestic sphere of marriage, home and children. Alan Menhennet's 'A Goethe Reference in *Cranford*' (*GSJ* 8.111–12) traces the influence of Goethe upon Gaskell's aesthetic, while Valerie Wainwright's 'Discovering Autonomy in *North and South*: Elizabeth Gaskell, John Stuart Mill, and the Liberal Ethic' (*ClioI* 23.149–65) compares the liberalism of Gaskell with Mill's ideological positions. Ian Campbell's 'Scottish Writers, Elizabeth Gaskell, and the Industrial Revolution' (*GSJ* 8.98–110) discusses the fictional place of the industrial revolution, while Anna Unsworth's 'Elizabeth Gaskell and German Romanticism' (*GSJ* 8.1–14) explores the influence of the German Romantic movement upon Gaskell's fictions.

It is refreshing to note works on hitherto neglected authors. In *The Myth of Aunt Jemima: White Women Representing Black Women*, Diane Roberts explores the treatment of American slavery in the works of Frances Trollope and Frances Wright, among others. Roberts identifies 'mythic spheres of race' and their place in the prevailing cultural inscriptions of race during the nineteenth century. Marilyn D. Button's 'Reclaiming Mrs Frances Trollope: British Abolitionist and Feminist' (*CLAJ* 38.69–86) also traces the role of Frances Trollope in the British abolitionist movement. Mary Jean Corbett's 'Public Affections and Familial Politics: Burke, Edgeworth, and the "Common Naturalization" of Great Britain' (*ELH* 61.877–98) discusses the ways in which the marriage plot of Maria Edgeworth's *The Absentee* addresses the nature of the Irish familial experience and its need for reform and stability during her era. Joseph Andriano's '"Our Dual Existence": Archetypes of Love and Death in Le Fanu's "Carmilla"' (49–55), collected in Michele K. Langford's *Contours of the Fantastic: Selected Essays from the Eighth International Conference on the Fantastic in the Arts*, examines the treatment of death and love in the fictions of Joseph Sheridan Le Fanu, while also addressing their relationship with vampirism and lesbianism in his 'Carmilla'. In 'Breaking in Englishness: *Black Beauty* and the Politics of Gender, Race, and Class' (*Women* 5.34–52), Moira Ferguson investigates the treatment of slavery and gender and their interconnections with national identity in the fiction of Anna Sewell. Joseph S. Salemi's 'The Canvas of His Life: Epitaphs in Samuel Butler's *The Way of All Flesh*' (*VIJ* 22.165–77) discusses the places of epitaphs and mourning in *The Way of All Flesh*. Using the novels of Bulwer-Lytton, among others, Fiona Stafford interestingly explores the literary appropriation of the myth of 'the Last of the Race'. In *The Last of the Race: The Growth of a Myth from Milton to Darwin*, she discusses the myth-making abilities of Bulwer-Lytton and other writers and the scientific, political and religious underpinnings of their texts regarding the plights of endangered peoples. Oxford's WC series published the first critical edition of Geraldine Jewsbury's *The Half Sisters* in 1994. Edited and introduced by Joanne Wilkes, this edition marks the growing contemporary interest in the career of this often neglected journalist, novelist and author of *Zoë: A History of Two Lives.*

The well-produced and annotated *An Expression of Character: The Letters of George MacDonald*, edited by Glenn Edward Sadler, selects from nearly 3,000 letters penned by writer and lecturer George MacDonald (1824–1905), the nineteenth-century author whose works inspired such writers as G. K. Chesterton, C. S. Lewis and J. R. R. Tolkien, among others. In addition to tracing the writer's life from his boyhood in Huntly and his student days at Aberdeen University to his American lecture tour and his final years in Bordighera, Italy, MacDonald's correspondence reveals the development of his religious views and the spiritual struggles that marked the balance of his lifetime. Sadler's is a significant work of scholarship and addition to our knowledge of Victorian life and letters. Reiko Aiura-Vigers's 'The Link between George MacDonald and the Grimms' Fairy Tales' (*SwR* 'Writing and the Nation' 113–20) establishes the influence of the Grimms upon MacDonald's aesthetic.

GBB 8 features a selection of essays devoted to his work, including David Chandler's 'Onus Probandi (More on the Dingle)' (16–28), which details the historical and geographical details inherent in Borrow's *Lavengro* and *Romany Rye*. Angus Fraser's 'On the Fringes of the George Borrow Canon' (29–33) attempts to validate Borrow as the author of a twenty-four page pamphlet, the *Life and Adventures of the Famous Colonel Blood*, a matter of debate among Borrow enthusiasts. Kedrun Laurie's 'W. R. Hudson and George Borrow' (33–5) assesses Borrow as a possible influence upon Hudson's aesthetic, while Paul Watkins's 'George Borrow's Tomb – Past and Present' (36–9) details the epitaph on Borrow's tomb and discusses the current, neglected state of Borrow's dilapidated grave-site. R. C. Fiske's 'Whitwell Elwin Tells James Hooper about George Borrow' (40–2) relates Whitwell Elwin's account of the author's final years, as well as his critical response to *Lavengro* and *Romany Rye*.

This year has been a rich one for Thackeray scholarship. Two new important and thoroughly annotated editions of Thackeray's novels include John Sutherland's edition of *Pendennis* for the Oxford WC series, as well as Peter L. Shillingsburg's edition of *Vanity Fair*, published in the NCE series. Sutherland chooses as his copytext a resetting of the 1864 Saintsbury edition reprinted by Oxford in 1908. His appendix lists differences between the 1850 and 1864 texts. He reinstates the illustrations to *Pendennis* removed by Thackeray's publishers: 'reading *Pendennis* without the illustrations is to get only half the novel'. On the other hand, Shillingsburg chooses as his copytext the serialized instalments rather than the bound-up February 1853 'cheap edition', into which crept over 350 errors. He supplements his edition with a selection of criticism, including essays by such critics as Ina Ferris, Catherine Peters and James Phelan, in addition to commentary regarding the novel's composition and critical reception. The seminal work of the year – and perhaps of the decade – is Edgar F. Harden's *The Letters and Private Papers of William Makepeace Thackeray: A Supplement to Gordon N. Ray's 'The Letters and Private Papers of William Makepeace Thackeray'*. Harden's edition encompasses superlative editorial scholarship with consummate Sherlock Holmes detection. Fourteen hundred and sixty-four hitherto uncollected and mostly unpublished letters appear, with a full textual apparatus and notes identifying hundreds of persons and events related to the novelist's life and work. Ina Ferris's 'Thackeray and the Ideology of the Gentleman', in Richetti's *Columbia History of the British Novel*, offers an account of Thackeray's work, focusing upon his 'special interest in – even obsession with – the figure of the gentleman'.

Alison Byerly's '"The Masquerade of Existence": Thackeray's Theatricality' (*DSA* 23.259–86) argues that Thackeray's 1840 essay in *Fraser's Magazine* regarding the public execution of the murderer Courvoisier informs much of his fiction, particularly *Vanity Fair*, while Thomas McKendy's 'Sources of Parody in Thackeray's *Catherine*' (*DSA* 23.287–302) traces the sources of Thackeray's *Catherine* to works by Dickens, William Harrison Ainsworth and Bulwer-Lytton, among others. Peter L. Shillingsburg's judicious 'Thackeray Studies: 1983–1992' (*DSA* 23.303–36) details a decade's worth of scholarship devoted to Thackeray's life and work. John Peck's 'Middle-Class Life in *Vanity Fair*' (*English* 43.1–16) explores the ways in which Thackeray's narrative voice functions upon the disturbing darkness of the novelist's moral vision. Victor R. Kennedy's 'Pictures as Metaphors in Thackeray's Illustrated Novels' (*M&SA* 9.135–47) and Stephen Canham's 'Art and the Illustrations of *Vanity Fair* and *The Newcomes*', collected in Bill Katz's *A History of Book Illustration: 29 Points of View*, explore the power of illustration as a metaphorical narrative construct in Thackeray's novels.

Robert R. Wark's 'Thackeray's Drawings for *Cornhill to Cairo* in the Huntington Library' (*HLQ* 57.27–44) discusses the archive of the novelist's drawings housed at the Huntington Library. In 'Thackeray and the Sirens: Autobiographical Fiction and the "Talking Cure"' (*CCTES* 59.5–11), Joe K. Law discusses the role of autobiography in Thackeray's texts, while Charles J. Heglar's 'Rhoda Swartz in *Vanity Fair*: A Doll without Admirers' (*CLAJ* 37.336–47) examines racial differences in the characterization of Rhoda Swartz. Of interest to students of Thackeray is William Baker's assessment of the achievement of the great Thackeray scholar Gordon N. Ray (1915–86) in Joseph Rosenblum, ed., *American Book-Collectors and Bibliographers, First Series*, volume 140 in the *Dictionary of Literary Biography* series. The late Lillian F. Shankman's *Anne Thackeray Ritchie: Journals and Letters*, edited by Abigail Burnham Bloom and John Maynard, assembles the personal memoirs written in 1864–5 and 1878 by Anne Thackeray Ritchie, Thackeray's daughter. In addition to detailing the nature of the London social and literary scene during that era, Anne Thackeray Ritchie's journals offer valuable commentary regarding both her father's and her own literary endeavours. Shankman's framing narrative provides readers with an introduction to Anne Thackeray Ritchie's career in letters.

Work on Dickens continues to proliferate. In *Dickens and the Grown-Up Child*, Malcolm Andrews examines Dickens's career-long preoccupation with childhood and its uneasy and unresolved relationships with the adult world. While also considering the problematic cultural status of childhood in nineteenth-century England as well as Dickens's own private childhood experiences, Andrews offers an expansive psychoanalytic treatment of Dickens's biographical and literary life, including specific psychological discussions of the fictive treatment of children in landmark Dickensian texts such as *Hard Times*, *David Copperfield* and *A Christmas Carol*. Using such novels as *Bleak House*, *The Old Curiosity Shop*, *Little Dorrit* and *Oliver Twist*, Gail Turley Houston's *Consuming Fictions* discusses Victorian representations of gender, class and hunger in the novels of Charles Dickens. Houston also emphasizes the consumer limitations placed upon women and the disenfranchised lower classes by Victorian society, as well as Dickens's depictions of historical and economic disparities in his fictions.

Brian Murray's *Charles Dickens*, aimed at an undergraduate audience, surveys the life and work of Dickens, particularly the tragic proportions of his personal life and his fascination with the theatre. In addition to exploring the structural and narratological strategies endemic to Dickens's work, Murray includes specific analysis of the dramatic and satiric elements in novels from *The Pickwick Papers* and *Nicholas Nickleby* to *David Copperfield* and *The Mystery of Edwin Drood.* In *The Philosophy of Literary Amateurism*, Naomi Lebowitz contrasts what she regards as a philosophy of literary 'amateurism' that allows writers – in contrast to their professional counterparts – to engage and represent experience with a vulnerable subtlety and imagination. Drawing upon the works of Dickens, among a host of others, Lebowitz explores their texts in relation to the works of more self-consciously 'professional' writers such as Flaubert, Rousseau and Proust. For Lebowitz, a moral sense of complexity and richness undergirds the texts of all great writers in the Western literary tradition. John Kucich's chapter on 'Dickens' (in Richetti, *Columbia History of the British Novel*) surveys Dickens's achievement and assesses his profound and pervasive influence, paying particular attention to the ways in which 'Dickens's vision crossed social boundaries'.

In *Critical Theory and the Novel: Mass Society and Cultural Criticism in Dickens, Melville, and Kafka*, David Bruce Suchoff traces the historical roots of cultural criticism in the novel since the mid-nineteenth century, and includes close readings of Dickens's *Little Dorrit* and the social economic response of the novelist's nineteenth-century audience to the text. In his detailed *The Night Side of Dickens: Cannibalism, Passion, Necessity*, Harry Stone, a distinguished Dickensian, explores the dark side of the novelist's creative powers, focusing in particular upon Dickens's thematic use of cannibalism, unbridled passion and inexorable fate. Stone offers close readings of much of Dickens's immense canon – particularly *A Tale of Two Cities*, *Great Expectations* and *David Copperfield* – and draws upon a variety of contemporary theoretical approaches, including biographical, psychological, sociological, historical, linguistic and archetypal critical insights. Stone's is an important contribution to Dickens scholarship and criticism.

Anny Sadrin's *Parentage and Inheritance in the Novels of Charles Dickens* investigates the dramatized rituals of succession upon which Dickens's plots function, while also tracing the quests for parentage that undergird the narratives of such works as *Oliver Twist*. Sadrin argues that Dickens employs themes of lineage and inheritance in an effort to account for the complex processes that enable the disinherited to assume their proper places within familial and societal structures. A fascinating and neglected facet of Dickens's life appears in Sidney P. Moss and Carolyn J. Moss's *Charles Dickens and his Chicago Relatives: A Documentary Narrative*, which examines the life of Augustus Dickens, the novelist's brother, who settled in Chicago after causing an international scandal through his extramarital affair with Bertha Phillips. The authors afford particular attention to the ways in which the affair and Augustus Dickens's subsequent escape to the United States impinged upon Dickens's life and work. John Cunningham's 'Christian Allusion, Comedic Structure, and the Metaphor of Baptism in *Great Expectations*' (*SoAR* 59.35–51) discusses the sacrament of baptism and its role in the comedic narrative of Dickens's novel, while George B. Bryan and Wolfgang Mieder's '"As Sam Weller Said, When Finding Himself on the Stage": Wellerisms in Dramatizations of Charles Dickens' *Pickwick Papers*' (*Proverbium* 11.57–76) surveys various dramatic productions of *Pickwick Papers*. James A. Davies's 'Dickens and the Region in *David Copperfield*' (*SwR* 'Writing and the Nation' 187–96) examines the treatment of geography and regional characteristics in *David Copperfield.* Juliet John's 'Dickens's Deviant Women: A Reassessment' (*CR* 34.67–84) re-explores the representation of female characters afflicted with insanity in the novelist's works, while Natalie McKnight's 'Making Mother Suffer, and Other Fun in Dickens' (*DQu* 11.177–86) addresses incidents of familial abuse in Dickens's novels. Additionally, temporal constructions in Dickens's narratives receive attention in Soultana Maglavera's *Time Patterns in Later Dickens: A Study of the Thematic Implications of the Temporal Organization of 'Bleak House', 'Hard Times', 'Little Dorrit', 'A Tale of Two Cities', 'Great Expectations',* and *'Our Mutual Friend'*.

Roger D. Sell's collection of reprinted essays devoted to the study of *Great Expectations* includes A. L. French's 'Beating and Cringing: *Great Expectations*'; Lucy Frost's 'Taming to Improve: Dickens and the Women in *Great Expectations*'; Jack Rawlins's 'Great Expiations: Dickens and the Betrayal of the Child'; Peter Brooks's 'Repetition, Repression, and Return: *Great Expectations* and the Study of Plot'; Robin Gilmour's 'Pip and the Victorian Idea of the Gentleman'; Jeremy Tambling's 'Prison-Bound: Dickens and Foucault'; Eiichi Hara's 'Stories Present and Absent in *Great Expectations*'; Steven Connor's 'The Imaginary and the Symbolic in *Great Expectations*'; James Phelan's 'Reading for the Character and Reading for the Progression: John Wemmick and *Great Expectations*'; Anny Sadrin's '*Great Expectations* as Romantic Irony'; Thomas Loe's 'Gothic Plot in *Great Expectations*'; and Linda Raphael's 'A Re-vision of Miss Havisham: Her Expectations and Our Responses'. The Pierpont Morgan Library has published a facsimile edition of Dickens's autograph manuscript of *A Christmas Carol* with thirteen of John Leech's illustrations. Introduced by John Mortimer, the well-produced facsimile of Dickens's text suitably commemorates the 150th anniversary of its original publication. Most welcome is the first instalment of four projected volumes of Dickens's journalistic endeavours, the Dent Uniform Edition of Dickens publishes *Sketches by Boz and Other Early Papers, 1833–39*, edited with an introduction by distinguished Dickensian Michael Slater. The four volumes will be an important tool for students of Dickens. This year Dent also published Norman Page's edition of *A Tale of Two Cities*.

Nancy Aycock Metz's 'Dickens and "The Quack Architectural"' (*DQu* 11.59–68) reads *Martin Chuzzlewit* in terms of the novelist's employment of architecture as a thematic device. Metz emphasizes the novel's depictions of issues of professional identity and the abuses of apprenticeship/competition systems in her analysis. Graham Benton's '"And Dying Thus Around Us Every Day": Pathology, Ontology, and the Discourse of the Diseased Body. A Study of Illness and Contagion in *Bleak House*' (*DQu* 11.69–80) explores the role of contagious disease and prevailing public health standards in the narrative of *Bleak House*. Drawing upon such historical issues as the Public Health Act of 1848, Benton discusses Dickens's narrative representations of disease as metaphors for the social ills that problematized the English society of his day. Piya Pal Lapinski's 'Dickens's Miss Wade and J. S. Le Fanu's Carmilla: The Female Vampire in *Little Dorrit*' (*DQu* 11.81–7) explores the manner in which Dickens's character anticipates Le Fanu's female vampire and her penchant for sexual violence. Lapinski argues that both characters shared in the creation of a social and cultural vampirism that drains the life and energy from its victims. In 'Minding the Wheel: Representations of Women's Time in Victorian Narrative' (*RMR* 48.45–59) Elizabeth Campbell discusses Dickens's temporal structures in *Little Dorrit* and their relevance to the interpretation of his female characters.

Dickensian (90) features a host of essays that explore Dickens's massive canon. Elsie Karbacz and Robert Raven's 'The Many Mysteries of *Edwin Drood*' (5–18) addresses the many questions regarding plot and conclusion propounded by Dickens's last, unfinished novel, while Mary G. McBride's 'Contemporary Economic Metaphors in *Dombey and Son*' (19–24) discusses the image of the sea and its relation to the various interpretations of *Dombey and Son* as a study of the nature of spiritual value and the human condition. Sharon Kubasak's 'Reflexive Delight' (25–35) assesses the various mysteries and delights that Dickens provides for his readers in his novels, while Stanley Friedman's 'Heep and Powell: Dickensian Revenge' (36–43) attributes Dickens's villainous characterization of Uriah Heep in *David Copperfield* to his attempt to seek fictional revenge upon Thomas Powell, a former friend of the novelist's. Interesting sidelights upon Dickens are revealed in Robert Vine and Sheila Smith's 'John Overs: Family Tradition, Poetry, and Memorabilia' (85–94), which discusses the place of cabinet-maker John Overs in the biographical life of the novelist. Don Richard Cox's 'The *Every Saturday* Page Proofs of *The Mystery of Edwin Drood*' (95–101) identifies a second set of partially corrected page proofs of the novel, while Sidney P. Moss and Carolyn J. Moss's 'Frederick Dickens: From Courtship to Courtroom' (102–12) discusses the life of the novelist's brother, particularly regarding the writer's objections to his brother's marriage. Takao Saijo's 'T. W. Hill and "Tom King and the Frenchman"' (121–4) establishes the textual history of 'Seven Dials' from *Sketches by Boz*, while Pamela Long's 'Fagin and Monopodio: The Sources of *Oliver Twist*' (113–20) explores the influence of Cervantes's *Rinconete y Cortadillo* upon Dickens's novel. John B. West's 'Krook's Death by Spontaneous Combustion and the Controversy between Dickens and Lewes: A Physiologist's View' discusses G. H. Lewes's challenge to the veracity, and, indeed, scientific possibility, of Krook's unusual demise.

Mara H. Fein's 'The Politics of Family in *The Pickwick Papers*' (*ELH* 61.363–80) examines the elements of innocence, benevolence and stability that undergird Dickens's treatment of the family in his novel. In 'Dickens's "The Signalman"' (*Expl* 53.i.26–9), Graeme Tytler attributes the short story's narrative to Dickens's personal knowledge regarding mental illness. In addition to interpreting the linguistic role of signalling in the story, Tytler notes that the story depicts a type of partial insanity known in the nineteenth century as 'lypermania' and 'monomania'. Howard W. Fulweiler's '"Dismal Swamp": Darwin, Design, and Evolution in *Our Mutual Friend*' (*NCL* 49.50–74) argues that Dickens structures his novel on a Darwinian pattern that functions upon themes of predation, mutual relationships, chance and inheritance – central issues in both Victorian fiction and Darwin's *Origin of Species*. Dona Budd's 'Language Couples in *Bleak House*' (*NCL* 49.196–220) examines the relationship between language and the politics of gender in Dickens's novel, especially emphasizing the relationship between Esther and the anonymous narrator. Budd argues that such relationships underscore the unsettling power of patriarchal authority during Dickens's era. Rodney Stenning Edgecombe's 'Two Oblique Allusions in *Our Mutual Friend*' (*N&Q* 41.352–3) addresses the riddles and comic circumlocutions that mark Dickens's narrative, while Edgecombe's 'The "Waters" in *Bleak House*, Chapter I' (*N&Q* 41.353) establishes a textual connection between a passage in Leigh Hunt's *The Town* that refers to the biblical myth of the Flood and the role of water in *Bleak House*. Charles Forsyte's 'Charles Dickens Junior, Harold Macmillan, and *Edwin Drood*' (*N&Q* 41.353–4) attempts to account for the mysterious introduction by Charles Dickens Jr to an 1896 edition of *The Mystery of Edwin Drood*. Edgecombe's 'Topographic Disaffection in Dickens's *American Notes* and *Martin Chuzzlewit*'

(*JEGP* 93.35–54) assesses the roles of geography and topography in Dickens's fictions. Lynette Felber's '"Delightfully Irregular": Esther's Nascent *écriture féminine* in *Bleak House*' (*VN* 85.13–19) discusses the gendered qualities of the discourse of Esther Summerson in Dickens's novel and its ideological properties that underscore the Victorian era's sexual-textual politics. John M. Dundek's 'A New First American Edition of *Great Expectations*' (*BC* 43.298–9) identifies the first American edition of Dickens's classic novel as the text published by James G. Gregory in New York in 1861, while also noting that the libraries at Harvard and Yale both currently house copies of the volume.

The editors of *DSA* (23) include a variety of essays in their latest volume that employ a diversity of critical approaches in their analyses of Dickens, including historical, biographical, feminist and narratological critical methodologies. Murray Roston's 'Dickens and the Tyranny of Objects' (1–16) addresses the operation of 'things' as metaphors of tyranny in the hands of such Dickens characters as Miss Havisham of *Great Expectations* and Mrs Gamp in *Martin Chuzzlewit*, among others. Barry Thatcher's 'Dickens's Bow to the Language Theory Debate' (17–48) ascribes the 'divisive and puzzling' nature of *Hard Times* to its reflection of the language theory debate regarding nineteenth-century conceptions of language. Thatcher concludes that the novel's language strategies demonstrate the injustices of the Victorian social and economic structures. Robert Newsom's '*Pickwick* in the Utilitarian Sense' (49–72) associates Dickens's novel with the fundamental properties of utilitarianism, while Sylvia Manning's '*Nicholas Nickleby*: Parody on the Plains of Syria' (73–92) reads the narrative pace of Dickens's novel as a brand of self-parody that creates a sense of uncertainty regarding morality and ethics. Kerry McSweeney's '*David Copperfield* and the Music of Memory' (93–120) explores the ways in which Dickens attempted to imitate the movements of memory and imagination in his novels, while Carrol Clarkson's 'Alias and Alienation in *Bleak House*: Identity in Language' (121–36) draws upon Plato's *Cratylus* in an attempt to demonstrate that language creates the nature of personal identity in *Bleak House*, particularly in regard to the characterization of Esther Summerson. Razak Dahmane's 'A Mere Question of Figures: Measures, Mystery and Metaphor in *Hard Times*' (137–62) discusses the manner in which moral decency is propounded through language and metaphor in *Hard Times*. In 'Domestic Transformation in Dickens's "The Haunted Man"' (163–82), Wendy Carse investigates metaphors of power that manipulate structures of domesticity in Dickens's Christmas narrative, while Katherine Retan's 'Lower Class in the Middle Class House: The Domestic Woman's Progress in *Hard Times* and *Ruth*' (183–204) discusses Dickens's portrayal of female sexual identity in his works, particularly emphasizing his attempts to characterize the place of women in Victorian familial relationships, and contrasts Dickens with Mrs Gaskell.

In what is perhaps a lean year for Trollopians, Richetti's *Columbia History of the British Novel* includes N. J. Hall's chapter on 'Trollope' surveying Trollope's life, work and writing habits, which 'were complex and various, as were, naturally, his attendant reputations during his lifetime and since' (457). For Hall, 'the question of what constitutes the peculiar excellence of . . . [the] "essential Trollope" is . . . unanswerable,' although the answer 'probably lies in some elusive and complex mix – the proportions varying with each reader' (477). Christine S. Wiesenthal's 'The Body Melancholy: Trollope's *He Knew He Was Right*' (*DSA* 23.227–58) explores the novelist's self-conscious employment of the plot of Shakespeare's *Othello* as a relevant commentary on the nature of Victorian society.

Glynn-Ellen Fisichelli's 'The Language of Law and Love: Anthony Trollope's *Orley Farm*' (*ELH* 61.635–54) explores the competing roles of legal and romantic rhetoric in Trollope's novel, particularly regarding the manner in which language often both reveals and conceals the truth in *Orley Farm*. In 'A Woman's Best Career: Choices for Women in Selected Novels by Anthony Trollope' (*CrM* 4.37–54), Sheila Burgar addresses the treatment of choice by women in Trollope's works, while George Watson's 'Tolstoy's Master: The Case of Trollope' (*VQR* 69.666–75) explores the influence of Tolstoy upon Trollope's aesthetic. Wendy Jones's 'Feminism, Fiction, and Contract Theory: Trollope's *He Knew He Was Right*' (*Criticism* 36.401–14) discusses the role of the marriage contract in a relatively ignored Trollope novel. Charles Calder's '"A Novel Country": The England of the *Pallisers*' (*SwR* 'Writing and the Nation' 147–55) explores the treatment of England by Trollope in the well-known *Palliser* novels.

The Brontë highlights are Juliet Barker's massive *The Brontës*, which traces the history of the tragic Brontë family and challenges the prevailing biographical myths regarding their dysfunctionality, and Lyndall Gordon's important and well-written *Charlotte Brontë: A Passionate Life*. In addition to drawing upon correspondence and manuscripts from every member of the family, as well as newspaper accounts from the era, Barker portrays the Brontës as a family that thrived upon culture and religion – elements that provided the foundations for the family's innovative contributions to Victorian literature and aesthetics. Gordon addresses the novelist's works as autobiographical treatises regarding her incipient Victorian feminism. Using unpublished letters, the 'Roe Head Journal', early stories, the manuscript of *Villette*, and the writer's last, unfinished novel, Gordon interestingly investigates the elements of Charlotte Brontë's life that resulted in the active, feminist voice that marks her novels. Jill Dix Ghnassia's *Metaphysical Rebellion in the Works of Emily Brontë: A Reinterpretation* draws less heavily upon primary sources and offers a reassessment of Emily Brontë's poetry and French essays, affording particular attention to the writer's thematic concerns with the nature of the universe, divine creation and the fate of humanity. Dividing Brontë's work into four chronological periods, Ghnassia demonstrates the manner in which she matured aesthetically during the production of her poetry and French essays and reveals the ways in which Brontë's literary evolution culminates in *Wuthering Heights*. Steven Vine's 'The Wuther of the Other in *Wuthering Heights*' (*NCL* 49.339–59) discusses Brontë's novel as a drama of instabilities that captures the disruptive nature of the social, psychological and ideological dilemmas of her era. Drawing upon Marxist, feminist and deconstructive arguments, Vine explores issues of desire, identity and sexual difference as they are illustrated by the relationship between Cathy and Heathcliff. In 'The Sublimity of Catherine and Heathcliff' (*VN* 86.24–30), Patrick Kelly argues that Catherine and Heathcliff, despite their destructive acts in *Wuthering Heights*, approach sublimity because of their monumental suffering and moral indignation. Sheryl Craig's 'Brontë's *Wuthering Heights*' (*Expl* 52.iii.157–9) identifies the relationship between the cuckoo and Heathcliff in Brontë's novel. An international perspective is revealed in Lingguo Lin's 'On Three Chinese Versions of *Wuthering Heights*' (*Waiguoyu* 5.26–30, 76), which critiques three Chinese-language translations of *Wuthering Heights*.

James Phelan and Peter J. Rabinowitz's *Understanding Narrative* features essays that offer a variety of approaches to the theory and interpretation of narrative, including Elizabeth Langland's 'Dialogue, Discourse, Theft, and

Mimicry: Charlotte Brontë Rereads William Makepeace Thackeray.' Carol-Ann Farkas' '"Beyond What Language Can Express": Transcending the Limits of the Self in *Jane Eyre*' (*VR* 20.49–69) investigates the depiction of the female self and Charlotte Brontë's employment of the Gothic romance in *Jane Eyre*. Amanda B. Witt's '"I Read It in Your Eye": Spiritual Vision in *Jane Eyre*' (*VN* 85.29–33) re-addresses the nature of the female gaze in Charlotte Brontë's novel, arguing that Jane's gaze functions as an emblem of individual confidence and spiritual insight rather than an indication of sexual conquest and desire, as a number of critics have posited. Elizabeth McIntyre's 'Charlotte Brontë's New Corinne: Re-Reading *The Professor*' (*VN* 85.34–39) challenges prevailing arguments regarding the relationship between the heroine of the novel and the schoolmaster. In 'Apocalypse When?: *Shirley*'s Vision and the Politics of Reading' (*SNNTS* 26.350–72), Sally Greene contextualizes Charlotte Brontë's life within the narrative of *Shirley* and its apocalyptic ideology. Laura E. Ciolkowski's 'Charlotte Brontë's *Villette*: Forgeries of Sex and Self' (*SNNTS* 26.218–34) explores the qualities that mark Victorian notions of female selfhood in Brontë's novel.

Margaret L. Shaw's 'Narrative Surveillance and Social Control in *Villette*' (*SEL* 34. 813–34) investigates the ways in which Brontë's heroine Lucy Snowe assesses the character of her compatriots through her intense powers of observation. Marianne Thormählen's 'The Brontë Pseudonyms' (*ES* 75.246–56) discusses the employment of pseudonyms by Anne and Emily Brontë, while Christine Alexander's detailed and scholarly 'Readers and Writers: *Blackwood's* and the Brontës' (*GSJ* 8.54–69) explores the serialization of works by the Brontës in *Blackwood's Edinburgh Magazine*. Marianne Hirsch's 'Jane's Family Romances', collected in Margaret R. Higonnet's *Borderwork: Feminist Engagements with Comparative Literature*, explores the treatment of motherhood in Brontë's text. In 'Edward Rochester and the Margins of Masculinity in *Jane Eyre* and *Wide Sargasso Sea*' (*PLL* 30.235–56), Robert Kendrick explores the treatment of masculinity in Charlotte Brontë's novel and Jean Rhys's twentieth-century parody of the text. Fiona Morphet's 'Playing with *The Professor*' (*CLAJ* 37.348–57) discusses pedagogical approaches to teaching Brontë's novel, while Susie O'Brien's 'Lying Back and Thinking of England: Sex and Nationalism in Charlotte Brontë's *Shirley*' (*FrontenacR* [1994]54–79) investigates the places of race and gender in the construction of English national identity.

Richetti's *Columbia History of the British Novel* features the essay, '"Speak What We Think": The Brontës and Women Writers' (352–80), in which Barry V. Qualls surveys the fiction of Charlotte and Emily Brontë and argues that 'the questions they repeatedly ask, . . . escape the confinements of Victorian realism, haunt the history of the novel'. For Qualls, Charlotte Brontë requests 'woman to have the power both to express her desire through choosing its domestic enclosure, and to patrol the moral territories that encircle it. Emily Brontë sets the limitation of this choice' (379–80). Edward Flintoff's 'Branwell at the Heights: An Investigation into the Possible Influence of Branwell Brontë upon *Wuthering Heights*' (*DUJ* 86.iii.241–52) examines the contribution of Branwell Brontë to the linguistic development of Emily Brontë's replications of the Worth Valley dialect in *Wuthering Heights*. Elizabeth Hollis Berry's *Anne Brontë's Radical Vision: Structures of Consciousness* addresses the narratological and psychological issues inherent in such Anne Brontë volumes as *The Tenant of Wildfell Hall*, among others.

Re-reading the primary materials at the Beinecke Library, Yale, and drawing upon the biographical and literary insights of the author's vast and expansive correspondence, Rosemarie Bodenheimer's *The Real Life of Mary Ann Evans: George Eliot, Her Letters, and Fiction* sheds new lights upon the relationships of George Eliot with her stepsons and with those people who sought her literary assistance. One of the highlights of George Eliot scholarship this year, Bodenheimer's volume demonstrates the manner in which reading Eliot's letters in context with her novels, stories and verse reveals the paradoxes that defined her fictional characters and narrative style. Another important contribution, Carol A. Martin's *George Eliot's Serial Fiction*, reviews the publishing and manuscript history of several Eliot novels, including *Romola*, *Scenes of Clerical Life*, *Adam Bede*, *The Mill on the Floss*, *Middlemarch* and others. Martin affords special attention to the analysis of the ways in which serialization affected the novelist's composition strategies, particularly regarding the development of character and plot in her fictions. Martin also addresses the manner in which publishing her novels in instalments impinged upon the consumption of Eliot's work in the Victorian literary marketplace. Using insights from a variety of psychoanalytic theorists and at times pushing her theories too firmly into readings, Peggy Fitzhugh Johnstone argues in *The Transformation of Rage: Mourning and Creativity in George Eliot's Fiction* that George Eliot's thematically rich prose finds its roots in her unconscious sense of loss stemming from traumatic family separations and deaths during her childhood and adolescence. Johnstone interestingly explores the manner in which this internalized rage and mourning result in a constructive response in Eliot's novels and stories.

Dorothea Barrett's provocatively titled 'The Politics of Sado-Masochism: Swinburne and George Eliot' is featured in Rikky Rooksby and Nicholas Shrimpton's *The Whole Music of Passion: New Essays on Swinburne*, a collection of essays that explore Swinburne's textual examinations of such issues as morality, politics, gender and aesthetics. Drawing upon recent developments in moral philosophy and literary theory, David Parker's *Ethics, Theory, and the Novel* problematizes many currently influential movements in literary criticism and reveals their silences about ethical issues. Using such texts as George Eliot's *Middlemarch*, Tolstoy's *Anna Karenina*, and several novels by D. H. Lawrence, Parker demonstrates the efficacy of this new evaluative discourse and its larger implications for the future of literary theory.

Drawing upon Eliot's fiction, intellectual journalism and published correspondence, Bernard Semmel's *George Eliot and the Politics of National Inheritance* attempts to explain the author's controversial relationship to the ideas of Auguste Comte and the Positivists. Ploughing well-trodden ground, Semmel examines Eliot's interest in the notion of inheritance in her work, while also considering other significant issues of political import in *Felix Holt*, *Middlemarch* and *Impressions of Theophrastus Such*. Karen L. Pangallo's *The Critical Response to George Eliot* contains a rather unselective variety of contemporaneous newspaper and periodical responses to the novels of George Eliot, including *Adam Bede*, *The Mill on the Floss*, *Silas Marner*, *Romola*, *Felix Holt, the Radical*, *Middlemarch* and *Daniel Deronda*. Ingrid Kuczynski's 'Das Konstukt des Judentumas in George Eliot's Roman *Daniel Deronda*', collected in *Jüdische Kultur und Weiblichkeit in Der Moderne*, edited by Inge Stephan, Sabine Schilling and Sigrid Weigel, reviews scholarship on George Eliot's sources utilized in her last published novel. Gillian Beer's 'George Eliot and the Novel of Ideas' (in Richetti, *Columbia History of the British Novel*) places Eliot's novels within the tradition 'of ideas realized in fiction'.

For Beer, Eliot's 'novels have a passion for the commonplace – by which, her fiction leads us to understand, is meant not only the phatic repetitions but also the hidden ferment of others' daily life to which no one can have access, save through the form of fiction'.

The September issue of *GEGHL* (26–7) for this year includes essays that explore Eliot and Lewes's work from a variety of critical perspectives. In 'Eliot's Spanish Connection: Casaubon, the Avatar of Quixote' (1–6), Chester St H. Mills compares the characterization of Don Quixote with that of Casaubon in *Middlemarch*. Mills concludes that each character functions as a narratological critique of the social conventions inherent in their respective societies. Lesley Gordon's 'George Eliot and Theocritus' (6–14) usefully traces the influence of Theocritus through a variety of allusions in Eliot's novels. Gordon affords special attention to such works as *Adam Bede*, *Felix Holt* and *Middlemarch*, among others. Julian Wolfreys's 'The Ideology of Englishness: The Paradoxes of Tory–Liberal Culture and National Identity in *Daniel Deronda*' (15–33) explores the manner in which Deronda questions the Tory–Liberal culture that functions within the pages of Eliot's novel. The issue concludes with '*Middlemarch* on TV – A Symposium' (36–81), in which a host of scholars and critics, including Graham Handley, Donald Hawes, U. C. Knoepflmacher, Sebastian Knowles and Anne Wallace, among others, critique, often most humorously, the BBC television production of Eliot's novel.

Sharon Deykin Baris's essay, 'George Eliot as Revenant in Faye Kellerman's Mysteries: An American Daniel is Alive and Well in Southern California' (*Prospects* 19.491–511), draws extensive parallels between character, plot and motifs in *Daniel Deronda* and the contemporary detective writer, Faye Kellerman, and especially in four of her works, including *The Ritual Bath*, *Sacred and Profane*, *Milk and Honey* and *Day of Atonement*. Baris demonstrates the manner in which 'we are drawn to the ways in which their characters' life stories are so uncannily alike' (493), especially the story of Kellerman's hero, Peter Decker, who discovers after he has fallen 'in love with the orthodox Jewish mikvah woman' (493) that he was born Jewish. For Baris, 'the mystery that emerges in both Faye Kellerman and George Eliot refers to the nature and origins of a culture's repressive forces' (497). Although it remains a neglected area of George Eliot's achievement, her narrative poem *The Spanish Gypsy* sheds much critical light upon her novels, as demonstrated by James Krasner's '"Where No Man Praised": The Retreat from Fame in George Eliot's *The Spanish Gypsy*' (*VP* 32.55–74). Krasner discusses the treatment of self-denial, ambition and fame in Eliot's poem – elements inherent in her novels that often find their origins in her verse. Gail Marshall's 'Actresses, Statues, and Speculation in *Daniel Deronda*' (*EIC* 44.117–39) explores the similarities between Ovid's Galatea and Victorian-era actresses, as well as their roles in the interpretation of the narrative of *Daniel Deronda*.

Kathleen Adams and William Baker's 'Alfred Austin and George Eliot: Two Unpublished Letters' (*GEFR* 25.29–31) provides Eliot scholars with two letters that she wrote in the late 1870s to the future poet laureate. In the twenty-second George Eliot Memorial Lecture, which he delivered in 1993 (*GEFR* 25.22–31), Baker offered an expansive account of the more than 450 letters of George Henry Lewes that will appear in his forthcoming edition of Lewes's correspondence. Christopher Date's 'George Eliot and the British Museum Reading Room' (*GEFR* 25.32–3) assembles the Register of Readers' Names for 14 November 1861 – which reveals that Eliot and Lewes were admitted to the Reading Room on that date. Gerlinde Röder-Bolton's 'George Eliot's Weimar' (*GEFR* 25.51–5) describes

Eliot's visit to Weimar and the surrounding district with Lewes in 1854 and 1867, while Carolyn J. Moss's 'Kate Field and Anthony Trollope: Re George Eliot and George Henry Lewes' (*VN* 86.31–3) addresses the manner in which Lewes prompted Eliot to publish *Scenes of Clerical Life*. Joyce Quiring Erickson's 'Multiculturalism and the Question of Audience: *Adam Bede* as a Test Case' (*VN* 85.20–5) discusses Erickson's experiences while teaching *Adam Bede* at three different institutions, and demonstrates the diversity of responses that she received regarding the novel. In 'A Novel Sympathy: The Imagination of Community in George Eliot' (*Novel* 27.5–23), Forest Pyle addresses *Adam Bede* and *The Mill on the Floss* in terms of each novel's didactic and narratological qualities.

Lesley Gordon's 'Tito, Dionysius, and Apollo: An Examination of Tito Melema in *Romola*' (*GEFR* 25.34–8) reveals the influence of Dionysius and Apollo in Eliot's characterization of Tito Melema, while Bruce K. Martin's 'Fred Vincy and the Unraveling of *Middlemarch*' (*PLL* 30.3–24) assesses Eliot's favourable treatment of Fred Vincy in *Middlemarch*. J. Jeffrey Franklin's 'The Victorian Discourse of Gambling: Speculations on *Middlemarch* and *The Duke's Children*' (*ELH* 61.899–921) discusses capitalism in the novel, particularly as manifested in the form of gambling, a predominant theme in *Middlemarch*. As the above issue of *GEGHLS* demonstrated, the recent BBC television production of *Middlemarch* received abundant treatment in this year. David Gervais's 'Televising *Middlemarch*' (*English* 43.59–64) concludes that the novel's tragic tone is problematized by the medium of television, while Bernard O'Keefe's 'The "Soaping" of Middlemarch' (*ER* 5.7–12) argues that the television production of the novel simplifies and mollifies the novel's narrative achievements. Ian Mackillop's 'The BBC *Middlemarch*' (*GEFR* 25.73–5) dismisses the production as a 'bland' adaptation of a novel that functions upon the subtleties of the human imagination.

In 'Metafiction and Metaphor: Daniel Deronda as Golem' (*GEFR* 25.39–44), Saleel Nurbhai addresses the role of aspects of Judaism in Eliot's *Daniel Deronda*, while Pam Hirsch's 'Women and Jews in *Daniel Deronda*' (*GEFR* 25.45–50) explores the parallels in the novel between the social positions of Jews and those of women. In '*Daniel Deronda* and Wordsworth's *The White Doe of Rylstone*' (*ELN* 31.43–53), Shifra Hochberg examines the thematic influence of Wordsworth upon *Daniel Deronda*. P. E. Easterling's 'George Eliot and Greek Tragedy' (*GEFR* 25.56–67) traces the echoes of Greek tragedy in *Silas Marner*, *Adam Bede* and *Felix Holt*, and demonstrates Eliot's self-conscious infusion of mythology into her novels. Katherine Sorensen's 'Conventions of Realism and the Absence of Color in George Eliot's "The Sad Fortunes of the Reverend Amos Barton"' (*VIJ* 22.15–31) discusses Eliot's employment of visual imagery in her short fiction. Mark Warren McLaughlin's '*Adam Bede*: History, Narrative, Culture' (*VIJ* 22.55–83) employs a sociopolitical critical approach in an analysis of Eliot's novel. Eva Fuchs's 'Eliot's *The Mill on the Floss*' (*Expl* 52.i.79–80) examines the false ending and the representation of autonomy in *The Mill on the Floss*.

Tony E. Jackson's *The Subject of Modernism: Narrative Alterations in the Fiction of Eliot, Conrad, Woolf, and Joyce* investigates the place of the self and impulses of self-preservation in *Daniel Deronda*. Drawing upon the psychoanalytic theories of Lacan, Jackson argues that psychologically realistic terrain of Eliot's novel and its various elements of self-analysis contributed to the emergence of the narrative experimentation that marks the texts generally associated with literary modernism. Andrew Brown's superb edition of *Romola* is reprinted in the Oxford WC series; Brown contributes a new introduction. Nancy Henry's widely praised text of the neglected *Impressions of Theophrastus Such* has been published, along with an extensive introduction and textual apparatus, in P&C's WC series. Her introduction makes a welcome case for the subtlety and complexity of George Eliot's final work.

In *The Novels of Mrs. Oliphant: A Subversive View of Traditional Themes*, Margarete Rubik reads the novels of Margaret Oliphant as texts that the author created expressly to subvert the prevailing ideals and values of the era in which she lived. In addition to addressing the manner in which Oliphant challenged Victorian stereotypes regarding gender roles, marriage and family life, and religious issues, Rubik argues that the novelist posited narratives that intentionally dispensed with conventional textual models to craft instead new and subversive fictions. Elisabeth Jay's 'Mrs Oliphant: The Hero as Woman of Letters, or Autobiography, a Gendered Genre' (*Caliban* 21.85–95) discusses the treatment of sex roles in Oliphant's work, particularly in comparison to the ideologies of such contemporary figures as Thomas Carlyle. Peter G. Christensen's 'The Aestheticized Image of Aphrodite in George Moore's *Aphrodite in Aulis*' (*CML* 14.127–40) discusses the place of mythology in Moore's neglected fictions, while Stacia L. Bensyl's 'Cecilia: Irish Catholicism in George Moore's *A Drama in Muslin*, 1886' (*Éire* 29.65–76) assesses the treatment of Irish Catholicism in Moore's works.

Ronald B. Thomas's lengthy 'Wilkie Collins and the Sensation Novel' (in Richetti, *Columbia History of the British Novel*, 479–507) places Collins's works within the tradition of the history of sensation fiction. Special attention is paid to *The Woman in White* and the lesser-known *The Dead Secret*. For Thomas, *No Name* is 'one of Collins' greatest sensation novels'. Other novels considered are *Hide and Seek*, *Basil*, *Armadale*, 'one of Collins' most effective novels of the 1860s', and *The Moonstone*. Thomas also considers the work of other writers such as Miss Braddon and Charles Reade. Of special interest is Thomas's observation that 'after his astonishing success in the 1860s, the rapid decline of Collins' literary production in the subsequent decades has been variously attributed to some combination of gout (which crippled him with pain), Charles Reade (who encouraged him to write his less effective protest novels), and laudanum (which he consumed daily in quantities that would have killed most men)'. And it is worth quoting in full Thomas's observation that 'these biographical details suggest that in creating a genre of sexual secrets, double identities, domestic intrigues, legal difficulties, and medical confinement, these prominent authors may have been playing out the mysteries of their own private lives as those lives collided with the repressive force of established social conventions'. Thomas's is indeed a most provocative analysis, for he suggests that 'those collisions were produced by . . . specific conditions of mid-nineteenth-century England, conditions which carried profound implications for the identities people were able to assume . . . within the culture'.

Ian Duncan's stimulating and well-written '*The Moonstone*, the Victorian Novel, and Imperialistic Panic' (*MLQ* 55.297–320) discusses Collins's depiction of colonial India in his novel, arguing that *The Moonstone* remains one of the most significant Victorian representations of empire during the nineteenth century. Harry Mead's 'On the Trail of Yorkshire's *Moonstone*' (*WCSJ* [1994]26–31) discusses Wilkie Collins's 1868 novel in terms of its Yorkshire locale and its place as one of the earliest entries in the genre of detective fiction. In addition to addressing Collins's influence upon such writers as Dickens and Conan Doyle, Mead explores the remarkable role of the Yorkshire terrain in Collins's narrative design. Mark Ford offers a new edition of Wilkie Collins's *No Name* in the Penguin

Classics series. Based upon the 1864 edition of the novel housed in the British Library, Ford's volume includes an introduction to the life and work of the novelist. Also reprinted this year was Collins's *The Evil Genius*, a novel dealing with 'a woman's struggle to resist legal and ideological subjection' and edited with a perceptive introduction by Graham Law. Law's text is that 're-set from Volume XXIV of the Collier collected edition' with silent correction of 'obvious printer's errors'. American spellings are retained. Chris Tiffin and Alan Lawson's *De-Scribing Empire: Post-Colonialism and Textuality* includes Jo-Ann Wallace's 'De-Scribing *The Water-Babies*', an essay that explores the textual fabric of colonialism and its legacies, as well as its historical and literary implications in Charles Kingsley's novel. Lynn E. Wolf's 'A Bracing Corrective: Women and Comedy in George Meredith's "Case of General Ople and Lady Camper"' (*ELWIU* 21.68–81) discusses Meredith's depiction of women in his novels, arguing that female characters in his fictions often employ comedy as a means for dissecting male egoists. The treatment of rites of passage in the works of Sir Henry Rider Haggard receive attention in Marysa DeMoor's 'Ritual Celebrations as Rites of Passage in Rider Haggard's Dark Romances' (*CVE* 39.205–17). Lloyd Siemens's 'Rider Haggard's Neglected Journal: "Diary of an African Visit"' (*ELT* 37.155–61) investigates the contents of Haggard's African travelogue.

Drawing upon a variety of linguistic approaches, Jean-Jacques Lecercle's *Philosophy of Nonsense: The Intuitions of Victorian Nonsense Literature* attempts to account for the role of nonsense in Victorian literature, particularly within the work of Lewis Carroll (see also section 3 below). In addition to his interest in explaining the mythical constructs of nonsense, Lecercle offers chapters that examine the linguistics, pragmatics, philosophy and polyphony of nonsense. In *Sir John Tenniel: Aspects of His Work*, Roger Simpson investigates the early works of the celebrated illustrator Sir John Tenniel, and the influence of the debate regarding the English school of history painting during the 1840s upon his art. Simpson also features discussion about Tenniel's best-known works, including his illustrations for Lewis Carroll's *Alice in Wonderland* and *Through the Looking-Glass*. Robert M. Polhemus's 'Lewis Carroll and the Child in Victorian Fiction' (in Richetti, *Columbia History of the British Novel*) offers an extensive reading of *Alice's Adventures in Wonderland* and *Through the Looking Glass*. Polhemus affords particular attention to 'Carroll's originality and importance', and the way in which 'through the child' he 'pushed the limits and conventions of fiction, expanded them, and made fantasy probing, speculative, radically comic, and intellectually rewarding'.

Charlie Lovett edits the *Proceedings of the Second International Lewis Carroll Conference*, held in June this year in Winston-Salem, North Carolina. Selections include Lovett's 'Opening Remarks – *Alice* and America'; Morton N. Cohen's 'Reeling and Writhing with Lewis Carroll'; Christina Björk's 'What Was Behind Alice's Nursery Door: Behind the Making of *The Other Alice*'; Edward Wakeling's 'Mrs. Hargreaves Comes to the USA'; Julie Grossman's 'Escape from the Real: Lewis Carroll, "Alice," and Henry James' *Watch and Ward*'; Stephen Haedicke's 'The Tea Party that Hit Light Speed: Order, Relativity, and Chaos in the *Alice* Books'; Selwyn Goodacre's 'The Nineteenth-Century American *Alice*'; Donald Rackin's 'Mind Over Matter: Sexuality and Where the "Body Happens to Be" in the *Alice* Books'; Stan Marx's 'Memoirs of the Lewis Carroll Society of North America: The First Twenty Years'; Maxine Schaefer's 'My Twenty Years as Secretary of the Lewis Carroll Society of North America'; Francine F. Abeles's

'Algorithms and Mechanical Processes in the Work of Charles L. Dodgson'; Elizabeth Sewell's 'What Took *You* Through the Looking Glass?'; Donna White's 'The Game Plan of *The Hunting of the Snark*'; Frankie Morris's 'Tenniel's American Cartoons: A Civil War Extravaganza'; Yoshiyuki Momma's 'Why is *Alice* Popular in Japan?'; Anashia Plackis's 'Lewis Carroll as a Pioneer of Whole Language Philosophy'; Jan Susina's 'Imitations of *Alice* – Lewis Carroll and the Anxiety of Influence'; and Anne Clark Amor's 'C. L. Dodgson: An Englishman Abroad'. Lovett supplements his volume with a valuable appendix for Carroll scholars, 'Notes on an Exhibition of Mathematical Works by Charles L. Dodgson'. Carroll's mathematical texts also saw publication in book form as *The Pamphlets of Lewis Carroll.* Vol. 2: *The Mathematical Pamphlets of Charles Lutwidge Dodgson and Related Pieces*, edited with an introduction by Francine F. Abeles.

In another rich year for Hardy studies, students of his novels should refer to Frank G. Healey's 'Proust and Hardy: An Update' (*THJ* 10.51–7), an essay that addresses the novelist's influence upon Proust's *À la recherche du temps perdu.* Tod E. Jones's 'Michael Henchard: Hardy's Male Homosexual' (*VN* 86.9–12) explores the characterization of Hardy's alleged homosexual protagonist in *The Mayor of Casterbridge*, arguing that he seeks atonement for his past while resisting self-punishment. In 'Hardy's Vocabulary' (*ContempR* 265.90–3), the distinguished Elizabethan scholar A. L. Rowse turns his attention to the arcane parlance inherent in Hardy's poetry and prose, arguing that 'sublime passages of description' are often followed by 'a paragraph of jargon, clumsy rhetoric or novelistic cliché'. Rowse opens his essay by admitting, 'I have always loved Hardy, but not uncritically.' Byron Caminero-Santangelo's 'A Moral Dilemma: Ethics in *Tess of the D'Urbervilles*' (*ES* 75.46–61) argues that T. H. Huxley's *Evolution and Ethics* influenced the ethical possibilities and desire for community propounded by Hardy's narrative. Roger Craik's 'Hardy's *Tess of the D'Urbervilles*' (*Expl* 53.i.41–2) addresses the novelist's use of language – particularly the nineteenth-century vernacular – in his classic work. Jeanette Shumaker's 'Breaking with the Conventions: Victorian Confession Novels and *Tess of the D'Urbervilles*' (*ELT* 37.445–62) traces the history of the confessional novel as a genre through an analysis of Hardy's *Tess.* Richard W. Noland's 'The Migrating Anima in Thomas Hardy's *The Well-Beloved*' (*JEP* 15.104–11) explores the psychological foundations of Hardy's novel, while Laura Otis's 'Organic Memory: History, Bodies, and Texts in *Tess of the D'Urbervilles*' (*NCS* 8.1–22) discusses Hardy's treatment of the human body in his text and its relation to the function of organic memory.

Drawing upon a diversity of critical approaches, the essays in Charles P. C. Pettit's collection, *New Perspectives on Thomas Hardy*, explore a wide range of selections from Hardy's immense canon of poetry and prose. Originally presented at the Tenth International Thomas Hardy Conference in 1992 in Dorchester, the selections include James Gibson's '"The Characteristic of All Great Poetry – The General Perfectly Reduced in the Particular": Thomas Hardy'; Peter J. Casagrande's '"Something More to be Said": Hardy's Creative Process and the Case of *Tess* and *Jude*'; Michael Slater's 'Hardy and the City'; Trevor Johnson's '"Thoroughfares of Stones": Hardy's "Other" Love Poetry'; Peter Widdowson's '"Moments of Vision": Postmodernising *Tess of the d'Urbervilles*; or, *Tess of the d'Urbervilles* Faithfully Presented by Peter Widdowson'; Lance St John Butler's '"Bosh" or: Believing Neither More Nor Less – Hardy, George Eliot, and God'; Raymond Chapman's '"Good Faith, You Do Talk!": Some Features of Hardy's Dialogue'; Timothy Hands's '"A Bewildered Child and his Conjurers": Hardy and the Ideas of his Time'; Craig Raine's 'Conscious Artistry in *The Mayor of Casterbridge*'; Pettit's 'Hardy's Vision of the Individual in *Tess of the d'Urbervilles*'; and F. B. Pinion's 'Questions Arising from Hardy's Visits to Cornwall'. P. V. Mallett and R. P. Draper's *A Spacious Vision: Essays on Hardy* includes essays by Robert Schweik, Rosemarie Sumner and Draper that focus on *Jude the Obscure* and *The Return of the Native*, with particular emphasis upon Hardy's relationship with modernism. In addition to material on Hardy's verse, Mallett and Draper's volume includes Dale Kramer's interesting essay, 'Hardy's Style of the Moment', which deals with minutiae in *The Mayor of Casterbridge*.

Drawing upon linguistic and literary criticism, Valerie Shepherd's *Literature about Language* discusses the interface between language and literary studies in Hardy's novels. The distinguished German Victorian critic and scholar Paul Goetsch, in *Hardy's Wessex-Romane*, addresses the role of English geography and culture in Hardy's 'Wessex' novels. Hopefully, Goetsch's insights will be translated into English. Martin Seymour-Smith's *Hardy: A Biography* challenges the prevailing assessments of Hardy as a misogynist and snobbish pessimist by such Hardy biographers as Robert Gittings and Michael Millgate. Seymour-Smith argues instead that Hardy was a sensitive, profoundly ironic man who cared deeply for the women in his life. Drawing upon a host of psychoanalytic theories, Seymour-Smith affords special emphasis to the nature of Hardy's sexual relationships, while also exploring the writer's composition methods and his attitude towards his audience and publishers. George Levine's 'Shaping Hardy's Art: Vision, Class, and Sex' (in Richetti, *Columbia History of the British Novel*) argues 'that the distinctive character of Hardy's fiction grows from the way his remarkable powers of sensuous responsiveness play off against the contingencies of society and biology'. Levine focuses upon the manner in which Hardy's 'acute powers of observation . . . complicate his attitudes toward the class structures that govern society and the powerful sexual drives that govern human behavior'.

Philip V. Allingham's 'Six Original Illustrations for Hardy's *Tess of the D'Urbervilles* Drawn by Sir Hubert Von Herkomer, R.A., for *The Graphic* (1891)' (*THJ* 10.52–70) discusses the illustrations for *Tess*, while William Bonnell's 'Broken Communion in *Tess of the D'Urbervilles*' (*ELN* 31.63–71) examines Hardy's treatment of the sacrament of the Eucharist in the novel. In 'Insects in Hardy's Fiction' (*THJ* 10.54–63), Michael Irwin assesses the role of insects in Hardy's narrative, while F. B. Pinion's 'Hardy and Scott' (*THJ* 10.71–77) remarks upon the influence of Sir Walter Scott upon Hardy's fictions. Martin Heusser's '*Déjà vu* with a Difference: Repetition and the Tragic in Thomas Hardy's Novels', collected in Andreas Fischer's *Repetition*, discusses the iterative nature of tragedy and its function in Hardy's works. Bernard Jones's 'An Absentee Patron' (*THJ* 10.66–77) discusses Hardy's treatment of the patronage, while David Jones's 'The One Believed-In Thing' (*THJ* 10.48–53) explores the role of religion in Hardy's works and its relationship with the nature of art. In 'The Trumpet Major's Signal: Kinship and Sexual Rivalry in the Novels of Thomas Hardy' (*CEA* 56.43–61), William J. Mistichelli investigates Hardy's fictional treatment of sexuality and the family. Toru Sasaki's 'Viewer and Victim in *Desperate Remedies*: Links between Hardy's Life and His Fiction' (*THJ* 10.77–86) offers a biographical approach to Hardy's volume, while Simon Gatrell's '*Far from the Madding Crowd* Revisited' (*THJ* 10.38–50) traces the critical reception of Hardy's novel. In 'Ethelberta: Portrait of the Artist as a Young Woman – Love and Ambition' (*THJ* 10.87–99), Patrick Roberts employs a biographical analysis of *The Hand of Ethelberta*. James

J. Snow's 'Two Different Ethics: Philosophy and Literature' (*Mosaic* 27.75–94) assesses the relationship between philosophy and literature through an analysis of *Jude the Obscure*.

The principal achievement in the year's work in Robert Louis Stevenson studies are the long-awaited four volumes of *The Letters of Robert Louis Stevenson* edited by the late Bradford A. Booth and continued by Ernest Mehew. Begun in the 1950s and tracing Stevenson's biographical and literary life from 1854 to June 1884, this definitive edition of the writer's correspondence features invaluable material related to Stevenson, including a family tree and extensive background materials regarding Stevenson's correspondents. The work is richly annotated and researched, with an extensive introduction, and Stevenson emerges as a fascinating correspondent. This edition will form the foundation for future Stevenson biographical, critical and other studies. Booth and especially Mehew have assembled a mine of information of use not only to students of the Victorian novel but to those concerned with genius, nationalism, post-colonialism and many other issues. Hunter Davies's *The Teller of Tales: In Search of Robert Louis Stevenson* chronicles the travels of Stevenson, from his birthplace in Edinburgh to France, California, and his final home on the Pacific island of Samoa. In addition to tracing the composition and publication history of such novels as *Kidnapped*, *Catriona*, *Treasure Island* and *Dr Jekyll and Mr Hyde*, Davies discusses Stevenson's enigmatic persona in terms of the novelist's extant personal correspondence. Frank McLynn's *Robert Louis Stevenson: A Biography* employs a more conventional approach to the life and work of the novelist. In *Robert Louis Stevenson in France*, Louis Stott investigates Stevenson's love affair with France, while also establishing its place within both his artistic and his personal development. Written as a companion piece to his earlier work, *Robert Louis Stevenson and the Highlands and Islands of Scotland*, Stott's latest volume affords particular attention to Stevenson's compositional achievements during his forays in France, including such works as *Prince Otto*, *Black Arrow* and *A Child's Garden of Verses*, among others.

Daniel L. Wright's 'The Prisonhouse of My Disposition: A Study of the Psychology of Addiction in *Dr Jekyll and Mr Hyde*' (*SNNTS* 26.254–67) draws upon psychoanalytic insights while discussing Stevenson's depiction of addictive behaviour in his novel. Burton R. Pollin and J. A. Greenwood's 'Stevenson on Poe: Unpublished Annotations of Numerous Poe Texts and a Stevenson Letter' (*ELT* 37.317–49) addresses Stevenson's marginal commentary on the works of Poe, while Bryan Bevan's 'The Versatility of Robert Louis Stevenson' (*ContempR* 264.316–19) assesses the wide-ranging nature of the novelist's narrative achievements. Brian Rose's 'Transformations of Terror: Reading Changes in Social Attitudes through Film and Television Adaptations of Stevenson's *Dr Jekyll and Mr Hyde*', collected in Richard Chapple's *Social and Political Change in Literature and Film: Selected Papers from the Sixteenth Annual Florida State University Conference on Literature and Film*, examines the role of social change in several recent television adaptations of Stevenson's work, while Annette Federico's 'Books for Boys: Violence and Representation in *Kidnapped* and *Catriona*' (*VIJ* 22.115–33) discusses the places of masculinity and violence in Stevenson's novels.

This year *CVE* (40) offered a special issue devoted to the works of Robert Louis Stevenson. Jenni Calder, an authority on Stevenson and his genre, in 'Story and History: R. L. Stevenson and Walter Scott' (21–36) discusses the ways in which both Stevenson and Scott employed history in their novels, particularly as a means for exploring the psychological and moral terrain of their narratives. Max Sutton's

'Jim Hawkins and the Faintly Inscribed Reader in *Treasure Island*' (37–50) ascribes the power of Stevenson's novel to the manner in which Hawkins wins the reader's respect through his respect for his audience, while Ian Campbell's 'Jekyll, Hyde, Frankenstein, and the Uncertain Self' (51–62) examines Stevenson's visual and often melodramatic medium of story-telling in *The Strange Case of Dr Jekyll and Mr Hyde*. Chris Foss's 'Xenophobia, Duality, and the "Other" Side of Nationalism: A Reading of Stevenson's *Jekyll and Hyde*' (63–76) argues that Stevenson's novel critiques dualism as a dangerously reductive force, finding its origins in the ethnocentrism promulgated by the fear of one's own self. Edwin M. Eigner's '*The Master of Ballantrae* as Elegiac Romance' (99–106) reads Stevenson's text as a precursor to the twentieth-century sub-genre of elegiac romance, arguing that the protagonist typifies such narratives through his image of the self, through his attitude to other more heroic figures, and in his personal development. Christine Persak's 'Spencer's Doctrines and Mr Hyde: Moral Evolution in Stevenson's "Strange Case"' (*VN* 86.13–17) argues that Herbert Spencer's theory of evolution, rather than Darwin's, influences the cultural anxiety that manifests itself in Stevenson's writing.

William H. P. Crewdson and Robert D. Crewdson's 'Hesba Stretton' (*ABMR* 21.20–3) discusses the life and work of the often neglected Victorian writer, Hesba Stretton (1832–1911), the author of more than fifty volumes. Anthony Hope's *The Prisoner of Zenda*, edited with an introduction by Tony Watkins, was published in Oxford's WC series. Drawing upon the insights of feminist and psychoanalytic criticism, Lynda Hart's 'The Victorian Villainess and the Patriarchal Unconscious' (*L&P* 40.1–25) discusses the treatment of the female villain in Mary Elizabeth Braddon's *Lady Audley's Secret*. Jeanette Shumaker's 'Deathbed Confessions: Sacrifice Eroticized in Victorian Fiction' (92–106), included in Justus George Lawler's *The 1994 Annual of Hermeneutics and Social Concern*, discusses the treatment of deathbed repentance and its relationship to desire in Charles Reade's *The Cloister and the Hearth*, among other novels. Linda Hunt's 'Amy Levy and the "Jewish Novel": Representing Jewish Life in the Victorian Period' (*SNNTS* 26.235–53) discusses Levy's depiction of Jews and Judaism in her novel *Reuben Sachs: A Life*.

Christina Sjöholm's *'The Vice of Wedlock': The Theme of Marriage in George Gissing's Novels* discusses the evolving theme of marriage in Gissing's novels, from a one-dimensional institution in the 1880s to a psychologically complex union in the 1890s. In addition to demonstrating the influence of other writers upon Gissing's aesthetic, Sjöholm answers the prevailing critical attacks upon Gissing for alleged elements of ambiguity and misogyny in his novels. She offers close readings of such works as *The Emancipated*, *New Grub Street*, *The Odd Woman*, *In the Year of the Jubilee* and *The Whirlpool*, while also placing Gissing's novels in the historical and literary context of the late nineteenth century. *The Collected Letters of George Gissing*. Vol. 5: *1892–1895*, edited by Paul F. Mattheisen, Arthur C. Young and Pierre Coustillas, offers scholars a vital research tool for understanding Gissing's years of growing literary production, as well as his profitable association with his publishers, Bullen and Lawrence. In addition to publishing such works as *Denzil Quarrier*, *The Odd Women*, *In the Year of the Jubilee* and *Eve's Ransom*, Gissing continued to enjoy during this era a growing reading audience. Using a diversity of sources, including newspapers, the author's memoirs, biographies and sales catalogues, the editors provide a valuable context for understanding this significant moment in the aesthetic shift between the

Victorian age and the advent of modernism. Fully annotated, this important edition of Gissing's work should serve for years to come as a central resource to Gissing scholars and students of late Victorian culture.

Vol. 30 of *GissingJ* includes a variety of essays of interest. The January issue this year includes Constance D. Harsh's 'George Gissing's *Thyrza*: Romantic Love and Ideological Co-Conspiracy' (1–12), an essay that contends that the writer intentionally constructed narratives that consider the problems that women experience in a patriarchal society. In '*The Emancipated*: A Comedy in Italy' (12–25), Françoise Dupeyron explores the Italian terrain that marks the setting of Gissing's novel, while in 'The Critical Response to Gissing and Commentary about him in the *Chicago Evening Post*' (26–37), Robert L. Selig continues in his effort to assess the American journalistic and critical response to Gissing's work. The April issue includes Pierre Coustillas and Xavier Pétremand's edited version of 'London Homes and Haunts of George Gissing: An Unpublished Essay by A. C. Gissing' (1–14), which reproduces an essay by the novelist's son. The July issue includes the doyen of Gissing scholars, Pierre Coustillas, with '"Found Him a Genial Fellow, Well Disposed": The Relationship between Gissing and Herbert Heaton Sturmer' (1–26), an essay which, drawing upon a font of knowledge, details the professional and personal relationship between the novelist and Sturmer. Sydney Lott's 'Gissing in Sussex' (26–8) discusses perhaps too briefly Gissing's life in Sussex in the late 1880s. The October issue includes Bonnie Zare's '*The Odd Women*'s Creation of a Desire for Romantic Fulfillment' (1–18), which examines Gissing's depiction of the marriage plot in his novel as an inherently destabilized entity. Pierre Coustillas's 'Arthur Waugh Reminisces about Gissing: A Letter to Herbert van Thal' (19–24) reveals Arthur Waugh's reflections about dining with Gissing in 1895. Constance D. Harsh's 'Gissing's *In the Year of Jubilee* and the Epistemology of Resistance' (*SEL* 34. 853–76) addresses the manner in which Gissing resisted the aesthetic movement in the nineteenth century towards unified works of art.

Ian Small's new edition of Oscar Wilde's *Complete Short Fiction* features selections from the writer's *The Happy Prince and Other Tales*, *A House of Pomegranates*, *Lord Arthur Savile's Crime and Other Stories*, and *Poems in Prose*, as well as such well-known Wilde stories as 'The Portrait of Mr W. H.', among others. In addition to referring to Wilde's periodical publications in such journals as *Blackwood's Edinburgh Magazine* and the *Fortnightly Review*, Small employs the texts of Robert Ross's collected edition of Wilde's works in this volume. Christopher Lane's 'Framing Fears, Reading Designs: The Homosexual Art of Painting in James, Wilde, and Beerbohm' (*ELH* 61.923–54) examines the problem of desire in the fictions of Henry James through an analysis of contemporary accounts of painting in works such as Wilde's *The Picture of Dorian Gray*, among others. Karl Beckson's 'Oscar Wilde's Celebrated Remark on Bernard Shaw' (*N&Q* 41.360–1) attempts to account for the remark about Shaw often attributed to Wilde: 'Mr Bernard Shaw has no enemies but is intensely disliked by all his friends.' Beckson argues that the remark actually finds its origins in the 1891 edition of *The Picture of Dorian Gray*. Talia Schaffer's '"A Wilde Desire Took Me": The Homoerotic History of *Dracula*' (*ELH* 61.381–426) studies the influence of Bram Stoker's friendship with Oscar Wilde upon the composition of his narrative.

Garrett Stewart's '"Count Me In": *Dracula*, Hypnotic Participation, and the Late-Victorian Gothic of Reading' (*LIT* 5.1–18) examines the Gothic properties inherent in the narrative of Stoker's novel. David Thompson's 'Supinely Anticipating Red-Eyed Shadows: A Jungian Analysis of Bram Stoker's *Dracula*' (*JEP* 15.289–301) applies the theories of Jung to Stoker's volume. Joel N. Feimar's 'Bram Stoker's *Dracula*: The Challenge of the Occult to Science, Reason, and Psychiatry' (165–71), collected in Langford's *Contours of the Fantastic,* explores Stoker's appropriation of the occult in his novels. Robert A. Smart's 'Blood and Money in Bram Stoker's *Dracula*: The Struggle Against Monopoly' (253–60), collected in John Louis DiGaetani's *Money: Lure, Lore, and Literature*, addresses the role of money and capitalism in *Dracula*. A further significant contribution to Richard Jefferies studies by Hugoe Matthews is this year to be found in his and Phyllis Treitel's *The Forward Life of Richard Jefferies: A Chronological Study*, which assembles 'the events of [his] life in the order in which' it was lived. This work is indispensable for the understanding of Jefferies, his writings, and their context. Richard Marsh's forgotten *The Beetle*, first published in 1897, the same year as Stoker's *Dracula*, is reprinted with an introduction by William Baker, who argues that Marsh 'draws upon literary traditions of fantasy and transformation, having their roots in the Gothic and the mid-Victorian Sensation Novel, as well as in Stoker, Conan Doyle, and Stevenson'.

Miles A. Kimball's '"A Benefactor of the Race": Sherlock Holmes, Voyeurism, and Victorian Readers' (*KPR* 9.16–22) explores the treatment of voyeurism in the Sherlock Holmes mysteries of Sir Arthur Conan Doyle. James Griffith's 'From a Certain Point of View in "A Scandal of Bohemia": Outsmarting Mr Sherlock Holmes' (*VN* 86.7–9) problematizes the television adaptation of Conan Doyle's tale because it neglects to capture the essence of the author's penchant for adventure. Ronald R. Thomas's 'The Fingerprint of the Foreigner: Colonizing the Criminal Body in 1890s Detective Fiction and Criminal Anthropology' (*ELH* 61.655–84) explores the relation between the individual body and the body politic in Conan Doyle's detective fiction, particularly regarding the ways in which the study of criminality links issues of personal identity with the prevailing late nineteenth-century crisis in national identity. *Sherlock Holmes: The Major Stories with Contemporary Critical Essays*, edited by John A. Hodgson, features a variety of essays that critique Conan Doyle's short fiction. Selections include Martin Priestman's 'Sherlock Holmes: The Series'; Peter Brooks's 'Reading for the Plot'; Gian Paolo Caprettini's 'Sherlock Holmes: Ethics, Logic, and the Mask'; Hodgson's 'The Recoil of "The Speckled Band"'; Alastair Fowler's 'Sherlock Holmes and the Adventure of the Dancing Men and Women'; Stephen Knight's 'The Case of the Great Detective'; Catherine Belsey's 'Deconstructing the Text: Sherlock Holmes'; Rosemary Hennessy and Rajeswari Mohan's '"The Speckled Band": The Construction of Woman in a Popular Text of Empire'; and Audrey Jaffe's 'Detecting the Beggar: Arthur Conan Doyle, Henry Mayhew, and "The Man with the Twisted Lip"'. Robert F. Fleissner's 'Conan Doyle's "Woman of Mystery"' (*SherHR* 4.167–70) examines the treatment of Jewish identity in regard to selected female characters in Conan Doyle's fictions.

In *Rudyard Kipling: A Study of the Short Fiction*, Helen Pike Bauer explores representative short stories from Kipling's massive fictional canon in an effort to reveal the complexity and sophistication of the writer's narrative technique and the enduring value of his thematic concerns. In addition to examining Kipling's treatment of men and women in crisis, Bauer discusses the author's understanding of the pleasures and pains of childhood and their particular place within his fictions. Michael Gorra's 'Rudyard Kipling to Salman Rushdie: Imperialism to

Postcolonialism' (in Richetti, *Columbia History of the British Novel*) discusses Kipling, whose 'emphasis . . . as a whole is on subduing the subcontinent to description, on making it "knowable"'. Phillip E. Wegner's '"Life as He Would Have It": The Invention of India in Kipling's *Kim*' (*CulC* 26.129–59) discusses the representation of India in Kipling's novel and explores the manifestations of British imperialism in its pages, while Phillip Mallett's 'Rudyard Kipling: Narrating India' (*SwR* 'Writing and the Nation' 358–68) examines the manner in which Kipling appropriates India in his fictions.

In an important article on Kipling, Rolf P. Lessenich's 'The Mission of Empire: Romantic Humanitarianism in Rudyard Kipling's Earlier Work' (*SN* 66.[1993]197–211) examines *Puck of Pook's Hill*, *Rewards and Fairies*, *The Jungle Book*, *Kim*, *Plain Tales from the Hills* and *Stories in Life's Handicap* in order to demonstrate the 'humanitarian' ideological basis underlying Kipling's imperialism, which 'was a religious mission enjoining combative self-sacrifice for what [Kipling] believed would guarantee a more peaceful and steady world, stabilized by Britain's cultural contribution of law and order'. Lessenich's analysis, especially of the role Kipling gives to Spanish Jews in, for instance, *Puck of Pook's Hill*, goes some way towards mitigating charges of anti-Semitism levelled at Kipling. Lessenich writes, 'Kipling was not a racist in any pseudo-scientific or ethnocentric sense, but a firm believer in Anglo-Israel.' This year R. K. R. Thornton and Ian Small also provided readers with a new edition of Kipling's *Barrack-Room Ballads, 1892*.

3. Poetry

In the year of the centenary of the death of Christina Rossetti, it is not surprising that we find a number of significant publications on this major Victorian poet. Fresh controversy is injected into debates about the motivation behind Rossetti's writing by Jan Marsh's biography, *Christina Rossetti*. This is a substantial, six-hundred-page publication which usefully draws together research into Rossetti's life and career that has accumulated through the tradition of biography developed since the 1890s. Marsh resists one of the besetting sins of the tradition in that she eschews the image of the poet as a secluded spinster, writing in grand isolation, and takes seriously Rossetti's position at the heart of Victorian literary culture and of some of the most important political and social debates of her day. Marsh draws on her extensive knowledge of the pre-Raphaelites to establish Rossetti's artistic as well as personal links with the brotherhood and its associates. By tracing Rossetti's relationships with Dora Greenwell, Jean Ingelow, Caroline Gemmer, Augusta Webster, Lisa Wilson and other women poets of her period, Marsh also makes admirably clear that Rossetti was not part of an oppressed minority, whose work was received only on sufferance, but was part of a distinct group with a clear mandate to produce poetry which was seen as having an important cultural role. The publication history and her relationships with her publishers and critics are traced in detail. Marsh's Rossetti is deeply imbricated with the politics of her contemporary period. The complexity of her opposition to female suffrage, her association with the feminist Langham Place Group, her work with 'fallen' women at the Highgate Penitentiary and her enthusiastic support of the anti-vivisection campaign are given due consideration. Marsh is also perhaps the first biographer to investigate the politics of Rossetti's religious writing, emphasizing that her extensive and increasing commitment to the composition of devotional poetry and exegetical prose texts was envisaged by Rossetti as having a 'public' as well as a 'private' significance, that she 'took seriously her role as an influential and Christian writer'.

However, this clear-sighted meticulousness is compromised by the fact that Marsh is unable to stop herself from falling prey to the second besetting sin of Rossetti biography – of offering wild and unsubstantiated speculation as to the existence of a central 'secret' within the poet's life. The most notorious example of this phenomenon to date has been Mona Losk Packer's hypothesis, expounded in her biography of 1963, that Rossetti sustained an intense and illicit romantic attachment with the (married) minor pre-Raphaelite William Bell Scott. Marsh's thesis, for which there is equally a total absence of direct evidence, is that the mental breakdown which Rossetti suffered at the age of 14 and the recurrence throughout her adult writing of images of monsters, devils and terrifying physical and moral assault, are due to repressed memories of sexual abuse she suffered from her father in her thirteenth and fourteenth years. Marsh explains the domestic circumstances which allowed for the perpetration and concealment of the incest by reference to a housebound, infirm and depressed Gabriele Rossetti who, in the absence of his wife (forced to seek work to supplement the family income), sought sexual solace from his youngest child. Marsh makes her diagnosis by reference to the contemporary literature of childhood abuse, specifically the work of Alice Miller, pointing to a similarity between Rossetti's episodes of depression and physical self-mutilation and patterns of behaviour modern psychotherapists and counsellors find in their patients who confess to childhood incest. Quite apart from the obvious problem that the verification of these accusations is impossible, Marsh seems unaware of the huge controversy which has surrounded the work on recovered memories of incest, and that many practitioners and analysts have argued that in some cases they are a symbolic language which represent other kinds of violence and psychic process. Marsh does not consider the possibility that there is quite enough within Victorian culture to give a middle-class adolescent girl a mental breakdown. To view the whole of Rossetti's *oeuvre* as a kind of therapeutic process, working through the legacy of a specific personal event, compromises the clear view of the complex significance of that culture for her work. The forcing of her material into the grand narrative of the 1990s will date Marsh's biography more quickly than its otherwise solid scholarship deserves.

Marsh's edition of Rossetti's *Poems and Prose*, which appeared alongside her biography this year, will have a longer shelf life. This Everyman paperback is the first of a number of editions of Rossetti which will appear over the next few years. Marsh arranges her texts by genre, rather than by chronology of publication (although date of composition is usefully recorded at the foot of each text), subdividing into four sections: 'Lyrics, Ballads and Shorter Poems'; 'Poems for Children, from *Singsong*'; 'Narrative and Longer Poems'; and 'Sonnet Sequences'. Her choice of texts is slightly conservative, weighted in favour of Rossetti's earlier, secular poems, which twentieth-century critics have always been more interested in than her later devotional work. It is interesting to see a substantial selection of Rossetti's secular prose, including the well-known story of adolescent religious melancholia *Maude* and four stories from the far less accessible collection *Commonplace and Other Short Stories* (1870). The major shortcoming of the edition is the neglect of the devotional prose. Only a few short passages from *Letter and Spirit* (1883) and *Time Flies: A Reading Diary* (1885) with particular autobiographical significance are reprinted in the section of the edition devoted to correspondence. Only when this material is accessible will it be possible to consider Rossetti's significance as a writer fully, but this edition is an important step towards that destination, making available as it does a substantial range of texts to those without access to a research library.

Marsh's work is also represented in the third major volume devoted to Rossetti this year, the special double issue of *VP* (32.iii-iv) edited by A. H. Harrison. Marsh's essay,'Christina Rossetti's Vocation: The Importance of "Goblin Market"' (233–48) discusses the context of the production of the poems in Rossetti's first published volume, *Goblin Market and Other Poems* (1862). Much of the article is devoted to the context of the title poem, including Rossetti's extensive knowledge of Keightley's *Fairy Mythology* and other European and English works of fairy and folklore, and her work at the Highgate penitentiary. Lorraine Jazen Kooistra also focuses on Rossetti's most famous poem. In 'Modern Markets for "Goblin Market"' (249–78) she points out the appropriateness of looking closely at the way in which this poem, which deals with a sexually and socially charged commercial transaction, has been exploited by three distinct markets in the twentieth century: the markets for children's literature, for pornography, and for academic discourse. This meticulously documented study, which works through publication and illustration history, opens up some fascinating observations on the poem, not the least of which is the fact that the text of the poem 'whether produced for children, or for adult fantasist, does not change significantly'. Extending a line of inquiry in Victorian studies which seeks to scrutinize the 'other Victorians', Kooistra demonstrates the insistence of Rossetti's poem on the proximity of investments and interests, which her culture tried to demarcate. Several essays focus on Rossetti's position as part of a developing tradition of women's poetry in the nineteenth century. In 'Sisters in Art: Christina Rossetti and Elizabeth Barrett Browning' (339–64) Marjorie Stone focuses on a specific dialogue. Diane D'Amico's essay, 'Saintly Singer or Tanagra Figurine: Christina Rossetti through the Eyes of Katharine Tynan and Sara Teasdale' (387–407), is addressed to the topic of Rossetti's considerable influence on the women poets who followed her in the nineteenth and earlier twentieth centuries. In '"Poet's Rights": Christina Rossetti as Anti-Muse and the Legacy of the "Poetess"' (365–386), Susan Canley takes a broader view of Rossetti's position within the development of nineteenth-century women's poetry, which encompasses both what she took and what she gave to poets including Letitia Landon, Elizabeth Barrett Browning and 'Michael Field'. Kamilla Derman and Sarah Smith's essay, 'Christina Rossetti's copy of C. B. Cayley's *Divine Comedy*' (315–38), concentrates on the poet's interaction with a male contemporary, describing the 'editorial diligence' she addressed to the translation of her one-time suitor. Linda E. Marshall's '"Abstruse the problems!": Unity and Divisions in Christina Rossetti's *Later Life: A Double Sonnet of Sonnets*' (299–314) is a close-reading of one of Rossetti's sonnet sequences, in particular its revisionary interaction with Petrarchan tradition.

This volume demonstrates the way in which Rossetti studies is coming of age, with critics no longer restricting themselves to the narrow corpus of her earlier, secular poems. Several articles dealing with the later, devotional poetry and prose offer competent observations on this underscrutinized aspect of her work. In 'Restoring the Book: The Typological Hermeneutics of Christina Rossetti and the PRB' (209–27) Linda H. Peterson explores the way in which Rossetti utilizes Christian typology – using the signs of the world in order to model aspects of the nature of God – to challenge the account of women as 'relative creatures', current in the art of her brother Dante Gabriel Rossetti and other male Victorian artists and thinkers. In *The Girlhood of Mary Virgin* (1849), Dante Gabriel Rossetti's painting, he required Christina as a model to pose embroidering, rather than reading a book as was traditional in representations of the Virgin; but 'Goblin Market' and 'The Prince's Progress' poems, Peterson argues, reassert the validity of typology as a mode of reading, to produce an account of women as the correct readers of scriptural and social tradition, to challenge the reductive masculinist view of women's relationship with art. Mary Arsenau's 'Pilgrimage and Postponement: Christina Rossetti's "The Princes's Progress"' (278–98) has a closely related theme. Making the link with Rossetti's commitment to seeing the phenomena of this world as signs of heaven, Arsenau sees the poem as 'primarily concerned with the individual for whom incorrect interpretation of symbolic events and figures has dire and mortal consequence', and argues that it constitutes an implicit criticism of Dante Gabriel Rossetti's (non-typological) 'Symbolic technique' and its foundation in his agnosticism. In what is perhaps the most ground-breaking essay in the collection, Colleen Hobbs addresses herself to the devotional prose. In 'A View from "The Lowest Place": Christina Rossetti's Devotional Prose' (409–28), she argues that the huge investment which feminist criticism has made in the vindication of sisterhood of 'Goblin Market' is challenged by the explicit critiques of militant feminism found in the devotional texts. Rather than simply ignoring this divergence, as most critics have done, or wringing her hands over the 'false consciousness' the poet was induced into by her religious faith, Hobbs explores the complex sexual politics of these texts. Through an account of Rossetti's vindication of female celibacy and the link of her texts with a tradition of English female mysticism (Julian of Norwich and Margery Kempe), she points out that a (feminist) vision of heavenly sexual egalitarianism underlies Rossetti's self-effacement.

Virago have reprinted Frances Thomas's biography, *Christina Rossetti*, for the first time this year. It was originally self-published in 1992 (and reviewed in full in *YWES* 73.452–3). The adoption by a major feminist publishing house of this somewhat limited study, whose beleaguered and rather fey heroine is in sharp contrast with the competent artist and intellectual of Marsh's more sophisticated account, indicates nothing so much as the considerable commercial interest this Victorian poet now represents within a variety of markets.

As this survey of the field of Rossetti studies indicates, publication in the area of women's poetry of the period continues to grow apace. This year saw the appearance of Jennifer Breen's anthology *Victorian Women Poets: 1830–1900*, a companion volume to her edition *Women Romantic Poets: 1785–1832* (*YWES* 73.340–1). The volume is the first of several such collections to appear over the next few years, which will open up the study of this poetry, dramatically altering, as Breen points out, the understanding of the traditions both of women's writing and of Victorian poetry. The anthology includes extracts from the work of thirty poets, prefaced by brief biographical notes. A useful bibliography lists relevant nineteenth-century editions of each poet and twentieth-century critical works which will aid further study. Breen's introduction provides some useful contexts to bring to our reading, describing important social and legislative changes which affected women's access to education, employment and property, and thus allowed for the development of an understanding of poetry as a vocation and a living, rather than just an accomplishment for women. She also discusses the very different model of literary history inscribed by women's poetry. The period break between Romanticism and Victorianism which most critics accept in men's poetry is not there in women's poetry to anything like the same degree. Several poets wrote across both the chronology and the thematics of the two categories. Breen argues that within the period 1830–1900 two clear categories of women's poetry are discernible, which she terms 'post-Romantic' poetry (concerned with the articulation of a new language of female sexual desire) and 'New Woman' poetry (preoccupied with social and political reforms which affected women's lives and opportunities from the mid-nineteenth century). The large number of poets included in such a short volume means that we get only a tantalizing glimpse of many. Breen is honest about the fact that her selection is weighted in favour of those poets, such as the Brontës, Barrett Browning and Rossetti, who already have an established and intelligible place within the 'canon'. At the start of a major work of canonical reconstruction, which the wide dissemination of Victorian women's poetry represents, it is always difficult to justify a radical challenge to the understanding of relative status of particular poets. As the project progresses the substantial reprint of poets like August Webster, Amy Levy, Mary Elizabeth Coleridge and Mathilde Blind alongside that of Rossetti and Barrett Browning will be recognized as perfectly justified. Breen's anthology is an important opening into a major new arena.

Vol. 12 of *The Brownings' Correspondence*, edited by Philip Kelley and Scott Lewis, covering January–April 1846, is published for the first time this year. As usual an index and biographical sketches of principal correspondents are included, as well as all locatable reviews which appeared in the period covered in the volume. An additional bonus is the reprint of W. J. Fox's 'Lecture on Elizabeth Barrett and Sarah Flower Adams', delivered in February 1846 to the Working Men's Association in Holborn, London. It reveals the way in which certain kinds of women's poetry were perceived as having an imperative moral role. Fox argues that whereas society and its institutions are utterly indifferent to the suffering of children, and 'philanthropy tenders its useless, its degrading almsgiving', poetry (Fox has just been discussing Barrett Browning's poem of protest against child labour, 'The Cry of the Children') 'lends them its own voice to claim their rights, to describe their wrongs and sufferings'.

Two major volumes of interest to Tennyson scholars appeared this year. First is Matthew Rowlinson's *Tennyson's Fixations*, a psychoanalytically informed study by a young critic keen to demonstrate the application of contemporary literary theory to Victorian poetry (to be reviewed in full in *YWES* 76). The second major study, *Anglo-American Antiphony: The Late Romanticism of Tennyson and Emerson*, by Richard E. Brantley, takes up a rather different position within the debate about the relevance of contemporary theory to the poet. Brantley's is a late-career study, which stands on the foundation of several decades of scholarship, and provides a summary and summation of concepts and concerns central to his previous work, principally his argument for the existence of a specifically Anglo-American intellectual tradition, discernible in the dialogue between and progressive unification of empiricism and evangelicalism. The book is divided into two discrete sections, with the first and largest portion of the study being devoted to Tennyson. Nine chapters work through a close reading of *In Memoriam*, exploring a clear and sometimes fascinating account of its dialogue with varieties of scientific, philosophical, theological and spiritual thought and experience current in its period. Brantley considers tradition as well as contemporaneity, the discussion is well documented, and the often rebarbative dialogue with 'postmodern' critics is conducted with information and insight into the positions with which he is in disagreement. Brantley's relationship with modern literary and cultural theory is much more complex than the dismissal of a traditionalist. He acknowledges and endorses the influence on his criticism of Bakhtin and of a new historicism derived from Foucault (although his account of these theorists and their significance might be considered eccentric by some). Yet he retains a fierce stance against postmodernism, declaring himself a 'modern realist' and arguing, *contra* Rorty, 'that philosophical, religious and literary experiences are grounded in and refer to natural (as well as spiritual) existences beyond culture'. His is an ethical as well as an epistemological stance. Brantley's justification for his work is that the optimistic resolution of the dialectic he finds in his two writers has something to offer to modern dilemmas. In recent years, such protest against the ethical sterility of postmodernism and an attempt to reimagine critically the definition of value and distinction have seen a resurgence in the work of philosophers such as Martha Nussbaum and Gillian Rose. Paradoxically, Brantley's volume may take up an eccentric dialogue with the cutting edge of contemporary cultural theory.

Enthusiasts of the poetry of Lewis Carroll and Edward Lear will wish to take a detour to the philosophy of language shelves to consult Lecercle's *Philosophy of Nonsense* (see also p. 453 above). There has long been a philosophical discourse of immense seriousness attached to nonsense literature, the most famous example perhaps being Martin Gardner's *The Annotated Alice* (1965). Through particular reference to 'Jabberwocky', a selection of Lear's limericks and other Victorian nonsense texts, Lecercle pursues his thesis that nonsense literature lays bare something crucial about the contracts, conditions and paradoxes of language and thus ultimately of culture. The genre is 'conservative-revolutionary . . . structured by a contradiction . . . a dialectic, between over-structuring and de-structuring, subversion and support', which allows it to become a kind of reflexive meta-language. The bulk of the text is devoted to a meticulous working through of the proposition in relation to different aspects of generative linguistics (phonetics, morphology, syntax, semantics, pragmatics). Shifting from the synchronic to the diachronic, the final chapter focuses specifically upon the Victorianism of the texts. Lecercle's thinking here is also dialectical. Utilizing Bakhtin's concept of the *cronotope*, the 'literary form of [historical] intuition . . . the locus for the plurality of voices and points of view to develop', he traces the intertexts of Carroll and Lear in various discourses of Victorian culture (philosophy of language, logic, natural history, madness), emphasizing that nonsense literature is not just interpolated by them; nonsense itself interpolates and interprets Victorian culture. A strenuous read for the literary critic without an advanced grasp of Chomsky's linguistics and continental philosophy, the study is nevertheless well worth the effort, for its convincing and sophisticated demonstration of the centrality of nonsense poetry to the discourses which structured Victorian culture.

An equally strenuous but far less rewarding read is Franco Marucci's study *The Fine Delight that Fathers Thought: Rhetoric and Medievalism in Gerard Manley Hopkins*, which is translated into English from the author's native Italian for the first time this year. The original version came out in 1981, and bears the burden of many of the problems of the application to literary texts in that era of the semiotic theory of the French structuralists and others, with which Marucci declares an affiliation. Whilst it is refreshing to see a critic attempting to grapple with the complexity of Hopkins's 'sprung rhythm', as Marucci does in the first section of the study, devoted to rhetorical strategies of the poetry, it is often difficult to extract the direction of Marucci's argument from his abstruse prose. Whilst the quality of the translation, and whether it does justice to the force of the original text, is clearly an issue here (one into which I am not in a position to intervene), it seems difficult to find anything to justify the inclusion of the following formulation, typical of many passages in the text:

> If ['The Wreck of the Deutschland's'] 'genotext' is a problematic oxymoronic statement ('death is life and life is death'), the genotextual oxymoron active on the paradigmatic axis will necessitate and involve, on the syntagmatic axis, an amplification and confirmation in metaphor, so that a modelling of the 'phonotext' could be the following alogorithm:
> $D = n\,(0\ .\ M)$ or $D = (0.\ M)^{n}$'

The second section of the volume, devoted to medievalism, is more engaging. Through close readings of the poetry supported by reference to Hopkins's prose, Marucci explores the thesis that the conventional debate within Hopkins studies, as to whether Hopkins's poetics is best considered in relation to Victorian or modern poetry, is misconceived. Marucci points to theological, philosophical and aesthetic patterns in the poetry which can be usefully compared to those current within medieval culture.

A more accessible contribution to the understanding of Hopkins's relationship with his culture is Gerald Roberts's succinct study *Gerard Manley Hopkins: A Literary Life*. The Macmillan Literary Lives series, edited by Richard Dutton, within which this publication appears has done a great deal to rehabilitate the genre of the literary biography and demonstrate its usefulness to literary criticism in the era of theoretical reconstruction. Roberts's contribution to the series is typical in that, whilst quite making clear that biographical knowledge is not an indispensable key to or ultimate destination of criticism, 'to set and evaluate Hopkins' poetry within the context of his own life, particularly that part of it which was spent as a Jesuit, when his major work was written' can illuminate reading greatly. Whilst locating his conversion to Jesuism as also the most important moment of 'conversion' within the form and style of his poetry, Roberts also gives due regard to the earlier impact of Tennyson, Keats and Coleridge on the younger poet's 'ear for sound'. He offers interesting origins for the metaphor of 'inscape' – noting that Hopkins may have developed Pater's dictum that 'failure is to form habits' into the awareness that 'a fleeting experience impresses itself on the consciousness with a new intensity and freshness'. The centre of the study, both conceptually and physically, is Hopkins's entry into the Society of Jesus at the age of 24 and the nine-year hiatus this induced in his writing career. Roberts argues that Hopkins's realization of his religious vocation, although temporarily interrupting his output, turned him from a minor poet into a major one because Jesuism intensified the internal conflict central to his poetry, between his great attraction to beauty on the one hand and his call to subordinate it to moral and spiritual values on the other. Roberts sees the sonnet as the form which correlated with this conflict most fully for Hopkins – imposing, like his religious commitment, a discipline upon an unstable emotional temperament. This literary biography amounts in the end (like so much Hopkins criticism authored by the members or the friends of the Society of Jesus) to an apology for Jesuism. But it is none the worse for this, maintaining as it does throughout a clear-sighted view of the impact of the agony and energy of Hopkins's religious life on the development of his poetics.

Two valuable additions to *fin de siècle* scholarship appeared this year. Catherine Reilly's annotated bibliography *Late Victorian Poetry, 1880–1899* is the first instalment of a three-volume series which will provide a comprehensive bibliography of Victorian poetry. A considerable indication of the benefits to scholars of this ambitious project is given from this publication, which lists alphabetically almost 3,000 British poets. Reilly has dug deep not only into existing bibliographies and the holdings in British copyright libraries but also into the major British civic libraries, which were endowed with volumes in the late nineteenth century that would have been passed over as not of sufficient intellectual weight by the academic institutions, and the valuable collection, 'Minor British Poets 1789–1918', at the University of California. Brief biographical notes, where available, and a list of each writer's publications follow. The bibliography demonstrates the class-diversity of the full-time occupations followed by poets in the period, indicating the impact of mass education from the mid-nineteenth century. A little less than a third of those listed are directly identifiable as women, and Reilly acknowledges that there may be many more who are concealed by publication under initial rather than forename.

The diverse and useful series of facsimile reprints from the Woodstock Press, Decadents, Symbolists, Anti-Decadents: Poetry of the 1890s, edited by R. K. R. Thornton and Ian Small, saw its second instalment this year. Volumes appearing this year include Ernest Dowson's *Verses* (1896) bound with his *Decorations* (1899); *Silverpoints* (1893) together with *Spiritual Poems* (1896) by John Gray; Thomas Hardy's *Wessex Poems* (1898); A. E. Housman's *A Shropshire Lad* (1896); the 1892 and 1894 editions of *The Book of the Rhymers' Club*, bound together; and Theodore Wratislaw's two collections *Caprices* (1893) and *Orchids* (1896) in one volume. This year's crop of texts demonstrates the meritorious aim of the series: to present the work of poets who have fallen out of the canon alongside that which has survived into the late twentieth century, thus allowing both for a revaluation of the period as a whole through the discovery of forgotten voices and for a fresh perspective on work which has long been subject to intense scrutiny. Victorian scholars will be looking forward to the completion of the series in 1996 when, except in respect of its inexplicable neglect of the work of women poets of the period – a problem which stands out particularly sharply in the year which sees the publication of Reilly's anthology – it will prove to be a valuable resource for scholars and students of the *fin de siècle*.

Another facsimile reprint list from the Woodstock Press, Revolution and Romanticism 1789–1834, under the editorial control of Jonathan Wordsworth, demonstrates a more adventurous enthusiasm for exploring the significance of the work of women after 1830 in its publication this year of two interesting volumes. Caroline Norton's *A Voice From the Factories* (1836) is a polemic protest against the conditions of industrial child labour. It is one of several poems by women in the 1830s and 1840s to respond directly to the reports of the parliamentary commissions of 1834, and its reprint provides a useful resource in the reconstruction of a tradition of nineteenth-century female political poetry. *Phantasmion* (1837), the prose-poem fantasy by Sara Coleridge, provides an important new perspective on a staple of late twentieth-century feminist criticism, the effect on nineteenth-century female writers of their relationships with male Romantics. Whereas most critics, even feminists like Virginia Woolf, have viewed Sara Coleridge in terms of her relationship with her father Samuel Taylor Coleridge, and concentrated on her effort to edit and promote his work, Wordsworth chooses to take her seriously as an independent artist and reprints her extended creative work. Scholars will wish to explore the relationship of the fantasy world depicted in *Phantasmion* with the Angria and Gondal sagas produced contemporaneously with it.

Finally, this and last year have been particularly rich in new selected editions of the poetry of Thomas Hardy. Three new volumes, representing three different approaches in conception of the poet, editorial practice and copytexts, provide new opportunities to reconsider many aspects of his work. First is Tim Armstrong's edition, *Thomas Hardy: Selected Poems*, which appeared last year in the Longman Annotated Texts series, and provides both the largest selection of texts and the most extensive notes and editorial apparatus. Deciding on an editorial practice with Hardy's poems is a complex matter, as Hardy himself made extensive and continual (if, to the eyes of most critics, artistically minor) revisions to his poems right up until his death. Armstrong takes as his copytext the 1930 *Collected Poems*, which consolidated most of the revisions that had been made to successive editions of the poems from the time of their first publication. Armstrong's introduction is also the most extensive of the three and the most intellectually challenging. The Hardy who emerges from this account is as much an intellectual in a state of strenuous and mostly painful dialogue with some of the most pressing social, religious and cultural issues of his period as an artist engaged in bold experimentation with the structure of poetic language. Whilst avoiding the flabby sentimentality which often creeps into criticism of the writing of Hardy's declining years, Armstrong does give a full and creative account of the significance of the personal griefs and changes in Hardy's life for the poetry, including an interesting discussion (via Freud) of death, ageing and melancholia. Armstrong includes a wide range of different kinds of poem, including the 'core' texts about which there is critical consensus of their centrality, but also a selection of aspects of Hardy's work which is sometimes under-represented in anthologies: elegiac and narrative verse; ballads; classical experiments; dialogues; epitaphs; and translations. He preserves the structure and chronology of Hardy's first editions, rather than arranging the texts thematically or generically, believing that it is essential to represent changes and developments in style (comparatively minor as they are) across time. I am perhaps not alone in finding the format of the Longman series, which prints the notes about the context and provenance of the poem and textual annotations on the page with the poem (rather than in a separate section at the back of the volume), slightly coercive and distracting. The reader has to work hard to preserve the integrity of her or his own reading over the insistence of the scholarship of the editor. But of the three new editions, this is the most challenging and stimulating, opening up new perspectives on the poet.

The second volume, *Selected Poems* edited by Andrew Motion, under the Everyman imprint, follows almost the same tradition of copytext, taking its texts from James Gibson's 1976 edition *Thomas Hardy: The Complete Poems*, which was compiled from the 1930 and 1928 editions. Motion also honours the integrity of Hardy's chronology, organizing his edition as a succession of selections from each of the first editions. A brief introduction sketches out some of the most important cultural issues with which Hardy was in dialogue, and also considers something of the 'critical bafflement' which has dogged the reading of the poetry throughout the twentieth century. Motion argues that this is partly due to the unusually interrogative nature of the poems, the fact that they often appear to appropriate 'to themselves the job which is normally undertaken by a critic . . . they often depend on arguments and interior dialogues which make the purpose of a poem not just to re-create something but to elucidate it'.

Taking a different approach to the production of copytext is the third volume, *Thomas Hardy: A Selection of his Finest Poems* edited by Samuel Hynes in the Oxford Poetry Library series. The edition is abridged from Hynes's own five volumes of *The Complete Poetical Works of Thomas Hardy* (1982–95), also published by Oxford University Press. Hynes takes his copytexts from the first editions and then records the subsequent revisions in his notes. His introduction fully acknowledges the impact of the scientific and social changes of his period, indeed going as far as to claim that '[m]ore than any other writer of his generation, Hardy grasped what the ideas of the great Victorian scientists implied for the human imagination: that Lyell, Darwin, and Huxley had stretched Time and Space, and by so doing had diminished Man, and made God an unnecessary hypothesis'. Yet Hynes's claim for the importance of Hardy rests on the poems' explorations and understanding of 'private' rather than 'public' dilemmas. His genius is 'expressed most purely in his short lyrics – poems written, as it seems, for himself alone to give a private order to his feelings, so that he might live with them'. Hynes's useful edition, like its fellows (all of which are accessible in paperback), will give critics a fresh opportunity to consider the relationship between social crisis and individual pain explored in the fascinating poetry of this late Victorian.

4. Victorian Drama and Theatre

Last year's and this year's work has been dominated by critical re-evaluations of the life and dramatic *oeuvre* of Oscar Wilde. Certainly this has been the case in the year under review, and it would be appropriate, therefore, to begin with the issue of *NCT* 21[1993] which appeared too late to be included in *YWES* 74. Joseph Donohue's overview, 'Oscar Wilde Refashioned: A Review of Recent Scholarship' (117–32), begins with Norbert Kohl's *Oscar Wilde: The Works of a Conformist Rebel*, originally published in German in 1980 and translated into English in 1989, and ends with Joel H. Kaplan and Sheila Stowell's *Theatre and Fashion: Oscar Wilde to the Suffragettes* (published this year and reviewed below). Donohue points out that although scholars have tried to demythologize Wilde in recent years, the shadow of Richard Ellmann's definitive biography of 1988 with its insistence on the tragic ethos of Wilde's life continues to influence their thinking. He feels that Ian Small in *Oscar Wilde Revalued* perhaps most usefully captures the latest developments in Wilde interpretation by the simple expedient of providing a detailed bibliography of primary and secondary materials, together with samplings and a commentary which deconstructs Wilde, his assiduously self-cultivated myth and the reality of a hard-working writer within his late nineteenth-century context. Much of the material surveyed by Donohue relates to aspects of Wilde that only touch upon his persona as a dramatic writer. Kerry Powell, whose *Oscar Wilde and the Theatre of the 1890s* (CUP, 1990) Donohue regards as one of the most useful contemporary books on Wilde within his theatrical context, contributes an interesting gloss on the relationship between Wilde and Elizabeth Robins in the same issue of *NCT*, '"Oscar Wilde: An Appreciation": An Unpublished Memoir by Elizabeth Robins', 101–13). Elizabeth Robins began writing it probably about 1950. The memoir is unfinished and breaks off in the middle of a sentence as, sixty years after the events, Robins was unable to come to an understanding of Wilde's 'personal tragedy' (112). Powell comments on the complexity of the relationship between Wilde and Robins as she tried unsuccessfully to marshal his support for her ideal Theatre of the Future. The memoir amplifies and extends the relationship depicted in Robins's autobiography, *Both Sides of the Curtain*, although there is little new in the memoir itself. Perhaps Robins felt that she needed to make a public acknowledgment of her debt to Wilde at a time when she was a struggling actress in the 1880s. This article should be viewed in conjunction with Powell's fuller contextualization, which appeared this year and to which reference is made below. George Rowell corrects some misunderstandings about Wilde's first play, *Vera* ('The Truth about *Vera*', 94–100). He points out there is little to support the contentions that the play was in rehearsal in 1881, or that Dion Boucicault had agreed to produce it, or that it was withdrawn due to the play's nihilist message at a time when there was public dismay at the assassination of Tsar Alexander II. Rowell's explanation of why the play never achieved its London première is persuasively mundane: Wilde was in no financial position to underwrite even a matinée of the play and Boucicault, however willing, had commitments which took him to Dublin and New York at the time when such a matinée might have been possible.

The special issue of *MD* (37.i) explores and crystallizes aspects of the debates surrounding Wilde's plays, and contributes to the way 'in which Oscar Wilde, at our century's close, has re-entered the popular imagination, as artist, commodity, and cautionary figure'. The issue begins with Russell Jackson and Ian Small's plea ('Oscar Wilde: A "Writerly Life"', 3–11) to disengage Wilde from the essentially Victorian and modernist determination to see his life and his writings as an interwoven detective novel, in which each clue is ultimately seen to contribute to an eventual unmasking, at which the biographer-as-detective or the text-editor-as-detective triumphantly demonstrates the working out of a personal or social tragedy or the creation of a definitive and authentic play-text. Rather, Jackson and Small suggest Wilde's life and his attitude towards his plays (as demonstrated in the numerous revisions and emendations to them) may be perceived as a series of conscious masks, which he assumed sometimes with bewildering speed and apparent inconsistency. As in life Wilde was prepared to fashion a series of social and personal masks as a self-conscious artifice, so in his plays he would refashion his texts in response to managerial demands and his own perceptions of what worked best on stage. It is a persuasive postmodern interpretation, which at the same time is immensely liberating. Lawrence Danson's 'Wilde in Arden, or the Masks of Truth' (12–31) discusses Wilde's inconsistent attitudes towards realism and truth. The vacillation can be found in Wilde's essays about Shakespeare and his acceptance as well as rejection of the principles of scenic decoration championed by E. W. Godwin. The focus of the essay is the production of *As You Like It* at Coombe Park in 1885 by Godwin, and especially the performance of Orlando by Lady Archibald Campbell. This, together with Wilde's allusions in his notice in the *Dramatic Review* to Gautier's *Mademoiselle de Maupin* in which a production of the play occurs, prefigures a fascination with androgyny and gender transgression that Danson suggests can be found in the later social comedies. Alan Sinfield ('"Effeminacy" and "Femininity": Sexual Politics in Wilde's Comedies', 34–52) offers a timely caution against inscribing modern values on late nineteenth-century audiences, particularly those relating to concepts of effeminate men and feminine women. He reminds us that 'the feminine woman, as Wilde represents her, together with the effeminate man, effects a disturbance of categories that reaches beyond the oppressive terms in which both are framed': and urges us to consider Wilde before the 1895 trial rendered him the 'most notorious homosexual of modern times'. Joseph Bristow revisits the subversive handling of character types by Wilde in the society comedies ('Dowdies and Dandies: Oscar Wilde's Re-fashioning of Society Comedy', 53–70). Inevitably this involves the structural changes of *Lady Windermere's Fan* and the contradictory signals which the characters send to audiences (Bristow takes their costuming into account), but ultimately he finds the plays structurally outdated and repetitious. Wilde's value-system does not transcend the models which he aims to subvert. The criteria which Bristow uses, however ('unity of purpose' and 'consistency'), seem curiously literary and perhaps themselves no longer appropriate.

Two of the essays specifically focus on *Salome*. From differing perspectives they see the play as an epitome of Wilde himself responding to his own evaluation of drama as the most objective of the arts. Austin Quigley ('Realism and Symbolism in Oscar Wilde's Salome', 104–10) uses this to launch a discussion about the role which realism plays in a work labelled as the most original symbolist play to have emerged out of the *fin de siècle* British theatre. Symbolist theatre offered audiences a different mode of perception, and the fascination with these differing modes in *Salome* serves not only to clarify character and develop the narrative, but also to relate the techniques of symbolism to and distinguish them from those that characterize the preceding and succeeding movements of naturalism and expressionism. Joseph Donohue discusses the play within the context of Wilde's sources and addresses the complaints about his alleged derivativeness ('Salome and the Wildean Art of Symbolist Theatre', 91–103). In so doing Donohue shows the affinities between contemporary continental *avant garde* theatre practice and its attractiveness for Wilde, but emphasizes that one should recognize 'for Wilde, treatment of a quasi-mythological subject is no different in its essentials from dealing with the highly conventionalized subjects of society comedy and farce'. Thus one may expect the same inherent paradoxes which characterize his other plays. The play 'emerges as an elaborate, extended epigram, a paradox in the sphere of thought transformed into perversity in the sphere of passion'. Perversity and passion, claims Donohue, are the terms which 'confer ultimately a genuine rather than a spurious originality upon his work (as upon his life)' and which undermine the arguments about derivativeness or artistic plagiarism.

Richard Dellamora discusses the separate ideals of virtue and duty held for women and men and Wilde's determination to subvert and change these ('Oscar Wilde, Social Purity, and *An Ideal Husband*', 120–38). Paradoxically, the erosion of the double standards so inextricably tied to Victorian domestic values, he suggests, threatened Wilde's own semi-protected status as a man able to act without let or hindrance in his own society. The play forms a site where issues such as self-development and a concomitant need for a transformation of bourgeois society might be discussed. Dellamora brackets his theoretical discussion by reference to Mona Caird's important 1888 essay on marriage and Walter Lippmann's 1914 prophetic book *Drift and Mastery*, which 'identifies the tension between self-development and the demand for purity as a leading problematic within contemporary feminist politics'. Dramatically, Wilde's play is part of an ongoing discussion about sex and gender, and Dellamora suggests parallels between its philosophy and that embodied in Shaw's *The Quintessence of Ibsenism*. Wilde's strategies in the play are latent and subversive but prefigure the belief held by

Edwardian feminists that, through dramatic performance, a transformation of the audience could be achieved.

Peter Raby's essay on 'The Origins of *The Importance of being Earnest*' (139–47) considers the manoeuvres with actor-managers, particularly Alexander and Frohman, which Wilde undertook while thinking about the shape of the play, and suggests some of the elements which he included as he wrote – especially his use of names and places, which make his work so 'relentlessly self-referential'. Raby concludes that the play is a genuinely new experiment infused with a desperate gaiety which Wilde was hard-pressed at the time to find in his own life. This self-reference is further explored by Karl Beckson in his examination of the significant narcissistic mirror as object and medium for self-evaluation in all Wilde's work ('Narcissistic Reflections in a Wilde Mirror', 148–55).

John Stokes's and Richard Allen Cave's essays are concerned with Wilde in the theatre. Both essays suggest the centrality of design as providing keys to his interpretation. Wilde was a considerable influence upon Charles Ricketts's creative imagination, and Cave uses this as a lead into the discussion of the role of design in some recent British productions ('Wilde Designs: Some Thoughts about Recent British Productions of his Plays', 175–91). Stokes, on the other hand, works backwards. Using Jonathan Miller's comment in *Subsequent Performances* that 'the bequests of the past arouse our interpretative energies as never before', Stokes investigates a number of recent British productions to determine whether they indeed identify current trends and new meanings within the texts themselves. ('Wilde Interpretations', 156–74). He also sets out to see whether this consideration of Wilde in the 1990s might illuminate elements of the theatre of the 1890s. Stokes draws attention to the lavish sets used in the West End productions which he surveys, and the ways in which they mediate between action and audience and emphasize the ambiguities which are today regarded as intrinsic to Wildean interpretation. Perhaps the most interesting part of the essay, however, is his account of the performances and place of Lady Bracknell, from Rose Leclercq's original performance in 1895 to Maggie Smith's in 1993, which suggested some new directions in the depiction of female behaviour on stage.

J. L. Wisenthal draws a connection between Wilde and Shaw in their commitment to the free play of the mind upon all subjects ('Wilde, Shaw, and the Play of Conversation', 206–19) and the way in which both express this commitment in their theoretical and theatrical writings. Examining and comparing Wilde's and Shaw's plays he concludes that 'it was Shaw who fulfilled the promise in Wilde's work, of a dramatic form that embodies the value of play and of mind' (217). Kerry Powell's contribution expands that which appeared in *NCT* 21 (see above) and explores in greater detail the relationship between Wilde and Elizabeth Robins already suggested in the earlier article. Robins's inauguration of a feminist critique of Victorian theatre and Wilde's relationship to it 'became the crux of his friendship with Elizabeth Robins in the 1890s' ('Oscar Wilde, Elizabeth Robins, and the Theatre of the Future', 220–37). In the course of this account we read about Robins's vision of a new theatre run by empowered women, and the feeling of intense disappointment which accompanied her realization that Wilde, while prepared in principle to support her, ultimately threw in his lot with an entrenched and dismissive enemy.

Joel Kaplan, who was the editor of this special issue, has shown elsewhere how Wilde accommodated the demands of his actor-managers and the extent to which playwrights remained disadvantaged despite their marketability. He contributes a further note on Wilde's financial arrangements in 'Oscar Wilde's Contract for *A Woman of No Importance*' (*TN* 48.i.46–8), on a contract in which Wilde agreed to financial terms dictated by Tree in 1892. Donohue concluded his survey of recent Wilde scholarship (see above) by referring to Joel H. Kaplan and Sheila Stowell's *Theatre and Fashion: Oscar Wilde to the Suffragettes*, an account of the complex interplay between the fashion and stage industries and how this affected both the production and reception of theatre texts from *Lady Windermere's Fan* to 1914. Kaplan and Stowell suggest the strategies by which some playwrights and performers used clothes and the characters who wore them to argue a subversive and condemnatory case, especially in the last years of the Victorian period and in the context of the Edwardian preoccupation with the processes and products of *haute couture*. Wilde was able to use the elaborate dress codes of society to reinforce his moral and social paradoxes, and to destabilize dramatic types and the audience's moral expectations, in such plays as *Lady Windermere's Fan* and *A Woman of No Importance*. Perhaps the most elaborate critique of society appears in Henry Arthur Jones's *The Liars*, where the women's costumes (by Lucile) presented the audience with 'troubling uniforms, intended to catch the attention and consciences of the Criterion's more affluent spectators'. 'Dressing Mrs Pat' charts the contradictions which Mrs Patrick Campbell embodied in *The Second Mrs Tanqueray, The Notorious Mrs Ebbsmith* and *Pygmalion,* the last itself a Shavian attack on the theatrical fashioning of Mrs Pat on stage. There exist, suggest the authors, inherent contradictions between the glitter of society and its drama and the problem play and its issues. These were addressed by the plays of Ibsen, in which he physically removed the theatrical milieu to one which was uncompromisingly middle-class. The chapter title 'The Ghost in the Looking Glass' is taken from the caption of a *Punch* cartoon of 1863 showing the exhausted seamstress reflected in the mirror before which a society lady is being fitted for her dress. In this chapter *haute couture* is seen from the perspective of those whose sweated labour brought it about. Inevitably the discussion is tied in with the efforts of those writers who were active in the suffrage movement. Particular attention is paid to Edith Lyttleton's *Warp and Woof* (1904) – in which Mrs Pat played Theodosia Hemming: Lyttleton attempted in the play to reach those who benefited from exploitation by casting a performer identified with society plays – and to Cicely Hamilton's *Diana of Dobson's*, which confronted audiences with images of industrial oppression. Granville Barker's *The Madras House* is referred to as a site for debate about the economic and social implications of the Edwardian fashion world. At the same time theatrical techniques were being appropriated by fashion houses and department stores like Harrod's and Selfridge's, and the stage was used to flaunt the latest fashions – mannequins in *Our Miss Gibbs,* for example, were dressed by Harrods. In their chapter on 'The Suffrage Response', the authors point to a nice twist of irony when suffragists responded to popular stereotypes of the New Woman by dressing fashionably and making this into a political act. Their organized buying power enabled suffrage feminists to influence the look of goods sold, and this was taken very seriously by magnates such as Selfridge, resulting in a curious alliance between suffrage supporters and fashion retailers. The cumulative effect of this volume is a fascinating re-visioning of the role and function of theatre costume and its relationship to issues of industry, as well to the shifting *fin de siècle* perceptions of gender and sexuality.

Tracy Davis's *George Bernard Shaw and the Socialist Theatre* is intended to place Shaw's practice as a playwright within the contexts of political theory at the end of the nineteenth century and *realpolitik* in the twentieth. It traces attempts to identify an audience for a socialist theatre, and the study is illuminated by the feminist and post-colonial critiques of recent literary history. As well, the inherent paradoxes and contradictions in Shaw's make-up and in his pronouncements make him, like Oscar Wilde, an ideal postmodern object of attention. Davis makes it clear that she is not aiming at a biography. The book, in fact, is aimed at students wishing to make their way through the labyrinth of Shavian scholarship and to come to terms with the various strategies Shaw employed to exert his influence in both the social and political spheres. The first three chapters of Davis's book cover the Victorian period. They document Shaw's attraction to playwriting as a mode of political expression from the early works to the publication of *Plays Pleasant and Unpleasant* (1898) and from then to the production of *Pygmalion* (1914). Though Davis disclaims any attempt at biography, the first three chapters do trace Shaw from the days before he began playwriting, through his apprenticeship to his theatrical heyday. Until 1884 Shaw considered himself a novelist. Between 1884 and 1892, he absorbed the influences which would shape his development as a playwright, in which he was guided principally by Ibsen and William Archer. Although first introduced to the possibilities within Ibsen's dramaturgy for intervening in the leisure industry in 1885 by Eleanor Marx Aveling, it was not until 1888 that Shaw became an active Ibsen apostle. Davis subsequently considers *Widower's Houses, The Philanderer* and *Mrs Warren's Profession*, with their rejection of conventional femininity, and their documentation of social realities. Davis particularly approves of Shaw's depiction of the social dimension of sexual prostitution in the last play and the way in which he relates this to the lack of economic choices for women in the period. As she points out, Shaw's anti-moral stance was at this time revolutionary. However, as Shaw moves into his 'pleasant' phase, Davis becomes more critical of his adoption of melodramatic models in favour of overt propaganda. In a sense Shaw becomes tarred by the same brush which Elizabeth Robins used on Wilde – the failure to look to the future and the courting of the highest actor-managers of the period. Davis recognizes that 'influencing public policy by reaching the influential suited the Fabian preference for gradualist and strategic reform'.

The complete Shaw is for Davis a disappointment. The Fabian connection with the Stage Society, and subsequently the Royal Court seasons from 1904 to 1907, demonstrate for her an uncomfortable willingness on the part of Shaw to address 'the elite mandarin segments of the intellectually inclined middle classes' and a failure to threaten their vested interests and aesthetic preferences. Shaw's marriage to Charlotte Payne Townshend in 1898 and the increasing royalties derived from his plays after this period allowed him to make generous gestures. Though he challenged family values, political theatre and particularly feminist theatre was directly involved in the issues of suffrage and the economic deprivations of women, issues in which Shaw took little part. His withdrawal from political involvement in the period to 1914 placed him at a distance from the socialist drama, while the debate about women was confined by him to the private realm of sex and reproduction rather than to the public realm of the struggle for the franchise. Davis's disappointment with Shaw culminates with his 'surrender' to the establishment by agreeing to the production of *Pygmalion* by Beerbohm Tree in 1914 and the publication of his tract *Common Sense about the War*, in which Shaw's inveterate love of irony and irreverence again got in the way of his social and political effectiveness. The book then moves out of the Victorian context to Shaw's responses to and in the twentieth century. Davis covers the late Victorian period impressively and is particularly at home in her analysis of Shaw within the Edwardian and post-Edwardian periods.

One of the virtues of Tracy Davis's recent work relating the practices of Victorian theatre to the economic conditions of the time has been to compel scholars working in the fields of British economic and social history to take serious cognizance of the theatre's role in the debates about class, economic status and gender. Just as important has been her advocacy of the significance of social and economic history to the theatre historian. Her article 'Laborers of the Nineteenth-Century Theater: The Economics of Gender and Industrial Organization' (*Journal of British History* 33.32–53) takes her into the heartland of the North American Conference on British Studies. As we have grown to expect, it offers a piece of meticulous research in which the theatre serves as a focus for the examination of a whole 'gamut of nineteenth-century manufacturing occupations including textiles, metallurgy, leather, chemicals, paper, engineering, building, and service trades'. She illustrates the growth in unionization, the effect of the shift from the stock company's rapidly changing repertoire to the long-running single show on employment opportunities, and the move from workers employed by theatre companies to the growth of specialized contractors upon whom theatres increasingly relied, transforming theatre in the Victorian period from 'a system of medium-sized workshops full of craftspersons to a classic model of the factory system'. The article is an excellent piece of labour history.

Performers on the Victorian stage have been well represented in this year's work. Joyce Green MacDonald in her article 'Acting Black: Othello, Othello Burlesques, and the Performance of Blackness' (*TJ* 46.ii.231–49) takes as her starting points the appearance of Ira Aldridge on the English stage as Othello in 1833, the first performance of the role by a black actor, the performances of Kean in the role, and the burlesque of *Othello* by Maurice Dowling performed in Liverpool in 1834, and examines what it meant 'to perform race during Aldridge's theatrical career' and 'white responses to the self-authorization of blackness'. She also examines Aldridge's performance as Mungo in Bickerstaffe's *The Padlock*, which he performed regularly throughout Britain and the Continent. The travesty version of *Othello,* in which all ends happily, MacDonald suggests, 'works to perform a kind of communal forgetting of just how closely the Shakespearean spectacle approached the sexual and racial fears of white audiences'. While we undoubtedly find the smugness of Victorian attitudes towards supposed black inferiority to be offensive, the inscription of a deep-seated audience resistance to black performance in the Victorian period still needs further investigation. The other two articles of note and one major book concern themselves with significant female performers on the Victorian stage.

Shaw tried his damnedest to seduce Ellen Terry away from Irving. What is perhaps less well known is that he tried the same strategy with Ada Rehan by systematically destroying, between 1885 and 1899, the credibility and status of the Shakespeare seasons of Augustin Daly, whose relationship to Rehan was closer and much more obvious than that of Terry to Irving. Russell Jackson examines Shaw's strategy in 'Shaw's Reviews of Daly's Shakespeare: The Wooing of Ada Rehan' (*TRI* 19.203–13). In this case Shaw's plan went completely awry, through his callous handling of matters immediately after Daly's death and his total disregard for Rehan's feelings. More illuminating than any account of Shaw's ineptitude with women, however, is Jackson's description of the extensive venality practised by the two theatre critics Clement Scott and William Winter, who at one stage were both directly employed by Daly as part of his marketing department.

Over the years David Rinear has helped scholars understand the careers of some significant performers, notably William Farren and Alfred Wigan. His article '"To submit and patiently to wait": The Career of Mrs Stirling' (*TLS* 35.ii.57–71) helps to make understandable the career of Mrs Fanny Stirling, whose career spanned the period 1829–86 and who was one of the most respected and admired performers on the Victorian stage. What makes her interesting to us, and, equally, frustrating to the critics of her day, was her refusal to be categorized, by assuming a wide range of characters and not allowing herself to be straitjacketed by traditional 'lines of business'. The failure of her marriage to Edward Stirling after 1832 and the consequent need to be self-reliant, assertive and versatile, suggests Rinear, shaped her acting style. She developed her abilities to encompass both the pathetic and comic roles of the repertoire, which placed her apart from performers who decided to perfect their abilities within a relatively narrow range. Rinear sets Mrs Stirling's apogee in her time with the Olympic company between 1848 and 1853. During this period she became identified with a sequence of strong-willed women who were 'more than a match for the men in her life', which culminated in her performance as Peg Woffington in Reade and Taylor's *Masks and Faces*. Although she was never identified as a star in her lifetime, her influence upon notable performers like Ellen Terry and Alice Wright was indelible. She was 'the first early modern actress to be lauded for both her credible psychological approach to acting and her vocal skills'.

Claire Tomalin's *Mrs Jordan's Profession: The Story of a Great Actress and a Future King* once more scrutinizes the enigma of Dorothy Jordan. Despite the book's title and the stature of its author, however, this is not a story about a great actress juggling her professional commitments with her domestic responsibilities, but a rather dreary account of 'an unmarried working mother' who from the age of 14 was committed to looking after a large family – her mother's in the first instance and then her own. The book chronicles Dorothy Jordan's tormented relations with the royal family and her succumbing to the 'irresistible glamour in being loved and courted by a real prince of the blood'. To be sure, Tomalin tries to do justice to Jordan's story and to redress the unsympathetic narrative about her which appears in the recent edition by A. Aspinall of her letters. Tomalin finds his omission of material relating to Jordan's daily life at Bushy, as well as that of the evidence of Jordan's conscientious care for her children by the Duke of Clarence, objectionable. In this regard Tomalin makes good use of the hitherto unused letters between Jordan and the Duke of Clarence at the Huntington Library. Just as useful and interesting is Tomalin's inclusion of illustrations, many of them little known paintings and caricatures, which show the differing perceptions of Jordan and her relationships in the period. In redistributing the light and shade, Tomalin has domesticated Dorothy Jordan and sentimentalized her to the point where it becomes hard to reconcile her coruscating comedic brilliance away from Bushy with her infatuation for a man whose absence from her seems to have been his salient characteristic.

Provincial performers are also noted in *Scenes from Provincial Stages: Essays in Honour of Kathleen Barker*, edited by Richard Foulkes.This volume is a timely celebration of the life of Kathleen Barker, and a reminder of the huge debt which theatre historians of the British nineteenth-century theatre owe to her pioneering work. The essays which comprise this volume touch upon personalities, companies and issues of the provincial stages from the eighteenth century virtually to the present. Shirley Brown's essay, for instance, picks up the history of Bristol's Theatre Royal where Barker left it in 1966, and takes it to 1993. Much of the material, however, relates to the eighteenth century and the rise of provincial theatres. J. S. Bratton's essay, 'The Making of a Character', discusses the life and reputation of Sarah Baker, who managed the Kent theatre circuit at the end of the eighteenth century. Derek Forbes focuses on William Grossmith of Reading, who was the founder of a theatrical dynasty and whose circuit provided some of the earliest examples of illustrative playbills in their promotional material. Tracy Davis's '"Let Glasgow flourish!"' illustrates a particular Scottish example of the monopoly wars in her account of the opposition to the building of the City Theatre in 1845. Carol Carlisle and Josephine Harrop both examine examples of other theatrical dynasties, the former that of the Faucit Saville brothers (which gains a degree of piquancy from its inevitable inclusion of Helen Faucit, whose mother ran off with William Farren in 1821), and the latter that of the Holloways (whose longevity, mainly in North Wales and the Midlands, stretched from the 1830s to the 1930s). M. Glen Wilson, in 'Charles Kean at Bristol and Bath', provides an interesting background to the enmity between Macready and Kean. Macready's strong ties to Bristol ensured a critical hostility there to Kean from 1828 until 1862, while a mere seven miles away in Bath, Kean did well. The volume is an obvious labour of love and the editor has performed a signal service.

More exotic performers are discussed in two chapters of *Crossing the Stage: Controversies on Cross-Dressing*, edited by Lesley Ferris. Laurence Senelick's 'Boys and Girls Together' and Lynn Garafola's 'The Travesty Dancer in Nineteenth-Century Ballet' are concerned with the glamour drag artist and the male impersonator on stage (and off) in the former, and the female dancer of male roles in the latter. Senelick links the presence of drag artists to performances of plays at single-sex male schools, the use of feminine disguise by male performers in the circus, and the performance of wench roles in minstrel shows in the Victorian period. These elements helped condition the public to accept a new genre in which men frankly portrayed lovely women. But he also maintains that there co-existed a 'thriving transvestite demi-monde impinging on the norms of popular entertainment'. Senelick refers to the notorious Boulton and Park case of 1871 and contrasts the prosecution in the street of deviant behaviour with the acclaim accorded it on stage. He describes the popularity, especially in North America, of male impersonators and concludes that 'male impersonation responded to woman's longing for the freedom and license available to young men. Female impersonation responded to man's longing for woman's colorful trappings and the strategy of vulnerability. Vicariously they could experience the potential offered by changing sex.' Garafola's article really focuses on the ballet dancers of the Paris Opera, although there is a passing reference to the English stage through the influential visits of Taglioni and Fanny Elssler. The article shows the decline of the male dancer in France during the nineteenth century and his replacement often by a *danseuse en travesti.* Garafola relates this to the decline of the courtly male dancer, who was reduced 'to comic character and occasional "lifter"', which, in turn, became validated by contemporary attitudes towards concepts of masculinity. Garafola take pains to show how ballet dancers in particular were the objects both of an aggressive male gaze and, at least in Paris, of unashamed male sexual trading. Almost no research has been done on the ballet in England during the Victorian period, and Garafola's article suggests that this needs to be addressed.

Playwrights too are well represented, and a mark of the seriousness with which Victorian dramatists are now treated is the inclusion of those not usually considered as part of the canon in the playwrights volume of the *International Dictionary of Theatre*, edited by Mark Hawkins-Daly. The dictionary covers 485 writers. Among these, the Victorian period is represented by Dion Boucicault, Edward Bulwer-Lytton, H. J. Byron, Gilbert, Jerrold, Henry Arthur Jones, Arthur Wing Pinero, James Robinson Planché, Charles Reade, Tom Robertson, Shaw, Wilde and Tom Taylor. Disappointingly, the notable exceptions are William Thomas Moncrieff and Edward Fitzball, but this is understandable given the immense scope of the undertaking. As well, the book includes American nineteenth-century authors such as Augustin Daly, Anna Cora Mowatt and Langdon Mitchell, and the Irish playwright and co-founder of the Irish Literary Theatre, Edward Martyn. The editorial principles which have determined the editor's selection appear to have been governed by the 'rediscovery' of the playwrights as important in recent criticism or by an evaluation of intrinsic historical importance. From this perspective the omissions are understandable as well, since Moncrieff and Fitzball have yet to be given their proper place within the corpus of Victorian drama. The entries themselves are something of a mixed bag. On the one hand there are some excellent accounts which stimulate the reader to want to know more about the playwrights in question – Jim Davis's entries on H. J. Byron and Gilbert, Martin Banham's on Taylor and Pinero, Katherine Worth's on Wilde, Richard Foulkes's on Bulwer-Lytton and Donald Roy's on Planché are instances. There are those, however, which either misrepresent the playwrights or actively discourage further investigation – Howard McNaughton's entry on Boucicault claims his sole innovation as that of an adaptor of the novels of Dickens, Reade and Wilkie Collins, and completely ignores the long tradition of dramatic 'intervention' which forms part of the history of Victorian theatre practice. Valerie Grosvenor Myer does little to justify Reade's inclusion in the dictionary when she characterizes his writing as possessing little more than the 'sentimental clichés of melodrama', with 'little real action and no character development'. John D. Hurrell's entry on Robertson mentions nothing of his debt to the Bancroft management, thereby refusing to acknowledge the work practices of Victorian playwrights. On the other hand, Margery Morgan's entry on Shaw, which perforce extends into the modern period, gives a very useful account of Shaw's indebtedness to his Victorian models.

The reference to Tom Taylor in the *Dictionary* is complemented by two essays which appeared in *TN* 48.iii, offering insights into his work practices with particular reference to two plays, *The Contested Election* (1859) and *Arkwright's Wife* (1873). Martin Banham discusses the question of plagiarism which dogged Taylor towards the end of his life. In this case, a Mr Davies of Warrington suggested that *The Contested Election* was an adaptation of his own play *Our Town*, and Banham concludes, on the plays' internal evidence and that of the close friendship which Taylor had with the actor Frederick Robson, to whom Davies had sent his play, that Davies may well have been right ('Tom Taylor and Mr Davies of Warrington', 164–9). Tim Fort's 'An Opening at Leeds in 1873: Tom Taylor's *Arkwright's Wife*' (157–64) is more concerned with the uncomfortable relationship between Taylor as director and the young Steele MacKaye, who was trying his hand as an actor performing the role of Peter Hayes in the play. The article brings to scholarly attention the more than forty letters between Taylor and MacKaye which exist in the Dartmouth College Library.

Similarly, T. W. Robertson continues to exercise critical minds, and the debate about the extent to which he was merely an inheritor of older theatrical traditions or the harbinger of naturalism is further explored in Patricia D. Denison's 'Victorian and Modern Drama: Social Convention and Theatrical Invention in T. W. Robertson's Plays' (*MD* 37.401–20). Robertson is a frustrating writer, because we want him to be a revolutionary playwright and there are indications of a fresh approach to both social issues and their theatrical realization in his plays. Critical frustration is further exacerbated by our own stances, especially as we come to reject the traditional teleological paradigm of theatre of the second half of the nineteenth century. Denison admits that there exists a tension between invention and convention in Robertson's plays, but usefully concentrates on the implications of his pictorialization for his thematic and structural concerns: 'Rather than asking whether or not specific elements have been used before, we need to clarify the precise functions they serve in particular plays and how Robertson relates their current use to the history of their former use as well as to contemporary theory and practice.' Although Denison refers to his other plays in passing, she focuses on *Caste* and particularly the tableaux at the end of the acts and the characterizations of the male characters in the play. Her thesis is that Robertson constantly subverts audience expectations about the action and the characters by providing unexpected twists, which 'thicken', in her word, the texture of the play. All of which, she suggests, helped to promote 'an active rather than an accepting scrutiny by the audience'. While we may cavil at Denison's own reduction of theatre before Robertson to one of mere spectacle and histrionic conventionality, and at her anachronistic use of the term 'naturalism' at this time, the idea that Robertson's contribution lay in his determination to expand the audience's perceptions, by forcing it to 'read' the stage picture anew, appears to me to be a valuable insight. Robertson's reputation tends to be filtered through the appreciations by the Bancrofts. Denison rightly urges a caveat that we should differentiate between Robertson's actual achievements and the ambitions of the Bancrofts as actor-managers.

David Mayer always has the ability to surprise, and his book *Playing out the Empire: 'Ben Hur' and other Toga Plays and Films. A Critical Anthology* is no exception. In fact what is surprising is that no one has previously compiled an anthology of plays about the most enduring binary melodramatic opposition of the twentieth century, that of the conflict between evangelical Christianity and the vicious luxury of post-Republican Rome. Roman history struck a responsive chord in the Victorians. Republican Rome embodied values with which many could identify – stoicism, frugality and intellectual rigour – while imperial Rome provided object lessons of profligate excess and the corruption of family and civic values. Within this trope of empire, the role of Christianity was complex and contradictory. To some the image of weak Christians opposing the might of Rome and claiming ultimate victory in defeat might appear as a parable of working-class struggle and opposition. To feminists, the heroines stood in opposition to imperialism and the constraints of patriarchal authority. Without question, new audiences were drawn to the theatre through the plays with which Mayer provides us. He points out that these plays were measurably different from the earlier paradigms provided by such plays as Joseph Addison's *Cato* and Sheridan Knowles's *Virginius*. The Roman world of the toga plays was that filtered through the imagination of such writers as Sienkiewicz, whose *Quo Vadis?* was published in 1896, while its realization on stage owed much to the scenic conventions established by the production of Tennyson's *The Cup* (1881). The volume includes an essay by Katherine Preston on the music of toga dramas.

Mayer provides the scripts of *Claudian,* the Wills and Herman variant on the story of the Wandering Jew condemned to eternal youth through his thoughtless acts of cruelty; *The Last Days of Pompeii,* the longest enduring of outdoor melodramatic pyrodramas; Barrett's own *The Sign of the Cross*, whose London season at the Lyric in 1896 attracted 70,000 per week; William Young's 1899 version of Lew Wallace's *Ben Hur*, which addressed American perceptions and issues; and an account of *The Charioteer*, which figured as part of a Coliseum entertainment in 1905. Finally Mayer provides us with the remnants of D. W. Griffiths's filmic adaptation of Maria Lovell's version of the German play by Friedrich Hahn, *Ingomar the Barbarian* (1908). All these plays have required considerable editorial intervention to bring their experience to life. The most difficult have obviously been *Claudian* and *The Sign of the Cross*. Neither of these were published, and Mayer's very successful versions have made extensive use of licensing copies, those in the Lord Chamberlain's collection, and, in the case of the latter, the novel which Barrett wrote on the basis of the play – arguably the first occurrence of a play providing the 'prequel' to a novel. Mayer's is a splendid achievement, and will be seen to be a milestone in our understanding of Victorian drama in its period and its enduring legacy to the twentieth-century cinema.

The title of Roxanna Stuart's book, *Stage Blood: Vampires of the 19th Century Stage*, is something of a misnomer. While the first part of the book concerns itself with various manifestations of the vampire on the Parisian, London and American stages, the second part is only tangentially and somewhat speciously connected to the nineteenth-century stage in that it concerns itself with the figure of Dracula, who remained unperformed as a stage character until Hamilton Deane's famous version of 1924. To be sure, there are suggestions that the trappings of Dracula may well have been influenced by the on-stage persona of Henry Irving in such performances as Macbeth and Mephistopheles, but Bram Stoker's vision of the vampire is very different from that realized on the nineteenth-century stage. The title is also a misnomer because, curiously, there is no evidence of stage blood at all. This raises an interesting question for theatre historians in that, despite the many instances of violent death on stage in Victorian drama, there appears to be little indication of the appearance of the most recognizable manifestation of such violence. The book is intended more for the interested general reader than for the scholar, and the author's enthusiasm for the subject makes her a persuasive advocate for taking the sub-genre of Gothic vampire dramas seriously. To assist the reader, she provides plot summaries of the relevant plays and excerpted scenes which help to make her discussion intelligible. Moreover, she aims to communicate some understanding about theatre practices in the period from 1820 to 1897, and to provide a psychological and social insight into popular taste. Although Stuart appears to contribute little new to the vast corpus of scholarly output on vampirism, the value of the book lies in its compilation of French and English sources, and in its documentation of the evolution of the vampire as a figure on stage from Charles Nodier in 1820. There is much in the book which is not directly theatrical, although a literary contextualization is perfectly justifiable.

Stuart traces the origins of the characteristics of the vampire. She refers to models drawn from the Bible and from classical mythology, little of which appears in their stage versions. Inevitably the discussion draws heavily on Freudian interpretation, and the fascination with the vampire is linked inextricably to psychosexual drives and the fear of death and sexual violence. Stuart then traces the evolution of the vampire theme from Polidori's novella, the first treatment of the vampire in English fictional prose. She suggests that the immediate popularity of the work reflects a contemporary guilt, which inevitably accompanied the decline in religious feeling, and that vampirism became a Romantic metaphor for the predatory nature of human relationships generally. The connection with the stage really commences in chapter 3 with an account of the huge popularity as well as critical condemnation in the French theatre of Nodier's *Le Vampire* in 1820. Nodier's play was almost immediately adapted by Planché for the English stage as *The Vampire; or, the Bride of the Isles* at the Lyceum in August 1820. Planché took great exception to the vampire being portrayed as a Scottish character, but the vogue for Scott and Scotland as a Gothic site demanded that this element, present in the French original, remain. Having posited the psychosexual underpinning of the vampire story, Stuart is somewhat disappointed to discover its absence in Planché's version. She misses the erotic relationship between vampire and victim and is puzzled by the wholly English incongruity of the comic characters in the play. She is, moreover, completely wrong when she attributes the success of melodrama to its appeal to a subliterate audience deserted by the educated and middle classes. None the less, the success of this manifestation of melodrama was immediate, and Planché's play opened in New York in October of the same year. Continuing the historical account, chapter 5 discusses Moncrieff's *The Vampire* and Planché's burletta *Giovanni the Vampire* during the years 1821–3. It is in this period that Stuart suggests the vampire figure becomes reduced from the complex Romantic to merely another, more exotic stage villain. On the other hand, the German influence, especially the performance of Heinrich August Marschner's opera *Der Vampyr* (1828), introduced a more viscerally disturbing character.

The most influential version of the vampire story, Stuart feels, is that of Boucicault, who adapted Dumas's *Le Vampire* at the Princess's theatre in June 1852. The play appeared in a version called *Ruthven* at the Grecian Theatre, adapted by Augustus Harris (senior), and subsequently as *The Phantom* in Philadelphia in 1856 and then in New York in 1857. Stuart argues that the female characters in the play are the prototypes for Stoker's heroines and du Maurier's Trilby, and attributes to Boucicault as well the development of the theatrical accoutrements of the vampire's cloak and nocturnal existence. In the last chapter of the book's first part, 'Satire and Misogyny, 1872–1887', Stuart refers to the shift in interest from male to female sexual predator and its appropriation by symbolists and the pre-Raphaelites, but the chapter forms chiefly a coda which, in describing the burlesques of the vampire story (such as Reece's at the Strand in 1872 and, more significantly, *Ruddygor*e [sic] at the Savoy), parallels the increasing self-consciousness felt by Victorian audiences about melodrama generally. Stuart argues persuasively that Gilbert was deliberately parodying Boucicault's version of the story, but does not really explain why its performance was greeted so ambivalently. At least Gilbert's title suggests the awareness that stage blood forms an integral part of the vampire's make-up. The second part of Stuart's book concerns itself with stage and screen versions from 1897 to 1985 and 1992 respectively. Stuart notes that Stoker's *Dracula* may well have been originally intended to provide a vehicle for Irving. Certainly some kind of reading was given to a version for copyright purposes at the Lyceum in 1897. Irving did not care for it – hardly surprising since, by this stage in his career, it would have offended the seriousness of artistic purpose to which his recent knighthood was a tribute.

Finally, the history of nineteenth-century theatre practice attracts two articles which examine the function of the new proscenium arch in the early part of the century. They explore the ways in which the desire for the new pictorialism in the early nineteenth century was met by the Grieve family of designers, especially in their manipulation of the arch's conventions (Nancy J. Doran Hazelton, 'The Grieve Family: Frame and Icon on the Nineteenth-Century Stage', *NCT* 21.ii.[1993]76–93), and the ways by which Benjamin Wyatt's 1812 reconstruction of Drury Lane may have affected an audience's perceptions and its experience in the theatre (Anastasia Nikolopoulou, 'Panopticism and the Politics of the Proscenium Frame Theatre: Benjamin Wyatt's Drury Lane, 1812', *ET* 12.ii.141–56). Hazelton's article continues her interest in the huge Grieve collection of theatre designs at the University of London. She analyses the subtle way in which the Grieve designs played with the audience's perceptions and either erected or collapsed 'the distinction between the real and the represented'. There is a strong sense of design experiment with the new pictorial possibilities of the proscenium arch, and the Grieve collection shows the extent to which designers and painters in the Victorian period shared a virtuosity of technique through which they were able to manipulate the onlooker's perceptions. Nikolopoulou sees the manipulation of audiences as a managerial conspiracy in which the designer, in this case the architect Benjamin Wyatt, is wholly implicated. Unfortunately, her inadequate grasp of theatre history and understanding of the composition and experience of theatre audiences do little to persuade the reader about the viability of imposing a Foucaultian model of control upon aesthetic decision making by nineteenth-century designers or architects.

Books Reviewed

Abeles, Francine F., ed. *The Pamphlets of Lewis Carroll.* Vol. 2: *The Mathematical Pamphlets of Charles Lutwidge Dodgson and Related Pieces.* UPVirginia. pp. 420. $65. ISBN 0 9303 2608 3.

Altholz, Josef L. *Anatomy of a Controversy: The Debate Over 'Essays and Reviews'.* Scolar. pp. 198. $59.95. ISBN 1 8592 8040 4.

Andrews, Malcolm. *Dickens and the Grown-Up Child.* UIowaP. pp. 214. $29.95. ISBN 0 3335 9435 5.

Armstrong, Tim, ed. *Thomas Hardy: Selected Poems.* Longman Annotated Texts. Longman (1993). pp. 385. hb £42, pb £16.99. ISBN 0 5820 4051 5, 0 5820 4061 2.

Bailin, Miriam. *The Sickroom in Victorian Fiction: The Art of Being Ill.* Cambridge Studies in Nineteenth-Century Literature and Culture, 1. CUP. pp. 179. £30. ISBN 0 5214 4526 4.

Baker, William, ed. *Richard Marsh. The Beetle.* Sutton. pp. 277. £5.99. ISBN 0 7509 0688 X.

Baldridge, Cates. *The Dialogics of Dissent in the English Novel.* UPNE. pp. 203. $39.95. ISBN 0 8745 1060 8.

Barker, Juliet. *The Brontës.* W&N. pp. 280. £25. ISBN 0 2978 1290 4.

Barnes, Geraldine, Margaret Clunies Ross and Judy Quinn, eds. *Old Norse Studies in the New World: A Collection of Essays to Celebrate the Jubilee of the Teaching of Old Norse at the University of Sydney, 1943–1993.* USydP. pp. 155. $10 (Australian). ISBN 0 8675 8914 0.

Barreca, Regina. *Untamed and Unabashed: Essays on Women and Humor in British Literature*. WSUP. pp. 188. $29.95. ISBN 0 8143 2136 4.
Bauer, Helen Pike. *Rudyard Kipling: A Study of the Short Fiction*. Twayne. pp. 162. $23.95. ISBN 0 8057 8345 8.
Berry, Elizabeth Hollis. *Anne Brontë's Radical Vision: Structures of Consciousness*. ELS. pp. 122. $10.50 (Canadian). ISBN 0 9206 0474 9.
Bodenheimer, Rosemarie. *The Real Life of Mary Ann Evans: George Eliot, Her Letters, and Fiction*. CornUP. pp. 320. $32.50. ISBN 0 8014 2988 9.
The Book of the Rhymers' Club (1892, 1894). Intro. R. K. R. Thornton and Ian Small. Decadents, Symbolists, Anti-Decadents: Poetry of the 1890s. Woodstock. £28.50. ISBN 1 8547 7136 1.
Booth, Bradford A., and Ernest Mehew, eds. *The Letters of Robert Louis Stevenson*. 4 vols. YaleUP. Vol. 1: *1854–April 1874*. pp. 525. $45. ISBN 0 3000 5183 2. Vol. 2: *April 1874–July 1879*. pp. 352. $45. ISBN 0 3000 6021 1. Vol. 3: *August 1879–September 1882*. pp. 372. $45. ISBN 0 3000 6187 0. Vol. 4: *October 1882–June 1884*. pp. 326. $45. ISBN 0 3000 6188 9.
Brake, Laurel. *Subjugated Knowledges: Journalism, Gender and Literature in the Nineteenth Century*. Macmillan. pp. 228. £12.99. ISBN 0 3336 0672 8.
——. *Walter Pater*. Writers and their Work. Northcote. pp. 62. £6.99. ISBN 0 7463 0716 0.
Brantley, Richard E. *Anglo-American Antiphony: The Late Romanticism of Tennyson and Emerson*. UPFlor. pp. 352. £36. ISBN 0 8130 1247 3.
Breen, Jennifer, ed. *Victorian Women Poets: 1830–1900*. Dent. pp. 276. pb £5.99. ISBN 0 4608 7457 8.
Brown, Andrew. *George Eliot. Romola*. WC. OUP. pp. 622. £5.50. ISBN 1 8519 6086 4.
Bullen, J. B. *The Myth of the Renaissance in Nineteenth-Century Writing*. OUP. pp. 336. £40. ISBN 0 1981 2888 6.
Bulwer-Lytton, Rosina. *A Blighted Life: A True Story*. Subversive Women. Intro. Marie Mulvey Roberts. Thoemmes. pp. 111. £10.75. ISBN 1 8550 6248 8.
Cannell, D. M. *George Green: Mathematician and Physicist (1793–1841): The Background to his Life and Work*. Athlone (1993). pp. 265. £35. ISBN 0 4851 1433 X.
Chapman, Raymond. *Forms of Speech in Victorian Fiction*. Longman. pp. 263. £30. ISBN 0 5820 8746 5.
Chapple, Richard. *Social and Political Change in Literature and Film: Selected Papers from the Sixteenth Annual Florida State University Conference on Literature and Film*. UPFlor. pp. 136. $15.95. ISBN 0 8130 1286 4.
Coleridge, Sara. *Phantasmion (1837)*. RevR. Intro. Jonathan Wordsworth. Woodstock. pp. 404. £42. ISBN 1 8547 7166 3.
Copley, Stephen, and Peter Garside, eds. *The Politics of the Picturesque*. CUP. pp. 304. £35. ISBN 0 5214 4113 7.
Craft, Christopher. *Another Kind of Love: Male Homosexual Desire in English Discourse, 1850–1920*. UCalP. pp. 233. $30. ISBN 0 5200 8492 6.
Davies, Hunter. *The Teller of Tales: In Search of Robert Louis Stevenson*. Sinclair-Stevenson. pp. 290. £17.99. ISBN 1 8561 9263 6.
Davis, Tracy C. *George Bernard Shaw and the Socialist Theatre*. Contributions in Drama and Theatre Studies 65. Greenwood. pp. 184. hb £53.95, pb £15.95. ISBN 0 3132 7611 0, 0 2759 3764 X.
DiGaetani, John Louis, ed. *Money: Lure, Lore, and Literature*. Greenwood. pp.

268. $59.95. ISBN 0 3132 9219 8.

Dowson, Ernest. *Verses (1896) and Decorations (1899)*. Intro. R. K. R. Thornton and Ian Small. Decadents, Symbolists, Anti-Decadents: Poetry of the 1890s. Woodstock. £25. ISBN 1 8547 7142 6.

Ferris, Lesley, ed. *Crossing the Stage: Controversies on Cross-Dressing*. Routledge (1993). pp. 198. hb £40, pb £12.99. ISBN 0 4150 6268 3, 04150 6269 1.

Fischer, Andreas. *Repetition*. Narr. pp. 268. DM78. ISBN 3 8233 4682 2.

Ford, Mark, ed. *Wilkie Collins. No Name*. Penguin. pp. 617. £2.99. ISBN 0 1404 3397 X.

Foulkes, Richard, ed. *Scenes from Provincial Stages: Essays in Honour of Kathleen Barker*. STR. pp. 194. n.p. ISBN 0 8543 0055 4.

Fraser, Robert. *Proust and the Victorians: The Lamp of Memory*. Macmillan. pp. 272. £40. ISBN 0 3335 8473 2.

Ghnassia, Jill Dix. *Metaphysical Rebellion in the Works of Emily Brontë: A Reinterpretation*. St Martin's. pp. 352. $39.95. ISBN 0 3121 0221 6.

Goetsch, Paul. *Hardy's Wessex-Romane*. Narr. pp. 316. DM108. ISBN 3 8233 4275 4.

Goldman, Paul. *Victorian Illustrated Books, 1850–1870: The Heyday of Wood-Engraving*. BMP. pp. 148. £14.95. ISBN 0 7141 2600 4.

Goradia, Nayana. *Lord Curzon: The Last of the British Moghuls*. OUP (1993). pp. 309. £17.50. ISBN 0 1956 2824 1.

Gordon, Lyndall. *Charlotte Brontë: A Passionate Life*. Norton. pp. 416. $27.50. ISBN 0 3930 3722 3.

Gray, John. *Silverpoints (1893) and Spiritual Poems (1896)*. Intro. R. K. R. Thornton and Ian Small. Decadents, Symbolists, Anti-Decadents: Poetry of the 1890s. Woodstock. £25. ISBN 1 8547 7144 2.

Greenslade, William. *Degeneration, Culture, and the Novel, 1880–1940*. CUP. pp. 369. £37.50. ISBN 0 5214 1665 5.

Hall, Donald E., ed. *Muscular Christianity: Embodying the Victorian Age*. CUP. pp. 258. £35. ISBN 0 5214 5318 6.

Harden, Edgar F., ed. *The Letters and Private Papers of William Makepeace Thackeray: A Supplement to Gordon N. Ray's 'The Letters and Private Papers of William Makepeace Thackeray'*. 2 vols. Garland. pp. 1,557. $165. ISBN 0 8240 3646 8.

Hardy, Thomas. *Wessex Poems (1898)*. Intro. R. K. R. Thornton and Ian Small. Decadents, Symbolists, Anti-Decadents: Poetry of the 1890s. Woodstock. £32.50. ISBN 1 8547 7145 0.

Harsh, Constance D. *Subversive Heroines: Feminist Resolutions of Social Crisis in the Condition-of-England Novel*. UMichP. pp. 192. $37.50. ISBN 0 4721 0566 3.

Hawkins-Daly, Mark, ed. *International Dictionary of Theatre*. Vol. 2. *Playwrights*. St James. pp. 1,218. £99. ISBN 1 5586 2096 6.

Heinzelman, Susan Sage, and Zipporah Batshaw Wiseman, eds. *Representing Women: Law, Literature, and Feminism*. DukeUP. pp. 400. $49.95. ISBN 0 8223 1495 9.

Henry, Nancy, ed. *George Eliot. Impressions of Theophrastus Such*. PWC. P&C. pp. 187. £14.95. ISBN 0 1928 2964 5.

Heyns, Michiel. *Expulsion and the Nineteenth-Century Novel: The Scapegoat in English Realist Fiction*. Clarendon. pp. 293. £30. ISBN 0 1981 8270 8.

Higonnet, Margaret R., ed. *Borderwork: Feminist Engagements with Comparative*

Literature. CornUP. pp. 335. $44.95. ISBN 0 8014 2869 6.
Hodgson, John A., ed. *Sherlock Holmes: The Major Stories with Contemporary Critical Essays*. St Martin's. pp. 452. $9.50. ISBN 0 3335 3137 X.
Housman, A. E. *A Shropshire Lad (1896)*. Intro. R. K. R. Thornton and Ian Small. Decadents, Symbolists, Anti-Decadents: Poetry of the 1890s. Woodstock. £22.50. ISBN 1 8547 7147 7.
Houston, Gail Turley. *Consuming Fictions: Gender, Class, and Hunger in Dickens's Novels*. SIUP. pp. 256. $29.95. ISBN 0 8093 1953 5.
Hynes, Samuel, ed. *Thomas Hardy: A Selection of his Finest Poems*. Oxford Poetry Library. OUP. pp. 266. £5.99. ISBN 0 1928 2268 3.
Jackson, Tony E. *The Subject of Modernism: Narrative Alterations in the Fiction of Eliot, Conrad, Woolf, and Joyce*. UMichP. pp. 224. $39.50. ISBN 0 4721 0552 3.
Johnstone, Peggy Fitzhugh. *The Transformation of Rage: Mourning and Creativity in George Eliot's Fiction*. NYUP. pp. 207. $45. ISBN 0 8147 4194 0.
Jones, Roger Walton. *Larry McMurtry and the Victorian Novel*. TexA&MUP. pp. 112. $19.50. ISBN 0 8909 6621 4.
Kaplan, Joel H., and Sheila Stowell. *Theatre and Fashion: Oscar Wilde to the Suffragettes*. CUP. pp. 240. hb £32.50, pb £12.95. ISBN 0 5214 1510 1, 0 5214 9950 X.
Katz, Bill, ed. *A History of Book Illustration: 29 Points of View*. Scarecrow. pp. 690. $72.50. ISBN 0 8108 2742 5.
Kelley, Philip, and Scott Lewis, eds. *The Brownings' Correspondence*. Vol. 12: January–April 1846. Athlone. pp. 426. £65. ISBN 0 4853 0032 X.
Kipling, Rudyard. *Barrack-Room Ballads, 1892*. Ed. and intro. R. K. R. Thornton and Ian Small. Decadents, Symbolists, Anti-Decadents: Poetry of the 1890s. Woodstock. pp. 208. $49.50. ISBN 1 8547 7150 7.
Kopelson, Kevin. *Love's Litany: The Writing of Modern Homoerotics*. StanfordUP. pp. 194. $27.50. ISBN 0 8047 2299 4.
Kucich, John. *The Power of Lies: Transgression in Victorian Fiction*. CornUP. pp. 304. $39.95. ISBN 0 8014 2842 4.
Langford, Michele K., ed. *Contours of the Fantastic: Selected Essays from the Eighth International Conference on the Fantastic in the Arts*. Greenwood. pp. 232. $55. ISBN 0 3132 6647 6.
Law, Graham, ed. *Wilkie Collins. The Evil Genius*. Broadview. pp. 379. $12.95. ISBN 1 5511 1017 2.
Lawler, Justus George, ed. *The 1994 Annual of Hermeneutics and Social Concern*. Continuum. pp. 319. $19.95. ISBN 0 8264 4605 1.
Lawrence, Karen. *Penelope Voyages: Women and Travel in the British Literary Tradition*. CornUP. pp. 288. $38.95. ISBN 0 8014 2610 3.
Lebowitz, Naomi. *The Philosophy of Literary Amateurism*. UMissP. pp. 152. $29.95. ISBN 0 8262 0970 X.
Lecercle, Jean-Jacques. *Philosophy of Nonsense: The Intuitions of Victorian Nonsense Literature*. Routledge. pp. 288. hb £40, pb £13.99. ISBN 0 4150 7652 8, 0 4150 7653 6.
Lovett, Charlie, ed. *Proceedings of the Second International Lewis Carroll Conference*. Lewis Carroll Society of North America. pp. 191. $27.50. ISBN 0 9303 2610 5.
Machann, Clinton. *The Genre of Autobiography in Victorian Literature*. UMichP. pp. 191. $37.50. ISBN 0 4721 0565 5.

Maglavera, Soultana. *Time Patterns in Later Dickens: A Study of the Thematic Implications of the Temporal Organization of 'Bleak House', 'Hard Times', 'Little Dorrit', 'A Tale of Two Cities', 'Great Expectations', and 'Our Mutual Friend'*. Rodopi. pp. 251. $40. ISBN 9 0518 3690 2.

Mallett, P. V., and R. P. Draper, eds. *A Spacious Vision: Essays on Hardy*. Patten. pp. 149. £9.95. ISBN 1 8722 2912 3.

Manos, Nikki Lee, and Meri-Jane Rochelson, eds. *Transforming Genres: New Approaches to British Fiction of the 1890s*. Macmillan. pp. 272. £27. ISBN 0 3336 2657 5.

Marsh, Jan. *Christina Rossetti: A Literary Biography*. Cape. pp. 634. £25. ISBN 0 2240 3585 1.

——, ed. *Christina Rossetti: Poems and Prose*. Everyman. Dent. £5.99. pp. 488. ISBN 0 4608 7536 1.

Martin, Carol A. *George Eliot's Serial Fiction*. OSUP. pp. 348. £44.50. ISBN 0 8142 0625 5.

Marucci, Franco. *The Fine Delight That Fathers Thought: Rhetoric and Medievalism in Gerard Manley Hopkins*. CUAP. pp. 267. £39.95. ISBN 0 8132 0778 9.

Mason, Michael. *The Making of Victorian Sexual Attitudes*. OUP. pp. 272. £17.95. ISBN 0 1981 2292 6.

——. *The Making of Victorian Sexuality*. OUP. pp. 338. £17.95. ISBN 0 1981 2247 0.

Mattheisen, Paul F., Arthur C. Young and Pierre Coustillas, eds. *The Collected Letters of George Gissing*. Vol. 5: *1892–1895*. OhioUP. pp. 371. $60. ISBN 0 8214 1067 9.

Matthews, Hugoe, and Phyllis Treitel. *The Forward Life of Richard Jefferies: A Chronological Study*. Petton. pp. 239. £15. ISBN 0 9522 8130 9.

Mayer, David. *Playing out the Empire: 'Ben Hur' and other Toga Plays and Films. A Critical Anthology*. OUP. pp. 321. £37.50. ISBN 0 1981 1990 9.

McLynn, Frank. *Robert Louis Stevenson: A Biography*. RandomH. pp. 567. $30. ISBN 0 6794 1284 0.

Mendes, Peter. *Clandestine Erotic Fiction in English 1800–1930: A Bibliographical Study*. Scolar (1993). pp. 479. £75. ISBN 0 8596 7919 5.

Mitchell, Judith. *The Stone and the Scorpion: The Female Subject of Desire in the Novels of Charlotte Brontë, George Eliot, and Thomas Hardy*. Greenwood. pp. 228. $49.95. ISBN 0 3132 9043 1.

Morris, William. *'Hopes and Fears for Art' and 'Signs of Change'*. Intro. Peter Faulkner. Thoemmes Press William Morris Library. Thoemmes. pp. 140. £14.75. ISBN 1 8550 6254 2.

Mortimer, John, ed. *Charles Dickens. A Christmas Carol.*YaleUP, Pierpont Morgan Library. pp. 168. $30. ISBN 0 3000 5843 8.

Moss, Sidney P., and Carolyn J. Moss. *Charles Dickens and his Chicago Relatives: A Documentary Narrative*. Whitston. pp. 186. $23.50. ISBN 0 8787 5444 X.

Motion, Andrew, ed. *Thomas Hardy: Selected Poems*. Everyman. Dent. pp. 276. £5.99. ISBN 0 4608 7458 6.

Murphy, Paul Thomas. *Toward a Working-Class Canon: Literary Criticism in British Working-Class Periodicals, 1816–1858*. OSUP. pp. 208. $39.50. ISBN 0 8142 0654 9.

Murray, Brian. *Charles Dickens*. Continuum. pp. 198. $19.95. ISBN 0 8264 0565 7.

Nelson, Claudia, and Lynne Vallone, eds. *The Girl's Own: Cultural Histories of the*

Anglo-American Girl, 1830–1915. UGeoP. pp. 304. $45. ISBN 0 8203 1615 6.
Norton, Caroline. *A Voice From the Factories (1836)*. RevR. Intro. Jonathan Wordsworth. Woodstock. £21. ISBN 1 8547 7169 8.
Novy, Marianne. *Engaging with Shakespeare: Responses of George Eliot and Other Women Novelists*. UGeoP. pp. 288. $50. ISBN 0 8203 1596 6.
Nunokawa, Jeff. *The Afterlife of Property: Domestic Security and the Victorian Novel*. PrincetonUP. pp. 152. $24.95. ISBN 0 6910 3320 X.
Page, Norman, ed. *Charles Dickens. A Tale of Two Cities*. Everyman. Dent. pp. 448. £3.99. ISBN 0 4608 7451 9.
Pangallo, Karen L., ed. *The Critical Response to George Eliot*. Greenwood. pp. 256. $55. ISBN 0 3132 8773 2.
Parker, David. *Ethics, Theory, and the Novel*. CUP. pp. 218. $54.95. ISBN 0 5214 5283 X.
Pawley, Margaret. *Faith and Family: The Life and Circle of Ambrose Phillipps de Lisle*. Canterbury (1993). pp. 457. £25. ISBN 1 8531 1073 6.
Pettit, Charles P. C., ed. *New Perspectives on Thomas Hardy*. St Martin's. pp. 213. $59.95. ISBN 0 3121 2036 2.
Phelan, James, and Peter J. Rabinowitz, eds. *Understanding Narrative*. OSUP. pp. 256. $59.50. ISBN 0 8142 0633 6.
Polhemus, Robert M., and Roger B. Henkle, eds. *Critical Reconstructions: The Relationship of Fiction and Life*. StanfordUP. pp. 370. $42.50. ISBN 0 8047 2243 9.
Preston, Peter, and Paul Simpson-Housley, eds. *Writing the City: Eden, Babylon, and the New Jerusalem*. Routledge. pp. 352. £40. ISBN 0 4151 0667 2.
Pykett, Lyn. *The Sensation Novel: From 'The Woman in White' to 'The Moonstone'*. Northcote. pp. 82. £6.99. ISBN 0 7463 0725 X.
Reilly, Catherine W. *Late Victorian Poetry, 1880–1899: An Annotated Bibliography*. Mansell. pp. 577. £70. ISBN 0 7201 2001 2.
Reynolds, Kimberley, and Nicola Humble. *Victorian Heroines: Representations of Femininity in Nineteenth-Century Literature and Art*. NYUP. pp. 195. $40. ISBN 0 8147 7361 3.
Richetti, John, ed. *The Columbia History of the British Novel*. ColUP. pp. 1,064. $69.95. ISBN 0 2310 7858 7.
Roberts, Diane. *The Myth of Aunt Jemima: White Women Representing Black Women*. Routledge. pp. 230. £30. ISBN 0 4150 4918 0.
Roberts, Gerald. *Gerard Manley Hopkins: A Literary Life*. Macmillan Literary Lives. Macmillan. pp. 153. hb £40, pb £9.99. ISBN 0 3335 6820 6, 0 3335 6821 4.
Rooksby, Rikky, and Nicholas Shrimpton, eds. *The Whole Music of Passion: New Essays on Swinburne*. Scolar (1993). pp. 300. £39.50. ISBN 0 8596 7925 X.
Rosenblum, Joseph, ed. *Dictionary of Literary Biography*. Vol. 140: *American Book-Collectors and Bibliographers, First Series*. Gale. pp. 408. $125. ISBN 0 8103 5399 7.
Rowlinson, Matthew. *Tennyson's Fixations: Psychoanalysis and the Topics of the Early Poetry*. Victorian Literature and Culture. UPVirginia. pp. 224. £31.50. ISBN 0 8139 1478 7.
Rubik, Margarete. *The Novels of Mrs. Oliphant: A Subversive View of Traditional Themes*. Lang. pp. 352. $54.95. ISBN 0 8204 2209 6.
Sadler, Glenn Edward, ed. *An Expression of Character: The Letters of George MacDonald*. Eerdmans. pp. 416. $29.99. ISBN 0 8028 3762 X.

Sadrin, Anny. *Parentage and Inheritance in the Novels of Charles Dickens*. CUP. pp. 182. £30. ISBN 0 5213 9086 9.

Sell, Roger D., ed. *Great Expectations: Contemporary Critical Essays*. Macmillan New Casebooks. Macmillan. pp. 276. hb £37.40, pb £10.99. ISBN 0 3335 4606 7, 0 3335 4607 5.

Semmel, Bernard. *George Eliot and the Politics of National Inheritance*. OUP. pp. 168. £30. ISBN 0 1950 8567 1.

Seymour-Smith, Martin. *Hardy: A Biography*. St Martin's. pp. 886. $35. ISBN 0 3121 1819 8.

Shankman, Lillian F. *Anne Thackeray Ritchie: Journals and Letters*. Eds Abigail Burnham Bloom and John Maynard. OSUP. pp. 370. $62.50. ISBN 0 8142 0638 7.

Shepherd, Valerie. *Literature about Language*. Routledge. pp. 192. £32.50. ISBN 0 4150 6996 3.

Shillingsburg, Peter L. *W. M. Thackeray. Vanity Fair*. NCE. Norton. pp. 876. $11.95. ISBN 0 3939 6595 3.

Simpson, Roger. *Sir John Tenniel: Aspects of His Work*. AUP. pp. 187. $32.50. ISBN 0 8386 3493 1.

Sjöholm, Christina. *'The Vice of Wedlock': The Theme of Marriage in George Gissing's Novels*. Uppsala. pp. 144. £12.15. ISBN 9 1554 3258 1.

Slater, Michael, ed. *Charles Dickens. Sketches by Boz and Other Early Papers, 1833–39*. Dent Uniform Edition of Dickens. OSUP. pp. 371. $18.95. ISBN 0 4608 6076 3.

——, ed. *Charles Dickens. The Christmas Books*. Vol. 2. Penguin. pp. 398. £4.50. ISBN 0 1404 3069 5.

Small, Ian, ed. *Oscar Wilde. Complete Short Fiction*. Penguin. pp. 288. £1.99. ISBN 0 1404 3423 2.

Stafford, Fiona J. *The Last of the Race: The Growth of a Myth from Milton to Darwin*. OUP. pp. 326. £37.50. ISBN 0 1981 1222 X.

Stephan, Inge, Sabine Schilling and Sigrid Weigel, eds. *Jüdische Kultur und Weiblichkeit in Der Moderne*. Hatje. pp. 351. DM29.80. ISBN 3 4120 0492 8.

Stockton, Kathryn Bond. *God between their Lips: Desire between Women in Irigaray, Brontë, and Eliot*. StanfordUP. pp. 273. £11.95. ISBN 0 8047 2344 3.

Stone, Harry. *The Night Side of Dickens: Cannibalism, Passion, Necessity*. OSUP. pp. 726. $65. ISBN 0 8142 0547 X.

Stott, Louis. *Robert Louis Stevenson in France*. Creag Darach. pp. 128. £6.99. ISBN 1 8745 8503 2.

Stuart, Roxanna. *Stage Blood: Vampires of the 19th Century Stage*. BGUP. pp. 377. hb $49.95, pb $29.95. ISBN 0 8797 2659 8, 0 8797 2660 1.

Suchoff, David B. *Critical Theory and the Novel: Mass Society and Cultural Criticism in Dickens, Melville, and Kafka*. UWiscP. pp. 224. $43. ISBN 0 2991 4084 9.

Sutherland, John, ed. *W. M. Thackeray. Pendennis*. WC. OUP. pp. 1,061. £6.99. ISBN 0 1928 3168 2.

Thomas, Frances. *Christina Rossetti: A Literary Biography*. Virago. pp. 448. £9.99. ISBN 1 8538 1681 7.

Tiffin, Chris, and Alan Lawson, eds. *De-Scribing Empire: Post-Colonialism and Textuality*. Routledge. pp. 240. hb £40, pb £12.99. ISBN 0 4151 0546 3, 0 4151 0547 1.

Tomalin, Claire. *Mrs Jordan's Profession: The Story of a Great Actress and a Future*

King. Viking. pp. 474. £18. ISBN 0 6708 4159 5.
Watkins, Tony, ed. *Anthony Hope. The Prisoner of Zenda.* WC. OUP. pp. 177. £3.99. ISBN 0 1928 2933 5.
Watson, Nicola J. *Revolution in the Form of the English Novel, 1790–1825: Intercepted Letters, Interrupted Seductions*. OUP. pp. 220. £25. ISBN 0 1981 1129 7.
Weyant, Nancy S. *Elizabeth Gaskell: An Annotated Bibliography of English-Language Sources, 1976–1991*. Scarecrow. pp. 209. $29.50. ISBN 0 8108 2890 1.
Wilkes, Joanne, ed. *Geraldine Jewsbury. The Half Sisters*. WC. OUP. pp. 409. £6.99. ISBN 0 1928 3114 3.
Winnifrith, Tom. *Fallen Women in the Nineteenth-Century Novel.* Macmillan. pp. 178. £35. ISBN 0 3335 9191 7.
Wolfreys, Julian. *Being English: Narratives, Idioms, and Performances of National Identity from Coleridge to Trollope*. SUNYP. pp. 243. $49.95. ISBN 0 7914 2102 3.
Wratislaw, Theodore. *Caprices (1893) and Orchids (1896)*. Intro. R. K. R. Thornton and Ian Small. Decadents, Symbolists, Anti-Decadents: Poetry of the 1890s. Woodstock. £25. ISBN 1 8547 7160 4.
York, R. A. *Strangers and Secrets: Communication in the Nineteenth-Century Novel.* UDelP. pp. 165. £25. ISBN 0 8386 3533 4.
Youngs, Tim. *Travelers in Africa: British Travelogues, 1850–1900*. ManUP. pp. 235. $69.95. ISBN 0 7190 0369 X.

XIV

The Twentieth Century

JULIAN COWLEY, MACDONALD DALY, RICHARD STORER, MARK RAWLINSON, STUART SILLARS, IAN SANSOM and TREVOR R. GRIFFITHS

This chapter has the following sections: 1. Fiction; 2. Poetry; 3. Drama. Section 1(a) is by Julian Cowley; section 1(b) is by Macdonald Daly and Richard Storer; section 1(c) is by Mark Rawlinson; section 2(a) is by Stuart Sillars; section 2(b) is by Ian Sansom; and section 3 is by Trevor R. Griffiths.

1. Fiction

(a) General Studies

Preface to Modernism should not be mistaken for a history of modernist art and literature; indeed, Art Berman describes as 'quite casual' his approach to date and sequence. In fact, his book builds upon a set of hypotheses, working towards 'an extended conceptual definition'. His fundamental contention is that modernism developed within modernity in reaction to its dominant empiricism, and he argues that in the process it transformed not only its romantic inheritance, but also its capitalist context. Berman has opted to exclude supporting quotation from primary sources, on the basis that he wished to present coherent beliefs about modernism, rather than suggesting modernism to be a coherent set of beliefs itself. The picture is painted, therefore, using broad brush strokes, and this might be viewed as a methodological weakness. But although allusive and assertive, it is a substantial work, written with eloquence and authority, offering well-defined perspectives to stimulate further work in the field.

The relationships of art and commerce are touched upon in the course of Berman's book. They receive much fuller treatment in Robert Jensen's *Marketing Modernism in Fin-de-Siècle Europe*, a detailed study of the close links between commercial concerns and aesthetic practices in that period of art history when Impressionism was claiming legitimacy. His case, broadly put, is that 'market discourses' were ubiquitous in 'the ideological defense of both aesthetic modernism and avant-gardism', and were indeed 'bound to modernist art from its inception to its demise'. This challenge to any vestigial sense of the aesthetic purity of modernist practice is clearly provocative. Jensen is emphatic that he wishes not to diminish the actual works of art, but to highlight those institutions which came into existence to promote and define aesthetic modernism. His carefully constructed account is a substantial addition to study of the emergence of the modernist paradigm.

Daniel C. Melnick, in *Fullness of Dissonance*, engages with the thorny yet potentially fruitful area of inter-art comparison. He examines the ties between modern literature and music, taking as his focus the dissonant narrative practice of early twentieth-century writers. Following Adorno, he argues that self-conscious use of dissonance, by novelists and composers, produced destabilization of form that activated readers' capacity for 'freed, independent consciousness and judgment'. Melnick assumes an historical perspective on the grounds that 'the flow of ideas about music from the Romantics to the Symbolists and to Nietzsche constitutes a crucial revelatory source of modernism'. After brief consideration of Conrad, he proceeds to the work of Proust, Mann and Joyce, with the dual presence of Nietzsche and Beethoven looming dominantly from the nineteenth century. As a defence of modernist practice the book makes its point emphatically and convincingly; as inter-art comparison it reads as a long, suggestive essay rather than a detailed study, and raises numerous issues that beg for further investigation.

In a letter to Edwin Abbey, Henry James commented: 'Look into Ruskin and he's all about Nature – splendidly often, but loathing Art.' George Leonard's *Into the Light of Things* boldly identifies a cultural vector passing from Wordsworth to the radical American composer John Cage, by way of Ruskin and Carlyle. His argument is that dematerialization of the object in conceptual art, far from being an errant postmodern practice, culminates a line of aspiration that runs from Romanticism. In tracing the art world that emerged from natural supernaturalism, he incidentally presents useful corrective insights into the West's adoption of Zen Buddhism as an aesthetic influence. A subtle and suggestive study, this book provides a framework for revisionary assessment of the aspirations and accomplishment of modernism, the cultural phase which it passes over in significant silence.

Hypertext has raised a spectre of the imminent dematerialization of the printed book. George Landow has established himself as the leading figure amongst devotees endeavouring to imbed electronic textuality within a matrix comprising critical theory, literary history, and the practices of academic research and pedagogy. In *Hyper/Text/Theory*, he has gathered essays both speculative and assertive under the headings 'Nonlinearity', 'The Politics of Hypertext' and 'The New Writing'. The contributors assume a wide range of approaches, drawing authority from literary sources (such as Ford, Woolf and Joyce), and from philosophers (including Wittgenstein, Habermas and Deleuze). They converge in affirmation that, while the technology is still developing, it is already clear that hypertext has profound implications for the future of literary study, and that it invites our engagement.

'Who is to *design* books now that computers are *making* books?' asks John Dreyfus in the penultimate essay of *Into Print*. This handsomely produced volume collects articles and texts of lectures by the distinguished historian of printing, mainly addressing twentieth-century topics. His commentaries on private presses, type designers and typographers are by no means exhaustive; rather they offer glimpses into the printer's workshop, infused with his considerable enthusiasm. The significance of Eric Gill's achievement is a touchstone throughout.

The materiality of print is the crucial concern of *The Visible Word*, Johanna

Drucker's impressive examination of the interface of literature and visual art in the period 1909–23. Wyndham Lewis's BLAST being noted as an exceptional example of typographic play in English literature of the period, Drucker's attention is directed largely to the work of Mallarmé and Apollinaire, the Dadaists, and the Italian and Russian Futurists. But proceeding from the paradoxical ontological status of the Imagist poem, simultaneously being and meaning, she does investigate the foregrounding of self-conscious poetics as a more general characteristic of modernist writing.

'Whose Modernism?', asks the opening chapter of Bridget Elliott and Jo-Ann Wallace's excellent *Women Artists and Writers: Modernist (Im)Positionings*. The authors' commitment is 'to rethinking modernism as a discursive and historical *field*' by examining ways in which women have been positioned within it. They acknowledge a methodological debt to Pierre Bourdieu's work on cultural production. In practice, this results in an approach where less emphasis is placed on recuperation of neglected figures than on investigation of acquisition of power to define modernism, at the time and in our present. This they perform most effectively. Following Toril Moi's observation of 'the immense *variability* of gender as a social factor', they work with telling couplings: Natalie Barney and Romaine Brooks; Virginia Woolf and Vanessa Bell; Gertrude Stein and Marie Laurencin; Djuna Barnes and Nina Hamnett. These case studies produce fine readings comprising an accomplished addition to work in this field.

The same terrain is traversed in the final instalment of Sandra M. Gilbert and Susan Gubar's *No Man's Land* trilogy, entitled *Letters from the Front*. This is without doubt a major work of feminist literary history, characterized by the critical incisiveness one has come to expect from the authors. The passing of Woolf's Mrs Ramsay, the 'Great Mother of Victorian Culture', is taken as a signal event, establishing a point of view from which to read the situation of women novelists and poets from the 1920s to the 1980s. A substantial first chapter examines Woolf herself, caught between an untenable past and an uncertain future; subsequent chapters present Mrs Ramsay's female descendants, 'newly aware of the arbitrariness of sex *roles*', engaged in assumption of masks and in acts of impersonation. Additional edge is granted the discussion by disclosure of 'regressive or nostalgic sexual ideologies', which, under the cloak of progressive and innovative writing, have contained the doubts and fears of many male writers. The majority of women considered in this book are American, but it is necessary reading for all who will engage with its claim that 'what had been a single tradition has become many traditions, as women's spheres have widened and the certainties of men's worlds have crumbled'.

Graham Dawson's *Soldier Heroes* explores the construction of masculinity in relation to the notion of adventure, as defined within the legacy of imperialism. Dawson's contention is that 'the history of Empire continues to maintain a determining influence over cultural and political life in modern Britain'. His aspiration is to enhance our understanding of that influence. He draws on literary, historical and autobiographical materials, underpinned by psychoanalytic concepts derived from Melanie Klein, to effect a shifting focus on national and personal identity, and the conditions (factual and fictional) for their formation. The result is an ambitious and bold book, which sustains its coherence and analytical edge, while venturing across disciplines in order to show that 'the modern tradition of British adventure has furnished idealized, wish-fulfilling forms of masculinity to counter anxieties generated in a social world that is deeply divided along fracture-lines of ethnicity and nation, gender and class'. T. E. Lawrence is the main literary figure under scrutiny.

Jean Paulhan's place in modern literary history is secured by his editorship of the influential *Nouvelle Revue Française*. Christine Moneera Laennec and Michael Syrotinski have translated five of Paulhan's short fictions, *Progess in Love On the Slow Side*, written around the time of World War I. The volume also contains Maurice Blanchot's gnomic essay of tribute, 'The Ease of Dying'.

It was Blanchot who enjoined us (in *The Writing of the Disaster*) to 'learn to think with pain'. A comparable injunction emerges from *Intimate Violence: Reading Rape and Torture in Twentieth-Century Fiction*, where Laura E. Tanner explores 'the issues at stake in the process of reading fictional representations of rape and torture'. As readers we enter into the uneasy relationship between represented violence and its actual existence, and Tanner investigates the implications of this engagement. Her aim is to establish a critical perspective enabling readers to resist 'the kind of intimate violence that certain texts would perpetuate through the act of reading'. The examples of classical Marxist criticism and of feminist film criticism help her to address the materiality of violation in relation to the disembodiment threatened by textuality. The book includes sensitive and acute readings of Orwell's *Nineteen Eighty-Four* and D. M. Thomas's *The White Hotel.*

Lois McNay's *Foucault* is a splendid critical introduction to the work of the author of *Discipline and Punish*, which traces the development of his thinking to 'the addition of the idea of government to the theory of power' and to 'the move from a problematization of the subject to the idea of an "ethics of the self"'. McNay draws on the insights of his critics to acknowledge some of the weaknesses in Foucault's work, while reaffirming strengths in the light of his capacity to rethink and revise earlier positions. This is a fine introduction for students, and a sound platform on which to base assessment of this influential writer.

Kevin Kopelson contends in *Love's Litany* that while Foucauldian analysis of homosexuality identifies the constructive role of certain cultural discourses, it overlooks another: love, or erotic philosophy. Writers have, of course, long explored the relationship of love to sexuality, and of late it has become increasingly the subject of critical scrutiny. Kopelson's book, examining how love inflects homosexual texts, is a concise, witty and critically discerning addition to that scrutiny. One chapter boldly pairs Ronald Firbank with Gide. Others couple Woolf and Gertrude Stein, Marguerite Yourcenar and Mary Renault, while Wilde occupies the opening chapter, and Roland Barthes the last.

Foucault's view of Victorian sexuality is touched on in Stephen Kern's *The Culture of Love*, a history which draws upon sources from nineteenth- and twentieth-century art, literature and philosophy. Kern's claim is that modern lovers reflect more than did their Victorian counterparts on the meaning of their love, and so make it more their own. Whether or not one agrees with this argument, the book is compellingly readable, rich in detail, and packed with shrewd insights. Primary materials are most judiciously chosen, and are subtly located within chapters that reflect aspects of courtship, from anticipation, through sexual consummation, to loss. Heidegger's identification of authenticity provides a key analytical tool, used with consistent clarity and purposefulness. It is an exemplary work of cultural history, readily comparable to his earlier *The Culture of Time and Space* (1983).

Platonism and the English Imagination, edited by Anna Baldwin and Sarah

Hutton, is offered as the first comprehensive overview of the influence of Platonism and Neo-Platonism on English literature. Its comprehensiveness is in terms of chronological range, with a series of general accounts for particular periods punctuating case studies that trace the 'changing thread' from King Alfred to Iris Murdoch. It is, of course, a selective survey, but it maps the principal strands and major transformations through brief yet authoritative chapters. The scope of the collection makes it a convenient resource. The persistence, under threat, of Platonic thought into the current century is traced through essays on Yeats, Woolf's *Jacob's Room*, Eliot, Pound and Auden, while Anne Varty's contribution on Pater's Plato is also relevant.

David Holbrook's *Creativity and Popular Culture* is a rearguard attempt to affirm that the business of English studies is to preserve 'truth' and 'meaning'. For Holbrook, true creativity is a moral force that runs through authentic folk art as well as the great tradition in Western literature and music. In contemporary society this force for the good is perceived to be imperilled, and Holbrook invokes not only the cultural criticism of F. R. Leavis, but also the philosophy of Suzanne Langer and the psychology of D. W. Winnicott in his attempt to counter the corrupting influence of pop songs and children's comics. The author's earnest concern for the damage wrought by rampant commercialism may be worthy, but, as he recognizes, his alarm at the popularity of the Beatles is out of date, and there are too evident limits to his comprehension of the targets for his attack.

Holbrook's book has the virtue of an unmistakable purpose. This could not really be argued for Jack Hodges's *The Heart of the Writer*, a peculiar assemblage of snippets concerning the lives, loves, proclivities and destinies of a selection of English writers. The principle of selection seems to have been primarily availability of source material; names recur regularly, yet the overall organization of biographical and anecdotal fragments appears disarmingly haphazard, and the information they convey rarely rises above the trivial and inconsequential.

An Appointment with Somerset Maugham is a far more coherent treatment of authors and their lives, ranging from the personal encounter of the title to praise for Richard Ellman's biography of Joyce. Richard Hauer Costa has written critical biographies of H. G. Wells and Malcolm Lowry, and both receive substantial coverage here, but the real subject of the book is Costa himself, looking back on his shift from journalism into academic life, and musing on his fascination with literary figures, their trials and their achievements. It appears to be a book written above all for its author, and it is likely that others readers will find it diverting rather than penetrating.

The Correspondence of Ford Madox Ford and Stella Bowen is a fascinating supplement to current biographies, attentively edited by Sondra Stang and Karen Cochran. The letters cover the period 1917–39, and chart the distinct phases of the couple's relationship. It is surprising that Ford, so pivotal a figure of the time, makes so little reference here to his theories and practices as a writer. There are occasional allusions to dealings with publishers, and occasional mention of encounters with other writers and artists: Pound, of course, and Gertrude Stein, and a tantalizing allusion to a dinner where Ford was to meet with Duchamp and Brancusi. But the contents of the correspondence are overwhelmingly domestic, the record of an affair which, in the manner of Ford's fiction, evokes passionate lives, if one can read between the lines.

'Writing influences life, and life influences writing – indeed they become inextricable': this truism identifies the common thread that runs through Kathleen

Wheeler's series of studies in *'Modernist' Women Writers and Narrative Art*. Her approach reinstates mystery as a crucial element in the transformatory processes by which life becomes words, and words become fiction; but this does not compromise her insightful analyses of work by Jean Rhys, Katherine Mansfield and Stevie Smith (as well as Edith Wharton, Willa Cather and Jane Bowles). Wheeler's essential concern is to examine how those writers have responded to their perception of the limitations of realist convention, through disruption of familiar narrative structures. The result is a shrewd work of literary criticism.

Galya Diment's *The Autobiographical Novel of Co-Consciousness* is a curious choice as initial volume for a new James Joyce series. Diment's line of investigation is, broadly speaking, the translation of life into art, where the complexity of the author's sense of self demands representational dispersal through two, or more, characters. A parallel between Joyce and Woolf is readily made, enabling fruitful contrasts between their views on male and female identities. A case is made for the inclusion of Goncharov, but it is less convincing, and seems in significant ways unnecessary. A chapter on co-consciousness in *Don Quixote*, *Pamela* and Andrei Bely's *Petersburg* only adds to the sense of a rather forced alignment. Taken as an addition to current research into the nature and status of biography, however, this does make its case clearly and concisely.

Suzanne Nalbantian's *Aesthetic Autobiography* opens with a survey of autobiographical practices, focusing on signal figures since Augustine. The second chapter presents an overview of theories developed since the 1970s, identifying a gap in criticism which this book is intended to fill, concentrating on 'the transformation of autobiographical data into literary *écriture*'. The third chapter sets out the author's theory of aesthetic autobiography, and is followed by case studies of Proust, Joyce, Woolf and Anaïs Nin. Unlike Flaubert, whose source for *Madame Bovary* was a newspaper report, these are writers 'who construed major "events" from the minor occurrences of their *own* personal lives'. Nalbantian's argument that their writing is to be read as art, rather than mined for its sociological content, highlights her implied aim of preserving the validity of the category 'art' as that act of transmutation which produces work of universal and perennial value.

Nalbantian's goal might be interpreted as unfashionably neo-Kantian. Post-structuralism's radical relativism is challenged from a different position in *The Dematerialisation of Karl Marx* by Leonard Jackson, a non-Marxist materialist. He offers a pungent critique of what he sees as the left-wing posturing of literary theorists, who have forsaken the materialist and economistic base of Marxism proper, and have assumed a new idealism. The scope of the book is ambitious, and inevitably at times Jackson's critical instrument seems rather too blunt. Questions are posed that are timely and well formulated, but they clearly await appropriate response. As a liberal humanist defence of 'literature', the book mounts a substantial case, and it offers a coherent advocacy of cultural materialism, in its anthropological as opposed to its cultural studies guise.

An essay on the Gulf War entitled 'Support Our Tropes', making reference to Kant's *To Perpetual Peace*, might be taken as the ideal target for Jackson's attack on certain tendencies in post-structuralist writing. The essay can be found in Avital Ronell's *Finitude's Score*, a collection of deconstructive pieces 'for the end of the millennium'. It will doubtless be received by some as a dazzling performance of intellectual agility and resourcefulness, by others as the worst kind of postmodern posturing, a professor of comparative literature making pronouncements on political and ethical issues in language that combines the arcane and the populist, for an exclusively academic readership. The factions are most likely to concur in approval of an essay on Kafka's *The Castle*.

Michael Levine writes with insight on Kafka and Ovid, Baudelaire and Walter Benjamin, on Heine, and on Freud, in *Writing through Repression*. The title suggests his concern with both the restrictive and the enabling aspects of censorship, in literature and in psychoanalytic discourse. Crucially, he refuses to take Freud's legacy as an instrumental body of knowledge, emphasizing instead how psychoanalysis and literary texts mutually inform one another. Censorship is examined, then, within the context of a dialogue between disciplines. Levine's sophisticated investigation should counter any tendency to seek a crude distillation of complex ideas that facilitates their deployment as mere critical tools.

Patrick O'Neill's *Fictions of Discourse* invokes Zeno as the first postmodernist on account of his demonstration that all discourse 'at least potentially subverts the story it sets out to narrate, and thus ultimately itself also'. His specific concern is with narratology as itself a form of narrative, which in this perspective becomes inescapably problematic. The discussion is conducted with welcome clarity and with regular reference to a range of literary narratives, (especially those of Kafka). It is a sane and lively account of the relationship between the ultimate self-reflexivity of theory, and the viability of its constructive application.

Charles E. May has edited *The New Short Story Theories*, extensively revising his 1976 collection, which fuelled a revival of interest in the genre that is reflected here. The essays address both formal and historical issues, beginning with basic problems of definition and concluding with discussion, in cognitive terms, of readers' reception of short stories. There is a helpful annotated bibliography, and essays by practitioners including Elizabeth Bowen, Nadine Gordimer and Julio Cortázar. Suzanne C. Ferguson's 'Defining the Short Story: Impressionism and Form' is an essay that is particularly noteworthy in a collection that will be of considerable assistance to teachers and students of the genre.

Criminal Practices brings together selected reviews and essays from the past three decades of Julian Symons's involvement with crime writing. The musings and observations of a practitioner and an *aficionado*, these pieces are low on theory, but rich in informed insight. Symons's unparalleled familiarity with crime fiction gives weight to his measured defence of Agatha Christie, and his critical consideration of John le Carré. He casts light on the enduring appeal of Conan Doyle's work, and considers the relative merits of masters of technique, such as Eric Ambler, and of prodigiously energetic writers, such as Edgar Wallace. Other British writers examined are Erskine Childers, Margery Allingham, P. D. James, Ruth Rendell, Dick Francis, John Mair and John Creasey. In addition, Georges Simenon features here, together with the major American crime novelists, and a sample of Symons's judgements on the writing of accounts of 'real-life' crime.

The kinds of theoretical concern neglected by Symons are the essential matter of Heta Pyrhnen's *Murder from an Academic Angle*. This book aims to present a comprehensive account of how literary critics have analysed detective fiction. In little over one hundred pages it achieves an admirably clear exposition that embraces a range of responses, including structuralist accounts, political readings, psychoanalytical interpretations, feminist analyses and deconstructive studies. As an introduction, it will enlighten the general reader, or the undergraduate commencing engagement with the fiction or with modes of analysis. At the same time, it provides a concise reference guide for readers with an established grasp of the materials.

In *Murder by the Book?*, Sally Munt explores 'the diversity of feminist crime novels which offer some challenge to the view of crime fiction as an intrinsically masculine – and by implication innately conservative – literary form'. As this quotation indicates, the terms of her readings are clearly delineated, but in execution there is a tendency for a priori assumptions about the gendered nature of crime fiction to appear somewhat crude. This tendency is perhaps unavoidable in a survey, which at times becomes cluttered, leaving little space for fine tuning. The following categories are used: 'Mainstream women crime writers'; 'Liberal feminist crime fiction'; 'Socialist feminist crime fiction'; 'Race politics in crime fiction by women'; 'Lesbian crime fiction'; 'Psychoanalysis and feminist crime fiction'; and 'Postmodernism'. The book is a convenient source of information about work done by feminist crime writers.

Joseph Slade provides insights into 'Technology and the Spy Novel' as 'a cultural response to what is sometimes called the Information Age'. The essay, which deserves the attention of anyone seriously interested in the genre, is included in *Literature and Technology*, edited by Mark L. Greenberg and Lance Schachterle as part of a series devoted to Technology Studies. Consciously avoiding facile parallels, they have assembled a fascinating collection of essays which scrupulously establish the terms for a philosophy of technology, and proceed to explore how technology has shaped literary texts, and how literature has formed perspectives on technology. Its methods are versatile, as is evidenced by the range of the essays, from medieval to contemporary topics. It is to be hoped that this accomplished work of interdisciplinarity will generate more studies of this kind and quality. Rosalind Williams writes splendidly on Jules Romains's *Unanimisme* and urban systems. David Porush's contribution is an authoritative survey of 'Literature as Dissipative Structure', drawing on the work of Ilya Prirogine to elucidate literary structures employed by Roussel, Woolf and Joyce, and developed by postmodernists such as Beckett, William Burroughs and Donald Barthelme.

To observe that Donald Bruce and Anthony Purdy's collection, *Literature and Science*, is more tentative in tone is not to diminish what is a particularly fine series of controlled experiments investigating the terms of this interdisciplinary encounter. There is accomplished literary analysis in Anthony Wall's 'Developing a Taste for Metaphors', and in William Paulson's 'Chance, Complexity, and Narrative Explanation'. But to isolate these is unfair to a collection that is uniformly stimulating. It is again evident that the activity of Prirogine in the field of chaos theory is found relevant by an increasing number of literary theorists.

Laura Otis ranges confidently across disciplinary boundaries in *Organic Memory*, examining an idea in its ascendancy between 1870 and 1918, now discredited by science, yet retaining significant discursive power in areas ostensibly remote from that of its formation. She begins by looking at attempts to justify organic memory as a scientific theory, attending especially to Samuel Butler, Ewald Hering and Thodule Ribot. She then considers the cultural implications of the assumption that history determines both personal and collective identity, before examining representative writers including Zola, Mann, Hardy, Unamuno, Freud and Jung. Otis demonstrates, skilfully and substantially, how the concept has been linked with forms of nationalism, and other constructions of community as value.

Raymond Williams suggested that 'nature is perhaps the most complex word in the language'. This is cited by Michael Mayerfeld Bell in *Childerley*, his sociological study of an English country, or 'exurban', village, and exploration of the 'social experience of nature', of 'nature as a form of cultural and moral understanding'. This embraces, of course, literary treatments of 'pastoral nature', which, Bell suggests, continue to form a dominant English tradition. The book in fact contains little direct treatment of literary issues, being primarily a record of fieldwork, but as a study of the cultural meaning of place, it may prove of interest to readers engaged with matters of location and of identity formation.

In *Comic Transactions*, James F. English brings the study of humour and the theory of community to bear on a selection of novels in order to elucidate the politics of literature in twentieth-century Britain. His choice of texts is surprising in its general avoidance of the overtly comic: *The Secret Agent*, *The Apes of God*, *Between the Acts*, *The Golden Notebook* and *The Satanic Verses* are scrutinized, along with *Lucky Jim*. English's provocative point of departure is the claim that literature is constantly making jokes, and that 'community' is regularly the topic of those jokes. His conclusion is that 'we need to stop positing community as the missing term of value whose restoration will assure the improvement of culture'. Considerable intellectual weight underlies his argument, and he produces vigorous and sophisticated readings in a virtuoso performance that must stand as one of the major achievements of the year.

Imagination of alternative worlds, where communities may exist that evade familiar limitations based on gender, is the domain of *Utopian and Science Fiction by Women*, a collection of essays edited by Jane L. Donawerth and Carol A. Kolmerten. Starting from Margaret Cavendish's *Blazing World* (1668) and passing via *Cranford* to contemporary utopian fiction, the volume is perceived by its editors as ground-breaking in its identification of a distinct literary tradition, within which diverse fictions 'historically speak to one another'. The majority of twentieth-century writers treated are American, but Sarah Lefanu contributes 'Difference and Sexual Politics in Naomi Mitchison's *Solution Three*'.

'Heterogeneity is the dominant characteristic of postmodern utopian thinking', asserts Tobin Siebers in his rather slick, playful introduction to *Heterotopia*, in which contributors ponder a variety of utopias imagined within postmodernism, reflecting the nature of desire in our time. The essays explore in various ways the continuing need for community in an age distrustful of the means for its attainment. In effect they address the future projected by James English, 'rigorously unimagined and freed of its obligations to a community of the past'. The latter half of the book deals specifically with the politics of the human body framed by contemporary discourses. For such a committedly postmodern volume, individual essays demonstrate surprising dedication to forms of historical awareness, and while characteristically eclectic they are refreshingly free from terminological jargon. Particularly notable are Carol Thomas Neely's 'Woman/Utopia/Fetish', drawing Cavendish's *Blazing World* into a discussion of contemporary utopian writing by women, and Samuel R. Delaney's 'The Rhetoric of Sex, the Discourse of Desire', where the novelist discloses an enthusiasm for the work of Raymond Roussel.

Heterogeneity is to be expected from a collection of essays entitled *Writing the City*, and in terms of its diversity of topics the volume assembled by Peter Preston and Paul Simpson-Housley meets that expectation. Essays explore cities ranging from early eighteenth-century Osaka to Bernard MacLaverty's Belfast and Helsinki as found in contemporary Finnish literature. There is a tendency, however, for the urban landscape to be treated as 'background' to narrative action or to characterization. Some essays, such as Emily Gilbert's 'Transgressing Boundaries: Isabel Allende's Santiago de Chile', succeed well in fusing literary with geographical concerns; but a number of others are simply expository, rather than engaging with the various investigative theoretical models available to this kind of interdisciplinary work.

An alternative way to present the writing of urban space is the anthology, where juxtaposition may suggestively render diversity of experience offered by the city. Gladys Mary Coles has edited, in *Both Sides of the River*, an unpretentious compilation of prose and poetry generated by the Merseyside conurbation. The quality of the pieces (ranging from translations of medieval texts to work by Alan Bleasdale and Willy Russell) varies considerably, but the editor's twin aims, to evoke a specific place and to reflect its contribution to literature, are well met. There are numerous accompanying pictorial illustrations.

The Virago Book of Women Travellers extends the invaluable service the publishers have performed in rediscovering neglected travel writing by women. Mary Morris, with Larry O'Connor, has assembled a chronological sequence of extracts running from Lady Mary Wortley Montagu to Leila Philip, and including Freya Stark, Rebecca West, Rose Macauley and Dervla Murphy, among many others. The pieces are well chosen, but the introductory notes are rather too brief to be genuinely helpful, and the absence of a supporting bibliography, which would enable readers to pursue particular interests, is regrettable.

Karen Lawrence, in *Penelope Voyages*, takes 'travel writing' to embrace not only Mary Wollstonecraft's account of Scandinavia, and Mary Kingsley's of West Africa, but Woolf's *Orlando* and *The Voyage Out*, and fiction by Christine Brooke-Rose and Brigid Brophy. It is testimony to Lawrence's skill and critical resourcefulness that this expansiveness does not diminish, indeed enhances, her analysis of these 'fantasies of errancy'. This book is a considerable addition to the steadily growing number of studies of travel writing, and it is an important work of criticism well beyond the parameters suggested by that classification.

An essay on, and an interview with, Christine Brooke-Rose form the centrepiece of *British Postmodern Fiction*, edited by Theo D'haen and Hans Bertens. The volume starts with the assumption that British literary tradition has been 'staunchly anti-postmodern', on account of its commitment to mimetic modes of writing. Such stark identification of postmodernism with the non-mimetic, and with technical and formal experimentation, is problematic, and this is acknowledged in a number of essays that wrestle with issues of definition and taxonomy. This results in a certain unevenness, compounded by the fact that some pieces were originally conference papers. Catherine Bernard contributes a noteworthy essay, 'Dismembering/Remembering Mimesis: Martin Amis, Graham Swift'. The Brooke-Rose materials are interesting, although her atypicality itself tests the collection's underlying assumption.

Framing the Margins is a study of American fiction, but its terms of analysis might fruitfully be consulted in conjunction with a reading of *British Postmodern Fiction*. Phillip Brian Harper identifies literary postmodernism with presentation of a decentred subject, and suggests that comparable decentredness can be found in earlier fiction, dealing with 'the socially marginalized and politically disenfranchised'. This suggestion retains a sense of the postmodern as disruptive of received forms, while endorsing another definition which acknowledges the emergence of previously unheard voices. *Mrs Dalloway* is discussed as exemplifying modernist rather than postmodern practice, in that it supposedly 'thematizes the aestheticist hedge against experiential fragmentation'.

There is no sign of Christine Brooke-Rose in Carol McGuirk's 'Drabble to

Carter: Fiction by Women, 1962–1992', an essay to be found in *The Columbia History of the British Novel*, edited by John Richetti, Deidre David, John Bender and Michael Seidel (see also section 1(b) below). This monumental volume constitutes (in the words of contributor Jill Campbell) 'a collective inquiry into the emergence and evolution of one profoundly influential literary form'. It is easy enough to identify omissions from such an enterprise (where, for instance, is Henry Green?), and to criticize the limited nature of departures from the canonical focus, which so evidently furnishes an organizing principle for this inquiry. But it is equally easy to acknowledge the strengths of the book. Individual essays will serve as helpful introductions to students seeking a reliable and convenient guide. The standard of contributions is uniformly high. Each provides a summary view, rather than a summary of views, so they form substantial accounts to fuel debate amongst readers concerned with contesting histories of the novel.

Gavin Wallace and Randall Stevenson have edited *The Scottish Novel since the Seventies: New Visions, Old Dreams* (1993), a collection of essays that does valuable and appropriate service to the creative maturity and consistency of the contemporary Scottish novel, from Robin Jenkins and Muriel Spark to James Kelman and Janice Galloway. It includes a useful bibliography, compiled by Alison Lumsden, and will surely stimulate further critical activity. This uniformly intelligent and incisive series of essays is characterized by a balanced sense of indebtedness to tradition and of significant innovation. This is exemplified by Edwin Morgan's fine 'Tradition and Experiment in the Glasgow Novel'. The 'chorus of opinion' offered here has the great virtue of making one wish to read further.

Comparative study of twentieth-century British and American literature has resulted in *Forked Tongues?*. Ann Massa and Alistair Stead have assembled essays predictably various in both method and matter. The variety is arguably a weakness; some contributors offer broad surveys, others home in on small groupings, others address a single author. To redress discontinuities thrown up by this shifting focus, and conscious of the demand from students for more coherent mapping of major issues, the editors supply occasional brief interjections that aim to place these essays in relation to other work in the field, and they suggest (after the fashion of Julio Cortázar) other orders than the printed sequence for reading of chapters. The volume is useful; it might have been more so, had more essays performed the kind of focused comparison found in Bryan Cheyette's chapter on Philip Roth and Clive Sinclair (and Cynthia Ozick and Elaine Feinstein). Overall the range of authors examined is surprisingly limited: Angela Carter and John Fowles loom large, and attention is paid to Martin Amis, Ian McEwan, Jeanette Winterson and Zöe Fairbairns. David Seed's 'Party-going: The Jazz Age Novels of Evelyn Waugh, Wyndham Lewis, F. Scott Fitzgerald and Carl Van Vechten' is a fine, ingenious and suggestive essay. Alistair Stead's all-too-brief 'Pastoral Sexuality in British and American Fiction' is another of the book's highlights.

The problem faced by Kimberley Reynolds in *Children's Literature in the 1890s and the 1900s* is how to handle adequately, within the confines of a small volume, complex issues of literary production and consumption, of periodization, and of cultural construction of 'the child'. Her recognition of the problem is evident in regular citation of other works her readers might fruitfully consult, but rather too much of the available space is none the less expended in tentative discussion of issues dealt with more fully elsewhere. Ideology is taken as her ostensible analytical focus, but that category is too broad to be of notable assistance. Compounding the sense that not all is satisfactory here is the fact that remarkably little time is spent discussing texts from the specified decades, and one is left wondering why they were selected. A different focal point might have helped this project; for example, the practice of stylistic and formal innovation in recent literature for children, an area that furnishes the most intriguing section of this book.

(b) Individual Authors: 1900–45

Northcote House have produced a *Joseph Conrad*, by Cedric Watts, in their WTW series. This is a revamp of the old British Council series (indeed, it is still produced 'in association with the British Council') and, although allowing authors a slightly broader canvas on which to account for the entire writing lives of their subjects, remains awkwardly poised between the devil of the pamphlet and the deep blue sea of the monograph. Watts is as compromised by the format as anyone would be, forced to economize drastically on quotation or, where he does not, having to curtail comment. Take his treatment of *Almayer's Folly*: in four and a half pages he has to account for Edward Garnett's involvement with it as publisher's reader, T. Fisher Unwin's view of it as publisher, the kite-flying that was done in advance of publication, and its fate at the hands of reviewers, as well as summarizing the plot and attempting to give some account of its themes and evaluation of its style. Watts manages this with admirable conciseness, but the very imperative to be so concise is what makes the entire enterprise so unsatisfactory. Something along the same lines has to be said of Daniel R. Schwarz's thirty-page chapter on Conrad in Richetti et al., *The Columbia History of the British Novel* (see also section 1(a) above, and this section, below). Forced similarly to telescope his discussion, Schwarz cannot find the space sufficient to distinguish *Almayer's Folly* from *An Outcast of the Islands*, and so in the two pages he has available he understandably lumps them both together as texts which share a locale and omniscient narration. This information might just be useful – but it would also be misleading – to someone who has read neither text.

At the other end of the scholarly scale, things are salvaged for *Almayer's Folly*, at least, by its long-awaited appearance in that prolonged tooth-pulling exercise, the Cambridge Edition of the Works of Joseph Conrad. The text is edited by David Leon Higdon and Floyd Eugene Eddleman, and introduced by Ian Watt, and comes replete with maps, explanatory notes, textual apparatus and an essay on the texts, the editorial material totalling roughly the same number of pages as the text of the novel itself. One only wishes that Cambridge would get its act together on Conrad in the way it has with Lawrence: this is only the second Conrad novel to emerge from a project that began in the seventies. One other edition of Conrad this year did not, predictably, include *Almayer's Folly*. Norman Page includes *Heart of Darkness, The Secret Agent* and *The Shadow-Line* in Macmillan's omnibus *Joseph Conrad: Three Novels*. There is no real textual work to speak of (with few exceptions the edition reproduces the Dent texts), and the explanatory notes are thin to say the least (only five pages of notes for all three novels). There is, however, a glossary of nautical terms and a brief chronology of Conrad's life, and a twenty-page introduction. The intellectual rationale for such an edition is not clear. But as these three texts are probably the most in demand of Conrad's *oeuvre*, the commercial motives are patent.

Alicia Pousada individualizes Ronald Wardaugh's definition of language planning as a 'longterm, sustained, and conscious effort to alter a language's function in a society for the purposes of solving communication problems' to help her produce a fascinating exploration of Conrad's linguistic development in

'Joseph Conrad's Multilingualism: A Case Study of Language Planning in Literature' (*ES* 75.iv.335–49). Pousada surveys the arguments for Conrad's ultimate choice of English as the language of his texts, and briefly accounts for the effects this had on his French and Polish. The starting point for Jeremy Hawthorn in 'Joseph Conrad's Theory of Reading', in Andrew Kennedy and Orm Øverland, eds, *Excursions in Fiction: Essays in Honour of Professor Lars Hartveit on his 70th Birthday* (see also below, this section and section 2(a)), is the contention that, unlike the lyric poet, 'a struggling novelist such as Joseph Conrad – desperate for the sales that will solve his pressing financial problems, and having to obtain these in a culture and set of traditions to which he was not born – is likely to think both long and deeply about how what he writes will be read'. He looks particularly at Conrad's implicit theory of the 'suggestiveness' of literary as opposed to non-literary texts, and dredges up a number of good and bad readers from the Conrad character list to enable this scrutiny, concluding 'Conrad seems to have believed that the issues which face the reader of fiction are comparable to those facing any human being who has to respond to and interpret the world: tact, moral integrity, and risk-taking are unavoidable.'

The case for a link between Conrad and Schopenhauer is eloquently made by Owen Knowles in '"Who's Afraid of Arthur Schopenhauer?": A New Context for Conrad's *Heart of Darkness*' (*NCL* 49.75–106). It is the '*indirect* manifestation of Schopenhauer through the host of popular legends and icons of the time', rather than a concrete tie, which interests Knowles. One notices this kind of strategy as an increasing trend in modernist literary scholarship: the direct influences having been investigated exhaustively, attention is now being switched to the more penumbral associations which major cultural figures generate. Thus 'Joseph Conrad did not read the works of his contemporary Sigmund Freud', writes Catharine Rising in 'Conrad and Kohut: The Fortunate Oedipal Fall' (*P&CT* 17.i.107–20). 'Nevertheless, this paper will attempt to show that Conrad's "The Lagoon," which seems to essay a racial comparison, can be better understood as a psychic debate in which the desire for freedom from the Oedipus complex conflicts with a Freudian appreciation of its essential role, as the basis of morality, in human development.' This is a fruitful turn in the old debate about Conrad's Western allegiances. He clearly believed, Rising demonstrates, that conscience and the Oedipus complex were exclusively Western experiences. In 'The Lagoon', she argues, there is a subtext in which these shackles to passionate living are repudiated, which, in theory, as they are not conceived as universal, is a possibility.

Katarzyna Sokołowska has a pretty debatable comparison of *The Secret Agent* with *The Devils* in 'Verloc and Stavrogin: Two Versions of Personality Disintegration' (*EiP* 19.ii.34–44). To claim, as she does in conclusion, that 'Conrad and Dostoevsky . . . belong to the opposed cultures of the West and East' is rather outrageous. But quite what this basic character study, and its concomitant traditional emphasis on morality, are doing in 'the journal of the British neo-formalist circle' is a more fundamental question. Sokołowska's endnotes give a clue to her old-fashionedness: most of the critical texts she cites were published in the sixties and seventies. Colin Milton has an interesting but not terribly original paper on 'Region, Nation, and Empire in *Heart of Darkness*' in a special number of *SwR* devoted to 'Writing Region and Nation' (408–26) (see also this section, below, and section 2(b)). The conception of national development which he sees as implicit to *Heart of Darkness* envisages 'the birth and growth, the maturing and decline of nations as a slow, organic, evolutionary process'.

Conradiana continues to appear on time, although numbers ii and iii of volume 26 were published within a single cover. This remains one of the better single-author journals available, although some of the contributors inevitably seem to be doing the literary equivalent of basket weaving. Thus 'Lieut. Cdr. Andrew K. M. Browne, R.N. (Ret.)' offers us 'An Original for "Gentleman" Brown' (26.i.76–9). The purported original turns out to be the author's uncle, and one cannot help feeling that the overwhelming wish to claim some personal connection with Conrad has got the better of the author here. Weak articles like this tend to make one read the rest of a journal with undue scepticism, which is a pity, for all the main articles in the first number of this volume of *Conradiana* – Lesley Heywood writing on 'The Unreadable Text: Conrad and "The Enigma of Woman" in *Victory*' (3–19), Rita Bode on '"They . . . Should Be Out of It": The Women of *Heart of Darkness*' (20–34), Monika M. Elbert on '"Freya of the Seven Isles" and the Heart of Male Darkness' (35–55), Jennifer Shaddock on 'Hanging a Dog: The Politics of Naming in "An Anarchist"' (56–69), and Charles Ponnuthurai Sarvan and Paul Balles on 'Buddhism, Hinduism, and the Conradian Darkness' (70–5) – are all worth reading. The high point of numbers ii and iii is the opening essay on 'The Politics of Irony in Reading Conrad' (85–101) by Paul B. Armstrong, but it is well accompanied by Gudrun Kauhl's 'Strategies of Reappraisal: Joseph Conrad's *The Secret Agent*' (103–18), which shares its dual focus on *The Secret Agent* and irony. It also contains a fascinating attack on Conrad biography, 'Requiem for Biography: The Case of Joseph Conrad' (211–17), by Joyce Wexler. This is a plea for the implementation of 'the structuralist paradigm', in which biographers 'do not seek the genesis of literary texts in the writer's unique experiences but in the author's public career', and an arraignment of Conrad biography for being far too interested in Conrad's private life and psychology. Wexler lapses herself, however: 'When Conrad realized the limits on the public's ability to construe his texts', she tells us, 'he tried to make his fiction more explicit not because he suddenly decided to write for money, but because he chose to use his hard-won technical skill to communicate with others.' But how does Wexler know, and why does she wish to announce, Conrad's private choices, when, in practice, they cannot be known and, according to her theory, do not really matter? In the end, mapping sociology/psychology too strictly onto the objective/subjective divide proves too restrictive for Wexler's argument, because, as her discussion unwittingly demonstrates, a sociological approach needs to account in some way for subjectivity too.

Wexler's article was written too late to deal with John Batchelor's *The Life of Joseph Conrad*, but there is very little doubt that it would incur her wrath. For example, the narrative hostility to Winnie Verloc's mother in *The Secret Agent* is claimed to be a direct transference of Conrad's hostility to his own mother-in-law. But one could easily make a case for the narrative being much less hostile to Winnie's mother than Batchelor thinks it is. The association of Verloc with Conrad and of Stevie with his own child seems even more wilful. Elsewhere, Batchelor allows himself to free-associate on the recurrence of the letter 'K' in the manuscript of *Under Western Eyes*, and sums up: 'K. stands for the dead father and the displaced son in Conrad's life and for the absent, hidden father and the displaced son in his novel.' But it would not be hard to manipulate the associations of virtually *any* letter in the way Batchelor does to arrive at this conclusion. But *The Life of Joseph Conrad* is not all psychobiography with a vengeance: there is a good deal of textual analysis, a lot more responsible scrutiny of the manuscripts, and solid research around the facts. It does not have the scale of some Conrad biographies, but it is considerably more up to date than some of them.

The year threw up *yet another* Lawrence biography, Brenda Maddox's *The Married Man: A Life of D. H. Lawrence*. Ironically, this points up a glaring gap in what seems to be an overpopulated field. Since the deficiencies of even the revised edition of Harry T. Moore's *The Priest of Love* (1974) have been made glaringly clear by a sequence of commentators, there is no decent one-volume biography of Lawrence. There are several bad ones, of which I have had cause to complain before in these pages, but the good ones (Paul Delany's *D. H. Lawrence's Nightmare: The Writer and his Circle in the Years of the Great War* [1979], say, or John Worthen's *D. H. Lawrence: The Early Years: 1885–1912* [1992]) focus on a period of Lawrence's life rather than the whole. Maddox herself remarks that Lawrence's 'life is often sliced into fragments of time, place or topic, as if his forty-four years on earth were too extraordinary to be squeezed into a single volume'. She has the added advantage over her academic competitors of being published by a commercial rather than an academic publisher and being extremely well connected in the media. The journalistic coverage which this biography of a somewhat unpopular author has consequently received has been little short of staggering. Foreign publishers are no doubt queuing up for the translation rights already in a way that they are surely not for the Cambridge biographies, making this *the* force to be reckoned with in Lawrence biography, the book that, for good or ill, will have more influence on popular understanding of Lawrence's life than any other. It is consoling to be able to report, therefore, that Maddox could have done a much worse job, and has done a better one than my predispositions led me to expect. The emphasis on Lawrence's marriage being the central relationship of his life certainly exorcizes the Oedipal spectre which haunts most Lawrence biography: exit the shade of Lydia Lawrence. But Maddox does not romanticize this marriage in the slightest: she calls it, memorably, 'a mismatch made in heaven', and sets out to try to account for the mystery of its not having cracked into pieces. But she does not do this by arrogating to Frieda Lawrence a position of influence far in excess of her meagre intellectual credentials (as some Lawrence scholars have unforgivably done). Frieda does not, in fact, have a great deal of depth in Maddox's account, which is exactly the impression that Frieda's own writings, and what we know of her from most others, give of her.

Those writings themselves, in all their superficiality, banality and awkwardness, are made available again in Rosie Jackson's *Frieda Lawrence*. This curiously organized volume prints Frieda's highly unreliable memoir, *Not I, But the Wind* (with some of the Lawrence material omitted which had padded out the original volume of 1934), and excruciatingly bad 'extracts from Frieda's fictionalized memoirs', *And the Fullness Thereof . . .* . To be sure, these evaluations are not Jackson's: she thinks *Not I, But the Wind* is all passionate sincerity ('written from the heart') and that the fictional passages 'show [Frieda] to be a potentially talented writer'. These judgements are offered in the first half of the book, a rather rambling, condensed, impressionistic biography of Frieda, hashed together from a variety of diverse sources, written by Jackson herself. At no point is Jackson candid enough really to explore her own personal reasons for her unique empathy for Frieda: namely that Frieda, like herself, suffered the guilt and pain of choosing to separate from her children (Jackson's own book on the subject, *Mothers Who Leave: Behind the Myth of Women Without Their Children* [1994], is listed in her bibliography). Such shared experience obviously gives as much scope to indulgent identification as it does to inward understanding. Creditable biography usually requires more critical detachment than this permits.

Peter Preston's excellent *A D. H. Lawrence Chronology* does not entirely supplant Keith Sagar's *D. H. Lawrence: A Calendar of His Works* (1979), as the latter incorporates many quotations from Lawrence's letters and marries them to a checklist of his manuscripts (itself now somewhat out of date, however). But it does update most of the information one uses Sagar's book for (i.e. checking when precisely Lawrence was working on a particular draft or text) and thus performs its main function. It also doubles as a full-scale chronology, summarizing Lawrence's movements and activities day by day (something Sagar managed only synoptically). Lawrence scholars will want to acquire this book as a constant resource.

Robert E. Montgomery displays a commendably sensible attitude to literary influence in *The Visionary D. H. Lawrence: Beyond Philosophy and Art*: 'In order to establish influence, the critic must first prove that A actually read certain works by B; he then must resist the powerful temptation to find evidence of B's influence where it does not exist; he must also not ascribe to B ideas and formulations that could just as well have come from C or D or any number of others, not to mention the possibility that A may have had an idea of his own.' The many Lawrenceans who have flouted these principles have failed to do justice to the fact that 'the strands making up the web of Lawrence's thought are hopelessly tangled'. Montgomery unravels where he can, but is conscientious in simply explaining the tangles. We just cannot gauge, for example, how much Lawrence's interest in Schopenhauer and Heraclitus was mediated by Nietzsche, who was haunted by both. Though Montgomery is admirably unafraid to strew major difficulties like this in his own path, the bizarreness of his approach comes out in a discussion of Lawrence and Coleridge. 'I do not think of Coleridge as a direct influence', he frankly admits, adding, 'there is no evidence that Lawrence read any of his philosophical works.' What Montgomery does is take an astonishing leap of faith across the gulf he has thus acknowledged: 'I assume that, as A. C. Bradley said of Wordsworth and Hegel, we find "the same mind" in Lawrence and Coleridge.' If Lawrence and Coleridge have 'the same mind' history is entirely negated, and the importance for Lawrence of post-Coleridgean philosophers paradoxically neutralized. The process whereby Lawrence achieved a mental identity with his Romantic precursor is much more evidentially mystified than the constructions of the Lawrence influence-mongers Montgomery berates. But then, the book's limitations are hardly surprising: Lawrence studies have seldom been the province of the historically inclined. As a lucid, informative discussion of Lawrence's philosophical relations, *The Visionary D. H. Lawrence* is a very good book indeed. Montgomery, unlike Lawrence, presents philosophical ideas with tremendous clarity, and relates them to literary texts (particularly *The White Peacock* and *Women in Love*) in sensitive and insightful ways.

Cynthia Lewiecki-Wilson's *Writing Against the Family: Gender in Lawrence and Joyce* is a comparison of family relations as represented in the works of Joyce and Lawrence. A long chapter on Freudian, Lacanian, Marxist, feminist and object-relations theories of the family precedes a fifty-page analysis of how the sexual struggle displaces the class struggle in Lawrence's work. There is little attempt at comprehensive coverage of texts: twenty-four pages are devoted to *Sons and Lovers*, a mere seven to *The Rainbow*, and fourteen to *Women in Love*. A sixty-page chapter on Joyce follows, and then there is a sixty-seven page comparative chapter which surveys the common interests of Lawrence, Joyce and (for some reason) Freud in – wait for it – Egyptology. This troublingly dull chapter is doubly problematized by the fact that it bears only the most tenuous link to the familial focus declared by Lewiecki-Wilson at the outset. The subtitle of the short concluding chapter – 'Resituating Lawrence and Joyce within Modernism and Postmodernism' – threatens an even more digressive tendency, but thankfully draws us back to a comparison of how Lawrence and Joyce rethink family and gender.

In 'Calling in the Realists: The Revision and Reputation of Lawrence's *Sons and Lovers*' (*Novel* 27.233–56), David M. Thompson demonstrates how Lawrence's early realist novel has divided critics into those who regard it as the first of his major novels or those who see it as the last of his novelistic apprenticeship, and those who view it as a salutary example of editorial assistance or a regrettable instance of editorial vandalism on the part of Edward Garnett. Thompson's position is not to take sides in these polarities, but to examine 'the processes by which these questions have come to seem like the questions that need to be asked'. In doing so he does offer a powerful and timely critique of the ideological predispositions behind the Cambridge edition of Lawrence's works and, in particular, of Cambridge's 1992 edition of *Sons and Lovers* (see *YWES* 73.491–2). Dent Everyman have produced an edition of *Sons and Lovers*, edited by Macdonald Daly, which shares Thompson's scepticism about the Cambridge project, and offers an alternative text based on the 1913 edition. Had David Trotter's Oxford WC edition of the same novel been published nineteen days earlier it could have been discussed in this rather than the next volume of *YWES*: as it is, I propose to hold comparison of the three editions over until *YWES* 76, especially as the text of the Cambridge *Sons and Lovers* (eds Helen Baron and Carl Baron) is now also in paperback, one of four Lawrence titles published this year by Penguin, who have reputedly paid the Lawrence Estate alone over £600,000 for the rights to the Cambridge edition. The other three texts were *Lady Chatterley's Lover* (ed. Michael Squires), *The Trespasser* (ed. Elizabeth Mansfield), and *The Fox; The Captain's Doll; The Ladybird* (ed. Dieter Mehl).

The Penguin editions reproduce (sometimes with corrections) the texts of the Cambridge edition, with the same pagination, but without the line numbering. Each has a newly commissioned literary critical introduction and annotation which are distinct from but lighter than those of the Cambridge texts. Under the general editorship of John Worthen, the Penguin Lawrence is a much more consistent and coherent series than several of those in the same publisher's list. As no other paperback house is seriously taking on Lawrence, the Penguin texts will without doubt become the standard, despite the controversy which has raged about the Cambridge principles. Predictably, they do not contain the editorial apparatus which, in theory at least, allows dissenters from those principles to reconstruct alternative texts. In that respect at least, the Cambridge edition is not redundant. Its value continues to be exhibited in the two excellently edited volumes which appeared this year: *Twilight in Italy*, edited by Paul Eggert, and *Kangaroo*, edited by Bruce Steele. Had Simon Leys read Bruce Steele's earlier work on *Kangaroo* before writing 'Lawrence of Australia' (*NYRB* 41.viii.29–35) he might not have so slavishly reproduced Robert Darroch's unfounded speculations (in *D. H. Lawrence in Australia* [1981]) that Lawrence was actually in touch with a secret army organization when he was writing *Kangaroo*. Among others, Steele so convincingly put this matter to rest in 'Kangaroo: Fiction and Fact' (*Meridian* 10[1991].19–34) that he justifiably alludes to Darroch only once in passing in his edition. More welcome attention to Lawrence's unduly neglected Australian novel can be found in Gisèle Marie Baxter's '"After such knowledge, what forgiveness?": Exile, Marriage and the Resistance to Commitment in D. H. Lawrence's *Kangaroo*' (*JNT* 24.127–40), which explores the narrative consequences of the notion that the protagonist's dual refusal of social integration and ideological commitment is a strategy for personal survival.

David Ellis writes on 'Lawrence, Wordsworth and "Anthropomorphic Lust"' (*CQ* 23.230–42). The phrase is taken from Lawrence's essay '. . . Love Was Once a Little Boy', where it is used to condemn the incorporation into the ego of elements of nature which are a source of passionate desire. Ellis surveys 'Lawrence's tendency to overflow his own boundaries and saturate his surroundings with his own feelings' and suggests that in this he has a 'strong affinity' with Wordsworth. Ellis's fellow Lawrence biographer, John Worthen, adds a supplementary note to his excellent account of Lawrence's early years (see *YWES* 72.371–2) in 'D. H. Lawrence and the Society for the Study of Social Questions' (*N&Q* 41.364–6). The Society in question was probably, he thinks, 'formed of Nottingham University College students' in 1908, and he suggests the informed hypothesis that its study 'almost certainly meant adopting – or taking into consideration – a socialist point of view'. Lawrence's early relationship with socialism is more fully explored in two publications by Macdonald Daly: 'D. H. Lawrence and Labour in the Great War' (*MLR* 89.19–38) and 'D. H. Lawrence and the 1912 Miners' Strike' (*ES* 75.133–45)

Gerald Doherty continues his prolific stylistic examinations of Lawrence's fiction, reviewed in recent volumes of *YWES*, with 'Death and the Rhetoric of Representation in D. H. Lawrence's *Women in Love*' (*Mosaic* 27.i.55–72). Here, he applies Roman Jakobson's metaphor/metonymy opposition to 'different approaches to dying, and different evaluations of death' in Lawrence's novel, with his customary taxonomic structuralist dryness. Lucas Carpenter, in 'The Name "Minette" in *Women in Love*' (*ELN* 32.70–3), explains the name change from 'Pussum' to 'Minette' in the Secker edition of Lawrence's novel by reference to the erotic connotations of the latter in French, and calls it 'a cunning and ultimately successful alteration that better highlights some of the central concerns of the novel'. He considers it regrettable 'that current trends towards establishing an authoritative edition of *Women in Love* neglect to include it'.

Thérèse Vichy sees an opportunity to 'explore the relationship between poetry and fiction' in 'Autobiography, Poetry and Fiction in *Look! We Have Come Through!* and *Mr Noon*' (*CVE* 39.101–12). There is a problem with treating *Mr Noon* as autobiography, of course, as it is only in part two that one could claim, as Vichy does, that 'Lawrence turns his life into fiction'. Her solution – to ignore part one altogether – is convenient, but not intellectually acceptable. Is this any different from claiming that *Sons and Lovers* is autobiographical if you ignore the major narrative elements which are demonstrably imagined? Moreover, Vichy does not actually get round to making any general statement about the relationship between poetry and fiction which she claims to be exploring. Her conclusion is staggeringly banal: 'I shall say in conclusion that, if what is fascinating with Lawrence is his creative imagination rather than his life-story, it is equally obvious that what fuels the imagination is the living man in his dividedness.' Perhaps the obvious does not require stating.

Howard Mills gives himself rather a large canvas in '"The World of Substance":

Lawrence, Hardy, Cézanne and Shelley' (*English* 43.209–22). Mills wants to use the word 'substance' as Lawrence uses it in 'Introduction to These Paintings', to designate the life of the body without reducing its sense to 'flesh' or 'sex'. As usual, if you start by accepting Lawrence's terms, your intention is usually to celebrate them. Hardy, Cézanne and Shelley are here not in their own right (as Lawrence is), but because Lawrence had things to say about them, and the notion of 'substance' is useful to Mills in summarizing and evaluating what these things were, and being lyrical about Lawrence generally in a winsome, old-fashioned way. Earl Ingersoll, meanwhile, thinks 'Lawrence's development of his two couples within the framework of references to eyes and seeing' in *Women in Love* is interesting enough to devote thirteen pages to it in 'Staging the Gaze in D. H. Lawrence's *Women in Love*' (*SNNTS* 26.268–80). Although he had not read Freud's 'Instincts and their Vicissitudes', Lawrence, Ingersoll believes, 'had independently developed insights into the complexities of visual exchange' which offer 'the opportunity for what might be termed a New Psychoanalytic Criticism'. It is good to know that Lawrence is contributing in this fundamental way to such wholly ingenious new critical industries.

A special number of *SwR* on 'Writing Region and Nation' offers the proceedings of the Fourth International Conference on the Literature of Region and Nation, held at the University of Wales, Swansea, in 1992 (see also this section, above, and section 2(b) below), and throws up four papers on Lawrence. Wendy Vacani writes on 'D. H. Lawrence's Perception of Mexico: A Meditation on Consciousness' (535–47), discussing Lawrence's relations with animism in particular; Michael Herbert offers an original paper on Lawrence's construction of 'nations or races or other human collectives' in 'D.H.Lawrence's Peoples' (299–310), is quick to note that he is 'prone to extreme generalisations', but in the end, somewhat predictably, lets Lawrence off the hook: 'he is also very even-handed; and surely we can forgive him a lot for the honesty so often attested to'. What was that – forgive Lawrence for the *honesty* with which he deploys stereotypes? H'm. Catherine Greensmith writes on 'Movements in European Art: A Lawrentian Perspective' (243–58), but does not think any kind of scholarly references are necessary in doing so: quotations tumble out without any attributed source beyond the title of the text (and on one occasion not even that), and the paper is full of breezy generalizations. Mark Kinkead-Weekes does better in 'Re-placing the Exiled Imagination: D. H. Lawrence and Bessie Head', although their respective exiles were so different that it remains unclear what precise grounds there are for comparing these two writers.

In Elizabeth Hayes, ed., *Images of Persephone: Feminist Readings in Western Literature*, Virginia Hyde's '"Lost" Girls: D. H. Lawrence's Visions of Persephone' deals synoptically with the recurrence of the Persephone myth in Lawrence's works. Andrew Kennedy's 'The Myth of Rebirth' (in his and Øverland's edited volume, *Excursions in Fiction* – see also above, this section, and section 2(a) below) investigates the possibilities of writing fiction with a religious dimension in a post-Christian age by means of a brief examination of *The Man Who Died.* Vincent P. Pecora contributes a twenty-five-page chapter on Lawrence to Richetti et al., eds, *The Columbia History of the British Novel* (see also above, this section and section 1(a)). The level of generalization required of an enterprise such as this has the potential to render any contributor helpless. In the days of the British Council pamphlet it may have been considered possible to *do* Lawrence in twenty-five pages, but in these days of narrower and narrower specialism the prospect is unenviable. Pecora's implied solution to the problem – to treat many of Lawrence's occasionally expressed prejudices (anything from his 'hatred' for his father to his aversion to internal plumbing) as if they were permanent resolutions – is not encouraging. Carol Siegel's 'Border Disturbances: D. H. Lawrence's fiction and the Feminism of *Wuthering Heights*', in Thaïs E. Morgan, ed., *Men Writing the Feminine: Literature, Theory, and the Question of Genders*, points out that much feminist criticism is in danger of 'ignoring – or worse, over-simplifying – the dialogue that has always existed between men's and women's fictions', and believes that the 'unusual' relationship between *Wuthering Heights* and Lawrence's novels 'both marks and obscures a border between the genders'. The Lawrence novel which gets the most attention is the lamentably immature *The White Peacock*, although *The Ladybird* and *John Thomas and Lady Jane* get a look in.

The assuredness of a text's cultural importance can often be gauged by the presence of later attempts at parody or rewriting. Orwell's *Nineteen Eighty-Four* has been singularly successful on this count: to Anthony Burgess's *1985* (1978) and György Dalos' *1985* (1982) is now added Peter Huber's *Orwell's Revenge: The 1984 Palimpsest*. Formally, Huber owes a great deal to Burgess (he seems unaware of Dalos): he offers both a literary critique of Orwell's novel (in which, essentially, his laboured point is that Orwell was too pessimistic about computer technology) and rewrites the plot (so that a character called 'Blair' discovers the diary of a character called 'Orwell', previously vaporized because he developed the cellular potential of the telescreen, thus transforming it into a potentially liberatory technology). The critique and the rewrite alternate chapter by chapter, although the critique gradually assumes centre stage. Huber is occasionally aware of the abyss of technological determinism on which his central argument sometimes teeters, but he eventually falls into it because this argument is firmly tied to a very heavy weight in the form of a somewhat simplistic need to defend free market principles. It is possible to accept the limitations of Orwell's technological thinking while considering it highly unlikely that his ideas, driven to a rational conclusion, would imply so enthusiastic an embrace of even the most regulated forms of capitalism. That said, *Orwell's Revenge* is a rich and provocative text, precisely the kind of thing that would get students debating, not only the ideas of Orwell's novel, but the potential forms which literary criticism can take. Huber does not, for instance, just talk in the abstract about the vast potential of the personal computer: he *demonstrates* it by feeding Orwell's entire works through an optical scanner, thus allowing himself to search and plunder them in the most thorough manner imaginable. The resultant footnotes reveal a virtually totalitarian command of Orwell's *oeuvre*.

Every year there are other indicators that *Nineteen Eighty-Four* proves to be of some utility to intellectuals whose concern is not literature. The text routinely pops up in discussions taking place in other disciplines. Michael Bukowski, David B. Kronenfeld, William Peterman and Lynn Thomas oblige this year by using Orwell 'as a convenient starting point for our considerations' of the language of the 1989 revolutions in Eastern Europe in 'Language, *Nineteen eighty-four* [*sic*], and 1989' (*LSoc* 23.555–78). As is usual in cases like these, however, the article could have been written without reference to Orwell. On the other hand, one wonders what the impulse to write certain papers on Orwell is. Geoffrey Heptonstall contributes four negligible pages on 'Orwell and Bohemia' to *ContempR* (264.1539.211–14), while Henri Astier presents a journalistic comparative survey of Orwell and the philosopher-turned-journalist Jean-François Revel (a parallel first pointed out by

Mario Vargas Llosa as long ago as 1979) to the same journal (264.1541.292–302).

Much more interesting is Peter Davison's 'Orwell: Balancing the Books' (*Library* 16.ii.77–100), 'the results of an examination of the records of the publishing history of Orwell's books and journalism to 1945 [which] offers conjectural estimates of what Orwell earned from 1922 until the end of 1945'. The main sources are a notebook Orwell kept for tax purposes between 1943 and 1945 and the records of his publisher, Gollancz. Davison admirably tabulates his findings across a two-page spread, allowing for fascinating comparisons. The trend across the twenty-four years in question is not inexorably upwards. From an estimated £70 income in 1932, Orwell's fortunes soared to £345 in 1933, largely due to British and American sales of *Down and Out in Paris and London*, only to slump again below £250 in each of the next three years. To intensify the irony of Orwell's sporadic well-offness accruing from books about poverty, the next big surge was provided by *The Road to Wigan Pier* in 1937 (£631). This was followed by further lean years until 1941 (£573), after which something closer to affluence beckoned: £706 (1942), £807 (1943), £1,179 (1944), £1,514 (1945). Davison cleverly puts all of this into perspective by comparing Trollope's earnings four years before his death from books alone (almost £67,000, equivalent to £500,000 in 1945) with Orwell's total book earnings at the same point in his life (£2,200 in 1945). One wishes biographers in general gave as much attention to this kind of nitty-gritty as Davison does.

A much less assured performance is Ramón Magrán's 'Anti-Totalitarism [*sic*] in *Animal Farm* and *The Time of the Hero*', in Ana María Hernández de López, ed., *Mario Vargas Llosa: Opera Omnia*. There are three misprints in the first paragraph of the article alone (one of them in the first word), and a generally poor grasp of English idiom: Orwell and Vargas Llosa are said to 'exhibit communion' and 'to cling to an irresistible vocational flame' (can one cling to a flame, and can a flame be vocational?). These basic linguistic problems get worse rather than better: 'opaque' is used as a verb, 'obstinance' appears in place of 'obstinacy', adjectives are left unattached to nouns. One wonders what Orwell, with his belief in linguistic transparency, would have made of it all. In so far as a case is argued, it is no more developed than that there are some similarities between the two novels. Why the author chose to construct this minimal argument in English, rather than the Spanish used by almost every co-contributor to the volume, is a mystery. Why the editor failed to have the text checked by a mother-tongue speaker of English is another.

Paul Peppis writes on 'Anti-Individualism and the Fictions of National Character in Wyndham Lewis's *Tarr*' (*TCL* 40.ii.226–55). He reads considerable significance into the fact that *Tarr*, conceived of as 'a critical assault on English Individualism', originally appeared in the *Egoist*, an 'Individualist Review'. More challenging on *Tarr* is Ann L. Ardis, who in 'Reading "as a Modernist"/ Denaturalizing Modernist Reading Protocols: Wyndham Lewis's *Tarr*' (in Lisa Rado, ed., *Rereading Modernism: New Directions in Feminist Criticism*) is interested in 'the dialectic between modernism and mass culture that is sustained throughout *Tarr* but that is epitomized . . . in the scene in Part IV in which Otto Kreisler rapes Bertha Lunken'. She argues persuasively that this scene concentrates a number of stylistic practices associated with modernism, and then offers this for consideration as a grave problem: 'Does Lewis's narrative invite us to appreciate the modern artist's formal treatment of material while at the same time bracketing off or delegitimizing any other response we might have to the actions represented here?' This is precisely, she concludes, what Eliot and Pound did in their early appropriation of Lewis's text as modernist over and against the features of mass culture which they derided. The whole of this excellent article deserves attention from more than simply Lewis specialists: it addresses in exemplary fashion a major unresolved issue in modernist poetics. The reader might do well to turn from it to Geoffrey Gilbert's long article, 'Intestinal Violence: Wyndham Lewis and the Critical Poetics of the Modernist Career' (*CritQ* 36.iii.86–125), in which modernism is understood 'not as an independent writing practice, whose formal laws are understood to be immanent in its *own* development – not, that is, as a variety of literature – but always as the reflection of an emergent crisis in other discourses'. In 'Blasting the Bombardier: Another Look at Lewis, Joyce, and Woolf' (*TCL* 40.iii.365–78) Kelly Anspaugh dismantles Bonnie Kime Scott's construction of 'male modernism' (associated with Lewis) and 'female modernism' (aligned with Woolf). [M.D.]

In her short conference report, 'Industry or Community? Joyce and the Social Function of Criticism' (*JJQ* 31.ii.17–20), Helene Myers raises some interesting questions about the current condition of Joyce studies – not just whether 'industry' or 'community' is the more appropriate label but also 'what it means when we tell students Joyce is subversive, and they agree'; and what difference it makes to discuss issues of Irish nationalism in California rather than in Dublin or Belfast.

The tensions arising from this last issue – the apparent recolonization of Irish politics and experience by overseas scholarship – were dramatized in a heated exhange at the conference Myers attended, and they also provide an important dynamic for Emer Nolan's new study *James Joyce and Nationalism*. Writing from an Irish perspective, Nolan challenges the attitude of 'detached ambivalence' towards Ireland which 'the international James Joyce critical industry' has always attributed to Joyce, and argues that such a reading represents 'a crucial failure . . . to attend to the full complexity of nationalism in the political culture of modernity'. Liberal and post-structuralist readings alike have tended to empty Joyce's texts of any meaning which can be productively related to the question of how the Irish can actually 'live out their political desires'. Nolan attempts to correct this by re-examining the different implications of modernity for nationalism, and by re-reading some of the key texts in previous accounts. She suggests it is misleading, for example, to read 'Cyclops' as a vindication of the heroically moderate Bloom against the caricatured 'Citizen': some positive values should be attributed to the 'Citizen', whose views partly correspond to Joyce's own published account of Irish history and whose voice is 'probably the funniest in the book'. At times the analysis in *James Joyce and Nationalism* seems rather overcooked: so much of the book is given over to mildly ironic explorations of other critics' positions it becomes difficult at times to distinguish Nolan's own. But resistance to oversimplifying accounts of nationalism is her main point, and this is clearly an important and authoritative contribution to the growing body of work that aims to recontextualize Joyce in terms of Irish and/or post-colonial history.

Enda Duffy's *The Subaltern Ulysses* is another strong contribution to this project, although at first glance his approach would seem to represent the worst excesses of that 'failure . . . to attend to the full complexity of nationalism' which Emer Nolan warns against. Some may find his opening question, for example – 'Might an IRA bomb and Joyce's *Ulysses* have anything in common?' – in doubtful taste. As the book develops, however, Duffy does show that he is sensitive to the different inflections of nationalism and the way they are explored and tested in

Ulysses. Where his approach may seem more suspect, from Nolan's point of view, is in his dominant concern to make Irish history fit a global model of 'post-colonial' experience and to present *Ulysses* as 'the first postcolonial novel'. The book is overloaded with post-colonial jargon (as the title itself suggests) and it is difficult at times to make sense of some of the conclusions Duffy claims to have reached. Some stimulating insights are provided on the way, however. Duffy makes a point of correlating the process of writing *Ulysses* with the upheavals in Irish history of 1916–22, rather than seeking correspondences with the novel's fictional setting in 1904, and this approach endows some familiar figures with an intriguing new significance: thus the man in the macintosh becomes a possible IRA terrorist, the narrator of 'Cyclops' a police informer, and the blind man in 'Sirens' the 'type of a new potentially independent postcolonial flaneur'. It is unfortunate that two such important books as *The Subaltern Ulysses* and *James Joyce and Nationalism* should have come out at the same time, apparently without knowledge of each other – some further dialogue would enhance the value of both works.

Dialogue between different critical approaches as part of the teaching of canonical texts is the main aim of the Case Studies in Contemporary Criticism series, which combines the original text with a collection of essays each representing a different approach. This year's volume on Joyce's 'The Dead', edited by Daniel R. Schwarz, is not as strong as the volume on *A Portrait of the Artist as a Young Man* (reviewed in *YWES* 74.474), but it is still a very useful package. The essays include John Paul Riquelme (representing 'A Deconstructionist Perspective') on 'For Whom the Snow Taps: Style and Repetition in "The Dead"'; and Margot Norris's analysis of the way a feminist reading can be produced by detaching the patriarchal narrator from the (often silenced) voices of the women in the narrative. Kelly Anspaugh's '"Three Mortal Hour[i]s": Female Gothic in Joyce's "The Dead"' (*SSF* 31.1–12) is strongly influenced by an earlier version of this interpretation. Anspaugh relates Norris's critique of the narrator to the 'Gothic' elements in the story (the ghostly figure of Michael Furey, for example), which enact a similar 'implicit feminist critique of patriarchal culture'. Reading the ambiguous last paragraphs with this interpretation of the 'Gothic' in mind, Anspaugh argues, it becomes clear that the final note is not one of paralysis and death but 'the movement toward rebirth'.

Still on *Dubliners*: in '"Derevaun Seraun!": Resignation or Escape?' (*JJQ* 32.102–4) Wim Tigges suggests a new interpretation of the mother's mysterious words in 'Eveline', based on the fact that when he quoted the untranslatable expression out of context to an Irish-speaking colleague she 'spontaneously' translated it as 'I have been there; you should go there!'. This does seem to speak more directly to Eveline's situation than other versions – although, as Tigges acknowledges, the impossibility of settling this question is probably the real point of the utterance. *Narrative Con/Texts in Dubliners*, by the late Bernard Benstock, is a series of rather indeterminate musings on the way the individual stories interact with each other to produce complex networks of associations across the book as a whole. The standard theme for this kind of exercise – prompted by Joyce himself – has always been 'paralysis'. But Benstock extends this in some interesting ways. He suggests, for example, that the various images of fire, birds and air – even the rusty bicycle-pump found in the wild garden in 'Araby' – can be seen as ironic symbols of the 'great disappearance' of the Holy Spirit from paralysed Dublin. The interest here, for the reader and for Benstock, is all in the expert marshalling of significant detail rather than the development of a new big idea about Joyce.

Benstock applies his expertise in a similar non-assertive way in 'Middle-Class Values in *Ulysses* – and the Value of the Middle Class' (*JJQ* 31.439–54), in which he browses through 'the shoddy world of Joyce's petty bourgeoisie' and observes its shaky hold on respectability.

Mitzi Brunsdale's *James Joyce: A Study of the Short Fiction* contains two substantial sections on *Dubliners* and *Portrait* plus a useful selection from Joyce's letters and criticism. More than just a superficial survey, it provides some interesting detailed readings, and takes as its central theme the presence in Joyce's work of images from ancient Celtic culture. The myth-making of the modern Celtic Revival is William O'Neill's focus in 'Myth and Identity in Joyce's Fiction: Disentangling the Image' (*TCL* 40.379–91). O'Neill traces Joyce's changing attitude to this movement, from the contempt expressed in 'Stephen Hero' to the more subtle exploration found in *Portrait*. On a similar theme, there is a section on Stephen's 'Irish shadow' in Weldon Thornton's *The Antimodernism of Joyce's Portrait of the Artist as a Young Man*, the major new book on *Portrait* this year. Thornton applies the term 'Irish shadow' to a 'complex' of interrelated images that evoke a primitive 'Irishness' and that Joyce uses to reveal 'how fearful Stephen is of those elements that confound his attempts to be totally self-aware and self-determining'. But it is this question of the limits of Stephen's consciousness, rather than the issue of 'Irishness', which is Thornton's main preoccupation in his book. He takes a long view of 'modernism' as a philosophical and psychological framework, coming down to us from the Enlightenment, that perniciously denies the existence of a 'collective psyche' and asserts that the individual psyche can and should be 'totally self-aware and self-determining'. The significance of *Portrait* (though Thornton sees all great literature as fulfilling a similar function) is that 'while Stephen Dedalus subscribes to a simplistic idea of individualism that deserves to be called modernist, Joyce shows us the costs and limitations of such a view, and thus should be seen as antimodernist'. Thornton's book is carefully argued and extensively annotated (the notes take up almost a quarter of the total length) but it seems oddly distanced from other recent work on Joyce and *Portrait*. His reading of Stephen in terms of Joyce's 'sympathetic irony' is not particularly new. And he strongly resists any assimilation of his concept of 'antimodernism' to 'postmodernism' or to scepticism about the idea of 'the self': 'Joyce's criticism of the insufficiency of the Humean view of the self does not mean that he disavows the idea of a self, but rather that he wishes to lead us to a more holistic and sufficient view.'

The sixtieth anniversary of the first official American edition of *Ulysses* produced two new studies of the circumstances surrounding this publication – particularly the trial and famous judgement that preceded it. In 'Lifting the Ban on *Ulysses*: The Well-Intentioned Lies of the Woolsey Decision' (*Mosaic* 27.4.179–97), Paul Vanderham examines the theoretical principles on which Judge Woolsey's decision in favour of publication was based, noting that 'decisions in literary censorship cases ... are inescapably forms of literary criticism'. He concludes that Woolsey 'misrepresented the nature of *Ulysses* and, implicitly, literature in general' by basing his judgement on the theory that a work of literature was an aesthetic object and had no power to influence readers' actions or beliefs. Although it achieved the desired result in 1933, this 'aesthetic' defence of freedom of speech set a precedent which has proved inadequate in more recent censorship controversies. Brook Thomas's essay, '*Ulysses* on Trial: Some Supplementary Reading', is in *The Administration of Aesthetics: Censorship, Political Criticism, and the Public Sphere*, edited by Richard Burt. Thomas compares the trial of *Ulysses* in 1933 with the controversy surrounding the Gabler text of *Ulysses*, and notes that both the Random House edition of 1934 and the Gabler edition of 1986 contain supplementary material, including a letter from Joyce in 1934, and a preface by Richard Ellmann in 1986. These supplements are ostensibly there to 'authorize the texts of which they are a part', but, Thomas suggests, their effect is actually to problematize authorship as a legal and aesthetic concept.

The Landmarks of World Literature series, to which Vincent Sherry's *James Joyce: Ulysses* belongs, claims to offer 'concise and lucid introductions to major works'. But this is a rather misleading gloss in Sherry's case, as his book provides very little in the way of basic explanation or orientation (it also fails to provide an index or a proper apparatus for its non-Joyce references, which does not help anyone). What it really offers is a *re*introduction to *Ulysses* for readers who already know their way round – a short, sophisticated overview, which draws on recent scholarship and has some interesting ideas of its own. Sherry's main concern is to reinterpret the epic structure of the novel as Joyce's vindication of 'civic' over individualist values. Bloom rather than Stephen is therefore the hero of Sherry's reading. This provides an interesting contrast with Robert Spoo's more heavyweight study, *James Joyce and the Language of History: Dedalus's Nightmare*, which 'rehabilitates Stephen as the novel's hero by showing that the persistent historiographical concerns of *Ulysses* are ultimately *his* concerns'. As this suggests, Spoo's basic premise is that *Ulysses* can be read as a study in historiography: 'notions of history are both figured and resisted in the Joycean text'. He is wrong to claim that there has been no previous book on this subject: James Fairhall's *James Joyce and the Question of History* (reviewed in *YWES* 74.478) attempted something similar. But Spoo is much more scrupulous than Fairhall in providing, as he puts it, 'historiographic (as distinct from historical) criticism'. He does not combine historiographic readings of *Ulysses* with attempts (like Fairhall's – or Enda Duffy's) to reconstruct the sociopolitical context in which it was written. He is more interested in constructing 'intellectual contexts for the Dedalian nightmare' and in tracing possible connections between notions of history figured in *Ulysses* and Joyce's reading of European philosophers and historians, including Nietzsche, Vico, W. E. H. Lecky and Guglielmo Ferrero. The result is a book of considerable erudition and insight, but one which comes to the rather melancholy conclusion that Stephen can never awake from his nightmare: 'language . . . cannot be the vehicle for escape or transcendence, even though it may express the desire for transcendence, because language is where the enthrallment to history begins'.

This year's work on *Ulysses* also includes John Somer's 'The Self-Reflexive Arranger in the Initial Style of Joyce's *Ulysses*' (*JJQ* 31.65–79), which reviews David Hayman's concept of 'the arranger', and uses it to highlight the way the style of the first six chapters prepares for the variations that follow. *Molly Blooms: A Polylogue on 'Penelope' and Cultural Studies*, edited by Richard Pearce, is a collection of twelve essays which Pearce describes as looking at the last chapter of *Ulysses* 'through the lenses of cultural studies – which include feminism, new historicism, popular culture, postcolonialism, and postmodernism, and which therefore produce a multiplicity of Molly Blooms and illuminate the multiplicity of positions she occupies within the novel'. In many ways the most interesting essay is Kathleen McCormick's 'Reproducing Molly Bloom: A Revisionist History of the Reception of "Penelope" 1922–1970', which outlines the critical history of 'Penelope' *before* this era of 'multiplicity' dawned. McCormick uses the concept of the 'text-in-use' to highlight two earlier phases in the male-dominated construction of Molly Bloom: in the first twenty years or so after publication, critics were so concerned to establish *Ulysses* as a canonical text that they transformed Molly into an 'Earth Mother' figure as a way of coping with her sexuality; once *Ulysses* was secure, however, a backlash began that participated in post-war gynophobia and identified Molly with the dangers of promiscuity and the threat of world destruction. The other essays in this collection tend to explore ways in which Molly can be read as a figure of resistance to these and other repressive discourses. In 'Molly's Resistance to the Union: Marriage and Colonialism in Dublin, 1904', Carol Shloss explores the correspondences between the status of married women in 1904 and that of the whole Irish population 'in thrall to a colonial government': both are in a situation of 'corporate powerlessness within a supposedly benign partnership'. Cheryl Herr adopts a more sceptical tone in '"Penelope" as Period Piece', where she states that she is no longer prepared to grant Molly 'any reality-value whatsoever – not as Earth Mother, not as Celtic Goddess, not as ordinary Dublin Hausfrau . . . For me, "Penelope" projects simply an actor reading a script, a star singing an aria.' Other sections extend the range by looking at 'Molly as Consumer' and 'Molly as Body and Embodied'. This will clearly be an important book for anyone working on or teaching 'Penelope'.

This year's other major collection of essays to note is a special issue of *JJQ* on 'Joyce and Homosexuality', edited by Joseph Valente. The various approaches to this topic include Joseph A. Kestner's illustrated article, '"Youth by the Sea": The Ephebe in *A Portrait of the Artist as a Young Man* and *Ulysses*' (*JJQ* 31.233–59), and Jennifer Levine's study of the innuendo and connotations of homosexuality in 'Eumaeus', 'James Joyce, Tattoo Artist: Tracing the Outlines of Homosocial Desire' (*JJQ* 31.277–99). In 'The "unhappy mania" and Mr Bloom's Cigar: Homosexuality in the Works of James Joyce' (*JJQ* 31.357–73), David Norris writes as someone for whom homosexuality is part of 'lived reality' and 'not just a sophisticated literary construct or an exotic metaphor to be projected onto a text'. From this perspective he concludes that Joyce 'did not devote a great deal of attention' to the issue. Norris's judgement provides an important counter-balance to the other essays, but it is very effectively challenged by the most impressive study in this collection, Joseph Valente's 'Thrilled by his Touch: Homosexual Panic and the Will to Artistry in *A Portrait of the Artist as a Young Man*' (*JJQ* 31.167–88). Valente argues that Joyce's reluctance to speak of homosexuality can be seen as a form of denial which becomes a 'fundamental determinant' of Stephen's development in *Portrait*, and he presents a detailed reading of the novel in terms of its homoerotic energies and the inseparability of Stephen's sense of artistic vocation from homosexual anxiety. Not surprisingly, Oscar Wilde is a key reference in several of the essays in this collection. Valente discovers numerous allusions to Wilde in *Portrait* and suggests that the title itself is derived from a passage in *The Picture of Dorian Gray*.

The Steadfast Finnegans Wake: A Textbook, by Grace Eckley, is one of those books that claim to have discovered a new master-key to the difficulties of Joyce's last work. For Eckley this key is found in the unlikely figure of W. T. Stead, the English journalist who controversially exposed child prostitution in Victorian London, edited a journal which charted 'the Progress of the World', and died on the *Titanic* in 1912 (hence, according to Eckley, Joyce's use of the Tristram-and-Iseult myth). *Finnegans Wake*, it turns out, is all about Stead and his career: 'With Stead for epic hero, the *Wake* can be acclaimed as a socio-historical novel set primarily in the years 1885–1922 . . . Stead provides a narrative for the reading of the *Wake*, bridges the spaces of nonsense, and fills the words with sense.' The material evidence for Eckley's theory of 'the Stead source' seems rather thin, consisting mainly of a few dark hints by Joyce's friends and a note in his papers. Circumstantial evidence, on the other hand, as relentlessly downloaded by Eckley throughout her argument, proves abundant in all Joyce's works. But it could hardly be otherwise, given the nature of *Finnegans Wake* and the fact that Eckley can seize on any word in the texts that corresponds to any detail in Stead's life or even vaguely resembles his name ('Stand me now and ever in good *stead*', as Stephen prays at the end of *Portrait*). It is useful to be reminded of Stead, a now largely forgotten figure, as a presence in Joyce's early reading and as a possible source for some later references in his work. But it is hard to imagine Eckley's larger claims being taken seriously by *Wake* readers. Her case is weakened by some careless editing, a baffling appendix format, and a rather abrupt manner: 'Other sources are not disproved but subsumed', she bluntly announces. The real eccentricity of her approach to *Finnegans Wake* surely lies in her concern to reduce it to a form that 'bridges the spaces of nonsense and fills the words with sense', since for most *Wake* readers the spaces and the nonsense define what the text has to offer.

Incoherence is the starting point for Susan Shaw Sailer's new study, *On the Void of to Be: Incoherence and Trope in Finnegans Wake*, and she confesses that she is 'puzzled' by responses which do not acknowledge that reading Joyce's text is initially marked by this experience. Rather than look for an external referent to explain this, however, Sailer seeks to understand *Finnegans Wake* 'as a practice of language' and to account for incoherence 'as an integral dynamics of the text'. As part of this project, she experiments with Kristevan and Derridean notions of language and assesses their usefulness in the Joycean context: she also analyses the process by which readers 'discover the *Wake*'s coherence evolving from what may have seemed its chaos' in terms of four major tropes – metaphor, metonymy, synecdoche and irony. Though her subject is incoherence, Sailer never confuses her own discourse with Joyce's, and her analysis remains admirably coherent throughout. The same can certainly not be said for Jennifer Bloomer's *Architecture and the Text: The (S)Crypts of Joyce and Piranesi*. This is a series of essays on some etchings by the eighteenth-century architect Piranesi, using deconstructive strategies 'dissected out of the text of *Finnegans Wake*'. The writing is outrageously playful and oblique, and the book is probably best described by Bloomer herself as 'an object of mind-boggling ideational intricacy'. Other essays on *Finnegans Wake* this year include Jack Vespa, 'Another Book at the *Wake*: Indian Mysticism and the *Bhagavad-Gita* in I.4 of *Finnegans Wake*' (*JJQ* 31.81–7); and Kelly Anspaugh, 'How Butt Shot the Chamber Pot: *Finnegans Wake* II.3' (*JJQ* 32.71–81), a reading of 'How Buckley Shot the Russian General' in terms of Joyce's 'cloacal obsession'. Anspaugh extends this interest to the whole of Joyce's work in 'Powers of Ordure: James Joyce and the Excremental Vision(s)' (*Mosaic* 27.i.73–100).

Speculating on the significance of characters' names has always been a good way of filling a few paragraphs in an essay. In *Names and Naming in Joyce* Claire Culleton has elevated this practice to the status of 'onomastics' and made a short book out of it. Culleton actually claims not to be offering 'an annotated catalogue of names' but 'a theoretical and conceptual study of onomastics in Joyce' (elsewhere we read of 'Joyce the onomastician' practising 'onomancy'), and to a certain extent this claim is vindicated by her quite sophisticated intertextual analyses. But the overall argument has a tendency to collapse into such banalities as 'Joyce was one of those writers on whom nothing was lost' or 'names resonate in many different and complex ways in Joyce's *Ulysses*'. The book is really most worth reading, despite its pretensions, for those parts which most resemble an 'annotated catalogue of names': in the chapter on 'Naming and History', for example, Culleton outlines the mosaic of Irish history that can be pieced together from the various names of HCE in *Finnegans Wake* or from Joyce's rendering of the string of names belonging to the real Dublin eccentric 'Endymion' who figures in *Ulysses*.

As usual this year's work includes various interesting or unlikely 'Joyce and . . .' combinations. In 'Joyce and Boxing: Famous Fighters in *Ulysses*' (*JJQ* 31.21–9) J. Lawrence Mitchell documents the real fights referred to in 'Wandering Rocks' and 'Cyclops'. Matthew Campbell's 'Changing Habits: James Joyce and Drunken Catholics' is included in *Beyond the Pleasure Dome: Writing and Addiction from the Romantics*, edited by Sue Vice, Campbell and Tim Armstrong. Campbell reflects on the relation between drinking, narratives of religious conversion and Joyce's vocation as an artist, and identifies three important converts who 'hover before James Joyce and his own conversion from Catholic to priest of eternal imagination': Augustine, Newman and his own brother Stanislaus (a 'temperate atheist'). The connections between Joyce and theoretical physics are usefully reviewed and discussed in Thomas Jackson Rice, '*Ulysses*, Chaos and Complexity' (*JJQ* 31.41–54). Concentrating on what is popularly known as 'Chaos Theory' (which needless to say Joyce turns out to have 'uncannily anticipated'), Rice argues that this new approach to science can provide a model for understanding the 'emergent design' of *Ulysses*: 'No random phenomenon, *Ulysses* nevertheless strays from the ordered and static world of the stable system, not into chaos, but to the borderline of complexity, the edge of chaos, where small causes have large effects and where both life itself and great works of literature are found.' Two more studies on a similar theme, but focusing on earlier scientific developments that Joyce himself would have been aware of while writing *Finnegans Wake*, are 'The Joyce of Silence: Quantum Physics in *Finnegans Wake*' (*IUR* 24.272–82) and 'The Relativity Theory in *Finnegans Wake*' (*JJQ* 32.61–70), both by Andrzej Duszenko.

In their illustrated article 'James Joyce in the Netherlands: Fish or Fiction?' (*JJQ* 32.23–43), Gene M. Moore and Ton Hoenselaars scrutinize the single paragraph in Richard Ellmann's *James Joyce* dealing with Joyce's holiday in the Netherlands in 1927. Comparing this with the available historical evidence they provide a 'corrective gloss' on the inevitable distortions and omissions in Ellmann's narrative. Two other minor corrections to classic textbooks are Danis Rose, 'Solider than Most: John Joyce's House in North Richmond Street' (*JJQ* 31.105–111), which identifies a different original for the house described in 'Araby'; and Stephen Derry, 'The Sex of Sceptre: An Error in '*Ulysses* Annotated' (*N&Q* 41.371) which notes that the famous racehorse on which Blazes Boylan bets and loses in *Ulysses* was in fact, despite the phallic suggestions of its name, a mare.

Several essays on Joyce this year use Virginia Woolf as a reference point for favourable and unfavourable assessments. Kelly Anspaugh's 'Blasting the Bombardier: Another Look at Lewis, Joyce, and Woolf' (*TCL* 40.iii.365–78) attempts to correct the view that Joyce had more in common with Woolf ('the modernist critics love to love') than with Wyndham Lewis ('the modernist critics love to hate') and warns against misleading biographical constructions of Joyce as a feminist.

Caroline Webb also finds Joyce lacking, as a critic of patriarchy, compared to Woolf. In 'Listing to the Right: Authority and Inheritance in *Orlando* and *Ulysses*' (*TCL* 40.190–204) Webb compares the list of names in 'Cyclops' with the acknowledgements in the parodic preface to *Orlando*, and suggests that whereas Joyce's purpose in debunking spurious claims to authority is to reinforce his own, Woolf somehow manages to position her subject and her reader outside 'the traditional system of literary exchange'. Joyce's feminist credentials are reaffirmed, however, in Jennifer Wicke's 'Lingerie and (Literary) History: Joyce's *Ulysses* and Fashionability' (*CritQ* 36.ii.26–41), which also includes a brief comparison between *Ulysses* and *Orlando*. Wicke notes that both books deal with 'history, modernity and gender' but whereas *Orlando* is almost silent on fashion, *Ulysses* can be seen as 'obsessed' with it – particularly in the representations of Molly Bloom and of Gerty McDowell in 'Nausicaa': 'the rich archaeology of fashion arcana is unmatched by any other modernist text'. Far from being an ephemeral issue, or one which is simply used by Joyce to expose Gerty McDowell as a fashion victim, Wicke argues that 'a fashion intelligence' is partly constitutive of the 'new womanly manhood' of Joyce's text.

The centenary of Aldous Huxley's birth was marked by a reissue of his works in paperback (Flamingo), but only one book attempting a significant critical reassessment. This was *The Hidden Huxley: Contempt and Compassion for the Masses 1920–36*, a new collection of Huxley's journalism, edited with a substantial introduction and other material by David Bradshaw. The other material includes a study of the correspondence between Huxley and H. L. Mencken, focusing particularly on the 'imprint' of Huxley's admiration for Mencken on *Crome Yellow*; and a reassessment of Huxley's attitude to the utopianism of H. G. Wells, which Bradshaw argues was at times more sympathetic than *Brave New World* implies. Bradshaw's overall aim in this collection is to correct the image of Huxley as (in his own words) an 'amused, Pyrrhonic aesthete', and document 'the authentic 1930s Huxley' – a much more Orwellian figure – who has 'languished misunderstood and unread for over fifty years'. That he has remained misunderstood so long is partly due, Bradshaw suggests, to the inadequacies of the standard bibliography. He attempts to remedy this situation in a separate publication, 'A New Bibliography of Aldous Huxley's Work and its Reception, 1912–1937' (*BB* 51.237–55).

Helen Pike Bauer's *Rudyard Kipling: A Study of the Short Fiction* is in the same Twayne's series as Mitzi Brunsdale's study of Joyce, mentioned above. But it does not really provide the same quality of analysis, and consists mainly of an undemanding thematic survey – though Bauer's summaries do at least make one aware how much interesting material the stories contain. Their potential is tapped more effectively in Philip Mallett's short study, 'Rudyard Kipling: Narrating India' (*SwR* 'Writing and the Nation': 358–68). Mallett agrees with Bauer in suggesting that the Anglo-Indian stories should be read as fables of men at work, but insists that this approach should not 'push into the background the political realities of the British presence'. He analyses the way the confidence of the narrator, in many of the stories, is 'ironised' to produce the 'sense of a narrative failing to bring its material to order' and relates this to the 'model of knowledge' – of racial difference – on which the imperial administration was based. Reading Kipling's narratives in terms of ironizing frames, splits, or disorders, is one way of coping with their overt imperialism. A related feature of his writing, which Mallett touches on, is his tendency to play poetry and prose against each other within and around his narratives – in his epigraphs, for example, which often serve to 'ironise' the prose narrative. There is an interesting chapter on this habit in Peter Keating's *Kipling the Poet*, in which Keating notes that while much of Kipling's poetry stood alone 'there was comparatively little of the prose that he did not feel was incomplete without being given some connection with poetry'. This interconnectedness helps to make *Kipling the Poet* a useful general introduction, not just to Kipling's poetry but to his whole career as a writer.

The *Powys Journal* for this year includes a very well-documented study, by Stuart Marriott and Janet Coles, of 'John Cowper Powys as University Extension Lecturer, 1898–1909' (*Powys Journal* 4.7–50). This draws on the relevant administrative records (rather than the autobiographical material) to reconstruct the details of Powys's career as an extension lecturer, and incidentally provides some interesting insights into the conditions under which these 'travelling salesmen of knowledge' worked. In the same volume, a great deal of research is condensed into J. Lawrence Mitchell's '"Lift up Thine Eyes to the Hills": The Visionary World of T. F. Powys' (*Powys Journal* 4.93–123). Mitchell discusses, among other things, the 'Geography of Powysland', the traces of Hardy's influence, and the merging of the natural world with a 'biblical' vision in Powys's fiction. There are numerous references to T. F. Powys in Claire Harman's edition of *The Diaries of Sylvia Townsend Warner*. This is a single-volume selection from thirty-eight diaries spanning fifty years, and should provide a valuable new resource for anyone working on Sylvia Townsend Warner or her associates. [R.S.]

(c) Individual Authors: Post-1945

Many academics publishing in the field of near-contemporary literature share an apologetic strategy. Monographs are justified by some evaluative injustice. As one of the authors under review observes, inclusion in Twayne's English Author Series 'seemed to confirm' a writer 'belonged in the canon of English authors'. Reading for an annual bibliography is a relatively atypical pattern of academic behaviour, but this estranging perspective is not uninstructive about the state of English studies. Although one might at first assume that the field is incoherent because consensus has not been established, and everyone is doing something different (i.e. doing a different author), what emerge are strong patterns of convergence. Whether this indicates the success of the discipline, or the fact that contemporary scholars, in fulfilling their duty to serve their author-subjects, are serving themselves and their institutions by pursuing lines of least resistance, is for users to judge.

After surveying this year's crop of single-author studies, it is the question, 'To whom is this book or article addressed?' that most insistently demands an answer. Not only is the quality of execution widely divergent, so too are the ways in which items are conceived and planned. Often one is left wondering how far the supposed or intended audience could overlap with the population of likely readers or users (different classes in themselves). Who acknowledges the gap between the buoyant spirit of advocacy with which an author's worth, or even existence, is broadcast and the lowly destiny of such publications, which is to be closeted in the archive until someone else decides to write a critical re-evaluation? The critical archive is of course used by students and their teachers, as well as by publishing scholars, but you would not always be able to gather this simple fact from the material annually added to it. What publishing scholars are writing for, apart from an ISBN number for an audit, is a very significant measure of the state of English studies, and of higher education. On the basis of the books and articles I have seen this year, one can conclude that, given the scale of operations of English Inc., the best is hard to find amongst the merely instrumental. Functional work is, however, to be welcomed when it knows itself to be so. But it is rather discomforting to find so much that reveals neither a knowledge of its function, nor an inkling of its own value.

To begin with the properly functional, York Press of New Brunswick is issuing a series of 'Authoritative Studies in World Literature' – confined, so far, to nineteenth- and twentieth-century European and North American writers – which are 'designed to help students of literature and young scholars in their investigations'. A. F. Cassis's volume on Graham Greene contains, in its forty pages of printed text, a biography, a chronological list of Greene's works, a critical essay surveying Greene's output of fiction, a brief survey of major trends in Greene criticism, and, finally, an annotated bibliography of work about Greene, running to just under sixty items. Committing an eight-page 'life' to print in the year in which appeared a controversy-courting Greene biography by Michael Shelden *Graham Greene: The Man Within* and the year before the second instalment (vol. II, 1939–55) of Norman Sherry's trilogy *The Life of Graham Greene* (Penguin, 1995), might be considered naive, if the latter's depth of research did not make his work virtually unreadable. (Shelden's rapid progress through Connolly, Orwell and now Greene implies that he has other priorities.) Sherry's project may end up as an important work of reference, but what does anyone needing a chronology or outline of Greene's life do with an as yet incomplete narrative in excess of one thousand pages? (Sherry himself must periodically produce an abstract in order to restart his archive-narrative.) 'Authoritative Studies' have the merit of routing the reader through the landmarks of career, reception and bibliography, thus making it possible to organize a distinct and focused investigation more quickly, and with greater confidence than when presented with a shelf-ful of books bought in the old days, or scrolls of CD-ROM hard copy. The volume under review was accurate and judicious, and in an era of overproduction and of underfunded libraries, it represents a valuable resource for enabling better undergraduates and postgraduates as they embark on independent research. But what it will not do is inspire anyone who has not already found an interest in or line into Greene. A. F. Cassis's *Graham Greene: Man of Paradox* (LUP) was not seen.

In terms of the question of use, 'Authoritative Studies' invite comparison with the new Northcote House series, WTW. The value of the original series grows as one relies on them less as an objective intellectual resource and more as historical and literary documents in their own right. For this reason it turns out to be a good thing that the series was not penned by academics, and that an outsider like Jocelyn Brooke was commissioned to write pamphlets on Bowen and Huxley. The format has not been substantially changed, but the new series comes out of universities rather than the private study. With the change of intellectual gear, and at around sixty pages, these are short books rather than long essays. Three volumes came my way, and they are representative of the strengths and weaknesses of the WTW concept. Lorna Sage's *Angela Carter* is brilliant, arguably more interesting and certainly more consistently intelligent than her collection of Carter pieces for Virago (1995). The writer is present throughout in the quotations from correspondence with Sage that are woven through the book. The chronological format is wittily renewed as 'Beginning', 'Middle' and 'Ending', but Sage also narrates Carter's struggle to be read, a perspective which numbers among the casualties of the forgetfulness implicit in her canonization. Literary theory is handled with the same kind of unsolemn seriousness that Carter achieves in the later fiction. For Sage, the Carter of the vagrant, alternately female and male points of view in the first five novels is a writer for whom transformation and constructedness are dimensions of a camp 'theatricalization of experience'. Carter's fantasy is nevertheless revealed to be a rigorous and cunning mode of thought. Sage is good at showing us why early novels like *Love*, *The Passion of New Eve* and *The Infernal Desire Machines of Doctor Hoffman* were and should remain, despite glib reductions of Carter's art, difficult. The readings of the late fiction are informative, and have the kind of zest to shake teachers and students alike out of too ready an acceptance of the ready-made critical and literary historical formulations about her work. This is a lot for a little book to achieve.

Reading Elizabeth Maslen's *Doris Lessing* is a less bracing experience. The name 'Bakhtin' is a leaden leitmotif, and different aspects of Lessing's fiction-making are being dubbed, seemingly indifferently, as Bakhtinian. The overall argument is sound. Lessing's *oeuvre*, like the 'book' of Yeats's poetry, manifests a revisionary development. New work augments, rather than negates, the earlier novels, with which it exists in a kind of (doubtless 'Bakhtinian') dialogue. This framework enables Maslen to suggest ways in which Lessing remains contemporary whilst reviewing the forms and ideologies embodied in work that is now in the past. Narrating and analysing the disjunctions in Lessing's fiction – how the writing of *The Golden Notebook* reconfigures the Martha Quest sequence, and then, to cap the displacement of realist conventions in the sixties, the turn to 'the discourse of space fiction' as an alternative set of devices for dealing with 'inner space' – was never going to be easy, given the space available. But there are too many gestures at sociolinguistic analysis which are unconsummated, and too few detailed readings which earn their keep. The coverage, in aiming to be as complete as possible, also undermines the worthy intention of uncovering the integrity of Lessing's experimental career, making this a useful, but less than entirely successful addition to the series. But it would serve as a helpful guide to someone starting out to explore Lessing's (to some) disconcertingly inconsistent output.

The case for Kevin McCarron's *William Golding* is less easy to make. Saying something new about Golding while surveying his work is a challenge this book does not live up to. This disappointment seems to have coloured the prose, which cannot animate the rather pedestrian and plot-based accounts of the novels. Does anyone need any more interpretations of *Lord of the Flies* and *The Inheritors*? It is unlikely unless this is the only thing one ever reads about Golding. But if it tells us nothing new, does it tell us accurately and with verve? There is little of the latter, and when we are told that 'Wells' "The Grisly Folk" is optimistic in an evolutionary, Darwinian way', confidence in the book's handling of contexts falters. By contrast, Leon Surette has produced a very effective reading in 'A Matter of Belief: Pincher Martin's Afterlife' (*TCL* 40.ii.205–25). Starting out from an account of the resistance on the part of early readers and critics to the idea that Golding's *Pincher Martin* entertains the idea of persistence of self and consciousness after death, he goes on to discuss the novelist's 'official beliefs' in relation to the treatment of the afterlife, and of the numinous, in twentieth-century literature. He considers hostility to the ego in 'alternative religious speculation', his coinage for the kind of unorthodox faith which lies behind Golding's fictions, and offers to read *Pincher Martin* as a Schopenhauerian allegory, an awakening into the noumenal realm on the rock. This is suggestive, taking account as it does of both the fabular and affective qualities of Golding's work. Surette also tries out a 'precursor' for *Pincher Martin* in the form of Swedenborg's 'circumstantial account of the world after death'.

Shadia S. Fahim's *Doris Lessing and Sufi Equilibrium* examines the 'rationale' of Lessing's development from 'Classical Realism . . . towards mysticism and forms of science fiction which verge on myth and Oriental fable', thus addressing the same offence against the myth of authorial consistency which Maslen deals with under the sign of Bakhtinian dialogism. Here, by contrast, we are presented with a biographically grounded thesis highlighting Lessing's search for models of equilibrium, drawing in particular on Sufism, a mystical branch of Islamic thought with a doctrine of the annihilation of the individual in God. Lessing's public interest in Sufism goes back to 1964, but Fahim opens her account with a discussion of *The Grass is Singing* (1950). This is primarily to assert a continuity of 'preoccupations' with the later fiction which transcends (but also underwrites, such are our notions of development) the evolution of Lessing's *oeuvre*. Fahim argues that the thematic core of this early novel is the overcoming of Freudian and Marxian determinism in a journey to awareness of inner self, which, it is suggested, can be the source of a 'healthy relationship with the collective'. On *The Golden Notebook*, Fahim is both more ambitious and less sure-footed, as she attempts to show how both rational and mystical apprehension is required of the reader who succeeds in apprehending the falseness of the opposition of inner and outer life. The *Memoirs of a Survivor* of 1964, which she sees as picking up the threads of the Martha Quest sequence which *The Golden Notebook* had interrupted, provides another chance at running this analysis. Lessing has written of a desire to write a book which could 'talk through the way it was shaped': for Fahim, *Survivor* is a model for meditation, and 'a strategy designed to prepare the one-dimensional mind for such activity'. Everything is thus set for a demonstration of the merits of the *Archives*, Lessing's science fiction series, and a rejoinder to critics who label the novels 'indulgences in escapism and decadence'. In this longest section of the book, many Sufi concepts are employed not so much to explore the resonance or provenance of Lessing's vision as to provide the basis of a philosophical parallel to the way Lessing confounds science fiction conventions, 'to establish a critical relation with and . . . [provide] a solution to the limitation of the realistic genre of writing'. In the final analysis, Fahim's interest in Lessing's formal strategies for transcending the one-dimensional, and Maslen's eye for the dialogic, come down to very much the same thing. Both books are concerned above all with essentially formalist and generic approaches, and as a consequence do not bring much resistance to bear on what Lessing gets to say with her evolving, multivocal or multidimensional forms.

Robert Boschman's 'Excrement and "Kitsch" in Doris Lessing's *The Good Terrorist*' (*ArielE* 25.iii.7–27) takes its co-ordinates from Freud, Swift, Norman O. Brown and Milan Kundera, with whose epigram from *The Unbearable Lightness of Being* – 'kitsch is the absolute denial of shit' – it begins. Lessing is said to take up Swift's aim to expose the way kitsch is employed to conceal shit, to 'closet the truth'. The heroine, Alice, is caught between the kitsch of middle-class decency and the kitsch of terrorism's violent bourgeois-bashing. The literal shit that fills the squat becomes a symbol of everything that is unacceptable to its denizens. The postmodern turn comes in this article with the identification of Alice's situation as 'undecidable', and the thesis that those characters in the novel who most vociferously pronounce their freedom from a culture of kitsch are most deeply imbued with the more universally closeting kitsch which Lessing takes as a synonym for contemporary willed ignorance.

Harriet Kramer Linkin offers a lucid reading of Angela Carter's reading of the Romantics in 'Isn't it Romantic?: Angela Carter's Bloody Revision of the Romantic Aesthetic in "The Erl-King"' (*ConL* 35.305–23): 'Carter's reimagining of the subject's position in Romantic poetics and ideology offers a more complex analysis than the simple identification of blatant oppression.' Linkin is interested in Carter's reshaping of the Romantic myth of creation to restore a voice to the figure of the silenced female, and how the narrative puts to the test Romantic ideology's fitness to embody 'a female aesthetic form'. Linkin picks up Carter's allusions and citations, and makes them the starting point for reflections on the figurations of the female in nineteenth-century writing, and on Carter's attempts to evade the 'gilded cage' to which female creativity is condemned by Romantic aesthetic theory. On the negative side, the categories and concepts employed are rather rigid, and they also tend to acquire a meaningless agency and autonomy in a way which will be familiar to readers of contemporary theoretical prose.

M. Daphne Kutzer's 'The Cartography of Passion: Cixous, Wittig and Winterson', appearing in *Re-Naming the Landscape* (edited by Jurgen Kleist and Bruce A. Butterfield), seemingly pits gender theory against fictional practice. While the theorists argue, it is claimed that 'novelists have made the imaginative leap to re-mapping the female body'. In fact the discussion of Wittig and Winterson is parasitic on theoretical discourse about 'sexuality and textuality'. Winterson's 'resistance to naming the gender of the narrator' is revealed to be a way of transcending the violent binary of male and female on which phallocentrism is predicated. By creating the illusion of an 'ex-gendered' narrator, Winterson can 'look at the truly human': but the 'remapping' that is claimed to be a consequence of Wittig's and Winterson's fiction-creating is a well-trodden exegetical path.

Salman Rushdie is being established as a key figure in recent fiction; in part only, this is a function of the dissemination of the concepts and critiques associated with post-colonial studies. David W. Price, in 'Salman Rushdie's "Use and Abuse of History" in *Midnight's Children*' (*ArielE* 25.ii.91–107), argues that the controversy surrounding *The Satanic Verses* has drawn attention away from Rushdie's philosophical examination of history. Accordingly, *Midnight's Children* started out as a Proustian project, but turned into an Orwellian one as Rushdie sought to oppose the increasingly sophisticated weapons with which the truth is manipulated. The novel is written to 'slightly increase the sum of what it is possible to think', in Rushdie's words. Nietzsche's 'On the Uses and Disadvantages of History for Life', with its tripartite conception of historical representation – antiquarian, monumental and critical – is employed to sharpen what, since Linda Hutcheon's *The Poetics of Postmodernism*, seems a commonplace remark about postmodern fictional narratives. Saleem Sinai, the narrator of *Midnight's Children*, is a critical historian, performing a narration which opposes both the 'nostalgic, antiquarian vision of British imperialism' and the process of self-mythification undertaken by Indira Gandhi's dynasty. This focus on the politics of the subcontinent is the article's most significant offering. Similar issues arise in Elaine Yee Lin Ho's 'How Not to Write History: Timothy Mo's *An Insular Possession*' (*ArielE* 25.iii.51–65). Here Mo is taken to task for being insufficiently self-conscious about a dilemma thrown up by his use of the 'reconstructed idiom of the nineteenth-century novel'. Does this strategy involve imitation or 'mimicry as radical revision'? Mo's novel 'casts doubts on traditional historiography' by employing the heteroglossic strategy for which Maslen praises Lessing (a narrative constructed out of bits of other putative texts), and hence exposes the 'constructed or fictional nature of history'. But Mo, in his treatment of the Chinese (the novel is a history of the colony of Hong Kong), apparently falls for the risk of reproducing the ideological norms of his nineteenth-century discursive models. Readers interested in this kind of argument might also take a look at Suzanne Kehde's 'Engendering the Imperial Subject: The (De)construction of (Western) Masculinity in David Henry Hwang's *M. Butterfly* and Graham Greene's *The Quiet American*', in *Fictions of Masculinity* (edited by Peter F. Murphy). Mujeebuddin Syed's 'Warped Mythologies: Salman Rushdie's *Grimus*' (*ArielE* 25.iv.135–49) similarly takes Rushdie to task for his first novel, which 'falters in its failure to countenance postcolonial concerns'. Rushdie, alongside authorities like Said and Fanon, is cited as reproving culture which is ungrounded, lacking roots. The bottom line of the article is that the novel, which is not usually given much attention by Rushdie criticism, is brilliantly plural without ever transcending its topos, and hence cannot achieve a practical resolution of Rushdie's 'insider/outsider location at the interstices of both metropolitan and indigenous societies'.

Nevertheless, stalwarts of the domestic literary scene continue to attract reverent attention. 'Vandalizing Time: Ian McEwan's *The Child in Time*', by Jack Slay Jr (*Crit* 35.iv.205–18), considers McEwan's images of time and childhood, in relation to other near-future fiction by Amis, Carter, Hoban and Ballard. Unlike McEwan's earlier work, *The Child in Time* embarks on a 'search for the lost child within every adult', a search which throws up examples of affirmative as well as regressive experience. Broaching the novel's treatment of theory in science, Slay argues that time is not a certainty, a reality of the world; rather it is as difficult and ambiguous as life itself. In a manner which goes beyond the solipsism and shock of earlier fiction, in this novel adult alliances strengthened by acknowledgement of the inner child point towards an 'acceptance of the innocent joy of life and love'. Such an approach can seem rather quaint in the company of more contemporary critical idioms, but it need not be underpowered, as Jack Turner shows in 'Iris Murdoch and the Good Psychoanalyst' (*TCL* 40.300–17). Here he sets out to answer Harold Bloom's query about *The Good Apprentice*: 'whether the comic story and the spiritual kernel can be held together by Miss [*sic*] Murdoch's archaic stance as an authorial will'. Murdoch has, in this novel, according to Turner, found her limits and honoured them, and he is duly responsive to the way the book poses questions it cannot resolve. This is traditional fiction criticism, commending its subject for creating 'real' characters and for writing well ('the fine shape of the prose'). The article turns on Murdoch's critique of Freud (unlike in *A Severed Head* and *The Sacred and Profane Love Machine*, she has not caricatured the analyst she puts into *The Good Apprentice*). Turner's conclusion raises some very interesting, but purely speculative, questions about power, gender and the novel.

In 'We all have something to hide': Muriel Spark, Autobiography, and the Influence of Newman on the Career of a Novelist' (*DUJ* 86.ii.281–9), Leon Litvak provides an account of Spark's conversion in the late fifties, and the influence of Newman on the process by which her beliefs find their way into her fiction. He traces a progression from *The Comforters* to *Symposium*, by which narratorial doubt has an increasingly significant and disturbing role, if we assume Spark to be a moralist. The postmodern void of 'certainty' is seen to rescue the novelist from the limbo of her readers' uncertainty about how to take her. 'It has always been difficult for readers to understand Spark's detachment, her evasiveness; yet her technique is, perhaps, more enlightening and acceptable in our postmodern and post-colonial world, with its abrogation of constraining power and the appropriation of language and writing for new and distinctive uses. She has a coherent religious vision, and religion still appears in her novels, but it seems that she wishes to destabilize structures and to force her readers to consider the seemingly uncentred, pluralistic, and multifarious nature of society, and the effect of this trend on their own existences.'

Postmodernism gets to do an awful lot of work, without anyone stopping to ask just how relevant the terms of an intellectual debate might be to analysis of the forms and themes of recent British fiction. Thus Roberta Rubenstein's 'Fragmented Bodies/Selves/Narratives: Margaret Drabble's Postmodern Turn' (*ConL* 35.i.136–55) addresses the shift in the novelist's work from a 'concentration on moral and domestic dilemmas' to 'narratives that reflect . . . a problematic, violent and arbitrary universe'. That these categories can be juxtaposed in this way says much about the consequences of contemporary literary studies' exiling of the ethical. Drabble, it is averred, has adopted an increasingly pessimistic outlook and the yen to experiment with postmodern narrative structures. 'Disjunctive narrative' is presented as a consequence of a world that 'can be neither understood nor represented through a single moral code or vision'. There are a number of difficulties here. The first is to mistake the 'post' of postmodernity or post-colonial as signalling a rupture in the historical process as discrete as that which critical theory's self-engendering polemic must detect within the institutions of learning. The second is the pretty preposterous notion that complexity is a contemporary phenomenon, and that anyone in the past who ventured an explanation expected to see the world in 'a single moral code or vision'. This article presents a competent interpretation of Drabble's more recent, world-historically orientated novels as examples of postmodern fiction, but remains unreflective about its own credentials: does such a reading exemplify its own form of 'nostalgia for meaningful connection'?

Brian Diemert, in 'The Pursuit of Justice: Graham Greene's Refiguring of the Detective Story in *It's a Battlefield*' (*PLL* 30.iii.285–308), begins his discussion of what Greene called his 'first overtly political novel' from the perspective of the author's disenchantment with the ideological shortcomings of the country-house detective narrative. He is also concerned with metaphorical texts: the clues that the detective must read, the city as text and so on. Interpretive undecidability, it is suggested, is a generic characteristic of the American hard-boiled thriller, whereas the detective novel promotes the authority of the detective, an authority which Diemert links, rather speculatively, to thirties' consciousness of the rise of Nazism. Although it is only belatedly acknowledged that *It's a Battlefield* is not about detection, the argument makes some useful assertions about the blurring of the figures of the detective and the murderer. Diemert concludes by counting the novel as Greene's first effort at a 'popular literature that could suggest moral values', and hinting that this establishes a 'new kind of thriller' taken up more recently by John le Carré. Diemert does not tell us much about these values, however, focusing instead on those Greene is supposed to subvert in his portrayal of a metropolitan war-zone. But then the yield from a hermeneutics of suspicion remains more difficult to state than the perils such scepticism is claimed to wrest us from.

Thomas S. Foster, in *Understanding John Fowles*, argues that it is Fowles's belief 'that fiction should engage readers dramatically and morally even in the midst of experiment' that makes him critically and popularly successful. His Fowles is both postmodernist and existentialist. The former claim is merely fashionable; the latter, worked through some cogent and helpful analyses of individual novels, is more relevant to Foster's case. However, the book could have benefited from more attention to what existentialism actually was, so that readers could gain a sense of why Fowles's treatment of its moral and metaphysical topics might be significant. As it is, we are shown how themes such as alienation, absurdity and freedom are explored in, for instance, *The Magus*; although these elements are not woven into a higher-order thesis, Foster does fulfil his aim of showing how important story-telling is to Fowles's art. His method is to provide a well-condensed paraphrase in six chapters on seven novels, and then to offer a critical discussion of each. There is a mix of overview and detail in these necessarily brief chapters suggestive enough to interest undergraduate readers, and the book is accurate and reliable enough to be useful as a work of reference for those seeking to reactivate memories of reading Fowles in more casual circumstances. But there is little here for those interested in the relations of fiction and the history of ideas, or indeed, Fowles's place in post-war British writing.

Richard Pine's *Lawrence Durrell: The Mindscape* is a massive, serious and well-written appraisal of Durrell's contribution to the development of the novel in the twentieth century, and a sequel to Pine's earlier *The Dandy and the Herald*, which investigated Durrell's 'literary genealogy'. Pine, who corresponded with his subject in the seventies and eighties, is as intimate with Durrell's unpublished writings as he is authoritative about the external details of the writer's life. This book opens with a good biographical narrative which is richly informed; best of all, it balances objectivity with sympathy and enthusiasm. This bodes well for the chapters that follow, in this densely argued analysis of the experiential basis of Durrell's fiction – 'I find art easy. I find life difficult' – and the strategies he employed in the making of it. Rather than applying theory and the generalities of literary history to his subject like a critical space blanket, in the vain hope that fashionable concepts will warm up an unfashionable *oeuvre*, Pine presents Durrell's career as an allegory of modernism and of theory. This has the advantage of capturing the simultaneous centrality and marginality of this 'extraterrestrial' writer. Rather than leaping on the bandwagon of an epistemological relativism, Pine offers the following thoughts on Durrell's narrative forms: 'The technique of multiple narratives and personal landscapes, capable of expanding and contracting at will, is central to Durrell's own psychology. In psychological terms, the need to be elusive, to have many meanings, was as important as, in philosophical terms, the need to embrace many possibilities, many occasions of access to truth.'

The book is partially structured around an Audenesque opposition between the city as symbol of the fallen, historical world and the island as that of wished-for redemption. Pine sees Durrell's career as an alternation between the islomane's repose and the action of the marketplace. He writes at length about *The Alexandria Quartet*, *The Revolt of Aphrodite* and *The Avignon Quintet*. By the time Durrell came to compose the latter, writes Pine, there was little more for him to say about human nature, but he continued to contribute 'to the debate on modern aesthetics'. The *Quintet* risks being an 'unreadable book' because Durrell aimed at the vantage created by stasis and circularity rather than occasion and sequence. The *Quartet* had at least cultivated the reader's complicity, if it had not fulfilled her (but more likely his) 'sexual curiosity and metaphysical speculation'. Pine's book requires concentration and patience, but will reward those who want to find out more about

Durrell and the impact of his fiction on one astute and sympathetic critic. This is an informative kind of advocacy: one might want to argue vigorously with the book, but it will be harder now to contest the application of so much critical and imaginative energy to this writer. Pine succeeds, where many studies published in the last two or three years have failed, in making a case for his subject.

Orphia Jane Allen's *Barbara Pym: Writing a Life* is further evidence of the North American fascination with a fictional world which Larkin judged not 'likely to have held its own in the Swinging Sixties'. He regretted that its 'unpretentious adherence to the Church of England, the absence of self-pity, the scrupulousness of one's relations with others, the small blameless comforts' had been neglected in the 'reign of Lady Chatterley'. But twenty years on from his puff, Pym has acquired the status of a (minor) Jane Austen, especially in post-Reagan America. The present work is aimed at being a kind of *summa* of that writing career and the academic reception that belatedly acknowledged it, designed to 'distil an essence of Pym that will encourage further study'. One could be forgiven for being left in doubt as to whether Pym is a 'leading post-World War II British novelist' because of her novels' literary and historical value, their 'treatment of feminist topics', or because 'there exist sixteen books about Pym and her work, more than seventy articles in scholarly journals and collections'. Once this might have been reason enough to remain silent. There are four sections to this latest Pym book: the first is a biographical essay, drawing on the work of earlier Pym specialists, notably Anne Wyatt-Brown. Then follows a chronological survey of the novels, each treated at once too generally and too briefly – the thesis of this section seems to be that the novels 'represent her lifelong need to write her life' (it is not obvious what 'represent' might mean here). There is little literary criticism, and little by the way of new light on Pym, and Allen does not follow up on her claims about Pym's special angle on the 'contradictions implicit in the social narrative by which many women live'. These lacks might be compensated for by section three, where Allen tells us what everyone else has said about Pym. Reception histories of the purely documentary kind can be interesting when they also tell the story of academic English, but they struggle to be of more than practical value (but to what end?) when the material described is all from the same stable, stretching back over only a few years. The discussion is divided up into 'Topics of Scholarly Discussion' – Bibliography; Themes; Narrative Technique – which should at least simplify matters for those who want to cut down on the effort of reading Pym criticism. Again, the level of commentary is not inspiring, of either confidence or the yen to add to the Pym secondary bibliography. Allen lists dissertations on Pym, as well as contemporary reviews. Maybe she should have thought harder about the last item in her survey of the Pym commentary, John Bayley's remarks on the futility of trying to 'fix our gaze' on that 'Pym World', which Larkin just wanted to see in print.

Isabelle Joyau opens *Investigating Powell's 'A Dance to the Music of Time'* with the rider that 'No artist can be critically imposed by argument upon a reluctant and prejudiced public', but she nevertheless seeks to counter the usual objections about the upper-middle-class-Englishness, preciousness, indirectness, snobbishness and unreadableness of his *roman fleuve*. She seeks, quite rightly, to redeem these volumes, finding instead of orotundity, meticulousness and humour, and where others have condemned evasiveness, the wary honesty of exploration for truth. Indeed, Nicholas Jenkins begins to sound fashionably postmodern when the 'involutions' in his narrative are described as 'apposite to a halting semiological quest, to consistently tentative exegeses since Man's epistemological aim is constantly up against evidential gaps and the absence of warranted assertability in a world immediably [*sic*] replete with obscurities'. Joyau, however, delivers more than this gesture might imply in the ensuing chapters. Narrating, and time, are almost obligatory topics, which are dealt with informedly, and with the effect of putting flesh on the concept of Jenkins's 'interminable quest'. These preoccupations are present also in the analysis of Powell's conservatism and prejudice (for traditional values), and of the alleged incoherence of the sequence, which, as Joyau shows us, is in fact a state of 'permanent incompleteness'. There is interesting stuff, too, on the play of surface and depth, on Powell's predilection for balance and paradox, and on the question of whether *A Dance* is satire or comedy. One of the book's strengths is the way in which the chapters reinforce each other in illuminating, with critical authority, the qualities of Powell's sequence.

Doris T. Myers, in *C. S. Lewis in Context*, wants to rescue Lewis for 'serious study', by proposing an alternative to the biographical and Christian/mythopoeic approaches that dominate both British and American work on this author. She succeeds in this by reading Lewis in the light of the linguistic and especially semantic theories which were debated between the wars: I. A. Richards's work with the philosopher C. K. Ogden, and Owen Barfield's study of metaphor in his *Poetic Diction*. This focus is not as narrow as it might sound, because Richards in particular was addressing the consequences of World War I when he undertook theoretical resistance to the linguistic hoodwinking of wartime and peacetime propaganda in *The Meaning of Meaning*. Richards's Basic English, from which the non-disjunctive messiness of metaphorical signification was supposedly expunged, ended up parodied as Newspeak in Orwell's *Nineteen Eighty-Four* (but it also resembled Orwell's war on dead metaphor in 'Politics and the English Language'). Owen Barfield, by contrast, propounded the view that, in Myers's words, 'our knowledge of the universe depended on metaphor'. Sacramentalism versus instrumentalism, and Myers's Lewis opts for the former. Another chapter, on 'Language Control' – that is, what Richards was attempting, rather than warning against (an ambivalence, also, in Orwell's writing on language, and in literary culture's responses to World War II propaganda) – follows up Lewis's fictional response, in *That Hideous Strength*, to Richards's influence on education. One would be right to query whether the 'context' supplied by this book really does show us a new Lewis, or whether it is just another way of generating the same kinds of claim about the need to 'recover an appreciation of his craftsmanship'. When it comes to the Chronicles of Narnia and the World Wars, the 'context' part of the discussion becomes somewhat thinner: Myers does not really show why *The Last Battle* should be read, alongside *Nineteen Eighty-Four*, as a picture of England after 1945 (this sort of thing is very much better done in Sebastian Knowles's *A Purgatorial Flame* of 1990). There is, however, a useful chapter weighing up Cambridge vigilance against low culture in the light of Lewis's interesting *An Experiment in Criticism*, and his and other Inklings' tastes and practices in low-brow fictional genres. This is a more patient and responsible book than Kath Filmer's study from 1993, in part because of its author's historical awareness, but it does not rescue Lewis from the C. S. Lewis societies.

2. Poetry

(a) Poetry: 1900–50

The work of compiling this review was, as in the last volume, aided by the staffs of the libraries of the University of the Incarnate Word and Trinity University, both of San Antonio, Texas. That said, I should make clear that many works were not seen because of publishers' reluctance to supply review copies.

Philip Gardner's *A. E. Housman: The Critical Heritage* follows the approach familiar from earlier volumes in this series, and offers a selection of critical responses to the poet's work from the first unsigned reviews of *The Shropshire Lad* to John Crowe Ransom's verdict of 1951. To some the writer may seem a curious choice for this treatment, but recent reassessments of Edwardianism make this a timely volume. That apart, it reads like a collection of essayists of the period. As well as the familiar Cyril Connolly, E. M. Forster and William Empson pieces there are notices by J. C. Squire, Holbrook Jackson, Lascelles Abercombie, Geoffrey Grigson and F. L. Lucas. It is good to have so many pieces so easily available as a history of the changing public taste – and also, of changing levels of awareness of irony – during the decades that are covered.

Two articles by Dennis Shrubsall about W. H. Hudson appeared this year. The first, 'W. H. Hudson's Pilgrimage for a Poet' (*ELT* 37.52–5), records a trip to Troston in Suffolk, which village was the original of 'Norton' in *Afoot in England* and provided material for other essays. 'Hudson's Norfolk Connection: A Note on a Visit to "New Farm"' (*ELT* 37.350–4) relates a visit to Hunstanton to the writer's essays.

Ann P. Linder's 'Landscape and Symbol in the British and German Literature of World War I' (*CLS* 31.351–69) is a suggestive article which continues the recent trend of seeing writing of World War I in a comparative context. She asserts that, while British writers see landscape as a distillation of pity and the lost past, emblematized in the poppy, the Germans see it through the filter of Herder's idea of the historical destiny of nations attained through struggle. In particular, the German landscape combines a *völkische* sense of community with the legacy of German Romanticism, especially in *Märchen*. She discusses in Stramm, Junger and Remarque the image of the *Stahlhelm* as heroic emblem which takes the place of the British poppy. This is a valuable extension of our view of the period. Important, too, is Mark Graves's 'Wilfred Owen's "The Letter" and the Truth of War' (*ELN* 31.59–66). The poem is both a statement on propaganda and evidence of the soldier's inability to articulate his predicament, and Graves discusses both these 'texts' in the context of propaganda and censorship and explores the variety of meanings to be found in this neglected but fascinating poem. 'Faulkner and Sassoon' (*N&Q* 41.377–8) by Andrew Hook shows the novelist's use of part of 'The General' in his short story 'Victory' (*These Thirteen*, 1931), as well as in his 1925 essay 'Literature and War'.

At first sight, *The Great War and the Missing Muse: The Early Writings of Robert Graves and Siegfried Sassoon* by Patrick J. Quinn appears to rest on an intriguing concept: that, since the two writers' biographical work is their best known, a paired biographical approach will illuminate their poetry. This is not quite borne out by deeper inquiry, since Quinn deals with the two poets in turn and only unites them in the last chapter. Much of the book is devoted to fairly straightforward literary biography of the two figures, and there is an annoying tendency to summarize other critics' ideas at the drop of a text. That said, there is much of importance here, in the discussion of material that is often overlooked, and in the stress laid on the complete careers of both poets rather than the sectioning that so often goes on with writers of their generation. The final chapter, though, could have said far more: not for the first time I find myself longing for a critic to cast aside the usual bounds of attribution and risk having some ideas.

Two books on Yeats offer introductory studies from a biographical standpoint. Edwin Malins's *A Preface to Yeats* has been sensitively revised by John Purkis. The volume follows the usual form of the series, with sections on the life and other elements of 'background', and there are also sections on Yeats's family, Gaelic place-names, the poetry's most common symbols and further reading. In a book of this length, aimed to assist confused undergraduates making a first reading of Yeats, there is much of value; though a minor cavil is the lack of explanation of the pronunciation of Gaelic words and place-names, so we are probably doomed to hear still the leaden English fall of 'Deirdre' in place of the rich Gaelic original. The volume is handsomely illustrated. Alasdair D. F. Macrae's *W. B. Yeats: A Literary Life* is aimed at a slightly different audience, and its larger extent allows it somewhat greater depth. What is apparent right from the start is the writer's deep acquaintance with and easy manipulation of all of the frighteningly large number of source materials available for a Yeats biographer. Much of the material will be familiar, but not to the intended readers, and the book progresses thoughtfully through the phases of the poet's life with authority and poise. There are separate chapters on 'Yeats and the Theatre' and 'Yeats and Politics', and one called 'Masks and Developments', which lucidly addresses the introspective phoenix aspect of the poet's growth. A concluding chapter on 'Yeats and Modern Poetry' reflects on his place within modernism, posing the important questions with precision and frequent qualification. Overall this is a book that will be a fine introduction for those who already have a sure footing in critical reading: for those on the lower slopes, the *Preface* volume makes an excellent point of departure.

The winter 1994 *YER* (12.iii-iv) is a double issue containing papers from the National Poetry Foundation Yeats Conference in 1990. Laura Cowan's 'Introduction' (67–76) comments on the volume's focus – *At the Hawk's Well*, *A Vision* and the early poems – as representing current Yeats studies, and this certainly suggests new directions in criticism. Hugh Kenner's 'At the Well of the Universe' (71–80) is primarily concerned with the first of these three texts. The piece is concerned with 'singularity', events quite isolated from all else, and uses the concept to illuminate the play and several poems including 'The Wild Swans at Coole' and 'Among School Children'. That Yeats's syntactic completeness must be seen as an ironic rendering of the inaccessibility of the singular is only one of many brilliantly suggestive thoughts in this lucid, witty essay. Karen Foster's 'Decoding the Female in *The Only Jealousy of Error*' (77–80) looks at motivation through examining proxemics, to argue that the women characters mediate between mythic and real worlds.

To Cowan's list of topics should be added a concern for Yeats's philosophy, in particular his ideas of what we might term attainable ecstasy, which has been prominent in several articles. 'Yeats's "Unity of Being" in the Perspective of Upanishadic States of Turiya and Sushupti' by Shalini Sikka (81–8) argues that the two states correspond to the full and dark phases of the moon, the former representing complete unity in a turning inward of the senses. Sikka looks at Yeats's annotations of the Upanishads and offers illuminating readings of 'Among School Children' and 'Sailing to Byzantium' in a detailed and important recontextualizing. Louis L. Martz writes on 'Yeats and Pound: From Reverie to Prophecy' (107–14), discussing the transformation in Yeats's style, with parallels and squibs from Pound, from the Stone Cottage years to the later poems of prophetic engagement with contemporary reality and with history – which is, as Martz points out, the setting of much of Yeats's earlier reverie. A similar concern to relate realism and transcendence is apparent in M. L. Rosenthal's 'Early Yeats: Poems before 1900, with Some Glances Ahead' (115–20). Valuable close readings of the early poems are followed by discussions of the use of dialogue and 'pivotal moments of concrete description' in the later work. 'Plato's Ghost and the Vision of Yeats and Pound' by Angela Elliott (93–6) uses Yeats's annotations of Plato and larger similarities to discuss ways in which the poet's encounters with the otherworldly may be regarded as Platonic. A similar topic is tackled from another direction by Natalie Crohn Schmitt in 'Ecstasy and Peak-Experience: W. B. Yeats, Marghanita Laski, and Abraham Maslow' (*CompD* 12.ii.167–81). Laski related ecstasy to images of the context that triggered it; Maslow gave accounts to encourage ecstatic experiences; and Yeats's plays do both. All three have further in common the links between ecstasy, love and death. As contextualizing this may be helpful, but I am not sure what it adds to a reading of the plays or poems.

In 'Revision and Closure in Yeats's "The Rose"' (*YER* 12.121–4), David Holdeman emphasizes ambiguity and question instead of resolution at the end of the mature poems, relating this to the poet's concern for symbolism. The early 'Fergus and the Druids' is contrasted with the later version, in which open-endedness replaces closure. Linda Ray Pratt, in 'Yeats and Metaphor: Making the Modernist Arcadia' (*YER* 12.125–9), defines the poet's awareness of the peculiarly modernist nature of metaphor in comparison with the theories of Frank Kermode and Paul de Man, seeing the trope as used in 'The Song of the Happy Shepherd' as 'the process by which words remake the world'. More specific analogies concern Rachel V. Billigheimer in 'Symbolic Birds in Yeats's Cyclic Vision of History' (*YER* 12.89–92). From 'Leda and the Swan' through the dove in 'The Mother of God' and the 'brazen winged beast' of 'The Second Coming' to the culmination in the golden birds of Byzantium, birds articulate the stages of Yeats's fundamentally Spenglerian view of history. Another metaphor, that of the city, is examined by Russell Elliott Murphy in 'Byzantium as the Center of History: Yeats and the Quest for Cosmopolis' (*YER* 12.103–6). This is a reflective piece on Yeats's grasp of the real Byzantium as well as its mythic importance as synthesis of disparate hopes within its ideal Pantokrator. Helen Vendler's concern is with much larger historical patterns in 'Fin-de-Siècle Lyric: W. B. Yeats and Jorie Graham', an essay in Elaine Scarry's collection, *Fins de Siècle*. In it she explores how Yeats finds a suitable form in which to reconcile epic history and lyric moment in shorter poems, most particularly 'Leda and the Swan', 'The Second Coming' and 'The Magi'.

Dwight H. Purdy's *Biblical Echo and Allusion in the Poetry of W. B. Yeats: Poetics and the Art of God* fills a gap in the current critical panoply surrounding the poet. After stressing the importance of biblical allusion in poetry before the twentieth century, it processes through the work from the nineties poems that subvert the Bible to promote Celticism, through the increasingly secular and ironic uses of biblical language, to the poems that use biblical language in a manner that is at once 'ironic and integrative'. It then turns to explore a new sensuality in Yeats's biblical references after 'Vacillation', and the use of scriptural tones in his criticism, and offers a final chapter on other modernist and Romantic uses of the Bible as source. The book has many interesting things to say, although it needs to be seen as a further reference tool rather than a wholly new reading of the poetry.

Biographical articles also appeared this year. Gerry Dukes's 'Yeats and Some Irish Ambiguities' (*YER* 12.130–3) discusses the ambivalence of the poet's attitude towards home rule and post-treaty politics, shown in 'Easter 1916' and *The Dreaming of the Bones*. 'A Biographical Footnote on Yeats' by Carroll F. Terrell (*YER* 12.134–5) reveals, with the aid of contemporary reviews, that the poet visited Bowdoin College in November 1932 to speak on the Irish renaissance. Donald Pearce's 'Hours with the Domestic Sibyl: Remembering George Yeats' (*YER* 12.136–43) is reprinted from *SoR* 28.3 (see *YWES* 73.518). George Surette's study of 'Yeats, Pound and Nietzsche' (*YER* 12.97–102) looks at the ways in which Yeats saw and did not see Pound as the Nietzschean 'Forerunner' in the Stone Cottage years and after, but also discusses Blake and Swedenborg and their inclusion in Yeats's synopticism.

Mastery and Escape: T. S. Eliot and the Dialectic of Modernism is a collection of essays by Jewel Spears Brooker that have appeared in various journals since 1979. The volume's title is also that of a new essay which forms the introduction, and which defines the key principle of modernism in psychology, history and literature as a tendency to look forward by looking back in a dialectic that combines Hegel with Marx – a proposition that Brooker effortlessly expounds here and throughout the volume, with repeated reference to Eliot's doctoral work on F. H. Bradley as underpinning to clarify both Eliot's ideas and their larger intellectual context. The essays cover Hulme, Bradley, Mallarmé and Frazer, with a new one on Sandra Gilbert and Susan Gubar as readers of Eliot, a discussion of form in the *Quartets* reprinted from the Lobb anthology reviewed below, and two essays on teaching 'The Waste Land'. This is far more than a collection of separate approaches to its topic: it is a lucid and exciting diagnosis of the whole condition of modernism and Eliot's place within it.

Marianne Thormählen's collection *T. S. Eliot at the Turn of the Century* begins with a survey of 'The Mind of Europe in T. S. Eliot' by A. David Moody, which shows Eliot's linguistic and cultural involvement with the Continent. This is followed by Nancy D. Hargrove's '"Un présent Parfait": Eliot and La Vie Parisienne, 1910–1911', which looks entertainingly at what Eliot may or may not have seen when in Paris with Alain-Fournier and Pierre Verdenal – although, resting wholly on the columns of *Le Figaro*, it is at best purely speculative. In the next essay, 'Eliot's Cities', Bernard Bergonzi locates 'Prufrock', 'The Waste Land' and sections of the *Quartets* within a tradition of metropolitan distancing that embraces Tennyson, Symons and others, as well as Baudelaire's *flâneur*, yet sees hints of the *sancta civitas* at the close of Little Gidding. It says as much about the larger literary history of the twentieth-century city as about Eliot's use of it. Lois A. Cuddy draws on John Fiske, John Boodin and other philosophers as well as Dewey and Darwin to explore Eliot's use of evolution in 'Making a Space in Time: T. S. Eliot, Evolution, and the *Four Quartets*', to suggest that the poet used the philosophy and language of evolutionary theory. Ideas and influences are listed, if not exploited through discussion of the poems' ideas and movements. Rudolf Germer's survey of 'T. S. Eliot's Religious Development' begins by reviewing earlier and more limited treatment of the topic, including that by Lyndall Gordon, then reminds us of how much material is still kept away from the scholarly gaze, and finally suggests the poet's changes in belief. This, too, is the first foray for a larger study; but the discussion is serious and complex, leading one to hope for good things when Germer's researches are complete. M. Teresa Gibert-Maceda's

'T. S. Eliot on Women: Women on T. S. Eliot', which follows, is a survey with little that is new or analytically challenging. By contrast, Marianne Thormählen's '"My Life for This Life": T. S. Eliot and the Extinction of the Individual Personality' is a tautly argued account of the kinds of self-erasure found in the poetry and plays, from the flight from self in 'Prufrock' to the effacement of personality as a facet of love in the later writing.

The central parallel of Stephen Medcalf's contribution to the Thormählen volume, 'T. S. Eliot's Punk Poems: Sweeney and the Quatrains', may or may not work – the desire for violent disruption through new structures as common to punk culture of the 1970s and Eliot's quatrains is not at first sight the most suggestive notion. But the essay has much to say about the poetry, its structures and stances. Next, Kristian Smidt looks afresh at 'Eliot and the Victorians', finding many of the differences in quality between these poets and the Metaphysicals less pronounced than Eliot claims in his essays, and suggesting that his preference is the result of his liking for 'subtle, complicated, and surprising emotions'. A compelling and convincing article. Barbara Everett's 'How Unpleasant to Meet Mr Eliot' argues that Eliot's poetry is unpopular because of its great achievement, the drawing together of separate worlds, which inevitably results in its being found unacceptable by political thinkers of all persuasions. On the way, it offers intriguing and detailed insights into some passages of the poems and their critics, including Christopher Ricks and John Carey. Thormählen's collection also contains a valuable review – or perhaps performance-record is nearer the truth – of '*Murder in the Cathedral* at Stratford' by Emrys Jones, and an essay on *The Cocktail Party* by Grover Smith. It concludes with a panel discussion on 'Eliot's Standing and Eliot Studies', in which some of the problems of criticism are explored. If the collection is uneven, that should not detract from the value of its finest essays, which are more than worthwhile extensions of the tradition of Eliot criticism.

Clay Daniel claims that 'T. S. Eliot's "A Cooking Egg"' (*N&Q* 41.374) borrows the rhyme of 'Sidney' and 'kidney' from Walter Savage Landor's 'Excommunication'. Tougher meat is Eric P. Levy's 'The Romance of Self-Doubt and Self-Pity: A Study of *The Love-Song of J. Alfred Prufrock*' (*YER* 12.1–6). This sees the poem's celebrated opening 'you and I' as representing self-doubt and self-pity and reads the text as resting on these twin foundations. Only self-pity can remedy self-doubt's deficiency, and Prufrock 'knows himself only through the need to hide his insecurity from others'. Thomas Gibbons examines '"The Waste Land" in the Light of the "Cross-Correspondence" scripts of the Society for Psychical Research' (*YER* 12.7–16). He suggests that these scripts provide the unifying principle of the poem, in offering a dialogue between several spirit mediums that is interconnected through its use of recurrent words and phrases, many of which are quotations, in several languages. This may be a source, though there is no evidence of Eliot's having seen the scripts, and cynics might well think that the unconscious speech of Cambridge academics would inevitably contain unintelligible fragments and quotations. Conscious, too. 'Eliot, Pound and Expatriate Authority' (*Raritan* 34.106–22) by James Buzard sees the expatriation of 'Eeldrop and Appleplex' as anthropological tourism rather than exile, suggesting that the outsider's privileged view of the whole culture is something it creates as Jamesian 'sublime synthesis', and offering valuable larger insights about the idea of modernism as exile.

Words in Time: New Essays on Eliot's Four Quartets, edited by Edward Lobb, is an important collection of new essays which should do much to refocus critical attention on these texts which have, as Lobb's introduction points out, suffered as a result of shifts in critical currents since their first appearance. The volume begins with Denis Donoghue's 'On Burnt Norton', a fluid and delightful essay which explains our difficulty with the poem through the failure of our grasp of 'a poetics of discourse', and also explores levels of meaning in parallel with *Murder in the Cathedral* and the poems of Mallarmé. Edward Lobb's contribution is 'Limitation and Transcendence in "East Coker"'. This explores, with both meticulousness and imagination, the closed-room metaphor as synecdochic of humankind's limited experience and the acceptance of it which is the first stage in transcending it, something as true of the poem's form as of its ideas. Lyndall Gordon next ruminates on 'The American Eliot and "The Dry Salvages"', having more to say on the man than the work but suggesting that his poetry is a version of the American dream of self-transformation, owing its impenetrability to the early American forms of soul history and sermon.

'"If I think, again, of this place": Eliot, Herbert and the Way to Little Gidding' by Ronald Schuchard is the longest essay in Lobb's collection. It is a thoughtful and detailed piece about Eliot's spiritual and poetic pilgrimage towards Little Gidding and George Herbert, commendable for its human breadth as well as its scholarly precision. A different kind of progress is masterfully chronicled by Jewel Spears Brooker in 'From "The Waste Land" to *Four Quartets*: Evolution of a Method'. The essential difference of the *Quartets* is in their use of 'a key pattern instead of a key myth', a model that is both synchronic and diachronic, both musical and mythic, in which aporias become gateways. The concern for form remains from the early works, but it is now transformed into something Lévi-Straussian in its relating of myth and pattern. Louis L. Martz's 'Origins of Form in *Four Quartets*' approaches similar ideas but reaches different conclusions. It addresses 'Burnt Norton' from the viewpoint of the original readers, and then moves through a choreographic pattern of allusion and reference to show the origins of the later poems in 'The Waste Land' and other earlier work. Together, the essays of Martz and Brooker make a remarkable approach to the structure of the later Eliot.

'Intelligence pushed to its depths leads to mysticism' is a statement by Eliot that forms the basis of Donald J. Childs's 'Risking Enchantment: The Middle Way between Mysticism and Pragmatism in *Four Quartets*' (also in Lobb's collection). This draws together Eliot's early interests in the philosophy of Bradley with a discussion of pragmatism and metaphysics, reaching its conclusion with a calm inevitability: 'we must construct something upon which to rejoice'. The complexity of basing such a construction on apophasis, or 'the negative way', while not denying the possibility of the positive way, is the basis of Cleo McNelly Kearns's 'Negative Theology and Literary Discourse in *Four Quartets*: A Derridean Reading' (in the same volume). With the aid of the Buddhist writer Nagarjuna and of Derrida's 'How to Avoid Speaking', Kearns addresses the complexity of thought and structure in the poems to show how they can 'trace both the way up and the way down'. Michael Levenson's 'The End of Tradition and the Beginning of History' explores Eliot's changing ideas, and asserts that, in the *Quartets*, 'going in search of the timeless Eliot discovered the past' – that is, the unaccommodating actuality of past events rather than the consolatory presence of tradition that he constructed in the earlier essays. It is an original and persuasive approach to the endlessly variable topic of time in the poems. A. Walton Litz looks at 'Repetition and Order in the Wartime *Quartets*', finding in them a wholeness that reflects Coleridgean ideas of unity in converting a series into a whole, offering symmetry and balance in the tradition of Romantic creative theory. This is, in a larger sense, true of Lobb's collection, for, good as the individual essays in it are – and some of them are very good indeed – they take on when read as a whole something of the nature of the *Quartets* themselves, repeating and reworking around certain central themes of philosophy and criticism that allow us to see the texts and their contexts within several new dynamics. For this reason, the collection is an outstanding contribution to Eliot scholarship.

Of more specialized interest is *T. S. Eliot and Hispanic Modernity (1924–1993)*, edited by K. M. Sibbald and Howard Young. Young's introduction briefly surveys translations of Eliot into Spanish, and is complemented by a bibliography of texts and criticism. C. Brian Morris discusses 'The Cultural Underground of Eliot, Alberti, and Lorca', exploring the effect of the poet's 'compound ghost' on these later writers: John C. Wilcox writes on 'T. S. Eliot and Juan Ramón Jiménez: Some Ideological Affinities', exploring similarities of outlook and attitude. K. M. Sibbald's '*Kulturkritik*: T. S. Eliot, Jorge Guillen and Pedro Salinas' finds parallels between the three writers' cultural criticism, and two articles in Spanish discuss matters of similarity and influence: '*The Cocktail Party* de T. S. Eliot y *El Director* de Pedro Salinas: Notas de un Cotejo', by Carmen Pérez Romero, and 'La Influencia de T. S. Eliot en la Poesía de Jaime Gil de Biedma: Tradicion como ruptura', by Juana Sabadell Nieto. Not only does this collection reveal much about an unexpected facet of Eliot's Europeanism; it also does something to enhance the study of Eliot in Spanish-speaking countries.

Eliot's criticism was a popular subject this year. '"The Present Self-Conscious Century": Eliot on Valéry' (*YER* 12.42–7) by Gareth Reeves traces Eliot's approach to the French Symbolist, from 'Tradition and the Individual Talent' to 'From Poe to Valéry', concluding that he found the poet disturbing but representative of the 'cool scientist' in his self-consciousness. David Pascoe finds 'A Source for the "Auditory Imagination"?' (*N&Q* 41.374–6) in Egerton Smith's *The Principles of English Verse* (1923), of which Eliot might have seen a review – though Pascoe's discussion of Eliot's recollection of the tentative nature of some of his coinages may negate the strength of the source. 'T. S. Eliot's Criticism of Nineteenth Century Fiction' by Kristian Smidt (in Kennedy and Øverland, *Excursions in Fiction* – see also above, section 1(b)) is a worthy survey of the poet's opinions, but it does not consider at all how these might be reflected in the poetry. 'Reading T. S. Eliot reading D. H. Lawrence: The Significance of Gender' (*CentR* 37[1993].355–68) attributes Eliot's preference for *Aaron's Rod* and *Mornings in Mexico* to his fear of modern woman as threat to a wholly male unity of being. To both Eliot and Lawrence, woman is the instrument of transcendence through romance and duality through child-bearing: the late works of both reject modern woman because of the threat she presents.

William H. Klein looks at 'Aspects of Time in Eliot's *Four Quartets*' (*YER* 12.26–36), exploring ideas of music and dance as temporal measures in each poem in turn. This offers a model of music and time, not of music and poetry, for decoding the text's movement, and an exploration of how dancer and dance unite, time dissolves as a sequential reality, and personal and eternal, individual and God, are one.

Arthur Sherbo's 'Envoy: Reviews of Spender, Auden and Stein' (*N&Q* 41.371–3) finds reviews of *The Cocktail Party*, Spender's *The Edge of Being*, Auden's

Collected Shorter Poems and a work by Stein in *Envoy*, a Dublin small magazine, between 1949 and 1951, and is valuable in offering hitherto undiscovered contemporary responses. David Renaker and Edwin Williams write on 'W. H. Auden's *Memorial for the City*, Part IV, Line 12, *Let our weakness speak*' (*RomN* 34.ii[1993].155–6), glossing the line with reference to Don Quixote's 'candid earthiness'. The special number of *CS* on Auden has not been available and will be reviewed next year.

In 'Dylan the Durable' (in Phillip Lopate, intro., *The Ordering Mirror*), Seamus Heaney explores the central conflict in Thomas's poetry, that between 'suffered world' and 'conscious craft', finding it in some of the later poems yet throughout praising the endeavour in an essay that is as lyrically intoxicating as it is intellectually rigorous: an ideal starting point in any consideration of the poems. 'Semiotics and the Poetry of David Jones and Geoffrey Hill' by Kathleen O'Gorman (in C. C. Barfoot, ed., *In Black and Gold* – see also section 2(b) below) explores the similarities between the two poets by looking at 'The Tutelar of the Place' and 'Tenebrae'. She concludes that, while both use sign-systems to give form to their texts, they do so in different ways, the former gravitating towards the Christian ritualistic use of language, the latter with far less ordered a purpose.

(b) Poetry: Post-1950

This year was the year in which poetry hit the headlines: 'Dead Poet is Groovy Due to Hit Movie' ran the story in the *Sun*. The dead poet was of course W. H. Auden and the hit movie was *Four Weddings and a Funeral*, in which Auden's poem 'Funeral Blues' was read as an oration at the funeral of a gay character. The film was a box office hit, and Faber and Faber rushed out a pamphlet of ten of Auden's poems, titled *Tell Me the Truth About the Love*, to cash in on the success. The pamphlet eventually sold over 200,000 copies, and Faber even decided to produce a long-awaited paperback edition of Auden's *Collected Poems*. Auden and his poetry received much media attention, and Peter Forbes dedicated an editorial in *PoetryR* (83.iv.3) to a discussion of what he called the new 'Auden cult' and its implications for the packaging of poetry. *CS* 6.iii was devoted to Auden, with Stan Smith in his 'Introduction' rightly asserting that 'Auden's great gift to twentieth-century poetry was . . . to depose the patriarchal metropolis as source of power and poetic authority, to affirm instead that "The marginal grief/ Is source of life" ', and Mark Currie ('The Hectic Quest for Prelapsarian Man: The Adamic Myth in Late Auden') and Mihaela Irimia ('The Art of Losing: W. H. Auden and Elizabeth Bishop') both providing accounts of Auden's later post-war work. Peter Porter, in a review essay on Anthony Hecht's *The Hidden Law* ('The Magician and the Censor', *PoetryR* 83.iv.4–8), asserted that 'Auden was prefiguring a new Europe: not the EC which we have, but the Europe-absorbed-by-America which is the real culture of our time', and James Fenton summed up the whole *Four Weddings and a Funeral* phenomenon in his article 'Four Weddings and a Circle of Poetry', which appeared in the *Independent* on 30 May.

The year 1994 was, then, Auden's, but it was also Fenton's, who succeeded Seamus Heaney as Oxford Professor of Poetry. For some reason Fenton's poetry has never received much critical attention, and the only detailed published account of his work this year came from Ellen Kreger Stark, in 'An American's Confession: On Reading James Fenton's *Out of Danger*' (*CritQ* 36.ii.106–10), an appreciative review of Fenton's 1993 collection, in which Stark states her admiration for Fenton's un-American reticence.

There was of course no such paucity of response to Fenton's predecessor as Oxford Professor. One is sometimes reminded, on reading criticism of Heaney's work, of Terence's *Nullumst iam dictum quod non dictum sit prius* ('Nothing has yet been said that's not been said before'), yet Kevin McGuirk managed a variation on an old theme in 'Questions, Apostrophes, and the Politics of Seamus Heaney's "Field Work"' (*ArielE* 25.iii.67–81), in which he identified *Field Work* as Heaney's most 'questioning' of volumes and argued that the book outlines 'a specific tropology that articulates the conflict between the disruptions of politics and the lyric impulse', which 'finds its fulfilment . . . in the triumph of the apostrophe'. Describing Heaney enthusiastically as an 'apostrophizing poet' who 'turns himself into a transhistorical and transnational bard', McGuirk argues none the less that apostrophizing is 'radically an act of solipsism' which fails to offer 'genuine answers to the problems raised' in the poems.

There was a similar ambivalent tone in Eamon Halpin's 'Seamus Heaney and the Politics of Imagination' and Michael Bernard-Donals's 'Governing the Tongue: Seamus Heaney's (A) Political Aesthetic' (*CJIS* 20.ii.20–8 and 75–88). Halpin argues that Heaney is a nationalist poet, 'but one who reveals to us some of the complexity of his tradition', while Bernard-Donals asserts that 'Heaney's own theory of the political aspects of poetry . . . does not do justice to his poetic sensibility' and attempts to show how Heaney's 'theory downplays the political force (and the political source) of all language . . . and instead emphasizes a counterbalancing romantic notion of poetic "inspiration" operating "at the moment of lyric conception"'.

Other articles about Heaney included a typically allusive and swashbuckling piece by Stan Smith, 'Darkening English: Post-Imperial Contestations in the Language of Seamus Heaney and Derek Walcott' (*English* 43.39–55), which discusses the decolonization of English in Heaney and Walcott, and argues that their use of 'linguistic hybridisation' is a key element in their polemic. The article is engaging and memorable partly because Smith himself cannot resist polemic of his own, such as his assertion that 'elocution, in the British system, is itself a form of class struggle, as the synthetic tones of Lady Thatcher's anxiously over-corrected speech remind us'. Brian Gibbons's 'Heaney's "Clearances", Hopkins and Vaughan' (*NPQ* 1.15–20) is rather more restrained in its argument that 'Heaney's turning to the sonnet in the "Glanmore" sequence is a deliberate step and one that is significant in his development', while R. J. C. Watt's 'Seamus Heaney: Voices on Helicon' (*EIC* 44.iii.213–34) is an old-fashioned piece of literary detective work, which identifies the statement by the third unnamed 'fosterer' in Section V of Heaney's 'Station Island' ('For what is the great / moving power and spring of verse? Feeling, and / in particular, love') as Michael McLaverty quoting Gerard Manley Hopkins. Watt moves beyond mere sleuthing in the second part of the article to argue that Hopkins, 'consonantal as opposed to vowelly, full of craft as opposed to instinct, willed and masculine as opposed to emotional and feminine', is both 'Heaney's alien' and his 'secret sharer too'.

Laurent Milesi, in 'Archaeologies of Localism in Seamus Heaney and Charles Olson' (*SwR* 'Writing and the Nation': 369–92 – see also this section, below, and section 1(b) above), makes connections of another kind, suggesting how 'Heaney's position as a Catholic Ulsterman or "inner émigré" on either side of the border may . . . somehow be seen as his more private version of the feeling of exile experienced by post-Poundian American poets within European culture'. In particular, Milesi compares Heaney and Olson in their 'conception of writing as digging' and their belief in poetry as an excavation 'grounded or anchored, whether it be Heaney's bogland or Olson's local fishing community of Gloucester'. (For further Irish-American encodings see Paul Bowers, 'John Montague and William Carlos Williams: Nationalism and Poetic Consciousness', in *CJIS* 20.ii.29–44.)

Michael R. Molino explores such themes further in his book *Questioning Tradition, Language and Myth: The Poetry of Seamus Heaney*, which focuses on 'Heaney's excavation of, interaction with, separation from, alteration of, and responsibility toward the complex and, at times, contradictory traditions he finds himself a part of'. Molino's competent overview of Heaney's work was, however, outdone and overshadowed by the publication of Bernard O'Donoghue's long-awaited and magisterial *Seamus Heaney and the Language of Poetry*. O'Donoghue combines common sense and an easy-going manner ('If Seamus Heaney proves to be as important a figure in the annals of English poetry as currently seems likely, it will be because he combines with his sense of poetic mission a strong suspicion that poetry is not the most important thing in the world') with a rigorous analytical method which he calls 'political formalism'. His formalism he defines as 'an approach founded entirely on the terms of traditional linguistic analysis', but which is not 'a New Critical claim for placing poetry in a hermetically sealed environment, uncontaminated by non-literary circumstance'. The book's 'guiding subjects' are 'the changes in Heaney's poetic language and his poetic commentary', and the focus is on Heaney's abandonment of Irish metrical forms and a 'pseudo-learned diction' and his adoption of English disyllabics and a more straightforward and colloquial diction. It is a book which should prove to be of lasting value to researchers, students and teachers.

O'Donoghue is of course himself a poet, and this year saw a number of books and articles by Irish critics who are also themselves practitioners. Gerald Dawe, for example, continued his process of self-analysis in *False Faces: Poetry, Politics and Place* (for a discussion of Dawe's poetry see David Gardiner's 'Uneasy Domesticity: The Poetry of Gerald Dawe', in *Éire* 29.ii.146–59), while Eavan Boland produced another of her scorching prose pieces, 'Making the Difference: Eroticism and Ageing in the Work of the Woman Poet' (*PNR* 20.iv.13–21), in which she stated that she has 'come to believe that the woman poet is an emblematic figure in poetry now in the same way the Modernist and Romantic poets once were' because 'she internalizes the stresses and truths of poetry at a particular moment'. It is a bold claim, but one supported by Sheila C. Conboy, in 'Eavan Boland's Topography of Displacement' (*Éire* 29.iii.137–46), who describes the ways in which Boland attempts to 'renovate Irish poetic tradition by giving a written place to her personal and personalized experience'.

The poet and critic Brendan Kennelly asked some searching questions in the introduction to *Journey into Joy: Selected Prose*, edited by Åke Persson, including 'why do we continue to dare presume to expect so much of literature?' and 'what effect does it have on oneself after several decades' immersion in it?', the answer to the latter being 'Not a great deal, I suspect', although with the telling parenthesis, '(But this tendency not to lie automatically to oneself may well be one of its deepest consequences.)' The selection of essays includes 'Derek Mahon's Humane Perspective', 'James Joyce's "Humanism"', and 'W. B. Yeats: An Experiment in Living', all of which demonstrate Kennelly's belief that the critic's task is to bear witness to 'the accuracy and courage with which other people reveal their experiences of this world'. A companion volume, *Dark Fathers into Light: Brendan Kennelly*, edited by Richard Pine, includes essays about Kennelly's work by

Augustine Martin, Terence Brown and Kathleen McCracken, among others, as well as a (select) bibliography and an interview.

Like Kennelly, Thomas Kinsella and Austin Clarke are poets perhaps better known in Ireland than outside, and Maurice Harmon's 'Ancient Lights in the Poetry of Austin Clarke and Thomas Kinsella' (*Éire* 29.i.123–40) provides much useful background information on their work (see also Brian John's '"Brothers in the Craft": Thomas Kinsella and the Yeats Inheritance', *IUR* 24.ii.247–63, which charts Kinsella's gradual coming to terms with the Yeatsian inheritance). In contrast, the accomplishments of certain Irish women writers are now as well known outside Ireland as in, and Eileen Cahill, in '"Because I never garden": Medbh McGuckian's Solitary Way', (*IUR* 24.ii.264–71), goes some way towards explaining why. Cahill attempts to define McGuckian's appeal with a riddling formula ('In Lacan's words, McGuckian doesn't know what she is saying . . . Because she is not saying what is known') and describes in some detail her frequent 'sins against the laws of logic, syntax, congruity, grammar, causality, linear structure and unity'. Meanwhile, Linden Peach's 'Contemporary Irish Women Writers and the Gendered Construction of Space' (*SwR*, Special Number:450–61) examines work by McGuckian, Anne Hartigan, Boland, Paula Meehan and Mairéad Byrne, and praises its determination to offer alternatives to 'functional, oppositional structuring of space'.

Many of the essays in Edna Longley's *The Living Stream: Literature and Revisionism in Ireland* have already appeared elsewhere ('The Rising, the Somme and Irish Memory', 'No More Poems about Paintings?', 'The Room Where MacNeice Wrote "Snow"'), but two of them – one new, one republished – deserve special mention. Longley might be described as both the scourge and grandame of Irish letters, and in the long and tightly-argued introduction to the book, 'Revising "Irish Literature"', she sets out her claim that 'it may be the case that perceptions of Irish literature are unduly determined by assumptions – mainly Nationalist assumptions – about Ireland', and strenuously warns against the 'obsession with politics' and the 'chimera of secure Irishness' that characterized the *Field Day Anthology*. In the provocative 'From Cathleen to Anorexia' (first published as a pamphlet by the Attic Press, Dublin, 1990), she argues that 'Anorexic patients pursue an unreal self-image – in practice, a death-wish. Similarly, the Irish Nationalist dream may have declined into a destructive neurosis.' Longley keeps up the prodding and questioning in 'Northern Irish Poetry: Literature of Region(s) or Nation(s)?' (*SwR* Special Number:63–83 – also reviewed elsewhere in this section and in section 1(b) above), reading a number of poems (including Derek Mahon's 'Glengormley', Heaney's 'A New Song', the third sonnet from Paul Muldoon's 'Armageddon, Armageddon', Ciaran Carson's 'Hamlet' and McGuckian's 'Marconi's Cottage') in relation to the concept of the 'parish', as defined by Patrick Kavanagh in his description of the 'parochial mentality' as 'never in any doubt about the social and artistic validity of his parish'.

Parishes and parochial mentalities are also at issue in Tamar Hagar's 'British Poetry and National Identity: The Representation of Scottish, Irish and Welsh Poets by Literary Institutions of England Proper' in (*SwR* Special Number:259–73) which examines 'some institutional strategies by means of which the English introduce themselves to "other" British nations and those others to themselves'. Hagar looks at a number of anthologies, and finds for example that Douglas Dunn has been persistently classified as a working-class poet rather than a Scots poet, leading Hagar to conclude that 'By transferring Scottish poets from their national periphery to English social and cultural peripheries or to the English literary core, English literary institutions incorporate a distinct Scottish identity into an Anglo-British culture.' M. Wynn Thomas reverses the appropriation principle in 'Anglo-Welsh Poets and the Welsh Language during the 80s' (*SwR* Special Number:511–21), arguing that the work of a number of Welsh poets demonstrates how 'English can be turned, by creative force or cunning, into a Welsh language', concentrating on acts of 'guileful reconstruction' in work by Nigel Jenkins, Tony Conran, Oliver Reynolds and Peter Finch.

Turning from the Irish, the Scots and the Welsh to the English, Joseph Bristow in 'The Obscenity of Philip Larkin' (*CritI* 21.i.156–81) argues that the 'hostile comments' in his letters 'have made it impossible to feel that Larkin's meager output of poetry . . . can now stand as a central component of late-twentieth century English cultural consciousness' and explores 'what it is about Larkin's obscenity that has become posthumously so anachronistic in its "chummy democratic" appeal'. Bristow argues that Larkin 'made obscenity form the basis of an antimodernist understanding of the authenticity of male sexual desire' and reads three poems – 'Deceptions', 'Sunny Prestatyn' and 'Love Again' – as embodying an ambivalent aesthetic, 'Controlled, yet ruthless; condescending yet self-loathing; antimodernist yet elitist; anti-intellectual but nonetheless literary'. Patrick Swinden, in 'Larkin and the Exemplary Owen' (*EIC* 44.315–32), follows a trickle of para-rhyme from Owen through Auden to Larkin, and argues that in his early work 'By copying the worst features of Owen's practice Larkin produced a bland and undemonstrative pastiche of Auden's more vigorous style', whilst in his later work he moved towards 'less strident, less voiced, and above all less regularly imposed patterns of half-rhyme'. Swinden also examines Larkin's 'preoccupation with states of existence, or beyond existence, that refuse to identify themselves as rich or impoverished, occupied or vacant'.

In 'On Geoffrey Hill's Decade of Reticence' (*PNR* 20.vi.51–4) S. J. Ellis charts the development of Hill's recent work, detecting 'intimations of joy alongside encroaching melancholia' and even 'An increasing emphasis by Hill on fragmented utterance which expresses something of a "postmodernist" sensibility'.

Keith Sagar's *The Challenge of Ted Hughes* gathers together a number of essays on Hughes's poetry, including Alexander Davis's 'Romanticism, Existentialism, Patriarchy: Hughes and the Visionary Imagination', Terry Gifford's 'Gods of Mud: Hughes and the Post-Pastoral', and Rand Brandes's 'Hughes, History and the World in Which We Live'. Sagar himself claims that Hughes's work is a source 'of great psychic or spiritual power', which defies 'the coordinates provided by an enlightened literary education' and requires from the reader a background reading in Schopenhauer, Castaneda and alchemical texts. Gotz Schmitz, in 'Local Myth in the Poetry of Ted Hughes' (*SwR* Special Number:470–81 – see also above, this section and section 1(b)), requires reading only in local myth, analysing two poems, 'Esther's Tomcat' and 'Churn-Milk Joan', in which Yorkshire lore and legend play a part. (It is worth mentioning that this year also saw the publication of Hughes's own *Winter Pollen: Occasional Prose*, a collection of reviews, articles and essays from over a quarter of a century on subjects ranging from the ur-language of Orghast to Dylan Thomas.)

Jacqueline Banerjee writes about Sylvia Plath in 'Grief and the Modern Writer' (*English* 43.17–36), comparing work by Anne Sexton and Virginia Woolf in order to 'bring out the different strategies they employed to cope with their grief in their art, and to consider the value of such efforts'. Antony Easthope, in 'Reading the

Poetry of Sylvia Plath' (*English* 43.223–35), attempts to make explicit 'the point of view from which I would approach Plath's poetry, one that accords special attention to the operation of the signifier, to the formal properties of poetry, and the place of her poetry . . . within the developing and uneven tradition of twentieth-century poetry in English'. Easthope argues that the 'lyric-confessional mainstream' in verse in English relies on 'an endeavour to represent the empirical individual, staged in terms of the depths of the inward self, with corresponding necessity to deny, contain or . . . to recuperate the operation of the signifier'. He criticizes Plath's 'Daddy' for being 'a humanist poem, and a pretty old-fashioned one . . . aiming as it does to put at the centre of writing a dramatisation of the unified self'.

Alison Light, in 'Outside History? Stevie Smith, Women Poets and the National Voice' (*English* 43.237–59), examines Stevie Smith's 'brisk' and 'brittle' Englishness and discusses the implications of her 'refusal to separate the internal spaces of fantasy, the often bizarre imagery and dreamlike visions which make up much of the ambivalent psychic drama of the poetry, and what is usually called the "real world"'. Light argues for 'another history of Englishness which can include its domestic history and the history of its domestication (or perhaps privatisation or interiorisation)'.

Two books published by Carcanet bring together the English, the Scots, the Welsh, the Irish, the male and the female. C. B. McCully's *The Poet's Voice and Craft* grows out of lectures at the Manchester Poetry Centre in which poets were asked to respond to a number of questions about sound-structure and metrics ('How conscious are you of metrical considerations in your work?'), syntax ('Are you conscious of manipulating the syntax of your poems to achieve particular effects?') and lexis ('What principles are at work in your choice of words?'). The book contains responses from Donald Davie, on 'The Rudiments of Verse', Peter Scupham, on 'Poetic Practice', Douglas Dunn, on 'Writing Things Down', and Fleur Adcock, on 'The Way it Happens'. Clive Wilmer's *Poets Talking*, meanwhile, consists of 'Poet of the Month interviews' from Radio 3, and rounds up all the usual suspects, including Heaney and Raine, with a few unexpected appearances from the likes of Stephen Romer and Ken Smith.

Other round-ups and rag-bags included Barfoot's *In Black and Gold* (see also section 2(a) above), which contained essays not only on Hill and Harrison (David Gervais's 'Home-Made England: History and Nostalgia in the Poetry of Geoffrey Hill and Tony Harrison', Helmut Haberkamm's '"These Vs Are All the Versuses of Life": A Reading of Tony Harrison's Social Elegy *v*'), Larkin (Paul Moeyes's, 'The Return to the Native: Time and Tradition in the Poetry of Philip Larkin', David Punter's, 'Philip Larkin: Humiliation and Survival'), and Muldoon (Paul Goodby's 'Hermeneutic Hermeticism: Paul Muldoon and the Northern Irish Poetic'), but also on Ian Hamilton Finlay (by Peter Davidson), Peter Reading (by Dennis O'Driscoll) and C. H. Sisson (E. M. Knottenbelt).

The 'Anglo' in Dennis Brown's title, *The Poetry of Postmodernity: Anglo/American Encodings*, was covered by discussions of Ted Hughes's 'Crow', Geoffrey Hill's 'Mercia' and R. S. Thomas's 'Amen', which Brown reads 'for what they can tell us about the postmodern world'. Brown defines postmodernism as characterized by features such as 'Generic instability, "theatrical" fictionality, surface interplay, anamnesis, eschatological anxiety or the relativisation of language games', and argues that 'modernism and postmodernism are more nearly synonyms than antonyms'.

John Greening offers an alternative overview of the contemporary scene in 'The Quest for the Seven Virtues' (*PoetryR* 84.iv.64–7). According to Greening, the best contemporary poetry answers to the following: '1. It is driven by the elemental and the unseen. 2. It displays a command of narrative and conceptual thought. 3. It is sensually charged. 4. It is in the voice of one person speaking to another. 5. It sings both from the inside and the outside. 6. It has its roots in the land and in its history. 7. It is a reflection of its time.' Peter Forbes is rather more specific but much more negative in 'Talking About the New Generation' (*PoetryR* New Generation Poets Special Issue:4–6), in which he claims that the only unifying feature amongst the new generation of British poets is 'their relative disdain for English poetry of the 20th century and their enthusiasm for American and European poetry'.

Final mention should be given to Peterjon and Jasmin Skelt's *Alive in Parts of This Century*, a seventieth birthday tribute to Eric Mottram, who died shortly after the book's publication. The book includes poems and essays from Gilbert Adair, John Ashbery, Charles Bernstein, Thomas A. Clark, Elaine Feinstein, Roy Fisher and Wendy Mulford. Mottram was an indefatigable champion of contemporary poetry and the small presses, and would undoubtedly have welcomed 1994 as an important year in the history of English poetry, with *Poetry Review* celebrating its eighty-fifth birthday, the *London Magazine* its fortieth, *Agenda* being thirty-five, *Poetry Wales* thirty, Eddie Linden's *Aquarius* twenty-five, and *Outposts* fifty (see Wolfgang Gortschacher, James Hogg and Roland John's *Salute to Outposts*). For Mottram knew, as T. S. Eliot once put it, that 'It must be the small and obscure papers and reviews, those which are hardly read by anyone but their own contributors, that will keep critical thought alive and encourage authors of original talent.'

3. Drama

This section has two categories: (a) General Studies; (b) Individual Authors, in alphabetical order. Coverage of film and television is confined to works by writers with a substantial theatrical reputation. An author who is considered in a general work and is the subject of an individual study may appear in both sections. *MD* and the specialist journals such as *PinterR* and *ShawR* should be consulted for their bibliographies, which may cover items not available to me.

(a) General Studies

John Bull's *Stage Right* is an important study of what its subtitle describes as 'Crisis and Recovery in British Contemporary Mainstream Theatre'. A companion piece to Bull's *New British Political Dramatists* (*YWES* 65.579), it trenchantly teases out the history of English theatre between 1979 and early 1993. There are illuminating essays on the artistic achievements of Alan Ayckbourn, Alan Bennett, Michael Frayn, Simon Gray, Peter Nichols and Tom Stoppard, but Bull's great strength is a comprehensive approach that firmly locates theatrical phenomena in the cultural and ideological matrices of their period.

Fidelis Morgan continues her excavations of theatrical work by women in *The Years Between*, a collection of plays and revue sketches from 1908 to 1949. She includes Cicely Hamilton's *Diana of Dobson's*, Clemence Dane's *Will Shakespeare*, Margaret Kennedy's *The Constant Nymph*, Daphne Du Maurier's *The Years Between* and Lesley Storm's *Black Chiffon*, as well as revue sketches by Hermione

Gingold, Nina Warner Hooke and Diana Morgan. Fidelis Morgan contributes brief introductions to the authors and their works. The book is a useful contribution to the beginnings of a general reassessment of a generally underresearched period of theatrical activity.

Two volumes in the New Directions in Theatre series deal with important issues in regrettably opaque prose. Unfortunately, both semiotics and postmodernism have acquired critical discourses that sometimes seem to equate the lucid with the simplistic. *A Semiotics of the Dramatic Text* by Susan Melrose is a hefty but often impenetrable exploration of a range of issues in theatre practice and analysis; Nick Kaye's *Postmodernism and Performance* deals with what is currently called 'Live Art', with specific reference to works by the Wooster Group, Karen Finley, Robert Wilson and Richard Foreman.

One Night Stands is a collection of Michael Billington's *Guardian* reviews from 1971 to 1991. Newspaper reviews are an important source for theatre historians, so the opportunity to read a selection of one person's reviews is valuable, as are Billington's own brief introductory and concluding remarks, which offer some important insights into the practices and principles of newspaper criticism.

Oscar Lewenstein's memoirs, *Kicking Against the Pricks*, record the professional life of a key figure in modern British theatre and film. However, despite Lewenstein's pivotal role at the Royal Court as producer, manager and artistic director, and his involvement in many significant productions and many of the defining moments in post-war developments, the book is relatively uninformative and rather general.

David Ian Rabey's 'The Bite of Exiled Love: Abjective Protagonists in Some Contemporary Anglo-Irish Dramas' (*EiTET* 13.29–43) looks at works by David Rudkin, Thomas Kilroy and Ron Hutchinson, which, he argues, use 'protagonists whose self-performative reflexes and unforgivable effects simultaneously problematise Irish and British definition alike'. He contrasts the dramaturgy of these works with that of writers like Brian Friel, Graham Reid and Billy Roche, which can be 'supportive of both nations' presumptions of inevitabilities'. The point is well made, and the essay offers some illuminating comments on the individual plays, but the argument is presented in a Kristevan matrix which does little to focus it.

Lionel Pilkington's interview with Dan Baron Cohen, entitled 'Resistance to Liberation with Derry Frontline Culture and Education' (*TDR* 38.iv.17–47), is an interesting record of a theatre-based group which combines opposition to British rule with a questioning of nationalist beliefs.

As usual, *NTQ* (10) is replete with interesting and important essays: Mick Wallis's important 'Pageantry and the Popular Front: Ideological Production in the Thirties' (132–56) explores the 'politics, aesthetics, and logistics of a long neglected form of popular performance'; James Ross Moore offers a perspective on a different form of the popular in 'The Gershwins in Britain' (33–48); William W. Demastes's 'Re-Inspecting the Crack in the Chimney: Chaos Theory from Ibsen to Stoppard' (242–54) is a stimulating account of its topic; Caroline Gardiner's 'From Bankside to the West End: A Comparative View of London Audiences' (70–86) has some fascinating material on the current London audience; and Nicholas Whybrow examines the crisis in Theatre in Education and Theatre for Young People in two essays (198–9 and 267–80).

Anna-Marie Taylor's 'The Germans in Britain' (in Brian Docherty, ed., *Twentieth-Century European Drama*) is a useful brief survey of the presence of German drama in the British repertory, with some interesting points about modes of cross-cultural exchange. Although it does not offer a complete list of productions and the companies that staged them (Foco Novo's significant contribution, for example, remains anonymous), the essay could prove a valuable starting point for more detailed examination of a whole range of issues.

(b) Individual Authors

Instead of the usual tendency to discuss the respective contributions of Behan and Joan Littlewood to the first production of *The Hostage*, Michael Patrick Gillespie's 'Violent Impotence and Impotent Violence: Brendan Behan's *The Hostage*' (*Éire* 29.i.92–104) suggests that it may be more fruitful to read it as underscoring disorientation, so that the play's refusal 'to assign primacy to any polemical or rhetorical position' means that 'the inevitable irresolution of the topic – political turmoil in Ireland – stands as the drama's concern'.

Daphne Turner's examination of Alan Bennett's use of landscape in 'North and South: Two Landscapes of Alan Bennett' (*MD* 37.551–67) shows how he associates specific (often stereotypical) characteristics with different landscapes, but neither wins his full approval. This is a well-argued and subtle reading of Bennett's work.

Ian Stuart has two pieces derived from the workshops Edward Bond conducted with Royal Shakespeare Company actors in 1992. In his 'Interview with Edward Bond' (*JDTC* 8.ii.129–46) he concentrates on Bond's views on Shakespeare and his theories on central situations and theatre events; in 'A Political Language for the Theatre: Edward Bond's RSC Workshops 1992' (*NTQ* 10.207–16) he concentrates on the workshops themselves and their attempt to 'explore a post-Stanislavsky, post-Brecht, anti-happening drama'.

In '"I am cast as a monster": Shelley's *Frankenstein* and the haunting of Howard Brenton's *Bloody Poetry*' (*MD* 37.588–602) Jennifer A. Wagner usefully reads Brenton's play in the light of feminist re-reading of Mary Shelley.

Graham Holderness's 'Weiss/Brook: *Marat/Sade*' (in Docherty, *Twentieth-Century European Drama*) is a deft rehearsal of the ways in which Peter Brook stressed some elements in Weiss's play in line with his own Artaudian interests at the expense of Weiss's more dialectical approach.

Agatha Christie's *Witness for the Prosecution* is a sturdy thriller last revived in 1992. Frank Ardolino's valuable account of its genesis in '*Witness for the Prosecution*: Agatha Christie's Autobiographical Revenge Play' (*Clues* 15.79–92) explores the difference between the original short story and the much-altered theatrical version in terms of Christie's own personal marital traumas. He draws on Christie's autobiography and her autobiographical novel *Unfinished Portrait* to flesh out the picture, with many precise, detailed and convincing comparisons.

In '"Make us the Women We Can't Be": Cloud Nine and the Female Imaginary' (*JDTC* 8.ii.7–22) Marc Silverstein draws on Herbert Blau, Lacan, Irigaray, Mulvey, Kristeva and Foucault to discuss how, in Churchill's play, 'our negotiation of the lived experience . . . of sexuality and gender is mediated, if not governed, by representational and signifying economies'. Donna Soto-Morettini's informative and insightful 'Revolution and the Fatally Clever Smile' (*JDTC* 9.i.105–18) shows how *Mad Forest* is an examination of the complex challenges of the Rumanian attempt to remove 'a long-running hegemony of paranoia and double-think' and that its method 'reflects a disorganised subjectivism that must glimpse historical forces through a much smaller lens' than the one Brecht used.

Susan C. Haedicke compares two modern plays that explore the exploitation of women at home and at work in 'Doing the Dirty Work: Gendered Versions of

Working Class Women in Sarah Daniels' *The Gut Girls* and Israel Horovitz's *North Shore Fish*' (*JDTC* 8.77–88). She argues that whereas Daniels challenges patriarchy and calls for the overthrow of the dominant ideology, Horovitz tends to see capitalism and patriarchy as the best available system.

William Jent tries to rescue Brian Friel from what he sees as 'a systematic oversight that leads to a crucial misapprehension of the play's central concern' in 'Supranational Civics: Poverty and the Politics of Representation in Brian Friel's *The Freedom of the City*' (*MD* 37.568–87). He argues a case for the centrality of the insights into poverty of the American sociologist character, Dodds, rather than the overtly political responses that have tended to dominate responses to the play. This is a useful corrective, but the evidence of responses to actual performance does suggest that there is some validity in the more usual readings.

Jonathan Bignell analyses 'Trevor Griffiths's Political Theatre: From "Oi for England" to "The Gulf Between Us"' (*NTQ* 10.49–56), a thoughtful and perceptive analysis both of the texts in performance and of institutional and audience reception issues: the audience for *Oi* sometimes hardly recognized that they were watching a play at all; the audience for *Gulf* tended to view structural irresolution as 'an effect of bad writing or direction'.

Seamus Heaney is not well known as a dramatist, so Matthew M. DeForrest's 'Seamus Heaney's *The Cure at Troy*: Individuality and the Psychological' (*Éire* 29.ii.126–36) is particularly welcome. He offers a useful reading of Heaney's characterization in terms of the relationship between the universal and the individual, with Freudian readings of the characters as 'iconic representations of psychological archetypes'.

Interest in Ann Jellicoe remains low. Laura Snyder tries to read Jellicoe's current community play concerns back into an analysis of 'Learning to Play the Game: Learning and Teaching Strategies in Ann Jellicoe's *The Knack*' (*MD* 37.451–60). The results are unstartling, although the emphasis on learning strategies is a useful corrective to the usual stress on sex and gender.

'Worlds Elsewhere: The Plays of Thomas Kilroy' (*Éire* 29.ii.123–38), by Christopher Murray, locates Kilroy's work in a modernist context, drawing attention to his affinities, with Ibsen in particular.

'D. H. Lawrence and the 1912 Miners' Strike' (*ES* 75.133–45), Macdonald Daly's well-informed account of how Lawrence uses strikes in his early work to 'embody concepts of marital and work relationships as areas both of mutual aid and of conflict', touches briefly on *The Daughter-in-Law*.

Fintan O'Toole's *Tom Murphy: The Politics of Magic*, a major study of a major Irish writer who has made little impact in Britain, has now been revised to cover the period since 1987, when it first appeared. As O'Toole points out, there were no British-originated professional productions of one of Murphy's plays between 1961 and 1991, a curious omission given the attention paid to Brian Friel in particular. This study serves as an excellent introduction to Murphy's achievement, locating it in both personal and Irish cultural contexts.

I saw two essays on Sean O'Casey, neither of them centrally concerned with the plays: Patricia Angelin traces the importance of O'Casey's friendship with George Jean Nathan in 'Comrades in Arms: George Jean Nathan and Sean O'Casey' (*Éire* 29.iv.7–23) and J. D. Scrimgeour examines 'Song and the Artist in the Autobiographies of Sean O'Casey' (*Éire* 29.iii.93–108), drawing useful distinctions between the methods of the first two volumes of autobiography.

Göran Nieragden's 'Comedy and Menace: A Gricean Look at the Dialogue in

Joe Orton's *Loot*' (*GRM* 44.77–86) is a straightforward account of how Grice's theories can be applied to and may account for some of the comic effects created by Orton's characteristic dislocations of expected conversational strategies.

In 'Still Looking Back: the Deconstruction of the Angry Young Man in *Look Back in Anger* and *Déjàvu*' (*MD* 37.521–9), Graham A. Dixon does his best to rescue John Osborne's *Déjàvu* from almost universal condemnation of its marathon self-indulgence. There are some good points about the detailed operation of the play but the overall argument did not convince me.

In 'Adulteration as Clarity: Dramaturgical Strategy in Peter Nichols's *Passion Play*' (*MD* 37. 437–50) William Storm offers a lively reading of an important but generally undervalued play that pinpoints the ways in which its dramaturgical boldness transcends the limitations of the bourgeois adultery play.

'Stream of Consciousness and Freud's Primary Process: Comprehending Pinter's *Old Times*' (*L&P* 40.71–80), by Evelyn Schreiber, attempts to use her two title concepts to elucidate Pinter's play. It is a careful and helpful reading that substantiates her opening claim that Pinter 'presents characters coping with uncertainty about their security and identity', whether we see the play as 'a presentation of unconscious thought processes or a play of sparse dialogue between distracted characters', but also raises some tentative questions about the nature of theatrical pleasure. If there are times when the essay seems to be straining too hard to invest its close reading with theoretical gravitas, the same might also be said of Michael Lynch's ambitiously titled 'Pinter and Foucault: Duologues as Discourse' (*SSEng* 20.104–16), which makes some perfectly reasonable, if often not unfamiliar, points about the ways in which power relations are expressed through speech in Pinter's work. Gene Fendt offers 'A Medieval Reading of Pinter's *Homecoming*' (*L&T* 8.47–63), suggesting that 'Pinter moves Freud's symbology from the level of archetypes of the unconscious to that of a myth about the soul.' It is a detailed and sophisticated account, with many incidental insights, even if references to the play being set in the rubble of World War II and living 'on the north end' of London do suggest an imperfect grasp of the nuances of English life. As with many readings of Pinter, the difficulty lies in relating some of the points directly to the play's theatrical effectiveness. Mel Gussow's *Conversations with Pinter*, which reprints interviews from 1971 to 1993 covering a wide range of topics relating to Pinter's output from *Old Times* onwards, including his work as a director, has no such difficulties.

In 'Disparaging Freud: The Negative Function of Psychoanalysis in Peter Shaffer's *Equus* and John Pielmeier's *Agnes of God*' (*JEP* 15.22–8), Daniel Wright takes issue with his authors' repetition of the 'rather tired insight' that 'it is man's unhappy inclination always to destroy that which he does not understand', particularly 'when it merges uncomfortably with other dramatic themes to create unnecessary confusion and needless distraction'. Wright's anger with what he sees as the plays' negative approach to Freudian insights is not unfamiliar, but this is a minor example of the genre.

Apart from the usual coverage in *ShawR*, which I have not seen this year, Philip O'Leary's 'Lost Tribesman or Prodigal Son? George Bernard Shaw and the Gaelic Movement' (*Éire* 29.ii.51–64) is an illuminating and well-illustrated account of Shaw's usually stormy relationship with the Gaelic movement and of the difficult status of Anglo-Irish literature. Sheila Stowell locates Shaw's interest in Joan of Arc in the context of the Women's Social and Political Union (particularly the activities of Christabel Pankhurst) and the important pioneering work of Cicely Hamilton and Elizabeth Robins, in '"Dame Joan, Saint Christabel"' (*MD* 37.421–36).

David Storey attracts attention again this year. Rakesh H. Solomon offers a convincing overview of 'Man as Working Animal: Work, Class and Identity in the Plays of David Storey' (*FMLS* 30.193–203), showing how physical labour is privileged over mental labour throughout Storey's work. Comradeship between manual labourers can be more cohesive and sustaining than family relationships, particularly where working-class parents have produced educated offspring who find themselves alienated both from their roots and from their own situations. Malcolm Pittock addresses rather different ground in 'Storey's Portrayal of Old Age: *The March on Russia*' (*Neophil* 78.329–41). His title describes his content succinctly enough and his method is a straightforward account of the play through a close reading of characters and situations.

I saw one essay on Synge. Daniel Davy's 'Tragic Self-Referral in *Riders to the Sea*' (*Eire* 29.ii.77–91) offers an economic and effective synopsis of the continued dispute about 'the nature of the tragic experience expressed in the play'. He sees Maurya's vision of Bartley and Michael as a key factor in creating a tragic scheme which is similar to the Aristotelian model, but also differs from it, offering 'participation in an experience which is simultaneously natural and transcendental; and which ruthlessly reduces the protagonist to the status of object even as it expands his awareness and status as a participatory subject'.

Books Reviewed

Allen, Orphia Jane. *Barbara Pym: Writing a Life*. Scarecrow. pp. 261. $35. ISBN 0 8108 2875 8.

Baldwin, Anna, and Sarah Hutton, eds. *Platonism and the English Imagination*. CUP. pp. 357. £40. ISBN 0 5214 0308 1.

Barfoot, C. C., ed. *In Black and Gold: Contiguous Traditions in Post-War British and Irish Poetry*. Rodopi. pp. 332. $31.00. ISBN 9 0518 3660 0.

Baron, Helen, and Carl Baron, eds. *D. H. Lawrence. Sons and Lovers*. Penguin. pp. 498. £5.99. ISBN 0 1401 8832 0.

Batchelor, John. *The Life of Joseph Conrad*. Blackwell. pp. 335. £19.99. ISBN 0 6311 6416 2.

Bauer, Helen Pike. *Rudyard Kipling: A Study of the Short Fiction*. Twayne's Studies in Short Fiction. Twayne. pp. 165. £15.95. ISBN 0 8057 8345 8.

Bell, Michael Mayerfeld. *Childerley: Nature and Mortality in a Country Village*. UChicP. pp. 279. £11.95. ISBN 0 2260 4198 0.

Benstock, Bernard. *Narrative Con/Texts in Dubliners*. Macmillan. pp. 171. £35. ISBN 0 3335 8739 1.

Berman, Art. *Preface to Modernism*. UIllP. pp. 354. hb $39.95, pb $15.95. ISBN 0 2520 2103 7, 0 2520 6391 0.

Billington, Michael. *One Night Stands*. Hern (1993). pp. 382. £17.99. ISBN 1 8545 9185 1.

Bloomer, Jennifer. *Architecture and the Text: The (S)Crypts of Joyce and Piranesi*. Theoretical Perspectives in Architectural History and Criticism. YaleUP (1993). pp. 236. hb £27.50, pb £10.50. ISBN 0 3000 4927 7, 0 3000 6302 4.

Bradshaw, David, ed. *The Hidden Huxley: Contempt and Compassion for the Masses 1920-36*. Faber. pp. 255. hb £17.50, pb £7.99. ISBN 0 5711 7259 8, 0 5711 7620 1.

Brooker, Jewel Spears, *Mastery and Escape: T. S. Eliot and the Dialectic of Modernism*. UMassP. pp. 274. $33.25. ISBN 0 8702 3905 8.

Brown, Dennis. *The Poetry of Postmodernity: Anglo/American Encodings*. St Martin's. pp. 146. $35. ISBN 0 3121 2093 1.

Bruce, Donald, and Anthony Purdy, eds. *Literature and Science*. Rodopi. pp. 179. $34. ISBN 9 0518 3762 3.

Brunsdale, Mitzi M. *James Joyce: A Study of the Short Fiction*. Twayne's Studies in Short Fiction. Twayne. pp. 288. $23.95. ISBN 0 8057 0854 5.

Bull, John. *Stage Right: Crisis and Recovery in British Contemporary Mainstream Theatre*. Macmillan. pp. 251. hb £40, pb £12.99. ISBN 0 3333 9596 4, 0 3333 9597 2.

Burt, Richard, ed. *The Administration of Aesthetics: Censorship, Political Criticism, and the Public Sphere*. UMinnP. pp. 381. hb £35, pb £15.95. ISBN 0 8166 2365 1, 0 8166 2367 8.

Cassis, A. F. *Graham Greene: Life, Work and Criticism*. YorkP. pp. 45. ISBN 0 9199 6689 6.

Coles, Gladys Mary, ed. *Both Sides of the River: Merseyside in Poetry and Prose*. Headland. pp. 305. £17.95. ISBN 0 9030 7465 6.

Costa, Richard Hauer. *An Appointment with Somerset Maugham and Other Literary Encounters*. TexA&MUP. pp. 227. hb $35, pb $15.95. ISBN 0 8909 6618 4, 0 8909 6619 2.

Culleton, Claire A. *Names and Naming in Joyce*. UWiscP. pp. 148. hb £34.50, pb £13.50. ISBN 0 2991 4380 5, 0 2991 4384 8.

Daly, Macdonald, ed. *D. H. Lawrence, Sons and Lovers*. Dent Everyman. pp. 472. £5.99. ISBN 0 4608 7453 5.

Dawe, Gerald. *False Faces: Poetry, Politics and Place*. Lagan Press. pp. 104. £6.95. ISBN 1 8736 8720 6.

Dawson, Graham. *Soldier Heroes: British Adventure, Empire and the Imagining of Masculinity*. Routledge. pp. 350. hb £50, pb £14.99. ISBN 0 4150 8881 X, 0 4150 8882 8.

D'haen, Theo, and Hans Bertens. *British Postmodern Fiction*. Rodopi (1993). pp. 179. $23.50. ISBN 9 0518 3663 5.

Diment, Galya. *The Autobiographical Novel of Co-Consciousness: Goncharov, Woolf, and Joyce*. UFlorP. pp. 199. £26.95. ISBN 0 8130 1304 6.

Docherty, Brian, ed. *Twentieth-Century European Drama*. Macmillan. pp. 228. £13.99. ISBN 0 3335 3284 8.

Donawerth, Jane L., and Carol A. Kolmerten, eds. *Utopian and Science Fiction by Women: Worlds of Difference*. LiverUP. pp. 260. hb £27.50, pb £15. ISBN 0 8532 3269 5, 0 8532 3279 2.

Dreyfus, John. *Into Print: Selected Writings on Printing History, Typography and Book Production*. BL. pp. 339. £45. ISBN 0 7123 0343 X.

Drucker, Johanna. *The Visible Word: Experimental Typography and Modern Art, 1909–1923*. UChicP. pp. 298. $35. ISBN 0 2261 6501 9.

Duffy, Enda. *The Subaltern Ulysses*. UMinnP. pp. 213. hb £30, pb £12.95. ISBN 0 8166 2328 7, 0 8166 2329 5.

Eckley, Grace. *The Steadfast Finnegans Wake: A Textbook*. UPA (1993). pp. 335. £43.50. ISBN 0 8191 9273 2.

Eggert, Paul, ed. *D. H. Lawrence. Twilight in Italy*. CUP. pp. 327. £55. ISBN 0 5212 6888 5.

Elliott, Bridget, and Jo-Ann Wallace. *Women Artists and Writers: Modernist*

(Im)Positionings. Routledge. pp. 204. hb £40, pb £15.99. ISBN 0 4150 5365 X, 0 4150 5366 8.

English, James F. *Comic Transactions: Literature, Humor, and the Politics of Community in Twentieth-Century Britain*. CornUP. pp. 269. £17.54. ISBN 0 8014 8166 X.

Fahim, Shadia S. *Doris Lessing and Sufi Equilibrium*. Macmillan. pp. 279. £37.50. ISBN 0 3121 0293 3.

Foster, Thomas S. *Understanding John Fowles*. USCP. pp. 186. ISBN 1 5700 3003 0.

Gardner, Philip. *A. E. Housman: The Critical Heritage*. Routledge (1992). pp. 438. $150. ISBN 0 4150 3298 9.

Gilbert, Sandra M., and Susan Gubar. *No Man's Land: The Place of the Woman Writer in the Twentieth Century, Volume 3: Letters from the Front*. YaleUP. pp. 476. £25. ISBN 0 3000 5631 1.

Gortschacher, Wolfgang, James Hogg and Roland John, eds. *Salute to Outposts*. USalz. pp. 167. £8.95. ISBN 3 7052 0404 1.

Greenberg, Mark L., and Lance Schachterle. *Literature and Technology*. LehighUP, AUP (1992). pp. 322. £34.95. ISBN 0 9342 2320 3.

Gussow, Mel. *Conversations with Pinter*. Hern. pp. 158. hb £12.99, pb £9.99. ISBN 1 8545 9201 7, 1 8545 9206 8.

Harman, Claire, ed. *The Diaries of Sylvia Townsend Warner*. C&W. pp. 384. £25. ISBN 0 7011 3659 6.

Harper, Phillip Brian. *Framing the Margins: The Social Logic of Postmodern Culture*. OUP. pp. 233. hb £27.50, pb £12.95. ISBN 0 1950 8238 9, 0 1950 8239 7.

Hayes, Elizabeth T., ed. *Images of Persephone: Feminist Readings in Western Literature*. UPFlor. pp. 212. £26.95. ISBN 0 8130 1262 7.

Hernández de López, Ana María, ed. *Mario Vargas Llosa: Opera Omnia*. Pliegos. pp. 439. £15.25. ISBN 8 4884 3512 6.

Higdon, David Leon, and Floyd Eugene Eddleman, eds. *Joseph Conrad. Almayer's Folly: A Story of an Eastern River*. Intro. Ian Watt. CUP. pp. 260. n.p. ISBN 0 5214 3205 7.

Hodges, Jack. *The Heart of the Writer: Private and Public Lives of English Writers*. Sinclair-Stevenson. pp. 446. £20. ISBN 1 8561 9379 9.

Holbrook, David. *Creativity and Popular Culture*. AUP. pp. 279. £32.50. ISBN 0 8386 3473 7.

Huber, Peter. *Orwell's Revenge: The 1984 Palimpsest*. FreeP. pp. 374. £15.99. ISBN 0 0291 5335 2.

Hughes, Ted. *Winter Pollen: Occasional Prose*. Ed. William Scammell. Faber. pp. 465. £8.99. ISBN 0 5711 7426 4.

Jackson, Leonard. *The Dematerialisation of Karl Marx: Literature and Marxist Theory*. Longman. pp. 312. hb £36, pb £16.99. ISBN 0 5820 6654 9, 0 5820 6655 7.

Jackson, Rosie. *Frieda Lawrence*. Pandora. pp. 240. £14.99. ISBN 0 0444 0915 X.

Jensen, Robert. *Marketing Modernism in Fin-de-Siècle Europe*. PrincetonUP. pp. 367. $29.95. ISBN 0 6910 3333 1.

Joyau, Isabelle. *Investigating Powell's 'A Dance to the Music of Time'*. Macmillan. pp. 217. £40. ISBN 0 3121 0670 X.

Kaye, Nick. *Postmodernism and Performance*. Macmillan. pp. 180. hb £42.50, pb £13.99. ISBN 0 3335 1917 5, 0 3335 1918 3.

Keating, Peter. *Kipling the Poet*. S&W (1994). pp. 270. £25.00. ISBN 0 4362 3249 9.

Kennedy, Andrew, and Orm Øverland, eds. *Excursions in Fiction: Essays in Honour of Professor Lars Hartveit on his 70th Birthday*. Novus. pp. 260. ISBN 8 7709 9224 0.

Kennelly, Brendan. *Journey into Joy: Selected Prose*. Ed. Åke Persson. Bloodaxe. pp. 271. £10.95. ISBN 1 8522 4210 8.

Kern, Stephen. *The Culture of Love: Victorians to Moderns*. HarvardUP. pp. 458. $16.95. ISBN 0 6741 7959 5.

Kleist, Jurgen, and Bruce A. Butterfield, eds. *Re-Naming the Landscape*. Lang. pp. 290. £36. ISBN 0 8204 2465 X.

Kopelson, Kevin. *Love's Litany: The Writing of Modern Homoerotics*. StanfordUP. pp. 194. £10.95. ISBN 0 8047 2345 1.

Landow, George P. *Hyper/Text/Theory*. JHUP. pp. 377. £12.50. ISBN 0 8018 4838 5.

Lawrence, Karen R. *Penelope Voyages: Women and Travel in the British Literary Tradition*. CornUP. pp. 268. £12.50. ISBN 0 8014 9913 5.

Leonard, George J. *Into the Light of Things: The Art of the Commonplace from Wordsworth to John Cage*. UChicP. pp. 249. $24.95. ISBN 0 2264 7252 3.

Levine, Michael G. *Writing through Repression: Literature, Censorship, Psychoanalysis*. JHUP. pp. 220. £29. ISBN 0 8018 4835 0.

Lewenstein, Oscar. *Kicking Against the Pricks*. Hern. pp. 210. £17.99. ISBN 1 8545 9171 1.

Lewiecki-Wilson, Cynthia. *Writing Against the Family: Gender in Lawrence and Joyce*. SIUP. pp. 301. ISBN 0 8093 1881 4.

Lobb, Edward, ed. *Words in Time: New Essays on Eliot's Four Quartets*. Athlone. pp. 240. hb £35, pb £14.95. ISBN 0 4851 1389 9, 0 4851 7074 7.

Longley, Edna. *The Living Stream: Literature and Revisionism in Ireland*. Bloodaxe. pp. 302. £9.95. ISBN 1 8522 4217 5.

Lopate, Phillip, intro. *The Ordering Mirror: Readers and Contexts*. FordUP. pp. 304. $30. ISBN 0 8232 1515 6.

Macrae, Alasdair D. F. *W. B. Yeats: A Literary Life*. Macmillan. pp. 204. hb £37.50, pb £9.99. ISBN 0 3334 8584 X, 0 3334 2050 0.

Maddox, Brenda. *The Married Man: A Life of D. H. Lawrence*. Sinclair-Stevenson. pp. 652. £20. ISBN 1 8561 9243 1.

Malins, E., and John Purkis. *A Preface to Yeats* (2nd edn). Longman. pp. 218. £13.99. ISBN 0 5820 9093 8.

Mansfield, Elizabeth, ed. *D. H. Lawrence. The Trespasser*. Intro. and notes John Turner. Penguin. pp. 284. £5.99. ISBN 0 1401 8800 2.

Maslen, Elizabeth. *Doris Lessing*. WTW. Northcote. pp. 70. £6.95. ISBN 0 7463 0705 5.

Massa, Ann, and Alistair Stead. *Forked Tongues?: Comparing Twentieth-Century British and American Literature*. Longman. pp. 384. hb £34, pb £13.99. ISBN 0 5820 7554 8, 0 5820 7555 6.

May, Charles E., ed. *The New Short Story Theories*. OhioUP. pp. 337. £15.95. ISBN 0 8214 1087 3.

McCarron, Kevin. *William Golding*. WTW. Northcote. pp. 66. £6.95. ISBN 0 7463 0735 7.

McCully, C. B., ed. *The Poet's Voice and Craft*. Carcanet. pp. 200. £12.95. ISBN 1 8575 4020 4.

McNay, Lois. *Foucault: A Critical Introduction*. Continuum. pp. 196. $27.95. ISBN 0 8264 0778 1.
Mehl, Dieter, ed. *D. H. Lawrence. The Fox; The Captain's Doll; The Ladybird.* Intro. and notes David Ellis. Penguin. pp. 241. £5.99. ISBN 0 1401 8779 0.
Melnick, Daniel C. *Fullness of Dissonance: Modern Fiction and the Aesthetics of Music*. AUP. pp. 159. £25. ISBN 0 8386 3525 3.
Melrose, Susan. *A Semiotics of the Dramatic Text*. Macmillan. pp. 338. hb £42.50, pb £13.99. ISBN 0 3334 1943 X , 0 3334 1944 8.
Molino, Michael R. *Questioning Tradition, Language and Myth: The Poetry of Seamus Heaney*. CUAP. pp. 215. £26.95. ISBN 0 8132 0796 7.
Montgomery, Robert E. *The Visionary D. H. Lawrence: Beyond Philosophy and Art*. CUP. pp. 248. £32.50. ISBN 0 5214 5213 9.
Morgan, Fidelis, ed. *The Years Between: Plays by Women on the London Stage, 1900–1950*. Virago. pp. 460. £9.99. ISBN 1 8538 1620 5.
Morgan, Thaïs E., ed. *Men Writing the Feminine: Literature, Theory, and the Question of Genders*. SUNYP. pp. 207. $16.95. ISBN 0 7914 1994 0.
Morris, Mary, with Larry O'Connor. *The Virago Book of Women Travellers*. Virago. pp. 438. £16.99. ISBN 1 8538 1836 4.
Munt, Sally R. *Murder by the Book?: Feminism and the Crime Novel*. Routledge. pp. 262. hb £37.50, pb £11.99. ISBN 0 4151 0918 3, 0 4151 0919 1.
Murphy, Peter F., ed. *Fictions of Masculinity: Crossing Cultures, Crossing Sexualities*. NYUP. pp. 324. $18.95. ISBN 0 8147 5498 8.
Myers, Doris T. *C. S. Lewis in Context*. KSUP. pp. 248. £24.95. ISBN 0 8733 8497 0.
Nalbantian, Suzanne. *Aesthetic Autobiography: From Life to Art in Marcel Proust, James Joyce, Virginia Woolf and Anaïs Nin*. Macmillan. £37.50. ISBN 0 3334 6001 4.
Nolan, Emer. *James Joyce and Nationalism*. Routledge. pp. 219. £30. ISBN 0 4151 0343 6.
O'Donoghue, Bernard. *Seamus Heaney and the Language of Poetry*. HW. pp. 172. £10.95. ISBN 0 7450 0716 3.
O'Neill, Patrick. *Fictions of Discourse: Reading Narrative Theory*. UTorP. pp. 188. £35. ISBN 0 8020 0468 7.
Otis, Laura. *Organic Memory: History and the Body in the Late Nineteenth and Early Twentieth Centuries*. UNebP. pp. 297. £35. ISBN 0 8032 3561 5.
O'Toole, Fintan. *Tom Murphy: The Politics of Magic* (expanded edn). Hern, New Island. pp. 272. £9.95. ISBN 1 8745 9775 8.
Page, Norman, ed. *Joseph Conrad: Three Novels: Heart of Darkness; The Secret Agent; The Shadow-Line*. Macmillan. pp. 455. £9.99. ISBN 0 3336 1096 2.
Paulhan, Jean. *Progress in Love On the Slow Side*. UNebP. pp. 142. £23.95. ISBN 0 8023 3705 7.
Pearce, Richard, ed. *Molly Blooms: A Polylogue on 'Penelope' and Cultural Studies*. UWiscP. pp. 291. hb £39.95, pb £22.50. ISBN 0 2991 4120 9, 0 2991 4124 1.
Pine, Richard. *Lawrence Durrell: The Mindscape*. Macmillan. pp. 452. £45. ISBN 0 3334 7077 X.
——, ed. *Dark Fathers into Light: Brendan Kennelly*. Bloodaxe. pp. 224. £10.95. ISBN 1 8522 4276 0.
Preston, Peter. *A D. H. Lawrence Chronology*. Macmillan Author Chronologies. Macmillan. pp. 208. £42.50. ISBN 0 3335 3133 7.
——, and Paul Simpson-Housley, eds. *Writing the City: Eden, Babylon, and the*

New Jerusalem. Routledge. pp. 351. £40. ISBN 0 4151 0667 2.
Purdy, Dwight H. *Biblical Echo and Allusion in the Poetry of W. B. Yeats: Poetics and the Art of God*. BuckUP, AUP. pp. 169. $32.50. ISBN 0 8387 5254 3.
Pyrhnen, Heta. *Murder from an Academic Angle: An Introduction to the Study of the Detective Narrative*. Camden House. pp. 134. £39.50. ISBN 1 8797 5181 X.
Quinn, Patrick J. *The Great War and the Missing Muse: The Early Writings of Robert Graves and Siegfried Sassoon*. SusquehannaUP. pp. 297. £34.50. ISBN 0 9456 3649 0.
Rado, Lisa, ed. *Rereading Modernism: New Directions in Feminist Criticism*. Wellesley Studies in Critical Theory 4. Garland. pp. 395. $60. ISBN 0 8153 1189 3.
Reynolds, Kimberley. *Children's Literature in the 1890s and the 1900s*. Northcote. pp. 100. £6.99. ISBN 0 7463 0728 4.
Richetti, John, Deidre David, John Bender, and Michael Seidel, eds. *The Columbia History of the British Novel*. ColUP. pp. 1,200. £54. ISBN 0 2310 7858 7.
Ronell, Avital. *Finitude's Score: Essays for the End of the Millennium*. UNebP. pp. 368. £32.95. ISBN 0 8032 3911 4.
Sagar, Keith, ed. *The Challenge of Ted Hughes*. St Martin's. pp. 190. £35. ISBN 0 3336 1063 6.
Sage, Lorna. *Angela Carter*. WTW. Northcote. pp. 77. £6.95. ISBN 0 7463 0727 6.
Sailer, Susan Shaw. *On the Void of to Be: Incoherence and Trope in Finnegans Wake*. UMichP. pp. 217. £19.95. ISBN 0 4721 0414 4.
Scarry, Elaine, ed. *Fins de Siècle: English Poetry in 1590, 1690, 1790, 1890, 1990*. JHUP. pp. 142. hb £32, pb £11.50. ISBN 0 8018 4928 4, 0 8018 4929 2.
Schwarz, Daniel, ed. *James Joyce, 'The Dead': Complete, Authoritative Text with Biographical and Historical Contexts, Critical History, and Essays from Five Contemporary Critical Perspectives*. Case Studies in Contemporary Criticism. Macmillan. pp. 248. £7.50. ISBN 0 3336 1849 1.
Shelden, Michael. *Graham Greene: The Man Within*. Heinemann. pp. 400. hb £20, pb £8.99. ISBN 0 7493 9521 4, 0 7493 9848 5.
Sherry, Vincent. *James Joyce: Ulysses*. Landmarks of World Literature. CUP. pp. 123. hb £19.95, pb £6.95. ISBN 0 5214 2075 X, 0 5214 2136 5.
Sibbald, K. M., and Howard Young, eds. *T. S. Eliot and Hispanic Modernity (1924–1993)*. Society of Spanish and American Studies. pp. 106. $25. ISBN 0 8929 5075 7.
Siebers, Tobin, ed. *Heterotopia: Postmodern Utopia and the Body Politic*. UMichP. pp. 274. £34. ISBN 0 4721 0557 4.
Skelt, Peterjon, and Jasmin Skelt, eds. *Alive in Parts of This Century: Eric Mottram at 70*. North and South. pp. 168. £8.95. ISBN 1 8703 1426 3.
Spoo, Robert. *James Joyce and the Language of History: Dedalus's Nightmare*. OUP. pp. 195. £30. ISBN 0 1950 8749 6.
Squires, Michael, ed. *D. H. Lawrence. Lady Chatterley's Lover*. Penguin. pp. 365. £5.99. ISBN 0 1401 8786 3.
Stang, Sondra J., and Karen Cochran, eds. *The Correspondence of Ford Madox Ford and Stella Bowen*. IndUP. pp. 479. £55. ISBN 0 2533 5494 3.
Steele, Bruce, ed. *D. H. Lawrence. Kangaroo*. CUP. pp. 493. £60. ISBN 0 5213 8455 9.
Symons, Julian. *Criminal Practices: Symons on Crime Writing 60s to 90s*. Macmillan. pp. 229. £7.99. ISBN 0 3336 1446 1.

Tanner, Laura, E. *Intimate Violence: Reading Rape and Torture in Twentieth-Century Fiction.* IndUP. £17.50. ISBN 0 2533 5648 2.

Thormählen, Marianne, ed. *T. S. Eliot at the Turn of the Century.* LundU. pp. 244. Sek 288. ISBN 9 1796 6272 2.

Thornton, Weldon. *The Antimodernism of Joyce's Portrait of the Artist as a Young Man.* SyracuseUP. pp. 233. hb £39.95, pb £19.95. ISBN 0 8156 2587 1, 0 8156 2613 4.

Vice, Sue, Matthew Campbell and Tim Armstrong. *Beyond the Pleasure Dome: Writing and Addiction from the Romantics.* ShaP. pp. 316. £40. ISBN 1 8507 5378 4.

Wallace, Gavin and Randall Stevenson. *The Scottish Novel since the Seventies: New Visions, Old Dreams.* EdinUP (1993). pp. 254. £14.95. ISBN 0 7486 0415 4.

Watts, Cedric. *Joseph Conrad.* WTW. Northcote. pp. 67. £6.99. ISBN 0 7463 0737 3.

Wheeler, Kathleen. *'Modernist' Women Writers and Narrative Art.* Macmillan. pp. 220. £12.99. ISBN 0 3336 1732 0.

Wilmer, Clive. *Poets Talking.* Carcanet. pp. 156. £12.95. ISBN 1 8575 4075 1.

XV

American Literature to 1900

HENRY CLARIDGE, KEVIN MCCARRON and JANET BEER

This chapter has the following sections: 1. General; 2. American Literature to 1830; 3. American Literature 1830 to 1865; 4. American Literature 1865 to 1900 (including Edith Wharton). Sections 1 and 2 are by Henry Claridge, section 3 is by Kevin McCarron and section 4 is by Janet Beer.

1. General

Current bibliographical listings for the field and the period continue to be available quarterly in *AL* and annually in *MLAIB*. *AmLS* for 1992, under the editorship of David Nordloh, enters its thirtieth year. Nineteen ninety-two saw the appointment of some new contributors: Leland S. Person Jr now covers Hawthorne, Tom Quirk now covers Mark Twain, and Albert J. DeFazio III now covers Fitzgerald and Hemingway. Very little misses the meticulous eye of *AmLS* and the standard of critical reviewing here is consistently informed and intelligent.

The most important general work of the year is, unarguably, the first volume of *The Cambridge History of American Literature* under the general editorship of Sacvan Bercovitch. The series is projected to run to eight volumes and to bring the story of America's literature up to 1990. This first volume has the widest chronological scale, covering the period 1590–1820, though contriving, somehow, to bring James Fenimore Cooper into the 'frame' (*Precaution*, his first novel, was published in 1820). I shall leave my commentary on some of the material in this volume to later, and more appropriate, points in my essay, but for the moment I want to confine my comments on the first volume of this ambitious project to general matters of design and methodology. The project, of course, supersedes the older *Cambridge History of American Literature* (1917) and, in the words of Bercovitch, 'embodies the work of a generation of Americanists who have redrawn the boundaries of the field and redefined the terms of its development'. This notion of development is, to put it simply, one that has 'substantially enlarged the meanings as well as the materials of American literature', so much so that 'American literary history is no longer the history of a certain, agreed group of American masterworks'. Such a redefinition will, necessarily, involve considerable enlargement, since once one gets away from literary history as a matter of the enumeration of, and commentary on, 'masterworks', the explicit absence of discrimination opens up potentially unlimited areas of intellectual inquiry. This history, therefore, 'is fundamentally pluralist: a federated histories of American literatures'. Fair enough, one might say, but when so *much* has claims (or, to put it more accurately, we are *told* has claims) on our attention, such a history is bound to be indifferent to notions of tradition and to the notions of relations that tie significant authors together, for a writer's historical importance is not the same thing as granting to him or her an enduring value. In *The Cambridge History of American Literature* the notion of tradition is replaced (I might even say usurped) by the notion of 'America' ('these volumes', Bercovitch writes, 'make "America" intrinsic to the *literary* history of the United States'.) 'America' is construed as something different from 'Americanness', a term which, for all its vagueness, was commonly understood by an older generation of scholars as designating a struggle to find a body of native American materials worthy of artistic expression and a native voice in which to express them. 'America' is here construed as a necessarily fissiparous concept of nationhood, something which is neither a 'narrative premise' nor an 'objective background', and, perhaps unsurprisingly, it is more a tool of the critic than of the creative writer, for it directs us towards 'the historicity of the text and the textuality of history'.

This first volume in what will obviously become a major series is a collection of long essays (five contributors in all) on early American literature. Myra Jehlen writes on 'The Literature of Colonization' and is followed by Emory Elliott on 'New England Puritan Literature', David S. Shields on 'British-American Belles Lettres' (the shortest section in the book), Robert A. Ferguson on 'The American Enlightenment, 1750–1820' and Michael T. Gilmore on 'The Literature of the Revolutionary and Early National Periods'; my comments on these sections are offered below. The apparatus appended to the volume includes a very thorough chronology (running to some 70 pages), though it has some peculiar omissions, and a good selected bibliography. Those interested in reading a long, trenchant but dismissive review of this first volume are referred to William C. Spengemann's 'E Pluribus Minimum' (*EAL* 29.277–94). This history reflects, of course, those agitations about the 'canon' and pedagogical methods that have beset the study and teaching of American literature over the past two decades, and anyone eager to pursue this debate is referred to the 'Forum' in *AL* for December 1994, which is given over to essays by various hands, amongst them those of Carolyn Karcher and Cary Nelson, on 'Repositionings: Multiculturalism, American Literary History, and the Curriculum'. Similarly *AmLH* for fall 1994 devotes its whole issue to 'Curriculum and Criticism', the contributors addressing both theory and practice in the study of American literature; included here are essays by David Levin and Carolyn Porter, and a lively, if ultimately intractable, 'dialogue' between Gerald Graff and Christopher Looby.

Robert F. Sayre's *American Lives: An Anthology of Autobiographical Writing* is an invaluable contribution to our understanding of, and, indeed, our teaching of, American autobiography. The volume is historically organized and presents fifty-five 'American' voices from John Smith and Anne Bradstreet to Maxine Hong Kingston, Richard Rodriguez and bell hooks. Major longer works in the genre such as Franklin's *Autobiography* and Mary McCarthy's *Memories of a Catholic Girlhood* have been excluded, and the general policy has been 'not to take excerpts from classic longer works', but what *is* included offers a remarkable range of representative (and, at times, arguably unrepresentative) American voices. The volume is arranged in eight sections, each with its own introductory essay in which

Sayre explores the weaving together of history and the personal; the introduction to the volume as a whole, 'On Reading and Writing Autobiography', is an exemplary general account of the nature of the genre. Headnotes to the selections provide critical and biographical information, and there is a useful 'Select Bibliography' at the end. This is an impressive resource for both scholar and student, and UWiscP are to be congratulated on an indispensable addition to the Wisconsin Studies in American Autobiography series. Daniel A. Cohen's *Pillars of Salt, Monuments of Grace: New England Crime Literature and the Origins of American Popular Culture* (OUP, 1993) has not been made available for review.

2. American Literature to 1830

I begin with brief mention of those works of historical and political scholarship of interest to students of the literature of the period. Chief among these is J. C. D. Clark's *The Language of Liberty, 1660–1832: Political Discourse and Social Dynamics in the Anglo-American World.* This is a work that has generated a good deal of controversy among historians of the colonial period, largely because of Clark's contention that the American Revolution is best understood as a war of religion, more specifically as a 'civil war' within English Protestantism in North America. Relatedly, Steven M. Dworetz's *The Unvarnished Doctrine: Locke, Liberalism, and the American Revolution* (first published in 1990) now appears in paperback, returning us to that important debate about the place of John Locke's ideas in American revolutionary thinking. Dworetz challenges the interpretations of historians such as Bernard Bailyn and J. G. A. Pocock who see Locke, primarily, as an apologist for capitalism. He suggests that Locke was understood by his American readers (notably the New England clergy) as a theistic liberal and, as such, is the 'historically appropriate Locke for an investigation of American Revolutionary thought', for the 'Revolutionists formulated and expressed their grievances and aims in Lockean-liberal terms' and 'the essential questions and answers in Revolutionary argument . . . were the essential questions and answers of Locke's political theory'.

Jack P. Greene's *Negotiated Authorities: Essays in Colonial, Political, and Constitutional History* draws together fourteen essays Greene has published separately (either as articles or as chapters in books) over the last thirty years or so; to these are added an introductory essay, 'Negotiated Authorities: The Problem of Governance in the Extended Polities of the Early Modern Atlantic World', and a previously unpublished essay, 'The Gifts of Peace: Social and Economic Expansion and Development in the Periodization of the Early American Past, 1713–1763'. The essays are held together by Greene's 'early and continuing interest in the history of colonial public life'. This is an important collection.

Social history is at the centre of Darrett B. Rutman and Anita H. Rutman's *Small Worlds, Large Questions: Explorations in Early American Social History, 1600–1850*, which, again, draws together previously published essays. Two of these are particularly noteworthy for literary scholars: 'The Mirror of Puritan Authority' lays down an important challenge to the domination of intellectual history in Puritan studies, arguing that New England's intellectuals were isolated from reality and 'clung for almost half a century to ideals that grew more outdated with the passing of each day'; and 'Magic, Christianity and Church in Early Virginia' juxtaposes magic and Christianity as 'competitive systems' in the religious life of colonial Virginia.

Donald Skaggs's *Roger Williams' Dream for America* seeks to correct the view of Williams as 'a secular political philosopher' by putting an emphasis on his religious beliefs and, more particularly, on his role in the attempt to construct a 'Zion in the New World'; Skaggs's book is clearly written and well informed, though at times a little simplistic, but it provides an important re-evaluation of Williams's place in American history as well as being of use to the reader coming to Williams for the first time. *Paine, Scripture, and Authority: The Age of Reason as Religious and Political Idea* by Edward H. Davidson and William J. Scheick examines Paine's attack on religion in *The Age of Reason* in terms of its 'intellectual context and the authorial pretext of its representative identity'; scholars interested in Paine's thought and his reading will find the chapter on his biblical learning especially valuable.

Myra Jehlen's 'The Literature of Colonization' and Emory Elliott's 'New England Puritan Literature' make up the first two (substantial) sections in Bercovitch's *Cambridge History of American Literature. Vol. I: 1590–1820* (reviewed above). Jehlen's interest is in the languages of 'discovery, exploration, and settlement', addressing what she calls 'the implications of imperial origins for the national literary culture'. One chapter here, 'Three Writers of Early America', looks in some detail at Thomas Harriot's *A Brief and True Report of the New Found Land of Virginia* (1588), John Smith's *The General History of Virginia, New England, and the Summer Isles* (1624), and Roger Williams's *A Key into the Language of America* (1643), reading these works as formative texts of American imaginative writing (or 'theaters of self-development'), rather than as objective, or semi-objective, exploratory essays. Jehlen's concluding chapter, 'The Final Voyage', is a more general, and more theoretical, account of the literary and ideological implications of colonization, its central thesis established through a paradox: 'The United States shed its colonial status after it had successfully colonized America, a paradox resolved by casting the new nation as an empire to end all empires.' Thus she suggests that 'U.S. literature has seemed from the start to display more tension than European literature in mediating between centrifugal creative impulses and the conservative needs of cultural continuity.' I suppose the force of this generalization will all depend on what one understands by 'European literature'. Elliott's 'New England Puritan Literature' takes its point of departure from the witchcraft trials in Salem village in 1692, isolating the 'verbal tactics' of the magistrates for close analysis. 'In many ways', he argues, 'the story of the literature of Puritan New England reads as a cautionary tale of how – through grand design, through conscious decisions and unconscious delusions, through sincere or self-serving verbal stratagems – the utopian dream of joyful fellowship metamorphosed into the realities of confusion, accusation, terror, and lamentation of 1692'. Other chapters here are devoted to particular bodies of literature – personal narrative and history, poetry, and the jeremiad. This overview is informed and clearly written, a good starting point for the student or general reader.

David M. Robinson's 'The Cultural Dynamics of American Puritanism' (*AmLH* 6.739–55) is a review essay dealing, primarily, with Stephen Foster's *The Long Argument: English Puritanism and the Shaping of New England Culture* (UNCP, 1991) and Amanda Porterfield's *Female Piety in Puritan New England: The Emergence of Religious Humanism* (OUP, 1992); but what Robinson has to say will be of value to readers unfamiliar with these works, for his essay usefully summarizes the conclusions of a good deal of other recent work in the field, particularly with regard to scholarship on the place of women in Puritan society and more general issues in feminist cultural studies.

Writing about the early poetry is somewhat thin on the ground this year. Pattie Cowell's 'Early New England Women Poets: Writing as Vocation' (*EAL* 29.103–21) discusses 'the uses to which early New England writing women put their skills', arguing that these varied 'enormously with social status and geographical location' and that women often 'wrote poetry with little attention to an audience beyond family and friends and no thought of publication'. Her paper explores 'the act of writing rather than the substance of it', and while it is arguably of greater historical than literary interest its account of the obstacles that confronted women writers in the period is of considerable value. Surprisingly, only one article has appeared on Edward Taylor: J. Daniel Patterson, in 'The Last Unpublished *Preparatory Meditation* from Edward Taylor's "Poetical Works" Manuscript' (*EAL* 29.273–5), prints an unemended version of Meditation 153 for 'scholars and students who do not have convenient access to the manuscript'. A more minor poet, Samuel Danforth, is the subject of Michele Valerie Ronnick's brief note, 'A Horatian Influence on the Verse of Samuel Danforth (1626–1674)' (*ELN* 32.37–9), in which she explores possible sources in Horace's *Odes*. I have not seen Jeffrey A. Hammond's *Sinful Self, Saintly Self: The Puritan Experience of Poetry* (UGeoP, 1993).

The case is similar, unfortunately, with the early prose writings, and there is little article work of value to report on this year. The eighteenth century fares somewhat better, though even here writing on major figures such as Jonathan Edwards and Benjamin Franklin is, by comparison with some recent years, scanty. Before turning to the article literature and work on individual authors, however, I should first of all say something about those sections in *The Cambridge History of American Literature*. The concluding three sections take this history from the close of the seventeenth century into the early nineteenth century. David S. Shields's 'British-American Belles Lettres' discusses a small body of what he, and others, call 'polite letters', concentrating on the writings of Henry Brooke, Benjamin Colman, William Byrd II, James Franklin, Dr Alexander Hamilton and Robert Bolling, amongst others; a body of writing that, he argues, was of little use to those other writers 'who came forward to speak for the new nation' in the years following the revolution. The two concluding sections have much greater amplitude than Shields's relatively short essay. Robert A. Ferguson, in 'The American Enlightenment, 1750–1820', draws on a very diverse body of materials in seeking to address his central proposition that understanding the American Revolution 'is a literary pursuit', for the Revolution is 'itself the greatest literary achievement of eighteenth-century America'. Predictably, a good deal of the literature discussed here is not imaginative but belongs instead to political and religious thought, and as one reads Ferguson's section one might innocently assume that he has not found any American 'literature' worth talking about – his chapter on 'The Literature of Public Documents' is a striking case in point. The concluding section by Michael T. Gilmore, 'The Literature of the Revolutionary and Early National Periods', returns us to more recognizably 'literary' territory: there are chapters here on drama, poetry and the novel as well as on individual writers, notably Washington Irving, Charles Brockden Brown and James Fenimore Cooper. Gilmore, generally, seeks to redress 'the persistent neglect of postrevolutionary culture', a neglect, he argues, that arises from 'the supposition that the writing of the federal era defies sympathetic understanding because it lacks intrinsic merit'. Gilmore invites us to challenge, or reject, the 'ahistorical notion of what constitutes literary achievement, one that gives absolute primacy to aesthetic value', though quite what he asks us to put in its place remains something of a mystery, for it seems misguided to press the claims of the works and writers he discusses solely on the basis of their historical significance and regardless of literary merit.

Volume II of *The Works of Jonathan Edwards, The Typological Writings*, edited by Wallace E. Anderson and Mason I. Lowance Jr, with David H. Watters, is a major contribution to Edwards scholarship. This volume reprints the texts of 'Images of Divine Things' and 'Types of the Messiah', and prints for the first time the essay on 'Types'. These texts extend and enlarge our understanding of Edwards's theoretical contribution to typology and metaphysical thought, and the editing and annotation is, as we have come to expect from Yale editions, exemplary. In 'Jonathan Edwards and the Reconstruction of "Feminine" Speech' (*AmLH* 6.185–212) Sandra Gustafson addresses Edwards's reclamation of 'the medieval heritage of sanctified female self-starvation for Calvinist America'. Her essays turns very much on a reading of *A Faithful Narrative of the Surprising Work of God* (1737) which she sees as inaugurating 'an American sentimental tradition of feminine spiritual autobiography which flowered in the nineteenth century. Edwards's pious females dominate *A Faithful Narrative*, opening new representational possibilities and performance options for evangelical women.'

Two articles on Thomas Jefferson have been seen: David Haven Blake Jr, in '"Posterity Must Judge": Private and Public Discourse in the Adams-Jefferson Letters' (*ArQ* 50.1–30), considers Jefferson's letters to and from John Adams in the light of their negotiation of the private and public realms of American politics. Andrew Burstein and Catherine Mowbray in 'Jefferson and Sterne' (*EAL* 29.19–34) assess Jefferson's response to the writings of Laurence Sterne, who 'more than any other writer', they argue, 'prompted Jefferson to use his imagination', particularly in his familiar letters, where he expresses 'his desire for friendship and intimacy as a human being who bound himself to an ever-widening world'. Samson Occom, the first 'Native American to be ordained a minister of the Christian gospel', is the subject of Michael Elliott's '"This Indian Bait": Samson Occom and the Voice of Liminality' (*EAL* 29.233–53), where Elliott reads Occom's *A Sermon Preached at the Execution of Moses Paul, an Indian* in the light of Occom's 'liminal presence within society', one which, he argues, requires Occom 'to make and remake himself continually in order to fashion his multiplicity into a permanent presence'. This essay raises interesting questions about Occom, but whether its central thesis (which at times reads like an attempt to rescue Occom from the force of his own conclusions) is persuasive is another matter. In '"Remarkably Emancipated from Bondage, Slavery, and Death": An African American Retelling of the Puritan Captivity Narrative, 1820' (*EAL* 29.122–40), John Saillant discusses *Mystery Developed*, the account written by Lemuel Haynes, a black New England minister, of the trial, imprisonment and liberation of Stephen and Jesse Boorn, who 'were condemned to death by hanging for the murder of their sister's husband'. Saillant argues that Haynes 'mapped his account of the Boorns' ordeal onto the coordinates and language of a prominent American literary genre, the Puritan captivity narrative', with, however, one important 'inversion' of the original narrative pattern; for 'in Haynes's captivity narrative the captors are representatives of white society and executors of its laws', a change which allows Haynes 'to focus the Puritan captivity narrative on the enslavement of black Americans'. Arguably, Saillant makes rather too much of this 'inversion', but his essay is valuable for its analysis of the new life breathed into captivity narratives in the early nineteenth century.

Three essays on Philip Freneau have appeared this year. That by Michele Valerie Ronnick, 'A Note on the Text of Philip Freneau's "Columbus to Ferdinand": From Plato to Seneca' (*EAL* 29.81–2), briefly addresses the text of Freneau's poem of 1779, which first appeared in the *United States Magazine*. Ronnick points here to lines in the June issue that are drawn from a translation of Seneca's *Medea*. In '"The Posture that We Give the Dead": Freneau's "Indian Burying Ground" in Ethnohistorical Context' (*ArQ* 50.1–30), Phillip Round explores Freneau's treatment of Indian burial rites (particularly the use of a sitting posture for the dead) from historical and ethnographic perspectives. 'The Rising Glory of America', which Freneau co-authored with Hugh Henry Brackenridge, is the subject of Eric Wertheimer's 'Commencement Ceremonies: History and Identity in "The Rising Glory of America", 1771 and 1786' (*EAL* 29.35–54), which examines 'the poem's recurring obsession with the bordered, discretely national elements of New World History'. This student effort (Freneau and Brackenridge were graduating seniors at the College of New Jersey, later Princeton University) is read as a kind of prescription for what America will become, rehearsing 'stories that would be crucial to the prospective national identity' in a visionary mode 'that is saturated with the ordaining energies of historical greatness and the undeniable potential of geographical prospects while it attempts to erase racial components that might complicate the new American'. Wertheimer's essay turns on intelligent comparisons of the 1771 and 1786 versions of this blank verse epic cum ode. One essay of note on Phillis Wheatley's poetry has appeared – Helen Burke's 'Problematizing American Dissent: The Subject of Phillis Wheatley', in Carol Colatrella's and Joseph Alkana's collection, *Cohesion and Dissent in America* (SUNYP, 1993) – but this has yet to be received for review.

This year sees the publication of a new book-length study of Charles Brockden Brown, Steven Watts's *The Romance of Real Life: Charles Brockden Brown and the Origins of American Culture*. This is, in effect, an interpretive critical biography, one that calls itself a 'cultural biography', eschewing 'the hoary "life and times" approach of the traditional historian, which assumes too much about each partner in this analytic construct'. I am afraid I am not familiar enough with the details of Brown's life to judge whether Watts adds, substantially, to what we know about him, but it quickly becomes clear that Watts's account does not really turn on this kind of scholarship. His study 'aims to reconstruct historically the life and writings of Charles Brockden Brown in terms of their cultural connection', and to show that he 'embodied many of the social and psychological pressures resulting from the wrenching development of market relations in post-Revolutionary decades'. Watts contends that in both his private life and his public writings Brown 'delineated a fragmentary personality type as the ultimate expression of a liberal capitalist society increasingly separated by economic interests, gender expectations, moral values, and political organization', and that Brown, 'partly by way of compensation, became an exemplary and pivotal figure in the articulation of an American "culture" in the early years of nationhood'. The opening chapters of this book examine the early writings, including the much-neglected 'dialogue', *Alcuin* (1798), before moving on to those works which have helped secure Brown's reputation as one of the most important figures of late eighteenth-century American literature.

Two chapters are given over to 'The Major Novels', which are construed as constructing 'a kind of foundation for American literary effort later in the nineteenth century'. In these chapters Watts's book becomes more conventionally literary critical, and he usefully summarizes, and analyses, the implications of Brown's authorial principles; though he is eager, particularly in the case of *Wieland*, to 'psychologize' both text and author in a characteristically late twentieth-century way, and to read Brown's treatment of what he calls 'patriarchal decay' in the light of what he later describes as 'the schizoid quality of liberal bourgeois civilization', words that seem far removed from the first impressions of Brown's fiction most readers will have. The book is, I think, something of a mixed bag, strong in the areas of theoretical discourse about the making of American literature in a republican culture, disappointing when it turns to literary criticism. The concluding 'Bibliographic Essay' is, however, strongly recommended as a guide to Brown scholarship. Michael T. Gilmore also discusses Brown in *The Cambridge History of American Literature*. He considers Brown's representativeness as a man 'trying to become a self-supporting author . . . in a society dominated by republican ideals', suggesting that his writing 'destabilizes the epistemological certitudes of republican culture'. His reading of Brown is, at times, not dissimilar to that of Watts, both of them stressing Brown's dramatization of 'the triumph of individualism in society' and offering quasi-Marxist insights into the close relations between property and sexuality in the fiction. One obvious criticism of Gilmore's essay, however, is that one cannot quite read it as an introduction to Brown's writing for someone unfamiliar with his work – there are better, less demanding things to read than this chapter – but this is, arguably, a weakness of the *Cambridge History* as a whole. Several other essays on Brown have appeared this year, three of them devoted to *Edgar Huntly*. Jared Gardner in 'Alien Nation: Edgar Huntly's Savage Awakening' (*AL* 66.429–61) reads Brown's treament of the Native American in the novel as a response not to the problems of civilization but to those of national identity, and in this his argument echoes similar preoccupations in Watts and Gilmore. In 'Penn's Elm and *Edgar Huntly*: "Dark Instruction to the Heart"' (*AL* 66. 463–84), Sydney J. Krause explores a rather arcane matter that arises from Brown's short story, 'Somnabulism: A Fragment' (first published in Brown's *Literary Magazine* in 1805 but, Krause surmises, written earlier), and the novel: the transformation of an oak tree to an elm tree is deemed significant for those 'eighteenth century Philadelphians at all mindful of the role of an elm in the city's origins', for it was under an elm tree ('the Treaty Elm') that William Penn negotiated a treaty of friendship with the Delaware Indians. Krause's interpretation turns, yet again, on matters of national identity; Paul Vatalaro returns us to more recognizable scholarly territory in his '*Edgar Huntly*: Charles Brockden Brown's Early American Fairy Tale' (*JEP* 15.259–68), where he reads the novel in the light of considerations of the elements of fantasy and romance in German *Märchen*. One further article on Brown has appeared, Nicholas Rombes Jr's '"All Was Lonely, Darksome, and Waste": *Wieland* and the Construction of the New Republic' (*SAF* 22.37–46). This has not been seen and will be reviewed in *YWES* 76.

Michael T. Gilmore's essay on Washington Irving in *The Cambridge History of American Literature*, like those chapters in his section on Brown and James Fenimore Cooper, is broadly introductory in character but contrives to go from remarks to the effect that Irving 'belonged to an outdated phase of culture . . .' to ones such as '[his] instrumentality in validating and commodifying the autonomous aesthetic helps us to explain his fascination with death', with barely a pause for breath. Given the kind of theoretical urgency Gilmore shows elsewhere in his section of the book, the readings of Irving's 'two most memorable stories', 'Rip Van Winkle' and 'The Legend of Sleepy Hollow', are brief and rarely rise above statements of the obvious. Oddly enough, no mention is made here of Irving's sojourn in Spain or of the beguiling *The Alhambra: A Series of Tales and Sketches of the Moors and Spaniards* (1832), popularly known as the *Tales of the Alhambra*, that issued from it, or of the influence of Addison, Goldsmith and Scott on his writing; perhaps the later stories are to be covered in the next volume of this history.

James Fenimore Cooper's treatment of the Native American is intelligently assessed by Gary Ashwill in relation to contemporary Indian narratives, in his 'Savagism and its Discontents: James Fenimore Cooper and his Native American Contemporaries' (*ATQ* 8.211–27). The current interest in adaptations of *The Last of the Mohicans* for the screen (prompted by Michael Mann's film of the novel) is addressed in Gary Edgerton's '"A Breed Apart": Hollywood, Racial Stereotyping, and the Premise of Revisionism in *The Last of the Mohicans*' (*JAMC* 17.1–20), where cinematic patterns of stereotyping are compared in the versions of Mann and Maurice Tourneur. E. W. Pitcher's brief note on the novel, 'Anticipated Torments and Indian Tortures in *The Last of the Mohicans*' (*ANQ* 7.215–19), offers a source study of Native American methods of torture. More generally, Thomas S. Gladsky in 'James Fenimore Cooper and American Nativism' (*SAR* 18.43–53) considers the treatment of 'nativist' matters across a range of Cooper's writings. Finally, Michael T. Gilmore's chapter on Cooper concludes *The Cambridge History of American Literature*, thus taking the volume a little beyond its end-date. Gilmore focuses on Cooper's 'early novels through *The Pioneers* (1823), which can be read as complex meditations on his anxious effort, as a contemporary reviewer put it, to lay "the foundations of American romance."' One might legitimately wonder why novels are called 'meditations' and ask where one is to find the complexity in these early works of Cooper, but a more serious criticism of this chapter is that Gilmore takes so little account of those writers whose influence meant so much to Cooper in the years when he was struggling to master the art of fiction: Jane Austen gets only a brief mention and the role Sir Walter Scott played in his career is consistently understated: what model was more important to Cooper than that provided by *Waverley*? Yet that novel is not mentioned, an oversight one hopes will be corrected in any subsequent criticism of Cooper in this history. There are, it has to be said, better introductions to Cooper's work than this. Beyond these there is, perhaps surprisingly, little to report on in Cooper criticism and scholarship this year.

3. American Literature 1830 to 1865

A remarkable number, over half, of the books received this year were not single-author studies, but discussed several writers and covered large periods of time. Given that all the writers considered in these books are canonical (Emerson, Thoreau, Melville, Poe, Hawthorne, Whitman) and in previous years would certainly have had a book each to themselves, it is interesting to speculate on some of the possible reasons for this: are publishers insisting that scholars increase the potential readership of a book by considering more authors, or are critics themselves, perhaps influenced by the 'New Americanism', currently more concerned with tracking issues across lengthy periods of American history than within the work of a single author?

Cindy Weinstein, in *The Literature of Labor and the Labors of Literature*, begins her excellent book with an illuminating discussion of allegory and argues, convincingly, that we can best understand allegorical characters of the period by rethinking traditional, ahistorical formulations of allegory, in order to see the powerful conjunction among the discourse of allegory in nineteenth-century America, the representation of persons as mechanical and undeveloped in the discourse of labour, and a burgeoning market economy. She suggests that the work ethic gave both ontological and epistemological identity, and in the course of a brilliant reading of the figure of Cadwallader Cuticle in Melville's *White-Jacket* equates the lust for work with the lust for death. Weinstein is particularly perceptive in her recognition of the paradox that, in the middle of the century, American culture represented and celebrated the valiant struggle to attain virtue through industrious behaviour, while that same culture simultaneously disdained literary texts that represented their own labour. In four separate chapters Weinstein evaluates the work of Hawthorne, Melville, Twain and Henry Adams. Each of these sections focuses on representations of labour and, pre-eminently, allegory, and she argues that allegorical characters reveal themselves as dialogically engaged with the developing market economy of antebellum America. In her chapter on Hawthorne she focuses on 'The Celestial Rail-Road', which is also read as a conceptual look ahead to a reconfiguration of allegory, while 'The Birth Mark' similarly calls attention to the problematic consequences of authorial invisibility developed in *The Scarlet Letter*. Weinstein argues that Melville is, of all the writers she considers, the most self-conscious about constructing a model of literary labour that differs from the predominant ideal of erasure. Her reading of a whale's dismemberment in Melville's chapter 'Stowing Down and Clearing Up' in *Moby-Dick* is inspired: 'By cleaning up after itself, the whale is made to participate in mystifying the process of its own disembodiment and eventual commodification. All evidence of labor seems to be completely erased by the whale himself/itself except for the fact that he does not "consume his own smoke".' This is an outstanding book, and of value not only to Americanists but to anybody interested in work, labour and cultural symbiosis.

In the introduction to *Revisionary Interventions into the Americanist Canon*, edited by Donald E. Pease, one of the best known of the 'New Americanists', Pease offers a very useful consideration of the opposition between the Old and the New Americanists, although there are moments when one wonders whom he is writing for, as when he says of Hawthorne that he is 'a canonical figure in the field of American Studies'. The word 'Studies' rather than 'Literature' here prefigures the book's theoretical stance, and Pease's introduction offers a brilliantly concise evaluation and criticism of the ways in which readings of American literature have been constructed over the past hundred years. John McWilliams, in a chapter entitled 'The Rationale for "The American Romance"', also devotes most of his time to an assessment of canonical critical texts, in particular Richard Chase's *The American Novel and its Tradition* (1957), before considering Hawthorne's four romances. In 'Scarcity, Subjectivity, and Emerson', Wai-chee Dimock gives a close reading of the opening paragraph of Emerson's essay 'Experience' and uses the writings on political economy of Malthus and Ricardo to suggest that the Emersonian self, as the site of constitutional scarcity, would also seem to be the site of vigilant proprietorship. Priscilla Wald, in 'Hearing Narrative Voices in

Melville's *Pierre*', uses Emerson's 1844 lecture 'The Young American' to suggest that *Pierre* is Melville's deconstruction of the national script of identity, while Susan Mizruchi argues that *Billy Budd* represents and criticizes the rationalization of social life that absorbed sociologists of the period. The book also contains stimulating chapters on Chopin, Douglass and Twain, and, overall, provides valuable insights into the literature and cultural life of the nineteenth century, while also functioning as a provocative contribution to the increasingly contentious field of American studies.

Priscilla Wald's own book, *Constituting Americans: Cultural Anxiety and Narrative Form*, makes a further contribution, and in her introduction she suggests that the book 'attends to the anxiety evident in the language of legal, political, and social debates concerning personhood and national identity'. Wald writes particularly well on Lincoln's imagery, especially in the Gettysburg Address, and the ways in which his tropes and figurative language work towards establishing a specific American identity. Interestingly, and somewhat unusually for a New Americanist, she focuses on 'the uncanny' (using Freud's essay) and on American Gothic to suggest that the uncanny helps us to understand what inaugurates narratives of identity and what haunts them. She discusses Brockden Brown, Poe, Hawthorne and Melville as practitioners of American Gothic, and suggests that characteristically these authors recast the supernatural as a richly ambiguous authorship in which characters produce spectres, from an unacknowledged and internalized script, that haunt and often destroy them. Her particular emphasis is on Melville's *Pierre* and Harriet Wilson's *Our Nig*, and she writes of the former text: 'In *Pierre*, the relationship between authorship and the market dramatizes the implications of an ideology of American liberalism that defines the self as free because self-owned.'

As the subtitle of Terence Martin's *Parables of Possibility: The American Need for Beginnings* indicates, this is a book concerned with 'beginnings'. Martin concisely surveys a range of eighteenth- and nineteenth-century histories, of individual colonies and of America, noting of them in general that they take dates of discovery and first settlement as logical points of departure, and move from the 'known to the known' with a faith in the divine ordering of events that sustains their narrative structure. He then writes that Washington Irving converted the role of historian to burlesque, and offers an illuminating reading of Irving's *A History of New York, from the Beginning of the World to the End of the Dutch Dynasty* (1809), stressing that its tone of comic *gravitas* mocks the pretensions of many of the histories Martin has himself just surveyed. In what is perhaps the best section in the book, Martin analyses the function of negatives in American society, and suggests that American negatives constitute a secular version of the body of apophatic theology by means of which certain medieval thinkers formulated their ideas of a prime cause. Martin persuasively links negative mysticism to Hawthorne and Henry James's celebrated lists of negatives, and quotes from an essay Emerson wrote after Thoreau's death, which describes Thoreau's life as a series of ongoing renunciations and is itself constructed almost entirely in negatives: 'He had no temptations to fight against; no appetites, no passions, no taste for elegant trifles.' Martin's own enthusiasm for his subject and his pleasure in constructing an argument can be seen when he writes: 'A few paragraphs later Emerson concludes (and I bless him for his phrasing), "No truer American existed than Thoreau".' Martin concludes this stimulating and scholarly book with an appraisal of Whitman, noting his tactic of deferring, structuring time so as to privilege the future.

In *The Trivial Sublime: Theology and American Poetics*, Linda Munk concentrates on Emerson, Melville, Whitman, Dickinson, Frost and Flannery O'Connor. She argues for the importance of the ostensibly trivial by suggesting that the Puritans had sufficient confidence in God's design to believe that no fact was without significance, and that it has always been American rhetorical practice to treat every detail as if it were equal to anything else. Her assessment of Emerson stresses his reliance on analogy and metonymy, and she writes well on his characteristic reliance on images of transformation and conversion, which enable him to view the trivial as simultaneously the sublime. In her discussion of Melville's *Billy Budd* she plays with the pun on 'hand/handsome', and links the story to Hawthorne's 'The Birth Mark' to construct an ingenious reading of a much-discussed text. In the chapter on Whitman she argues that, by insisting upon the correspondence between the male body and the natural world, Whitman also insists on analogies between the body and the text, including its exegesis.

While not particularly succinct, the subtitle of Robert M. Greenberg's *Splintered Worlds: Fragmentation and the Ideal of Diversity in the Work of Emerson, Melville, Whitman, and Dickinson* gives a very good idea of what is discussed in the book. While Munk focuses on the ways in which the trivial is transformed into the sublime by nineteenth-century American writers deeply influenced by the Puritan legacy, Greenberg is preoccupied with portraying a representative relationship between 'splintered worlds' in certain literary texts and the 'historical text'. In a strikingly aggressive introduction, he launches a scathing attack on 'ideologically oriented historical scholars', and in an endnote specifically cites Donald E. Pease: 'Bashing dead, dated critics such as F. O. Mattthiessen, whose only real error may be that they wrote the most influential books of their day; ignoring evidentiary obligations when making claims of identity between literary and historical motivation; maligning writers based on how the critic thinks he or she would have acted if he or she were the writer; or, really no better, praising writers for a presumed attack on social evils – all these practices constitute two steps backward for one step forward.' Greenberg devotes a lengthy chapter to New York, noting that in the middle of the nineteenth century multiplicity and individual separation were at the heart of urban life, as well as of religious life. He focuses on Emerson's belief in the possibility of uniting the spiritual life with the secular, while in his evaluation of Emerson's essay 'Compensation' he concentrates not on its moral and consolatory aspects but on its delineation of the polarities of psychological life. In his chapter on *Moby-Dick*, Greenberg writes that Melville saw in an exhaustive method using differing epistemologies and their working methods a form for communicating the philosophic conflict and disarray at the centre of the mid-century crisis of disbelief. He further suggests that Whitman's poetry constitutes a response to segmentary and atomistic fragmentation, and he offers a sophisticated reading of 'As I Ebb'd with the Ocean of Life' to support his claim. Greenberg concludes this engaging and confident book with an analysis of Emily Dickinson and an impassioned plea for what he calls 'open reading'.

America and the Sea: A Literary History, edited by Haskell Springer, is, perhaps surprisingly, the first literary history of the United States to explore exclusively the presence of the sea in American writing. Its structure is sensibly chronological, moving from the Puritans to the present day, covering various genres, locales, ethnic groups and related arts. Donald P. Wharton's chapters 'The Colonial Era' and 'The Revolutionary and Federal Periods' are extremely informative on the subject of 'deliverance' in the earlier period, and on the ways in which the expanding commercial might of the colonies and a growing sense of American nationalism were reflected in the narratives, poems and emerging fiction of the sea in the 1700s. In 'Cooper and his Contemporaries', Hugh Egan notes that Cooper's early sea novels embrace the radical oppositions implicit in the form and reminds us of Melville's indebtedness to Cooper, while he also notes that Melville was profoundly influenced by Hawthorne's story 'Footprints on the Sea Shore' (1838). Haskell Springer and Douglas Robillard devote an entire chapter to Melville, which briskly covers all his nautical fiction, including the collection of poems *John Marr and Other Sailors* (1888). The book contains a fascinating chapter, with illustrations, on American seascape art, in which Roger B. Stein offers perceptive and illuminating readings of many seascapes, including Edward Blackett's *Shipwrecked Mother and Child* (1851), James Hamilton's *The Pack off Sylvia Headland* (1856), and Albert Ryder's *Jonah* (*c*.1885).

Stanley Cavell's *In Quest of the Ordinary: Lines of Skepticism and Romanticism*, first published in 1988, was reissued in paperback this year. Essentially Cavell's Beckman Lectures, the book constitutes a sustained and compelling argument for the philosophical basis of Romanticism, particularly in its American rendering. Cavell's book has some similarities with Munk's *The Trivial Sublime* in that Cavell, too, is interested in the devotion of Emerson and Thoreau to 'the thing they call the common'. Cavell's concern throughout most of the book is to argue that American Transcendentalism is a response to European, specifically Kantian, scepticism. He focuses on Emerson's essay 'Self Reliance' and claims that it presents, ultimately, a theory of reading; he links it to Poe's 'The Imp of the Perverse', noting that for Poe, however, philosophy only exists as a parody of philosophy. He is interested in the 'sound' of Poe's stories and compares the opening lines of 'The Black Cat' with some early sentences from Descartes's *Meditations*. This is a book which will be of interest to readers who are not philosophers, not least because of Cavell's accomplished writing style. He can be aphoristic: 'Philosophy cannot say sin'; comical: 'Thoreau goes to extravagant lengths – that is, his usual lengths'; or shrewd: 'One of [Thoreau's] most innocuous, hence suspicious, sentences'; and he is always capable of disrupting a complex line of thought with a striking comment such as this, describing inquiries concerning the origins of thought: 'the philosophical waltz of obviousness and obscurity'. William Rossi, in 'Poetry and Progress: Thoreau, Lyell and the Geological Principles of *A Week*' (*AL* 66.275–300), shares an interest in epistemology with Cavell. Rossi draws on Charles Lyell's *Principles of Geology* (1830–3) to establish analogies between Lyell's geological principles and Thoreau's thought processes. Rossi suggests that in its representation of the process of knowing as discontinuously progressive and perpetually incomplete, *A Week on the Concord and Merrimack Rivers* attempts to render dynamic natural law even in the lapses to which it subjects its readers. In 'Emerson's "Domestic and Social Experiments": Service, Slavery, and the Unhired Man' (*AL* 66.485–508), Barbara Ryan gives a close biographical account of Emerson's relationships with servants, culminating in an evaluation of Thoreau's stay with the Emersons in 1841. She concludes by suggesting that Emerson eventually saw that the payment of wages helped maintain hierarchies pertinent to privacy, that wages enforced distance by insisting on the relative power of the server and the served, and that, at least for a capitalist, wages relieved guilt. Martin Buckman, in 'From Emerson to Dewey: The Fate of Freedom in American Education' (*AmLH* 6.385–408), takes Emerson's *The American Scholar* (1837) as his starting point. In effect, he reviews the book and then points out how wildly short of the Emersonian ideal of education the reality is – and always has been: 'One needs to explain, then, why, with Emerson's position as a cultural spokesman and his popularity as a lecturer, there was so little connection between his ideas and the actual practice of American education.' Buckman goes some way to answering the question, noting that Emerson's emphasis on the spontaneous, the immediate and the individual worked against translating this epistemology into actual institutions. He analyses the methodology of Dewey to note his failure too, and concludes this stimulating article by offering ideas himself about teaching.

Robert D. Richardson Jr's biography *Emerson: The Mind on Fire* was certainly the most enjoyable book received this year. It begins dramatically, with Emerson opening the coffin of his recently deceased wife, and Richardson writes of the event: 'The act was essential Emerson. He had to see for himself.' This biography is, overall, as the subtitle indicates, very much concerned with the two strands of Emerson: intellect and passion, and their continuous points of interaction. Fortunately, Richardson spends little time on Emerson's childhood and, in addition, the initial chronology of the book is unconventional; the second chapter opens, for example: 'Eleven years earlier, in the Spring of 1821'. Such strategies, combined with Richardson's consistent use of short chapters, ensures that this 670-page book is never tedious, and by adroit cross-referencing the author always gives a sense, despite the disrupted chronology, of Emerson's intellectual consistency. Richardson's biography is very informative on Emerson's time at Harvard and especially so on his reading, and his heavy reliance on it throughout his career; there is a splendid section on Emerson's indexing methods for his journals and notebooks, which eventually came to over 263 volumes. Richardson offers comprehensive, if unproblematic, readings of Emerson's most celebrated works, and brief appraisals of everything else he wrote. The chapters on Emerson in England are extremely well documented, and Richardson also writes well on the considerable amount of satire levelled at Emerson throughout his public life. Although Richardson quotes often and illuminatingly from Emerson's work, the quotations are rarely annotated, which, at times, is irritating. However, given the sheer bulk of quotation it would be ungenerous to complain too much; doubtless to incorporate comprehensive annotation would have added immeasurably to the intense labour already evident in the composition of this excellent biography, and it would certainly have impeded its brilliantly self-assured narrative flow.

John Irwin's *The Mystery to a Solution: Poe, Borges, and the Analytic Detective Story* is a work of remarkable scholarship, and contains not only superb readings of individual stories by Poe and Borges but also numerous perceptive observations on the perennial appeal of the analytical detective story. Irwin begins by claiming that Poe created the dominant modern genre – the primary genre of an age dominated by science and technology, an age characterized by mental work as analysis. Irwin's book has some similarities with Weinstein's *The Literature of Labor and the Labors of Literature*, as Irwin, too, is interested in work: 'In the detective scenario and the figure of the mastermind Dupin, Poe gave us at once the most appealing format and the most glamorous mask for mental work and the mental worker.' Irwin gives excellent summaries of the three best-known readings of 'The Purloined Letter' – Lacan's, Derrida's and Johnson's – and suggests himself that part of the peculiar force of hidden-object and locked-room detective stories is that they present us with the physical embodiment, the concrete spatialization, of the mechanism of logical inclusion/exclusion on which rational analysis is based. Irwin writes perceptively on Poe's infamous 'Dying Women' stories (1835–41), and with ingenuity and formidable erudition on subjects such as the relationship between mathematics and politics, game theory, and the connection between Sir Thomas Browne's rhomboidal network of interlocking quincunxes and the functioning of human intelligence. Joan Dajan, in 'Amorous Bondage: Poe, Ladies and Slaves' (*AL* 66.239–73), is particularly interested in Poe's relationship to slavery, and scrutinizes his review of Paulding's *Slavery in the United States* (1836). Referring to Poe's use of Gothic as 'racialized', she reads his love poems so as to emphasize the ways in which they can be seen as actually engaging with slavery, and argues that in them Poe articulates a specific relationship of domination, where the speaker who has defined himself as possessor is, in turn, defined by his possession. In *Critical Desire: Psychoanalysis and the Literary Subject*, Linda Ruth Williams suggests that Poe's stories are preoccupied with the 'exquisite' impossibility of acquiring fixed knowledge in a world in which truth is not fixed. She argues persuasively that Roger Corman's films of Poe's stories, in which he often conflates texts, are readings of his work and draw out from Poe both the horror of traditional Gothic and the horrors of the family structure itself. Like Irwin, although less extensively, Williams also discusses the readings of 'The Purloined Letter' by Lacan, Derrida and Johnson, and in an illuminating section on 'Psychobiography and Dream Analysis' she considers Marie Bonaparte's *The Life and Works of Edgar Allan Poe: A Psycho-analytical Interpretation* (1949). Williams argues for a more intertextual way of situating Bonaparte's work, while acknowledging that through Bonaparte's reading Poe begins to show how the literary is already at stake in the most basic terms of psychoanalysis.

In *Reinventing Cotton Mather in the American Renaissance: Magnalia Christi Americana in Hawthorne, Stowe, and Stoddard*, Christopher Felker suggests that the principal effort of New England writers during the American Renaissance was directed at creating an audience of democratic readers capable of modelling their individual gestures as readers on the contingent realities of American Puritanism. Felker argues for the 'tutor text' potential of Mather's *Magnalia Christi Americana*, and claims that the issues Mather brings to light become sites of negotiation that, through form and theme, record the archive of the past. This is a new historicist account of the 'embedding' within nineteenth-century texts whose aims were to express American 'governmentality' properly, and to renegotiate Mather's explicit thematic concerns in *Magnalia* with the historical consequences of Puritanism. Felker writes well on Harriet Beecher Stowe's *The Minister's Wooing*, arguing that Stowe used Mather to negotiate a cultural space for the practice of her authorship, and on Elizabeth Stoddard's *The Morgesons,* noting that Stoddard, like Mather, locates the historical consciousness outside a unified self; but his section on Hawthorne is particularly impressive. He observes of his work in general: 'Characteristic in Hawthorne's fiction is the display of an object rescued from antiquity followed by a displacement of the object into a drama of resonance', and then focuses on *Grandfather's Chair*, conventionally read as a story for children, claiming that in it Hawthorne turns key moments in Massachusetts history, recast from a variety of historical sources, into exempla of intolerance, suffering and violence that puzzle his juvenile auditors. This scholarly and meticulously argued book should be of interest not only to readers interested in Hawthorne, Stowe and Stoddard, but also to those interested in Mather, Puritanism, and new historicism.

In his introduction to *Nathaniel Hawthorne: The Contemporary Reviews*, edited by John L. Idol Jr and Buford Jones, Idol notes: 'Well over four thousand reviews and notices resulted from the publication of Nathaniel Hawthorne's writing in the time from the self-withdrawn *Fanshawe* (1828), through the Riverside edition of his collected works (1883).' This book offers 'representative reviews' in chronological sequence, and each section contains a 'Checklist of Additional Reviews'. In his introduction, Idol surveys Hawthorne's critical reception and notes that 'a zeal to have American writers recognized as peers of their European counterparts informs the appraisals of many of Hawthorne's countrymen'. This book will be a valuable resource for scholars, and a consistent pleasure for anybody interested in Hawthorne's work, as well as for those concerned to study the trajectory of critical reception in nineteenth-century America. The book contains reviews by Longfellow, Margaret Fuller, Evert Duyckinck, William Henry Channing, Orestes Brownson and Charles Weller, as well as two reviews, Poe's of *Twice Told Tales* (1842) and Melville's of *Mosses From an Old Manse* (1850), which are themselves now almost as well known (better known to some) than the books they discuss. While so big a collection of reviews spanning half a century can hardly fail to offer the reader an illuminating insight into the cultural preconceptions and intellectual preoccupations of the period, a large number of the reviews are wonderfully entertaining in their own right, as when Charles Hazewell begins his review of *The Scarlet Letter* with these words: 'The critic in the *Examiner* is an ass.' Orestes Brownson, in his review of the same novel, raises an issue that still preoccupies critics today, perhaps more than ever, when he writes: 'we are more disposed to analyze an author's work than the author himself', and it is instructive for the modern reader to ask if any critic could make a statement such as the following about any modern novel: 'As everybody will read *The Scarlet Letter*, it would be impertinent to give a synopsis of the plot.'

In 'Delia Bacon: Hawthorne's Last Heroine' (*NHR* 22.1–10), Nina Baym gives an interesting account of Hawthorne's meeting in 1856 with Delia Bacon, who was writing a book contesting Shakespeare's authorship of the plays attributed to him. Baym details the financial and editorial assistance that Hawthorne provided, thereby enabling Bacon to publish *The Philosophy of Shakespeare's Plays Unfolded* in 1857. Baym makes it clear she believes Bacon to have been deluded in her beliefs, and while this article appears an objective appraisal of an act of great generosity on Hawthorne's part, it also reads very much as a warning against the dangers of purely textual scholarship – in any period. In the same issue, Klaus P. Stich discusses the Saturday Club as an intertext in Hawthorne's *Elixir of Life Manuscripts* (11–20), and Carmen Valero-Garces gives a comprehensive list of Spanish translations of *The Scarlet Letter*. In the spring edition of the review, Margaret B. Moore, in 'Elizabeth Manning Hawthorne: Nathaniel's Enigmatic Sister' (*NHR* 20.1–10), discusses the relationship between Hawthorne and his sister. She is informative on their collaborative writing projects, and it is interesting to note that she rejects Philip Young's suggestion, in *Hawthorne's Secret: An Untold Tale* (1984), that their relationship was incestuous, on the grounds that 'there is little evidence'. In the same issue, J. Lasley Dameron, in 'Faust, the Wandering Jew, and the Swallowed Serpent: Hawthorne's Familiar Literary Analogues' (10–17), suggests that Hawthorne's short fiction relied on analogues familiar to readers of popular journalistic literature, while Arnold G. Tew, in 'Hawthorne's P.P.: Behind the Comic Mask' (18–23), argues that Hawthorne drew on Alexander Pope and John Gay's 'Memoirs of P.P., Clerk of this Parish' for comic inspiration because their text offered situations and characters relevant to his novel and to the particularly difficult time of his life during which he wrote *The Scarlet Letter*.

AL 66 was a Melville Special Issue; it contains six new essays, which, as Cathy Davidson notes, 'represent the full generational spectrum of our profession, from a new graduate student to a professor emeritus'. Paul Lauter, in 'Melville Climbs the Canon' (1–24), attempts to account for Melville's (depressingly familiar) lack of appeal to undergraduates, and argues that the rise in Melville's critical reputation is linked to modernism: 'For them [students], the modernist preference for difficult, indeed obscure, texts is no virtue; it may, in fact reflect a process deeply inflected by class standards, whose effect is to marginalize them culturally.' In 'Lovers of Human Flesh: Homosexuality and Cannibalism in Melville's Novels' (25–53), Caleb Crain links these two taboo subjects, suggesting that they both share the trope of preterition and the topos of the South Seas in the culture at large. From this, however, Crain shifts to equating cannibalism with homosexuality in Melville's letters to Hawthorne, and writes of one featuring this subject, from June 1851: 'Through the metaphor of cannibalism, Melville expresses his desperate love for Hawthorne, ingeniously capturing at once the most physical and the most spiritual aspects of that love.' Not only is such speculation, rhetorically announcing itself as fact, seemingly blind to 'evidentiary obligations', it lacks any obvious purpose other than to 'claim' a canonical author. The word 'desperate' would seem more applicable to this reading than to Melville's feelings for Hawthorne. Crain's article, however, is for the most part excellent, unlike Elizabeth Renker's 'Herman Melville: Wife Beating, and the Written Page' (123–50), which may well be the worst article published on Melville in recent years. Renker rancorously sets out to prove that Melville regularly beat his wife, and that his wife abuse 'is one crucial element in a network that also includes his tortured relationship to writing and his simultaneous dependence on and resentment of the Melville women whose labor he needed to produce his texts'. Oddly, therefore, Renker refers to Melville throughout as 'Herman', doubtless for reasons connected to the demystification of patriarchal power and authority. She goes on to adduce a conspiracy on an immense scale, claiming that her article intends to draw attention to the wife beating that 'scholars have either silenced or failed to confront'. There seems little point in objecting to a form of criticism that seems itself, at best, totally pointless, but it does seem necessary to object to being told what issues must be discussed. Scholars should not be criticized for refusing to ride another's hobby-horse, especially when, as in this case, the horse has been fed on a diet of misandry. In 'The Eden of Saddle Meadows: Landscape and Ideology in *Pierre*' (55–81), Samuel Otter argues that Melville's excesses in *Pierre* do not simply subvert Romantic convention: 'the excess breathes new life into it, conveys its particular intense antebellum American invocation'; while Nancy Ruttenberg, in 'Melville's Handsome Sailor: The Anxiety of Innocence' (83–103), suggests of *Billy Budd* that it offers Melville's retrospective and metaphorical account of his own professional failure. The most provocative article in the journal is surely Julian Markels's 'The *Moby-Dick* White Elephant' (105–22), which is a scathing attack on the editors of the 1988 Northwestern-Newberry *Moby-Dick*. Markels writes of them: 'Honorable men these editors are, yet they have discharged an intellectual public trust in an unwittingly self-serving manner, and it is the ideological inadvertence in their methodology that I want to focus on here.' Markels's central objection is to what he sees as the editors' use of this edition 'both to promulgate and at the same time insulate their interpretations from engagement with rival interpretations that can be as knowledgeable as theirs'. The article lists numerous instances of what Markels sees as 'ideological inadvertences' and these, combined with his own thorough knowledge of the text, raise crucial questions about the vexed issue of editorship. In 'Towards the Promethean Ledge: Varieties of Sceptic Experience in Melville's *Clarel*' (*L&T* 8.30–46), Zephyra Porat considers the role of Judaism in Melville's poem and suggests that, at least in this work, the God who is revealed is responsible for evil, while humanity is seen to be a source simultaneously of satisfaction and redress. Porat then reads *Billy Budd* with this view of the specific religiosity of *Clarel* in view and suggests that, glossed by the elaborate Gnostic, sceptic and atheist voices in *Clarel*, *Billy Budd*'s deceptive, defiant double-voicedness surfaces more audibly, and the moral implications of its metaphysical ambiguities seem more legible.

Like Julian Markels, Walter Grünzweig, in *Constructing the German Walt Whitman*, is interested in the agendas carried into editing, and, in particular, translating. He writes of Karl Knortz, one of Whitman's earliest translators, for example: 'Knortz interprets *Leaves of Grass* as a guide to American democracy from which Germans should learn.' Grünzweig is emphatic concerning Whitman's importance to the Germans, and argues that Whitman is 'central' to an understanding of German culture between 1890 and 1933. The first ten chapters of the book concentrate on individual translators of Whitman, while the second part focuses on the critical reception of Whitman's work in Germany. Grünzweig covers Whitman's influence on German naturalism and expressionism, and there is an especially interesting chapter on the uses German anarchists and the Nazis made of Whitman's work. Grünzweig concludes this informative book with a well-researched account of the ways in which the debate surrounding Whitman's homosexuality shows to what extent 'non-literary' categories influenced the German reception of Whitman – and to what degree they, too, involve literature and fiction. Mark Maslan, in 'Whitman and his Doubles: Division and Union in *Leaves of Grass* and its Critics' (*ALH* 6.119–39), says of D. H. Lawrence's comment on Whitman in *Studies in Classic American Literature*, ('He confuses sympathy with self-sacrifice') that it prefigures a remarkable amount of subsequent criticism of Whitman's work. This is a review article which concentrates on the following four books: Kerry C. Larson, *Whitman's Drama of Consensus* (UChicP, 1988); Betsy Erkilla, *Whitman the Political Poet* (*YWES* 70.596); Michael Moon, *Disseminating Whitman: Revision and Corporeality in Leaves of Grass* (*YWES* 72.450–1), and Robert K. Martin, ed., *The Continuing Presence of Walt Whitman: The Life After the Life* (*YWES* 73.568). Maslan notes that each book presents a politicized and historicized version of the Lawrentian conflict between the autonomous soul and an all-encompassing identity. He is particularly struck by the ways in which all the writers site Whitman culturally, and notes, in particular, an interest in Whitman's sexual orientation, which is, in turn, linked to capitalism. In 'Whitman's Tale of Two Cities' (*ALH* 6.633–57), M. Wynn Thomas investigates the ways in which Whitman's journalistic New York differs from his poetic version (Mannahatta) of the same city. Thomas gives particularly enthusiastic readings of 'Song of Myself' and 'Give Me the Splendid Silent Sun', noting of the latter poem that the 'parallelism of syntactical structure' between the city and the country causes city life to become naturalized; part of an organic process.

Ed Folsom, in *Walt Whitman's Native Representations*, has rejected the temptation to present a totalized Walt Whitman. Instead, he assesses Whitman's work, and to some degree his life, by investigating four important American cultural developments that occurred during the poet's lifetime. He begins his study of Whitman's cultural influences by recounting the 'war of the dictionaries', between Webster's *American Dictionary of the English Language* (1828) and Worcester's *Comprehensive, Pronouncing and Explanatory Dictionary of the English Language* (1830), and he is a gifted enough writer to make this somewhat unpromising-sounding topic one of the most fascinating chapters in the book. The following chapter, devoted to baseball, is as interesting for its discussion of the sport in general as it is on Whitman's relationship to it. Folsom records, for example, that in 1862 a Christmas game attracted an audience of forty thousand soldiers, and that in 1869 the Cincinnati Red Stockings became America's first fully professional side. Folsom suggests that Whitman was particularly enthusiastic about the game because of its non-European, specifically American nature, and because of the huge crowds which the game drew, delighting him with the opportunity this provided to celebrate democracy. It is impossible not to agree with Folsom when he writes that Whitman was probably the first writer to 'recognize the vital significance of baseball to America'. The section called 'Whitman and American Indians' contains a reproduction of John Mulvaney's famous painting *Custer's Last Rally*, and Folsom illuminatingly records Whitman's response to the work. Folsom reads Whitman's own poem about Custer's defeat as indicative of the poet's deeply ambivalent feelings about the American Indian. He points out that there are no Indians in Whitman's poem, and then reminds us that Whitman lived with a George Catlin painting of Osceola, the Seminole warrior, given to him by Catlin. He also notes that Whitman was the only major American poet actually to work in the Indian Bureau of the Department of the Interior. The final section, on photography, contains reproductions of some truly fascinating photographs of Whitman, spanning most of his life. Whitman reached his maturity, Folsom points out, just as photography began to transform sight. This chapter, like the earlier one on baseball, is very informative on the general history of its subject in America, as well as on Whitman's relationship with the technology of the camera. Folsom concludes his excellent book by suggesting that, while photography had a powerful impact on Whitman's understanding of the complex interplay between art and reality, its principal appeal for him lay in the fact that it was a truly democratic art form.

4. American Literature 1865 to 1900

American Trajectories: Authors and Readings, 1790–1970 by Warner Berthoff, bringing together lectures and also essays which have been published in a variety of journals over the course of the last forty years, yields both particular and general interest. The individual nineteenth-century authors who feature in Berthoff's collection are Brockden Brown, Twain, Dickinson, O. Henry and Kate Chopin, and the discussion of the last named includes an account of *At Fault*, Chopin's first novel. Joan Burbick's account of *Healing the Republic: The Language of Health and the Culture of Nationalism in Nineteenth-Century America* ranges between narratives of health written by practitioners – both professional and lay – as well as by health administrators, social reformers and literary artists, which, in some way or other, purport to claim the 'cultural authority to represent the body'. The first part of Burbick's study sets up an opposition between interventionist or 'heroic' medicine, the 'bleeding, purging, and dosing' of the patient which made the authority of the physician supreme, and the claims of common sense, the right of every individual to practise healing of the self and others. This dialectic is then extended into moral and ideological spheres, with Thoreau's *Walden* serving as supporting text as a narrative of health which 'demands a new economic order'. A chapter on 'Biodemocracy in *Leaves of Grass*' positions Whitman in contradistinction to those, like Catharine Beecher and William Alcott, who would alert the mid-century nation to the fact of its ill health. Whitman as the prophet of a healthy nation, affirming the 'ability of the "subject" to govern the body' and 'privileging the human body as the key to democratic meaning', thereby sanctions the body as a trope sufficient to encompass the diversity and unity of the nation. The second part of *Healing the Republic*, 'Fictions of the Body Politic', looks at the way in which values attached to the specific body parts of brain, heart, nerves and eye become freighted with cultural meaning and even conflict, as each offers a different 'key' to social order and health, with Poe, Dickinson, Warner, Stowe, Hawthorne, Holmes, Emerson and Melville variously invoked as practitioners of narratives of health.

The Ethos of Romance at the Turn of the Century by William J. Scheick is grounded in classification; he seeks to denote and exemplify subgenres of romance as a means towards a taxonomy of both writer and reader. Works by English and American turn-of-the-century practitioners of the art of romance are discussed through single short stories or novels, these texts being positioned within types of romance according to their 'generic reflexivity'. Whilst Scheick is careful to acknowledge the alternate genres within which his chosen texts can be located – tales of the supernatural, of adventure and mystery and the farce are all considered – they are here repositioned to illustrate the richness, variety and complexity of the romance. Audience reaction is a crucial constituent in definition of author and text for Scheick, and it is, in some form or other, factored into his readings of romance in all its forms. The artists under discussion are divided into eventuary, ethical and aesthetic romancers; sharing a commitment to the 'ethos' of romance, they nevertheless divide along subgeneric lines. As a prelude to his discussion of these subgenres Scheick reads Hawthorne's 'Roger Malvin's Burial' as paradigm, posing questions about 'Hawthorne's romance about romance' that remain substantially unanswered and unanswerable. The endless circularity of the genre itself – 'Romance necessarily conceals certain elusive truths about existence even as it tries or pretends to reveal them' – is shown to be richly represented in Hawthorne's story. Aesthetic romances, here represented by Henry James's *The Turn of the Screw*, disregard their audiences in the fashioning of what James himself described as the 'self-referential artifact', so as to reflect the genre itself in being composed of 'character, mood and effect hermetically sealed in a cryptic pattern, design, or form'; being, in other words, an end in and unto itself.

A History of the 'Atlantic Monthly', 1857–1909: Yankee Humanism at High Tide and Ebb by Ellery Sedgwick is an indispensable guide to the editors and contributors who gave the journal its character during its most influential years. This study covers the period in which the journal was edited by James Russell Lowell, James T. Fields, William Dean Howells, Thomas Bailey Aldrich, Horace Scudder, Walter Hines Page and Bliss Perry, and, whilst the cultural hegemony of the Yankee humanist is obvious in this line-up, Sedgwick is effective in making the point that this did not mean that there was an absence of diversity in editorial approach or ideological standpoint. It is this very diversity which, Sedgwick claims, allowed 'the magazine to adapt and survive the decline of the New England tradition and the rise of mass culture'; and he traces the development of the magazine from its essentially liberal, literary character, through the more reactionary years of Aldrich and Scudder, to the editorial transformation of the journal, under Page's hand, towards journalism and away from literary high culture. Howells's period of office, between 1871 and 1881, saw radical changes not only in the magazine but in the editor himself, Sedgwick describing Howells's development from 'a sentimental, imitative, romantic poet to a major practitioner, theorist, and advocate of realistic fiction' as contiguous with the transformation of the journal into a more national and democratic organ, with a wider readership and list of contributors, including local colourists and, of course, a whole-hearted championing of Henry James. Sedgwick dedicates a chapter to each of the seven editors and, whilst Howells and Page are clearly the outstandingly influential figures, the contribution of each individual is given full acknowledgement and distinction; even the deeply conservative Aldrich took, and sometimes solicited, work which expressed views in opposition to his own, and he was the editor responsible for first publishing fiction by Charles Chestnutt.

This year brought a new Norton critical edition of *Uncle Tom's Cabin*, edited by Elizabeth Ammons, as well as second editions of *The Awakening* and a third of *The Red Badge of Courage* (both reviewed below). The 'Backgrounds and Contexts' to Stowe's novel contains material from Stowe's 'Key to *Uncle Tom's Cabin*', copies of contemporary documents like slave sale bills, runaway advertisements, some of Cruikshank's illustrations from the first British edition of the novel, and contemporary reviews, one of which is a panegyric penned by George Sand. The critical essays range between the condemnation of Stowe by James Baldwin, the familiar but absolutely indispensable Jane Tompkins (who, more than any other commentator, has redrawn the terms of critical engagement with the text around the concept of 'cultural work'), and Robert Levine, who provides an analysis of the contemporary reception of the novel as reflected in the debates and responses published in *Frederick Douglass' Paper* between 1852 and 1854. Christina Zwarg discusses the discourse of patriarchy in the novel in a provocative essay 'Fathering and Blackface in *Uncle Tom's Cabin*', whilst in a piece that effectively draws together all points of the argument of and around the text, 'Changing the Letter: The Yokes, the Jokes of Discourse, or, Mrs. Stowe, Mr. Reed', Hortense Spillers critiques the terms of engagement of Stowe scholarship in a wide-ranging discussion of the novel, juxtaposing Stowe's work with Ishmael Reed's *Flight to Canada*, and positioning Reed 'not so much "rewriting" Stowe as he is intimating a repertory of strategies that denote, that circumlocute, a particular cluster of discursive acts'.

S. P. Rosenbaum's revised edition of *The Ambassadors* reprints the New York text of 1909 along with James's preface and textual notes; also included is the story of the publication of the novel, editions and revisions, and an invaluable chapter called 'The Author on the Novel', featuring notebook entries and the 'Project of Novel by Henry James'. There are five critical essays new to this edition (though they have been previously published elsewhere), amongst which is an essay by Maud Ellmann, revised for republication here, on 'Power and Representation in *The Ambassadors*', and extracts from books on James by Nicola Bradbury and Millicent Bell. A Norton *The Red Badge of Courage* last appeared in 1976, and a large quantity of critical material is new to Donald Pizer's 1994 edition. The editor offers a new guide to criticism on Crane (up to and including 1992) and provides his own essay, 'Text, Theme and Form', to take up the debate about the textual authenticity of the first edition (1895) as against the Hershel Parker/Henry Binder text, which restores portions cut from Crane's manuscript before its first publication. Pizer seeks to prove through exegesis of Crane's textual strategy the will of the author – not his contemporary editor – in the revision and cutting of the Appleton text; the extensive bibliography also includes a section dedicated to the textual controversy. Margo Culley's important 1976 edition of *The Awakening* is extended here to include extracts from some of the most significant writing on Chopin of the last twenty years, the list of contributors – Elaine Showalter, Sandra Gilbert, Helen Taylor, Nancy Walker and Elizabeth Ammons amongst them – indicating the current high critical esteem in which Chopin's work is held and, indeed, the dynamic condition of Chopin scholarship. All these Norton editions are outstanding as teaching texts, providing the right balance between textual and critical apparatus and presenting a clear agenda which supports independent research by the student.

The Ethnicity and Representation in American Literature special issue of *YWES*, edited by Lionel Kelly, includes an essay on Kate Chopin and the enactment of ethnic stereotypes in her fiction. As I am its author I shall do nothing other here than to mention that the essay treats of Louisiana as a post-colonial rather than an American post-bellum society, and discusses 'La Belle Zoraïde', 'A Matter of Prejudice', 'Athénaïse', 'A Dresden Lady in Dixie' and 'Désirée's Baby' as they reflect Chopin's ability to illuminate and dissect the power and value structures of her society. Michele A. Birnbaum also discusses the 'abuses and uses of the color line in the postwar South' in her article ' "Alien Hands": Kate Chopin and the Colonization of Race' (*AL* 66.301–23). Birnbaum seeks to interrogate assumptions which place *The Awakening* in the context of a 'traditionally Western conceptual duel (and duality) of self against culture, the idealization of the self-sufficient individual', and to redirect our attention to the distinctively 'colonial production of selfhood and sexuality in the novel'. Chopin also features substantially in Richard Fusco's *Maupassant and the American Short Story: The Influence of Form at the Turn of the Century*, alongside Ambrose Bierce, O. Henry and Henry James, as amongst those writers significantly indebted to Maupassant. Fusco is insightful in his treatment of Chopin's work, bringing to the discussion of her stories an intimacy with Maupassant's form and content which can do nothing other than illuminate Chopin's own practice in the genre of the short story. He is particularly acute on Chopin's alteration and innovation of the Maupassantian model, and has, as a result, fresh things to say about 'Désirée's Baby' and 'The Story of an Hour'. The first half of his study is dedicated to theorizing Maupassant's fiction and provides a complex but useful ontology of the short story form, which is illustrated by close reading of a selection of stories. This is followed by a discussion of the four American writers wherein Fusco shows how Bierce and Henry took too literally the 'surprise-inversion story', doing the 'twist in the tale' to death by inflexibility and overuse, whereas Chopin and James used the various Maupassantian models as a licence to adapt and change whilst learning both structural and thematic principles from the Master. Linda Wagner-Martin's *Telling Women's Lives: The New Biography* looks intelligently, though briefly, at the different influences under which the biographers of Kate Chopin (and also Edith Wharton) wrote their *Lives*; the very brevity of this account of the differences between Daniel Rankin, Per Seyersted and Emily Toth, however, means that Wagner-Martin cannot do much more than point to the most obvious divergences in their approaches.

The Sermon and the African American Literary Imagination by Dolan Hubbard is chiefly concerned with the influence of the sermon upon twentieth-century black writers, but Hubbard does begin his study in consideration of the work of Frederick Douglass and his use of the rhetorical structures of black oratory. Hubbard examines the integration of the 'preacherly voice' into the *Narrative* of 1845 in both linguistic and structural terms, and illustrates cogently and compellingly the ways and means by which 'Douglass's phraseology carries cosmological weight; the ethos of black culture authorizes the black preacher to foster intellectual anarchy – a tradition of protest and resistance – in the face of a morally bankrupt system'.

A collection of writings by Margaret Fuller, *Woman in the Nineteenth Century and Other Writings*, edited by Donna Dickenson, includes a variety of reviews, poetry and excerpts from *Summer on the Lakes* as well as a critical introduction and bibliography. Dickenson's useful introduction provides a context in which to read Fuller as well as details of her background, development and political thought; those seeking more flesh on Fuller's bones should then proceed to Dickenson's biography, *Margaret Fuller: Writing a Woman's Life* (*YWES* 74.551). In a year without much critical activity in Gilman studies, Denise D. Knight offers an invaluable collection of short fiction in *'The Yellow Wallpaper' and Selected Stories of Charlotte Perkins Gilman* as well as *The Diaries of Charlotte Perkins Gilman* in two volumes which cover, respectively, 1879–87 and 1890–1935. In the collection of stories Knight divides the fiction thematically and generically, provides an introductory biographical sketch, details of Gilman's magazine *The Forerunner*, and an examination of Gilman's didactic intentions, considers her work as a sociologist as well as writer of fiction, and explains the rationale for the choice of stories in the collection. This is a very welcome addition to works in print by Gilman, making available many obscure pieces and extending the possibilities for further work on the full range of Gilman's fiction. The diaries are similarly indispensable for Gilman scholars, providing, as they do, direct access to her private reflections on the traumatic events of her life as well as the more mundane conditions of her existence. Knight also adds appendices to the diaries which include a variety of other personal writings by Gilman, among them poetry and letters. The editing here is of a very high standard, the index is well-organized and capacious, the annotation is helpful and, whilst the diaries cannot in themselves be described as a riveting read, Knight's scholarship turns them into a brilliant resource for reference purposes.

This year proved not to be a very good one for book-length studies of Henry James, although *HJR* continues to offer a wide and interesting range of short critical essays as well as a number of articles of the notes-and-queries species. *HJR* 15.i includes Wai Chee Dimock on 'Gender, the Market, and the Non-trivial in James' (24–30), a James conference address which places *The Bostonians* in the context of 'the postulate of equivalence . . . and the tyranny of explanation' as set up by Adorno and Horkheimer, in order to scrutinize the 'limits of explanation', both as thematic and as narrative affectation. Also in this issue, Julie Olin-Ammentorp puts a case for 'The Feminization of Merton Densher' (38–54), Lewis O. Saum offers 'Christopher Newman: *The American* as Westerner' (1–9), and Beth Sharon Ash performs a detailed psychoanalytic reading of *The Golden Bowl* (55–90). In *HJR* 15.ii Nancy Bentley's essay 'James and the Tribal Discipline of English Kinship' (127–40) reads *The Spoils of Poynton* to brilliant effect in an anthropological context, particularly in the light of late nineteenth-century kinship studies, where James is considered as presenting 'a cultural order in which the bonds linking kin are indistinguishable from their relations to property'. The same novel is considered by Carol Faulkner in her 'Reconsidering Poynton's Innocent Patriarch' (141–51), an essay which seeks to wrest critical attention away from the struggles enacted between Fleda, Mona and Mrs Gereth and toward Owen and the crucial issue of primogeniture. Essays on *The Golden Bowl*, 'The Beast in the Jungle' and *A Small Boy and Others* also feature in this issue. Craig A. Milliman opens *HJR* 15.iii with an essay on 'The Fiction of Art: Roderick Hudson's Pursuit of the Ideal' (231–41), in which he argues that in the novel James is conducting an attack on 'the popular stereotype of the artist'. The issue contains two essays on *The Ambassadors*: 'Typical Tales of Paris: The Function of Reading in *The Ambassadors*', by Allen W. Menton (286–300), examines Lambert Strether's experiences of Paris through his reading in nineteenth-century literature about life in the city whilst 'Dining with *The Ambassadors*' (301–8), by Jan van Rosevelt, continues the phenomenological strain of the journal with a discussion of the 'metaphoric or depicted acts of eating or tasting' in the novel. Also of note is Julie Grossman's essay '"It's the Real Thing": Henry James, Photography, and *The Golden Bowl*' (309–28), which puts James in dialogue with the art of the camera to the extent that he is deemed to have invented 'new strategies for representing the real that . . . appropriate aspects of photography'.

Henry James and Masculinity: The Man at the Margins by Kelly Cannon is concerned to establish an alterity for James's portrayal of the masculine; it has the writer constructing a series of 'marginal males' who 'by their very existence challenge the status quo: they devote the majority of their energy not to public life, but to marginal activities whose source is the imagination'. Whilst Cannon offers some insights into individual works, notably *The Ambassadors* and certain of the short stories, the study labours under the unassimilated weight of both critical theory and prior James scholarship, and has something of a mission to mark and name James himself amongst those who people his fictions, using bits and pieces of 'evidence' from biography and the Jamesian *oeuvres*. Cannon glides between the criticism, the life and works and renders all three anodyne. In contrast to the majority of critical work being produced on James at the moment, *Henry James and the Real Thing: A Modern Reader's Guide*, by Virginia Llewellyn Smith, proclaims its unpretentious aims from the outset. Instead of obfuscating or sectionalizing the work of the Master, Smith here offers to provide assistance to 'those persons under no obligation to read novels, let alone criticism, who have tactfully said to me that they might become James enthusiasts if they had some idea where to start'. Enough said.

T. J. Lustig's account of *Henry James and the Ghostly* is, unsurprisingly, much taken up with *The Turn of the Screw*, but the wider ambition declared here is to demonstrate the centrality of the ghostly 'to the great dynamic forces which play throughout [James's] work in its entirety'. Lustig refuses to work with the generic or with predictable interpretative strategies, preferring instead to proceed from James's 'deployment of the frame', whereby the 'frame' and its adherents – the threshold, the window, the door, and the narrative form itself – 'displace or obscure "vulgarity" . . . [and] defend against readings which reduce the text to sexual and aesthetic clichés'. The first chapter sets the scene for Lustig's redefinition of the ghostly as predicated by James, by scrutinizing pre-Jamesian versions of the supernatural from Plato and Aristotle, through Hobbes and Locke, to Freud and Girard, whilst the second broaches the function of the ghostly in the context of James's use of his literary predecessors, especially Mérimée and Hawthorne, in discussion of 'The Romance of Certain Old Clothes', 'De Grey', 'The Ghostly Rental' and 'Sir Edmund Orme', amongst others. Having arrived at the point where the much-maligned governess becomes the 'medium of exchange, crossing borders and enabling borders to be crossed', Lustig moves on to *The Ambassadors*, but extends and informs his argument with extensive references to most of the major novels and their affiliations to the uncanny. Thomas Galt Peyser, in a lucid and compelling article, 'James, Race, and the Imperial Museum' (*AmLH* 6.i.48–70), positions *The Golden Bowl* at the heart of a debate which establishes intimacy between aesthetic and political concerns, so that 'James's manner of treating the world as a museum and its inhabitants as curators and exhibits joins his artistic labor to the assimilative labor that lay ahead for his native country'.

Volume 3 of *The Correspondence of William James, William and Henry, 1897–1910*, edited by Ignas K. Skrupskelis and Elizabeth M. Berkeley, completes the letters between the brothers and contains multiple pleasures for those entranced by the omissions and commissions of Jamesian communications. The period covered by this volume is one of massive professional productivity for both brothers, but the correspondence is dominated by the more mundane business of bowel efficiency – William to Henry in July 1902: 'I keep finding "shredded wheat" a great *relaxer*'; social life – Henry to William in June 1905: 'These 3 fell *absences* (after Friday: viz: to Howells on 17th, to Masons on 20th & to Mrs. Wharton (with her knife in my flesh & at my throat,) for later all crowd me up so'; Fletcherism and banting – Henry to William in July 1904: 'his precious little munching message; for which I go on not ceasing to bless him . . . For the first few weeks I in fact felt I *was* thinning, but this consciousness, so enchanting, has since then sadly dropped'; as well as travel, both European and American, gardens, houses, family and so on. On fraternal criticism of each other's work there is little harmony; the whole give and take of family interchange of criticism being neatly encapsulated within Henry's response to William's criticisms of *The Golden Bowl* in November 1905: 'I mean to try to produce some uncanny form of thing, in fiction, that will gratify you, as Brother – but let me say, dear William, that I shall greatly be humiliated if you *do* like it, & thereby lump it, in your affection, with things, of the current age, that I have heard you express admiration for & that I would sooner descend to a dishonoured grave than have written.' The temptation for the reviewer, of course, is to go on and on endlessly quoting from the letters, but suffice it to say that the volume yields immeasurable delight in terms of reading the relationship, the rivalries, the harmonies, the mundanities as well as the felicities of style and subjects.

Transcendent Daughters in Jewett's Country of the Pointed Firs by Joseph Church is a detailed psychoanalytic study of Jewett's Dunnet Landing stories; in addition to the novel he discusses 'The Foreigner', 'The Queen's Twin', 'A Dunnet Shepherdess' and 'William's Wedding', before concluding with some remarks on 'The Landscape Chamber', a story of 1887. Church relies upon a number of psychoanalytic theorists, beginning with Melanie Klein and utilizing insights from Freud, Janine Chasseguet Smirgel and Luce Irigaray, so as to focus upon mother-daughter relations in a 'preoedipal realm' – specifically here, the narrator's relationship with Almira Todd – in conjunction with 'patrilineal identification' in exegesis of the relationships with the three elderly gentlemen who feature in the novel. Church is absolutely transparent in his aims and intentions and provides a thorough account of both his methodology and the route to his conclusions, which are concerned with the achievement of 'transcendence' through the 'reworking of the paternal figure and reestablishing her association with the maternal one'. *The Country of the Pointed Firs* joined the list of texts featured in CUP's American Novel series this year, with a volume of essays edited by June Howard. This collection is of more general interest and use than Church's study and the introductory essay by the editor provides a useful survey of the trends in critical opinion on Jewett, including contemporary reviews of her work, detailed discussion of Jewett's network of literary women friends, the development of the *Atlantic Monthly*, Jewett's view of authorship and an outline of the rationale for the volume. The various contributors offer readings which amply illustrate the critical terrain Howard maps out, where Jewett is considered 'in terms of gender, genre, region, and nation', following the ground-breaking work on these areas in recent years by Eric Sundquist, Richard Brodhead, Philip Fisher, Amy Kaplan and Michael Davitt Bell (the last named a contributor to the volume under discussion). In her essay '*Country*'s Portrayal of Community and the Exclusion of Difference', Sandra Zagarell treads a fine line between what she terms the 'inclusive and restrictive' in the novel, critiquing readings which posit Jewett's construction of community as universal by invoking 'the figurative exclusion of those significantly different from community members'. In 'Gender and American Realism in *The Country of the Pointed Firs*', Michael Davitt Bell offers Jewett in constructive relationship with Howellsian realism, making plain the risks of forcing her text into a reading which excludes multiplicity, and concluding: 'The book itself is capable of affirming its community of women without conspiring in the assumption that women should inevitably be hemmed and marginalized.' The prolific Elizabeth Ammons adds to the influential work she did on the text in her *Conflicting Stories: American Women Writers at the Turn into the Twentieth Century* in an essay which takes on 'Material Culture, Empire, and Jewett's *Country of the Pointed Firs*', whilst Susan Gillman completes the collection in a discussion of 'Regionalism and Nationalism', placing Jewett's text in a historicized context in order to examine the role and function of 'reunion' – both local and national – within the narrative structure.

Harriet Beecher Stowe was the subject of much good work in this year, including an outstanding new biography of the writer. In an article, 'Puritan Providences in Stowe's *The Pearl of Orr's Island*: The Legacy of Cotton Mather' (*SAF* 22.i.61–79), Dorothy Z. Baker demonstrates the structural and thematic debt which Stowe's novel owes to the sixth book of Cotton Mather's history of New England, Baker claiming a single voice for Mather and Stowe in their articulation of the desire 'for a society unified in its mission to march toward spiritual perfection in this world and salvation in the next'. Joan Hedrick's *Harriet Beecher Stowe: A Life* is a nicely judged, non-judgmental, always compelling but never sensational account of the life of the woman she demonstrates as one of the most important American writers of the nineteenth century. Stowe is communicated in all the strength of her enthusiasms and evasions; her attention to and her neglect of her family, the multiple contradictions which inspired both the radical energies and the innate conservatism of this native of that most American of institutions, the Beecher family, are here put on full display. The family is given space to flourish in Hedrick's book but not at the expense of the detail of Stowe's life; her many and varied social and professional endeavours are documented, and her part in the founding of the *Atlantic*, the breathtaking and reckless extent of her journalism, leader and letter writing as well as her fiction are all detailed alongside her reforming activities, first among which was her commitment to the expansion of educational opportunities in America, in both geographical and social terms. The semi-detached nature of Stowe's commitment to abolition as well as to the cause of women's suffrage is illuminated by Hedrick's account of the compromises and shifts of Stowe's diurnal reality, the demands made upon her by husband and children, as well as the pursuit of cures and treatments or foreign travel made for reasons of personal preference. More detailed discussion of the fiction would have been welcome, but Hedrick's account of the changing cultural context for Stowe's fiction, and, indeed, for the work of other women writing in the gilded age, as literary activity became more and more professionalized, is outstanding and deserves to be read as a portrait as much of the age as of the woman.

The three informing principles, *Message, Messenger, and Response: Puritan Forms and Cultural Reformation in Harriet Beecher Stowe's Uncle Tom's Cabin*, named in Gladys Sherman Lewis's formulation of Stowe's work are ruthlessly interrogated here for their effectiveness in provoking social change. In other words the triad of Puritan genre, voice of the story-teller, and audience shape and determine the course of Sherman's investigation of the novel's success as polemic. The sermon, the captivity narrative, the spiritual autobiography and the propaganda tract are rendered schematically as Puritan forms in fulfilment of the first principle, whilst the second is constituted by means of 'The Preacher's Tone' and 'The Storyteller's Style', where the 'preacher's voice contributes design and authority to the storyteller voice which shows how individual time and experience conflict with rules once grounded in the ideology of the culture'. The section of the book which deals with audience response addresses 'three reading communities . . . the religious; the sentimental; and the socio-political', with another magic triad, 'the Bible, the sentimental novel and the melodrama', shaping and structuring the 'transference of Stowe's antislavery message'.

Discussions of Harriet Beecher Stowe also feature in two Routledge publications: *The Discourse of Slavery: Aphra Behn to Toni Morrison*, edited by Carl Plasa and Betty J. Ring, and *The Myth of Aunt Jemima: White Women Representing Black Women*, by Diane Roberts. In her book Roberts conducts an extensive inquiry into the ways in which white women write about race, and she moves from Stowe to pro-slavery writers and their responses to *Uncle Tom's Cabin*, through British woman travel writers – Frances Trollope, Frances Wright, Harriet Martineau and Frances Kemble – and also considers the work of Lydia Maria Child, and in particular her espousal of race-mixing or 'amalgamation'. Roberts's chapter on *Uncle Tom's Cabin* concentrates on Stowe's use of Orientalism and Gothic representations in the text, as the enabling principles in thematic development of 'the sins of slavery: rape, incest, miscegenation, adultery, dead children, stolen children, absent spouses, split families, broken marriages', which lead ultimately to the triumphant closure of the Christian story of redemption. The critical responses to Stowe's work are analysed in terms of the grounds upon which respondents made their attack: first in terms of personal assaults upon the author's womanhood, including her Christianity and her wifehood and motherhood, then the denigration of her picture of the South as 'sensationalist', and finally the substitution of an alternative picture of the happy South with contented slaves 'redeemed from barbarity and heathenism' by their benign masters. The chapter on the work of Lydia Maria Child also incorporates some discussion of Harriet Jacobs's *Incidents in the Life of a Slave Girl, Written by Herself*, which Childs edited, and which is seen alongside Child's own work as mediating 'between the states of sexual black body and asexual white body' as a means to push at the limits of the debate about female sexual morality in the context of slavery.

In Plasa and Ring's volume, Stowe is contextualized in an Anglo-American relationship with Mrs Gaskell by Elizabeth Jean Sabiston, who argues that the narrative structures of *Uncle Tom's Cabin* and *Mary Barton* are mutually illuminated by making a close comparison between them; Sabiston also analyses Stowe's indebtedness to the British social problem novel as a means to illustrate the limits of its usefulness as model for the portrayal of slavery. Harriet Jacobs is also the subject of an essay in this volume, 'Perilous Passages in Harriet Jacobs's *Incidents in the Life of a Slave Girl*' by Jon Hauss, who contends that the tales of oppression and resistance told within this text offer 'the ritual storytelling of slave-women as cultural model for an expanding struggle to produce tentative understanding, and political alliance, across the cultural schisms of America'. Betty J. Ring offers Frederick Douglass engaged in what she terms 'semantic intervention', used here as a means to critique both his text and the critical hierarchy which constructs Douglass as 'representative slave-narrator'. [Plasa and Ring's collection also contains the following discussions: Anne Fogarty on Aphra Behn's *Oroonoko*; Jane Moore on Mary Wollstonecraft; Steven Vine on William Blake's 'Visions of the Daughters of Albion'; Carl Plasa on *Jane Eyre*; David Lawrence Rogers on William Faulkner; and April Lidinsky on Toni Morrison's *Beloved*. The contributions by Vine and Moore are especially interesting. This is a good collection of essays on a current topic. The editors, however, have chosen to remain within the usual post-colonial canon, and a more comprehensive and adventurous volume could have been produced. Additional review material by PJK.]

Greg Camfield's *Sentimental Twain: Samuel Clemens in the Maze of Moral Philosophy* begins by making connections between Harriet Beecher Stowe and Mark Twain, not only the physical connection between them as neighbours in Hartford but in their ethical positions. Camfield offers a Mark Twain caught between sentimental and naturalistic versions of morality, and grounds his discussion in the dialectical oppositions which follow. He examines responses to *Huckleberry Finn* which focus on the question of race as a means of 'setting the stage' for his wider study of a whole-cultural ambivalence to sentimentalism, and goes on to explore, in some detail, the origins and development of sentimental moral philosophy as it features in American literary activity. Twain's work is shown to provide evidence of his changing and contradictory attitudes to the uses of sentimentality, with the journalism viewed as the 'beginning of his serious moral use of domestic ideology in his writing'; discussions of *The Innocents Abroad*, the collaboratively written *The Gilded Age* and *A Connecticut Yankee* follow, and Camfield devotes a chapter to a re-reading of *Pudd'nhead Wilson* which follows the genesis of the novel in terms of the 'tension between humour and irony, between play and serious moral purpose', where Twain's original burlesque – on the Siamese Twins – falls victim to an 'accidental' gravity of subject. Camfield's findings, that Twain's writing career negotiated 'a strange transmission to the twentieth century of sentimental ideas packaged in an anti-sentimental rhetoric', are amply illustrated and coherently argued, with the obscure and reviled writings discussed as seriously as the well-known, to which he also brings fresh insights. In *Mark Twain in the Company of Women*, Laura E. Skandera-Trombley seeks to address a default in Twain criticism: the absence of proper attention to the part played in the professional as well as private life of Samuel Clemens by the women with whom he lived in close relation. Drawing extensively upon Twain's letters, notebooks and journals, Skandera-Trombley lays the ghosts of 'androcentric scholarship' systematically, examining the effects of mother, wife, daughters and other close women associates by challenging the prevailing notions of their individual roles in his life. Skandera-Trombley's portrait of Twain's wife, Olivia, is a particularly compelling one, detailing as it does the extent of her power and influence in the organization of the family and home as well as providing details of her childhood, the women who were influential in her life, and the ideological register of her family background, her father being a 'conductor' on the underground railroad. The account given here of Olivia Langdon's home town, Elmira, is full and engaging: the Elmira water cure, a therapeutic regime established by the doctors Gleason, Elmira's Independent Congregational church, which had Thomas Kennicut Beecher as its minister and abolitionism as one of its chief tenets, Elmira's temperance crusade and the establishment of the Elmira Female College provide an intriguing cross-section of Olivia's social context. As Skandera-Trombley says in her 'Epilogue', the purpose of the book is to 'trace the dichotomy present within Twain scholarship owing to the schools of Brooksian "dualism" and DeVotoian "integration" and their subsequent critical offshoots . . . to examine the social and cultural influences of the women closest to Clemens . . . and . . . to investigate the background and feminist influences of the one person who inarguably had the greatest effect on Clemens, his partner, Olivia'; all of which is managed to good effect.

Martha Banta's essay 'The Ghostly Gothic of Wharton's Everyday World' (*ALR* 27.i.1–10) locates Wharton's work in the ghost story within the 'cultural context of [the] flourishing science of ethnography', paying particular attention to 'Afterward', to *The Decoration of Houses* and its capacity to reveal Wharton as a part of the 'long train of those who "read" interiors as inventories of separated selves and family secrets', and to *Ethan Frome*, where the past and present merge in the hellish final scene, which finds the 'Frome family ghosts in dominion over the present'. The literary particularities of time and place are also to the forefront in Donna M. Campbell's 'Edith Wharton and the "Authoresses": The Critique of Local Color in Wharton's Early Fiction' (*SAF* 22.ii.169–84), which examines Wharton's repudiation of likeness with writers like Jewett and Freeman through close readings of the early stories, 'Mrs. Manstey's View' and *Bunner Sisters*, which render an account of 'the literary shift from local color to naturalism'.

Eleanor Dwight's lavishly illustrated *Edith Wharton: An Extraordinary Life* structures its biographical endeavour around Wharton's dwelling places, moving from New York, through the various landscapes she inhabited, to Paris and the south of France, detailing Wharton's domestic arrangements – in particular her gardening – her social life, her writing and her travels. In bright, enthusiastic prose Dwight moves between the fiction and the life, the travels and the travel writing, providing a detailed commentary on the numerous photographs of Wharton, her contemporaries, the places she lived and visited, illustrations from contemporary magazines, postcards, garden plans and society portraits. It is in the illustrations that Dwight's account of Wharton's life can be distinguished from other biographies, and it is from the photo-plates that most pleasure is to be gained. Dwight does not treat the fiction in sufficient detail to warrant attention, but she does provide fascinating snippets of detail about Wharton's diurnal existence and her extra-literary projects; the chapter on the Mount, Wharton's Lenox home, is of particular interest, as is the account of her adventures in planting the gardens of her two last homes: Chateau Sainte-Claire and the Pavillon Colombe.

A special 'Wharton and the Gothic' issue of the *EWhR* (11.i) features articles by Kathy Fedorko, Richard Kaye, Monika Ebert and Kristin Lauer. Fedorko takes '"Forbidden Things": Gothic Confrontation with the Feminine in "The Young Gentlemen" and "Bewitched"' (3–9) in order to examine the Gothic as 'a kind of psychic theater, a means for dramatizing the conflict between female and male selves in a "dialogue with the unconscious"', whilst Kaye (18) scrutinizes Wharton's five 'homosexual' ghost stories: 'The Eyes', 'The Triumph of Night', 'A Bottle of Perrier', 'Afterward' and 'Pomegranate Seed', dividing the stories between those set in all-male environments, where 'women are absent and male rivals malevolently vie for attention', and those that 'explore marriages seemingly threatened by the possibility of a male outsider beckoning superficially upright husbands'. Monika Ebert also considers 'A Bottle of Perrier' (19–23), but in comparison with T. S. Eliot's *Waste Land* 'as Modernist Gothic in describing the fragmentation of the modern mind'; whilst the final essay, Kristin Lauer's 'Is this Indeed "Attractive"? Another Look at the "Beatrice Palmato" Fragment' (26–9), seeks to reorientate our reading of the famous fragment away from the Freudian bias of most critics and towards the insights offered by psychoanalyst Karen Horney in order to scrutinize the text as a continuation of the 'rescue scenario ubiquitous in male–female relationships in Wharton's fiction'.

Edith Wharton's Inner Circle by Susan Goodman is a study of the close friends whom Edith Wharton designated in her autobiography, *A Backward Glance*, as the 'inner group', and whom Nicky Mariano, the long-time secretary/mistress of Bernard Berenson, called Wharton's 'male wives': Henry James, Percy Lubbock, John Hugh Smith, Walter Berry, Robert Norton, Gaillard Lapsley, Howard Sturgis and, from time to time, Bernard Berenson. In her study Goodman seeks to make the case for their membership in some sort of definable body, with closer ties than those of casual membership of a transatlantic class of aesthetes who had either Henry James or Edith Wharton in common. One of the means by which she makes a case for the existence of such a group is in comparison with Bloomsbury, and although she struggles valiantly to identify an Edith Wharton circle, its most substantial testament remains in the discreet pages of Wharton's autobiography, where anodyne tribute is paid to large numbers of friends and acquaintances. Goodman communicates a fine sense of the particular manifestations of neediness that were Wharton's: the intellectual and the emotional never managing quite to balance either within her own sense of self or in her public persona. What Goodman cannot avoid – and does not – is the communication of a sense that Wharton was not as important to this 'circle' as it was to her. The chapter which Goodman provides on the Bloomsbury Group, its membership and role as the paradigmatic inner circle, both fleshes out the period and acknowledges Bloomsbury's interest in Henry James and resistance to Wharton. Finally Kenneth M. Price and Phyllis McBride's article, '"The Life Apart": Text and Contexts of Edith Wharton's Love Diary' (*AL* 66.663–88), reproduces in full the text of Wharton's diary of her affair with W. Morton Fullerton. The diary is held in the Lilly Library at Indiana University, and is here prefaced with remarks upon the biographical and literary context, a brief character sketch of Fullerton, discussion of the relationship between the diary and Wharton's fictions. Ultimately this article makes a claim for the diary's capacity to reveal Wharton in the act of 'self-analysis, self-questioning, self-creation'.

Books Reviewed

Anderson, Wallace E., Mason I. Lowance Jr with David H. Watters, eds. *The Typological Writings of Jonathan Edwards. Vol. II: The Works of Jonathan Edwards*. YaleUP (1993). pp. 432. £50. ISBN 0 3000 5352 5.

Ammons, Elizabeth, ed. *Harriet Beecher Stowe: Uncle Tom's Cabin*. Norton. pp. xviii + 584. £6.95. ISBN 0 3939 6303 9.

Bercovitch, Sacvan, ed. *The Cambridge History of American Literature. Vol. I: 1590–1820*. CUP. pp. 829. $69.95. ISBN 0 5213 0105 X.

Berthoff, Warner. *American Trajectories: Authors and Readings, 1790–1970*. PSUP. pp. 200. £26.95. ISBN 0 2710 1051 7.

Burbick, Joan. *Healing the Republic: The Language of Health and the Culture of Nationalism in Nineteenth-Century America*. Cambridge Studies in American Literature and Culture. CUP. pp. 368. £37.50. ISBN 0 5214 5434 4.

Camfield, Greg. *Sentimental Twain: Samuel Clemens in the Maze of Moral Philosophy*. New Critical Studies. UPennP. pp. 296. £32.95, $34.95. ISBN 0 8122 3285 2 .

Cannon, Kelly. *Henry James and Masculinity: The Man at the Margins*. St Martin's. pp. 176. £30. ISBN 0 3336 1980 3.

Cavell, Stanley. *In Quest of the Ordinary: Lines of Skepticism and Romanticism*. UChicP. pp. 200. $10.95. ISBN 0 2260 9818 4.

Church, Joseph. *Transcendent Daughters in Jewett's Country of the Pointed Firs*. FDUP, AUP. pp. ix + 202. £26.50. ISBN 0 8386 3560 1.

Clark, J. C. D. *The Language of Liberty, 1660–1832: Political Discourse and Social Dynamics in the Anglo-American World*. CUP. pp. 404. hb £35, pb £13.95. ISBN 0 5214 4510 8, 0 5214 4957 X.

Culley, Margo, ed. *Kate Chopin: The Awakening*. Norton. £5.95. ISBN 0 3939 6057 9.

Davidson, Edward H. and William J. Scheick. *Paine, Scripture, and Authority: The Age of Reason as Religious and Political Idea*. AUP. pp. 144. £22.50. ISBN 0 9342 2329 7.

Dickenson, Donna, ed. *Margaret Fuller: Woman in the Nineteenth Century and Other Writings*. WC. OUP. pp. 304. £6.99. ISBN 0 1928 3085 6.

Dwight, Eleanor. *Edith Wharton: An Extraordinary Life*. Abrams. pp. 296. £24.95. ISBN 0 8109 3971 1.

Dworetz, Steven M. *The Unvarnished Doctrine: Locke, Liberalism, and the American Revolution*. DukeUP. pp. 247. £14.95. ISBN 0 8223 1470 3.

Felker, Christopher. *Reinventing Cotton Mather in the American Renaissance: Magnalia Christi Americana in Hawthorne, Stowe, and Stoddard*. NortheasternU. pp. 309. $42.95. ISBN 1 5555 3187 3.

Folsom, Ed. *Walt Whitman's Native Representations*. CUP. pp. 197. $35. ISBN 0 5214 5357 7.

Fusco, Richard. *Maupassant and the American Short Story: The Influence of Form at the Turn of the Century*. PSUP. pp. 395. £36. ISBN 0 2710 1081 9.

Goodman, Susan. *Edith Wharton's Inner Circle*. Ed. Thomas F. Staley. UTexP. pp. 192. $24.95. ISBN 0 2927 2771 2.

Greenberg, Robert M. *Splintered Worlds: Fragmentation and the Ideal of Diversity in the Work of Emerson, Melville, Whitman, and Dickinson*. NortheasternU. pp. 258. $45.50. ISBN 1 5555 3167 9.

Greene, Jack P. *Negotiated Authorities: Essays in Colonial, Political, and Consti-*

tutional History. UPVirginia. pp. 488. hb £53.95, pb £17.95. ISBN 0 8139 1516 3, 0 8139 1517 1.

Grünzweig, Walter. *Constructing the German Walt Whitman*. UIowaP. pp. 274. $22.95. ISBN 0 8774 5482 5.

Hedrick, Joan. *Harriet Beecher Stowe: A Life*. OUP. pp. 544. $35. ISBN 0 1950 6639 1.

Howard, June, ed. *New Essays on The Country of the Pointed Firs*. American Novel. CUP. pp. 160. hb £27.95, pb £10.95. ISBN 0 5214 1574 8, 0 5214 2602 2.

Hubbard, Dolan. *The Sermon and the African American Literary Imagination*. UMissP. pp. 192. hb £26.95, pb £7. ISBN 0 8262 0961 8, 0 8262 1087 2.

Idol Jr, John L., and Buford Jones, eds. *Nathaniel Hawthorne: The Contemporary Reviews*. CUP. pp. 518. $95. ISBN 0 5213 9142 3.

Irwin, John. *The Mystery to a Solution: Poe, Borges, and the Analytic Detective Story*. JHUP. pp. 481. £30.50. ISBN 0 8018 4650 1.

Knight, Denise D., ed. *The Diaries of Charlotte Perkins Gilman*. 2 vols. Vol. I. 1879–87. Vol. II. 1890–1935. UPVirginia. pp. 1,096. £79.95. ISBN 0 8139 1524 4.

——, ed. *'The Yellow Wallpaper' and Selected Stories of Charlotte Perkins Gilman*. UDelP. £28. ISBN 0 8741 3479 X .

Lewis, Gladys Sherman, *Message, Messenger, and Response: Puritan Forms and Cultural Reformation in Harriet Beecher Stowe's Uncle Tom's Cabin*. UPA. £43.50. ISBN 0 8191 9607 X .

Lustig, T. J. *Henry James and the Ghostly*. Cambridge. CUP. pp. 541. £40. ISBN 0 5214 5378 X.

Martin, Terence. *Parables of Possibility: The American Need for Beginnings*. ColUP. pp. 263. $27.50. ISBN 0 2310 7050 0.

Munk, Linda. *The Trivial Sublime: Theology and American Poetics*. Macmillan (1992). pp. 196. £35. ISBN 0 3120 8561 3.

Pease, Donald E., ed. *Revisionary Interventions into the Americanist Canon*. DukeUP. pp. 342. £15.95. ISBN 0 8223 1493 2.

Pizer, Donald, ed. *Stephen Crane: The Red Badge of Courage*. Norton. £6.95. ISBN 0 3939 6430 2.

Plasa, Carl, and Betty J. Ring, eds. *The Discourse of Slavery: Aphra Behn to Toni Morrison*. Routledge. pp. 226. hb £40, pb £11.99. ISBN 0 4150 8151 3, 0 4150 8152 1.

Richardson Jr, Robert D. *Emerson: The Mind on Fire*. UCalP. pp. 670. £27. ISBN 0 5200 8808 5.

Roberts, Diane. *The Myth of Aunt Jemima: White Women Representing Black Women*. Routledge. pp. 230. hb £35, pb £12.99. ISBN 0 4150 8247 1, 0 4150 4919 9.

Rosenbaum, S. P., ed. *Henry James: The Ambassadors*. Norton. £8.95. ISBN 0 3939 6314 4.

Rutman, Darrett B., and Anita H. Rutman. *Small Worlds, Large Questions: Explorations in Early American Social History, 1600–1850*. UPVirginia. pp. 316. hb £49.50, pb £16.50. ISBN 0 8139 1529 5, 0 8139 1530 9.

Sayre, Robert F., ed. *American Lives: An Anthology of Autobiographical Writing*. Wisconsin Studies in American Autobiography. UWiscP. pp. 732. hb £51.95, pb £19.95. ISBN 0 2991 4240 X, 0 2991 4244 2.

Scheick, William J. *The Ethos of Romance at the Turn of the Century*. UTexP. pp. 216. $30. ISBN 0 2927 7673 X .

Sedgwick, Ellery. *A History of the 'Atlantic Monthly', 1857–1909: Yankee Humanism at High Tide and Ebb.* UMassP. pp. 352. £38. ISBN 0 8702 3919 8.
Skaggs, Donald. *Roger Williams' Dream for America.* Lang (1993). pp. 240. £30. ISBN 0 8204 1870 6.
Skandera-Trombley, Laura E. *Mark Twain in the Company of Women.* UPennP. pp. xvi + 219. £28.50. ISBN 0 8122 3218 6.
Skrupskelis, Ignas K., and Elizabeth M. Berkeley, eds. *The Correspondence of William James. Vol. 3: William and Henry, 1897–1910* UPVirginia (1993). pp. 576. $45. ISBN 0 8139 1414 0.
Smith, Virginia Llewellyn. *Henry James and the Real Thing: A Modern Reader's Guide.* St Martin's. pp. xi + 247. £42.50. ISBN 0 3336 1139 X.
Springer, Haskell, ed. *America and the Sea: A Literary History.* UGeoP. pp. 414. $40. ISBN 0 8203 1651 2.
Wald, Priscilla. *Constituting Americans: Cultural Anxiety and Narrative Form.* DukeUP. pp. 390. £16.95. ISBN 0 8223 1547 5.
Wagner-Martin, Linda. *Telling Women's Lives: The New Biography.* RutgersUP. pp. 200. $22.95. ISBN 0 8135 2092 4.
Watts, Steven. *The Romance of Real Life: Charles Brockden Brown and the Origins of American Culture.* JHUP. pp. 246. £30. ISBN 0 8018 4686 2.
Weinstein, Cindy. *The Literature of Labor and the Labors of Literature.* CUP. pp. 268. £40. ISBN 0 5214 7054 4.
Williams, Linda Ruth. *Critical Desire: Psychoanalysis and the Literary Subject.* Arnold. pp. 212. £11.99. ISBN 0 3405 6816 X.

XVI

American Literature: The Twentieth Century

LIONEL KELLY, PAT RIGHELATO, HENRY CLARIDGE, DEBORAH PARSONS, PETER VERNON and STEVEN PRICE

This chapter has four sections: 1. Poetry; 2. Fiction 1900–45; 3. Fiction Since 1945; 4. Drama. Section 1 is by Lionel Kelly and Pat Righelato; section 2 is by Henry Claridge and Deborah Parsons; section 3 is by Peter Vernon; and section 4 is by Stephen Price.

1. Poetry

(a) General

This section covers books and journal articles published in 1993 and 1994. There are many fine studies to record for these two years, as will be seen, and it is a pity to have to start on a negative note, but the truth is that Amittai F. Aviram's *Telling Rhythm: Body and Meaning in Poetry* is one of the dullest books ever to have been published. Aviram draws on Nietzsche and Nietzschean psychoanalytic revisions by Freud, Lacan, Nicolas Abraham, Julia Kristeva and Philippe Lacoue-Labarthe, and argues that rhythm can make the physical world manifest with a power which is not in words, a sentiment to which the bosom of every poetry reader would return an echo. Aviram aims to address the problem of the decline of poetry, but in a heavily theory-laden argument some dull close readings are delivered, curiously immune to rhythm, so that his comments on Wallace Stevens's 'Sunday Morning' and Emily Dickinson's lyrics induced this reader to echo the latter's 'Had but the Tale a warbling Teller'.

As a woman poet educated in a tradition dominated by male poets Sharon Bryan invited other women poets to respond to a series of questions about their sense of their relationship to literary tradition, citing Eliot's 'Tradition and the Individual Talent' as an implied exercise in gender exclusion. The answers to her questions are gathered in the replies of twenty-three contemporary women poets in *Where We Stand: Women Poets On Literary Tradition.* Happily, I think, no gender-based conclusions emerge from these responses, though many of these poets express their sense of exclusion with a vigorous joviality which suggests that being on the outside is no bad thing, a sense that Emily Dickinson's cherished obliquity of vision is a good perspective to have, and one which increasingly constitutes a tradition of its own, a woman's tradition. At the same time Bryan's questions recall many of these writers to a specific historical urgency associated with the political, social and aesthetic enterprise of American feminist writing over the past three decades. Amy Clampitt, for example, records her failure with the editors of *Aphra* and other periodicals and acknowledges that the first person to hear her 'voice' was a male editor, and that she has been helped more by men than women over the years. And Clampitt takes up something of Dickinson's situation, when she argues that 'perhaps to be anomalous is finally inseparable from what makes a poet, of either sex?' Similarly, Alicia Ostriker persists in her admiration of the male tradition, exemplified for her by William Blake, without surrendering her prerogatives as a woman writer. This anthology is a remarkably peaceful document, persistently affirming an inclusive view of the act of writing, even as it rehearses the conditions of exclusion felt by many of these women, an exclusion they have, of course, overcome.

There is a paradox at the heart of Don Byrd's *The Poetics of Common Knowledge*, an encyclopaedic endeavour to engage with the condition of posteriority – a coming after the cultural edifices which brood over our late twentieth century ways of knowing ourselves and our world. The paradox is that Byrd is antagonistic to most system-building intellectual monuments which impose their authority on our consciousness: at the same time, he shows himself incapable of reading those signal instances of particularity which refuse these system-building imperatives as they are manifest in the practice of twentieth-century American poetry. Byrd begins with the confident proposal that he will challenge the dominant orthodoxies of Cartesian, Hegelian and Freudian abstractions – 'their simplistic representationalism, their implicit doctrines of force, their submissions of the individual to generalized, abstract formulations' – in favour of an account of *being* centred in the 'radical uniqueness' of individuals. For Descartes, Hegel and Freud, other trinities of authority may be substituted, such as Spinoza, Darwin and William James, or Locke, Hume and Whitehead, or Newton, Darwin and Farraday: or, from more recent examples, Derrida, whose work is seen as a late refinement of Enlightenment sentimentality, a figure whose carriage of personal authority 'removes him from the company of the common world', a writer whose texts 'can be read but not shared'. When he moves to those whose practice is poetry, Byrd shows himself an inept reader, strategically imputing obscurity to those texts he dislikes because they make no surrender to the common expectations of 'readability': thus, for Wallace Stevens, 'personal reality is permutative and statistical', and 'Sea Surface Full of Clouds' and 'The Man with the Blue Guitar' are mere anticipations of 'computer poetry'! Byrd admires the poetry of individuality and place, even where it appears recalcitrant to common experience and knowledge, and therefore advocates the poetry of William Carlos Williams and those who might be said to work in his tradition, which here would include Louis Zukofsky. When Byrd deploys bewilderment as a critical strategy his exploitation of perplexity can often be telling: on the other hand, this is a preposterously self-advertising book about a subject barely definable, with a resolution which denies the power of reason without fully articulating the contrary authority of intuition.

Those who were in a position to buy the books of poetry under the Wesleyan University Press imprints – Wesleyan New Poets, Wesleyan Poetry Program and Wesleyan Poets in Translation – over the past four decades would have an enviable collection. An anthology from these publications now appears edited by Michael

Collier, *The Wesleyan Tradition: Four Decades of American Poetry*, and reading through it decade by decade provides a perspective on literary tastes over this time. However, this collection is essentially about a press and its work, and the selection by decade gives an odd perspective on those poets who have gone far beyond their early work as represented here, such as Ashbery who gets five poems from *The Tennis Court Oath* of 1962. On the other hand it is useful to have this access to so many poets, especially for British readers who are least likely to have the original publications.

Robert M. Crunden's *American Salons: Encounters with European Modernism 1885–1917* covers some of the same ground as Steven Watson's *Strange Bedfellows: The First American Avant-garde* (*YWES* 72.462), but its leaden biographical and anecdotal narrative lacks any of Watson's verve and lucidity. Crunden's account is broader and is organized around cities (Philadelphia, New York, Chicago, Baltimore, Paris, Los Angeles) and familiar names such as the Arensbergs, Mabel Dodge Luhan, Stieglitz, Leo and Gertrude Stein. His literary judgements are of the following order: Henry James was a 'writer of books, not a man of critical theory', and Wallace Stevens 'gloried in the retinal and then used it as a deceptive surface that hid the depths of his own implicit nihilism'. The book brings together a good deal of information, but it is useful rather than enlightening.

Stephen Cushman's *Fictions of Form in American Poetry* argues two important issues arising from de Tocqueville's view of the absence of a national American literature in the 1830s and 1840s and his prescriptive forecasts of the forms that literature would take in due course, severed from classical and European models in matters of form and style. Against de Tocqueville, Cushman argues that American poets have been obsessed with the formal aspects of their art, investing these with 'tremendous significance' as they negotiate the conflict between innovation and tradition in matters of technique and style in response to the demands of a truly national literature. In addition, Cushman argues that these 'fictions of form' have led American poets to 'overestimate the synecdochic relationship between those formal aspects and various ideas of America' in relation to the 'general characteristics – social, economic, political, psychological – of democracy'. This ambitious study is most rewarding for Cushman's commentary on form in Whitman, Pound, Ammons, Dickinson and Bishop, a group of writers chosen for their heterodox formal practice, called on here to dispute the 'traditional taxonomic histories' which divide American poetry into a conflict between 'formalists' and non-formalists. Cushman redefines 'formalism' as a mastery of all the particulars of the elements which make poetry what it is – 'the nature of lineation, the presence or absence of meter and rhyme, the cooperation of sound and sense, syntactic and rhetorical patterns' – whether the poetic mode is traditional or not, and shows through a series of agile readings of individual poems how these five poets are all 'formalist' within the terms of his definition. This is an ambitious and rewarding study, though the argument about the imputed relationship between poetic form and American democracy really requires a book in itself.

The Dark End of the Street: Margins in American Vanguard Poetry by Maria Damon offers an eclectic version of *avant-garde* writing in American poetry of this century, in a book which deliberately subverts historical continuity in favour of the ruptures of linearity evidenced in the work of her chosen poets. Thus, positioning Gertrude Stein as the programmatic 'first' in this narrative, she is actually discussed in the final part of Damon's book after chapters on Bob

Kaufman, Robert Lowell and three 'unknown' teenage women writers in a South Boston Housing Project educational programme, and Robert Duncan with Jack Spicer. For Damon chronology is another index of the vertical praxis of the Great Chain of Being, which she reads as a 'metaphor . . . underlying most Western poetic texts up through the modernist mode', a trope of hierarchy she rejects in favour of 'postmodernism's return to the lateral and cofoundational'. Her chosen figure for this is the 'Street' of her title, 'which functions both as border of exclusion and of access, as a trope of circulation and as a dividing line. As an image of potential pluralism, it also works against an easy equation of different kinds of exclusion.' In addition, because the 'Street' itself is a 'devalued image' through its verbal association with the 'harsh exigencies of a border life', she uses it strategically in a book designed to 'valorize the devalued'. If Stein, Kaufman and the women of the South Boston project fit easily into this programme, the cases of Lowell and Duncan are surely more problematic. Damon justifies Lowell's inclusion because of the 'new terrain' explored in *Life Studies* and *For the Union Dead*, and Duncan's because his experimental poetics is taken to 'represent the constitution of a poetic community within the gay subculture of the 1950s and 1960s', mediating the 'problems of community and isolation, physicality and spirituality, democracy and the self-protective elitism of a cultural ghetto'. This is a remarkable book, passionate in argument and wide-ranging in focus, but it suffers from a vocabulary which persistently seeks to register every notation of the 'either–or' dichotomy endemic to debates about the inside–outside, mainstream–vanguard, centre–margin paradigms of cultural theory.

Leonard Diepeveen's study of the use of quotation in modern poetry – as opposed to allusion, intertextuality, and borrowing – is an original exploration which makes his *Changing Voices: The Modern Quoting Poem* a welcome addition to the study of modernist poetics. In his preface Diepeveen identifies his concern with the properties of 'exactness' involved in the use of quotation as distinct from the variousness of reference entailed in allusion, for if allusion exploits potentiality, quotation's power lies in its specificity. This serves to disrupt its parent body and radically changes the way we read the poem in which quotation is a component, introducing what Pound called 'planes of relation' into the construct of the poem, which works against its linear development and imperils the enterprise of a 'perfectly stable' unifying structure. Furthermore, quotation impedes the utterance of lyric subjectivity in its muffling of personal expression, extending the vocal range of a poem to a point slightly out of reach of the intelligence which drives it. Diepeveen's central analyses deal with T. S. Eliot, Ezra Pound, Marianne Moore and E. E. Cummings, and ends with a rather cursory conclusion which briefly looks at *Paterson*, Adrienne Rich, John Ashbery and the Language poets. On Eliot and Pound Diepeveen's commentary is least innovative, reminding us of Pound's use of quotation as an instrument for incorporating history into the *Cantos*, and of Eliot's enactment of the struggle between the lyric and the dramatic, though *en route*, the notion that 'finding and losing' denotes the crucial timbre of voice in *The Waste Land* is provocative. He is at his best on the relationship between polyphony and authorial power in Marianne Moore, a fertile reading of one of the most adroit users of quotation as a strategy of discovery and hesitancy in modernist poetics.

In *The Wicked Sisters*, Betsy Erkkila writes on Emily Dickinson, Marianne Moore, Elizabeth Bishop, Adrienne Rich and Gwendolyn Brooks: her subtitle is *Women Poets, Literary History, and Discord*, where 'discord' marks the creative relations between these women poets in this version of literary history, for the terms of engagement between women writers are seen as a 'site of dissension, contingency, and ongoing struggle'. In the case of Dickinson, the dynamics of intimacy with and difference from other women and women writers is explored through her social relations and her reading. Erkkila takes the increasingly common view of Sue Gilbert as central to Dickinson's emotional and creative life and sees this relationship, along with the sisterly intimacy of other women friends and correspondents, as providing the bonds which enabled Dickinson's resistance to patriarchy and her refusal of publication: at the same time her response to published women writers is debated through the ways in which Dickinson's reading of affinities and rivalries with others is enacted in the poems. On Marianne Moore and Elizabeth Bishop, Erkkila finds discord where others have found a less ruffled creative sympathy, and she sees Bishop's poetry of homoerotic desire as a challenge to Moore's aesthetic morality. The arc of Rich's career is read through the evolution of her responses to Dickinson, whose historical priority as a poet, woman and sister provokes the profound changes in Rich's ways of articulating her own situation as a woman poet. On Gwendolyn Brooks, Erkkila reads a conflict between the early poetry, which defines her as a black woman poet, and the later work, which responds to the essentially male project of a 'separatist poetics' to speak for the African-American community. This provocative study radically challenges the idealization of women writers in much feminist scholarship, and offers an alternative literary history to the kinds most commonly on offer.

In 1983 Stephen Fredman published a much admired study of prose written as poetry by American poets, *Poet's Prose* (*YWES* 71.565), a work notable in particular for the thoroughness of his analysis of Ashbery's *Three Poems*. In his latest book, *The Grounding of American Poetry*, Fredman returns to his preoccupation with the prose writings of American poets to explore an argument about tradition and innovation in American poetry since Emerson, organized around the concept of 'grounding', defined here as 'assuming the work of tradition' by conceptualizing its possibility within the conditions of its absence. This is a version of American exceptionalism as it applies to poetics and aesthetics, and Fredman's study is adjacent in its interests to Stephen Cushman's *Fictions of Form* (see above). However, where Cushman argues that American poetry is over-theorized in its search for a substitute traditionalism, Fredman sees such theorizing as the necessary prolegomena to the poetry itself, and uses the prose writings of his elected poets as the material 'bulwarks' which support the enterprise of their poems, 'staging' or creating the contexts in which their work can be seen and understood. The implicit argument from American exceptionalism is vulnerable here, because the scenario Fredman pictures has its antecedents in British poetry, and no doubt in most other national literatures, as new poets seek to clear a space for themselves in spite of the traditions they inherit. The nub of the matter Fredman confronts seems to have its origins in a paradox bequeathed by Emerson, for if his essays underwrite a belief in spiritual individualism, in 'The Poet', he anticipates the poet who will speak not of himself, but of his 'Commonwealth', and this negotiation of a voice which mediates between self and commonwealth seems to be at the heart of all the material Fredman, like Cushman, brings to our notice. In this study the prose writings and poetry of Charles Olson form the centre-piece of Fredman's argument, in which Olson's enterprise is read within a frame provided by Thoreau's *Walden*: later chapters read Robert Duncan in similar relation to Emerson, and Robert Creeley in relation to Whitman, following an opening chapter on the somewhat obligatory distinctions between Eliot's 'traditionalism' and William

Carlos Williams's 'localism'. The governing argument about 'grounding', and its subsequent refinements as Fredman develops this notion, are considerably less impressive than the detailed analyses of the relationship between theory and practice which this book offers. And I am not at all sure that Olson or Duncan would be pleased to find themselves caught in this exceptionalist framework: surely, for them, the local and particular were indicative not exemplary conditions, signs of the universal rather than the exceptional.

Mick Gidley's *Modern American Culture* is designed for students of American studies and for the general reader, and has essays by some notable British Americanists (Stephen Fender, Martin Crawford, Douglas Tallack, Robert Lawson-Peebles, David Murray and Richard H. King). Murray's essay on 'Poetry and Poetics' addresses the varieties of American poetry and elects to dwell on the line of Whitman and modernist reactions to it, where his entry is through Whitman's voicing of a 'primordial sense of self' as superior to the spatial and temporal limitations of the sense of 'social self', particularly since this primordial self becomes the agency of 'a critical and political resource' in relation to the idea of America itself 'as an inclusive and utopian project'. Murray's all-too-brief pages on Whitman's inclusive poetics and epic intentions lead into abbreviated commentaries on early Pound, William Carlos Williams and Objectivism, the long poem in Pound, Crane and Williams, Charles Olson, Robert Duncan and Denis Levertov, and a final section on Stevens and Ashbery.

James A. W. Heffernan in *Museum of Words: The Poetics of Ekphrasis from Homer to Ashbery* is concerned with the verbal representation, 'the dynamic and obstetric' delivery from the 'pregnant moment of visual art in its embryonically narrative impulse', and, following W. J. T. Mitchell, traces the paragonal impulse, the struggle for dominance between word and image in texts selected from a long chronological sweep. The fourth chapter, 'Modern and Postmodern Ekphrasis', is of particular interest to readers of this section: it brings into play Derridean notions of ergon and parerga. arguing that whereas the passages in Homer's *Iliad* about Achilles's shield might be considered marginalized adornment to the epic text, William Carlos Williams's Breughel poems represent silent compositions by telling us how 'the eye of the art-book-reading museum-goer wanders through them'. John Ashbery's 'Self Portrait in a Convex Mirror' takes the process further by advertising its ekphrastic sources and making explicit the implication of ekphrasis, the pressure of the experience of the viewer in his or her interpretation of the work of art. Heffernan provides detailed readings of these poems and an extensive bibliography on the topic.

Daniel Hoffman's *Words to Create a World* comes in the excellent Poets on Poetry series and gives a selection of Hoffman's essays and reviews. The collection is framed by two essays on the *avant-garde* and its relation to tradition, the first using Alfred Kreymborg's 1916 anthology *Others* as an instrumental text (because Kreymborg's choice went beyond the contemporary fashion for imagism and included a catholic range of poetic forms), the second debating with varieties of contemporary practice over the past decade in the ongoing conflict between formalism and its alternatives. Hoffman's position seems to be one of cautious tolerance for experiment, but it is what he calls the 'felt continuities' of experience and tradition which command his greatest respect. In these two pieces and in the many reviews included Hoffman shows himself as a versatile and responsible critic.

Paul Hoover's anthology of *Postmodern American Poetry* for Norton is a very welcome addition to Norton's list and makes available in this convenient format a wide range of poets from Charles Olson to Diane Ward. Hoover works with the simplest definition of the 'postmodern', here defined as the 'historical period following World War II'. It represents the experimental practices of post-war American poetry from 'the oral poetics of Beat and performance poetries to the more "writerly" work of the New York School and language poetry'. Used in this way 'postmodern' and 'experimental' are both generous terms of inclusion, but also, inevitably, oddly exclusive in view of the poets of this period who are not represented here, such as Elizabeth Bishop, John Berryman, Robert Lowell, W. S. Merwin, Sylvia Plath and Rita Dove, for example. Apart from these contestable omissions – do Berryman's *Dream Songs* fail the 'experimental' test? – Hoover gives a good sampling of writers in the post-Poundian tradition, with Olson, Creeley, Dorn, Duncan, Mac Low and so on, through to more recent poets from the varieties of ethnic literatures, the Language poets, and other contemporaries. An especially useful feature of this anthology is the closing section, which gives extracts from statements of poetics by many of these poets, including Olson's 'Projective Verse', O'Hara's 'Personism', Amiri Baraka's 'How You Sound??', Ron Silliman's 'Of Theory, To Practice', and Victor Hernandez Cruz's 'Mountains in the North: Hispanic Writing in the U.S.A'.

Walter Kalaidjian's *American Culture Between the Wars* is in part a complex study of the radical tradition of cultural production in the domain of popular culture and socialist politics found in American little magazines between the wars, such as *The Masses* and its successor *New Masses*, *Liberator*, *Partisan Review*, the magazines of the Harlem Renaissance, and a variety of other ephemeral publications. The familiar aspect of this project is in Kalaidjian's explicit challenge to the canonical version of high modernism developed in the academy over the past forty years, which has 'largely silenced the century's complex and contentious social context', reducing the scene of twentieth-century cultural production in the United States to an 'incredibly narrow focus on a select group of seminal careers', and in this agenda Kalaidjian's work follows on Cary Nelson's *Repression and Recovery* (*YWES* 70.615–16). Whilst Kalaidjian's initial gaze is on what he calls the 'historical avant-garde', the 'formalist and politicized aesthetic schools and movements that once flourished between the world wars', he adds a further dimension to this study in his desire to read this historical *avant-garde* through the instruments and ideologies of postmodern cultural pluralism, and vice versa, a critical 'crossing' which promises a 'postindividualistic solidarity among sexual, racial, class, and ethnic subject positions, at once formally sophisticated and critically responsive to America's cultural diversity'. This ambitious programme explains why Kalaidjian moves, for example, from the historical *avant-garde* to the 'Guerilla Aesthetics' of Diego Rivera, Muriel Rukeyser's 'Book of the Dead', Kenneth Fearing's poetry, the Language poets, and the oppositional art of Hans Haacke, to name only those most prominently discussed in this book. The common link in this dazzling array of literary and visual texts is one version or another of the art of protest, against the institutions of high culture, of corporate power, of government, or of all these together.

Poetics of the Feminine: Authority and Literary Tradition in William Carlos Williams, Mina Loy, Denise Levertov and Kathleen Fraser is a revisionary feminist study of modernism which then seeks a 'maternal' line through to Kathleen Fraser. Linda A. Kinnahan traces the stimulus of Loy's 'Love songs I–IV' in the first issue of the *avant-garde* journal, *Others*, for Williams's early expression of the interplay between erotic sexuality and gendered authority. She argues that the alignment with a feminine poetics is an important element in Williams's opposition to the classical model of modernism offered by Pound and Eliot. Surprisingly, Marianne Moore is only briefly touched upon (and in a later chapter), although Kinnahan states that she 'stands explicitly as his poetic model'. Moore certainly complicates Williams's negotiation with feminine poetics, but our understanding of it is surely incomplete without her considerable revision of what it might entail. The second half of the book amply demonstrates that Levertov and Fraser continue to develop a feminine poetics but is less effective in establishing, for example, that Fraser's 'recasting of modernism' is a useful strategy for rereading *Spring and All.*

New moralism is in evidence in Mary Kinzie's *The Cure of Poetry in an Age of Prose: Moral Essays on the Poet's Calling*. The poet is, in fact, recalled to soul-making and redemptive tasks and reprimanded both for 'prosaism' and for the 'rhapsodic fallacy', which 'nourishes such aimlessness, such provisionality, such nonsense'. Yet if Kinzie is eager, in Ashberyan phrase, 'to praise this, blame that', she is also, in these nine essays revised from journals, engaged with the issue of the invasion of the poem by prose in contemporary verse and with the poet's struggle to restore language to its 'aboriginality'. There is, for example, a long chapter on Ashbery's poem 'Houseboat Days', a linguistic analysis of how it is and is not like Henry James's prose in the ultimate destination of its grammatical shifts. A detailed analysis of Lowell's 'Waking Early on Sunday Morning' reveals Kinzie's didactic energy, like Jacob with the Angel, wrestling productively with the poem. Other essays are on Louise Bogan and Theodore Roethke, Howard Nemerov, Randall Jarrell and Elizabeth Bishop. Working much the same ground as Shetley (see below) in diagnosing ills and prescribing cures, Kinzie is more diffuse and haphazard in overall direction.

Nathaniel Mackey explains the title of his book *Discrepant Engagement: Dissonance, Cross-Culturality, and Experimental Writing* as an expression that signifies the 'imperfect fit between word and world' and reminds us of the root meaning of *discrepant* – 'to rattle, creak': Mackey reads it as signifying a primal noise, the 'noise upon which the word is based'. In a political frame 'discrepant engagement sings "base", refuses to be drowned out, and thus becomes the means by which the excluded, the voiceless, the unheard may challenge the social positings of identity and meaning'. Mackey's study is about the oppositional writing of black writers from the United States and the Caribbean, and the Black Mountain poets, a cross-cultural mix of writers whose distance from the cultural norm, either by exclusion or by dissent, underlies their experimental practice and their 'valorization of dissonance, divergence, and formal disruption'. Amiri Baraka is a crucial figure in this study, a 'bridge figure' as Mackey calls him, the only black writer associated with the Black Mountain group and the only black writer included in Donald Allen's *The New American Poetry: 1945–1960*. Furthermore, Baraka has 'long held black music to be a relevant model for a truly black writing, for a truly American writing', and this perspective is ably developed by Mackey in the uses he makes of black music in this book, especially in the chapter on Baraka's poetry and the later chapter on 'Sound and Sentiment, Sound and Symbol'. This draws on the work of the musician and anthropologist Steven Feld, whose own *Sound and Sentiment* is dedicated to the memory of Charlie Parker, John Coltrane and Charles Mingus, and Victor Zuckerkandl's *Sound and Symbol*, in which Zuckerkandl attempts 'a critique of our concept of reality from the point of view of music'. Mackey's discussion of the Black Mountain poets includes an account of Charles Olson's celebration of the typewriter as a technology which gave the poet an instrument of composition akin to the musician's 'stave and bar'. The other writers discussed include Clarence Major, Robert Duncan, Robert Creeley, Edward Kamau Brathwaite and Wilson Harris, and this excellent study succeeds in expanding the frame of 'oppositional' writing as it is commonly pictured.

The eighteen essays on the differences between twentieth-century British and American writing, edited by Ann Massa and Alistair Stead under the 'allusive' and 'a little playful' title of *Forked Tongues?,* contains several contributions relevant to this section. Mark Jarman pursues the 'Americanness' of Pound and Eliot beyond the defining image formulated by Louis MacNeice, that they were 'first and foremost American tourists' who wished to shake off the vulgarity of America 'to become European, cosmopolitan'. Jarman writes on the ideas and conditions which describe their Americanness for him, and its effect on their poetry, itemized as their iconoclasm, their desire for unity or syncretism, their anti-Semitism, and the influence of their American childhood on them, in an essay notable for its generous view of the American idealism at the heart of Pound's search for a perfect society, and Eliot's belief in a transcendent religious reality. William A. Johnson writes a brief comparative study of Robert Bly, John Silkin, Geoffrey Hill and Seamus Heaney, to show how Bly's confrontation with what Johnson calls 'collective violence' on the international and national scene took him away from his 'profoundly isolated and private' early work into a 'horizon of cultural politics' that 'has not been attainable by English poets since the thirties'. In reading these poets Johnson looks for a poetry of engagement which avoids 'the mirror-popularities of resistance and consent', a site where poetry's contact with sectarian positions becomes an enabling critical reflection on collective violence without assuming a position superior to it. Finally, the late Eric Mottram writes on 'American Poetry and the British Poetry Revival 1960–75', recalling the context and outcome of two mid-1970s conferences on this topic in London.

In *The Regenerate Lyric: Theology and Innovation in American Poetry*, Elisa New repudiates the view that much canonical American poetry has Emerson as its source: her counter-argument is to insist on the Calvinist inheritance of those poets familiarly identified as writing within the Emersonian tradition, such as Whitman, Frost, Stevens, Crane and Lowell, who all wrote poems 'fruitfully exercised by all those appurtenances of the Logos Emerson foreswore: purity and the Incarnation, idolatry and God's unnameability; awe, dread, and the lure of the Nations; sin, Doom and the Fortunate Fall'. New's argument with Emerson is to dispute the grounds of his idealizing of the figure of the poet into an oracular speaker of transcendental truths, and to propose that the achievements of his successors were founded upon an awareness of human limitation, sin and divine ineffability. Frost and Lowell would seem to fit easily enough into this programme but the cases of Whitman and Stevens are surely more problematic. Indeed, New argues that Stevens was 'most the heir to Emerson' and developed an Emersonian poetics to its logical end, an hypothesis verifiable for New in her view of Stevens's work as guilty of an 'elision of the person', an 'a-personalism' which 'dramatizes the consequences implicit in rejecting the patrimony of Adam'. Such an argument will not persuade those who take pleasure in Stevens precisely because of his 'a-personalism', his power to abstract into imaginary figures the human crises of longing, desire and despair. And it does seem as though New's version of Emerson is unequal to the later development of his work, as though the optimism of the early essays represents the whole of his case. None the less, this is an engrossing revisionary study, and New has much to show us of the sustaining power of the vocabulary of religious and theological doctrine as it inhabits the work of these poets.

Robert Pack and Jay Parini have combined in an anthology of contemporary American 'nature' poetry in *Poems for a Small Planet*, in this addition to the Bread Loaf series of anthologies. This collection gives us some 250 poems by 83 poets including A. R. Ammons, Wendell Berry, Amy Clampitt, Rita Dove, Robert Pinsky, Gary Snyder, Richard Wilbur and Nancy Willard. Anthology making is a pleasurable business and it can be carried on under virtually any pretext, but one would expect the occasion for a collection such as this to have a more vigorous defence than Parini allows himself in a very brief introduction; this task is left to his co-editor Robert Pack in a more extensive 'afterword', which seeks to place these contemporary nature poems within the long tradition of nature poetry in Western culture. The vague appeal to contemporary ecological and environmental anxieties used as the formative principle of this anthology does little to militate against the sense that this compilation is an exercise in book making.

The *Columbia History of American Poetry* edited by Jay Parini and Brett C. Millier devotes three-quarters of its eight hundred pages of critical commentary to the poetry of this century, ranging from Jeanne Larsen's account of five early twentieth-century women poets (Amy Lowell, Sara Teasdale, Elinor Wylie, Edna St Millay and Louise Bogan) to the concluding chapter by Edward Hirsch on the visionary poetics of Philip Levine and Charles Wright. There is more than a hint of political correctness, both in the structure of this book and in individual chapters, in the way in which women poets and poets of other than Euro-American origins are foregrounded at the expense of some familiar names, and through the relative attention given to particular poets. For example, Lynn Keller's chapter on 'The Twentieth-Century Long Poem' identifies three categories of long poem as a way of dealing with the multiplicity of this kind, though these categories exist in a rather arbitrary relationship to each other: the first is conceptual and dwells on the collage-based texts of the early to later phases of modernism; the second is chronological, covering poets born between 1910 and 1930; and the third examines some long poems of the seventies and eighties, 'an era in which poetic decentralization and pluralization render text selection particularly difficult'. Within this frame Keller manages at least to name almost every long poem of substance in this century but too often she has little space to tell us much about them. Zukofsky's 'A' and Williams's *Paterson* are disposed of in one or two short paragraphs, a treatment on the same scale as her account of Melvin B. Tolson's long poems, and whilst one must admire the egalitarian motives of this editorial practice, the critical commentary on these very complex works becomes sparse to the point of poverty.

Elsewhere in this volume Marianne Moore features both in Margaret Dickie's revisionary reading of 'Women Poets and the Emergence of Modernism' – a chapter notable for Dickie's attention to Gertrude Stein and H. D. within the frame of early modernism – and also in Jeredith Merrin's chapter on 'Marianne Moore and Elizabeth Bishop'. This relative level of repetition and overlapping – Whitman has a chapter to himself and also features briefly in Keller's chapter on the long poem, and Pound not only has a chapter on his imagist aesthetics but features prominently in two other chapters – is at the cost of certain exclusions. For example, there is very little on Edwin Arlington Robinson, W. S. Merwin or Rita Dove, and no chapter on the Language poets, though Ron Silliman, Charles Bernstein and Lyn Hejinian are cited briefly in a number of chapters. British readers will be gently surprised to find W. H. Auden here appropriated as a New York poet, whilst that native New Yorker Frank O'Hara is ignored, beyond naming him as one of Ashbery's early compatriots in the New York School. However, it must be said that Claude J. Summers's account of what he calls 'American Auden' is an exemplary performance, and fully justifies this reading of Auden in an American context. Similarly, W. S. Di Piero's brilliant short account of the 'Public Music' of Pound's *Cantos* and George Oppen's poetry accomplishes a difficult task with great skill, in a stylish commentary on Pound and Oppen's working of the essential relationship between the political order and the poetic imagination. Patricia Wallace's account of Robert Penn Warren, John Crowe Ransom and Allen Tate manages an impressive completeness within the small frame allowed her, and John Shoptaw's authoritative essay on James Merrill and John Ashbery will do much to make these poets accessible to new readers.

There is something of a revisionary enterprise about the whole of this volume, an endeavour to read three centuries of American poetry from new perspectives and with new insights, as in Dana Gioia's astute essay on Longfellow in relation to the aesthetic of modernism. Finally, there is a curious, unexplained, ahistorical disruption of conventional chronology throughout the book. For example, the chapter on Dickinson precedes that on Whitman, and that on Poe (whose dates incidentally are given as 1809–1949), whilst Elizabeth Bishop (because yoked to Marianne Moore) precedes Stevens, William Carlos Williams, Hart Crane, the Harlem Renaissance, and so on. Perhaps these idiosyncracies of placing are of no great importance, but they give a peculiar look to this particular history.

In the Shadow of Parnassus: Zoe Akins's Essays on American Poetry, edited by Catherine N. Parkes, comprises twenty-three articles which came out between February and August 1915 in the weekly *Reedy's Mirror*. Written before her career as a dramatist took off, the essays exemplify Akins as a self-styled new woman commenting with a distinctive verve upon a new generation of poets. The collection includes her responses to Amy Lowell, Sara Teasdale, Ezra Pound and, in the eleventh article (7 May, 1915), a comparative review of Robert Frost's *North of Boston* and Edgar Lee Master's *Spoon River Anthology*. Parkes provides a detailed introduction to each article.

In the exchanges about poetry between William Carlos Williams and Louis Zukofsky there came a moment when Williams, despite his profound admiration for the other's work, admitted that he found some of Zukofsky's poems to be 'a dangerous sort of writing' that 'makes too often no sense'. Marnie Parsons does not cite this moment in her book *Touch Monkeys: Nonsense Strategies For Reading Twentieth-Century Poetry,* but she might have done, for Zukofsky features prominently in this absorbing study. Parsons's primary title seems to come from an injunction in the Talking Heads film *Stop Making Sense*, which in turn derives from the *Bandar-log* or Monkey Folk of Kipling's *The Jungle Book*, creatures who 'have no speech of their own, but use the stolen words which they overhear when they listen, and peep, and wait up above in the branches'. However, as we all know, nonsense, like stolen words, is a serious matter, and Parsons relates these beasts and their impish activities to Julia Kristeva's *Language: The Unknown*, with its citing of the invention of writing and language by the Egyptian god Thoth, and the legend that scribes were represented as writing 'while squatting in front of an image of Thoth's sacred animal, the baboon'. Thus for Parsons, the 'lawless, playful, and ultimately destructive' Monkey-Folk are 'animate versions of Kristeva's idiosyncratic "semiotic"'. When I add that this book naturally opens with the Mad Hatter's Tea Party from *Alice's Adventures in Wonderland*, and makes appropriate gestures to Mervyn Peake, Monty Python, John Lennon and others, something of its range is suggested: however, Parson's longest address is to the theorizing of nonsense by Kristeva and Gilles Deleuze, and its practice in Charles Olson, Charles Bernstein, Ron Silliman, Steve McCaffery, Louis Zukofsky, Lyn Hejinian, Daphne Marlatt and others. It is a dazzling read, a bravura performance which leaves one with a decided antipathy to 'sense'.

The notion of 'genius' seems an unpromising topic in the current climate of literary debate, yet Bob Perelman overturns this apparent disadvantage in his absorbing study *The Trouble with Genius: Reading Pound, Joyce, Stein, and Zukofsky*. Perelman's interest is in the conflict between the social reach of the work of these four writers and its inherent difficulty for the reader, and for other writers, difficulties which follow from the technical and formal innovations in this body of poetry and fiction. Perelman nicely cites the contrary case of Dickens, 'where criticism disturbs the consumable clarity of the surface to reveal additional meaning beneath', whereas with these four writers 'unreadability is the raw material that is turned into the finished product of significance, which then gives the works their social importance', from which 'an aura of illegible authority surrounds the modernist genius, offering a lure for endless study': they have achieved the status of 'post-Arnoldian' touchstones of 'embodied critical value'. Perelman's subsequent readings of each writer pursue the ways in which the communal reach of their work is meshed in with the innovative forms and practices that makes the reading of them so exacting: his chapter on Pound is especially good, urging poetry's debt to Pound for the ways in which his language 'presents a charged image of speed and lucidity', even if what it illuminates 'is always accompanied by a phobic shadow'. Joyce's unwillingness to let *Ulysses* stand by itself in his subsequent 'passion for explanation' is related to the 'antipathy of modernist genius to linear, social plot' in favour of circularity, and as evidenced in Zukofsky's 'A' through the method of musical recurrence. If for Perelman the promise of a humane social vision is insufficiently achieved in the work of these writers, he ends by advocating a balanced view of them, 'neither dismissive nor monumentalizing'. This excellent book makes the case for and against them with commendable vigour and clarity.

Jahan Ramazani's *Poetry of Mourning: The Modern Elegy from Hardy to Heaney* is of great interest to Americanists. Chapter 3, devoted to Wallace Stevens, is a subtle account of the mock-elegies of *Harmonium*, the war elegies and the final self-elegies of *The Rock*, arguing that 'Stevens helps us to divulge an intense but covert dialogue between modernist poets and elegiac tradition.' Chapter 4 is on Langston Hughes, the 'African-American elegy' and the Blues; chapter 6, 'American Family Elegy I', is devoted to Lowell, Berryman, Ginsberg and Harper; chapter 7 on Sylvia Plath argues that she attacks the dead, the elegiac tradition and herself more persistently than any other poet and that her self-elegies expose the confessional mode; chapter 8, 'American Family Elegy II', is on Anne Sexton, Adrienne Rich and Amy Clampitt. Ramazani's 'critical narrative of psychohistorical change' in the elegiac genre is a work of sensibility, always acute in the readings of individual poems, yet extensive in range, providing a valuable book on modern poetry.

For Nathan A. Scott Jr, 'poetic vision' provides the refutation of deconstruction's ideology, replacing its erasure of 'presence' and the absolute of its 'nothing' beyond language. Citing the French Catholic philosopher Gabriel Marcel, Scott defines 'presence' as a loving of 'the concrete, the particular, the individual', a recognition of what is beyond the self in the acknowledgement of what is other, the '*Thou*' of things, which signals and ignites reciprocity. Scott, a professor of religious studies and of English, moves from these reflections to an account of the central tradition of American poetry in this century as he reads it in *Visions of Presence in Modern American Poetry*, with chapters on Wallace Stevens, W. H. Auden, Theodore Roethke, Elizabeth Bishop, Robert Penn Warren, Richard Wilbur, A. R. Ammons, James Wright and Howard Nemerov, who in various ways maintain the tradition of the American sublime, and whose work has a sacramental drive. With due respect, this is the sort of book which marks the generational divide between scholars of an older humanist tradition and those nurtured in the differently exacting practices of European theory over the last thirty years. Scott's intentions are to restore poetry to us and to give to contemporary consciousness an 'intimacy of relationship with reality' through this restoration. These admirable ambitions are supported by intelligent commentaries on most of his chosen poets, though his denial of Bishop's value – 'She intends to receive the world sacramentally . . . though being without myth or religious commitment, hers is a sacrament without warrant or justification' – may be taken as indicative of his commitment to a white male canon.

After the Death of Poetry: Poet and Audience in Contemporary America is a lucid, witty, toughly argued book whose author, Venon Shetley, is not afraid of the personal note and tests his claims through close readings of individual poems. He explains, with admirable cogency, why contemporary poetry in America has lost its readers and he offers prescriptions to enable it to regain cultural vitality. He takes up the issue of 'difficulty' and 'common readers', who 'seem to have been driven ever closer to extinction . . . last sighted in large numbers . . . refreshing themselves in the New England landscapes of Robert Frost'. Poetry, according to Shetley, has divided into two camps: lyricism and lucidity. Whereas New Formalists rely on conventional form as a kind of 'natural magic' (Shetley notes that both *Beowulf* and rap songs are written in a four-stress accentual line, but the former is unlikely to gain the broad popular appeal of the latter), Language poets, in seeking 'unreadability' are too cerebral in their demands. The solution is neither of these polarities; neither is it to abandon difficulty. Only poets such as Bishop, Merrill and Ashbery (there is an excellent chapter on each one), who have disavowed the heroic attitudes of modernism and have subjected their imaginative stances to genuine questioning by the sceptical consciousness, who have the ability to mix free and fixed forms and (incidentally, via their homosexuality) to express an opacity and enlargement of sympathy, are sufficiently tough *and* tender-minded to create a way forward. The last chapter, 'Directions for Poetry', considers some contemporary poets who have the 'resistant individuality' to combine lyric apprehension with tough-mindedness. Shetley sounds the new mid-nineties note of jargon-free, theoretically clarified, moral renewal, aware that critics need to regain readers too.

John Taggart takes the title of his collection of eighteen essays on contemporary poetry and poetics, *Songs of Degrees*, from Louis Zukofsky's series of seven short Valentine poems gathered under this title, fit tribute from the younger poet-theorist, as he is called, to his dominant creative mentor, Zukofsky. This borrowing of Zukofsky's title identifies Taggart as a writer within the Objectivist 'tradition', if there be such a thing, one whose critical practice grows outward from his reading of the poems before him and not from a pre-existing method, or ideology, or critical circuit of thought. Thus, in her introduction to these essays, Marjorie Perloff distinguishes Taggart as a 'poet-theorist', unlike his predecessors such as Robert Lowell, Robert Duncan and Robert Creeley, 'poet-critics' 'who regarded the production of critical essays as a kind of left-handed activity, a holiday from their "real" poetic vocation'. It is almost certainly pointless to argue with such discriminations, though Creeley, it should be remembered, brings the skills and responsibilities of textual scholarship to bear on his recent selection of Olson's poems, and one would not normally think of Lowell or Duncan as casual in their critical practice. If the description of the 'poet-theorist' smacks of contemporary fashionableness, Perloff's deeper argument is that Taggart's writing on poetry and poetics is about poetry as spiritual value, and his method one which cleaves as close as possible to the verbal, syntactic and structural particulars of the work he addresses. Such practice is everywhere apparent in these instructive essays on Zukofsky, Oppen, William Bronk, Bruce Andrews, Susan Howe, Robert Duncan, Charles Olson and Theodore Enslin. Thus, Taggart's claim in the centre-point essay, 'Louis Zukofsky: Songs of Degrees', that his endeavour is both to give a reading of this complex suite of poems and to offer 'something of an introduction to the poetics and poetry of Louis Zukofsky', is fully justified in the ways he moves from the short suite of poems into 'A', and the powerful relation in Zukofsky's work between poetry and music. It is a pleasure to have this collection of intelligent, articulate essays, responding to the variety of one strain of contemporary American poetry and poetics. I note here two recent articles on Susan Howe, Ming-Qian Ma's 'Poetry as History Revised: Susan Howe's "Scattering as Behaviour toward Risk"' (*AmLH* 6.716–37), and Bin Ramke's '"Between Ourself and the Story": On Susan Howe' (*DQ* 28.89–96).

Milton Teichman and Sharon Leder's *Truth and Lamentation*, a new anthology of writing on the Holocaust, make clear their omission of Sylvia Plath from this collection on the grounds that 'Daddy' and 'Lady Lazarus' do not 'treat the Holocaust as their central subject' but use Holocaust imagery as 'metaphors for internal horror and female victimization'. Perhaps so, but this decision further problematizes the relationship of all writing on this subject, as Milton Teichman and Sharon Leder acknowledge in their introduction when they admit that many believe that all artistic responses to the Holocaust are inadequate, even untenable. It remains difficult to see why Plath's imagery does not bear witness in its own way if we compare her poems to some included here, such as Louis Simpson's 'A Story About Chicken Soup', if only because Simpson's poem openly addresses the impossible dilemma between bearing witness and going on. Teichman and Leder order their introduction around a series of topics such as 'Historical Truth-telling', 'Psychological Truth-telling', 'How to Live in the Aftermath', and so on, categories which seem neither exclusive of each other nor clinical enough to define the parameters of the imaginative response to the Holocaust, if indeed it is a possible project. American poets included in this anthology are Richard Fein, Irving Feldman, Jacob Glatstein, Anthony Hecht, William Heyen, Randall Jarrell, Cynthia Ozick, Marge Piercy, Charles Reznikoff, Adrienne Rich, May Sarton, Anne Sexton, W. D. Snodgrass, Ruth Whitman and C. K. Williams. Of the many European writers included, the most notable are Giorgio Bassani, Paul Celan, Primo Levi and Czeslaw Milosz. The book includes a useful bibliography of Holocaust literature.

Introducing a Penguin anthology of verse translations, George Steiner proposed that without translation we would live 'in ignorant parishes, bordered by silence', an eloquent affirmation of our need to hear the literatures of other peoples. But of course the problem has always been, what is it that we read when we read translations? How many of Pound's contemporaries thought they were hearing a Chinese voice in his *Cathay* poems of 1915? And we know the fate of his *Homage to Sextus Propertius* at the hands of his academic critics when it first appeared. For Pound, who knew some other languages, if not Chinese, in 1915, as for Robert Lowell and others later, the concept of the 'imitation' proved a fertile strategy. Wai-Lim Yip, who published a study of Pound's *Cathay* versions in 1969, and is an authority on Chinese verse modes and genres, returns to the representation of China and its literature in the Western world (in English) in *Diffusion of Distances: Dialogues Between Chinese and Western Poetics*. In part an idealist agenda for an integrative poetics in place of the 'dominant–marginal' paradigm of cultural appropriation and misrepresentation which he reads in the West's 'treacherous representation of the OTHER', this book is most valuable for Yip's commentary on Chinese poetry and theories of reading, illuminating Chinese cultural differences in the composition and reception of poetry which seem to anticipate a variety of modernist and postmodern practices in the West. Yip tells us that the poem in Chinese is not a unitary entity but an intertextual, interlinear polyphony, comprised of many other poems and voices, replete with a system of internal and external correspondences, and his central chapter on this topic is full of illuminating evidence of how Chinese poets composed their work and how their readers and scholars responded to it. Inevitably, Yip's investigation of the acts of translation and the attempts at writing in a Chinese mode by modern American poets shows him most sympathetic to the innovative aesthetics of Pound, Williams, Olson and their successors, whose openness to formal experiment he reads as co-existent with a desired cultural pluralism and a respect for the 'other' he finds absent in much of the Western literary tradition.

(b) Individual Authors

A book-length study of A. R. Ammons is to be welcomed for its rarity, and Steven P. Schneider's *A. R. Ammons and the Poetics of Widening Scope* does valuable service in its wide-angled gaze on the whole of Ammons's career up to 1993. The central preoccupation of this study is on the relationship between what the eye sees and what the mind imagines, the play of oracular vision between the optics of literal sight and the figures of the imagination in Ammons's work, informed by the poet's extensive scientific knowledge. Schneider begins by relating practices of vision in Ammons to his nineteenth-century predecessors, Emerson, Thoreau and Whitman, and then considers the 'visual calisthenics' in poems which seem to impel the eye to see beyond its customary reach, to achieve the 'widening scope' which provides this study's title, and the contraries of telescopic and microscopic vision. Schneider's commentary on these topics is informed by his own special knowledge of optometry, and he writes with confidence on astronomy and quantum physics as these disciplines provide Ammons with ways of picturing the relationship between the personal and the cosmic, the local and the universal. In his final chapters Schneider provides brief commentaries on all the Ammons volumes published since 1974, and if this bold enterprise means a too cursory treatment of many of these collections, readers will find this a helpful overview of the scale of Ammons's achievement over the last twenty years.

A. R. Ammons is currently being published in Britain by Norton, who have made two of his collections available here in paperback, *Tape for the Turn of the*

Year, originally published in 1965, and *Garbage*, the 1993 collection which won the National Book Award for that year. As indicated above, Nathan Scott has a chapter on Ammons in *Visions of Presence in Modern American Poetry*, and while he admits Ammons's distance from traditional figurings of the Sublime and the 'Christian mythos', Scott none the less finds Ammons recoiling from the 'ennui of the human' in a desire for some 'otherness' in reality 'that cannot be made subservient to the engines of our planning and our manipulation', and finds these desires embodied in the visionary vocabulary of the final poem of *Lake Effect Country* and elsewhere in Ammons's work. David Jarrawy writes on self-reflexiveness and the poetics of 'The Bleak Periphery' in 'Ammons Beside Himself' (*ArQ* 49[1993].99–116).

Three major studies of Ashbery have recently appeared: Edward Haworth Hoeppner's *Echoes and Moving Fields: Structure and Subjectivity in the Poetry of W. S. Merwin and John Ashbery*, John Shoptaw's *On the Outside Looking Out*, and Geoff Ward's *Statutes of Liberty: The New York School of Poets* (1993). Hoeppner draws on structuralism, phenomenology and deconstruction in considering issues relating to identity and time in the two poets. Hoeppner argues that their formal affinities with Dickinson and Whitman are philosophically and linguistically suggestive: Merwin's 'grave economy' has recourse to the vertical axis of Dickinson, whereas Ashbery parodically sets Whitman's successive mode 'on its ear' yet retains a commitment to the horizontal axis. The deconstructionist aspect of this argument is that the two poets generate indeterminacies for different reasons: Merwin's formal strategies preserve the self's intensities and resist outward movement; Ashbery decentres in a movement to the periphery. This theory-laden study is heavy going at times, not a book to place in the hands of the average undergraduate, although difficult poems and issues are tackled, sometimes rewardingly. Hoeppner concludes that both Merwin and Ashbery question whether it is possible to reach beyond the isolate self.

Shoptaw's *On the Outside Looking Out* covers the range of Ashbery's *oeuvre* from *Some Trees* to *Flow Chart*, guided by a view of Ashbery's enterprise as a poetry of 'misrepresentation', a term which allows him to see Ashbery within the inclusive representative poetics of the line of Whitman, and the exclusive, restrained misrepresentativeness of Dickinson with her celebration of circularity and her compulson to tell the truth 'but tell it slant –'. In charting the narrative of Ashbery's poetry as representative of the self it speaks for and the selves it speaks to, Shoptaw reads Ashbery's major misrepresentation as his avoidance of himself and his homosexuality as subject matter: at the same time Shoptaw reads these poems as 'homotextual' through the otherness of their behaviour, 'their distortions, evasions, omissions, obscurities, and discontinuities', a strategic misrepresentativeness conditioned by Ashbery's poetic evolution in the forties and fifties during McCarthy's reign of homophobic political terror. From this, Shoptaw's analysis of individual poems is determined by a suggestion from Ashbery that substitution, revision or replacement of words and phrases in his process of composition conceals a 'crypt word' or phrase which is the given from which the words of the finished poem radiate, and the uncoding of what he calls this 'lyric cryptography' forms the substance of Shoptaw's approach throughout this book, defined predominantly as the products of sonic, visual or associational misrepresentation. Shoptaw has had privileged access to Ashbery in the composition of this book, and through this access, and his own energetic researches, *On the Outside Looking Out* is bound to become a major source for all students of

Ashbery: it is immensely informative in particular details, and is an eloquent and challenging study, even if the argument about lyric cryptography will seem to many readers to add a further barrier to an understanding of this deeply influential but difficult poet.

Geoff Ward's *Statutes of Liberty: The New York School of Poets* has chapters on James Schuyler, Frank O'Hara and John Ashbery, and if Ward's attention to Ashbery occupies almost two-thirds of this book, that reflects upon the range and extraordinary late flourishing of his work, rather than a sense of his priority as one of the New York School, for this book is a generous critique of all three poets. At the end, O'Hara is as much the presiding genius of this 'school' as Ashbery is its most famous poet. Ward is especially good on the wit and comedy of these poets, one element which constitutes their particular identification with the verbal idioms of New York life, and one which allows him to theorize Schuyler's work through Paul de Man's 1969 essay 'The Rhetoric of Temporality', with its opposition between symbol and allegory. In this reading New York becomes for Schuyler 'one massively networked Symbol', and a 'honeycombed text of anecdote, remembrance and common knowledge under sentence of death from Time disguised as the construction industry'. Ward's view of Schuyler thus makes over an entropic anxiety into a comedic engagement with a passing world registered for its people, its places and what Ward calls its 'layered spaces', which are also the spatial drama of these poems, and denotes the condition and mode of voice in Schuyler's work, as in O'Hara's. For Ward, O'Hara is a poet of Whitmanesque quality, a Promethean jester in the city–court, whose comedic idiom translates into, even as it formally refuses, the grand manner and the tragic mode. This is perhaps the best writing on O'Hara currently available, and should do much to rescue his work from the cultish enthusiasm which generally marks a taste for O'Hara in Britain. Ward challenges Harold Bloom's cherished version of Ashbery as the belated exponent of an agonistic high seriousness and therefore addresses those aspects of Ashbery which most oppose Bloom's version, celebrating his comedy, the influence of Auden's urbane manner upon him, and his fascination with Surrealism. As Ward acknowledges, this is a selective view of the New York School, deliberately framed to appeal to a British audience unfamiliar with the names and work of those who might otherwise have featured in this book. *Statutes of Liberty* will be required reading for everyone interested in the New York School as a specific cultural phenomenon, or in Ashbery as its most lasting voice. I note two articles this year on Frank O'Hara, William Weaver's 'Remembering Frank O'Hara' (*SWR* 79.139–46) and Michael Hettich's 'The Avoidance of Abstractions: The Poetry of Frank O'Hara' (*ArkR* 3.80–5).

Recent articles on Ashbery include Frank Lepkowski's 'John Ashbery's Revision of the Post-Romantic Quest: Meaning, Evasion, and Allusion in "Grand Galop" ', (*TCL* 39[1993].251–65); Garcia Rodrigo Lopes's report of an interview with Ashbery in 'Notes about the Process' (*HFR* 12[Spring–Summer 1993].27–33); Stephen Paul Miller's ' "Self-Portrait in a Convex Mirror", the Watergate Affair, and Johns' Crosshatch Paintings: Surveillance and Reality-Testing in the Mid-Seventies' (*Boundary*, 20.ii.[1993].84–115); Seija Paddon's 'John Ashbery and Paavo Haavikko: Architects of the Postmodern Space in Mind and Language' (*CRCL* 20.iii-iv.[1993]. 409–16); Susan Schultz's 'The Lyric Crash: The Theater of Subjectivity in John Ashbery's *Three Poems*' (*Sagetrieb* 12.ii.[1993].137–48); and Benjamin Sloan's 'Houseboat Days and "Houses Founded on the Sea": An Example of Emerson as Source for Ashbery' (*NConL* 23[1993].5–16). Journal contributions to Ashbery studies for 1994 include a short supplement in the British journal *PNR* where David Herd reports 'John Ashbery in Conversation' (*PNR* 21.i.32–7); Daniel Cottom discusses 'Getting It: Ashbery and the *Avant-garde* of Everyday Language' (*SubStance* 73.3–23); and Martin Kevorkian discusses *Flow Chart* in 'John Ashbery's *Flow Chart*: John Ashbery and the Theorists on John Ashbery Against the Critics against John Ashbery' (*NLH* 25.459–76).

Luke Spenser's 'Mistress Bradstreet and Mr. Berryman: The Ultimate Seduction' (*AL* 66.353–66) is an account of the sexual politics of Berryman's poem. He contrasts Eileen Simpson's version of its genesis as the 'ultimate seduction', in a period when Berryman sought relief from his creative frustration by years of manic womanizing, with a view of the poem as Berryman's way of appropriating Bradstreet's difficulties and achievements as woman, wife, mother and poet to himself: thus if the intention is to heroize Bradstreet, the outcome affirms the historical partriarchal victimization of women beneath the rhetoric of male respect. Elsewhere Carol Frost contributes 'Berryman at Thirty-Eight: An Aesthetic Biography' (*NER* 16.iii.36–53), and Claudia Keelan gives 'Last Rites of the Orphan: John Berryman and César Vallejo' (*Pequod* 37.39–45).

C. K. Doreski chooses an appropriate title for her study *Elizabeth Bishop: The Restraints of Language*, for 'restraint' is a specially apposite word to use in connection with this poet. In the event Doreski's work disappoints, and lacks critical restraint in her dispute with other recent commentaries on Bishop, which she believes 'portrayed an Elizabeth Bishop unknown to me: alcoholic, asthmatic, repressed cipher'. In fact, psychobiographical readings of Bishop are not notably evident in the recent body of work on her, so that Doreski's complaints seem both unrestrained and inappropriate. Doreski's own approach is to read the poems as though they come into existence in some impersonal way, divorced from the particulars of Bishop's experience, whilst at the same time she argues that Bishop creates 'a convincing narrative of childhood and social development' as a way of reintegrating herself 'into a society in which, in fact, she never assumed a full role'. If the critical practice here contradicts Doreski's alleged dislike of the biographical import, the vocabulary is vague and the conceptions dubious, and the want of any sustained formal reading of the poems undermines Doreski's evident appreciation of them.

Remembering Elizabeth Bishop: An Oral Biography by Gary Fountain and Peter Brazeau consists of 120 interviews between 1984 and 1992 with the poet's relatives, friends, colleagues and students, edited to follow her life chronologically. Seventy interviews were conducted by the late Peter Brazeau, to which Gary Fountain has added a further forty and incorporated them all into a narrative researched from published and unpublished writings. There are, necessarily, significant omissions: Lota de Macedo Soares and Robert Lowell died before the project was under way, although there are a number of commentators on Bishop's relationships with these two central figures; Alice Methfessel declined to participate, but distinguished literary luminaries – John Ashbery, James Merrill, and Helen Vendler among others – all have their say. Only rarely do we get close to the poem-making, as when Frank Bidart recalls Bishop wrestling with the last stanza of 'Poem', searching for a way to put a 'skin' on the abstraction. The comments of her Harvard students are revealing of her ways of thinking: about Stevens's 'The Emperor of Ice Cream' she asked the class if they knew what 'deal' was. They did not. Some of the reminiscences of the earlier New York years have a period feel: the pianist, Arthur Gold, evokes a dinner party in which Marianne Moore and Bishop, 'like two butterflies deliciously hovering', expatiated on the 'celestial' meat loaf, or, as Gold refines the image, 'like two iron butterflies'.

The value of Victoria Harrison's *Elizabeth Bishop's Poetics of Intimacy* lies in its careful tracing of the workings of memory through a succession of manuscript drafts in Bishop's struggle with the 'terrible oxygen' of the past: the manuscripts show how often the 'blank' of her mother's illness blocked her expression. Harrison places Bishop in the pragmatist tradition and draws on Spivak, de Lauretis and Geertz in her readings of subjectivity and the politics of gender and culture, most particularly in her discussion of the Brazilian period. Bishop herself is more subtle than the theorists who are set on to her, and Harrison is most discerning when she follows the poet's lead in registering the localized and the specific. Bishop was not inclined to simplify the politics of culture, and she could also adopt the large historical view. Harrison's command of the manuscript versions of 'Brazil, January 1, 1502' enables her to add to Lowell's appreciation of the poem's transformations – from jungle to picture to history – that of gender, when she notes the change to identifying the Indians as women. The last chapter of this excellent book includes an examination of the manuscripts of some of Bishop's unpublished love poems.

Elizabeth Bishop: The Geography of Gender, edited by Marilyn May Lombardi, contains essays by many of the best recent contributors to Bishop criticism: Lee Edelman, Joanne Feit Diehl, Bonnie Costello, Lorrie Goldensohn, Jacqueline Vaught Brogran, Victoria Harrison, Brett C. Millier, Thomas Travisano, Jeredith Merrin and Barbara Page. Many of these essays are reprinted from their first appearance in book-length studies of Bishop, or as articles, and there are several new essays. Lombardi's collection is unified by its attention to gender issues approached from a variety of perspectives, though there is considerable critical difference in the versions of Bishop offered throughout. This is an invaluable collection for readers who want a view of the current state of Bishop criticism.

Susan McCabe's *Elizabeth Bishop: Her Poetics of Loss* adds to the growing tide of Bishop monographs a new focus on her postmodernism in a gendered reading which draws on Freud, Lacan and both French and Anglo-American feminist theory. By emphasizing loss as the premise of Bishop's poetics in her fashioning of a rhetoric of indeterminacy, McCabe threads the vulnerabilities of the life into a comprehensive explication which includes prose, letters, translations and select manuscript material as well as poetry. McCabe calls her method 'eclectically untraditional' and assumes the '*bricoleur* or assemblage sensibility – of making do with what is at hand and partaking of diverse materials'; the *bricolage* is sometimes awkwardly patched together, but there are compensations in the openness of these readings. They endorse positively Bishop's 'gift of alterability', ascribe to her the quality of language which 'teases us out of our sense-making petrification', and applaud her postmodernist and feminist choice 'not to hierarchize or enclose or limit signification'. This is a very humane book, theoretical but not overtheoretical.

Brett C. Millier's indispensable critical biography, *Elizabeth Bishop: Life and the Memory of It,* focuses on the personal aspects of her subject, rather than taking a wider cultural frame, and is frank about the difficulties with asthma, alcohol and depression that Bishop faced in an existence in which early trauma made her 'a chronically displaced person'. Yet this is not a sensationalist exercise; extensive archival research brings Bishop's own voice to the fore through notebooks and letters, and Millier has also interviewed her colleagues and friends: 'I do have some nice friends and that's a mercy', she wrote during one of her alcoholic binges, and although relationships with lovers deteriorated, a nucleus of friends was loyal in spite of many lapses. Millier does not foreground literary relationships (the relationship with Lowell is treated on the personal level) or examine the effects of the cultural and ideological constraints of the era on Bishop's lesbianism, so it is difficult to know the extent to which these contributed to her famous reticence, overcome only in the love poems in manuscript, which she might well have chosen not to publish. There is indeed an irony in so much revelation about a writer who deflected biographical inquiry and eschewed the confessional mode. Millier shapes her narrative of this stumbling life (Bishop, literally, frequently fell over and injured herself) to show how it was sifted into the finely wrought poems, with an elegance which her subject might have approved.

Journal articles on Bishop include the following: Susan McCabe's 'Writing Loss' (*AI* 50[1993].69–110) on Bishop's treatment of loss in relationship to the authorial self; Margaret Dicke's 'Seeing Is Re-Seeing: Sylvia Plath and Elizabeth Bishop' (*AL* 65[1993].131–46) comparing the treatment of the visual perception of women between Plath and Bishop; and John Palattella on '"That Sense of Constant Re-Adjustment": The Great Depression and the Provisional Politics of Elizabeth Bishop's *North & South*' (*ConL* 34[1993].18–43). Journal entries for 1994 are as follows: Margaret Dickie on 'Elizabeth Bishop: Text and Subtext' (*SoAR* 59.iv.1–19) and on 'Race and Class in Elizabeth Bishop's Poetry' (*YES* 24.44–58); William Logan's 'The Unbearable Lightness of Elizabeth Bishop' (*SWR* 79.120–38); Mutlu Konuk Blasing on 'From Gender to Genre and Back: Elizabeth Bishop and "The Moose"' (*AmLH* 6.265–86); Robert Giroux on 'The Making of "The Moose"' (*PULC* 55.400–10); and Xiaojing Zhou on 'The Oblique, the Indirect Approach: Elizabeth Bishop's "Rainy Season: Sub Tropics"' (*ChiR* 40.iv.75–92).

Langdon Hammer's *Hart Crane and Allen Tate: Janus-Faced Modernism* tells of the broken friendship of two writers whose brief intimacy was fractured by their opposing ideas of modernism, their antithetical life-styles and their sexual disposition in a quarrel which led to Crane's being kicked out of Tate's farmhouse home in Patterson, New York, in 1926, a severance repeatedly drawn upon in this book for its 'emblematic' status. In reading these two writers as crucial figures in the narrative of modernist literary culture in America, Hammer subverts the impersonal idiom integral to modernism and reads the lives and texts of Crane and Allen 'conjointly', a way of working which enables his later calling in of Lowell's *Life Studies* (the occasion of another famous literary quarrel involving Tate) as a text which seeks to 'get outside modernism precisely by making the personal literary', and to argue that the 'postmodern is made out of the modern'. Eliot and the 'authority' of *The Waste Land* are crucial to Hammer's telling of what became of Crane and Tate after the fracture of 1926: Crane's role is that of an 'outlaw genius' opposed to the negation he read in *The Waste Land*, and, denied the male companionship inherited as an ideal from Whitman, becoming an embittered and isolated romantic 'addressing modernist readers in the strange tongue of the high style'; by contrast Tate took to the role of 'poet-critic', read *The Waste Land* as proof of the death of traditional cultural forms, shared Eliot's traditionalism and political conservatism, and sustained a career as a critic and teacher who 'brought modernism into the American university'. Hammer makes good his case for reading these two writers together as a way of understanding their paradigmatic importance to the question of 'what it means to write "after modernism"'. This highly recommended book addresses many more issues than this brief notice suggests. Jean Guiget's *The Poetic Universe of Hart Crane* (NPF) was published in 1993 but has not been seen for review. Elsewhere, John T. Irwin writes a comparative study of female figures as images of transcendence in Crane and Goethe in 'The Triple Archetype: The Presence of Faust in *The Bridge*' (*ArQ* 50.i.51–73), and Jeffrey J. Folks writes on Tate's autobiographical poetry in 'The Archeologist of Memory: Autobiographical Recollection in Tate's "Maimed Man" Trilogy' (*SLJ* 27.51–60).

H.D.: A Bibliography 1905–1990 by Michael Boughn is published for the University of Virginia Bibliographical Society and is the first bibliography of her. It is a necessary volume given the complexity of her publication history, and Boughn's labours look as thorough as one could hope. The first part covers work by H.D., the second part work on her from reviews through to miscellaneous documents. Of course it is a pity that the closing date of this work is 1990, so that the substantial body of writing on her in recent years is not included in this edition. In 'The Muse's Dance: H.D'.s "The Dancer" as Spiritual Metaphor' (*W&Lang* 16[1993].49–52) Joyce Owens discusses H.D'.s uses of the figure of the dancer as a metaphor for the spiritual, and Rose Lucas writes on H.D'.s relationship to Pound and her treatment of memory and desire in 'Something Left Over: Memory and Desire in H.D'.s "Winter Love" and *End to Torment*' (*L&P* 39[1993].28–64). Susan Edmunds's *Out of Line: History, Psychoanalysis, and Montage in H.D'.s Long Poems* (StanfordUP) was published this year but has not yet been seen for review.

Articles on Rita Dove this year include John Keene on 'Rita Dove's *The Darker Face of the Earth*: An Introductory Note' (*Callaloo* 17.371–3); Helen Vendler's 'Rita Dove: Identity Markers' (*Callaloo* 17.381–98); and William Walsh's interview with Dove, 'Isn't Reality Magic' (*KR* 16.142–54).

A selection of Robert Duncan's poems is issued by Carcanet, edited by Robert J. Berthoff, with a sampling from the early poems of 1939–46 through to *Ground Work II: In the Dark* of 1987. Berthoff's introduction acutely situates the nature of this poetry when he writes that 'Duncan's poetry is filled with immediate details and fanciful discoveries; statements of the daily enterprise and prophecies of world order'. He gives a summary account of Duncan's life lived in and for poetry, in the company of fellow poets and painters, and distinguishes between the elegiac idiom of the early work and Duncan's pervasive interest in myth in the later poems. It is a pity the introduction is so brief, for when Berthoff comments on the 'serial form' of *Medieval Scenes* (1950) and Duncan's return to serialism in the later poems, general readers will need more information on the distinctive nature of this form than is allowed for here. That said, this is a welcome edition giving us some of the best of Duncan. Elsewhere Greg Hewett writes on 'Revealing "The Torso": Robert Duncan and the Process of Signifying Male Homosexuality' (*ConL* 35.522–46), and Thomas P. Peterson writes on 'Parallel Derivations from Dante: Fortini, Duncan, Pasolini' (*SoAR* 59.iv.21–45).

T. S. Eliot's series of eight Clark Lectures, 'On the Metaphysical Poetry of the Seventeenth Century with Special Reference to Donne, Crashaw and Cowley', delivered at Trinity College, Cambridge, in 1926, and the abbreviated and revised sequence given as the three Turnbull Lectures, 'The Varieties of Metaphysical Poetry', at Johns Hopkins University in 1933, are published for the first time, edited, annotated and introduced by Ronald Schuchard. Eliot had intended to revise the Clark lectures as a book to be entitled *The School of Donne*, but abandoned the project. They are an important document of his intellectual and emotional life written in the year that preceded his religious conversion, more spacious and revelatory than in the lectures familiar to readers of *Selected Essays*. Eliot works through the permutations of Donne, 'a mind of the trecento in disorder', and Dante, the one as fellow traveller in the 'fraction of thought into innumerable thoughts', the other as the beacon of multiplicity in unity. Readers of the 1990s will no doubt trawl the lectures for autobiographical revelation as severely as the original audiences, which included a scholarly tribunal, J. G. Frazer, A. N. Whitehead and G. E. Moore. The Turnbull lectures are more relaxed and offguard and include an autobiographically revealing distinction between Milton's '*self-dramatisation*' in *Samson Agonistes* and 'the metaphysical poet' who 'deals with his feelings directly, and more as if they were someone else's, only happening to be available to his inspection. One is the attitude of the theatre, the other that of the confessional.'

The Cambridge Companion to T. S. Eliot edited by A. David Moody is a substantial and carefully co-ordinated volume with seventeen contributions from an international group of scholars. The emphasis of the first seven chapters is to situate Eliot in relation to philosophical, cultural and religious issues. Peter Dale Scott's essay 'The Social Critic and his Discontents' argues that if claims for the unity and importance of Eliot's art are to be made, 'the social criticism cannot be . . . marginalized'. These opening chapters are accomplished but, at times, intimidating and stern, a rather daunting assault course for a student looking for help with the poetry, who might be grateful for Eric Sigg's 'Eliot as a Product of America', which is instructive yet sympathetic and lively. Chapters 8–11 do cover the poetry with useful essays, open in approach, on the early poems by J. C. C. Mays, *The Waste Land* by Harriet Davidson and *Four Quartets* by the volume editor. An excellent chapter on Eliot's theatre by Robin Grove makes a good case for *Sweeney Agonistes*; James Longenbach writes on Eliot's allusive practice; Charles Altieri's distinguished contribution, 'Eliot's Impact on Twentieth Century Anglo-American Poetry', is notably insightful on Eliot and John Ashbery; Bernard Sharratt gives an overview of 'Eliot, Modernism, Postmodernism and After'; and finally Jewel Spears Brooker provides a demystifying review of Eliot studies.

Mastery and Escape: *T. S. Eliot and the Dialectic of Modernism* by Jewel Spears Brooker is a cultural study of international modernism, of the emergence of dialectical patterns in the disciplines of history, psychology and philosophy which collectively gave shape to high modernist literature. The characteristic dialectical pattern of Eliot's work, a movement forward by spiralling back and refiguring the past, a 'mastery' followed by an 'escape' to a broader perspective, is argued to be exemplary of this process. Brooker's book consists of a series of related essays mostly previously published in journals or collections. It is divided into four sections: the first includes essays on Mallarmé and T. S. Hulme; the second relates Eliot to Bradley and Frazer; the third is primarily on Eliot and Bradley, but includes an essay on Sandra Gilbert and Susan Gubar's readings of Eliot; the fourth section has essays on teaching *The Waste Land*. The approach throughout is pedagogical, clear and brisk, devoted to the clarification of the relationships of ideas and literary texts.

T. S. Eliot at the Turn of the Century edited by Marianne Thormählen consists of twelve papers from a 1993 colloquium at Lund University. Contributors include Bernard Bergonzi, M. Teresa Gibert-Maceda, Nancy D. Hargrove on Eliot's life in Paris, 1910–11, A. David Moody, and Kristian Smidt. The outstanding essay is by Barbara Everett, 'How Unpleasant to Meet Mr Eliot!', which tackles head-on the overall concern of the colloquium, the current hostility to Eliot amongst theoretical critics. Everett argues that Eliot's complexity arises from his ability to caricature the lowest social aggressions, as distinct from countenancing such aggressions, and that he takes risks: we meet Mr Eliot and ourselves 'and the meeting is something other than pleasant. But what is met isn't truthfully enough described as hatred of women and of Jews.' Everett traces the allusions through Eliot's own, 'How delightful to meet Mr. Hodgson' and Edward Lear's 'How pleasant to know Mr. Lear' to show the echo-chamber modernism, but also how it is, via Lear, transgressive, and in the change of verb from 'know' to 'meet' challengingly social; and further, how in the 'broken brilliance' of this and other poems Eliot brings together divided worlds in violent and naked feelings of betrayal and surrender, dignity and indignity. This is an essay which all critics must reckon with and which returns them to what Samuel Beckett called 'the power of the text to claw'.

John H. Timmerman's *T. S. Eliot's Ariel Poems: The Poetics of Recovery* is a descriptive, non-theorized account of the 1927–1931 phase of Eliot's career, concentrating on the religious source material which assisted his search for new forms. Virginia Woolf wrote to her sister, Vanessa Bell, reacting to his religious declaration of 1928, 'poor dear Tom Eliot . . . may be called dead to us all from this day forward'; Timmerman argues, however, that the Ariel poems are major poems, unduly neglected, in which Eliot successfully extricates himself from Pound's version of modernism and recovers a sense of history as process, as a pattern for the individual, guided by religion, to appropriate. To express his religious renewal, Eliot moved towards a more patterned symbolism and a more unified poetic voice.

Dennis Brown writes on 'Plato and Eliot's earlier verse' in *Platonism and the English Imagination*, edited by Anna Baldwin and Sarah Hutton, a collection of essays on the impact of Plato on the English literary tradition. Brown works with the familiar distinction between Eliot's earlier and later poetry, in which *Four Quartets* is seen as 'affirmatory and declarative' against the 'dialogical and sceptical manner and tone of the earlier poems', and reads these poems as questioning the 'nature of Platonism' through the ways in which they participate in a 'quasi-sceptical journey into ultimate mystery'. Brown finds a Socratic manner at the heart of many of the earlier poems, appropriate to the 'exercise of questioning' which informs them, and the humility of tone which characterizes many of their speakers. Murray McArthur's 'Deciphering Eliot: "Rhapsody on a Windy Night" and the Dialectic of the Cipher' (*AL* 66.509–24) takes up Lyndall Gordon's intuition that the poem is some form of cipher, arguing that it was produced by a 'dialectical drive governed not by the necessity of a unifying synthesis, but by the necessities of cipher itself', and finds supportive evidence for this approach in Eliot's own essay of 1917, 'Reflections on Contemporary Poetry'. This fascinating article argues that the figure of the pentagon is a 'master signifier' in Eliot, and from post-Lacanian theory takes the number 'five' as that of maternity or paternity in which the Oedipal triangle can be studied in inverted forms in adult life. This reading, which calls on the widespread use of patterns of fives in Eliot, reads this number-figure as a cipher for the 'place of the creation of the subject' in Eliot, and a clue to the ways we should read the 'Rhapsody'.

To deliver a version of Frost which sees him firmly anchored to his nineteenth-century American precursors yet aligns him to his modernist peers is both a difficult and a fashionable enterprise. This is the task George F. Bagby sets himself in *Frost and the Book of Nature*, and if the nineteenth-century anchorage looks the more secure part of his achievement, this is not to deny the value of his proposition that we read Frost's nature lyrics 'as part of an over-all imaginative drama' in the manner of the modernist long poem. In addition, Bagby agues that if much of

Frost's nature poetry follows in an Emersonian tradition in which the poem is an instrument for the interpretation of nature, he also argues for Frost as a poet of 'the visionary uses of lostness', where his antecendents are, if differently, Shelley and Thoreau, giving us a Frost of Promethian ambition and Thoreauvian excess. These are, as Bagby acknowledges, the outer limits of Frost's imaginative world, so that in this work he more frequently assumes his familiar role as the interpreter of nature's daily reality. The innovative aspects of this study follow from Bagby's analysis of the differing types of lyric structure Frost works with, differences determined by the experiences they confront.

The Frost Family's Adventure in Poetry by Robert Frost's granddaughter, Lesley Lee Francis, is an account of the adventures of the spirit which this close-knit, hard-up family encountered from the early years on the farm in Derry, New Hampshire, to the 1912–15 period in England during which Frost became publicly recognized as a poet. For a good deal of their childhood, the four children were not at school, but were educated at home by Robert and Elinor, an education which involved long botanizing walks, picnics, writing, drawing, and evenings listening to their parents reading poetry aloud: all very much a collective family experience. Francis's account is based on the notebooks of her mother, Lesley, published and previously unpublished letters of family and friends, and six surviving issues of the magazine, the *Bouquet*, which the Frost children produced from 1912 to 1915. Contributions were invited from parents and friends, and Edward Thomas's first step towards publishing was the poem, 'Nettles', in the children's magazine. The period of Frost's friendship with Thomas, 'the closest I ever came in friendship with anyone', until Thomas's death in 1917 was of intense significance for both poets. Francis's aim is corrective; her book is written because she did not recognize her grandfather in the single neurosis theory of Lawrence Thompson's biography. She does not sentimentalize, however, but shows how what Frost called 'a life that goes rather poetically' was a family enterprise, courageous and active, out of which great poetry came.

The author of 'Home Burial', 'The Silken Tent' and 'Maple' was alive to the imperatives and compromises of gender, and Katherine Kearns's *Robert Frost and a Poetics of Appetite* has a volatile terrain to explore. She draws on feminism, psychoanalytic theory and deconstruction to propose that Frost's poetry enacts a contest between the feminine metamorphosing power of metaphor and the masculine 'heautocratic' (Foucault's term) control of form. She argues that the ambiguities and instabilities which ensue force a deconstructive reading of the poems. This is a very dense, at times laboured and congested study, not for the student new to Frost's work; the method of circulating brief quotations from a large number of poems in a variegated theoretical orbit is directed to the knowing. The sexuality of the poetry is rather dulled when it is so endlessly recycled and explicated, but the focus on the tension between the feminine and masculine aspects of Frost's sensibility is timely.

It is good to know that William H. Pritchard's *Frost: A Literary Life Reconsidered* is available now in a second edition, with a new preface by the author regretting his publisher's setting up in 1984 the Pritchard 'benign sage' versus Thompson 'monstrous megalomaniac' polarized versions of Frost. Pritchard's emphasis upon the volumes of poetry rather than Frost's temperament has evidently had an influence in the intervening years, which have seen Frost's modernist credentials firmly established, putting him on a level with his poetic peers of the first half of this century.

Journal articles in 1993 on Frost include the following: Christopher E. Jones's review of 'Current Frost Scholarship, 1990–1993' (*RFR* Fall.[1993].103–10); George Monteiro's introduction to 'Three New Robert Frost Letters, an Inscription, and an Unrecorded Emendation' (*PLL* 29[1993].111–13); Kyle Norwood's 'The Work of Not Knowing: Robert Frost and the Abject' (*SWR* 79[1993].57–72); James R. Dawes's 'Masculinity and Transgression in Robert Frost' (*AL* 65[1993].297–312); Sheldon W. Liebman's 'Frost on Criticism', using Frost's prose writings for what they reveal of his view of literary theory and criticism (*NEQ* 66 [1993].399–415); and Mark Richardson's 'Robert Frost and the Motives of Poetry' (*ELWIU* 20[1993].273–91). Articles for 1994 are as follows: Daniel Hoffman on 'Robert Frost: The Symbols a Poem Makes' (*Gettysburg Review* 7.101–12) and George Monteiro in the same journal with his 'Introduction to "For Glory and for Use": Robert Frost at Brown University' (89–99); Helen H. Bacon on Frost's sources in Horace in 'Getting among the Poems in Horace's *Fons Bandusiae* and Robert Frost's *Hyla Brook*' (*CML* 3.259–67); and George Monteiro again on 'Robert Frost's "On Talk of Peace at This Time": A Third Version of an Uncollected Manuscript Poem' (*ANQ* 7.26–8).

The brief introduction to Denise Levertov in Paul Hoover's anthology *Postmodern American Poetry* mentions her commitment to organic form and represents her as a poet of 'intense lyricism' and 'visionary Christianity'. It is against this kind of restricted version of Levertov's canvas that Audrey T. Rodgers says she writes in *Denise Levertov: The Poetry of Engagement*, where Levertov's poetry of 'social consciousness' is to be foregrounded. Given the critical animus against the ways in which Levertov politicized her work from the early 1960s, especially in the anti-Vietnam war poems, Rodgers has a well-defined subject, and had she kept to it this might have been a much better book than it is. In the event her focus on Levertov's political engagement becomes subsumed within a view of the poet's whole career, and Rodgers is drawn as much to the ecological and visionary poetry as to anything else. This could be argued as an appropriate strategy, locating the socially 'engaged' work within the frame of Levertov's post-Romantic practice, and there are occasions when this synthesis pays dividends through close analysis of individual poems. The problem is that Rodgers's approach is eulogistic in manner, impelled by an enthusiasm for Levertov which is almost wholly uncritical, so that all the poet's pronouncements about poetics and politics go unchallenged. This simple, expository account draws heavily on Levertov's essays in *The Poet and the World* (1973) and Rodgers's own interview with the poet of 1988. In addition, although there are tedious paragraphs full of lists of other writers who have taken up the cause of political engagement – a problematic category in this book – the isolation of Levertov from her contemporaries is very marked, as though she has always worked in a self-sustaining cultural vacuum. Elsewhere, Dorothy Nielsen compares Levertov's treatment of environmental issues with Gary Snyder's in 'Prosopopoeia and the Ethics of Ecological Advocacy in the Poetry of Denise Levertov and Gary Snyder' (*ConL* 34 [1993].691–713).

Paul Mariani's *Lost Puritan: A Life of Robert Lowell* is a patient and sympathetic account of the poet who turned his own life and family history to creative purpose in the middle of his career and in the process alienated many of his friends and companions, even as *Life Studies* significantly enlarged his national and international audience. Mariani pays due credit to Ian Hamilton, who went before him in the writing of Lowell's life, and signals the difference in emphasis in his own approach in 'giving Lowell more of his own words and in recognizing Lowell as a major poet at every step of his development . . .'. Even as we note the modest implications of '*A Life*' in Mariani's title, it must be said that this biography is likely to survive as the definitive version for many years to come. At the core of Mariani's book is a belief in the 'dramatic dark' at the centre of Lowell's personality which is neither the product of nor the agent of his mental illnesses, but the consequence of his 'Calvinist upbringing'. This burden affected all aspects of his life, and of course, conditioned his creative temperament, so that, drawn as he was to Yeats's ideals of creative joy or ecstasy, 'he knew he was still a puritan at heart'. Yet, as Mariani ably demonstrates, Lowell was a flamboyant and attractive personality in public and in private, a man whose warm personality shines through this book even in those moments when Mariani's materials force him to record the marital and familial fractures of a life lived on the edge. This is a fine biography.

Journal articles on Lowell in 1993 are as follows: William Doreski considers Lowell's influence in his Confessional mode in '"My Mind's Not Right": The Legacy of Robert Lowell' (*ArQ* 49[1993].93–106); Henry Hart writes on 'Robert Lowell, Emerson, and the American Sublime' (*ESQ* 39[1993].iv.279–307); Daniel Hoffman reminisces in 'Afternoons with Robert Lowell' (*Gettysburg Review* 6[1993].480–9), and in the same issue Richard Tillinghast contributes 'Robert Lowell: The Vagaries of a Literary Reputation' (441–52); and Terri Witek writes on a biographical approach to Lowell in 'The Boy with the Raspberry Sherbet Heart' (*Shenandoah* 41[1993].107–20). Witek's book *Robert Lowell and Life Studies: Revising the Self* (UMP) was published in 1993 but has not been received for review. Articles in 1994 are as follows: David M. Bethea on 'Joseph Brodsky and the American Seashore Poem: Lowell, Mandelstam and Cape Cod' (*HudR* 6[1993].115–22); Antoine Cazé on 'Polyphony in Robert Lowell's Poetry' (*JAms* 28.385–401); Richard Tillinghast on 'Robert Lowell's *Day By Day*: "Until the Wristwatch Is Taken from the Wrist"' (*NER* 16.iii.54–63); and William Doreski on 'One Gallant Rush: The Writing of Robert Lowell's "For the Union Dead"' (*NEQ* 67.i.30–45).

The uses of spiritualism in modern poetry are rehearsed in Helen Sword's 'James Merrill, Sylvia Plath, and the Poetics of Ouija' (*AL* 66.553–72), with specific reference to Merrill's *The Changing Light at Sandover* and Plath's 'Dialogue over a Ouija Board', this latter written in 1957 but not published until 1981. Sword reminds us of the fascination with the occult and spiritualism in Yeats, Rilke and others, and sees Merrill and Plath's uses of the ouija board as a means of transposing the age-old prophetic mode of the visionary utterance into the 'cynical, subversive, ludic realm of the postmodern'. Conversely, C. A. Buckely discusses *The Changing Light at Sandover* in relation to quantum physics in 'Quantum Physics and the Ouija-Board: James Merrill's Holistic World View' (*Mosaic* 26[1993].39–61). Eric Murphy Selinger writes on Merrill's love poetry in 'James Merrill's Masks of Eros, Masques of Love' (*ConL* 35.30–65).

In addition to Edward Hoeppner's book on Merwin and Ashbery reviewed above, we record the following articles on Merwin: Jane Frazier on 'W. S. Merwin and the Mysteries of Silence' (*SDR* 32.116–25), and Floyd Collins on 'Forms Open and Closed: The Poetry of W.S. Merwin' (*Gettysburg Review* 7.144–62).

Articles on Marianne Moore in 1993 included Vicki Graham's 'The Power of the Visible: Marianne Moore and the Mimetic Fallacy' (*Sagetrieb* 12[1993].ii.33–50); Stacy Carson Hubbard on 'The Many-Armed Embrace: Collection, Quotation, and Mediation in Marianne Moore's Poetry' (*Sagetrieb* 12 [1993].7–32); Linda Leavell on Moore's treatment of modern art in 'When Marianne Moore Buys Pictures' (*AmLH* 5[1993].250–71); and Robin Riley Fast's comparative account of Moore and Bishop's treatment of the sea and notions of motherhood in 'Moore, Bishop, and Oliver: Thinking Back, Re-Seeing the Sea' (*TCL* 29[1993].364–79). Journal articles in 1994 are as follows: Elizabeth Gregory on 'Stamps, Money, Pop Culture, and Marianne Moore' (*Discourse* 17.123–46); Lisa R. Myers on 'Precision and Illusion: The Objects of Marianne Moore's Affections' (*Rev* 16.135–44); Carol J. Pierman's 'An Air of Gaiety and Zest' (*IowaR* 24.153–60); and Charles Swann's 'Gardens and Toads or, Milton – Another Fly in Marianne Moore's Amber?' (*N&Q* 41.376–7).

Jenny Penberthy's selection of the correspondence of Lorine Niedecker and Louis Zukofsky survives a particular difficulty, the refusal of the executor of the Zukofsky estate to permit quotations from his letters to Niedecker, or quotation from his published shorter poems. Despite this, Penberthy's *Niedecker and the Correspondence with Zukofsky: 1931–1970* is a triumph, an eloquent testament to the enduring creative relationship between two poets separated by place, creed and ethnic identity yet united in the common cause of a scrupulous poetic form and language, even if that commitment exacted its costs in the exchanges between them, particularly in his critique of her work. Because the first few years of Niedecker's letters are missing, Penberthy provides what she calls a reconstruction of the line of development Niedecker's poetry followed during the years from 1931 to 1941, a document which occupies one third of this book and must stand as one of the best available introductions to this poetry. Additional material describes aspects of the Zukofsky archive at Texas; this includes Niedecker's letters and the original documents that were to form her selection from his letters to her, which she had planned to publish, a project for which Zukofsky had no enthusiasm. Penberthy's editing of the letters included in this volume is detailed but unobtrusive, and this collection can only add to the current level of interest in Niedecker, a poet described by Basil Bunting as 'easily the finest female American poet' and 'one of the finest American poets at all'.

In the company of twentieth-century American poets no one is better fitted to introduce Charles Olson's work than Robert Creeley, the dedicatee of *The Maximus Poems*, who now gives us a selection of the poems in a handsome edition from UCalP. Creeley approaches Olson's distinctive enterprise through a brief account of the system-building imperative in the poetics of this century, especially in Pound, Eliot and Williams, through to Olson's fieldwork, defined as his attempt to answer this question: 'what is humanness, call it, what are its parameters, its givens, its determining histories, its collective biology, its company and investment upon the earth?'. Creeley stresses that this selection is entirely his, though the text follows George Butterick's editions of *The Maximus Poems* and *The Collected Poems* except for particular occasions itemized in Creeley's introduction. To have this selection of Olson's work made by one so intimately bound up with Olson's poetics and who had an instrumental part in the final shape of some of these poems is a particular pleasure.

Nancy D. Hargrove's *The Journey Toward Ariel: Sylvia Plath's Poems of 1956–1959* does valuable service to the Plath industry in this account of the chronological order of the composition of Plath's poems between 1956 and 1959. Treading gently over Ted Hughes's acknowledgement of his insecurity about the dating of many of these poems in his introduction to *The Collected Poems*, Hargrove argues her case for a more accurate chronology in support of the view that this is important to a true sense of Plath's development. The effect of Hargrove's discoveries in a variety of manuscript collections is to challenge the critical readings of many of these early poems, such as 'Moonrise', inaccurately attributed to 1959, which has led several commentators to suggest that it reflects Plath's responses to her pregnancy: Hargrove shows that it was written in late July 1958 and therefore argues that it is about Plath's sense of creative sterility at the moment of composition: it looks as though one of these readings is at fault, and Hargrove's confident dating of 'Moonrise' to July 1958 suggests her view is more accurate, though it must be acknowledged that the final verse of the poem lends itself to the argument from pregnancy. Hargrove's sources are principally the Plath Collections in the Lilly Library at the University of Indiana, the Smith College Library Rare Book Room, and the Cambridge Manuscript, a collection of forty-three poems submitted towards part II of the English tripos in the late spring of 1957, and some of these sources have yielded rich discoveries, such as the 'two tiny and unassuming datebooks in the Lilly Collection' which 'clearly establish the exact dates of composition for thirty-six poems in 1956, drastically altering the established chronology for that year'. Plath scholars will need to take account of Hargrove's revision of the chronology of these poems.

Plath's work has become a notoriously public literary property in recent years, appropriated with fervour by competing critical and biographical persuasions. Janice Markey's *A Journey Into the Red Eye: The Poetry of Sylvia Plath – A Critique*, published by the Women's Press, seems determined to force a view of Plath unwarranted by any documentary evidence we have of her, and written in a style unconstrained by a sense of critical perspective and responsibility. This is a study which reads Plath as a vociferous anatagonist of 'patriarchal culture', a candidate for lesbian sexual relations, an existentialist, and a belated enthusiast for Unitarianism on the grounds that 'conventional religion' was seen by her as an extension of patriarchal ideology. We might agree with Markey that Plath's suicide was 'an ill-timed cry for help', but it is difficult to accept the lapse of taste that can then argue for Plath's interest in mysticism and her curiosity about the 'afterlife' as 'nevertheless firmly rooted in an appreciation of life in the here and now'. The intense drama of the last poems, addressing the 'here and now' of lived experience, seems to have failed her both at the level of imaginative possibility and in reality. And Markey's uncritical denigration of Marianne Moore and Elizabeth Bishop, as role models whose treatment of 'personal relations' Plath left far behind, suggests the approach of an ideologue more concerned to convince us of an opinion than a critic interested in the persuasive possibilities of argument. Janet Malcolm's biographical study *The Silent Woman: Sylvia Plath and Ted Hughes* has been so widely reviewed in the national press that comment on it here would seem redundant at this stage, but this record of publications on Plath would be incomplete without citing this latest foray into the Plath–Hughes story.

The Plath Collection at Smith College Library has also proved fertile for Susan R. Van Dyne in her study *Revising Life: Sylvia Plath's Ariel Poems*, in which she is largely concerned with the poems written during the autumn and winter of 1962. Her interest is in examining the 'proliferation of masks and performances that Plath produced in her poetry' and her approach is feminist, exploring the 'relation between a woman's life and her artistic revision, between her sexuality and textuality, between a psychosexual identity and cultural authority'. Her method is to set three 'kinds of texts' in play: Plath's journals and letters, the interpretive strategies of feminist theory, and the poet's revision of the *Ariel* poems. Van Dyne's use of the manuscripts of these late poems yields the greatest interest of this important book. She takes us to the compositional centre of Plath's last creative drive to reveal the extraordinary and heroic drama of the making of these powerful and haunting poems, made all the more compelling by what Van Dyne shows of their process of becoming. This is one of the best recent studies of Plath.

Elsewhere, Richard Tillinghurst discusses the biographical representations of Plath in 'Digging for the Truth about Sylvia Plath' (*Gettysburg Review* 6[1993].124–35), and Kathleen Margaret Lant writes on the treatment of the female body in Plath in relation to male power in 'The Big Strip Tease: Female Bodies and Male Power in the Poetry of Sylvia Plath' (*ConL* 34[1993].620–69). Jahan Ramazani writes on Plath's 'Daddy' as an example of the modern elegy (*PMLA* 108[1993].1142–56); Sherry Lutz Zivley considers 'Schizophrenic Behaviour, Perception, and Logic in Plath's Poetry' (*JEP* 14[1993].238–49); whilst William Freedman discusses the treatment of the female self as monstrous in 'The Monster in Plath's "Mirror"' (*PLL* 29[1993].152–69). Journal entries for 1994 include Mary Lynn Broe's 'Plathologies: The "Blood Jet" is Bucks, Not Poetry' (*Belles Lettres* 10.i.48–62); Anthony Easthope (*English* 43.223–35) admires Jacqueline Rose's reading of Plath's 'Daddy', but against Rose reads the poem as a comprehensive privileging of the personal, which follows from Plath's failure to challenge the 'lyric confessional mode' in which it is written. Ted Hughes provides some biographical information about Plath in 'On Sylvia Plath' (*Raritan* 14.1–12), and Susan Bohandy gives a comparative study of Plath in 'Defining the Self through the Body in Four Poems by Katerina Anghelaki-Rooke and Sylvia Plath' (*JMGS* 12.i.1–36).

The Letters of Ezra Pound to Alice Corbin Henderson, edited by Ira B. Nadel, gives a vivid sense of the entrepreneurial activity of Pound in the early years of American modernism through the agency of his job as foreign correspondent of Harriet Monroe's journal, *Poetry: A Magazine of Verse*. For example, Pound's letter of 14 October 1913 argues that *Poetry* should publish as much of Yeats and himself as it could lay its hands on, responds cautiously to the use of Frost, Skipwith Cannell and John Gould Fletcher in the issue of May 1913, acknowledges an admiration for Edwin Arlington Robinson's 'Miniver Cheevy' but is horrified at some of the other poems in *The Town Down by the River* (1910), and explains his relationship to the *New Age* – 'I write in only occasionally' – and the *Freewoman* (later the *Egoist*) – 'I'm more or less running, I don't mean all of it. . . . but I'm somewhat a guiding star and I choose about a third, sometimes more sometimes less of the contents. Loosely, for we haven't a red cent to pay authors. It is just run *pour effarer le mouffle*, and to keep ourselves from being utterly idle.' A subsequent letter of December 1913 proposes that Henderson suggests to Harriet Monroe that she print 'Aldington. H.D. (american) Frost (") Fletcher (") and Bezruc *at once*. It would make a fairly decent number. There will be some *me* in April, & some Yeats in May. & possibly some Sturge-Moore – if America (non-expatriated) can't produce something better. The Lawrence will do for Feb. if it aint in before then. And thereafter what I send over marked definitely to go in, will appear within two months.' The advisory imperatives of this note merely require editorial approval – and who could blame Pound in the circumstances – though it is a pity that we do not have Henderson's response to this, as to so many of the other letters herein, and her part in this correspondence is limited to the nine surviving letters Nadel has been able to find. Pound's view of Henderson as the enabling intelligence in the offices of *Poetry* has long been known, and this edition of their correspondence confirms the fact of Henderson's priority for him. Nadel has done a valuable service in unearthing these letters, most of which are very well annotated. Still, I should like to know something about Bezruc!

According to David M. Gordon the archive of correspondence between Pound and James Laughlin amounts to 2742 items, and from these he has selected some 350 items for this edition of their *Selected Letters*. The materials are nicely framed by glimpses of Marianne Moore, as Pound writes in 1933 of his *Active Anthology* how Basil Bunting finds 'Marianne better on rereading', and Gordon in an editorial note to Pound's visit to New York in 1969 with Olga Rudge, to attend a meeting of the Academy of American Poets, records how Laughlin told Dorothy Pound that the poet 'seemed in excellent shape' and that though he was 'saying almost nothing, but shaking hands, graciously. He talked a little with Marianne Moore at the meeting of the academy.' One would give a great deal to have overheard that conversation. The materials in this selection relate to the way Pound and Laughlin's relationship developed, the genesis of Laughlin's career as a publisher, an outline of Pound's publishing history after he met Laughlin, their personal and professional relationship as it developed over Pound's lifetime, some representation of Pound's aesthetic, political and economic interests within the frame of this relationship, and an appendix giving Rolfe Humphries's 'Introduction' to Pound's 1946 *Selected Poems,* unused in the event because of Humphries's stated objections to Pound's politics. The Pound–Laughlin relationship is one of the extraordinary narratives in the publication history of high modernism, and this excellent selection of their correspondence gives pleasure and information in equal proportion.

Platonism and the English Imagination, edited by Anna Baldwin and Sarah Hutton, is a collection of essays on the influence of Plato on the English literary tradition from the early Christian period and the Middle Ages through to this century, and includes an account by A. D. Moody of Platonism in its Neoplatonic form in the *Cantos*. Moody provides a helpful itemization of the allusions to and citations from some dozen philosophers writing within the compass of Platonic thought, but insists that the *Cantos* offers the practice of Neoplatonism, not an exposition of it, and requires an interactive participation by its readers to experience the poem's arguments about the power of light and of love, as agencies central to Platonic thought which are 'made new' in the *Cantos*.

Pound is a 'case study', along with Beckett, Twain, Mailer and Kleist, in Albert Cook's *Canons and Wisdoms*, a book written in defence of the conviction 'that a profound wisdom inheres in poetry' and that indeed we should displace the concept of the canon from our discourse and replace it with wisdom, itself a deliberately undefined term in this book. From these unpropitious beginnings Cook eventually moves to an important issue, the relationship between aesthetics and ethics, grounded here in the question of whether a writer of bad faith may produce a work of ethical value – which is where Pound comes in. Do his doctrinal support of the politics of fascism, and his anti-Semitism – strangely relegated here to what Cook calls 'fairly rare effusions' in the *Cantos* – militate against the ethical ambition of the poem? Impressed by the lyric power of some of the *Pisan Cantos* and the 'Seven Lakes' canto, Cook can only answer his question by the unhelpful assertion that on balance 'the unacceptability of one key part of its ethics does not irreparably vitiate the poem'.

Pound in Multiple Perspective, edited by Andrew Gibson, gives seven substantial essays addressed to the diversity of Pound and his work: in his introduction Gibson argues that within their own diversity of topic and approach, all these essays have common concerns, particularly in relation to two questions which repeatedly recur in this study as in many others on Pound – 'how far is it possible to think of Pound and his work (especially the *Cantos*) in terms of wholes; and if we can't, does it matter?' These lively and provocative essays by non-Poundians – with the marginal exception of the late Eric Mottram – debate the chameleon-like manoeuvrings of Pound's personality as it dips and bows to the persuasions and interests of his peers, at once imitator and mimic, companion and adversary of the manners and aesthetics of his famous contemporaries, such as W. B. Yeats, Wyndham Lewis, Ford Madox Ford, Joseph Conrad and T. S. Eliot. On the completeness of Pound's poetic and aesthetic enterprise these essays offer predictable responses, given the central interests of these contributors in the other major modernists: Warwick Gould and John Harwood share a view of the *Cantos* as a flawed work lacking coherence or a distinctive pattern of development, whilst Robert Hampson and Andrew Gibson find ways of defending the poem through its 'decentred' nature, which yields a postmodern subversion of authoritarianism and the totalizing convictions that go with it. On a different note John Woolford celebrates Pound as a Bloomian strong poet in his repudiation of Browning's version of poetic wholeness, and Eric Mottram reads the *Cantos* within the American epic tradition, a tradition here seen as open-ended in form and intermediate in its ideological withholding of conclusion. Finally, Peter L. Caracciolo locates representations of Pound and Yeats in Wyndham Lewis's *Apes of God*, in an essay which traces the personal, anthropological and literary sources Lewis turned to in composing this complex satire.

None of Pound's biographers has so far provided an account of his education to equal that of Herbert Howarth's *Notes on Some Figures Behind T. S. Eliot* (1964). Gail McDonald goes some way towards satisfying this need in her *Learning to be Modern: Pound, Eliot, and the American University*, though in the end the breadth of her focus still leaves us short of a thorough history of Pound's university years. McDonald's argument is that the dynamic tension between tradition and innovation which underwrites the modernist aesthetic of these poets can be read in the history of the American educational system as they experienced it, a system divided by two educational philosophies represented by the convictions of Irving Babbit and John Dewey. She argues that if Pound and Eliot were drawn to the powerful conservative idealism of Babbit, who saw the traditions of learning as a coherent, ordered pursuit of absolute and eternal truths, they were equally drawn to Dewey's lifelong project to dismantle the conventional opposition between abstract thought and experience. In McDonald's reading these conflicting philosophies of education and their implications for the practices of the poet are everywhere apparent in the prose and poetry of Pound and Eliot, a claim she supports though extensive citations of their work and her wide reading in the primary and secondary sources on the American higher educational system.

Fred C. Robinson's major essay on Pound's Anglo-Saxon studies and his route to his version of *The Seafarer*, 'The Might of the North: Pound's Anglo-Saxon Studies and *The Seafarer*', is now reissued from its first publication in *YR* in 1982, in a collection of Robinson's essays, *The Tomb of Beowulf*. Largely on the basis of archival researches at Yale, Robinson was able to show that Pound had been a student of Anglo-Saxon at Hamilton College, and that his knowledge of *Beowulf* and *The Wanderer* was genuine, thus disposing of the widespread scholarly view that *The Seafarer* version was an extraordinary anomaly in a writer largely educated in Romance languages and literatures. Robinson provides a detailed exposition of the strategies of translation used by Pound in his *Seafarer* version and relates these to Pound's early attention to the music and metrics of Anglo-Saxon poetry.

Niall Rudd has a chapter on Pound and Propertius in his study *The Classical Tradition in Operation*, materials originally given as the Robson Classical Lectures at the University of Toronto, and with chapters on Chaucer and Virgil, Shakespeare and Plautus, Pope and Horace, and Tennyson and Lucretius. Rudd investigates Pound's claims for Propertius's anti-Augustanism and anti-imperialism, and finds Pound's representation of the Latin poet's view only partially valid, and the *Homage to Sextus Propertius* hardly the 'incisive, hard-hitting, anti-imperialist satire' it is claimed to be, and a 'strangely inadequate response to the disasters of 1914–17'. In an appendix Rudd defends Pound's adversary, William Gardner Hale, from Pound's gratuitously aggressive responses to Hale's 'trenchant and witty' 1919 article on four sections of the *Homage* where he argues that Hale's article was based not on the appreciation of poetry but on what he excelled in, an expertise in Latin developed over half a century of study of the written words of Latin authors. Rudd rightly sees Hale's work as indicative of the modes of scholarship existing at that time, and does his best by Pound through a brief summary of the ways in which later classicists, responding to differing idioms of cultural practice, have made claims for the *Homage* which Hale could never have supported.

In *Ezra Pound, Wyndham Lewis, and Radical Modernism*, Vincent Sherry confronts a crucial question: what is the relationship between the *avant-garde* aesthetics of Pound and Lewis and their reactionary politics? The question has been asked before, but Sherry's answer to it follows from an original reading of a change of aesthetic values in European cultural history from the French Revolution to the onset of modernism, a change from the primacy of 'musical empathy' as the condition of the aesthetic to one which privileges the visual over the aural, the eye over the ear. His tracing of this shift in the writings of T. E. Hulme, for example, is particularly telling and leads into an account of the importance of Julian Benda, Ortega y Gasset and Remy de Gourmont, where the aesthetic and the political unite in an anti-democratic and aristocratic ideology. Sherry's reading of Pound, and of Lewis's paintings and writings, situates them within the ideological framework of the 'antique state', a totalitarian site where the unity of art and politics finds its centre. The forceful study adds significantly to our understanding of Pound's disastrous involvement with fascism.

G. Singh's *Ezra Pound as Critic* is a labour of homage from a scholar once on familiar terms with the poet, and intimate with his work. That said, it has to be acknowledged that this is a curiously ill-informed and outdated study of Pound's criticism, apparently ignorant of much of the most recent work on Pound's aesthetics and his critical practice. For example, there is no reference in Professor Singh's book to I. F. A. Bell's seminal study *Critic as Scientist* (1981) – the foremost study of Pound's prose writings within the frame of his modernist aesthetics – or to any subsequent contribution to these matters. In his bibliography, Singh cites Hugh Kenner's critical study *A Homemade World* (1975) within his list of 'Select Biographies', an odd place to discover Kenner's remarkably influential study of American writing, and the general bibliography lists no work on Pound published later than 1981. In the intervening fifteen years commentary on Pound, his poetry, aesthetics and criticism, has been transformed by radical re-readings of his work, none of them cited in this sadly redundant book.

Demetres Tryphonopoulos's study of Pound and the occult, *The Celestial Tradition* (*YWES* 73.604), acknowledged a debt to Leon Surette's *A Light from Eleusis* (1979): Surette's new work *The Birth of Modernism: Ezra Pound, T. S. Eliot, W. B. Yeats, and the Occult* now appears with a tribute to Tryphonopoulos, Surette's student and companion in these studies for several years. Surette spreads his net wider, and proposes that many other modernists – D. H. Lawrence, Joseph Conrad and Wallace Stevens, for example – were variously involved in some aspect of occultism. Surette properly asks the question, 'What is the Occult?', and in answer cites Denis Saurat's characterization of it as the 'strange and monstrous alliances' of 'all the conquered religions: Gnostic beliefs, Neo-platonism, Hermeticism, Manicheanism, Mithraism, Zoroastrianism'. Surette adds that the occult is 'metaphysical speculation – speculation about the nature of ultimate reality and of our relation to it' and that if it is less coherent than theological or philosophical practices, it is 'perhaps more interesting'. Furthermore, it is typically 'nontheistic and monistic' and 'typically mystical', and assumes 'the possibility of direct contact between living human beings and ultimate reality, the noumenal, the transcendent, or the divine'. As I noted in *YWES* 73 (604), there is no doubt that Pound had some knowledge of these unorthodoxies, though Surette argues that Pound kept a sceptical distance from the wilder reaches of occultism, and sees it confined to the venerable kind articulated in *A Light from Eleusis*. Yeats's intimacy with the occult is familiar property, if a persistent embarrassment to Yeatsians. On Eliot, Surette's most important argument is about Pound's editing of *The Waste Land*, where Surette proposes that Pound's editorial task was primarily to advise on its thematic coherence and perspicuity 'as much as, or more than, on its rhetorical structure', and its thematic coherence had to do with Eliot's use of occult materials derived substantially from Jessie Weston, whose *From Ritual to Romance*, Surette shows, has become the derided and ignored 'source' of the poem. Surette adduces considerable evidence in support of this claim, and for this reason alone, his arguments about the role of the occult in the emergence of modernism will have to be taken seriously.

Walter Sutton has edited *Pound, Thayer, Watson, and The Dial*, an edition of a considerable cache of letters from Pound to Scofield Thayer, editor of the *Dial*. This is a valuable edition of materials which further enlarges our knowledge of Pound's editorial labours on behalf of his contemporaries, of his tirelessness in this capacity and of the nature of his relationship with Thayer.

Papers from the International Pound Conference of 1992 under the title *Ezra Pound and Europe*, edited by Richard Taylor and Claus Melchior, includes contributions from many well-known Poundians and some younger scholars entering this endlessly proliferating industry. This volume has Ronald Bush on 'The Composition of Ezra Pound's *Drafts and Fragments*', John Xiros Cooper on 'Music as Symbol and Structure in Pound's *Pisan Cantos* and Eliot's *Four Quartets*', Helen Dennis on Pound and Arnaut Daniel, Helen V. Emmitt on Pound and European aestheticism, A. D. Moody on 'Bel Esprit and the "Malatesta Cantos"', Peter Nicholls on Pound's 'Idea of Italy', Mary de Rachewiltz on Pound's library, Leon Surette on Pound and Cavalvanti, John Solt on Pound's relationship to Kitasono Katsue, Richard Taylor on his major project of a Variorum *Cantos*, 'Edition, Manuscript, Archive, Reading Text', and Demetres Tryphonopoulos on Pound's correspondence with Olivia Rossetti Agresti.

J. J. Wilhelm has completed his expansive biography of Pound with the publication of *Ezra Pound: The Tragic Years 1925–1972*, the third volume of this composite study. When we think of the enormous body of work Pound produced between 1925 and the late 1960s, then his life can hardly be called 'tragic' throughout the range of the titular period, though obviously enough the culmination of his fascist sympathies in the prison cage at Pisa and the madhouse of St Elizabeth's does cast a long shadow over his last quarter of a century. This volume is rich in detailed information and sympathetic in its presentation of a misguided genius whose work somehow survives the terrible error of his political views in his admiration for Mussolini. Wilhelm's life competes easily with Carpenter's, both in what it reveals of the intimacies of Pound's personal and intellectual relationships, and in the patient understanding it exhibits of its subject's enormous ambition and achievement.

There is a moment in Cary Wolfe's study of Pound and Emerson, *The Limits of American Literary Ideology,* when he locates the 'permanent property' left to society by Pound's 'donative artist' to an economy of value Pound found 'in the paradigms and authority of nature', the materials of common substance – wheat, sunlight, corn, saffron – which offer a glimpse of 'visionary essence' or 'transcendent radiance', forms of 'naturalized gold' entirely different to the 'debased gold of Pound's own economic context'. These quotations come from Wolfe's chapter called 'Visionary Capital', where lyric and epic poetry, coin and paper money, and the value-laden transactions of aesthetic and economic exchange are his subject. Much of this vocabulary is naturally associated with the author of 'Nature', especially with the moment where he writes of property and possession and reminds us that no one owns the landscape though it has a property, that of unity, visible to the poet. Elsewhere, Emerson employs the vocabulary of imperialism to designate the poet, who is not 'any permissive potentate, but is emperor in his own right'. The ideas common to Emerson and Pound and the contiguity of their vocabularies are Wolfe's subject, the evidence which supports his central proposition – that of Pound's closeness to Emerson's brand of American liberal individualism – a way of reading Pound which Wolfe offers as a 'reframing' of his more widely acknowledged interests in American history and culture through figures such as Thomas Jefferson and John Adams. Wolfe argues that if the disturbing consequences of liberal individualism are held in check by Emerson's idealism and his separation of culture and politics, Pound transformed the ideological symptom of Emersonian individualism 'into the full-blown condition of authoritarian egoism and fascism'. This is an intriguing study which repays close attention.

Journal articles on Pound in 1993, other than those in *Paideuma*, are as follows: Stephen Hartnett on 'The Ideologies and Semiotics of Fascism: Analyzing Pound's *Cantos* 12–15' (*Boundary* 20[1993].i.65–93); Burt Kimmelman on 'Ezra Pound's Medievalism and the American Avant-garde' (*ArkQ* 2[1993].213–41); Frank Lentricchia on 'Ezra Pound's American Book of Wonders' (*SAQ* 92[1993].387–415), an absorbing essay on Dante's treatment of Florence as a model for Pound's treatment of American history; Richard Taylor on 'Canto XLIX, Futurism, and the Fourth Dimension' (*Neoh* 20[1993].337–56) on Futurism and the paranormal and its relationship to this Canto; David Kadlec on 'Pound, Blast, and Syndicalism' (*ELH* 60[1993].1015–31); and Ming Xie on 'Elegy and Personae in Ezra Pound's *Cathay*' (*ELH* 60[1993].261–81). Journal articles for 1994, other than in *Paideuma*, include: Robert Casillo on 'Ezra Pound: The Marxist Anti-Semitic Zionist?' (*JAmC* 17.iii.49–54); Narayana K. Chandran on 'Ezra Pound and Sir Walter Raleigh: Allusions to "The Lie" in some *Lustra* and *Blast* Poems' (*Neophil*

78.497–503); and Peter Nicholls on 'A Consciousness Disjunct: Sex and the Writer in Ezra Pound's *Hugh Selwyn Mauberley*' (*JAmS* 28.61–75). Readers with an interest in Carl Rakosi should know of a collection not received for review, *Carl Rakosi: Man and Poet* (NPF, 1993), edited by Michael Heller.

The publication in a handsome volume at reasonable cost of Adrienne Rich's *Collected Early Poems 1950–1970* brings together her first six volumes from *A Change of World* (1951) to *The Will to Change* (1971), with a few additional poems of this period. In her foreword, Rich notes that the word 'change' occurs in the titles of both the first and last books in this collection and, looking back on this phase of her poetic career, regards the poems in *Snapshots of a Daughter-in-Law* (1963) as the ones in which she broke free from imitation of her predecessors and 'began trying, to the best of my ability, to face the hard questions of poetry and experience'. And so she did, a cultural seismograph of American powers of reinvention. It is interesting, therefore, that in *The Will to Change* she remained in touch with that 'Sinner of the Florida Keys', Wallace Stevens, looking back as well as forward: 'I watched the lights on the shore I had left for a long time; each / one, it seemed to me, was a light I might have lit, in the old days.' This is an important book because it enables the complexity of Rich's early poetic development to be traced fully by those, particularly her many younger admirers, who missed the opportunity to acquire the early volumes.

What is Found There: Notebooks on Poetry and Politics is a title Adrienne Rich partly takes from William Carlos Williams's love poem to his wife, 'Asphodel, That Greeny Flower'. In this collection Rich gives us a fertile mix of journals, letters and responses to established and contemporary poets which shows her consumed with the desire to find in poetry the instrument of change and diversity: 'I see the life of North American poetry at the end of the century as a pulsing, racing convergence of tributaries – regional, ethnic, racial, social, sexual – that, rising from lost or long-blocked springs, intersect and infuse each other.' Rich gives attention to many of these voices including the half Chicano, half Apache poet Jimmy Santiago Baca, the Muskogee Creek Joy Harvo, the unknown people who scratched graffiti on the boarded-up house of Pablo Neruda after his death – to all those struggling into language. She also unflinchingly assesses Irena Klepfisz's poetry about the ghetto, arguing that Adorno's statement, 'After Auschwitz, to write a poem is barbaric', has 'to be severely parsed'. Rich, as always is strenuous, but this is complicated and intensified by her sense of language as desire: there is a running engagement with Wallace Stevens throughout these essays, an attraction–repulsion response which castigates the Stevens who could write 'do not use the rotted names' but was nevertheless so complacent about the 'old racist configurations', yet percipiently identifies the politics of his 'Yellow Afternoons' and Elizabeth Bishop's 'Chemin de Fer'. Rich describes how 'The Idea of Order at Key West' offered her something absolutely new, 'a conception of a woman maker'. This book shows that Rich quite rightly made of what she found in her American poetic predecessors a vision beyond their imaginings, a vision more convinced of the political as well as poetical roots of language.

Alice Templeton's *The Dream and the Dialogue: Adrienne Rich's Feminist Poetics* (UTennP) appeared in 1994, though we have not seen it for review. Recent journal articles on Rich include Elissa Greenwald's 'The Dream of a Common Language: Vietnam Poetry as Reformation of Language and Feeling in the Poems of Adrienne Rich' (*JAmC* 16[1993].iii.97–102); Sandra Runzo on 'Intimacy, Complicity, and the Imagination: Adrienne Rich's *Twenty-One Love Poems*'

(*Genders* 16[1993]. Spring. 61–79); Alice Templeton writing on 'Contradictions: Tracking Adrienne Rich's Poetry' (*TSWL* 12[1993].333–40); and Kevin McGuirk's consideration of Rich's lyric idiom in 'Philoctetes Radicalized: "Twenty-One Love Poems" and the Lyric Career of Adrienne Rich' (*ConL* 34[1993].61–87).

The first volume in the American Poetry Recovery series is an edition of *Edwin Rolfe: Collected Poems* edited by Cary Nelson and Jefferson Hendricks. The aim of this Recovery series is to collect and anthologize the work of poets who have not made their way into the traditional literary canon, 'labor poets, feminist and minority poets, and socialist and anarchist poets', a necessary enterprise as argued for in Nelson's major study *Repression and Recovery: Modern American Poetry and the Politics of Cultural Memory, 1910–1945* (*YWES* 70.615–16). In a preface to this *Collected Poems*, his editors note that several of Rolfe's poems are due to appear in the second edition of *The Heath Anthology of American Literature*, a small but significant sign of the effects of their labours in recovering this poet to contemporary view, for there is nothing like Heath (or Norton) for determining, in the most practical terms, a consensus understanding of what constitutes the 'tradition' of American writing. The degree of editorial prerogative in this edition is also made evident in the preface, where Nelson and Hendricks make clear that this collection does not reprint all the poems Rolfe published, and includes only a few of the unpublished poems from the Rolfe archive. In effect this is to give us a 'selected' *Collected Poems*, where the intention is to affirm the relationship between Rolfe's socialist politics and his practice as a poet, and to preserve this version of him as representing the case for his importance in the history of modern American poetry. To this end the editors include a section called 'Early Poems' which suggests something of the routes Rolfe might have taken as a poet in the late twenties and early thirties, had his poetry resisted the imperatives of his political vision. Nelson's introductory essay on Rolfe's 'Lyric Politics' is a work of sober advocacy, urging the unity of principle and method which enabled Rolfe to make 'decisive political and moral judgments' in these poems. Cary Nelson also relates the case of Rolfe in 'What Happens When we Put the Left at the Center?' (*AL* 66.771–79).

A Muriel Rukeyser Reader edited by Jan Heller Levi with an introduction by Adrienne Rich is an enterprising publishing venture much to be welcomed. The editor's principle of selection is to give the sense of the 'journey' rather than a 'greatest hits' approach: Levi has thus included material from all phases of Rukeyser's career, with a generous selection of her prose writing. This accentuates Rukeyser's role as a multi-faceted thinking activist, successor to Margaret Fuller and precursor to Adrienne Rich, but always entirely her own woman. This is most notable in the ideological integrity of her work in the 1930s. The prose selections are well chosen to illustrate her range: the chapter 'The *Amistad* Mutiny', from the 1942 biography *Willard Gibbs*, is a fine instance of her power to connect across cultural divisions; in contrast, the short prose piece 'College Radicals' incisively assesses the process by which youthful radicals surrender to the 'foam of rewards', knowing 'only the floors of their own forgetting'. There are also generous selections from *The Life of Poetry* (1949), which speaks for the multiplicity of experience and for poetry as an index of cultural possibilities. Some of the short poems included have what Rukeyser herself called the 'Breathe in experience, breathe out poetry' quality which will be valued differently by different readers. For this reader, some of the most impressive poems were the longer ones, including the 'Lives', well represented here by 'Gibbs' (misprinted as '7ibbs' in the contents page) and 'Ann

Burlak' (the labour organizer), which are reprinted in full. Rukeyser is most powerful in the 1938 selection from the long poem 'The Book of the Dead', an indictment of the cover-up of the silicosis damage to miners in West Virginia: the juxtaposition of documentary evidence from the inquiry, blues-like rhythms and formal verse patterns acquires an earned resonance questioning how Americans created this 'breathed in America', these 'unmade boundaries of acts and poems'. This very laudable book deserves to be available in paperback. It is an important act of recovery.

Delmore Schwartz and James Laughlin: Selected Letters is edited by Robert Phillips in the Norton series of Laughlin's correspondence with his *New Directions* writers. Their relationship was founded on Laughlin's response to Schwartz's unsolicited offer in July 1937 of five poems and two short stories for the new annual, *New Directions in Prose and Poetry*. After the serious hiccup over Schwartz's sending one of these poems – 'In Dreams Begin Responsibilities' – to *PR*, which accepted it, whilst Laughlin was still making up his mind about it, their relationship blossomed, and for some years Schwartz was sustained by a job as Laughlin's assistant at *New Directions*. These letters date from 1937 to 1963 and give ample evidence of Laughlin's generous handling of his gifted but difficult friend. They contain an absorbing mix of detail about Schwartz's and Laughlin's creative projects, the business affairs of *New Directions*, and literary gossip. Phillips has added a brief coda covering the last desperate years of Schwartz's life, a sobering narrative of his paranoia, destitution and death.

Work on Anne Sexton includes Cathryn Essinger's 'Recreating Fairyland – A Feminist Perspective: Transformations by Anne Sexton' (*MAR* 14.ii.14–19); Ann Mikhail Long's psychological approach to suicide in 'As If Day Had Rearranged Into Night: Suicidal Tendencies in the Poetry of Anne Sexton' (*L&P* 39[1993].i-ii.26–41); John Hruschka's 'Anne Sexton and Anima *Transformations*: *Transformations* as a Critique of the Psychology of Love in Grimm's Fairy Tales' (*Mythlore* 20.45–7); and Rose Lucas also turns to *Transformations* in 'A Witch's Appetite: Anne Sexton's *Transformations*' (*SoRA* 26[1993].73–85). Diane Wood Middlebrook has an article, not seen, on Tillie Olsen and Anne Sexton in *Listening to Silences: New Essays in Feminist Criticism* (OUP, 1994) edited by Shelley Fisher Fishkin.

With *Modernism from Right to Left: Wallace Stevens, the Thirties and Literary Radicalism*, Alan Filreis extends the research undertaken in *Wallace Stevens and the Actual World* (*YWES* 72.478–9) to a reappraisal of the poet's responses to political events and literary politics in the preceding decade. The present study is broader in scope and more avowedly new historicist in approach: Filreis aims 'to come at Stevens from the ideological commingling, the circulating playground' of the poets, editors, reviewers who constructed the debate within which he read himself. This is a sophisticated feat of historical recovery which shows Stevens renegotiating the status of a modernist aesthetic challenged from the left: at the time when *Harmonium* was reissued, Stevens, in poems such as 'Anglais Mort à Florence', was responding to the pressures of literary radicalism and moving on. Filreis lines up 'The Men That Are Falling', which received the *Nation*'s poetry prize for 1936, with, in Stevens's phrase, 'what one reads in the newspapers', showing how the fact that it was so early a response to the war in Spain structures its ideology; it was the militancy of the contending partisan voices which honed Stevens's poetics. The most brilliant and assured section of Filreis's analysis is devoted to 'The Man with the Blue Guitar', a poem produced in a 'red' atmosphere;

he identifies it as the key poem of the thirties and demonstrates that canonical modernists like Moore and Stevens did not sit it out in rarefied seclusion but worked within that partisan decade.

David Jarraway's *Wallace Stevens and the Question of Belief* traces the evolution of Stevens's 'genealogy of belief', arguing that the poet's early attempts to explore the possibilities of a substitutive humanism for faith developed into a postmodern investigation, assisted by his reading of Heidegger and Nietzsche, of the 'different intelligence' involved in post-metaphysical questions of 'belief' rather than 'faith'. The Nietzschean slant brings to mind B. J. Leggett's *Early Stevens: The Nietzschean Intertext* (*YWES* 73.606), which played the poetry with such lambent intelligence; Jarraway, in contrast, is ponderous and dull, shored up by theoretical sandbagging and given to pronouncements such as '"An Ordinary Evening in New Haven" . . . can begin to suggest the process of semiosis more primordially anterior to the products of mimesis, when the rhetoric of representation in both of its paradigmatic forms becomes deregulated.' Who would want to return to the poem after this? Jarraway tells us that Stevens moves from a 'poetry of transcendence to a poetry of immanence', and he makes a wearying journey of it.

As the title suggests, Glen MacLeod's *Wallace Stevens and Modern Art: From the Armory Show to Abstract Expressionism* records Stevens's deep and continuous preoccupation with the art world, in particular the world of collectors and gallery directors, and shows how developments in his poetic theory paralleled developments in modern art from 1910 to the 1950s. It was Stevens's friendship with Walter Arensberg which gave him privileged access to the 'art-crowd' during the *Harmonium* years, and MacLeod suggests that the abrupt end of that friendship in 1921 was a contributory factor to Stevens's poetic silence in the ensuing years. When he took up writing again in the thirties, the Wadsworth Atheneum in Hartford was the most modern museum in the United States, presenting the first Picasso retrospective in 1934. MacLeod's discussion of the post-*Harmonium* period shows that Stevens 'speaks the dialect of the art world' and that 'It must be abstract' is spoken from within the Abstract Expressionism controversy. After 1939, Henry Church replaced Arensberg as the wealthy art collector friend, 'the figure of capable imagination'; Filreis's research on the 1940s might have been drawn on to round out the registration of the 'actual world' of art in which Stevens liked to dwell, but MacLeod has, in any case, given us not just information, but Stevens, the man, alive in his time.

Wallace Stevens and the Feminine edited by Melita Schaum, a collection of ten essays, is divided into two parts. The first, 'Texts', comprises essays which argue for the centrality of the feminine in Stevens's poetry: the Jungian interpretations of the first three essays by Jacqueline Vaught Brogan, Mary B. Arensberg and Barbara M. Fisher move rather ponderously through the poems. Daniel O'Hara's Kristevan model of the semiotic recovery of 'the lost thing' is more responsive to Stevens's lyric power. Paul Morrison's 'The Fat Girl in Paradise' is an assured Derridean reading of 'Notes' as a 'Beginnengans Wake', witty and stylish about Stevens's relation to the Miltonic figuration of the feminine. Part 2, 'Contexts', examines the intersection of gender with religion and poetics. C. Roland Wagner interprets Stevens's deathbed conversion as a return to the 'nurturing pre-Oedipal' mother, whereas Rosamond Rosenmeier finds that Stevens's 'mothers' include the 'Divine Female' of the wisdom-seeking Pennsylvanian pietists of his family heritage. The best essay in this collection, by Celeste Goodridge, a barometer of the changes in aesthetic and political pressures of the period, shows how Marianne Moore's reading of Stevens in the 1930s evolved from early caution to an endorsement of his distancing from mass politics. Melita Schaum compares the political agendas of the critics of Stevens in the 1940s and 1950s with those of H.D. Lisa M. Steinman finds in both Emerson and Stevens a celebration of the private domain in art, but a tendency to internalize commonplace gender roles in order to distance themselves from domesticity in life. It is curious that, with the exception of Fisher, not one of these contributions responds to the eroticism with which Stevens's language, 'Since the imperfect is so hot in us', is so often imbued.

Daniel R. Schwartz in *Narrative and Representation in the Poetry of Wallace Stevens* puts into play a pluralist ideology of reading, a dialogue between a humanist concern with voice, character, narrative and a modernist-deconstructive interest in rhetoricity. Furthermore, Stevens's personae, 'exfoliations of himself' (in a phrase from 'Someone Puts a Pineapple Together'), are invested with a Whitmanesque largess and his preoccupation with representation is read within a modernist eclecticism, most notably in the visual arts. In one sentence alone, Stevens is likened to Monet, Yeats, Joyce and Matisse. What we are given is a carnivalesque poet, sexy, fecund, with an overflowing, rich narrative palette, at once a Divine Comedy and a Prelude, Arnoldian yet Joycean, whose 'Anecdote of the Prince of Peacocks' is his 'Circe', whose 'Blue Guitar' is his 'Scylla and Charybdis'. Such a broad scope has disadvantages: the comments on political context, for example, have obviously not benefited from Filreis's scholarship, and, in general, the theory is sketchily applied. But the discussion fizzes along; the mode is pedagogic, interrogative, as if an ongoing seminar session, generating bold and extensive commentary on individual poems unchecked, with a 'metaferocity' in the rapid sequences (as Schwartz describes Stevens) changing gear frequently from new criticism to deconstructive readings, always stimulating, never dull.

Wallace Stevens: An Annotated Secondary Bibliography compiled by John N. Serio, editor of the *Wallace Stevens Journal*, surveys the criticism, books, essays and dissertations on Stevens from 1916 to 1990. The 1,875 entries are chronologically arranged and Serio summarizes the critical approach and topic of each item. There are also four indices: Author, Journal, Subject and Title, with effective cross-references. One of the unwitting revelations of the chronological organization of recent contributions is that the reader is given the opportunity to note the exigencies of publishing practice in the academy: material processed through essays towards the goal of the book. The contours of the Stevens industry are evident from the single dissertation entry for 1957 through to the nine entries for 1990. The layout also makes readily accessible interesting facts such as how consistently appreciative Marianne Moore was of Stevens's poetry, or which writers (a distinguished collection) reviewed *The Auroras of Autumn* in 1952. Serio, in his preface, writes that his inspiration was J. M. Edelstein's landmark study, *Wallace Stevens: A Descriptive Bibliography* (1973), and that his aim was to 'complement Edelstein's work'. He is unduly modest. Serio's book is in itself a landmark study, a monumental labour accomplished with grace and urbanity, an essential resource for Stevens scholars and a testament to the continuing life of the poetry.

The spring 1993 *WSJour* (17.i) is a special issue on 'Poets Reading Stevens', contributions which guest editor Joseph Duemer has arranged as an 'extended composition of four movements'. The overture consists of previously published poems, including Roethke's 'A Rouse for Stevens' and Berryman's 'So Long? Stevens'. This is followed by a 'prose interlude', which includes contributions from

John Updike (13–15) and Robert Pinsky (31–4), the latter a beguiling, stylish response to Stevens's 'pastoral' or 'charms and spells'. The 'central suite' of short lyrics, some with related prose, includes a cento of Stevens's phrases by Robert Mezey (19–21)and 'Notes on the Reality of the Self' by Jori Graham (22–6). Robert Dana, surveying the modern-day tackiness of Florida, reprimands Stevens for his 'travel poster Florida', for his perorations that 'could just as well be delivered to an orchid' (44–6). It is difficult for the poems in this section to live up to the titles, which are often witty as is Paul Mariani's 'Wallace Stevens Returns from Paris Ruined' (65), but more often just wacky. The best poems such as David Young's 'Putting it Mildly' (63), are affectionate and do not attempt too much. The last section of critical essays includes a reading by Mark Irwin of 'Large Red Man Reading' (126–8), registering the title 'as human as it is mythic, and as sweaty as it is serene'.

In the fall 1993 *WSJour* (17.ii) Helen Vendler discusses Stevens's allegorical personae as 'indices of potential discourses, "cartoons" of conceptual play' (147–61). She focuses primarily on *Notes*, arguing that allegorical pairings such as Canon Aspirin and his sister are exercises in self-portraiture, poetic desire and its antithesis or banal parody. Their function is to oust the classical god, Apollo, and the Christian angel who haunt the poem. Alan Filreis gives a detailed account of the relationship of Stevens and J. Ronald Lane Latimer, founder of the Alcestis Press, in the thirties (180–202). The most notable contribution is Bonnie Costello's 'Wallace Stevens: The Adequacy of Landscape' (203–18), which charts how the poet moved away from the scenic structures of Romanticism and questioned the European painterly traditions of spatial mastery. *Parts of a World* is, to Costello, the key volume in which Stevens rejects dominion but makes 'gestures of habitation' in the contingent. Clive Watkins picks up a poem from the spring issue, in 'Some Reflections on Donald Justice's Poem "After a Phrase Abandoned by Wallace Stevens"' (236–44), to meditate further on Dana Gioia's discussion of its use of 'generative quotation'.

The spring 1994 *WSJour* (18.i) opens with Janet McCann's essay on material relating to Stevens's conversion to Catholicism: the letter she received from Father Hanley stating that Stevens 'was baptized absolutely' is reproduced (3–5). It is interesting to read her essay in conjunction with the first two items in the fall 1994 issue, which are also concerned with Stevens and Catholicism. Karl Precoda's 'The Noble Rider on the Terminal Beach' (6–18) traces the derivation of the poet's aesthetic from the sea sounds and the shifting material ground (both economic and ecological) of Florida and the Keys. Jonathan Strange reproduces and comments upon six unpublished letters from Stevens to various correspondents (19–26). Thomas L. Martin, writing on 'Someone Puts a Pineapple Together', notes how 'threeness' is integral to the poem's structure and argues that its process of decreation is exemplary of Stevens's thought (27–49). Howard Needler discusses the Shakespearean and biblical incorporations of 'Peter Quince at the Clavier' as multiple voices that 'bespeak different phases and degrees of awareness' (50–62). Mervyn Williams writes on Stevens's 'sound cosmology' (63–80). Fred Hoerner's 'Gratification and its Discontents: The Politics of Stevens' Chastening Aesthetics' (81–105) is an enterprising, highly theorized Lacanian psychoanalytic and gender reading of several poems, including an extended discussion of stanzas vi and vii of 'Sunday Morning' and 'A Postcard from the Volcano'. The issue concludes with a current bibliography of criticism of Stevens.

The fall 1994 *WSJour* (18.ii) opens with two contributions related to Thomas

McGreevy. Mary Joan Egan's 'Thomas McGreevy and Wallace Stevens: A Correspondence' (123–45) traces their long epistolary friendship on matters of art and spirit from 1948 until Stevens's death. Stevens wrote of McGreevy to Barbara Church, 'He is . . . a blessed creature, sustained by a habit of almost medieval faith'; to a self-styled 'dried up Presbyterian' like Stevens, this abundant religious spirit was attractive. It is good to know that when they finally met in 1954 at a dinner party given by Mrs Church, at which the fourth guest was Marianne Moore, they got on famously, all cheeping together, in McGreevy's phrase, 'just like so many canaries'. Lee Jenkins's 'Thomas McGreevy and the Pressure of Reality' (146–56) covers some of the same ground concerning the artistic relationship of the two men, but also undertakes a brief assessment of McGreevy's poetry, noting, as does Egan, that Samuel Beckett admired it. Michael Hobbs's 'Stevens' Gunman Lover: Readers in *The Rock*' (157–69) is a rather heated Bakhtinian study of the poet's ' "conception of the listener" – in the form of his intra-textual readers' in the late poems. Hobbs argues that Stevens's imagined reader in 'Notes on Moonlight' is 'between the slouchings of a gunman and a lover', an indeterminate being with whom Stevens cultivates a dialogic exchange. Hobbs also finds the gunman/lover as reader in 'Final Soliloquy', a guise in which some readers might find themselves surprised. Stephen J. Adams claims that 'The Ordinary Women' is a playful fantasy on Longfellow's 'Hymn to the Night' (170–3). Edward Marx's 'The Comedian as Colonist' (175–95) is a reading of the exotic, focusing primarily on 'The Comedian as the Letter C'. Chris Beyers's 'Wallace Stevens and Ludwig Richter' comments on Stevens's allusion to the German Romantic painter and illustrator in 'Chaos in Motion and Not in Motion' (197–206).

Other journal articles on Stevens from 1993 are Thomas Austenfeld's 'Rituals of Reading in the Poetry of Wallace Stevens' (*SoAR* 59[1993].67–83); Timothy Bahti's 'Palm Reading: A Response to Eleanor Cook' (*Connotations* 3[1993].90–4) and John Hollander's commentary on this debate in 'A Note on Eleanor Cook, From Etymology to Paranomasia' (*Connotations* 3[1993].95–8) followed by Cook's responses in 'Paronomasia Once More' (*Connotations* 3[1993].99–102); Lorraine C. DiCicco's ' "The Comedian as the Letter C": Stevens's Successfully Failed Initiation Poem' (*WascanaR* 28[1993].i.23–39); William Doreski's 'Wallace Stevens in Connecticut' (*TCL* 39[1993].152–65); Mary Joan Egan's finding of an echo of Goethe's *Faust* in 'Wallace Stevens's "Homunculus et la belle étoile" ' (*ELN* 31[1993].59–62); and Sherod Santos's discussion of Stevens and Rilke in 'Eating the Angel, Conceiving the Sun: Toward a Notion of Poetic Thought' (*APR* 22[1993].vi.9–13). Articles in 1994 include Stanislaw Baranczak's 'The Unwelcome Modernist: The Paradox of Wallace Stevens's Reception in Poland' (*HudR* 6.92–103), and James Longenbach's 'Leaving Things Out' (*SWR* 79.574–90), on Stevens's relationship to the painter Claude Monet.

Robert Penn Warren was the subject of the summer 1993 issue of *SoR* (31.iv) with the following: J. Larry Allums on 'Robert Penn Warren's Fugitive Years: A Revaluation' (75–85); James H. Justus on 'Wisdom on the Slant: Warren Over the Long Haul' (37–50) and R. W. B. Lewis on 'The Great Dragon Country of Robert Penn Warren' (13–36); James A. Grimshaw Jr on 'Biographical Trends in Warren Criticism: The 1980s' (51–67); and Thomas H. Winn on Warren's novel *The Night Rider* (68–74). Daniel Duane writes on 'Of Herons, Hags and History: Rethinking Robert Penn Warren's *Audubon*: *A Vision*' (*SLJ* 27.25–35), and Anthony Szczesiul takes the same text as his subject in 'Robert Penn Warren's *Audubon*: Vision and Revision' (*MissQ* 47.3–13).

Barry Ahearn's *William Carlos Williams and Alterity* argues that too little attention has been paid to the paradoxes and contradictions of Williams's early poetry, which he sees as governed by the spirit and practice of 'alterity', the exploitation of contradiction as a creative strategy. He points to the unstable state of many of the poems in the early collections, subjected to Williams's repeated revisions, and the innovative format of the verse and prose books with their disruptions of generic conventions. Ahearn's argument is that Williams developed his own poetic voice through manipulating the anxious, crisis-ridden, contending voices of the early poems and that this was a self-conscious strategy, necessary to the conditions of his creativity. Ahearn develops this view through close examination of the poems as 'expressions of Williams's personal struggles with himself, his parents, his domestic role and his social position', an appropriate way of connecting the poems with Williams's aesthetic belief in the primacy of the local and particular. Ahearn devotes three chapters to thematic topics, Williams's handling of his public personae in the revolutionary poetics of early modernism, love and marriage, and his negotiations with various social communities, both artistic and civic; these are matched by later chapters on style and technique in relation to the governing idea of 'alterity' as the copestone of Williams's practical aesthetic. This is an enjoyable and instructive book, especially useful for its clear view of the relationship between the life and the poetry.

In Brian A. Bremen's *William Carlos Williams and the Diagnostics of Culture*, Williams becomes a savant for our own times, a figure whose cultural criticism not only had its purchase throughout his long life, but anticipated the conditions of late twentieth-century cultural anxiety and spoke to those conditions through his innovative poetics, which is said to 'embrace ideas about literature, history, medicine, gender relations, and politics that are currently finding expression in the contemporary critical enterprise of "cultural studies"'. This proposes a more radical re-reading of Williams's political and social thought than Bremen actually delivers, for we learn very little of the poet's involvement with politics in his time beyond a sense of his difficult relations to socialist politics in the thirties and forties and his abhorrence of Communism and fascism. In this context, Bremen's use of Eliot as a diehard traditionalist against Williams's enlightened liberalism becomes an unexamined thesis, lacking sophistication and a sufficient sense of the different constituencies they addressed, a strange failure to embrace adequately the specificity of place in the work of both these modernists. This looks all the more peculiar given Bremen's valuable researches into the source material for *Paterson*.

In Williams's red wheelbarrow poem there is a propositional ambiguity in the use of the word 'depends' in the line 'So much depends', an ambiguity which rescues the poem from its mere representation of objects as simply there. In his *Ideas in Things: The Poems of William Carlos Williams*, Donald W. Markos commits himself to the view that 'Williams' focus on particulars is a way through to the universal, bypassing – as far as possible – stale, conventional conceptions of what the universal is.' It seems a legitimate question then to ask what 'universal' is revealed in 'The Red Wheelbarrow', a poem very much dealing in things. Yet that qualifier 'depends' seems to come between the reader and the universal or essence, which must be present in the poem according to the kind of reading Markos brings to Williams's work. For Markos, Williams is an Emersonian visionary who seeks ways of overcoming the dualism of mind–nature and whose experimental verse line and form adumbrate the role of language in the 'renewal of perception'. These notions, along with Markos's commentary on the problematic relationship of nature and the imagination in Williams, provide a structural scheme which underpins his belief in the ethical programme of this body of poetry, whose purposes, it seems, are to reveal the universal in concrete particulars. This does seem at odds with other claims of particularity in Williams, his celebration of the rooted and local, in terms of both place and language. If the central thesis of this book seems of questionable value as a way of reading Williams's total enterprise, Markos's close attention to matters of prosody and line in a substantial number of poems offers an alternative centre of value in this ambitious study.

The Last Word by Elizabeth Murrie O'Neil is an edition of the letters between Marcia Nardi and William Carlos Williams, who used excerpts from three of Nardi's letters in books I and II of *Paterson*, under the attribution 'Cress'. On the evidence of O'Neil's introduction, Nardi's life was one of almost unremitting hardship, with long periods of ill-health, a failed marriage, a series of short-lived love affairs, and a son born out of wedlock who finally abandoned her because she would not reveal his father's identity. What kept her going was her commitment to poetry, and Williams's early faith in her work – which he thought to be 'some of the best writing by a woman (or anyone else) I have seen in years'. This correspondence is in two phases and gives some forty letters from April 1942 to the late spring of 1943, when Williams sought to bring their relationship to an end, oppressed by the variety of Nardi's written demands upon him. The second phase of letters runs from March 1949, following Nardi's chance discovery of excerpts from her letters in *Paterson*, and continues to October 1956, when Williams writes to congratulate her on the publication of her book *Poems*, issued in Alan Swallow's New Poetry Series that year. At the present time Nardi seems to be chiefly known through this association with Williams, and her place in the history of mid-twentieth-century American poetry is still insecure: O'Neil's excellent book will surely generate an interest in Nardi's work for its own qualities, independent of the difficult relationship recorded in these letters.

Papers from an international conference in Italy on Williams, which took place some years ago, have now been published under the title *The Rhetoric of Love in the Collected Poems of William Carlos Williams*, edited by Cristina Giorcelli and Maria Anita Stefanelli. Many notable Williams scholars from the United States are published in this collection along with their European counterparts, including Joseph Riddel on 'Cupid's Arrow – "Asphodel" and the Dynamics of Language', Peter Schmidt on '*Kora in Hell*: The Sewer Venus, Sexual Politics, and Williams's Improvisation "Rome" (1924)', Christopher MacGowan on 'Noah F. Paterson and *The Wedge*', Marjorie Perloff on 'The Fallen Leaf and the Stain of Love: The Displacement of Desire in Williams's Early Love Poetry' and Terence Diggory on 'Williams between St. Venus and St. Francis'. This collection offers expansive consideration of its topic throughout the range of Williams's work, developed from a variety of critical perspectives and methods.

WCWR 19 (1993) appeared as a double issue opening with essays in honour of Mary Ellen Solt and Hugh Kenner, acknowledged here as two of Williams's best critics. We are reminded of the value of Solt's essay 'The American Idiom' for its patient account of Williams's theories of 'relative measure' and 'variable foot', and Kenner's celebration of Williams as 'the best theorist the Paris decade had', and his unrivalled understanding of the workings of Williams's poems. Tributes to Solt follow in the form of essays by Theodora Rapp Graham, Terence Diggory, Barry Ahearn and T. Hugh Crawford, variously exploring the variety of Williams's poetics, and essays for Kenner by Marjorie Perloff, John Slatin, M. L. Rosenthal and Will Goodwin. Perloff's tribute to Kenner is especially telling for the way she handles Kenner's current marginalization from the theory-centred versions of contemporary critical discourse, and really has little more to do than to cite the range of his critical preoccupations in his published work to make the case for his standing declare itself, virtually without argument, though Perloff argues passionately enough for his value in this admirable piece. Where, indeed, should we be without him? This issue also carries a short essay by Paul Mariani 'On the 200th Anniversary of the Founding of Paterson'.

The critical essays in *WCWR* (20.i) open with Andrew Lawson's reading of 'The Wanderer' (1–22), Williams's 'rite of passage into the turbulent waters of modernity'. Lawson disputes with the prevailing critical commentaries on this poem and argues for it as 'a critical engagement with modernity in a specific form: that of alienated labour. Labour appears in Williams's poem against the grain of its initial romantic aesthetic, in a form so spectacular and degraded that it amounts to a return of the repressed.' Lawson's reading of this poem within the frame of modernist and political opportunities in 1913, the year of its composition, is innovatory and persuasive. Daniel Morris (23–37) uses the Williams–Laughlin correspondence to discuss the poet's dissatisfaction with Laughlin's publicizing of his work in relation to Williams's desire for a popular audience, and relates these matters to Williams's response to promotional displays on behalf of Charles Sheeler and Ernest Hemingway in the picture magazine *Life* in 1938 and 1941. Morris's essay gives us a picture of this anti-materialist modern poet in his ambition to challenge the 'elitist assumptions about the economics of modernism' and its relation to popular culture. Sergio Rizzo (38–60) writes on the 'Beautiful thing' of *Paterson*, a representation of African-American femininity Rizzo shows to be but one version of a 'series of textual attempts on Williams' part to grapple with the reality of black femininity and the highly personal significance it held for him'. Rizzo charts these other textual representations of black femininity in Williams's work in an essay which follows Aldon Lynn Nielsen and Toni Morrison in averting the critical gaze 'from the racial object to the racial subject; from the described and imagined to the describers and imaginers; from the serving to the served'.

'Williams and History' is the subject of the fall *WCWR* (20.ii), guest edited by Richard Frye, and gathering papers from an ALA 1993 conference on 'Williams and the "Poem Including History"'. Frye opens this issue with an essay on the poem 'Impromptu: The Suckers' (2–14) based on the Sacco–Vanzetti case: if this poem is generally ignored by Williams's commentators Frye finds its 'historicity' pointed, and discovers in it an indictment of the Anglo-American system of criminal justice, a rejection of the myth of American innocence and a repudiation of the bourgeois political bias of the Rutherford townspeople, whose response to the case is read as a 'defection of democracy'. Burton Hatlen (15–29) confronts the various editions of *Spring and All*, those with the prose and those without it, to argue for the importance of the text in its completest state, where the prose adds to the 'variables' in the ways we may read the poems, and suggests that Williams's willingness to allow *Spring and All* to appear in quite different states indicates something of the duality of his creative make-up, the creator of *avant-garde* experimental texts and the lyric poet. Linda A. (Taylor) Kinnahan (30–51) warns against any totalizing endeavour to characterize Williams's engagement with history, and reads a variety of prose works and early poems to argue that Williams rejects the 'objective' eye of the historian for a 'recognition of the relationship between cultural power, the construction of history, and the language of its narratives', through the textual process in which historical events and facts are 'ideologically mediated and discursively shaped'.

Other articles on Williams from 1993 include Thomas F. Bertonneau's 'Consecrated in Blood/Unjustly Accused: The Ethical Paradox of WCW's *In the American Grain* (An Anthropoetics)' (*Sagetrieb* 12[1993].i.7–30); Joseph Coroniti's 'An Assembled Order: William Carlos Williams's Music of the Imagination' (*AntigR* 92[1993].83–90); Sharon Dolin's 'Enjambement and the Erotics of the Gaze in Williams's Poetry' (*AI* 50[1993].29–52); and Jeff Poggie and Sergio Rizzo's 'The Novel Poetry of *Paterson*' (*Sagetrieb* 12[1993].i-ii.81–7). In 1994 Susan Ayres wrote on 'Women in the Later Poems of William Carlos Williams: "What Should You Do? But Love Them?"' (*JEP* 15.iii-iv.168–75) and Neil Easterbrook contributed '"Somehow Disturbed at the Core": Words and Things in William Carlos Williams' (*SCRev* 11.iii.25–44).

A new book on Louis Zukofsky is a rare but welcome event, and this is especially so in the case of Sandra Kumamoto Stanley's *Louis Zukofsky and the Transformation of a Modern American Poetics*, which brilliantly situates Zukofsky at the start of his career through his responses to Eliot and Pound, and takes us through to Ron Silliman's celebration of Zukofsky as the 'first to read Pound & Williams with what we wld recognize as modern eye & ear'. This brief book sets out to reveal Zukofsky's 'historical importance as a poet who links the Modernist revolution with a postmodern aesthetics', and Stanley's fascinating chapter on the exchange of ideas about poetry and poetics between Zukofsky and William Carlos Williams shows how well these two poets enact this transition. Stanley's name must now be added to that small but impressive group of writers who have risen to the challenge of Zukofsky's work, and made his strangeness accessible to us.

2. Fiction 1900–45

(a) General

Louise K. Barnett's *Authority and Speech: Language, Society, and Self in the American Novel* from 1993 analyses some canonical American novels of the nineteenth and twentieth century through the discourses of speech-act theory and sociolinguistics. Barnett argues that the confident use of a public language by Cooper, Hawthorne and Stowe, for example, gives way to a transitional period in which the reliability of a common language becomes problematized in the work of Melville and subjected to verbal scepticism by Twain, developments echoed in various ways by the work of James, Fitzgerald, Hemingway, Faulkner and Hurston. In the fictions of postmodernism the viability of a public language becomes the focus of parody. Barnett's study is a valuable account of the interaction of the linguistic, the social and the personal in the development of modern American literary culture in the novel: covering a wide range of materials, her argument is carefully structured and ably presented.

Also from 1993, Barbara Foley's *Radical Representations*: *Politics and Form in U.S. Proletarian Fiction 1929–1941* investigates the uses of the novel for the articulation of class consciousness in the 1930s, analysing the work of politically radical authors such as Tillie Olsen, William Attaway and Josephine Herbst, and examines the benefits and obstacles of four genre forms appropriated by proletarian literature: the fictional autobiography, the *Bildungsroman*, the social novel and the collective novel. Foley wishes to reconstruct the conventional understanding of the relation of class, gender and race in the ideology of the political left as it is reflected in the work of these writers, and appeals for a positive recognition of the value of their work. *Radical Representations* is a provocative re-reading of the relation of narrative and politics and the historically assumed conflict in the uses of art for propaganda: this is a stimulating contribution to the study of proletarian fiction.

What some critics see as the 'grey area' between fiction and non-fiction (particularly of the journalistic kind) is the subject of Phyllis Frus's *The Politics and Poetics of Journalistic Narrative: The Timely and the Timeless*, where she 'investigates the textuality of all discourse' and argues that 'the ideologically charged distinction between "journalism" and "fiction" is socially constructed rather than natural'. Frus suggests that the literary text is determined as 'nonpropositional' and thus is 'unlikely to be a factor in the politics of ordinary life, the domain of social experience and public expression where change is possible'. Her introductory chapter 'What Isn't Literature?' is theoretical, challenging, but, in many ways, deeply problematic, for in seeking to erode the distinctions between fiction and non-fiction she strikes a blow at some of our most cherished aesthetic and ontological certitudes about narrative art. One of her most important propositions here is that 'fictional narrative cannot be distinguished from nonfictional narrative on the basis of the fictivity of any of its elements, for even fictivity must be represented in language'; and, a little later, she remarks to the effect that 'all narratives have the same status: that they are textually indistinguishable and that their fictionality or literariness depends on the way they are read and in what context'. 'Depends' here is the operative word, though it disguises the illogicality of Frus's position, since it is precisely because 'fictionality or literariness' *depends* on the ways, and contexts in which, we read narratives that they cannot have 'the same status' in our experience of them, and Frus's formulation of the problem is at odds (and always will be) with what we can only call our commonsense understanding of the 'modes of being' of fictional and non-fictional texts. Obviously her thesis works best with those texts of non-fiction that utilize fictional techniques, which were loosely deemed examples of 'the New Journalism' by Tom Wolfe – many of Mailer's autobiographical reports, Truman Capote's *In Cold Blood* (subtitled, we might remember, 'A True Account'), Wolfe's own journalistic writings – but the boundary between Hemingway's journalism and the way in which he adapted it for narrative fiction is not easily torn down and, unfortunately for Frus, many of Hemingway's remarks on the distinctions between fiction and journalism, and the crafts involved in the composition of both, forcefully insist upon the ways in which he sought to raise the timely piece of reportage into the timelessness of art. The opening chapter considers Stephen Crane and other chapters take in John Hersey, Janet Malcolm and Philip Roth. The book as a whole, however, is more preoccupied by theory than exemplification and in this it disappoints, but it is frequently suggestive and is a useful addition to the available commentary on a number of modern American writers. [H. C.]

Carla Cappetti's *Writing Chicago: Modernism, Ethnography, and the Novel* assays in what is, to my knowledge at least, largely neglected territory. Her subject is the influential Chicago School of Sociology (notably the work of Horace Cayton, Robert Parks, Robert Redfield and Louis Wirth) and its connection with Chicago novelists of the 1930s, primarily Nelson Algren, James T. Farrell and Richard Wright (Algren is more properly speaking a novelist of the 1940s and 1950s, but as Cappetti is addressing the interaction between literary and sociological ideas about the city in the inter-war years, it seems reasonable that he should be included here). Her study is marked by arguments from affinity rather than influence, though in her chapter on Farrell's *Studs Lonigan* trilogy ('Ethnographers at Home') she successfully shows how closely Farrell's development of Studs's story and its Chicago backdrop 'tracks' Farrell's familiarity with the work of Chicago sociologists (he was an undergraduate student at the University of Chicago); she concludes the chapter by suggesting that in sociology 'Farrell found a theoretical framework that allowed him to recognize this process [economic and spiritual destruction allied to moral dissipation] and understand why a Studs remains trapped even as he appears to be defying the norms of his community'. Cappetti's approach works particularly well with Farrell, and, though to a lesser extent, with Algren, given their obvious similarities, but the work of Richard Wright raises larger questions of race and the African-American inheritance that make an approach to him through ethnography and sociology, and the attendant emphasis on the conflict between group and individual, somewhat less conclusive. The book as a whole, however, has much to recommend it and while the readings of individual novels frequently fail to rise above the statement of the obvious (there is, perhaps, too much plot summary here), the intellectual context in which these writers are placed is constructed with a good deal of scholarly acumen, and our knowledge of Chicago literature is considerably enlarged by Cappetti's book. Her bibliography, it might be noted, is a valuable research tool. [H. C.]

(b) Individual Authors

Rewriting the South: History and Fiction, edited by Lothar Honnighausen and Valeria Gennaro Lerda, is an interdisciplinary collection of essays with a section on the influence of southern history on Faulkner's authorial vision. Honnighausen's 'Faulkner Rewriting the Indian Removal' analyses Faulkner's moral and ideological purpose in recovering and recreating the results of Jackson's Indian policy, and concentrates on the short story 'Lo!' as a grotesque comedy that both draws on and expands historical detail to explore the roots of the human condition. Faulkner's practice of rewriting history suggests affinities with historiography, and in 'The Novelist as Historian in *Requiem for a Nun*', Andre Bleikasten describes Faulkner as both novelist and historian, relating his manner of narrative to that of the historical chronicle and yet suggesting that he denies the linearity of this mode, instead reading history as constantly recurring events that emphasize the continuity of the human psyche. Thomas L. McHaney's 'Faulkner's Cosmos and the Incarnation of History' posits Proust and Bergman as influential in Faulkner's shift from writing narratives of an objectified past to the refiguration of history in *Light in August*, the fluid sense of time in the Faulknerian cosmos resulting in the incarnation of the past through the characters of the present.

A set of *New Essays on The Sound and the Fury* is a welcome addition to the well-established series of contemporary study guides, the American Novel. Edited by Noel Polk, this collection reassesses the novel in terms of contemporary critical interest in continental feminism, deconstruction, and the racial and regional context of the novel, and through the novel's linguistic and syntactical experimentation. After Polk's summary of traditional critical responses Dawn Trouard questions the traditional reading of the text as centred on a unified image of Caddy, and draws on the work of Luce Irigaray to suggest that the Compson women resist presentation in terms of coherence and narrative closure. Donald M. Kartiganer also takes up the notion of intratextual resistance, claiming that, in incorporating a range of irreconcilable literary styles and perspectives, Faulkner also parodies them by denying the authoritative value of each, therefore at once encouraging and denying pluralistic readings. Polk also analyses tensions within the written text in his study of the antagonism between linguistic signifiers and their associated meanings, exemplified in the monologues of the Compson brothers. Richard Godden takes a different approach, with a social reading of the relation of incest and miscegenation that rejects psychological interpretations, reading incest within the politics of white Southern Radicalism as an attempt to support the social hierarchy and avoid the threat of blood-crossing.

A special issue of *MissQ* (46[1993].iii.) offers fresh readings of Faulkner's work. 'The Passion of Margaret Powers: A Psychoanalytic Reading of *Soldiers' Pay*' by Michael Zeitlin (351–72) concentrates on the stylized female figures of Faulkner's early prose and the tension between the author's presentation of women as iconographic object and woman as human subject, suggesting that, with Margaret Powers, the latter impulse prevails. Adopting the modernist concern with the representation of consciousness, and influenced by Freud's psychopathologic theories, Faulkner analyses the 'otherness' of women, and in so doing creates Margaret Powers as an autonomous identity. Continuing this psychoanalytic focus, Deborah E. Barker and Ivo Kamps in 'Much Ado About Nothing: Language and Desire in *The Sound and the Fury*' (373–93) apply Lacan's theories of ego formation in analysing the position of each of the Compson brothers in the transition from the Imaginary to Symbolic realms, arguing that in their desire for the absent and therefore unrepresentable, the brothers fail to approach the Symbolic; Barker and Kamps suggest that the brothers are trapped within personal worlds structured by futile, empty signifiers. This issue also takes up the subject of Faulkner's concern with the representation of history in John Lowe's positive reading of *The Unvanquished*, in 'Faulkner's Nietzschean Skirmish with the Civil War' (407–36), paralleling Bayard Sartoris's understanding of the relevance of the past with Nietzsche's tripartite formulation of historical perception, and arguing that Sartoris moves beyond all three modes to a Nietzschean 'super-history', in which obsolete traditions are redefined and the past realigned for the positive development of the future. Turning to shorter works, Michael Lahey in 'Trying Emotions: Unpredictable Justice in Faulkner's "Smoke" and "Tomorrow"' (447–62) provides an interesting slant on traditional studies of the status of truth and objectivity in Faulkner, looking at the presentation of community justice and law and suggesting that it is through perceptions of the interplay of courtroom action and emotion that Faulkner comments on the questionable ethics of legal procedure. In 'Reconsidering Maggie, Charles, and Gavin in *The Town*' (463–77), Anne Colcough Little departs from accepted readings of the Mallison marriage, arguing that the apparently stable and healthy relationship of Maggie and Charles that is initially presented is subsequently undercut by a progressive tension between the couple with implications of sibling incest, a suggestion she supports with a close analysis of the verbal interaction between Maggie, her husband and her twin, as well as the observations of Chick, the Mallison son. Finally, this issue also includes the first full publication of three letters written by Faulkner to Ben Warren in the summer and autumn of 1924. Philip Cohen reviews these in '"This Hand Holds Genius": Three Unpublished Faulkner Letters' (479–83), remarking on their interesting revelation of an early intuition of literary acclaim.

MissQ features another special on Faulkner by way of homage to Cleanth Brooks, and the essays included are appropriately provocative and informative. In

'Cross-Dressing in Yoknapatawpha County' (47.369–90), Michael Williams uses the psychoanalytic theory of the masquerade and transvestism to explore the conception of gender in Faulkner's female characters, analysing three figures that epitomize cross-dressing and masculinity: Drusilla Hawk Sartoris, Joanna Burden and the mature Linda Snopes. In a stimulating discussion of the dynamics of clothing, occupation and behaviour, Williams studies the motive for female cross-dressing from necessity to liberated choice. Particularly interesting is his suggestion that it is the mask of femininity, rather than the costume of masculinity, that constitutes the real masquerade. Robert Merrill in 'Faulknerian Tragedy: The Example of *As I Lay Dying*' (403–18) proposes that, of all Faulkner's novels, *As I Lay Dying* is the purest example of his mastery of modern tragedy and exhibits the motifs of the modern tragic structure in the flawed central characters of Addie and Darl, the macabre comedy of Jewel and the anticipation of inevitable doom. He suggests, however, that Faulkner presents the tragic fate of his characters as the result of a distinctly modern awareness of the isolation of the human condition, and the inevitably ineffectual attempt to protest against this isolation. 'The Abjection of Addie and Other Myths of the Maternal in *As I Lay Dying*' (419–39) by Diana York Blaine continues the reading of the novel as contemporary tragedy, yet perceives Addie as a female version of the informing patriarchal authority rather than the tragic protagonist. Blaine reads the permutations of the postmodernist, ontological and symbolic instability that results from the position of a woman as the dead/absent head of the family, and suggests that the multiple-narrative, non-linear text represents at once our cultural rejection of the relevance of the maternal and its importance as a stabilizing identity. Voyeurism provides the focus of Andrew J. Wilson's 'The Corruption in Looking: William Faulkner's *Sanctuary* as a *Detective* Novel' (441–60), which examines the dispassionate isolation of the detached observer. Through the motif of the doubled figure of the lawyer/criminal, Wilson argues that Horace Benbow and Popeye are detached, impotent spectators of life, one a metaphoric voyeur, the other a literal one. The constant references to the act of seeing throughout the novel, however, and the final image of the previously active Temple Drake as a *flâneur* in the Luxembourg Gardens, implies that the impulse to detachment is a universal one. In 'The Riddle of *Absalom, Absalom!*: Looking at the Wrong Blackbird?' (461–88), Nancy E. Batty argues beyond the narratological approach that claims Henry Sutpen's murder of Charles Bon is the only indisputable fact of the novel. Tentatively and carefully she argues that the identities of murderer and victim are ambiguous, and that consequently even the ghostly figure at Sutpen's Hundred poses a riddle, an 'assumed fact' which she also reads as possibly indeterminate. This special issue includes two 'Essay-Reviews', 'Desire and Interpretation: Reading *The Sound and the Fury*' by James M. Mellard, and 'Female, Feminist, Femme, Faulkner?' (521–45) by Anne Goodwyn Jones.

'*Absalom, Absalom!*, Haiti and Labour History: Reading Unreadable Revolutions' (*ELH* 61.685–720), by Richard Godden, is an extended version of an earlier note in *MissQ*. Here Godden writes that Faulkner's chronological 'mistake' in having Thomas Sutpen subdue a slave uprising in Haiti in 1827, twenty-three years after the island had become an independent black state, is actually another example of the writer's interest in the construction of history through its narrative transmission. Through the free black Jacobins of Haiti, Faulkner represents the continuous revolutionary potential of the slave class that reaffirms the authority of the white master, and yet also indicates the similarities between Sutpen and his slave force, an interdependence that Sutpen recognizes but has to suppress in retelling his story as a plantation owner in 1835. Historical analysis also informs Barbara Ladd's essay '"The Direction of the Howling": Nationalism and the Color Line in *Absalom, Absalom!*' (*AL* 66:525–51). Ladd's detailed examination of the classification of miscegenation in the Deep South, and of the complex status of the 'Creole' caught between French colonialist policies and United States nationalism, emphasizes the significance of Charles Bon for the self-perception of James and Quentin Compson, and their respective interpretations of the *post-bellum* world. Also worthy of mention is Ineke Bockting's 'Mind Style as an Interdisciplinary Approach to Characterisation in Faulkner' (*L&L* 3.iii. 157–74), which uses psychostylistics (an interdisciplinary discourse derived from psychology, psychiatry and the linguistic theories of Roger Fowler), to study Faulkner's construction of fictional characters, an approach that is particularly appropriate to *The Sound and the Fury*.

Of the few articles on F. Scott Fitzgerald in 1994, 'Medium of Exchange: The Blue Coupé Dialogue in *The Great Gatsby*' (*PLL* 30.73–87) by Lauraleigh O'Meara is noteworthy. O'Meara analyses Fitzgerald's use of the automobile as a symbol of modern technology and commodification, concentrating on the exchange values attributed to objects by the consumer culture of the 1920s. Her close reading of the developments in the transaction between Buchanan and Wilson, coupled with her study of motor-car advertisements from the twenties, provides an informative, contextualized study of how the value of objects in a capitalist economy is determined by consumer desire rather than material worth. And Jeffrey Louis Decker gives an original slant on Fitzgerald's portrayal of the twenties in 'Gatsby's Pristine Dream: The Diminishment of the Self-made Man in the Tribal Twenties' (*Novel* 28.52–71), where he reads *The Great Gatsby* in the context of Fitzgerald's professional association with the nativist *Saturday Evening Post* and the popularity of theories of White American Nordicism. Decker argues that the ethical conflict between Gatsby's own vision and his connections with immigrant crime is informed by nationalist beliefs that strove to preserve White American Nordic purity. Opposed interpretations of *The Great Gatsby* can be found in Thomas Pauly's 'Gatsby as Gangster' (*SAF* 21[1993].225–36), in which he argues that in Jay Gatsby, Fitzgerald portrays a believable criminal based on dandified gangsters such as Arthur Rothstein, and suggests that Gatsby, although a romantic idealist, is fundamentally self-interested and manipulative, his extreme wealth testifying to his success at exploitation. In comparison, Jeffrey Hart in 'Anything Can Happen: Magical Transformation in *The Great Gatsby*' (*SCR* 25[1993].37–50) argues that Gatsby is presented as a divinity in his own economic world of magic and witchcraft, where he epitomizes the powers of transformation and transcends his futile attempts to alter the reality of the physical world by becoming a hero of the imagination.

The latest volume in Michael Reynolds's lively and emotive biography of Ernest Hemingway, *Hemingway: The American Homecoming*, published in 1993, concentrates on the period 1926–8, the greater part of which Hemingway spent in Paris, and much of this material would therefore seem to be more appropriate to Reynolds's previous volume, *The Paris Years*. This aside, Reynolds presents the growth of Hemingway's notoriety and public persona in a style that continues to be both informative and accessible. The latter half of the 1920s was a transitional period for Hemingway in many ways, during which his life altered dramatically due to his divorce from Hadley and his marriage to Pauline Pfeiffer, the suicide of his father, and his developing cult status following the publication and reception of *The Sun Also Rises*. These familiar events become immediate and poignant under Reynolds's creative hand, supported by a wealth of documentary information. Reynolds deals predominantly with the relation of Hemingway's personal life to his compositional process, particularly the details of his Parisian social world and the break with the literary environment of the Left Bank that ultimately resulted in his return to the United States. It is somewhat unfortunate that the comments on the work itself are rather limited in scope and infrequent, perhaps the result of the compact chapter lengths of this book, which is clearly aimed at a popular audience.

Wendolyn E. Tetlow's *Hemingway's In Our Time: Lyrical Dimensions* (1993) argues for *In Our Time* as a coherent and integrated work that follows the structure of the modernist sequential poem as defined by M. L. Rosenthal and Sally Gall in *The Modern Poetic Sequence*, and evident in the works of Pound and Eliot. Analysing language patterns and emotive tone, Tetlow suggests that the stories of *In Our Time* are lyrically rather than dramatically presented. She supports her argument with a theory of Hemingway's aesthetics drawn from a comparison of the early publications in the *Little Review*, the 'in our time' pieces and *In Our Time*, all of which she reads as stages towards the integrated narrative structure of *A Farewell to Arms*. By a careful reading of manuscript material Tetlow suggests that Hemingway consciously structured *In Our Time* to create an intensifying atmosphere, and notes the influence of Pound and Eliot in the coherent representation of feeling rather than action achieved by compressed description, recurring images and the objectification of emotion. Tales of war, bullfighting and personal relationships are concerned less with particular conflicts than with a sterility and lack of communication that is universal, and it is in this respect that they parallel and intensify each other. Tetlow's book is a valuable and detailed analysis of the works that lead to *In Our Time* and plausibly argues for its integrated nature, yet emphasizes the lyrical tone of Hemingway's early work rather to the negation of narrative. There are several misinterpretations of technical references, links between stories and inter-chapters sometimes seem forced, and the continuation of Tetlow's argument to cover *A Farewell to Arms* results in conclusions that are less than convincing.

Several journal articles illustrate the currently obsessive biographical concern with Hemingway. One example is 'Hemingway's *The Garden of Eden*' (*TexasSLL* 35[1993].198–225) by Rose Marie Burwell, who attempts to establish the autobiographical context of the posthumously published novel by studying the original manuscript, claiming that the juxtaposition of the androgynous and masculine narratives in the work of the character David Bourne reflects Hemingway's own ambivalence towards the role of androgyny in the creative act. In 'Hemingway's Gay Blades' (*Differences* 5[1993].116–39), Robert Scholes and Nancy R. Comley also concentrate on the author's concern with homosexual desire and, analysing *Death in the Afternoon*, convincingly argue that the tradition of the bullfight provides a cultural context within which to explore gender issues and forms sympathetically, suggesting that the matador is an androgynous figure combining extremes of bravery and gracefulness. In an original biographical perspective, Marc Baldwin's stimulating discussion of literature as an ideological discourse in 'Hemingway's Political Unconscious' (*JNT* 23[1993].170–87) analyses the social politics of the very forms of literature, taking *The Sun Also Rises* as an example of artistic strategies of irony and impressionism that repress or obscure political content, and suggests that Hemingway, in intentionally employing such techniques in order to avoid political classification, creates a silent discourse beneath the studied detachment of the surface text. In 'The (Hi)story of their Lives: Mythic Autobiography and "The Lost Generation"' (*JAmS* 27[1993].35–56), Marc Dolan attempts to deflate common objections to the relevance of autobiography as historical evidence by employing the techniques of new cultural historians and argues, through a searching analysis of works by Hemingway, Cowley and Fitzgerald, that, by treating autobiography as 'myth', historical information can be gained about the perception of the past age from the present. Continuing this perspective, Debra A. Moddelmog's 'Reconstructing Hemingway's Identity' (*Narrative* 1[1993].187–206) surveys the recent propensity of biographical criticism that attempts either to substantiate or to reassess the 'Papa Hemingway' image, and, concentrating on conventional interpretations of gender and sexuality in *The Sun Also Rises*, argues for the recognition of an interdependent relationship between author and text, suggesting that authorial identity does not lie behind a text but is instead constantly constructed and reconstructed from the interaction of text, biography and changing cultural codes.

Of the articles on Hemingway in 1994, two from *PULC* 56 relate to the presentation and availability of Hemingway's work and the archives now open to scholars. In 'Hemingway: A Publisher's Perspective' (15–23) Charles Scribner III celebrates the publication of Hemingway's work by four generations of Princetonian Scribners by reproducing a lecture given by Charles Scribner Jr in 1985 to the Princeton Club Library in New York, a refreshingly personal and unassuming assessment of the importance Hemingway placed on his own professionalism, and the successful publication of his fiction and journalism. Rose Marie Burwell's 'The Posthumous Hemingway Puzzle' (25–45) notes the importance of the opening of the Scribner's Archives in 1992, previously closed to academics on Hemingway's request since 1953. These materials provide a wealth of previously unknown information, and as a result Burwell confirms the rumour of the Ritz Hotel Papers reputedly found by Hemingway in 1957, building up a plausible context for the writing of the four posthumously published novels. She painstakingly details the discordance between Hemingway's intentions as to the meaning and presentation of these works, evident in the manuscripts and letters he sent to Scribner Jr, and the published versions of *Islands in the Stream*, collected and edited by Mary Hemingway and Carlos Baker, and *A Moveable Feast*, edited by Mary Hemingway and Charles Scribner Jr. Margot Norris in 'The Novel as War: Lies and Truth in Hemingway's *A Farewell to Arms*' (*MFS* 40.iv.689–710) suggests that the juxtaposition of the love story of Catherine and Frederic with the violence of the war story exposes the conventional ideology of the former and is analogous to the actual tensions between the abstraction and reality of war itself. She argues that the war is represented in the textual dynamics of the novel, which can therefore be read as a carefully euphemistic and controlled rationalization of human fate that employs a reciprocity of deceit to shield the characters and the reader from the horrors of war.

A collection of essays edited by Donald R. Noble, *The Steinbeck Question: New Essays in Criticism*, is an attempt to rectify the paucity of critical writing on this writer. That Steinbeck is an enduringly popular writer who is yet attributed little status by literary scholars is the topic of 'The Favourite Author We Love to Hate', in which Jackson J. Benson suggests the cause of this situation to be the traditional reading of Steinbeck as a Western, often sentimental, political novelist. Emphasizing new concerns in Steinbeck's fiction are several essays on the representation of women, notably Charlotte Hardella's discussion in 'Steinbeck's Cloistered Women' of the author's interest in the unnatural repression of women that results from the demand of the American Eden myth for female sexual purity. 'Steinbeck's War', by Robert E. Morsberger, studies Steinbeck as the major American author writing on World War II, and argues with reference to *The Mood is Down*, *Bombs Away* and *Lifeboat* that his work not only fulfils a propagandist role but is also sensitive to the effects of war on all concerned. Continuing the interest in Steinbeck's studied observation of human nature is Sylvia J. Cook's article 'Steinbeck's Poor in Prosperity and Adversity', which analyses the writer's varying perspective on the poor and defines certain underlying qualities of primitive ingenuity, vitality and adaptability that set the mark of heroism on those with the instinct to survive.

Last year Tetsumaro Hayashi edited two further collections on Steinbeck. One is *A New Study Guide to Steinbeck's Major Works, with Critical Explanations* (1993), an updated addition to Hayashi's previous guides, containing eleven introductory essays and aimed at the student market. Each essay is organized into a background, synopsis and critical analysis formula, and also offers a comprehensive bibliography as well as stimulating suggestions for basic research. Contributors include Michael Meyer on *Cannery Row* and *The Winter of Our Discontent*, Louis Owens on *East of Eden* and *The Grapes of Wrath*, and Hayashi in a concluding essay on Steinbeck's art and technique. The other collection is *John Steinbeck: The Years of Greatness, 1936–1939*, papers from the Third International Steinbeck Congress of 1990, offering a wealth of original and well-researched commentary on Steinbeck's work in the late 1930s. Divided into two sections, the first on 'Steinbeck's Women' concentrates on the influence of the feminine on Steinbeck's work. In 'Your Own Mind Coming Out in the Garden: Steinbeck's Elusive Woman' (3–19), John Ditsky focuses on the short stories of *The Long Valley* and studies the repeated image of the Edenic garden landscape as a symbol of both female sexuality and narrative creativity. A fascinating contribution is Robert DeMott's 'After *The Grapes of Wrath*: A Speculative Essay on John Steinbeck's Suite of Love Poems for Gwyn "The Girl of the Air"' (20–45), which quotes extensively from the love poems, not previously publicly available, that DeMott suggests are evidence of biographical influence on Steinbeck's idealized and reductive fictional portrayals of women. The second section, 'Steinbeck's Worker Trilogy', analyses his representation of the Depression years. Of particular note is Thomas Tammaro's argument for *In Dubious Battle* as an example of an important yet overlooked genre, in his essay 'Sharing Creation: Steinbeck, *In Dubious Battle*, and the Working-Class Novel in American Literature' (95–105). Mimi Gladstein and Susan Shillinglaw both write on *The Grapes of Wrath*, the former undertaking a personal reading that connects the problems of the Joad family with the experiences of immigration, and Shillinglaw on the literary resistance to the novel in a study of the historical and ideological background of its production and reception. Concentrating on the period of Steinbeck's rise to international acclaim, *The Years of Greatness* is an invaluable addition to Steinbeck studies.

Gertrude Stein Remembered, edited by Linda Simon, gathers together twenty memoirs by people who knew Stein, some of them previously unpublished, and provides us with a series of portraits of her in contexts ranging from her undergraduate years at Radcliffe College to her final days in Paris at the end of World War II. Linda Simon adds a brief introduction and there are headnote comments covering each contributor. The volume reprints three famous photographs of Gertrude Stein (those by Alvin Langdon Coburn, Man Ray and Carl Van Vechten), Paul Tchelitchew's 1930 drawing and Jacques Lipchitz's bronze bust of 1920. [H.C.]

Neil A. Grauer's biography of James Thurber, *Remember Laughter: A Life of James Thurber*, offers itself as of interest to the scholarly and non-scholarly alike, though those who enjoy reading Thurber will wonder about the point of making such a distinction between prospective customers in the first place. Suffice it to say, however, that this is, happily, not a scholarly biography: Grauer tells the story of Thurber's life clearly, concisely and (given the obvious advantage that accrues from his subject) entertainingly, without recourse to any 'thesis' about the man or any attempt to read a hidden significance into his writings and drawings. The biography is written from the perspective of a great admiration of Thurber's achievement, but it remains disinterested and unsentimental, and the less attractive aspects of Thurber's character are given due consideration. I am too unfamiliar with Thurber biography to know whether Grauer adds considerably to what we know of the man but I found this an immensely readable and informative book. [H.C.]

3. Fiction Since 1945

(a) General

Hyper/Text/Theory, ed. George P. Landow, is a collection of essays that follows his ground-breaking work on *Hypertext: The Convergence of Contemporary Critical Theory and Technology* (JHUP, 1992) and, in electronic format, *The Dickens Web* (1992). Landow is interested in the similarities of hypertext (defined as 'an information technology consisting of individual blocks of text, or lexias, and the electronic links that join them') and recent work by post-structuralists such as Roland Barthes and Jacques Derrida (can Barthes be described as a post-structuralist?). Also brought into the equation are Kristeva's notions of intertextuality, Bakhtin's emphasis on multivocality, Foucault's networks of power, and Deleuze and Guattari's 'rhizomatic, nomad thought' – the only fashionable guru missing from the cocktail party would seem to be Lacan, but then he is wheeled on later in Terence Harpold's 'Conclusions' to the first section. Landow's concern, then, is the way in which theory and new technology emerged at the same time and grew out of 'a dissatisfaction with the related phenomena of the printed book and hierarchical thought'. As someone in no way dissatisfied with the printed book as form (only in individual items like this one – which could well have included an index), I am suspicious of the argument and do not understand what Landow is driving at by relating the printed book to hierarchical thought, any more than I follow Charles Ess in 'The Political Computer: Hypertext, Democracy, and Habermas', who argues for information technology's potential for true democratization. To take Landow's point first: it seems to imply an extraordinarily pedestrian approach to reading; true enough, there might be some application if our text is 'Jack and Jill went up the hill', but I doubt that an absence of book or hierarchical thought would help us much in attempting to read *À la Recherche du Temps Perdu*. There seem to be elements of both the emperor's new clothes and a quasi-religious belief that since one, theoretically, could interrogate and have access to limitless knowledge through the Web and hypertext, this is, necessarily, 'a good thing'. It looks like yet another example of what Daniel Berrigan called 'distraction as a way of life'. I would argue that some things are more important than other things (like life and death); that some words, in context, are more important than other words in certain texts ('The horror! The horror!) – whether they be called nodes, cruces or touchstones; and that the *Commedia* is more important than tabloid journalism. The machines on which we write and work, as I am doing now on a little portable, are machines, no more, no less. Unless significant relief is given, and given by us, then we end up with theoretical nonsense, buried under a weight of meaningless trivia. As far as Ess's argument goes, it would seem to have nothing to do with real men and real women, but more to do with virtual shopping and virtual sex. As far as true democratization goes, in the USA 54 per cent of long-term sentences are passed on blacks (12 per cent of the population); the life expectancy in certain ghettos is less than that of Bangladesh (*La Chronique d'Amnesty*, Juillet 1996: 9). It may well be that students of medicine or languages, for example, can benefit from interactive hypertext. But to imply that hypertext is in any way an improvement on or substitute for reading literature, and thinking, reflecting and meditating upon it, is absurd.

Historiographic Metafiction in Modern American and Canadian Literature, eds. Bernd Engler and Kurt Müller, is a hefty tome by thirty-one different hands and covers the classic writers of historiographic metafiction – Nabokov, Vonnegut, Barth, Pynchon, DeLillo, Coover, Doctorow et al. – and also treats such diverse figures as Henry Adams, John Dos Passos, Larry McMurtry (*Lonesome Dove*) and Art Spiegelman (*Maus*). There are important articles on re-reading Henry Adams (Julika Griem), Doss Passos (Gerd Hurm), Nabokov (Herbert Grabes), Pynchon (Hanjo Berressem) and many others. But of particular importance is the theoretical groundwork supplied by the editors. Bernd Engler discusses the philosophic implications of the historiographic endeavour, while Kurt Müller writes of the development of the historical novel in America. Engler, in 'The Dismemberment of Clio', points out that distrust in claims to authenticity and objectivity of all factual representations of reality imposes two aims on this book: one, a necessary analysis of the premises of the shift in epistemes in the philosophy of history; and, two, a necessary inquiry into the intellectual preconditions for the rise of historiographic metafiction. Drawing on Hayden White and Linda Hutcheon in particular (there are comparatively few references to Barthes or Derrida), Engler usefully reviews the arguments of postmodern positions in art (the representation acknowledges its position *as* representation and thus cannot give access to the referent; the representation is based on cultural conventions; the authority of such conventions is at best provisional). Engler goes on to deal with what might be called 'lingering mimesis' when it comes to historiography, journalism, biography, etc. Thus, he writes, there is a false distinction between so-called fictional discourse and non-fictional discourse. He takes to task those historiographers who claim to deal with verifiable historical events rather than imaginary realities; which seems to me to slide over the argument. The essay continues by examining 'Fictions of a Factual Representation of Reality', pointing out that nineteenth-century historians produced as many reports and explanations of past events as there were historians. However, Engler argues, 'Thinkers such as Hegel, Droysen, Nietzsche and Croce challenged the belief in the empiricist notion of historical authenticity.' Since the purpose of true historiography is the *interpretation* of historical data, history came to be understood as the result of a dialogue between past and present which is inspired by the historian's present interests. Now, following Lévi-Strauss and White, Engler concurs that history is never history, it is always 'history for' some interest or vision. Historical narrative cannot, according to Engler, be constituted from *a priori* constructive imagination. Likewise, historical events do not have intrinsic meanings; if they appear tragic it is 'only because they are emplotted in a manner which we as readers might perceive as being tragic'. Doubtless this would have been of great consolation to Paul Celan and Primo Levi, not to mention the countless victims of history's bloody career. There is, in all this, an admitted hopelessness: the triumph of relativism and pure fiction over base fact destroys objectivity and any discovered meaning. Thus, Engler concludes, 'historiographic metafiction becomes an oxymoronic endeavor'.

Kurt Müller in 'The Development Towards Historiographic Metafiction in the American Novel' begins with Sir Walter Scott and traces his influence to the writings of James Fenimore Cooper, who introduces a note of historical pessimism. This note is continued through the works of Hawthorne, Melville, Mark Twain and Stephen Crane. From Crane we are brought to Henry Adams, whose historical writings reveal a tension between fact and fiction: his effort to 'make sense' is seen as a parody. From Adams we come abruptly to Dos Passos and Faulkner, who, despite their impressive achievements, are seen to be marginal to the main movement of modernism. The development since the sixties 'historicizes' the novel: the Kennedy assassination, the escalation of the Vietnam war, counter culture, etc. These events, or their images, have overtaken the imagination of the novelist. As Philip Roth writes: 'The actuality is continually outdoing our talents, and the culture tosses up figures almost daily that are the envy of any novelist' ('Writing American Fiction').

I would like to single out for further consideration Franz Link's 'In Search of the Figure in the Carpet of History' because of its historical grasp; and Richard Martin's 'Art Spiegelman's *Maus* or "The Way it Really Happened"' because of the intrinsic interest in the subject matter and the subtle analysis of mask in the cartoon. For Link, James's 'The Figure in the Carpet' is the starting point for an examination of secrets trembling on the brink of discovery, which may be present in the text but are just as likely to be projected by the narrators. Link briefly looks at *V, The Crying of Lot 49* and *Gravity's Rainbow*, and defines the search for the 'lost message' as paranoiac. Ishmael Reed's *Mumbo Jumbo* is considered next. Though the text of the *Book of Thoth* is lost (burned by a black Muslim), the protagonist Papa La Bas decides, like Borges, to create a future text. The paper concludes with an examination of *Foucault's Pendulum* which is of interest to readers of historiographic metafiction in that it claims to reinterpret history *ad absurdum*, and also draws heavily on Pynchon and Reed in the search for a 'true text'. Historical fact becomes subverted and reality increasingly absurd. 'With Eco's novel the paranoia of the contemporary novel has become a metaphor of the paranoia of the contemporary world.'

Richard Martin begins his analysis of *Maus* by comparing Adorno's notorious statement 'poetry after Auschwitz is barbaric' with Hayden White's definition of 'the greatest historians' as being those who deal with the traumatic aspects of society. Spiegelman, according to Martin, aligns himself to White by illustrating not just the chronology of his parents but particularly their survival of the Holocaust. The moral and narratological problems are solved by a number of increasingly subtle strategies. In the first place Jews, Germans and Poles are seen as comic-book animals: mice, cats and pigs respectively. Second is the frame device, in which Art Spiegelman interviews his father Vladek, who gives limited information from the past and also comments from the present. Third, Spiegelman constantly draws attention to his own presumption in adapting the Holocaust to the medium of comic books. Of particular interest is the discussion on metafiction as a method for overcoming the narrative dilemma (not the *what* next, but the *how* next), by concentrating on Spiegelman, wearing a mouse mask, drawing himself drawing his father's story. Some consideration of metalepsis might have been useful here. However, this is a finely argued and stimulating article.

There are gaps in *Historiographic Metafiction*: for example, there are only two, fleeting, references to Gabriel Marquez's *One Hundred Years of Solitude* and, astonishingly, no one sees to have thought of mentioning Sterne or Borges, who would seem to be important background figures to this whole discussion. The index is faulty and limited: at one point George Steiner becomes Sue Steiner; a list of works cited would have been more useful than the sometimes indigestible footnotes. Perhaps as a result of clumsy translation, the style is somewhat rebarbative. However, despite the quibbles raised above, this is a valuable book which will be essential reading for anyone researching historiographic metafiction from the North American continent.

In a good article on Spiegelman, Michael Rothberg in '"We Were Talking Jewish": Art Spiegelman's *Maus* as "Holocaust" Production' (*ConL* 35.661–87) connects Philip Roth's *Patrimony* with *Maus*: 'what goes into survival isn't always pretty', as Roth writes in *Patrimony*. Like Martin, Rothberg comments on the levels of representation found in *Maus*: 'the same pictorial space literalizes the artist's position – backed by the industry, but everywhere confronted with the detritus of the real'. Rothberg points out that *Maus* took thirteen years' work, which he connects to what Marianne Hirsch has called 'the aesthetic of the testimonial chain – an aesthetic that is indistinguishable from the documentary'. *Maus* hovers uneasily between highbrow and lowbrow, between painful present and even more painful past, between futile documentary and effective fiction.

A number of books have been published this year on gender studies: in *Feminist Nightmares: Women at Odds*, Susan Ostrov Weisser and Jennifer Fleischner have set themselves the brave, and worthwhile, task of examining portrayals of women at odds with themselves. They were told, early on in their venture, that feminists should concentrate on how men oppress women, not how bad women are to each other; but, happily, they pursued their task, for there is much of interest in this work. The tone of 'the sisterhood' is occasionally irritating, as the editors merge into one voice: they cannot remember who had the idea first, they had long talks in which the personal, the professional and the political merged seamlessly, they listened to and learned from each other, etc. (given such a subject, how much more satisfactory it would have been to find an expression of disagreement and difference). There is also, in some of the essays, a defensive strategy which perceives all women as oppressed – given the eloquent fact of these articles, this is hard to sustain. However, this apart, there are a number of useful articles in this book. Tuzyline Jita Allan writes about 'Women and the (Ab)use of Power in *The Color Purple*', examining 'the unequal distribution of power in the novel with a view to broaching the vexing issue of woman-abusive women'. Despite some unnecessarily ugly formulations ('womanist', 'womanism', 'solidarist', etc.), the article enables the reader to rethink *The Color Purple* in terms of predatory femininity contrasted with patriarchal white power structures: female characters, both white and black, collude in these structures, but there is also an uneasy sense of an inherently destructive female power at work. Jennifer Shaddock, meanwhile, examines women's relations in Louise Erdrich's *Tracks* and Leslie Silko's *Ceremony*. Fleur and Tayo, the redemptive protagonists of these two novels, refuse to engage with their oppressors and thus are virtually invulnerable. Shaddock argues that *Tracks* and *Ceremony* determine women's realities through language and thus enable women to struggle against patriarchal values and, most importantly, to overcome various stereotypes of the powerlessness of women, which are often fostered, paradoxically, by women themselves. The programme put forward by Shaddock is that from works like *Tracks* and *Ceremony* women will find a regeneration through women's oral history, story-telling, myth and language. The gem in this interesting collection of essays is Eileen Gillooly's 'Rehabilitating Mary Crawford: *Mansfield Park* and the Relief of "Throwing Ridicule" ', but regrettably the subject is beyond the scope of this chapter.

Communication and Women's Friendships, edited by Janet Doubler Ward and Joanna Stephens Mink, continues the feminist theme and approach, but, unfortunately, with nothing of the rigour of *Feminist Nightmares*. The editors begin with what seems to be developing into a trope of symbiosis and collective amnesia: 'sharing a desk, class notes, cigarettes. Something happened, we don't recall exactly what – some crisis about a seminar paper deadline or some man – but, as a result, we became good friends.' One can only hope that all these feminist critics have a somewhat better recall of their scholarly material. After some discussion of the criteria of selection, one perceives that the papers collected here are arranged in roughly chronological order, beginning with primary sources of nineteenth- and twentieth-century diaries, which lead on to a discussion of the portrayal of women's friendships in literature. Of interest to readers of this chapter are 'Female Friendship in the Contemporary *Bildungsroman*' by Katherine B. Payant, and 'Women's Community and Survival in the Novels of Louise Erdrich' by Julie Tharp. Payant, after a brief mention of earlier women's learning novels such as *Fear of Flying*, moves on to a consideration of *During the Reign of the Queen of Persia* by Joan Chase, *Rumors of Peace* by Ella Leffland and *The Color Purple*. Her point is that in these novels 'the protagonist's relationship with other women – friends, sisters and other female relatives – is a key force in shaping her'. In *Queen* and *Color* traditional patriarchy is seen as different for men and women: 'because in their shared oppression and lack of power, women often excluded men, who found themselves on the fringe of the family unit'. *Rumors of Peace* (which I have not read) reads, in this account, like children's literature '[it] says that love redeems and hatred kills, and the love and guidance young women provide each other can provide that redemption'. The account of *Color* is also very basic: 'This epistolary form, seldom used by contemporary writers [really?], is an important and unusual feature of the novel, and is particularly suitable for a novel of development.' Indeed. Julie Tharp, meanwhile, examines the novels of Louise Erdrich, in which she finds that 'Female friendship enables women . . . to recreate an empowering matrix that was frequently lost or disrupted through colonization and acculturation.' The tone of the essay is sometimes unintentionally funny; here is a description of a mother-daughter relationship from *Tracks*: 'That Leopolda should lock Marie in closets, scald her with hot water, brain her with an iron pole and skewer her hand with a meat fork suggests that, like Lulu, Marie has a difficult relationship with her mother.' However, anyone who wishes to read about contemporary American feminist thought will find some useful material in this collection of essays, though it is a pity that there is no index.

In contrast, Nancy J. Peterson in 'History, Postmodernism, and Louise Erdrich's *Tracks*' (*PMLA* 109.982–94) has written an excellent article which begins by pointing out Erdrich's difficulties in writing a historical saga in a postmodern, post-representational era. Writers like Erdrich, she continues, write their own stories of the past only to discover that they must find a new way of making history. In telling the poignant story of the Turtle Mountain Chippewa's struggle to keep their land in the late nineteenth century, a story which Erdrich tells in the late twentieth century, the writer would seem to be reacting against the excesses of postmodernism, which attempts to reject the referential function of language: '*Tracks* takes up the crucial issue of the referentiality of historical narrative in a postmodern epoch and creates the possibility for a new historicity by and for Native Americans to emerge.' In 'African-American Women Writers, Black Nationalism, and the Matrilineal Heritage' (*CLAJ* 38.143–61) Joan S. Korenman writes of the difficulties faced, in the sixties and seventies, by African-American women who had been active in the civil rights and black nationalist movements. The article focuses on three works of short fiction: Alice Walker's 'Everyday Use', Toni Cade Bambara's 'My Man Bovanne', and the 'Kiswana Brown' chapter from Gloria Naylor's *The Women of Brewster Place*. Korenman argues that in these works one finds a tension between the claims of black nationalism and the claims of feminism. Ironically, women writers' wariness of black nationalism may very well come from an esteem for traditional African respect for older women, as the bearers of their culture. Walker, Bambara and Naylor all have young women protagonists, and Korenman suggests that this may be not simply a criticism of the male-dominated nationalist movement, but also a warning to the younger generation not to forget the importance of the matrilineal heritage.

Fictions of Masculinity: Crossing Cultures, Crossing Sexualities, ed. Peter F. Murphy, continues the feminist interest, but this time specifically related to fictions of masculinity. The premise of the book is that masculinity, like femininity, is a fictional construct, and the book claims that it 'examines the deep structure of masculine codes in fiction and asks the question "Who are the men in modern literature?"'. Though there is little evidence of the deep structure of masculinity, there is far too much description and too little analysis, and often the 'men in modern literature' examined here appear a pretty nauseating bunch; nevertheless the book is a brave attempt to discover why men have accepted travesties on their nature and role in life. Thus men are portrayed as cowards and alcoholics, and most remarkably, 'men who die when most needed are the men who victimize women in American literature'. Ranging in subject from Crane to Mahfouz, and from Natty Bumppo to Batman, there are interesting discussions of Barthelme, John Hawkes and the *roman noir*. Peter Schwenger, in 'Barthelme, Freud and the Killing of Kafka's Father', applies Freud and Derrida to Kafka's *Letter to his Father* and then considers Donald Barthelme's *The Dead Father* (1975). Barthelme is found to write consistently about texts and contexts, arranging surreal battles between them, which undermines the authority of all texts including his own – unsurprisingly this is seen as a basic ploy in postmodernism. In turning authorities against themselves, the postmodern vision allows one to '*sidestep*' the figure of the father and finally come of age oneself. In 'Male Heterosexuality in John Hawkes's *The Passion Artist*', Peter F. Murphy looks at Hawkes's dark allegory, and decides, rather too comfortably, that Vost becomes a better man through confronting the ordeal of women's lives. Murphy concludes his piece with the depressing notion that as one moves towards becoming a liberated man so one becomes less socially acceptable as a man, but then his idea of 'liberated' man is as limited as his definition of society: a 'homophobic and sexist society that fears and hates female sexuality, especially when embodied in a man'. The article is occasionally bolstered with very dubious, but unquestioned, statistics: 'More than half of the men surveyed in a recent poll said they would rape a woman if they were absolutely sure they would get away with it.' The best article in the collection is 'Living Degree Zero: Masculinity and the Threat of Desire in the *Roman Noir*', by Christopher Metress, who compares and contrasts the 'hardboiled' fictions of Chandler, Hammett et al. with a sub-genre of works by James M. Cain (*The Postman Always Rings Twice*), Horace McCoy, Cornell Woolrich, Jim Thompson and David Goodis. Whereas Chandler's and Hammett's detective is a complete man and a hero ('down these mean streets a man must go who is not himself mean'), the protagonist of the *roman noir* is fragmented and finally has only two options: to annihilate himself or to erase himself – the zero degree. The collection as a whole will be worth reading for scholars of cultural studies; it is of less interest to scholars of literature.

Images of the 'real' America and the hardboiled school are well captured in 'The Dream of the Empty Camera: Image, Evidence, and Authentic American Style in *American Photographs* and *Farewell, My Lovely*' (*Crit* 36.415–57) by Ronald R. Thomas. Both the hardboiled school and the photographs of Walker Evans challenge the evidentiary value of literal documents and bring into question truth-telling authority; they both reach to a larger category of truth than straightforward documentary. It is a pity that Thomas did not include James Agee's prose as contrast and counterpoint to Chandler's novels and Evan's photographs, but, nevertheless, this is a thoughtful, and thought-provoking article.

On the same theme as Murphy's *Fictions of Masculinity*, but very much more achieved, is Thaïs E. Morgan's collection of essays, entitled *Men Writing the Feminine: Literature, Theory, and the Question of Genders*. Morgan asks the big questions: 'What does it mean to say that a male author writes the feminine? Is he writing as (identifying with) a woman? Or writing like (mimicking, and perhaps mocking) a woman? Or writing through a woman (an Other that confirms his own identity as the Same)?'. The book has excellent essays on George Herbert, Wordsworth, Lawrence, Faulkner, Randall Jarell and John Berryman, amongst others, as well as a theoretical discussion, 'Postmodern Theories: Beyond Gender', which contains an interesting short piece by Jonathon Culler, 'Five Propositions on the Future of Men in Feminism'. Peter F. Murphy rehearses several of the points on John Hawkes he had made in his discussion of *The Passion Artist* previously noticed, but here they are related to *Virginie: Her Two Lives.* Towards the end Murphy rather tritely suggests that even today 'The woman writer still struggles to secure a room of her own, a receptive publisher, and an audience who takes her seriously.' I think most men writers could say the same themselves. Following Derrida and Foucault, there is a continuing interest, in the essays gathered together here, in what Morgan describes as 'the tension between the sexed body of the author (male) and the double gender-marking of his discourse: performatively feminine but politically masculine'. One could have wished for an essay on Tolstoy and another on Henry James here. The most far-reaching thought in the book is enunciated in Culler's remarks to the 1988 MLA Convention. He states that there is no such thing as *a* feminist view or position; that for a man to call what he is doing 'feminism' or a 'feminist reading' is to obscure *énoncé* and *énonciation*; and he shows how his own views on *Madame Bovary* have perforce been changed by feminist criticism – I think we could probably all agree, and have experienced similar changes ourselves. This is a valuable collection of essays, which, on the whole, are of high quality; I could have wished for some contrast in terms of Virginia Woolf's criticism of George Eliot's prose, for example, or a consideration of Anaïs Nin, particularly thinking about the blurred boundaries between being a woman, acting like a woman and, above all, writing like a woman, but, as the editor could justifiably remark, that is the subject of another collection.

John A. McClure's *Late Imperial Romance* is an engaged, engaging, stimulating and sometimes infuriating book which has its intellectual roots (fully acknowledged) in Jameson's *The Political Unconscious* and Said's *Orientalism*. McClure reads the novels of Didion, Stone, DeLillo and Pynchon as late imperial romances and argues that, except for Pynchon, they put forward the interests and policies of romance rather than arguing for or against American foreign policy. The author describes 'late imperial romance' as emerging towards the end of the nineteenth century when 'the partnership between romance and imperial expansion was under strain'. This is a world in which the hero flies from the quotidian world – the ultimate enemy of romance – in order to find 'the other' in some unmapped part of the globe.

McClure's aim in chapter 1 is to establish 'the ideological and geopolitical developments that gave rise to late imperial romance, the problematics that define it, and the features that characterize it'. This large task is not fully achieved, and perhaps it could not be in the scope of one chapter. However, McClure usefully underlines the symbiotic relationship between romance and imperialism, and the images of mapping and ordering which control the wilderness and deny the wilderness its romance. The problems begin to emerge in the discussion of McClure's paradigmatic texts: *Heart of Darkness, A Passage to India* and *Kim*. These texts are seen as anti-imperial, 'But in their determination to preserve the non-Western world as the locus of magic and mystery, they perpetuate a Western tradition of "othering" the subjects of imperialism and repudiate all attempts on the part of these subjects to assimilate "Western" ways.' Having set up his grid of Western imperialism vs. exotic otherness, romance vs. the quotidian, McClure then goes on to allot blame or praise. Thus Conrad, though writing a masterpiece, has an 'aristospiritual ascetic view'; Forster's novel is 'a vision offered in place of any political program for positive change'; Kipling is a committed imperialist; etc. McClure's argument here is precisely the same as that for which he criticizes the writers of imperial romance: it is a Manichean view that praises engagement and blames any supposed identification with empire. The argument is dangerously simplistic. For McClure 'otherness' in *Heart of Darkness* is outside and the struggle with otherness is redemptive. But this is to miss the point: Marlow finds otherness within himself and his struggle lies there. McClure's engaged view reaches a nadir when we find *Gravity's Rainbow* celebrating an 'eco-spiritual alternative to the deadly codes of Western rationality and Western spirituality'. *Gravity's Rainbow* is, of course, a fine work but not for this reason – the whole of Western thought and spirituality *cannot* simply be dismissed as 'deadly codes'.

It is in the second chapter, when he is not primarily discussing literary texts, that McClure comes into his own. In order to place the novels in their historical context, McClure examines the discourses of Kennedy's call for action on 'new frontiers'; the revolutionary romances of Fanon and Che Guevara; and the apocalypse of Anglo-American modernism. The material collected here is valuable for a consideration of Didion, Stone and DeLillo – I am less sure of the application to Pynchon's narrative. In a detailed analysis of some of Kennedy's acceptance address it is good to be reminded that the American frontier moved from space to time: 'the frontier of the 1960s' when Kennedy asked his fellow Americans to be 'new pioneers on that New Frontier'. The excitement of Kennedy's rhetoric is contrasted to the march forward of Che Guevara, whose chilling and uniform view of the future is justly contrasted to the much more subtle analysis of Fanon; and Fanon is then further contrasted to those modernists who see the future as a journey into darkness.

McClure's treatment of Pynchon seems the most interesting. Though McClure early on admits Pynchon is a special case, his analyses of *V* and *Gravity's Rainbow* distort these complex texts. For example: 'Pynchon offers anarchism as a potentially effective political response to the threat of global gridding that sponsors late imperial romance'; *V* makes sense, and its argument makes sense, 'because it calls for a stand down from the absolute affirmations and apocalyptic intensities of political romance'. Pynchon's novels are unrecognizable in statements like the above, just as Stencil is unrecognizable as a belated and confused knight of espionage, who is engaged in a half-hearted search for the Lady V. But Stencil is defined as the man who searches for V, and he has stencilized the world to fit his obsession. (Of course Stencil is recognizable as a Don Quixote figure – but then Tony Tanner made that point some fifteen years ago.) McClure is surely right to stress Pynchon's concern for humanity in the grip of imperial design and the conspiracies of multinationals operating throughout the century. It is a shame that he should have so mapped his territory that he takes his final stand on banality. He concludes, quoting Rigoberta Menchu, 'the whole truth is not to be found in the Bible, but neither is the whole truth in Marxism'.

Carol Colatrella and Joseph Alkana have edited a useful collection of essays entitled *Cohesion and Dissent in America*, which have all been influenced by the work of Sacvan Bercovitch, who, in works like *The Puritan Origins of the American Self* (YaleUP, 1977), *The American Jeremiad* (UWiscP, 1978) and, most recently, *The Office of the Scarlet Letter* (JHUP, 1991), focused on texts which describe Americans to themselves. In *Puritan Origins*, Bercovitch looked at two terms 'America' and 'self': America is shown to be moving towards an ideal, and the term 'America' conveys a sense of both promise and anxiety about the shortcomings of the present. In the *Jeremiad* Bercovitch looks more closely at the self and community, with particular reference to *Walden*; his examination shows that we no longer have a situation in which literary works are seen as either an expression of individual consciousness, or debased expressions of conformist thought, but rather 'a *dynamic* relationship between individual and community, one that accommodates individual protest by highlighting the quintessentially American function of protest'. Finally, in the *Office*, Bercovitch attempts to integrate ideological and aesthetic criticism. All of the essays gathered here deal with the implications of Bercovitch's thought, both for the canon and for how one understands literary studies. The essays also deal with the fundamental problem in Bercovitch, carefully expressed in the editors' introduction: since Bercovitch brings to light underlying processes, his system has the capacity to 'generate critical formalism, one that would advance a deterministic vision of American culture and pessimism about the possibility of change'. The editors wriggle out of this impasse of pessimistic determinism by bringing on the concept of pedagogy: since academics will use Bercovitch in the classroom we may find a counterbalance to the logic of determinism; but this does not sound very convincing.

The first essay in the collection is by Bercovitch himself, who charmingly expresses his discovery of America as cultural artefact through a reading of Kafka's

'Investigations of a Dog'. There are a number of fine essays on such diverse subjects as 'Jewish Critics and American Literature' and 'Romance Theory of American Fiction'; and there are essays on individual writers such as T. S. Eliot, William James and Melville; but I would like to concentrate on 'Norman Mailer and the Radical Text' by Kathy Smith. In 1986 Norman Mailer, then president of the PEN club, invited US Secretary of State George Schultz to deliver the keynote address to the forty-eighth conference in New York. Smith analyses this notorious event as a making visible of what is normally invisible in art, which, through its form, hides the affiliations between the world of ideas and brute politics. (It also gained a lot of publicity for Mailer, of course.) Smith points out that 'Bercovitch suggests that a peculiar feature of our cultural history is that the need for consensus is played out in a vital interchange between politics and culture.' However, no vital interchange occurred between Schultz and Mailer because they had diametrically opposed views of the state: Schultz perceiving state and individual as divided and uncontaminated; Mailer seeing the state as a dynamic creature with imagination in which the individual plays a vital part. Bercovitch points out that in creating America, the Puritans saw a process that continually invested the secular with the sacred; Smith examines Mailer's questioning of this fiction in *Armies of the Night*. Mailer's aim is dual: 'to produce change in the way we come to knowledge and to avoid being disarmed and commodified by the ideological machine of consensus'. Mailer's analysis of himself, the war, history, and himself playing a part in history and the war fulfils what Bercovitch has shown to be at the heart of the American experiment, 'a convergence of state acts and cultural expression'; Mailer perceives the war in Vietnam as evil, but at the same time perceives that it is a source of energy for him. This essay and the others in the collection make stimulating reading and will be of interest to anyone interested in contemporary literature and American cultural studies.

Amritjit Singh et al. have edited a useful collection of essays devoted to ethnic American literatures, entitled *Memory, Narrative, and Identity*. The essays explore the construction and narration of the past; the politics of remembrance; collective and mythic memory; story-telling and the role of the story-teller. The essays may be grouped under a number of topics: the first group approaches issues of memory, narrative and cultural politics in defining American ethnicity; the second group focuses on time and orality in validating historical and narrative experience; the third concerns the ways in which immigrants' memory or racial memory filters through the expanding net of language consciousness; the fourth group looks at a re-reading of documentary and photographic evidence; and the last group is concerned with the transformation of memory in both the individual and the culture. Most of the articles are of a high standard, and I would single out 'Memory and Silences in the Work of Tillie Olsen and Henry Roth' by Jules Chametzky, 'Nostalgia, Amnesia, and Grandmothers: The Uses of Memory in Albert Murray, Sabine Ulibarri, Paula Gunn Allen, and Alice Walker' by Wolfgang Karrer, but of particular importance are Sharon Jessee's '"Tell me your earrings": Time and the Marvelous in Toni Morrison's *Beloved*' and Debra Shostak's 'Maxine Hong Kingston's Fake Books'. Jessee perceives that Beloved haunts her mother and others because they repress their memories of slavery; she haunts because she has not been remembered. Quoting Morrison, Jessee recuperates Beloved in terms of *sasa* time (a West African concept whereby the community is responsible for maintaining the temporal continuum). The dead in Africa wish to be remembered and be 'familiar' with their relatives until they pass away from *sasa* time. The disorientation, the hesitant, eked-out narrative of *Beloved*, has often been commented on, but I have seldom been so convinced of the necessity of this broken rhythm to the narrative. The reader is forced to remake the time, as Beloved returns to force a collective sharing of memory. As Morrison says, very ambiguously, at the end of *Beloved*, 'This is not a story to pass on.' In looking at the work of Maxine Hong Kingston, Debra Shostak points out that the books are woven out of Kingston's own memories and a mixture of story, lore and fantasy. After a brief discussion of memory and history, Shostak states that in each of her books Kingston shows that 'memory becomes an obvious source of the past both when the past remains undocumented in conventional ways and when the events of the past have been played out thousands of miles distant from those who would recover and retell them'. Shostak is particularly good at reconstructing the Chinese literature and legend, both in its original form and as translated into drama and story by nineteenth-century Chinese immigrants, and how these operate, together with Western materials, in *Tripmaster Monkey: His Fake Book*. Shostak is at pains to show how Kingston is uneasy and uncertain with the changeability of some of these oral legends, as well as with historical 'fact'; this is a well-researched, well-argued essay, which will be essential reading for Kingston scholars.

The effects of voice (which to a certain extent continue an examination of identity) are carefully considered in *Effets de Voix*, edited by Pierre Gault, who opens the discussion with a masterly reading of James Agee. Gault's argument is that Agee's 'impossible innocence' rediscovers the world of the real through poetic language: 'l'ultime recours de la voix face à l'ordre mortel du langage'. There is a lengthy interview by Guy Davenport, and Joseph McElroy writes well about attempting to define voice: 'if you're going to talk seriously about voice as something that exists and as perhaps a key to understanding the force of a writer or the distinctiveness of a writer, you're going to have to be poetic about it, that is to say you're going to have to find the best possible words for it because it's so difficult to pin down'. There is an excellent debate with Jerome Charyn, entitled 'Desperately Seeking for the "Undersong"', by which he means the particular language or voice that runs through the text – a music or pulse, not between the lines, but in the lines. Danièle Pitavy-Souques has written a fine article concerning Welty, particularly Welty describing the finding of voice in literature in *One Writer's Beginnings*. Meanwhile, Noëlle Batt in 'À la Recherche de la Voix de Son Texte' presents a theoretical survey of 'voice' and concludes that 'voice' needs to be seen under three sub-sections: 'le fait de style' (linguistic); 'l'effet de voix' (the material realization – sound and rhythm – which characterize the ideolect of the author); and 'le sens du texte' (which puts together the linguistic, stylistic, symbolic, etc., as influenced by the epistemology of the contexts of production and reception).

In *Talking Up a Storm: Voices of the New West*, Gregory L. Morris has interviewed fifteen writers working in the West today, including Gretel Ehrlich, Richard Ford and Amy Tan amongst others. The emphasis here is on the *new* West, an area which Morris sees as in transition from the old stereotypes into something more problematical. In contradistinction to the old certainties, the writers interviewed all 'stand in new and tense relation to the place of which they write'. Morris is not afraid to play with the clichés, however, and reports that the old range wars have given way to literary range wars, where much time and effort is spent fencing off aesthetic territory. Whether Morris is right to classify these writers as postmodernist and post-regionalist is something that might well be debated. His avowed aim, however, is to represent 'various Wests' (though no doubt Montana is the privileged area) and to allow the writer to speak directly of a tradition and a place within that tradition. There is an undoubted attraction in listening to these various voices talk about their work and their place in the West of America, but I wonder if this is not simply a voyeurism that seems to lead somewhere, but in fact leads nowhere. Morrison asks Gretel Ehrlich: 'Do you consider yourself a political writer?' Ehrlich replies 'Oh, God, no! I avoid politics like the plague.' Ehrlich does not really give any sound-bites, but is touching and real when she writes about the gestation of *The Solace of Open Spaces*: 'I wasn't writing *The Compleat Book of Ranchlife in Wyoming*, which is what everyone seems to want. . . . I was also naïve in that I didn't think, first of all, that anyone would ever publish the book, and second of all, that anyone would ever read it if it did get published. I *certainly* didn't think I was writing about anything of any particular interest to anybody.' In reply to a question about place, Richard Ford replies that he might just as well be writing about Nebraska as Montana, and he strongly resists the notion of regionalism. 'My life has simply shown me that we're more in the same boat wherever we are, and that recognizing that fact might enable us to adapt to our situations more successfully.' Morris always remarks upon writers who smoke: 'As we talked, [Amy] Tan smoked; her responses were often hushed, always careful and considered.' Morris asks Tan if she writes out of tensions generated by race and relationships: 'I guess I'm interested in your storytelling technique, in the pressures that exert themselves on that technique and shape it.' To which Tan replies, 'My storytelling technique is probably undefined. It often starts with a question about life; coupled with that is an image of something, or of several images, that are interesting to me.' Morris has, undoubtedly, put together a series of fascinating interviews, and the individual writers come across as generous and talented individuals. Whether any generalizations can be made on their views of 'the West' seems to me doubtful, since their voices and experiences are so idiosyncratic. Likewise doubtful is that these interviews can lead to any serious analysis of their novels.

(b) Individual Authors

Jakob Köllhofer has edited a useful collection of articles on James Baldwin, entitled *James Baldwin: His Place in American Literary History and his Reception in Europe*. Michel Fabre writes, with deep knowledge, of Baldwin's relationship with France, of his meetings with students from French African colonies, whose attitude to their own sense of identity and tribe forced Baldwin to define himself as an American, someone from the New World, even though he had black skin; it was these encounters which gave birth to 'Encounter on the Seine' (1950). Fabre writes that Baldwin, after flirting with the USIS and American Liberalism, came more and more to view himself as black, having little to do with European culture. Baldwin sailed for France on Armistice Day 1948; when he arrived he was something of an innocent, but by the 1970s he was very much more politicized, pointing out changes in French feeling towards all blacks since the fall of Dien Bien Phu and the Algerian rebellion. Though Baldwin always maintained he was in exile, never an expatriate, which to him was an impossible condition, nevertheless it was in Paris that he found the key to 'unlock the trap of color'. Other essays in the volume include those by Peter Freese, who writes on the reception of Baldwin's work in Germany, and who comes to the unusual conclusion that Baldwin will be remembered for the role he played in articulating the plight of black America, rather 'than the enduring artistic achievement of his contradictory and uneven fictional oeuvre'; and by Hélène Christol, who examines aspects of gender and race in Baldwin. Altogether this is a good introduction to Baldwin in Europe.

The Stories of Raymond Carver by Kirk Nesset is a nicely produced (Gill's 'Joanna' font and Hopper's 'Cape Cod Evening' cover), though meanly margined book, and it is a fair introduction to Carver's stories. It will help the undergraduate get a grip on what Herzinger has called an 'equanimity of surface', and rightly points out Carver's roots in Anderson, Cheever, and above all Chekhov. Disarmingly, Nesset writes that he does not come to these texts armed with a 'methodology', but immediately seems to want to claim a theoretical base by referring to 'phantom methodologies emerging from the subtextual shadows of this study'. Certainly Barthes, Derrida et al. form part of the bibliography – though, as far as I can see, they are not referred to in the study. *The Stories of Raymond Carver*, then, is mercifully free from critical jargon, and relies on 'close reading', which Carver's fiction in 'a characteristically modernist way *invites*'. It is not, therefore, that the method is unsound, but that there is no method at all (to borrow from *Heart of Darkness* and *Apocalypse Now*). This might not be a problem if the reading were more 'close', more open, more fine. In 'Fat', for example, we read 'the royal "we" not only evokes regalness [regality?], . . . it evokes even more immediately a kind of complicity, a victimization common to fat man and waitress both'. It may be true that the fat man and the waitress are complicit, but it is in terms of plurality and birth (the spilled water, the feeling coming over her, the last sentences: 'My life is going to change. I feel it') – some discussion of process, change, and necessity would have been welcome. In his analysis of 'So Much Water So Close to Home', Nesset writes that Claire identifies herself with 'a raped and murdered woman found naked in a creek, the corpse ignored by her husband and his friends until their fishing trip is conveniently over'. Nesset closes the text by determining 'raped and murdered'; it *may* be so, but does not have to be. But Nesset has missed the point: the fishermen do *not* ignore the corpse – they are obsessed by it. When the moon comes up, they talk about the girl; they keep the body from drifting away; they wade in and get her; they tie her to a tree; they even wash their dirty dishes 'where the girl was'! The last thing they do is ignore her. The lack of intellectual rigour in this introduction to Carver's stories is disconcerting, but Nesset has made a start, and it is to be hoped that someone will continue the work, which Carver's prose so richly deserves.

In '*Libra* and the Assassination of JFK: A Textbook Operation' (*ArQ* 50.i.109–32), Joseph Kronick examines what DeLillo makes clear: 'the assassination is a text, which is to say that it is anything but clear'. Kronick's argument is that *Libra* operates like Borges's stories; the novel is a proposition about fiction and it holds in its scales the undecidable balance between history and language. Kronick spends some time looking at Paul de Man's reading of *Labyrinths*, particularly 'Theme of Traitor and Hero', and links this reading to *Libra* – experience (history) is bound to fall into narrative, and in a sense is bound to repeat itself. Kronick spends rather too long on models of fiction generated by cybernetics and quantum theory, and rehearses the well-known links between information theory and physics: entropy dictates that any system must behave in a sufficiently random way for there to be a distinction between past and future. The article concludes with a linguistic analysis where the formalizing powers of narrative determine history; the appeal of fiction is to turn death into the telos of narrative; and all plots end in death because all plots resolve themselves in the privileged perspective of destiny. In contrast, Magali Cornier Michael looks at 'The Political Paradox within Don DeLillo's *Libra*' (*Critique* 35.146–56). Like Kronick, Michael uses Linda Hutcheon as a theoretical base (history is not made obsolete by postmodern fiction, really it is being remade as human construct) and finds *Libra*, like *Gravity's Rainbow*, emphasizing patterns of coincidence. Michael seems to hedge her bets at the end: at one point she says that the novel is not apolitical, rather it demonstrates the pervasiveness of all types of politics, but she concludes her paper by writing that *Libra* is neither apolitical nor ahistorical 'in its overt engagement with politics and history'. Some attempt to resolve this apparent contradiction would have been welcome. Meanwhile John Johnston in 'Superlinear Fiction or Historical Diagram?: Don DeLillo's *Libra*' (*MFS* 40.319–42), argues that *Libra* brings DeLillo's work full circle, and, more importantly, the novel confirms the crucial significance of genre to DeLillo's fiction. Johnston uses Deleuze's notion of intensive systems, and sees Oswald and Kennedy as simulacra. DeLillo according to Johnston thus implies that conventional history may be only one possible system. Therefore, while DeLillo's treatment of Oswald and his relationship with the CIA is supposedly 'fiction', in the light of suspicions of the official version of events, DeLillo's account is seen as a historically more responsible version.

Meanwhile, John N. Duvall, in 'The (Super)Marketplace of Images: Television as Unmediated Mediation in DeLillo's *White Noise*' (*ArQ* 50.iii.127–53), states that *White Noise* treats both academic and domestic life comically and that these subjects 'serve as a vehicle for DeLillo's satiric examination of the ways in which contemporary America is implicated in proto-fascist urges'. As chair of the department of Hitler studies, Jack Gladney is blind to the world mirrored back to him: a postmodern, decentralized totalitarianism. Duvall's point is that for the National Socialists ideology was conscious choice, whereas in proto-fascist America it is 'more like the Althusserian notion of ideology as unconscious system of representation'. I doubt that Duvall is right about contemporary America, but his comments on Nazi Germany are certainly facile. With *White Noise*, DeLillo created a series of memorable images that show America anaesthetized by television, a much more effective way of forgetting death than Dylar; but to conclude, therefore, that fascism is diffused throughout America, its mass media and its representations, is to fall into conspiracy theory. In contrast, Mark Conroy in 'From Tombstone to Tabloid: Authority Figured in *White Noise*' (*Critique* 35.97–109) begins his analysis with a consideration of Gladney's visit to 'the old burying ground', which, unlike 'the most photographed barn in the world', is right off the tourist track, unphotographed, unvisited, and yet having an authority of the past, the past of ancestors with 'great strong simple names, suggesting a moral vigor'. Conroy finds it facile to see *White Noise* as a simple critique of American materialism; he sees DeLillo putting forward a view that the spirituality that preceded consumer culture still exists, though in a degraded and superstitious form. Thus he concludes, 'If the supermarket is indeed the point of intersection between profane consumption and sacred celebrity, it is the tabloids that make it so.' It is no accident that Gladney is last seen looking at the tabloid rack. Arthur M. Saltzman continues the debate with a thoughtful article entitled: 'The Figure in the Static: *White Noise*' (*MFS* 40.807–26). Saltzman ranges far and wide in DeLillo's work, and writes with some elegance: 'Anxiety is awareness that remains on the far side of enlightenment.' He argues that the linguistic implication is the desolate voice of the novel, as the gleaming artefacts of today shimmer momentarily only to settle back into the collective hum. We can no longer use metaphor because it implies a greater command of hierarchy, resonance and relation than we can achieve. 'Thus, white noise is literally an anaesthetic, paving the imagination for the transportation of sanctioned simulations.' Saltzman cogently argues that DeLillo, more than any of his contemporaries, is alert to the pre-constructions and prior manipulations of language and inevitably sets his fictions in environments hostile to the individual's capacity to use words. Maurice Couturier, meanwhile, argues that *White Noise* is concerned with history in the making: 'L'histoire et la refiguration de l'instant: *White Noise* de Don DeLillo' (*RFEA* 62.383–92). Couturier argues that the present becomes fiction because of its instant recycling by the media. In choosing the title *White Noise* (over two previous titles 'The American Book of the Dead' and 'Panasonic'), DeLillo was not just thinking about sound waves 'mais aussi à l'ecriture elle-même : une cacophonie de voix sur des pages blanches'.

Michael Kaufman, in 'The Textual Body: William Gass's *Willie Master's Lonesome Wife*' (*Critique* 35.27–42), has written an interesting paper on the implications of Gass's use of the physical form of text, typography and pagination. Throughout the work, Gass shows the problematic nature of reality, its represented character. The textuality of the world is apparant from the beginning as a bare arm extends from the left margin and almost touches *Willie Master's Lonesome Wife*, the title of the book – the flesh made word. In truth it is the reader that makes these words live. The final piece of the world introduced into the novel is the coffee-cup ring, the author's mark on the page. Kaufman analyses this well: 'She leaves a ring with her coffee cup, a sort of kiss on the page, returning us to the lips that formed the words we read. But "all contact . . . [is] impossible . . . a wall divides us like the wall which grew between Pyramus and Thisbe".'

In *The Ethics of Indeterminacy in the Novels of William Gaddis*, Gregory Comnes has made a brave effort at coming to terms with Gaddis's difficult prose. The book is underpinned by a reading of quantum mechanics and there are frequent references to Bohr and Heisenberg; the indeterminacy in Gaddis's prose, signed by his frequent lacunae, is given form in Comnes's book: each section opens with a lacuna, as though to imply that this is merely one way of putting it, or we might as well pick up the story here as anywhere else. Einstein does not figure much because, apparently, God *does* throw dice, maybe even loaded dice. Comnes argues that 'Gaddis shows how ethical choice, rather than conformity and passivity, is possible, even when the absolute has been replaced with the probable as the basis of judgement.' The ethics of indeterminacy means trying 'to recover some provisional sense of *agapé* in a world that remains intractably "agape"' (the terms are taken from Gaddis's *J R* [1975]). Beneath the carapace of modern physics and postmodern theory, something rather basic, something ideal and visionary, is trying to get out: at one point it becomes the work ethic: 'difficult books always teach their readers the virtue of hard work' (do they? always?). At other moments it seems to be 'love' or humanistic values vs. the capitalistic state (here some consideration of George Eliot's moral aesthetic might have been useful, particularly as Comnes stresses the didactic quality of Gaddis's novels); and throughout Gaddis preaches that 'to live deliberately' means, in Keats's terms, to live in perplexity and doubt. Unfortunately this fairly basic concept, in which the poet's intuition precedes the physicist's theories, is turned, in Comnes's rebarbative prose, into something virtually incomprehensible: 'the reader learns to enact an agapistic ethics of indeterminacy in a postmodern landscape and to recover through hermeneutic exploration and risk and dialogical transactions a redemption that necessarily remains open to further risk-taking'. (What I take this to mean is the very dubious concept that a reading of Gaddis's novels will teach the inquiring reader how to act properly in the modern world.) There would seem to be an inherent contradiction in trying to derive ethics from an indeterminate world, but Comnes's aim, like Gaddis's, is didactic. However, whereas Gaddis's novels would seem to be open, Comnes's methodology leads to closure. His goal is 'to delineate a set of narrative methods so that informed readers can then read the novels for themselves, deriving (as I believe Gaddis intends) how the idea of postmodern ethics in these novels is grasped through experiencing the texts rather than reading criticism about them'. Disregarding the intentional fallacy, Comnes here seems to want to determine our reading patterns. There is much throwing about of philosophical brains here, but little that will help the first-time reader of Gaddis's novels.

In 'The Properties of Desire: Forms of Slave Identity in Charles Johnson's *Middle Passage*' (*ArQ* 50.ii.73–108), by Ashraf H. A. Rushdy, we have a good article which compares Morrison's *Beloved* with Johnson's *Middle Passage*: in both, the value of self can be counted in dollars. Thus Paul D learns his price in *Beloved*: 'the dollar value of his weight, his strength, his heart, his brain, his penis, and his future'. Rutherford responds to the same knowledge in *Middle Passage* by becoming a thief, but in the latter case he is operating philosophically and politically: 'Theft, if the truth be told, was the closest thing I knew to transcendence.' Rushdy carefully argues that Rutherford integrates his three careers and that by a rewriting of the documents of the slave trade 'Rutherford finally learns what to steal and how best to steal it.'

Alan J. Rice, in 'Jazzing It Up a Storm: The Execution and Meaning of Toni Morrison's Jazzy Prose Style' (*JAmS* 28.423–2), points out that *Jazz*, though the most recent, and the novel in which jazz influence is most obvious, is not Morrison's only work which is influenced by jazz music. Rice claims that Morrison consciously uses a 'jazz aesthetic' throughout her work, and that central to both the jazz musician and Morrison's technique is (there are no surprises here) 'Repetition'. Rice castigates David Cowart for an analysis that likens Morrison's style to Faulkner's, because, according to Rice, although her style might owe something to the Anglo-American modern tradition, 'its major debt is to African-American expressive forms'. Rice tries to support his argument with recourse to 'the riff', defined as a repeated melodic phrase, without melodic development, in order to stress the melodic development outside the short phrase. But, I am afraid, the argument is nonsensical – and indeed it strikes me as a kind of reverse racism. There is only space to pick up two examples of the 'argument' in practice: quoting from *Sula*, Rice comments on the repetition of 'Lonely', 'Morrison embeds her riffs in dialogue so they literally become the basis for a character's solo expression. The second example is taken from *Tar Baby*, where Rice comments on the extended use of the word 'waste' – 'That was the sole lesson of their world: how to make waste, how to make machines that made more waste, how to make wasteful products – that this is obviously a riff and that its function is hyperbole for Morrison's polemic purpose. Of course, the astute reader realises that we do not need the concept of 'riff' to analyse these words, and that if this is what the 'riff' describes then clearly Dickens, like Morrison, was strongly influenced by jazz: consider Mrs Gummidge's 'Lone, lorn, creetur' or Dickens's great extended riff on fog at the beginning of *Bleak House*.

In contrast to the literal-minded argument of Rice, Paula Gallant Eckard, in

'The Interplay of Music, Language, and Narrative in Toni Morrison's *Jazz*' (*CLAJ* 38.11–19), offers a more subtle analysis in which jazz is personified and operates as the narrator; this clearly has implications for the narrative structure. In effect Morrison has created a postmodern novel in which the 'jazz narrator' admits to inventing the stories of everyone in the city, and directly exhorts the reader to bring the text to life by reading 'Say make me, remake me. You are free to do it and I am free to let you because look, look. Look where your hands are. Now.'

Marilyn Sanders Mobley in *Folk Roots and Mythic Wings in Sarah Orne Jewett and Toni Morrison: The Cultural Function of Narrative* extends our knowledge of the cultural background and folk roots of these two writers. As Morrison has said, 'I write what I have recently begun to call village literature, fiction that is really for the village, for the tribe.' Mobley finds that both Jewett and Morrison have an abiding interest in myth and folklore, which they utilize to reclaim lost and forgotten experience that will then be imparted to their readers: they have 'a shared literary aesthetic and narrative intention of cultural affirmation'. (I cannot comment on whether this is true or not for Jewett, but it seems to make Morrison more didactic than she is.) Though both Jewett and Morrison approve of progress, they are also 'redemptive scribes': Jewett redeems the values of country life opposed to the city, whereas Morrison apparently has a mission to correct cultural misapprehensions, and to 'defend the cultural integrity of her people' against those who marginalize narratives about African-Americans. As the title of the book indicates, it has three *loci* of argument: one, a fusion of folklore and myth; two, that this fusion reveals a narrative function in both writers; three, that the narrative function is meant to validate people and places that have been undervalued. So baldly stated, the problems with the book become obvious – it is trying to do too much. On the question of folklore and myth, these writers are so different: Jewett, white, writing in the nineteenth century about Maine, and Morrison, black, writing today about the South and Midwest. In a sense what these writers have in common is what any two writers may have in common; one could probably make the same case for, say, Thomas Hardy and Graham Swift, in that both write about almost forgotten rural areas and both have an equivocal approach to the past. On the question of narrative and narrative method, Mobley admits that her approach is 'somewhat eclectic'; she uses 'narrative' synonymously with 'story' and 'story-telling', which seems a very dangerous confusion; and although she includes a number of critical theorists from Bakhtin to Hayden White in her bibliography, the index reveals that she makes very little appeal to them. On the last question of whether these writers have a palpable aim on their readers, all readers have to decide this themselves; but for me, Morrison does not work in that simplistic manner. Essentially Mobley examines three texts: Jewett's *The Country of the Pointed Firs* (1896), and Morrison's *Song of Solomon* (1977) and *Tar Baby* (1981). The first chapter deals with 'The Cyclical Journeys of Jewett's female characters', the second with 'The Complex Response to Loss in *The Country of the Pointed Firs*', whereas the third and fourth chapters are separate treatments of Morrison's novels. Of these the discussion of *Song of Solomon* is the most achieved because Mobley is a much better analyser of myth than she is of narrative, and her treatment of *Tar Baby* is more concerned with narrative than it is with myth. Despite the fact that this book tries to go in too many directions at once, it has valuable insights about Morrison; the curious reader may also learn something about Sarah Orne Jewett.

Michael Wood's *The Magician's Doubts: Nabokov and the Risks of Fiction* is, quite simply, the best book on Nabokov yet written. The subject, 'our subject', as Wood puts it, 'is Nabokov's restless and stylish insubordination' and also our own insubordination as readers. The disconcerting pleasures of reading Nabokov raise questions of curiosity and reading beyond Nabokov and are concerned with philosophy and language. Reminding us of Benjamin's 'The Task of the Translator', Wood quotes, in the chapter on *Eugene Onegin*, 'Languages are not strangers to one another, but are, a priori and apart from all historical relationships, interrelated in what they want to express.' Wood's great interest is Nabokov's language: a language created out of the loss of another language. Forcing himself, with great pain, *not* to write in Russian, Nabokov was able to create 'a fabulous, freaky, singing, acrobatic, unheard-of English', which enables 'the sly idiot, the haughty mandarin and the great doubting magician to get along together' in works like *Lolita* and *Ada* (as Edward Said has also pointed out). Throughout the exceptionally fine analyses of Nabokov's work, the reader has a sense of fun and adventure, and experiences a tough-minded dialogue with complex and provocative texts. *The Magician's Doubts* is beautifully written, and mercifully free from all pedantic jargon; the great learning behind the work is gracefully subsumed into a light and supple prose – very much as Wood describes Nabokov's prose. Anyone, from the greenest first-year student to the sere and yellow emeritus, interested in Nabokov and reading will be enthralled by this book.

Michael Kokonis in '"Meaning Upon Meaning, and Voice Upon Voice": Competing Discourses in V. Nabokov's *Lolita* and W. Allen's *Zelig*' (*Logomachia*, ed. E. Douka-Kabitoglou, 441–53), applies Bakhtin's *Dialogic Imagination* to both works. *Lolita* is seen as a chameleon text with a proliferation of literary forms and genres. There is some fair analysis of Nabokov's prose, but, regrettably, Kokonis takes Humbert too much at face value, finding him, towards the end of the novel, capable of humane qualities. A reading of *The Magician's Doubts* would have put him right. Gennady Barabtarlo was born in Moscow and teaches Russian at the University of Missouri; in *Aerial View: Essays on Nabokov's Art and Metaphysics*, he has written a book that claims to unlock Nabokov's metaphysics as well as his Russian. Of the latter I am no competent judge, but the former attempt is surely wrong-headed. As Barabtarlo paraphrases, for Nabokov style *is* matter, so to claim that Nabokov 'probed the mysteries of the hereafter' is to get him wrong: Nabokov does not write about philosophy, he writes philosophy. The book is comprised of chapters on the early story 'Revenge'; *Invitation to a Beheading*; *The Enchanter*, *English Short Stories*; *The Russian Lolita*; and *Pnin*; and a final chapter entitled '*Entrefilets*', which concerns Nabokov's cryptography. There are in addition various documents reproduced, including the MS of a poem written on 25 October 1917 – the first day of the Soviet era. Barabtarlo seems to be searching for clues, which he finds in palindromes and anagrams (the terms are sometimes confused) from Russian to English and vice versa. The argument throughout is tendentious: for example, in discussing 'Revenge', the ghost 'perhaps arranged the professor's elaborate revenge ploy'; but then, over the page, we read that the professor 'is being steered by the ghost of the very man whom he imagines alive'; and a few lines later Barabtarlo withdraws from the assertion, as the professor 'designs, or is driven to design, his revenge plan'. In trying to find clues or keys, in trying to determine a metaphysic which does not exist, in utilizing chop-logic, and in relying too much on his Russian expertise, Barabtarlo's *Aerial View* never really takes flight. I am very sympathetic to someone trying to write in a language not his own; it is not, finally, Barabtarlo's fault that the book is riddled with solecisms, which should have been picked up, and corrected, by the editor. In contrast, Martine Hennard in 'Playing a Game of Worlds in Nabokov's *Pale Fire*' (*MFS* 40.299–317) is a much more sophisticated reader. She argues that *Pale Fire* dramatizes the Derridean 'infinite drift of meaning' whereby a text, once cut off from its originating source and circumstances, becomes prey to a paranoid scholar and his far-fetched interpretations. *Pale Fire* can thus be seen as an allegory of reading in which there is no access to an original authorized meaning: 'In other words, language is shown to exceed an intended meaning irretrievably lost as soon as materialized in discourse – a tenet crucial to much post-structuralist theory.'

Part social history, part popular culture, part literary criticism, Jon Lance Bacon's *Flannery O'Connor and Cold War Culture* is an excellent introduction to O'Connor; a book which, for once, almost fulfils the blurb's claim of 'a radical new reading'. The value of the book is to set O'Connor's narratives within the intertext of the Cold War. The Cold War manifests itself in popular culture by a series of invasion narratives, whether these be from the Communists or from outer space, and Bacon clearly relates their structures and themes to O'Connor's rural parables. Bacon points out that though O'Connor was one of the few to criticize consumerism and the American Way of Life, this certainly did not imply any sympathy for the extreme left. What Bacon overwhelmingly achieves is to set O'Connor's work within a political context; the theological argument, he states correctly, has been well worked over, and, while it has deepened our understanding of O'Connor's imaginative power, it has marginalized her work. Bacon's interest is not therefore to separate religious ideals (particularly where these concern the Catholic church) and political realities. The book is richly illustrated with comic strips and cartoons from the 1940s and 1950s, campaign ads from the Midgeville *Union-Recorder*, film stills, and reproductions of paintings, by Hopper, Grant Wood, Wyeth, etc. In fact the only weak point of the book is Bacon's analyses of the illustrations. Two examples will have to suffice: Grant Wood's *Stone City, Iowa* presents a rural idyll, a cultivated landscape that is virtually depopulated, and Bacon writes 'The near absence of human figures in Wood's painting suggests that the stability of the community derives as much from the natural setting as from human action.' This misses the point. Wood has cancelled out agency; work has occurred – ridges, buildings, cultivation etc. – but no one is there to do it; this begs to be linked to a myth of America as a prelapsarian world. Likewise, Hopper's *People in the Sun*; according to Bacon, these people survey a natural world that seems not to intimidate them; they are far from helpless. But the painting is much more ominous than that: the formal suits and ties for the men, a hat for the woman, the recumbent position on deck-chairs, the white sanitized building to the left, all make one think of TB patients or, more ominously, witnesses to an atomic bomb (brighter than a thousand suns). However, apart from these very small criticisms, the book is well produced, meticulously researched, usefully indexed, and essential reading for anyone interested in O'Connor's work.

With twenty-one collections of short stories, twenty-two novels, five volumes of poetry and seven collections of essays already published, Joyce Carol Oates may well be 'America's most prolific writer', as the blurb claims – indeed if she carries on like this it will be worse than Sainte-Beuve and Ruskin put together. *Joyce Carol Oates: A Study of the Short Fiction* by Greg Johnson is an ideal introduction to her short stories. The book has a useful chronology, excellent bibliography and index, and is broken into three sections: 'The Short Fiction', 'The Writer' (various statements by Oates) and 'The Critics' (four original and three reprinted pieces on Oates's work). It will thus be the starting point for anyone researching into Oates's shorter fiction. However, the problem with the book is palpable from the first sentence: 'Among contemporary writers, Joyce Carol Oates is the unrivalled American master of the short story.' This is simply silly. Joyce Carol Oates, in stories like 'The Dead' or 'My Warszawa', is a good short-story writer, but she is not in the same league as Carver. Likewise, 'it should be stressed that her assimilation of literary tradition is more wide-ranging than that of any other American writer' (than Melville, Hawthorne, James?). This is a worthwhile book, certainly, but one could have done without the hyperbole.

The best joke in *Cynthia Ozick's Comic Art*, by Sarah Blacher Cohen, runs as follows: 'Let's talk about something more cheerful. What's new with the cholera in Odessa?'. Unfortunately, it is not by Cynthia Ozick but by Sholom Aleichem. 'All that is not Law is levity' is the epigraph to the book, and there is a considerable amount of Law (as well as lore), but not a great deal of levity: we are introduced to *misnagids, schlimazels* and *schlemiels* as well as the difference between *Halachah* (Law and Consensus) and *Aggadah* (tale and lore). Ozick is a *midrash*-maker and her liturgical literature is not hackneyed nor formulaic 'it is *Aggadigic*, utterly freed to invention'. Cohen makes the obvious connections between Bellow and Ozick, but, from the evidence of this book, does not make the important distinction that while Bellow is a writer who happens to be Jewish, Ozick is very much a Jewish writer. According to Cohen she is marginalized as a 'Jewish writer in the Christian world'; I do not think that Ozick is in any way marginalized, and of course there is extraordinary insularity in defining the world as Christian. It is notoriously difficult to analyse the light touch of comedy, but I am afraid Cohen gets nowhere close. The theoretical introduction, 'Cynthia Ozick's Comic Art of Truth-Telling', is based partly on an article by Nathan Scott entitled 'The Bias of Comedy and the Narrow Escape into Faith' (1961), but even more on a letter Cohen received from Ozick in 1992, which is cited half a dozen times, and often throughout the book; the letter is taken entirely on trust. There seems to be no critical distance established at all and the analysis, apart from the occasions when it sets Ozick's work into the context of Jewish culture, is of the most rudimentary. It is hard to think whom this book is intended for; I suspect it is only for the converted – it will not gain Ozick new readers, which is a pity.

There is a fine article by Lewis A. Lawson on Walker Percy, entitled 'The Dream Screen in *The Moviegoer*' (*PLL* 30.25–56). Lawson establishes that the time sequence in the novel is more subtle than is usually thought; it represents, in fact, selected events from an eight-day period, over one year in the past. The epilogue of *The Moviegoer* establishes that Binx has been representing events and feelings which he may not have been able to articulate in the past. Lawson states that the technique is illuminated by Charles Sanders Peirce's model of consciousness, 'the self-which-is silently converses with the self-which-is-just-coming-to-be'. Walker Percy had earlier written an essay entitled 'The Man on the Train' (collected in *The Message in the Bottle*, 1975), and Lawson's argument is that by conversion to Christianity, Binx is still the man on the train but his destination is now the city of God.

Anne Rice has written two historical novels, and five works defined by Bette B. Roberts in *Anne Rice* as 'erotics', by which I suppose she means pornography. However, she is best known for her Gothic fiction: *Interview with the Vampire* (1976), *The Vampire Lestat* (1985), *The Queen of the Damned* (1988) and *The Tale of the Body Thief* (1992). There has been some critical debate on Rice, and Roberts claims that the decision as to whether to take this work seriously 'rests primarily on our placing her Gothic novels in the history and context of the genre'. This introductory statement seems just as illogical as her conclusion: 'except for the erotic fiction, all of Rice's novels may be taken seriously on the grounds provided by new critical theories of historicists and culturalists, who use the popularity of a work to come to terms with the nature of the times in which it was created and the values of its readers'. Why then exclude the erotic novels from this equation? Roberts argues that Rice has philosophical substance, stylistic richness and impact on the genre of the Gothic, but such claims do not emerge from a reading of this book, whose turbid plot outlines and lack of analysis make one wonder what all the fuss is about. There may be scope for yet another book on American Gothic, in which Rice may go down as a minor practitioner of the Southern variety, whose popularity emerges from a mélange created out of historical window-dressing, contemporary settings, a *frisson* of horror, and a titillation of the erotic. It was this potent combination that accounted for the popularity of Dennis Wheatley from the thirties to the fifties. No matter how much *Faust*, *Frankenstein*, Blake, Yeats, etc., Roberts throws over Rice's work, this book is still no more than a series of plot outlines covered by a superstructure of scholarship.

Anne Tyler was awarded the National Book Circle Award in 1985 for *The Accidental Tourist*, and the Pulitzer Prize in 1988 for *Breathing Lessons*, and not before time Dale Salwak has edited a useful collection of essays, *Anne Tyler as Novelist*. Often connected with Eudora Welty, Tyler has acknowledged her debt, since, as she writes, Welty 'showed me that very small things are often really larger than the large things'. Stella Nesanovich in 'The Early Novels: A Reconsideration' points out that Tyler's earliest attempts at fiction dealt with the struggle of the individual within a family setting, and that one of her major themes is the isolation of the individual within the family and the growth of self-awareness that emerges from such isolation. Tyler is interested in the possibilities of change and growth within a very limited space, and though this change and growth may entail loss, Tyler cannot be considered as pessimistic. Alice Hall Petry, in 'Tyler and Feminism', quotes Tyler on novels written by liberated women: 'I hate them all.' The essay is an uneasy balance between an appreciation of Tyler's work and concern at its politically incorrect message. Lamenting the loss of the strong woman character in Tyler's later work, Petry seems worried as to what will happen to the American novel in the future; but I think she misses the point of Tyler's irony, which seems often closer to Austen than anyone else, particularly in the self-awareness of the fictional world. In contrast, Kathleen Woodward in 'Forgetting and Remembering: In Praise of Tyler's Older Women' engages personally with the wit, courage and sometimes wisdom with which Tyler's middle-aged women characters face the world. Given Tyler's celebration of middle America it is unsurprising to find her approved of by John Updike: 'This writer is not merely good, she is *wickedly* good.' We have mentioned Welty and Austen, but perhaps George Eliot too could come into the picture with Tyler's infectious delight in 'the smell of beautiful, everyday life'. This unpretentious collection of papers will be of interest to anyone familiar with Tyler's work, and will be a good introduction for anyone coming to Tyler for the first time.

Since 1946, when he published *Williwaw*, to today Gore Vidal has virtually fifty titles to his credit. As Jay Parini, editor of *Gore Vidal: Writer Against the Grain*, writes: 'One has to wonder at the lack of critical response to this extraordinary body of work.' Parini comes up with a number of reasons why Vidal has been ignored by critics: first, the sheer volume of the work; second, Vidal's unpredictability – the novels, plays and detective stories do not fall into an easily identifiable pattern; third, Vidal is not trendy, he is not postmodern (indeed he may be anti-postmodern), and he fills in all the narrative gaps; fourth, Vidal's tone is mandarin, not intimate — he is a formal host, not a relative. Brought up in the American aristocracy, friends with Huey Long, Eleanor Roosevelt and, through Hugh D. Auchincloss, the Kennedys, Vidal has, from the inside, a real knowledge of the workings of power; he may be something of a hack, but he is also one of the finest stylists in America today. This excellent collection of essays is long overdue. Italo Calvino writes of Vidal in Ravello, where he has kept a house since 1972, and half wants (Calvino is also attacked by cold sweats at the thought) Vidal to write an Italian novel whose pages 'can take their place in the great *humour noir* tradition from Swift onward'. With references to Shakespeare, Jonson, Waugh and Mailer *inter alia*, William H. Pritchard subtly investigates 'Vidal's Satiric Voices' and concludes that he is a first-rate creative satirist. In 'Gore Vidal: Private Eye' Stephen Spender, in the gem of the collection, muses on Vidal's talents as an essayist, celebrating his wit, his lightly worn learning, and his 'style', with which he elevates brashness through satire; above all Spender celebrates Vidal's ability to create an anti-self, a Yeatsian negative, to the positive 'Senator Vidal'. There is a quite wonderful description of Ronald Reagan, of which I can only quote a few lines: 'Ronald Reagan is a well-preserved not young man. Close-to, the painted face is webbed with delicate lines while the dyed hair, eyebrows, and eyelashes contrast oddly with a sagging muscle beneath the as yet unlifted chin, soft earnest of wattle-to-be.' As Spender says, this is written with 'the diamond lens of hell's least kind recording angel'. In 'The Central Man: On Gore Vidal's *Lincoln*' Harold Bloom honestly records how badly he underestimated Gore Vidal: Bloom writes that *Myra Breckenridge*, together with West's *A Cool Million* and Waugh's *Scoop*, 'will outlive many of the more celebrated visions of our century'. It is with *Lincoln*, however, that Vidal has found his truest subject, which is 'our national political history during precisely those years when our political and military histories were one'. There are twenty-one articles here, most of good quality and some quite exceptional; there is a useful bibliography; the book is well indexed; and anyone working on Gore Vidal could usefully start with the various views expressed in it.

In 'Into the Secret Chamber: Art and the Artist in Kurt Vonnegut's *Bluebeard*' (*Critique* 35.16–25), David Rampton wittily connects a work of art that is destroyed by carelessness in Vonnegut's novel with a W. C. Fields film. The Fields character knocks over and decapitates a statue, during an erratic drive to California: 'She ran right in front of the car', Fields replies to his nagging wife. In *Bluebeard*, Rabo Karebekian's painting is destroyed, but this time because the medium, Sateen Dura-Luxe, self-destructs. Rampton argues that Vonnegut is still being innovative, that his moral targets are a little less crude than usual, and that the novel is a 'resonant meditation on the morality of representational art itself'. Rampton makes high claims for Vonnegut's right to be taken seriously by the academy: *Player Piano* is a more ominous dystopia than those of Orwell and Huxley; no American writer has written more clear-eyed accounts of World War II. This is certainly hyperbolic (what about *Catch 22*?), but nevertheless, Rampton is probably right to castigate those po-faced academics who studiously snub Vonnegut.

Two new books on Eudora Welty testify to a continuing interest in her work.

Ruth D. Weston in *Gothic Traditions and Narrative Techniques in the Fiction of Eudora Welty* examines Welty's debt to the Gothic tradition. In particular Weston looks at themes of enclosure and escape amidst settings, particularly the Natchez Trace wilderness of Mississippi, that generate mystery and magic. Given that Welty has consistently rejected the 'Gothic' label, this may seem rather a perverse enterprise, but Weston has much of interest to say about Welty's indebtedness to European and North American Gothic tradition (though, as will be seen later, she is much less sure about the European tradition). Weston is careful to discriminate between Welty's fiction and that of other Southern women writers, such as O'Connor and McCullers, and determines that Welty cannot be placed in the category of 'Southern Gothic', though she is necessarily a 'Southern' writer in the sense that the South provides a natural source of place in her fiction. According to Weston, one of Welty's strongest points is the ability to construct plots that serve as signifying patterns which correspond to cognitive processes, the most basic of which involves a recognition of similarity and difference. Weston concentrates particularly on Welty's female characters: Rosamond in *The Robber Bridegroom*, Virgie in *The Golden Apples* and Laurel in *The Optimist's Daughter*. Overall, Weston argues that Welty has followed 'a subtly feminist track'. This again is slightly worrying, because, as is well known, Welty has consistently refused a feminist stance. The narrative patterns generated by Welty's debt to the Gothic involve aspects of enclosure and escape, and Weston's valid point is that Welty's narratives escape from the 'thralldom' of the romance plot, and reveal a new openness for her protagonists.

The first chapter deals with Gothic space as narrative technique. Moving from archetypal folk-memory of sun-worship and sacrifice, which linger on in the Natchez Trace, Weston makes a transition to Gothic labyrinthine enclosures such as cathedral or castle dungeons (as far as I know cathedrals do not have dungeons, though they may well have crypts). But I find the logic and connection unconvincing: the whole point about these European architectural structures, in terms of Gothic fiction, is that they are usually in ruin and *thus* leave space for the viewer's/reader's imagination. Some consideration of Goethe's 'Essay on Strassburg Cathedral' or Byron's *Manfred* might have been of use here, since Weston could then have pointed out the liberating power of the incomplete on the imagination. (Another disturbing aspect of Weston's appreciation of European Gothic is that Scott's *Marmion* is classified as a Gothic *novel.* This kind of misapprehension raises serious doubts as to her control over the European background to this study.) In the second chapter Weston examines space in the short story; this is particularly useful in its reminder of the tradition of Cooper, Hawthorne, James et al., who lay the imagination onto an actual landscape and thus produce a 'neutral territory'. (That this is, essentially, a Wordsworthian concept goes unmentioned.) However, the analysis of the short stories in terms of Hawthorne and Chekhov is particularly well achieved.

The heart of the book is to be found in the chapter entitled 'Patterns of Enclosure, Exposure, and Escape', which draws on Foucault and Bentham and at some level is concerned with the reform of society. At moments the critical judgement seems shaky: thus we read that 'The primary images of a Gothic novel are those of "dammed up" characters.' But this begs the question, certainly in the European tradition, of damned-up characters breaking out and seizing power. However, when not dealing with the European tradition, and in particular in examining Welty's debts to and affiliations with Faulkner, Weston is on safer ground and makes a convincing case for the 'mysterious and eternal' worlds, both human and natural. Despite some dreadful neologisms, such as '[Welty's] canonwide themes', this is, by and large, a useful scholarly book on an important subject.

In contrast, Gail L. Mortimer's *Daughter of the Swan: Love and Knowledge in Eudora Welty's Fiction* does not seem, quite, to know its addressee. We read, for example, that 'Welty would find the Nietzschean vision of art as an interplay of Dionysian chthonic energy and passion with Apollonian imposition of order to be entirely congenial' and are given a note to one hundred-odd pages of *The Birth of Tragedy*; whilst two pages later we find basic definitions of simile and metaphor. The tone of the book thus tends to oscillate between address to the learned scholar and to the inquiring first-year student. Another problem is that Mortimer places too much weight on Welty's biography, and then hedges her argument around with 'perhaps' and 'maybe'. This said, however, Mortimer has written a worthwhile book, taking as its controlling image Yeats's view of schoolchildren, as a pattern for Welty's protagonists finding in children a search for fuller understanding. The most interesting aspects of the book are Mortimer's probing examination of Welty's epistemology, and, in chapter 1, her consideration of the themes of love and separateness seen through Nancy Chodorow's psychoanalytic object-relations theory. Whereas Weston discussed Welty's debt to Faulkner in terms of the Gothic, in contrast Mortimer uses Faulkner as a counterpoint to Welty's fiction: the key difference being that Welty's characters are capable of empathy, while in Faulkner, the character's isolation is absolute. There is room for considerable work yet on the relation of Faulkner and Welty, but certainly both Weston and Mortimer make a number of valid, though quite different, points. Perhaps inevitably, there is some overlap between these two books, particularly in terms of characterization, themes of entrapment, etc., but both, in their different ways, are well worth reading.

4. Drama

(a) General

The American Stage: Social and Economic Issues from the Colonial Period to the Present, edited by Ron Engle and Tice L. Miller, is a fascinating and diffuse collection. Although framed by Oscar G. Brockett's very brief introduction to American theatre history scholarship and Don B. Wilmeth's alphabetical and unannotated 'checklist' of selected books on American theatre from 1960 to 1990, this collection quite consistently explores areas generally marginalized or overlooked in previous studies. Good examples of this kind of detailed research are Vera Mowry Roberts's discussion of six nineteenth-century 'lady managers'; Marvin Carlson's account of the development of the American theatre programme, which is particularly interesting in revealing the proleptic phenomenon of a form of publication in which the text is there to support the advertising; Errol Hill's painstaking reconstruction of the lives and careers of the Hyers Sisters, 'pioneers in Black musical comedy'; Felicia Hardison Londré's discussion of turn-of-the-century women playwrights, which focuses not on the plays but on journalistic obsession with financially successful authors, who were nevertheless reinscribed by the popular press within conventional domestic roles; Brooks McNamara's examination of comedians' source books of jokes and routines, which finds in them predictable expressions of popular prejudices against women, racial minorities and the rich; Stephen M. Archer's entertaining reconstruction of Sarah Bernhardt's 1905–6 tour; and Thomas Postlewait's sceptical account of the demonization of Hollywood in the recent autobiographies of major figures of the theatre. The financing of the Federal Theatre Project is considered by Barry B. Witham, while Margaret M. Knapp's Sontag-like 'Narrative Strategies in Selected Studies of American Theatre Economics' notes that such studies have a tendency to assume that the theatre is in trouble and to describe the problem in metaphors of organic disease and of industry, metaphors which practically guarantee that the continued existence of theatre can only be justified in terms of profitability. Related to these is Daniel J. Watermeier's account of the failure of the American Repertory Theatre of 1946–7: although the project failed in part for reasons of quality, direction and leadership, Watermeier doubts the practicability of the repertory ideal in the absence of substantial subsidy. Two essays on the commercial drama of a specific decade, Ronald H. Wainscott's on the 1920s and Alan Woods's on the 1980s, are perhaps a little too pat in finding such close parallels between the drama and the political, social and economic climate, although Wainscott does provide a fairly flexible taxonomy which reveals a variety of dramatic responses to the business world. (In this connection, see also Cynthia McKown's '*The Great God Brown*: A Diagnostic of Commercialism's Ills' [*EONR* 17.53–9].)

The essays on developments in the early American theatre are the most challenging. Douglas McDermott finds that changes in social, political and religious structures were emulated in developments in theatre organization, from the eighteenth-century democratic rebellion against the British, aristocratically governed company, to the nineteenth-century star system, the specialized roles of the combination company, the turn-of-the-century Syndicate, and finally the reforming, rebellious alternatives developed regionally after 1920. Peter A. Davis argues that the Continental Congress's anti-theatre act of 1774 was a sign not so much of religious as of commercial moral fervour, part of a boycott of imported British goods in which theatre came to be seen as a symbol of English oppression and theatre-going as economically wasteful. Rosemarie K. Bank provides a fascinatingly detailed, Foucaultian account of the circulation of prostitutes and the regulation of the audience in the Jacksonian era, suggesting that these are indicative of social transformations more complex than a simple binary division between vice and respectability would allow; while Bruce A. McConachie examines the attempt by P. T. Barnum and Moses Kimball to promote respectability as a sign of class equality in their museum theatres.

Inevitably, some essays are less impressive than others. Walter J. Meserve's account of 1850s plays dealing with money, gambling, temperance, slavery, religion and women's suffrage would be more convincing if his conclusions about the reception of these plays were not drawn almost entirely from a single periodical, the *Spirit of the Age*; Charles H. Shattuck's essay is little more than an extended synopsis of a largely forgotten novel, *Quicksilver*; and Stephen Langley's discussion of the recent impact of multiculturalism and 'technoculturalism', although pertinent, is rather journalistic in tone and less penetrating than many recently published analyses of these developments. More generally, it is a little surprising that many (but by no means all) of the essays find that the social, economic or political climate tends to be reflected straightforwardly in the drama; and one could do with a more extensive editorial overview to forestall the impression of an overly eclectic collection. But the eclecticism is one of the things that makes the collection so valuable, along with the detailed research and the substantial amount of new and fascinating information on social, commercial and dramatic exchange. This important volume plugs many gaps in our understanding of nineteenth-century American theatre in particular.

Not content with assembling his *American Musical Theatre: A Chronicle*, or with writing *The Oxford Companion to American Theatre* (*YWES* 73.613), the amazing Gerald Bordman has now embarked on the mammoth task of chronicling the history of straight plays on the American stage. The first volume to appear is *American Theatre: A Chronicle of Comedy and Drama, 1869–1914*. Year by year, Bordman gives a narrative survey of well over three thousand plays, providing details of playwright, cast, theatre, plot and critical reception. The approach is far from schematic, with some plays discussed at considerably greater length than others, but this adds to the immense readability of what in other hands could have become a rather arid project. Sheer weight of detail aside, perhaps the greatest value of Bordman's research is that any given play can be situated in its immediately contemporary theatrical context. The emphasis is on full-length American and non-American plays performed in New York's first-class houses: Bordman notes that many of the most interesting plays dealing with contemporary American problems would have been performed in lesser houses, making details hard to come by, but this hardly detracts from an astonishing achievement.

Jeffrey D. Mason valuably recognizes in *Melodrama and the Myth of America* a circular self-contradiction, whereby the nineteenth-century melodramatic sentimentality presented perfectibility as a natural progression towards a condition of original virtue which had already lapsed. However, his concluding remarks, which argue for the essential conservatism of theatre in general, overlook many serious objections, and this awkwardness in generalization is characteristic of a certain weakness in the book as a whole. The arguments are often obvious (form cannot be detached from the wider discursive field, melodrama presents a set of binary oppositions, it is part of the ideological work of melodrama to present a simplified and monolithic America, etc.); we do not need the brief and rather jarring summaries of theories of ideology (for example) to get the point, especially as Mason invariably proceeds to more fluent explanation 'in other words'. The bulk of the book consists of five chapters, each of which considers how a given nineteenth-century play helped transform social and political experience into myth: John Augustus Stone's *Metamora* and the 'Indian' question; W. H. Smith's *The Drunkard* and the temperance movement; George L. Aiken's adaptation of *Uncle Tom's Cabin* and the politics of race and slavery; Bartley Campbell's *My Partner* and the West; and Bronson Howard's *Shenandoah* and the Civil War. Mason shows how each play adapted the form to its own concerns, and notes that in most cases the events depicted had already passed into mythic closure. Sometimes his critical analysis sparks, as when he shows how *Metamora* could both transform a figure who had historically been represented as savage into a kind of American patriot, and simultaneously vindicate the exploitation and removal of the indigenous population; but for the most the plays as Mason presents them are insufficiently complex to repay detailed consideration, with the consequence that his mostly second-hand accounts of historical events are significantly lengthier and more interesting than his treatment of the plays.

In *The Dawning of American Drama*, Jürgen C. Wolter has compiled a list of 496 pieces of American dramatic criticism from the period 1746–1915, and reprinted around a third of them in whole or in part, thereby creating a valuable resource for future scholars. A short introductory chapter provides a historical, cross-referenced overview of this criticism, and argues (as have many others; see, for example, Gary Richardson's volume for Twayne, below) that what proved to be at stake was the possibility and nature of a national drama. Wolter is more interested in broader questions like this than in the plays and performances themselves, but it is still surprising that he should state that James A. Herne's *Margaret Fleming* (1891) and Anna C. Mowatt's *Fashion* (1845) were received 'with equal enthusiasm', since these are two of the best-known plays of the century and the generally vituperative response to Herne's play has been well documented. A more significant drawback of Wolter's approach is the absence of commentary on individual critics and journals, since without this information the reader can have no understanding of the personal, editorial or ideological influences which may or may not have determined the nature of any given piece of criticism. Wolter's book provides some valuable materials, but their significance will have to be judged by others.

AmDram devoted a special issue (3.ii) to American drama before 1920. Two outstanding contributions historicize the reception of well-known plays: Gary A. Richardson, in 'The Greening of America: The Cultural Business of Dion Boucicault's *The Shaughraun*' (1–28), contextualizes the play within the ethnic tensions between New York's Anglo-American and Irish-American populations, and suggests that Boucicault subverts the figure of the 'stage Irishman' by revealing it as an effect of the contemporary Irish condition; while Lucy Rinehart's 'A Nation's "Noble Spectacle": Royall Tyler's *The Contrast* as Metatheatrical Commentary' (29–52) explores the subtleties of the play's engagement with post-revolutionary republicanism and contemporary anti-theatrical feeling, before exploring its self-reflexive commentary on author, actors, audiences and critics. Thomas M. Kitts's 'An Argument for Boker's *Francesca da Rimini*' (53–70) is a more straightforward, textually-embedded evaluation, although it contains an interesting discussion of manuscript variants. (Quite why Mary Ellen Jordan's 'Lyle Kessler's *Orphans* and "The Father's Breasts"' [71–88] is included in this issue is a mystery: Jordan defends this recent play as going further than Pinter's *The Caretaker* or Shepard's *True West* in its exploration of father–son relationships.) In the following issue, J. L. Styan gives a detailed account of 'Chekhov and American Drama in the Early Twentieth Century' (*AmDram* 4.i.3–20), suggesting that he could be claimed as 'the step-father of American drama' because of the transmission of his style via Stanislavsky and the Moscow Art Theatre, and the influence of his work on many of the major American dramatists of the period.

Three volumes of Twayne's Critical History of American Drama series have now appeared, with a fourth and final volume, by Matthew C. Roudané, due shortly. In reviewing the course of *American Drama from the Colonial Period through World War I*, Gary A. Richardson has chosen a necessarily selective path, foregoing consideration of '[n]ative American rituals, treaty ceremonies, farces, minstrel shows, vaudeville skits, musical theater, civic pageants, and non-English language ethnic drama', and focusing his attention on specific authors and genres, each of which tends to be examined by way of one or two representative plays (around sixty in all), most of them available in the standard anthologies. He also provides a brief theoretical rationale for eschewing an 'organic history' or 'totalizing, teleological narrative' in noting that post-revolutionary drama in particular is characterized by 'disjunctions, discontinuities, and variety'. That said, Richardson's method and style are more traditional than his prologue would suggest: each section on a genre or period is framed by condensed but helpful historical material at the beginning, and a brief summary of the argument at the end, while the sections on individual dramatists usually follow a somewhat dry schema of career summary, plot summary, commentary, and a conclusion which relates the play or playwright to the developing picture of the genre or period which Richardson has been building up. This is not the most arresting way of treating the material, but it may be the most appropriate for an introductory volume on such a large subject; and although it would be beyond the scope and purpose of the book to provide extensive analyses of the relations between form and ideology or theatre and society along the lines explored in the Engle and Miller collection, Richardson nevertheless succeeds in giving a clear impression of how and why certain forms developed as they did. Although there is much evaluative commentary, Richardson rarely wastes time defending on aesthetic grounds those plays which need to be considered more as social and political interventions: in considering the colonial and revolutionary periods, for example, Richardson notes the frequent contradiction between the call for an independent American drama on the one hand, and the tendency of that drama to adhere to established European forms on the other. Similarly, the perceived need for the legitimation of American drama in the period from 1814 to the Civil War led both to the experiments in Romantic drama of John Howard Payne, Robert Montgomery Bird and George Henry Boker, who tended to accept the dominant European aesthetic, and to the more populist, specifically American genres created around the frontier, the Yankee, the noble savage, and the institution of slavery. These genres in turn informed the development of American melodrama in the plays of Daly and Boucicault, and finally the emergence of realism through the criticism and plays of James, Howells, Gillette and others. Although the book entails certain necessary compromises in method and scope, Richardson succeeds both in demonstrating the historical specificity of the aesthetic contradictions and defamiliarizations around which he has organized his material, and in maintaining a consistent balance between generalization and illustration.

This balance is equally apparent in the second volume of Twayne's series, Jordan Y. Miller and Winifred L. Frazer's *American Drama Between the Wars: A Critical History*. The greater familiarity of this period's drama reduces the need for extensive plot summaries, allowing for a broader range of contextual material (especially in the relation of the stage to other media), but the increased number of important plays in turn has led the authors to a sometimes ruthless evaluative rigour. Again, this is probably necessary in a study of this kind, but comes across as curiously old-fashioned when, as often, it is combined both with a certain moralizing idiom (O'Neill's Anna Christie, for instance, is a 'thoroughly fallen woman' with a 'sordid past') and a humanism which often applauds the verisimilitude of character while manifesting a blind spot in regard to broader issues (it is simply not true, for instance, that O'Neill has never been accused of racial stereotyping in the creation of the 'thoroughly human' Brutus Jones: the most recent example, Peter R. Saiz's subtle and illuminating 'The Colonial Story in *The Emperor Jones*' [*EONR* 17.31–8], was published after this book appeared, but there are many precedents). Nevertheless, the selective approach to the most familiar dramatists (O'Neill, Odets, Rice, Wilder, Hellman, Maxwell Anderson) means that Miller and Frazer have been able to give due weight to the most significant plays of such mainstream writers as Sidney Howard, S. N. Behrman, Robert E. Sherwood, George Kelly, Sidney Kingsley, Philip Barry, George S. Kaufman, Paul Green, etc. The relation of individual writers and plays to the theatrical context of the period is kept clearly in view, and reinforced by the full coverage of the little theatres, the Theatre Guild, the Group Theatre, the Federal Theatre Project, and Orson Welles's Mercury Theatre.

The most critically penetrating of the three Twayne volumes is Thomas P. Adler's *American Drama 1940–1960: A Critical History*. Again, there are good reasons for this: where Richardson is hampered by the relative weakness and unfamiliarity of the material, and Miller and Frazer by the inescapable pre-eminence of O'Neill, the series' division of the century into periods allows Adler to begin with the finest plays of O'Neill and a reconsideration of Hellman, before moving on to discuss the early, most significant phases of the careers of Miller and Albee, and the work of Inge, Hansberry, and other distinctive figures like Robert Anderson, Arthur Laurents, Jerome Lawrence and Robert E. Lee, William Gibson and Paddy Chayevsky. Given the division of O'Neill's career between two volumes in the series, the decision to survey the whole of Tennessee Williams's *oeuvre* in this volume appears arbitrary, especially as Adler himself distinguishes two halves to that career and considers the second phase in a separate chapter; presumably Matthew C. Roudané, in the concluding volume, will have to cover the same ground or significantly misrepresent the American drama of the 1960s and 1970s. More irritating is that Adler often fails to provide references for important quotations. These niggles aside, the book is detailed and penetrating, and engages the plays at a higher critical level than is generally the case with introductory surveys. The decision to devote a chapter or chapters to each of a few significant playwrights, and to explore those playwrights in depth, allows for a reasonably detailed analysis, and many sections of the book read very well as incisive critical essays rather than as stages in a narrative survey.

The Twayne series stands up quite well alongside its obvious competitors. Each volume is more flexible and detailed in its critical approach than Gerald M. Berkowitz's single-volume *American Drama of the Twentieth Century* (*YWES* 73.616), and overall the series is comparable in critical orientation and depth to the survey volumes in Macmillan's Modern Dramatists series, while providing more comprehensive coverage. Its consistent readability perhaps makes it preferable, but only as a strictly introductory survey, to C. W. E. Bigsby's three-volume *Critical Introduction to Twentieth-Century American Drama* (CUP, 1982–5), which remains the benchmark and by far the most analytically dense account. The quality of the photographic reproductions in the Twayne volumes is pretty poor, however, and there is a disconcertingly high number of misprints throughout, while cost and availability are likely to limit the appeal to its target audience.

A highly condensed but very readable survey of Broadway, up to and including the work of the Theatre Guild and the Group Theatre, is provided in the opening chapters of Andrew B. Harris's *Broadway Theatre*, although the aim here is not primarily to provide an overview but to contextualize the circumstances under which Broadway plays characteristically achieve their final form in stage production. To this end, Harris then devotes a chapter to each of six plays, one from each decade from the 1930s through to the 1980s: George S. Kaufman and Moss Hart's *You Can't Take It With You*, Arthur Miller's *Death of a Salesman*, Tennessee Williams's *Cat on a Hot Tin Roof*, Edward Albee's *Who's Afraid of Virginia Woolf?*, David Mamet's *American Buffalo*, and Neil Simon's *Broadway Bound*. In each case, Harris discusses the process of composition and revision, the roles of director, producer and set designer, the choice of cast, the rehearsal process, and reviews of the first performance, to give a lucid and non-technical account of the materiality of production and the collaborative work involved in bringing a play to the Broadway stage. Much of this is familiar, of course, not only in general outline but in relation to some of the plays themselves; for example, Brenda Murphy recently provided a critical and very full account of the Williams–Kazan–Mielziner production of *Cat on a Hot Tin Roof* in her *Tennessee Williams and Elia Kazan: A Collaboration in the Theatre* (*YWES* 72.625). But elsewhere the detail adds considerably to one's understanding of the plays, and particularly of *You Can't Take It With You*, which depended for much of its effect on decisions of casting and scenic composition difficult or impossible to recuperate today from the text alone. This concise, detailed and very helpful book concludes with a discussion of Broadway today, which provides a less downbeat perspective than many on the likely consequences of current trends in theatre financing. See also 'The "Oriental" Musicals of Rogers and Hammerstein and the U.S. War in Southeast Asia' (*TJ* 46.385–98), by Bruce A. McConachie, which explores an important aspect of the ideological role of Broadway and argues that these shows display the same narrative structure and range of metaphors (notably of containment) as those used to legitimate American foreign and military policy in the 1950s and 1960s.

In his dense, combative and contentious *Get the Guests: Psychoanalysis, Modern American Drama, and the Audience*, Walter A. Davis argues that contemporary literary theory deploys a range of *a priori* displacements, denials and repressions designed to prevent the critic from confronting the 'Crypt', 'the place or psychic register of . . . primordial anxieties and affects', which literature threatens to expose. Theatre especially 'is dangerous because it publicly stages the truths about society which that society wants to conceal', but to get at these truths Davis has to repudiate the conventions both of a psychoanalytical 'regression in the service of the ego' and of Aristotelian catharsis, which offer spurious forms of release instead of undertaking what he calls 'the proper task of aggression: the act of committing within the murder of the internal saboteur who controls and harms the psyche most when operating in the guise of beloved object'. In five startling accounts of canonical American dramas, Davis delves progressively deeper into the crypt: the group psychology of *The Iceman Cometh*'s bar-room drunks is an act of collective 'death-work', that process whereby deeper, disruptive truths are denied, culminating in the exorcism of Hickey; a calculatedly provocative chapter on *A Streetcar Named Desire* refuses to see in the rape an opportunity for interpretive closure, an exposure of the brutalities of a patriarchal society, instead arguing that the play 'places these problems in a larger structure in which the mutual cruelty between men and women is the prior ideology from which sexual ideologies derive'; *Death of a Salesman* reveals the family as society's breeding ground for psychic disorder and policing, and bourgeois tragedy as a repressive form constantly disrupted by the revelations of expressionism, although for Davis the conclusion of the play shows Miller's ideological refusal to turn the insights of regression back onto the institution of the family. *Long Day's Journey into Night* is obviously amenable to Davis's concerns, and his discussion of it is therefore a little predictable, but the chapter on *Who's Afraid of Virginia Woolf?* is outstandingly successful in uncovering the psychodynamics of onstage and offstage audiences, and in its account of the functions of game-playing and of George and Martha's fantasy child. This remarkable book cuts far deeper than most in exposing the means by which an audience becomes ensnared in plays whose meanings it will attempt to deny; but, quite needlessly, Davis often achieves this depth by the familiar strategy of stereotyping the responses of others, especially feminist critics (usually unnamed), thereby creating the very repressions his analyses are designed to expose; so that at times, particularly when it is accompanied by an excessive and misogynistic rhetoric, his theory threatens to describe the kind of self-referential circle for which he castigates others. Following a discussion of 'the things *any woman worthy of the name* wants', for example, we are told that '[t]he audience this paragraph offended is . . . one of the primary ones that the play [*Streetcar*] snares in a mousetrap that refers its ideological imperatives to their repressed'; elsewhere we discover that '*[p]erhaps the nicest thing one can say* about Linda [Loman] is that she's an anal obsessional' (all italics mine).

More pressingly political are the critical problems posed by ethnic and multicultural drama, which were the subjects of several studies. In *Blueprints for a Black Federal Theatre, 1935–1939*, Rena Fraden unearths much first-hand testimony from those involved in the Federal Theatre Project's (FTP's) 'Negro units', launched as part of Roosevelt's New Deal, to provide an inside account of a debate mainly focused on the question of whether black drama should be separationist or integrationist: whether the theatres should, in the words of W. E. B. Du Bois, produce only work 'of, by, for and near' the black community, a serious, moralistic drama of propaganda; or whether, as Du Bois's theatrical antagonist Alain Locke believed, plays should engage with the aesthetics of modernism, aim at a more universal significance, and examine scientifically the relation between white and black American history. In an exceptionally lucid account both of the complex development of these debates between Du Bois, Locke, Theophilius Lewis, Charles Johnson and other African-American theatre critics in the inter-war years, and of their relation to the development of the FTP, Fraden argues that while many of the participants conceived of the black audience as unified, a 'people', in actuality ' "they" were plural and didn't exist except in the minds of everyone working in the theatre'. This recognition leads her to a postmodernist rejection not only of master narratives but of authenticity in the presentation of black experience. She easily demolishes the 'natural', 'spontaneous' actor, but more provocatively floats the idea of masking in the minstrel stereotype as something potentially subversive, projecting two (or more) meanings to its divided audience, and notes the tendencies towards essentialism and a kind of cultural policing in competing critics. In deconstructing authenticity, Fraden exploits Cornel West's theories of hybridization to suggest that 'cultural, even racial identity [might] be seen as always in the process of borrowing, adopting, adapting, appropriating, changing', so that 'separate theatrical traditions cannot be managed'. This book is itself an unusually successful hybrid of scholarship, theatre history and postmodern theory, raising important questions of methodology and representation.

Samuel A. Hay's *African American Theatre: An Historical and Critical Analysis* begins with a table of no fewer than fifty-two 'schools, periods, classes, subclasses and types', an 'outline' fleshed out in the course of a 120-page account of the drama which fails to notice either that these categories are merely provisional constructions which privilege similarity over difference, or that the typology gives no vital sense of development or disjuncture – which one might have assumed would be the whole point – because Hay is more interested in dragging everything back into the oversimplified binary opposition between Du Bois and Locke on which his whole history depends. Time and again a challenging, resistant play will poke its head up; time and again Hay fearlessly batters it back into a little box. He can write without irony, for instance, that '[s]uch a large number of New Consciousness plays supplanted the older group that the Unified Flow class subdivided into Serious and Musical subclasses'. The categories are self-generating and self-referential, oblivious to the complexities of intertextual dialogue: there is no sense at all even of the ways in which certain mid-century African-American plays engaged the hegemonic contemporary form of white, middle-class domestic realism, which Hay completely overlooks in pulling Lorraine Hansberry's *A Raisin in the Sun* (for example) into his 'Binding Relationships' group, a group which he nevertheless bizarrely contrasts to 'English domestic melodramas and tragedies of the seventeenth and eighteenth centuries'. The typologies further privilege content over form; when it comes to style, Hay is almost embarrassingly ill at ease, so that difficult playwrights like Ntozake Shange or Adrienne Kennedy become marginalized, as do directors: Lloyd Richards, for instance, gets a single mention in the course of a ten-page discussion of August Wilson, despite his active collaboration in the work and a record of major achievement stretching back to the fifties. The second part of the book adopts the rhetoric of the self-help manual in the kind of patronizing appeal to a unified audience that Fraden so carefully critiques: thirty-six pages are devoted to 'inspiring stories' of individuals who have overcome tribulation, as Hay collapses first into sheer banality, noting that while the second of his 'Sayings' 'is no less trite than the first, yet the most fascinating thing about the saying is its truth', and then into evangelizing mode, proposing that African-American theatre companies 'might reorganize themselves so that they were more like church organizations', whose audiences 'would subscribe to services, not only to plays', and whose 'Performance Services' would follow church ritual. What is particularly disappointing about this is that Hay's misleadingly titled book has appeared at a time when African-American playwrights are receiving more sustained critical attention: Lorraine Hansberry, Adrienne Kennedy, August Wilson and Ntozake Shange have all been the subject of at least one recent full-length study, while even some of the more recent dramatists mentioned by Hay, such as Suzan-Lori Parks, have been considered in rigorous and provocative critical articles.

In seeking an alternative to what he sees as the plot-based and essentially melodramatic tradition of O'Neill, Miller, August Wilson and so many others, Marc Robinson, in *The Other American Drama*, has rediscovered the plays of Gertrude Stein, whose work focuses more attention on the individual moment, word, line, sensation. In detailing related emphases in Tennessee Williams, Sam Shepard, Maria Irene Fornes, Adrienne Kennedy and Richard Foreman (and, in the afterword, Wallace Shawn, David Greenspan, Suzan-Lori Parks and Mac Wellman), Robinson 'describes a loose cluster or a set of affinities rather than something so dogmatic as a tradition, and aims to demonstrate a way of looking at drama more than a way of classifying it'. His 'way of looking' is suitably fresh and eclectic, deliberately falling short of anything so definite as a theory, which may be no bad thing; but it does mean that the discussion becomes, at times, assertive, while failing to clarify what is so novel about Williams in particular, who is considered predominantly through the heroines of three of his best-known plays, which hardly represent a major challenge to the mainstream. Shepard is another figure who features prominently in more orthodox histories, although Robinson sees the later career as consonant with Shepard's commitment to change and to a presentation of the self as image, and he provides an excellent discussion of the plays as enactments of creativity. More importantly, the book provides probably the best available accounts of three writers: Fornes, whose best work receives the kind of nuanced attention to detail it requires; Kennedy, whose stage spaces are illuminated by reference to Gaston Bachelard's *Poetics of Space*; and Foreman, whose works Robinson characteristically examines for their performative strategies. This is a versatile and powerfully written study, offering simultaneously an introductory overview and a detailed critical analysis, while catching the moment in arguing for the primacy of Stein.

The title of Stanton B. Garner Jr's *Bodied Spaces: Phenomenology and Performance in Contemporary Drama*, a study of Western drama from the early 1950s to the present, refers variously to relationships of space, to the materiality of the human body, and to the perceptual interaction of actor and audience in stage presentation. Such a project immediately suggests not only a critique of Appia and Craig, which we get, but a theoretical position opposed to the questionable scientific objectivism of semiotics, and to the deconstruction of the subject and the privileging of text over speech in various forms of post-structuralism which, Garner argues, have tended to critique Husserl's essentialism at the expense of engaging with later philosophers of phenomenology, such as Merleau-Ponty, on whom Garner has drawn extensively. It is of course not unusual to see this kind of destabilization of binary oppositions in deconstruction itself, but nevertheless Garner's grounding in phenomenology often breathes new life into familiar debates; in perhaps the most successful chapter, for example, Garner shows that the prop on the realist stage can be defamiliarized by its very materiality, its 'objectness', an argument which allows both for a particularly illuminating discussion of Shepard's later plays and for several adroit passages on Beckett's 'ghostly paradox of a subjectivity whose traces are multiplied at the moment of its dispersal'. The chapter on post-Brechtian political drama highlights the preoccupation with the suffering body on the twentieth-century stage, and although perhaps too neat a distinction is drawn here between the carnivalized body of Brecht's early plays and the body subjected to rational analysis in his later work, few would take issue with the suggestion that Peter Weiss's *Marat/Sade* dramatizes a tension between political transformation and its physical embodiment which Brecht never fully confronted, or that the explicitly un-Brechtian 'aggro effect' in Edward Bond's work highlights the complex relation between the visceral and the rational in the post-Brechtian theatre. However, although Garner argues persuasively in his introduction for the historical specificity of phenomenology, he gives insufficient attention to the historical and material conditions of production in attempting to account for the impact of successive generations of political dramatists; and while the concluding chapter on the theatres of Maria Irene Fornes, Caryl Churchill and Ntozake Shange interestingly foregrounds the potentially transgressive presentation of the female body on stage, it is nevertheless surprisingly thin in considering the implications of the many feminist theories of the male gaze. These, however, are minor objections to a book which bears comparison with the recent work of Bert O. States and W. B. Worthen, and productively engages some of the most stimulating theoretical debates in contemporary drama.

Garner's book usefully complements the growing literature on postmodern performance on the American stage. Some of the work in this field takes its cue from Philip Auslander's 1992 study *Presence and Resistance: Postmodernism and Cultural Politics in Contemporary American Performance*. The first part of the book provides a critical survey of some of the main theories of the postmodern and seeks to escape from the familiar polarity between postmodernisms of 'resistance' and 'reaction' by suggesting, surely correctly, that 'even the critical, resistant postmodernism of the 1980s positioned itself *within* dominant cultural discourses and ran the necessary risk of being co-opted by them'. Throughout the book, Auslander explores the possible erasure of any *a priori* distinction between critical 'distance' and mere 'representation'; there is an 'undecidability' in the act of 'miming', for instance, and a 'continuum' of discourses has replaced fixed and definable categories. If much of this is now familiar in general terms, Auslander's analysis is nevertheless valuable in exploring and historicizing the implications for performance, showing for example how the apparently radical gestures of corporeal presence in the 1960s gave way to commodification and manipulation of that presence, and finally to a 'refusal of presence' by performers who are 'engaging mediatized culture critically from within its own terms', and whose work the book proceeds to explore: the Wooster Group, Spalding Gray, Laurie Anderson, Andy Kaufman and Sandra Bernhard. These are detailed and exciting studies; although developments since publication have rendered the discussion of digital technology and copyright law a little out of date, I still found this chapter fascinating, while Auslander's account of the late stand-up comedian Andy Kaufman has set me off on an as yet futile search for any performances preserved on video.

Many further articles on performance artists and theatre groups were published. John Brockway Schmor's 'Confessional Performance: Postmodern Culture in Recent American Theatre' (*JDTC* 9.i.157–72) argues that the influences of confessional realism and feminist performance art have impacted variously on three kinds of confessional performance: 'monologue-drama' (e.g. the plays of Ntozake Shange, or Henry David Hwang's *M. Butterfly*), in which monologue becomes a central action; 'transformational comedy', especially in the multiple personae of the stand-up artist; and 'autobiographical performance art' (e.g. Karen Finlay, Spalding Gray). Schmor suggests that the confessional artist obscures the boundaries between fantasy and reality, conflating a fascination with celebrity and a consumerist delight in vicarious experience. Celebrity aside, and with an appropriate emphasis on the problematics of speaking in the shadow of the Holocaust, a broadly similar range of performance strategies is identified by Deborah R. Geis in the work of Leeny Sack, Beatrice Roth and Rachel Rosenthal in '"And This Strength Is in Me Still": Memory in Works by Jewish Women Performance Artists' (*YES* 24.172–9). In 'The Emerging Ensemble: The Vieux-Colombier and the Group Theatre' (*ThS* 34.i.60–70), Richard Alan Whitmore explores parallels rather than influences between Jacques Copeau's ensemble and the Group. In 'Uprising of the Beast: An Interview with Peter Schumann' (*Theater* 25.i.32–43), the founder of the Bread and Puppet Theatre discusses with John Bell the centrality of eco-sensitivity in the Theatre's work. Postmodernism clearly also problematizes and historicizes the *avant-garde*, which receives a retrospective in 'Ages of the Avant-garde' (*PAJ* 16.i.9–57), in which twenty-one eminent theatre performers, writers, etc., aged 50 and over present their thoughts on the recent history of the theatre, and in particular on their responses to the ageing process and its impact on their work.

Articles like these, and critical books like Auslander's, create something of a problem for a contributor to *YWES*, since they indicate the extent to which theatre criticism is moving away from the text-based studies and performances normally associated with 'English studies'. Journals like *TDR* and *PAJ* today seem less distinct than previously from *MD*, for example, since performance art has become more mainstream and dramatists working with scripts and texts appear less prominent than ever before, and notions of the 'canon' continue to evaporate. In 'Going, Going, Gone: Theatre and American Culture(s)' (*TDR* 38.i.98–105), Bradley Boney notes that today's theatre no longer aspires to cohesive national institutionality, but has come to represent subcultures which, however, 'ultimately desire to participate in *mass* cultural spin' (the success of gay African-American writer-producer George C. Wolfe is given as an example) and will probably themselves move out of theatre into film and television. Nevertheless, notions of the canon still exert a powerful hold, as is illuminatingly demonstrated by William Sonnega's '*Dutchman* Destabilised: Ideology and Multicultural Discourse' (*TheatreS* 38.5–15). Sonnega takes as his starting point the placement of Amiri Baraka's play within an otherwise all-white drama anthology, in which context *Dutchman* appears to explore questions of marginalization and autonomy in the construction of the literary and dramatic canon.

These and related issues are engaged pointedly in *Negotiating Performance: Gender, Sexuality, and Theatricality in Latin/o America*, edited by Diana Taylor and Juan Villegas. The idea for this all-new collection of essays stemmed originally from the meetings in Irvine, California, of a group of scholars working on US Latino and Latin American drama and performance, although others are represented in the published book. Alongside extensive debates concerning the appropriateness of terms such as 'Latino', and the difficulties of 'negotiation', the collection focuses particularly on the problems of 'theatre' (texts for staging in conventionally enclosed spaces) as a sign and instance of economic exclusivity and hegemony, and the alternative possibilities of many kinds of 'performance' (for which, interestingly, there is no word in Spanish). For the purposes of this volume this word includes various forms of 'culture as performance' and 'public performance', so that we get essays not only on marginalized, though clearly theatrical, forms (Alberto Sandoval discusses the staging of AIDS, Kirsten F. Nigro considers Mexican feminist theatre, and both Donald Frischmann and Cynthia Steele write on Mayan theatre, for instance) but also on such topics as the construction of Puerto Rican 'casitas' or workers' shacks in the Bronx (Juan Flores), 'Carnaval in Santiago de Cuba' (Judith Bettelheim), Argentinian drag culture (Jorge Salessi and Patrick O'Connor), and gendered performance in political resistance (Diana Taylor's essay on Madres de la Plaza de Mayo; on this, see also Stratos E. Constantinidis's interview with Lavonne Mueller in *JDTC* 9.i.145–56, which concludes with Mueller's suggestion that plays should make 'a social statement', of which her own anti-militaristic *The Mothers of Plaza de Mayo* is given as an example).

An uninhibited critique of current dramatic and academic responses to multiculturalism is given by Robert Brustein in *Dumbocracy in America: Studies in the Theatre of Guilt, 1987–1994*, another collection of his articles and reviews, the most significant of which are drawn from the *New Republic*. This is one of Brustein's best books, as his restatement of what might otherwise appear an innocuous position has been given new bite in the context of political correctness. Broadly, Brustein argues (as often before) that mainstream American drama has been impaired by a victim complex: the American theatre of guilt takes the form not of an Ibsenite struggle within the self but of a struggle between the self and an Other (which may be unspecified, as in *Death of a Salesman*) which torments it. Brustein notes that this same structure is repeated in many contemporary plays dealing with multiculturalism, sexual oppression, disability and so forth. Although one could argue that Brustein oversimplifies many of the plays mentioned, or the arguments of some of those on the other side of the fence (it is not every day that Stanley Fish gets dismissed as a 'fellow-traveling academic'), his book is valuable not so much for its dramatic criticism as for its polemical journalism, which traces the connections between the mainstream, the fringe, and a stifling conformism in the arts and the academy.

Brustein is one of the critics interviewed in *Who Calls the Shots on the New York Stages?*, in which Kalina Stefanova-Peteva presents the responses of most of the well-known New York theatre critics to a series of questions she put to them, principally about how they became critics and how they perceive their role. She also asked for the views on theatre criticism of a number of playwrights, producers and others involved in the theatre. It is a badly-presented book, hampered by the curious autobiographical introduction (something of a paean to Frank Rich), the author's awkward written style, and some gruesome misprints; but it does provide a useful overview of a crucial influence on the contemporary American stage.

(b) Individual Authors

Probably the single most interesting development this year was the apparently simultaneous discovery (one cannot even say rediscovery) by several excellent critics of Gertrude Stein as a major dramatist. As noted above, Marc Robinson's *The Other American Drama* takes its cue from Stein, but Robinson is not alone. In 'Saint Gertrude' (*PAJ* 16.xlvi.107–12), Bonnie Marranca compares Stein to Maurice Maeterlinck, and notes that in her work horticulture and landscape are combined with an interest in 'theological space', evident both in the subversion of 'plot', and in her interest in saints, ecstasy and aura. The same ideas inform Marranca's 'Presence of Mind' (*PAJ* 16.xlviii.1–17), an essay which is to appear as the preface to an edition of Stein's *Last Operas and Plays*, and which offers an overview of her dramatic achievement: her formal experimentation, her interest in the role of the spectator, and her influence. Like Marranca, Elinor Fuchs's 'Play as Landscape: Another Version of Pastoral' (*Theater* 25.i.44–51) compares the dramatic aesthetics of Stein and Maeterlinck, creators of plays which combine 'nonlinear spatial structure, imagery from natural landscape, hints of the thematics of pastoral'. In pursuing this 'new configuration', Fuchs then examines four works by more recent dramatists: Robert Wilson's *Alcestis*, Reza Abdoh's *Tight Right White*, Suzan-Lori Parks's *The Death of the Last Black Man in the Whole Entire World*, and Charles Mee's *Orestes*. This is drama 'that encourages and relies on the faculty of landscape surveyal'; 'we are interested in the entire *field*, the whole *terrain*, the total *environment* of the performance, both as performance and as imaginative construct'. One of these works is considered also in 'Unfinished Business: Reconfiguring History in Suzan-Lori Parks's *The Death of the Last Black Man in the Whole Entire World*' (*TJ* 46.447–61), in which Alice Rayner and Harry J. Elam Jr give a theoretically dense, multi-layered, but very readable account of this play's reconfiguration of time and history, regarding its structure as that of a 'vertical spiral rather than a horizontal line', and finding in its patterns of loss, reappearance and repetition a complex articulation of African-American history and speaking subjects, which the latter part of the essay examines by way of Lacanian psychoanalysis.

Critical work on women dramatists of the period from 1900 to 1930 included not only the studies of Gertrude Stein, but also Mary Maddock's 'Alice Gerstenberg's *Overtones*: The Demon in the Doll' (*MD* 37.474–84), which suggests the play resists the stereotypes it presents by its use of doubles to indicate how patriarchy 'breeds demons'; and Jennifer Jones's 'In Defence of the Woman: Sophie Treadwell's *Machinal*' (*MD* 37.485–96), which takes a fresh look at a play which is beginning to attract concerted critical attention, and argues that Treadwell follows the criminal case on which it was based more closely than has previously been supposed, the deviations being the product of an attempt to capture the psychological subtext of the character and events.

As ever, a large number of books and articles was devoted to Eugene O'Neill, many providing documentary rather than critical material. The most important of these is Limelight's reissue of Travis Bogard and Jackson Bryer's 1988 *Selected Letters of Eugene O'Neill*. This indispensable volume brings together 560 of more than three thousand surviving letters. Although rather unrevealing about the plays themselves, they provide a detailed picture of O'Neill's relationships, and do much to support the view recently taken by Joel Pfister in *Staging Depth* (UIowaP: to be reviewed in *YWES* 76) that the common perception of a brooding interiority in both the plays and the private life overlooks O'Neill's artistic manipulation of 'depth'. The O'Neill who emerges from the letters is, as the editors remark, a rounded and often good-humoured figure, contextualizing his private life within the public concerns of law, finance, commerce, theatre, publishing and media attention.

Bogard and Bryer provide some prefatory comments to a newly discovered letter of 1949 from O'Neill to Arthur Miller (*EONR* 17.121–3), which is followed in the same issue by Dan Isaac's 'Founding Father: O'Neill's Correspondence with Arthur Miller and Tennessee Williams' (124–33). This contains the Miller letter to which O'Neill's is a response, and an account of some lost correspondence between O'Neill and Williams. This double issue of *EONR* otherwise contains a lesser proportion of archival documents than is commonly the case with the journal, and a correspondingly greater proportion of critical discussions. In 'McTeague's Dream and *The Emperor Jones*: O'Neill's Move from Naturalism to Modernism' (21–9), Brenda Murphy suggests the pattern of regression and flight in Frank Norris's novel is a source for O'Neill's play, and notes the modernist direction in the latter's focus on subjective experience instead of scientific explanation; while in 'O'Neill's Beginnings and the Birth of Modernism in American Drama' (11–20), Frank R. Cunningham argues for a similar direction at the very outset of the playwright's career. It is hardly surprising, then, that in 'Modern and Postmodern Wastelands: *Long Day's Journey into Night* and Shepard's *Buried Child*' (106–19) Laurin R. Porter should conclude that the former is modernist and the latter postmodernist. This is yet another example of what seems to be something of a sub-genre in studies of American drama: the untheorized and arbitrary comparison. James R. Keller, for example, managed it twice with the same play: he compares *The Hairy Ape* to *Paradise Lost* in 'Rage Against Order: O'Neill's Yank and Milton's Satan' (*EONR* 17.45–52), initially noting only 'similarities', but concluding by speaking of 'O'Neill's decision to borrow from *Paradise Lost*'; and the same unsubstantiated shift occurs in Keller's 'Eugene O'Neill's Stokehole and Spenser's Cave of Mammon' (*ELN* 31.66–73), which starts by suggesting a 'potential influence' for the opening scenes of *The Hairy Ape* in the *Fairie Queene*, II.vii, and concludes that this is an 'allusion', a 'borrowing from Spenser'. There are clearly problems in the suggestion that the same image is simply 'borrowed' from two different sources; it would have been more useful had Keller written a single article differentiating as necessary between intertextuality, allusion and source (for starters), because as they stand these piecemeal comparisons seem both dubious and rather pointless.

The remaining articles in *EONR* 17 cover a variety of topics. D. G. Kehl provides a close reading in 'The "Big Subject" in *The Hairy Ape*: A New Look at Scene Five' (39–43). In 'O'Neill and the Old Ham' (77–81), Stephen A. Black contradicts the commonly held view that O'Neill was left emotionally wrecked by his father's death; in fact, 'Eugene followed exactly the course of normal mourning, and he clearly was headed towards separating his own self-image from his image of his father – which is the principal task of mourning.' Approaching a related topic from a very different angle, James R. Dawes, in his ambitious and wide-ranging 'Drama and Ethics, Grief and Privacy: The Case of Eugene O'Neill' (83–92), argues for a correspondence between the corporeal and the textual body, perceiving in plays such as *Long Day's Journey* and in O'Neill himself a loss of the self, a dying, in the act of expression. Brad Field's 'Corrections in O'Neill' (93–105) enumerates the typical variations on this characteristic aspect of the playwright's dialogue. James Fisher details the personal and professional relationship between two major writers in 'Tender Men: The Acquaintanceship of Eugene O'Neill and Sherwood Anderson' (135–47). Stephen A. Black considers the realism and tragedy of *The Iceman Cometh* before writing more extensively 'On Jason Robards as O'Neill's Nietzschean Iceman' (149–56) in a 1960 production directed by Sidney Lumet; Dru Dougherty and María Francisca Vilches de Frutos detail the textual and performative reception of 'Eugene O'Neill in Madrid, 1918–1936' (157–64); and George Monteiro contributes a short piece on 'Jorge de Sena, Eugene O'Neill's [Portuguese] Critic and Translator' (165–6).

William M. Peterson's 'A Portrait of O'Neill's Electra' (66–75) reproduces a colour portrait of O'Neill's wife-to-be Carlotta, which Peterson argues may have influenced the playwright in creating the figures of Christine and Lavinia Mannon. Vance Philip Hedderel compares the mother–daughter relationship in the same play to that in Lillian Hellman's work, in 'Sibling Rivalry in *Mourning Becomes Electra* and *The Little Foxes*' (60–5), which also notices the attempt to invest a melodramatic structure with Freudian depth psychology. A related conjunction of forms is the subject of a book-length study, Kurt Eisen's *The Inner Strength of Opposites: O'Neill's Novelistic Drama and the Melodramatic Imagination*. The central premise of Eisen's book is clear and uncontentious: O'Neill was heavily indebted to nineteenth-century melodramatic forms, but challenged their simplistic dualities by adopting novelistic techniques, some of which are common to both melodrama and the novel. In O'Neill's work of the 1920s and 1930s, for example, there is much literal or metaphorical use of masks, interior monologues, doubling and so forth; and if in the weaker plays this conjunction is mannered and awkward, Eisen's separate chapters on *Long Day's Journey into Night* and *The Iceman Cometh* argue for a more successful treatment of the melodramatic roles on which *Iceman*'s characters are nevertheless dependent for any sense of integrity. Eisen's approach also allows for a fruitful examination of the 'marriage' of forms in relation to O'Neill's presentation of the family, and provides a metaphor by which other characteristic oppositions such as that between the spiritual and the material may be understood. The book contains many lengthy discussions on the history and theory of character, melodrama and Bakhtinian novelization; although these discussions could have been abbreviated, they are nevertheless interesting and valuable condensations of essential theoretical debates, and Eisen does convincingly historicize form to show how O' Neill's dramatic experiments relate to his reading of history (*Hughie*, for example, is in some ways a meditation on the possibilities of dialogue in an era arguably dominated by modernistic solipsism and totalitarian monomania). If the book contains few startling re-readings, this is because Eisen's understanding of O'Neill is, for the most part, so obviously sound; and within this framework he covers the full range of the plays and effectively contextualizes them within the history and theory of the drama and the novel.

O'Neill's plays have been the subject of many properly edited and systematically organized critical anthologies; John H. Houchin's *The Critical Response to Eugene O'Neill* is not one of them. The book brings together a mish-mash of contemporary reviews and more recent critical essays, but aside from chronology there appears to be no organizing principle at all: Houchin's thin and cliché-ridden introduction provides no clue and mentions only a few of the pieces he has included, and then only in passing. There is certainly a lot of good stuff here, and it is always useful to have some material like this to hand, but one has to wonder why so many of the critical essays are taken from the most obvious sources, such as *MD*. In its random pointlessness the book brings to mind the dubious pleasures of the budget-priced pop hits anthology, except that those things are more fun, and do not cost £53.95.

O'Neill's *Bound East for Cardiff* is one of twenty-one pieces collected by Barbara Ozieblo in *The Provincetown Players: A Choice of the Shorter Works*. Ozieblo provides a solid account of the genesis of the Players and of the thematic concerns of the plays, although the primary interest of the collection of course lies in the texts themselves. These include some significant works (most notably Susan Glaspell and George Cram Cook's *Suppressed Desires* and Edna St Vincent Millay's oft-anthologized *Aria Da Capo*), alongside pieces by major figures such as John Reed, Djuna Barnes, and Edna Ferber. The literary reputations of others represented here have not lasted or were never made, but at least their sex lives can be rediscovered in the pages of Leona Rust Egan's *Provincetown as a Stage: Provincetown, the Provincetown Players, and the Discovery of Eugene O'Neill*, which tells a rather different story from the one implied in the title. This is not an academic account of the early O'Neill, or of the dramatic and theatrical significance of the Provincetown Players, but a racy account of the multifarious affairs of a bohemian and sexually liberated community, interspersed with Baedeker-like digressions on local history and topography. Egan is an obsessive accumulator of gossipy detail, and although this is a minor study when placed alongside the voluminous biographical studies of O'Neill, for the most part it is, as they say, a good read. A later incident in O'Neill's career is well documented in Madeline Smith and Richard Eaton's *Eugene O'Neill in Court: Documents in the Case of Georges Lewys v. Eugene O'Neill, et al.* This 1931 case concerned an allegation that in *Strange Interlude* O'Neill had plagiarized an earlier, privately printed work by an unknown writer. The editing creates quite a compelling narrative, of which the most interesting section is a 138-page parallel text, with the allegedly plagiarized passages placed between Lewys's 'original' on one side, and O'Neill's withering comments on the other. The legal arguments over textual details are equally fascinating at times. Not surprisingly, O'Neill was acquitted.

Of the other articles published on O'Neill the only silly one is 'The Bitch Archetype' (*JDTC* 9.i.119–33), in which Ibry Theriot, in his remarkably simplistic and uncritical 'analysis using Jungian psychological theory as applied to literature', demonstrates to his own satisfaction that Ibsen's Hedda Gabler, O'Neill's Abbie, and Tennessee Williams's Maggie are . . . well . . . *bitches*. *LFQ* printed two essays on filmed versions of *Long Day's Journey*. Following a justification of the cutting of around a quarter of the text in 'Sidney Lumet's *Long Day's Journey into Night*'

(*LFQ* 22.ii.78–92), deletions which diminish the work only in so far as they sometimes lessen our understanding of Mary, Donald P. Costello argues for the cinematic strength of Lumet's version by analysing the shot selection in a range of scenes focusing on the Tyrones individually and in their relationships with one another. In the same issue, Edward T. Jones's 'The Tyrones as TV Family?' (93–7) compares Michael Blakemore's videotaped version of Peter Wood's National Theatre production of 1971, and Jonathan Miller's record of his own production of 1986.

Also published in *LFQ* (22.ii.72–7) is Linda Costanzo Cahir's 'The Artful Rerouting of *A Streetcar Named Desire*', which argues that the difficulties Elia Kazan faced in filming Tennessee Williams's play were finally turned to advantage: the personality and stylistic clashes between the method actors and Vivien Leigh's stylized/classical acting worked in terms of character, while the changes demanded by the Breen office led Kazan to develop poetic, ambivalent scenes which in some ways improved on Williams's work, especially the 'heavy-handed and obvious' ending. Philip C. Kolin published a number of articles on this play: in 'On a Trolley to the Cinema: Ingmar Bergman and the First Swedish Production of *A StreetcarNamed Desire*' (*SCR* 27.277–86), he provides a detailed reconstruction of the production and suggests that Bergman was attracted by 'the play's psychological themes, its experimental staging, and the status and personality of its heroine artist-victim'; while in '"Cruelty . . . and Sweaty Intimacy": The Reception of the Spanish Premiere of *A Streetcar Named Desire*' (*ThS* 35.ii.45–56), the same critic, besides unearthing a wealth of reviews, suggests that the delayed premiere (the play was not performed in Spain until 1961) can be accounted for by cultural and political factors as well as by confusion over whether Williams's agents had withheld permission. Kolin's 'Bonaparte Kowalski: Or What Stanley and Napoleon Have in Common (and What They Don't) in *A Streetcar Named Desire*' (*NConL* 24.iv.6–8) interestingly notes that Stanley's invocation of the Napoleonic Code encourages the comparison, which Kolin traces in Stanley's physical stature, despotic behaviour, military record, and Italian campaign (winning at Salerno).

Nicholas Pagan's *Rethinking Literary Biography: A Postmodern Approach to Tennessee Williams* is uneven but intermittently valuable. Pagan is right to emphasize that Barthes and Derrida did not deny but reorientate the relation between author, text and the biographical subject, but the entry-level discussions of biography and theory at the start of the book could have been greatly condensed and more fluently presented; and he seems barely aware of the obvious, theatre-specific destabilization of the authorial subject in the act of collaboration, a phenomenon explored in depth in some recent studies of Williams. On the other hand, when Pagan comes to focus more particularly on Williams's texts he provides two fascinatingly detailed sections, first on the multifarious intertextual associations of the name 'Blanche DuBois', and second on the tracing of Williams's 'stylistic signature' in the opposition between words containing the 'phonic signifiers' *st* and *bl*. Although other critics have explored each of these associative webs, Pagan here reintroduces the biographical subject in ways which usefully complement his theoretical concerns. Nevertheless, the overriding impression is of a certain sketchiness not wholly explicable in terms of the problematics of postmodern biography; it is a shame, for example, that although Pagan mentions Foucault's work on sexuality he does not mention that philosopher's directly relevant work on author and subject. Indeed, James Miller's brilliant *The Passion of Michel Foucault* (S&S, 1993) is much more rigorous in examining the possibilities of recuperating a biographical subject in the teeth of popular misconceptions of post-structuralism, and although this may be an unfair standard of comparison, one of the difficulties with Pagan's book is that it does not identify any similar correlation between the theoretical concerns and the choice of subject, so that aside from the two excellent sections highlighted above one comes away without any greatly enriched understanding of author, texts or theory.

Kaarina Kailo's 'Blanche DuBois and Salome as New Women: Old Lunatics in Modern Drama' (*TD* 15.119–36) is less interesting for its opening statement of purpose, 'to compare the two classic lunatic women of modern drama . . . who occupy the opposite ends on the spectrum of "female" madness', or for the familiar and questionable concluding remark that Williams and Wilde were 'forced to express their feminine self through their female characters', than for its use of the Demeter and Kore myth to reveal complex allusive and poetic structures in the plays while, more interestingly still, positing a Jungian mythic psychoanalysis as arguably more feminist than the Freudian Oedipal myth. Gender issues of a very different kind are engaged in Susan Koprince's 'Tennessee Williams's Unseen Characters' (*SoQ* 33.i.87–95), which shows how Williams, through dialogue, sensory images and the appearance of surrogates, evokes the personalities of five figures who never appear onstage, and more interestingly notes that these figures share certain similarities: all are male, young, homosexuals or philanderers, and generally the victims of violent death, and inspire an almost idolatrous devotion in those who suffer their loss.

Little was published on Thornton Wilder this year aside from Sidney Feshbach's 'Deeply Indebted: On Thornton Wilder's Interest in James Joyce' (*JJQ* 31.iv.495–518), which provides a chronological inventory of Wilder's works and their references to Joyce, including many notes on *Finnegans Wake* unearthed in Wilder's archives. Feshbach speculates that reading *Finnegans Wake* and writing *The Skin of Our Teeth* were a kind of therapeutic response to the war, and defends Wilder from the charge that he stole from Joyce. A play by a slightly later and much lesser-known figure is the subject of 'Robert Ardrey and *Thunder Rock*' (*THStud* 14.41–8), in which Ronald A. Willis focuses on the contemporary reception of various productions of this 1939 play in New York, London and Berlin, and shows how Ardrey revised the ending several times both during and after the war to take account of audience reception, particularly in relation to differing political sensibilities.

James J. Martine's *The Crucible: Politics, Property, and Pretense* is an introductory account which briefly places Arthur Miller's play in a literary and historical context before proceeding to such traditional subjects as structure, themes, characters, etc. The book is very competently presented, and would be useful for schools, but even novices at undergraduate level are likely to find it insufficiently challenging. More stimulating, despite the occasionally predictable argument and hackneyed terminology, is Wendy Schissel's 'Re(dis)covering the Witches in Arthur Miller's *The Crucible*: A Feminist Reading' (*MD* 37.461–73), which uncompromisingly accuses the 'dishonest' playwright of a misogynistic prejudice against Abigail and Elizabeth, who should more properly be seen as victims.

The Crucible is one of the texts considered in *Censored Books: Critical Viewpoints*, a tragi-comic collection of mostly new essays edited by Nicholas J. Karolides, Lee Burress and John M. Kean. The scope is a little more restricted than the title suggests: following six 'perspectives', including Arthur Miller's 'On

Censorship', the bulk of the study is devoted to fifty-seven defences of fifty-three censored books, which here means those which have most frequently been challenged in America, from one quarter or another, as being unacceptable for the classroom. Miller gets into the chart twice, in Joan DelFattore's 'Fueling the Fire of Hell: A Reply to Censors of *The Crucible*', and in Harry Harder's '*Death of a Salesman*: An American Classic'. The nature of the book almost inevitably means that the discussions of the texts themselves are less interesting than the factual information: it is alarming to discover that, for example, *The Crucible* was one of sixty-four books banned in 1987 in Bay County, Florida, after the superintendent of schools 'announced that he considered his election a sign from God that he was to return conservative Christian values to the Bay County schools', and salutary to be reminded that Miller was asked to approve a short film, to be screened before cinema audiences could watch *Death of a Salesman*, which explained that 'nowadays selling [is] a fine profession with limitless spiritual compensations as well as financial ones'. The book is bursting with gems like this, often so outrageous that in a saner climate the well-intentioned but often dull 'defences' of the texts would have been superfluous. But that, unfortunately, is the point.

Helge Normann Nilsen's 'From *Honors at Dawn* to *Death of a Salesman*: Marxism and the Early Plays of Arthur Miller' (*ES* 75.ii.146–56) considers the influence of Marxist thought on three unpublished works (*Honors at Dawn*, *The Great Disobedience* and *They Too Arise*), arguing that their anti-capitalistic thrust persists in the impact of economic pressures on the individual's sanity in *The Man Who Had All the Luck*, *All My Sons* and *Salesman*. In '*Death of a Salesman* and American Leadership: Life Imitates Art' (*JAmC* 17.ii.49–56), political scientist John S. Schockley describes former General Electric salesman Ronald Reagan as 'the successful Willy Loman', but the comparison, while intermittently funny, adds little to an understanding of either figure.

Rakesh Solomon notes that Edward Albee can be a problematic interviewee, but nevertheless extracts a great deal from the playwright in 'Text, Subtext, and Performance: Edward Albee on Directing *Who's Afraid of Virginia Woolf?*' (*ThS* 34.ii.94–110). Albee considers the specifics of staging at some length, commenting on different productions and the rationale behind textual revisions. Related matters of text and performance are considered in Carlos Campo's exploration of 'The Role of [Henry Blanke's film] *Beyond the Forest* in Albee's *Who's Afraid of Virginia Woolf?*' (*LFQ* 22.iii.170–73).

TCG have reissued *Joseph Chaikin and Sam Shepard: Letters and Texts, 1972–1984*, edited by Barry Daniels. This is an invaluable collection of materials relating to a series of performed and unperformed collaborations between the two artists, including Shepard's contributions to a 1972 project called *Nightwalk* and another short piece from 1976–7; the better-known collaborations, *Tongues* and *Savage/Love*; and pieces from a 1984 workshop in Cambridge, Mass., on the theme of the 'captured angel', ideas which after Chaikin's stroke found their way into *The War in Heaven*. Besides the texts themselves, Daniels has provided detailed prefatory remarks for each section, and included working notes and variants for *Tongues, Savage/Love* and the Cambridge pieces, some critical reviews and essays, and a large number of letters between Shepard and Chaikin. The collection is incomplete (in particular, we do not have Chaikin's side of the correspondence between 1972 and 1976), and for this reason and others it would have been helpful to have more detailed editorial notes, especially as Shepard will often refer to books and to works in progress which are not identified. But perhaps clarification was impossible, and objections to such an important collection seem churlish. One of the collaborations is the subject of Johan Callens's 'Reciprocity and the Transformational Generation of Shepard's and Chaikin's *Savage/Love*' (*REALB* 9.242–69), which traces in the piece the transformational techniques of the Open Theatre and the influence of Beckett, via an extensive comparison with Barthes. Callens finds in the work a now-familiar tension between the holistic search for authenticity and a postmodernist destabilization of the self, a principle of 'recurrence and mutuality, without identity'.

Following a survey of how some of the mainstream American dramatists have used stage-time, Enoch Brater, in 'American Clocks: Sam Shepard's Time Plays' (*MD* 37.603–12), suggests that what distinguishes Shepard in this respect is an avoidance 'of the dramatic trap of his predecessors, where the past is fetishized and essentialized as some sort of historical/psychological explanation for what takes place in the theatrical "now"'. In 'Authorization and Subversion of Myth in Shepard's *Buried Child*' (*MD* 37.509–20), Tucker Orbison argues that the play validates the vegetation myth of the Corn King in the renewal of the natural world, but that the Holy Grail legend is treated ironically, as there is no comparable renewal in the human world, which cannot contain its potential for violence. Suzy Clarkson Holstein's '"All Growed Up" in the *True West*, or Huck and Tom Meet Sam Shepard' (*WAL* 29.i.41–50) is a rather whimsical and overextended comparison of Twain's characters to Lee and Austin in Shepard's play, although the remarks about the theme of escape and its relation to fictions and story-telling are valid.

In 'Today I am a Fountain Pen: An Interview with Richard Foreman' (*Theater* 25.i.82–6), the playwright discusses with Elinor Fuchs his lack of interest in a character-based theatre, relating his attempts at a constant deferral of meaning on the stage to a Derridean critique of the metaphysics of presence. Foreman instances his tendency to 'add layers' to the work on stage (for example in the use of commentary and texts), and his interest in Jewish mysticism, letters and numbers, which forestall conclusive interpretations. The same issue contains the text of a new Foreman play, *My Head was a Sledgehammer* (87–101), prefaced by the playwright's introductory remarks, in which he invites open directorial interpretations, and followed by Paul McKinley's review of the first production (102–4).

Anne M. Dean's *Discovery and Invention: The Urban Plays of Lanford Wilson* offers a similar approach to that provided in the same author's 1990 study of David Mamet: a biographical chapter is followed by a general survey of themes, language, development and reception in the career as a whole, while the core chapters are devoted to extensive discussions of selected plays, in this case three 'urban' plays: *Balm in Gilead*, *The Hotel Baltimore* and *Burn This*. Dean explains that these works demonstrate the full range of Wilson's abilities; but the book is a short one, and a more rounded picture of Wilson might have emerged had room been found for chapters on *The Rimers of Eldritch* and *Talley's Folly* at least, although the second chapter does contextualize these plays within Wilson's general thematic and stylistic concerns. (Coincidentally, the plays chosen complement very well those studied in detail in Philip Middleton Williams's *A Comfortable House: Lanford Wilson, Marshall W. Mason and the Circle Repertory Theatre* [McFarland, 1993], which will be reviewed in *YWES* 76, having come to my attention too late for inclusion this year.) Dean's extensive use of reviews and interviews with many of those involved in staging the plays, including Wilson himself, has many obvious advantages, but also the disadvantage of engaging the works largely on the dramatist's own terms. To take a characteristic example: we are told that 'Wilson portrays people *as they are*; refusing to glamourize or falsify them in any way, he depicts them as individuals', but this describes an effect of the work, and a critical analysis (as opposed to review) could devote more space to accounting for how that effect is achieved in terms not just of style but of the problematics of form, ideology and representation. But of course this is to ask for a different kind of book; in theatre studies in particular, Dean's approach is not unusual, and it has the advantage of documenting an impressively wide range of otherwise ephemeral or unobtainable material. Dean's style is certainly fluent and engaging, and one can expect this well-researched book to prove as fruitful a source for subsequent accounts of its subject as her study of Mamet has been.

Mamet's own collected essays are reprinted in *A Whore's Profession: Notes and Essays*. Most of the important pieces on dramatic theory and practice are to be found in *Writing in Restaurants* and *Some Freaks*, while *The Cabin*, although it contains some material on writing, is more consistently autobiographical. Also included is the excellent *On Directing Film*, based on a series of lectures and seminars at Columbia, which contains some wonderful demolitions of the pretensions of film-makers. There is now a newsletter, the *David Mamet Review*, devoted to the playwright, which publishes reviews and information. Critical articles on Mamet were rather thin on the ground this year: David Worster's 'How to Do Things with Salesmen: David Mamet's Speech-Act Play' (*MD* 37.375–90) convincingly demonstrates the appropriateness of J. L. Austin's theories of language to *Glengarry Glen Ross*, a play saturated with references to talking and speaking, although Worster does not consider the implications of the many deconstructive critiques of Austin; and Leslie Kane's '"In Blood, in Blood Thou Shalt Remember": David Mamet's *Marranos*' (*YES* 24.157–71) gives the first critical account of this unpublished play, the playwright's earliest work on the subject of Jewishness.

Ntozake Shange is now regularly considered in studies of American drama (see the books by Garner and Hay in the section 4(a) above). But the only journal essay I unearthed this year was Philip U. Effiong's 'The Subliminal to the Real: Musical Regeneration in Ntozake Shange's *boogie woogie landscapes*' (*TheatreS* 39.33–43), which restates largely familiar accounts of the non-verbal elements of her drama before noting that the more prominent role of men and dialogue in *landscapes* makes it less of a 'choreopoem' than some of the other works.

Two book-length studies of August Wilson were published or received too late for review this year: these were *May All Your Fences Have Gates: Essays on the Drama of August Wilson*, edited by Alan Nadel (UIowaP, 1993) and *August Wilson: A Casebook*, edited by Marilyn Elkins (Garland, 1994). Both will be reviewed in *YWES* 76. Recent critical articles on Wilson include Mary L. Bogumil's '"Tomorrow Never Comes": Songs of Cultural Identity in August Wilson's *Joe Turner's Come and Gone*' (*TJ* 46.463–76), which gives a critical-historical analysis of the complex displacements enacted in the songs and dances of Wilson's play; and Mark William Rocha's 'Black Madness in August Wilson's "Down the Line" Cycle' (*TD* 15.191–201), which similarly engages the centrality of blues music in considering a black community's response to the notion of 'madness' in the five plays from *Ma Rainey's Black Bottom* to *Two Trains Running*. Rocha argues that the plays demonstrate the 'African principle of inclusion that dictates acceptance of the madman'.

Daniel Larner has long championed the work of Barrie Stavis, who has been writing since the 1930s but whose plays have been more successful in Europe than in America or Britain. 'Anywhere but Home: The Life and Work of Barrie Stavis' (*AmDram* 4.i.39–61) is a detailed, descriptive and critical survey, while Larner's interview with the playwright (*AmDram* 4.i.62–91) explores his ideas and fears for the future. Daniel Kiefer's wide-ranging essay on Tony Kushner's '*Angels in America* and the Failure of Revelation' (*AmDram* 4.i.21–38) should similarly be seen as a critical introduction to this playwright, whose work is certain to receive more extensive attention.

Articles appeared on several other recently produced playwrights and performers. A currently heated debate is engaged in William H. Sun and Faye C. Fei's 'Masks or Faces Re-Visited: A Study of Four Theatrical Works Concerning Cultural Identity' (*TDR* 38.iv.120–32). The authors are interested in works which attempt to transcend the dichotomy between a 'color-strict rhetoric' and a 'color-blind vision', which they perceive in Henry David Hwang's public pronouncements and in his *Face Value*. Having found problems in Sherwood Xuehua Hu's 'transcultural' *The Legend of Prince Lanling* and in the 'cultural amnesia' of Han Ong's *The L. A. Plays*, Sun and Fei find in the performances of Anna Deavere Smith (the example is *Fires in the Mirror*) a means of transcending the divide between single-ethnic and racially mixed plays. A detailed and fascinating account of Smith's method, which involves the re-presentation by Smith, as performer, of tape-recorded interviews with observers of actual events such as the Los Angeles riots, is given in Charles R. Lyons and James C. Lyons's 'Anna Deavere Smith: Perspectives on Her Performance within the Context of Critical Theory' (*JDTC* 9.i.44–61). The essay sometimes gets bogged down in non-issues (are the works Brechtian, feminist, postmodernist, etc.), but is interesting for its speculations on how Smith challenges received notions of performance. Again, a reading of Auslander's book (above) is helpful here. Hwang gets a more sympathetic hearing in Kathryn Remen's 'The Theatre of Punishment: David Henry Hwang's *M. Butterfly* and Michel Foucault's *Discipline and Punish*' (*MD* 37.391–400), although the general remarks concerning the relation between theatre and the Foucaultian prison, and the suggestion that the role of the audience in Hwang's play is especially amenable to this theorization, both seem a little forced.

Books Reviewed

Adler, Thomas P. *American Drama 1940–1960: A Critical History*. Twayne's Critical History of American Drama. Twayne. pp. 251. £20.95. ISBN 0 8057 8957 X.

Ahearn, Barry. *William Carlos Williams and Alterity: The Early Poetry*. Cambridge Studies in American Literature and Culture 75. CUP. pp. 183. £37.50, $59.95. ISBN 0 5214 5200 7.

Ammons, A. R. *Tape for the Turn of the Year: A Poem*. Norton (1993). pp. 205. £8.95, $11. ISBN 0 3933 1204 6.

—— *Garbage: A Poem*. Norton (1993). pp. 121. £7.50, $.9. ISBN 0 3933 1203 8.

Auslander, Philip. *Presence and Resistance: Postmodernism and Cultural Politics in Contemporary American Performance*. UMichP (1992). pp. 206. hb $39.50, pb $15.95. ISBN 0 4721 0299 0, 0 4720 8278 7.

Aviram, Amittai F. *Telling Rhythm: Body and Meaning in Poetry*. UMichP. pp. 324. £30, $39.95. ISBN 0 4721 0513 2.

Bacon, Jon Lance. *Flannery O'Connor and Cold War Culture*. CUP. pp. 174. £30. ISBN 0 5214 4529 9.
Bagby, George F. *Frost and the Book of Nature*. UTennP (1993). pp. 217. $28.95. ISBN 0 8704 9805 3.
Baldwin, Anna, and Sarah Hutton, eds. *Platonism and the English Imagination*. CUP. pp. 357. £40, $59.95. ISBN 0 5214 0308 1.
Barabtarlo, Gennady. *Aerial View: Essays on Nabokov's Art and Metaphysics*. Lang. pp. 301. FF346. ISBN 0 8204 1892 7.
Barnett, Louise K. *Authority and Speech: Language, Society, and Self in the American Novel*. UGeoP (1993). pp. 293. $45. ISBN 0 8203 1520 6.
Berthoff, Robert J., ed. *Robert Duncan: Selected Poems*. Carcanet (1993). pp. 147. £9.95. ISBN 1 8575 4037 9.
Bogard, Travis, and Jackson R. Bryer, eds. *Selected Letters of Eugene O'Neill*. Limelight. pp. 602. £16.99. ISBN 0 8791 0181 4.
Bordman, Gerald. *American Theatre: A Chronicle of Comedy and Drama, 1869-1914*. OUP. pp. 793. £70. ISBN 0 1950 3764 2.
Boughn, Michael. *H.D.: A Bibliography 1905–1990*. UPVirginia (1993). pp. 229. £35.50. ISBN 0 8139 1412 4.
Bremen, Brian A. *William Carlos Williams and the Diagnostics of Culture*. OUP. pp. 231. $39.95. ISBN 01950 7226 X.
Brooker, Jewel Spears. *Mastery and Escape: T. S. Eliot and the Dialectic of Modernism*. UMassP. pp. 274. £33.25. ISBN 0 8702 3905 8.
Brustein, Robert. *Dumbocracy in America: Studies in the Theatre of Guilt, 1987–1994*. Dee. pp. 276. $12.95. ISBN 1 5666 3098 3.
Bryan, Sharon, ed. *Where We Stand: Women Poets On Literary Tradition*. Norton (1993). pp. 200. £8.95. ISBN 0 3933 1209 7.
Byrd, Don. *The Poetics of Common Knowledge*. SUNYP (1993). pp. 404. $49.50. ISBN 0 7914 1685 2.
Cappetti, Carla. *Writing Chicago: Modernism, Ethnography, and the Novel*. Social Foundations of Aesthetic Form Series. ColUP (1993). pp. 320. hb £40, pb £14.95. ISBN 0 2310 8128 6, 0 2310 8129 4.
Cohen, Sarah Blacher. *Cynthia Ozick's Comic Art*. IndUP. pp. 193. $25. ISBN 0 2533 1398 8.
Colatrella, Carol, and Joseph Alkana, eds. *Cohesion and Dissent in America*. SUNYP. pp. 252. $21.95. ISBN 0 7914 1718 2.
Collier, Michael, ed. *The Wesleyan Tradition: Four Decades of American Poetry*. UPNE (1993). pp. 276. $29.95. ISBN 0 8195 2210 4.
Comnes, Gregory. *The Ethics of Indeterminacy in the Novels of William Gaddis*. UPFlor. pp. 188. £22.50. ISBN 0 8130 1251 1.
Cook, Albert. *Canons and Wisdoms*. UPennP (1993). pp. 213. $31.50. ISBN 0 8122 3204 6.
Creeley, Robert, ed. *Selected Poems of Charles Olson*. UCalP (1993). pp. 225. $25. ISBN 0 5200 7528 5.
Crunden, Robert M. *American Salons: Encounters with European Modernism 1885–1917*. OUP (1993). pp. 493. £30. ISBN 0 1950 6569 7.
Cushman, Stephen. *Fictions of Form in American Poetry*. PrincetonUP (1993). pp. 217. $24.95. ISBN 0 6910 6963 8.
Damon, Maria. *The Dark End of the Street: Margins in American Vanguard Poetry*. UMinnP (1993). pp. 305. $17.95. ISBN 0 8166 1987 5.
Daniels, Barry, ed. *Joseph Chaikin and Sam Shepard: Letters and Texts, 1972–1984*.

TCG. pp. 255. $10.95. ISBN 1 5593 6095 X.

Davis, Walter A. *Get the Guests: Psychoanalysis, Modern American Drama, and the Audience*. Wisconsin Project on American Writers. UWiscP. pp. 286. hb £39.95, pb £17.95. ISBN 0 2991 4150 0, 0 2991 4154 3.

Dean, Anne M. *Discovery and Invention: The Urban Plays of Lanford Wilson*. AUP. pp. 139. £23. ISBN 0 8386 3548 2.

Diepeveen, Leonard. *Changing Voices: The Modern Quoting Poem*. UMichP (1993). pp. 196. $37.50. ISBN 0 4721 0369 5.

Doreski, C. K. *Elizabeth Bishop: The Restraints of Language*. OUP (1993). pp. 180. £22.50, $35. ISBN 0 1950 7966 3.

Egan, Leona Rust. *Provincetown as a Stage: Provincetown, the Provincetown Players, and the Discovery of Eugene O'Neill*. Parnassus. pp. 296. $21.95. ISBN 0 9401 6157 9.

Eisen, Kurt. *The Inner Strength of Opposites: O'Neill's Novelistic Drama and the Melodramatic Imagination*. UGeoP. pp. 256. £35.95, $40. ISBN 0 8203 1595 8.

Engle, Ron, and Tice L. Miller, eds. *The American Stage: Social and Economic Issues from the Colonial Period to the Present*. CUP (1993). pp. 320. £45, $54.95. ISBN 0 5214 1238 2.

Engler, Bernd, and Kurt Müller, eds. *Historiographic Metafiction in Modern American and Canadian Literature*. Schöningh. pp. 511. n.p. ISBN 3 5067 0823 6.

Erkkila, Betsy. *The Wicked Sisters: Women Poets, Literary History, and Discord*. OUP (1993). pp. 279. hb $35, pb $15.95. ISBN 0 1950 7212 X, 0 1950 7211 1.

Filreis, Alan. *Modernism from Right to Left: Wallace Stevens, the Thirties and Literary Radicalism*. CUP. pp. 376. £37.50. ISBN 0 5214 5384 4.

Foley, Barbara. *Radical Representations: Politics and Form in U.S. Proletarian Fiction 1929–1941*. Post-Contemporary Intervention Series. DukeUP (1993). pp. 484. hb £52.50, $55, pb £17.95, $19.95. ISBN 0 8223 1361 8, 0 82231394 4.

Fountain, Gary, and Peter Brazeau. *Remembering Elizabeth Bishop: An Oral Biography*. UMassP. pp. 408. £33.25. ISBN 0 8702 3936 8.

Fraden, Rena. *Blueprints for a Black Federal Theatre, 1935–1939*. Cambridge Studies in American Literature and Culture 80. CUP. pp. 243. £37.50. ISBN 0 5214 4359 8.

Francis, Lesley Lee. *The Frost Family's Adventure in Poetry*. UMissP. pp. 236. £26.95. ISBN 0 8262 0945 9.

Fredman, Stephen. *The Grounding of American Poetry: Charles Olson and the Emersonian Tradition*. CUP (1983; reprinted1993). pp. 170. £30, $49.95. ISBN 0 5214 4303 2.

Frus, Phyllis. *The Politics and Poetics of Journalistic Narrative: The Timely and the Timeless*. CUP. pp. 320. £40. ISBN 0 5214 4324 5.

Garner Jr, Stanton B. *Bodied Spaces: Phenomenology and Performance in Contemporary Drama*. CornUP. pp. 260. hb £29.50, pb £12.50. ISBN 0 8014 3039 9, 0 8014 8218 6.

Gault, Pierre, ed. *Effets de Voix*. Groupe de Recherches Anglo-Américaines de Tours. UTours. pp. 156. FF100. ISSN 0997-4970.

Gibson, Andrew, ed. *Pound in Multiple Perspective: A Collection of Critical Essays*. Macmillan (1993). pp. 256. £40. ISBN 0 3335 1227 8.

Gidley, Mick. *Modern American Culture: An Introduction*. Longman (1993). pp. 407. £13.99. ISBN 0 5820 5110 X.

Giorcelli, Cristina, and Maria Anita Stefanelli, eds. *The Rhetoric of Love in the*

Collected Poems of William Carlos Williams. Edizioni (1993). pp. 317. L68,000. ISBN 8 8267 0196 2.
Gordon, David M., ed. *Ezra Pound and James Laughlin: Selected Letters*. Norton. pp. 313. £23. ISBN 0 3930 3540 9.
Grauer, Neil A. *Remember Laughter: A Life of James Thurber*. UNebP. pp. 226. £19. ISBN 0 8032 2155 X.
Hammer, Langdon. *Hart Crane and Allen Tate: Janus-Faced Modernism*. PrincetonUP (1993). pp. 277. $32.50. ISBN 0 6910 6877 1.
Hargrove, Nancy D. *The Journey Toward Ariel: Sylvia Plath's Poems of 1956–1959*. LundU. pp. 293. SEK211. ISBN 9 1796 6238 2.
Harris, Andrew B. *Broadway Theatre*. Theatre Production Studies. Routledge. pp. 180. hb £35.00, pb £10.99. ISBN 0 4150 6039 7, 0 4151 0520 X.
Harrison, Victoria. *Elizabeth Bishop's Poetics of Intimacy*. CUP (1993). pp. 252. £37.50, $59.95. ISBN 0 5214 3203 0.
Hay, Samuel A. *African American Theatre: An Historical and Critical Analysis*. Cambridge Studies in American Theatre and Drama. CUP. pp. 287. hb £35, pb £13.95. ISBN 0 5214 4522 1, 0 5214 6585 0.
Hayashi, Tetsumaro, ed. *A New Study Guide to Steinbeck's Major Works, with Critical Explanations*. Scarecrow (1993). pp. 312. £31.50, $35. ISBN 08108 2611 9.
——, ed. *John Steinbeck: The Years of Greatness, 1936–1939*. UAlaP (1993). pp. 240. £26.95, $29.95. ISBN 0 8173 0692 7.
Heffernan, James A. W. *Museum of Words: The Poetics of Ekphrasis from Homer to Ashbery*. UChicP (1993). pp. 249. $29.95. ISBN 0 2263 2313 7.
Hoeppner, Edward Haworth. *Echoes and Moving Fields: Structure and Subjectivity in the Poetry of W. S. Merwin and John Ashbery*. BuckUP. pp. 250. £30. ISBN 0 8387 5279 9.
Hoffman, Daniel. *Words to Create a World: Interviews, Essays, and Reviews of Contemporary Poetry*. Poets on Poetry. UMichP (1992). pp. 240. hb $39.50, pb $13.95. ISBN 0 4720 9505 6, 0 4720 6505 X .
Honnighausen, Lothar, and Valeria Gennaro Lerda, eds. *Rewriting the South: History and Fiction*. Francke (1993). pp. 439. DM136. ISBN 3 7720 2003 8.
Hoover, Paul, ed. *Postmodern American Poetry: A Norton Anthology*. Norton. pp. 701. £14.95. ISBN 0 3933 1090 6.
Houchin, John H. *The Critical Response to Eugene O'Neill*. Critical Responses in Arts and Letters. Greenwood. pp. 318. £53.95. ISBN 0 3132 7617 X.
Jarraway, David R. *Wallace Stevens and the Question of Belief*. LSUP (1993). pp. 339. £32.95. ISBN 0 8071 1759 5.
Johnson, Greg. *Joyce Carol Oates: A Study of the Short Fiction*. Twayne. pp. 235. $24.95. ISBN 0 8057 0857 X.
Kalaidjian, Walter. *American Culture Between the Wars: Revisionary Modernism and Postmodern Critique*. ColUP (1993). pp. 316. $18.50. ISBN 0 2310 8279 7.
Karolides, Nicholas J., Lee Burress and John M. Kean, eds. *Censored Books: Critical Viewpoints*. Scarecrow (1993). pp. 498. $49.50. ISBN 0 8108 2667 4.
Kearns, Katherine. *Robert Frost and a Poetics of Appetite*. CUP. pp. 228. £37.50. ISBN 0 5214 4485 3.
Kinnahan, Linda A. *Poetics of the Feminine: Authority and Literary Tradition in William Carlos Williams, Mina Loy, Denise Levertov and Kathleen Fraser*. CUP. pp. 285. £37.50. ISBN 0 5214 5127 2.
Kinzie, Mary. *The Cure of Poetry in an Age of Prose: Moral Essays on the Poet's*

Calling. UChicP (1993). pp. 341. £39.25. ISBN 0 2264 3735 3.
Köllhofer, Jakob. *James Baldwin: His Place in American Literary History and his Reception in Europe*. Lang (1991). pp. 140. £17. ISBN 3 6314 0726 2.
Landow, George P., ed. *Hyper/Text/Theory*. JHUP. pp. 377. £14. ISBN 0 8018 4838 5.
Levi, Jan Heller, ed. *A Muriel Rukeyser Reader*. Norton. pp. 294. £19.95. ISBN 0 3930 3566 2.
Lombardi, Marilyn May, ed. *Elizabeth Bishop: The Geography of Gender*. UPVirginia (1993). pp. 264. hb £33.95, $37.50. pb £14.50, $12.95. ISBN 0 8139 1444 2, 0 8139 1445 0.
Mackey, Nathaniel. *Discrepant Engagement: Dissonance, Cross-Culturality, and Experimental Writing*. CUP. pp. 313. £35, $54.95. ISBN 0 5214 4453 5.
MacLeod, Glen. *Wallace Stevens and Modern Art: From the Armory Show to Abstract Expressionism*. YaleUP (1993). pp. 253. £25. ISBN 0 3000 5360 6.
Malcolm, Janet. *The Silent Woman: Sylvia Plath and Ted Hughes*. Picador. pp. 213. £14.99. ISBN 0 3303 3578 2.
Mamet, David. *A Whore's Profession: Notes and Essays*. Faber. pp. 412. £12.99. ISBN 0 5711 7076 5.
Mariani, Paul. *Lost Puritan: A Life of Robert Lowell*, Norton. pp. 527. £24. ISBN 0 3930 3661 8.
Markey, Janice. *A Journey Into the Red Eye: The Poetry of Sylvia Plath – A Critique*. WP (1993). pp. 216. £7.99. ISBN 0 7043 4316 9.
Markos, Donald W. *Ideas in Things: The Poems of William Carlos Williams*. FDUP. pp. 236. £29.95, $39.95. ISBN 0 8386 3518 0.
Martine, James J. *The Crucible: Politics, Property, and Pretense*. Twayne's Masterwork Studies. Twayne (1993). pp. 126. £7.95. ISBN 0 8057 8584 1.
Mason, Jeffrey D. *Melodrama and the Myth of America*. IndUP (1993). pp. 268. £25, $31.95. ISBN 0 2533 3686 4.
Massa, Ann, and Alistair Stead. *Forked Tongues? Comparing Twentieth-Century British and American Literature*. Longman. pp. 384. hb £37, pb £14.99. ISBN 0 5820 7554 8, 0 5820 7555 6.
McCabe, Susan. *Elizabeth Bishop: Her Poetics of Loss*. PSUP. pp. 273. £40.50. ISBN 0 2710 1047 9.
McClure, John A. *Late Imperial Romance*. Verso. pp. 187. hb £39.95, pb £12.95. ISBN 0 8609 1447 X, 0 8609 1612 X.
McDonald, Gail. *Learning to be Modern: Pound, Eliot, and the American University*. Clarendon (1993). pp. 241. £27.50. ISBN 0 1981 1980 1.
Miller, Jordan Y., and Winifred L. Frazer. *American Drama Between the Wars: A Critical History*. Twayne's Critical History of American Drama. Twayne. pp. 280. £20.95. ISBN 0 8057 8950 2.
Millier, Brett C. *Elizabeth Bishop: Life and the Memory of It*. UCalP (1993). pp. 602. $28. ISBN 0 5200 7978 7.
Mobley, Marilyn Sanders. *Folk Roots and Mythic Wings in Sarah Orne Jewett and Toni Morrison: The Cultural Function of Narrative*. LSUP. pp. 193. £10.95. ISBN 0 8071 1964 4.
Moody, A. David, ed. *The Cambridge Companion to T. S. Eliot*. CUP. pp. 259. £11.95. ISBN 0 5214 2127 6.
Morgan, Thaïs E., ed. *Men Writing the Feminine: Literature, Theory, and the Question of Genders*. SUNYP. pp. 207. $16.95. ISBN 0 7914 1994 0.
Morris, Gregory L. *Talking Up a Storm: Voices of the New West*. UNebP. pp. 246.

£11. ISBN 0 8032 8224 9.
Mortimer, Gail L. *Daughter of the Swan: Love and Knowledge in Eudora Welty's Fiction.* UGeoP. pp. 213. £35.95. ISBN 0 8203 1633 4.
Murphy, Peter F., ed. *Fictions of Masculinity: Crossing Cultures, Crossing Sexualities.* NYUP. pp. 324. $18.95. ISBN 0 8147 5498 8.
Nadel, Ira B., *The Letters of Ezra Pound to Alice Corbin Henderson.* UTexP (1993). pp. 256. $34.95. ISBN 0 2927 1134 4.
Nelson, Cary, and Jefferson Hendricks, eds. *Edwin Rolfe: Collected Poems.* American Poetry Recovery. UIllP (1993). pp. 337. $34.95. ISBN 0 2520 2026 X.
Nesset, Kirk. *The Stories of Raymond Carver: A Critical Study.* OhioUP. pp. 131. hb £32.95, pb £13.95. ISBN 0 8214 1099 7, 0 8214 1100 4.
New, Elisa. *The Regenerate Lyric: Theology and Innovation in American Poetry.* CUP (1993). pp. 278. £35, $54.95. ISBN 0 5214 3021 6.
Noble, Donald R., ed. *The Steinbeck Question: New Essays in Criticism.* Whitston (1993). pp. 300. $29.50. ISBN 0 8787 5424 5.
O'Neil, Elizabeth Murrie. *The Last Word: Letters Between Marcia Nardi and William Carlos Williams.* UIowaP. pp. 242. $34.95. ISBN 0 8774 5445 0.
Ozieblo, Barbara, ed. *The Provincetown Players: A Choice of the Shorter Works.* ShaP. pp. 304. £12.95. ISBN 1 8507 5725 9.
Pack, Robert, and Jay Parini, ed. *Poems for a Small Planet: Contemporary American Nature Poetry, A Bread Loaf Anthology.* UPNE (1993). pp. 301. hb $35, pb $16.95. ISBN 0 8745 1621 8, 0 8745 1620 X.
Pagan, Nicholas. *Rethinking Literary Biography: A Postmodern Approach to Tennessee Williams.* AUP (1993). pp. 150. £23. ISBN 0 8386 3516 4.
Parini, Jay, ed. *Gore Vidal: Writer Against the Grain.* ColUP. pp. 321. hb £23.50, $30, pb £12.95, $16.95. ISBN 0 2310 7208 2, 0 2310 7209 0.
——, ed., and Brett C. Millier, associate ed. *The Columbia History of American Poetry.* ColUP (1993). pp. 894. £46, $59.95. ISBN 0 2310 7836 6.
Parkes, Catherine N. *In the Shadow of Parnassus: Zoe Akins's Essays on American Poetry.* AUP. pp. 273. $27.50. ISBN 0 9456 3660 1.
Parsons, Marnie. *Touch Monkeys: Nonsense Strategies for Reading Twentieth-Century Poetry.* UTorP. pp. 262. £32.50, $50. ISBN 0 8020 2983 3.
Penberthy, Jenny. *Niedecker and the Correspondence with Zukofsky: 1931–1970.* CUP (1993). pp. 378. £40, $59.95. ISBN 0 5214 4369 5.
Perelman, Bob. *The Trouble with Genius: Reading Pound, Joyce, Stein, and Zukofsky.* UCalP. pp. 263. $16. ISBN 0 5200 8755 0.
Phillips, Robert, ed. *Delmore Schwartz and James Laughlin: Selected Letters.* Norton (1993). pp. 382. £21. ISBN 0 3930 3471 2.
Polk, Noel, ed., *New Essays on The Sound and the Fury.* American Novel. CUP (1993). pp. 182. hb £24.95, $34.95, pb £9.95, $12.95. ISBN 0 5214 5114 0, 0 5214 5734 3.
Pritchard, William H. *Frost: A Literary Life Reconsidered.* UMassP (1993). pp. 286. £13.50. ISBN 0 8702 3838 8.
Ramazani, Jahan. *Poetry of Mourning: The Modern Elegy from Hardy to Heaney.* UChicP. pp. 419. £16.95. ISBN 0 2267 0340 1.
Reynolds, Michael. *Hemingway: The American Homecoming.* Blackwell (1993). pp. 264. $24.95. ISBN 0 6311 8481 3.
Rich, Adrienne. *Collected Early Poems 1950–1970.* Norton (1993). pp. 435. £18.50. ISBN 0 3930 3418 6.

——. *What is Found There: Notebooks on Poetry and Politics*. Norton. pp. 304. £14.95. ISBN 0 3930 3565 4.

Richardson, Gary A. *American Drama from the Colonial Period through World War I: A Critical History*. Twayne's Critical History of American Drama. Twayne (1993). pp. 320. £22.95. ISBN 0 8057 8956 1.

Roberts, Bette B. *Anne Rice*. Twayne. pp. 173. $25.95. ISBN 0 8057 3961 0.

Robinson, Fred C. *The Tomb of Beowulf and Other Essays on Old English*. Blackwell (1993). pp. ix + 335. £45. ISBN 0 6311 7328 5.

Robinson, Marc. *The Other American Drama*. Cambridge Studies in American Theatre and Drama 2. CUP. pp. 216. ISBN 0 5214 5437 9.

Rodgers, Audrey T. *Denise Levertov: The Poetry of Engagement*. AUP (1993). pp. 234. £32.95. ISBN 0 8386 3494 X.

Rudd, Niall. *The Classical Tradition in Operation*. UTorP. pp. 186. £35, $55. ISBN 0 8020 0570 5.

Salwak, Dale, ed. *Anne Tyler as Novelist*. UIowaP. pp. 226. $14.95. ISBN 0 8774 5487 6.

Schaum, Melita, ed. *Wallace Stevens and the Feminine*. UAlaP (1993). pp. 243. $25.50. ISBN 0 8173 0666 8.

Schneider, Steven P. *A. R. Ammons and the Poetics of Widening Scope*. FDUP. pp. 246. £29.95, $38.50. ISBN 0 8386 3507 5.

Schuchard, Ronald, ed., *T. S. Eliot: The Varieties of Metaphysical Poetry*. Faber (1993). pp. 343. £25. ISBN 0 5711 4230 3.

Schwartz, Daniel R. *Narrative and Representation in the Poetry of Wallace Stevens*. Macmillan (1993). pp. 242. £40. ISBN 0 3120 9488 4.

Scott Jr, Nathan A. *Visions of Presence in Modern American Poetry*. JHUP (1993). pp. 298. $26. ISBN 0 8018 4537 8.

Serio, John. *Wallace Stevens: An Annotated Secondary Bibliography*. UPittP. pp. 435. $100. ISBN 0 8229 3836 7.

Sherry, Vincent. *Ezra Pound, Wyndham Lewis, and Radical Modernism*. OUP (1993). pp. 228. £35. ISBN 0 1950 7693 1.

Shetley, Vernon. *After the Death of Poetry: Poet and Audience in Contemporary America*. DukeUP (1993). pp. 209. £12.95. ISBN 0 8223 1342 1.

Shoptaw, John. *On the Outside Looking Out: John Ashbery's Poetry*. HarvardUP. pp. 386. £14.95. ISBN 0 6746 3613 9.

Simon, Linda. *Gertrude Stein Remembered*. UNebP. pp. xv + 195. £19. ISBN 0 8032 4240 9.

Singh, Amritjit, Joseph T. Skerret Jr and Robert E. Hogan., eds. *Memory, Narrative, and Identity: New Essays in Ethnic American Literatures*. NortheasternU. pp. 349. £32.95, $50. ISBN 1 5555 3203 9.

Singh, G. *Ezra Pound as Critic*. St Martin's. pp. 176. $29.95. ISBN 0 3121 2056 7.

Smith, Madeline, and Richard Eaton. *Eugene O'Neill in Court: Documents in the Case of Georges Lewys v. Eugene O'Neill, et al.* American University Studies. Lang (1993). pp. 293. £26. ISBN 0 8204 1907 9.

Stanley, Sandra Kumamoto. *Louis Zukofsky and the Transformation of a Modern American Poetics*. UCalP. pp. 198. £28, $35. ISBN 0 5200 7357 6.

Stefanova-Peteva, Kalina. *Who Calls the Shots on the New York Stages?* Contemporary Theatre Studies. Harwood. pp. 172. hb £28, pb £12. ISBN 3 7186 5437 7, 3 7186 5438 5.

Surette, Leon. *The Birth of Modernism: Ezra Pound, T. S. Eliot, W. B. Yeats, and*

the Occult. McG-QUP (1993). pp. 320. $34.95. ISBN 0 7735 0976 3.
Sutton, Walter. *Pound, Thayer, Watson, and The Dial*. UPFlor. pp. 383. $39.50. ISBN 0 8130 1316 X.
Taggart, John. *Songs of Degrees: Essays on Contemporary Poetry and Poetics*. UAlaP. pp. 254. $29.95. ISBN 0 8173 0713 3.
Taylor, Diana, and Juan Villegas, eds. *Negotiating Performance: Gender, Sexuality, and Theatricality in Latin/o America*. DukeUP. pp. 368. hb £52.50, $54.95, pb £17.95, $18.95. ISBN 0 8223 1504 1, 0 8223 1515 7.
Taylor, Richard, and Claus Melchior, eds. *Ezra Pound and Europe*. Internationale Forschugengen zur Allegemeinen and Vergleichenden Literaturwissenschaft. Rodopi. pp. 242. £27.75, DM75. ISBN 9 0518 3521 3.
Teichman, Michael, and Sharon Leder, eds. *Truth and Lamentation: Stories and Poems on the Holocaust*. UIllP (1993). pp. 432. hb $49.95, pb $17.95. ISBN 0 2520 2028 6, 0 2520 6335 X.
Tetlow, Wendolyn E. *Hemingway's In Our Time: Lyrical Dimensions*. BuckUP (1993). pp. 158. $28.50. ISBN 0 8387 5219 5.
Thormählen, Marianne, ed. *T. S. Eliot at the Turn of the Century*. LundU. pp. 244. SEK288. ISBN 9 1796 6272 2.
Timmerman, John H. *T. S. Eliot's Ariel Poems: The Poetics of Recovery*. BuckUP. pp. 203. £29.95. ISBN 0 8387 5282 6 1.
Van Dyne, Susan R. *Revising Life: Sylvia Plath's Ariel Poems*. UNCP (1993). pp. 206. $27.50. ISBN 0 8078 2102 0.
Ward, Geoff. *Statutes of Liberty: The New York School of Poets*. Macmillan (1993). pp. 208. £40. ISBN 0 3334 7389 2.
Ward, Janet Doubler, and Joanna Stephens Mink, eds. *Communication and Women's Friendships: Parallels and Intersections in Literature and Life*. BGUP. pp. 201. hb $42.95, pb $15.95. ISBN 0 8797 2643 1, 0 8797 2644 X.
Weisser, Susan Ostrov, and Jennifer Fleischner, eds. *Feminist Nightmares: Women at Odds, Feminism and the Problem of Sisterhood*. NYUP. pp. 405. hb £44, $55, pb £15.25, $18.95. ISBN 0 8147 2619 4, 0 8147 2620 8.
Weston, Ruth D. *Gothic Traditions and Narrative Techniques in the Fiction of Eudora Welty*. LSUP. pp. 202. £23.95. ISBN 0 8071 1897 4.
Wilhelm, J. J. *Ezra Pound: The Tragic Years 1925–1972*. PSUP. pp. 390. £44.50, $49.50. ISBN 0 2710 1082 7.
Wolfe, Cary. *The Limits of American Literary Ideology in Pound and Emerson*. Cambridge Studies in American Literature and Culture 69. CUP. pp. 290. £37.50, $54.95. ISBN 0 5214 4555 8.
Wolter, Jürgen C., ed. and comp. *The Dawning of American Drama: American Dramatic Criticism, 1746–1915*. Contributions in Drama and Theatre Studies. Greenwood. pp. 328. £53.95. ISBN 0 3132 9028 8.
Wood, Michael. *The Magician's Doubts: Nabokov and the Risks of Fiction*. C&W. pp. 252. £18. ISBN 0 7011 6197 3.
Yip, Wai-Lim. *Diffusion of Distances: Dialogues Between Chinese and Western Poetics*. UCalP (1993). pp. 246. $29.95. ISBN 0 5200 7736 9.

XVII

New Literatures in English

FEMI ABODUNRIN, BRIAN KIERNAN, EVA-MARIE KRÖLLER, PAULA BURNETT, PHILLIP LANGRAN and CAROLE DURIX

This chapter has six sections: 1. Africa, by Femi Abodunrin; 2. Australia, by Brian Kiernan; 3. Canada, by Eva-Marie Kröller; 4. The Caribbean, by Paula Burnett; 5. India, by Phillip Langran; 6. New Zealand and the South Pacific, by Carole Durix.

1. Africa

(a) General

This year *JCL* included 'a Bibliographic Listing of Nigerian plays in English, 1956–1992' by Chris Dunton (29.i.103–13), and 'South Africa (1992 & 1993)' compiled and introduced by Dorothy Driver (29.iii.125–238). Special issues of journals included *Matatu* (11) on 'Southern African Writing: Voyages and Explorations'; *SAQ* (93) on 'The Writings of J. M. Coetzee', ed. Michael Valdez Moses; *ALT* (19) on 'Critical Theory & African Literature'; *RAL* (29.iii) on 'Women as Oral Artists', eds Omolara Ogundipe-Leslie and Carole Boyce Davies; and *RAL* (29.iv) on 'South African Writing'.

While praising the new critics (mainly American) of the 1940s and 1950s for being able to rescue literature from generalizations which paid insufficient attention to the text and often concerned themselves with biographical irrelevancies, Eldred Jones has also rekindled (deliberately?) the ongoing debate between so-called traditional and modern aesthetics at the heart of 'Critical Theory and African Literature Today'. In his editorial article entitled 'Critics and Creators' (*ALT* 19.1–7), Jones asserts that 'a poetic which limits an African work to one which participates in the outward manifestation of the traditional African culture will be an inadequate vehicle for the portrayal of the truth of African contemporary life'. While the question as to what we may consider 'outward manifestation of traditional culture' remains unanswered, Jones asserts barely two paragraphs later that 'in traditional African societies there is no ambiguity about the centrality of the author/presenter, and from this tradition it is easy to derive Achebe's "novelist as teacher"'. The sentence preceding the one just quoted praises recent critics for restoring the centrality of literary texts, while describing their other obsession, the elimination of the author, as not just hedonistic but unaccomplished.

Introducing the special issue of *RAL* on 'Women as Oral Artists', Ogundipe-Leslie and Davies locate a conceptual blind spot in what they have termed the construction of the field of African oral literature as conflict-less, or at least, a tendency to let it develop without major consideration of women as oral artists. Even among leading commentators (Finnegan, Okpewho, etc.), virtually none is free of this blind spot: the exception is Harold Scheub, whose *African Oral Narratives, Proverbs, Riddles, Poetry and Song* identifies a female emphasis in South African orature tradition and actually locates it along a female line: 'and our grandmothers said that oral narratives had been created years before by their grandmothers'.

Such debates might be informed by Kenneth Harrow's book-length study of what he calls *Thresholds of Change in African Literature: The Emergence of a Tradition.* Acknowledging Dennis Duerden's 1975 effort in *African Art and Literature: The Invisible Present*, 'in which he [Duerden] avoids the "Bolekaja" fallacy that would have us look to oral literature as an answer to all questions of sources and influences on written literature', Harrow states that theoretical assumptions about 'Change' constitute the main basis of his study. A contemporary syncretism, most especially one which combines tradition with modernism, is the only means through which simplistic binary oppositions, especially those that equate Africa with tradition and modernism with Europe, can be avoided. In chapters like 'Literature of the *Temoignage* and the Foundations for Change', Harrow offers convincing descriptions of how responsive criticism could assist the pioneering works of African literature – like the *temoignage* itself – or how a literature that bears witness to individual lives and to social, cultural and historical realities could be regarded as the basic threshold for change. Harrow suggests that V. Y. Mudimbe has located the problematic area for us (or at least an integral aspect of it, especially the love–hate syndrome for the West symbolized by the Bolekaja fallacy) when he proffers the following philosophical approach:

> Really to escape from the West presupposes an exact assessment of what it costs to become detached from it: that presupposes knowing how far the West, insidiously perhaps, has become close to us; that presupposes knowing, in what is permitted us to think against the West, what is still Western; and to measure the extent to which our recourse against it is still perhaps a ruse that it uses against us and at the end of which it awaits us, unmoving and distant.

Alain Ricard's 'Post-Colonial Reader Lost in a Bush of Ghosts: Theories of Africans by Christopher L. Miller' (*RAL* 24.i.101–6) and Bill Ashcroft's 'Africa and Australia: The Post-Colonial Connection' (*RAL* 24.iii.161–70) are two review essays focusing on different aspects of what is still Western in ideological and polemical terms, and above all, what it costs the post-colonial subject (a problematic term, recontextualized by Ashcroft) to be detached from it.

Essays on African Writing 1: A Re-evaluation, edited by Abdulrazak Gurnah and published in 1993, is another important collection of essays inadvertently missed on these pages last year. Fielding a healthy mixture of both established and well-known critical voices like Mark Kinkead-Weekes, Derek Wright, Simon Gikandi and Gurnah himself, as well as currently evolving and forceful ones such as Adewale Maja-Pearce, Frank Chipasula and Belinda Jack, to mention just a few, Gurnah describes the joint preoccupation of these critics as a timely attempt to re-read those texts gradually congealing to form the African 'canon'–that authoritative list of books accepted as 'literature'. In his lucid critical introduction to the volume, Gurnah traces the linear processes in the evolution of African literary/critical discourse, and observes how an 'originary essence' still pervades critical attitudes, like those of Soyinka and Achebe for example, even when they are presented as attitudes that seek to take us some way from the manichean propositions of high négritude. In 'Negritude and African Poetry' (*ALT* 19.22–43) Isaac Eliminian agrees more or less with Gurnah and cites Eldred Jones's 1971 assertion that 'Soyinka has little or no basis for attacking the Negritude writers since "his work exhibits all that Negritude was essentially about, bar the shouting".' In *Essays on African Writing 1*, however, Gurnah summarizes, discursively, this and related critical issues, ranging from 'the Poetics of Location' in Achebe's fiction examined by Gikandi; to that of the costly oversight, in the male-dominated cultural space of African letters, where issues of gender differentiation are concerned, which is examined by Rashidah Abubakar using the prism of Mariama Bá; to Nuruddin Farah's legendary exemption, one which Derek Wright has dubbed, not uncritically, 'Fabling the Feminine'. He concludes that in spite of the rabid tone in which many of the debates (such as the one on language) in African literature are conducted, the major texts of the tradition 'self-consciously spoke above differences, to other "Africans" whose language they did not share and whose cultures they did not fully grasp'. Referring to the language issue, Ezenwa Ohaeto, a practitioner of creative writing in Pidgin and an irrepressible critical voice, in 'Pidgin Literature, Criticism and Communication' (*ALT* 19.44–52), repostulates a familiar challenge to writers and critics of African literature. In 1975, Chinua Achebe, echoing the proverbial dictum of the Igbo people, 'those whose palm-kernel has been cracked for them by benevolent spirits should not forget to be humble', urged the European critic of African literature to cultivate the habit of humility. Ten years later, in 1985, Mineke Schipper, feeling that the pendulum had swung far enough, made the same appeal to the increasingly swollen tribe otherwise known as the male writers and critics of African literature. Ezenwa Ohaeto now feels that the assertion is in need of a long overdue revision, or at least, rephrasing, and presents the following restructuring of Achebe's and Schipper's commentaries: 'The *elitist* critic of African literature must cultivate the habit of humility appropriate to his (and her?) limited experience of the pidgin world and purged of the superiority and arrogance which history so insidiously makes him heir to.' Finally, anyone who has studied the intricacy, politics and poetics involved in what we may term the movement of the voluptuous pendulum may find Robert Philison's suggestive commentary, 'The Making and Unmaking of a White Africanist' (*RAL* 24.i.95–9), harrowing but instructive.

If the overriding paradigm, according to Gurnah, could be summarized as 'ignorant accounts of Africa written by arrogant Europeans', then one such account, written, ironically enough, by a man who never physically trampled the African landscape, is Shakespeare's celebrated play *The Tempest*. In their introduction to *The Postmodern, the (Post-)Colonial, and the (Post-) Feminist*, Theo D'haen and Hans Bertens observe how Shakespeare's play has served as source and target for both post-colonial and women writers. Chantal Zabus's 'Prospero's Progeny Curses Back: Postcolonial, Postmodern and Postpatriarchal Rewritings of *The Tempest*' is another critical articulation of the second part of Abdulrazak Gurnah's useful summation of the post-colonial paradigm: how the 'ignorant accounts of Africa [. . .] were followed by insider accounts that wrote back at them'. Shakespeare, who is described by Zabus as a Renaissance magus, and his four-centuries-old play have produced the paradigmatic double yoke of colonialist prosperity – one post-colonial, the other feminist – through the remote kinship between Caliban and Miranda respectively. According to Zabus, the former has become, at least in Africa and the Caribbean, the inexhaustible symbol of the colonized insurgent; whereas in English Canada, Caliban's relevance appears secondary to the Prospero–Miranda or Miranda–Ferdinand relationships, conventional metaphors of parental and romantic relations. In 'Margins and Metaphors: The Politics of Post-***', on the other hand, Sylvia Soderlind is merely stating the obvious in asserting that we seem to live in a world of posts – ranging from postmodernism and post-structuralism to post-colonialism. Soderlind engages the three major posts of the tail end of the twentieth century, and postulates the quintessential dilemma with which every potential commentator has to grapple: 'what are asterisks, in place of what are they and what comes after, post- them?' What seems certain, however, is that whether as a temporal marker or as an indicator of a challenge/subversion, the debate over the prefix 'post' is set to continue for some time. Eva Hunter's '"What Exactly Is Civilization?": "Africa", "The West" and Gender in Buchi Emecheta's *The Rape of Shavi*' (*ESA* 37.i.47–61) upholds a view of the post- as challenge/subversion through her critical identification of Emecheta's fable as a provocative view of colonial and neocolonial intercourse between 'Africa' and 'the West'. In view of the widespread ambivalence over the proper meaning of the prefix, and the seemingly affordable luxury of the postmodern imperative to let the word lead where it may, Hunter reiterates that, from the vexed issue of clitoridectomy to that of fond 'notions of tradition' or a usable past, critics appear slow in realizing that one way of perceiving the post- is as a 'typographical sign connecting the margin to the centre – and as such, a sender-away'. The asterisk, according to Soderlind, 'is a visual deictic, telling the reader where to go, which is away from the centre'. Soderlind's thesis would appear in this sense to be in perfect agreement with that of Hunter, who admonishes the centrist critic, or one who badly needs to jettison expectations of what either an 'African' or a 'feminist' woman ought to be writing.

Thus, when a major Nigerian/African playwright and critic, Olu Obafemi, in 'Towards Feminist Aesthetics in Nigerian Drama: The Plays of Tess Onwueme' (*ALT* 19.84–100), commences critical appraisal of the work of a female counterpart with lengthy preambles about the 'paucity of information on the feminist experience of the black people', no one can pretend not to understand the source of his critical disquiet. Obafemi confesses to being 'intrigued as well as amused reading a major study recently, on feminism. The book has only one chapter on Black Feminism – and that chapter was shared with Lesbianism. With copious apology.'

(b) West Africa

In 'Griottes: Female Voices from West Africa' (*RAL* 24.iii.71–91) Thomas Hale wonders why, during nearly two decades of what we might term the post-*Roots* era, there has been such a silence on griottes in scholarship about the oral tradition of the West African region. Besides serving as a useful indicator of Sahelian and Savannah civilization, the female wordsmith, in the context of that civilization, is as real as her male counterpart; and the function of both griot and griotte, which many would regard as stirring controversy, according to Hale can only 'help to distinguish more clearly female griots from those who, like Alex Haley, did not know of the existence of these women wordsmiths'. Hale's remarkable research effort in this lengthy essay is described as the starting point for a longer and more detailed chapter that will be part of a book on griots and griottes now under way. In spite of this, Hale describes his modest purpose in the present essay as fourfold:

> First, to offer preliminary responses to the question of why we know so little about griottes; second, to report on work now being done by other scholars; third, to give some examples of the verbal art of griottes; and fourth, to suggest some avenues of research for a new generation more aware of the dangers of long-held assumptions that have prevented many of us in the past from taking a less biased view of the subject.

Thomas Hale's present effort does not merely fulfil these lofty aims but also complements the other essays in the special issue of *RAL* (24.iii) on 'Women as Oral Artists'. Above all, it situates us, in critical terms, within the parameters set by the editors of the volume: 'to contribute to areas of theory in African gender theory which is as new a territory as is the study of women'. And, besides the euphemistic prodding, or as they put it, 'collegial humour', of the declaredly feminist editors of the volume, the other choice essays focusing pre-eminently on the West African region include Ropo Sekoni's 'Yoruba Market Dynamics and the Aesthetics of Negotiation in Female Precolonial Narrative Tradition' (33–45); Chinyere Grace Okafor's 'From the Heart of Masculinity: Ogbodo-Uke's Women's Masking' (7–17); and Ode S. Ogede's 'Counters to Male Domination: Images of Pain in Igede Women's Songs' (105–20).

If the issue of 'Griottes', as Ogundipe-Leslie and Davies inform us, constitutes a conceptual blind spot in African literature, the politics of 'revisionism' itself (a major creative and critical project embarked upon by the now canonized writers and critics of African writing) is also being problematized by leading post-colonial theorists and feminists. Simon Gikandi's 'Achebe and the Politics of Location: The Uses of Space in *Things Fall Apart* and *No Longer at Ease*' (in Gurnah, *Essays on African Writing 1*) echoes the Foucaultian observation that we seem to live in the epoch of space, and examines how the African cultural space, in the handling of Achebe, functions as a paradoxical 'space of emplacement'. If this 'doubleness' accounts for the chronotopic disjuncture that leads to the triumph of colonialism at the end of *Things Fall Apart*, an excellent discussion of masculinist ideologies in the same novel, according to Gikandi, can be found in Rhonda Cobham-Sander's 1991 essay 'Making Men and History: Achebe and the Politics of Revisionism'. Another leading author deserving an eminent position within the sparsely populated canonical space of (West) African letters is J. P. Clark-Bekederemo. According to Dan Izevbaye, in his characteristically erudite 'J. P. Clark-Bekederemo and the Ijo Literary Tradition' (*RAL* 24.i.1–21), 1991 'was a year of harvest for Clark-Bekederemo, a man of letters whose pioneering work and continuing creativity was rewarded with an honourary degree of the University of Benin and a Nigerian National Merit Award'. From the time he presented his scathing attack on what was then construed as an incipient US imperialism, *America their America*, to the moment he pitched his creative tent with the federal side during the Nigerian civil war, leading to the publication of his highly controversial post-war poems *Casualties*, a marked ideological assault on Clark-Bekederemo's literary reputation had been evident. Izevbaye invites us to perceive the overriding ambivalence in his writing 'as a reflection of the theme of psychic wound in his early poetry'. From this premise Izevbaye avers that Clark-Bekederemo's 'production of the Ozidi Saga may be seen not only as a mark of cultural restitution, but also an act of healing, one which bridges the sense of cultural exile expressed in "Agbor Dancer" (1959), when he was John Pepper Clark, and the homecoming of J. P. Clark-Bekederemo in "Heroes of Funama" (1981)'.

Still trampling the canonical space like a colossus is Wole Soyinka, first African recipient of the coveted and highly controversial Nobel prize. Apart from the numerous essays, three book-length studies of Soyinka's *oeuvre* are available this year. Rather appropriately, Oluwole Adejare's *Language and Style in Soyinka: A Systemic Textlinguistic Study of a Literary Idiolect* and Tanure Ojaide's *The Poetry of Wole Soyinka* concentrate on two areas where Soyinka could be said, in critical terms, to be inherently problematic (language) or grossly underestimated (poetry); while *Wole Soyinka: An Appraisal* edited by Adewale Maja-Pearce is a collection of essays which (according to its editor) represents a critical 'appraisal to mark Soyinka's sixtieth birthday [which] hardly requires any justification'. Critical responses to Soyinka's writing remain as passionate and divergent as ever. Niyi Osundare, for example, in 'Wole Soyinka and the Atunda Ideal: A Reading of Soyinka's Poetry' (in Maja-Pearce) locates the essential Soyinka within the parameters of Yoruba culture and philosophy, albeit via a circuitous route, or what he calls the Atunda ideal: 'creative and re-creative, iconoclastic, rebellious, libertarian, and frequently revolutionary, an instinct almost natural, opposition to "constituted authority", especially of the inhuman totalitarian kind'. Another second-generation poet, Tanure Ojaide, argues in his book-length study of Soyinka's poetry that it is only after rigorous discussion of the voice and viewpoint in Soyinka's poems that the poet's persona can be established. In '*Death and the King's Horseman*: A Poet's Quarrel with His Culture' (*RAL* 24.i.47–60), however, Wole Ogundele offers two rather illuminating critical suggestions in a bid to transcend the traditionalism/modernism binary opposition which has been the lot of this major drama of existence. First, Ogundele suggests that critical focus should dwell on the extant features of the play (metaphysical confrontation, human vehicle, and universe of the Yoruba mind), features which suggest that the experience enacted is fundamentally that of ritual; second, and perhaps more importantly, Ogundele invites us to understand Elesin's ritual negating actions, and not Olunde's salvaging gesture, as the paradoxical motif which makes possible a new beginning, after the exhaustion. Kwame Anthony Appiah's 'Myth, Literature, and the African World' (in Maja-Pearce) returns to the controversial issue of language or the use of it, and one of his primary conclusions is that 'in reading Soyinka we hear a voice that has ransacked the treasuries of the English literary and vernacular diction with an eclecticism that dazzles without disconcerting, and has found a language that is indisputably his own'.

In 'Kofi Awoonor as Critic' (*ALT* 19.8–20), Obi Maduakor focuses on another first-generation modern (West) African writer who has been engaged in creative activity since the publication by Mbari of his first book of verse, *Rediscovery*, in 1964. According to Maduakor, Awoonor (like Soyinka, Achebe, Clark-Bekederemo, and his own contemporary, the Nigerian poet Christopher Okigbo), 'is one of the creators of the style and technique of modern African poetry'. In this essay, Maduakor assesses Awoonor as a critic, one who has argued consistently that the overwhelming aspiration of African art is the condition of wholeness – but

Awoonor as critic has also stated that second-generation writers like Ayi Kwei Armah and Yambo Ouologuem epitomize an era of intense despair, aggravated by their status as writers in exile. In 'Ayi Kwei Armah and the Harbingers of Death' (in Gurnah), Adewale Maja-Pearce examines integral aspects of Armah's work, and observes that Armah is a visionary writer in the strict sense. However, Armah's vision, according to Maja-Pearce, is also a racist one, and 'if his work has so far escaped the charge of racism, it is because the depth of the African humiliation to the fact of their enslavement has blinded African commentators, along with their Western apologists, from seeing the thing for what it is'.

Olu Obafemi's 'Towards Feminist Aesthetics in Nigerian Drama: The Plays of Tess Onwueme' (*ALT* 19.84–100); Ify G. Achufusi's 'Feminist Inclinations of Flora Nwapa' (*ALT* 19.101–14); and Rashida Ismaili Abubakar's 'The Emergence of Mariama Bá' (in Gurnah) address what Obafemi has termed 'paucity of information on the feminist experience of the black people'. Emerging from a society that is both African and Islamic, for Abubakar, Bá's writing is without doubt worth celebrating as an art which 'takes women out of the parenthesis, and offers a direct and clear account to replace the variations which imply the pitiable position of African women in general and Islamic women in particular'. Achufusi's thesis agrees more or less with Abubakar's, and sees the ostensible demonization of feminist inclinations among African intellectuals, both male and female, as the hallmark of societies which have not internalized the notion that the woman's self-actualization is no longer dependent on her social and biological reproductive roles. Olu Obafemi, on the other hand, insists that a position of relative independence should be reserved for the critic, if she or he is going to function creatively and autonomously. This position of independence, according to Obafemi, has been reaffirmed by Wole Soyinka in a keynote address to the 1989 Calabar Annual International African Literature Conference, 'Beyond Insularity: Beyond Rushdie: Prescription for the Terminal Critica'; and in his assessment of Onwueme's creative output, Obafemi argues that both the extraverted and silent ideological persuasion of the dramatist must be transcended in order to evaluate a work independently of the views and positions which the artist may or may not hold.

Ulli Beier's *The Return of Shango: The Theatre of Duro Ladipo* is a critical appraisal of the historical as well as cultural origins of Yoruba popular theatre. This important book is focused pre-eminently on the theatrical career of one of Nigeria's foremost theatre practitioners, the enigmatic Duro Ladipo of the Shango/*Oba Koso* fame. Its wealth of information makes it a necessity for everyone interested in Nigerian theatre history, chronicled and accounted for by a cultural/literary scholar whose modesty only accentuates the depth of his contribution. It revisits, among other pulsating moments, the period in which the relatively unknown 'sleepy backwater' called Oshogbo attained an enviable status as one of the thriving centres of Nigerian arts, from the time the idea of an Mbari or Theatre Club was proposed to Ulli Beier by the late Duro Ladipo. The analysis of Ladipo's short but intense career in the theatre, and the formidable challenge that the legacy of his numerous achievements poses to succeeding generations, can be described as Beier's overriding purpose in writing this very important book.

(c) East and Central Africa

Abdulrazak Gurnah's 'Transformative Strategies in the Fiction of Ngugi wa Thiong'o' (in Gurnah, *Essays on African Writing 1*) focuses on the paradigmatic themes in Ngugi's fiction, themes which include 'expropriation of African land and subsequent rupture of "whole ways of life"; the inhumanity or "unnaturalness" of the European settler; the cynicism of "neocolonial" capital and the grotesque complicity of African elites'. Besides epitomizing the essential Ngugi, these paradigms enact a post-colonial discourse that constructs, among other things, Ngugi's 'Kenya', which like all 'nations' in Africa and elsewhere has plural existences in the imagination. This dominant discourse in which history, for example, functions as an enabling code of recognition, in conjunction with 'the calamity which has befallen the African people', Gurnah sees as constituting the characteristic landscape of Ngugi's fiction – 'a characteristically bleak landscape – a dystopia'. In Ngugi's writing, land has come to acquire a metonymic function, and integral aspects of the 'transformative strategies' involved in its narrativization include the substance and symbols of Gikuyu creation myth, deployed as they are in order to reiterate and legitimize the African claim to ownership. Very often, these strategies transform the Europeans and their neocolonial African allies into monsters, and through repeated re-enactment of the 'heritage' of Gikuyu and Mumbi, for example, women are also depicted figuratively as both capriciously cruel and weak. Ostensibly, even for the most patriotic among Ngugi's women characters, according to Gurnah, 'deliverance into "the patriot" state arrives as a mystical experience, a sudden burst of irresistible knowledge under the agency of an appropriate man'.

Ngugi's predecessor, the legendary Gakaara wa Wanjau, about whom he speaks in glowing terms in his prison diary *Barrel of a Pen*, receives attention of a more adulatory kind in Cristiana Pugliese's critical commentary, 'The Organic Vernacular Intellectual in Kenya: Gakaara wa Wanjau' (*RAL* 24.iv.177–87). Unlike Ngugi, the self-taught Gakaara never belonged to the academic circle, and although constantly ignored by those Pugliese described as 'the accredited Kenyan literary critics', Gakaara's writing has been steadily supported by his Gikuyu readership. Epitomizing, at the beginning of his writing career in the 1940s, the spokesman for the restricted class of educated and politicized Gikuyu, Gakaara, according to Pugliese, 'became in the sixties a "popular" author, writing for the growing number of literate Gikuyu with primary or secondary education and addressing those ethical issues about which majority [*sic*] of his people felt strongly'. In critical terms, Pugliese's aim is to situate Gakaara's writing within the popular and realist mode, and she sees Gakaara's winning of the Noma Award for Publishing in Africa in 1984 as one interference too many by those she has branded Gikuyu academics. Apart from muddling Gakaara's moderate political views in the diary he had written while in detention in the fifties, and which won for him the Noma Award, 'the editor and the translator of Gakaara's diary', according to Pugliese, 'transposed the writer's vivid language in clumsy and rhetorical Marxist idiom, thus completely distorting his ideology and spoiling his style'.

In 'Fabling the Feminine in Nuruddin Farah's Novels' (in Gurnah), Derek Wright explores the political implications of Farah's assertion that he sees 'women as the symbol of the subjugated self in everyone of us'. According to Wright, the well-known attempt 'to endow gender with political significance', or read Woman as Nation in the Somali context, finds its *reductio ad absurdum* in the eccentric telescoping of Nation and biological fates in *Maps*. Derek Wright has also published, during the year under review, a book-length, comprehensive study of Farah's published novels in English, *The Novels of Nuruddin Farah*. Farah's Somalia, which he fled in 1974, was under the grip of the totalitarian regime of

General Muhammad Siyad Barre from 1969 to 1991, and the oppression of his land and people has ever since constituted the reverberating subject to which Farah has returned novel after novel. In eight concise chapters, Wright provides an extremely useful critical introduction to the writing of one of Africa's most multilingual, multicultural and multiliterate writers – a literary nomad, whose relentless proclivity manifests on a global scale.

Helen Nabasuta Mugambi's 'Intersections: Gender, Orality, Text and Female Space in Contemporary Kiganda Radio Songs' (*RAL* 24.iii.46–70) returns us to issues of gender, especially how contemporary Kiganda radio songs dramatize gender politics. Mugambi studies how these songs constitute a rich nexus for traditional and emergent constructions of gender in Buganda. As with Gurnah's critical focus on the 'Gikuyu' and 'Mumbi' paradigm above, Mugambi anchors her critique of these images of power and powerlessness in the woman's experience around what she calls the paradoxical moments for the woman in the Kiganda founding myth, 'the story of Kintu'. Two key paradigms of the construction of womanhood, *silencing* and *deletion*, are derived from the premise of this founding myth and used in analysing the radio songs. From neighbouring Kenya, Awuor Ayodo in 'Definitions of the Self in Luo Women's Orature' (*RAL* 24.iii.121–9) extends Okpewho's assertion that 'the characters and events contained in [African folklore] are fundamentally symbols illustrating various moral and philosophical issues relating to the people', to suggest that the representative animals involved in the tales told by Luo women 'attempt to explain and account for male behaviour within male/female relationships'. According to Ayodo, the animals employed to represent the male protagonists are symbolically powerful. In many of the tales recorded by Ayodo, animals like the snake and the hyena are recurrent, and the latter, for example, 'is characterized by its voracious appetite, its odour, its powers of divination on occasion, the strength of its jaws, its naivety, lack of grooming, and cowardliness. In a pack it can be powerful; on its own it dare not show its face.'

In 'Jean-Baptiste Tati-Loutard: Death and Identity' (in Gurnah), Belinda Jack engages in critical dialogue with what she calls 'an important element in the dense fabric of Jean-Baptiste Tati-Loutard's writing: death'. As with many other African poets writing in French, Tati-Loutard's work, according to Gurnah (introduction to *Essays on African Writing 1*), 'has been foreshadowed by Leopold Sedar Senghor's capacity of functioning as the focus of attention on African poetry in French'. However, the salient features of Tati-Loutard's writing, according to Jack, include its coherence 'in terms of its social, political, and philosophical correlatives and its poetic coherence' amidst seemingly disparate elements and symbols such as the River Congo, water, the sea, movement, light and darkness, birds, dreams, slavery, time and history, legend, social and political concern, over which death holds a privileged position 'as a point of interchange among them'.

(d) Southern Africa

A paucity of 'ideologically-free space and societal positions', according to Michael Chapman, runs through the entire corpus of critical writing on the new South Africa, and by implication the Southern African region. For the second year running, apologies have to be tendered for the relative lack of space in the *YWES* to accommodate the explosion of writing on the new South Africa. The term 'free-fall', favoured by economists to describe a situation of utter chaos in the currency market, perhaps best summarizes what *Current Writing* (6.iii) experienced when it asked those academics still empowered in the academy, and their paradigmatic 'Other', still disempowered under the same dispensation, to contribute to power-broking antics under the general headline: 'democratizing culture'. Michael Chapman's brief but concise preface to the volume captures the prevailing critical attitudes: 'we continue to hear liberals berating Marxists and vice-versa, Africanists haranguing Eurocentrics and vice-versa, and – currently fashionable – creolised Afro-Westerners or Westernised Africanos lauding black Atlantic anti-romantics as a check on unfeeling economics: can the Rasta-man block the machinations of Anglo-American?'. During the year under review, *SAQ* dedicated a volume of essays to 'the writings of J. M. Coetzee'; *Matatu* 11's coverage was broader, extending to what it called 'Southern African Writing: Voyages and Explorations'; *RAL* (24.iv) contributed a 'Cluster on South African Writing'; and of course, *Current Writing* (6.ii) continued its excellent coverage, focusing on 'Democratising Culture'.

In '"My Turn, Now": Debunking the Gordimer Mystique in *My Son's Story*' (*RAL* 24.iv.105–16) Jorshinelle T. Sonza raises the spectre of the somewhat over-orchestrated division among critics in their evaluation of Nadine Gordimer as a woman writer. However, Sonza's essay also argues that 'the ambivalence or the mystique surrounding Gordimer's works is the appropriate response to the South African experience'. Critics who have constructed simple binary oppositions, according to Sonza, have forgotten that 'reconciling racial and gender conflicts is a complicated process that defies simplistic political solutions'. One of the primary themes of Sonza's essay concerns its identification of a major change that evolved over forty years in Gordimer's political and feminist outlook, as indicated in *My Son's Story*. It is here, for the first time, according to Sonza, that Gordimer valorizes the black woman's participation in the South African struggle by providing it with the centrality it deserves.

In 'Sharp Knowing in Apartheid?: The Shorter Fiction of Nadine Gordimer and Doris Lessing' (in Gurnah, *Essays on African Writing 1*) veteran ex-South African academic and critic Mark Kinkead-Weekes rouses another ghost: the tendency in certain quarters to pit Gordimer, in creative and political terms, against her Southern African contemporary, Doris Lessing. A profound irony, according to Sonza, can be observed in the odyssey of a writer who is dismissed as 'colonial' in certain quarters, and simultaneously holds the unflattering compliment of seeing her novels banned in her own country. Juxtaposed, the two extremes make Michael Chapman's summation of the prevailing critical milieu appear severely understated. Kinkead-Weekes re-examines all the superstructural and economic bases of the arguments for and against in the protracted debate. On the one hand, we are confronted with a writer who has always been 'safe', because she broke no law, and one whose reputation in the outer world was sufficient to protect her from brutal arrest and imprisonment without trial. On the other hand, our *feminine terrible* confronts us, seemingly uncompromising, one whose sense of political commitment came much earlier and more radically, though it took her abroad. Kinkead-Weekes's essay is morally and philosophically weighed and balanced, and therefore unflinching in its primary conclusion that:

> Between those who stayed in South Africa, believing that the work they could do would justify the privilege they could not afford; and those who went, believing that their best work lay outside, and unable to feel that attempting it on South African terms would justify the

> 'privilege' of remaining, there is no intrinsic moral superiority one way or the other.

In 'Nadine Gordimer, J. M. Coetzee and the Politics of Interpretation' (*SAQ* 93.i.11–32), Ian Glenn contends that within South Africa itself comparisons between Gordimer and Coetzee have become a staple of literary analysis. Such comparisons, according to Glenn, often draw on Gordimer's reaction to Coetzee, with a view to determining his political allegiances and commitment – what one might polemically call his 'political correctness'. 'The Writings of J. M. Coetzee', to which *SAQ* devotes a volume of essays during the year under review, have, in Glenn's view, 'overtaken Gordimer's work as the subject of academic analysis not only in South Africa, but in mainstream academic journals in the United States as well'. The challenge that Coetzee represents is clearly manifest on many fronts: as both critic and novelist, Coetzee threatens Gordimer's pre-eminence as realist novelist, and by implication the realist tradition at large. In 'A Bored Spinster with a Locked Diary: The Politics of Hysteria in *In the Heart of the Country*' (*RAL* 24.iv.33–49), Chiara Briganti articulates the manner in which Coetzee 'in fact, stretches the boundaries of realism' – on the one hand, by taking the stuff for the story from literature, and on the other, by creating a narrator who is able to find evidence only in her own writing. The heart of the matter reposes in what Ian Glenn has termed 'the politics of interpretation', and every essay in this special issue of the *SAQ* addresses different aspects of the protracted debate. In 'Silence and Mut(e)ilation: White Writing in J. M. Coetzee's *Foe*' (*SAQ* 93.i.111–29), for example, Richard Begam problematizes Coetzee's fabled preference for the 'aesthetics of deconstruction' as opposed to the 'politics of reconstruction', within a contemporary critical milieu that readily proclaims the former as a synonym for postmodernism, while the latter is often invested with metonymic properties in relation to post-colonialism.

Malawian poet and critic Frank M. Chipasula, in 'A Terrible Trajectory: The Impact of Apartheid, Prison and Exile on Dennis Brutus's Poetry' (in Gurnah, *Essays on African Writing 1*), remains undaunted in his conviction that the major casualty of this regime of extra-literary postulations is, ironically enough, literature itself. As a result of what Chipasula describes as this 'terrible trajectory', many who would have earned their worth and praise in other spheres have been projected into the literary and canonical limelight. Dennis Brutus, a veteran of the life-and-death battle against injustice, has, according to Chipasula, 'garnered rewards for an art that might not have attracted a stare had it been otherwise'. Chipasula submits further that without the dedicated and sympathetic grooming of a group of critics willing to suspend negative observations on the shortcomings of his work, the veteran poet and sports politician would not have found himself in print so effortlessly.

According to Ian Glenn, 'the debate on what the canon could or should be' is an essential component of the French-based, largely homogeneous and monolingual model contained in the work of Pierre Bourdieu. Presenting what amounts to a drastic summation of Bourdieu's argument, Glenn describes the literary field as the product of struggles for dominance. However, Geoffrey Davis's introduction to *Matatu*'s coverage, entitled 'South African Writing: Voyages and Explorations', proffers a critical and creative scenario in which every aspect of South African life has become the subject of intense debate, and one in which 'writers, artists and cultural workers are faced with the real possibility of creating a culture for a post-apartheid society'. Anne Fuchs's 'The Market Theatre: Drama for a New Society? Targeting the Spectator' (*Matatu* 11.13–24) reiterates a pertinent paradigm, and one which, according to Fuchs, demonstrates 'how recognition of diversity has become the hallmark of the Market Theatre's current view of what should constitute drama for a new society'. The quandary which Fuchs identifies at the end of the essay is not peculiar to the Market Theatre, but epitomizes the dilemma facing the entire critical and creative milieu in the new South Africa. Fuchs's open-ended conclusion encapsulates this basic dilemma: should the Market (and by implication all the other writers, artists and cultural workers) concentrate on its/their work at the laboratory, decentralize, give up its/their European-style theatre venue traditions, or should it/they serve the formation of the new black middle classes which are already taking their seats with their white peers in a conventional, first-world, *class*-segregated theatre audience?

Geoffrey Davies's 'From Soweto to Gorée: A South African Writer in Search of the African Heritage' (*Matatu* 11.25–37) does not contain a straightforward solution to the cultural dilemma highlighted above. On the contrary, Davies's essay problematizes further the quandary, articulated by Fuchs, by focusing on the odyssey of a South African writer in search of the African heritage, and on what are described as two of the more interesting publications of recent years on South African Literature. The first is entitled *Crossing Borders: Writers meet the ANC*; the second publication, *Spring is Rebellious*, according to Davies, 'documents the debate provoked by Albie Sach's – by now notorious – paper on "Preparing Ourselves for Freedom"'. While the second publication urges South Africans to forsake the notion that culture could be 'a weapon of struggle', the first, in the light of the views and opinion of one of the writers who met the ANC (a former exile, Baleka Kgotsitsile) advocates the need to create a new literature for South African children – a literature that emphasizes the African identity of South African, 'and one that sees it as a positive thing to be in Africa'. Matsemela Manaka's play *Gorée: The Spiritual Journey in Search of African Dance* springs from Manaka's visit to the West African state of Senegal, along with other South African artists such as Breytenbach, Miriam Tlali, Miriam Makeba and Johnny Clegg. The visit remains a clear testimony to the fact that, with the years of cultural isolation truly over and done with, the road is clear to erect the all-important dialogic imagination which South Africa badly needs to project itself into the twenty-first century, as the country/region abandons the manichean aesthetics foisted on it by decades of racial/cultural segregation and stagnation. The abiding theme of 'voyage', and a new-found freedom to explore – in short, to journey away from the erstwhile morbid direction of the apartheid state – is given critical attention in all the essays in this volume of *Matatu*. Thus, while Marcia Blumberg dwells on 'Women Journeying at the South African Margins: Athol Fugard's *The Road to Mecca*' (11.39–50); Rowland Smith focuses on 'The Voyage Out: Exile, Escape and Obligation in Nadine Gordimer's Fiction' (11.51–7); Rosemary J. Jolly's essay concentrates on the related theme of 'Voyages in the Novels of J. M. Coetzee' (11.61–70); and Helen Cooper's paper describes as 'Voyagers' (11.71–80) both the Nigerian Buchi Emecheta and her Southern African counterpart, Bessie Head.

Finally, the Study Guide to Shimmer Chimodya's *Harvest of Thorns* by Beverley Abrahams and Lesley Humphrey, as well as Pat Made's and Beverley Abrahams's Guide to Alex La Guma's *In the Fog of the Season's End* (both directed at literature students working for the O-level examination), though published in

1993, deserve mention here, most especially as they appear to offer appropriate responses to Baleka Kgotsitsile's call for a drive to create a new literature for South African children. The sociohistorical background to what used to be known as the federation of Rhodesia and Nyasaland which Chimodya's novel invokes; together with the many transformations which South Africa has witnessed since the inception of European colonization in 1652, culminating in the pseudo-democratic dispensation that brought the National Party to power for the first time in 1924, as well as the rapid transformation of the socioeconomic and political landscape into a full-blown apartheid state by the same party in 1948 – all of which reiterate the essential background to La Guma's novel – are adequately covered by the authors of the Study Guides as moments to be firmly ingrained in the social and cultural psyche of South African youths, on all sides of the racial divide.

2. Australia

(a) General

The 1993 essay for this section attempted to summarize the climate of ideas, and the institutional circumstances, in which studies were appearing. Many were seen as sharing an impulse to revise previous accounts and understandings of 'Australian Literature' by engaging with issues of race, ethnicity, gender and regionalism. While the influence of 'Theory' could readily be perceived, these issues are not only of theoretical, or academic, interest but have their correspondences with national (and post-colonial) political concerns. The tendency discerned was for literary studies to participate in wider, and multidisciplinary, Australian studies. This tendency continues, with literature providing a focus for revised understandings, or deconstructions, of 'Australia' past and present.

This year the major scholarly publication might have been expected to be the second, revised and expanded, edition of *The Oxford Companion to Australian Literature*, eds William H. Wilde, Joy Hooton and Barry Andrews. Unfortunately, 'revised' is to be understood primarily in an historiographical sense, in the new edition's recognition of 'the greater influence and volume of women's and multicultural writing', rather than in any scholarly sense (as will become clearer below). The first edition in 1985 departed from OUPAus's corresponding volumes for English and American literatures by providing – in addition to *information* on authors, titles, famous characters, literary institutions, common allusions, etc., arranged alphabetically on the dictionary principle – extended entries that further organized some texts into fields of *knowledge* on the principle of the encyclopaedia or handbook. Thus, while in Hart's *Companion to American Literature*, 'Blacks' is a paragraph-length entry only (but numerous black authors have their own entries), the Australian equivalent now has fifteen pages in succession on Aboriginal subjects: 'Aborigine in Australian Literature', 'Aboriginal Song and Narrative in Translation' and 'Aboriginal Writing/Testimony in English'. To essays on 'Feminism and Australian Literature', 'Science Fiction' and 'War Literature', all updated, have been added 'Crime Fiction' and 'Immigrant Experience in Australian Literature'. 'Shakespeare in Australian Literature' occupies slightly more space than 'Shakespeare' in Margaret Drabble's English *Companion*. However, this urge to categorize and organize Australian literature into fields of institutionally sanctioned knowledge (with the contemporary agenda governed by 'difference' of all kinds) is indulged inconsistently. Inconsistent encyclopaedism should be a contradiction in terms; but we find, for example, an entry on the 'Turf' in literature though none on 'Politics' or 'Religion'. And, given the dutiful representation of minorities, it seems even odder that still the only Gay is William (1865–97), especially as lesbian writing is explicitly acknowledged in numerous entries, and in 1993 Oxford itself published Robert Dessaix's *An Anthology of Australian Gay and Lesbian Writing*.

Intrinsically valuable as these survey essays can be, increasing their number, and length, while at the same time attempting to accommodate new knowledge of the past, the continuing careers of contemporaries included in the first edition, and the many who have come into prominence since it appeared, has forced a reduction in the random particles of literary information trapped according to the dictionary principle. Some useful, if miscellaneous, information which made the first edition more a 'stand-alone' ready reference has been omitted, together with many of what – for a *Companion* rather than an encyclopaedia or a handbook – are the all-important cross-headings for titles and characters; and some of the cross-references carried over from the first edition no longer relate to the revised entries. One resort in an attempt to fit around five hundred new entries into only seventy-seven more pages is to direct readers to *The Oxford Companion to Australian Children's Literature*, with page references provided. If this principle had been followed consistently readers could similarly have been sent off to other Oxford publications, including their *Companion to Australian Folklore*, *Companion to Australian Sport*, *Concise Oxford Dictionary of Australian History* and *Literary Guide to Australia*. Incidentally, place-names are highly inconsistent: 'Adelaide' has been replaced by 'Adelaide, Debra'; Brisbane and Hobart have disappeared, as has 'New South Wales' (but 'Victoria' and 'Perth' survive). Lawson's Eurunderee is still in, although no township remains there, but his ambivalently remembered Gulgong (the town that used to be on the ten-dollar bill) has been replaced by 'Gunew, Sneja'. Similarly with political figures: John Curtin, prime minister during World War II and the subject of numerous writings, has been replaced by social historian Ann Curthoys; but the entry on Anglophile post-war prime minister R. G. Menzies has been expanded.

Given the always relentless restrictions on space which editors ritualistically appeal to in anticipation of criticisms (though these editors now have not many fewer pages than Drabble or Hart), the repetitiveness and prolixity of many entries are puzzling. To update 'Criticism', one of the survey essays, the contributor concentrates on feminist theory (most of his examples having little to do with the *Companion*'s basic understanding still of 'literature' as poetry, fiction and drama), and repeats much the same information as appears, more appropriately and informedly, in 'Feminism and Australian Literature'. The well-considered author entry on Patrick White deals with each of his novels, which also have their own extended title entries. Peter Carey's fiction too is well covered in his author entry, but his only novel to receive a title entry is *Bliss* (not the Booker-Prize-winning *Oscar and Lucinda*), because this has been carried over from the first edition when it *was* Carey's only novel. Many of the new entries suffer from a lack of proportion – and, indeed, patent puffery. These are not all new writers. Editor Joy Hooton's researches into autobiographies have no doubt contributed to the many new authors from the past included in this edition, though some of them wrote only their autobiographies; see 'Mann, Dame Ida' as an instance of the most marginal 'literary' interest. With new entries on contemporary authors, the language is too often that of publishers' blurbs, or a friend's euphemistically enthused review – or (see preface) could it be the writer's own? The inconsistency in content and style between the crisp biographical and bibliographical entries that, fortunately, most receive and the soggy puffs bestowed on others is dismaying. Some writers, it seems, are 'distinguished', make 'important contributions to the Australian literary scene' or are in other ways 'significant' – a word which, by dint of repetition, fails to signify and becomes mere cant. Vincent Buckley's *Cutting Green Hay* is 'absorbing', 'fascinating'; Gary Catalano has a reputation as 'one of Australia's finest prose writers'. This is not the austerely factual style expected in a *Companion*; nor do we expect such padding as a list of one writer's unpublished plays, 'some of which have been performed' (p. 438). On the other hand, describing the university magazine *Hermes* as 'populist' could simply be excused as a failure to check the OED. Spelling, also, could have been checked: Don'o Kim appears as 'Kim, D'Ono'.

The flyleaf claims each entry retained from the first edition has been re-examined as well as revised and expanded if necessary. One wonders, though, what the entries have been checked against when one finds the same mistakes faithfully retained from the first edition (in the essay on 'Criticism': 'Craft' for 'Craftsmanship' in the titles of A. A. Phillips's essays on Lawson and Furphy) and when the description of Donald Horne's *The Education of Young Donald* no longer relates to the current *revised* edition of this work. The revision of Bernard Smith's entry unaccountably omits his *Noel Counihan* (1993), a work of considerable literary interest because of the painter's friendships with writers, and also a work published by Oxford. The entry 'Australian Literature to 1900: A Guide to Information Sources', which refers to bibliographies published in the United States, is carried over from the first edition unrevised but could appropriately have accommodated mention of Robert Ross's *Australian Literary Criticism 1945–1988: An Annotated Bibliography* (1989). While other entries are impressively up to date, even including works published this year, they are not always accurate: Andrew Riemer's monograph on Peter Goldsworthy appeared in 1994 not 1993.

The editors' policy is to omit contemporary critics, scholars and biographers unless they are also creative writers or have been around for a 'significant' period; unfortunately, the example they give for the latter is A. A. Phillips, who died the year the first edition appeared. Contradictorily, by observing this principle in the case of literary scholars but at the same time 'taking a broad definition of "author" [. . .] and "literary work"' to include historians and social commentators, the editors have dug a very large hole into which to bulldoze the many on whose work a compilation like this depends. Thus we find the convener of women's studies at the Australian National University, who has written 'a study of the historical construction of femininity in twentieth-century Australia', is in (and, if space allowed, why not?), but the professor of English at the Australian Defence Forces Academy, the editors' own institution, is not – even though he has thirteen authored or co-authored titles on Australian literature in the current *Australian Books in Print*, including the biography of Peter Porter (also published by OUP). With many others, he is filed away under the subject of his biography rather than being considered a true author – like those who have penned their autobiographies or unpublished and unperformed plays. No doubt this edition, like its predecessor, will be found to be 'indispensable' over its allotted span; it certainly reflects, in its dutiful filling and balancing of quotas, today's institutionally desiderated 'consensual' perception of Australian literature. One can only hope that the mistakes and misconceptions incurred in the pursuit of this higher editorial aim will not be legitimized in the minds of users who might innocently consult it for information – rather than for the opinions it seeks to promulgate.

Australian Civilization, ed. Richard Nile, deliberately has the same title as the often-quoted collection of essays edited by Peter Coleman thirty years ago, and the same 'stock-taking' purpose. Of direct literary interest are John Barnes's chapter 'Legend', Bruce Bennett's 'Myth' and Andrew Milner's 'Culture'. Each shows how the 'narratives' that circulate today differ from those presented in Coleman's collection. Milner traces the reception of 'Theory' in Australia and provocatively questions the crucial post-colonial assumption that colonies were 'Other' to Europe: he contends that instead they were 'Self', 'imagined precisely as overseas extensions of Europe', and for critics today to imagine otherwise is to reinscribe a discredited 'radical nationalism' by detecting post-colonial 'subversion' everywhere. Internationally, post-colonial criticism continues to be a growth area, in which Australian writing and commentary are prominent. *De-Scribing Empire: Post-Colonialism and Textuality* edited by Chris Tiffin and Alan Lawson includes Simon Ryan's 'Inscribing the Emptiness: Cartography, Exploration and the Construction of Australia', an historical overview of the processes of mapping and naming the continent. (Ryan's 'Voyeurs in Space: The Gendered Scopic Regime of Exploration' appears in *Southerly* [54.i.36–49], his 'The Aborigines in Journals of Australian Exploration' in *ArielE* [25.iii.95–112], and his 'Discovering Myths: the Creation of the Explorer in Journals of Exploration' in the special 'focus on exploration issue' of *ACS* [12.ii.1–13].) Robert Dixon contributes 'The Unfinished Commonwealth: Boundaries of Civility in Popular Australian Fiction of the first Commonwealth decade', which argues that such 'ripping yarns' as Alexander MacDonald's *The Island Traders*, Ambrose Pratt's 'invasion' narrative *The Big Five*, and Louis Becke's *The Pearl Divers of Roncador Reef* 'centre the nation by narrating it from the limits of territoriality and civility'. (With Phillipa Kelly, Dixon also contributes '"Meaningless Chatter": Hybridisation in Two North Queensland Texts' to *JAS* [41.79–87].) Helen Gilbert's 'Describing Orality' discusses 'Carnival' and the hybridization of language in Aboriginal performance texts. Other Australian contributions to *De-Scribing Empire* will be discussed under individual authors below. *'Return' in Post-Colonial Writing*, ed. Vera Mihailovich-Dickman, includes Gay Raines's '"Return" in Australian Fiction' – an imaginative thematic reading of White's *A Fringe of Leaves*, Mudrooroo's *Wild Cat Falling* and *Doin Wildcat*, and Moorhouse's *Forty-Seventeen* – and David Coad's 'Platonic Return in Patrick White's *The Eye of the Storm*' (referred to below under individual authors). *Recasting the World: Writing After Colonialism* (1993), edited by Jonathan White, contains passing references to a number of Australian writers as well as essays focused on Carey and Malouf (also referred to below; and see section 5(b) below).

Two locally published general collections of essays touch at a number of points on the problematics of reading in a relativized 'postmodern' world: *Tilting at Matilda: Literature, Aborigines, Women and the Church in Contemporary Australia*, dedicated to Veronica Brady and edited by Dennis Haskell, and *Identifying Australia in Postmodern Times*, edited by L. A. C. Dobrez and Bill Ashcroft. While specifically literary contributions to these will be referred to below, both collections are of topical interest for presenting coincidences among what would otherwise seem heterogenous concerns. Historian David Goodman's essay 'Australian Identity, Postmodernism and History' in the Dobrez collection ends with a set of questions – about how much longer we can go on negatively deconstructing the past without beginning to reconstruct it rewardingly in relation to the present – which are relevant also to literary history, or simply the reading of earlier literature. Coincidentally, Michael Ackland's *That Shining Band: A Study of Australian Colonial Verse Tradition* provides an example of how Goodman's 'new, pluralised imagination', informed by feminism, multiculturalism and post-colonial theory, can engage empathetically with the past. Ackland has established himself as this generation's foremost published scholar on colonial poetry, and *That Shining Band* reworks and interrelates essays which he has published over a decade or more to offer a re-reading of colonial literary culture. Ackland locates the emergence of the indigenous poetic tradition in the 'dialogue' he discerns between poets, especially with Kendall's 'rewriting' of Harpur. Most previous commentators, he claims, have read the individual poets in isolation. Seen together, and in their contexts, a different understanding of tradition becomes available. Yet, while steeped in those historic contexts, Ackland is also writing consciously within the postmodern ideological context. Important to his 'study of colonial verse tradition' are women who wrote against or uneasily within 'the male-prescribed, thematic canon and code of acceptable female poetic practice'. These include Mary Hannay Foott, Emily Manning and Emma Anderson; and Ada Cambridge and Catherine Martin are the subjects of separate chapters. (Ackland discusses colonial women's poetry further in 'The Iphigenia Complex: Repression and Empowerment in Australian Colonial Women's Verse' [*Westerly* 39.ii.17–31] and '"Wrecked Through All Eternity": Faith and Gender Issues in Catherine Martin's *The Explorers and Other Poems*' [*Southerly* 53.ii.149–68].) *That Shining Band* is not structured around a single argument; instead it offers many arguments, or opens up many different interpretative possibilities, as it follows its essayistic course. But Ackland's revisionist claim that most other literary scholars are still 'focussed on balladists of the 1890s as the first major expression of national identity' is exaggerated and ignores at least a generation of attempted recuperation by others.

The persistence of tropes and topoi from the colonial period to the present is discussed in a number of essays. Elizabeth Webby's 'The Grave in the Bush' (in Haskell, *Tilting at Matilda*) argues that this recurring image in literature and painting usually functions as an indicator of ownership of the land, or the desire to legitimate occupancy. Noel Macainsh's '"Ah, to be by Mooni now": History and Melancholy in Early Australian Poetry' in Manfred Jurgensen, ed., *Riding Out: New Writing from Around the World*, a literary yearbook (formerly *Outrider*), traces through, and beyond, Murdoch's *Oxford Book of Australasian Verse* (1918) and Perceval Serle's *An Australasian Anthology* (1927) a persistent note of regret that the promises of history have not been fulfilled. David Carter's 'Modernity and Belatedness in Australian Critical Discourse' (*Southerly* 54.iv.6–18) finds, from Marcus Clarke on, a proclivity among cultural critics to discover 'the possibility of a radical originality in the peripheral [colonial] culture in which the very absence of history makes modernity our own'; 'a kind of primitive, originary postmodern, scarcely conscious of itself – indeed requiring European/North American postmodernism to name and know itself'. Horst Priessnitz's 'Dreams in Austerica: A Preliminary Comparison of the Australian and the American Dream' (*Westerly* 39.iii.45–64) ranges over an even longer time-span and contains some unfamiliar references. Also bridging the centuries is Ros Pesman's 'Some Australian Italies' (*Westerly* 39.iv.95–104), an engaging, anecdotal account of visitors' responses to Italy. Colonial writing is represented in the special 'Australian Writing Today' issue of *CS* by Lucy Frost's discussion of Barbara Baynton and Annie Baxter

Dawbin, 'A Shape to Suit Desire: Re(Reading) Nineteenth-Century Australia' (6.i.14–19). While the literary is only one of multiple historical interests in *Pioneering Culture: Mechanics Institutes and Schools of Art in Australia*, eds Philip C. Candy and John Laurent, the nineteen contributions contain much in passing that adds to an understanding of the cultural milieu for many earlier writers, particularly Elizabeth Webby's chapter on the early institutes and John Laurent's on how Australian institutes departed from the UK model by being most influential in rural areas.

General studies specifically related to the earlier twentieth century include two fiercely feminist revisionist essays. Donna Coates's 'The Digger on the Lofty Pedestal: Australian Women's Fiction of the Great War' (*ANZSC* 10.1–22) takes issue with Robin Gerster for leaving women writers out of *Big Noting*, his account of Great War literature; however, her own survey of women writers who adopted the 'bushman into Anzac' myth leads but to the sorry conclusion that their 'intense and cloying adulation of the Anzac' only shows 'how easy it was for the bastards to win the homefront war'. Joy Hooton's 'Australian National Identity and Self-Identity: Four Post-Colonial Autobiographies' (in Dobrez and Ashcroft, *Identifying Australia in Postmodern Times*) discusses Arthur Lynch's *My Life Story* (1924), Lionel Lindsay's *Comedy of Life* (1961), Randolph Bedford's *Naught to Thirty-Three* (1944) and George McIver's *A Drover's Odyssey* (1934). She reads the first three autobiographies as quintessentially (Russel) 'Wardian' exemplars of the masculinist 'national legend', but finds the obscure last redeemed by its contrastingly positive attitudes to women and Aborigines. As was noted last year, the reviled 'legend' is still capable of returning to haunt revisionists, even in these pluralized 'postmodern' times. Also in *Identifying Australia in Postmodern Times* is Ivor Indyk's 'On "the Land" as a Relative Absolute', which discusses the depiction of landscape by novelists of the thirties and later – Palmer, Prichard, Davison, Herbert, Dark, Barnard Eldershaw, Tennant – and argues that what might seem a return to an earlier tradition by way of nostalgia for 'the pioneering condition', or anticipation of a glorious future, was instead a means of testing social values during the contestation of ideologies that preceded the World War II and the subsequent Cold War. *Wallflowers and Witches: Women and Culture in Australia 1910–1945*, ed. Maryanne Dever, contains both general essays (which also refer to a number of the writers Indyk discusses) and studies of individual authors that will be noted below; the collection as a whole is welcome for its rethinking of 'some of the fundamental conceptual models to analyse women's relationships to cultural production' (painting as well as writing) and its interrogation of sweepingly simplistic assumptions of 'patriarchal' suppression.

Among general studies in the contemporary period, Graham Huggan's *Territorial Disputes: Maps and Mapping Strategies in Contemporary Canadian and Australian Fiction* is of more than usual interest (see also section 3(b) below). Lucidly and through constant illustration he argues not only that the topos of the map is 'a mainstay' of Australian and Canadian writers but also that it functions metaphorically as a means of tracing the heterodoxies of 'two post-colonial societies in a state of flux, transition and [productive] dispute'. These 'heterodoxies' include the indigenous, the ethnic, the feminine and the regional, and these diverse conceptions of territoriality 'have clearly been used to undermine or remodel the "standard" representations of patriarchal and nationalist discourses'. Australian writers discussed include Thea Astley, Murray Bail, Marion Campbell, Peter Carey, Helen Garner, Rodney Hall, Nicholas Hasluck, Christopher Koch,

Mudrooroo, Gerald Murnane, David Malouf and Patrick White. Given that cartography as a trope for a range of current preoccupations is apparent in numerous other studies this year – among them, David Callahan's 'The Narcissism of Distance – Australia and the Rhetoric of Extension of Distance' and Patrick Morgan's 'Australian Literature Through Time and Place' (*Antipodes* 8.101–4 and 115–19 respectively) – Huggan's sustainedly insightful study seems set to be cited frequently. It would be unfortunate, though, if such citation lent authority to his uncritical acceptance of the contention that Australian literary discourse remained repressively 'patriarchal' until the advent of our own brave new world (a glance at H. M. Green's *History*, published during the height of 'radical nationalist' fervour, should indicate the dubiousness of this contemporary myth). Essays on White and Malouf, and on the poetry of Les A. Murray and Rosemary Dobson, are included in Veronica Brady's collection *Caught in the Draught*. The subtitle of the *Tilting at Matilda* collection dedicated to Brady, *Literature, Aborigines, Women and the Church in Contemporary Australia*, suggests the range of her cultural and social concerns, concerns which intrude on the ostensibly literary essays here and make them read more like sermons than studies.

Sneja Gunew's *Framing Marginality* in UMel's Interpretations series is a concise account of post-structuralist theorizing of Australian 'multicultural', 'ethnic' or 'migrant' writing by its most influential and prolific proponent, and includes discussion of works by Antigone Kefala, Ania Walwicz, Rosa Cappiello and Anna Couani. A more critical consideration of multicultural literary theorizing is provided by David Carter's 'The Outsider with Inside Knowledge?: Migrant Writing, Assimilationism and Recent Theory' in *Australia in the World: Perceptions and Possibilities*, papers from the Outside Images of Australia Conference, Perth 1992, eds Don Grant and Graham Seal. Carter deconstructively queries and complicates some of the now-conventional pieties of multiculturalism by employing novelist Judah Waten as a test case. Annette Robyn Corkhill makes constant reference to Gunew and other theorists in her *Australian Writing: Ethnic Writers 1945–1991*, but her concerns are primarily literary historical and she presents a valuable analysis of developments (official policy and authors' manifestos) and a comprehensive account of key figures and their works since World War II. Susan Ballyn provides English readers with her necessarily more cursory survey of migrant writing, 'The Voice of the Other', in the special Australian issue of *CS* (6.i.91–7); other general essays in this issue include Geoff Page's 'Loaded Canons: Australian Poetry Anthologies' (20–7); Dennis Haskell's 'Iambic Pentameters and the Platypus Duck: Trends and Traditions in Contemporary Australian Poetry' (28–42); David Gilbey's 'The Dance of Metaphors: Notes on Some New Australian Poems' (43–52); and Michael Wilding's 'The Modern Australian Short Story' (112–13), which amplifies his observations on this period in his introduction to *The Oxford Book of Australian Short Stories*. That introduction and his selection of fifty stories, from Marcus Clarke to Tim Winton, are intended to counter various kinds of exclusiveness in previous anthologies. Kevin Hart's *The Oxford Book of Australian Religious Verse* similarly entails a fresh appraisal of tradition and a number of individual reputations. Another well-introduced and well-selected anthology is Laurie Hergenhan and Irmtraud Petersson's *Changing Places: Australian Writers in Europe 1960s–1990s*. The only general monograph on drama this year is *Converging Realities: Feminism in Australian Theatre* by Peta Tait, with contributions from five collaborators – a not obviously coherent attempt to marry abstract theorizing with performance studies of fringe productions. Richard Nile's 'Cartels, Capitalism and the Australian Book Trade' in *Commonwealth Literary Cultures* (1993), papers from the 1990 European Association for Commonwealth Literature and Language Studies conference (eds Giovanna Capone, Claudio Gorlier and Bernard Hickey), is a substantial historical study of its subject to the near present.

Serial bibliographies remain the same as in recent years: the monthly and annually cumulated *Australian National Bibliography*, Thorpe's bi-monthly *Guide to New Australian Books*, the annual *ALS* bibliography of studies in Australian literature, the *JCL* bibliography for Australia and New Guinea (xxiv.13) which amalgamates 1992 and 1993, and *Antipodes*' annual bibliography of Australian literature and criticism published in North America. Not seen are John Loder's *Australian Crime Fiction: A Bibliography 1857–1993*, published by Thorpe in association with the National Centre for Australian Studies, Monash, and Toby Burrows 'Australian Comics and Comic Strips: An Introductory Bibliography' in Tony Burrows and Grant Stone (eds), *Comics in Australia and New Zealand: The Collections, the Collectors; the Creators* (Haworth, New York).

(b) Individual Authors to 1920

Three biographies of women fiction writers whose international reputations overlapped provide interesting detail over a wide span of literary-cultural history. In *Tasma: The Life of Jessie Couvreur*, Patricia Clarke proudly presents the results of her assiduous researches into the life (1848–97) and career of the writer who became a celebrated lecturer on Australasia in France and Belgium and a correspondent for the London *Times*. The biographer's accounts of her genealogical discoveries frequently delay the telling of a good story, but her scholarly thoroughness is seen to advantage when she cautiously suggests how gaps in the subject's personal and emotional record might be filled by imaginatively interpretating themes in her fiction. (Couvreur's public persona as 'Tasma' and her novel *The Penance of Portia James* [1891] are the subject of Fiona Giles's '"The Softest Disorder": Representing Cultural Indeterminancy', a discussion of constructions of post-colonial female subjectivity [in Tiffin and Lawson, *De-Scribing Empire*]). Ethel Turner (1870–1958) was a generation younger, yet only five years separated the publication of her *Seven Little Australians* (1894) from that of 'Tasma''s *Uncle Piper of Piper's Hill* (1889), their best-remembered novels. Whereas Clarke had only some of 'Tasma''s diaries to draw on, A. T. Yarwood had his subject's already published diaries, as well as other extensive records, available for his *From a Chair in the Sun: The Life of Ethel Turner*, and consequently, his is a more seamless integration of life and career. Turner's aspirations to break away from English and American models of children's fiction and to celebrate a distinctive Australian character is the focus of Ron Shepherd's 'Larrikinism and Ethel Turner's Fiction: The Sand-Patch and the Garden' (in Haskell, *Tilting at Matilda*), which finds that the celebration turns out to be markedly ambivalent. Also well researched and of literary historical interest is Alison Alexander's *A Mortal Flame: Marie Bjelke Petersen: Australian Romance Writer 1874–1969*. Her subject published nine novels with Australian settings in London and New York between 1917 and 1937, and was at that time one of the country's most successful authors. Two other biographies of prominent women have literary connections: Brenda Niall's *Georgiana: A Biography of Georgiana McCrae, Painter, Diarist, Pioneer*, and Judith A. Allen's *Rose Scott: Vision and Revision in Feminism*. McCrae (1804–90) was the grandmother of poet Hugh McCrae, who edited and published her 1840s

Melbourne journals, and Scott (1847–1925) was a pioneering suffragette who numbered many of Sydney's literati among her wide circle of influential acquaintances.

The earliest writings from Australia, Watkin Tench's chronicles of settlement in New South Wales, published in London in 1789 and 1793, are contextualized within eighteenth-century European culture by Adrian Mitchell in the 'Solving History's Problems' issue of *ANZSC* (11.23–33). The title, 'Watkin Tench's Sentimental Enclosures: Original Reactions from the First Settlement', alludes to the educated Marine captain's disappointed Enlightenment expectations of a new world. Mitchell's perceptive re-reading of these familiar texts is refreshingly free of post-colonial jargon (he even manages to avoid the word altogether). Other early writers discussed this year are two convict poets, in Ian Syson's 'John Grant: Australia's First *Really* Radical Poet' (*ALS* 16.297–311) and Veronica Brady's 'The Innocent Gaze: John Boyle O'Reilly's "The King of Vases"' (*Kunapipi* 16.iii.1–6), the latter referring to a seven-hundred-line poem about first encounters between whites and Aborigines in Western Australia. Judith Johnston's '"Woman's Testimony": Imperialist Discourse in the Professional Colonial Travel Writing of Louisa Ann Meredith and Catherine Parr Traill' (*ANZSC* 11.34–55) pursues parallels between Meredith's *Notes and Sketches of New South Wales* (1844) and *My Home in Tasmania* and Traill's contemporaneous accounts of colonization in Canada. Published by Mulini Press in 1993, but not seen, are two reprints of works by John Lang, the first native-born novelist: the short stories *Botany Bay: Or, True Tales of Early Australia* (1859) and the verse tales *The Rose Garden: Translation from the Persian of Sadi of Shiraz* (1845).

Anne Allingham's 'Challenging the Editing of the Rachel Henning Letters' (*ALS* 16.262–79) moves beyond detailing deficiencies in editions of Henning's mid-nineteenth-century letters (first published in 1952) to a sweeping attack on the poor standards for editing documents prevailing in Australian publishing. While the attack is well supported by instances and comparisons with UK and US practice, it is not made clear whether scholars or publishers' editors have been responsible for the deficiencies. In 'Representing Failure: Gender and Madness in Henry Kingsley's *The Hillyers and the Burtons*' (*AUMLA* 82.35–48), Christopher Lee interprets Kingsley's colonial immigrant novel, usually dismissed for its 'failure of aesthetic form', as a cultural document revealing contradictory mid-Victorian preoccupations. Bernice McPherson's 'Colonial Feminine Ideal: Feminity and Representation' (*JAS* 42.5–17) discusses photographic images and short stories by Ada Cambridge and Ethel Catilla (who published *An Australian Girl and Other Verses* in 1900). McPherson sees the ideals of womanhood circulating in colonial society and adapted to Australian nationalism as being derived from English models but, curiously, makes no mention of the perhaps more pertinent American models prevalent at that time. After his omission from last year's *The Penguin Book of 19th Century Australian Literature*, ed. Michael Ackland (*YWES* 74.624–5), it is gratifying to find Furphy has not been completely supplanted by Ada Cambridge. María Suárez-Lafuente's 'The Creative Gaze on Life Manifold: Furphy and Cervantes' (in Haskell, *Tilting at Matilda*) offers a brief, broad but suggestive comparison of *Such is Life* and *Don Quixote*; and in the special two-volume issue of *SPAN*, Manfred Mackenzie's '"The Mighty Pipe Smoking Me": Imposture in *Such is Life*' (36.533–40) suggests imposture offers a paradigm for the post-colonial as well as the colonial writer's attempts to reconcile the demotic with the European literary tradition. Mackenzie's post-colonial instance is White's

The Solid Mandala, and his discussion of both novels as he outlines his general hypothesis is most stimulating.

Barbara Holloway's 'White Steps on the Way to the International Year of Indigenous People: The Difficulties and Lines of Flight of Mary Gilmore' (*SPAN* 37[1993].93–107) is an historically informed contextualizing of Gilmore's verse which reveals the strategies she adopted in seeking to include the Aborigines in 'the nation', and the ideological binds these involved. Christopher Lee's 'The Emasculation of Henry Lawson' (*Meridian* 13.3–14) focuses on A. G. Stephens's criticism of this author to trace a more general shift from the initial hailing of the young Lawson as the representative Australian realist to disappointment with his later, more subjective, and therefore 'feminine' writing, and to consider this critical shift as expressive of a decline in national, or masculine, confidence during this period. It is a bold argument, persuasive on Stephens's attitudes to Lawson but recklessly speculative in generalizing beyond them. While there was personal antagonism between Stephens and Lawson (not considered by Lee), the literary editor had among his protégés John Shaw Neilson, who could equally have been considered 'feminine' in accordance with the period's gender stereotypes. In '"The Green Singer": Neilson's Pastoral Poetry' (*Southerly* 54.ii.82–96) Carmel Gaffney argues that Neilson's contribution to the local adaptation of the pastoral tradition has not been adequately recognized, and that the duality his verse conveys is as much part of the ancient pastoral tradition as the moments of transcendence it expresses on occasions. Nan Bowman-Albinski's 'Helena Sumner Locke – Careful! She Might Hear You' (*Antipodes* 8.47–53) provides a profile of the life, fiction, plays and verse of the writer now best remembered as the mother of novelist Sumner Locke-Elliott.

(c) Individual Authors since 1920

Two autobiographies of considerable literary-cultural interest are Geoffrey Dutton's *Out in the Open* and Peter Coleman's *Memoirs of a Slow Learner*. Dutton, poet, novelist, biographer, critic of art as well as literature, and a prolific editor of others' writings, has been an influential figure for over three decades, and his autobiography is rich in details of his contacts with artists and writers throughout the world (and his long friendship with Patrick White). In his considerably shorter memoirs, Coleman, editor of the original *Australian Civilization*, and a former editor of the *Bulletin* and *Quadrant*, provides a participant's account of the 'culture wars' of the 1950s and 1960s. These enter large into Dorothy Hewett's autobiography, discussed by Joan Newman in 'Dealing it Out: Dorothy Hewett's *Wild Card*' (*CS* 6.i.133–9). Unseen is a consideration of other autobiographies that encompass this period: Joy Hooton's 'Australian Autobiography and the Question of National Identity: Patrick White, Barry Humphries and Manning Clark' (*ABSt* 9.i.43–63). In 'Parents, Crisis and Education: Jill Ker Conway's *The Road from Coorain*' (*ANZSC* 11.91–102) David McCooey compares and contrasts this autobiography with some of the great late nineteenth-century examples by males, and concludes that Conway's demonstrates how 'a crisis with a parent can be related to the autobiographical impulse, and how such stories are linked by a sense of guilt and the importance of education as a response to guilt'.

The major edition for the year is Dennis Haskell and Geoffrey Dutton's *Kenneth Slessor: Collected Poems*. The editors claim that theirs is only the second documented and annotated collection of an Australian poet's work, the first being Colin Roderick's of Lawson (though this overlooks the fact that Roderick's is a variorum edition). However, if this is their way of making the point that there is the need for more scholarly editions of such widely prescribed texts as Slessor's poems (or Rachel Henning's letters), it would be one eagerly agreed with by scholars, though less enthusiastically by publishers. Unfortunately, the annotations which distinguish this edition – most of the previously uncollected verse is light and occasional – are not keyed to the pages on which the poems appear: a considerable inconvenience in a volume of 327 pages of verse and 144 of annotation, which could have been overcome by following the common practice of making the running head 'Notes' indicate the preceding pages to which the notes beneath refer. An indication of Slessor's continuing representation on syllabuses as a 'modern', if not indeed a 'modernist', is his being the first discussed in Noel Rowe's *Modern Australian Poets* in OUPAus's Horizon series for senior secondary school students; the other prescribed poets Rowe discusses in an unpretentious but theoretically aware way are Rosemary Dobson, Bruce Dawe, John Tranter and Lee Cataldi. In the light of the *oeuvre* Haskell and Dutton have collected, Slessor's reputation as a 'modern' begins to look in need of some qualification.

Stephanie Trigg's *Gwen Harwood* is not as stylish as previous contributions to OUPAus's Australian Writers series. Her agonizing over what can be said about texts these days seems less theoretical sophistication than a failure of confidence, and it is doubtful if Harwood enthusiasts will find it any advance on other recent book-length studies, such as Jennifer Strauss's *Boundary Conditions* (1992). Strauss provides an elegant introduction to this recently deceased poet's work with 'Playing in Time: The Poetry of Gwen Harwood' (*CS* 6.i.81–7). Gary Catalano's 'The Figure in the Doorway' (*Quadrant* 38.x.28–32) discusses the relationship between poetry and painting in Rosemary Dobson's imagination.

In UQP's Australian Authors series, *Christina Stead: Selected Fiction and Non-Fiction*, expertly edited by R. G. Geering and A. Segerberg, includes the novella 'The Puzzleheaded Girl', multiple extracts from *Seven Poor Men of Sydney*, *For Love Alone* and *The Man Who Loved Children*, and a selection of her short fiction, unpublished prose, book reviews, interviews and letters. Jennifer Gribble's *Christina Stead* appears in OUPAus's Australian Writers series of critical monographs. She confronts the formidable task of offering some fresh observations on such an extensive, and by now intensively discussed, *oeuvre*, by drawing attention to Stead's foregrounding, from her first book *The Salzburg Tales* to the posthumous *I'm Dying Laughing*, of 'the revelatory importance of stories, how they tell themselves through people, what they tell us about the tellers and their beliefs and cultures'. This approach, influenced by Bakhtin's 'dialogic' narratology, proves most effective for discussing Stead's narrative inventiveness simultaneously with her concerns for those cultural formations – power, politics, class and, not least, gender – that have most often preoccupied recent commentators. Coincidentally, Susan Lever in '"The Night of Which No One Speaks": Christina Stead's Art as Struggle' (*SPAN* 37[1993].108–19) also sees Stead's characters in *The Man Who Loved Children*, *Cotters' England* and *I'm Dying Laughing* as story-tellers, 'structuring their experiences into narratives which provide their lives with meaning', and sees the kinds of experience they share as eluding 'any programmatic solution to human political problems, whether Marxist or feminist'. However, after apparently having thrown ideology out the front window, Lever allows it to re-enter through the back door by seeing Stead's 'formal disruption' as her way of subverting the 'phallogocentric', of being unprogrammatically feminist. With their overlapping interests in narrative *and* ideology, both these studies should stimulate fresh feminist readings of Stead's avowedly non-feminist work. In the special 'Australian Writing

Today' issue of *CS* (6.i.118–24), Ann Blake's 'Ocean of Story' provides an introductory overview of Stead's novels, appropriately drawing English readers' attention to *Cotters' England*, which Blake also writes on in 'Christina Stead's Tyneside Novel' (*DUJ* 86.271–9). Not available for review was Brooke Allen's '"A Real Inferno": The World of Christina Stead' *NCrit* (13.ii.23–32).

Stead's first books were published in the mid–1930s, as were Brian Penton's 'sagas' of pioneering, *Landtakers* and *Inheritors*, though Penton is better remembered as editor of Sydney's *Daily Telegraph* and a pamphleteer. In *The Scandalous Penton: A Biography of Brian Penton*, Patrick Buckridge meticulously details Penton's life; most of the literary interest is found in early chapters dealing with his relations with the Lindsay circle in Sydney and London during the 'roaring twenties'. Sydney literary culture between the world wars is a topic common to a number of contributions to *Wallflowers and Witches*, including editor Maryanne Dever's '"Conventional Women of Ability": M. Barnard Eldershaw and the Question of Cultural Authority', and Michael Sharkey's '"Dear Beppo": Recuperating "Margaret Fane"', a study of a forgotten minor writer that reveals some fascinating literary and sexual entanglements. Reappraisals of Katharine Susannah Prichard continue. In 'Aboriginal Subjectivities and Western Conventions: A Reading of *Coonardoo*' (*ANZSC* 10.23–9), Susan Lever nicely summarizes the divided responses among post-colonial and feminist readers of this novel and steers a considered course between them in attempting to defend Prichard from extremist charges of racism and sexism. On the other hand, Leigh Dale's contribution to *Tilting at Matilda* (ed. Haskell), '*Coonardoo* and Truth', is concerned not with Prichard's agency but with offering a fresh, detailed reading of the text as manifesting 'the operation of colonial and patriarchal power upon the bodies of indigenous women'. Together, these two articles, which engage specifically with the more-usually theorized problematics of reading literature from pre-postmodern periods, should stimulate future discussion of this key work. In *Westerly*, Ric Throssell, Prichard's son, revisits the question of the autobiographical basis, or not, of *Intimate Strangers* in 'The Stranger Fiction' (39.i.45–9), and Brenton Doecke contextualizes Prichard's goldfields trilogy in 'Australian Historical Fiction and the Popular Front' (39.iii.25–36). Julie Wells's '"Red Witches": Perceptions of Communist Women Writers', also in *Tilting at Matilda*, focuses on the other best-known Communist woman writer, Jean Devanny, who is the subject of Kay Ferres's much more specialized 'Written on the Body: Jean Devanny, Sexuality and Censorship' (*Hecate* 20.i.123–34). Also in this issue and seemingly for specialists only (because it discusses Eve Langley's unpublished novel 'Wild Australia') is Robyn Colwill's 'Eve Plays her Wilde Card and Makes the Straight Flush' (10–27), but the delightfully punning title – Langley changed her name to Oscar Wilde – suggests the entertaining way in which the article claims Langley as a postmodernist *avant la lettre*.

For the media, the literary event of the year was the publication of *Patrick White: Letters* edited by David Marr. In preparing his celebrated biography of White, Marr had drawn from 2,000 of his letters, most of which he had located himself; in preparing this volume he unearthed a further thousand, and the diary White kept in Africa during the war. His selection presents 620 of the letters, and the diary, with a linking commentary and generous footnotes which frequently quote from letters not included. As well as being a natural companion to White's 'self-portrait', *Flaws in the Glass*, and Marr's biography, *Patrick White: Letters* is a major contribution to scholarship, containing much destined to surface in the notes to books and articles by others for generations to come. However, there is no entry for Marr in the Oxford *Companion* (eds Wilde, Hooton and Andrews), biographers being referred to only within their subjects' entries. Some of White's private correspondence and letters to the press are included by Alan Lawson in his *Patrick White: Selected Writings* in UQP's Australian Authors series. In his introduction Lawson argues that White's work should be seen as a whole without separating 'the kinds of writing that he did over a long career', as these were 'merely different locations for the act of writing'; and his selection departs from the original 'portable authors' conception of the series by containing no extracts from White's major body of writing, the novels. Instead, as well as letters, there are short stories (some of them previously uncollected), extracts from White's autobiography, uncollected poems and revue sketches, interviews, essays and speeches. The selection usefully gathers in many often-referred-to fugitive pieces but, unlike the companion Stead volume, it is clearly not intended to serve as an introductory sampler.

In A. L. McLeod, ed., *R. K. Narayan: Critical Perspectives*, H. H. Anniah Gowda's 'R. K. Narayan and Patrick White as Short-Story Tellers' contrasts the two writers in terms of the constrictiveness of the form for White's ambitions to encompass a whole society but its compatability with Narayan's religious vision. In '*The Twyborn Affair*: Beyond 'the Human Hierarchy of Men and Women' (*ALS* 16.289–96), Susan Lever lucidly and insightfully elaborates on how indeterminancy of gender functions as a metaphor for the whole novel: 'E's several changes of sexual identity insist that E's body can never fully represent E., while the novel's self-reflexive strategies suggest that language can never fully represent reality.' Terry Goldie's 'The Man of the Land/The Land of the Man' (*SPAN* 36[1993].156–63] compares *The Twyborn Affair* with Canadian novelist Scott Symon's *Contact Journal for Place D'Aumes*, seeing both as 'concerned to discover a particularly homosexual way of belonging'. Michael Giffin in 'Judaism between *Torah*, *Haskalah* and *Kabbalah:* The Revealed Imagination in the Novels of Patrick White' (*L&T* 8.i.65–79) discounts this author's avowals that he was no intellectual and sees him as informedly engaged, in a modern and postmodern way, with the mythical systems of 'the Primitive, the Classical, the Jewish, and the Christian imagination' throughout his major fiction. Giffin persuasively supports this sweeping perception by a detailed discussion of the 'imaginative horizon' of the Jewish characters in *The Living and the Dead*, *Riders in the Chariot*, *The Solid Mandala* and *The Eye of the Storm*. White's consciousness of the classical is considered in David Coad's contribution to *'Return' in Post-Colonial Writing* (ed. Mihailovich-Dickman), 'Platonic Return in Patrick White's *The Eye of the Storm*', which interprets Mrs Hunter's return to 'the world of the cave' after her moment of illumination as an example of epistrophe.

In 'Family Affairs/National Fictions, and *The Tree of Man*' (*SPAN* 36[1993].164–73), Manfred Mackenzie sketches out the bold but suggestive proposal that, like Hawthorne's and Melville's novels, White's might be read as allegories of nationalism, though with the difference that White's reveal an 'incestuous return' to 'Mother/England'. Thomas L. Warren's 'Patrick White's *The Living and the Dead* – A Struggle for Identity' (*Antipodes* 8.37–40) interprets this early novel as evidence of its author's similar struggle at that stage of his life. Geneviève Laigle's thematic reading, 'La Symbolique de l'arbre dans l'oeuvre romanesque de Patrick White' (*EA* 47.iii.95–306), ranges over White's novels, and her 'The Reality of Illusion and the Illusion of Reality' (*CE&S* 16[1993].i.77–8) discusses *Memoirs of*

Many in One. Unavailable for review this year were David Merrington, '*The Twyborn Affair*: Patrick White's Allegory of Fiction' in Loes Nas and Lesley Marx, eds, *InterAction* (University of Cape Town Press), and Andrew Elfenbein, 'Narrating Australia: Competing Heroisms in *A Fringe of Leaves*'(*CNIE* 6[1993].i/ii.358–76).

ALS 16.iv, 'Oodgeroo: A Tribute', is a special issue devoted to the late Aboriginal poet (who first published as Kath Walker), guest-edited by Adam Shoemaker and including the following commentaries on her work, each of which engages with the issue of the appropriate criteria, or context, for evaluation: Mudrooroo's 'The Poetemics [*sic*] of Oodgeroo of the Tribe Noonuccal' (57–62), Bob Hodge's 'Poetry and Politics in Oodgeroo' (64–76), Angela Smith's 'Long Memoried Women: Oodgeroo Noonuccal and Jamaican Poet, Louise Bennett' (77–91), Anne Brewster's 'Oodgeroo: Orator, Poet, Storyteller' (92–104), and Eva Rask Knudsen's 'From Kath Walker to Oodgeroo Noonuccal? Ambiguity and Assurance in *My People*' (105–18). The most authoritative assessment, from a foremost white poet and longstanding acquaintance, is 'The Poetry: An Appreciation by Judith Wright', included in *Oodgeroo*, a collection of memoirs, speeches and verses edited by Kathie Cochrane.

The contemporary author who appears to have attracted the most critical attention this year is David Malouf. *Provisional Maps*, a collection of essays on Malouf, ed. Amanda Nettlebeck, spans a wide range of interests. Some of the contributions – Thomas Shapcott's informative 'insider' account of Malouf's place in Australian poetry since the early 1960s, Beate Josephi's interview with him after the appearance of *The Great World*, Samar Athar's survey of the theme of exile throughout his *oeuvre*, and Annie Patrick's account of his libretti – might suggest that this is a 'case book' for the 'general' market. But most of the essays assume a close familiarity not only with Malouf's fiction and poetry but also with what amounts to a checklist of post-structuralist, including post-colonial, interests: in language, culture, history, place; subjectivity, sexuality, the body; boundaries, borders, margins. Dennis Haskell writes on individual identity in the poetry; Andrew Taylor on history in the fiction, especially *The Great World*; Gillian Whitlock on Malouf and regional writing; Leigh Dale and Helen Gilbert on his topographies of the body, the editor on his narration of space, and Maryanne Dever on its politics; Paul Kavanagh on Malouf, Heidegger and language; Patrick Buckridge on sublime discourse in the fiction, and Peter Pierce on problems of history and form in *Remembering Babylon*. Those in command, rather than the grip, of ideas communicate their interests more coherently. In White, *Recasting the World*, Carolyn Masel writing on 'Late Landings: Reflections on Belatedness in Australian and Canadian Literature' concentrates on Malouf and Atwood to explore her theme, which she defines as a 'perceived lack of authenticity in relation to place' on the part of white settlers. *CE&S* (16[1993].ii) contains four substantial studies of Malouf. Bill Ashcroft's 'The Return of the Native: *An Imaginary Life* and *Remembering Babylon*' (51–60) compares both novels in terms of the 'Lost Child' figure in Australian culture, 'the enduring allegory of the settler society's sense of vulnerability and displacement', but finds that Malouf's lost children do return, 'to announce the possibility of a different life, a different kind of invention of Australia'. Gareth Griffiths's '*An Imaginary Life*: The Post-Colonial Text as Transformative Representation' (61–9) elaborates on the correspondences implied between the classical world presented in this novel and contemporary Australia. Whereas many of the younger contributors to the Nettlebeck collection of essays on Malouf give the impression they would be more comfortable writing in French, the French contributors on Malouf in this issue of *CE&S* not only write in the most elegant English but also unembarrassedly within an unfashionable 'humanist' framework: Geneviève Laigle with '"Entering the Dimensions of my Self": Malouf's *An Imaginary Life*' (70–8) and Xavier Pons with 'Broken Lines, Broken Lives: Discontinuities in David Malouf's *The Great World*' (79–87). The highly literary Malouf's ambiguous relation to humanism is taken up, demandingly but suggestively, by American critic Anthony Winner in 'David Malouf's *Child's Play*: Narrative Traditions in a Postmodern Game' (*Southerly* 54.iv.116–30); in comparison, Veronica Brady's 'Redefining Frontiers – "Race", Colonizers and the Colonized' (*Antipodes* 8.93–100), ostensibly a discussion of *Remembering Babylon* directed to North American readers, is but pious panegyric.

While Peter Carey has for long been among the most prominent of fiction writers, locally and internationally, sustained attention to his work has been sparse until this year. Anthony J. Hassall's *Dancing on Hot Macadam: Peter Carey's Fiction* in UQP's Studies in Australian Literature series is the first monograph to discuss his *oeuvre* in detail (up to *The Unusual Life of Tristan Smith*). Hassall is interested in both Carey's literary affiliations, the networks of texts into which Carey inserts his own, and the diffused 'cultural text', the national myths, dreams and nightmares, with which his fictions engage. The result is a well-rounded overview, theoretically aware but also unembarrassed about seeing Carey's engagements with a referential (not merely a textual) world as essentially 'moral' – a term not often so frankly encountered in academic literary discourse today. Geoff Stokes, ed., *Australian Political Ideas*, contains two studies by M. D. Fletcher: 'Peter Carey's Post-Colonial Australia I: *Illywhacker*: Lies, Dependence, and Political History' and 'Peter Carey's Post-Colonial Australia II: *Oscar and Lucinda*: Misunderstanding, Victimisation, and Political History'. That their author is a political scientist indicates that Carey is beginning to be seen as more than the inventive advertising copy-writer turned entertainer he was for long taken to be by more than a few in the local literary culture. Unseen is Fletcher's 'The Theme of Entrapment in Peter Carey's Fiction' (*Commonwealth Review* 3.ii[1993].74–9). Patrick Fuery's contribution to *Recasting the World*, ed. White, 'Prisoners and Spiders Surrounded by Signs: Postmodernism and the Postcolonial Gaze in Contemporary Australian Culture', takes the first half of its title from *Illywhacker*, but discussion of Carey is very general and sees his 'historical pastiche' as representative of a shift towards postmodern styles and concerns, especially in Australian film. Fuery does not indicate that Jameson, from whom he borrows the term, employs it in a derogatory sense, distinguishing it from 'true' parody; 'historiographical parody' might more accurately categorize Carey's practice in the novels Fuery refers to in passing. Phil McClusky's 'The Handsomest Drowned Man in the Outback: Contextualizing a Structural Magic Realism' (*SPAN* 36[1993].88–94) compares Carey's seeming 'magic realism' with South American models and finds that, rather than sharing their 'fictional manifestation of immediate reality', his mode in *Illywhacker* 'underlines the self-destructive effects of a continually shifting colonization'. In *Overland* 137, the late Bob (D. R.) Burns's 'Feasibility Through Fictional Means: Peter Carey's Accord with Stephen Potter' (39–44) is a characteristically quirky discussion of *Illywhacker*, which, none too clearly, seems to imply that the novel's discordant elements of 'ultra-Australian realism' are rather glibly reconciled at its end by an 'ultra-Anglo', Potteresque irony.

Elizabeth Jolley has also attracted substantial critical attention this year. As their title suggests, Helen Thomson's 1993 Colin Roderick Lectures, *Bio-Fictions: Brian Matthews, Drusilla Modjeska and Elizabeth Jolley*, offer a wide-ranging discussion of 'the textual intersections of autobiography, biography, history and fiction'. Thomson writes forcefully as an avowed, and theoretically informed, feminist; but always individually and insightfully about the texts under consideration. Her approach to Jolley's 'Vera' trilogy in the culminating lecture is a major contribution to the still-emerging discourse about this writer's work. More schematically, Julie Carr invokes French feminist theorists to consider 'The Dancing Body – Somatic Expression in Elizabeth Jolley's fiction' (*Westerly* 39.ii.75–80); and, responding to the same theorists, Kerry Goddard writes on 'Women Off the Market: Possession and Desire in Elizabeth Jolley's *The Well*', in the special 'Postcolonialism and Feminism' issue of *SPAN* (37[1993].201–11). This is an illuminating reading, which happily accommodates the novel's narrative 'vertigo', as also is Silvana Caporaletti's contribution to *Commonwealth Literary Cultures* (eds Capone et al.), 'The Echoes of the Echoing Well', a psychosexual inquiry into the workings of the novel's central symbol. Jennifer Livett's 'Against the Grain: Dream Narrative in Elizabeth Jolley's *Foxybaby*' (*SPAN* 36[1993].211–19) identifies Jolley with women writers who employ dream narrative to assert the power of women to reinvent their places in literature and culture. Anne-Marie Soulier provides French readers with a brief general introduction, 'Elizabeth Jolley et le Pays des Autres', (*CE&S* 17.i.45–50).

In *CS*, Bill Perrett's 'The Novels of Mudrooroo'(6.1.105–11) introduces English readers to the work of the most prominent Aboriginal writer; in *NLitsR*, John Fielder's 'Wildcat Reading: *Wild Cat Falling*, Assimilation and Ambivalence' (27.16–27) expounds on the incontestable proposition that official attitudes towards Aborigines differed from today's when Mudrooroo's (Colin Johnson's) first novel appeared in 1965; and in *SPAN* (36[1993].647–60), Justin MacGregor's 'A Dialogue Between Margins' compares *Wild Cat Falling* and the later autobiographical narrative *Doin Wildcat*. David Foster is the subject of two articles this year: A. (Andrew) P. Riemer, providing a general introduction to his novels and those of Robin Wallace-Crabbe in 'Maverick Voices' (*CS* 6.i.125–32), opines that both these authors maintain the 'larrikin tradition' in Australian culture against a rising tide of gentility; and in *LiNQ* (21.ii.63–70) Narelle Shaw's 'It's a Small Martial Arts World' relates Foster's *Mates of Mars* to his earlier novels. Andrew Riemer is also author of *The Ironic Eye*, a monograph on the poetry and fiction of Peter Goldsworthy, which unfortunately omits any bibliography of this emerging author's work. In 'Frank Moorhouse and Michael Wilding – and Internationalism' (*Antipodes* 8.15–20), Frank Parigi introduces two established fiction writers to American readers by observantly comparing, and contrasting, stylistic nuances and cultural attitudes in *The Americans, Baby* and *Pacific Highway*.

Kunapipi 16.i is a bumper special issue on women's post-colonial writing, with articles on Australian fiction predominating. Amin Malak's '"The World is your People": *The Time of the Peacock* and the Evolution of an Australian Identity' discusses this collection of short stories about Muslim Indians in Australia, first published in 1965 (43–47). Elaine Lindsay, in 'Women Rising: Spirituality in the Writings of Barbara Hanrahan' (13–21), argues that although discussions of spirituality in Australian literature all but ignore the writings of women, they also portray the world as a 'paradise garden' where the divine is immanent, rather than celebrating the 'desert spirituality' of male pilgrims: she instances Hanrahan's five books of 'autobiographical fictions', five of 'fantastic fictions' and five of 'biographical fictions'. Joan Kirkby's '"The Vertigris of Glory": The Lure of Abjection in Thea Astley's *The Acolyte*' (27–43) offers a Kristevan reading of this novel which might equally have been titled 'The Vertigo of Theory'; whereas French scholar Xavier Pons, in 'Blood and Water: Feminine Writing in Beverley Farmer's *The Seal Woman*' (74–86), shows once again how theoretical inquiry – here into *écriture feminine* – and observant attention to a text can be brought together illuminatingly. Melissa Boyde and Amanda Lawson's 'Diving for the Read Pearl: Surfacing and Setting the Centre in *Working Hot*' (119–24) perceives Mary Fallon's text as pivotal in the development of lesbian experimental writing in Australia; and Anne Brewster's 'Ania Walwicz's Vagrant Narration: Cosmopolitanism vs Nationalism in Australia's "Migrant Writing"' (181–6) hails the 'political strategy' implicit in *red roses*: 'namely the strategy of migrants and minority constituencies reinscribing themselves not in terms of fixed identities of an originary, nativist or ethnicist discourse such as multiculturalism, but through mimicry and pastiche of dominant representations' – which seems at least to accommodate most of the key terms in the lexicon of multiculturalism.

Connoisseurs of the post-colonial lexicon will relish Gareth Griffith's contribution to *De-Scribing Empire* (eds Tiffin and Lawson), 'The Myth of Authenticity', which de-scribes Sally Morgan's *My Place* as 'a classic text-case for [the] kind of presentation of Aboriginality as legitimated by a process of subversive mimicry and displacement rather than as an overdetermined replication of the sign of the authentic'. In *SPAN* 36[1993], Wenche Ommundsen's 'Engendering the Bicentennial Reader: Sally Morgan, Mark Henshaw and the Critics' (251–63) sees the incest theme in *My Place* and Henshaw's novel, *Out of the Line of Fire*, linked to that of identity. In 'Tactics of Evasion' (*SoRA* 27.178–86), Sue Gillett argues sharply that Henshaw's postmodern pastiche, which so seduced the (male) reviewers, amounts to no more than an irresponsible indulgence in the clichés of pornography. Female desire is the focus of Philippa Kelly's 'The Language of Subversion: Discourses of Desire in *Painted Woman*, *The Children's Bach*, and *Messages from Chaos*', in which she discusses novels by Sue Woolfe, Helen Garner and Susan Johnson (*Southerly* 54.i.143–56). Marion Campbell's *Not Being Miriam* (1988) is 'perhaps the most overtly experimental women's novel to have been written in Australia in recent years', according to Colleen Keane who, in 'Post-Humanism, Plurality and *Not Being Miriam*' (*Meridian* 13.27–37), provides a thematic and stylistic reading which, like the novel itself, is informed by feminist theory; as also are Sue Gillett's 'Away from the Gaze, Into the Maze' (*Southerly* 54.ii.47–57), which sees the novel articulating 'the repressed semiotic', and Valerie Spence's 'Representations of Subjectivity in *Not Being Miriam*' (*SPAN* 37[1993].33–47), a philosophically disposed analysis of Campbell's narrative technique.

Poetry provides a fascinating instance of how the multidisciplinary 'Australian studies' approach can illuminate a text in Leo Scheps's 'Unkelling Quiros: A Gloss on Part II of James McAuley's "Captain Quiros"' (*JAS* 42.18–31). Scheps reads McAuley's attempt at an epic against the records both of Quiros's Christianizing mission and of Australia's policy towards Papua New Guinea (a protectorate at the time the poem was composed), finding that McAuley's 'infatuation with antique themes of empire and crusade' determined his views as an administrator on PNG's development, and led him as a poet to suppress the brutal accounts of colonization in his sources. Les Murray is the subject of three thoughtful articles:

in 'This Country is My Mind' (*Westerly* 39.i.67–79), Carmel Gaffney discusses his work in relation to pastoral traditions (as she does Neilson's in the *Southerly* article referred to above); Martin Leer innovatively explores the relationships between intimately known landscape and an oral rural culture in '"Contour-Line by Contour": Landscape Change as an Index of History in the Poetry of Les Murray' (*ALS* 16.249–61); and in 'Fullness of Being in Les Murray's "Presence: Translations from the Natural World"' (*Antipodes* 8.123–30), Bert Almon provides a closely detailed discussion of this central sequence in Murray's most recent collection. Andrew Johnston's 'Surviving Desire' (*Landfall* 187.45–58) is an excellent general introduction to John Tranter's poetry, while David Brooks's 'Feral Symbolists: Robert Adamson, John Tranter, and the Response to Rimbaud' (*ALS* 16.280–8) is a closely focused study of intertextuality across the centuries and continents, and an individual contribution to the literary history of 'the generation of '68'. (As a poet himself, and fiction writer, Brooks is discussed by Gary Catalano in 'Poised Upon a Border' [*Imago* 6.i.65–8].) Fay Zwicky is featured in *Southerly* 54.iii, with Ivor Indyk writing on 'Fay Zwicky: The Poet as Moralist' (33–50) and Elsa Linguanti offering some scattered observations on her work in 'On the Shifting Sands of Our Experience' (51–64). In the same issue is Michael Griffith's 'Peter Skrzynecki: "the revelation of a Landfall beyond any known map"' (119–28), a discussion of Christian imagery in this poet's latest collection. Somewhat uninspiringly for potential readers of her subject, Michelle Tsokos's general introduction to the poetry of Antigone Kefala, 'Memory and Absence' (*Westerly* 39.iv.51–60), finds 'darkness and a lack of meaning' as the dominant notes of this poet's work.

A much more positive approach is taken in the only monograph on a playwright this year, Elizabeth Perkins's *The Plays of Alma De Groen* in Rodopi's Australian Playwrights series. Perkins is clearly an enthusiastic admirer of De Groen's experimentation with theatrical forms and her simultaneous engagement with a wide range of, and especially feminist, themes. Both are analysed lucidly in this first comprehensive study of De Groen's work. The employment of the Medusa myth in De Groen's *The Rivers of China* and Sarah Cathcart's *The Serpent's Fall* is discussed by Helen Gilbert in 'The Serpent's Gaze: Re-Working Myths for a Feminist Australian Drama' (*ANZSC* 10.30–9). Gilbert has published prolifically on other contemporary playwrights this year. Her 'Monumental Moments: Michael Gow's *1841*, Stephen Sewell's *Hate*, Louis Nowra's *Capricornia* and Australia's Bicentennary' (*ADS* 24.29–45) discusses these plays as 'counter-texts' to bicentennial fervour, which attempt to 'recuperate marginalised, muted or silenced histories'. (Joanne Tompkins's 'Celebrate 1988: Australian Drama in the Bicentennial Year' [*ANZSC* 11.102–12] surveys relevant productions during 1988, but unaccountably fails to note the premiere at the Sydney Opera House of David Malouf's *Blood Relations*.) Gilbert considers other plays by Nowra in 'Postcolonial Grotesques: Re-Membering the Body and Louis Nowra's *Visions* and *The Golden Age*' (*SPAN* 36[1993].618–33), which rewardingly considers his 'deployment of the carnivalesque as a decolonizing strategy', and in 'Ghosts in a Landscape: Louis Nowra's *Inside the Island* and Jan Balodis's *Too Young for Ghosts*' (*SoRA* 27.432–47). In the special 'Theatre in Southeast Asia' issue of *ADS* (25.177–87), Gilbert's 'Occidental (Sex) Tourists: Michael Gurr's *Sex Diary of an Infidel*' sees this play's ostensible subject of the sex trade between Australia and the Philippines as a metaphor for 'all kinds of other neoimperialism'. Read together (and one can envisage them soon being brought together in a book), Gilbert's essays offer a stimulating perspective on recent drama even if, most often, she emphasizes heavily theorized political rather than performance values. *CS* (6.i) contains introductory essays on the pre-eminent Aboriginal playwright, the pre-eminent woman playwright, and the unqualifiedly pre-eminent playwright (whose most recent success is titled *Dead White Males*): Bob Hodge writes on 'Jack Davis and the Emergence of Aboriginal Writing' (98–104), Elizabeth Schaffer on 'Golden Girls and Bad Girls: The Plays of Dorothy Hewett' (140–5), and Brian Kiernan on 'The Ways We Live Now: David Williamson's Recent Plays' (146–52). Davis's *No Sugar* is discussed as a play that explores 'in complex ways the notion of inside/outside in the pursuit of a new, self-assertive Aboriginal identity' by Brian Dibble and Margaret Macintyre in 'Looking at Them Looking at Us' (in Grant and Seal, *Australia in the World*). Hewett's *The Chapel Perilous* is considered, unproblematically, in relation to contemporary Australian feminist writing by Joanne Tompkins in '"I was a rebel in word and deed"' (*ANZSC* 10.41–55). Tompkins, who makes no acknowledgement of the complicating structural ironies in this play, writes much more interestingly on 'Re-Orienting Australasian Drama: Staging Theatrical Irony' (*ArielE* 25.iv.117–33), discussing Buzo's *Norm and Ahmed*, Romeril's *The Floating World* and New Zealander Vincent O'Sullivan's *Shuriken*, plays that engage with attitudes towards Asia and which she argues complicate Edward Said's influential but reductive binary definition of the Oriental as 'Other'. Veronica Kelly's 'Enright's *Mongrels* as Intervention in the Canon of Contemporary Australian Drama' (*Southerly* 54.ii.5–22) draws some interesting observations on current drama in the course of discussing this recent play based on the careers of two 'new wave' playwrights of the 1970s, Jim McNeill and Peter Kenna. An even earlier stage of modern theatrical history is revisited by Frances de Groen in her contribution to Haskell, *Tilting at Matilda*, 'Dymphna Cusack's *Comets Soon Pass*: The Genius and the Potato Wife', which contextualizes this play from the early 1940s within the ideologies and personal interactions of that time.

Despite pessimistic perceptions that 'cultural studies' are replacing traditional literary studies, and that publishing outlets for the latter are diminishing, it could be observed, once again, that much thoughtful criticism and valuable scholarship appeared during this year. When, as is most often the case, 'cultural studies' engage with 'Australia' (no matter how heavily that term is placed under erasure), imaginative writing – from the early colonial period to the present, especially fiction and poetry – continues to furnish most of the texts felt to be in need of decoding, deconstruction, demystification (even though on occasions it might seem more like mystification). This year offers plenty of evidence that, rather than replacing traditional literary interests with undifferentiatedly theorized 'cultural studies', the institutional tendencies (in education and publishing) towards a more multidisciplinary 'Australian studies' has revitalized them, and given them new relevance in a society preoccupied by the same issues of post-colonialism, multiculturalism, gender equity, etc., as enter into literary discourses.

3. Canada

(a) General

A major topic in the 1994–5 Canadian literary scene was the lives – and deaths – of some of its 'Mandarins', notably Earle Birney, Robertson Davies and Northrop Frye. Elspeth Cameron's biography *Earle Birney: A Life* was the most controversial of the resulting publications, but one suspects that the objections to Cameron's allegedly prurient coverage of Birney's many love affairs say more about residual puritanism among Canadian reviewers than about the quality of the book itself. By any standards, *Earle Birney* is a major achievement, thoroughly researched and compellingly narrated. For the duration of the poet's long life, Cameron documents the Canadian (and international) literary scene: she writes about university careers in times of economic depression and personal patronage; about the business of editing, publishing and reviewing; the cabals and coteries among writers (especially the kind who also hold academic posts), and the effects of such intrigue on their students; and the substantial role of the Canada Council in fostering Canadian culture by funding reading tours and providing poets with exotic holidays. At least as engrossing as Birney's love life is the extent to which he controlled his literary reputation by brow-beating magazine and newspaper editors into reviewing his books and taking noisy issue with assessments of his work that were not to his liking. As is often the case in biography, discussion of the author's work and its qualities tends to be smothered in documentary detail or else is somewhat arbitrary and glib, but it is perhaps for specialized symposia to fill that particular gap. Thus Northrop Frye receives excellent attention in *The Legacy of Northrop Frye*, eds Alvin A. Lee and Robert D. Denham, a collection based on a 1992 symposium held at the University of Toronto. The book features a substantial section on 'Frye and Canada', with contributions by Linda Hutcheon, James Reaney, Sandra Djwa, Milton Wilson, David Staines and Clara Thomas, and a 'Norrie Banquet Ode' by Margaret Atwood. Addressing, in Hutcheon's words, 'the magisterial, totalizing work of Frye, the "Mandarin", modern, Canadian theorist', several essays analyse the ideas and rhetoric that inform his influential poetry reviews in *UTQ*, thus paying close attention to the *ways* (rather than the long-established fact) of Frye's influence on the Canadian literary canon.

It is a far cry from Birney's working-class origins, socialist leanings and bohemian demeanour to Frye's world at Victoria College and to Robertson Davies's at Massey College, but there are also remarkable similarities. As Cameron explains, his erudition as a Chaucerian placed Birney in 'Apollonian' contrast to his 'Dionysian' contemporaries, many of them by several decades his juniors. The members of the Vancouver TISH group, for example, found it difficult to accept his experimentation in concrete and performance poetry as proof that, although in retirement age, he could swing with the best of them. Davies's insistence on ceremonious civility in literary and personal matters, his old-world preferences, and his patriarchal beliefs made him even more suspect than Birney to the rebellious students who accused Massey College and its first master of fostering anachronistic elitism. Judith Skelton Grant's *Robertson Davies: Man of Myth* is particularly good in recreating the historical and cultural context that made Davies a man of (and occasionally *out* of) his times, ranging from his involvement in patriotic theatrical projects in the centennial year, his failure to win the Governor General's Award for *Fifth Business* (losing to Dave Godfrey's *The New Ancestors*, a book now of mostly historical interest), to his repeated nominations for the Nobel and Booker Prizes – all of which remained unsuccessful. Although Grant's book is marred by its overly reverential attitude toward its subject, this is outstanding work nevertheless, bringing to life periods in Canadian theatrical and intellectual history which have not received this kind of attention so far.

A somewhat less daunting but no less interesting figure is Leo Kennedy, member of the 'Montreal Poets' clustered around the *McGill Fortnightly Review*.

A. J. M. Smith, F. R. Scott and especially A. M. Klein have already received a great deal of critical and biographical attention; Patricia Morley fills in an important gap by tracing the career of the fourth, Leo Kennedy, in *As Though Life Mattered: Leo Kennedy's Story*. The details of the 1920s literary scene in Montreal are generally well known, but Morley also vividly describes Kennedy's origins in working-class Liverpool and his work as a copy-writer in leading US advertisement agencies. In the latter in particular, Morley sketches an intriguing chapter in cultural studies, as well as tracing the employment history of an intellectual who frequently crossed the border between Canada and the US. Kennedy's slim poetic *oeuvre* acquires additional resonance against the details of a life apparently ruled by family loyalties, and Morley's interview with Kennedy's cantankerous son, who praises his father for his 'ability to budget' but has little respect for his literary achievement, is a suitably sad and ironic conclusion.

While the works on Birney, Frye, Davies and Kennedy are substantial tomes, ECW continues to issue short biographies of major Canadian writers. Among this year's publications are Gary Boire's *Morley Callaghan: Literary Anarchist*, Ira Nadel's *Leonard Cohen: A Life in Art*, Ed Jewinski's *Michael Ondaatje*, Carol Roberts's *Timothy Findley: Stories from a Life*, and Stella Algoo-Baksh's *Austin C. Clarke*. The wisdom of writing the biography of a writer like Ondaatje who has always questioned the relevance of an author's life to his work may be debatable, but these are useful first (and sometimes even pioneering) efforts nevertheless.

As a winner of the Booker Prize, Michael Ondaatje might also be said to have joined the ranks of the 'Mandarins'. In *Oppositional Aesthetics: Readings from a Hyphenated Space*, Arun Mukherjee presents an anatomy of the literary reputations of Michael Ondaatje and Neil Bissondath respectively, and introduces East Asian writers who have found it more difficult than these two to establish themselves. Including all of the essays from her previous book *Towards an Aesthetic of Opposition: Essays on Criticism and Cultural Imperialism* (1988) as well as new discussions and reviews, *Oppositional Aesthetics* is an often angry manifesto reading current critical practices through the biographical lens of a 'hyphenated' Canadian academic. Mukherjee passionately resists the universalizing tendencies of her profession, insisting on detailed observations instead. The results include alternative readings of such classics as Birney's poem 'The Bear on Delhi Road' and Margaret Laurence's story 'The Perfume Sea'. For her methodology Mukherjee draws on elements of the very approaches she criticizes, but she affirms that doing so is an act of volition not subservience.

The work of 'hyphenated' Canadians is also introduced in two special issues of *CanL* on 'East-Asian–Canadian Connections' (140) and 'Hispanic–Canadian Connections' (142–3). Writers like Joy Kogawa, Sky Lee, Evelyn Lau, Paul Yee and those of the active Latino literary community, especially in Quebec, are often not (yet) adequately covered in the standard reference works of Canadian literature, and these special issues help to fill the gap by offering introductions, sketching critical paradigms, and outlining necessary revisions to received notions of literary history. 'East-Asian–Canadian Connections' (*CanL* 140) features an interdisciplinary essay, by Marilyn Iwama, '"If you say so": Articulating Cultural Symbols of Tradition in the Japanese-Canadian Community' (13–29), on the construction of cultural symbols in the Japanese-Canadian Community; a comparison, by Graham Huggan, of 'Representations of Chinese Canada in Bowering's *To All Appearances a Lady* and Lee's *Disappearing Moon Café*' (34–48); an introduction, by James Doyle, to the Eaton sisters, Eurasian writers whose work is among the earliest to describe Chinese working-class life in North America ('Sui-Sin-Far and Onoto-Watanna: Two Early Chinese-Canadian Authors' [50–8]); a travel sketch by George Woodcock ('The Woman on the Treadmill: A Collective Pastiche on Cambodia, 1964' [62–70]); and a spirited biographical essay by Frances Itani on the tribulations of a biracial marriage ('Transforming the Insult' [73–8]).

A more substantial and varied publication, 'Hispanic–Canadian Connections' (*CanL* 142–3) will be particularly interesting to those who, in the wake of the recent separatist referendum in Quebec, wish to take a closer look at the troublesome ethnic component which has helped to shape the cultural (and political) life of the province. Lake Sagaris introduces Chilean-Canadian writing ('Countries like Drawbridges: Chilean-Canadian Writing Today', [12–20]); Mayte Gómez discusses the Chilean exile Alberto Kurapel and his theatre ('Infinite Signs: Alberto Kurapel and the Semantics of Exile' [38–48]), and Hugh Hazelton describes 'Québec Hispánico: Themes of Exile and Integration in the Writing of Latin-Americans living in Quebec' [120–35])'. Memoirs and travel writing by George Woodcock, George McWhirter, Matt Cohen and P. K. Page complement these and other critical essays. Like 'East-Asian–Canadian Connections', 'Hispanic–Canadian Connections' also contains a lengthy review essay discussing publications pertinent to the topic at hand.

The critical neglect of ethnic writing that makes special issues such as these necessary has also been evident in the university curriculums of Canadian literature. Margery Fee's article on 'Canadian Literature and English Studies in the Canadian University' (*ECW* 48[1993].20–40) has been ground-breaking in investigating the ethnic and other factors. All of the essays in *OpL* 9's issue entitled 'The Failure? of Canadian Literature' refer to Fee's work, but few are as accomplished in combining painstaking research with penetrating analysis. Sarah King applies Fee's methods to a case study of the University of Western Ontario; Robert Lecker continues his work on canon-building with 'Anthologizing English-Canadian Fiction: Some Canonical Trends'; Linda Lamont-Stewart takes yet another look at the infamous 1978 Calgary Conference, at which a list of the 'best' Canadian novels was drawn up; and Paul Martin investigates the teaching of Canadian literature in French in departments of English. Whereas the precision of the methods used is often impressive (Lecker and Martin in particular provide numerous tables to support their assertions), the evaluation of the data is occasionally less so. Lecker, for instance (whose readings of the Canadian literary canon have previously been challenged by Frank Davey and Tracy Ware as too reductive), lists Alice Munro as one of 'those whose work can be used, in the classroom, to reinforce New Critical assumptions about unity, coherence, and closure, as well as modernist assumptions about the power of metaphor and symbol', a judgement which amounts to a serious misreading of Munro's work in particular and of 'modernist' writing in general. Similarly, Martin rightly observes that certain French-Canadian texts are preferred in the classroom over others, but he fails to probe the reasons for these preferences (which may have something to do with, among other factors, available translations and the preference, in their turn, of translators and the agencies that fund them for certain authors over others). He also omits to investigate, satisfactorily, the role of interdepartmental diplomacy in determining curriculums and syllabuses. He is right to suspect departments of comparative literature of harbouring practical or even self-serving motives in claiming courses comprising texts in both English and French as *their* territory, but omits to acknowledge the role of French departments in protecting *their* turf against encroaching English departments. The number of questions raised by these articles is, however, a good indicator of their value, and anyone interested in the larger social and political contexts of Canadian literature will be well served by them. Readers interested in reading more by Lecker on issues of canonicity may wish to consult his 'Professionalism and the Rhetoric of English-Canadian Criticism' (*ZGKS* 25.i.87–103), which in a measure vindicates thematic criticism for having more successfully bridged the gap between town and gown than the more formalist varieties.

The issues raised in 'The Failure? of Canadian Literature' often impinge on the disciplines of sociology, history and aesthetics. The recent flourishing of cultural studies ought to renew an interest in those journals which have always taken an interdisciplinary approach, even if they do not always subscribe to the theoretical and ideological underpinnings of cultural studies. A recent issue of *JCSR* (28.iv), for instance, carries articles on 'Native People and the Tourist Industry in Ontario' by Patricia Jasen (5–27) and on the travels of a 'maternal feminist' in 'An English, Protestant, Upper-Class Feminist on the Grand Tour: Elizabeth Smith Shortt in Great Britain and Europe, 1911' by Peter E. Paul Dembski (72–87). Both essays are by historians, but literary scholars with an interest in travel writing, women's writing and popular culture will find much pertinent information here. A special issue of *JCSR* (29.iv) on the Dionne quins explores these complex national icons from a number of unexpected angles. A particularly brilliant piece is David Welch's 'The Dionne Quintuplets: More than an Ontario Showpiece – Five Franco-Ontarian Children' (36–64), which traces the construction of identities as fictional as those in a novel, but also records the quins' eventual rebellion when they refused to speak English or perform 'There'll Always Be an England' on command. Another national icon, the Avro Arrow interceptor, features in Eva-Marie Kröller's 'Fear of Flying? The Myth of Daedalus and Icarus in Canadian Culture' (*JCSR* 28.iv.102–16), an essay which also discusses the late London painter Greg Curnoe's airport art and John Gray's play *Billy Bishop Goes to War*.

(b) Fiction

Perhaps the most substantial book on Canadian fiction to appear in this year is Arnold Davidson's *Coyote Country: Fictions of the Canadian West*. It provides a perceptive update of earlier readings of the Canadian West by McCourt, Ricou and Harrison. Detailing the generic characteristics of the Canadian Western as opposed to its American counterpart, Davidson expands existing definitions to include Native, ethnic and feminist versions. He analyses classics such as *Tay John*, *The Double Hook* and *Badlands*, but also potboiler romances that helped establish the clichés of the Western in the first place. Davidson ranges with ease through the vast amount of criticism on questions of appropriation, race and gender. Only his comments on Gabrielle Roy's *La Petite Poule d'eau* may give cause for concern: quoted in English and insufficiently related to its own literary context, the book seems 'appropriated' in a manner contrary to the intentions that inform the book elsewhere.

An excellent companion volume to Davidson's books is 'Critical Visions: Contemporary North American Native Writing', a special issue of *ArielE* (25.i) featuring critical essays, interviews, memoirs, poems and a review article. Helen Hoy's essay on Beatrice Culleton's *In Search of April Raintree* (' "Nothing But the Truth": Discursive Transparency in Beatrice Culleton' [155–84]) speaks of the pedagogical and critical complexities involved in teaching the novel; the article comes with thorough footnotes and bibliography, documenting in some detail the different versions of the novel, its publication history and its critical reception. Helen Hoy is one of the very few critics who know how to practise the self-reflexivity she discusses without self-destructing in the process. Still, Lee Maracle's complaint, in an interview with Jennifer Kelly, over the impenetrability of much post-structuralist jargon also tempers Helen Hoy's remarks. Another noteworthy contribution to 'Critical Visions' is Gail Valaskakis's analysis of the media coverage of the Oka crisis in 'Rights and Warriors: First Nations, Media, and National Identity' (60–72). Using a cultural studies model, Valaskais takes the media to task for their central role in 'creating a powerful fictive identity in which the disproportionately large number of Indian youth who are not in school and unemployed are invested'.

Among the chief creators of Western fictions is Robert Kroetsch, whose deconstructions of traditional plots and characters have made him a favourite among Canadian post-structuralist critics. In *'The Old Dualities': Deconstructing Robert Kroetsch and his Critics*, Dianne Tiefensee takes Kroetsch and his critics to task for only seemingly disentangling themselves from 'the hegemony by which we in the Western World are governed'. Tiefensee's apparently unquestioning allegiance to Derrida the Almighty Sage is worrisome, as is her categorical (and contradictory) assertion that 'Metaphysics and the oppressive violence it fosters cannot be escaped, but it can be resisted [. . .] by our rigorously contextualizing the metaphysical concepts that govern our thought, our actions, and our lives.' The book displays the humourless pedantry that sometimes characterizes postgraduate essays, and one is not surprised to learn that the book is an adapted doctoral dissertation. The fact remains, however, that Tiefensee conducts intelligent, observant readings of her texts and that her conclusions are often both courageous and apt. She targets the 'lazy and sloppy scholarship in the name of groundbreaking innovation' which often goes by the name of postmodern theory, and she earnestly proposes to teach the practitioners of such scholarship a timely lesson.

While Tiefensee chastises her subject(s) for failing to conform to the categories they have set out for themselves, Ajay Heble takes an entirely different approach in *The Tumble of Reason: Alice Munro's Discourse of Absence*. Heble 'does not seek specifically to theorize the relation between Munro's absences and the complex but systematic formation for a discursive trajectory which operates as both an instance and a criticism of representationalism'. This may be a mouthful, but for the most part Heble provides an admirably lucid commentary to Munro's fiction from *Dance of the Happy Shades* to *Friend of My Youth*, dwelling on the ways in which 'epistemological issue[s] [. . .] lead [. . .] to a kind of ontological questioning'. Heble proposes that this connection becomes increasingly complex in Munro's later fictions, thus redefining the nature of 'realism' as it is most frequently understood. His point is well taken, but once Heble's central statement has been made, it is then somewhat repetitively asserted throughout the remaining chapters and insufficiently accounts for Munro's subtleties. Munro's literary lineage has been traced to such American writers as William Faulkner and Carson McCullers. Heble does not dwell on these connections, but two other recent books explore Canadian-American literary connections. Irene Gammel's *Sexualizing Power in Naturalism: Theodore Dreiser and Frederick Philip Grove* is an important contribution to criticism on Grove and to the study of Canadian-American literary relationships. Re-reading naturalism through Foucault's lens and that of the French feminists, Gammel emphasizes the decadent aspects of Grove and Dreiser's fiction without restricting herself to their aesthetic dimensions. The result is a densely argued, if occasionally ponderous, book that rests on a broadly comparative and multilingual base.

Context North America: Canadian/US Literary Relations, ed. Camille R. La Bossière, published as part of the University of Ottawa Reappraisals series, contains some excellent pieces. Like all of her work, Carole Gerson's 'Canadian Women Writers and American Markets, 1880–1940' is distinguished by its impeccable scholarship and feisty argument; the essay contains enough information about neglected women writers and their literary (and financial) fortunes to generate several doctoral dissertations. James Doyle's 'Literary Magazines and the Cosmopolitanism/Nationalism Debate in Canada' rightly points toward the arbitrariness with which literary critics have defined the 'essence' of Canada or the United States respectively. Arbitrariness also emerges as a leitmotif in Laurie Ricou's 'Two Nations Own These Islands: Border and Region in Pacific–Northwest Writing', which, in a series of questions and answers, explores assumptions and conjectures about an amorphous literary region.

UTorP has added two new titles to its theory/culture series, both – like several previous volumes – adaptations of doctoral dissertations. Once its theoretical premises have been sketched out, Graham Huggan's *Territorial Disputes: Maps and Mapping Strategies in Contemporary Canadian and Australian Fiction* presents, in a somewhat mechanical series, analyses of cartography as an important *mise-en-abyme* motif in self-reflexive fiction (see also section 2(a) above). The contextualization of the literatures considered is, however, not detailed enough to seem to warrant a comparison in the first place, a deficiency particularly striking in Huggan's comments on Quebec literature. As a result, one comes away from *Territorial Disputes* with a long list of books to read and many questions unanswered. The comparative basis of David Jordan's *New World Regionalism: Literature in the Americas* is somewhat more complex, but much in this 149-page book remains tantalizingly brief. The cursory remarks on Grove, for instance, characterizing his fiction as 'illustrat[ing] not only the realist approach to domesticating the environment through naming, but also the naturalist tendency to seek determinist explanations for regional identity', fail to acknowledge Grove's by now well-established connections to symbolism. Similarly, the chapter on *As For Me and My House* largely ignores the complex critical history of the book. Still, Jordan's efforts to relate Anglo-Canadian fiction by Grove, Ross, Watson and Kroetsch to Latin-American novels are original enough to warrant attention. Huggan and Jordan's books make one wonder, however, whether the directors of the 'theory/culture' series would not do well to re-examine its premises. There is little culture here, considerable sameness in the theory, and too many dissertations insufficiently revised for publication.

(c) Poetry and Drama

Because they are so rare, any study of a Canadian woman poet qualifies as good news. Nadine McInnis's *Dorothy Livesay's Poetics of Desire* is a competent volume professing to read Livesay's poetry through 'her struggles with her female experience and identity'. McInnis finds fault with most previous critical work on Livesay for either dwelling unduly on its biographical aspects or imposing feminist or, for that matter, masculinist frameworks onto it which an attentive reading fails to sustain. This book attempts no less than 'a complete reading of the psychic journey of a poet as she grapples through the various stages of her life', paying attention to 'the individual perceptions of the persona and [conveying] a knowledge of the social-political context'. McInnis makes many astute observations, but 114 pages are hardly enough to fulfil such an ambitious programme, and there is still much room for commentary on Livesay's work. Women poets such as Phyllis Webb and Daphne Marlatt also feature in Frank Davey's *Canadian Literary Power*. Part of NeWest's Writer as Critic series, which has included books devoted to Stephen Scobie, George Bowering and Aritha van Herk, Davey's book contains a compelling piece on the literary reputation of Phyllis Webb. Women writers will not take kindly to Davey's lecturing that, in rejecting previous readings, they 'are not only overlooking that all "Phyllis Webbs", even the "Phyllis Webb" of the person or "writer" are textual constructions', and they would be right to ask how, given that premise, Davey can still assert the validity of one 'Phyllis Webb' over another. Still, Davey's essay makes for a thought-provoking case study in the history of Canadian literary taste.

The work of Webb, Avison and Page has been compared to that of the seventeenth-century 'metaphysical poets'. A study exploring these connections to an essentially male tradition in some detail remains as yet to be written, but there is a book discussing A. J. M. Smith's indebtedness to the metaphysicals. Anne Compton's *A. J. M. Smith: Canadian Metaphysical* deliberately places the poetry at its centre, not the man or 'the theoretical conflicts ongoing among contemporary critics and theorists'. The result is a careful reading of much of Smith's work, embedded in a survey of his critical reception and literary contexts. Based on a doctoral thesis, *A. J. M. Smith* is somewhat too eager to quote rather than analyse the evidence, but the book is nevertheless a welcome discussion of a poet whose strongest influence appears to have been exerted more through the anthologies he edited than through his own work.

A different work altogether is Stan Dragland's *Floating Voice: Duncan Campbell Scott and the Literature of Treaty 9*. A mongrel sort of book which is part history, part critical study, part autobiography, *Floating Voice* subscribes to postmodern self-reflexiveness while attempting to avoid its pitfalls. Chief among these efforts is Dragland's insistence on 'textual theory [as] generated by raw material and not by other theory' and on seeing his subject in historical context rather than assigning the self-satisfied blame bestowed by hindsight. The result is a complex, stimulating book which places a reading of Scott's best stories and poems against a scrupulous and often painful analysis of the documents detailing his work in the Indian Affairs department, of his letters and photographs. *Floating Voice* makes for time-consuming and sometimes awkward reading, but it is well worth the trouble.

While Scott's work, because of its relevance to issues of racism and appropriation, remains relevant (if only, as Dragland repeatedly claims, to academics), D. M. R. Bentley's *Mimic Fires: Accounts of Early Long Poems on Canada* covers a field mostly thought to be of historical interest. Bentley's devotion to his topic is thus all the more impressive, as is his attentive scholarship in establishing the visions of Canadian nationhood evoked by poets ranging from Henry Kelsey, Oliver Goldsmith and Joseph Howe to Isabella Valancy Crawford and Archibald Lampman.

If critical studies of Canadian poetry are scarce, then work on Canadian drama appears to be even more so. However, *Playwriting Women: Female Voices in English Canada* by Cynthia Zimmerman is a noteworthy exception. Featuring essays on Carol Bolt, Sharon Pollock, Margaret Hollingsworth, Erika Ritter, Anne

Chislett and Judith Thompson, Zimmerman's book is an unassuming but useful compendium that does not pretend to advance a unifying idea for its subject.

4. The Caribbean

(a) General

Taxonomies, which tend to appear so lucid, are always tricky, and particularly so in this cultural context. *WLT* for instance, with its worthy attempt at global coverage, lists Caribbean texts nationally, by island, under the geographical heading 'Africa and the Caribbean' but worryingly elides writing from the USA, Canada and Britain under an undifferentiated and centrist heading of 'English'. Taxonomies are acutely problematic in the Caribbean region with its various political, geographical, cultural and linguistic units and groups. Now that we have become sensitized to old categories such as 'West Indian' there is a tendency to resort, for an equivalent, to 'Caribbean' without always specifying 'anglophone'. In his Nobel lecture Derek Walcott reintroduced the term 'Antilles' (in English, long relegated to geographical discourse), which is one way of circumventing the problem. There is an obscured problematic in the idea of 'English studies' too; if the study is in English, is that sufficient to qualify it for review here? It is noticeable that since (it seems) the recent founding of the polyglossic Italian journal *Caribana*, studies of the region's literature are tending to cross the language barriers which had seemed insurmountable only a few years ago. Increasingly, critical monographs, collections and individual essays are making connections across the water separating the complex sociocultural groupings marked out by language. Now a growing number of journals are starting to offer, in English, critiques of writings not just in English, encouraged perhaps by the fine American example (in relation to the Caribbean) of *Callaloo*, which recently published a special issue on Maryse Condé, for instance. Even as squarely anglocentric a journal as *JWIL* has now branched out with an article on French Caribbean women novelists (*JWIL* 6.i).

The tendency to bring out special themed editions of journals which function as scholarly, book-length symposia is intrinsically useful for the focus these deliver, and is also a way of circumventing the commercial market's innate conservatism, so that perceived minority topics can see the light of print. This year has seen editions of *MR, RAL, CRNLE* and *Matatu* devoted to Caribbean writing, a special edition of *WLT* devoted to Kamau Brathwaite, and a *Kunapipi* special, subsequently reissued as a book, on post-colonial women's writing, including the Caribbean.

Edited by Anna Rutherford, Lars Jensen and Shirley Chew, the *Kunapipi* special (16.i), *Into the Nineties: Post-Colonial Women's Writing,* fascinating as it is with its wealth of creative writing, and informative, with its photographs and brief biographies of contributors, is heavily skewed towards writing from the settler countries of Australia and Canada, with the Caribbean only getting a glance in (see also section 5(a) below). The imbalance is acknowledged (in relation to Africa) by Rutherford (who has made *Kunapipi* a much-respected forum for consistently high-quality work). She attributes it to difficulties of communication, but this is not wholly convincing. It remains a pity that only Erna Brodber, Lorna Goodison and Olive Senior feature in the Caribbean section, although Claire Harris and Joan Riley slip in under Canadian and British headings. Brodber, Harris and Riley all offer reflections on their role as writer – Rutherford clearly having invited her contributors to do so. Harris's is of particular power and subtlety:

> I have to know which strands of thought and practice are essential Africa, which strands are Europe, which are/were designed in the white hot cauldron of the Caribbean to ensure the survival of the human spirit. How did we come to the incredible, private, life-saving cynicism that enables us to watch the manoeuvres of the Euro-American Axis to ensure continued domination without turning into bombs? [. . .] This is the rocky ground of the writing I do.

Riley's essay is fired by the race and gender politics of fiction. She identifies the 'lack of an independent and representative black critique' not dominated by Eurocentric values, and tackles criticism of her work, defending, for instance, her refusal to accept upbeat closure, which would be a betrayal, 'providing, from the struggle of a community, a voyeur's view, safe, tidy and packaged as just another digestible, environmentally polluting commodity, to go with the television dinners and no deposit bottles'. Brodber explains that she writes because she is not a good talker; her story 'One Bubby Susan' is usefully reprinted. The volume is most useful, however, from the Caribbean point of view for the essay 'Anglophone Caribbean Women Writers' by Denise deCaires Narain and Evelyn O'Callaghan, one of a series of eight 'Overview' articles on regional literatures. These close the volume, but they might more helpfully have opened it, or at least been juxtaposed to the sections to which they relate. As it is, they are set in painfully small type and buried at the end, which is a pity, as the Caribbean one is an excellent piece, thoughtful, well informed, clear and interesting. It can be recommended to new students of the topic and old hands alike. After suggesting a number of recurrent concerns and approaches it concludes with the 'striking variety' of the writing:

> Like the culture from which it springs, this writing epitomizes the features of the creolization process: inclusivity, polyphony, syncreticity and hybridity; imposing any totalizing label on the literature would be to ignore its deconstructive thrust which seeks to undo simplistic binary oppositions of any kind. It is this fracturing of hierarchised ways of reading the Caribbean, that is particularly liberating to regional women's writing.

RAL's special edition on Caribbean literature, ed. Abiola Irele (25.ii) – the taxonomy of 'African' coming into question here – has two articles on the Martiniquan writer Edouard Glissant, one on his compatriot Joseph Zobel's *Black Shack Alley* (on which the film *La Rue Cases Nègres* is based), and one on 'West Indian Mythology and its Literary Illustrations' which proves, interestingly, to be about francophone writing despite the 'West Indian' title. The editor, Irele, has also assembled illuminating articles on Lamming's *Of Age and Innocence* and Walcott's play *Dream on Monkey Mountain*, long due for a contemporary reading; but one of the most fascinating contributions to the volume is that of Raoul Granqvist, who deconstructs the Swedish discourse around the award of the Nobel Prize to Derek Walcott. In a comment which re-enacts precisely the imperial seizure of chronology, Sweden's cultural attaché in France is reported as designating 1993 year '1 after Nobel' for Caribbean literature (presumably not counting St. John Perse, on the grounds that he could be co-opted – culturally or racially? – to metropolitan France rather than the Caribbean). Drawing on Walcott's Nobel lecture (published as *The Antilles: Fragments of Epic Memory*) Granqvist applies one of its memorable images to *Omeros*, which he sees as 'local and impure, a hybrid [. . .] a fragmented vase made whole, whose fragments and glue are visible and beautiful', and reads Walcott's 'I am not your city, your culture' as 'a near-desperate attempt to challenge and refute the bias of his hosts'. He anatomizes three different versions of Walcott's appropriation by 'universalism' in the Nobel discourse of those hosts, one presenting him as 'classicist', one as the 'radical, black man', and the third as '*l'homme moderne*, at the romantic Edenic crossroads where history has become an exotic foreground'. The way in which the literary text can be overdetermined by the elaborate systems of cultural production in which it participates was never more clearly set out.

More closely focused is Rodopi's special edition of *Matatu* (12, published in book format), eds Marlies Glaser and Marion Pausch, collecting a range of articles, interviews, creative writing and reviews, under the title 'Caribbean Writers: Between Orality and Writing'. Once again a publisher from continental Europe (Amsterdam) is taking the lead in pan-Caribbean studies: this is a bilingual edition, with half of its critical articles and a third of the interviews in French, while it includes a piece (in English) on Dutch-Caribbean writing and, in its review section, three anglophone reviews of German-language publications and a critique of *Caribana*, the Italian-published multilingual journal. The editors have collected contributors from all over the Caribbean and Europe, as well as Africa. The creative writing offered is, however, all in English, and is dominated by Jamaicans and by poetry, though, while some of the writing employs a distinctively oral style, no dub poetry is included. The interviews alone make the book worthwhile: the Canadian dub poet Lillian Allen, Jamaicans Mervyn Morris, Olive Senior and Pamela Mordecai, and Martiniquans Patrick Chamoiseau and Xavier Orville, are all given enough space to produce really interesting explorations of their personal creative predicament and their view of the wider context. In an article on 'Oral Tradition and Recent Caribbean Poetry', Emilio Jorge Rodriguez, from Cuba, draws refreshingly on all the language traditions of the region, although he does not have anything particularly new to say as he celebrates its 'cultural polyphonia'. Charles Bodunde, too, covers some familiar ground with his 'The Black Writer in the Multicultural Caribbean – The Vision of Africa in Edward Kamau Brathwaite's *The Arrivants*', but Moya Jones Petithomme offers a provocative and engaging study, 'Forty Years Hence – Immigrants and Yardies in Selvon and Headley'. The penetrating comparison of Selvon's *Lonely Londoners* of 1956 with Headley's phenomenal popular success, *Yardie* (published by X Press in 1992 and marketed in unconventional retail and service outlets), is a reminder of the scale of the changes in the London-Caribbean experience: while Headley's bleak vision is only a part of the contemporary picture, its popularity demonstrates its relevance to second-generation Caribbean-British people, many of whose parents were probably not reached by the Selvon with its oh-so-innocent humour.

Developing the theme of orality – of particular significance in the region's cultures – is Carolyn Cooper's *Noises in the Blood: Orality, Gender and the 'Vulgar' Body of Jamaican Popular Culture*. Anything from Cooper is worthy of close attention. This volume is no exception, presenting nine essays on aspects of Jamaican popular culture from song through performance poetry (Cooper's preferred term, which she credits to Mervyn Morris) to drama and dance hall, and examining the complex interactions of textuality and orality all along the continuum. She develops the familiar idea – gendering imperialism as patriarchal, which projects the colonized as feminized – taking the trope of womanism on to a specifically Jamaican position, that of 'slackness'. Citing Nettleford, Cooper illustrates the 'assumption of an almost instinctual correlation between linguistic "slackness" and sexual (im)morality that is thoroughly bred into the Jamaican psyche'. This she interprets as characteristic of the oral culture, with its roots in resistance to oppression, its inclusive acceptance and its flexibility, as well as its contemporary repudiation of systems of control. The eighteenth-century woman-voiced song with its line 'Me know no law, me know no sin' is taken as paradigmatic. Cooper has fun with the oral/sexual wordplay as marker of what she presents as her transgressive culture. Speaking of herself as 'guided by a missionary instinct for interpretation that attempts to reclaim the often derided "gibberish"/ verbal creativity of "illiterate" Jamaicans', she defines her project as 'womanist': 'to reproduce a body of subversive knowledge that originates in the centres of consciousness of the historically dehumanised peoples of the region'.

But the overall thesis of the book could have been better presented. The majority is, in fact, a putting together of a number of separately written essays from the mid-eighties, which, she says, she has 'resisted the temptation to rewrite'. While this can be a legitimate decision, in this instance, given her introduction to the whole project, Cooper might have been better advised to revise her material to present her overall argument more coherently. The individual chapters, however (mostly reprinted from *JJ*), make fascinating reading, and towards the end the unifying theme emerges more strongly with incisively original readings of Michael Thelwell's novel from the film *The Harder They Come*, and of the lyrics of Bob Marley and the dance-hall DJs, although her womanist thesis is projected uneasily, and in the end unconvincingly, on the rampantly sexist 'vulgar' culture of the DJs. The irony of subjecting such lyrics to the weight of academic discourse is not lost on Cooper. In an act of 'experimental Jamaican subversion of the authority of English as our exclusive voice of scholarship', she switches codes to give (in Frederic Cassidy's orthography) a critique in the local vernacular – which she prefers to call simply 'Jamaican' – of Sistren's *Lionheart Gal.*

For all her acuteness, she misses the irony of her preference for Cassidy's (relatively unfamiliar) spelling system on the grounds of its 'internal consistency, one symbol or pair of symbols always representing the same sound' – surely a case of Western scientific rationalism casting its homogenizing net over yet another beleaguered cultural heterogeneity. Brathwaite has, of course, for years been experimenting with a critical discourse which Others the dominant, not just orally and syntactically but typographically too. Cooper is undoubtedly mistress of the dominant convention when she chooses to be, but when she changes languages in the middle of her essay on Sistren, it is extremely interesting to observe the way the nature of the critique changes as the code shifts. This is not a 'translation' in any conventional sense, but a quite different kind of utterance (as perhaps one should expect). But in that it is characterized by appeals to the personal, by the emotive, by the metalanguage of proverb, and by a tendency to refrain from assertion: 'Mi no nuo; mi jos a wanda', it might be taken to confirm the concerns of such as Victor Chang that expression in the vernacular is necessarily limited: that perhaps 'the very spoken nature of the Creole, its very physicality, militates against its use for inner reflection and introspection'. Cooper, of course, is unable to stand truly in the shoes of a Jamaican-speaker without academic English, and it is impossible to know whether there is an unconscious négritude syndrome present.

One of the book's strengths, however, is its nimble unpicking of orality's presence in print, and vice versa, alive to the complexity of the interpenetration, as the social function of biblical text – the hierarchical Book which none the less reaches a huge audience as spoken language – neatly illustrates. In a witty discussion, in Jamaican, of the signing of the literary within the oral, Cooper homes in on the literary-English-influenced stories of two members of Sistren, which Honor Ford-Smith herself acknowledges 'sounded stilted when spoken, full of jargon, and hollow'. But Cooper adopts an inclusive and generous stance: 'wat iz fi-yu kyaan bi on-fi-yu! An muor taim dem stil kech wan nais likl ruuts vaib ina di Inglish.' Although the capital 'I' seems out of place, the remark is a nice reminder that standard English cannot easily translate phrases such as 'roots vibe' (to use the more familiar spelling).

Once again the bibliographical edition of *JCL* (29.iv) regrettably lacks a Caribbean section. *Callaloo* (16.iv, 17.iv) thankfully continues to make good the deficiency. *CRNLE* in its special Caribbean edition (1.1994) provides a useful though not exhaustive range of reviews of new writing. *MD* (38.ii) in its 'Post-Colonial and Asian' bibliography includes a short section on Walcott's drama – and on Césaire's, for those who are interested. Comment on Judy Stone's exhaustive bibliography of anglophone Caribbean drama will be found below. The major new two-volume reference work, Eugene Benson and Leonard Conolly's *Encyclopedia of Post-Colonial Literatures in English*, from Routledge (a press which is setting a good standard in this critical field), is an invaluable new resource for all kinds of information (see also sections 5(a) and 6(a) below). It is just a pity that at £160 it is too expensive for individuals to have on their shelves at home. It does, however, return us to the question of taxonomies. The meaning of the term 'post-colonial literatures' is far from self-evident; I incline increasingly to the view that 'post-colonial' is probably only defensible as a description of a reading practice. No doubt the debates about what we are engaged on here will continue for a good while yet.

In the meantime the cultural practice seems pretty clear at the pragmatic level, although certain new crossings may still surprise us. Easily missed but significant is an address given by Rex Nettleford as his contribution to South Africa's new regime, which in examining that country's cultural predicament addresses that of his own region. Published as 'Multiculturalism, the Arts and Nation-Building: The New South Africa' (*CW* 6.ii), it distinguishes the term 'multiculturalism' – 'concerned more with mechanical encounters affording ready retreats to the base of the original culture' – from 'creolisation', which describes a 'symbiotic interaction between people and cultures' producing 'a radically new dimension of reality' – the Caribbean process of 'becoming an identity'. In South Africa the task is not, he argues, to substitute black culture for white culture, but as Manley saw, to 'mould the clay of the old order into new forms that could have new purpose'. While warning against revisionism – 'The modernising elites are in constant danger of remaining tenaciously Eurocentric, and in this respect South Africa is not likely to be different' – he calls for an inclusive aesthetic to 'demarginalise' those who have grown up alienated within their own homeland. The builders of the new South Africa should see themselves 'as artists moulding a new nation', for as 'the conscience of the free society, the arts provide an excellent means of self-cleansing, self-reflection, and self-criticism, uncomfortable though this at times may be to the government and to the wider society'. That gurus such as Nettleford should offer the hard-won pluralism of Caribbean culture as model for other societies is perhaps not as new as it seems; the message of Walcott's Nobel lecture *The Antilles: Fragments of Epic Memory* is essentially the same, and it was probably part of the vision of 'Caribbean renaissance' with which those of his generation began as artists around the middle of the century.

(b) Fiction

Sadly it is not until they die that some of the region's pioneering artists tend to receive the critical attention they have long deserved. Selvon, although the subject of a couple of recent books, is likely to be a case in point. Below Eric Tabuteau's intriguing comparative study of the representation of interracial sexual politics in writings by Selvon and Fanon, who were both born in the mid-twenties ('Love in Black and White: A Comparative Study of Samuel Selvon and Frantz Fanon [*CE&S* 16[1993].ii.88–95]), is Jean-Pierre Durix's obituary notice for Selvon, who died on 16 April 1994: 'Like his own Moses, he knew how to laugh at others but also at himself. We cannot quite believe that there will not be another episode of the saga featuring his favourite trickster figure'. Kenneth Ramchand in his obituary tribute writes 'I think of him as the man who wrote the greatest love story in our literature, because it is the story of a man, a city, a woman, the world and that man's unending work of hearing thunder and re-creating its silences' (*CRNLE* 1.1994). *JWIL* 6 is dedicated to his memory, though not about him; a special edition of *Kunapipi* will be devoted to him next year.

The recent death of Andrew Salkey is (coincidentally) marked by an in-depth and unusual comparative study of his work. Peter Nazareth's *In the Trickster Tradition*, written in 1988, examines Salkey's five adult novels (as opposed to those written for children) in parallel, interestingly, with the work of the Maltese writer Francis Ebejar and America's Ishmael Reed. The book offers the first in-depth reading of the Salkey novels, some eighty pages long, but given the thematic approach indicated in the title it is a pity that Nazareth did not extend his compass to include Salkey's brilliant contemporary Anansi stories, *Anancy's Score* (1973), which we owe to the excellent small press, Bogle, publishers of this new study. Nazareth mentions the introduction to *Anancy's Score* but does not engage critically with Salkey's use of the genre. His argument in relation to the novels is based on the need for a particular reading practice, presenting Salkey, typically, as 'doing an Anancy on us; giving us a tricky story which we misread if we read it "straight"'. His critique bears down on the closures of the stories, which tend to thwart expectations, levering the reader into re-evaluation and the kind of interrogation Brecht sought. Nazareth, who as an African of Indian descent living in the USA carries a pluralist awareness to his work, brings a wide range of texts to bear on his thesis, making illuminating reference to writers and thinkers as various as Fanon, Jung and Albert Wendt, Umberto Eco and Ayi Kwei Armah. Of particular interest is his reading of the gender agenda in colonialism. He observes that there are few father figures in Salkey's novels; but, in identifying in the world at large a particular post-colonial problematic for constructions of masculinity, risks a masculinist bias in his own explication. While his overall argument is that the texts demand a tricksy reading which can get us 'to come to terms with our complex selves so that we can deal with and master a complex and dangerous world', at times he betrays a lack of the very multilayered awareness he claims is needed. He asserts, for instance, that 'Literature written by a member of the working class or peasantry about and to that class will naturally be straightforward' – will it? – and gives a very shallow reading of Salkey's dagger-sharp ironic phrase from *The Adventures of Catullus Kelly*, in which Catullus 'narrowed his eyes, arrogantly, heroically, like Othello before the handkerchief'. Nazareth has some important primary material, from corresponding with Salkey himself over the book, and at his best can turn a witty phrase: the works of his three authors, for instance, 'are tricksters, light-bringers because they want to bring things up from the depths, they want us to stop feeding history peanuts, because they want us to take hold of our history, control it and change it'. But it is difficult to avoid the thought that Salkey himself would have been so much more trenchant, and would have served the political objectives that much more effectively.

Mervyn Morris also revisits Salkey's work. In 'Re-Reading *A Quality of Violence*' (*JJ* 25.ii), a novel published in 1959 and controversial for its presentation of folk culture and in particular pocomania (a case of 'blackism', according to Sylvia Wynter in a 1972 critique), Morris examines Salkey's use of biblical language and his eschewal of 'rigid oppositions, simple certainties' to explore 'the interaction between African and European influences in Jamaican culture'. He concedes that in the novel pocomania is 'seen as a sensational spectacle', but wisely celebrates the multiplicity of unfolding reader/writer exchanges with his typical economy of phrase: 'We write, and read, from where we are.' Salkey was of his time, as indeed are we all.

Another commemorative publication is the first collection of stories by Frank Collymore, the founding editor of *Bim* and one of the founding fathers of the Caribbean literary renaissance. The editors Harold Barrett and Reinhard Sander have collected eighteen stories published in *Bim* between 1942 and 1971, and Heinemann now make them available to a wider readership. There is a need for republication of other early work which first saw the light of day in journal and small-press format and is now increasingly rare.

Collymore was a popular writer of a kind, who had a light touch with social mores although he also explored what Barratt in his 'Afterword' calls 'the dark underside of human beings'. A rather different kind of populist is East-Indian-Trinidadian-Canadian Neil Bissoondath. In 'Positioning Neil Bissoondath: Post-Colonial, Multicultural and National Formations' (*NLitsR* 27), Penny Van Toorn observes wryly that the 'enormous' advances he can command, and the fact that his work is being translated into French and German and widely reviewed in conspicuous places, indicate that a writer's mixed cultural heritage is not necessarily a disadvantage, but 'may well give his/her work broader relevance'. She takes on Helen Tiffin's strictures in a *CRNLE* review; while Van Toorn accepts that his texts 'reinscribe colonialist ideology and neocolonial political and economic relations' she does not see them doing so naively or straightforwardly. Citing Bissoondath's assertion of his Canadianness – 'I'm a Canadian writer [. . .] It's a wonderful big box. You can put just about anything into that' – she reads his work in the context of the Canadian multiculturalism debates of the 1980s and 1990s and finds him implicitly opposing 'both the exclusionists and the romanticists by abjuring the role of "other" – as both irrelevant and as exotic – and insisting instead on the universal relevance of his work'. The case is well argued that his work is above all not simple, but 'part of a considered response to the Canadian Multicultural Act and the many and diverse modes of its implementation'. Steve Harney in 'Neil Bissoondath and Migrant Liberation from Nation' (*JWIL* 6.i) also repudiates the hostile stereotype of Bissoondath. He takes a mellower view of his recent work, seeing signs of a 'new and more honest vision'.

Another East-Indian-Trinidadian expatriate who could use some recuperative criticism is, of course, Naipaul. Timothy Weiss's monograph on Naipaul attempts that increasingly rare phenomenon, an inclusive review of his *oeuvre* (up to and including *India: A Million Mutinies Now*). In a critical climate which tends to unhelpfully separate 'fiction' and 'non-fiction' – categories which Naipaul deliberately troubles – it is refreshing to see a study which from the outset refuses snap generic distinctions, and frequently places books of various types under one chapter heading. Weiss chooses an historical approach, distinguishing early, middle and late phases in the writing, characterized respectively by 'mediation, alienation and syncretism'. The book is titled *On The Margins* but it might more helpfully have borne just its long title, *The Art of Exile in V. S. Naipaul*, which is more indicative of its preoccupations. Weiss sees Naipaul's 'exile' as 'an ambiguous two-way journey': 'A split exists between the narrator as experiencing and knowing self, or between the third-person narrator and the authorial narrator. The use of irony and satire allows the author to say one thing yet mean another, thus creating a duality that depicts a two-sided colonial world and engages differing aspects of the author's colonial and metropolitan selves.' The rather flat delivery might have been sharpened by Homi Bhabha's theorization of ambiguity, but it is to Bakhtin that Weiss turns, invoking his idea of double-voicedness from 'Discourse in the Novel'. Weiss speaks of the 'basic idea that one can better know the center from the margins' – a hardly novel idea, which might usefully have been set against Said's privileging of exile as vantage point – although he proceeds to examine the intricate inversions of Naipaul's positions with considerable shrewdness. In some ways this is an illuminating study; in others, it is irritating – in its tendency to change gear suddenly into disquisitions on social history or economics or politics, and in its habit of plot summary. However, the *oeuvre* is so extensive now that few have read it all, and perhaps the summaries have their place. Generally Weiss is no stylist, tending to put his sentences down like suet puddings on a refectory table, but occasionally a vivid image catches the imagination, even as it tumbles into another: as in his portrait of Naipaul 'always standing on the fault line of his split as exile; he is always going over a crumbling bridge that is also a world unmaking itself'. Also memorable is his characterizing of the works of the 1970s as 'Afro-Gothic', a term which could prove serviceable in discussions of other texts: Conrad's, for example. Overall, however, the book's strength lies in its sensitivity and balance, making a compassionate and affectionate attempt to read Naipaul whole, with all his human contradictions teased out into the daylight. College libraries should add this book to their Naipaul collections as a useful addition to undergraduate studies. It is a reminder of how far Naipaul is established as literary institution that Weiss's bibliography lists fourteen critical monographs already, without King's, Nixon's and Shashi Kamra's, published presumably since his book went to press.

The growing corpus of Asian readings of Naipaul is extended by two Sri Lankans working in Hawaii. Wimal Dissanayake's and Carmen Wickramagamage's book on his travel writing, *Self and Colonial Desire*, had the misfortune to have gone to press before Rob Nixon's rather more convincing study of the same field, *London Calling* (*YWES* 74.667–8), was published, but to have emerged after it. In addition the Swiss-based publisher, Peter Lang, has unaccountably sent the book out into the world disadvantaged not only by a rather slight, summary approach, but by an absence of annotation, although the debate seems pitched at an intendedly academic level, and quotations are clearly referenced to a short bibliography. A good editor would have brought the text in line with current scholarly practice and tidied up stylistic tics such as the ubiquitous use of 'imbricated'. Unfortunately the authors take too much time out from their argument for excursions into general exegesis of its theoretical background, and the meat of each chapter is soon consumed. The thesis is the unremarkable one that Naipaul is 'a postcolonial writing about postcolonial societies using the implicit theorizations and signifying practices of the imperial powers', informed by an Enlightenment concept of 'civilization'. Far from the self constructing the narrative, 'as Naipaul would have us believe', they argue (which is far from self-evident), it is 'the narrative that constructs the self'. If only, they complain, he had seen fit to 'probe into the dialectic between the colonial self and the colonized other more productively'. But in examining what he does explore, they exhibit some blind spots, and appear intent on reading Naipaul's commitment to the Western Enlightenment project as a single-minded fanaticism at least equivalent to any religious fundamentalism.. For instance, after quoting, usefully, a 1991 article of Naipaul's from the *NYRB* (31.i.22–5) titled revealingly 'Our Universal Civilization', in which he writes of his time researching *Among the Believers* as a period of contact with those 'who wished to be pure' – a wish he deplores in a clear repudiation of the cultural privileging of purity – the authors go on to accuse him of aligning himself against 'epistemologies which celebrate plurality, difference, and heterogeneity', without noticing the discrepancy. Nor do they take account of the way *The Enigma of Arrival* is very much about celebrating precisely the mutual creolization of interpenetrating cultures. There is a lot of intelligent analysis in this book which is useful, but, after Nixon, it can only take a rather redundant second place.

Rana Kabbani, a Syrian Muslim, has revised her *Imperial Fictions: Europe's Myths of Orient*, adding a preface which gives a devastating account of the sexism and racism she encountered at the university of Cambridge in the early eighties, though not bringing her short section on Naipaul up to date. Naipaul features as the end point of her discussion of orientalism, serving as whipping boy to her chastening indictment. Examining briefly *An Area of Darkness* and *Among the Believers*, she anatomizes his hostility to Islam, and berates him for his confirmation of the worst aspects of European myths of the orient and for his blinkeredness: 'The East was a construct that had been whole in his mind before he ever embarked on the journey to it, and one that would hardly alter at all despite the journey taken.' While such readings of Naipaul as these two undoubtedly reflect an aspect of his writing, they miss an important ambivalence in it, particularly where India is concerned – which features as an object of love and awe rather than of scorn – and pay scant attention to the way in which his attitude has shifted, as he has obsessively written and rewritten his story of it over the decades.

Reading more sensitively against the grain is Laura Lomas in 'Mystifying Mystery: Inscriptions of the Oral in the Legend of Rose Hall' (*JWIL* 6.ii). In a finely worked study she adduces a wide range of non-literary historical texts to reveal a discourse around the Great House story which she then uses as a springboard from which to deconstruct DeLisser's novel. Her intention is 'to read past the claim that the *White Witch of Rose Hall* represents national culture or Jamaican history'. Rather, she argues, 'The oral voice, as encoded in the written testimony about the legend, render[s] DeLisser's tale suspicious.'

Another historical text features in Barbara Lalla's interesting essay 'Unmasking Deviance: Theme and Language in the Jamaican Novel' (*JWIL* 6.ii), which reads two recent novels against *Marly, or the Life of a Planter in Jamaica*, published in

1828. Bringing in Roger Mais's 1971 novel *Brother Man* to support her thesis about John Hearne's *The Sure Salvation* (1981) and Anthony Winkler's *The Lunatic* (1987), she identifies instability of meaning as 'a device for tearing away society's mask of sanity and normalcy and, through absurdity, for revealing madness'. The early text, on the other hand, inverts the process, staying with conventional representation even though it 'records gross distortion', in order to support the values of its society.

Spirit thievery features in Faizal Forrester's 'Who Stole the Soul in *Wide Sargasso Sea*' (*JWIL* 6.ii) and in Sandhya Shetty's 'Masculinity, National Identity, and the Feminine Voice in *The Wine of Astonishment*' (*JCL* 29.i). Earl Lovelace, who tends to be in line for positive critical evaluation, here comes in for some feminist flack over his ghosting of the female voice as narrator: 'Although it appears to empower and centre Caribbean women's voice, the narrative voice is also hostage to the pressure of a constituency that claims priority for its own male-centred programme of narrative and political recovery.' Shetty questions Lovelace's intentions in recruiting the feminine voice, since the text 'does not extend itself to any perception of gender as a locus of colonial oppression and nationalist resistance'. Although he is conceded to be good on race, Lovelace is found wanting on gender, as 'the story of the village girls and women gets consistently displaced'. I am not convinced, however, that Shetty follows her own argument through, when she asserts that 'Rather than problematize the mutual construction of racial and gender ideologies within colonial discourse, the novel is seduced by it.'

An indubitably eminent writer who has acknowledged his own increasing awareness of gender issues (the kind of awareness which, one might have thought, the deploying of a female narrator might signal) is Wilson Harris, who began, as did all Caribbean men over a certain age, in a culture of unrestructured masculinity. In Morris's phrase, mentioned above, we have to begin where we are. In his 'Profile of Wilson Harris' (*Kyk-Over-Al* 45), Fred D'Aguiar helpfully makes available to a wider public a *Kaleidoscope* programme first broadcast on BBC Radio 4 in 1993, which can serve as a stimulating and accessible introduction to his work. It offers contributions from fellow Guyanese writers Pauline Melville and David Dabydeen, as well as from D'Aguiar, in conversation with Harris, and from the English poet Edward Blishen. The comments from Dabydeen are particularly illuminating, but of course it is Harris himself who steals the show, talking about Guyana and its landscapes, and those of Essex where he now lives, and about writing *Palace of the Peacock* and most recently *Resurrection at Sorrow Hill.* He speaks of his use of archetypes and myth, and of his perception of the spiritual, offering a new definition of a term which much exercises post-colonial critics, 'home': 'I think that "home" signifies soul: that without a sense of soul, which reaches through us and beyond us, there is no home for humanity. Humanity is utterly lost.' Harris's writing may not be particularly 'fashionable' just now, but it is not difficult to envisage it enduring to earn respect and affection from a wider readership when most of today's criticism is long forgotten. As Blishen recalls, reading Harris's work for the first time – for all its 'tough sensibility' – is 'like reading a splendid dream'.

(c) Poetry

As a further exploration of orality, Rodopi of Amsterdam, seemingly always willing to take on non-mainstream studies, has brought out in its valuable Cross/Cultures series an important evaluation of dub poetry, Christian Habekost's

Verbal Riddim: The Politics and Aesthetics of African-Caribbean Dub Poetry. Habekost, a German poet who performs as Ranting Chako and is known academically for his 1986 anthology *Dub Poetry: 19 Poets from England and Jamaica* (*YWES* 68.752), offers a survey and critique of an as yet little understood phenomenon of huge cultural significance. His study, which originated as a doctoral thesis for the university of Mannheim, is scholarly without alienating the general reader, and benefits from Habekost's inside knowledge of dub. It brings off the difficult trick of writing engagingly in print about a culture of performance. It is a key source-book for primary material which is difficult to access, and includes a useful bibliography and discography.

Interviews with the poets illuminate their self-perceptions and should help to dispel some misconceptions and centrist criticisms. Benjamin Zephaniah, for instance, is quoted here as saying, 'I admit freely: some of my work is slogan poetry. If I am performing I want to whip up emotions. That's what I want to do. I am guilty.' The fundamental contract between an aesthetics and a politics is negotiated differently from the way it informs much canonical poetry – or the bulk of commercial lyric-writing, for that matter. Oku Onuora puts it well: 'The aim and purpose of what I'm doing is to dub *out* the unconsciousness out of people head, and to dub *een* consciousness.' That consciousness-raising is primarily about an awareness of black politics. Habekost traces the background from which the dub explosion springs, with an historical analysis which reads dub as 'coming up through the middle, as it were, of reggae's moribundity' in the early eighties, after the collapse of the militant optimism nurtured by the Manley government in Jamaica. But he recognizes from the outset that what began as a Jamaican phenomenon has diversified in other cultural contexts, instancing not just metropolitan Jamaican-diaspora activities, but new creolizations, for instance in South Africa and among North American First Nation people. The distinctively British interculturalism of bangra-reggae-dub synthesis from young performers such as Apache Indian could be added to the list, and the chapter on Trinidad rapso invites questions about the omission of other performers such as Abdul Malik (Delano Decoteau).

After definitions of 'Basic Dub', 'Defined Dub' and 'Critical Dub', the book moves to an historical and then geographical survey, looking at Linton Kwesi Johnson as the 'pioneer' and Oku Onuora as the 'originator', and moving out from Jamaica to sections on the British, Canadian and Trinidadian scenes, as well as further afield. The next part of the book, which engages with musical and linguistic connections, and contextualizes dub in orality and Rastafarianism, leads well to the third section, which gives a hard look at the technical business of performance and print. The second half of the book offers close readings of exemplary works under largely political section headings. It is here that women's dub is given a rather cursory survey, centred on Lillian Allen and Jean Binta Breeze. Habekost is aware of the feminist politics, and quotes Afua Cooper as saying:

> We can't liberate ourselves in just one way [. . .] When you fight racism you have to fight all the other 'isms' as well, and men are caught up in these 'isms' they have created throughout history [. . .] of course I'm gonna look at it from an Afrocentric perspective but definitely I'm gonna have to look at it from a female-centric perspective as well. That is crucial [. . .] feminism means empowering people who are oppressed. Not just women but also children who are

> oppressed and abused. And men, too, but for me women and children come first.

A more extensive examination of the female contribution to dub would have helped to redress an historical imbalance and the sensitive ongoing difficulty in addressing black sexism. Habekost's tokenism unfortunately serves as much to aggravate a sore point as to heal, but in other respects this is a useful and illuminating survey.

Himself a long-time nurturer of performance poets and explorer of orality in his own work, Kamau Brathwaite (who now drops the 'Edward') has been awarded the 1994 Neustadt Prize for Literature, which is commemorated by a special edition of *WLT* (68.iv). Offering 120 pages on Brathwaite, this makes an important contribution to study of his work and should help to restore him to prominence, as the price of Walcott's limelight seems to have been the eclipse of Brathwaite. The volume opens with a piece by Brathwaite himself, and includes a formal tribute from the Barbadian ambassador to the USA, and fascinating items such as family photographs and an account from his sister, as well as fourteen critical articles by, among others, Gordon Rohlehr, Elaine Savory, Abena Busia, Anne Walmsley and Abiola Irele. These will be discussed in more detail in *YWES* 76 alongside Seren Books's *The Art of Kamau Brathwaite*, which will become only the second monograph on his work.

Bruce King in 'Writing Walcott' (*CRNLE* 1.1994) deplores the paucity, likewise, of studies of the better known of the two, Derek Walcott. Enumerating five monographs, he goes on: 'Perhaps we need fewer critics arguing about theories of postcolonialism and more hard work reading the major writers and trying to make sense of their careers and what they have written?'

Critical engagement with Walcott's poetry finds a prominent place as the end point of the argument Homi Bhabha sets out in his study *The Location of Culture* (see also section 5(a) below). Bhabha begins emphatically: 'Nowhere in contemporary postcolonial poetry have I found the concept of the right to signify more profoundly evoked than in Derek Walcott's poem on the colonization of the Caribbean as the possession of a space through the power of naming.' The poem on which he focuses is 'Names', which unusually for such a work is quoted at length. As he acknowledges, bravely, *avant garde* thinking has sometimes been guilty of reductionism: 'It is too easy to see the discourses of the minority as symptoms of the postmodern condition.' He reads the poem as an example of his theory of the 'lag' of cultural translation – the 'intimate differences that lie between genealogies and geographies' – but gropes towards an understanding of Walcott's project using concepts such as 'solidarity' and 'a sense of culture's belonging' which, appropriate as they are, seem to belong in a different book. Earlier, Naipaul figures briefly in relation to Bhabha's discussion of mimicry (a concept adduced in Terada's title for her book on Walcott). Defining mimicry provocatively as that which 'conceals no presence or identity behind its mask', Bhabha gives a mimic-man genealogy which runs 'Kipling, Forster, Orwell, Naipaul', but surely Naipaul's self-aware engagement with the idea of the mimic-man should let him off Bhabha's particularly sharp hook.

Walcott provides the ground from which Susan Gingell approaches one of the lesser-known poets of the next generation whose work merits critical attention, Dionne Brand. In 'Returning to Come Forward: Dionne Brand Confronts Derek Walcott' (*JWIL* 6.ii) she intriguingly presents Brand's work as a radical revision of Walcott's: she 'confronts Walcott's vision of history and how things are, a vision hostile to her feminist and socialist politics' and 'begins to break the hold of that vision by critiquing his work in review form and by rewriting such key texts as "Ruins of a Great House", "A Far Cry From Africa", *Another Life*' and other works. Unfortunately there is a reductionist tendency at work here in the feminist preference for holding earlier work of Walcott's firmly in foreground view, at the expense of rendering invisible later, rather different works, where the gender criticism is less applicable. While the works mentioned by Gingell clearly have a continuing canonical importance, and the idea of Brand's creative project being in a sense to rewrite them is a helpful one, strictures on Walcott's gender representations should in fairness recognize the phenomenon of change over his now nearly half a century of work.

Lorna Goodison, a Jamaican poet of growing significance, comes in for a sympathetic reading from Christine Pagnoulle. Under the title 'Pilgrimage out of Dispossession' (*CE&S* 17.i.100–5), Pagnoulle explores Goodison's mining of both personal and collective experience to trace a movement from 'spoliation and subjugation' to a state of 'responsible self-possession in which the world is ours to protect'. Identifying the influence of T. S. Eliot as well as of local myth, she charts her expanding worlds, from the personal/ancestral through the progressively political, in which the past functions as 'a springboard for the future', but sees Goodison's second collection – although 'more outwardly concerned with collective issues' – as paradoxically more inward, about 'inner illumination'. Goodison's concept of 'heartease' (the title of her second collection) is explained by Pagnoulle as 'a sense of well-being which makes it possible to act positively upon the world' – a quiet phrase, but just.

Fred D'Aguiar is another young poet, of more variable output perhaps than Goodison. He was interviewed by Frank Birbalsingh (*Kyk-Over-Al* 45) in Toronto in 1992 when working on his collection *British Subjects*, before he reinvented himself as a novelist. The interview covers informative biographical and artistic matters of relevance to his whole *oeuvre*, which now includes poetry, drama and prose.

Andrew Salkey leaves us with a gem of a review of the latest collection, *Examination Centre*, by the fine Jamaican poet, Mervyn Morris (*WLT* 68.i.193–4). In a compact, many-faceted, sparkling piece he pinpoints the particular genius of Morris's deceptively quiet style, which carries a tightly packed depth-charge. He begins by offsetting Morris's style against that of Walcott: if the latter is the 'ultimate embellisher of the poetic line', Morris is 'the complete whittler': 'The one is a painter in lavish oils; the other an engraver with short, sharp slashes that go deep.' Or, drawing on local speech, his poems are 'Lickle but Talawa'. Morris's work is long overdue for careful critical attention. Such contributions as Salkey's here remind us that he was not only an important poet himself (author, among other works, of the epic poem *Jamaica*) as well as an impressive novelist, but an inspired critic too.

(d) Drama

Two very different but welcome publications take the study of theatre in the Caribbean a large step forward, and will facilitate further detailed research. Both offer general surveys, but they approach their task from different angles. *The Cambridge Guide to African and Caribbean Theatre* (eds Martin Banham, Errol Hill and George Woodyard) is an encyclopaedic handbook, with individual entries alphabetically arranged under geographical divisions. On the other hand there is

Judy Stone's *Theatre*, the first volume in Macmillan's series Studies in West Indian Literature (general ed. Kenneth Ramchand), part of Macmillan's valuable ongoing commitment to its Macmillan Caribbean imprint. Stone's book is the first academic monograph on the subject since Omotoso's 1982 study. Eschewing geographical organization, it presents an overall critical thesis engaging with the old regionalist question of what a West Indian theatre is or might become. Stone's book, therefore, is the place to seek considered critical assessment of individual playwrights' work within the wider phenomenon of anglophone Caribbean theatre, while the *Cambridge Guide* is a handy reference work for compact information about theatre companies and performers as well as plays and playwrights. Inevitably what tends to emerge from the *Cambridge Guide* is a sense of distinct cultural phenomena in different geographical locations, while a regional concept is tacitly promoted by the Macmillan book.

Stone, whose long career in Caribbean theatre has involved, among other things, review journalism, here embarks on a scholarly work of great readability, which puts before a wider public a great deal of hitherto inaccessible material. She is very well informed about interviews and early reviews, revisions and adaptations, and her critical evaluations of individual plays are always of interest, but her overall thesis leaves something to be desired, with its uncritical acceptance of Errol Hill's idea that originality of form is essential for the definition of a national or regional theatre. By analogy with the twin Japanese traditions of Kabuki and No, she argues that the West Indies may also develop 'two unique theatres – the one perhaps a total theatre with folk orientation, playing for the entertainment of the popular audience, the other a serious and more socially conscious theatre of ritual, drawing form and symbolism from the same folk heritage, but created out of a more considered craftsmanship, and affording a greater intellectual reward'. This seems to be a particularly off-beam application of the Western preoccupation with classification by division. Any distinctive genius of the theatre of the anglophone Caribbean (which the series is content to refer to as the West Indies) may be expected to reside rather in syncretism than in difference.

To support her conclusion Stone organizes her material – after a couple of initial chapters on the history of the early years from the sixteenth century to the pioneering work in the twentieth, focused on Errol Hill – under generic chapter headings. These are unsatisfactory, particularly when the title is examined against the content: 'Theatre of Realism' has the long title 'Yard plays and the social conscience: Errol John, Trevor Rhone, Alwin Bully', while 'Theatre of the People' turns out to be about the women's theatre of Sistren and Pat Cumper, and 'Total Theatre' proves to be about the musical, as instanced by the work of Roderick Walcott and Earl Lovelace. Progress through the generic chapters culminates in one on 'Theatre of Ritual', which presents the (clearly admired) work of Dennis Scott, Rawle Gibbons and Michael Gilkes – the equivalent, apparently, of the No plays in the Japanese analogy. This grouping of exemplary writers under each (unfortunately arguable) chapter title tends to be arbitrary and unhelpful. The most untenable of the distortions is the presentation of a chapter on Derek Walcott's drama under the heading 'Classical Theatre', which is both highly misleading and inappropriate to Stone's own argument within the chapter.

Yet the content of the chapter is fascinating – fresh, knowledgeable, and illuminating to students of Walcott, whose reputation as a poet tends to have travelled better than knowledge of his vast experience as a playwright and man of the theatre. Stone, who was with Walcott's Trinidad Theatre Workshop for several years, speaks with authority of the drafts and revisions of his plays and other drama work, such as screenplays, about which very little has hitherto been written. She also gives a forceful portrait of him as a man 'of powerful charisma, as demanding of perfection in others as in himself, staunchly loyal, caustic in tongue, quick to jest but slow to forgive, and capable of implacable rage'. From the book as a whole there emerges an acute sense of the will-power needed to overcome obstacles, and to make theatre happen in the region at all. Stone's tribute to Walcott, who 'by force of personality, by the genius of his artistry, by mutual affection and admiration, had welded together the finest theatre ensemble in the Caribbean', can be seen as marking the collective effort by dedicated artists throughout the region in the decades before and after independence.

Most chapters focus on two or three playwrights whose work is given critical evaluation as text for performance, as well as assessment based on actual performance and contemporary reviews. The emphasis is thus on the dramatic content of plays, rather than on an historical survey of theatre companies, productions or performers. Stone, who knows her material at first hand, makes available her extensive personal knowledge, and brings a professional's eye to bear on her critiques of individual plays. The study's structural uncertainties culminate in a final geographically orientated chapter investigating the work of diaspora playwrights Edgar White, Mustapha Matura and Caryl Phillips, under the heading 'Black British Theatre' (although White has worked in the USA for many years, and Phillips has now joined him). But for all its quirky organization, the volume will be invaluable for its serious critical evaluation of the best-known Caribbean dramatists, for its record of unpublished plays in performance, and for its extensive bibliography, which lists – in separate, rather confusingly presented, sections – published, performed and unperformed plays as well as radio plays and screen-plays, non-dramatic literature, and critical works (chiefly Caribbean-published reviews).

The *Cambridge Guide*, on the other hand, has a clear organizational principle, with introductory essays on the three main language communities of the Caribbean, and, within the anglophone region, geographical subsections on Barbados, the Eastern Caribbean States, Guyana, Jamaica, and Trinidad and Tobago. Each section has a very useful prefatory essay which places the development of theatre of all kinds in its historical context (including a lot of original data, particularly of the early period), followed by individual entries on theatre people including dramatists and actors, popular dramatic traditions, drama groups and theatres. This enables a clear sense of a Jamaican tradition, for instance, as opposed to a Trinidadian tradition of theatre to emerge. Since the distinct histories of the geographically separate communities have given rise to cultural difference, this enables the drama to be related clearly to folk traditions as diverse as Trinidadian carnival, Jamaican pantomime, St Lucian Rose and Marguerite bands and Barbadian crop-over festivities. But the structure has difficulty in accommodating federalist enterprises such as Derek Walcott's *Drums and Colours*, a truly regional drama commissioned for the opening of the federal parliament in Trinidad in 1958, and Walcott himself is entered under the Eastern Caribbean section, although most of his theatre life has been spent in Trinidad. The volume is extensively illustrated with black-and-white photographs of individuals and productions.

One thing missing from the *Cambridge Guide* entry for Trinidad and Tobago is the Hindu 'Ramleela' folk drama, made famous by Walcott in his Nobel lecture, but it does mention the Muslim 'Hosay' festival. This is given a detailed, illustrated investigation, tracing its relationship to equivalents in Pakistan, in Frank Korom and Peter Chelkowski's 'Community Process and the Performance of Muharram Observances in Trinidad' (*TDR* 38.ii).

Individual dramatists or plays (like poetry) tend to be less popular choices for critical essays than prose, presumably because prose tends to be the fuel on which the pedagogic establishment mostly functions. Drama is in a particular cleft stick, in that relatively few texts are readily available in print (as Stone's bibliography reminds us, it is not that Caribbean drama itself is a meagre phenomenon), and those that are available in print often alienate the reader from that very text, which serves only as a trigger for desire of a production experience. Two articles represent the conundrum from different perspectives.

First, Kwame Dawes is clearly unperturbed by the inevitable restriction of reader interest imposed by writing about a play which has not been published – and rightly unperturbed. His study 'Politics and Violence in Dennis Scott's *Dog*: A Study in Political Pessimism' (*JWIL* 6.ii) demonstrates that perceptive criticism can be of compelling interest to readers without access to the text under review, either as text or performance; and, of course, the whole journalistic business of theatre reviews functions mostly to inform readers who have not (yet) seen the play, so there is nothing especially new in this. Some writings of Scott's – both poetry and drama – are, however, available, and overdue for extended critical attention (his death in 1991 has not, regrettably, sparked off a commemorative, themed issue of a journal). His work is important and valuable, and should not be allowed to slip into oblivion. Dawes's subject, *Dog*, an unpublished drama from the 1970s, presents symbolic groups of humans, animals and a mixed breed, mapping them against the real social conditions of Jamaica at the time: 'Scott basically carries the threat of a society ruled and shaped by a violent imposition of social order on the basis of colour to its logical and bizarre extreme.' While regarding it as 'a clever and disturbing parable', Dawes asserts that 'As a political piece it lacks a coherent articulation of alternatives and answers.' In other words, it warns against the fascist tendency among the affluent, but fails to 'understand all of its characters and their motivations' – particularly damaging in the portrayal of the focal dog–human, Finger. This is particularly ironic, argues Dawes, since Scott himself is in an analogously ambiguous position: a shrewd point which it would be good to test against the text.

Derek Walcott has tackled the problem by writing verse plays, such as *The Odyssey*, which was rushed, deservedly, into print after its production by the Royal Shakespeare Company, first at Stratford-upon-Avon and then in London. Reading reviews of it as text curiously inverts the experience of reading the Dawes article, for one who saw the RSC production. It is already evident that the play will reach a much wider public of readers than of playgoers. Edward Baugh in a generally perceptive review, 'The Walcott Version' (*CRNLE* 1.1994), misses the extent to which Walcott has revolutionized the gender roles. For him, 'Walcott's is the stereotypical Penelope, wish-fulfilment of male fiction', when in fact she is a radical revision (within the confines of the given story) of Homer's. But Baugh also has the rare gift of capturing the elusive and the profound. He sees the play as the 'perfect complement' to *Omeros*: 'Together [. . .] they make one kind of fitting culmination to the career of the poet–playwright, the fulfilment of a lifetime's admiring, loving *agon* with Homer and the classics. It is an act of homage that has no obsequiousness about it, one free spirit's creative acknowledgement of the greatness of another.' This drama, unlike some play-texts, offers a rich experience simply as a book in the hand.

Perhaps we should educate ourselves to the pleasures of play-reading: plays have the advantage of being usually absorbable at a sitting, unlike most novels (a powerful recommendation, it would seem, in our time-pressed culture). Then the publishers might be more willing to make available to us in paper covers dramatic texts which have played an important part in shaping the region's literature, and once in print, they could again be staged as food for thought for coming generations.

5. India

(a) General, Poetry and Drama

Shyamala A. Narayan's introduction to her extensive bibliography of works published in 1993 (*JCL* 29.iii.53–85) briefly notes some critical works as well as reviewing fiction, poetry and drama. As a guide to the Indian literary and academic scene Narayan's annual contribution is indispensable. *The Encyclopedia of Post-Colonial Literatures in English*, eds Eugene Benson and L. W. Conolly, is a substantial work of reference featuring a good coverage of Indian subjects and writers (see also sections 4(a) above and 6(a) below). The range of contributors (some of whom, such as C. D. Narasimhaiah and M. K. Naik, are given entries in their own right) is impressive, as is the scope of the contextual, generic and thematic material. The entries on individual authors include brief factual details and, in many cases, interesting critical commentaries. The editors have encouraged contributors to offer some comparative analysis in these sections, and whilst this leads to an occasional overstating of critical orthodoxies (for example, the categorization of Raja Rao, Mulk Raj Anand and R. K. Narayan as, respectively, spiritual, political and 'uniquely personal' writers), this is more than compensated for by the contextual detail that emerges. Sweeping statements are perhaps inevitable in a project of this kind, but in general enough space is devoted to each entry to avoid oversimplification. The regional surveys offer useful discussions of Indian fiction, poetry and drama, as well as entries on, for example, 'Literary Magazines', 'Criticism', 'Anthologies', 'Children's Literature', 'Feminism', 'Film and Literature', 'Folklore', 'Language', 'Short Fiction', 'Science Fiction and Fantasy', and 'Translation'. There are also some thematic entries that deal with specifically Indian topics, such as those discussing Gandhi, myth, mysticism, and orality in Indian literature in English. Overall, Indian writing has been well served by this project, which manages to combine sound scholarship with readability.

Into the Nineties: Post-Colonial Women's Writing, eds Anna Rutherford, Lars Jensen and Shirley Chew, is a special issue of *Kunapipi* (16.i) and is also available in book form (see also section 4(a) above). It features a good selection of creative pieces by Indian writers, prefaced by short sections entitled 'Why I Write'. The contributors include Shashi Deshpande, Githa Hariharan, Sunetra Gupta, Bharati Mukherjee and Kanchana Ugbabe. Ranjana Sidhata Ash contributes a brief overview, 'Indian Women's Writing in English' (614–17), which considers contemporary fiction and poetry written by authors resident in India. She offers a summary of recent developments in publishing, notes some of the thematic concerns of Anita Desai and Nayantara Sahgal, among others, and draws particular attention to the multilingual features of works by Deshpande, Hariharan, Rukmini Bhaya Nair and Ruth Vanita.

Dipesh Chakrabarty's 'Postcoloniality and the Artifice of History: Who Speaks for "Indian" Pasts?', which investigates the subalternity of the academic discourse of 'Indian' history, with brief reference to Salman Rushdie and Nirad Chaudhuri, is included in *The New Historicism Reader*, ed. H. Aram Veeser.

Homi K. Bhabha's *The Location of Culture* collects together a number of influential pieces, including 'DissemiNation: Time, Narrative and the Margins of the Modern Nation', which briefly considers Salman Rushdie's *The Satanic Verses*, as does 'How Newness Enters the World: Postmodern Space, Postcolonial Times and the Trials of Cultural Translation'. Bhabha also refers to Adil Jussawalla's poetry, in 'Interrogating Identity: Frantz Fanon and the Postcolonial Prerogative' (see also section 4(c) above).

While it is, strictly speaking, beyond the scope of this review, it is worth noting that Sangam have reprinted Sujit Mukherjee's *Translation as Discovery and Other Essays on Indian Literature in English Translation*. Originally published in 1981, this new edition has a revised and updated bibliographical supplement, listing a selection of works translated into English for the period 1930 to 1992. Mukherjee's ten very readable and pragmatic essays ably justify the academic study of Indian writing in English translation. He also draws attention to the problems of definition raised by Rabindranath Tagore's *Gitanjali*, a work in which the author appears to be offering his own translation of the Bengali original, but which on closer examination reveals a process 'which should be regarded as transformation'. Anita Desai's 'Re-reading Tagore' (*JCL* 29.i.5–13) offers an interesting re-evaluation of Tagore's work, and a useful biographical account.

Ten essays on Indian writing are included in *From Commonwealth to Post-Colonial* (1992), ed. Anna Rutherford. These are drawn from the papers given at the Silver Jubilee conference of the Association for Commonwealth Literature and Language Studies in 1989. Those on fiction will be reviewed in the following section. Nayantara Sahgal's 'The Schizophrenic Imagination' examines India's 'plural culture', and discusses the writer's own experience and work. Bruce King's 'The Commonwealth Writer in Exile' is concerned with a wide range of writers 'who exist some place between the new national literatures and the new immigrant communities and their literatures', including Salman Rushdie, Meena Alexander and A. K. Ramanujan. These are 'likely to be most sensitive to and representative of the contemporary post-modern condition'. In 'Canons and Canon-Making in Indian Poetry in English', Rajeev S. Patke explores the problems and processes of canon formation in general and makes particular reference to the work of recent poet-anthologists, concluding that 'Anthologies too, like canons, are necessary evils.'

P. P. Raveendran's 'Text as History, History as Text: A Reading of Kamala Das's *Anamalai Poems*' (*JCL* 29.i.47–54) discusses the historicity of Das's sequence of poems, arguing that 'notwithstanding the apparent posture of self-absorption in the text of *Anamalai Poems*, there is a historical subtext at work in the series that resists its assimilation to a voice of pure interiority'.

(b) Fiction

From Commonwealth to Post-Colonial (1992), ed. Rutherford, includes seven essays on Indian fiction. In keeping with the theme of the volume, 'Trans-Formations: Cross-Cultural Communities, New Forms and Functions of Commonwealth

Literature', there is a particular concern with the diaspora. Amin Malak's 'From Margin to Majority: Minority Discourse and "Third World" Fiction Writers in Canada' examines a selection of writers of Caribbean and South Asian origin. There is a brief reference to Bharati Mukherjee, and a more detailed consideration of Rohinton Mistry's ironic method in 'Squatter', from *Tales from Firozsha Baag*. In 'Troubled Journeys: Indian Immigrant Experience in Kamala Markandaya's *Nowhere Man* and Bharati Mukherjee's *Darkness*', Emmanuel S. Nelson searches for 'the practical value of these texts to the immigrant communities that Markandaya and Mukherjee write about'. Whilst admiring the 'remarkable accuracy and flair' with which these writers articulate the experiences of subcontinental immigrants in the West, Nelson is critical of their 'analysis of racism' and their tendency to universalize experience through symbolism, a reflection, presumably, of their 'resolutely apolitical stance'. Ishrat Lindblad's 'Salman Rushdie's *The Satanic Verses*: Monoism *contra* Pluralism' analyses the narrative structure of Rushdie's novel to argue against many critics' unwillingness 'to grant the book artistic unity'. The basic argument is that the form of the novel reflects and reinforces its content and artistic purpose, questioning 'by its very plurality all forms of monoism'. In 'The Cross-Cultural Experience of a Pioneer Indian Woman Writer of English Fiction', Chandani Lokuge offers a detailed commentary on the life and work of Krupabai Satthianadhan, and in particular her novel *Kamala*, published in 1894. Satthianadhan's work explores the 'split personality of the Indian female psyche caught in the cross-currents of two cultures', and is therefore seen to anticipate the concerns of contemporary writers such as Kamala Das, Namita Gokhale and Bharati Mukherjee, initiating, 'in English fiction by Indian women writers, the female identity's metamorphosis from tradition to modernity'. Dorothy Jones's 'Decolonizing Women's Romance' offers an interesting comparative study of novels by Margaret Atwood, Jean Rhys and Namita Gokhale (*Paro*), in which 'the writer interrogates the genre of romantic fiction within a post-colonial context'. Ganeswar Mishra sounds a cautionary note in 'Problems of Transmissibility of Culture: A Comparative Study of an Oriya Novel and its English Translation'. Here the wisdom of using translations in academic work is thrown into serious doubt as Mishra, through a detailed comparison of K.C. Panigrahi's *Matira Manisha* (1931) with its English rendering, Lila Ray's *A House Undivided* (1973), shows how little the latter resembles the Oriya text. Finally, Viney Kirpal's contribution to the collection, 'Has the Indian Novel Been Understood?', gives an admirably lucid view of the narrative structure of fiction written in English and indigenous languages. Kirpal questions the reliability of Eurocentric readings which treat the Indian novel simply as a derivative form, and suggests that greater attention should be paid to the influence of indigenous oral narratives. A methodical survey of the episodic and digressive elements that the Indian novel shares with the Sanskrit classical tradition and the popular, folk tradition leads to the conclusion that these elements 'are the two outstanding attributes (and not the defects) of the Indian novel'.

Sudhakar Pandey and R. Raj Rao are the editors of *Image of India in the Indian Novel in English, 1960–1985*, a collection of thirteen contributions to the 1986 conference at the University of Poona. The introduction discusses questions of categorization and canon formation, partly prompted by Nissim Ezekiel's insistence at the conference that contributors say whether or not they regard each text under consideration as 'a good novel'. The essays each focus on one novel and are somewhat uneven in quality. Makarand Paranjape's 'Critique of Communism in Raja Rao's *Comrade Kirillov*' offers a clearly contextualized reading, and Viney Kirpal's 'The Perfect Bubble: A Study of Anita Desai's *In Custody*' is balanced and readable, but elsewhere the approach of some contributors is rather limited; for example, in 'The Hothouse Cactus: A Note on R. K. Narayan's *The Painter of Signs*', Ramesh Dnyate discusses the ways in which the novelist's 'interfering mind [. . .] seems to preclude his men and women from growing', whilst K. R. Shirwadkar's 'Literature as Ideology: Raja Rao's *The Serpent and the Rope*' finds Rao's novel to be overly metaphysical. The other writers discussed in this collection are Manohar Malgonkar, Kamala Markandaya, Arun Joshi, Rama Mehta, Salman Rushdie and Shouri Daniels. Four of the essays consider the work of Anita Desai.

Harveen Sachdeva Mann's '"Cracking India": Minority Women Writers and the Contentious Margins of Indian Nationalist Discourse' (*JCL* 29.ii.71–94) analyses Bapsi Sidhwa's *The Ice-Candy Man*, Nina Sibal's *Yatra*, Kamala Das's *Alphabet of Lust*, and Suniti Namjoshi's *The Mothers of Maya Diip* 'not only to underscore their contestations of the dominant, patriarchal national discourse but also to articulate the heterogeneity and plurality operative within subcontinental women's resistances'. The choice of novels prompts an interesting discussion of marginalization, since it includes the work of Sidhwa, who since 1947 has assumed Pakistani citizenship and whose novel largely deals with pre-Partition India, but Mann contends that the other writers can also variously be regarded as 'marginally constituted by the hegemonic culture'. The article as a whole is an ambitious and persuasive analysis of the ways in which these narratives '"crack" the unified Indian nationalist discursive tradition to establish the complexity of the modern Indian nation-state'.

The work of Bharati Mukherjee has received considerable critical attention in a variety of contexts. Emmanuel S. Nelson has edited *Bharati Mukherjee: Critical Perspectives* (1993), an interesting collection of twelve essays which examine the whole range of her work from a number of critical perspectives. The editor's introduction acknowledges that Mukherjee's *oeuvre* 'can be read in the national context of Indian writing in English and in the international context of the literature of the Indian diaspora', but in claiming her as 'a major American writer' Nelson highlights her achievement as 'a singular voice in the tradition of immigrant writing'. The essays themselves are largely concerned with viewing her work in an American context. All of the contributors offer useful insights, but the following are worth noting as interesting in their own right and as indicating the range of the collection. Carole Stone's 'The Short Fictions of Bernard Malamud and Bharati Mukherjee' offers a good comparative analysis, finding some striking similarities between the two writers' work. Janet M. Powers, in seeking 'a critical theory which will take into account the functions of multiple cultural codes', adopts a Barthesian approach to the fiction, in 'Sociopolitical Critique as Indices and Narrative Codes in Bharati Mukherjee's *Wife* and *Jasmine*'. Pushpa N. Pareke's 'Telling Her Tale: Narrative Voice and Gender Roles in Bharati Mukherjee's *Jasmine*' sees that text as thematically and structurally related to the Indian oral tradition of 'woman-centred' tales. Mukherjee, 'the writer of immigrant tales in America', reinvents this ancient form. Alpana Sharma Knippling's 'Toward an Investigation of the Subaltern in Bharati Mukherjee's *The Middleman and Other Stories* and *Jasmine*' is especially interesting. It offers an analysis of Mukherjee's 'representations and homogenizations of the Other', arguing that her fiction's 'assertedly radical critique of mainstream American literary-cultural productions is not as radical as it might be'.

Florence D'Souza Deleury's 'The Perception of the Self in Bharati Mukherjee's *Jasmine*' (*CE&S* 17.i.10–17) offers a positive view of Mukherjee's recent novel. Jasmine migrates from passivity to self-determination, following a 'path of inner liberation' that leads to integration into American life and 'the exciting new ethics of "adventure, risk and transformation"'. In *Reading Asian American Literature: From Necessity to Extravagance* (1993), Sau-ling Cynthia Wong views Mukherjee as a writer who can usefully be considered in an Asian-American context. There is a brief consideration of *Jasmine*, and the suggestion that 'Mukherjee is perhaps the first Asian American writer to exhibit a full awareness of the global context of contemporary Asian immigration', with tales set 'against a background of intertwined, transnational economic activities and mass uprootings caused by proxy wars in the Third World'. Geeta Ganapathy-Dore's 'Mapping Continents: The Journey Home in Salman Rushdie, Michael Ondaatje and Bharati Mukherjee' (*CE&S* 17.i.3–9) traces connections between three writers who have migrated to the West, offering a brief but useful survey of a variety of recurring themes and techniques in their work such as historical dislocation, images of family and childhood, intertextuality and juxtaposition of place.

Rushdie's migrant status has, like Mukherjee's, led to some interesting critical repositioning, with his work being evaluated in global as well as more specifically Indian contexts. Jonathan White has edited *Recasting the World: Writing After Colonialism* (1993), which includes essays on subjects ranging from African popular music to Australian film (see also section 2(a) above). White's own contribution, 'Politics and the Individual in the Modernist Historical Novel: Gordimer and Rushdie', is concerned with the way in which 'the modern novel has taken on the role of witness to the shaping histories of our era'. In a very readable analysis, White sees *Midnight's Children* as offering 'a profoundly useful breakdown of categories [. . .] whereby history is no longer a solid edifice [. . .] but is allied with dream, invention, myth and prophecy'. History then becomes 'not a polar opposite of fiction but its mirrored other, as Saleem Sinai is of India'. David W. Price's 'Salman Rushdie's "Use and Abuse of History" in *Midnight's Children*' (*ArielE* 25.ii.91–107) seeks to identify Rushdie's philosophy of history. Price uses Nietzsche's essay 'On the Uses and Disadvantages of History for Life' as 'an interpretive grid' to argue that Saleem Sinai (and, by extension, Rushdie) is a 'critical historian' in the Nietzschean sense, rejecting 'the monumentalist "history" constructed by Indira Gandhi and her followers [. . .] and the nostalgic, antiquarian vision of British imperialism'. Mujeebuddin Syed's '*Midnight's Children* and its Indian Con-Texts' (*JCL* 29.ii.95–108) takes as its starting point an increasingly familiar concern of Rushdie criticism – 'the characteristic hybridity of [his] work' – and then proceeds to an examination of the more specifically Indian aspects of the novel, which in themselves reflect the 'eclectic hybridity' of the Indian tradition. The article interestingly pursues some of the mythological and philosophical aspects of the novel, and concludes that 'Saleem's account of Indian history [. . .] is an alternative history, a tale of the marginalized [...] and an assertion of his polyglot identity as an Indian.' Another article by Mujeebuddin Syed, 'Warped Mythologies: Salman Rushdie's *Grimus*' (*ArielE* 25.iv.135–51), considers the hybrid nature of Rushdie's first novel and its 'characteristic heterogeneity'. The use of allusion is explored in some detail, together with a brief consideration of the 'one-dimensional representation of women' in the novel. The conclusion distinguishes *Grimus* from the later work in its minimal concern with 'questions of postcolonial identity and exile'.

Teresa Hubel's 'Devadasi Defiance and *The Man-Eater of Malgudi*' (*JCL* 29.i.15–28) offers an interesting perspective on R. K. Narayan's novel, by focusing on the character of Rangi, the female temple dancer. Hubel discusses the cultural background of the devadasi tradition, and the changing status of its practitioners, and clearly locates Rangi in an Indian context. The novel itself 'is wildly ambivalent about Rangi', who shows 'the potential [. . .] to unsettle the dominant mythic, ahistorical, conservative and patriarchal flow of Narayan's narrative'. The analysis, in insisting on the political and historical specificity of the text, runs counter to the tendency amongst many critics to regard Narayan's work as 'repressively timeless', and also suggests that other women characters in the Malgudi novels 'are made to bear on their persons and in their experiences the marks of Indian history'. Steve Carter's 'Narrative Ostranenie in R. K. Narayan's *The Painter of Signs*' (*JCL* 29.ii.109–16) argues that in Narayan's novel 'a process of defamiliarization [. . .] is being employed, albeit mildly, to estrange the reader from the act of narration itself'. As with Hubel's analysis, this is an idea that might fruitfully be applied to other narratives of Malgudi. In 'Breaking the Borderline: A Note on Narayan's People' (*LCrit* 29.ii.18–24), R. Ramachandra explores Narayan's frequent use of liminal characters in his fiction. Also worth noting is Urbashi Barat's 'Fictions About Fiction: Graham Greene's *Our Man in Havana* and R. K. Narayan's *Talkative Man*' (*LCrit* 29.iii.23–36).

LCrit has offered a good variety of articles on Indian writers this year. In 'Gita Mehta's *A River Sutra*: Two Views' (*LCrit* 29.iii.1–15), C. N. Ramachandran gives a useful analysis of the technique of framed narratives which places Mehta's novel 'at the centre of the Indian narrative tradition'. A. G. Khan, in the same piece, is chiefly concerned with establishing the novel's formal scheme through an analysis of character types. Syd Harrex's 'Shakespeare: "Almost an Indian of my India"' (*LCrit* 29.iv.1–14) interestingly explores the impact of Shakespeare on some Indian writers, highlighting the dynamic and creative appropriation of Shakespeare, chiefly in the work of Raja Rao and G. V. Desani, but with some reference to R. K. Narayan. K. C. Belliappa gives an enthusiastic commentary on a work of 'supreme intellectual synthesis' in 'Amitav Ghosh's *In An Antique Land*: An Excursion Into Time Past and Time Present' (*LCrit* 29.iv.15–24).

6. New Zealand and the South Pacific

(a) General Studies

In his introductory essay to the 'Annual Bibliography of New Zealand Literature 1993' (*JCL* 29.iii.87–114), John Thomson emphasizes the strong production of fiction which displays a great variety of modes ranging from travel writing, represented by Jean Watson's novel *Three Sea Stories*, to Anne Kennedy's *Musica Ficta*, which challenges many of the accepted conventions of fiction. Having discussed the new works of Stead, Shadbolt and Gee, Thomson highlights Damien Wilkins's *The Miserables* and Vincent O'Sullivan's *Let the River Stand*, works which were awarded the top New Zealand literary prizes in 1993. Thomson chooses to mention Anderson, Renée and Duckworth in women's writing while *Te Tangi Aroha* by Apirana Taylor is, in the critic's opinion, the only representative of Maori writing of note. For Thomson, the most ambitious novel of the year is Graham Billing's *The Chambered Nautilus*, which presents an incredible range of experience and much matter for intellectual reflection. Thomson's selection within the vast poetry production has to be small: among the established poets he chooses Tuwhare and Baxter; he admires the niceties of Elizabeth Smither's happy choice of words; he admits difficulty in approaching the complexity of Gregory O'Brien's work and wholeheartedly supports the choice of Andrew Johnston's *How to Talk* for the New Zealand Book Award for Poetry. Among the enormous number of plays published, Thomson selects Robert Lord's *Joyful and Triumphant*, since it was a testament of this author who died shortly before the first performance, David Geary's *Lovelock's Dream Run*, which 'exploits the make-believe which lies at the heart of all theatre', and Lorae Parry's *Frontwomen*, which champions the rights of women to pursue career and personal emotional happiness. Finally the bibliographer welcomes the two latest volumes of Ihimaera's compendium of Maori writing *Te Ao Marama*. The *JCL* bibliography provides invaluable information on the literary production of 1993, while the 'Checklist of Theses on New Zealand Literature: Supplement No. 1' (*JNZL* 12.161–5) completes Thomson's listing of published material.

New Zealand has been well represented in the larger general reference works of recent years. The *Encyclopedia of Post-Colonial Literatures in English*, eds Eugene Benson and L. W. Conolly, is invaluable and has a deliberately comparative approach to literature which involves critics world-wide (see also sections 4(a) and 5(a) above). Besides the critical articles on many individual authors and general surveys of the different literary genres, there are background essays on the history and geography of the country and some very informative overviews of aspects pertaining to literature such as anthologies, literary magazines and prizes, translations and film adaptations, which all contribute to the distribution of literature from the South Pacific, an essential factor that enables authors to live from their work. Robert Ross is the editor of *International Literature in English: Essays on the Major Writers* (1991), which includes long introductory articles on some of New Zealand's major writers. Each entry includes both biographical and literary elements and is accompanied by a bibliography of the author's published work and a selected critical reading list. Carole and Jean-Pierre Durix's *An Introduction to the New Literatures in English* (1993) is a survey of the literary history of the areas concerned and includes selections of texts by the major authors. It provides a good initiation for undergraduate students of post-colonial literature and discusses the major issues which characterize this field of studies. The chapter on New Zealand and the South Pacific illustrates the most important landmarks with extracts from representative writers such as Mansfield, Curnow, Sargeson, Frame, Baxter, Ihimaera, Grace and Wendt.

JNZL has had great difficulty in keeping up with its policy of yearly surveys of the various genres. While some must welcome this systematic reviewing as a way of keeping abreast of literary production in general, others will have regretted the lack of those close critical analyses which should appear in any critical journal of repute. In order to fulfil both these demands, the editorial committee have decided to bring out two issues per year from now on. Meanwhile the 1994 journal includes a survey of literature in 1990 with Lisa Warrington on theatre (see section 6[d] below) and Charles Croot on poetry (see section 6[c] below). Starting from Albert Wendt's title 'Pacific Maps and Fiction(s)', Ralph J. Crane and June Ellis explore the ways in which short stories confronted colonial and post-colonial precepts in 'Re-Writing Maps: The New Zealand Short Story, 1990' (*JNZL* 12.55–66): three texts are chosen to represent the new directions: Bill Manhire's postmodern *The New Land* remaps New Zealand's position in relation to the colonial centre,

Elizabeth Smither's *Nights at the Embassy* charts a different role for women, while Apirana Taylor's *Ki Te Ao* uses literature to propagate political and educational ideas. Each example shows the reconstruction of literary landscapes in the modern short story. In 'Some Other Countries: The Novels of 1990' (*JNZL* 12.67–101), Lawrence Jones surveys over two dozen novels published in 1990. He examines them within the ever-growing framework of 'worlds' (future worlds, overseas worlds, the world of historical events, the bicultural Maori/Pakeha world, the realm of marginal groups or that of daily life) that centre on New Zealandness rather than on questions of fictional style. Nevertheless he concludes that the realist tradition of the 1930s is still very much alive in today's writing. Jones's shortlist for the most impressive novels of that year is Gee's *The Burning Boy*, Shadbolt's *Victoria in Maoriland*, Anderson's *Girls High*, Duff's *Once Were Warriors*, McAlpine's *Farewell Speech*, McNeish's *Penelope's Island* and Mann's *Wulfsyarn: A Mosaic*.

In her perceptive article 'A Story of Land: Narrating Landscape in Some Early New Zealand Writers or: Not the Story of a New Zealand River' (*ANZSC* 11.1–11), Lydia Wevers presents a convincing discussion of how the land in early New Zealand texts is viewed through the closed frameworks of the various characters' visions of their surroundings; they are incapable of giving accounts of New Zealand without using the filters of their own experience, and Wevers argues that the descriptions of the new land become meaningful only when it has been transformed from its original state into an area that has been worked upon to satisfy the aspirations of the colonizer: 'the otherness of the new land is continually transformed into the landscape of colonialism'. Such descriptions either are rigidly controlled by the author or reveal the alienation of his situation.

Juniper Ellis compares and contrasts James Cowan's *The New Zealand Wars: A History of the Maori Campaigns and the Pioneering Period* (1922–3) with James Belich's *The New Zealand Wars and the Victorian Interpretation of Racial Conflict* (1986) in her well-reasoned article 'Race, Historiography, and the Colonial New Zealand Wars' (*SPAN* 38.86–103). Ellis demonstrates the ways in which politics and history are intimately related and shows how 'discourse or the dialogue of historiography is produced in a colonial text'. While Cowan focused on the action and adventure of colonial conquests, Belich endeavours to revise existing accounts in order to include the Maori point of view, which was originally absent from Cowan's accounts. In short, Belich bases his work on a close analysis of varying versions of the events, whereas Cowan's work was distorted by the Victorian ideology of the times.

Heather Murray's second part of her essay 'Celebrating Our Writers: 1936, 1951 (Part II: 1951)' (*JNZL* 12.119–34) describes the event of the 1951 Writers' Conference with verve; the rifts between the 'old' colonial writers, the 'middle-aged' Phoenix group and the 'young men' appeared to matter more than literary questions, but the differences were considerably narrowed by J. K. Baxter's brilliant performance, which was to impress young and old alike. Debates on the required standards to be set were heated and continued well after the conference; discussion of the aims and function of poetry produced diametrically opposed views, but what Murray considers the most outstanding difference between this conference and the 1936 Writers' Week is the evacuation of women and their writing from the literary circles. This, she believes, was due to the dominant influence of the Phoenix group on literary criticism, on anthologizing New Zealand literature, on the selection of texts for publication and on the editorial decisions for literary journals. Although a few women were published regularly in the fifties, it was only in the seventies that they regained the place in the literary canon that they had occupied in the thirties. Heather Murray concludes that literary history will prove that 'Authors' Week 1936 reflects the norm; the 1951 Writers' Conference reflects the aberration.'

The year 1951 was a pivotal date in New Zealand history for more than one reason: it divides the century in two; it was a political watershed for the government; and it was a turning point in the literary canon, as Heather Murray's article demonstrates. Consequently it is hardly surprising that the events of that year have inspired much literary creation. In 'From Fretful Sleepers to Juice Extracters: Versions of the 1951 Waterfront Dispute in New Zealand Writing, 1952–1986' (*JNZL* 12.135–60), Laurence Jones competently traces the development of the many texts based on the 1951 Waterfront Dispute over the years. The Authors' Week 1951 provided a platform for much discussion about the nature of New Zealand literature; meanwhile in London, Bill Pearson was writing his fundamental essay 'Fretful Sleepers', which became a starting point for so many artists. This critical piece, together with those of Baxter, Brasch and Chapman, was to transform the Dispute from history into legend. For Jones, the works of Shadbolt and Gee illustrate a changed attitude to history. The playwrights Thompson and Renée provide a working-class view of the events. Stead, however, has utilized 1951 in two contrasting ways: *Smith's Dream*, written in 1971 with the possibility of retrospective reflection, gives a futuristic view of the dangers that threaten New Zealand; while *All Visitors Ashore*, a novel published in 1984, 'can consciously use historical distance to gain an all-inclusive romantic irony, a pervasive mode of having it both ways'. Jones believes that Stead uses postmodern metafictional techniques to make his 'fiction' more credible by commenting on its own fictionality.

Annabel Cooper's review article 'Gate-Crashing Public Space: Desire and Masculine Romance, 1900–1950' (*JNZL* 12.101–18) deals with *Disputed Ground: Robin Hyde, Journalist*, with Jane Tolerton's biography, *Ettie: A Life of Ettie Rout*, and with Rachel Barrowman's *The Arts and the Left in New Zealand, 1930–1950*. Cooper achieves the feat of drawing these three texts together by analysing the ways in which Hyde and Rout found a public space to voice their opinions at a time when women were mainly confined to domestic duties while men alone exercised power. The link between these texts and Barrowman's work is more tenuous: Cooper believes that the feminine voice, together with those of the left and the artists between 1930 and 1950, all expressed a feeling of alienation. Her conclusion is that all these protagonists 'produced a variation on a nostalgic romance of masculinity'.

In 'Where to From Here? Contemporary New Zealand Women's Fiction' (*Hecate* 20.ii.217–25) Laurel Bergmann declares that the eighties were a decade when women writers were at last able to compete on equal terms with their male counterparts. This she believes is due to the establishment of the New Women's Press and the greater importance of the university presses; the Queen Elizabeth II Arts Council and the Women's Book Festival have also had decisive roles. Many new writers have joined Janet Frame and Keri Hulme on book lists. The hallmark of women's writing in the eighties has been diversity 'of style, subject matter, approach and form', and many taboos and generic boundaries have been transgressed. Bergmann believes that the production of all these women writers has been remarkable, and would hate to see their creative energy quelled by the present economic crises in the publishing world.

Janet Wilson's 'Contemporary Women's Writing in New Zealand' (*Kunapipi* 16.i.603–4) supplies a brief history of women's publications. Once the male-dominated editorial boards were overcome, women writers were free to become more experimental. Thus Maori artists such as Grace, Hulme and Renée are now well established world-wide. Short-story anthologies enabled many women to publish. For Wilson, women's contributions to the New Zealand novel have been diverse rather than memorable since Keri Hulme's *the bone people*. This critic believes, on the whole, that 'Contemporary New Zealand women writers are more experimental, witty and urbane than their predecessors.'

In 'Beyond Barbed Wire and Mirrors: The Contemporary New Zealand Short Story' (*LHY* 33.i [1992].40–9) Lawrence Jones claims that the critical realists and the modernist impressionists have been joined by the 'new story' – metafictional and postmodernist – in which questions of gender and race are more and more pressing.

Linda Tuhiwai Smith's 'In Search of a Language and a Shareable Imaginative World: E Kore Taku Moe Riro I A Koe' (*Hecate* 20.ii.162–74) reaffirms the necessity for a Maori academic to speak out on behalf of her people. According to her, language and education in New Zealand have always been based on imperial premises, a reality which distorts any comment or thesis put forward by Maori intellectuals about their way of thinking, reacting or imagining. She questions the West's tendency to perceive the Other in dual terms, and the imposition of texts and language embedded in the dominant colonial discourse. Finally she admits that she herself is partially 'colonised' and has not to date found a satisfactory way of freeing herself from this self-imposed but inevitable conformity to the Western world.

Lydia Wevers's 'Short Fiction by Maori Writers' (*CE&S* 16.ii.26–33), a detailed study of the evolution of Maori short fiction since the days of *Te Ao Hou*, sees in this production a continuation of the traditional oral literature with its themes of displacement and dispossession. She concludes that modern Maori short fiction, while addressing itself as much to Pakeha as to Maori readers, has become more confrontational, which does much to enhance the richness of New Zealand short fiction in general.

After a useful discussion of the concept of interculturality as opposed to bi- or multiculturality in the new literatures, Hartwig Isernhagen's enlightening paper 'Contemporary Maori Narrative as Intercultural Text' (*LWU* 24.ii[1993].135–51) opposes language and culture. He argues that English, with its accompanying cultural connotations, has become, in many postcolonial countries, the vehicle of literatures based on indigenous culture even if the discourse is somewhat 'borrowed' from Western literary traditions. Isernhagen subsequently attempts a typology of contemporary Maori narrative in this context, examining works by Patricia Grace, Witi Ihimaera and Keri Hulme. While Patricia Grace and Witi Ihimaera were initially concerned with the transmission of knowledge, this writing has developed into a literature of rehabilitation in order to avoid the creation of stereotypes. Isernhagen establishes that these three Maori writers are now trying to strike a balance between their protest against white domination and reconciling the old traditions with the demands that modern life places on the younger Maori generations.

Continuing this line of thought, Hartwig Isernhagen wonders about the appropriateness of using conventional generic terms for the study of the new literatures in his polemical article 'Why Novels? Why Short Stories? A Note on the

Use of Genres in the Works of W. Ihimaera and A. Wendt' (*CE&S* 16.ii.34–7). He believes that the relative openness of literary circles in New Zealand has led to English realism imposing its mark on indigenous writers. Yet he discerns that, while apparently adopting this genre, both Witi Ihimaera and Albert Wendt subvert it in innovative ways by using contrasting individual and group perspectives to produce multifarious voices that express diverging rather than converging opinions. The use of these Western genres is consequently quite alien to their original form.

In a controversial contribution 'A (Roundabout) Comment on New Zealand Literature' (*LHY* 33.i [1992].67–72), Alan Duff rails at the 'bores' who according to him have always dominated literature in New Zealand. He polemically argues that in *Once Were Warriors* he gave the country its first real insight into the major social issue called 'Maori'. For Duff, the Maori people are a race of losers and failures, and he provocatively adds that this has never been said because the writers of New Zealand are 'gutless'.

Another fierce controversy this year involved the launching of *The Faber Book of Contemporary South Pacific Stories* edited by C. K. Stead. Such a volume was long overdue. Yet, if the publishers had been better informed about literary politics in New Zealand, they would have saved themselves the trouble of a number of Maori and South Pacific writers of the first order withdrawing their texts from the collection. The book as it stands is not a true reflection of South Pacific fiction, and the uncalled for 'Note on Absences' unnecessarily contributes to the polarization of the New Zealand intellectual scene by drawing attention to the lopsided nature of the selection.

In his provocative but stimulating piece 'Narrativity, or the Birth of Story' (*Landfall* 186[1993].211–28) C. K. Stead challenges some of the theses of French critical theorists, particularly those of Roland Barthes, who claimed that fiction was neutral and without authorial voice. Stead proves that the author is ever-present and shows through the philosophies of Moravia, Borges and Grass that their influence has modelled his own work as a fiction writer. Stead makes a vibrant plea that good fiction should not be governed by the theorizing straitjacket of any critical school – especially that of the French *nouveau roman*.

(b) New Zealand Fiction

Nina Nola believes that Amelia Batistich, who wrote in the forties, was the first to challenge the homogeneity of New Zealand identity. In 'Migrant Women's Writing in New Zealand: Amelia Batistich's Three-Dimensional World' (*Hecate* 20.ii.140–59), Nola examines the isolation of migrant authors and their attempts to modify the binding ideas that govern the concept of nationhood. Batistich paved the way for artists from other marginal groups such as Maori and women. Nola points out that if Batistich's work is read within the framework of bi-cultural precepts, her multicultural renderings of migrant experience illustrate admirably the dislocation and isolation of cultural exile, no matter what the 'difference' from the mainstream community may be.

The idea of 'difference' in New Zealand literature has often been associated with Janet Frame. Nancy Potter's 'The Voyage between Self and Society' (in Ross, *International Literature in English*) provides a well-informed introduction to the works of this writer whose fiction investigates the nature of reality, art, sanity, memory, truth, life and death. Having examined the novels, Potter goes on to study Frame's three-volume autobiography; while the tragedy of her supposed mental record governed her early writing, the discovery that her schizophrenia had never existed was a major revelation. Yet it did not change Frame's ambition for her writing, which was 'to connect the events and myths of her two worlds, inner and outer'.

In 'An Angel at My Table' (*CE&S* 17.i.79–87) Claire Bazin examines how Janet Frame cultivated her difference and isolation to enhance her creative impulse. Bazin points out that Frame's desire for invisibility and fear of exposure in her youth could only lead to a death wish. Her internment at Seacliff appeared as a punishment for her lack of normality, and indeed, the treatment that aimed at a smoothing out of difference could only lead to a disidentification of the patients. When Frame was eventually released, however, she felt extremely vulnerable, for the atmosphere of Seacliff had protected her from the outside world. Her difference was that of a poet; by appropriating her illness and proving the diagnosis wrong, Janet Frame assumed a new-found identity of nonconformity which finally enabled her to put the world of her imagination into words and find new meaning to her life as a writer.

Marc Delrez parallels Janet Frame's 'Snowman, Snowman' with Milan Kundera's *Immortality* in 'The Unbearable Burden of Being: Janet Frame's "Snowman, Snowman"' (*CE&S* 17.i.88–98). He perceptively explores the concepts of 'living' and 'being' and their rapport with death and mortality. While Kundera's outlook is pessimistic, Frame believes that the dead live on in memory and it is the artist's role to remember them.

A number of critical works were published to coincide with Janet Frame's seventieth birthday. *I Have What I Gave* (1992) by Judith Dell Panny contains a chronological analysis of Janet Frame's novels but also includes her novella 'Snowman, Snowman'. For Panny, this author has subverted both language and literary forms. The allegorical component of the novels is systematically examined and shown to be essential to Frame's use of irony and parody. Gina Mercer further explores the idea of subversion in her book *Janet Frame: Subversive Fictions*, where she uses the feminist theories of Luce Irigaray and Hélène Cixous to highlight this aspect. Her thesis of the multiplicity of Frame's writing is anchored initially in the polyphony of critical appraisals that her books have raised. Analysing each novel separately, she provides a thorough and stimulating re-reading of the artist's works. For her, Janet Frame's revolutionary approach to language and form bears witness to the very forceful creative powers characteristic of feminine creation. Finally, Elizabeth Alley has brought together an amazing number of varied personal appreciations in *The Inward Sun: Celebrating the Life and Work of Janet Frame*. The result is a very entertaining and readable book which throws light not only on the life and works of Janet Frame but also on the contributors themselves who have responded so wholeheartedly to the call for tributes to Janet Frame on this occasion.

Margery Fee's 'Keri Hulme: Inventing New Ancestors for Aotearoa' (in Ross, *International Literature in English*) places Hulme's writing within the context of 'nation-building' novels. The analysis of *the bone people* is based on an examination of narrative techniques, the use of fantasy and a description of the interdependence of the different characters. In 'No Country for Towers: Reconsidering *the bone people*' (*Landfall* 186[1993].277–90), Rod Edmond discusses the different levels of psychological realism and myth and contrasts various critics' reactions to and unease with the novel's ideological aims. Edmond discerns a parallel movement in 'the novel's cultural and mythic levels' that 'involves neither a sentimental looking backwards nor a turning away from history. Instead, the novel offers an interrogation of myths of origin, and the relation of these to a possible myth of rebirth, without losing sight of a history of violence and dispossession.' This, Edmond points out, generates an interesting illustration of the connections between Maori culture and that of the colonizers. Comparing the novel with Wole Soyinka's play *Death and the King's Horseman*, this critic concludes that 'it seeks an inclusive vision based on the acceptance of otherness and difference, on facing rather than denying the past, on contemplating the results of several hundred years of violence and expropriation, on drawing myth and history into some intelligible relation'. Also concerned with various critics' responses to *the bone people*, Mary Ann Hughes in 'Transgressing Boundaries' (*SPAN* 39.56–68) closely analyses this work and rejects both C. K. Stead's appraisal of the contradictions in this novel and the classification of the novel as post-colonial rather than Maori by Simon During. She convincingly argues that Keri Hulme puts forward a series of varying boundaries which are transgressed, retraced and reinforced as the narrative progresses. This stems from Hughes's perception of Hulme as an interstitial writer – neither Pakeha nor Maori – who has consequently learnt to circumnavigate barriers instead of forcing them down. *The bone people* follows a similar path; its numerous cultural references defy partisan definition, literary categorization or thematic direction. The novel oscillates between 'two sets of thematic possibilities rather than moving toward a resolution', and consequently progresses spirally so that the reader can erect new relationships between the strands of narrative and between the varying modes of communication, be they written, oral or musical, Maori or English.

In 'Witi Ihimaera: Glimpses of Childhood' (in Ross, *International Literature in English*), Nan Bowman Albinski provides a good introduction to the life and works of this author and shows how the political changes have led to a hardening of the tone of Ihimaera's novels. Albinski traces the changes from the innocence of *Pounamu Pounamu* through the urban difficulties described in *A New Net Goes Fishing* to the confrontational epic work *The Matriarch*.

Although Mansfield's writing was multiform, Patrick Morrow emphasizes first and foremost her mastery of short fiction. In 'Katherine Mansfield: The Idea of the Perfect Short Story' (in Ross, *International Literature in English*), he examines the underlying techniques of her story-telling that have often been overlooked by the superficial reader.

After briefly discussing the more significant phenomena of New Zealand's literary and cultural nationalism in the 1930s, Stuart Murray goes on to reposition John Mulgan's writing within the context of the socioeconomic problems of the period in 'Oxford Man: John Mulgan and National Discourse' (*SPAN* 39.17–28). Murray claims that Mulgan's involvement with the English literary circles considerably 'complicates his position within the New Zealand nationalist canon'. Drawing on the theoretical writings of Bhabha and Spivak, he concludes that Mulgan's exploration of varying frontiers – political, historical, psychological and physical – are less stably defined than New Zealand critics have believed, and prefers to place Mulgan's *Man Alone* within the context of a challenge to the boundaries of nationalist canons as they were being developed in New Zealand at the time.

Alex Calder's 'An Interview with Bill Pearson' (*Landfall* 185[1993].51–77) draws this reserved intellectual into a fascinating discussion of his life, his ideals and his work. The history behind his two landmark publications – 'Fretful Sleepers' and *Coal Flat* – is carefully plotted. We learn of his religious searchings as a student, his well-thought-out attachment to New Zealand, his Marxist ideals and subsequent questionings, his engagement in the various peace movements and finally his fight against racial discrimination. It is particularly interesting to follow his account of his early explorings of relationships with the Maori community in a country which in the early sixties possessed two very separate communities. Pearson is never afraid to disclose his unwitting *faux pas*, and his account bears witness to his sensitive recuperation of such difficult situations. His respect for the other is unwavering and his candid modesty about his literary role quite refreshing.

Patrick Holland's '"A Virtue in Shedding Light": An Interview with Maurice Shadbolt' (*ANZSC* 11.68–73) traces the genesis of Shadbolt's New Zealand Wars trilogy, and underlines the importance of accuracy for the author, who, while not attempting to give a documentary account of events, aims to evoke the atmosphere of certain historical periods.

In his article 'C. K. Stead and the New Literary Order' (*Meanjin* 4.695–703), Mark Williams examines the work and the turbulent career of C. K. Stead as a writer and critic. Stead's stances have always stimulated heated discussion and his influence, whether good or bad, seems to have spread world-wide. While Simon During and Jonathan Lamb have, according to Williams, done much to draw international interest in race, culture and discursive power in New Zealand's literature, Stead's reputation is essentially derived from his criticism of British and American poetry. Williams illustrates the decline of Stead's influence in New Zealand by describing the editorial politics behind *The Oxford Book of Short Stories* (1966) and *The Faber Book of Contemporary South Pacific Stories*. The former was published in a period which favoured nationalistic preoccupations in a country which was moving away from Eurocentrism, whereas the latter epitomizes the colonial backlash of Maori and women who have felt excluded from the male Pakeha literary circles so powerful in the middle of the century. Williams believes that Stead's position has not evolved greatly since the fifties, while the profound shift in New Zealand letters has marginalized him. Yet, for Mark Williams, C. K. Stead remains one of the country's most important writers, as his latest novel *The Singing Whakapapa* proves.

For J. C. Sturm 'the roses' and 'the taupata' are the two elements of her make-up, namely her Pakeha and her Maori heritage. The undefined area between the two represents that special place in which she works as an artist. In this interview 'Between the Roses and the Taupata: J. C. Sturm Interviewed by Briar Wood' (*Hecate* 20.ii.175–82) Sturm gives an account of her early married life with James K. Baxter. She finds it difficult to talk about the Maori since they cannot be reduced to generalizations; she claims that she is a Maori writer, which need not mean writing about things Maori. For her, Maori as a metaphorical language approaches problems obliquely. Consequently she finds Alan Duff's confrontational attitude out of keeping with traditional ways.

(c) New Zealand Poetry

Charles Croot on 'New Zealand Poetry in 1990' (*JNZL* 12.45–54) gives an exhaustive account of the thirty poetry publications of that year. *Sport* and *Takahe* have provided occasional outlets for poets after the disappearance of the *Listener*'s weekly poem, so the first two issues of *PoetryNZ*, he believes, are well timed; he expresses the hope that this publication will concentrate on the work of promising poets rather than on those who are already established.

In 'Opening the Archive: Robin Hyde, Eileen Duggan and the Persistence of Record' (*Hecate* 20.ii.193–216), Michele Leggott rehabilitates these important early women writers in the foundation of a national literature. Leggott convincingly analyses the sexual innuendos and the strategies of concealment that are so much part of Hyde's work in the thirties. The second part of her article deals mostly with Eileen Duggan's ongoing disputes with Allen Curnow, the editor of *The Penguin Book of New Zealand Verse*. Leggott draws tenuous feminist connections between these fragmented parts of her argument but fails to establish a convincing conclusion.

In her informative article 'The Varieties of Cultural Nationalism: *Landfall in Unknown Seas*, 1945 to 1995' (*SPAN* 39.29–55), Sarah Shieff traces the history of various forms of national culturalism since the 1930s. Using the successive performances of Allen Curnow's poem 'Landfall in Unknown Seas' and Douglas Lilburn's incidental music composed to accompany the poem's performance in 1942, Shieff illustrates how both have contributed to the formation of a national cultural identity. She studies the historical collaboration with Beaglehole, the artistic connivance with Lilburn, the emergence of a sense of independent nationhood against the background of World War II, and the colonial celebrations of Waitangi. In her conclusion she shows that the recent disagreement between Curnow and Ian Fraser over the choice of Sir Edmund Hillary as narrator in the latest CD recording of 'Landfall in Unknown Seas' is an ironic comment on the making of a national identity.

In 'How to Read Curnow: "A Note on the Parakeets at Karekare"' (*LHY* 33[1992].i.9–12), C. K. Stead asserts that, for the poet, there is a reality out there which we share and yet, in the absence of God, that certainty must rest on the fleeting perceptions of 'the walking eye'. Lauris Edmond in 'Why I Write' (*Kunapipi* 16.i.197–8) describes her development as a poet and the author of a three-volume autobiography.

In 'Rapua te tumu – To the Point' (*CE&S* 16.ii.15–25) Reina Whaitiri emphasizes the importance of women's creativity in traditional Maori poetry. She claims that women have always fought against the constraints of tradition and male arrogance, sexual violence and abuse. A very special form of inner strength has resulted from these tribulations, which today has gained them a place of prime importance within the Maori community. Consequently their poetry has come to express both the power of their resistance in adversity and the influence they wield in Maori circles.

In 'Maori and Aboriginal Literature in Australia and New Zealand. Poetry Anthologies: Some Problems and Perspectives' (*NLitsR* 25[1993].23–36), Lawrence Bourke compares the two contact histories of these different indigenous peoples and suggests that 'whether the contemporary interest in Maori and Aboriginal writers as speaking subjects of their own discourse represents the abrogation of imperialist designs or the realisation of a universalism so supreme that difference can entertain but never threaten, it remains an open question'.

(d) New Zealand Theatre

Lisa Warrington's 'Theatre in 1990' (*JNZL* 12.5–44), an extremely detailed study, covers productions throughout the country. She also provides an extensive list of recent New Zealand plays, adaptations and comedy/cabaret/musicals performed that year together with bibliographical details concerning publications; a list of radio and television broadcasts and film releases is supplied.

Adrienne Simpson's 'Footlights and Fenians: The Adventures of a Touring Concert Party in Gold-Rush New Zealand' (*ADS* 24.182–96) is a light-hearted and lively account of the travels and adventures of the Simonsens and George F. Price, who put on numerous shows in the most isolated areas of the south island as well as in the larger towns of New Zealand between 1860 and 1870.

Joanne Tompkins in 'What We Want and What We Get: Renée's *Jeannie Once*' (*Hecate* 20.ii.243–50) is disappointed by what she perceives as a much weaker feminist statement in this play. While she concedes that Renée has collected 'the significant arguments and stagings of gender construction and patriarchal constraints on women', recognizes the playwright's vision of colonial New Zealand and finds the performance convincing, Tompkins judges that the play is an entertaining statement of 'women's theatre' but lacks feminist punch.

(e) The South Pacific

In 'Autobiography in the Pacific: Changing Functions of Self, Writing and Nations' (*NLitsR* 27.29–44), Michael Hayes argues that early autobiography was governed by colonial institutions which insidiously modified indigenous accounts: the forewords, footnotes and translations written by the missionaries aimed at giving a Christianized, acceptable version of local myths. Taking examples from three early autobiographies, *Joel Bulu: The Autobiography of a Native Minister of the South Seas. Translated by a Missionary* (1871), *Story of a Melanesian Deacon: Clement Marau Written by Himself* (1894), and *The Erstwhile Savage: An Account of the Life of Ligeremaluoga (Osea)* (1894), he argues that these texts are simultaneously the spiritual autobiographies of the European and the first indigenous writings to come into being.

In 'Two Autobiographical Responses to Decolonization in Papua New Guinea' (*NLitsR* 27.57–69), Ellerman shows that Wedega in *Listen My Country* (1981) regards politics as a world-wide affair and emphasizes the essential place of women in society, while Matane's *My Childhood in New Guinea* (1972) underscores the importance of education and uses the two culture systems to create an orderly world.

In 'Albert Wendt: The Attempt "to Snare the Void and Give it Word"' (in Ross, *International Literature in English*), Jean-Pierre Durix provides a detailed introduction to the artistic creation of the most significant writer in the South Pacific. Durix underlines Wendt's use of metafiction, and argues that his mastery of humour, irony and parody, together with his ability to contrast different voices, and deflate stereotypes about the South Seas, contributes to the exceptional vivacity of his narratives.

'Pages from Albert Wendt's Photograph Album' (*CE&S* 16.ii.1–6) is a transcript of this writer's commented poetry reading at the University of Burgundy, where an honorary doctorate was conferred on him in November 1993. The poems underline the importance of family ties for him. In 'The Travels of a Tusitala: Albert Wendt in Burgundy' (*CE&S* 16.ii.7–9), Wendt examines the role of hierarchy and power games in community life. For him, history and memory play a vital part in the constitution of a stable present. In his poetic sequence 'Nightflight', he evokes his journey to China. In an answer to the audience at his reading, Wendt gives an interesting account of his New Zealand education, of his beginnings and growth as a writer.

Jean Guiart's 'Albert Wendt's Anthropological Truth' (*CE&S* 16.ii.38–43) compares the research and expectations of anthropologists with Albert Wendt's literary evocation of Samoa. For him, these two points of view converge in their pessimistic diagnosis concerning the effects of colonialism on Samoan society, but they are both confident in the resilience of the *faa Samoa* to overcome these problems. For Jean Guiart (a world authority on anthropology in the South Pacific), though Wendt's writing does not pretend to be strictly true to reality, his fictional work faithfully reflects the more disturbing aspects of Samoan life, which suggests that fiction can be more truthful than documentary writing.

In 'A Postmodernism of Resistance: Albert Wendt's *Black Rainbow*' (*ArielE* 25.iv.101–13), an overview of this novel, Juniper Ellis explores how Wendt uses postmodern techniques to resist 'rigid concepts of cultural identity' and to escape the 'imposition of "high" culture and advanc[es] a complex conception of indigenous culture'. For her, this work questions its own status as fiction and the processes of representation. Unfortunately Ellis fails to spot some of the fairly obvious and highly amusing references to New Zealand's literati. She interestingly argues in her conclusion that 'Wendt's employment of postmodern and traditional techniques to attempt a decolonization of artistic and cultural realms suggests one way in which postcolonialism can modify postmodernism.'

Lynda Schulz's 'Theatre for the seven hundred: William Takaku's dream for the National Theatre of Papua New Guinea' (*ADS* 24.47–55) gives a brief history of the Papua New Guinea National Theatre Company established in 1974. In a country of such diversity, there is an increasing awareness of the dangers of the indiscriminate development of the environment, which may lead to the individual populations and traditions of PNG becoming uniform. Schulz's interview with Takaku underlines the creative adaptations ongoing during each performance. Takaku aims to create a federal national theatre in order to protect valuable differences and provide a solid organization to defend the interests of PNG traditional theatre better.

Books Reviewed

Abrahams, Beverley, and Lesley Humphrey. *Study Guide to Harvest of Thorns*. Academic Books (Pvt) Harare (1993). pp. 108. £3.75. ISBN 0 9492 2926 1.

Ackland, Michael. *That Shining Band: A Study of Australian Colonial Verse Tradition*. UQP. pp. 243. A$29.95. ISBN 0 7022 2686 6.

Adejare, Oluwole. *Language and Style in Soyinka: A Systemic Textlinguistic Study of a Literary Idiolect*. HeinemannNg. pp. 207. £16.75. ISBN 9 7812 9849 9.

Alexander, Alison. *A Mortal Flame: Marie Bjelke Petersen: Australian Romance Writer 1874–1969*. Blubber Head. pp. 276. A$29.95. ISBN 0 9085 2825 6.

Algoo-Baksh, Stella. *Austin C. Clarke*. ECW. pp. 234. n.p. ISBN 1 5502 2218 X.

Allen, Judith A. *Rose Scott: Vision and Revision in Feminism*. OUPAus. pp. 331. A$49.95. ISBN 0 1955 4846 9.

Alley, Elizabeth, ed. *The Inward Sun: Celebrating the Life and Work of Janet Frame*. DBAP. pp. 214. NZ$34.95. ISBN 0 9088 9639 5.

Banham, Martin, Errol Hill and George Woodyard, eds. *The Cambridge Guide to African and Caribbean Theatre*. CUP. pp. 261. £35. ISBN 0 5214 1139 4.

Beier, Ulli, ed. *The Return of Shango: The Theatre of Duro Ladipo*. Iwalewa-Haus. pp. 40. DM40. No ISBN.

Benson, Eugene, and L. W. Conolly, eds. *Encyclopedia of Post-Colonial Literatures in English*. 2 vols. Routledge. pp. 1,874. £160. ISBN 0 4150 5199 1 (set), 0 4151

1344 X (vol. 1), 0 4151 1345 8 (vol. 2).
Bentley, D. M. R. *Mimic Fires: Accounts of Early Long Poems on Canada*. McG-QUP. pp. 368. £35. ISBN 0 7735 1200 4.
Bhabha, Homi K. *The Location of Culture*. Routledge. pp. 285. hb £35, pb £11.99. ISBN 0 4150 1635 5, 0 4150 5406 0.
Boire, Gary. *Morley Callaghan: Literary Anarchist*. ECW. pp. 131. $9.95. ISBN 1 5502 2185 X.
Brady, Veronica. *Caught in the Draught*. A&R. pp. 310. A$24.95. ISBN 0 2071 7943 3.
Buckridge, Patrick. *The Scandalous Penton: A Biography of Brian Penton*. UQP. pp. 350. A$34.95. ISBN 0 7022 2602 5.
Cameron, Elspeth. *Earle Birney: A Life*. Viking. pp. 685. A$40. ISBN 0 6708 2874 2.
Candy, Philip C., and John Laurent, eds. *Pioneering Culture: Mechanics Institutes and Schools of Art in Australia*. Auslib. pp. 413. A$48. ISBN 1 8751 4525 7.
Capone, Giovanna, Claudio Gorlier and Bernard Hickey, eds. *Commonwealth Literary Cultures: New Voices, New Approaches*. Edizioni (1993). pp. 899. n.p. ISBN 8 8726 1056 7.
Clarke, Patricia. *Tasma: The Life of Jessie Couvreur*. A&UA. pp. 213. A$34.95. ISBN 1 8637 3519 4.
Cochrane, Kathy. *Oodgeroo*. UQP. pp. 235. A$16.95. ISBN 0 7022 2621 1.
Coleman, Peter. *Memoirs of a Slow Learner*. A&R. pp.168. A$16.95. ISBN 0 2071 8248 5.
Compton, Anne. *A. J. M. Smith: Canadian Metaphysical*. ECW. pp. 262. n.p. ISBN 1 5502 2225 2.
Cooper, Carolyn. *Noises in the Blood: Orality, Gender and the 'Vulgar' Body of Jamaican Popular Culture*. Warwick University Caribbean Studies. MacmillanC (1993). pp. 214. £13.95. ISBN 0 3335 7824 4.
Corkhill, Annette Robyn. *Australian Writing: Ethnic Writers 1945–1991*. Academia. pp. 234. A$35. ISBN 0 9589 6685 0.
Davey, Frank. *Canadian Literary Power*. NeWest. pp. 317. ISBN 0 9208 9757 6.
Davidson, Arnold. *Coyote Country: Fictions of the Canadian West*. DukeUP. pp. 223. ISBN 0 8223 1469 X.
Dever, Maryanne, ed. *Wallflowers and Witches: Women and Culture in Australia 1910–1945*. UQP. pp. 175. A$16.95. ISBN 0 7022 2607 6.
D'haen, Theo, and Hans Bertens, eds. *Liminal Postmodernisms: The Postmodern, the (Post-) Colonial and the (Post-) Feminist*. Rodopi. pp. 357. $69. ISBN 9 0518 3756 9.
Dissanayake, Wimal, and Carmen Wickramagamage. *Self and Colonial Desire: Travel Writings of V. S. Naipaul*. Lang (1993). pp. 161. DM30. ISBN 0 8204 1975 3. ISSN 1043-8586.
Dobrez, L.A.C., and Bill Ashcroft, eds. *Identifying Australia in Postmodern Times*. Bibliotech (ANU). pp. 176. A$20. ISBN 0 7315 2014 9.
Dragland, Stan. *Floating Voice: Duncan Campbell Scott and the Literature of Treaty 9*. Anansi. pp. 289. $24.95. ISBN 0 8878 4551 7.
Durix, Carole, and Jean-Pierre Durix. *An Introduction to the New Literatures in English*. LongmanF (1993). pp. 206. 120FF. ISBN 2 8664 4210 5.
Dutton, Geoffrey. *Out in the Open*. UQP. pp. 528. A$39.95. ISBN 0 7022 2681 5.
Gammel, Irene. *Sexualizing Power in Naturalism: Theodore Dreiser and Frederick Philip Grove*. UCalgaryP. pp. 262. $24.95. ISBN 1 8951 7639 5.

Geering, R. G., and A. Segerberg, eds. *Christina Stead: Selected Fiction and NonFiction*. Australian Authors. UQP. pp. 281. A$22.95. ISBN 0 7022 2520 7.

Grant, Don, and Graham Seal, eds. *Australia in the World: Perceptions and Possibilities*. Black Swan. pp. 385. A$35.95. ISBN 0 6461 6487 2.

Grant, Judith Skelton. *Robertson Davies: Man of Myth*. Viking. pp. 787. n.p. ISBN 0 6708 2557 3.

Gribble, Jennifer. *Christina Stead*. Australian Writers. OUPAus. pp. 133. $18.95. ISBN 0 1955 3370 4.

Gunew, Sneja. *Framing Marginality: Multicultural Literary Studies*. Interpretations UMel. pp. 158. A$19.95. ISBN 0 5228 4639 4.

Gurnah, Abdulrazak, ed. *Essays on African Writing 1: A Re-evaluation*. Heinemann (1993). pp. 192. £12.95. ISBN 0 4539 1762 5.

Habekost, Christian. *Verbal Riddim: The Politics and Aesthetics of African-Caribbean Dub Poetry*. Cross/Cultures 10. Rodopi (1993). pp. 262. Hfl.75, $46.50. ISBN 9 0518 3549 3.

Harrow, Kenneth. *Thresholds of Change in African Literature: The Emergence of a Tradition*. Heinemann, Currey. pp. 284. £12.95. ISBN 0 8525 5532 6.

Hart, Kevin, ed. *The Oxford Book of Australian Religious Verse*. OUPAus. pp. 268. A$39.95. ISBN 0 1955 3498 0.

Haskell, Dennis, ed. *Tilting at Matilda: Literature, Aborigines, Women and the Church in Contemporary Australia*. Fremantle Arts Centre Press, CSAL. pp. 219. A$19.95. ISBN 1 8636 8105 1.

——, and Geoffrey Dutton, eds. *Kenneth Slessor: Collected Poems*. A&R. pp. 497. A$24.95. ISBN 0 2071 7257 9.

Hassall, Anthony J. *Dancing on Hot Macadam: Peter Carey's Fiction*. UQP. pp. 204. A$24.95. ISBN 0 7022 2596 7.

Heble, Ajay. *The Tumble of Reason: Alice Munro's Discourse of Absence*. UTorP. pp. 210. £35. ISBN 0 8020 0617 5.

Hergenhan, Laurie, and Irmtraud Petersson. *Changing Places: Australian Writers in Europe 1960s–1990s*. UQP. pp. 296. A$14.95. ISBN 0 7022 2615 7.

Huggan, Graham. *Territorial Disputes: Maps and Mapping Strategies in Contemporary Canadian and Australian Fiction*. UTorP. pp. 198. $68.40. ISBN 0 8020 2923 X.

Jewinski, Ed. *Michael Ondaatje: Express Yourself Beautifully*. ECW. pp. 144. $9.95. ISBN 1 5502 2189 2.

Jordan, David. *New World Regionalism: Literature in the Americas*. UTorP. pp. 149. n.p. ISBN 0 8020 6989 4.

Jurgensen, Manfred, ed. *Riding Out: New Writing from Around the World*. Outrider/Phoenix Publications. pp. 471. $19.95. ISBN 0 9497 8021 9.

Kabbani, Rana. *Imperial Fictions: Europe's Myths of Orient* (2nd edn). Pandora. pp. 166. £7.99. ISBN 0 0444 0911 7.

La Bossière, Camille, ed. *Context North America: Canadian/US Literary Relations*. UOttawaP. pp. 166. $22. ISBN 0 7766 0360 4.

Lawson, Alan. *Patrick White: Selected Writings*. Australian Authors. UQP. pp. 304. A$22.95. ISBN 0 7012 2625 4.

Lee, Alvin A., and Robert D. Denham, eds. *The Legacy of Northrop Frye*. UTorP. pp. 353. hb $55, pb $24.95. ISBN 0 8020 0632 9, 0 8020 7588 6.

Made, Pat, and Beverley Abrahams. *Study Guide to In the Fog of the Season's End*. Academic Books (Pvt) Harare (1993). pp. 42. £4.95. ISBN 0 9492 2925 3.

Maja-Pearce, Adewale, ed. *Wole Soyinka: An Appraisal*. Heinemann. pp. 166. £9.95. ISBN 0 4359 1151 1.
Marr, David. *Patrick White: Letters*. RandomHAus. pp. 677. A$49.95. ISBN 0 0918 2992 5.
McInnis, Nadine. *Dorothy Livesay's Poetics of Desire*. Turnstone. pp. 114. $10.95. ISBN 0 8881 0181 4.
McLeod, A. L., ed. *R. K. Narayan: Critical Perspectives*. SterlingND. pp. 174. £24. ISBN 8 1207 1623 X.
Mercer, Gina. *Janet Frame: Subversive Fictions*. UQP. pp. 294. A$29.95. ISBN 0 7022 2459 6.
Mihailovich-Dickman, Vera, ed. *'Return' in Post-Colonial Writing: A Cultural Labyrinth*. Rodopi. pp. 173. $42.50. ISBN 9 0518 3648 1.
Morley, Patricia. *As Though Life Mattered: Leo Kennedy's Story*. McG-QUP. pp. 238. $29.95. ISBN 0 7735 1147 4.
Mukherjee, Arun. *Oppositional Aesthetics: Readings from a Hyphenated Space*. TSAR. pp. 189. £13.95. ISBN 0 9206 6142 4.
Mukherjee, Sujit. *Translation as Discovery and Other Essays on Indian Literature in English Translation*. Sangam. pp. 181. £8.95. ISBN 0 8631 1377 X.
Nadel, Ira. *Leonard Cohen: A Life in Art*. ECW. pp. 160. $14.95. ISBN 1 5502 2210 4.
Nazareth, Peter. *In the Trickster Tradition: The Novels of Andrew Salkey, Francis Ebejar and Ishmael Reed*. Bogle. pp. 262. £14.95. ISBN 0 9045 2197 4.
Nelson, Emmanuel S., ed. *Bharati Mukherjee: Critical Perspectives*. Garland (1993). pp. 236. $38. ISBN 0 8153 1173 7.
Nettlebeck, Amanda, ed. *Provisional Maps: Critical Essays on David Malouf*. CSAL. pp. 206. A$18. ISBN 0 8642 2300 5.
Niall, Brenda. *Georgiana: A Biography of Georgiana McCrae, Painter, Diarist, Pioneer*. UMP at Miegunyah Press. pp. 344. A$39.95. ISBN 0 5228 4513 4.
Nile, Richard, ed. *Australian Civilization*. OUPAus. pp. 260. A$24.95. ISBN 0 1955 3504 9.
Ojaide, Tanure. *The Poetry of Wole Soyinka*. Malthouse. pp. 140. £8.95. ISBN 9 7802 3006 8.
Pandey, Sudhakar, and R. Raj Rao, eds. *Image of India in the Indian Novel in English, 1960–1985*. Sangam (1993). pp. 143. £16.95. ISBN 0 8631 1347 8.
Panny, Judith Dell. *I Have What I Gave: The Fiction of Janet Frame*. DBAP (1992). pp. 194. NZ$34.95. ISBN 0 9088 9617 4.
Perkins, Elizabeth. *The Plays of Alma De Groen*. Australian Playwrights. Rodopi. pp. 183. A$38. ISBN 9 0518 3764 X.
Riemer, Andrew. *The Ironic Eye: The Poetry and Prose of Peter Goldsworthy*. A&R (1993). pp. 125. A$14.95. ISBN 0 2071 8250 7.
Roberts, Carol. *Timothy Findley: Stories from a Life*. ECW. pp. 135. $9.95. ISBN 1 5502 2195 7.
Ross, Robert, ed. *International Literature in English: Essays on the Major Writers*. Garland. (1991). pp. 762. n.p. ISBN 0 8240 3437 6.
Rowe, Noel. *Modern Australian Poets*. Horizon Studies in Literature. OUPAus. pp. 63. A$9.95. ISBN 0 4240 0195 0.
Rutherford, Anna, ed. *From Commonwealth to Post-Colonial*. Dangaroo (1992). pp. 450. £14.95. ISBN 1 8710 4942 3.
——, Lars Jensen and Shirley Chew, eds. *Into the Nineties: Post-Colonial Women's Writing*. Dangaroo. pp. 636. £14.95. ISBN 1 8710 4952 0.

Stead, C. K., ed. *The Faber Book of Contemporary South Pacific Stories*. Faber. pp. 286. £14.99. ISBN 0 5711 6765 9.

Stokes, Geoff, ed. *Australian Political Ideas.* UNSW. pp. 203. A$24.95. ISBN 0 8684 0094 7.

Stone, Judy. *Theatre*. Studies in West Indian Literature, general ed. Kenneth Ramchand. MacmillanC. pp. 268. £14.95. ISBN 0 3336 0078 9.

Tait, Peta. *Converging Realities: Feminism in Australian Theatre*. Currency. pp. 276. A$19.95. ISBN 0 8681 9376 3.

Thomson, Helen. *Bio-Fictions: Brian Matthews, Drusilla Modjeska and Elizabeth Jolley*. Colin Roderick Lectures 1993. Foundation for Australian Literary Studies (James Cook University of North Queensland). pp. 54. A$15.95. ISBN 0 8644 3513 4.

Tiefensee, Dianne. *'The Old Dualities': Deconstructing Robert Kroetsch and his Critics*. McG-QUP. pp. 225. £24. ISBN 0 7735 1191 1.

Tiffin, Chris, and Alan Lawson, eds. *De-Scribing Empire: Post-Colonialism and Textuality*. Routledge. pp. 254. A$32.95. ISBN 0 4151 0547 1.

Trigg, Stephanie. *Gwen Harwood*. Australian Writers. OUPAus. pp. 119. A$19.95. ISBN 0 1955 3280 5.

Veeser, H. Aram, ed. *The New Historicism Reader*. Routledge. pp. 376. hb n.p., pb £10.99. ISBN 0 4159 0781 0, 0 4159 0782 9.

Weiss, Timothy. *On the Margins: The Art of Exile in V. S. Naipaul.* UMassP (1993). pp. 276. £26.95. ISBN 0 8702 3820 5.

White, Jonathan, ed. *Recasting the World: Writing After Colonialism*. JHUP (1993). pp. 255. hb £37, pb £12.50. ISBN 0 8018 4605 6, 0 8018 4606 4.

Wilde, William H., Joy Hooton and Barry Andrews, eds. *The Oxford Companion to Australian Literature*. OUPAus. pp. 833. A$69.95. ISBN 0 1955 3381 X.

Wilding, Michael, ed. *The Oxford Book of Australian Short Stories*. OUPAus. pp. 348. A$39.95. ISBN 0 1955 3610 X.

Wong, Sau-ling Cynthia. *Reading Asian American Literature: From Necessity to Extravagance*. PrincetonUP (1993). pp. 258. hb n.p., pb $15.95. ISBN 0 6910 6875 5, 0 6910 1541 4.

Wright, Derek. *The Novels of Nuruddin Farah*. Bayreuth African Studies Series, vol. 32. University of Bayreuth. pp. 166. hb DM41.96, pb DM29. ISBN 3 9275 1017 3, 3 9275 1027 0. ISSN 0178-0034.

Yarwood, A. T. *From a Chair in the Sun: The Life of Ethel Turner*. Viking. pp. 392. A$39.95. ISBN 0 6708 3717 2.

Zimmerman, Cynthia. *Playwriting Women: Female Voices in English Canada*. Simon & Pierre. pp. 235. $22.50. ISBN 0 8892 4258 5.

Index I. Critics

Authors such as Seamus Heaney, who are both authors of criticism and subjects of discussion, are listed in whichever index is appropriate for each reference.

Index II. Authors and Subjects Treated

Notes

1. Material which has not been seen by contributors is not indexed.
2. Authors such as Seamus Heaney, who are both authors of criticism and subjects of discussion, are listed in whichever index is appropriate for each reference.
3. Author entries have subdivisions listed in the following order:
   (a) author's relationship with other authors;
   (b) author's relationship with other subjects;
   (c) author's characteristics;
   (d) author's works (listed alphabetically).
4. A page number in **bold** represents the main entry for that particular subject.